BOWLER HATS AND KINKY BOOTS

THE UNOFFICIAL AND UNAUTHORISED GUIDE TO THE AVENGERS

BOWLER HATS AND KINKY BOOTS

THE UNOFFICIAL AND UNAUTHORISED GUIDE TO THE AVENGERS

Michael Richardson

First published in the UK in 2014 by
Telos Publishing Ltd,
5A Church Road, Shortlands, Bromley, Kent, BR2 0HP
www.telos.co.uk

Telos Publishing Ltd values feedback. Please e-mail us with any comments
you may have about this book to: feedback@telos.co.uk

ISBN 978-1-84583-097-7

*Bowler Hats and Kinky Boots: The Unofficial and Unauthorised Guide to The
Avengers* © 2014 Michael Richardson

Foreword © 2014 Brian Clemens

Editor: Stephen James Walker
Index: Ian Pritchard
Typesetting: Sam Stone
Cover Design: David J Howe

The moral right of the author has been asserted.

British Library Cataloguing in Publication Data.
A catalogue record for this book is available from the British Library.

DEDICATION

Dedicated to Joan Richardson

ACKNOWLEDGEMENTS

I have to express extreme gratitude to the following, as without their endless enthusiasm and devotion, this project would have been much more difficult to achieve. Their support, assistance and encouragement pushed me forward to research further and make this volume more detailed than I ever could have imagined when I began writing:

Proof reader: Annette Hill; plus Alan Hayes, Anthony McKay, Andrew Pixley and Jaz Wiseman.

Over the years I have met, interviewed, corresponded and exchanged emails with a number of people who were associated with *The Avengers*, *The New Avengers*, ABC Television and *The Avengers* feature film, and their assistance (no matter how large or small) in writing this book is greatly appreciated:

Mick Audsley, Roy Ward Baker, Duncan Barbour, Richard Bates, Jeremy Burnham, Michael Chapman, Cyd Child, Brian Clemens, Jennifer Croxton, Peter Duffell, Cyril Frankel, John Hough, Gareth Hunt, Don Leaver, Patrick Macnee, Frank Maher, Roger Marshall, Rhonda Parker, Ron Purdie, Jon Rollason, Dennis Spooner, Julie Stevens, Robert Banks Stewart, Brian Tesler, Linda Thorson and Tony Williamson.

My thanks must also go to the following for their contributions:

Neil Alsop, Ian Beazley, Chris Bentley, BFI Special Collections, Simon Coward, Vince Cox, Nick Dando, Sam Denham, Geoff Dodd, Alan Field, Dandy Forsdyke, Des Glass, Piers Johnson, Gerald Lovell, Dave Matthews, National Media Museum, Stephen Pickard, Bob Rocca, Dave Rogers, Julie Rogers, David K Smith, Tony Sullivan and Paul Welsh.

I would also like to thank certain patrons of both *The Avengers: The International Fan Forum* and *Britmovie: British Film Forum*, who can be identified only by their usernames:

Christoph404, Hitchcock Scholar, Mark O, Mousemeat, Tavistock, Wadey and Whiskers.

All Peter Hammond quotes are courtesy of Jaz Wiseman.

The section of background information on the creation of the BBC's *Adam Adamant Lives!* was contributed by Stephen James Walker.

CONTENTS

FOREWORD

This is hardly a comeback. *The Avengers* has never really been away; since its inception as a filmed series in the '60s it has always been showing on some screen, somewhere in the world, and still is.

What is the reason for its longevity? Well, I think primarily, serendipity; its production coincided with the demise of our film industry, so suddenly an awful lot of top people became available. Hence I was lucky and privileged to work with directors such as Charles Crichton, James Hill, Roy Ward Baker, Sid Hayers etc, and still find time to encourage the likes of Bob Fuest, John Hough, Ray Austin. The series was lit by such as Gil Taylor (later to win an Oscar with Polanksi) and Alan Hume (who lit many of the Bond movies), designed by Robert Jones (who worked with Corman), Wilkie Collins (who worked with Hitchcock) and many others of the same ilk. Each episode of *The Avengers* was really a small feature film; individually scored by distinguished composer Laurie Johnson (*Tiger Bay*, Kubrick's *Dr Strangelove*, etc). Best of all we had Albert Fennell, my business partner and wonderful friend. Albert had behind-the-scenes masterminded movies such as *This Sporting Life*, *The Innocents* and *Tunes of Glory*, some of Britain's finest movie product. Albert, more by osmosis than lecture, taught me just about everything I know about pre- and post-production. Each filmed episode was shot on 35mm (essential when a lead is a woman, because beauty-enhancing lighting can be subtler). Each was cut and all stages of post-production heightened as in a major movie. That helped, as indeed did the era of the '60s we were spawned from. Life was (in the old sense of the word) gay then. People pursued happiness as an antidote to war – and *The Avengers* provided it with the right degree of naughtiness; I always said that you could watch the show with your maiden aunt, *but* if you had a really dirty mind there was much going on beneath the surface!

Another reason for our success was that we created our own world, in much the same way as pantomime, early Disney long-form movies and those Doris Day comedies provided. We were able to combine thrills and tension with humour – just as Hitchcock always did. And I am his greatest fan! In our series, death was treated in such a way that I hoped the viewer saw the actor die (usually without much blood in evidence) and then they could imagine the actor getting up, collecting his fee and going home unscathed! Talking of actors: in a way we were not unlike the later *Morecambe and Wise Show*; famous names actually *wanted* to work with/for us. What it meant was getting the chance to play someone outrageous. Amongst them were Donald Sutherland, Charlotte Rampling, John Cleese, Bernard Cribbins, Ronnie Barker … and many other talents. Halcyon days!

With revivals in the wind: *The Avengers* is to get an Australian DVD release for the very first time, and there are whispers it might present what are arguably some of the best episodes of all – the first 26 filmed black and white episodes – *in colour,* using unbelievable new technology. Others have discussed rerunning all the episodes on a major network, proof positive that you are *always* as good as your best product. *The Avengers* marches triumphantly on – forever entertaining. In light of this, Mike Richardson's scholarly retake on our seemingly imperishable series could be another touch of that serendipity – his perfect timing relaunching *The Avengers* one more time!

Brian Clemens
November 2013

INTRODUCTION

Welcome to *Bowler Hats and Kinky Boots*, which aims to serve as a definitive single-volume guide to the classic 1960s British television show *The Avengers* and its spin-offs and follow-ups, including *The New Avengers* and the 1998 movie adaptation.

The material in the following pages is split into a number of sections for ease of consumption. Broadly speaking, the first two-thirds of the book gives an in-depth chronological account of the production history of *The Avengers* and all related matters. Within this, each televised episode is accorded its own individual entry, detailing key behind-the-scenes aspects and developments, highlighting any points of special note – including items of trivia that tend to be of particular interest to aficionados, such as any firearms or classic motor vehicles featured – and briefly summarising the story content. (Detailed plot synopses have however been consciously omitted, not only because such information can be readily found elsewhere, both in print and online, but also because all the surviving episodes are available on DVD, and even the missing ones are being adapted as audio dramas by Big Finish, and it would be a shame to give away too many 'spoilers' for those who have yet to experience them.) The remainder of the book is then devoted to brief biographies of all the show's main cast members and production personnel, and finally a number of appendices giving more highly detailed production facts and figures and other information intended primarily for reference purposes.

It is now well over 50 years since *The Avengers* made its on-air debut, and yet still the show enjoys a cult following, not only in the UK but also in the USA and elsewhere around the world. This book will hopefully shed new light on its enduring phenomenon for its legion of long-time fans, and at the same time offer an accessible introduction for relative newcomers, all in the form of a single comprehensive overview.

But now, on with the action!

PART ONE
PRODUCTION HISTORY
THE AVENGERS

SEASON ONE

BROUGHT TO BOOK

The Avengers came about as a necessity to keep actor Ian Hendry working for ITV's London and Midlands weekend franchise-holder ABC Television[1], when their series in which he was already starring, *Police Surgeon*, was curtailed prematurely.

Police Surgeon

Writer Julian Bond originated *Police Surgeon* in the summer of 1960.[2] After doing some research and meeting with a real-life surgeon who worked with the police, he devised a format for a crime show in 30-minute episodes, incorporating aspects of two other popular television series of the time, ATV's soap *Emergency-Ward 10* and the BBC's police drama *Dixon of Dock Green*. Having come up with the idea and written most of the episodes, Bond was appointed series producer and story editor by the head of ABC's drama section, Sydney Newman. The writer carried out these duties while also working on other TV projects.

Ian Hendry was cast as the show's lead character, London-based Dr Geoffrey Brent, who was employed by the Metropolitan Police. The only regular supporting character was Detective Inspector Landon, portrayed by Australian actor John Warwick.

Police Surgeon began transmissions on Saturday 10 September 1960 with the episode 'Easy Money', featuring as the series theme tune composer Ivor Slaney's 'The Big Knife 2' – a stock recording sourced from the De Wolfe music library. Six days later, on Thursday 15 September, *The Stage and Television Today* featured a largely negative review of the programme, disliking everything about it except Hendry.

After the third episode, 'Lag on the Run', Julian Bond decided to relinquish the role of *Police Surgeon*'s producer, which by his own admission he was not enjoying. Leonard White, who had been the producer on another ABC show, *Armchair Mystery Theatre*, was brought in as his replacement, although the writer stayed on in the position of story editor until the end of production. Bond was concurrently writing and developing for Lew Grade's programme-financing company ITC another proposed television series called *Fleet Street* (aka *London Bureau*), based in a busy newspaper office. By this time, he had already been working on the *Fleet Street* concept for several months. However, in

---

[1] See Appendix Six for a brief history of ABC Television.

[2] According to the edition of *The Stage and Television Today* dated 30 June 1960, Bond was at that time engaged in researching and writing *Police Surgeon*, with four scripts already completed. The editions dated 14 July and 21 July indicated the same.

the event it would never progress any further than an outline.

In an effort to make *Police Surgeon* as realistic as possible, Bond had liaised closely with his actual police surgeon contact and written some episodes in collaboration with him. As a result, the surgeon, who used the pseudonym J J Bernard, received half of Bond's salary, with the exception of fees for screenplays. However, Bernard was not satisfied with this arrangement and threatened to take legal action against ABC, who managed to avert this by crediting him on the opening titles: 'Written in collaboration with "J J Bernard MBBS", pseudonym of a Police Surgeon in the London area.' In order to prevent any repetition of these events, ABC decided to cancel *Police Surgeon* in the same month it premiered and to dispense with the services of Bernard. However, it nevertheless produced a full season of 13 episodes, as the show was contracted to fill this number of slots on the ITV network.

Some confusion was caused when both newspapers and TV listings magazines of the time billed the *Police Surgeon* episode 'You Won't Feel a Thing' twice, on 15 October and again on 29 October. Many years later, researchers ascertained that the episode transmitted on 15 October was actually 'Diplomatic Immunity', written by Australian Peter Yeldham. 'You Won't Feel a Thing' went out on the second date, 29 October.

Genesis of *The Avengers*

ABC considered Ian Hendry to be the finest television actor of his generation, and they desperately wanted him to stay with them after the cancellation of *Police Surgeon*. Finding a new vehicle for him thus became a priority. At the time, Managing Director Howard Thomas felt there was an imbalance in the company's schedules and what they really needed was a thriller. Thomas passed his views on to Sydney Newman who, no doubt having seen the films *The Man Who Knew Too Much* and *North by Northwest*, suggested that the works of director Alfred Hitchcock could influence the direction in which a new series could go. Consequently, at the same time that Leonard White was called to Newman's office to be informed that production on *Police Surgeon* was to cease, he was asked if he could go away and come up with a format for a new light thriller to spotlight Ian Hendry's talents.

Returning to Newman sometime later, White presented him with an outline for a crime/espionage series that involved an enthusiastic general practitioner, who had a great sense of right and wrong, becoming involved in undercover work with a professional spy. This was the series outline for what became *The Avengers*, a title that Newman was initially unsure of, but changed his mind about when White explained that the two lead characters would be avenging on behalf of others.

Both Newman and White were responsible for developing the new series and the situations to be featured within it. It would begin with a medical doctor becoming involved in fighting criminals and organised crime following the killing of his fiancée by a gang of drug dealers. The doctor would be approached by a mysterious man with knowledge of criminal activities and experience of dealing with the underworld, who would go on to gain his trust in order to make him a partner against crime and assist in his investigations.

This format was passed on to Patrick Brawn, who was initially to be one of two story editors on the first season of *The Avengers*. Born in Walsall on 2 March 1919, Brawn had entered the film industry as a dialogue coach in the early '50s, before writing for the anthology series *London Playhouse* and the comedy show *I'm Not Bothered* and scripting the feature film *Chain of Events*. He then came to the attention of Sydney Newman, who had him write an instalment of *Armchair Theatre*, which obviously went well enough for him to become a part of the team putting *The Avengers* together.

The other story editor was to be a young Scotsman called John Bryce, whom Leonard White considered to be extremely helpful and a good team player. Bryce had performed the same function on *Armchair Theatre* and had previously worked in the script department for ABC's parent company, the Associated British Picture Corporation (ABPC).

Brawn provided a storyline that would cover the first two episodes of the new series. However, he would not write the actual screenplays: Ray Rigby would adapt the first half of the story as the debut episode, 'Hot Snow', then Brian Clemens would conclude events with the second episode, 'Brought to Book'.

In later interviews, Leonard White stressed that the drama department at ABC had a family atmosphere and that various different people contributed to the development of *The Avengers*, insisting 'No one person invented it'.

Ray Rigby had started out by writing TV plays for the BBC before moving across to ABC to become a contract writer for the company, penning several episodes of *Armchair Theatre*. However, 'Hot Snow' would be his only work on *The Avengers*. Brian Clemens, on the other hand, would become associated with this series more than any other he ever worked on, and would be instrumental in developing it into a worldwide success – but that was several years down the line.

So, with Ian Hendy confirmed as fronting the new series, attention turned to casting the second lead. One night during September 1960, Leonard White was attending a performance of the play *A Passage to India* at the Comedy Theatre in London, and during the interval the two friends he was with arranged to meet actor Patrick Macnee. White was already acquainted with Macnee, having crossed paths with him some years earlier when they were both actors in the same theatre company in London, and again when they both appeared together in several Canadian television productions. With a long string of acting credits behind him, Macnee had been a jobbing actor for ten years, but his profession had not made him wealthy or even a household name. In June 1960, he had jumped at the chance to become a producer on a documentary series called *Winston Churchill: The Valiant Years*, in light of the relatively high salary it offered.

White informed Macnee that Sydney Newman, with whom they had both worked in Canada, was now the Head of Drama at ABC and that together they were planning a new action-adventure-thriller series called *The Avengers*. White explained the format and then suggested that Macnee consider himself for the role of the then unnamed mystery man, who would draw the doctor into the seedy underworld. Macnee was unconvinced, pointing out that he was on better money as a producer, to which White replied that his salary as a regular on a television series would be substantially more than he was making at the time. Macnee asked White to get Newman to telephone him. This happened the following day. Attempting to get Macnee on board, Newman apparently came out with one of the all-time great television quotes: 'We're calling it *The Avengers*. I don't know what it means, but it's a hell of a good title.'

However, Macnee was more interested in the remuneration, and asked for what he considered to be the outrageous sum of £300 a week. Much to his amazement, Newman agreed to this. However, there had been some misunderstanding, as the Canadian meant £300 an episode, and this broke down to £150 a week, as each episode would be made over two weeks. Nevertheless, this was still three times the amount Macnee was getting for producing *Winston Churchill: The Valiant Years*, so he signed a contract with ABC and the production gained its second lead.

Sometime during these early days of preparing to begin production on *The Avengers*, one of the directors of ABPC, Robert Clark, made the board aware that there would be tax advantages if ABC's programmes were made by another company. Hence the in-house production company Iris Productions Ltd was formed, and all the technicians and crew were required to sign new contracts taking them off the ABC payroll. In time it would be discovered that this arrangement did not provide the tax benefits envisaged, and Iris Productions would be dissolved, but not before it had been the production company on the first three seasons of *The Avengers*.

On 21 November 1960, Leonard White circulated an internal memo at ABC formally indicating that production on *Police Surgeon* would stop but that Ian Hendry would front a new series to be transmitted in 1961 called *The Avengers*. Once again Hendry would play a doctor, this time David Dent, a completely different character from Dr Geoffrey Brent of *Police Surgeon*, and there would be no connection between the two series.

It was also confirmed that Patrick Macnee would be assuming the role of undercover secret service man John Steed and that the first three scripts were now on file, with four others in preparation. Several days later, Macnee made his first visit to ABC's Teddington Studios in Teddington, Middlesex, where the show would be recorded. He was welcomed by Newman and White and met Hendry and Don Leaver, who would direct the first episode, 'Hot Snow'.

Production routine

Production on the early series of *The Avengers* would generally follow a set pattern. Work on each episode would begin in earnest several months prior to its recording, when the writer would agree a storyline with Leonard White and the story editors, having already discussed their requirements at several preliminary meetings and submitted an outline of several pages. The writer would then draft a complete teleplay. Six weeks before the recording date, this teleplay would be scrutinised by both the director and the designer, who would point out any obvious problems. With four weeks to go, the director would decide what sets were required in order to tell the story, and the designer would then draw up plans for the carpenters to build them, making certain that they would all fit within the confines of the allocated studio.

Previously, ABC had mainly transmitted drama productions live from the former Capitol Cinema in Didsbury, Manchester. The sets had been constructed locally by a company called Watts and Corrie, who would continue to provide this service. Consequently, the sets for *The Avengers* would have to be transported to Teddington Studios by road, for assembly on site.

This was also the time when the director would call upon the assistance of the casting director in order to cast the various guest characters in the teleplay, trusting his knowledge of both actors and actresses and what range they had as performers.

With the countdown to recording continuing, the final two weeks would be filled with rehearsals. In the first week, the director and a story editor would supervise the cast as they went through all the dialogue. By the second week, Leonard White would be in attendance, making certain that everyone involved was up to speed and assuring himself that a professional recording would take place.

Also present at the rehearsals would be the camera operators and lighting and sound technicians, to familiarise themselves with proceedings and highlight any difficulties that could arise during recording. The places where furniture would stand on the set would be represented by shapes marked in strips of tape stuck to the rehearsal room floor, and the director would have to plan out all of the camera, lighting and microphone movements that would be needed on a scene-by-scene basis in the studio.

Other factors that had to be taken into account included making certain that the cables trailing behind the cameras would not get tangled up and restrict their mobility, and similarly that the cameras – which were pedestal-mounted and weighed approximately 77 kilos each – would not be pushed over any cables on the studio floor, which would cause damage. Furthermore, as each camera was equipped with four different four-and-a-half-inch lenses, calculations needed to be made regarding the length of time it would take the camera operators to switch between lenses, all this being incorporated into the running time of the episode. According to Don Leaver, all these permutations could be so complicated that directors would sometimes have to work until two or three in the morning to produce their final camera scripts.

Any location material needed for a given episode would be shot on film a few days in advance of the studio recording.

The day preceding the recording would be filled with camera rehearsals, as would the actual day of the event, which would culminate in a full dress rehearsal with both the wardrobe and make-up supervisors present, before the whole team launched themselves into actually making the episode.

The recording would be done 'as live', with any pre-filmed sequences played in at the appropriate points. All the sets would be erected in the studio and a floor manager would supervise the cast and crew as they moved between them, while being in constant communication with both the director and the producer, who would be in the control room (aka gallery) watching events unfolding on the video monitors there. The performers would hurriedly take up new positions between scenes, sometimes changing their costumes along the way, while the cameramen and technicians tracked their movements, following the director's camera script and blocking instructions. Meanwhile, the sound mixer in the control room would have to make certain that footsteps or other extraneous noises were not be picked up and recorded onto the soundtrack.

The theme and incidental music would be played in on cue from records. So too would some of the show's sound effects, although the simpler ones (such as doors being closed) would be achieved by having a member of the crew actually performing the required action off camera.

Due to an agreement with the actors' union Equity, the ITV companies had only one hour in which to record a 50-minute videotape production. Hence, with an attitude of 'It'll be all right on the night,' cast and crew would put themselves under extreme pressure and go for it in a single take, hoping to avoid any errors. In many ways, this was just like doing a stage play; and because there was no redubbing, post-synching or editing readily available, it meant that any fluffed lines, wobbling sets or props that failed to work would usually be fully apparent on screen. In fact, the making of any edits at all was very much discouraged, because if a tape had more than a handful of splices in it, it became prone to break when recorded over and was thus deemed unsuitable for further use – a serious matter, as due to the high cost of videotape in 1960

(£1,540 per reel in today's prices, adjusted for inflation) it was standard practice for old programmes to be taped over with new ones in order to minimise the number of reels that had to be bought.

1.01 – 'Hot Snow'

As *The Avengers'* debut episode, 'Hot Snow' was afforded a longer rehearsal period than usual. This began on 28 November 1960 on the second floor at RCA Records' re-recording theatre The Tower, on what was Bush Green Road (now part of Shepherd's Bush Road) in Hammersmith. The initial problem director Don Leaver encountered was Ian Hendry's dislike of the script, which early on the first day the actor tore in half and dumped in a wastepaper basket claiming, 'Its crap. It doesn't work, does it?' Hendry's quest for quality drama would cause plenty of rewriting over the course of the first season.

This draft script, dated 22 November 1960, carried no episodic title, being simply headed '*The Avengers*'. The rewriting of this teleplay resulted in a new draft in which the Dent name was dropped and Hendry's character became Dr David Keel. Likewise, his partner in the medical practice, Dr Reeding, underwent an alteration to become Dr Tredding. Vinsons the jewellers was called Finsons in the first draft, and neither version included any of the location scenes that were ultimately filmed in Chelsea for the beginning of the episode, which appear to have been added at the eleventh hour.

The 1 December edition of *The Stage and Television Today* informed readers that ABC Television was in the process of preparing a new thriller called *The Avengers*, with Patrick Brawn and John Bryce as story editors. Starring Ian Hendry, who had gained a following from *Police Surgeon*, Patrick Macnee and an actress of Viennese descent, Ingrid Hafner, the series would begin screening in January 1961.

Meanwhile, on 2 December, Leonard White sent another memo, confirming that he had managed to obtain the services of jazz musician Johnny Dankworth to compose and record both the theme tune and incidental music cues for the series.

Police Surgeon reached the end of the road as the last episode, 'The Bigger They Are', was transmitted on Saturday 3 December 1960. Its creator Julian Bond did later work on some other ABC shows, including *Out of this World*, but failed to become involved with *The Avengers*, preferring to write for higher-paying ITC film series such as *The Saint*, *Ghost Squad* and *The Sentimental Agent*.

On 15 December, rehearsals for 'Hot Snow' were continuing, now at a new venue nearer the studios, specifically the Regal Cinema on London Road in Twickenham.

The first ever footage for *The Avengers* was shot on film on 20 December at Upper Cheyne Road and Glebe Place in Chelsea, London SW3. This involved actor Godfrey Quigley, playing the character Spicer, a member of a drugs gang. It showed Spicer parking his 1959 Humber Hawk Mk IV and then walking around a corner and climbing over a gate to gain entrance to the rear of the Keel and Tredding surgery. Dankworth's opening theme would be played over this material during recording.

On the same day, Hendry, Macnee and Hafner – who would play the semi-regular character of Keel's nurse/receptionist Carol Wilson – were on location in Upper Compton Road in Westminster, London W3 for a photoshoot to capture publicity stills for the series.

The last week of December saw rehearsals well under way for both 'Hot Snow' and the subsequent episode, 'Brought to Book', in Rehearsal Room 3A at Teddington.

ABC's programme production no 3365, 'Hot Snow' was finally recorded between 6.00 pm and 7.00 pm on Friday 30 December in Studio 2 at Teddington, to start the ball rolling on what would become one of the most successful and stylish British television series ever.

The storyline of 'Hot Snow' revolves around a package of heroin that has been mistakenly delivered to the Keel and Tredding surgery by a gang member called Johnson. Spicer tries but is unable to recover the drugs for the gang. The leader of the gang, known to his associates as the Big Man, decides that Keel's fiancée and current receptionist Peggy, who accepted the package, would be able to identify Johnson and lead the police to them. Having arranged to meet Peggy by Vinsons the jewellers, Keel is unaware that the gang are also awaiting her arrival across the road in a car, where Spicer has taken aim with a rifle complete with telescopic sight. Peggy arrives and is promptly shot, dying in Keel's arms. The police fail to turn up any leads, so Keel takes it upon himself to investigate. In doing so, he encounters a mysterious stranger named John Steed, who offers to help. In line with ABC's standard practice of the time, the closing credit captions ended with one informing viewers of the transmission date and title of the following episode.

Don Leaver assembled a strong cast for 'Hot Snow' that included Philip Stone, Moira Redmond and, playing the part of Peggy, Catherine Woodville – who obviously made an impression on Patrick Macnee, as they were married in 1965, although unfortunately they divorced four years later.

Unlike most of the season one episodes, some of 'Hot Snow' still survives to be viewed today.[3] Specifically, this is the first of the three acts – i.e. the section before the first of the two commercial breaks that each episode would have – comprising all of the action up to the point where Peggy is shot and killed. This reveals some aspects of the production that would otherwise have been lost to history. For instance, in the studio-realised night-time exterior scene outside Vinsons, it can be clearly seen that wet plastic sheeting was used to represent the road surface in the shot where the car pulls up.

Into transmission

Nowadays it can take years for a television series to be developed. The company financing the project will generally demand that it be given across-the-board appeal to attract the largest possible audience, including people of a certain age and minority groups; as a result, extensive market research is often carried out before a single frame of film is shot. Even when an episode is made, there can be various test screenings to determine if revisions should be made. Did the audience like the characters? Could they follow the plot? What did they think about the ending? And so on. Behind all this there can be a hierarchy of producers, executive producers, associate producers, supervising

---

[3] For many years, it appeared that the only season one episode to have survived was the fifteenth, 'The Frighteners'. However, in 2001 the then-missing sixth episode 'Girl on the Trapeze' was located in the library of UCLA (University of California) in Los Angeles, California. This was followed by the discovery of the first act of 'Hot Snow' (21 minutes and 47 seconds) from the same source. UCLA had recently placed a catalogue of its entire archive online, and eagle-eyed television enthusiast Dave Wood noticed the material thought to have been lost forever. This resulted in copies being handed over to *The Avengers'* current copyright holder, the French company StudioCanal.

producers and consulting producers. *The Avengers* was taken from an idea to production in six weeks by just a head of department, a producer and two story editors, showing a real example of 'less is more'.

In anticipation of the on-air debut of the new series, the Midlands and North editions of the *TV Times* issue no. 270, which went on sale on 30 December 1960 and covered programmes for the week of 1 to 7 January 1961, featured *The Avengers* along with other shows on its front cover and gave a preview of 'Hot Snow'. There were quotes from Hendry, who said he had thought twice about assuming the role of another doctor after *Police Surgeon*, but felt that with *The Avengers* the accent was on the scripts and he knew it was going to be a lot of fun. Macnee meanwhile described Steed as a wolf with women and someone who revelled in trouble. Producer Leonard White added that the series would involve fast-moving action stories.

'Hot Snow' was transmitted at 10.00 pm on Saturday 7 January 1961, but disappointingly for ABC only in their own two ITV regions. ATV refused to show it in their prized London weekend region, and the other ITV companies followed their lead. ATV London and most of the other regions continued to use that Saturday evening slot to screen their own anthology series *Theatre 70*, which had been running since September 1960. ABC had dropped *Theatre 70* at the beginning of December, running episodes of a half-hour film series called *International Detective* and the cowboy series *Maverick* as a stopgap until *The Avengers* arrived. Meanwhile, the main competition over on the BBC was *Sports Special*, although the Corporation frequently varied its Saturday night scheduling to include films and one-off plays.

ABC Midlands and ABC North would be the only regions to show all 26 episodes of the first season of *The Avengers*.

1.02 – 'Brought to Book'

The storyline started in 'Hot Snow' was concluded in the next episode, 'Brought to Book', making this the only two-part story in the entire run of the series.

'Brought to Book' was recorded on Thursday 12 January 1961 under the direction of Peter Hammond. It began with a recap by Philip Stone as Dr Tredding, outlining the events of 'Hot Snow' against diverse shots of a grieving Keel and a cheerful Steed enjoying himself at a horse-racing track. The storyline of 'Brought to Book' sees Steed offer Keel the chance of bringing Peggy's killer to justice. However, in order to achieve this, the doctor has to appear corrupt in order to infiltrate the drug smuggling gang. Working together, Keel and Steed manage to bring about the downfall of the gang, after the doctor threatens Spicer with a lethal injection unless he confesses to killing Peggy. Keel's hypodermic syringe is actually full of harmless witch-hazel, but Spicer is unaware of this and his confession is overheard by the police. With Peggy's death avenged, Keel agrees to join Steed in his crusade against organised crime.

The episode title caption appeared over 35mm filmed horse racing stock footage, with a freshly-spoken commentary describing the race being added before being fed into the recording by telecine. At the time, ABC had three Rank Cintel flying spot telecine machines, which could handle both 16 mm and 35mm film. By increasing the number of frames per second, film could be made to run at the same speed as television and be slotted in wherever required without any noticeable difference in sound quality, although the picture quality was slightly clearer than videotape.

Peter Hammond was the director who pioneered a style for which *The Avengers* became renowned, which involved frequently using odd camera angles and shooting through foreground objects such as bookcases. This greatly impressed the designer on 'Brought to Book', Robert Fuest, who would adopt a similar approach years later when he himself became a director on the filmed episodes of the series.

1.03 – 'Square Root of Evil'

Ian Hendry had previously guest-starred in 'Return to Base', an episode of the ABC series *Inside Story* written by Richard Harris, and he and the writer had become firm friends. This led to Harris being asked to contribute to *The Avengers*. His script, entitled 'Square Root of Evil', was written from a story by John Bryce.

'Square Root of Evil' was notable for the fact that, unlike the previous two episodes, it was not pre-recorded but actually transmitted live from Studio 2 at Teddington on the evening of Saturday 21 January. This was necessitated by scripting and other production pressures. Live transmission would in fact become the norm for the following half-dozen episodes.[4] It would take until early March 1961 for the production team to resolve the problems and get completed scripts on file in good time, so that they could relieve some of the pressures and return to pre-recording episodes in advance of transmission.

Another stopgap measure decided upon at this point, also aimed at reducing production pressures, was to slant the storylines of forthcoming episodes toward one of the lead characters, with the other reduced to a supporting role. Once instigated, this would mean Keel and Steed alternating as the lead, reducing the amount of constant rehearsal time that Hendry and Macnee would each have to endure.

Patrick Downing was the designer for 'Square Root of Evil'. He had originally been lined up to take charge of the sets for all of the first three episodes, but found himself unavailable until now, having been kept busy working on other ABC programmes.

One significant element of the episode's plot – which involved a criminal organisation planning to flood Europe with forged banknotes – was a character known as Five, played by Heron Carvic. This was the first of Steed's various superiors seen in the series over the years, from whom he would receive his instructions.

The camera script reveals that another of the episode's characters, Steve Bloom, was subject to a last-minute casting alteration, director Don Leaver bringing in John Woodvine to replace Michael Robbins during the rehearsal period, for reasons unknown.

---

[4] In all, nine episodes of season one would be transmitted live. These would all however be videorecorded – as was later confirmed in an Iris Productions Ltd memo dated 30 March 1961 from Michael Chapman to ABC's director of programmes Brian Tesler. This communication, which was also sent to both Sydney Newman and Leonard White, pointed out that these episodes had not been screened by ATV, but speculated that they might be at a future date. When questioned regarding this situation in June 2011, White thought that the episodes would also have been copied onto film for possible overseas sales; but as the first season did not generate any foreign interest, the videotape copies would have been recorded over and the film copies disposed of.

Steed re-invented

It was around this time that Sydney Newman called Patrick Macnee into his office and voiced his opinion that the John Steed character was not working out. Macnee was naturally unhappy with this statement, feeling that he had acquitted himself well so far, but Newman insisted that the character was just too plain and simply not interesting enough.

Sometime during rehearsals for 'Hot Snow', director Don Leaver had enquired if Macnee had ever read any of Ian Fleming's James Bond novels, to which Macnee had replied in the negative. Thinking that it would assist the actor in getting into the correct frame of mind for *The Avengers*, Leaver had then given him a copy of the first 007 book, *Casino Royale*, which the actor had proceeded to read. However, Macnee had been horrified by the book's sadistic and graphic violence, not to mention Bond's lascivious attitude toward women, and decided that there was no way he could ever play Steed in such a manner. Clearly, though, in light of Newman's comments, he now had to make some kind of adjustment to his portrayal of the character.

Taking stock of the situation, Macnee returned home that evening and thought through what he wanted to do. He came up with a plan to incorporate the personalities of four different individuals into the character. Macnee's father, the racehorse trainer Daniel 'Shrimp' Macnee, came to mind, and particularly how he always wore a carnation in his buttonhole and had the collars of his overcoats covered in velvet; tailored effects that Steed would adopt. Macnee then borrowed elements of the fictional hero Sir Percy Blakeney, alias the Scarlet Pimpernel, a fashionable dandy who did not appear to be a threat and was consequently underestimated by all. The bravery side of the new Steed was drawn from two other individuals, the first being a man named Bussy Carr, Macnee's commanding officer from his wartime experience in the Royal Navy, and the second being the fictional character Major Hammond, played by Sir Ralph Richardson, from the 1939 spy movie *Q Planes*.

When Macnee arrived at Teddington Studios for the first time wearing his three-piece suit and bowler hat and carrying an umbrella, Hendry was so surprised at Steed's new look that he uttered an explitive. Newman's reaction was typical of the Canadian's outlook: 'Well, it's sure as hell different.' After a short while, ABC acquired a bowler for regular use in the series. This cost the equivalent of £6.10 in decimal currency, which would have been taken out of the wardrobe budget of approximately £60 per episode.

By this point in the series it had become apparent that John Steed was one of the good guys, although he had underworld connections and experience of moving in criminal circles without attracting attention. He was not a police officer; he worked for some unnamed government agency, but without the back-up of official colleagues, preferring to gain assistance by enticing people from everyday walks of life to become involved in fighting crime. Initially it was Dr Keel who fulfilled the latter role but – as we shall see later – there would be others who would be persuaded to become Steed's allies, putting themselves into considerable danger in the process. For Steed, the mission was everything; he was a ruthless professional in a dirty, vicious world of organised crime and espionage, and he knew what human dirt was and how to deal with it efficiently.

Hendry's Dr Keel, on the other hand, was an amateur in the crime-fighting stakes, but no less competent at rooting out evil-doers. Having been originally motivated by the death of his fiancée Peggy, his strong morals would not allow him to walk away when Steed required help in investigating the underworld. Ever resourceful, Keel did not hesitate to become involved in the action and used his extensive knowledge of medical matters to confuse and wilfully mislead villains with whom he came into contact.

Ian Hendry strived to make the series look impressive, and one day when he and Patrick Macnee were in The Anglers pub next to the studios on Broom Road, he was heard to voice his opinion that they should pull out all the stops to make *The Avengers* pure quality.

1.04 – 'Nightmare'

On Saturday 28 January 1961, the episode 'Nightmare' – involving someone trying to kill Dr Keel after mistaking him for a missing scientist called Professor Braintree – was transmitted live. It was penned by Terence Feely and utilised the director/designer combination of Hammond and Fuest, who had worked together on 'Brought to Book'.

The storyline of this episode was extensively rewritten, presumably by one of the story editors, before being handed back to Feely to provide the draft script. This procedure was something that producer Leonard White was extremely strict about, as he firmly believed that story editors should amend storylines only, and not screenplays. Any alterations required to be made to the script would either be done at short notice by the writer or more likely by the director with assistance from the cast at the rehearsal stage.

On Friday 3 February 1961, Leonard White issued an extensive memo regarding the series format, aimed mainly at his story editors, writers and potential writers; this was basically an outline that specified scripting requirements. White emphasised that Keel and Steed work undercover, identifying criminal activities and getting themselves into a position of trust, so that they can tackle the problem from the inside. He also pointed out that the series was not a typical private detective show, so a storyline where Keel and Steed use traditional investigation methods was not right for them. Further to this, White reinforced that our heroes had no special relationship with the police and that when the chips were down, they could rely on the forces of law and order only to the same degree as any other citizen would. So in dangerous situations the only help Keel, Steed and Carol could rely on was themselves.

The Carol Wilson character was fleshed out a little here. She was the link back to Keel's old life as nothing more than a general practitioner, and although she would sometimes get involved in proceedings, she was not officially part of the undercover team. Neither was she fully aware of the agreement between Steed and Keel, although White indicated that she might have her suspicions. (Due to the lack of surviving visual evidence, there's no telling if this element was ever followed up on by the writers.)

There was also some additional information given for Steed, describing him as being of upper-class background, owning a Rolls Royce, having expertise with firearms and having had some combat training. He was also said to be quick-witted and to ooze old-world charm.

A small section of White's memo was devoted to Steed's superior, One-Ten (who would not appear on screen for several weeks). He was characterised as a highly intelligent man who might have been a university don. He would be the face of the establishment, who gave Steed his assignments, knowing full well that Keel would become involved but considering him nothing more than an amateur.

The directives continued as White maintained that stories/scripts should contain attractive women, plus different and unusual settings that one would not normally expect to be the locale for a TV thriller. Other required inclusions were fleshed-out human characters, enough intrigue to make the audience have to think a little about the unfolding plot, some humour, camaraderie among the regular characters, and as much action as possible within the confines of a live studio production. The final directive reinforced the fact that *The Avengers* was a series and not a serial, and every script had to be a stand-alone presentation, hence no continuity such as running gags from episode to episode. The reasoning behind this was that viewers should be able to watch any episode and be able to get into the format and situations straight away; it was felt that intricate continuity could be alienating and cause them to switch off.

1.05 – 'Crescent Moon'

The next adventure, 'Crescent Moon', was scripted by the writing partnership of Geoffrey Bellman and John Whitney, though based on a story by Patrick Brawn, and was originally drafted under the title 'Kidnapping by Consent'. It involved a character named General Mendoza faking both his own death and the kidnapping of his daughter in order to foil a plot by his wife and another man named Vasco to seize his money.

Bellman and Whitney had experience in this genre, having already written scripts for the early ITV crime dramas *Shadow Squad*, *Crime Sheet* and *Knight Errant 59*. After *The Avengers*, they would go on to work for ATV, coming up with the format for a department store-set soap, which became *Harpers West One*, and serving as joint story editors on the medical crime drama *The Hidden Truth*. They would then work intermittently on shows like *The Plane Makers* and the undercover cop series *GS5*, before in 1967 creating for ATV the crime series *The Informer*, which became another vehicle for Ian Hendry. However, after this success the partnership would break up, with Whitney going on to become the Director General of the IBA and Bellman collaborating with his wife Rosemary as a writing team.

'Crescent Moon' went out live on Saturday 4 February 1961 under the control of director John Knight, whose experience of videotaped productions stretched back to 1955 on the BBC anthology series *Appointment with Drama*. After moving across to ABC, he had gained directing credits on *Hour of Mystery*, *Armchair Theatre* and all 39 episodes of the comedy film series *Glencannon*. Knight was another veteran of *Police Surgeon*, making him an obvious choice for *The Avengers*. The sets on this occasion were provided by in-house designer and jazz music expert Alpho O'Reilly, who had fulfilled the same role on 'Hot Snow' and was another who had worked on both *Police Surgeon* and *Armchair Theatre*.

Less than four weeks after his previous lengthy memo, White issued another one with additional comments. Dated 27 February, it stressed that, as a new series, *The Avengers* was facing competition from other shows that were already established and, as such, the episodes they were producing had not only to maintain a high quality, but also to improve on it. White also noted that the title *The Avengers* needed to be borne in mind, and thus the storylines ought to reflect the element of avenging.

White had observed that the Keel storylines were proving more difficult to write, so he helpfully suggested that the writers find a way to get the doctor closer to the victims of crime, hence giving him a legitimate reason for his involvement. Hence a Keel story and a Steed story should be two totally different scenarios and should not be transferable from one character to the other.

Finishing off, White once again reminded writers that the stories should take place in surroundings dissimilar to those of standard TV thrillers. He suggested that Macnee's horse racing background and Hendry's motorcycle stunt team experience could provide sparks of inspiration for an episode idea (though in the event neither would).

The Avengers comes to ATV

Ever since ITV had been formed in 1955, there had been a rivalry between ABC and ATV, which was not helped by some complicated inter-company financial arrangements regarding the showing of each other's programmes. If ATV London transmitted an ABC show over the weekend, then they had to pay a third of the production cost, but if the situation was reversed, ABC were expected to pick-up two-thirds of the cost, as they broadcast in two regions: the Midlands and the North. Not only did this situation give ATV a financial advantage, but ABC found themselves effectively obliged to screen ATV shows – otherwise, they would risk having their programming go unseen in London, the most important television market in the country.

The head of ATV, Lew Grade, liked the arrangement, but his opposite number at ABC, Howard Thomas, was naturally unhappy, and their weekly meetings at Great Cumberland Street, London, were usually long and loud. Grade would typically express the view that ABC should restrict themselves to religious and children's programmes plus sports coverage, for which he would gladly pay a third of the production cost; but when it came to drama, variety and comedy, he considered ATV was the natural ITV company to handle those requirements. Thomas would reply that ATV could make all the drama, variety and comedy programmes for the weekend, but only if they could do so better and less expensively than ABC could. At this point both men would produce various invoices that the other company had not yet paid. The meetings would generally conclude with harsh words on both sides. However, Grade never held a grudge and would often call Thomas on the telephone later in the day and not even mention the earlier meeting. Eventually, Grade conceded and scheduled *The Avengers* in the ATV London region. Ever the negotiator, though, he fought his corner, agreeing only on fortnightly transmissions, alternating with the second season of ATV's own press-room drama *Deadline Midnight*.

On Friday 10 February 1961, the production crew at Teddington were advised that the majority of the ITV regions that were not currently transmitting *The Avengers* would be coming on board, starting on 18 March with 'Hot Snow' and continuing on 1 April with 'Brought to Book'. Then, having shown their viewers how Keel and Steed came together in these first two episodes, they would join the current ABC transmissions on 15 April with the episode 'Dance with Death'.

1.06 – 'Girl on the Trapeze'

The following day, Saturday 11 February 1961, 'Girl on the Trapeze' was transmitted live, with filmed inserts fed into proceedings as and when required. These inserts included stock footage of a lion-taming act and other circus performers, and night-time location work filmed on Battersea Bridge, London SW10. Both actor Ian Gardiner (credited as a policeman) and Ian Hendry were on location, the latter performing his own stunt work by taking a run up to some locked gates, leaping onto them and then jumping down to gain access to the riverbank.

The episode's circus storyline had been suggested to the producers by Hendry, who had spent time earlier in his career working as a clown. He had outlined a scenario that omitted Steed altogether (although Macnee nevertheless received his customary credit on the opening titles), but still played as a two-hander, this time between himself and Ingrid Hafner.

Having the adventure centre around a circus fulfilled Leonard White's desire to have stories with unusual settings. The script was written by a newcomer to television, Dennis Spooner, who originally called his two page outline 'Man on the Trapeze'. Don Leaver returned to direct, and assembled a cast that included Kenneth J Warren, Edwin Richfield (in the first of six guest-starring roles in the series) and, in an early uncredited role, Patricia Haines playing the trapeze artist Katrina Sandor. An eleventh-hour casting change during rehearsals saw actress Nadja Regin replaced by Mia Karam in the role of Anna Danilov. The transmission did not run entirely to plan, as the cast and crew performed the teleplay quicker on the night than they had during rehearsals, and the episode ran under Leaver's estimated timing by a minute and 40 seconds.

Spooner appears to have drawn inspiration from the Moscow State Circus for his fictional Radeck State Circus, as the performers speak with East European accents. In the process he created the first espionage storyline for the series, which unsurprisingly was one of Hendry's favourites.

Hafner carries some of the plotline as Carol Wilson, who takes it upon herself to deal with Vera, the female member of the conspiracy, which she does with a mixture of stealth and action by injecting the circus performer with a sedative and rendering her unconscious. While Carol is not generally regarded as an official Avengergirl, this is possibly where the spark of the idea first came from and was tried out.

It seems that a piece of dialogue where Keel tells Superintendent Lewis 'not to take a powder,' indicating that he and his officers should stay in the proximity, was an afterthought, as the original script simply had the accompanying sergeant becoming suspicious with the situation at the circus. The fight scene at the episode's conclusion, devised by Leaver, looked both cluttered and haphazard and nothing like the slick ones to come later in the series. The caption at the end of the closing credits read, 'The Avengers – Next Week – Diamond Cut Diamond.'

1.07 – 'Diamond Cut Diamond'

As viewers had been advised, 'Diamond Cut Diamond', which was primarily a Steed story, was transmitted live on Saturday 18 February, with Anglia coming on board to start transmitting *The Avengers* in preference to *Theatre 70* from ATV London. The script – involving Steed posing as an air steward in order to infiltrate and put a stop to a diamond-smuggling racket – was penned by Max Marquis, who had been responsible for an episode of the ITC film series *Interpol Calling* the previous year, and would be his only contribution to *The Avengers*. The Hammond/Fuest combination worked together again on direction and design. Douglas Muir appeared for the first time as Steed's boss, One-Ten, showing that despite the agent appearing to be a law unto himself, there was someone to whom he was accountable. One-Ten replaced Five as presumably Heron

Carvic was unavailable to reprise that role. This resulted in Muir becoming a semi-regular in the series, and overall he would feature in 11 episodes.

Showing that he was available for productions other than *The Avengers*, Hendry assumed the lead in Granada's 'Ben Spray', an instalment of *Television Playhouse*, screened across the ITV network on Thursday 23 February. Written by Peter Nichols, this social comedy would spawn a sequel, 'Ben Again', two years later, though on that occasion Dinsdale Landen would play the title character.

1.08 – 'The Radioactive Man'

The cast and crew assembled at Teddington Studios again on Saturday 25 February 1961 to execute another live transmission, this time for an episode called 'The Radioactive Man'. The script for this was credited to Fred Edge and, unlike all the others written for *The Avengers* so far, was not an original but an adaptation, from a Canadian television play. The source material by Edge was an instalment of the CBC-produced *General Motors Theatre* plays strand. Also called 'The Radioactive Man', it was transmitted in Canada on Tuesday 14 January 1958. Subsequently, it was one of a number of CBC plays sold to the BBC, who then aired it under their *Canadian Television Theatre* banner on Wednesday 28 January 1959.

Originally planned as the fifth episode into production, 'The Radioactive Man' was delayed while Patrick Brawn adapted Edge's play script for *The Avengers* – which involved some major changes. The names Marko, Mary and Milan were used for characters in both productions, but the original's central role of Shore, played by Canadian actor Cecil (Cec) Linder, was split between Keel and Steed, resulting in the latter being missing for most of the episode. The plot involved an illegal immigrant, Marko, trying to avoid being found and deported by the authorities, who are actually trying to catch him because he is unwittingly carrying a radioactive isotope that could be fatal to anyone in his vicinity.

Robert Tronson directed the episode, his only work on *The Avengers*. He cast, amongst others, noted actors George Pravda and Gerald Sim. However, Sim became unavailable at short notice, prompting the hiring of Arthur Lawrence to take over his part. This change came too late to be reflected in *TV Times*, which had already been provided with a cast listing including Sim.

There were a number of 35mm film inserts fed into the recording by telecine, including footage of railway sidings and some night-time shots involving a red telephone box, an alleyway and a montage of police cars.

White produced another memo on 2 March, this one for the attention of Bill Thom, head of Teddington Studios' small film unit. This noted that filmed inserts were adding considerable quality to *The Avengers*, but pointed out that the production was restricted to arranging exterior shooting only after rehearsals were already under way, when the floor manager attached to the episode could begin consulting the owners of properties with regard to filming there. White considered that this situation needed altering, hoping that one of Thom's staff could assume the role of location manager whenever required and supervise arrangements for exterior filming well in advance.

1.09 – 'Ashes of Roses'

'Ashes of Roses' was the final episode to be broadcast live, and it went out on Saturday

4 March 1961. From this point on, the crew would revert to recording *The Avengers* in advance of transmission. The deal between ABC and ATV had proved to be beneficial in one way, as the production treadmill the crew were on had slowed down, the situation allowing them double the time they'd previously had to rehearse and prepare episodes. Another consequence of this was that the requirement for scripts that concentrated on one of the central characters at the expense of the other would now be dispensed with, so that henceforth Keel and Steed would generally feature as joint leads.

The screenplay for 'Ashes of Roses' came from the husband-and-wife writing team of Peter Ling and Sheilagh Ward, with Don Leaver assuming the director's chair once again to supervise a small cast, including actor Mark Eden. The plot concerned Steed enlisting Carol's help to investigate a scheme by Olive and Jacques Beronne to have their own hair salon burned down by an arsonist, Mendelssohn, in order to collect the insurance money.

This adventure also featured Steed's Great Dane, which Macnee had christened Puppy. The crew considered this name ludicrous, but Macnee claimed it was an example of reverse thinking, explaining that Robin Hood's sidekick Little John was his motivation. Juno was the animal's real name, and it had previously appeared in both *Ivanhoe* and *Mark Sabre*. It had been trained by Barbara Woodhouse, who at the time specialised in providing dogs for television productions but in the 1980s would become a minor celebrity in her own right by virtue of her short-lived series *Training Dogs the Woodhouse Way*. Juno was later killed in an accident on the London underground while on the way to Teddington Studios.

This episode was basically a two-hander for Macnee and Ingrid Hafner, with Keel's involvement reduced to a supporting one after Carol is enticed by Steed into assisting him with an investigation focusing on a series of arson attacks and then finding herself in great danger. Leonard White had indicated in a 23 December 1960 memo to Don Leaver that a future screenplay should feature Carol prominently, though originally this was envisaged as being played out with Keel. The plot element of Steed involving an innocent young woman in the criminal underworld would be expanded upon in the following season, with the character Venus Smith, and this episode could well be where the spark of that idea came from.

The camera script indicates that there was some night-time location filming done, it part to meet the requirement of a 50-second scene on a platform at Victoria Railway Station, Victoria Street, London SW1. This would have been captured prior to the taping of the episode by a small film unit minus any sound provision. The script also indicates that a promotional trailer was recorded in Studio 2 between 7.55 pm and 8.00 pm on 4 March, in advance of that evening's live transmission.

The production assistant for this episode was Verity Lambert, who would later transfer across to the BBC at the invitation of Sydney Newman to become the first producer of *Doctor Who*. All of the production crew for *The Avengers* at this time were drawn from a pool of staff and technicians based at Teddington Studios, who would work as and when required on whatever production needed their involvement. Another who was involved with the first season of *The Avengers* was senior cameraman Tom Clegg, who later became an actor, appearing in the well-remembered role of Oddbod in *Carry on Screaming*, and then a director on the various *Sharpe* television movies.

On 7 May Bill Thom responded to White's memo received five days previously, agreeing with his observations regarding the arranging of location filming. However, he regretted that due to increased workloads for his department, there was no way that he could accommodate additional duties for a member of his staff. Suggesting an alternative, Thom pointed out that a videotape floor manager based at Teddington could perform the function; or, if the budget could stand it, a freelance production manager could be drafted in as and when required.

1.10 – 'Hunt the Man Down'

Viewers in the two ABC regions, who had been watching *The Avengers* since December 1960, got a surprise on Saturday 11 March 1961 when, instead of their usual ration of weekly action and adventure, they were presented with the first episode of the second season of *Deadline Midnight*. A day later, it was all systems go again at Teddington, when Richard Harris's second script for *The Avengers*, 'Hunt the Man Down', was recorded under the direction of Peter Hammond, who was once again working in conjunction with designer Robert Fuest. The plot involved a man named Frank Preston, who upon his release from prison attempts to retrieve a stash of money hidden away from an earlier robbery, while avoiding the attentions of a group of thugs. With this episode, the production returned to pre-recording episodes in advance of transmission – which in this instance occurred six days later.

A memo from Leonard White brought about the construction of a new standing set for Keel's surgery. This made its initial appearance in this episode, resulting in the surgery sporting a darker colour scheme than before and having more of a medical look about it.

Location filming had taken place the week before in Wood Street, London EC2, for both day and night-time scenes, featuring Hendry and Hafner plus fellow actors Maurice Good, Gerry Duggan and Nicholas Selby. Utilising a small number of technicians out on location, Hammond captured the required footage on 35mm film using a tripod-mounted Arriflex camera.

After its low-key opening in the two ABC regions, *The Avengers* was about to get another bite at the cherry, as the date when the majority of the ITV regional companies began screening the show drew closer. Obviously wanting to make a good impression and eradicate any irregularities in the series before they had a chance to cause widespread problems on the ITV network, Leonard White distributed another memo at Teddington Studios. His major concern was the amount of alcoholic drink being consumed in the episodes by the lead characters, especially Keel, which he acknowledged had possibly been included in the scripts to pad them out to the required length. However, as it showed the characters in a bad light, he insisted that the practice cease immediately.

This brought him nicely to his next point, as he stressed to the whole crew that it was imperative that the episode timings taken during the rehearsal process be accurate, so they could produce the required running time of 53 minutes and 30 seconds when recording. White feared that an episode would run short on recording (as had happened with 'Girl on the Trapeze') and then, when transmitted, would leave the various ITV regional companies with a hole several minutes long in their schedules, which would not make either the production team or ABC very popular. As a counter measure to try to prevent this, the scriptwriters had been instructed to write slightly longer scripts; but this made it the responsibility of White as the producer, along with the director and the stage manager, to dictate a fast pace at the recording stage to make certain that the episodes did not overrun instead.

White also reminded the directors and story editors that daily alterations to the rehearsal script needed to be transferred to the master script, which was always located in the script department. Further to this, he felt that he should reinforce the basics regarding the narrative of scripts, warning writers, story editors and directors not to make plots overly complicated.

The second and bigger opening night for *The Avengers* was marked by the show being featured in a photographic cover on the London edition of the *TV Times* dated 12 to 18 March. This depicted Hendry, Hafner and Macnee. The magazine also included a short article on page 11 about the apparently-new series.

Then, on 18 March, while ABC Midlands, ABC North and Anglia showed *Hunt the Man Down*, ATV London, Southern Television, TWW (Television Wales and the West), Tyne Tees and Ulster all got to know Keel and Steed, as they screened 'Hot Snow'. However, after another episode of *Deadline Midnight* on 25 March, only ATV London, Southern and Tyne Tees followed through by screening 'Brought to Book' on 1 April; for some unfathomable reason, TWW and Ulster transmitted an episode of the American private detective show *77 Sunset Strip* instead. In short, TWW and Ulster made the strange decision not to screen what was the second part of *The Avengers'* pilot story.

1.11 – 'Please Don't Feed the Animals'

Dennis Spooner returned to the series with his second script, 'Please Don't Feed the Animals'. Taking White's memo regarding unusual story settings on board, this one would involve events taking place in a private zoo being used as a drop-off point for government secrets being leaked by compromised officials to a blackmailer. The director was Dennis Vance. Born on 18 March 1924 in Birkenhead, Cheshire, Vance was a genuine all-rounder in British television. Primarily known as both a director and producer, he also tried his hand at both acting and writing. At the time, he was working for ABC, having directed instalments of both *Armchair Theatre* and *Inside Story*, so his services were also called upon for 'Please Don't Feed the Animals', which would be his only contribution to *The Avengers*.

1.12 – 'Dance with Death'

The second offering from Peter Ling and Sheilagh Ward, 'Dance with Death' underwent recording at Teddington Studios on Thursday 13 April 1961. It was directed by Don Leaver, who brought together an impressive guest cast that included Caroline Blakiston, Angela Douglas and – previously used by Leaver in an episode of *Police Surgeon* – Geoffrey Palmer. The plot revolved around Dr Keel being framed for the murder of one of his patients; the real killer is a dance school pianist who electrocutes his victims in the bath.

In a scene where Keel visits the cinema, viewers were treated to a clip of the recently-released film *The Rebel* starring Tony Hancock, which had been made by ABC's parent company ABPC.

New to *The Avengers* this time was designer James Goddard, who would work on nine episodes altogether in this capacity, but would later make more of an impact in television circles as a director, eventually amassing a vast number of credits on many different series.

On Saturday 15 April, transmissions of *The Avengers* finally converged, as all eight ITV regions that took the series screened the same episode, 'Dance with Death', at the same time, 10.00 pm. Naturally ABC were relieved that their product was now reaching a wider audience. On the strength of this partial networking, both Hendry and Macnee were encouraged to contribute new ideas to the show, but the latter still saw it as only another acting job, as he reinforced when interviewed in the *TV Times* dated 21 April: 'I have a lovely little house right on the beach in Malibu, California. I'll be back there soon. I haven't any jobs lined up in the States, but who's worrying?'

1.13 – 'One for the Mortuary'

Brian Clemens' second screenplay for the series, 'One for the Mortuary', was recorded on Thursday 27 April 1961 between 6.00 pm and 7.00 pm, having had its first read-through at The Tower on 14 April, with Hammond and Fuest working together again. The episode dealt with typical '60s spy fare – a microdot containing a secret medical formula being smuggled to Geneva – with the majority of the action taking place in Switzerland, making it one of only a handful of episodes set in a foreign country, though in reality the production never left the UK. Hammond cast actor Steven Scott as a hotel concierge, a role that went unbilled on the closing credits and in television listings magazines.

'One for the Mortuary' was special in that it was the first episode to have a set of images taken of it on transmission by commercial photographer John Cura, who had developed a stills camera that could capture small but clear pictures directly from a television screen. Cura had launched his business, under the trading name Tele-snaps, in the late 1940s after first approaching the BBC and providing examples of his work. The Corporation's legal department had eventually concluded that the copyright laws of the time did not cover the televised image, and so had given permission for Cura to go ahead. They specified that he could photograph only those actors and actresses who had given their prior permission; but obviously, to amass the 250,000-plus images he made during his career, he must have in the main ignored that condition. He usually took around 70 to 80 snaps per episode of a show, and these became a standard reference source for both production personnel and performers who wanted a visual record of their work in an era before the advent of the domestic video recorder. Having becoming aware of the Tele-snaps service, Leonard White hired Cura to start photographing *The Avengers*, which resulted in a large amount of snaps covering the last 14 episodes of the first season. With the loss of the actual videotaped programmes, these are without doubt an extremely valuable source of information, giving an indication of what the series looked like on screen.

'One for the Mortuary' was transmitted at 10.00 pm on Saturday 29 April, with the eight ITV regions already taking the show being joined by the newly-formed Westward Television, who screened the episode as part of their opening night's programming.

1.14 – 'The Springers'

'The Springers' was the second script contribution by John Whitney and Geoffrey Bellman. The storyline involved Keel going undercover at Her Majesty's pleasure in a prison to help Steed uncover an escape route. Several 35mm film inserts were shot on location, including of Keel escaping from the prison and boarding a barge, and then of the vessel departing from its mooring.

Rehearsals for the episode got under way at The Tower in Hammersmith, London W6 at 2.30 pm on Friday 28 April – the day prior to transmission of 'One for the Mortuary' – with the first read-through of the script.

Camera rehearsals began in Studio 2 at Teddington at 10.30 am on 10 May. The recording took place the following evening between 6.00 pm and 7.00 pm. The episode took longer to complete than director Don Leaver's earlier timings suggested, overrunning by over a minute and a half.

After using him in the *Police Surgeon* episode 'A Home of Her Own', Leaver cast Frank Gatliff alongside Douglas Muir, appearing again as One-Ten, and Brian Murphy, who would later become famous for his roles in the ITV sitcoms *Man about the House* and *George and Mildred*.

ABC voiced concerns regarding this episode as it overspent its budget allocation by just over £500. Later in the season the company would acknowledge that the series was generally costing more to produce than originally estimated and would increase the budget to £4,500 per episode.

Mid-season developments

ABC publicist Marie Donaldson wrote to the *TV Times* features editor Eric Linden on 17 May 1961, suggesting that the magazine should run articles on both Ian Hendry and Patrick Macnee to promote *The Avengers*. Expanding the idea further, Donaldson offered the services of the series' story editors to assist in providing background to the Keel and Steed characters for an amusing piece that mixed fact with fiction. As a result of Donaldson's encouragement, the magazine would respond by running features on the series in both June and July.

Meanwhile, on the same day, Leonard White issued a further memo to his senior production staff, explaining that he would soon have to go into hospital, which he estimated would prevent him from participating in the production for two to three weeks. In White's absence, Sydney Newman would stand in as temporary producer, assisted by the story editors. White emphasised the importance of always having two episodes in rehearsal, to allow a choice of recording material, and warned that both the leads would be requiring time off for holidays sometime during the summer. An encouraging point of information in the memo was that on its 13 May transmission, 'The Springers' had attracted sufficient viewers to be the highest-rated programme in both the Midlands and North regions for that evening.

Further to this, White enumerated several items that he felt needed looking into. These included finding another script where Ingrid Hafner could play a sizeable role, after her impressive performances in 'Ashes of Roses' and 'Girl on the Trapeze'. The opinion was also expressed that the team needed to develop a 'doubles' episode involving Keel. It was noted, too, that the glamorous elements within the show were tending to be overshadowed by the gritty and lowlife qualities. White indicated it was imperative that the production should assemble a team of three or four writers who understood the show, but added that buying existing screenplays should not be out of the question. White also suggested, 'We should follow up the idea of using Angela Douglas again as a foil for Steed. You remember that she was the fair young dance instructress in "Dance with Death". She had a very good sense of comedy.'

Two days later, White sent a memo to Norman Kay, a noted composer who appears to have been acting as musical supervisor on *The Avengers* at this time, arranging for Johnny Dankworth to record another version of the theme tune and various incidental music cues and stings for use in the series. This was partly motivated by the fact that ABC were considering expanding the season from 26 to 39 episodes. White asked Kay to instruct Dankworth as to what type of incidental cues were required, the aim being to cut back the series' reliance on stock library tracks.

1.15 – 'The Frighteners'

'The Frighteners', recorded on Thursday 25 May 1961 and transmitted two days later, is one of only two complete first season episodes known still to survive – indeed it was for many years believed to be the only complete one, until the discovery of a copy of 'Girl on the Trapeze.'

The episode's script was credited to Berkeley Mather. According to the edition of *TV Times* published on Friday 21 April 1961, Mather was a pseudonym for Lieutenant Colonel Jasper Davies, who had served in the Royal Artillery and worked as an intelligence officer in Cyprus. He had already written for the television film series *African Patrol*. However, what *TV Times* failed to realise was that the name Jasper Davies was itself another pseudonym, for John Evan Weston Davies, who had indeed served as a Lieutenant Colonel in the Indian Army and had recently become a novelist. As Mather, Davies would supply various screenplays for both films and television throughout the '60s, as well as write espionage novels. However, perhaps Davies' greatest claim to fame was having a hand in the screenplay for the first James Bond movie, *Dr No*.

For research on his script for *The Avengers*, Davies ventured into the London underworld, accompanied by a couple of ex-high ranking police officers, to gain first-hand experience and thus ensure the authenticity of both characters and situations. The plot he came up with involved a wealthy businessman, Sir Thomas Waller, hiring a gang of thugs known as the Frighteners to scare off his daughter's unsuitable boyfriend.

The episode was again designed by Robert Fuest and directed by Peter Hammond, who put together a cast that included Stratford Johns and Philip Locke.

Stock film footage provided establishing shots of Berwick Street market plus night-time London, via shots of Coventry Street and Shaftesbury Avenue. These were all fed into the recording by telecine where required.

Hammond shot part of one scene through a parrot's cage and demonstrated further flair by the clever use of mirrors, first in a scene set in a restaurant and later with another one in Keel's surgery. Like Hendry, Hammond wanted to turn all the situations in the series on their head and present something as fresh and original as possible: definitely not clichéd or predictable.

The problems sometimes encountered when doing an 'as live' production are all too apparent in this episode. In one scene, Philip Locke got his lines confused, snapping 'And what about your flippin' neck?' when his character was supposed to be referring to another's face. Having fluffed the dialogue, Locke quickly recovered by ad-libbing the correct ending to the line, 'and face? One squirt of lemonade and you were screaming …' (This referred to a bluff by Keel involving a syringe supposedly full of acid.)

Hendry and Macnee were clearly enjoying themselves during recording of the episode, as after a line where Steed impersonates the character Moxon delivering a veiled threat with a cut-throat razor, both actors burst into laughter, although they managed to continue with their dialogue (only just, in Macnee's case) and proceed with the production.

The closing credits ended with the caption: 'Next Episode – June 10th – The Yellow Needle.'

1.16 – 'The Yellow Needle'

On Wednesday 31 May 1961, the company secretary of Iris Productions, C J Orr, forwarded a new contract for 13 episodes (with an option for 11 more) to Ian Hendry's agents, Fraser and Dunlop Ltd of Regent Street, London. Contained within the document was a provision for Hendry also to appear in two instalments of *Armchair Theatre*, whenever suitable roles became available, in which case he would be temporarily written out of *The Avengers* to allow both rehearsal and recording time. (In the event, Hendry would appear in only one *Armchair Theatre*.) Unlike his previous contract, where he was paid only for the actual recording of episodes, Hendry would now also receive a rehearsal fee.

The next episode, initially entitled 'Plague', came from Irishman Patrick Campbell, who had written film and television scripts throughout the '50s to augment his main career as a newspaper columnist and author. After *The Avengers*, he would continue briefly as a scriptwriter, contributing solitary screenplays to two other ITV shows, *Ghost Squad* and *The Sentimental Agent*, before starting to appear on television talk shows and then having a 12 year stint as a panellist on the BBC game show *Call My Bluff*.

The episode was renamed 'The Yellow Needle' after a rewrite by scriptwriter/ actor Reed de Rouen, who had by this point taken over from Patrick Brawn as *The Avengers'* second story editor. It concerned a plot to murder an African diplomat on a visit to London to try to negotiate independence for his country, Tenebra. Recording took place on Thursday 8 June. Transmission followed two days later. This marked *The Avengers'* debut on Scottish Television, who had decided to join the feed, although they declined to start with the introductory episodes 'Hot Snow' and 'Brought to Book'. Border and Grampian were now the only ITV regional broadcasters not taking the series.

This episode was another to feature Juno playing Steed's faithful Great Dane, Puppy. Location work involving actor Andre Dakar was done alongside the River Thames in London, using 35mm film that cost £150. Stock film footage of an airliner in flight was also utilised, to indicate Steed making a journey to Africa. A consultant, Dr Richard Yates, was employed by the production to make certain that all medical elements of the storyline were accurate. Unfortunately, this was another episode that went over budget, costing just over £180 more than allocated.

1.17 – 'Death on the Slipway'

'Death on the Slipway' by James Mitchell was the next episode into production. Its director, Peter Hammond, put together an excellent guest cast that included Frank Thornton, Nyree Dawn Porter, Tom Adams and Peter Arne, as well as Douglas Muir once again playing One-Ten.

The episode offered an espionage storyline dealing with a nuclear submarine and a foreign agent blackmailing a dockyard employee to plant a bomb on the vessel. It focused on Steed, hardly involved Keel and omitted Carol Wilson altogether – although it did feature the third and final appearance of Puppy.

Recording took place on Thursday 22 June. Transmission, as usual at this point, followed two days later; however, the series was now moved from its original time slot of 10.00 pm to the earlier one of 8.50 pm, indicating it was gaining in popularity. The rescheduling was part of a summer reorganisation that saw *The Avengers* effectively replacing *77 Sunset Strip* in most regions and now being transmitted opposite the BBC's popular US import courtroom drama *Perry Mason*.

Meanwhile, Hendry and Macnee had become drinking buddies and regularly got together to watch *The Avengers'* Saturday night transmissions, complete with a bottle of whisky, of which they consumed half each. Both believed the series to be exceptional – although Macnee would later reconsider, thinking that the alcohol had played a major part in their opinions. Macnee also reckoned that *The Avengers* was influenced by an American crime series called *New York Confidential*, which had been screened in the States in 1958 and in the UK the following year by Associated-Rediffusion. As a hard-hitting TV series that dealt with criminal lowlifes, *New York Confidential* attempted to incorporate elements of film noir; and to a degree so did *The Avengers* with its shadowy, confined sets.

1.18 – 'Double Danger'

Scriptwriter Gerald Verner (aka Robert Stuart Pringle) met both Hendry and Macnee sometime during April 1961 in order to discuss their characters and gain insight into the style of *The Avengers* in preparation for his forthcoming episode 'Double Danger' (working title: 'Confession from a Dead Man') – which was to prove a controversial one.

The plot involved Keel being held prisoner to treat a man injured during a diamond robbery, sending a prescription to Carol complete with a coded message for her to involve Steed and get him to investigate.

The first read-through of the episode's script took place on Monday 26 June at The Tower in Hammersmith. Rehearsals got under way later the same day. However, the script was considered unsatisfactory and was subjected to heavy revision by another writer, John Lucarotti, who was temporarily attached to *The Avengers'* production team at this point as an assistant story editor. Verner was unhappy with these rewrites, claiming that the story no longer made sense.

The following day, negotiations that were taking place between ITV and the actors' union Equity and the Variety Artistes' Federation regarding increased salaries ground to a halt. This raised the prospect of strike action disrupting production on *The Avengers* at some point in the future.

Camera rehearsals for 'Double Danger' started in Studio 2 at Teddington on Wednesday 5 July at 10.30 am. As usual, they continued until 9.30 pm, including two one-hour breaks during the day. The cast and crew reassembled the following morning at 10.00 am for additional rehearsals, ending with a full dress rehearsal at 4.30 pm. Then, after a break for tea and the application of make-up, the episode was recorded between 6.00 pm and 7.00 pm.

Roger Jenkins directed on what would be his first of only two episodes of the series. A jailbreak sequence was shot on location in advance on 35mm film. This was originally scripted to take place at night, though in the event it was done during daylight hours, probably to reduce costs. Additional location shooting did take place at night to establish a houseboat setting, though logically this would have been done somewhere close to the studio lot, alongside the River Thames.

Five days after the episode's transmission on Saturday 8 July, a review in *The Stage and Television Today* gave it a particularly negative assessment, describing it as 'reminiscent of a poor second feature film, with unrealistic gangster types ...' Gerald Verner was quick to defend himself. He sent the publication a letter that appeared in the subsequent issue, dated 20 July, stating that although his name was on the episode it bore little resemblance to his original script. Further to this, he pointed out that he had been writing for about 20 years, on a mixture of television productions, stage plays and novels, and so he should know all about plot construction, characterisation, dialogue and storytelling.

Although he had been pencilled in to write more episodes of *The Avengers*, this disagreement curtailed Verner's involvement. In fact he never wrote for television again, preferring to stick to novels and short stories, where he had much more control over the finished product.

1.19 – 'Toy Trap'

The nineteenth episode was entitled 'Toy Trap'. Australian writer Bill Strutton supplied a strong screenplay that dealt with adult themes and also contained a scene where Keel confronts Steed over his ruthless methods, Steed having used the doctor's ward Bunty Seton in an attempt to ensnare the leader of a vice ring pressurising young women into prostitution. In fact, Keel and Steed would be depicted almost coming to blows.

Camera rehearsals for the episode began at 10.30 am on Wednesday 19 July 1961 in Studio 2 at Teddington under the direction of Don Leaver. Recording then took place on Thursday 20 July, after the majority of the day had been filled with more rehearsals. The actual taping took place between 8.00 pm and 9.00 pm – a departure from the usual 6.00 pm to 7.00 pm slot.

The Avengers proved to be a stepping stone to success for this episode's floor manager, Mike Vardy, who later graduated to become a director on a great many television productions through to the end of the '90s.

Thinking ahead, Leonard White contacted his senior crew members on 27 July, suggesting that they should consider incorporating a lighter vein into the episodes scheduled to be transmitted over Christmas and the New Year, in order to reflect the festive season. The fact that this was under consideration indicated that – in reaction to the aforementioned threat of industrial action – plans had already been put in place for screenings of the series to be temporarily suspended at some point over the coming months and recommenced toward the conclusion of 1961. (In the event, no festive elements would actually be included in the forthcoming episodes.)

1.20 – 'Tunnel of Fear'

Recorded on Thursday 3 August 1961, 'Tunnel of Fear' came from the typewriter of John Kruse. This would be his only screenplay for *The Avengers*, although he would go on to be one of main scriptwriters on the popular series *The Saint*. This would also be director Guy Verney's only outing on *The Avengers*, after his recent work on other ABC productions such as *Inside Story* and the various *Pathfinders* children's serials and on Associated-Rediffusion's soap *Emergency-Ward 10*.

Having already used actor Murray Hayne in the ABC seaboard soap *All Aboard*, Verney cast him in 'Tunnel of Fear' as the character Harry Black, an ex-convict leaking top secret information into Europe under cover of a ghost train ride at a funfair in Southend. However, Hayne was ultimately unable to accept the part, and was replaced by Anthony Bate. This change must have occurred just before rehearsals began, as the *TV Times* and other listings magazines of the day, which were printed at least two weeks in advance, all showed Hayne as playing the part. Hayne, who was the son-in-law of One-Ten actor Douglas Muir, would eventually get to appear in *The Avengers*, though he would have to wait another seven years before being cast in the episode 'My Wildest Dream'.

1.21 – 'The Far Distant Dead'

Studio 2 at Teddington was once again the venue when camera rehearsals began on Monday 13 August 1961 for John Lucarotti's screenplay 'The Far Distant Dead', a now-rare solo outing for Keel, set partly in a cyclone-ravaged Mexico and partly in France. Peter Hammond was in control on his seventh episode, bringing together a cast that included Francis de Wolff, Tom Adams and the American writer, actor and story editor Reed de Rouen. As usual, recording took place between 6.00 pm and 7.00 pm the following day, after further rehearsals.

The episode's storyline – involving a crooked financier in France causing the cyclone victims in Mexico to be supplied with 'cooking oil' that is actually hydraulic fluid in wrongly-labelled tins – was unquestionably a strong one, but Sydney Newman considered the subject matter too tough for *The Avengers*; he preferred a balance of light and serious for the show.

The first tie-in merchandise

August 1961 saw the release of '*The Avengers* Theme' on a seven-inch vinyl single, credited to Johnny Dankworth and his Orchestra, on the Columbia label, serial number DB 4695. However, this was not a soundtrack recording, but rather a freshly-recorded version for Columbia's then distributor, EMI.

1.22 – 'Kill the King'

James Mitchell's second script for *The Avengers*, 'Kill the King', involved Steed being assigned to thwart an assassination attempt on King Tenuphon, the ruler of an unstable Far Eastern country called Shanpore, who is in London to sign an oil treaty. The episode went through the usual production process. Camera rehearsals ran from 10.30 am to 9.00 pm on Tuesday 29 August 1961; then, after further rehearsals, recording took place between 6.00 pm and 7.00 pm the following day in Studio 4 at Teddington. This was a sound studio usually dedicated to the recording of incidental music for ABC productions, although in order to have been used for videotape recording it must have had a lighting grid installed at some point. The lack of a control room probably meant that the crew improvised by using the gallery of one of the other studios on site, or even an outside broadcast van parked nearby. Despite proving that Studio 4 could be pressed into service if required, 'Kill the King' would be only episode of the series recorded there.

The recording was augmented with a small amount of 35mm stock film footage, providing establishing shots. Director Roger Jenkins put together a cast that included Burt Kwouk, Patrick Allen, Peter Barkworth and, making her second appearance in the series, Moira Redmond.

Five months after Puppy's first appearance in 'Ashes of Roses', consideration was now being given to Steed having a pet dog on a more regular basis. Leonard White sent both script editor John Bryce and director Don Leaver a press clipping and photograph of a pedigree Great Dane, suggesting that this dog, which went under the name Milady of Hornsgreen, would make the perfect pet for Steed. However, no decision would be taken regarding this proposal until the following season.

When 'Kill the King' was transmitted at 8.50 pm on Saturday 2 September, this brought to a premature end the initial on-air run of *The Avengers*, just as Border had begun showing the series. Following the breakdown several months earlier of negotiations between ITV and Equity regarding performers' salaries, the union had instructed its members not to sign any new contracts after 1 November. Consequently ATV, Granada, Associated-Rediffusion and ABC had decided to hold back – effectively to stockpile – as much pre-recorded material as possible, as when the industrial action started it would severely restrict any new programmes being made. Thus, while the regular transmissions of *The Avengers* were temporarily halted, production of further episodes continued unabated for the time being.

1.23 – 'The Deadly Air'[5]

'The Deadly Air' was the first screenplay by Lester Powell, who had previously been a novelist, news reporter and radio dramatist during his career. John Knight was on hand to direct his second and final entry for this series, attracting a cast that included Ann Bell, Geoffrey Bayldon, Allan Cuthbertson, John Stratton and Douglas Muir, the latter in his familiar role as One-Ten. The plot involved attempted sabotage of a project designed to develop a new vaccine.

1.24 – 'A Change of Bait'

Next came 'A Change of Bait', scripted by Lewis Davidson, who was born on 20 October 1926 in Squaw Valley, California, USA and had recently written screenplays for Associated-Rediffusion's *No Hiding Place* and ITC's *Ghost Squad*. The plotline revolved around corrupt import practices and insurance fraud, with Keel and Steed being alerted to the situation by Carol Wilson.

Camera rehearsals for the episode began on Tuesday 19 September 1961 in Studio 2, and followed the usual pattern. There were three blocks of rehearsals on the first day, lasting eight hours in total, separated by two food breaks of an hour each. There were then another four hours of rehearsals on the following day, with an hour and three-quarters' down time allowed altogether for lunch, tea breaks, applying make-up and additional procedures. There was then a dress rehearsal, followed by the taping of the

---

[5] The numbering of the episodes here and in subsequent entries in this book follows the production order, rather than the transmission order.

episode between 6.00 pm and 7.00 pm that evening

The production was completely studio-bound with the exception of a short piece of 35mm stock film footage of bananas being unloaded at a fruit and vegetable market.

1.25 – 'Dragonsfield'

Terence Feely returned to *The Avengers* with a story outline called 'The Case of the Happy Camper', which was later renamed 'Dragonsfield'. This was committed to videotape at Teddington on Wednesday 27 September 1961. Peter Hammond handled the direction, bringing together a top-notch cast that included Michael Robbins, Ronald Leigh-Hunt, Barbara Shelley and Alfred Burke. It appears that Douglas Muir was unavailable to play One-Ten, so for this one episode only, Steed acquired a temporary superior in the form of One-Fifteen, played by Eric Dodson, who had already portrayed Inspector Anthony in 'The Yellow Needle'.

However, One-Ten was not the only one missing; both Dr Keel and Carol Wilson were also absent, leaving Macnee to take the sole lead as Steed. This may perhaps account for the fact that, when transmissions eventually resumed, a decision was taken to make this episode the last in the first season's on-air run. The last in production order, 'Dead of Winter', would be pulled forward and shown before 'The Deadly Air'.

For the first time since he began working on *The Avengers*, Peter Hammond did not play a double-hander with Robert Fuest, as the design on this episode was entrusted instead to Polish-born Voytek Roman (always credited by his first name only), who had fulfilled the same function on many instalments of *Armchair Theatre*. There was a small amount of night-time location filming undertaken prior to the studio recording.

One notable aspect of the storyline – involving attempted sabotage of a research centre's development of a new material to shield astronauts from radiation – is Steed's ruthlessness, which borders upon the nasty as he threatens to crush a man's fingers in the gear cogs of a water mill unless he reveals the identity of a traitor at the centre.

Exit Ian Hendry

Ian Hendry's absence from 'Dragonsfield' was due to him being otherwise occupied, rehearsing for the role of David Simpson in the *Armchair Theatre* production 'Afternoon of a Nymph'. Sydney Newman, obviously wanting to keep Hendry happy by offering him other parts, had specifically asked Leonard White to rearrange the production schedule on *The Avengers* to accommodate this. Hendry thus spent several weeks away, before returning for the making of 'Dead of Winter'.

However, having taken stock of the situation, including the fact that an Equity strike now seemed inevitable, Hendry decided he would like to leave *The Avengers* altogether after the first season, despite having completed only ten of the 13 episodes he had been contracted for back at the end of May; and it appears that he was released from the series.

This development may not have been entirely unexpected. The concept of replacing Keel with a female character had already apparently been thought of, as when Barbara Shelley was at Teddington working on 'Dragonsfield', she was approached by White with a view to being Hendry's replacement on the show. Shelley thought the offer was a joke and did not take it seriously … and she heard nothing more.

1.26 – 'Dead of Winter'

Eric Paice's first screenplay for *The Avengers* had the original working title 'The Un-Dead'. It pioneered the plot element of a resurrected Nazi organisation, which would later feature in various ITC film series. Here, an ex-Nazi named Schneider plots to bring his Phoenix Party to power by placing its members in cryogenic suspension while all opposition is wiped out in a new world war that he intends to incite.

Robert Fuest returned to design the sets for this episode, working with director Don Leaver. Included in Leaver's guest cast were John Woodvine, in what would be the second of four appearances in the series, and Michael Sarne, who would go on to become both a recording artist and a film director.

The initial read-through began at 10.00 am on Monday 9 October at The Tower in Hammersmith, and production concluded with the end of recording at 7.00 pm on Wednesday 18 October in Studio 2 at Teddington.

'The White Rook'

'Dead of Winter' was not Eric Paice's only try at writing a first season episode for *The Avengers*. He also approached Leonard White with a three page outline for a proposed screenplay called 'The White Rook', in which espionage measures were calculated like the moves on a chessboard. This idea was ultimately rejected, but the plot ran as follows:

An eminent film director seeks to hire Keel's services and persuades him to travel to Berlin to treat his starlet, who is ill and unable to complete work on his current blockbuster. However, when Keel arrives in the German capital he finds that Steed is really the patient, having been shot in the leg while crossing the border between the Communist and Western sectors. For security reasons Steed could not go to hospital. An envelope of top secret information now needs delivering, and Keel agrees to take it on the Berlin underground railway, known as the U-Bahn. While on the train, Keel is attacked from behind and the envelope is stolen, although later Steed assures him it was not important, as there never was any secret information. The exercise – which also involved an American journalist called Bishop, who is a Communist spy – was really about discovering a double agent in the department for which Steed works. The action concludes on the U-Bahn. Steed tricks his traitorous colleague, Morgan, into thinking that they have stopped at an East German station, when in fact it is a West German one with fake signs. Hence, when Morgan is confronted and offers Steed the position of a double agent with the Communist bloc, he fails to realise that they are still in the free world.

In reality, passengers were not allowed to disembark at the East German stations on the West German-controlled U-Bahn, with just one exception: the Berlin Friedrichstraße station, which acted as a border crossing point. Steed's spy boss One-Ten was also included in Paice's scenario, though it never progressed as far as a rehearsal script.

The first season concludes

On 1 November 1961, members of Equity withdrew their services and officially went on strike. The view in *The Avengers'* production office echoed that of everyone else associated with ITV: that the dispute would be resolved in a matter of weeks. In the event, it took five months, during which time ITV programme production was brought to a virtual standstill.

This situation ended any possibility of *The Avengers'* first season being expanded to 39 episodes. It did however allow producer Leonard White and remaining story editor John Bryce – Reed de Rouen having now left the show – the opportunity to amass further scripts, so that there would be plenty of material to choose from when they were given the green light to recommence production.

The edition of *TV Times* dated 1 December 1961 featured a one-page interview with Ingrid Hafner regarding her experiences making *The Avengers*. She described Hendry as a practical joker and Macnee as modest and easygoing, adding that they were the sweetest men she knew.

Transmissions of *The Avengers* resumed on Saturday 9 December at 10.00 pm with 'Dead of Winter' receiving a partial networking. Scottish Television had now dropped the show, but the Grampian region had come on board.

Behind the scenes, Leonard White was busy reformatting *The Avengers*, as he outlined in a memo dated 11 December: '… we have now decided to go ahead with the nightclub singer as a new character for the series.' The nightclub singer was the culmination of months of development, after White had suggested back in May that Angela Douglas's character from 'Dance with Death' would make a good addition to the regular team. Liaising with composer Robert (Bob) Sharples, who had an association with ABC at that time, White sought his opinion regarding casting of the role, and also informed him that including a musical number in an episode would increase its budget by only £200.

'The Deadly Air' became the most watched episode of the season, with over five million households tuning in when it was screened the following Saturday, 16 December, taking it to tenth place in the weekly viewing chart.

'A Change of Bait', although it did not quite manage to match the previous week's figure, was watched by 4.9 million, giving it eighth place in the chart.

'Dragonsfield' kept up the momentum, maintaining the viewing average when it went out on 30 December. Even though this episode saw the show slip back to tenth place in the weekly chart, *The Avengers* appeared to have arrived as a permanent feature in the nation's viewing habits. Unfortunately, though, ABC had now run out of new episodes to transmit.

Keeping the public informed regarding the knock-on effect of the strike, the 29 December editions of both the *Daily Mirror* and the *Daily Express* confirmed that after that weekend both *The Avengers* and *Armchair Theatre* would cease transmissions until further notice.

Finding himself out of work due to circumstances beyond his control and not knowing when the strike would end, Patrick Macnee acquired himself an agent, Richard Hatton, who found him a part in a BBC production of Shakespeare's *A Winter's Tale*. Ian Hendry meanwhile had been searching for work in a different sphere, and had managed to secure himself a feature film contract. Macnee, aghast at the prospect of his friend not returning to *The Avengers*, arranged to meet him for a meal, where he attempted to persuade him to reconsider. Seeing his acting career going off in a new direction, Hendry declined; and without its initial driving force in place to push *The Avengers* forward, Macnee thought the show was finished.

SEASON TWO

INTERCRIME

Tweaking the format

Despite all Equity performers having withdrawn their services from ITV, several companies found ways of getting around the problem. Granada, for instance, managed to keep the sitcoms *Mess Mates* and *Bootsie and Snudge* in production, as the leads were not union members. The same company's *Coronation Street* also soldiered on with only 14 regulars and no supporting cast or extras. ATV meanwhile succeeded in keeping *The Morecambe and Wise Show* running. With their writers on strike, Eric and Ernie simply wrote their own material and did all the sketches themselves. ABC also had a small amount of success in this area, as they produced a second season of the sit-com *Our House* by simply replacing performers who were in the union with others who were not. To augment their meagre output, ITV also resorted to showing old films, American imports and game shows. The dispute eventually ended with both sides agreeing to a final settlement on 28 March 1962, paving the way for ITV to recommence full-blown production of both drama and comedy programming.

Back in December 1961, plans had been drawn up regarding the addition of a new semi-regular character for *The Avengers*, a young nightclub singer called Venus Smith, who was scheduled to make her first appearance in episode 27 of what was then envisioned as a 39-episode season. However, due to the industrial action brought about by Equity, this had been temporarily put on hold.

To compensate for Ian Hendry's departure, Sydney Newman and Leonard White convinced a sceptical Patrick Macnee that he could become the lead on the series, alongside with a new male character as the main sidekick. However, try as they might, Newman and White were initially unable to find an actor suitable to play the proposed new male character. Then one night, Newman watched a news programme on TV and was shocked by the story of a female settler in Kenya whose husband and two children had been murdered by machete-wielding terrorists in the Mau Mau uprising. The woman had had a baby on her back, a belt full of ammunition and a large pistol, which she knew how to use, and this image inspired Newman to start thinking that Steed's new partner need not necessarily be a man.

Taking the elements of courage and coolness under pressure from the woman in Kenya, Newman considered other females who had succeeded in what was then generally regarded as a man's world. Two came to mind: first the eminent American war photographer Margaret Bourke-White; and secondly the famous anthropologist

Margaret Mead, who was also from the States. The following morning, Newman sent White an internal memo in which he recommended a female character could fill the gap left by Hendry. This new character would have a background that included personal tragedy in Kenya, where she had learnt to handle firearms. In addition, she would have a strong sense of morality and be an expert photographer, and would first encounter Steed in her position of anthropologist at the British Museum. Further to this, the character would not scream for Steed's assistance when she got into trouble: instead, she would fight her own battles. Bringing such a radical concept to the series was without doubt a major gamble, and Newman therefore needed to consult Howard Thomas on it. Even ABPC's deputy chairman, Robert Clark, was informed. Ever the salesman, Newman sold the idea to both of them, insisting that his team at Teddington could make the new character work.

Given the green light, White proceeded to create Mrs Catherine (Cathy) Gale and assembled a complete characterisation overview to act as a reference guide for both writers and directors. Starting from the background that Newman had already established, White added that the character had a university education, had been part of an expedition to the Amazon, was sophisticated, though not upper class, and had a strong sense of humour. In addition, she would be a strong-willed and lively person who was equally adept at dealing with a baby or the mechanics of a car. Her motivation in becoming involved with Steed would stem from wanting to stop evil and injustice and to assist those unfortunate enough to have become victims.

With transmissions of season two scheduled to start at the end of September 1962, the team realised that they needed to begin producing episodes quickly, so as an interim measure they devised another male doctor character who could be slotted into already-commissioned scripts. Actor Jon Rollason would be employed to perform the role of Dr Martin King for three episodes, thus allowing Newman and White sufficient time to cast both Cathy Gale and Venus Smith. There would be virtually no rewriting involved with these first three scripts, as the name 'Dr Keel' would simply be crossed out and replaced with 'Dr King'.

In its edition of Thursday 3 May 1962, *The Stage and Television Today* reported that Leonard White was not only producing *The Avengers* but also serving the same function on a new science fiction plays anthology to be made by ABC. Production on the latter, which was subsequently given the title *Out of this World*, was scheduled to begin on 4 May. Season two of *The Avengers* was mentioned as being a major force within the upcoming autumn programming, and it was said that although Ian Hendry had departed the series, ABC hoped to entice him back for guest appearances.

2.01 – 'Mission to Montreal'

The initial groundwork for season two's first episode into production[6] appears to have been laid back at the end of 1961, before season one had even finished transmission. On 24 October, director Don Leaver met P A Hankin, the public relations officer of Canadian Pacific Steamships Limited, who was based in Trafalgar Square in London. Three days later, he followed this up with a letter. In response to a request from ABC for footage of an ocean liner to use in the episode, the Canadian company supplied

---

[6] As at the end of season one, the episodes would be transmitted out of production sequence – quite radically so in this season.

material of the latest addition to their fleet, the *MV Calpurnia*, aka the *Empress of Canada*. Leaver invited Hankin to Teddington Studios for lunch and an opportunity to watch rehearsals sometime during November, although he warned him that the proposed production was likely to be delayed – as ultimately proved to be the case.

The episode's working title was 'Gale Force', but the use of the word 'Gale' is thought to have been purely coincidental with no connection to Cathy Gale, as the episode was clearly written for Dr Keel originally. It was in the first week of May 1962 that rehearsals finally began on this initial outing for Jon Rollason, while the actor he had replaced, Ian Hendry, was busy at what was then MGM Borehamwood Studios in Hertfordshire making the feature film *Live Now – Pay Later*. The contract for 'Mission to Montreal' signed by Rollason on 1 May clearly showed the character name as Keel, but when approached on the subject in 2012, the actor indicated that this was simply because the King character had yet to be created. Obviously sometime during rehearsals, Newman and White thought up the latter as a substitute for Keel. Rollason confirmed: 'I was always going to be King, never Keel.'

On the morning of Friday 11 May 1962, the opening teaser sequence for 'Mission to Montreal', set in a film studio, was recorded in Studio 2 at Teddington. This involved an actress character named Carla Berotti, played by Patricia English, asking her understudy Peggy to fetch something from her dressing room, where Peggy is murdered in a case of mistaken identity. The storyline then continued with Berotti travelling to Canada on board an ocean liner, under guard by Dr King and an undercover Steed posing as a steward, waiting for the killer to make another attempt on her life.

As for season one, recordings for this season would all be done on two-inch Ampex videotape, which was compatible with ABC's RCA TRT-1B videotape recorder. The main recording for 'Mission to Montreal' took place in Studio 2 between 6.00 pm and 7.00 pm on Saturday 12 May from a screenplay by Lester Powell. The production designer was Terry Green, on the first of his nine episodes for the series. After casting him in the first season episode 'Ashes of Roses', Don Leaver rehired Mark Eden to guest alongside Pamela Ann Davy, Gerald Sim and Douglas Muir's daughter Gillian, who played Judy – Dr King's assistant, as Ingrid Hafner's Carol had been Dr Keel's. Gillian Muir had started her career four years previously with an uncredited part in the film *The Golden Disc*, before appearing in several instalments of *The Younger Generation* and the soap *Emergency-Ward 10*.

The crew utilised their own facilities and equipment to simulate the film studio setting. After Pamela Ann Davy's character Peggy was knifed, Leaver included a dramatic shot of the bloody murder weapon – something that would never happen again in the series. The half-dozen short pieces of film sourced from Canadian Pacific Steamships Limited showed *Empress of Canada* at the docks in Liverpool, leaving port, at sea and arriving in Montreal, plus an establishing shot of the ocean liner's funnel.

There was no introductory scene added to the screenplay; Steed and King are already acquainted at the start of the action. Only Patrick Macnee was credited on the opening titles, however, reinforcing the limited nature of Rollason's assignment on the series.

Johnny Dankworth specially composed 11 incidental cues, of which nine were described as 'linking music' and the other two as 'tension links' used to build suspense. The remaining cues heard throughout the episode were a mixture of library tracks taken from a tape provided by Frances, Day and Hunter and from records issued by production music suppliers Boosey and Hawkes and the mainstream label Decca.

This episode attracted 4.9 million viewers when it was part-networked on Saturday 27 October, making it the twentieth most popular programme for the week.

2.02 – 'Dead on Course'

Jon Rollason was enjoying his brief time on the series, and especially liked working with Patrick Macnee. The second outing for his Dr King character originally had the working title 'The Plane Wreckers', but the Eric Paice screenplay then underwent a change to 'Dead on Course', and it was as such that it was recorded on Saturday 26 May 1962. The Irish-set storyline involved a gang activating a fake landing beacon during a thick fog, resulting in an aircraft crashing and thus allowing them to steal a consignment of £250,000 from the wreckage.

Robert Fuest returned to design the sets for this episode, liaising with a director new to the series, Richmond Harding. Harding had started out in the late '40s as an uncredited third assistant director on various feature films, and just before arriving on *The Avengers* he had served as producer/director on one of the six-part crime serials that made up the BBC's crime drama *The World of Tim Frazer*. Later work of his would include episodes of *Z Cars* for the BBC and *Coronation Street* for Granada.

This story again shows Steed's ruthless side, when he virtually throttles the character Vincent O'Brien, played by Donal Donnelly, to obtain a confession regarding the conspiracy behind the air crash. Some background on Steed's wartime activities is also forthcoming, when he divulges that he flew bombers during his RAF service, giving him the experience required to pilot an airliner.

The original script included a secret passageway between an inn setting and a convent setting featured in the story, but this element was dropped and failed to make it through to the camera script. Another scene that caused some behind-the-scenes debate was one where the convent's Mother Superior garrottes an airline hostess with the waist cord of her habit. Having read this in the script, both Howard Thomas and ABC's script supervisor Anthony John were concerned it might offend viewers, and this led to memos being issued requesting reassurance that the violence would be carefully depicted on screen. This was indeed the case: the sequence was tastefully executed, with the garrotte being seen to go around the victim's throat, but the camera then panning away to show the victim's legs beginning to thrash wildly.

'Dead on Course' would be transmitted in most regions at 10.05 pm on 29 December 1962, clocking up 5.8 million viewers and making it the highest-rated episode for season two.

Casting Cathy

About to depart on several weeks' holiday in the summer of 1962, and realising that an actress still needed to be found to play Cathy Gale, Sydney Newman drew up a list of five potential candidates for the role. He passed this list to Leonard White, in order that the producer could arrange the casting in his absence. Newman's first choice at the top of the list was Nyree Dawn Porter, with Fenella Fielding somewhere in the middle and at the bottom an actress he did not really want, Honor Blackman. Following his superior's instructions, White attempted to secure the services of Nyree Dawn Porter, but she declined due to prior commitments. (The nearest she would ever get to being an

Avengergirl would be to play the similar role of Contessa Caroline di Contini in Gerry Anderson's *The Protectors* ten years later.) However, while Blackman was the actress that Newman was least keen on of all those listed, she was White's favourite for the role. The producer interviewed her, and explained how Cathy Gale would be an exponent of judo – to which she simply replied that she would require training. White offered Blackman the job, and she agreed to become Mrs Cathy Gale – a role that would redefine women in television action shows and create something new, different and revolutionary in *The Avengers*.

Blackman signed her contract in the first week of June 1962, initially for six episodes only, although there was a clause in the contract that allowed ABC to retain her services until January 1963 if required. When Newman returned, he was very surprised by the casting choice; yet despite initial misgivings he backed White's decision, and together they began planning how Blackman would play the part.

In order to make Cathy Gale work as a character, Newman and White realised that they required some female input, so they consulted Marie Donaldson, an ABC press officer, and Doreen Montgomery, who had now succeeded Reed de Rouen as *The Avengers'* second story editor. Having been a movie scriptwriter since the late '30s, Montgomery had moved across to ITV in the '50s, working on the anthology series *Douglas Fairbanks Presents* and then writing and editing on the historical series *William Tell*. Her brief on *The Avengers* was to evaluate all the elements that had been suggested for Cathy Gale and assemble a fully-rounded character. However, as she usually insisted on working from home, she was rarely available for production meetings, and inevitably this caused delays. A further source of friction arose when she put in an expenses claim to replace the carpet in her office at Teddington, because a writer she had interviewed had dropped some cigarette ash and burnt a hole in it. Michael Chapman, in charge of Iris Productions at the time, took great pleasure in refusing Montgomery's claim. Apparently unhappy with the situation, Montgomery stayed with ABC for no more than a few weeks and was never credited on screen as a story editor, although she did leave behind her screenplay for the forthcoming episode 'Warlock' and, perhaps more importantly, introduced writer Roger Marshall to the production.

2.03 – 'The Sell-Out'

Prior to 'The Sell-Out' being committed to tape on Saturday 9 June 1962, the largest amount of location filming for any episode to date was executed under the direction of Don Leaver. After some establishing shots of the British Museum in London, the action proceeded as follows. Steed, impersonating a diplomat named Roland whom he has been assigned to protect, leaves the Museum and walks the short distance to his AC Greyhound sports car (registration number 880 OPA), unaware that he is being followed by a character named Fraser, played by Michael Mellinger. Steed then drives along Great Russell Street, WC1, tailed by Fraser in a Ford Consul. He parks the AC in Endsleigh Street, WC1, and after placing some money in a parking meter walks up the street. Again he is followed by Fraser, who has parked his Ford some distance away on the other side of the road. Steed then enters the Tavistock Hotel in Tavistock Square, WC1, but later leaves the premises, still impersonating Roland. He gets into a 1953 Rolls Royce Phantom IV and is chauffeured away. The limousine moves away from the kerb in Bedford Place, WC1, taking the first road on the left into Tavistock Square, only to be followed by a potential assassin driving a Sunbeam Alpine convertible. As the two vehicles travel through central London, they move down a busy Tottenham Court Road, W1, before turning left into Maple Street, W1. The tailing comes to a conclusion when the chauffeur-driven Rolls Royce turns off Richmond Hill into the car park of the Richmond Hill Hotel in Richmond-upon-Thames, Surrey, followed by the Sunbeam. The Rolls Royce is then driven around the side of the building and stops behind the hotel.

There was also a substantial amount of night-time filming done for a sequence of Steed and King dashing in the AC to Heathrow Airport in order to prevent the assassination of Roland by a gunman masquerading as a journalist. Footage was shot of the sports car with Steed at the wheel travelling along the Hammersmith Flyover in London W6, passing the now-demolished Firestone tyre factory on the Great West Road in Brentford, Middlesex, and later negotiating the roundabout on Tunnel Road East at Heathrow before proceeding into a brightly-lit tunnel under one of the runways and taxi lanes to Terminals One to Three.

Some further day- and night-time location work was done in a leafy suburban street for exteriors of a house where the characters Lilian and Mark Harvey live. This material included the climax of the episode, where Mark Harvey herds Dr King away to kill him but Steed, having anticipated the situation, is waiting in the shadows armed with a .38 Colt Officer's ACP revolver, which he uses to kill the traitor and save his friend's life. This scene was concocted during rehearsals; as originally scripted, the conclusion was slightly different, being set in King's surgery, with Steed arriving in the nick of time to save the doctor's life but taking Harvey prisoner at gunpoint.

It appears that Douglas Muir was unavailable to play his usual role of One-Ten. Consequently Leaver cast Arthur Hewlett as the previously-unseen One-Twelve, who during the episode makes it clear that, for this mission, Steed is answerable to him.

Under the pressure of recording 'as live', some errors crept into proceedings. For instance, in a scene where Steed engages Lilian Harvey in conversation, the 'barn door' flap of one of the studio spotlights is visible for a short time in the top right-hand corner of the screen. Later, when Lilian, played by Anne Godley, takes away a tray containing cups and saucers, she balances it unsteadily with one hand while opening the door with the other, causing a teaspoon to fall onto the floor.

Writer Anthony Terpiloff and actor Brandon Brady collaborated on both the outline and teleplay for the episode, which had the working title 'Traitor'. Terpiloff would progress to writing for American shows such as *Ironside* and *The Alfred Hitchcock Hour*, and then in the '70s would get involved with Gerry Anderson on both *The Protectors* and *Space: 1999*. Brady was born in Johannesburg, South Africa and had a successful acting career in the UK, including a part in the season one *The Avengers* episode 'Toy Trap', but 'The Sell-Out' was his only venture into scriptwriting.

As this was the final episode for both Jon Rollason and Gillian Muir, the inclusion of a scene between Steed and King in the doctor's office where the physician has obviously grown tired of being used as an extension of the agent's department was very appropriate. 'Do I ever come round needing your help?' says King. 'I don't even know where you live and … Listen Steed, from now on I'm just going to be a doctor. I'm not going to be anything else. I'm not going to be an agent, a counterspy, a gunman, a cover for you or anything you can use in your business … So you can just leave me in peace.'

A tense episode, 'The Sell-Out' sports an unusual amount of location shooting (including some at night) making it quite a fast-moving adventure for the second season.

2.04 – 'Death Dispatch'

'Death Dispatch' was Honor Blackman's first taste of *The Avengers*, and it was recorded between 6.30 pm and 7.30 pm on Saturday 23 June 1962 in Studio 2 at Teddington, under the direction of Jonathan Alwyn. The production designer was newcomer Anne Spavin, who would go on to perform similar duties on other ABC series: *Out of this World*, *Armchair Theatre* and *Redcap*.

This episode provides an international adventure for Steed and Cathy Gale, as they investigate the murder of a diplomatic courier in Jamaica. The script by Leonard Fincham – also new to the series – underwent a few changes during production. Originally it featured a German character named Muller, as opposed to an American called Monroe in the final version, plus the Rosas characters lived in Buenos Aires instead of Santiago. Likewise, Steed's journey as a courier originally involved him travelling from Bogota to Santiago to Buenos Aires, but this was changed to have him go from Bogota to Lima to Santiago.

Steed is already acquainted with Cathy at the start of the action, and appears extremely pleased when One-Ten announces that she will be flying out from the UK to be his back-up on this mission. Although not officially an operative of the secret service department Steed works for, Cathy has obviously undergone some training in the art of espionage, smuggling her six-round Browning .38 ACP semi-automatic through customs in the false lining of her suitcase. At this point, the character has not yet been fully defined, being tolerant of Steed's sexist attitude toward her; something that would be unthinkable in later episodes. Probably in an attempt to attract a larger viewing audience, Cathy was shown in her underwear at one point; and some background was incorporated by having her speak Spanish when ordering drinks to be delivered to her hotel room.

Gerald Harper played a character called Travers, who was included as comedy relief, especially in scenes with Steed.

At one point in the action, Steed is relived of his .38 Colt revolver (as seen in the previous episode) by another character called Monroe at a hacienda.

Various pieces of both 16mm and 35mm stock footage were included to identify locales, showing Jamaica, an airliner in flight, planes touching down at the airports in Lima and Bogota and establishing shots of Santiago.

Leonard White was not impressed with the finished episode, pointing out similarities to Associated-Rediffusion's spy show *Top Secret*, which was also set in South America and was being transmitted by ITV at the time.

With everyone now on the production treadmill, there had been insufficient time to arrange any judo training for Blackman at this point, so she took matters into her own hands by asking around to see if anyone had any martial arts experience. Actor Geoff L'Cise, who was playing a secondary role in the episode, credited simply as Thug, showed her some basic throws. However, she would not really exhibit any great unarmed combat skills until the upcoming episode 'Propellant 23'.

This storyline of international adventure would prove to be the exception rather than the norm for the series, as due to the restrictive nature of making the series, UK based plots were far easier to accomplish. Further to this, they were also less expensive to produce not involving the buying in stock footage for use as establishing material of foreign locales.

2.05 – 'Warlock'

Doreen Montgomery's legacy, 'Warlock', was the next episode into production. In this story, Steed is called in when rocket fuel expert Neville becomes ill and falls into a trance, making the agent suspect that forces of the occult are involved.

'Warlock' had been written to introduce Cathy Gale, and it incorporated an idea from Sydney Newman's early outline for the character by having Steed encounter his new partner-against-crime at the Natural History Museum. Submitted under the working title 'Zodiac', it was clearly designed to show the characters' first meeting, as Cathy addresses Steed formally as 'Mr Steed' and the dialogue reveals a little of her background when she talks about her time in Africa. An initial indication of Mrs Gale's martial arts abilities is given in a sequence where she silently climbs through an open window into Neville's apartment and suddenly finds a hand on her shoulder as a voice demands, 'What are you doing here?' Cathy reacts instantly by taking the arm and executing an over-the-shoulder judo throw – leaving Steed on his back looking up at the ceiling.

Prior to recording the episode, Patrick Macnee was filmed on location on Cromwell Road, London SW7, entering the grounds of the Natural History Museum (also known at that time as the British Museum (Natural History)) through a gateway. There was also some footage shot on the junction of Covent Garden and Russell Street in Covent Garden, WC2, where Macnee walked past several men unloading fruit from a vehicle, as Steed proceeds to the nearby Floral Street to meet One-Ten in the White Lion pub. In addition, there was some night-time filming done of Steed driving a Triumph Herald (7081 MK), paying a nocturnal visit to Satanist Cosmo Gallion's bookshop and having to chloroform a vicious-sounding but playful German Shepherd dog guarding the back yard.

A scene where Cathy drives a slightly inebriated Steed home in her light-coloured MGA convertible (RVB 115) was videotaped on the studio lot behind Studios 2 and 3, with the recently-built technical block to the rear of the vehicle. This scene was captured during a 15-minute session beginning at 8.45 pm on the evening of Friday 6 July 1962, with cameras simply pushed outside through the scenery door at the rear of Studio 2. The new five-storey technical block was located between Studios 1 and 2 and contained additional facilities, including new control room suites for Studios 1, 2 and 3, rehearsal rooms, a sound recording room and a scene dock on the ground floor. From this point on, the majority of sets required for programmes would be manufactured on site at the studios, with only a small amount of material still being made in Manchester for transportation to Teddington. The main recording of the episode took place the following day between 6.30 pm and 7.30 pm in Studio 2.

Happy with Peter Arne's performance in 'Death on the Slipway', Hammond recast Macnee's friend as Gallion. In the scene of this character's initial meeting with Cathy, Arne accidentally dropped a clipboard he was carrying, but recovered the situation by ad-libbing 'So sorry,' before picking it up.

The episode's closing credits carried the additional credit 'Dance Direction by Pat Kirshner'. Kirshner's input had been required mainly for actress Pat Spencer's enthusiastic movement during sequences of black magic ceremonies.

With Dr Keel no longer in the series, Leonard White's ground rule against alcoholic drink being seen was relaxed a little, allowing Cathy to have a gin and tonic and Steed to indulge himself with a brandy and soda.

Besides his trusty bowler, Steed also wears a trilby hat (as he did in 'Death Dispatch'). He carries his Colt Officer's revolver again, in contrast to Cathy, who has a more compact and smaller-calibre Beretta 70 automatic. In a scene where Steed and the character Mrs Dunning are seen searching Neville's bedroom, a stagehand can be glimpsed through the open door behind them, sat with his arms folded and apparently unaware that he is on camera.

Besides Dankworth's incidental cues, there were a couple of library tracks included in the episode. These were 'Voice from Beyond' written by Van Phillips, and the Eric Siday-composed 'Musique Electronique', which would also be heard in the *Doctor Who* serial 'Inside the Spaceship' a couple of years later.

An optical effect seen to indicate the power of black magic was achieved by a century-old theatrical illusion called the Pepper's Ghost, created by John Pepper after he adapted an existing trick named the Dircksian Phantasmagoria. This is achieved by projecting a powerful light through a sheet of glass at an object, which then reflects back and off the glass through a second sheet of glass, causing a transparent image some distance away.

The original version of the script had Cathy being kidnapped by the Satanists to take part in their ritual, but this was later changed to have Gallion work out her horoscope and then use his power of the paranormal to summon her to the bookshop from her apartment.

Although 'Warlock' was initially planned to be the first second season episode transmitted, there was a change of mind, resulting in it being held back, presumably because Leonard White was not totally happy with it. As a consequence, a couple of scenes were remounted prior to transmission (see below for further details).

This episode proved to be a close encounter with fantasy for *The Avengers*, but only a taster of what would later become a staple diet of the series when it progressed to being made on film.

Having interviewed former French Resistance leader Rene Burdet for *Winston Churchill: The Valiant Years*, Macnee suggested that he would be ideal to teach both Blackman and himself some hand-to-hand combat techniques. White agreed, so Macnee and Blackman visited Burdet (who at the time was a London hotel proprietor) and he showed them some close-quarters fighting moves using the feet, as well as various dirty moves that proved too explicit to be used in a television series. Blackman asked Burdet how she should defend herself if attacked by a man, to which the Frenchman replied, in a deep accent, 'Kick zem in zee balls!'

Lighter and Faster

Even at this early stage in its development *The Avengers* was beginning to offer something different in television entertainment. The shadowy noir style seen in the first season was being left behind, as the series progressed into a lighter and faster action/adventure format, which included a. different style of approach and storytelling. This would all combine to make *The Avengers* a much more viewer-friendly series, which with more publicity would promote the show to a much wider audience, eventually including international exposure.

2.06 – 'Propellant 23'

Four scenes for 'Propellant 23', featuring Macnee and Blackman sat in a mock-up of Cathy's MGA convertible, were pre-recorded on videotape in the scene dock at Teddington Studios between 7.00 pm and 9.00 pm on Friday 20 July 1962. The main recording of the episode was then undertaken under the direction of Jonathan Alwyn the following evening in Studio 2, between 5.00 pm and 6.00 pm, from a teleplay by Jon Manchip White. White had started out writing for television by adapting a novel into a play for the BBC's *Sunday Night Theatre* in 1951. He went on to do a mixture of both television and film scriptwriting, including an episode of ATV's Victorian detective series *Sergeant Cork* and the sci-fi movie *Crack in the World*. However, 'Propellant 23' would be his only contribution to *The Avengers*.

After appearing in the pilot episode 'Hot Snow', Catherine Woodville was again amongst the guest cast here, along with Justine Lord, Nicholas Courtney and Geoffrey Palmer. The plot involves Steed and Cathy trying to retrieve a flask of top secret rocket fuel – the Propellant 23 of the title – stolen from a murdered courier. During the course of events, Steed gives Cathy a small, chrome-plated .22 Beretta 70 automatic, though later in the episode she produces a matt black example of this gun from her garter holster, to which he exclaims, 'You're full of surprises.' Steed's home address is revealed as 5 Winchester Mews, London, and in a sign of the times, both he and Cathy are witnessed smoking cigarettes – something that would not be allowed on television today. Cathy's fighting abilities are exhibited for the first time, when the knife-wielding character named Siebel confronts her in the apartment of one 'Curly' Leclerc, forcing her to block the weapon with her handbag before throwing him to the floor and knocking him out with a karate chop.

Casting Venus

Despite the initial plans to give Patrick Macnee another female co-star having been drawn up eight months previously, auditions for the role of nightclub singer Venus Smith were not arranged until the beginning of August 1962, when 51 women attended Teddington Studios. The line-up included Pamela Ann Davy, who had been there three months earlier when she guested in 'Mission to Montreal', plus three actresses who would appear in future episodes: Laurie Leigh ('Bullseye'), Angela Browne ('Intercrime') and Julie Paulle ('Killer Whale'). Amongst the others present were singers Anita Harris, Kathy Kirby, Joyce Blair and Millicent Martin and actresses Vera Day, Shirley Eaton, Angela Douglas, Gabriella Licudi, Sally Smith and Julie Stevens – although at the time the latter was known more as a presenter than anything else.

Having already appeared in the first season episode 'Dance with Death', Angela Douglas was the preferred choice of Leonard White, who felt that she would make a perfect partner for Steed. Douglas was offered the role, but at such short notice – she would have been required to start work the following day – was unable to accept it due to other commitments. Hence the second choice, Julie Stevens, was telephoned. Having only just arrived home from her audition, she was requested to return to Teddington Studios immediately. There she was informed that the role of Venus Smith was hers. The choice was not warmly received by Don Leaver, who would direct the first Venus episode. He was not totally convinced that he could get a competent performance from Stevens, and voiced his concerns to Leonard White.

White quickly assembled a fictional biography for Venus Smith for distribution to directors, writers, potential writers and the show's remaining story editor, John Bryce. This drew upon Stevens' own northern background for some of its detail. Venus was described as a bargee's daughter from Lancashire, who had left home at 17 to pursue her dream of being an entertainer. She would have a likeable nature, be outgoing, warm and friendly and would accept people as she found them. She would have no special abilities to assist her in the murky world of crime and espionage, being a traditional female character who would have to scream for help when the going got tough. The original outline indicated that Steed would refer to her as Smith, though her many friends and acquaintances would call her Vee for short. However, at a late stage in development, both these elements were dropped and everyone simply called her Venus.

Venus would not be a member of the secret service department Steed worked for; in fact she would not be aware of the full circumstances and often dangerous situations that she was getting herself drawn into. Her innocence and gullibility would make her easy for Steed to manipulate for his own ends, while generally keeping her in the dark; a situation highlighting the ruthless aspect of the agent's nature.

2.07 – 'Mr Teddy Bear'

The teaser sequence for 'Mr Teddy Bear', set in a television studio where a fictional talk show *The Man and the Place* is being made, was recorded between 8.45 pm and 9.00 pm on Friday 3 August 1962 in Studio 3 at Teddington. This served as a lead-in to a story where, in order to expose an infamous assassin, Cathy Gale pays to have Steed killed. As usual, the main recording of the episode was undertaken the following evening, between 6.30 pm and 7.30 pm in Studio 2. Three pieces of previously-filmed night-time location footage were fed in by telecine where required.

In this episode's action, Cathy is driving to Mantel's Holt in her MGA convertible (RVB 115) when she realises she is being tailed by a character called Farrow on his BSA motorbike. She stops and goes into a coffee bar, and he follows her. However, after leaving, she removes the spark plug lead from his motorbike, which then refuses to start. This differs slightly from the original camera script description of her swapping over the two plug leads on what was obviously meant to be a twin cylinder machine; presumably only a single cylinder bike was available. The rock and roll number playing on the jukebox when Cathy enters the coffee bar is 'Move Over Tiger' by Vince Taylor, which had been released on the Palette record label, number PG 9020, 13 months earlier in July 1961.

'Mr Teddy Bear' incorporates more humour into proceedings than normal. This works well in sequences such as where Steed reveals to Cathy that the cigarette box she has taken from Mantel's Holt is covered in fingerprints – but those of an adult chimpanzee. While practising their unarmed combat skills, Steed and Cathy grapple on a padded mat; Steed, applying a hold, gets too close for Cathy's comfort, so she places a hand in his face and simply pushes him away. At the episode's conclusion, Steed visits Cathy's apartment together with his pet Dalmatian called Freckles, causing her to comment humorously, 'Not on the furniture.'

An unintentionally amusing moment comes when Douglas Muir as One-Ten trips over a line of dialogue while in his office talking to Steed: '… and he's taken a good look at you … at you and Mrs Gale.' In a similar vein, under the threat of being killed by the assassin Mr Teddy Bear, Steed at one point has his clothing scrutinised for signs of poison and then, with the results negative, hurriedly dresses and leaves; but having failed to tuck his shirt into his trousers properly at the end of this scene, Macnee played the next one in a state of partial undress.

During the final confrontation with Mr Teddy Bear, Cathy is forced at gunpoint to hand over her small, chrome-plated pistol, but a short while later she reverses the situation by taking his Walther P38 automatic. Steed incidentally also uses this type of gun during the episode.

'Mr Teddy Bear' was written by Martin Woodhouse, who was born on 29 August 1932 in Romford, Essex and had become a scriptwriter the previous year, co-writing episodes of Gerry Anderson's puppet series *Supercar* with his brother Hugh. His other television work included contributions to the children's serial *Emerald Soup* and the crime dramas *The Hidden Truth* and *The Man in Room 17* for ITV, and *Dr Finlay's Casebook* for the BBC.

Despite *The Avengers* not yet being shown on American television, the weekly stateside entertainment journal *Variety* ran a positive review of 'Mr Teddy Bear' on Wednesday 10 October 1962, describing it as both energetic and satisfying.

Cathy's costumes

'Mr Teddy Bear' is also notable for marking the first time that Cathy Gale wears her soon-to-become-iconic leather two-piece fighting suit, designed by Audrey Riddle, head of the wardrobe department at ABC. This would be accessorised with her equally famous kinky boots. Problems had already been encountered regarding Blackman's clothing, which it was feared would not be up to the rigours of the longer fights that would be incorporated into upcoming episodes. Leonard White had suggested suede as a material that could withstand the rough and tumble envisaged, but then he realised that it absorbed light and would make it difficult to find the correct level of lighting on the set. Reconsidering, he had decided simply to reverse the thinking and use leather – an idea that apparently John Bryce also put forward on the strength of wearing leathers when riding his motorcycle. Further to this, after discussing the situation with fellow actor Peter Arne, Macnee is also said to have contributed toward the idea of Cathy wearing black leather trousers, although he was initially worried about approaching Blackman with his thoughts, because of the erotic nature of the outfit.

The fighting suit was designed to meet certain requirements. It needed to be hardwearing, allow plenty of movement and be easy to change into and out of. Also it had to be fashionable. Although it appeared to be black on screen, the leather used for this first fighting suit was actually dark green. Solid black clothing was generally avoided, as with the limitations of the old 405-line transmission system then in use it tended to reflect light and make the outline of the wearer appear fuzzy.

Blackman also wore a three-quarter blonde wig for the role, primarily for the fight scenes, as her own hair was extremely fine and a combination of all the movement and perspiration under the powerful studio lights caused the styling to drop out. When on set, the front quarter of Blackman's own natural blonde hair was visible, while the remainder was pinned up underneath the hairpiece.

Fashion designer Michael Whittaker had been approached by ABC back in May 1962 to provide a wardrobe of clothing for Cathy Gale. He had supplied this the following month, although his input was restricted to seven episodes made between

July and November. Whittaker had started out playing bit parts in films in the late '40s before switching to costume design in the early '50s. Later departing the movie business, he became a fashion show compère and then a designer. Whittaker said at the time: 'I have used such a lot of leather in Cathy's clothes and culottes; those divided skirts are just right for a woman who one minute has to look poised and serene and the next could be jumping into a shooting fray with a band of thugs.' However, ABC costume designer Ambren Garland disputes that any of Blackman's outfits were specially created by Whittaker, or by Frederick Starke in season three, as is commonly believed. She asserts that clothing associated with them was always off the peg. Garland does admit that both designers exerted some influence on fashions seen in *The Avengers*, but maintains that the clothing brought in from these outside sources was not always suitable, needing alterations that both she and Audrey Riddle would have to make. In short, the association with well-known fashion designers was really a marketing exercise thought up by ABC press officer Marie Donaldson to attract publicity to the series.

2.08 – 'The Decapod'

The first Venus Smith episode to go before the cameras was 'The Decapod', involving the murder of a private secretary of a Balkan republic while in London. Recording took place between 6.30 pm and 7.30 pm on Sunday 12 August under the direction of Don Leaver, who cast Wolf Morris again after using him previously in the first season episode 'The Yellow Needle'. Making the first of what would eventually be five appearances in *The Avengers*, Philip Madoc was also cast, along with stuntmen Douglas Robinson and Valentine (aka Val/Valentino) Musetti.

The screenplay, originally called 'End of Line', was by Eric Paice. It established the pattern for the Venus Smith episodes, whereby Julie Stevens would always perform at least a couple of songs. For this episode, she sang 'You're Getting to Be a Habit with Me' from the 1932 musical *42nd Street* and the 1941 jazz standard 'I Got It Bad' by Duke Ellington and Paul Francis Webster. These numbers were decided upon by Leaver during rehearsals; the rehearsal script indicated that Venus would be singing a song called 'Avenging Angel' in both nightclub sequences.

For her first three episodes, Stevens would be backed by the Dave Lee Trio, comprising Dave Lee on keyboards, Art Morgan on drums and Spike Heatley playing double bass. David Cyril Aarons, aka Dave Lee/David Lee, was born on 12 August 1926 in Newington, London and became a successful orchestra leader, arranger, songwriter and recording artist. He co-wrote the novelty songs 'Bangers and Mash' and 'Goodness Gracious Me' for Peter Sellers and Sophia Loren and composed some film scores, including the one for the horror movie *The Masque of the Red Death*.

A wardrobe of sophisticated fashions had been obtained for Stevens from several London fashion houses, including Wallis (who would later supply clothing for the ITC series *The Baron*). Stevens also initially wore a large blonde wig as Venus.

Contrary to White's original directive, Paice's rehearsal script did not have Steed call Venus 'Smith', although he did affectionately refer to her as 'Vee' on several occasions, indicating that they knew each other. This was later changed in the camera script to indicate that they were meeting for the first time.

Stevens proved adept at portraying the humorous side of Venus. In response to the villain Yakob Borb boasting that he has two muscle-bound bodyguards, she cracks the line, 'Wouldn't it be cheaper to get a dog?' At the conclusion of events, Venus realises that there never was a singing tour of the Balkans on offer, as she was told, and obviously feels used by Steed, who promises never to do it again (well not until next time ...)

Not only was this the initial Venus Smith adventure, but it was also the first episode of *The Avengers* to be recorded in the totally refurbished Studio 1 at Teddington, which at 8,891 square feet was largest stage on the lot. It had been mainly utilised as nothing more than a rehearsal space since ABC acquired the studio, but the company had recently invested greatly in converting it from film to television production and equipped it with several EMI 203 cameras, which would also become standard equipment in the other two television studios at Teddington. In ABPC's annual report, chairman Sir Philip Warner detailed the estimated £1.2 million upgrade that made ABC Teddington a state-of-the art television studio. Despite colour broadcasting being some years away, recording in this medium could now be achieved there, and additional facilities meant that the company could handle both the 405- and 625-line picture systems, plus the American 525-line format.

'The Decapod' again demonstrates care being taken to present the show's violent content sensitively: the karate blow that kills the wrester Giorgi in his match against the titular character happens off camera, leaving viewers to see simply his prone body, though the attack was described in the rehearsal script as a double-handed samurai chop to the neck.

Recording the scene where, having killed his opponent, the Decapod leaps over the ropes around the ring, the masked wrestler accidentally trapped one of his legs between the top and middle rope, but fortunately managed to untangle himself before dropping down into the crowd of spectator extras to make his escape.

The episode's rehearsal script gave the date of the first read-through in Room 2A at Teddington as Friday 31 August 1962. However, as it was actually recorded before that, on 12 August, it appears that this and the following episode, 'Bullseye', were transposed in production order. This probably came about as, after planning Venus's introduction for so many months, Leonard White wanted her debut episode recorded as quickly as possible. In the event, White was extremely pleased with Julie Stevens' performance, and Don Leaver was completely won over. Even ABC's Director of Programmes Brian Tesler echoed their sentiments in a memo where he voiced the opinion that the series was shaping up well and that the gamble with Venus Smith had paid off.

2.09 – 'Bullseye'

Eric Paice supplied the script for next adventure. Originally called 'Dead on Target', this Cathy Gale episode involving illegal gun-running to Africa was renamed 'Bullseye' and underwent recording in Studio 1 between 6.30 pm and 7.30 pm on Thursday 20 September 1962. Peter Hammond resumed the director's chair, and his casting included Ronald Radd in the first of his three guest roles in the series, plus, as Miss Ellis, Judy Parfitt, making the first of four guest appearances.

Two pieces of stock footage showing trading on the floor of the London Stock Exchange were included, along with eight seconds filmed at night to establish the character Young's houseboat, logically done nearby on the River Thames behind the studio.

A small error was made at the beginning of the episode. The office girl Jean, played by Mitzi Rogers, switches on a reel-to-reel tape player and a voice is heard, but the reels do not turn. Later, when the Brigadier character played by Charles Carson reloads and fires his handgun on a shooting range, no gunshot is heard, just a clicking sound, suggesting that the grams operator placed the stylus onto the wrong track on the sound effects record. Another slight error occurred during a scene where Felix Deebank as Young is making advances on Jean, who advises him that 'Miss Gale' (as opposed to 'Mrs Gale') is still around.

Again Cathy demonstrates her ability to handle a male assailant, when a character named Karl surprises her snooping about the houseboat and a fight ensues. Later she uses her ingenuity to gain access to the penthouse of a businessman named Henry Cade, claiming to be working for the fictional magazine *Woman about London*.

The banter between Steed and Cathy was already working very well by this point, thanks to Macnee, Blackman and some witty writing and rewriting, and the series was breaking new ground by starting to establish what American television would eventually term a 'dog and cat show' format – having a female lead character of equal standing to her male counterpart.

Season two starts transmissions

The front cover of the London edition of the 23 to 29 September 1962 *TV Times* (No. 360) bore the titles of various shows, including *The Avengers*, alerting viewers that it was about to return to their screens. Transmission of the second season began on 29 September with 'Mr Teddy Bear'. Both ABC regions, Tyne Tees, Ulster, TWW and their Welsh speaking service Teledu Cymru, which had started broadcasting only two weeks earlier, screened the episode at 10.05 pm. Anglia, ATV London, Grampian, Southern, Westward and the new Channel region, which had begun transmitting on 1 September, elected to schedule it a little later in the evening, at 10.30 pm. The Border and Scottish regions both declined to join the transmissions. The former would not begin to show the series until November 1962 and the latter would wait until April 1963.

Meanwhile, coinciding with the start of the new season, September 1962 also saw publication of the *TV Crimebusters Annual*, including a seven-page black-and-white *The Avengers* comic strip entitled 'The Drug Peddler'. This featured Dr Keel and Steed and was made up of both illustrations and photographs. This one-off hardback book, published by TV Publications Ltd for the Christmas market, also featured strips of other popular crime and action series of the time. It was the only spin-off merchandise involving the Keel and Steed combination of *The Avengers*.

2.10 – 'The Removal Men'

On Wednesday 3 October 1962, a sequence for 'The Removal Men' featuring Macnee, guest star Edina Ronay and Julie Stevens as Venus Smith was recorded between 2.00 pm and 2.15 pm in the stairwell of the technical block and the new foyer of Teddington Studios. This fitted into the storyline where, having infiltrated a gang of professional killers on the French Riviera and accepted a hit on Ronay's character Nicole Cauvin, Steed goes to Homeric Film Studios and leads her to safety, passing Venus on the way. The sequence was assembled by director Don Leaver, replacing one in the original outline where Steed simply ushers Nicole into a car before driving her away, though again not before being witnessed by Venus.

The recently-built foyer occupied the site of the original vehicle entrance to Teddington Studios; hence ABC also acquired Weir Cottage, situated between the studio lot and The Anglers pub on Broom Road, for further development. A large portion of the garden beside the cottage was removed, and a new access road constructed alongside Studio 3, complete with a security post.

'The Removal Men' was recorded in Studio 1 between 6.30 pm and 7.30 pm the following day. The script, by Roger Marshall and Jeremy Scott, had originally been called 'The Most Expensive Commodity'. Scott would do very little television scriptwriting after his involvement with *The Avengers*, and instead would concentrate more on his role as executive producer with a television advertising company.

Leaver again included Edwin Richfield in his guest cast, after using him in the first season episode 'Girl on the Trapeze', and brought in ex-story editor Reed de Rouen to play gang leader Dragna, with Douglas Muir reprising his role of One-Ten.

In a sequence in the Les Centaurs club, Venus is seen to rehearse the song 'I May be Wrong' for half a minute, backed by the Dave Lee Trio. Some of the lyrics were rearranged by Stevens and Dave Lee, from the original written in 1929 by Harry Sullivan and Harry Ruskin. Upon completion, Venus catches sight of Steed, who inquires how she is. Remembering their previous meeting in 'The Decapod' she replies, 'Great, up till now!'

The Dave Lee Trio also play an instrumental piece in the nightclub early in the episode, and later an easy-listening jazz number. The latter appears to have overrun as, part-way through, the expression on Edwin Richfield's face indicates that he was expecting the music to stop so that he could exchange dialogue with Ivor Dean, playing a French police officer.

Later, Venus sings 'An Occasional Man', penned in 1955 by Ralph Blane and Hugh Martin, again backed by Dave and the boys. Unfortunately, when Stevens began singing here, the boom microphone did not reach her in time, resulting in the first three words being extremely faint on the soundtrack. After this, the trio provide some background music as the club is being cleared, including several bars of 'Goodness Gracious Me'. As Dragna and his associate Siegel hold Steed at gunpoint, a tearful Venus accompanies herself on the piano to sing the 1938 ditty 'Sing for Your Supper' by Richard Rodgers and Lorenz Hart. Under the guidance of Dave Lee for a couple of weeks, Stevens had learnt how to play basic chords on the piano, and then simply executed them slowly and adjusted her singing to the pace.

In a sequence where Dragna visits the jeweller's shop of Charlie the fence, the accordion-based incidental music heard is a piece called 'Montmartre Mood', written by Dwight Barker and sourced from the Conroy music library.

The wall of the club set visibly sways several inches when Steed frantically hits a light switch, blacking out the place to avoid being shot by Dragna and Siegel.

During a break-in at Dragna's home, Steed carries a little insurance in the form of a .38 Smith and Wesson revolver.

Although Venus is referred to as 'Vee' throughout the camera script, she is never called this during the episode as transmitted, indicating that Leaver and the cast decided against using the shortened version of her name sometime late in rehearsals.

Shifting scheduling

Having transmitted 'Mr Teddy Bear' and 'Propellant 23' in a 10.30 pm slot, both Anglia and Southern then screened 'The Decapod' at 10.00 pm on Saturday 13 October 1962. However, they then joined the ABC transmissions, with all remaining episodes going out at 10.05 pm. ATV London also showed 'The Decapod' at 10.00 pm on 13 October and then switched to participate in the ABC feed, but only until the end of the year. Channel and Westward followed the trend with 'The Decapod', then they changed their transmission times randomly: 'Bullseye' went out at 10.30 pm on 20 October on both channels, while 'Mission to Montreal' was screened at 10.00 pm the following week on Channel and five minutes later on Westward. Things got back on course when 'The Removal Men' began at 10.05 pm in both regions, starting a run of episodes all transmitted at the same time, which would continue until the end of December.

Other differences occurred in the Grampian region. After screening 'Mr Teddy Bear' and 'Propellant 23', they took no episode of *The Avengers* on 13 October. The broadcasts resumed for one week when 'Bullseye' went out at 10.30 pm on Saturday 20 October. However, Grampian then declined to screen any further episodes until Sunday 6 January 1963, when they started another run with the episode 'Intercrime'.

2.11 – 'The Mauritius Penny'

'The Mauritius Penny', an episode from the writing duo of Malcolm Hulke and Terrance Dicks, went before the cameras in Studio 1 between 6.30 pm and 7.30 pm on Thursday 18 October 1962. In this story, the world of stamp collecting leads Steed and Cathy into contact with a neo-Nazi organisation who are planning the overthrow of several governments so they can dominate Europe.

Taking the director's chair this time was Richmond Harding, who having used actor David Langton in several episodes of the BBC adventure serial *The World of Tim Fraser* cast him here as the neo-Nazi Gerald Shelley. Also amongst the guest cast were Alfred Burke and Grace Arnold, making her only appearance in the series as Steed's housekeeper Elsie (credited as Charlady). This episode also sees the second and final appearance of Steed's pet Dalmatian, Freckles.

During a stamp auction scene, actor Richard Vernon missed his cue, causing the auctioneer to backtrack from £20 to £18 in the bidding and Macnee to give his fellow thespian a couple of quizzical looks as a prompt – which worked, as he then bid £25. The brief portion of organ music played as an incidental cue at the beginning of this scene was a Norwegian hymn, '*Den Store, Hvite Flokk*', which when translated becomes 'Behold a Host'. The outfit Cathy wears at the stamp auction – a scarlet Mary Quant suit with matching hat and black turtle-neck sweater with her famous leather boots – was Blackman's own, having been purchased days earlier from a fashionable London clothing outlet.

Later, at Steed's apartment, as he and Cathy discuss the stamp list being a code, the Spanish bullfighting music heard in the background is '*Suite Espanol*' written by J Enrique, played in live from a disc during recording.

The opening teaser sequence, involving the death of a stamp dealer named Peckham, is accompanied by another piece of library music, 'World of Plants', composed by Jack Trombey and played from a ten-inch De Wolfe Ltd library music record. 'World of Plants' had been the principal incidental music used in the ABC serial

Pathfinders to Venus the previous year and would be heard again in several years' time in the *Doctor Who* serial 'The Space Museum'.

At the beginning of act three, the usual commercial break sting is replaced by an orchestral fanfare, suggesting that the grams operator accidentally selected the wrong track on the record. Another error occurs in a sequence where Cathy opens the pages of Steed's stamp book *The World's Rare Stamps*, as unfortunately the text appears to be part of a biography and there is no mention of postage stamps.

Steed is seen to have his .38 Colt Trooper revolver locked in a drawer at his apartment, while in this episode Cathy favours an automatic in the form of an Italian 9mm Beretta Brigadier. As originally scripted, the episode was to have ended with Cathy and Steed training Sterling submachine guns on the villain Lord Matterley as he starts to address a meeting of the neo-Nazi group. In the final version, however, previously-summoned military forces arrive to break up the meeting and take the agitators into custody. During the confusion, Steed is mistakenly arrested, and the final scene features Cathy visiting him in prison and promising to rectify the situation and get him released … eventually.

Thirteen years later, Terrance Dicks would rework a scene of Cathy's infiltration of a paramilitary meeting for his *Doctor Who* serial 'Robot', for a sequence where the Doctor's assistant and journalist Sarah Jane Smith gains access to a meeting of the Scientific Reform Society, an organisation intent on imposing its will on the entire world.

Upon completion of 'The Mauritius Penny', Blackman's probationary period was over and, the production team being happy with her performances and the way *The Avengers* was progressing, her contract was extended.

Meanwhile, the London edition of *TV Times* dated 28 October to 3 November had a cover devoted to *The Avengers*, picturing Stevens, Macnee and Blackman. Other publicity around this time included a piece in the 27 October edition of the *Manchester Evening News* about Jon Rollason and his hobby of making pottery; this tied in with transmission of the episode 'Mission to Montreal'.

2.12 – 'Death of a Great Dane'

Between 5.30 pm and 6.30 pm on Wednesday 31 October 1962, a scene for 'Death of a Great Dane' was pre-recorded in Studio 1 at Teddington. This was set in Steed's apartment and involved him and Cathy debating the character Alexander Litoff's sudden withdrawal of charitable donations. Following the usual procedure, principal recording of the episode took place a day later, between 6.30 pm and 7.30 pm, once again in Studio 1. Peter Hammond was the director, and his guest cast included John Laurie and, making the first of his three appearances in the show, Frederick Jaeger.

The teleplay was by Roger Marshall and Jeremy Scott. The latter had come up with the basic outline of a millionaire dying and his employees keeping everything running as normal, allowing them time to sell off his assets. Elements of this plot would resurface in *The Saint* episode 'The Invisible Millionaire' when it was transmitted two years later, and another variation would be seen in 1968 in the *Man in a Suitcase* escapade 'Property of a Gentleman'.

The character Sir James Arnell's car was identified in dialogue by Steed as a 1961 Hirondel – a fictional manufacturer invented by Leslie Charteris as the mode of transport for his literary hero Simon Templar, aka the Saint, in his various books and short stories.

Having provided her pedigree Great Dane, Juno, as Steed's canine companion Puppy for the first season episode 'Ashes of Roses', dog trainer Barbara Woodhouse became involved with the series again, bringing Juno's sister Junia along to the studios to play Dancer. The other Great Dane in the episode, called Bellhound, was Macnee's own dog, Heidi. The rehearsal script had Cathy discover Bellhound in a back room at a joke shop, though this element was later rewritten to have a kennels employee arrive with the animal and, finding Mrs Gale present, mistakenly assume that she is the owner and simply hand the dog over.

In a sequence where she is attacked from behind in her apartment, Cathy defends herself with basic fighting skills and tripping her assailant, before quickly producing a chrome-plated .38 Smith and Wesson revolver from a drawer.

A fake gun prop in a joke shop scene refused to work correctly, leaving actress Clare Kelly with no option other than to take it off camera and physically pull out the flag with the word 'BANG!' printed on it, before bringing it back into shot. As the proprietor of the joke shop, Kelly delivered one of the best lines in the episode, noting with regard to her profession: 'I can live without plastic dog dirt!'

Though working independently, designer Patrick Downing and director Peter Hammond both came up with the concept of having the Litoff apartment suite as a large circular set. Litoff's two tickertape machines had seen service in the series two months previously when they had appeared in Henry Cade's penthouse in 'Bullseye'. In a scene where Steed and Cathy are trapped 14 floors up in Litoff's bedroom, they look out over the River Thames and the London skyline – the view being provided courtesy of a film insert fed into the recording by telecine. Macnee inadvertently changed some of his dialogue around during this scene, but not enough to cause any problems.

Toward the conclusion of events there is a frantic three-way discussion between the characters Getz, Gregory and Arnell. As Arnell, John Laurie got his one of his lines mixed up, saying 'Couldn't we take it with them,' before rectifying it with, '... them with us?'

Having decided to kill both Steed and Cathy because they know too much, Frederick Jaeger's character Getz arrives in Litoff's bedroom only to have the six-shot .38 Colt Officer's revolver he is carrying knocked from his grip. Having disarmed Getz, Steed waits for Cathy to scoop up the firearm and throw it to him so he can cover their adversary, while she produces her trusty Beretta 70 to take down Litoff's other two assistants in a mixture of gunplay and hand-to-hand combat. This sequence is indicative of the fact that, after several months of suggestions and ideas being thrown about by Sydney Newman, Leonard White, Don Leaver, Peter Hammond, Jonathan Alwyn and John Bryce regarding the depiction of Cathy, her fully-fleshed-out characterisation had now emerged in time for 'Death of a Great Dane'.

Originally, Mrs Gale was to have carried a small-calibre automatic in her handbag, but then it was decided against this, and the head of ABC's wardrobe department, Audrey Riddle, came up with a small leather inner thigh holster. This piece of equipment appeared in 'Propellant 23', but Honor Blackman disliked it, as with movement it tended to slide down her leg, and it was also felt that it was totally impractical for her to be raising her skirt to access her gun whenever faced with a dangerous situation. Another option considered was the use of an underarm holster, but this too was frowned upon as it was thought that Blackman's female attributes would restrict her ability to speedily draw the weapon. Also considered and rejected as unsuitable were a small wooden Japanese dumbbell-shaped weapon called a yawara stick, a dagger and a miniature sword. Eventually it was decided that, although she would carry a small pistol secreted in her pocket or waistband, Mrs Gale's main form of defence would be judo, which in effect took things back to Newman's initial outline. As mentioned, Blackman had already done some martial arts, but now she would go the whole hog, undergoing intensive training for five weeks with stunt man/actor Douglas Robinson (who had appeared in 'The Decapod') and his brother Joe at their gym near Leicester Square in London.

Patrick Macnee likewise received some judo coaching from the Robinsons, as it was felt that Steed should also be able to handle himself convincingly in fight scenes. For this season, Steed's Edwardian-style wardrobe was added to with hand-made Chelsea boots, a mixture of trilby and bowler hats, plus embroidered waistcoats from Macnee's own tailor, Bailey and Weatherill of Regent Street, London.

Meanwhile, Blackman had become confident in playing Cathy Gale. She had initially been unsure how to portray the character until doing a read-through of a script with her then husband and actor Maurice Kaufmann, who suggested that she play it like a man. This made logical sense, as Cathy was a tough woman, strong physically and emotionally, plus intellectually the equal of any male. After seeing Blackman's performance, the writers began writing to the character's strengths. Cathy's working relationship with Steed was at times abrasive, especially when he was trying to manipulate her into assisting him or when his ruthless streak appeared and he was callous and uncaring toward the innocent. She always had an answer for him and it became obvious that he would never be able to outwit or get the better of her. In many ways, Steed and Mrs Gale were direct opposites who worked together but used completely different methods to achieve a result.

Peter Hammond shot several scenes of 'Death of a Great Dane' reflected in a large mirror to give the impression of a set larger than it actually was. Roger Marshall was highly impressed by this and considered the episode to be the blueprint that the series should now follow. Also impressed by the episode was ABC chairman Howard Thomas, who had started thinking that producing the series on videotape was restrictive and that ABC's parent company, ABPC, ought to consider making *The Avengers* on film. Hammond and Patrick Downing took a copy of 'Death of a Great Dane' to ABPC's Elstree Studios to make a presentation to the board of directors in support of Thomas's proposal. However, the board decided against investing the larger amount of money required to produce the series on film. Downing would later cited the production team's lack of experience in dealing with celluloid as the stumbling block.

On Tuesday 13 November 1962, Leonard White issued a report in which he passed on Brian Tesler's congratulations to the crew for producing recent episodes, which in his opinion were as exciting as anything seen in the first season. However, White highlighted the need to depict a professional working relationship between Steed and Mrs Gale, pointing out to both writers and directors that the latter's character required suitable motivation to become involved in a storyline. He emphasised that Cathy cared about people who found themselves in trouble through no fault of their own and wanted to assist them in whatever way she could.

White also acknowledged the differing quality of the series' fight scenes, freely admitting that while some were excellent, others were poor and appeared unconvincing. To address this situation, he suggested that Doug Robinson be employed on a regular basis to choreograph the fights, as he had done very successfully in several previous episodes. In addition to this, White advised directors to take advantage of pre-recording fight scenes to avoid the performers being under pressure to get them right in one take, thus allowing already-completed action footage to be fed into the episodes during the main recording.

2.13 – 'Death on the Rocks'

The climax of 'Death on the Rocks' – an adventure involving a gang of criminals flooding the market with smuggled diamonds – was the first part to be taped. This was done in Studio 1 at Teddington on Wednesday 14 November 1962 between 11.45 am and midday. It featured a type of plot twist that would become more prevalent during the later filmed episodes, where the character that viewers least suspect turns out to be a villain. In this case it is a man named Daniels, but Cathy manages to hold him off with the aid of her trusty Beretta 70 until he has fired his own revolver six times and used up all his ammunition, leaving her free to disarm him. This sequence of events was not in the rehearsal script, which bore the working title 'Pillar of Salt'. In this earlier version, Cathy was to have dealt with Daniels by knocking him out with one of her hunting trophies, a stuffed animal head.

The main recording for the episode took place at the usual time, between 6.30 pm and 7.30 pm, on Thursday 15 November in Studio 1. Eric Paice provided the teleplay and Jonathan Alwyn returned to direct, putting together a cast that included, in the role of Daniels, Hamilton Dyce, whom he had used previously in the 1959 *No Hiding Place* episode 'Never Dine with Dead Men.'

As this episode features the first fully choreographed and longer Cathy Gale fight scene, it is no surprise that Blackman's black belt judo mentor Douglas (aka Doug) Robinson was also included in the cast to play her adversary, Sid. Against a background of Johnny Dankworth's screaming brass incidental music, Mrs Gale throws Sid around using moves later described in the actress's tome *Honor Blackman's Book of Self-Defence* as the spring wrist throw and the stomach throw. The latter was not a particular favourite of Blackman's, as despite the protection afforded by her leather fighting suit, falling backwards onto the concrete studio floor usually resulted in the friction removing layers of skin along her spine. Despite such problems, Blackman frequently pleaded with her male co-stars not to hold back during the fights, as the only way she could make them look realistic, and use judo techniques where their own momentum was used against them, was if they fought for real. In 'Death on the Rocks', there is a huge contrast between the spectacular Blackman/Robinson fight sequence and the Macnee/Robinson scuffle at the episode's conclusion, which unfortunately looks both haphazard and unconvincing.

The pressures of recording the episode 'as live' caught out the regulars on a couple of occasions. Macnee failed to get things word perfect in a scene where Steed discusses the diamond plot with Mrs Gale; he asks 'Have you ever hurled of a fella called Fenton?' instead of 'Have you ever heard of a fella called Fenton?' Later, after some illicit diamonds have been delivered to Cathy for Steed, Blackman also stumbled over a line of dialogue, beginning 'Let's hope that he doesn't mistake …' before quickly correcting herself and continuing, '… mistake it for talcum powder then.'

There was a little inconsistency in the commercial ad break bumpers for this episode, as they were accompanied by two different sections of Dankworth's theme.

The brass fanfare part was used at the conclusion of act one and the beginning of acts two and three, with the usual part heard only at the end of act two.

2.14 – 'Traitor in Zebra'

Perhaps the most technically challenging episode so far, 'Traitor in Zebra', was next into production. This contained seven location-filmed inserts, which were probably shot the week before the videotaping. Early in the episode, as part of his mission to investigate the jamming of a new satellite tracking system, an undercover Steed is impersonating a commander in the Royal Navy and drives a 1935 Alvis Speed 25 tourer (CPT 75) along Broom Road in Teddington to arrive at the security post of the naval base HMS Zebra – actually the main vehicle entrance to Teddington Studios. The main location was Weston Road and the adjoining parkland at Weston Green, Esher, in Surrey, about three miles from Teddington, where guest actors William Gaunt, Richard Leech, John Sharp and a terrier played out several scenes, during the course of which they went to a shop that now trades as the Esher Angling Centre. Night-time filming took place approximately a hundred metres down the road from the shop, at The Greyhound pub, which doubled as the Glen-Dower Arms in a scene where an anxious Lieutenant Mellors, played by Ian Shand, arrives in his Morris 1000 Traveller. Further night-time footage was shot at an unknown location of the Alvis being driven to a newspaper office with Steed and Mrs Gale – played by doubles – in the vehicle. This sequence was accompanied by the De Wolfe library stock music track 'Snap Decision', composed by Ivor Slaney and played in live from a record as the episode was being recorded.

Another De Wolfe-sourced track heard during the episode was a percussion piece used to accompany a fight scene between Steed and Leech's character, Joe Franks. Entitled 'Invention for Drums' and credited to Franz Mijts, this would be used again in the later episodes 'Conspiracy of Silence' and 'Killer Whale'. Also from De Wolf came the piece 'Naval Occasion' penned by Frank Spencer, which was utilised as background music to Steed arriving at Zebra.

Three videotaped scenes were pre-recorded between 8.15 pm and 9.00 pm in Studio 1 on Wednesday 28 November 1962, though one of these – a scene set in the office of naval commander Captain Nash, played by Noel Coleman, where he admits that the junior officer Sub-Lieutenant Crane, played by Danvers Walker, is innocent of the spying charge he faces – went unused. It should have been slotted in roughly five minutes from the end of the episode and was possibly excluded because of timing restrictions; if so, then obviously Leonard White and the episode's director, Richmond Harding, felt its omission did not detract from the narrative of the story.

Following the usual procedure, the main recording was completed on Thursday 29 November. The teleplay was by John Gilbert, who had a short writing CV and went on to supply only one more television script, for Associated-Rediffusion's *Crane*.

Steed's ruthless streak is again in evidence in this episode when, ignoring Cathy's objections, he locks the bomber Franks in with his own bomb, delivering the chilling line, 'It may not kill you, just mess you up a bit!' Left with no other option, Franks fortunately manages to defuse his device with seconds to spare.

While Steed is undercover, he and Cathy visit the Glen-Dower Arms. Mrs Gale drinks gin and tonic, but Steed settles for taking his gin straight. Later, when they are together at the bar, the unwanted sound of a door being opened and closed somewhere off camera can be heard on the soundtrack. Another minor glitch occurs in a scene where Captain Nash enters the naval laboratory to address scientist Dr Thom; during recording, the cameraman momentarily lost control of his pedestal-mounted camera and it collided with something on the set, resulting in a picture wobble. Unfortunately, these were not the only errors: recording a scene where Franks talks with the shop girl Linda, Richard Leech became confused and called her Cathy.

Although only a minor plot point, the concept of having the radar signals of an experimental satellite tracking system being jammed by a heat beam was a notable inclusion, marking the first time that science fiction had been featured in *The Avengers*.

The camera script was numbered as episode 37, but that was crossed out and a handwritten 40 applied, indicating that 'Traitor in Zebra' was pushed back in production order – although in the event it was actually the thirty-ninth episode to be taped.

2.15 – 'The Big Thinker'

'The Big Thinker', involving the ongoing sabotage of a new giant experimental computer called Plato, was the second episode of *The Avengers* to be scripted by Martin Woodhouse. It had a couple of scenes pre-recorded in Studio 1 between 8.00 pm and 8.30 pm on the evening of Wednesday 12 December 1962. These were the opening teaser sequence inside Plato, where the character Brensell, played by Johnson Bayly, is adjusting the system and a large cooling pipe begins leaking refrigerant gas, killing him; plus a scene at the Doctor Death Parlour amusement arcade, where Steed and Cathy discuss the situation and what their next move should be. Sticking with the usual production schedule, the main recording was undertaken the following evening between 6.30 pm and 7.30 pm, again in Studio 1. The director on this occasion was newcomer Kim Mills.

The previous episode having touched upon sci-fi, this one indulged in it further, thanks to Woodhouse incorporating cutting-edge technology into his writing and creating a computer that was more advanced than realistically possible at the time. The concept of a computer-controlled building was something that *The Avengers* would return to and expand upon several years later when the series was made on film.

No mention is made of Freckles the Dalmatian, as Steed has a new canine pet for this episode: Sheba the Whippet. During recording of a scene where he leaves the dog in the care of Mrs Gale prior to departing for the Middle East, the pressure of working 'as live' struck again, as Macnee fluffed a line of dialogue, saying, 'I've just dropped by to bring Sheba in for you. Will you look after me?' Obviously this should have gone, 'Will you look after her?' Sheba was actually owned by Macnee's girlfriend of the time, Catherine Woodville, who had appeared in a couple of episodes including the pilot 'Hot Snow'.

During the course of the episode, Cathy brandishes a Beretta 950 automatic and reveals that her husband was killed in Africa some years previously. She drinks her favourite tipple, gin and tonic, while at a gambling club with the character Dr Kearns, who Steed says is not her type, to which she replies, 'How would you know?' Wearing her leather combat suit, Mrs Gale later executes a shoulder throw on Kearns after he sneaks up and grabs her from behind in the computer room.

All change behind the scenes

Back in October 1962, Brian Tesler had been promoted to ABC's supervisor of features and light entertainment, which basically meant that he was now responsible for the overall running of the company and answerable only to chairman Howard Thomas. Two months later, in mid-December, Sydney Newman departed to join the BBC as their Head of Drama. He was replaced in the same role at ABC by one-time scriptwriter and script editor George Kerr. Meanwhile, Leonard White was offered the chance to assume Newman's former position as the producer of *Armchair Theatre*, a prospect that appealed to him greatly, and he accepted. Back on *The Avengers*, John Bryce was promoted to producer, filling White's shoes, and newcomer Richard Bates (son of novelist H E Bates) was brought in to take over as story editor. Bates had seen this job advertised in *The Sunday Times* two days after being made redundant by ABPC, for whom he had been involved in reading scripts and reporting on their potential at Elstree Studios. Having gone through separate interviews with Leonard White, Michael Chapman of Iris Productions and finally Sydney Newman, he had impressed them sufficiently for them to offer him the job. At the time, he knew absolutely nothing about *The Avengers*, but consulting Roger Marshall quickly brought him up to speed. Initially he became John Bryce's assistant, shadowing him for a couple of months in order to pick up the job. During the 16 months he would work on the series as story editor, Bates would invite 80 different writers to submit over 200 story ideas and outlines to the production office at Teddington.

2.16 – 'Intercrime'

No fewer than ten short scenes, which collectively made up a fast-moving fight sequence set in the office of a character named Felder and the adjoining rooms, were pre-recorded in Studio 1 between 8.15 pm and 9.00 pm on Friday 28 December 1962 for the final episode to be made that year, 'Intercrime'. The remainder of this adventure – in which Cathy finds herself in danger after taking on an assassin's identity in order to infiltrate a criminal gang – was videotaped in the same studio the following evening between 6.30 pm and 7.30 pm from a script credited to Terrance Dicks and Malcolm Hulke (the order of their being reversed from their previous episode). There was a small amount of location footage shot on 16mm film showing Her Majesty's Prison Holloway, on Parkhurst Road, London N7 – a location that would later be totally rebuilt in red brick.

During the course of the episode Cathy acquires and uses another different handgun: a .38 Smith and Wesson 10. When visiting her in Holloway, Steed wears black-rimmed spectacles as previously seen in 'The Mauritius Penny'.

A major glitch occurred during recording of a scene where Felder, portrayed by Kenneth J Warren, invites the assassin Hilda Stern, played by Julia Arnall, into his office to meet his superior, Manning: Arnall unfortunately left the door open behind her when she entered the set, revealing the sight of a cameraman pushing a pedestal-mounted camera along to get into position for the next scene.

The German character Kressler was an afterthought, being added at the rehearsal script stage to replace a Romanian named Lupescu.

The soundtrack included various stock tracks from the Conroy, Impress and De Wolfe music libraries, including composer Trevor Duncan's dramatic jazz piece

'Quotations for Murder', which would be reused in later episodes.

The cover for the London branch of Intercrime was originally meant to be a ten pin bowling alley, but this was later changed during a rewrite to become the Rifle Ranges International shooting range.

'Intercrime' was the first episode to air in 1963, being transmitted by ABC and some other regions on Saturday 5 January. ATV however decided to switch their screenings of *The Avengers* to Sunday nights at 10.35 pm, starting the following day, and this affected the other regions taking the line-feed from ATV's small studio in Foley Street, London W1. So, besides ATV London, the rescheduling affected the Channel, Grampian, Ulster, Westward and TWW regions. Border meanwhile declined to show any further episodes of the series until March.

'Warlock' revisions

The new production team combination of John Bryce and Richard Bates quickly arranged two replacement scenes for 'Warlock' as some of the episode's content was now considered irrelevant and potentially confusing to viewers. These new scenes, featuring Macnee, Blackman and Douglas Muir were recorded on 24 January 1963 and edited into place before transmission two days later. They comprised a piece of approximately two minutes' duration where Steed meets Cathy at the museum, and the end tag scene set in a pub, which was mostly rewritten, with Steed taking most of the lines originally delivered by One-Ten and the tone being made altogether lighter.

2.17 – 'Immortal Clay'

The first episode produced in 1963 was James Mitchell's 'Immortal Clay', which opens with the death of an apparent industrial spy in a factory where research into an unbreakable ceramic is taking place. Reports indicate that Jonathan Alwyn was originally lined up to handle the direction, but he became unavailable just before rehearsals began. Richmond Harding took over, and brought together a guest cast that included Douglas Muir making his tenth and final appearance as One-Ten.

When Steed mentions Mrs Gale, One-Ten registers his disapproval of amateurs getting involved in spying – although Cathy's specialist knowledge in ceramics comes in more than useful in this episode. Later, Steed advises Mrs Gale, 'It's bad to feel sorry for people in our business,' to which she promptly replies, 'I'm not in your business.'

Dialogue mentions Staffordshire and 'the five towns', indicating that the action takes place in Stoke-on-Trent, the capital of the Potteries, where clay found in the soil is ideal from making ceramics. In one scene where Cathy accompanies the villain De Groot and his burly assistant to the factory, they search her handbag and remove her nine-round Browning 1910 automatic.

The fight/struggle scene at the conclusion of events and the following scene were both pre-recorded between 8.30 pm and 9.00 pm on Wednesday 9 January in Studio 1, with the last few lines being ad-libbed by Macnee and Blackman. Adopting the same routine as used previously by Leonard White, John Bryce organised the main recording to take place the following day, in an early evening session that ran from 6.30 pm to 7.30 pm.

In a scene where Steed is attacked in the ceramics laboratory, the background music is the Bob Sharples-composed 'Waiting for Danger', supplied on record for the production by the Conroy music library. 'Quotations for Murder' surfaces again in a scene involving the packing of an unbreakable teacup, and another Trevor Duncan-written stock track called 'Passport to Soho' accompanies the conclusion of a scene where Steed gives some valuable figurines to Mrs Gale. A sequence where Cathy entices De Groot with the figurines concludes with a series of drumbeats, which were taken from another library track called 'Dissonance', composed by Norman Kay; this was used to bridge into the next scene.

The BBC gets worried ...?

On 12 January 1963, the *Manchester Evening News* reported that the BBC had begun scheduling their political satire show *That Was the Week That Was* earlier on Saturday evenings in an attempt to draw viewers away from *The Avengers* on ITV. In their defence, the BBC claimed that the difference in scheduling came about because a film was one of the regular weekly line-up of preceding programmes and, as different films ran to different lengths, this affected the start time of *That Was the Week That Was*.

2.18 – 'Box of Tricks'

With all the activity surrounding the development of Cathy Gale over the previous few months, Venus Smith had been neglected, not having appeared in an episode since 'The Removal Men' back in October 1962. However, this was rectified on Wednesday 16 January 1963 when three scenes were pre-recorded in Studio 1 for the finale of 'Box of Tricks'. The main recording, under the direction of Kim Mills, occurred the following evening, as usual between 6.30 pm and 7.30 pm.

The episode actually began life as a half-page outline for a first season adventure called 'Fifi and the Scorpion', submitted by Eric Paice. This featured Dr David Keel serving as a sports physician with a touring rugby team in Paris, where he is invited to a party set in a large property. The transmitted version was adapted from this outline by Peter Ling in a one-off writing collaboration with actor Edward Rhodes. The character Felicity (aka Fifi) in Paice's outline became Kathleen Sutherland, and the affliction suffered by her father, the General, was changed from gout to back pains. In the original, the General, who was working on secret NATO troop movements, requested a consultation with Keel as he was unhappy with the diagnosis of his French doctors. Keel would have carried the episode, with Steed – not even mentioned in the outline – in a lesser role.

The outline prepared by Ling and Rhodes for their revised version featured the trio of Steed, Venus and Cathy Gale, offering new possibilities within *The Avengers* format for having three lead characters working together. However, there was a huge rewrite before rehearsals began, and the final version includes just Steed and Venus. Steed is attempting to discover how top secret information is being passed to enemy agents, and gets Venus involved in his investigation after encountering her working as a magician's assistant in a club.

For her third appearance, Venus was transformed into a beat girl with much shorter hair. John Bryce was obviously aware of the growing pop culture and of new fashions inspired mainly by the Beatles, whose second single 'Please Please Me' entered the charts on 17 February. The revamped Venus still performed the same kind of songs as before though; in this instance the Cole Porter classic 'It's De-Lovely', and from 1946

'It's a Pity to Say Goodnight', written by Billy Reid, with additional lyrics provided by Stevens and Dave Lee. Back in full swing at Teddington, Stevens again gave her all for the musical numbers, backed as previously by the Dave Lee Trio, whose leader she found both helpful and humorous.

Stevens said in later interviews that she had preferred the original version of her character. By her own admission, a lot of the songs she sang in the show were chosen because they were ones she personally liked. The unused Venus Smith signature tune 'Venus', written by Bob Sharples, was not one of these, as its lyrics – credited to Sharples' pseudonym Robert Early – were awful. Choice examples included, 'My outline takes no Sputnik to span it,' and 'I'm no monolith, I'm no ancient Greek myth, I'm a Smith, Venus Smith.' Plans to record this song for a commercial single record release were drawn up, but Stevens refused to go along with them. She indicated that she was more than willing to do a more contemporary song, but nothing ever came of her request. She did record a version of 'Venus' at Teddington, presumably for possible inclusion as incidental music in the series, but this too was never used. Apparently, the sound department had at least two copies pressed on disc, one of which Stevens acquired and kept for several decades using it as a drinks coaster, until 2008 when it was eventually auctioned off at a charity event for £100.

There was no location filming undertaken for this episode, although there was some 35mm night-time stock footage used showing Piccadilly Circus and various nightclubs on Brewer Street, Dean Street and Wardour Street, all in London W1.

This time around, Venus comes across as more enthusiastic about getting involved with Steed and his shadowy undercover world, and he demonstrates genuine caring for her wellbeing, showing great relief when she emerges unscathed from a suspect magician's cabinet.

2.19 – 'The Golden Eggs'

Having quickly formed a working relationship with new story editor Richard Bates, Martin Woodhouse phoned him with an idea for an episode. Having gained his agreement, he proceeded to create 'The Golden Eggs', which dealt with items of germ warfare falling into the wrong hands. Once his outline had been accepted, he completed the teleplay within four weeks.

Woodhouse preferred character-driven stories, considering *The Avengers* as a different concept for an adventure series. He was very happy with the direction of this episode, assigned to Peter Hammond, whom he considered to be the best director on the series. Blackman also admired Hammond's work, later stating, 'He was so imaginative.'

The character of Cathy Gale was still being developed at this point, with John Bryce and Richard Bates obviously wanting to put their own stamp on the show. Her black leather image would come to the fore under the new producer/story editor combination, and generally the production would begin to look more slick and professional. Woodhouse later recalled meetings with Bates where he put forward the view that having both Steed and Mrs Gale as such complete characters was great – but what about making the villains interesting too?

Bryce instigated the construction of a new Cathy Gale apartment set, which meant that the old one had to be destroyed first – thus a plot device was concocted of having Cathy stay at Steed's place temporarily while he took accommodation in a hotel, in return for her cooking his meals. The new apartment set would not appear for another couple of months, making its debut in the season's last episode, 'Killer Whale', indicating that a decision had already taken to continue with the series after that.

In a scene where they are eating breakfast, both Steed and Cathy read the fictional newspaper the *Morning Post*. During recording of the subsequent action where they glue a broken porcelain vase back together, Blackman almost burst out laughing at Macnee's humorous observations regarding teeth and dentists.

Cathy latest handgun, seen at one point in this episode, is a Walther PPK automatic. In a later scene, she shows a ruthless streak similar to Steed's when she is faced with the armed villain Redfern, threatening him with virus-filled eggs and issuing the warning, 'Are you in the market for an handful of death!'

Having been satisfied with Peter Arne's performance in 'Warlock', Hammond cast him as Redfern in 'The Golden Eggs'; a somewhat unfortunate choice in one way, as in an unforeseen situation the two episodes were scheduled on consecutive weekends in most regions.

A small amount of night-time location footage was shot for this episode on 35mm film, showing the character Hillier, played by Robert Bernal, causing an ambulance to have an accident by making it veer off the road and onto some snow-covered rough ground.

Blackman's martial arts abilities were by this point beginning to attract plenty of interest in the press. *TV Times* No. 379, published Friday 1 February 1963, contained a two-page interview entitled *Gale Force!*, conducted with the actress at her home in Fulham. There were mentions for both Douglas and Joe Robinson as her judo trainers, and the actress noted that the cameramen at Teddington had never expected her to be able to throw a man over her shoulder. It was also revealed that Blackman had almost broken a finger when karate-chopping actor John Dearth in a fight scene in the episode 'Propellant 23', and had later needed hospital treatment.

2.20 – 'School for Traitors'

The production team were apparently beginning to struggle with their schedule by this stage, as the next episode, 'School for Traitors', was recorded between 6.30 pm and 7.30 pm on Saturday 9 February in Studio 1 and then transmitted in some regions later that same evening, at 10.05 pm. Taken from a teleplay by James Mitchell and directed by Jonathan Alwyn, this was another Venus Smith adventure; this one involving university students being blackmailed into becoming involved in anti-British espionage. The show's opening titles underwent a slight alteration, incorporating a new Julie Stevens caption card reflecting the character's changed appearance.

Stevens' usual musical collaborator Dave Lee was unavailable and was replaced by keyboard player Kenny Powell. The rest of her backing group, Art Morgan and Spike Heatley, remained unchanged, though the combo was now credited as the Kenny Powell Trio. They supported Stevens on a couple of numbers; 'Varsity Drag', a Charleston-inspired song from 1927 written by Buddy De Sylva, Lew Brown and Ray Henderson, followed by 'Put on a Happy Face', penned by Charles Strouse and Lee Adams, originally from the 1960 stage musical *Bye Bye Birdie*. However, Stevens did not sing the second verse of the latter song and worked out an improvisation with Powell to finish it early, as it obviously needed to fit into a timed slot. In a scene where she visits the university, Venus also gives an impromptu rendition of the calypso classic

'Yellow Bird', backed by a solitary acoustic guitar.

Recording a sequence where Steed arrives in the study of lecturer Jeff Roberts, Stevens stumbled over her dialogue, getting the introductions the wrong way round – saying 'This is a friend of mine, John Steed' when referring to Roberts. Looking at Macnee and Richard Thorp playing Roberts, she tried again, 'John Steed this is Jeff Roberts,' by which point all three performers were grinning broadly. Attempting to rectify the situation, Macnee chipped in, ad-libbing, 'Jeff Steed? This is marvellous. How do you do? Call me Bert, thank you. How do you do?' Later, actress Melissa Stribling as Claire also managed to get Roberts' name wrong, addressing him as 'Jack'. She fluffed another line, too, saying '220 guineas' instead of '220 pounds', which had the knock-on effect of making some calculations regarding a forged cheque inaccurate.

Frederick Farley made his only appearance here as Steed's latest and temporary superior One-Seven who, like his predecessor One-Ten, expresses great displeasure at amateurs becoming involved in matters of espionage – obviously meaning Venus. Farley was supposed to appear in two scenes, but although the second one with Macnee was in the camera script, it was omitted from the recording, possibly due to timing restrictions.

Toward the conclusion of the episode, Steed produces a Smith and Wesson 19 revolver, which he allows the student East, played by John Standing, to use to cover the villainous Claire Summers and Dr Shanklin.

2.21 – 'The White Dwarf'

Writing solo on the series for the first time, Malcolm Hulke came up with an imaginative teleplay involving a star on collision-course with Earth and the murder of an eminent astronomer. Hulke's concept of a heavenly body threatening to destroy the world pre-dated various big-budget feature films that explored and developed the idea in the following decades, including *Meteor*, *Deep Impact* and *Armageddon*.

The initial read-through of the script occurred at 10.30 am on Sunday 3 February 1963 in Rehearsal Room 2A at Teddington, with recording following between 6.30 pm and 7.30 pm on Saturday 16 February on eight sets in Studio 2. As with 'School for Traitors', the turnaround time between recording and transmission was extremely brief; 'The White Dwarf' was screened in Anglia, Southern, Tyne Tees and both ABC regions later that evening.

Filmed location footage was shot in Parliament Square SW1 on a misty day, showing the Houses of Parliament and a pan round to the H M Treasury building, doubling in the episode as the Ministry of Science: Division of Astronomy. A shot seen at the beginning of the episode to establish Tor Point Observatory was actually a still photograph of the University of London Observatory at Mill Hill, NW7. Additional filming was done for the shootout at the conclusion of events among the concrete supports and skylights on the roof of the technical block at Teddington Studios, as it was easier to get a 35mm Arriflex camera up there than one of the larger EMI studio cameras.

After arriving at Steed's apartment, Cathy discusses the headline on his copy of *The Daily World* – a fictional morning newspaper – while Sheba the whippet lies quietly on the sofa. The sign at the Tor Point Guest House points out that it is for vegetarians only; when Cathy requests a meal, the landlady offers carrot soup, herb omelette and baked bananas. Later, when Mrs Gale unlocks the outer door of the observatory from within, allowing Steed to enter surreptitiously and expecting a confrontation, he is armed with .38 Smith and Wesson 10 revolver. During recording of another scene at Steed's apartment, the overhead boom microphone became visible momentarily when Macnee stood up, as the boom operator failed to move it upwards in time to keep it out of shot.

In the rehearsal script, the end tag scene where Cathy browses through an astrology book had her inform Steed that her birth date was 13 November. However, someone noticed this was a continuity error, as she had previously stated in 'Warlock' that her birthday was 5 October, thus the dialogue was amended for the camera script so that the correct date made it into the episode.

2.22 – 'Man in the Mirror'

The next episode in production, 'Man in the Mirror', underwent recording in Studio 1 between 6.30 pm and 7.30 pm on Friday 22 February 1963 for screening in some regions the following night, in what would become standard practice until the end of the season. The writing of the teleplay was shared between Anthony Terpiloff and Geoffrey Orme. The latter had been scriptwriting for feature films since the mid-'30s, although his experience in television was somewhat less, having begun with *Ivanhoe* in 1958. After *The Avengers*, his career was quite short-lived, although he scripted a *No Hiding Place* episode and, perhaps his greatest claim to fame, the *Doctor Who* serial 'The Underwater Menace'.

This time around, Venus performs two songs in a recording studio: 'There's Nothing Like Love', written by Leo Robin and Jule Styne for the 1955 film *My Sister Eileen*, and 'I Know Where I'm Going', using a 1945 arrangement of a traditional tune. Stevens was backed by the Kenny Powell Trio again, although the line-up had undergone changes with the departure of both Art Morgan and Spike Heatley, to be replaced by orchestra leader Jack Parnell on drums, accompanied by his regular bassist Lennie Bush. Powell had worked with both Parnell and Bush previously, at Ronnie Scott's jazz club on Frith Street in London and at ATV's Elstree Studios.

The plot concerns a mystery surrounding the apparent suicide of a cipher expert. On the pretext of wanting information for a friend, Steed has Venus visit the Wonderland fun fair to take photographs (getting a shot of the dead man alive and well) and walk Sheba at the same time. Later, in the dressing room at the recording studio, Venus enquires further, and Macnee apparently forgot his dialogue for Steed's response, coming out with '… somewhere up near you live' instead of the scripted '… up in your part of the country'; however, before he had a chance to rectify things, Stevens came in with her next line, 'Manchester?'

Director Kim Mills cast Danish actor Michael Gover as another boss for Steed, One-Six. Steed receives a reprimand for turning up late for a briefing, although the agent defends himself, pointing out his long service and ability to stay one step ahead of the opposition.

The twangy electric guitar pop instrumental heard when Steed and Venus visit Wonderland is 'Boudaha', performed by the Belgian group the Cousins, which had been released on the Palette record label 19 months earlier under the serial number PG 9017.

In the climactic scene where the villain Victor Trevelyan starts a gramophone and informs Steed and Venus that when the record finishes it will activate an electrical circuit to detonate a bomb, he states that it will take three minutes. However, the camera script indicated ten minutes, suggesting that this must have been altered sometime during rehearsals on the day of recording to add tension to the episode's conclusion.

2.23 – 'Conspiracy of Silence'

Writer Roger Marshall returned to the series with 'Conspiracy of Silence', an adventure involving a Mafia drugs gang using a travelling circus as a front. This underwent recording in Studio 1 at Teddington on Friday 1 March 1963 under the direction of Peter Hammond, who cleverly framed one scene through the bars of a birdcage. A parkland sequence featuring Macnee, Sheba and guest actor Robert Rietty was pre-filmed on 35mm in the grounds of Chiswick House, off Burlington Lane, Chiswick, London W4, located about six miles from Teddington. This was a silent shoot with dog noises, silenced pistol shots and Dankworth's incidental music all dubbed on later. Several years on, the Beatles would use Chiswick House and its grounds as the location for promotional films for their single 'Paperback Writer' and its B-side 'Rain'.

The walls of the character James's office are seen to be plastered with circus posters, one of which advertises an act called the Diminutive Steed, although it's not known if this was purely a coincidence or an in-joke perpetrated by the crew. Recording the scene where Cathy arrives at the circus, Honor Blackman struggled to keep a straight face, obviously enjoying the antics of the clowns Leggo and Arturo. Later, while sat in the front row watching the clowns performing their routine, Steed places his bowler hat on the barrier in front of him and, as Leggo approaches, casually raises it to reveal a .38 short Webley revolver beneath. Mrs Gale meanwhile produces her Beretta 950 automatic at one point during in the action.

The same fake gun prop that failed to work in 'Death of a Great Dane' is used here by the clown Leggo, much to the amusement of the circus audience, as it works perfectly on this occasion, ejecting the flag with the word 'BANG!'

To add authenticity to the circus atmosphere, a real knife-throwing act called Elizabeth and Collins was included in the cast, billed on the closing credits as themselves. There was also a fully-grown caged tiger on set for several scenes, although the heat from the powerful studio lights made it somewhat lethargic. For the final sequence, the animal trainer's voice was captured on the soundtrack, calling the big cat's name, Cheshire, in an attempt to make it growl on cue.

2.24 – 'A Chorus of Frogs'

Two videotape inserts for the sixth and final Venus Smith episode, 'A Chorus of Frogs', were pre-recorded in Studio 1 between 10.00 am and 1.00 pm on Thursday 7 March 1963, with the bulk of the episode's recording being completed the following evening under the direction of Raymond Menmuir, who was new to the series. The first pre-recorded segment was a sequence of events in act one involving Steed and the characters Jackson, played by Alan Haywood, and Helena, played by Colette Wilde, on the deck of a yacht at night. This continued with Helena forcing Steed away at gunpoint and culminated in Anna, played by Yvonne Shima, killing Jackson with a spear gun. The second pre-recorded insert was of a shoot-out and struggle in a laboratory at the conclusion of act three, featuring seven performers.

Menmuir brought together a notable cast that also included Eric Pohlmann, John

Carson and, despite him having already appeared earlier in the season in 'The Sell-Out', Frank Gatliff, with Michael Gover making his second and last appearance as One-Six.

Martin Woodhouse provided the teleplay under the slightly shorter title 'Chorus of Frogs'. The plot involves Steed, on holiday in Greece, being asked to investigate the death of a deep-sea diver and smuggler. Woodhouse described it as 'A bit of fun,' and admitted that he rarely attended the recordings of his episodes at Teddington.

During a scuffle with a character named Ariston, Steed easily relieves him of his 9mm Beretta automatic, ejecting and keeping the magazine before throwing the now-harmless pistol onto a piece of furniture.

There were a couple of musical interludes included in the episode, with Julie Stevens performing the traditional number 'Hush Little Baby', in an arrangement created by Kenny Powell and herself, plus 'The Lips That Touch Kippers', written in 1924 by H M Burnaby and John P Long. The episode's dialogue reveals a little more background about Venus; specifically that she was born on her father's barge – though she is far from amused at finding stowaway Steed hiding in her cabin.

Stevens considered Macnee to be an absolute gentleman, who would make suggestions to make things easier for her on set. She never met any of the show's writers and only occasionally saw Blackman in the studio canteen. After 'A Chorus of Frogs', ABC declined to extend her contract, preferring to concentrate on the Steed and Mrs Gale combination. It was left to John Bryce to visit Stevens at her home to deliver the bad news that her time with *The Avengers* was over. According to Richard Bates, the Venus Smith storylines were more difficult to write. He said: 'The more girlie Venus did not really sit in a credible relationship with Steed. Looking at the episodes, one can see that neither of them was sparking off the other.' However, when interviewed at *The Avengers* at 50 event at Chichester University in 2010, Leonard White indicated that had he stayed with the series, then he would have definitely retained Stevens on the show.

On the afternoon of Saturday 9 March, Stevens returned to the nation's television screens when she took part in a celebrity ten pin bowling match against Roger Moore, whose series *The Saint* had begun transmissions in October the previous year. The contest had been publicised in the *TV Times* dated 1 March. With each celebrity partnered by a professional bowler, the contest was staged at a hotel near Heathrow Airport. Unfortunately, Stevens had never bowled before and struggled with technique, getting her fingers stuck in the holes of the bowling balls, leading to Moore's team taking a landslide victory.

2.25 – 'Six Hands Across a Table'

Having served as *The Avengers*' story editor for a time during season one, and having appeared in the episode 'The Removal Men' as Jack Dragna, Reed de Rouen, credited as Reed R de Rouen, provided season two's penultimate teleplay, 'Six Hands Across a Table', which cost £5,245 to produce. The storyline concerned a shipbuilding consortium resorting to murder to make certain that a nuclear powered liner was built in Britain, rather than being outsourced to a French shipyard.

An establishing shot supposedly of the head office of the Reniston Group shipbuilders of Glasgow was actually of Hampton House, situated on the Albert Embankment, London W4. The main recording of the episode took place in Studio 1 at Teddington on Friday 15 March 1963, augmented by three pre-recorded inserts. These were of a Renistone boardroom meeting at the beginning of the episode; the aftermath of the character Brian Collier's close call with a falling block and tackle outside the draughting office; and a fight between Mrs Gale and an unknown assailant.

After his performance in 'The Decapod', Philip Madoc was cast by director Richmond Harding for his second appearance this season. Harding also brought in Guy Doleman to portray shipyard owner Oliver Waldner, who initially provides a love interest for Cathy but is later revealed by Steed to be a murderer. Unfortunately, Doleman hit problems during the recording of a tense scene with Blackman, as he accidentally called her Ros instead of Cathy.

Continuity was maintained by having Mrs Gale confirm that she still works as an anthropologist for the British Museum, though the mocked-up interior of her car was given a roof, indicating that it could not be her MGA convertible seen in earlier episodes.

Attired in her leather fighting suit, Blackman executed her longest fight scene since 'Death of a Great Dane', using both the shoulder throw and body drop judo moves as shown in her self defence book published a couple of years later.

Steed at one point rescues Cathy from a tricky situation with the aid of a Smith and Wesson 18 revolver.

2.26 – 'Killer Whale'

The final second season episode, 'Killer Whale', penned by John Lucarotti, sees Steed and Cathy investigate a suspected link between a boxing gym and the illegal smuggling of ambergris – a valuable substance derived from sperm whales and used in the making of perfumes.

A couple of videotape inserts were pre-recorded on Thursday 21 March 1963 in Studio 1, with the main recording following the next day, under the direction of Kim Mills. The pre-recorded inserts were of a sparring session between two boxers at the gym, and the end tag scene set in Cathy's apartment, where Steed attempts to entice her to travel to the Caribbean with him. However, a decision was made not to use some of the latter. The cut material involved Steed making a devious telephone call to the airport to rearrange Mrs Gale's destination. This would account for the discrepancy between the episode's final duration of around 49 minutes and the timing of 50 minutes and 25 seconds noted by Mills on the camera script.

In the course of his investigations, Steed arrives at Fernand's boutique, where he is given a couple of magazines to look at by Denise the receptionist, one of them being a fictional fashion publication called *Svelte*. Under the pretext of wanting to purchase a complete wardrobe for his niece, Steed views various fashions from the collection of '60s designer Kenneth Sweet, modelled by three professional models of the time: June Hodgson, Diane Keys and Elaine Little. However, the models did not get individual name-checks on the closing credits; they were collectively billed as Models from the Kenneth Sweet Collection. Stuntman Valentine Musetti and actor Terry Brewer also went uncredited as the two boxers.

The teleplay called for Mrs Gale to engage in two fights, for which Honor Blackman donned her leather fighting suit once again. Steed loans her his Browning 1910 automatic so that she can cover the villains while he telephones the police using the false name Carruthers.

Mrs Gale's new, sparsely-furnished apartment set had finally been constructed in time for this episode, featuring upholstered benches, a bookcase, a drinks cabinet, sculptures, vertical blinds, an entry intercom system incorporated into a coffee table, a sliding outer door and a kitchen off to one side. This all gave it an ultra-modern '60s feel. The address was given as 14 Primrose Hill, London NW1.

Season two concludes

By the end of its second season, *The Avengers* had managed not only to consolidate its position in the nation's viewing habits, but also in the process to create something fresh, stylish and innovative. The kinky, black leather image of Cathy Gale had quickly become ingrained into British society, adding a new and exciting dimension to television entertainment. Unlike season one, this batch of episodes would not be junked by ABC; copies would be retained for overseas sale – they were transmitted in Australia and then in Canada the following year – and ultimately for future generations to enjoy. However, because at the time there was no satisfactory method of transferring British 405-line videotapes to American 525-line videotapes, the series was missing out on being screened in the most important television market in the world: the United States. This situation had not escaped attention at ABC. Howard Thomas, Patrick Macnee and Honor Blackman all thought *The Avengers* would work better if made on film rather than videotape, not least because it would make American broadcasters more inclined and able to transmit it. However, as season two concluded and pre-production began on season three, *The Avengers* would once again be recorded on videotape.

SEASON THREE

DRESSED TO KILL

The second season had captured the public's imagination with its combination of quirky storylines, raunchy black leather and offbeat humour, and *The Avengers* was quickly becoming a television and cultural phenomenon. However, all bar two episodes had overspent their allocated budget, prompting a costing executive at ABPC to recommend that action be taken to bring production costs under control. Patrick Macnee and Honor Blackman had both requested a salary increase before signing new contracts to continue for the third season, so ABC actually considered dropping one of them on financial grounds. One idea was that Steed could revert to working with a male colleague; Howard Thomas suggested that consideration be given to actor John Standing reprising his role of Ted East from 'School for Scoundrels'. Ultimately this did not occur, due to the tremendous impact Honor Blackman had created as Mrs Cathy Gale, making it unthinkable to dismiss her. Patrick Macnee was considered equally indispensable, having been with the show since day one. Recognising that a successful formula was at risk of being destroyed, Thomas overruled his colleague's advice and sanctioned a salary increase for both leads, which raised the budget to £5,100 per episode, ensuring that the series would continue.

3.01 – 'Brief for Murder'

There was only a six day break between the recording of the final series two episode, 'Killer Whale', on Friday 22 March 1963 and the start of rehearsals on the first season three episode, 'Brief for Murder', on 29 March; so there was no real respite for the behind-the-scenes team, or for Macnee and Blackman.

Recording resumed on Thursday 11 April in Studio 1, with Peter Hammond as director and James Goddard as designer. This episode marked the return of writer Brian Clemens to the series, with a teleplay about two corrupt solicitors, the eccentric Lakin brothers. Played by Harold Scott and John Laurie, these characters exhibited dark humour, giving a taste of the kind of villain that would almost become the norm in the later filmed seasons of the series. After using her talents in the first season episode 'Nightmare', Hammond gave another guest role to actress Helen Lindsay, who had also appeared in the *Police Surgeon* episode 'Man Overboard'.

A sequence where Steed rides a bicycle through a wooded area, getting into position to fire his Smith and Wesson revolver at Cathy on a motor cruiser, was filmed near the studios on the bank of the River Thames, between Teddington Lock and Ham

Dock. As Blackman was not a great swimmer, a stunt double performed Cathy's subsequent plunge into the water, which was done opposite some boat houses that backed onto Strawberry Vale in Strawberry Hill. Alice Fraser, who played the part of Miss Prinn, was also on location, using a small rowing boat to come ashore and discover Steed's bowler hat at the scene of the apparent crime.

Additional location filming was performed on New Street, London NW2, for a scene where Steed is taken through the Inns of Court to the chambers of the Lakin brothers. A couple of stills of the Old Bailey were also used to establish the location of Steed being placed on trial. The location work enhanced the episode considerably, although it would be one of the few examples this season, which would include somewhat less exterior shooting than the previous one, presumably to reduce costs.

Incidental music was sourced from both the De Wolfe and the Joseph Weinberger libraries, including 'Snap Decision' by Ivor Slaney, previously heard in 'Intercrime', and Frank Mijts' 'Invention for Drums', used when Steed quickly departs the riverbank. In one scene, Steed is witnessed reading the fictional publication *The Solicitors Gazette*.

Toward the episode's conclusion, when Miles Lakin telephones his assistant Bart to have him destroy incriminating evidence secreted in a wall safe, unfortunately Harold Scott transposed some of his words, saying 'In the bottom desk of the drawer is a bunch of keys,' instead of, 'In the bottom drawer of the desk is a bunch of keys.' Similarly, recording the scene where the verdict at Steed's trial is delivered, the pressure got to actor Walter Swash, playing the jury foreman, who got his only line of the episode wrong, blurting out 'Guilty!' when he should have said 'Not guilty!' No amount of ad-libbing could rectify this mistake, so in this instance the virtually unprecedented decision was taken to stop the recording and do a second take before continuing with the rest of the episode.

An early draft of Clemens' script gave a tantalising insight into Steed's background. It revealed that he was educated at Eton, and in the Second World War commanded a torpedo boat as a Royal Navy lieutenant. After hostilities ceased, he earned a living by smuggling items around the ports of the Mediterranean Sea, before returning to London and a position in the civil service. From there he then became an advisor to an oil-rich Sheikh in the Middle East and was involved in successful negotiations to avert a war in the region. Grateful for his efforts, the Sheikh awarded Steed a regular income of oil revenue, even when he came back to the UK and got involved with top secret work for the Ministry. Unfortunately none of this information actually made it into the episode; it was removed before the camera script was written.

The teleplay was vetted before rehearsals began by ABC's script supervisor Anthony John, who found several inaccuracies regarding the legal procedures it depicted. This resulted in both him and story editor Richard Bates correcting portions of it. The end product was so accurate that an impressed Law Society invited Clemens to speak at one of its events. However, due to his scriptwriting duties he declined the offer.

When the episode was transmitted by ATV London on Saturday 28 September 1963, John Bryce was disappointed to notice that the sound of a telephone ringing was omitted at one point, despite him having previously seen a copy where it had been dubbed on. Somehow the wrong tape had been supplied to ATV, who also fed their transmission through to Southern Television. Bryce registered his displeasure by sending an internal memo to various people at ABC, including George Kerr and Brian Tesler.

3.02 – 'Concerto'

On Saturday 13 April 1963, rehearsals got under way on the season's second episode, 'Concerto', which came from the Terrance Dicks and Malcolm Hulke writing partnership and involved Steed and Cathy protecting a visiting Russian concert pianist, Stefan Veliko. Recording was undertaken between 6.30 pm and 7.30 pm on Friday 26 April 1963 in Studio 1. The director was Kim Mills, whose distinctive visual style included plentiful use of close-ups. Among the cast assembled was Nigel Stock, who had also guest-starred in the *Police Surgeon* episode 'Wilful Neglect'. Terry Brewer and stuntman Valentino Musetti (first name given as Valentine on the camera script) played a pair of thugs, but went unmentioned in the closing credits.

Having already owned a variety of dogs – Puppy the Great Dane, Freckles the Dalmatian and Sheba the Whippet – Steed has acquired another canine pet in this episode in the form of a Great Dane called Junia – which was actually the animal's real name. Junia was supplied to the production by dog trainer Barbara Woodhouse and had been seen previously in a different role in the season two episode 'Death of a Great Dane'.

Commenting on an early draft of the script, Anthony John recommended that the strangulation of the character Polly White be toned down – which was achieved on recording by having her fall out of camera shot almost as soon as the attack began. Further to this, John insisted that the exterior set of a strip club featured in the episode be constructed minus the obscene images that were originally specified.

The commercial break bumper for the beginning of act two does not have the usual Johnny Dankworth-composed cue, but is accompanied by a recital that continues into the first scene with the character Stefan Veliko playing a piano.

In a scene where Steed visits Nigel Stock's character, Zalenko, Stock forgot his dialogue and covered by repeatedly drinking and toasting his visitor as Macnee nervously looked off set a couple of times, presumably at Kim Mills, eventually ad-libbing until his fellow actor remembered the next line.

3.03 – 'The Nutshell'

The day after 'Concerto' was recorded, rehearsals began on 'The Nutshell' under the direction of Raymond Menmuir. The script was by Philip Chambers, a writer new to the series, who had been discovered by Richard Bates. He had previously penned a screenplay for *Interpol Calling*, but his career as a television scriptwriter would be limited: after *The Avengers*, he would contribute only solitary scripts to the BBC's *Dr Finlay's Casebook* and *Adam Adamant Lives!*.

The story this time involves Steed apparently stealing state secrets and then being discovered, eventually allowing him and Mrs Gale to pinpoint a traitor in the secret underground base known as the Nutshell. Chambers dialled into the espionage genre perfectly with his script, picking up on the use of acronyms for television and film spies, started with the inclusion of the SPECTRE organisation in the James Bond film *Dr No*. For instance, the character designation Disco was an acronym of Director of Intelligence, Security and Combined Operations, and the file name Big Ben stood for Bilateral Infiltration of Great Britain, Europe and North America. The rehearsal script was again scanned by Anthony John for any potential problems, and he insisted that all references to the Soviet Union be removed prior to the camera script being written, in order to prevent any complaints from the Communist quarter that could embarrass ABC.

A small amount of night-time location filming was done for the episode, showing a dark-coloured Humber Super Snipe car travelling at speed. After the usual camera rehearsals the previous day, recording took place between 6.30 pm and 7.30 pm on Friday 10 May 1963 in Studio 1 at Teddington.

Having already had a new apartment set created for Mrs Gale, John Bryce proceeded to instruct the same for Steed, and the result, seen for the first time in this episode, was an up-market high-rise dwelling overlooking Parliament Square, though with the same address as his previous season's abode, 5 Westminster Mews, London SW1. The dual-level apartment included a large bookcase that acted as a room divider between the living space and the kitchen, plus hunting trophies, prints on the walls, a grandfather clock, three model ships in glass cases and a tiger-skin rug. There was also a large portrait of Steed's great grandfather and a telescope used to look out over the London skyline through a large plate glass window, which in the later episode 'The Gilded Cage' would be revealed to be bullet-proof.

Recording a scene where Steed visits the character Elin Strindberg, portrayed by Edina Ronay, Patrick Macnee accidentally dropped two small packages containing toothbrushes that she had produced from her bag while searching for some microfilm. Later he encountered problems leaving the set, as he attempted to walk backwards through the double doors, becoming uncoordinated and colliding with one of them. Another unforeseen hitch occurred with a radio secreted in Steed's apartment, which fell over after its short flex reached the end of its travel due to Macnee accidentally pulling the headphones too far. Ad-libbing again, Macnee simply made a sound indicating the problem before standing the radio back in the upright position. In a scene where Disco, played by John Cater, sees Steed in a surveillance photograph with Elin Strindberg, he is seen to exclaim a single word in surprise, but the soundtrack is silent at this point. According to the camera script, his exclamation should have been 'Good grief!', but clearly he must have said something different.

At one point in the action Steed packs the Smith and Wesson revolver seen previously in 'Brief for Murder'; but the 'Richard and Kerr' pistol mentioned in the dialogue was purely fictional, and presumably an in-joke reference to story editor Richard Bates and Head of Drama George Kerr. The 'Phoenix Square' referred to was similarly fictional, as there is no such place in Greater London. In a sequence where Cathy and the captive Steed have a pre-arranged scuffle, she slips him a Beretta 950 automatic. Later she uses a large-calibre revolver to shoot a villain she finds searching through Steed's apartment.

The *Daily Express* dated Saturday 19 October reported the strange situation of Ministry of Defence officials having vetted 'The Nutshell' before allowing it to be transmitted, fearing that it might reveal the location of a secret spy base. The episode's concept of the so-called Nutshell, a vast underground shelter beneath London where security forces would be based in the event of a third world war, had obviously caused someone in authority concern. However, an ITV spokesperson confirmed that there were no cuts made to the episode. Possibly the MoD had been searching for any references to Burlington Nuclear Bunker, a top secret bomb and radiation-proof Cold War installation built in the late '50s to house up to 4,000 government personnel in the case of nuclear war. Located at Corsham in Wiltshire, this fallout shelter was a 240 acre site, over a kilometre long and buried 120 feet underground. It remained a secret for decades until revealed in 1982 by journalist Duncan Campbell in his book 'War Plan'. Photographs of the interior of this complex can now be easily found on the internet, Burlington (aka Central Government War Headquarters) having been decommissioned in 2007.

3.04 – 'The Golden Fleece'

The following episode in production was 'The Golden Fleece', in which Steed accidentally discovers that a Chinese restaurant is being used as a front for a gold-smuggling operation with the surprisingly selfless motive of aiding needy ex-servicemen. This was recorded on Friday 24 May 1963 in the usual way in Studio 1, starting at 6.30 pm and concluding at 7.30 pm. The teleplay was by Roger Marshall, but credited as co-writer was Phyllis Norman, who possessed medical knowledge and had made certain that it was completely accurate in that respect. Marshall and Norman had previously worked together in the same manner on instalments of the soap *Emergency-Ward 10*. Before rehearsals commenced, Anthony John checked through the rehearsal script and recommended that work needed to be done to remove overt disrespect toward the British Army and the American President.

The director's chair was filled on this occasion by Peter Hammond, who cast Warren Mitchell in the first of what would eventually be four guest appearances in the series. Junia graced a solitary scene, to make this her second and final showing as Steed's pet.

For a scene where the doorbell of his apartment rings and, insisting on answering it, Steed throws Cathy her handbag and leather gloves, which she fails to catch, the action was captured in true Hammond fashion by shooting the reflection in a large wall mirror. Later, for a sequence where one character drives a car into another, Hammond utilised the novel effect of placing in front of the camera a sheet of glass representing the windscreen, which was made to crack and splinter upon the supposed impact of the collision.

Maintaining continuity, Steed is once again armed with his Smith and Wesson revolver, while Cathy relies on her Beretta 950. A scene of Mrs Gale fighting with a Sergeant Major involved Blackman propelling her fellow actor into some wire mesh fencing, tripping him up and performing a stomach throw, all on the restrictive exterior set of an army billet hut and security fence. While in his apartment, Steed was seen reading one of Herge's Tintin books; a French-language version of *Tintin and the Land of Black Gold*. At one point, another character is seen scanning through the fictional newspaper the *Hampshire Times*.

Some of the background music generally used to bridge between scenes came from library records provided by Keith Prowse (now KPM Musichouse) and the American company Major Records. This included the track 'Chopsticks' by the French composer Roger Roger. Additional material came from a tape courtesy of the De Wolfe library, which contained assorted drumbeat music and the piece 'Snap Decision' that had already been heard in 'Brief for Murder'.

Consolidating the format

Writer Roger Marshall had not rated the first season of *The Avengers* highly, because in his opinion it had lacked the distinctive style that had arrived with the second batch of episodes, mainly thanks to Macnee's refined portrayal of John Steed. He had originally become involved with the show with some apprehension, but had quickly realised that he had become part of a team, attending rehearsals and discussing characterisation and dialogue with Macnee and Blackman. In the second season, there had not been a writer's guide or series bible as such, simply a list of things Steed and Mrs Gale would and would not do. Richard Bates had expanded on this for the third season, and Marshall found that it allowed the writers quite a lot freedom to construct original storylines; though he also considered *The Avengers* to have been influenced by the late '50s American television series *The Thin Man*, based on the novel by Dashiell Hammett.

Having got the third season up and running, John Bryce also decided that the time was right to issue a new production directive. He created a seven page document, dated 1 June 1963, which was distributed to the crew. This basically constituted a reappraisal of the show and served as a reminder to all concerned about the format and regular characters, although it also covered some of the same ground as his predecessor Leonard White's earlier memos.

John Steed was described as a professional undercover man with a private income, who was dry-witted, debonair and enjoyed the finer things in life, appearing quite vulnerable so as to mislead his adversaries. However, it was emphasised that in order to complete his work Steed was ruthless, unscrupulous and dedicated, being able to call upon extensive training and experience in subjects as diverse as burglary, poisons, torture and murder. Bryce also pointed out that, above all, Steed exuded charm, and this quality applied equally if he was being menaced by villains or if he was the one doing the menacing.

Juggling her two vocations of anthropology and undercover agent, Mrs Catherine Gale was every bit as much of a professional as Steed. However, her description had her as a humanitarian whose moral attitude would not allow her to use people to achieve her own ends or perpetrate deceptions on the same level as her crime-fighting partner. Loyal and compassionate, Mrs Gale was more than qualified to become embroiled in the world of espionage, being an expert in both martial arts and firearms, though her different approach to their work would often bring her into conflict with Steed.

Bryce maintained that both Steed and Cathy were essentially undercover operatives and should not work like private detectives or police officers. In fact the forces of law and order should be included only as background and not feature prominently at all. With regard to the villains seen in the series, it was considered essential that they be worthy and intelligent opponents with viable motives for their actions. Further to this, Bryce thought that the episodes' teaser scenes were extremely important and that they needed to be original, bizarre and provocative, so that the viewer's attention was grabbed immediately and held. He went on to emphasise that the show had to capture its audience in the first five minutes; having an episode where acts two and three were good was irrelevant if no-one was actually left watching.

Regarding the popular fight scenes, Bryce stipulated that it was compulsory to have at least one physical altercation and some additional form of aggression in every episode. The different fighting styles were confirmed, with mentions of Mrs Gale's judo abilities and how she would throw an assailant, whereas Steed would trip them and generally disregard any form of fair play, being prepared to use anything at hand to give him an advantage, including his umbrella. The use of professional stuntmen for upcoming fight sequences was recommended, with the promise that future teleplays would be written accordingly to make casting such people practical. Toward that end, Douglas Robinson had apparently been placed on the payroll to make himself available for two rehearsal days or four half days per episode.

Policy regarding pre-recorded videotape inserts was reinforced, indicating that they should be reserved for fight scenes and important dramatic segments of an episode but definitely not for the convenience of costume changes. The restrictions surrounding the use of filmed exterior shooting were even more strict. It was indicated that this should never be considered for the conventional purposes of establishing shots or short linking segments to go between scenes. However, Bryce was open to what he referred to as self-contained filmed sequences and he offered some helpful examples: a motorcycle chase featuring Cathy; a shoot out on a golfing green involving Steed; or Cathy tied to railway tracks as an express train thundered closer and closer. (In the event, only the motorcycle idea would be incorporated into this season.)

Bryce also touched on the subjects of action, casting, music and sound effects and stated that he wanted writers to continue setting their storylines in different and unusual locales, instructing that realism should take a back seat to fantasy and glamour. On the plus side, he was open to experimentation in all areas of the series, thinking that pushing the envelope could only benefit and enhance *The Avengers*. On the minus side, writers and directors were advised that drinking and smoking should not feature prominently in episodes and that bad language and blasphemy were definitely not allowed.

For his part, Bates was encouraging the writers to have a closer working relationship with the performers, especially Macnee and Blackman, getting them to attend both rehearsals and recordings. Bates knew what he wanted, assembling a close-knit group of writers who had already contributed to the series and understood its requirements, relying mainly on Marshall, Clemens, Hulke, Woodhouse, Paice, Lucarotti and Mitchell. After having three different partners in his adventures in the previous season, Steed would have only Mrs Gale in this one, and Bates instructed his various writers to write for Blackman's character as if she were a man. Sometimes Bates would change the dialogue by having lines written for Macnee spoken by Blackman instead (and *vice versa*), and he admired Blackman for her willingness to have a go at anything a screenplay demanded.

Blackman was now receiving up to 500 items of fan mail every week, including risqué offers from various male admirers, some of whom sent her party invitations that insisted she wear her black leather and bring her whip! To eradicate the problem of Blackman dealing with this type of communication, ABC press officer Marie Donaldson started to open and vet all correspondence, disposing of any dubious items before passing the remainder on to the actress.

For this season, the caption card opening titles used for the previous two seasons were replaced by a series of cards depicting the silhouette of a man attempting to escape from between the letters of *The Avengers* logo.

3.05 – 'Death a la Carte'

The next episode into production, from the typewriter of John Lucarotti, was initially called 'Fricassee of Death' before being renamed 'Death a la Carte', and it saw Steed and Cathy trying to prevent the assassination of a visiting Emir. It included a sequence pre-recorded between 7.30 pm and 9.00 pm on Thursday 6 June 1963 involving Steed climbing up the exterior of the Emir's hotel at night. This was realised with the aid of a wind machine and having Macnee edging along a section of prop wall that was actually on the studio floor, with a large screen behind him on which film was projected showing a street from above. An earlier draft of the teleplay had a different version of this sequence, with Steed climbing down the building rather than up.

The main recording was undertaken between 6.30 pm and 7.30 pm the following evening in Studio 1, under the control of Kim Mills who, having previously cast Robert James in the children's sci-fi serial *Secret Beneath the Sea*, reused him here as the villain Mellor.

Ken Parry, playing the head of the hotel kitchen, Arbuthnot, tripped over one of his lines in an exchange of dialogue with Macnee, taking three goes to get it correct: 'I don't mind what they take from the silverware storage room, that's not my responsibility, but the cleaning room … room … cupboard is.' Blackman also fluffed slightly at the episode's conclusion, jumping in too soon with a line of dialogue giving the Latin name for some poisonous mushrooms, leaving a smiling Macnee to ad-lib a line in order to have her repeat it.

Bryce's production directive regarding the casting of stunt performers for fight scenes was adhered to, as Valentino Musetti was brought in to play Mellor's accomplice Ali. In a scene where Ali attacks Steed by clamping a stranglehold on him from behind, the agent extricates himself by dropping to one knee and executing an over the shoulder throw – a move Macnee had learnt from Douglas Robinson.

Earlier on 6 June, John Bryce sent a memo to Brian Tesler suggesting that *The Avengers* would make the perfect subject for a feature film, which in his opinion could be produced comparatively quickly and easily. Tesler agreed and, responding several days later, confirmed that he had consulted Howard Thomas and that the concept would be presented to the ABPC board of directors for their assessment.

3.06 – 'Man with Two Shadows'

Six inserts were pre-recorded on Thursday 20 June for James Mitchell's final episode for the series, 'Man with Two Shadows', the storyline of which was a variation on one of the standard plots in adventure fiction, involving eminent figures in society being replaced by doppelgangers. The inserts featured Steed and his double; a man named Gordon and his double; and two other characters, Cummings and Sigi. Following the standard procedure, the main recording took place the following day in Studio 1, though beginning earlier than usual at 5.15 pm. The director was Don Leaver, who cast Geoffrey Palmer in his third guest appearance in the series. This episode also saw the initial appearance by Paul Whitsun-Jones playing Steed's new regular superior, Charles, for whom the agent appears to have little respect, shouting at him to shut up when he interferes during an interrogation.

The episode's sets, including an impressive dual-level morgue and a wooden holiday camp chalet, were designed by Paul Bernard. A large matte painting was used to provide a view of the great outdoors as seen from within the chalet when Steed opens the door for Gordon.

Despite having been used on only a few episodes, the show's new opening titles were upgraded at this point, making them a little more spectacular; 'Man with Two Shadows' was the first episode to feature the upgraded version.

A fight scene between Cathy and the character Rudi Engel, portrayed by

Blackman's judo mentor Douglas Robinson, was longer and more complicated than usual, played out in the holiday camp ballroom set to an accompaniment of 'The Blue Danube' by Johann Strauss, played from a De Wolfe library record.

At one point, Cathy holds Steed at gunpoint with a .22 Colt Officer's Match revolver, mistakenly thinking that he is an impostor. This episode also sees her sport a couple of shorter hairstyles, one of which was first seen in 'Death a la Carte'. As in 'The Nutshell', Steed claims to be a non-smoker, despite the fact that in other episodes he has been witnessed smoking both cigars and cigarettes. While at the holiday camp he is seen reading another Tintin book, this time *Tintin in Tibet*.

The dialogue heard in the end tag scene, where Steed arrives at Cathy's apartment and enquires what is available for breakfast, to which she retorts, 'Cook it and see', was a late addition. These lines did not feature in the rehearsal script; presumably Macnee, Blackman and Leaver invented them and incorporated them into the camera script sometime during rehearsals.

Leaver enjoyed working with Blackman. 'It was terribly exciting,' he later said, 'the idea of having a woman in the role and its development into judo.' Loving everything about the sexy, emancipated Cathy Gale character, Leaver too had now joined the ranks of those who considered *The Avengers* ideal for feature film treatment.

3.07 – 'Don't Look Behind You'

Some pre-recording work for 'Don't Look Behind You' was undertaken between 7.30 pm and 9.00 pm on Thursday 4 July 1963 for the climactic confrontation between Mrs Gale and the villain Martin Goodman, with the bulk of the recording being started at 6.30 pm the following evening. With a teleplay by Brian Clemens, this adventure, originally called 'The Old Dark House', was something of a departure for the show, having psychological horror aspects. It was directed by Peter Hammond, who cast Maurice Good as Goodman after using him previously in the season one episode 'Hunt the Man Down'.

While visiting Cathy at her apartment, Steed announces that he has acquired a new car and arranges to drive her to Devon to visit Sir Cavalier Resagne. However, his 'new' car turns out to be a vintage Lagonda 3 Litre convertible (GK 3295). Location filming involving Macnee, Blackman and the Lagonda was executed on Ham Common and Sandy Lane, with a group of cheerful drinkers seen outside the Royal Oak pub on Ham Road, all across the River Thames from Teddington Studios in nearby Ham. The camera script indicates that the music originally intended to accompany this sequence was Lou Adler's harmonica theme from the film *Genevieve*, but in the event a piece of library music was used instead. The exterior of the fictional Resagne Hall was provided by Strawberry Hill House on Waldegrave Road, Twickenham – though this extremely large property now looks quite different, as in recent years it has undergone extensive renovations thanks to national lottery funding.

When interviewed for *Starlog* magazine in 1998, Blackman confessed to having had disagreements with Hammond about the part of this episode where Cathy has to be prepared to kill Goodman, who has been playing a macabre game of cat and mouse with her around the deserted house. During rehearsals Blackman found the scene so emotional that she began to cry, and felt there was no other way that she could play it. Hammond however insisted that he wanted Cathy to appear tough. Unable to give quite the performance the director wanted during the recording, Blackman did manage to scrape through it, although not without some obvious distress.

Cathy again wears her fighting suit and kinky boots in this episode, and carries her Beretta 950 automatic. She mentions having written an article about medieval clothing for the fictional magazine *Hers: For the Fashion Woman of Today*, of which a couple of prop copies are seen. Clemens' clever dialogue comes to the fore in a sequence where the character credited as Young Man asks Cathy 'How would you like me to tuck you in?', to which she replies, 'How would you like me to break your arm!'

Despite the fact that Steed hardly features in the storyline, Patrick Macnee rates 'Don't Look Behind You' as one of his favourite episodes. An earlier draft of the script was slightly different, in that it had Steed hide away somewhere in Resagne Hall until the final scene, whereas in the version as recorded he departs and returns later on, after reading about Goodman's escape from prison. Apparently Steed and Cathy tricked Goodman ten years previously due to his criminal activities, resulting in his arrest and consequent imprisonment by the Berlin police – though this does confuse continuity if one considers 'Warlock' to show the first meeting between the two crime-fighters.

'Don't Look Behind You' would be the only episode of *The Avengers* to be remade twice, first on monochrome film in the next season as 'The House That Jack Built' and again later in colour as 'The Joker', both co-starring Diana Rigg.

3.08 – 'The Grandeur that was Rome'

'The Grandeur that was Rome' went before the cameras for a slightly longer recording session than usual between 6.20 pm and 7.30 pm in Studio 1 on Friday 19 July 1963. It would be the only teleplay for the series by Rex Edwards, who had previously worked as script associate on 37 episodes of the BBC's *Dixon of Dock Green* but would not gain any further television credits until almost ten years later on some instalments of the early '70s ITV crime drama series *Six Days of Justice*.

Richard Bates considered Edwards' storyline to be a successful integration of classical characters into a contemporary setting. Sir Bruno Luker, played by Hugh Burden, would be the first in a long line of eccentric diabolical masterminds with illusions of grandeur to feature in the series, his scheme to poison the world's water supply also making him an early eco-terrorist. Slowly *The Avengers* was beginning to take on the surreal elements for which it would later become renowned, though at the time Macnee was uncomfortable with this, thinking that this was as far-fetched as things should go

The news bulletin that Sir Bruno watches on his television set at one point was stock footage of a violent demonstration in Trafalgar Square, London, fed in via telecine to a monitor on the set. Octavia, played by Colette Wilde, is seen to flick her way through a copy of the fictional *Hers* magazine, as also featured in the previous episode, 'Don't Look Behind You'. Steed attempts a mild disguise by donning thick-rimmed spectacles, as in both 'The Mauritius Penny' and 'Intercrime'. He also produces a hidden swordstick from his umbrella.

After 'The Grandeur that was Rome' was transmitted on Saturday 30 November, ABC received a number of telephone calls from viewers complaining that the resolution had been unclear. This prompted John Bryce to request a viewing copy of the episode, which he had missed when it went out. He found that the final ten minutes lacked a convincing plot explanation for Steed extricating himself from a swordfight with the character Lucius, and that Octavia and two other villains, Marcus and Eastow, all appeared to have escaped justice. He emphasised that, going forward, his team should create better narratives and that no loose ends should be left hanging at the end of an episode. In fact, the problems with 'The Grandeur that was Rome' appear to have arisen in rewriting during the course of production, as an earlier draft of the teleplay, when it was called 'The Glory that was Rome', had the swordfight between Steed and Lucius ending with the latter being killed and both Octavia and Marcus being apprehended.

3.09 – 'The Undertakers'

The ninth episode in the season's production order was 'The Undertakers', another offering from Malcolm Hulke, and this was assigned to Australian director Bill Bain, who was making his debut. The story involves an undertaker's premises and an exclusive rest home for the elderly being used as part of a scam to avoid inheritance tax.

'The Undertakers' features the longest piece of location filming yet seen in the series: a four minute chase and shoot-out in the grounds of York House and the adjacent York House Gardens, accessed by a footbridge over the road named Riverside in Twickenham. Bain would have captured this material using a tripod-mounted 35mm Arriflex camera, probably the week before recording the rest of the episode. The location's close proximity to Teddington Studios – only about two miles away – meant that it was a simple matter to transport the small unit to the location, along with Macnee, Blackman and guest actors Patrick Holt and Howard Goorney, and to arrange for a 1928 Rolls Royce Phantom 1 hearse to be in attendance as required. All the footage was shot minus sound, which was edited on later; in addition to various gunshots, this included the De Wolfe library track 'Invention for Drums', heard previously in other episodes.

The usual hour-long taping session took place in Studio 1 at Teddington on Friday 2 August 1963. Due to the light-coloured background used for it, the episode title lettering was done in black on this occasion as opposed to the usual white, making it the only one presented in this manner for the season. When Steed first visits Mrs Gale at her apartment, she is busy cleaning her Beretta 950 and reassembling an L1A1 self-loading rifle. Other firearms are also on view, including a couple of Walther P38 automatics.

After breaking into the undertakers' premises, Steed is attacked by a pallbearer named Frank, played uncredited by stunt performer Valentino Musetti, causing him to utilise his umbrella as an offensive weapon. At other points in the action Steed indulges himself with five-star Napoleon Brandy and also assists in consuming two bottles of champagne while at Cathy's abode – at one point appearing extremely eager to pour, resulting in a small spillage for which Macnee ad-libbed an apology. During recording of the end tag scene, Macnee fluffed a line, saying 'A couple of weeks ago' rather than the scripted 'It's two weeks off, isn't it?', leaving him no alternative but to correct himself by adding 'A couple of weeks ahead.' Blackman then ad-libbed in agreement, 'Ahead, yes.'

3.10 – 'Death of a Batman'

Roger Marshall provided the script for the next adventure, 'Death of a Batman', involving Steed attending the funeral of his wartime batman, Wrightson, and learning that the man has unexpectedly left him a large sum of money, which turns out to have come from an illegal share-dealing scheme.

This episode was recorded on Wednesday 14 August 1963 starting at 6.30 pm in Studio 1 at Teddington under the direction of Kim Mills, who gave Philip Madoc his third guest appearance in the series and also recast Ray Browne, having previously used him in the second season episode 'The Big Thinker'. Steed has acquired another Great Dane for this episode, by the name of Katie.

Fictional magazines abound at Steed's apartment, as Cathy reads *Miss* and he thumbs his way through *King*, which surprisingly has an advertisement on its back cover for Benson and Hedges cigarettes, at a time when product placement on ITV was strictly not allowed.[7]

Honor Blackman had problems with the door of a bedroom set at one point, as it refused to latch properly, resulting in her having to shut it three times before it remained closed. This episode also called for her to speak fluent Spanish (as previously heard in 'Death Dispatch') in a scene where Cathy makes a telephone call to Madrid. She had another demanding fight scene to perform as well. Using what was later described in *Honor Blackman's Book of Self-Defence* as the sweeping loin, Cathy throws the villain to the floor on his back, where he attempts to regain his feet only to receive a knee to the chest. Then, as he gets to his knees a second time, Cathy moves in and lands a karate chop to the neck, following up with a double-handed axe on the same target to knock the man out cold.

Scriptwriter Marshall had clearly remembered that Mrs Gale was supposed to have a background in photography, as he then had her produce a miniature camera and proceed to take photographs of some framed share certificates hung on the wall. The script also reveals some more details about Major Steed's army career, indicating that he was involved in military intelligence in Munich in 1945 after the Second World War.

The rehearsal script indicates that originally Geoffrey Alexander's character Gibbs was to have been named Grove, Andre Morrell's character Lord Teale was to have been Lord De Witt and the £180,000 left in Wrightson's will was to have been an even more substantial £480,000.

Considering 'Death of a Batman' to be representative of everything good in *The Avengers*, John Bryce would always choose this episode whenever ABC received a request from outside sources or potential buyers to view a sample of the series.

3.11 – 'Build a Better Mousetrap'

'Build a Better Mousetrap' was writer Brian Clemens' next contribution to *The Avengers*. In this adventure, Cathy goes undercover in a motorcycle gang – who accept her because she has passed their initiation test of doing the ton plus ten (110 miles per hour) on her machine – while Steed investigates an atomic plant that appears to be resulting in mechanical failures in the nearby area. The true cause of the failures is a device built by the late Professor Peck, whose two daughters live in the nearby watermill, but besides Steed and Mrs Gale, there are a number of foreign agents also searching for the cause of the disruption.

Recording took place in the usual fashion in Studio 1 at Teddington between 6.30

---

[7] Though *King* magazine did not exist in the '60s, a publication of this title did hit newsagents in 2003 as a spin-off from one called *XXL*.

pm and 7.30 pm on Wednesday 28 August 1963 under the direction of Peter Hammond. However, this was just about the only aspect of the episode that was usual as, without knowing it, the crew had effectively assembled a pilot for what *The Avengers* would become in the following season, when it would progress to being made entirely on film. Clemens' teleplay incorporated a number of components for which the series would later become famous: eccentric characters, a revolutionary invention with cutting-edge technology, and a liberal dose of humour, all set away from London in the English countryside. The episode also boasted a large amount of location filming, including some material shot at night.

The script required Blackman to ride a powerful 500cc Triumph Twin motorcycle (987 CAA), which luckily did not present any great problem as she had experience handling such machines, having at one time been a courier for the blood donor service. However, to get back up to speed she took a refresher course at Surbiton police station. This was arranged by the motorcycle club Riverhill Riders, whose members appeared on screen as the biker gang when on the road.

The daylight motorcycle footage was shot approximately eight miles south-west of the studios on roads situated within Chobham Common near the village of Chobham in Surrey. This also appears to have been the location used for a dusk photoshoot of Blackman astride a Royal Enfield twin motorcycle in her biking leathers and crash helmet, with Macnee complete with bowler hat and brolly as pillion passenger.

Some of the exteriors of the Vernon watermill featured in the plot were captured at Castle Mill in Dorking, Surrey. Toward the conclusion of the episode, a fight breaks out at the mill, and Cathy again gets into a struggle with a villain, Gordon, landing a knee to his chest and performing her famous stomach throw. With Gordon down, his accomplice Caroline jumps in to take his place, but she is no match for Mrs Gale's fighting abilities, being easily pushed away.

After John Tate's appearance in the second season episode 'Killer Whale', Peter Hammond cast him again in this episode, as the character Colonel Wesker.

Although the villains are never actually referred to as Soviets, Caroline's burst into Russian at one point – saying '*Niet!*' instead of 'No!' – gives the game away.

The studio sets, including the impressive courtyard exterior and adjoining barn interior of The Hunter's Horn pub, were constructed from designs by Douglas James, who had also worked on episodes of *Out of this World*.

'Build a Better Mousetrap' cost £5,235 to produce, with the largest outlay being for performers' fees, followed by set design and construction (including props) and then payment to the scriptwriter.

Blackman quits

With the premier of the third season on ITV now only a week away, the cogs of the ABC publicity machine started to rotate, resulting in media exposure in excess of anything witnessed previously for the series. The John Steed and Cathy Gale version of *The Avengers* also appeared in comic strip form for the first time, in weekly instalments in the pages of the television listings magazines *Look Westward* and *The Viewer*, published by the Dickens Press Limited, covering the Westward and Tyne Tees regions respectively. Both magazines began their run of strips with the first of a nine-part adventure, 'Operation Harem', on Saturday 14 September 1963. They would continue printing them until May 1964.

Everything seemed to be going smoothly for *The Avengers* until, on Thursday 19 September 1963, Honor Blackman dropped a bombshell by informing ABC executives that she would be departing the show upon completion of work on this season's final episode the following March. The actress had already signed a five-year film contract with Harry Saltzman and Cubby Broccoli, under which her first assignment would be to play a major role alongside Sean Connery in the next James Bond film, *Goldfinger*. Having suspected that something like this might happen, Howard Thomas had been lobbying the board of directors at the ABPC to give Blackman a film contract as a way of securing her involvement with *The Avengers*, but his request had been denied, and now his fear had become reality.

The Avengers' behind-the-scenes team found it difficult to believe that Blackman would abandon the show that had established her as a huge television star. However, even some determined pleading from Patrick Macnee made no difference, as the actress would not consider an extension to her contract.

Two days later, on Saturday 21 September, *The Weekly News* paper conducted an interview with Blackman where she ended by confirming that she would indeed be leaving the series. Strangely, however, the popular press ignored the story completely. In fact it would be another four months until the national dailies considered the loss of *The Avengers'* female lead a newsworthy item.

Meanwhile publicity continued for the third season's on-air debut. The edition of *Look Westward* published that same Saturday featured a two page article devoted to the series; then on Thursday 26 September *Reveille* magazine ran a piece concentrating on brown belt Blackman's weekly judo lessons.

3.12 – 'November Five'

Thursday 26 September 1963 also saw two videotape inserts being recorded between 7.30 pm and 9.00 pm in Studio 1 at Teddington for the next episode into production, 'November Five'. This story, scripted by Eric Paice, was basically a contemporary gunpowder plot scenario involving an atomic warhead. The pre-recorded elements were the end tag scene set in the lobby of the Houses of Parliament, plus an earlier scene involving Macnee, Blackman, guest actors David Langton, Ric Hutton, David Davies and various extras on the terrace of the same building.

Concern was raised by script supervisor Anthony John regarding the teleplay, which in his opinion contained several instances of political bias and elements that could potentially harm the integrity of ABC, such as the depiction of unscrupulous behaviour by Members of Parliament. This resulted in a large amount of rewriting to delete or alter the offending portions. John, Richard Bates and George Kerr then went through the camera script line by line until they were satisfied that all offending material had been removed.

Director Bill Bain supervised the main recording on Friday 27 September, which once again occurred in Studio 1 beginning at 6.30 pm. In addition to the videotape inserts, there was also a piece of stock film footage showing a night-time firework display, which was edited into the episode via telecine.

This was the first episode to carry the 'Honor Blackman's wardrobe designed by Frederick Starke' credit that would be used thereafter – a development that upset ABC costume designers Audrey Riddle and Ambren Garland, who felt it ignored their input.

The show's fight sequences had proved so popular with viewers that by this point the production team were striving to include two per episode, figuring that this would mean twice the spectacle and excitement. Blackman knew that when she heard the incidental music for a fight begin to play in the studio, there was no turning back: she would have to go through the pre-arranged moves with an attitude of 'It'll be all right on the night.' Cathy's first fight scene in 'November Five' comes in a gym where she is attacked with a ski-pole by the character Farmer, played in a series debut by stuntman Frank Maher; the second is with the character Max, portrayed by one of Blackman's judo associates, Joe Robinson.

With the anticipated increase in such combat sequences, Audrey Riddle quickly pointed out that a second leather fighting suit would be required for Blackman, as the first was beginning to show signs of wear. Designed and tailored by the wardrobe department at Teddington, the second suit had buttons down the right-hand side of the tunic and was black (as opposed to its green predecessor), as presumably lighting techniques had now improved. This new suit made its debut in 'November Five', for which Blackman also wore various other black leather items including boots, culottes, trousers and skirt. The wardrobe budget was now £100 per episode, up from £60 per episode in the previous season, but it is unknown if this increase was specifically to pay for the materials needed to make the new fighting suit.

As a security measure, Mrs Gale now has CCTV installed outside her apartment, giving her a picture of whoever wants access to her home. This was realised during recording by having a monitor fed by a live image from another camera on an adjoining set. Steed is once again armed with a Smith and Wesson revolver during the action. The identity of the paymaster or foreign power behind the hijacking of the warhead is never revealed.

Emphasising the gunpowder plot connection, 'November Five' was transmitted as close as possible to 5 November, going out on 2 November in the majority of ITV regions and on 3 November in the Grampian region.

'Berserk!'

Having had success co-writing the ABC sci-fi serial *Target Luna* and the follow-up *Pathfinders* trilogy, beginning with *Pathfinders in Space* in 1960, Eric Paice appears to have approached the company in late 1962 or early 1963 with an idea he envisaged forming another six-part serial, this one called *Berserk!*. ABC were interested enough to have him complete a single-page outline for the initial instalment, but ultimately decided against commissioning scripts. However, unwilling to throw the concept away, the writer then submitted it in a revised format as an episode of *The Avengers*.

This new version of 'Berserk!' still included the original opening from part one of the serial, where a body is discovered in one of the fountains in Trafalgar Square with a whaling harpoon protruding from its back. In his detailed four-page outline, Paice continued by having the authorities locate a letter written in Norwegian, sewn into the pocket of the deceased man. Investigating the situation, Steed and Cathy Gale come across two separate break-ins at the British Oceanography Institute, also located in Trafalgar Square. The second of these proves to be extremely baffling, as the night watchman's guard dog suddenly turned on him and viciously savaged him. Receiving a telephone call from a passer-by, two police officers then attended the scene, but before they could leave their vehicle, one attacked the other. The Avengers learn that some electrical devices were stolen from the Institute, and eventually discover that these create ultra-sonic waves that can brainwash people into committing acts of violence. The villains of the piece install the devices inside salon hairdryers and proceed to use them, discovering that the effect of the ultra-sound differs between men and women. Men can be programmed as assassins, but women simply kill themselves.

The scenario played out more like a filmed episode than one intended for videotape, with Paice absolutely excelling himself in the writing, but for some reason 'Berserk!' was never commissioned as a rehearsal script.

Season three starts transmissions

With a cover devoted to *The Avengers*, picturing Macnee on the courtroom set of 'Brief for Murder', the *TV Times* dated 22 to 28 September 1963 paved the way for transmissions of season three to get under way. Both ABC regions scheduled the episodes on Saturday evenings at 9.50 pm, and they were joined by Tyne Tees, Ulster, Anglia and both TWW regions. Five other regional companies – ATV London, Southern, Border, Westward and Channel – opted for a slightly later start at 10.05 pm, with Scottish Television opting for an even later 10.25 pm. This was the nearest to a co-ordinated network transmission that *The Avengers* had managed so far. The only outstanding region, Grampian, decided to go it alone and transmit on Sunday evenings, starting at 10.35 pm on 29 September. Every region began with the episode 'Brief for Murder'.

It was around this time that producer John Bryce decided to remind his team of some basics regarding the series. He issued another set of directives, indicating that the storylines should have a humanitarian angle to motivate Mrs Gale's involvement and generate interaction between her and Steed, whose often ruthless attitude would enrage her sense of morals and fair play. Bryce also considered that the resolution of each episode was extremely important; the way in which Steed and Cathy succeeded over their adversaries should be easy to understand, and the villains should be both intelligent and formidable opponents. Another issue covered by the producer was how violence should be portrayed on screen. He insisted that Steed and Cathy should be shown to fight only because they had no other option, and that the fighting should never appear sadistic or dirty. He added that in his opinion several episodes could have benefited from more glamour content, and that both writers and directors should remember to include and cast attractive female characters. He also voiced concerns regarding the way Dankworth's theme was being fed in over the ad-breaks, which meant that the first couple of notes were sometimes lost. To eradicate this, he insisted that in future the ad-bumper was to be faded up on screen first, before the music came in.

Also this month, the September issue of the fashion magazine *Harper's Bazaar* featured the results of a special photoshoot for *The Avengers*, with stills of both Macnee and Blackman taken by photographer Terence Donovan.

3.13 – 'Second Sight'

Another teleplay from Martin Woodhouse, 'Second Sight' was the next to be allocated space in Studio 1, recording taking place there from the usual start time of 6.30 pm on Friday 11 October 1963. Macnee's favourite director of the videotaped episodes, Peter Hammond, returned to supervise proceedings, having cast Peter Bowles in the first of his four guest roles in the show and John Carson in the second of his three. The white episode title lettering for this episode needed a drop shadow applied to it, as without that it would have been virtually invisible against the light-coloured background of the set.

The story this time concerns a multi-millionaire – Carson's character, Marten Halvarssen – who is apparently about to receive a corneal graft in a revolutionary new operation to treat his blindness. Steed calls in an eye specialist of his own – Dr Spender, played by Ronald Adam – who is subsequently murdered. It turns out that Halvarssen's associate Anstice – Bowles' character – is a criminal double-crossing him in a diamond smuggling scam.

The airfield building seen at one point in the action appears to be nothing more than a large wooden garden shed assembled in the studio, but its limitations are disguised by Hammond's inventive approach of shooting Blackman and Macnee from outside through one of the windows as heavy rain pounds against the glass. Another example of the director's imaginative approach can be found in the episode's opening scene, where the performers are seen via their reflections in the surface of a glass table.

The script called for Dr Spender to be shown falling hundreds of feet down a Swiss mountainside to his death – something seemingly impossible to achieve convincingly without resorting to location filming. However, the challenge inspired Hammond to be creative once more, cutting from an image of Ronald Adam falling out of frame to one of a figure spiralling away as reflected in the cornea donor's dark glasses. The latter was achieved by having a shot of a small, light-coloured artwork figure on a rotating caption slide superimposed over one of the dark glasses in close-up. This inexpensive effect interpreted the teleplay exactly, leaving viewers with no doubt as to what had happened.

A couple of production errors crept into the recording. At one point Steed is about to plug in a coffee percolator in his apartment when an overhead microphone appears briefly in shot. The same problem occurs again in a later scene at the Swiss clinic, when Anstice informs the cornea donor that she is about to have visitors.

An earlier draft of the screenplay had several subtle differences. Dr Spender was originally to have travelled to Switzerland against Steed's wishes, whereas in the episode as transmitted it is Steed who arouses his interest and then arranges for him to accompany Cathy to the clinic there. The circumstances of Spender's death were also changed. In the draft script, he is called to the cornea donor's room and goes out onto the balcony to see if anyone is there, only to be pushed over the guardrail. However, in the episode itself, the patient gets outs of bed and advances on Spender menacingly until he backs away so far that he overbalances backwards off the balcony.

3.14 – 'The Secrets Broker'

Taking John Bryce's advice regarding the staging of fight scenes, director Jonathan Alwyn arranged for the finale/action sequence of 'The Secrets Broker' to be pre-recorded. This was done between 8.30 pm and 9.00 pm on Friday 18 October 1963. Stunt man Valentino Musetti was cast in his fifth appearance in the series, adding a professional touch when the script required his character, the strong-arm man Bruno, to fight Mrs Gale. The main recording of the episode then happened the following day, beginning at the usual time of 6.30 pm, but in the smaller Studio 2 – the first time this had been used in the making of season three.

The teleplay was provided by newcomer Ludovic Peters and would be his only contribution to the series. The plot involves Steed investigating a wine shop, Waller & Paignton's, which he learns is being used as a front for espionage activities.

Mrs Gale has acquired some new furniture in her apartment this time, in the form of an Arne Jacobson-designed Egg Chair; a modern classic that can be found nowadays in some McDonald's restaurants after their 2006 refurbishment. The curse of the temperamental props struck again on the apartment set, however, as it took Blackman a couple of attempts to switch off a projector, prompting Macnee to ad-lib some dialogue in an effort to cover up the problem.

Another production glitch occurred in a scene where the character Marion Howard, played by Patricia English, leads Cathy into her husband's office; the first few words of Marion's dialogue are inaudible, indicating that the overhead microphone was slow in being moved to the correct position.

In a sequence where Steed is caught snooping around Waller & Paignton's premises by the young woman Julia Wilson, played by Jennifer Wood, she forces him into the wine cellar at gunpoint, only for him easily to disarm her and take command of her .38 Smith and Wesson revolver.

Ratings war

As with the previous season, *The Avengers* was pitted against the BBC's satirical comedy sketch show *That Was the Week That Was* (*TW3* for short) in the Saturday night schedules in ABC's two regions and others taking their line-feed. On Thursday 10 October 1963, *The Stage and Television Today* reported that *The Avengers'* move to a slightly earlier start time was apparently working, as it was commanding a larger audience than its rival. When the BBC announced that *TW3* would be discontinued at the end of the year because of the prospect of an imminent general election, ABC and others speculated that the competition from *The Avengers* had simply been too much and the Corporation was throwing in the towel. ABC's publicists certainly seemed to believe this, as they ran a quarter-page advertisement in *The Financial Times* on Tuesday 29 October with the headline '*The Avengers* Outsmart *TW3*'. The small print boasted of how *The Avengers* had stolen the majority of the Saturday night audience from *TW3*, with 12 million viewers across the ITV network tuning in on Saturday 12 October for the episode 'Man with Two Shadows', according to an estimate produced by Television Audience Measurement (TAM).[8] Predictably, these actions caused some friction between ABC and the BBC. When later approached on the subject, the director of BBC television, Kenneth Adam, described ABC's claims as laughable. Adam promised to replace *That Was the Week That Was* with another satirical sketch series – which would indeed materialise in 1964 as *Not So Much a Programme, More a Way of Life*.

Theatrical overtures

ABC received a somewhat strange approach at this time in the form of a letter dated 23 October 1963 from successful American theatre producer and director Cheryl

---

[8] At this time, ITV and the BBC both collected their own rival ratings data, and TAM was the agency that routinely performed this function for the former. It was only later that an independent body took on responsibility for operating a unified system covering all channels.

Crawford, who had been born on 24 September 1902 in Akron, Ohio. Despite never having actually seen an episode of *The Avengers*, Crawford thought that it offered great potential as the basis for a musical stage play. Her imagination had been captured by an article about it in a *Sunday Times* supplement, and she felt it could be adapted to a different medium without too much trouble. She had already met Leonard White while he was in New York and they had discussed the project. Now she was requesting scripts and tapes of selected episodes as research material.

Copies of three scripts were airmailed to Cheryl Crawford Productions in New York early in November, leaving ABC feeling out of their depth and Howard Thomas making the unprecedented move of seeking advice from his greatest rival, Lew Grade. To his credit, Grade gave all the assistance he could, arranging for ABC to use fellow ATV board member and theatre impresario Prince Littler as their negotiator. ABC were apparently willing to licence the series for the theatre, but stipulated that any production, musical or otherwise, would need to remain true to the original, with the leads maintaining the characterisations already established on television.

In a 24 December memo to Thomas, Brian Tesler reported that after acknowledging receipt of the scripts, Crawford had – in his own words – 'been markedly silent ever since.' Crawford never contacted ABC again, possibly because her then current Broadway musical, *Jennie*, flopped, closing after only nine weeks, when her company had invested approximately £44,000 in setting up the production. This figure was in fact only a quarter of the total finance involved in *Jennie*, giving some indication of the amount Crawford would have had to raise in order to get a musical version of *The Avengers* off the ground.

3.15 – 'The Gilded Cage'

Roger Marshall returned with a different angle for his next episode, 'The Gilded Cage', by having Steed and Cathy organise a gold bullion robbery – although this turns out to be just bait in a scheme to lure in and bring down a criminal mastermind, J P Spagge. The episode was recorded on Friday 25 October 1963 at Teddington, directed by Bill Bain.

The episode has some obvious similarities in story content to the subsequently-made James Bond movie *Goldfinger*, but the enormous budget difference between the two means that any like-for-like comparison will always be stacked in the latter's favour.

Cathy's home address is confirmed on screen as 14 Primrose Hill, and Steed's pet Great Dane Katie appears for the second and final time. Footage of a fly becoming trapped in a venus flytrap plant was from stock, played in via telecine during recording.

During a sequence where the robbers raided an underground vault, a telephone intercom is pulled off the set wall with such force that it unfortunately causes the wall to move. Two of the gang also have problems getting their pallet truck to run in a straight line along a corridor.

Against a background of frenzied drumbeat incidental music, the climactic confrontation between the gang and Steed and Cathy takes place in Benham's stonemason's yard – an intricate studio set. Picking off their adversaries with a mixture of unarmed combat skills and gunplay, the Avengers reduce their number until Steed can take a couple of them prisoner at gunpoint. However, the final gang member

Gruber, played by Geoff L'Cise, arrives and attacks Mrs Gale from behind, resulting in a martial arts fight scene that ends when she knocks him out cold with a couple of karate chops.

West Indian actor Edric Conner, who played the gang's field leader Abe Benham, was interviewed in *The Stage and Television Today* dated 25 June 1964, where he heaped praise on the production, saying, 'I was delighted with that part.'

Fashion show

On Tuesday 29 October 1963, an event involving fashions connected to Frederick Starke and *The Avengers* was arranged between 5.30 pm and 7.30 pm at The Garrison, Les Ambassadeurs Club at 5 Hamilton Place, off Park Lane, London. This served to create publicity for both parties. Three days later, issue no. 418 of *TV Times* featured a three-page article headed 'The Immaculate Avengers' that also turned the spotlight on fashions seen in the series and emphasised the connection to Starke. The Saturday 2 November editions of the television listings magazines *Look Westward* and *The Viewer* both featured an Honor Blackman cover – one of the Terence Donovan/*Harper's Bazaar* shots – and a chance for readers to obtain a Cathy Gale dress.

3.16 – 'The Medicine Men'

The pre-recording of three videotape inserts for the next episode, 'The Medicine Men', was completed between 7.30 pm and 9.00 pm on Thursday 7 November 1963. These comprised both of the required scenes set at a Turkish baths and the end tag scene. Following the standard procedure, the main recording of the episode was then undertaken in Studio 1 the following evening, with a 6.30 pm start, directed by Kim Mills from a Malcolm Hulke teleplay involving Steed and Cathy investigating a conspiracy to flood the market with counterfeit medicines.

The double fight scene at a print shop that concludes act two unfortunately features some movement of the set wall as Steed struggles against his assailant and they bump into it. Cathy wears a patch over her right eye for the remainder of the episode due to a bruise picked up in the course of the fight. An undercover Steed is later seen to smoke a large cigar while impersonating an art dealer from Reykjavik. At one point, despite being both gagged and tied to a chair with her arms behind her back, Mrs Gale still manages to become involved in a fight, tripping the gun-toting Miss Dowell and then pinning her on the floor with both feet.

Steed's morning reading habits have apparently changed, as in this episode he is seen looking at a copy of *The Financial Times*. He has placed golf balls around his apartment so that he can attempt to score a hole in one into his bowler hat. Mrs Gale also tries, and has considerably more success. When they leave for a golf course at the end of the episode, Steed admits to having a handicap of 24, but Cathy replies that hers is only 12.

Go-Go-Go

Issue no. 419 of *TV Times*, published on Friday 8 November 1963, continued its coverage of the series, with the first of a two-part feature concentrating on Blackman's hectic lifestyle, which had become the norm since she took on her role in *The Avengers*.

The concluding part, titled 'Life with Honor it's Go-Go-Go', appeared in the following week's edition and focused on fashion, judo and *The Avengers*' gruelling production schedule at Teddington.

The following evening, Saturday 16 November, both ABC regions, Anglia and Tyne Tees all moved the series to the earlier time slot of 8.55 pm, beginning with the episode 'Second Sight', and this would continue until the end of the year.

3.17 – 'The White Elephant'

John Bryce's earlier recommendation regarding the pre-recording of fight sequences was now being followed almost as standard practice. A couple of such scenes were taped between 7.30 pm and 9.00 pm on Thursday 21 November 1963 for 'The White Elephant', a story from John Lucarotti in which Steed and Cathy investigate illegal ivory smuggling following the theft of a rare albino elephant called Snowy. The first of these scenes was set at night in a cage-makers' foundry, where Steed comes into conflict with a man working there. The second was an extended gunshot and fight sequence at the episode's conclusion, where Steed takes on the villain Conniston, played by Scott Forbes, on the exterior set of a private zoo. Macnee considered this to be the toughest action sequence he ever did for the series; a statement reinforced by the fact that he managed to sprain an ankle badly during the course of it. The fight also greatly agitated the various caged animals and birds on the set. Among the different animals featured at the zoo were a leopard, a kangaroo, a fruit bat, a number of monkeys and various birds, including storks, pelicans and a toucan – although the original idea to have a tiger as well was not followed up on. This menagerie of creatures was supplied by exotic per shop owner Clive Desmond, who at the time was based in Colindale, London and specialised in providing birds and animals for both film and television productions. The setting of the climactic fight at the zoo was in fact a major change between the rehearsal script and the camera script; it was originally to have taken place in the cage-makers' factory.

The main recording for the episode took place between 6.30 pm and 7.30 pm on Friday 22 November, with Laurence Bourne making his directorial debut after graduating from an ABC scheme for trainee directors.

Guest actor Godfrey Quigley, in the role of Noah Marshall, had the challenge of performing some scenes with a macaw perched on his shoulder. He also encountered problems with a small snake he was handling, which decided to try to disappear under his jacket, prompting him to ad-lib, 'Come back here, Simba.'

At one point, Mrs Gale informs Steed that after her husband was killed she worked for a time as a big game hunter in Kenya – something that honed her concentration no end. A Colt Officer's Match revolver is seen to be hung on the room partition in Steed's apartment, where later he and Mrs Gale discuss the ivory smuggling over a game of chess and his telephone number is revealed as Whitehall 0011.

Steed calls in at a gunsmith's to drop off for repair a rare double-barrelled derringer belonging to Mrs Gale, who proves to be less than happy with him after becoming involved in another dangerous adventure, telling him: 'You always manage to win something, don't you, Steed? Whatever anybody else has lost, you pick-up your perks and off you go. Well, I'm an anthropologist, not one of your gang. If you want my help again you'd better have a very good reason.' Despite this outburst, Steed still manages to get a smile out of Cathy when he returns the repaired derringer.

Growing popularity

The Ulster and Teledu Cymru regions both rescheduled *The Avengers* to an 8.55 pm start time beginning with 'The Medicine Men' on Saturday 23 November 1963, while for one week only Westward went for a 9.50 pm start. As things transpired, however, 'The Medicine Men' went out several minutes late across the ITV regions as a result of extended news coverage of the assassination of US President John F Kennedy, which had occurred the previous day.

This month the first paperback novel based on the series was printed – and, due to high demand, reprinted – by Consul Books, an imprint of World Distributors of Manchester. Written by Douglas Enefer, it featured Steed, Mrs Gale and One-Six and was titled simply *The Avengers*. Enefer had previously written in various different fields, having scripted documentaries and instalments of *Coronation Street* and contributed stories to children's annuals. He would go on to provide a storyline for an episode of *The Saint* and to write many crime paperbacks. He also worked under the pseudonyms Sam Bawtry, Dale Bogard and Paul Denver, the latter of which he used for a number of novels based on the American private detective show *Cannon*.

World Distributors were also responsible for *Meet the Avengers*, a 40-page magazine issued in 1963 as part of their *Star Special* range, which mainly covered popular television shows and pop stars of the time.

Chain store F W Woolworth likewise saw the series' merchandising potential, producing a *The Avengers*-themed sketch pad through their Winfield subsidiary, with a colour photographic cover showing Macnee and Blackman on location for 'Build a Better Mousetrap'.

Also released in November was an updated version of the show's theme music, credited to Johnny Dankworth and his Orchestra, which was made available as a seven-inch vinyl record on the Fontana label, serial number TF422.

Viewing figures collected by TAM for October showed that *The Avengers* had been Britain's eleventh most popular television programme for the month, averaging 6.0 million viewers each week. By November the series had dropped down to the seventeenth most watched, but had still managed to increase its viewing average slightly to 6.3 million.

TV Post, the television listings magazine for the Ulster region, began running *The Avengers* weekly comic strip on Thursday 5 December, commencing with the six-part story 'Epidemic of Terror', and would continue with the weekly instalments through until late April the following year.

3.18 – 'Dressed to Kill'

Thursday 5 December 1963 was also the date when a couple of scenes were pre-recorded in Studio 3 between 7.30 pm and 9.00 pm for Brian Clemens' latest offering, which was originally called 'A Story of the New Year' before being retitled 'Dressed to Kill'. Under the direction of Bill Bain, the rest of the episode was committed to videotape during a standard hour-long recording the following evening in Studio 2. Unusually, the camera script revealed that the episode had already been given a scheduled transmission date, Saturday 28 December – no doubt necessitated by its seasonal content. The pre-recorded scenes were both set in Steed's apartment, which included a Christmas tree and decorations associated with the festive period. This also marked the first time – but not the last – that a tuba featured on the apartment set.

Clemens' storyline was an Agatha Christie-inspired whodunit with the plotline expanded to include espionage elements, presenting a scenario that would influence several other episodes when ABC later began making the series on film. 'Dressed to Kill' would be remade four years later as 'The Superlative Seven' and some of its plot elements would resurface again in both 'The Gravediggers' and 'A Funny Thing Happened on the Way to the Station'.

Half a dozen pieces of 35mm stock film footage were used for the episode, showing the wheels of a moving locomotive, various pieces of railway line, stations being passed through and the train stopping at Badger's Mount.

Bain brought together a dream guest cast including Leonard Rossiter, Alexander Davion, John Junkin, Anneke Wills making her first appearance in the series, Richard Leech making his second and stuntman Frank Maher.

The basic plot of the episode involves Steed and Cathy operating undercover after a false alarm triggers all bar one of Britain's nuclear attack early warning systems, and being invited to a bizarre fancy dress party on board a train where one of the other guests is a killer. The train departs from London's Paddington station, which was realised by a studio set. The same set was also used later in the episode for the deserted station at Badger's Mount. A small continuity error occurred as a belly dancer was seen to board the train twice.

Having chosen a Wild West Gambler's attire as his fancy dress outfit, Steed carries a fully-operational Colt .45 six shooter. However, Macnee's costume in these scenes seems slightly sub-standard, due to a dirty scuff mark on the back of his jacket.

The episode features some particularly fine direction by Bain, such as in a scene where someone touches the body of the murdered fancy dress Sherrif, played by Junkin, and he pitches forward to reveal a previously-unseen arrow in his back. In an earlier draft of the teleplay, the man's death was presented slightly differently, the partygoers discovering his body with the arrow sticking out of his back after hearing him scream and leaving their carriage to find out what has happened.

Another difference between the draft script and the final one was that in the earlier version, after they have escaped confinement from the stationmaster's office, Steed and Cathy overhear three of the villains – Napoleon, Newman and the barman – discussing their plans to jam the early warning system. In the actual episode, Cathy springs a trap for Robin Hood, played by Rossiter, only to discover that he is innocent, as Napoleon and the barman take them both prisoner.

Clemens' script is well crafted, including some nicely humorous dialogue. At one point Steed grabs the tail of the costume worn by the Pussy Cat, played by Wills, and she exclaims, 'Whoops, you'll make me purr.' Clemens could then not resist repeating this joke later on by having Robin Hood also yank on the Pussy Cat's outfit, in response to which she warns, 'Watch it, you'll have it off!'

There is a mixture of action and humour in a scene where Cathy fights the barman on the platform at Badger's Mount and throws him against an 'I Speak Your Weight' machine, which activates upon impact saying, 'You are six stone and two and have a strenuous day ahead.' The fight concludes with the barman, played by Maher, getting knocked unconscious over a table. During recording of this, the stuntman unfortunately suffering a bloody nose after Blackman accidentally struck him during the action. A few minutes later, Bain yelled cut as the recording was completed, allowing Blackman an opportunity to apologise and give Maher a long hug. He later commented, 'She was really, really concerned, but it was a hell of a fight.'

3.19 – 'The Wringer'

The next episode, Martin Woodhouse's 'The Wringer', explored brainwashing, interrogation and – as Mrs Gale puts it – 'Agents who have outgrown their usefulness' – to which Steed's reply is an extremely blunt 'Nobody retires ... ever!' After a number of British agents are killed in rapid succession, Steed finds himself wrongly accused by MI5 of being a traitor.

In what had now become standard procedure, two scenes were pre-recorded in a session lasting an hour and an half, which commenced at 7.30 pm on Thursday 19 December 1963. In addition to the end tag scene set in Steed's apartment, the other one involved him and Mrs Gale escaping from the MI5 facility and emerging into woodland through a culvert.

The bulk of the recording was undertaken the following evening, starting at the earlier-than-usual time of 6.25 pm to allow an additional five minutes for the rare occurrence of a planned recording break. With six pedestal cameras in Studio 1 for this episode – more than ever before – it appears that director Don Leaver had been unable to devise a way of keeping them all moving effectively in a continuous recording pattern. The only solution was to stop the recording for five minutes for the repositioning of cameras, lights and microphones. The break came about nine minutes into the episode, between a scene set in a shop run by the traitor Lovell and one of Steed arriving at a forest fire-spotting tower hide-out. After the break, the session was restarted, to finish at 7.30 pm.

Paul Whitsun-Jones made his second and final appearance in the series as Steed's superior Charles, though he would be seen later in other roles. Telecine was employed to feed in a couple of pieces of stock footage, used as a part of the interrogation techniques used by MI5 to break Steed while he is their prisoner. One was a shot of the ocean and the other a night-time Second World War artillery barrage.

A number of difficulties are apparent on screen with the set of a cell where Steed and Cathy are at various times held prisoner. Murdo, played by Douglas Cummings, has to take at least three attempts to unlock the door when he comes to let Cathy out; but worse still, part of the cage structure is clearly missing altogether, suggesting that the set had not been completely assembled.

At one point in the action, the character Bethune, played by Neil Robinson, shoots Cathy in the shoulder with his .38 Smith and Wesson revolver. The injured Cathy then has to spend the remainder of the episode with her arm in a sling. Another nugget of personal information is revealed, in the form of her telephone number: Primrose 0042.

The first movie proposal

On its partial network transmission on Saturday 21 December 1963, 'Death a la Carte' clocked up 7.3 million viewers, making it the most popular episode of the year and seventh most popular programme overall that week. Even more excitingly, however, sometime during the same month, ABC were approached by the American film company United Artists Theatres with a proposal to make a 65mm colour feature film based on *The Avengers*.

United Artists Theatres' intention was to use a variation on the Todd-AO lens system called Dimension-150. Todd-AO was a widescreen wide-angled lens system developed over a couple of years by Broadway and film producer Michael Todd, who had allied himself with other film industry professionals and eventually a company known as American Optical. Combining their resources, they had formed a new company, under the name Todd-AO, and managed in 1955 to get the rights to make a film version of the Broadway musical *Oklahoma*, which would be the first to be shot in the new format. As Todd and his associates lacked the necessary funding to produce the film, another deal was made, this time with United Artists Theatres, not only to secure finance, but also to create a co-owned subsidiary company called Magna both to handle motion picture distribution and to further develop Todd-AO.

Dimension-150 was one such further development, although at the time when the approach was made to ABC in 1963, no films had actually been produced in this experimental format.[9] Veteran American film producer Louis de Rochemont had an agreement with Todd-AO to make two features using Dimension-150 and, having no reservations about working in Europe, suggested this co-production with ABC. Born in Boston, Massachusetts on 13 January 1899, de Rochemont had made his name producing hard-hitting documentaries, especially propaganda films before and during the Second World War. After the War, he produced several espionage movies in the film noir style, with storylines based on real events of spying and infiltration by Nazi sympathisers and double agents. More recently, in 1961, he had produced the movie *The Roman Spring of Mrs Stone*.

ABC reacted very positively to the possibility of a film version of *The Avengers*. Howard Thomas devised a scenario that Brian Clemens wrote up as an outline in January 1964. Aiming for a more international appeal than the television series, the film outline, known as *The Pursuit of Evil*, had action set in several different countries, and not surprisingly a strong American element. In Beirut, the Lebanon, a group of trainee Western diplomats are gunned down by masked men. Steed receives instructions to travel from London to the Middle East, accompanied by Cathy Gale, to establish a branch of the British Secret Service in Beirut and more importantly to locate the killers of the diplomats and administer some permanent justice. Meanwhile, in Washington DC, an American agent, Drew Vernon, has received the same instructions, and together with his female college is also to embark to Beirut to rendezvous and work with his British counterparts.

The board of directors at the ABPC gave their blessing to the project and Brian Tesler was extremely enthusiastic, thinking that the regular production team led by John Bryce were the logical choice to actually make it. Meanwhile, de Rochemont's associate John Halas, of Halas and Batchelor Cartoon Films Limited, had contacted ABC acting as his UK agent and requested a sample episode in the 16mm film format to be forwarded to New York. In turn Tesler instructed Bryce to select an episode that showed the series at its best and arrange for a telerecording to be made; the one he chose was 'Death of a Batman'.

---

[9] Ultimately only three films would actually be made in this format. Any cinema showing a Dimension-150 picture needed to project it onto a curved screen for the system to work correctly, and given that such screens were not in general use at the time, it is perhaps unsurprising that it failed to take off.

For their part, Magna insisted that ABC should refrain from transmitting a new season of the television series until a mutually agreed interval had passed after the film's release in the United States – clearly they were keen to avoid the two competing with each other. Thus, while the remaining season three episodes could continue to be screened by the various ITV companies up to March 1964, ABC agreed in principle that, if the film version were to go ahead, the airing of any further episodes after that would be put on hold.

Correspondence during January 1964 between de Rochemont and the co-chairman of Todd-AO Marshall Naify, who was also the president of Dimension-150 Incorporated and United Artists Theatres, revealed that the producer wanted total control of the project. He also considered Macnee and Blackman unsuitable, particularly for the American market, and mentioned Sean Connery as a possible alternative star, although he thought it highly unlikely that Eon Productions would allow him to appear in any espionage films outside of their own James Bond franchise.

With a clear conflict in aims developing between the American producer and ABC, it seemed the project was in danger of collapsing, but discussions continued for the time being.

3.20 – 'The Little Wonders'

The first episode to enter production in 1964 was Eric Paice's 'The Little Wonders', in which Steed and Cathy investigate Bibliotek, an organisation of criminals masquerading as members of the clergy. Steed would go undercover as a high ranking official and attend a meeting of the criminal organisation, where their leader was standing down and his replacement would be decided on by either peaceful or violent methods.

The now-standard practice of pre-recording a couple of scenes in advance of the main session was continued. This took place between 7.00 pm and 9.00 pm on Thursday 2 January 1964 in Studio 1 under the direction of Laurence Bourne. The scenes in question comprised the conclusion of act two, with Sister Johnson, played by Lois Maxwell, brandishing a machine gun; and a school classroom shootout for the finale. Reverting to the usual start time of 6.30 pm, the main recording then took place the following evening, with an impressive guest cast that included David Bauer, Tony Steedman and, making his third appearance in the series, Kenneth J Warren.

While undercover at the school, Steed informs Bibliotek's leaders that his underworld nickname is Johnny the Horse, and he carries the Luger automatic of his predecessor Reverend Harbuttle.

Lois Maxwell had trouble with a line of dialogue in one scene, winging her way through it: '… to give the delegates a chance of straightening out er, straightening out any misunderstanding that may have occurred.' According to the camera script this should have been, '… so that delegates could have the opportunity to settle any little differences that might arise.'

When Steed and Cathy meet at a deserted sweetshop to compare notes, he voices a preference for brandy balls, while she has a sherbet fountain.

In a scene where two villains catch Cathy sneaking around the school and hold her at knifepoint, Steed saves the situation by thinking quickly and giving her long kiss, implying that she is his girlfriend. Predictably, this was something that the popular press seized upon. Three days after the recording, the *Daily Express* ran a story complete with two photographs under the title 'The Avengers Caught Kissing', the *Daily Mail* also reported the development and the *Daily Mirror* had a similar piece headlined 'At Last Avenger Cathy Gets a Kiss'. The latter went on to indicate that producer John Bryce had decreed that the characters should never indulge in a passionate kiss, but on this occasion it was a script requirement and essential to the storyline of having Steed save Cathy's life. Bryce was quoted as saying, 'The kiss may look romantic, but they aren't going to fall in love.'

Publicity and controversy

Meanwhile, on Saturday 4 January 1964, transmission of 'The White Elephant' saw *The Avengers* rescheduled to a new 9.10 pm time slot in all regions bar ATV London and Southern. The show was now a major programme commodity. Unlike the first two seasons, this third batch of episodes was shown across the board by the various ITV regional companies. The only exception was that Grampian for some reason omitted to screen 'The Medicine Men'.

The transmission of 'The White Elephant' prompted viewer Sydney Cox of Wilmslow, Cheshire to write a letter of complaint to ABC, as he considered the episode to have breached the Protection of Animals Act 1911. He advised that he had also taken the matter up with the Independent Television Authority (ITA) and intended obtaining the support of his MP, Sir W Bromley-Davenport, when responsibility had been established. Having acknowledged Mr Cox's communication, ABC informed both their company solicitor, Michael Brown, and Jan Choyce of the ITA. Anthony John however thought that there really was no case to answer. Having viewed the episode, he noted that although guns appeared to have been fired extremely close to a number of caged birds, the actual gunshots were in fact created off camera by a technician. An RSPCA official had also visited the set and been more than happy with the conditions there. The following day it was brought to John's attention that a hornbill had actually died on set during the production, leading its owner Clive Desmond to obtain a veterinary surgeon's report that indicated that the cause of death was a brain haemorrhage. However, there was no conclusive evidence that the action taking place around the birdcages in the studio was directly responsible for the bird's demise. Creating a memo for Brian Tesler, John warned that the situation could become extremely awkward should Desmond and Cox discover that they both had a complaint about the same incident. However, shortly afterwards, Jan Choyce viewed a copy of 'The White Elephant' and, besides enjoying it, assured ABC that the ITA would not be taking any official action against them regarding the matter.

The Avengers stayed in the news as, on Thursday 9 January, three of the national daily newspapers – the *Daily Mirror*, the *Daily Mail* and the *Daily Express* – finally ran stories about Blackman's imminent departure from the series to assume the role of Pussy Galore in the next James Bond film, *Goldfinger*. The *Daily Express* headlined their piece 'Cathy Is Bond's New Girl'. The publicity machine rolled on as, the very next day, the *Daily Mail* offering another short piece on Blackman, in which she was quoted as saying, regarding Cathy Gale: 'A large number of women like the anti-man aggressiveness and I seem to appeal to men because I'm dominant and independent.' Considering Blackman to be flavour of the month, the same newspaper began more in-depth coverage on Wednesday 15 January, with the initial part of 'The Honor Blackman Story', which ran for three days until the weekend and then another three the following week.

3.21 – 'Mandrake'

'Mandrake' was the latest episode from writer Roger Marshall. Marshall's usual approach was to agree a storyline with Richard Bakes and then provide a detailed five-page treatment. If the producer and story editor were happy with that, he would then have a rehearsal script ready in three weeks. In this instance, Marshall was asked by Bates if he had any storyline ideas and responded with the plot element of victims being murdered by arsenic poisoning, then being buried in ground high in arsenic content to hide the evidence. Further inspiration came to him after reading about Sir Sydney Alfred Smith, a New Zealander who lived in Edinburgh and developed forensic methods during the early part of the 20th Century. The plot he devised concerned a number of prominent businessmen dying suddenly and being buried in a cemetery near a tin mine in Cornwall, with Steed's suspicion being aroused when an old secret service colleague of his suffers the same fate.

Getting back into their production routine, the cast and crew occupied Studio 1 from 7.30 pm on Wednesday 15 January 1964 to pre-record three scenes for the episode, with Bill Bain in the director's chair. For once things failed to run smoothly, as Honor Blackman mistimed a kick during a fight scene on the cemetery set and split the nose of professional wrestler and sometime actor/stuntman Jackie Pallo. Blackman and Pallo had already gone through the choreographed fight four times before, but technical problems had prevented a complete recording of the action. They had been growing tired by that point, but had been asked to go for a fifth take – and it was on this that the mistimed kick occurred. When interviewed by *The Avengers* fan club On Target in 1986, Blackman recalled, 'I saw [Pallo's] eyes glaze over and I knew he wasn't properly conscious and I was panic stricken!' Both performers continued going through their pre-arranged moves for a few moments, but then Pallo simply fell back into an open grave on the set. In a delayed reaction, he had been knocked out cold. A doctor was called for, and it was seven and a half minutes before Pallo regained consciousness – much to the relief of a very upset Blackman, who at the time had vowed never to fight again. Upon his recovery, Pallo appeared no worse for wear, although the attending doctor insisted he not travel to Dover later that night to participate in a top-of-the-bill wrestling match.

Pallo's own take on the incident was somewhat different. He freely admitted it had been an accident, but was more bullish regarding any question of having been outfought by Blackman, saying that despite the padding provided to cushion his fall, he must have struck his head on something when he toppled backwards into the grave.

News travelled fast and the *Daily Mail* was hot off the press the following morning with the headline 'KO'd By Honor!' Meanwhile, the *Daily Mirror* was caught on the hop, not getting its report of the incident printed until the following day, Friday 17 January. In this, Pallo admitted to having his pride dented but generally made light of the situation. There was also a light-hearted report on the late-night ITN news bulletin, including footage of the fight scene.

The other scenes completed during the pre-recording session on 15 January were an opening funeral sequence in the churchyard and a final scene featuring Macnee and Blackman on the same set, which ran for approximately 20 seconds. Bain was not convinced that the sound effects in the opening scene were good enough to portray the required thunder storm, so he arranged some post-production work to have a picture filter added that showed lines descending to the ground representing falling rain.

The main recording of 'Mandrake' took place without further mishap in Studio 1 in the hour between 6.30 pm and 7.30 pm on Thursday 16 January. As usual for one of his stories, Marshall was present for this.

A sequence where Steed visits a Christmas cracker manufacturer was always meant to be amusing, but it appears that Macnee and Australian actress Annette André, playing the character Judy, agreed with Bain, perhaps as late as the day of recording, to go even further and play it for maximum laughs. André had to place boxes on top of some shelves four times, and each time she made certain something fell off, sometimes onto Macnee, with him ad-libbing his way through the sequence. The script simply indicated 'general confusion etc' at this point.

A cast iron spiral staircase prop last seen in 'The Gilded Cage' was used again here on the cracker factory set. Later, in a scene where Steed breaks into a doctor's consulting room, Macnee tipped his bowler to the skeleton hanging there and quietly ad-libbed, 'Good evening,' instead of the scripted line 'How's the wife?'

'Five Smooth Stones'

Roger Marshall also worked around this time on a teleplay for another episode, which he named 'Five Smooth Stones', with a scenario involving radioactive water. The writer believed he had been given the green light to produce a rehearsal script, and in fact had completed the whole of act one before Richard Bates informed him that the storyline was not what he required, obliging him to submit another one as a replacement.

Feature film developments

Discussions about the feature film proposal were still ongoing at this point. Howard Thomas sent Louis de Rochemont's agent John Halas a three-page letter on the subject on 22 January 1964, outlining the major points of a co-produced movie. The Lebanon had been chosen as the main overseas location, because it was felt that both the landscape and the vast array of historical buildings would be perfect for the panoramic images that the Diamension-150 system would create. Not only were Beirut, Baalbek and Byblos in the Lebanon mentioned, but so was the Syrian capital of Damascus. Thomas also acknowledged that American technicians would be essential to operate the cameras with the experimental wide-angle lens. The budget was set at one million dollars (at that time equivalent to approximately £350,000), which would be provided equally from American and British sources. The home-grown finance would come from ABPC and Leslie Grade, presumably from his Grade Organisation talent agency. Distribution would begin in movie houses equipped with a Cinerama screen to take advantage of the widescreen format, before moving on to traditional cinemas. Filming was expected to start on location and then continue at ABPC's Elstree Studios sometime late spring/early summer that year. Thomas concluded his communication by expressing the hope that arrangements could be finalised rapidly.

3.22 – 'Trojan Horse'

Pre-recording of two videotape inserts was completed in Studio 1 between 8.30 pm and 9.00 pm on Wednesday 29 January 1964 for 'Trojan Horse', an episode by Malcolm Hulke involving a horse-racing operation being used as a cover for a series of assassinations. One of these inserts was the finale, set in a stables tack room, where Steed becomes involved in gunplay with a Colt revolver. The other was a much longer sequence involving horse racing being shown by way of stock footage fed in via telecine onto on-set monitors. Both the small enclosure at the racetrack and the stables exterior, complete with a grey racehorse called Sebastian, were realised as studio sets. The horse, whose real name was Roy, was a placid 12 year old show-jumper of 16 hands that had been hired from his owners for a couple of days and was an established animal performer in both films and television. The stables exterior set was augmented by a horsebox and a large matte painting giving the impression of a long, enclosed cobblestone yard with various stable doors.

The main taping of the episode took place in Studio 1 between 6.30 pm and 7.30 pm on Thursday 30 January, directed by Laurence Bourne, who cast amongst others Basil Dignam and T P McKenna. This was the second and final episode to be recorded using six pedestal cameras at once. The opening scene was accompanied by the De Wolfe music library track 'Invention for Drums', heard previously in several other episodes. The newspaper seen during proceedings was the fictional *Evening Tribune*.

Back in February 1961, the then producer Leonard White had observed in one of his memos that Macnee's horseracing background could provide the basis for a storyline, though it had taken three years for this to occur. The rehearsal script differed from the final camera script in several ways. For instance, originally it was Steed who located the character George Meadows' body in a horsebox, whereas in the final version it is Cathy who discovers it there. Also the result of some significant rewriting was a scene in the final version where one of the villains, Major Pantling, manages to entice Mrs Gale away from the betting office to the stables by informing her that Steed wants to see her.

'Trojan Horse' was transmitted in most ITV regions at 9.10 pm on Saturday 8 February 1964, gaining 7.6 million viewers – the largest audience figure for this season, which also made it the ninth most popular programme of the week.

'Kinky Boots'

With public interest in the show at a high level, the *Manchester Evening News* began running *The Avengers* black and white weekly comic strip on Saturday 1 February 1964 from the first instalment of 'Operation Harem', and would continue with it until late September. A more famous piece of tie-in merchandise came about, however, when Patrick Macnee and Honor Blackman were approached with a suggestion that the show's leatherwear could be a passport to further success if they were to collaborate in singing about it on a novelty record. Macnee initially refused, but was eventually persuaded to go along with the idea. So, one Saturday night during the first eight days of February, after rehearsing for the next episode, 'The Outside-In Man', the two stars went to a sound studio and cut two tracks.

The A-side, 'Kinky Boots', was originally an instrumental piece written by Herbert Kretzmer and Dave Lee for the satirical BBC series *That Was the Week That Was*, to feature in a madcap look at leather footwear. Lyrics were added later specifically for

Macnee and Blackman. Macnee was so nervous about recording the single that he consumed plenty of brandy before entering the sound studio and then struggled with the timing of the song, resulting in an engineer nudging him every time it was his turn to sing a line. The B-side was another novelty number, 'Let's Keep it Friendly', also by Kretzmer and Lee, which was recorded on the same night and featured Macnee and Blackman more or less in character as Steed and Mrs Gale.

'Kinky Boots' was released as a seven-inch vinyl single later in February on the Decca label, serial number F11843, but failed to generate enough sales to enter the pop charts. Despite this lack of commercial success, Blackman was later enticed back to the sound studio by record producer Marcel Stellman to record a Decca album, *Everything I've Got*, which surprisingly failed to include either 'Kinky Boots' or 'Let's Keep it Friendly'. Released in the 12-inch LP format in November 1964, it had a photographic cover featuring one of the Terence Donavon shots originally taken for *Harper's Bazaar* the previous September. This showed a relaxed Blackman with the trappings of wealth, a light aircraft and Mercedes-Benz car.

No follow-up was forthcoming, but 16 years later, in December 1980, the album was reissued, under serial number 884 057-1, with 'Kinky Boots' added and retitled after that track. In May 1983, Cherry Red licensed both the 'Kinky Boots' single and the original album (minus the 'Kinky Boots' track) and reissued them again, but found only a minority audience. The single was reissued once more in November 1990 on Decca's subsidiary label Deram, complete with a *The Avengers* picture sleeve, under the number KINKY 1. This time it was also made available in the 12-inch vinyl format, as a cassette single and as a CD single. Thanks to disc jockey Simon Mayo breaking it nationally with numerous plays on his Radio 1 breakfast show, it eventually made the charts 26 years after being recorded, peaking at number five in December 1990.

3.23 – 'The Outside-In Man'

'The Outside-In Man' was directed by Jonathan Alwyn from the second and final teleplay written for the series by Philip Chambers, who had also contributed substantially to *The Sexton Blake Library* of pulp novels. The story involved Steed finding himself placed in the position of protecting a former defector to Aburain, General Sharp, who is now returning to Britain.

On Tuesday 11 February 1964, three videotape segments for the episode were pre-recorded between 8.30 pm and 9.00 pm in Studio 3, the smallest studio at Teddington at the time. These were all scenes on a cottage interior set.

The main recording was undertaken between 6.30 pm and 7.30pm in Studio 2 on Wednesday 12 February, featuring Ronald Radd in a one-off appearance as Quilpie, another new boss for Steed. Radd was an old friend of Alwyn's from the Northampton Repertory Theatre. Alwyn assisted both in devising the butcher's shop façade that serves as a cover for Quilpie's base of operations and in the naming of his secretary, Miss Alice Brisket. The government department for which both Quilpie and Alice work is named as PANSAC, standing for Permanent Agency for National Security and Counter-Intelligence. During the first scene featuring Macnee, Blackman and Radd, the latter momentarily lost his way with the dialogue, almost calling Cathy 'Mrs Steed', but paused to remember the line before adding 'Gale'.

The garter gun holster was reintroduced as a convenient way for Mrs Gale to store her small automatic pistol, though this was a different prop from the earlier example seen in the season two episode 'Propellant 23'. Later, when Cathy tracks the formerly-missing agent Mark Charter down to his cottage hideout there are two unexplained sounds in the background, suggesting that something was either dropped or knocked over accidentally off camera somewhere in the studio.

Steed is once again seen reading a Tintin book in his apartment – this time, *Tintin: The Secret of the Unicorn* – and there is a solitary piece of 35mm night-time stock footage used, showing a BOAC (now British Airways) airliner landing at what the camera script described as London Airport (renamed Heathrow Airport in 1966).

The episode was originally titled 'The Twice Elected'. In the rehearsal script, Charter is caught attempting to break into the Aburainian embassy, whereas in the transmitted version he hides in the boot of a car to gain admittance.

American overtures

By early 1964, plans for *The Avengers'* fourth season were starting to be laid. ABC's initial idea was to make this season on film as a co-production with fellow ITV regional company Associated-Rediffusion. According to *The Complete Avengers* book, published in 1989, if this deal had come to fruition, Iris Productions' staff would still have been responsible for the actual making of the episodes. In the event, however, it came to nothing.

ABC still wanted future episodes of the show to be made on film, however, and sometime during February Howard Thomas sounded out the possibilities of an American network sale. He had a meeting with Samuel C Cohen of the New York-based law firm Marshall, Bratter, Greene, Allison and Tucker, representing the General Artists Corporation (GAC), who wished to act as the exclusive agents for *The Avengers* in the USA. GAC proposed a 120-day trial period, in which they would attempt to locate a network buyer for the show and, if successful in attracting interest, would then have £26,000 or more made available for the filming of a pilot episode. The deadline for delivering any such pilot was 31 December. Should the network concerned then require a full season, GAC would receive approximately 30 percent of ABC's net profit from the sale. GAC strongly suggested that, in order for their objective to be achieved, the producer of any pilot needed to be American, and likewise the writers and performers, although they would defer the final decisions to ABC. This proposal was confirmed by Cohen to Thomas in a letter dated Wednesday 19 February. After some thought, ABC replied by airmail letter dated 6 March, declining GAC's offer to act as a go-between with the American networks.

The *Daily Express* dated Saturday 22 February once again reported Blackman's imminent departure from *The Avengers*, but also assured readers that Patrick Macnee would definitely be staying with the show for its next season. Two days later, Brian Tesler responded to a confidential memo that Head of Drama George Kerr had written three weeks earlier regarding recent steps toward *The Avengers* being produced as a film series. He agreed with Kerr's suggestion that story editor Richard Bates be given an opportunity to familiarise himself with film series screenplays, which seemed a logical thing to do, and indicated that arranging for him to scrutinise shooting scripts for the Independent Artists-produced ABC show *The Human Jungle* would not be a problem. However, Tesler feared that sourcing scripts used on ITC's *The Saint* would be much more difficult.

3.24 – 'The Charmers'

An action sequence comprising three scenes for the finale of the next episode, 'The Charmers', was pre-recorded in Studio 1 at Teddington in advance of the main recording, which occurred the following day on Thursday 27 February 1964. Having brought together a cast that included Warren Mitchell (appearing in his second episode this season) and Fenella Fielding, Bill Bain directed the usual hour-long taping between 6.30 pm and 7.30 pm from a teleplay by Brian Clemens. The story involves Steed and Mrs Gale co-operating with their Russian counterparts following the assassination of some Soviet agents by an unknown third party who is playing them off against each other. They eventually trace the villain Keller – Mitchell's character – to a charm school.

Six photographs stuck on a pinboard on the set of Keller's base, supposedly depicting the most dangerous enemy agents, were actually members of the show's behind-the-scenes team. Clockwise from the top they were Clemens, Macnee, Bates, Bryce, possibly Bain's personal assistant Eileen Cornwell, and Howard Thomas. The one of Macnee as Steed was taken from the filmed material for the episode 'Brief for Murder'.

Clemens included a subtle James Bond reference in the episode's dialogue: Cathy Gale is revealed to have been on the opposition's wanted list for some time, being second only behind 'J B'. Although Keller speaks with an East European accent, the opposition are never referred to as agents of the Communist bloc or Russian.

Steed has now incorporated an intruder alert security system on his apartment door, which causes a light bulb in the kitchen to flash indicating when someone – on this occasion the enemy agent Martin – is forcing the lock. After he gains entry, Martin is relieved of his Walther P38 automatic by a karate chop to the wrist from Mrs Gale, followed up by Steed pushing him down onto the floor of the lower level of the apartment.

During recording of a later scene where Steed and Cathy argue over his agreement with Keller to loan her out to the opposition, Macnee tripped over his lines, saying, 'Now Mrs Jowl … er, Mrs Gale.'

Cathy's small-calibre Beretta automatic is featured again in this episode, in a sequence where she trains it on Keller; and when Steed arrives at the charm school he is carrying a .357 Smith and Wesson 19 revolver.

This episode also provides an early example of gadgets being featured in the series, as trainee businessmen are seen using radios secreted in bowler hats, and swords hidden inside umbrellas.

Part of the charm school set was evidently rather fragile, as one of the walls sways badly when Steed throws Keller against it, and one of the double doors also falls from its hinges.

As a result of excessive judo training, Blackman was forced to miss a couple of days' rehearsal for 'The Charmers' to undergo a small operation to one of her feet. She returned to commence fencing lessons for her upcoming duel against actress Vivian Pickles, playing the character Betty Smythe.

Brian Tesler considered this to be one of the finest all-round episodes of the season. He was especially impressed with Fenella Fielding's performance as the actress character Kim Lawrence, having suggested her for the role as a tryout to see if she might make a suitable replacement for Blackman.

Taking stock

The edition of *The Stage and Television Today* published on Thursday 27 February 1964 featured several quotes from Tesler regarding the future of *The Avengers*. Pointing out that the crew had been on a pressurised schedule, recording an episode every fortnight and in some instances every week, he said that they would be stood down and allowed a six-month break after the completion of work on the current season. However, he reassured everyone, 'We are delighted that Patrick Macnee is to continue as [the male] star. John Bryce and story editor Richard Bates will continue to be associated with the programme.' After wishing Blackman well with her film career, he indicated that it would be autumn 1964 before production commenced on the next season, with transmissions not getting under way until 1965. Further to this, he stated that it would be necessary to introduce new characters and make changes to maintain the trend-setting reputation that the series had acquired. A couple of days later, some of the same quotes were carried in the 'Max North's Telereview' section of the *Manchester Evening News*. North was another who thought that Fenella Fielding would make the ideal on-screen partner for Steed.

3.25 – 'Esprit de Corps'

The Eric Paice-written 'Espirit De Corps' involves Steed and Cathy investigating the murder of a highland regiment soldier and uncovering an audacious plot to depose the British Government in a *coup d'état*. The script included several exterior scenes, and whereas these would normally have been shot on film and then inserted into the correct part of the episode via telecine, director Don Leaver saw an alternative. Boxed sockets had been installed at several locations around the Teddington Studios lot, enabling crews to utilise cameras, sound and lighting equipment for outdoors videotaping, and Leaver took advantage of this to pre-record four exterior videotape inserts of the regiment's Maroon Barracks on Tuesday 3 March 1964. As the pedestals on which the studio cameras were normally mounted were not ideal for smooth movement over the tarmac surface of the studio lot, this entailed the hiring-in of two dollies, a tripod, two gun microphones and additional equipment from Associated-Rediffusion. These items were collected by an ABC vehicle from the technical stores at Rediffusion's studios, 128 Wembley Park Drive, Wembley, on the morning of 2 March and returned there on the afternoon of 4 March. Three ABC cameras were temporarily mounted on the dollies and tripod for the recording. Leaver had arranged for staff vehicles to be parked in other places on the studio lot that day, so that they would not be seen in shot.

Three of the four inserts, consisting of two executions by firing squad and a scene where guest star John Thaw as Captain Trench walks through the camp followed at a distance by the firing squad and a piper, were taped at different points around the exterior of Studio 1. The fourth, in which Steed is accompanied by several soldiers escorting him to a court martial, was undertaken in front of Studio 1, with the group then entering the administration block.

The War Office had been approached in writing on 28 February to ask if they could provide genuine service personnel – a piper, a drummer and various soldiers – to act as extras, plus a number of army vehicles. These requirements were met by the 4th Battalion Queens Royal Surrey Regiment of the Territorial Army. No fees were paid for this assistance, although as a token of their appreciation ABC did make a contribution to regimental funds, sent along in cheque form with a letter of thanks from Don Leaver. Possibly with the forthcoming John Bryce-produced ABC military police drama *Redcap* in mind, Leaver added that he hoped the regiment would not object if he contacted them again sometime in the future should another suitable project arise.

Between 7.00 pm and 9.00 pm on Tuesday 10 March, three further videotape inserts were pre-recorded, this time indoors in Studio 3. They all took place on a gym set. One consisted of a two-and-a-half minute scene featuring Blackman, Thaw and – in the role of Sergeant Marsh – Douglas Robinson. The actors portraying two additional soldiers being put through their paces in this scene went uncredited on screen, but the one playing Private Collins was stuntman Billy Cornelius. The other two scenes were one in which Trench attempts to coach Mrs Gale in some unarmed combat techniques – which required Blackman to don her black leather fighting suit again – and one in which Cathy shoots and kills Sergeant Marsh. Douglas Robinson was so enthusiastic in recording the latter death scene that he overshot his mark, demolishing the supports of the on-set balustrade and knocking Blackman down.

The bulk of the recording for the episode happened in Studio 2 on Wednesday 11 March, beginning earlier than usual at 6.20 pm and running for an hour and ten minutes.

The newspaper Steed is seen reading while at a launderette was another made-up publication, *Battalion News*. Later, both he and Cathy sport .38 Smith and Wesson 10 revolvers. Mrs Gale smokes a slimline cigar at one point, and wears the same sequined evening dress seen previously in 'Death a la Carte'. She has also obtained some more '60s state-of-the-art furniture for her apartment in the form of a wicker bubble chair suspended from the ceiling.

John Thaw's well-received performance as Captain Trench was instrumental in him being cast as the lead character Sergeant John Mann in *Redcap* several months later. Also notable amongst the episode's guest cast, in the role of Private Jessop, was comedy actor Roy Kinnear, who was making his first appearance in *The Avengers* here but would return playing different eccentric characters on three further occasions.

'Espirit de Corps' was the final script for *The Avengers* by one-time Writer's Guild chairman Paice, and cost £5,630 to produce.

3.26 – 'Lobster Quadrille'

It had been agreed for some time that story editor Richard Bates would pen the third season's final episode, which became 'Lobster Quadrille'. Bates recruited Brian Clemens to assist him on the script, resulting in the episode being credited to the pseudonym Richard Lucas. As this was Blackman's last episode, there was some speculation that Cathy Gale would be killed off, and consequently two different endings were written as Bryce and Bates kept everyone (including Patrick Macnee) guessing as to the final outcome.

The episode's plot involves Steed and Cathy investigating a drug smuggling operation. A number of revisions were made to the script before recording. An earlier draft had both agents visiting a burnt out beach hut, whereas Steed does this alone in the final episode. Conversely, the earlier version had Steed returning alone to his apartment after a night out to discover that Mrs Gale is missing, whereas in the final episode he is accompanied by the character Katie Miles, played by Jennie Linden. In the draft, two bodies are discovered in the aftermath of a second fire – suggesting that

Cathy might be one of the victims – whereas in the camera script it is just one.

Designer Patrick Downing utilised black-and-white chessboard imagery on the floors of two sets, representing a chess shop and a mortuary respectively, plus various other surfaces, including table tops at the Alice Club. This monochrome theme would continue in the following season.

The taping of 'Lobster Quadrille' was completed on Friday 20 March 1964 under the direction of Kim Mills, whose other guest cast selections included Burt Kwouk, Leslie Sands and, making his seventh and final appearance in the series, Valentino Musetti.

Clemens penned the episode's end tag scene, in which Cathy tells Steed she is leaving the following day for a well-deserved holiday in the Bahamas, and reveals that she has already anticipated Steed attempting to manipulate this situation to his advantage. There follows an exchange of humorous dialogue, in which Steed assures Cathy that there is absolutely no danger involved in her doing a little investigation work for him while she is away: 'And as you're gonna be out there anyway, pussyfooting along those sun-soaked shores ...' He invites Cathy's reaction, and is surprised when she replies, 'Goodbye Steed.' 'But that isn't asking too much,' he protests. 'Oh yes it is,' she says. 'You see, I'm not going to be pussyfooting along those sun-soaked shores, I'm going to be lying on them.' And thus Cathy Gale departs *The Avengers* forever, leaving Steed to muse, 'Not pussyfooting. I must have been misinformed.' These repeated mentions of 'pussyfooting' were an in-joke reference to Blackman's upcoming role as Pussy Galore in the James Bond movie *Goldfinger*.

The episode ends with Steed making a phone call to an unseen third party, clearly a woman. After some pleasantries, he tells her that what she really needs is some sunshine, and that he needs a little job taking care of ... Obviously the series was going to continue, and logically Clemens knew that Steed would return for more adventures with a new female partner, but with hindsight it's easy to imagine that the woman on the other end of the phone was none other than Emma Peel.

No sooner was the recording of the episode finished than Macnee and Blackman were whisked away to the Dorchester Hotel in London to attend the Variety Club of Great Britain Awards, where they both accepted awards for independent television personality of the year. The event was televised by the BBC, and among the other celebrities in attendance were the Beatles, Dirk Bogarde, Julie Christie, James Fox and, to collect awards for their hit BBC sitcom *Steptoe and Son*, Harry H Corbett and Wilfrid Brambell.

With the transmission of 'Lobster Quadrille' across the ITV regions on the following evening, Saturday 21 March 1964, all initial screenings of season three ceased. Viewing figures for the final three months showed *The Avengers* to have been Britain's eleventh most popular programme in January 1964, averaging 6.8 million viewers for the month, rising to tenth position in February, with a record 7.5 million, but then falling to seventeenth in March, with only 6.0 million people watching.

The film proposal founders

The proposed feature film version of *The Avengers* was still under discussion when season three ended. With Blackman now unavailable, it appears that ABC were insisting on Macnee being included as Steed. Howard Thomas arranged for Macnee to meet Louis de Rochemont on Saturday 21 March 1964 at the Jumeirah Carlton Tower Hotel, Cadogan Place, Knightsbridge, where the American outlined the film's scenario in detail as his own work, leaving the actor quietly impressed. It was only some time later that Macnee discovered what he had heard was actually Brian Clemens' outline.

After returning from a trip to Paris, de Rochemont and fellow producer Lothar Wolff then held a story meeting on Thursday 26 March with Brian Clemens and Richard Bates, who together had produced a treatment that it was agreed Clemens would turn into a script. Intended to run to approximately 135 minutes, this retained the title *The Pursuit of Evil* and involved Steed's infiltration of the Mafia. The March issue of the American trade magazine *International Projectionist* announced that de Rochemont expected the release of the first D-150 feature film – presumably meaning *The Pursuit of Evil* – by early 1965.

Several internal ABC memos regarding the project were exchanged between Howard Thomas and programme administrator George Brightwell around the beginning of May 1964. Thomas's view appears to have hardened by that point, presumably because of the lack of progress. Referring to Clemens' screenplay, he wrote, 'It is up to Louis de Rochemont to accept or reject the script.'

According to Macnee's later recollection in his autobiographical tome *The Avengers and Me*, the film project was suddenly and inexplicably dropped, without any explanation: 'At the drop of a hat it was forgotten!' With the British side of funding arranged, it can only be assumed that the problem lay with the American companies involved: United Artists Theatres, Todd-AO and Magna.

Big changes in store

Meanwhile, on Wednesday 25 March 1964, programme controller Brian Tesler had sent Managing Director Howard Thomas a memo seeking confirmation that a new season of *The Avengers* could go ahead as a film production financed by the ABPC. The proposal was that it would be under the overall control of film producer Julian Wintle, but made in conjunction with ABC's own producer John Bryce, story editor Richard Bates and established writers. Tesler also pointed out to Thomas that they needed to move as soon as possible on the renewal of Macnee's contract and the commissioning of new scripts, as any delay of over two weeks would cause problems further down the line.

Thomas replied to Tesler's memo several days later, confirming that the production company for the film series would be jointly owned by ABC and Julian Wintle. He added his agreement that while the film series was being set up screenplays should be commissioned and negotiations should be opened with Macnee about his continuation in the role of Steed.

Sometime during March, Bryce and Bates had what would be their only meeting with Wintle regarding the series' future, at which nothing was decided. Bates' later interpretation of events was that Wintle was not impressed by their combined lack of film experience, and consequently they heard no more from him. Realising that they were in danger of being ousted from the show, the two men paid Macnee a visit at his home in Derwent Avenue in the Kingston Vale district of Kingston upon Thames, Surrey, and asked him to put in a good word for them with Wintle. At the time, however, the actor was distracted, struggling with regard to his contract for the new season, and he later admitted in *The Avengers and Me*, 'I certainly didn't fight their corner as well as I might have.'

In both of his later books, *Blind in One Ear* and *The Avengers and Me*, Macnee recalled that this was a difficult time for him. He felt that he was not being kept fully informed on developments regarding the series. Despite him attending several meetings at Elstree Studios, nothing of any substance was decided. Frustrated by the lack of progress, he sent Howard Thomas a letter dated Friday 10 April 1964, outlining his ideas for the next season. This went unanswered.

Feeling that there was no alternative, Macnee called in his agent Richard Hatton to negotiate on his behalf regarding an increase in salary. Hatton, a shrewd operator, asked for his client to receive five percent of *The Avengers'* future profits. A couple of days later, Macnee found himself summoned to a meeting with Wintle, who informed him that five percent was completely out of the question, but then offered him two and a half percent, which he gladly accepted.

Bryce at this stage obviously thought there was still a chance that he would be retained as either producer or associate producer of the series when it resumed on film, as on Thursday 2 April he issued a memo to most of the directors who had worked on the previous season. This offered his suggestions for Honor Blackman's replacement and included a shortlist of five names: Maggie Smith, Moira Redmond, Nyree Dawn Porter, Fenella Fielding and Millicent Martin.

The Friday 30 April edition of *Kine Weekly* reported that upon completion of *Goldfinger*, Honor Blackman's next part would be in a movie called *The Pass Beyond Kashmir*, based on a spy novel by Berkely Mather, with location filming in both India and Pakistan. This had already been mentioned in the *Daily Express* of 22 February as one of four features that Blackman was due to appear in over the next five years, the others being *Fings Ain't Wot They Used T'Be*, based on a stage play of the same title; *How to Succeed with Women Without Really Trying*, adapted from a novel published in 1957; and an original concept entitled *The Marriage Game*. Although producers Harry Saltzman and Albert R Broccoli did indeed have various plans to make these other films, they had failed to anticipate the mania that grew around their James Bond movies, and the consequent demand for further entries in the franchise. Hence they never found the time in the '60s to collaborate on anything other than additional exploits for Ian Fleming's secret agent, and the other projects earmarked for Blackman ultimately came to nothing.

By this time, however, Blackman had other business interests. As reported by the *Daily Express* of Thursday 14 May, she was one of six stars involved in the formation of a new production company called Six-Star Television, the others being Richard Attenborough, John and Hayley Mills, German actor Curt Jurgens and the project's main instigator, Herbert Lom. The basic idea behind the company was a collective approach to producing high-quality television film series, and initially Six-Star was thinking about developing both a comedy thriller and a sci-fi show.

Seven days later, on Thursday 21 May, *Kine Weekly* announced that producer/director Bryan Forbes had become associated with Six-Star as story supervisor to oversee finance from American sources. Through his connection with Herbert Lom on the first season of *The Human Jungle*, of which Lom was the star, producer-to-be Robert J Kahn had also become involved, acting as a liaison with contacts in the United States. The company was now looking toward producing an anthology series, with all six named performers appearing in both the first and last episodes and various combinations of them being seen in the remainder. However, due to their respective workloads, it appeared that the six stars could not actually schedule dates to get together for the filming of a pilot until sometime during the summer of 1965.

Ultimately, although Six-Star Television did acquire office space in London, very little more was ever heard from the company, and the planned projects failed to materialise.

Also in the Thursday 21 May edition of *Kine Weekly*, it was confirmed that Julian Wintle had entered into a long-term agreement with ABC / ABPC for the production of the third season of *The Human Jungle*, comprising 13 episodes, and the fourth season of *The Avengers*. Both shows would be based at ABPC's Elstree Studios in Borehamwood, Hertfordshire, but would be made consecutively rather than concurrently. The third season of *The Human Jungle* had a proposed production start date of September 1964 and – depending on how well the crew kept to schedule – it was thought that filming would continue until February/March 1965. Consequently season four of *The Avengers* would not enter production until after that.

Bryce and Bates had still not been officially informed as to whether or not they had a future on *The Avengers*, and naturally they were becoming frustrated with the situation. On 16 June 1964, Head of Drama George Kerr sent Brian Tesler a memo, marked 'Confidential' in red ink, requesting a meeting on their behalf whenever it was convenient for him to see them and 'clear the air'. It is not known what happened in response to that request, but an article in the 2 July edition of *Kine Weekly* stated categorically that Bryce and Bates would not be working on the film series at Elstree Studios.

Sometime between late May and the beginning of July a further significant development occurred, when a decision was taken not to proceed with the planned third season of *The Human Jungle*. Julian Wintle had convinced ABPC that *The Avengers*, in its new format as a film series, had a far greater potential for international sales. Furthermore, Herbert Lom, who later confessed to having never liked *The Human Jungle*, had declined to make another season, presumably seeing his future on television with the Six-Star concept. This left Wintle free to concentrate on the pre-production of season four of *The Avengers*; a state of affairs reported in the Thursday 2 July edition of *Kine Weekly*. As yet no suitable replacement for Honor Blackman had been decided upon, but Wintle was searching far and wide; and as a concession to a possible US network sale, he suggested that Steed's new partner might be an American.

Meanwhile, as a stopgap, a repeat season called *Best of the Avengers*, comprising seven (originally planned to be 13) second season episodes, commenced in some ITV regions at 10.20 pm on Saturday 4 July with 'Death of a Great Dane'. The same week, production started at Teddington Studios on the main run of ABC's *Redcap* series, with John Bryce occupying the role of producer. Richard Bates also found himself busy early in September, back in the position of story editor, when the private detective show *Public Eye* began recording.

The Avengers had progressed through each of its first three seasons from a realistic crime show with film noir undertones to a groundbreaking action spy series, leading the way with female equality and then blossoming into a stylish thriller. The videotape era of *The Avengers* had reached its conclusion, but the film era was about to begin, and in terms of both popularity and overseas sales, the series was about to enter its most successful period yet.

SEASON FOUR

THE DANGER MAKERS

Telemen

Upon conclusion of work on the second season of *The Human Jungle*, Julian Wintle dissolved the production company Independent Artists and then together with ABC Television formed Telemen Limited. This newly-established company would become responsible for making *The Avengers* at Elstree Studios, with Wintle and E W Wilford bringing Albert Fennell on board to make up the trio of company directors. Fennell's official credit would be 'In Charge of Production', though his duties included assembling the crew, deciding rates of pay for technicians, supporting performers and extras, writing up contracts, and hiring equipment and vehicles, making him a production manager in all but name.

Accomplished scriptwriter Brian Clemens, who had devised some of the most spectacular screenplays for season three of *The Avengers*, was recruited by Wintle for the forthcoming filmed episodes, his experience of both film and television making him the obvious choice. By the second week in July 1964, Clemens had been contracted to Telemen to become both associate producer and (uncredited) script editor on the series. The first matter of business was the creation of a new female character to replace Mrs Cathy Gale, which Clemens did by devising Mrs Samantha Peel, or Mantha for short.

On Friday 14 August 1964 Wintle submitted the draft script of the first episode, Clemens' 'The Town of No Return', for inspection by both Brian Tesler and legal expert Anthony John, wanting confirmation that it was the kind of screenplay they required for the new season. Tesler responded after the weekend, indicating that it was very promising and noting that the location shooting for the exteriors would exploit the full use of film. However, he also considered act one to be slow and recommended that it be tightened up and some action added. John agreed with his superior's sentiments, although he also voiced doubts over the Mantha name.

Fashion concept

It had been decided that Marie Donaldson would continue in her role as the series' press officer. Even though she would not be based at Elstree Studios, she would visit the production office at least once a fortnight to talk through publicity matters with the team. Having discussed with Clemens the fashions for the forthcoming series, Donaldson sent Tesler a memo dated 25 August 1964 regarding an idea that she had for the new jet-set Avengergirl. It was envisaged that Samantha Peel would have a vast wardrobe for various different countries, and when she required something to wear for a certain climate, all she would have to do was press the correct button on a computerised system, then the appropriate designer garments, stored behind electronically-controlled panels in her penthouse apartment, would simply appear and be ready to wear. However, this element could be played for comic effect, with Steed reprogramming the computer so that she would get, say, summer clothing for the Arctic. ABC obviously did not share Donaldson's sense of humour and the concept went no further.

Script consultations

After Wintle's submission of two more draft scripts, 'A Touch of Brimstone' by Clemens and 'The Disappearance of Admiral Nelson' by Philip Levene, Tesler recorded his views in writing on 15 September 1964. There was already some indication that 'A Touch of Brimstone' was going to be a controversial episode, Tesler describing it as, 'A good one, but showing dangerous tendencies toward violence and horror which would preclude the show from being transmitted before 10.00 pm, and I would dearly like this series to get away with a 7.30 pm slot.' Tesler listed six different aspects of the script that needed some rewriting, which were: a sequence of the electrified body of a character named Bates jerking and shuddering amidst a blaze of sparks; a macabre death scene where the character Darcy was pinned to his seat after being impaled from above by a heavy sword; an orgy sequence, which could not be allowed to become explicit; and three separate incidents involving the character Willy's false wooden hand, especially one where it was to be lopped off by Steed's sabre. 'The Disappearance of Admiral Nelson' fared even worse, with Tesler refusing to believe that the crew could manage to make the proposed miniaturisation of the characters look believable on screen, and instructing Wintle to forget about it.

Australian approach

On the same day, T L Donald of the London-based Global Television Services Ltd wrote to Howard Thomas on behalf of the Australian Broadcasting Commission (ABC), which was offering to contribute toward the cost of the series. In return for their funding of £1,500 per episode for up to 24 episodes, the Australian ABC wanted three or four episodes shot down under; the rights to transmit season four twice during a five year period, free of charge; and seven-and-a-half percent of net profits from any sales. Thomas replied two weeks later, agreeing in principle to most of the proposals, subject to a cost estimate of filming in Australia, but emphasising that profit-sharing was completely out of the question.

M-appeal

Meanwhile, Marie Donaldson had been considering the character of Samantha Peel and the ingredients needed to make her attractive to male viewers. Coming up with the phrase 'man-appeal', Donaldson shortened this to 'm-appeal' before finally using a play on words to coin the name Emma Peel. Both Wintle and Clemens were delighted, as they thought this had a much better ring to it for Steed's new partner. Thus all the screenplays were now altered to incorporate this new name.

Further script consultations

By Thursday 8 October 1964, the shooting script for 'The Town of No Return' had been forwarded to Tesler, who quickly returned it to Elstree for more amendments by Clemens before it was presented to him again. Wintle assured Tesler that the quirky tongue-in-cheek approach he required had now been incorporated into the screenplay and that they would have ten shooting scripts ready for filming when production started on 2 November. Further to this, he enclosed three more draft scripts for assessment: 'An Hour to Spare' by Roger Marshall, 'The Master Minds' by Robert Banks Stewart and 'Rip Van Winkle' by Martin Woodhouse. Both draft and shooting scripts were now regularly passing between Wintle and Tesler in this way. Four days later, Tony Williamson's teleplay 'The Murder Market' made its first visit to Teddington Studios for examination.

Having amassed a number of screenplays, Tesler returned them to Wintle with a two-page letter dated Tuesday 13 October, in which he went through them one by one. 'The Murder Market' he described as 'One of the best *Avengers* scripts I can ever remember reading.' Of 'A Touch of Brimstone' he said, 'I think this works well now,' although he still had reservations surrounding Willy's wooden hand, which he described as 'Horribly gruesome.' 'The Town of No Return' he thought was 'Very neatly tightened up.' 'The Master Minds' he considered 'Good.' Also included was a script by Roger Marshall called 'Strictly for the Worms', which Tesler was not totally convinced would work, suggesting that it required a major rethink and rewrite. Tesler also disliked the science fiction-based 'Rip Van Winkle', feeling that the concept of someone waiting in suspended animation for years until their shares accrued such a large amount in dividends as to bankrupt a company was too outlandish. He told Wintle: 'I feel we should shelve this one unless it can be radically reworked.' Wintle and Clemens presumably agreed that 'Rip Van Winkle' was unsalvageable, as it never progressed any further than a draft script.

Despite his positive outlook regarding 'The Town of No Return', Tesler received some amended pages for the shooting script the following day, along with the first draft of Philip Levene's 'The Man-Eater of Surrey Green'. Although he accepted the latter, he made it clear in his reply dated 16 October that he was becoming quite unhappy regarding the number of science fiction screenplays that were being presented to him.

Pre-production

By now Fennell was assembling his production crew, and in some instances he simply utilised key personnel from *The Human Jungle*, assigning them the same functions on *The Avengers*. Geoffrey Haine would become the production manager, Simon Kaye the sound recordist, A W Lumkin the recording director, Len Abbot the dubbing mixer and G B Walker the casting director. After serving in the same role on the first filming block of *The Saint*, June Randall was employed to handle continuity. George Blackler was assigned responsibility for make-up, and Pearl Orton took on the hairdressing, both having gained experience working on feature films.

Casting Emma mark one

There was still a missing component to the production: with filming imminent, there was still no leading lady. Sometime during the second week of October 1964, over 60 actresses took part in auditions to find Honor Blackman's replacement. The producers' initial choice was Eleanor Bron, whose previous experience was restricted to appearing on stage in the Cambridge Footlights revue and doing comedy sketches in Granada's *Second City Reports*. However, Bron turned down the part. Second choice was Londoner Elizabeth Shepherd, who had recently played a secret agent in an *Armchair Mystery Theatre* instalment entitled 'Time Out of Mind', co-starring Ian Hendry and written by Tony Williamson. Born on 12 August 1936, Shepherd had started her television career in 1959 with a segment of the BBC's *Saturday Playhouse*, followed up by a recurring role in the soap *Emergency-Ward 10*. She had then played various characters in different series and anthologies through to 1964, when she had graduated to the female lead in the horror film *The Tomb of Ligeia* alongside Vincent Price. When interviewed by *Time Screen* magazine in 1992, Clemens confirmed that Shepherd's casting had been a group decision between Wintle, Fennell and himself, after they had been impressed by her looks and screen test. The *Daily Mail* of Tuesday 20 October 1964 announced Shepherd's appointment to *The Avengers*, which had taken place several days previously, with the headline 'Steed's New Girl.' The report informed readers that Shepherd would play a totally new character (unnamed in the article), who would be the widow of a test pilot and (incorrectly, as it turned out) would not wear leather.

London repeats

Meanwhile, a mixture of second and third season episodes began being repeated in the London region, beginning on Thursday 22 October 1964 with 'Man with Two Shadows'. These were transmitted by Rediffusion, who had rebranded themselves six months earlier from Associated-Rediffusion.

Draft script

Also on 22 October 1964, Brian Tesler corresponded once more with Julian Wintle, this time regarding the draft script for 'Death at Bargain Prices,' with which he was extremely impressed. However, Tesler did not wish any repetition of its plotline and insisted that no further screenplays be written about mad scientists, businessmen or politicians who had plans of world conquest.

Proposed filming in Australia

Having scrutinised Wintle's findings regarding filming in Australia, Howard Thomas replied in writing to him on 27 October 1964, copying in both Brian Tesler and Marie Donaldson. Wintle's opinion was that the whole operation was not economically viable and that the Australian ABC would need to increase their proposed investment to £2,000 per episode in order to make it so. Thomas disagreed, stating that Wintle's figures were based on flying the two leads and a crew of ten or 12 people to Sydney, where space would be rented at the Supreme Sound Studios facility in the city. Thomas pointed out that the interiors could be filmed at Elstree Studios, leaving only a small unit to travel down under to film location footage for use as establishing shots. He also felt certain that a deal could be brokered with the Australian airline Qantas for reduced airfares.

'The Town of No Return' initial filming

Despite the earlier confirmation of a 2 November 1964 start date, location filming for 'The Town of No Return' actually commenced on the Norfolk coast on Thursday 29 October, directed by Wintle's close friend Peter Graham Scott. On the crew's return to Elstree, principal shooting on the episode was completed on Friday 13 November, allowing five working days for Elizabeth Shepherd to take part in various costume tests before the next episode entered production.

Fashions for the series on film

Intending to spotlight the fashion angle, ABC had entered into an agreement with American designer Bonnie Cashin to provide a range of ready-to-wear clothing for Emma Peel. Upon screen testing, however, this was found to be generally unsuitable. Marie Donaldson made Albert Fennell aware of the situation in a memo, where she summarised that Shepherd's clothing really needed to be tailored, offering numerous suggestions as to how the actress could be dressed to achieve the required look. As one option, Donaldson recommended using Bermans costumiers of London, who at the time were the top resource for both making and renting outfits for film and television productions. As an alternative, off-the-peg and less expensive options included Chanel, traditional Burberry and the high street chain Wallis.

'The Murder Market' initial filming

Filming on 'The Murder Market' began on Monday 23 November 1964 under the direction of Wolf Rilla, who had been born in Berlin, Germany, on 16 March 1920, going on to direct on early British film series such as *Fabian of the Yard*. Besides directing films and episodes of other television series, Rilla was also an accomplished writer, having provided the screenplay for the original *Village of the Damned* film in 1960. He would also pen a couple of the BBC's *Paul Temple* series.

The short reign of Elizabeth Shepherd

The problems encountered during the costume tests were about to fade into insignificance when the rushes of 'The Town of No Return' were screened and those present, including Howard Thomas, realised that there was a lack of rapport between the two lead characters. Both Patrick Macnee and Peter Graham Scott have since given their views on this matter in print, stating that there was no spark between Steed and Emma Peel mark one. The combination of Macnee and Shepherd failed to work on the level that Macnee and Blackman had done. It was decided that – despite the fact that it was going to cost a large amount of money – something needed to be done about it.

Filming on 'The Murder Market' was stopped and on Thursday 3 December 1964 Elizabeth Shepherd was dismissed from her role on *The Avengers*. According to her later recollection of events, she was simply told, 'We're letting you go!' The story had obviously been leaked to the *Daily Express*, as they managed an exclusive by running a piece regarding Shepherd's departure that day with the headline, 'I Quit, Says the Girl Who Followed Honor Blackman.' Reporting that only a single episode had been filmed, the newspaper quoted a spokesperson for ABC as saying, 'It was mutually agreed that Miss Shepherd should relinquish the role. The company admires her talent, but her interpretation of the role did not coincide with that envisaged by us.' The article continued by reporting that ABC were now actively searching for a replacement. It quoted Shepherd from her home in Duncan Terrace in Islington, London, as commenting, 'I don't want to say anything just now.' Despite the *Express* having stolen a lead, Julian Wintle did not make an official press announcement regarding events until the late hour of 11.30 pm that night.

Ironically, the edition of *Kine Weekly* published on the same day featured an update on the series that suggested all was going well. It reported that the crew were currently filming the second episode and that the production would be based at Elstree Studios for about a year. Season four would comprise 26 episodes with a budget of £750,000, and the famous William Morris agency of New York had been engaged by ABC in an effort to sell the series to one of the then three American television networks. A number of different writers were listed as having submitted story ideas and outlines, including Arden Winch – whose material must have been considered unsatisfactory, as none of his contributions even made it to a draft script. Perhaps even more ironic was a quote from Wintle in the issue: 'Beth Shepherd is quite fabulous and viewers throughout the world will go for her heavily … She more than adequately replaces Honor Blackman's Cathy Gale.'

The following week, *Kine Weekly's* television correspondent, Tony Gruner, filed a column noting that some readers had pointed out that the information regarding Elizabeth Shepherd had been out of date. The situation had come about because the issue had been printed two days before going on sale, making it an unfortunate coincidence that Shepherd left the series on the same day that the magazine appeared on newsagents' shelves.

During an overview of his career in a February 1997 issue of *The Avengers* fan club magazine *Stay Tuned*, Ray Austin recalled a loud conversation between Shepherd and Julian Wintle in a corridor at Elstree Studios. The production team was eager to introduce catsuits to Emma's wardrobe, but apparently Shepherd had informed the producer in no uncertain terms of her low opinion of this form of fashion and had then returned to her dressing room. This incident was possibly the straw that broke the camel's back, as Wintle summoned both Clemens and Fennell, and then Shepherd was – as Austin phrased it – fired, much to her and her agent's great surprise.

Elizabeth Shepherd never really told her side of events until she did a telephone interview in 2010 for the Optimum DVD box set *The Avengers: The Complete Series 4*. She stated that, upon being cast, she was informed by Julian Wintle that the producers would welcome her input into the character, as they saw Emma Peel as being much warmer and wittier than Cathy Gale. However, in Shepherd's opinion the screenplays did not reflect this, so she and her husband would rewrite lines of dialogue. She also suggested various different hairstyles for Emma. With an eye toward technology, she came up with an idea for a computerised wristwatch that could provide instant solutions to some of the problems Emma and Steed encountered. The wristwatch would have the ability to make time stand still for everyone except Emma – hence when she was caught in a tight spot by assailants, all she had to do was use the watch to freeze everything and then escape at ease.

All Shepherd's ideas were rejected except for her costume suggestion of a red leather fighting suit with matching boots, gloves, overcoat and hooded shirt, as seen in publicity photographs taken during the filming of 'The Town of No Return' (where it actually looks orange). Her opinion now is that the producers had already decided what *The Avengers* was going to be, recalling Albert Fennell's advice, 'You're going to be rich and famous. Just do as you're told.' Undoubtedly Shepherd was extremely enthusiastic and by her own admission would have loved to have done *The Avengers*. Sadly, the footage of her playing Emma Peel appears never to have been seen outside the small circle of ABC and Telemen staff who viewed it in 1964, giving rise to speculation that it no longer exists.

Global Television Services

Also on 3 December 1964, Howard Thomas wrote to T L Donald of Global Television Services, confirming that should the plans for filming in Australia go ahead then it would have to be limited to location footage for three episodes. The finance that the Australian Broadcasting Commission had offered to invest would stretch no further than that; and if this was unacceptable, then regrettably the idea would have to be abandoned. In the event, the plans progressed no further.

The Unusual Miss Mulberry

For a while it appeared that *The Avengers* would have some competition, as on Thursday 10 December 1964 the *Daily Express* reported that actress Diana Dors had signed to play the lead in a new Rediffusion series, *The Unusual Miss Mulberry*. Rediffusion described the title character as a glamorous private detective, and insisted that there would definitely be no leather or judo and that any similarities to Cathy Gale would be purely coincidental. Production of 13 episodes commenced in March 1965, but the edition of *The Stage and Television Today* published on 20 May indicated that Rediffusion had encountered problems: 'With six episodes already in the can, recording of Rediffusion's dramatic series *The Unusual Miss Mulberry*, starring Diana Dors, has come to a halt owing to legal difficulties over copyright.' Apparently this series was abandoned, as nothing further was ever heard of *The Unusual Miss Mulberry*.

Casting Emma mark two

Twenty actresses attended a second round of auditions for the role of Emma Peel, and eight of these were subsequently shortlisted to screen test. However, *Armchair Theatre* casting director Dodo Watts thought that she might already have the answer in a recently-recorded instalment entitled 'The Hothouse', featuring an actress named Diana Rigg. Clemens and Fennell watched a tape of the play and agreed that Rigg had a presence and could play comedy. Thus her name was added to the list. In fact Rigg had also attended the first round of auditions in October, but had failed to make an impression on the producers at that time.

The screen tests were held at Elstree Studios under the direction of Peter Graham Scott. Those hopeful of securing the role also included Shirley Eaton, Moira Redmond and Rosemary Martin. The tests consisted of some short Clemens-written scenes in which the various actresses had to interact with Patrick Macnee as Steed, followed by a formal interview. Clemens considered Moira Redmond to have tested better than the others, and at the time he would have chosen her, with Rigg second, although Rigg impressed enormously at the interview stage. Clemens recalled that the final casting choice was made by either Wintle or Thomas, who decided on Rigg because she was virtually unknown to the viewing public.

According to Rigg's recollection, the selection process included her taking part in a fight scene with a male stand-in and then having a long conversation with a producer (presumably Julian Wintle) in which she voiced the opinion that she was wrong for the part. According to Rigg, the producer agreed, so she was extremely surprised to receive a telephone call from ABC the following day offering her the role.

Media interest was so great that ITN conducted a short interview with Rigg (with Macnee in attendance) at Elstree Studios on Monday 14 December 1964. This made mention of her background as a Shakespearian actress. On the same day Rigg also posed for a number of publicity photographs wearing a black turtleneck sweater and matching trousers, holding a 9mm Walther P38 automatic.

The *Daily Express* dated Tuesday 15 December reported Rigg's appointment to succeed Blackman, stating that she had turned down the offer of a three-year contract worth £60,000 in favour of committing herself to the series for just one year. Brian Clemens was quoted as saying, 'She will wear a studded dog collar and we are experimenting with shiny jet black polythene materials.' For her part Rigg confessed, 'I'm slightly frightened about the whole thing.'

4.01 – 'The Murder Market'

'The Murder Market' was remounted with Rigg now in the role of Emma Peel, though it seems the original director Wolf Rilla declined to return – he subsequently went into semi-retirement and moved to France, where he ran a restaurant, directing only a further three projects over the next ten years. This put paid to Wintle's initial plan of only using two directors on the series, by having them direct alternate episodes, as outlined in the edition of *Kine Weekly* dated 3 December 1964. Once again it was Peter Graham Scott who came to the rescue. Picking up the pieces with Rilla's assembled guest cast, including Macnee's close friend Patrick Cargill, he set about finishing the principal shooting for this episode.

Brian Clemens had brought writer Tony Williamson onto *The Avengers* after meeting him through their mutual friend Dennis Spooner at the recording of a *Doctor Who* episode. 'The Murder Market' became Williamson's first contribution to the show. The storyline centres on a marriage bureau called Togetherness Incorporated, which is really a front for an assassination service. However, it is mostly played out on interiors, and as such does not really showcase *The Avengers'* move to 35mm film. There was obviously little time to develop Emma Peel mark two before the production was remounted, as her attitude toward Steed is basically that of a Cathy Gale clone. She loses her temper with him when she thinks he could have prevented the murder of the Togetherness client Henshaw; and when he describes himself as an eligible bachelor who is educated, charming and cultured, she retorts that he is ruthless, devious and scheming.

'The Murder Market' sees the first appearance of the standing set of Steed's new apartment, designed by art director Harry Pottle, who had been a part of Wintle's production team on both *The Human Jungle* and various Independent Artists films. Several steps lead down from the doorway entrance into a large living space, filled with Regency furniture and lavishly decorated with paintings and military prints. Antique weapons in the form of sabres and duelling pistols adorn the walls. There are numerous trophies and cups arranged on a bookcase, while above them are various framed photographs depicting horses. Several glass decanters stand on a wooden table behind the large sofa. Various ornaments, a large model of a galleon and a telescope finish off the agent's abode.

Steed's new address is revealed as 4 Queen Anne's Court, Tothill Street, Westminster – a real location, close to the Houses of Parliament and Westminster Abbey. In the original screenplay, one scene set in the apartment had Steed practising on the tuba while he and Emma discuss their investigation. However, during rehearsals, Macnee insisted that Emma should play the instrument instead, and Scott agreed. During post-production, tuba renditions of both Mendelssohn's 'Wedding March' and Wagner's 'Ride of the Valkyries' were dubbed on, matching up to Rigg's actions. In a piece of continuity going back to the videotaped episode 'The Medicine Men,' Steed indulges in some putting practice around the apartment, until his golf-ball accidentally lands in the horn of the tuba, preventing Emma from playing it anymore.

The marriage bureau's proprietor Mr Lovejoy at one point supplies Steed with a snub-nosed 9mm Walther P38 automatic complete with silencer, with a view to him carrying out a mission to assassinate Emma. Later, after Emma breaks into the Togetherness Incorporated offices, the latest victim's brother, Robert Stone, finds himself surprised by her, armed with her chrome-plated .38 Webley and Scott mark four revolver.

Diana Rigg continued the tradition of *The Avengers'* lead actress wearing black leather, as she sported a two-piece outfit and kinky boots for the fight scene at the episode's conclusion. The *Daily Mail* dated 15 December 1964 indicated that Rigg would be given judo lessons, but with the production schedule now running late it appears that initially stunt arranger Ray Austin simply coached her through the fight routines as he had done with Elizabeth Shepherd.

There was no way that Rigg was ever going to be allowed to participate in fight sequences to the same level that Honor Blackman had done as, given the amount of investment in the series, the consequences of her suffering a production-halting injury would have been too serious. In line with the standard practice for a film series, she would have a stunt double for the more dangerous sequences. This prompted Austin to bring in a slimly-built stuntman called Billy Westley. During the fight scene at the conclusion of 'The Murder Market' it is Westley, wearing a long wig, who is seen to perform a backwards stunt fall onto a desk when Emma is overbalanced off a shelf by the villainess Jessica Stone.

Some of the ingredients that would come to be viewed as essential components of *The Avengers* as a film series are already evident in 'The Murder Market'. These include some quirky, eccentric characters and Steed and Emma exhibiting a fondness for champagne. Another stylish device introduced by Clemens was that at the end of each adventure Steed and Emma would depart using a different mode of transport – in this instance a Rolls Royce Phantom hearse (BLX 20) in a sequence shot on location at Dagger Lane, near Elstree Aerodrome.

Although he would not begin working regularly on the series until the middle of April 1965, Laurie Johnson composed some memorable incidental music for this episode, including a haunting undertakers' piece (which would be heard again in the later-produced episode 'The Gravediggers') and a song called 'Togetherness', the lyrics to which were provided by Herbert Kretzmer, to co-writer of 'Kinky Boots'.

A bride and groom were portrayed by Penelope Keith and Colin Vancao, who both went uncredited on the closing credits and in television listings magazines.

The draft version of Williamson's script included an exchange of dialogue between Emma and murderer Barbara Wakefield when the former arrives at Henshaw's flat, but in the episode as transmitted Emma only sees the murderer quickly leave the premises. The scene in Steed's apartment where Emma plays the tuba was a replacement for one with similar dialogue in the draft, where the two of them discuss their investigations while playing a game in a billiards room. This version of the script incorporated several scene and page rewrites, as Mrs Peel was referred to as both Emma and Mantha in different sections.

Redefining Steed

Sometime during the early weeks of production on this season, Macnee spoke with Clemens regarding his dislike of firearms and suggested that Steed should use wits to think his way out of dangerous situations rather than resort to guns. Clemens agreed. Consequently, although Steed would still carry a gun occasionally, from now on he would tend to rely on hand-to-hand combat and use his umbrella as a weapon in confrontations. These elements were incorporated into a general reformatting of Steed, whose personality was mellowed for the filmed episodes, losing most of the ruthless and vicious traits, making him a more viewer-friendly character.

Macnee also suggested that Steed should have a different relationship with Mrs Peel than he had had with Mrs Gale, sharing the same sense of humour and having a much closer rapport. For her part, Emma would not berate Steed or deliver cutting remarks, even when drawn into dangerous and life-threatening situations. Unlike her predecessors Dr Keel and Mrs Gale, who were driven by compassion toward the victims of crime, Emma Peel's motivation would be completely different as she craved the excitement and danger her association with Steed brought her. Though not acknowledged in the series at the time, Mrs Emma Peel was an adrenalin junkie.

The next episode into production, 'The Master Minds', would showcase the revised format, depicting the leads working well together and including little touches of quirkiness such as Steed trying on a horse-guard's helmet.

4.02 – 'The Master Minds'

Principal photography on the revised version of 'The Murder Market' was complete by 18 December 1964, but Telemen were determined not to waste a second, and filming on the next episode to be made, 'The Master Minds', had already started the previous day. Again Peter Graham Scott assumed the director's chair, casting among others Patricia Haines and – having used him the previous year in an episode of *Zero One* – Bernard Archard.

The teleplay this time was by Robert Banks Stewart, who had met Brian Clemens when he was the story editor for *Interpol Calling* in the late '50s and had been invited by him to submit some ideas for *The Avengers*. Stewart's standard procedure entailed discussing a story idea with Clemens over the phone and then taking two to three days to construct an outline several pages long. If this presentation was satisfactory, then he would take two to two-and-a-half weeks to come up with a complete draft script. Then, if this was also approved, he would proceed to write the shooting script in about a week. In this instance the result was a story about a Mensa-type organisation called Ransack using intellectuals for subversive activities, including trying to steal a nuclear missile.

This screenplay required more exterior filming than the previous one. The main location used was Caldecote Towers (aka the Rosary Priory High School), situated on Elstree Road in Bushey Heath, Hertfordshire. Both the exterior and interior of the school became the Dorrington Dean College for Young Ladies, mentioned as being near Oxford, although in fact the location was only three and a half miles from Telemen's base at Elstree Studios in Borehamwood. The various wooden signs seen when Steed arrives at Ransack were manufactured in the carpenter's shop at the studio. The grounds of the school also provided ample space for the archery ranges featured in the plot.

For a sequence where Steed and Mrs Peel arrive in his vintage Bentley, Macnee and Rigg were filmed driving to the junction of Dagger Lane and Hogg Lane in Elstree before turning into the gateway of Pages Farm. However, when the car then pulls up in front of a house, this was actually on a soundstage set. This sequence introduced another of the Clemens-inspired contributions to the series: Steed's love of classic cars. Such vehicles had already been seen in a couple of the videotaped episodes, but they would now become a regular feature. Although Steed and Emma would always speak as if there was just one car, in fact no fewer than six different Bentleys would be used. However, apparently no-one on the production, not even Macnee, enjoyed driving these, as their large size, huge turning circle and lack of a synchromesh gearbox made them very impractical in traffic.

For this episode, the production hired a 1929 $4\frac{1}{2}$ Litre Bentley (UW 4887) from Kingsbury Motors, who at the time were based in Kingsbury, North London, but are no longer in business. This car is also the method of transport that Steed and Emma use to depart at the end of the episode, for which it was filmed going down Aldenham Road, Elstree, passing the buttressed wall of the grounds of the Haberdashers' Aske's School – a building situated in Aldenham Park, the estate of Lord Aldenham, an area covering approximately one mile by half a mile.

The episode's location filming was augmented with both day and night stock footage of Big Ben, the Houses of Parliament, River Thames and Westminster Bridge. A short scene showing a missile base break-in was filmed on the studio backlot.

The trampoline seen in the school gym proved to be a success with both Rigg and Macnee, who enjoyed themselves with it so much that Ray Austin persuaded Wintle to keep it at the studios to assist in keeping the leads fit.

Robert Banks Stewart thought Peter Graham Scott had done a marvellous job bringing his script to the screen, directing it like a mini feature film.

Unmade Wild West episode

Stewart also submitted an untitled story outline about a prize bull being rustled from a secret government experimental farm, and Steed and Mrs Peel finding a Wild West township in the English countryside, where people dress up in period costume to take a weekend break from everyday life. Stewart drew inspiration for this from a real-life establishment in the south of England[10], and the idea was that the episode would play out like a Western. However, the outline failed to find favour with Clemens and Fennell, who rejected it, although Stewart himself thought that it would have been perfect for the series.

'The Day it Rained Poets'

On 1 January 1965, Julian Wintle sent Brian Tesler another draft script in the form of 'The Day it Rained Poets' by John Kruse, who had contributed the first season episode 'Tunnel of Fear' and had both written for and script edited on *The Human Jungle*. Wintle stated that although this screenplay had shortcomings he felt these could be overcome. However, Tesler's reply on 5 January was mixed. He agreed that the script was a bit of fun but felt it was so far-fetched that he compared the finale to a *Tom and Jerry* cartoon. The concept appeared to conform to the science fiction approach adopted at times during this season; in his book *The Ultimate Avengers*, published in 1995, researcher Dave Rogers briefly summarised it as being about a brilliant young female scientist who creates mobile thinking machines that proceed to break free of their programming. Wintle confirmed to Tesler on 6 January that the screenplay had been passed to Clemens for rewriting. At some point, however, the production team obviously made the decision not to develop it any further, as it never progressed to a shooting script.

4.03 – 'Dial a Deadly Number'

Principal filming of 'The Master Minds' was completed on Friday 8 January 1965. After a break for the weekend, production commenced on Monday 11 January on Roger Marshall's 'Dial a Deadly Number', a story involving prominent businessmen dropping dead apparently from heart attacks, but actually being killed by a spring-loaded pin secreted in a lethal fountain pen carried in the breast pocket.

The director this time was Don Leaver, who had handled numerous videotaped episodes but had never worked on a film series before. Patrick Macnee – one of the series' few significant participants to have been retained in the move from videotaped episodes to filmed ones – was instrumental in getting Leaver this opportunity. However, the director found the transition a difficult one and struggled with the targets he had been set. It was obviously a steep learning curve; especially when pages of the screenplay were still being rewritten during the second week of the shoot. Perhaps fortunately, the only exterior location filming required was for the end tag scene, in which Steed and Emma are seen travelling in the back seat of an Austin FX3 cab, indulging in some wine tasting, as it travels from Trafalgar Square down Whitehall and then across a busy Westminster Bridge, London, SW1.

An underground car park sequence was shot on one of the Elstree Studios soundstages – although this was rather obvious on screen, as the stage's wooden plank flooring had simply had white parking bays painted onto it.

Marshall had obviously written the episode before Macnee and Clemens had their discussion regarding the use of firearms in the series, as Steed uses a .38 Smith and

---

[10] A similar place exists today. This is Wattlehurst Farm and Deadwood Western Town, situated at Paynes Green near Crawley in Sussex, where the management organise Wild West-themed weekends.

Wesson revolver at one point, to defend himself against some ambushing motorcyclists. Steed also helps himself to the villain Fitch's Beretta 950 automatic with silencer, and later kicks him into a chair that activates a gun concealed in a bicycle pump, killing him – though this doesn't make sense, as the nozzle is facing away from him.

The radiator grille of the parked Bentley is glimpsed a couple of times and reveals it to be the same 4½ Litre (UW 4887) seen in the previous episode.

A number of minor guest cast members went uncredited, including stuntman Alan Chuntz, playing a bank butler who falls off his motorcycle after it collides with a couple of wooden packing cases in the underground car park.

This episode is also notable for marking the first appearance of Emma Peel's black leather catsuit, incorporating several chrome zips and worn with boots from Anello and Davide. It was designed by Jan Rowell of the Elstree Studios costume department, with the actual cutting and stitching together of the garment being undertaken by Doreen Brown. Brown made two examples: one for Rigg and the other for stunt double Billy Westley.

Another on-screen first was the debut of the standing set of Steed's apartment kitchen, which included a Welsh dresser, units, shelving, table and various pans, crockery and cooking utensils.

Marshall drew part of his inspiration for the episode's plot from the pagers used in hospitals at the time, on which he consulted his sometime writing partner Phyllis Norman, who worked in the medical profession. Coupling this with his general interest in the stock market gave him the basics of the story outline, which Clemens prompted him to expand upon. Guest star Michael Trubshawe, who was apparently a wine expert, was allowed to rewrite dialogue for a scene involving a wine tasting session – although this actually made the factual content inaccurate, much to Marshall's disapproval.

Filming procedure

The differences between making the series on film as opposed to videotape were enormous. Whereas the taped episodes were recorded in one evening, generally in a single take, and had no post-synch or dubbing carried out, the standard shooting time for a filmed episode was ten days, and there was significant post-production work done. However, the taped episodes were preceded by several days of rehearsals, whereas the filmed episodes generally allowed for only a couple of run-throughs before each shot – although retakes could always be done if necessary. Directors working on a filmed series were expected to get at least five minutes of finished footage in the can every day, but it was not an all-or-nothing situation as with videotape. If the required footage was not captured in the allocated time, then the crew either continued filming until it was, or a smaller second unit would take over and finish things off.

Having worked extensively with film before, Patrick Macnee took well to the more relaxed method of production; and, having survived his baptism of fire, Don Leaver would return toward the conclusion of the fourth season to direct more episodes. However, Peter Hammond, who was actually the first director from the earlier taped seasons to be offered the chance to direct an episode on film, had a blunt response: 'I told them to get lost. There was nothing I could love in the new series of *The Avengers*!'

Beaconsfield Studios

A meeting regarding the series was organised at ABC's Hanover Square offices on Tuesday 2 February 1965, attended by representatives of both ABPC and ABC, including Howard Thomas, Brian Tesler, Julian Wintle and Gordon L T Scott. ABPC wanted to sell studio space at Elstree to film-makers, and it had therefore been decided by the board of directors that *The Avengers* should be transferred to another studio, such as Bray or Beaconsfield. After some discussion it was decided that Bray in Berkshire was unsuitable due to its limited facilities and small stages. However, consideration had already been given to taking over Beaconsfield in Buckinghamshire, which was currently empty, and staffing it from Elstree.

Wintle said that he was willing in principle to accept a move to Beaconsfield after March, but only if he was given an official decision within 24 hours, adding that there was no reason why the quality of the series should suffer. James Wallis of ABPC confirmed that all costs incurred due to any relocation, including those relating to personnel, the dismantling and reassembling of standing sets and transport, would be met by ABPC.

At the time, the six soundstages at Elstree were on the whole occupied, not just by *The Avengers* but also by the other two television series that were in production there, ITC's *The Saint* and *Gideon's Way*. The last feature film to have been made there was Hammer's historical adventure *The Brigand of Kandahar* starring Oliver Reed, which had been completed by the third week in November 1964. Despite a buoyant film industry, the ABPC would fail to attract another picture to the studios until the first week in April 1965 when, according to *Kine Weekly*, Hammer returned to begin filming with star actress Bette Davis on *The Nanny*. This lack of production companies wanting to take advantage of Elstree would ultimately gain a stay of execution for *The Avengers*; the mooted move to Beaconsfield would not take place, and the series would be allowed to stay at Elstree for the entire remainder of its production run.

Over budget

Also at the 2 February 1965 meeting, concern was expressed over the falling behind in the series' shooting schedule and the knock-on effect this was having on its budget. Wallis pointed out that episodes were costing £29,000 as opposed to the allocated £25,000. In his defence, Wintle said that the ten-day turnaround for principal filming was proving to be unrealistic for the series and that to make *The Avengers* a worthwhile show, it was essential to produce it to a higher standard than ITC's *The Saint*. Taking into account the Elizabeth Shepherd filming that had been written off, Wintle promised to compile a revised budget for the ABPC board as soon as he knew whether or not the production was to change studios.

Further to this, it was decided that Albert Fennell would assume overall responsibility for the series, including liaising with directors on the casting of episodes and overseeing some post-production work, such as assisting with the final editing of episodes. As a result of this decision, it was motioned that Gordon L T Scott would take over the supervision of the crew on the studio floor. It was later revealed in memos that Scott was unhappy with this directive, as he was an ABPC employee and not on the Telemen payroll, but the situation was apparently rectified in a personal meeting with Wallis.

4.04 – 'Death at Bargain Prices'

Next up before the cameras was another Brian Clemens episode, 'Death at Bargain Prices', concerning a plot to detonate an atomic bomb in the basement of Pinters department store in central London. Like 'Dial a Deadly Number', this was a largely studio-bound adventure, the only location footage featuring the cast being the tag scene of Steed and Emma peddling away on bicycles, filmed in Dagger Lane, Elstree. The transmitted version of this scene was actually a second attempt; the first, also featuring Steed and Emma cycling, included dialogue that was later deemed to make little sense; hence the dialogue was rewritten and the scene re-filmed. The beginning of the episode also features brief location footage of several London streets, all virtually deserted, to set the scene as early Sunday morning. These were Lombard Street and Fleet Street, EC3; Sloane Square, SW1; Marylebone Road, NW1; Oxford Circus, W1; and Notting Hill Gate, W11.

Making its debut in this episode was the Harry Pottle-designed Emma Peel penthouse apartment standing set, featuring a large living space dominated by a coal fire and stainless steel chimney directly in the centre. There are two large sofas (one of them L-shaped), a drinks cabinet and a few small items of furniture, several ceramic ornaments, and on the wall a few framed prints, which appear to be Greek. The outer door of the apartment incorporates a sophisticated spy hole in the form of a large human eye, complete with eyelid that opens whenever Emma wants to see who has rung her doorbell.

At one point during proceedings Emma is busy writing a paper on thermodynamics, proving that she has a good scientific knowledge. Clemens crafted some witty dialogue for a scene where Steed arrives at the counter where Emma has taken an undercover job in Pinters; after asking a supervisor for her whereabouts and being informed 'Our Mrs Peel is in ladies' underwear,' he adds, 'I rattled up the steps three at a time.' After Emma is transferred to work in the toy department, there are several interesting props on show, such as a puppet of Professor Matthew Matic from *Fireball XL5*, two clockwork Daleks and a number of assembled Airfix model plane kits.

Some fictional brands of ceramics featured in the Pinters scenes were given the names Royal Bates and Royal Crichton. The latter was obviously named after the episode's director, Charles Crichton; and as fashion designer John Bates had yet to become involved with the production, presumably the former was a nod to ex-story editor Richard Bates.

The final confrontation between Pinters' villainous management and Steed and Mrs Peel plays out as a deadly game of hide and seek, partly accompanied by eerie, suspense-building incidental music from Laurie Johnson. Mrs Peel's fight against the character Massey, played by George Selway, was choreographed to another Johnson track, 'Fisticuffs'. This was originally intended to be Emma's theme, pencilled in to accompany all of her action scenes; although the producers later dropped this idea, it works exceptionally well in this episode as a one-off. In 1975, 'Fisticuffs' would turn up on a KPM vinyl record album called *Metropolis*, serial number 1156, containing library music intended primarily for use by radio, television and film companies.

During the course of the action Steed is relieved of his .38 Smith and Wesson revolver, allowing Macnee to get his wish of having the agent fight using more impromptu weapons, including his umbrella and his bowler hat. Obviously inspired by the one worn by the character Oddjob in *Goldfinger*, Steed's bowler is a custom-made example incorporating a steel rim, which he later uses to knock out an opponent, Farthingale, with a single blow to the head.

'Death at Bargain Prices' concluded principal photography on Wednesday 17 February 1965. Macnee would later cite it as one of his favourite episodes.

Sometime during the 1980s, the then copyright holder of *The Avengers*, the American company Weintraub Entertainment Group, conducted some colourisation tests on black and white footage from this episode. However, it appears that the master tape of the colourised material was either disposed of or inadvertently lost, as the current copyright holder, the French company StudioCanal, possesses only a lower-quality copy of it.

Guidelines for scripts

As ABC always envisaged selling the filmed series to one of the American networks, Clemens issued a written directive to the writers and directors regarding censorship matters that had been brought to his attention. This was a heavily-condensed version of the American Television Code. Certain words such as 'idiot' and 'damn' were banned from being included in screenplays, and Mrs Peel was forbidden to fight dirty. There were also guidelines regarding the screen use of firearms; these could not be aimed at someone's head or directly at the camera, and telescopic sights were excluded completely. In addition, there were concerns over cigarettes appearing in the episodes, though not from a health point of view. As many cigarette companies were major advertisers on US television, it was thought wise not to antagonise them by showing tobacco abuse by characters under stress. Beer bottles and other branded commercial items were not to be mentioned by name, or be recognisable by their labels, and finally the American flag could not be defaced or ridiculed in any way, shape or form.

Clemens saw *The Avengers* as the perfect opportunity to push the envelope in storytelling, looking to take the genre that extra step, as evidenced by the science fiction and fantasy scenarios that were starting to appear. Interviewed in 1992 by the magazine *Time Screen* he said, 'A writer would come into the office with an idea and we'd talk it through, and as we went I would be typing a rough outline. By the end I would have three or four pages of major points, which might include amusing dialogue, and I would give the writer a copy. I always worked on the principle that if he got knocked down by a bus I could always write it myself. At that time we were working on a five to four ratio; commissioning five scripts to get four useable ones and have the funds to be able to write one off.'

Determined that *The Avengers* should steer clear of social realism, Clemens devised several ground rules to which he expected writers to adhere. These dictated that the episodes should include no killing of women, no blood, no police officers, and – more controversially, because Clemens did not want the series to touch on issues such as racism – no black characters. However, these rules could be broken if it helped to create a good storyline. For instance, black characters were featured in the episodes 'Small Game for Big Hunters', 'Honey for the Prince' and 'Have Guns Will Haggle'. Another ruling forbade the use of extras in background shots; hence the streets of what became known as Avengerland were usually unpopulated, as Clemens thought that Steed with his bowler and umbrella and Emma in her catsuit would look ridiculous in ordinary situations, such as stood in the middle of a bus queue. From now on *The Avengers* would deal exclusively with the upper classes.

4.05 – 'Too Many Christmas Trees'

A seasonal episode from the typewriter of Tony Williamson was next in production order, as filming on 'Too Many Christmas Trees' got under way on Friday 19 February 1965. This tale of foreign agents telepathically manipulating Steed in an attempt to obtain the secrets he holds in his mind definitely fitted Clemens' requirement of pushing the thriller format to another level, and was quite innovative for a British film series of the time.

The 4½ Litre Bentley (UW 4887) was hired again for location filming on both Butterfly Lane and Aldenham Road, Elstree, with doubles standing in for Macnee and Rigg; close-ups of the two stars were shot against back-projection at the studios and edited into the completed footage. The Bentley was also filmed turning off Aldenham Road into the gateway of the Haberdashers' Aske's School, and then pulling up outside Hilfield Castle, off Hilfield Road – which, although not apparent in the finished sequence, was actually three miles away. The episode's end tag scene, featuring Steed and Mrs Peel leaving via horse and trap, employed more back-projection, with film of the actors' doubles heading southbound from the direction of the village of Shenley toward Borehamwood.

At one point Steed receives Christmas cards from various female acquaintances including Cathy Gale; and in a tongue-in-cheek reference to Honor Blackman's role in *Goldfinger* he comments, 'Mrs Gale, how nice of her to remember me… What can she be doing at Fort Knox?'

Mrs Peel's intellectual capacity is emphasised again when it is revealed that she has written papers on psychoanalysis. After Steed is clubbed down by a villain, she quickly arms herself with his Smith and Wesson revolver, partly hidden in one of his boots, and deals with his attacker with a single shot.

For the elaborate Dickensian-themed Christmas party featured in the story, Steed dresses as Sydney Carton from the classic novel *A Tale of Two Cities* and Emma attends as the title character from *Oliver Twist*. In order to prevent his mind being read by the enemy, Steed concentrates on singing the nursery rhyme 'The Grand Old Duke of York', before being joined by Emma for verses of the folk song 'Green Grow the Rushes, O' and 'Oranges and Lemons.'

The designer of all the sets seen in the season so far, art director Harry Pottle, was initially unavailable for this episode, and was replaced by Robert Jones. However, in a strange turn of fate, Jones too suddenly became unavailable and, finding himself free again, Pottle rejoined the team, working on the rest of the season until production was completed.

Roy Baker directed *Too Many Christmas Trees* in an atmospheric fashion. It was the first of seven episodes he would handle this season. When interviewed at the Pictureville Cinema in Bradford in March 2000, at an event to promote his book *The Director's Cut*, Baker said that he was brought onto *The Avengers* to be the in-house director, and was also responsible for setting the visual style of the show on film.

4.06 – 'The Cybernauts'

Philip Levene's 'The Cybernauts' began filming on Tuesday 2 March 1965, with Albert

Fennell's friend Sidney Hayers brought on board to handle the direction. This was another screenplay that pushed the boundaries, not only in terms of its content but also in terms of its predictions of the future, with Levene accurately anticipating both the swipe card entry system and the integrated circuit. The storyline involves the brilliant inventor Dr Armstrong, played by Michael Gough, eradicating his rivals in the electronics industry with a seemingly unstoppable karate-chopping killer robot – the titular Cybernaut.

Levene had been brought onto the series by Brian Clemens, who had heard a science fiction radio play he had written for the *Just Before Midnight* anthology and thought it just the kind of story *The Avengers* needed. On discovering the writer's identity, Clemens realised they had already worked together on the television series *GS5*. Levene was held in high regard by Clemens, who considered him to have dialled into the style of *The Avengers* perfectly and to be a brilliant ideas man when it came to storylines. The only issue he had with Levene's scripts was his exchanges of dialogue, which as script editor he frequently rewrote and embellished upon.

Levene's draft script for 'The Cybernauts' had also been given a big thumbs up by Brian Tesler back in December 1964, despite it being another of the science fiction-based ones about which he had previously expressed reservations. In his own comments, Anthony John pointed out that the two Cybernauts featured in the storyline needed to have differences in appearance, otherwise viewers would become hopelessly confused. As a result, the first Cybernaut, dubbed Roger by Dr Armstrong, was given dark clothing and a trilby hat, while the maintenance Cybernaut had light coloured overalls and a flat cap.

This episode sees the arrival of Mrs Peel's personal transport for the series: a white Lotus Elan S2 convertible (HNK 999C). This was supplied by the manufacturers, who saw the chance for some free publicity and came to an agreement with Telemen. In a location-filmed sequence, Emma is seen driving the Elan into the car park at the Haberdashers' Aske's School, Elstree, where Steed is sat in a 1906 Humber Beeston veteran car, pondering over a newspaper crossword. Having assisted him with a nine-letter word beginning with C, Emma promptly departs in the Elan – although this footage actually shows the vehicle in a completely different location, south of Shenley travelling down Silver Hill toward Borehamwood. Surprisingly Steed's usual Bentley (UW 4887) is not featured in this scene, presumably as it was not available or had broken down.

The remaining exterior footage included in this episode was filmed on the Elstree Studios lot, featuring the Elan being driven past the cutting rooms before being parked outside the maintenance building doubling as United Automation.

Roger appears to be unstoppable, smashing through various doors and taking the full blasts from a double-barrelled shotgun at almost point-blank range. Bullets from Emma's Beretta 950 likewise have absolutely no effect on the robot. The dialogue features a clever play on the names of Julian Wintle and Albert Fennell when in one scene Emma claims to represent the company Winnel and Fentle.

Steed's umbrella conceals a miniature camera, which he casually uses to photograph industrialist Tusamo's list of appointments, and it is revealed that Emma's apartment contains a darkroom for processing such images.

One of Laurie Johnson's most memorable incidental music tracks accompanies shots of the stalking Cybernaut. This would be reused in later episodes and be made commercially available (albeit titled as the sequel, 'Return of the Cybernauts') on *The*

Music of Laurie Johnson Volume 1, issued in 2007.

Stuntmen Alan Chuntz, Billy Cornelius and Macnee's double Rocky Taylor all appear uncredited in some karate dojo scenes. Also uncredited are Katherine Schofield playing Oyuka – whose name means 'the immovable one' – and John Franklyn-Robbins portraying Gilbert, an expert from the ministry who visits Steed.

The shooting script dated January 1965 differed in several subtle respects from what actually appeared on screen. For instance it included a throwaway line from Mrs Peel after she defeats Oyuka in a martial arts bout, calling back to the head of the dojo, 'I think it's time you renamed her' – this was removed from the script before filming. Later, in a scene where a character named Jephcott demonstrates breaking a wooden block in half with a karate blow, it was Oyuka who was supposed to hold it in front of him and not one of the male martial artists, who eventually did. A visual joke in the transmitted episode of Emma pushing an immobile Roger the Cybernaut over with a single finger was not included in the script, suggesting that it was improvised on the day of filming. Scenes set in Emma's apartment, where Roger is homing in on the unsuspecting agent, were all originally scripted to be set in Steed's home; another alteration apparently made at the eleventh hour, as his name was simply crossed out and hers handwritten in. The closing tag scene started in the same way as in the episode itself, with Mrs Peel arriving in her sports car, but the scripted dialogue was completely different, leading to her and Steed preparing to go for a spin in a vintage car (though this was not indicated on paper as his Bentley).

Crew changes

Having handled the photography on the season so far, Gerry Turpin now departed for a career in movies. Alan Hume, who contributed his talents to a great many of the *Carry On* films, replaced him. Another new face arriving for this episode was Godfrey Godar, taking over as camera operator from Ronnie Taylor, who also preferred working on films. Previously, Richard Dalton and Claude Watson had alternated on episodes as assistant director, but from 'The Cybernauts' onwards only Dalton would occupy this position.

The Emma Peel fashions

Around this time, costume designer Jan Rowell left the production and ABC decided that they required a professional fashion designer on board – but not someone who would simply provide clothing off the peg, as on the Blackman episodes. On 24 March, ABC's head of press and publicity, Barry Wynne, wrote to Christopher Carr-Jones of the clothing brand Susan Small Limited to follow up several meetings that had taken place recently. The latest of these had occurred only two days previously, when Diana Rigg and fashion designer Jean Muir had got together to discuss what kind of fashions Emma Peel should wear. Wynne confirmed ABC's agreement to a deal whereby Muir would design a wardrobe of assorted garments for the character. These were required to be ready as soon as possible for use in forthcoming episodes. The communication continued, indicating that Muir would receive an on-screen credit on the episodes involved, and that there would be an introduction to shoe manufacturer Rayne to provide Rigg's footwear. However, this was only part one of the exercise. The second part was to market the clothing through high street outlets via the Susan Small-financed label Jane and Jane, with ABC receiving a five percent royalty payment on each item sold.

The plan included an option to extend the collection to various accessories, on the understanding that Jane and Jane were to be the exclusive producers of *The Avengers'* Emma Peel wardrobe. The letter confirmed that the agreement would also be valid for overseas markets, including the United States. It was stated that the new season would begin transmissions toward the end of September 1965, and that ideally the collection needed to be in the shops by then.

Thinking that they required additional assistance on the fashion front, ABC had at least one meeting with Anne Trehearne, the fashion expert with the advertising agency Collett Dickenson Pearce, with a view to hiring her as a consultant. As a result, Wynne wrote to Trehearne on 30 March 1965 outlining a proposal whereby if she agreed to become the fashion consultant and merchandising co-ordinator on *The Avengers*, ABC would give her a salaried position with reasonable expenses and expect her to work only three days a week. Trehearne accepted the offer.

4.07 – 'The Gravediggers'

The production schedule continued with Malcolm Hulke's 'The Gravediggers'. The draft script for this, with the title spelt slightly differently as 'The Grave Diggers', had been submitted to Tesler for approval on 23 February 1965, and Tesler had responded to Wintle on 1 March, commenting that it was very good. The draft required no rewriting and was transferred to a shooting script by Hulke in just over a week, that version arriving with Tesler by 10 March. The storyline presented a scenario in which Britain's missile early warning system is suffering failures, which Steed and Mrs Peel trace to jamming devices planted in coffins buried in cemeteries.

One script requirement called for Mrs Peel to be tied to a railway track and rendered helpless as a train speeds toward her at full steam – a scenario originally envisaged for Cathy Gale but too complicated to achieve in the studio at Teddington. Telemen obviously needed complete control over the shooting of this to ensure safety, and decided that a private railway would best suit their requirements. With almost two miles of track, the miniature railway at Lord Gretton's estate, Stapleford Park, near Melton Mowbray, Leicestershire, was chosen as the location for the fictional Winslip Junction. At the time, the stately home Stapleford Park was open to the public, and the miniature railway was an added attraction, along with a zoo and two ocean-liner-themed boats used for rides on the nearby lake. Instruction on how to drive the steam locomotive *John O Gaunt*, which was used in the episode, was given by Lord Gretton's son John to stuntman Ray Austin and to guest actor Ronald Fraser, both of whom by all accounts thoroughly enjoyed the experience. Macnee was also given some basics in controlling the loco for the end tag scene, where Steed and Emma reverse the engine along the track. On Sunday 4 April, as the sequence featuring the locomotive was being set up, a runner arrived from the main house with a message that someone wanted Rigg on the telephone. With his leading lady securely bound to the rails, director Quentin Lawrence quickly replied, 'Tell them Miss Rigg is tied up at the moment.'

This episode made greater use of exterior filming than any other in the season so far, with Macnee, Rigg, Austin, Fraser and additional guest cast members Paul Massie and Steven Berkoff all on location in Leicestershire. The 5 April edition of the *Daily Express* ran a report on the locomotive filming under the headline 'The Old Style Hero', quoting Rigg as saying, 'I have been asked to do some silly things in my career. This is the craziest.'

As a token of their gratitude to Lord Gretton, ABC awarded him with a metal plate that still resides beside the railway track, indicating that footage for *The Avengers* was shot there. However, the death of the second Lord Gretton in 1982 brought about the closure of both the stately home and the railway, with the house being sold three years later to become Stapleford Park Country House Hotel and Sporting Estate and the locomotives and rolling stock being placed in storage. When the third Lord Gretton passed away in 1989 it was feared that the railway would be broken up and sold off. However, in 1992 a group of local enthusiasts pooled their resources and became the Friends of the Stapleford Miniature Railway. After totally refurbishing the site, they now open it to the public on selected weekends. Over the years a number of modifications have been made to the *John O Gaunt*, and in 1995 the engine was renamed *John H Gretton*.

Although Lord Gretton's home is seen briefly on screen when Steed initially arrives, the establishing shot of Winslip Junction is actually of Oaklands College at Smallfield Campus, Hatfield Road, St Albans in Hertfordshire. When Steed visits the cemetery at Pringby, the sequence features a mixture of two locations. The light-coloured church was in the village of Aldenham in Hertfordshire, and the churchyard itself was at New Southgate Cemetery, Brunswick Park, Southgate, London N11. Hospital scenes involving the undertakers and a Humber hearse were shot in a courtyard and on one of the internal access roads at the Haberdashers' Aske's School in Elstree.

Stock footage of the three 40-foot diameter domes at RAF Fylingdales on the North York Moors in Yorkshire doubled as the early warning radar station visited by Steed and Mrs Peel. Locally referred to as giant golf balls, these structures were replaced in 1989 by a large pyramid to serve the same purpose of monitoring airspace in the northern hemisphere.

Apparently the Bentley (UW 4887) was still unavailable from Kingsbury Motors, as in this episode Steed drives a vintage 1924 Vauxhall 30/98 (XT 2275). While snooping around the Sir Horace Winslip Hospital for Ailing Railwaymen, he masquerades as a representative of the fictional trade union FFS (Footplateman's Friendly Society). Mrs Peel has her Beretta 950 automatic with her, but is able to defeat the villainous Miss Thirwell without firing a single shot. Later, in the sequence where she is tied to the railway tracks, the incidental music consists of a tinkling piano accompaniment reminiscent of those used for silent movies.

Thirwell and her accomplice Miller are not seen to be rounded up at the story's conclusion, though as half a minute was trimmed from the running time to bring the episode down to the correct length, it is possible that such a scene was filmed but ended up on the cutting room floor.

The Ronald Fraser-portrayed Sir Horace Winslip, who has filled his home with railway memorabilia, provides a foretaste of the type of eccentric characters who will often appear in season five.

Some of the sequence where Steed runs through the wooded area at Stapleford Park to meet up with the train was filmed at a slower-than-standard frame rate, in a technique known as undercranking, so as to appear speeded up when played back.

The unstable spiral staircase last seen inside Pinters department store in 'Death at Bargain Prices' was used again in this episode, this time on the funeral home set.

The pallbearers went uncredited, although some of them were played by stuntmen

Billy Cornelius, Alan Chuntz and Cliff Diggins. Aubrey Richards' performance as the head of the early warning station, Dr Palmer, likewise went uncredited.

A new theme tune

Telemen wanted a completely new theme tune for the series at this point. Initially they approached Johnny Dankworth to provide this, but he declined when he discovered that he would be required to supply the incidental score for each episode as well. Apparently his performing and recording schedule would not allow time for him to make such a big commitment to a television series. Bob Sharples was then contacted with a view to him taking on the task, presumably in light of his involvement with other ABC series including *Public Eye*. Responding to Telemen's request in February 1965, Sharples told them how much he would want to be paid, which was apparently more than they were anticipating. After considering the situation, Telemen then sounded out composer Stanley Black. However, they learned that Black's other work commitments would not allow him to take on another project for several months. Next to be contacted was Laurie Johnson, who had composed music for Julian Wintle's film *Tiger Bay* some years earlier. Wintle arranged an informal meeting with Johnson on Tuesday 16 March at the Pinewood Studios restaurant to discuss matters over a meal. This went so well that the composer signed a contract then and there. That same day, ABC accountant J M Tennent assured Howard Thomas by letter that Wintle would be writing to Sharples personally to advise him that his services would not be required.

Johnson had recently recorded the album *The Big New Sound Strikes Again* for Pye Records. Released in February, this contained a track called 'The Shake', which was later recorded again with a richer sound to become the new theme for *The Avengers*.

Ongoing publicity

On Monday 29 March 1965 Diana Rigg and John Thaw, in costume as Sergeant John Mann of *Redcap*, posed for a series of publicity photographs on the roof of ABC's premises in Hanover Street, London W1. On the same day, Patrick Macnee and Catherine Woodville were married at Hampstead Registry Office. The couple initially lived at Macnee's apartment in Swiss Cottage, London, before moving to a new family home in Richmond, Surrey in July.

4.08 – 'Room Without a View'

With filming on 'The Gravediggers' having been completed on Monday 12 April 1965, production on Roger Marshall's 'Room Without a View' then commenced. Roy Baker was now settling into his duties, which would see him direct every other episode until October.

In this episode, the sudden reappearance of a missing scientist after two years, only for him to disappear again, leads Steed and Mrs Peel to the high-class Chessman Hotel, where one floor is being used as a concentration camp. The draft script underwent an easy passage. In a Monday 8 March note to Julian Wintle, Brian Tesler simply described it as good and did not request any rewrites. He was sent the shooting script on Friday 2 April.

The 4½ Litre Bentley (UW 4887) is seen in a short location sequence filmed on

Packhorse Lane near the village of Ridge and at a large house called Rabley Willow, which stands in its own grounds approximately three miles from the studios. Additional footage, featuring two Chinese laundrymen placing a large wicker basket into the rear of their Austin van, was also shot here.

The only other location work carried out for this adventure was done on Silver Hill for the end tag scene, which this time involves a rickshaw being pulled along by Steed, with Mrs Peel as the passenger advising him about the speed limit.

Uncredited performers in this episode included stuntmen Terry Plummer and Romo Gorrara as guards, Anthony Chinn as an interrogator and Michael Chow as one of the laundrymen. Others in the Chessman Hotel scenes were Aleta Morrison as the daytime receptionist and Fred Stone as the head waiter.

4.09 – 'A Surfeit of H$_2$O'

'A Surfeit of H$_2$O' – in which Steed and Mrs Peel come up against a wine merchant, Dr Sturm, who is developing a way to control rainstorms powerful enough to wipe out armies and deluge whole countries – was the only episode of *The Avengers* to be credited to writer Colin Finbow. Born in 1941 in Ipswich, Suffolk, Finbow had entered the television industry in 1963 by scripting an instalment of the anthology series *Play of the Week*. However, after *The Avengers* he would switch to mainly directing films (some of which he also wrote), usually for the Children's Film Unit, clocking up his last credit on a short called *Awayday* in 1997.

The draft script had initially been sent for Brian Tesler's approval way back on Wednesday 11 November 1964, prompting a reply two days later in which the programme controller seemed unsure of the subject, commenting that it was not bad but lacking in both pace and excitement. As the premise was another science fiction one, perhaps his overall response was predictable: 'I wonder Julian if the scripts aren't on the whole veering too much and too often toward fantasy? Aren't we ever going to get any more good, fast, straightforward thrillers with action and wit?' A further draft of the script was passed to Tesler on Thursday 15 April 1965. This time he called for two further amendments, the last of which arrived with him on Monday 26 April.

When interviewed in the Tuesday 7 July 1992 edition of *The Stage and Television Today*, Brian Clemens was quoted as saying, 'Colin Finbow didn't write a word of "A Surfeit of H$_2$O".' He went on to explain that the writer had been commissioned on the strength of his *Play of the Week* but unfortunately had not lived up to expectations, indicating that a major rewrite had taken place.

Filming of a 'Room Without a View' having concluded on Thursday 29 April 1965, that of 'A Surfeit of H$_2$O' began the following day. Sidney Hayers was the director for an episode that incorporated plenty of exterior footage, most of which was captured at Kendal Hall Farm and adjoining fields off Watling Street near Radlett in Hertfordshire, approximately two miles north-west of Telemen's base of operations in Borehamwood. Besides Rigg and Macnee with an Austin Mini Moke (BOX 656C), Noel Purcell, John Kidd and an uncredited Terry Plummer were all on location here at the fictional village of Lower Storpington. The Mini Moke had previously featured in the film *Catch Us If You Can*, starring the pop group the Dave Clark Five. However, the end tag scene in which Emma and Steed depart used a different Moke (NKY 765C). This sequence was once again filmed along Silver Hill, though on this occasion further south by the junction of High Canons, near Well End.

The sequence where Mrs Peel explores the grounds of the wine distillery, Granny Gregson's Glorious Grogs, in her Jean Muir-designed black PVC outfit, was filmed at the rear of the studio lot and featured the larger of the two water tanks that was there in the '60s. Some wooden wine racks seen previously in 'Dial a Deadly Number' appear inside the distillery when it is paid an undercover visit by Steed – who for part of the episode wears a riding hat instead of his usual trusty bowler.

There is some particularly humorous dialogue in this script. When a man named Eli warns Mrs Peel of an impending downpour and floods, she casually replies, 'Yes, well I've put a down-payment on a canoe'. Then, when Steed and Jonah find the outline of the meteorologist Sir Arnold Kelly's dead body in a field, resembling a giant gingerbread man, the agent is prompted to remark, 'I had an auntie used to make biscuits like this'. Also amusing in the context of the plot is Dr Sturm's name, which when translated from German into English becomes Dr Storm. Jonah is at one point seen in his barn indulging in some over-the-top preaching to a small boy and his pet dog, while his wind-up gramophone plays the hymn, 'Eternal Father, Strong to Save', aka 'For Those in Peril on the Sea'. However, all this humorous content is balanced by the highly dramatic sequence where Sturm uses a wine press to torture Emma, threatening to kill her unless she talks.

In many ways 'A Surfeit of H_2O' pointed the direction the series would take in the following season: a bizarre situation to investigate (in this case a man drowned in the middle of a field), eccentric characters, a mixture of humour and drama and all done in the quaint English countryside.

4.10 – 'Two's a Crowd'

The next episode, 'Two's a Crowd', written by Philip Levene and directed by Roy Baker, proved to be problematic from a scripting viewpoint, undergoing more rewrites than any other this season. The draft script was submitted by Julian Wintle to Brian Tesler on Monday 1 February 1965. Unusually it was over three weeks before a reply came, and Tesler's two-page letter dated Wednesday 24 February found him less than impressed. He felt that the inclusion of deadly aircraft and battleship models pushed the screenplay into the realms of fantasy and in short made it absolutely ludicrous. He also noted that the villains were referred to as Russians, and strongly advised that in the cause of international relations this be altered to have them come from an unnamed state. Plus, he found the script's concept of Steed having a double confusing, and thought that viewers would also be confused. For his part, Anthony John pointed out that the duplicate Steed idea had been fully explored in the previous season with 'Man with Two Shadows', although in general he thought the script was okay. John, however, was overruled by Tesler, who requested a major rewrite.

Wintle replied on Thursday 4 March, indicating that the script had been passed to Brian Clemens for extensive work. Apparently this work was completed just a couple of days later, as on Monday 8 March Tesler communicated again regarding the amended version, which he still found substandard and lacking in plot explanations regarding the Steed double, Webster. In his opinion it still needed more work.

Clemens obviously gave this task his total attention, as he had another draft ready and back with Tesler the following day. Tesler responded to Wintle on Friday 12 March, saying that despite all the rewriting he still thought that the screenplay was unsatisfactory. He was now happy with the final explanation given to Mrs Peel regarding Webster, but thought that the latest rewrite had caused problems by making two other portions of the script nonsensical. By this point, he had at least accepted the inclusion of the model aeroplanes and battleship, on the understanding that the crew could make their inclusion look convincing, but he drew the line at a model helicopter complete with miniature television camera. Finishing his letter, Tesler added that he shuddered at the thought of rehearsals taking place at Elstree Studios with the giant models, because of their £500 each price tag.

Further amended drafts of the script were forwarded to Tesler on Monday 26 April and Monday 3 May. The latter was described by him as a great improvement, but pages of alterations were still coming through as late as Friday 21 May, with filming on the episode having already begun.

As per Tesler's suggestion, the actual nationality of the East European villains is never indicated in the finished episode. Footage of the exterior of their embassy was shot at Edge Grove School, Oakridge Lane, Aldenham, about six miles from the studio. In one of the embassy scenes, Webster (alias Steed) holds Mrs Peel at gunpoint with a 9mm snub-nosed Walther P38 automatic. Both Macnee and Rigg were on location in the school grounds for the sequence of an attack by a model Hawker Hurricane plane (described as a Spitfire in one pre-production letter), which Steed shoots down with an Enfield revolver taken by Emma from one of the embassy guards.

A second, larger model was identified in production correspondence before the episode started filming as an Avro Shackleton, but on screen it was actually an Avro Lancaster. Both radio-controlled aircraft were supplied by a company called Radio Controlled Services, who at the time owned a string of retail hobby shops and had their head office in Bedford.

In addition to the two military aircraft, the episode also features a model Cessna aeroplane, which flies across London, passing over Docklands and the Houses of Parliament before arriving at The Boltons, London, SW7, representing the home of the East European ambassador Brodny – a character who serves to provide some comic relief, such as in a scene where, upon meeting Steed in a bar, he insists on drinking vodka to prove his loyalty to the motherland, even though his demeanour clearly shows that he hates it!

The lake seen in the episode, complete with red-brick bridge, was actually Tykes Water Lake, situated behind the Haberdashers' Aske's School. In the episode it is supposedly situated in the embassy grounds, and is the place where Steed arranges to meet a character named Ivenko, portrayed by John Bluthal. Before their meeting can take place, a model submarine surfaces from the water and kills Ivenko with a single shot – a change from the original idea of him being blasted by a broadside from a model battleship, which fell victim to one of the many rewrites. Going beyond the call of duty for the filming of this sequence, Bluthal fell face down into the muddy water at the edge of the lake and remained motionless until Macnee as Steed arrived and turned his body over, allowing the actor to breathe again. The lake and bridge feature once more in the end tag scene, where Steed and Emma ride away on horseback.

The conference centre where Webster is seen arriving in a Humber Imperial (AWK 948B) was Watford Town Hall, situated on Rickmansworth Road, Watford, Hertfordshire.

The freestanding metal console complete with switches and dials seen in 'A Surfeit of H2O', where it was the control station for the wine press, reappears here as the direction controller for the lethal model aircraft. Also reused from an earlier episode is

Laurie Johnson's powerful Cybernauts incidental music, heard this time over a sequence where Steed and Emma escape from the embassy. The name of the secret master spy around whom the storyline revolves is given as 'Colonel Psev' in the script, yet box files in Steed's apartment are marked 'PZEV', suggesting that there may have been a change of spelling in the course of the rewrites that wasn't picked up by the prop-makers. Steed's height is quoted as six feet two inches at one point, although Macnee's height is actually six feet one. Arriving with Steed in her Lotus Elan to attend a party at the embassy, Mrs Peel enters the building alone while he drives the vehicle away.

Notable amongst the episode's guest cast is Warren Mitchell as Brodny. However, in a less successful move, director Roy Baker and casting director G B Walker gave German-born, French-based actress Maria Machado her only role in a British production as the enemy agent Alicia Elena. Machado subsequently returned to France, where she managed a long if not very successful career in both films and television, although she preferred to concentrate her efforts in the theatre.

4.11 – 'Man-Eater of Surrey Green'

Another Philip Levene episode, 'Man-Eater of Surrey Green', was before the cameras by the first week in June 1965, the draft script having been presented on Monday 10 May to Brian Tesler, who had apparently been happy enough to allow it to progress to a shooting script without any major rewrites. Once more Levene took *The Avengers* into the realms of science fiction, writing a pastiche of John Wyndham's *The Day of the Triffids* with some influences from Nigel Kneale's BBC serial *The Quatermass Experiment*. The result was his creation of an enormous alien plant with hypnotic qualities, enticing humans and then consuming them as food – an idea that also bore some similarities to the 1961 *Armchair Theatre* play 'The Trouble With Our Ivy'.

Like 'A Surfeit of H_2O' and 'The Gravediggers', 'Man-Eater of Surrey Green' made the most of 35mm film, with an abundance of exterior filming under the direction of Sidney Hayers. The main location used in the episode was known at the time as the British Rail Study Centre, based in Grove Park, off Hempstead Road, Watford in Hertfordshire. This represented the estate of Sir Lyle Petersen, whom Steed – posing as a member of the Tree Preservation Society – arrives to visit in his 1924 3 Litre Bentley (XR 6056). The then adjacent greenhouses and single-storey wooden buildings were the location used for botanist Alan Carter's research centre, and also the setting for a scene where the character Laura, under the hypnotic control of the alien plant, tramples through flowerbeds. The main building fell into extreme disrepair during the '90s, eventually undergoing eight years of renovation before reopening in 2004 as a five-star Ralph Trustees hotel complete with golf course.

The episode's derelict Moat Farm at Denbigh – which Emma and Steed investigate after their arrival in her Lotus Elan with the convertible top down – was realised by filming at Strangeways Farm on Rowley Lane on the outskirts of Borehamwood. The exterior of the Surrey Green Arms was actually The Three Horseshoes pub in Letchmore Heath, where additional footage was shot on the village streets, Back Lane and The Green.

The freestanding metal control unit seen in the previous two episodes, 'A Surfeit of H_2O' and 'Two's a Crowd', reappears again, this time with additional gauges supposedly intended to regulate both soil temperature and water supply for the embryonic plant. Steed again wears the riding hat seen previously in 'A Surfeit of H_2O', and actually uses his umbrella to keep dry when it is raining during his second visit to Carter's research facility. Mrs Peel at one point picks up a double-barrelled shotgun discarded by one of the villagers and defends herself, Steed and a researcher named Dr Sheldon from an attack by Peterson's trance-induced chauffeur, Lennox, armed with an identical firearm. Clocking up another uncredited appearance in the series was stuntman Alan Chuntz, as one of the soldiers seen in the background at Moat Farm.

Levene took plenty of writer's licence with the scientific elements of his storyline, such as Emma's speculation that the giant plant could have originated from Mars or the Moon. 'Recent photographs show whole areas of vegetation,' she says of the Moon – although even four years before the Apollo 11 Moon landing the scientific community was confident that astronauts would not find plant life there. Some dialogue where Dr Sheldon talks about a herbicide were also off the mark. 'Nothing more effective than propionic acid,' she says. 'A teaspoon of this would kill a large oak tree.' Actually propionic is not a herbicide, but a naturally-occurring fatty acid that restricts the growth of bacteria and mould.

'Man-Eater of Surrey Green' nevertheless features some of the most vivid images of the season, with people falling under the hypnotic control of the alien plant and then being enticed to their deaths. The horrific elements were toned down for a primetime television audience, though a scene where Steed, Emma and Dr Sheldon hear the screams of the villagers being consumed by the plant is chilling. Clemens' unwritten rule about no women being killed is also broken, albeit off camera, when Petersen – with a hearing aid in place to block out the plant's hypnotic effect – confirms to Steed and Emma that all the missing horticulturalists, including Laura Burford, have become plant food.

4.12 – 'Silent Dust'

Another Roger Marshall screenplay, called 'Strictly for the Worms' throughout principal filming, was being shot by the third week of June 1965, Brian Tesler having accepted the shooting script that had been passed through to him on Friday 21 May. Directed by Roy Baker, this episode involving a super-fertiliser gone wrong that wipes out all wildlife, and a group of people intending to hold the government to ransom against its use, was reminiscent of 'The Grandeur That Was Rome' from the previous season. Strategically placed in the production order to take full advantage of the mid-summer weather, it would feature more location filming than any other this season.

Shooting took place at nine different locales in the Hertsmere district. The crew returned to Tykes Water Lake to film a scene involving Macnee and Rigg punting, drinking wine and discussing the lack of martlets. A sequence of Steed and a government Minister travelling in the latter's chauffeur-driven Rolls Royce to the fictional village of Manderley is established by a shot of the limousine on Buckettsland Lane heading in the direction of Well End. This is followed by studio-filmed material in which back-projected location footage visible through the vehicle's rear window shows it moving along Summerswood Lane, turning off Earls Lane, passing Deeves Hall Cottage and continuing along Deeves Hall Road, all near the village of Ridge. The Rolls Royce is then seen reaching its destination on location at what is now a gateway to Willows Farm Village, situated on Coursers Road in London Colney, near St Albans.

Actors Conrad Phillips and Aubrey Morris, together with Diana Rigg, were on location outside the Stirrup Cup Inn, which was really Well End Lodge, on Well End Road in Well End, a small hamlet between Borehamwood and Shenley. This location appears somewhat different today, as a brick wall has since been erected in front of the property, giving it a front yard. The villainous Miss Snow, played by Joanna Wake, entices Steed around to the adjacent stables belonging to Wheatsheaf Farm, where a man named Croft, played by Norman Bird, attacks him with a scythe. In the ensuing fight scene, Macnee and Bird fought it out in close-up, although the more violent and dangerous aspects were performed by stuntmen Cliff Diggins and Ray Austin respectively, all done against a background of Laurie Johnson's 'Fisticuffs'.

Stock footage of an actual foxhunt was interspersed with newly-filmed material shot at Well End and in the fields adjacent to Kendal Hall Farm near Radlett, where exteriors for 'A Surfeit of H$_2$O' had also been shot. In a budget-saving move, the pub interior set used for 'Man-Eater of Surrey Green' had been left standing on the stage, going on to become the bar of the Stirrup Cup Inn.

An exterior scene in which the fertiliser developer's daughter Clare Prendergast paints a portrait of local landowner Omrod on the patio behind her home was actually filmed on one the stages at Elstree.

One rather clumsy piece of action comes when Steed picks up an apple and casually takes a bite out of it, despite having only just used his fingers to collect some of the white powder that he suspects is the deadly fertiliser, or 'silent dust'.

An unusual aspect of the episode is a humorous dream sequence prompted by Steed passing out after having been shot with buckshot by Omrod's gamekeeper Mellors. In his dream, Steed is a Wild West sheriff dressed in a pair of long johns, while Mrs Peel is the extravagantly-moustachioed town doctor, who sterilises a large hunting knife with a mixture of alcohol and fire before using it and a pair of water-pump pliers to remove a hugely out-of-proportion bullet from him.

The idea of having the climactic action set amidst a foxhunt opposed by anti-blood sports protestors appears to have been borrowed from the 1963 Kirk Douglas movie *The List of Adrian Messenger*. For the episode's various riding sequences Macnee mounted the same grey horse that Laurence Olivier had ridden 21 years previously in the film *Henry V*, finding the animal most agreeable and quite easy to handle. An earlier draft of the screenplay featured Steed on horseback using a large wooden 'For Sale' sign to accost the character Juggins, whereas in the actual episode he helps himself to a placard that the protestors have discarded. Emma carries her chrome-plated .38 Webley and Scott revolver, last seen in 'The Murder Market', though it is knocked from her hand by Mellors before she has a chance to use it.

The unusual mode of transport used by the agents to depart at this episode's conclusion is a hot air balloon.

On Monday 4 October 1965, some months after the completion of filming on the episode, Julian Wintle would raise an interdepartmental communication advising that it had undergone a change of title from 'Strictly for the Worms' to 'Silent Dust'. The latter was the title under which it would go out on transmission, although some publicity material would list both.

Crew changes

A number of further changes in the production crew occurred at this time. Having shared the assistant director credit with Frank Hollands on 'Man-Eater of Surrey

Green', Richard Dalton relinquished it to him completely from 'Silent Dust' (or 'Strictly for the Worms' as it then was). Hollands would hold the position until the season's penultimate episode, with Dalton returning for the final one to round things off. Ernest Steward, another former crew member on *The Human Jungle*, replaced Alan Hume as the show's director of photography from 'Silent Dust' onwards, and James Bawden took over from Godfrey Godar as camera operator, although Godar would be back for another run of episodes later in the season.

The Man from U.N.C.L.E.

Initially the main rival to *The Avengers* on film was ITC's *The Saint*, but at 8.00 pm on Thursday 24 June 1965 a new competitor arrived as the BBC unveiled their American import *The Man from U.N.C.L.E.*. Chronicling the exploits of secret agents Napoleon Solo and Illya Kuryakin of the organisation U.N.C.L.E. (United Network Command for Law and Enforcement), the show had been devised by producer Norman Felton. However, no less a person than James Bond creator Ian Fleming had provided some input into its format, including Napoleon Solo's name, helping to make it the most successful American spy show of the '60s.

The BBC could not afford to fund the production of television film series itself during this period, hence buying in was its only option if it wanted to have a credible stake in the current vogue for espionage series. Using the music chart show *Top of the Pops* as a lead-in to give Solo and Kuryakin a teenage and twentysomething audience, it saw viewing figures for *The Man from U.N.C.L.E.* steadily increase as the first and second seasons were run consecutively until May 1966. The fact that the show was mentioned in communications between Telemen and ABC suggests that both Brian Clemens and Brian Tesler were avid viewers, if only to see what the opposition was doing.

The Avengers in Italy

The first non-English-speaking country to buy *The Avengers* was Italy, where the state-owned television channel RAI screened season three, retitling the show *Agenti Speciali* and dropping the original Johnny Dankworth theme in favour of its own. The latter was written and performed by a beat group that called itself Avengers. At the heart of this were bass player Ares Tavolazzi and drummer Ellade Bandini, who both played in the backing band of Italian singer Carmen Villani. Villani performed uncredited on a vocal version of the theme – surprisingly sung in English – recorded for commercial release as a vinyl single on Thursday 1 July 1965, approximately six weeks ahead of the Italian transmissions actually beginning with 'Death of a Batman'. The single came out on the Italian independent label Bluebell Records, serial number BB.03138, and had an instrumental version on the B-side. It bore no credit for the theme's writers, although ABC Television, *Agenti Speciali*, Patrick Macnee and Honor Blackman were all name-checked. Promotion for the single seemed more than adequate as it came in a picture sleeve depicting Cathy Gale on the cover and John Steed on the reverse and an inner sleeve sporting umbrella, bowler hat and automatic pistol artwork.

4.13 – 'The Hour That Never Was'

Next to be scheduled – again to take advantage of the warmer summer weather, in view of the large amount of location shooting it required – was another Roger Marshall episode, initially known as 'An Hour to Spare'. The draft script, under that original title, had been dispatched to Brian Tesler for his comments on Friday 21 May 1965. Tesler replied seven days later, considering it first rate, intriguing and exciting. Marshall then finalised a shooting script, and this went for Tesler's approval on Saturday 26 June, although this time things did not run smoothly as amendments were requested.

Director Gerry O'Hara got the episode's filming under way on Monday 5 July, and it would continue until Tuesday 20 July. Minor script alterations were still being made on Tuesday 13 July and sent to Tesler as late as Thursday 15 July. Nevertheless, on his own website, O'Hara now cites this screenplay as the finest he ever directed.

In this episode, after swerving to avoid a dog and crashing their car, Steed and Mrs Peel visit RAF Hamelin, the base of 472 Squadron, where they uncover a plot to pre-condition RAF personnel into potential saboteurs.

The accident involving the 3 Litre Bentley (XR 6056) was filmed on the rough track leading down from Watling Street to Tykes Water Lake, with the vehicle swerving and then running head-on into the trunk of a tree. The front of the car was then raised higher by the crew and chocked into position, with steam emitting from the engine compartment to indicate damage to the radiator, and fitted with a severely cracked windscreen. The spare wheel carrier was unscrewed and the car given a general dirtying down to create the impression of impact damage.

Macnee and Rigg were also filmed crossing a bridge and proceeding through a wooded area, arriving at a wire mesh fence representing the secret back entrance to RAF Hamelin. However, for the scenes set inside the base, filming switched to the main location, RAF Bovingdon near Hemel Hempstead in Hertfordshire. This was used in preference to the disused RAF Bircham Newton airbase in Norfolk, which had inspired Marshall's story, as it was closer to Elstree Studios and therefore placed less strain on the series' budget.

The two leads effectively carry the first 22 minutes of the episode as a double-hander, building tension as they explore the deserted airbase. Both Macnee and Rigg climbed up the exterior of the base's control tower for a sequence where Steed and Mrs Peel, from the rooftop vantage point, witness the shooting of a milkman, played by an uncredited Ray Austin. Also featured in the filming was a Second World War de Havilland Mosquito fighter bomber, which was being stored at RAF Bovingdon after appearing in the movie *633 Squadron*, partly filmed there the previous year. The Mosquito (serial number RS 712) had been bought by ex-Group Captain Thomas Gilbert Mahaddie, the technical advisor on *633 Squadron*, and he would keep it at RAF Bovingdon until the early '70s. After appearing in another Second World War film, *Mosquito Squadron*, the aircraft then had various further owners until an American called Kermit Weeks acquired it and financed a total rebuild in 1986. It was then flown to Florida to be an exhibit in the Weeks museum. However, the museum later closed down, resulting in RS 712 being loaned to the EAA Air Venture Museum at Oshkosh, Wisconsin, where it is now on permanent display.

The Tuesday 13 July script alterations reworked a sequence involving an unconscious rabbit to include an 'old style plane', as presumably the crew had come across the Mosquito during their first week on location and wanted it written in.

Macnee also appears to have had a little script input, namedropping his wartime commanding officer Bussy Carr – a partial inspiration for his characterisation of Steed. Marshall's draft script had not included this, or any of the on-screen dialogue where Steed reminisces about a forces' rugby match and beer-drinking contest. There were other minor differences between script and final episode in both dialogue and settings. For instance Steed and Emma see a large cake through the window of a baker's shop on the base, when as scripted they were to have come across it in the cookhouse.

Consideration was given to using the wartime favourite 'We'll Meet Again' by Vera Lynn as background music in the episode, though eventually the production team decided against it. Roger Marshall's favourite guest star on the show, Roy Kinnear, was cast by Gerry O'Hara and G B Walker to play a vagrant named Hickey, who specialises in raiding and living off the contents of dustbins on RAF bases. 'Oh yes sir, certainly none of that Navy or Army rubbish for me,' he says. 'I'm loyal, I am. Loyal to the Airforce … Always have been. Best dustbins in the business.'

RAF Bovingdon is one of the locations seen in *The Avengers* that has completely changed since filming took place there. The airfield closed in 1972 and additional facilities were disposed of in 1976. The aircraft hangars, accommodation and administration blocks were all demolished, allowing for the building of Her Majesty's Prison The Mount, which opened in 1987. A permanent stock car track was also constructed at the end of one of the former runways, although due to falling attendances the promoter was forced to close this in 2008. The two remaining runways now play host to a large open air market every Saturday.

Speeded-up film controversy

On viewing a finished print of 'An Hour to Spare' at the end of August 1965, Brian Tesler was nothing short of outraged by its end tag scene, featuring speeded-up film of Steed and Mrs Peel chasing a runaway milk float. He wrote a complaint to Julian Wintle, who responded on Wednesday 1 September with a short note covering a longer one from Brian Clemens defending Telemen's decision to present the scene in such a manner. Clemens outlined four major reasons why it should remain intact. One: 'An Hour to Spare' was a taut mystery thriller with unknown elements, which he had countered by injecting humour in the form of a dénouement involving laughing gas, and the tag scene was simply a continuation of this lighter vein. Two: the tag scene should be regarded as separate from the main part of the episode. Three: the tag scenes had developed into a little amusing story of their own, adding a new and different dimension to a series that had always bent and sometimes broken the rules; in other words, they were a 'trademark' gimmick, in the same way that the closing credits of *The Man from U.N.C.L.E.* thanked the United Network Command for Law and Enforcement. Four: at worst the scene would generate conversation, which would then raise the profile of the series. Clemens ended his communication by stating that collectively Telemen and ABC should not be afraid of extending the style of the show on film.

Wintle appeared happy enough for Clemens to argue Telemen's case, simply adding his support and informing Tesler that they had decided to change the episode's title to 'Roger and Out'.

Tesler responded the following day and was far from happy, noting: 'It seems to me that there is a danger of losing perspective down there at Elstree among, admittedly, the workers.' Though he agreed with some of Clemens' statements, Tesler considered the production team to be responsible for bursting their own bubble of *The Avengers'* fantasy world, having used speeded-up footage not just for this episode's tag scene, but also for the one in 'Room Without a View'. Continuing, he branded the technique a phoney technical trick that belonged in the world of slapstick comedy, not in the sophisticated surroundings of *The Avengers*. Summing up, he added that surely the final memory of an episode should not be a cheap laugh. He agreed that *The Man from U.N.C.L.E.* credit was consistent with the series, but quickly pointed out that it was presented in a straightforward manner and not in Chinese graphics 'or stencilled on the behind of an elephant'.

Thinking that 'Roger and Out' failed to signpost what the episode was about, Tesler requested Wintle to devise another replacement title for 'An Hour to Spare', and wanted it to contain the word 'puzzle'. Wintle wrote back immediately, advising that the episode had been retitled 'The Hour That Never Was'; the word 'puzzle' was not mentioned.

Tesler subsequently agreed, as part of a compromise over another issue (see below), that the speeded-up film could be left intact in the tag scenes of both 'Room Without a View' and 'The Hour That Never Was', provided that there was no subsequent repetition.

John Bates – fashion designer

Although Jean Muir provided some clothing for Diana Rigg to wear in 'The Gravediggers', 'A Surfeit of H₂O', 'Two's a Crowd' and 'Silent Dust' (then called 'Strictly for the Worms'), the idea of her following this up by creating and marketing a line of *The Avengers* fashions came to nothing. On the recommendation of fashion consultant Anne Trehearne, fashion designer John Bates was approached to replace Muir. He was offered the same deal regarding the retailing opportunities, and grasped it with both hands.

With the September 1965 deadline looming, Bates rose to the challenge quickly, adopting the black and white theme of television pictures of the time and creating a mod-style two-tone wardrobe, some parts of which were based on clothing that his label Jean Varon was already producing. Putting together a collection of 35 garments and matching accessories, Bates subcontracted most of the manufacturing to other suppliers to produce the various items under licence and thus save time. Bates gave all his creations a name, resulting in Emma's catsuits being dubbed Black Bottom and Belt-up.

Despite her contributions and the letter she had received indicating that she would be given an on-screen credit, Muir never received any publicity for her involvement with *The Avengers*. The first episode to feature one of Bates' designs was 'Silent Dust', in which Rigg wore a snakeskin-print PVC jacket he had supplied, although this contribution also went uncredited. 'The Hour That Never Was' saw the designer receive his first on-screen credit, and the practice would then be continued for the season's final 13 episodes. Similarly Edward Rayne would from this point on receive an on-screen credit for providing Rigg's shoes and boots. Anne Trehearne would be credited as fashion consultant for only half a dozen episodes, after which she would return to one of her previous occupations as editor of the fashion magazine *Queen*.

Additional incidental music

On Friday 16 July 1965, Brian Tesler had dinner with Mort Werner, Vice President of Programmes for the American NBC network, who was a fan of the videotaped episodes of *The Avengers*, which he always watched whenever he was in London. Viewing some of the new filmed episodes, Werner considered Rigg to be the series' biggest selling point. He was however disappointed by the relatively sparse use of incidental music – though he liked what background cues there were. Thinking that this missing ingredient might make the difference between obtaining an American network sale and not, Tesler contacted Julian Wintle to provide a cost for putting additional music on all the episodes.

Wintle wrote back on Wednesday 21 July, informing Tesler that the proposed increase in incidental music would entail Laurie Johnson arranging additional recording sessions, increasing the budget by £300 per episode. Further to this, Wintle pointed out that eight episodes were already fully edited. He finished his letter by saying that an immediate decision on the matter would be desirable.

Tesler took a week to respond, then gave instructions to leave the eight episodes that were already in the can but to arrange for more incidental cues to be recorded and dubbed onto the remaining episodes.

4.14 – 'The Town of No Return'

A decision having been taken to remount the first Elizabeth Shepherd episode, 'The Town of No Return', a revised screenplay featuring Emma Peel mark two was sent to Brian Tesler on Thursday 3 June 1965, followed by some amendments on Thursday 1 July. The scenario involved Steed and Mrs Peel investigating the disappearance of colleagues in a remote coastal town, only to discover that enemy agents have assumed the identities of the local populace.

Filming commenced on Wednesday 21 July with Macnee, Rigg, guest actors Alan MacNaughton, Patrick Newell, Robert Brown and the crew all travelling to the Norfolk coast for location work under the direction of Roy Baker. Some of the footage from the original shoot done in October/November 1964 was still usable, however, and would be incorporated into the episode at the editing stage, so there was no need for that to be repeated.

The episode opens with another bizarre situation, as a figure concealed inside a large black vinyl bag wades ashore from the sea, then steps out from within and walks up the beach to where a local fisherman named Saul sits mending his nets. After obtaining directions to a place called Little Bazeley, the man heads off just as if this is a normal everyday occurrence. This scene was filmed on the Holkham National Nature Reserve at Gun Hill, near the small village of Burnham Overy Staithe.

The exterior and interior of The Inebriated Gremlin pub were both constructed on one of the soundstages at Elstree. Various Airfix model plane kits last see in 'Death at Bargain Prices' were hung above the bar, and the larger scale model of the Hawker Hurricane that attacks Steed and Emma in 'Two's a Crowd' was also suspended from the ceiling on a wire. In a continuity error, Newell's character Jimmy Smallwood fails to pay for his round of drinks before departing the pub to walk along the deserted street toward the church, with Saul following him at a discreet distance. The latter scenes were shot on location about two miles inland south-east of Wells-next-the Sea, in the village of Wighton, with filming taking place on the High Street and also at the local church situated on Kirkgate Lane.

A sequence where Smallwood is chased by Saul and his bloodhounds over the salt marshes was another of those shot on the Holkham National Nature Reserve. In the transmitted episode, it also incorporates a piece of footage showing someone running through a muddy drainage ditch while being chased – obviously one of the sections salvaged from the original shoot, as the build and hair colour of the fleeing man show that it was definitely not Newell.

For a sequence of Steed and Mrs Peel discovering Smallwood's body partly buried in the sand dunes the following morning, it appears that all the shots featuring Diana Rigg were filmed on a studio set against a back-projection screen. However, in his commentary on the Optimum DVD set *The Avengers: The Complete Series 4*, Brian Clemens insists that although it looks like a set, it was actually on location. Footage of Patrick Macnee was also shot on the sandy beach of nearby Holkham Bay, close to the small settlement of Holkham, about a mile west of the village of Wells-next-the-Sea.

The deserted airfield where Steed continues his investigations was actually RAF Bircham Newton. This had been decommissioned at the end of 1962, although some testing of the Hawker Siddeley Kestrel – the forerunner to the Harrier jump jet – was still taking place there in 1965. The whole site would later become the National Construction College.

The primary school exterior seen in the episode was really the block that housed the cutting rooms at Elstree, with Stage 5 – the main one used by *The Avengers* this season – visible in the background. The access point to some underground bunkers was actually the entrance to a disused air raid shelter at the studio, with both the carpenter's shop and Stage 5 providing the backdrop.

The end tag scene, featuring Emma and Steed on a Vesper GS scooter, was achieved partly through Rigg and Macnee being shot against a back-projection screen – the footage on the screen showing them passing through Well End – and partly through the use of doubles in a long shot of the scooter descending Silver Hill. The latter location would ultimately be used for no fewer than 12 of the series' end tag scenes, including a number supervised by Roy Baker for episodes on which he was not the principal director.

The train on which Steed and Emma travel to Little Bazeley was stock footage, initially of a Great Western Railways 6100 class steam locomotive and later of a Fowler-class loco built by the London Midland and Scottish Railway. During the journey Emma gets into her undercover character as a teacher by reading the magazine *Teacher's World*, while Steed engrosses himself in the book *Great Disappearing Acts*.

During the making of this episode Diana Rigg wore several of John Bates' newly arrived fashions, including a black stretch cotton catsuit with PVC panels, one of the first mini skirts and a target beret, plus Edward Rayne-designed white boots with a thin black central stripe.

Steed's ruthless side surfaces again when he sets fire to the handlebar moustache of a man masquerading as the airman 'Piggy' Warren, making him reveal the whereabouts of the missing Mrs Peel. When attacked by Saul wielding a sledgehammer in a blacksmith's, and later when trapped by four foreign invaders on the wrong side of an electronic shutter door, he defeats the villains using his steel-crowned and rimmed bowler hat as seen previously in 'Death at Bargain Prices'.

A matte painting was positioned over the end of the short section of darkened tunnel set leading to the bunker, creating the impression that it was longer than was actually the case.

Stuntman Rocky Taylor doubled for Macnee during a scene where Steed fences with Emma in her apartment.[11] Similarly Ray Austin doubled for guest actor Jeremy Burnham for a shot where Mrs Peel throws his character – a villain impersonating the local vicar, Amesbury – headfirst through a grating hole into the tunnel below.

In a sequence where Mrs Peel visits the church to look over the parish records book she is seen to be wearing gloves, but does not have them on in the close-up of her hands showing the missing pages in the book, suggesting that Elizabeth Shepherd did make it into the finished episode after all.

Brian Clemens was by this point already starting to give his scripts double-barrelled subtitles of the kind that would later appear on screen for the first 16 episodes of season five. The original version of 'The Town of No Return' was subtitled 'In which Steed finds a town full of strangers … and Emma teaches school'. This was changed on the revised version to 'In which Steed finds a town of ghosts … and Emma gets put into harness'.

When the Amesbury impostor has Mrs Peel at gunpoint after she discovers that his singing congregation is nothing more than a recording played on a reel-to-reel tape machine, Burnham ad-libbed his next line, 'A very appropriate piece of music, Mrs Peel. It's a requiem!' Apparently Clemens and Baker both liked the irony and delivery of this so much that they allowed its inclusion.

The small, round-rimmed spectacles that Mrs Peel wears when visiting the school were Rigg's idea.

Juliet Harmer was brought in to play the school's headmistress, Jill Manson, because Alison Seebohm, who had portrayed the character in the Shepherd version, was now unavailable; although while on the original shoot she had met her future husband, Ray Austin.

Clemens always intended that 'The Town of No Return' would be Emma Peel's introductory episode on transmission, and all the regional ITV companies bar one duly chose it as the season opener.

Budget concerns

On Monday 26 July 1965, ABC's accountant J M Tennent wrote to Howard Thomas raising concerns regarding a production overspend on *The Avengers*, which then stood at over £67,000. However, this figure did include the reshooting of segments of both 'The Town of No Return' and 'The Gravediggers', plus the cost of the screen tests to find Elizabeth Shepherd's replacement. Referring to a meeting they had had the previous week with Julian Wintle at his apartment in Bryanaston Square, London W1, Tennent asked Thomas when the economies they had discussed on that occasion would be implemented, should no American network sale for the show be forthcoming. Apparently the three men were planning a gearing-down process from what they called '*Danger Man* standard' to '*The Saint* standard'.

---

[11] This fencing match between Steed and Emma would be reworked for the 1998 feature film version of *The Avengers* starring Ralph Fiennes and Uma Thurman, even to the extent of recycling a 'flexibility in the wrist' line of dialogue.

4.15 – 'Castle De'Ath'

Writer John Lucarotti made his final contribution to *The Avengers* with a Scottish-set storyline called 'Castle De'ath', the shooting script for which was forwarded by Julian Wintle to Brian Tesler on Tuesday 20 July 1965. The plot revolves around two feuding brothers, one of whom is caught up in a scheme hatched by a foreign power to ruin the British fishing industry.

Reports in circulation around the beginning of the year indicated that there were plans in place actually to film exteriors at an ancient Scottish castle. However, these plans were later abandoned as budget concerns became paramount with ABC. Instead, the De'ath ancestral home was represented by several establishing shots of Allington Castle near Maidstone in Kent, with only a few extras and Mr Peel's Lotus Elan going on location. Some stock footage of the Scottish highlands was however mixed in to reinforce the impression that the action took place there.

With production on the remounted 'The Town of No Return' concluding on Friday 30 July 1965, principal filming on 'Castle De'ath' commenced on Monday 2 August, with director James Hill making his series debut. Hill had originally been pencilled in direct 'The Murder Market', but had been released from his contract when the opportunity arose for him to go on location in Africa to direct the feature film *Born Free*. However, he was obviously held in high regard by Wintle and Fennell, and sometime later was offered 'Castle De'ath', which he accepted.

Emma once again uses a combination of karate and judo to easily subdue an assailant in an early sequence set in the castle dungeon. Later though she shows her softer side by wearing a three-piece silver/blue lamé outfit called Flash, complete with matching boots. Flash was one of Patrick Macnee's favourites amongst the John Bates collection; he described it as both impudent and erotic. A couple of months later it would be made available to the public at a retail price of 29 guineas. Also in this episode Emma manages to open the antiquated lock on the large wooden door leading to the dungeon using nothing more complicated than a pencil; and she proves herself a dab hand with a crossbow. A sequence in which she confronts the De'aths' retainer McNab, who is playing the bagpipes and masquerading as the ghostly Black Jamie, was originally written to take place as an exterior scene on the battlements of the castle, and she was to have thrown him over the castle parapet. This was altered for the final episode, where it is McNab's own momentum in a misjudged attack on Emma that propels him over the balustrade of the first floor landing.

Other notable points: this episode boasts the longest acronym ever used in the series, ABORCASHAATA, short for the Advisory Bureau on Refurbishing Castles and Stately Homes as a Tourist Attraction; in a sequence where Emma sneaks back into the castle at night, the double used for Rigg in long shots clearly had much lighter hair; stunt arranger Ray Austin stood in for guest actor Robert Urquhart during the climactic scene where his character, Angus, fights Steed; and the matte painting depicting an underground corridor, last see in 'The Town of No Return', reappears here to perform the same function on the set of the tunnel beneath the castle.

A relatively novel kind of transport is seen to take Steed and Emma away in the end tag scene: a German-built convertible known as an Amphicar, which could be driven into a body water and then simply continue like a motorised boat. A number of these specialist vehicles had been imported into the UK in 1964. Once in the water, the driver simply had to shift the gear-stick into neutral and then pull a smaller lever to engage the two propellers mounted beneath. This tag scene was filmed, with doubles posing as the two leads, at Ruislip Lido, off Reservoir Road, Ruislip, in the London Borough of Hillingdon. Close-ups of Macnee and Rigg were shot against a back-projection screen in the studio and incorporated during editing.

ATV lose out to Rediffusion

Upon the completion of 'Castle De'ath' on Friday 20 August 1965 the crew was stood down for a two-week break in production; they would not reconvene until Monday 6 September. Having originally struggled to get ATV to transmit the series in a weekend slot in London, Howard Thomas thought that Lew Grade would not take kindly to *The Avengers* on 35mm film. After all, Grade's own ITC had a virtual monopoly on British film series at the time, and *The Avengers* was about to become its biggest rival. So, changing tactics, Thomas negotiated a deal with Rediffusion to give the series a weeknight transmission in the London region.

Things were not going to be plain sailing, however, as toward the end of August 1965 Rediffusion made the unusual request of having prints that ran for only 46 minutes and 45 seconds, in order to accommodate ten minutes of commercials in an hour-long slot. This meant that for Rediffusion's purposes Albert Fennell and the series' film editor Peter Tanner would have to cut down the standard-length episodes, which ran to approximately 50 minutes, to accommodate the new requirement.

Julian Wintle was extremely aggravated by this development, considering it nothing short of scandalous, and on Thursday 2 September wrote a two-page letter of complaint to Brian Tesler, with whom he was already in dispute over the issue of speeded-up footage in tag scenes (see above). He was concerned that removing material from the episodes might compromise the coherence of the storylines, and did not wish to establish a precedent whereby the ITV regional companies could simply demand prints of different durations.

After consulting both Wintle and Rediffusion on the telephone about the time slot situation, Tesler contacted Telemen again by letter dated Thursday 9 September to break the bad news that the editing of episodes would have to go ahead. The only alternative would have been for Rediffusion to screen the episodes later in the evening, when they could go out complete, but ABC desperately wanted an 8.00 pm start time. Tesler sympathised with the team having to make cuts to the episodes and understood the upset this had caused. He promised Wintle that ABC would not entertain any other ITV regions who might request episodes with other running times. This was also the point when, in a spirit of compromise, he agreed to the retention of the speeded-up tag scenes in 'Room Without a View' and 'The Hour That Never Was'.

Fashion show

The Jean Varon Avengers Collection was officially launched on Tuesday 24 August 1965 with a fashion show at Courtaulds Fashion Theatre, Celanese House, Hanover Square, London. Cameras from Associated British Pathé were present to capture events as news coverage. A smiling Patrick Macnee was present in the audience to see a fashion model wearing one of Bates' black jersey and PVC catsuits apparently throwing stuntman Ray Austin about. The event generated over £10,000 in advance orders. Samples of the collection would stay on display at Courtaulds until Friday 3 September.

The Avengers in print

Wednesday 25 August 1965 saw the publication by Hodder and Stoughton of an original *The Avengers* novel entitled *Deadline,* with Patrick Macnee's name emblazoned on the cover. Macnee was not in fact the book's author, but it had been his idea. Back in April 1964, he had liaised with agents International Literary Management (ILM), who had found an interested publisher in Hodder and Stoughton. By June that year, a meeting between Macnee, Howard Thomas, Sir Gerald Barry of ILM and John Attenborough of the publishers had ironed out an agreement for three books based on the series, to be written by a ghost writer, and initially intended to be published in hardback first and paperback later. Hodder and Stoughton figured that if the novels were ghost-written they could actually use a different writer for each, but they wanted them to have an up-market quality rivalling Ian Fleming's James Bond books. Thomas had no problem with Macnee setting up the deal, just as long as ABC were credited somewhere on the books' covers.

The ghost-writer chosen for *Deadline* was Peter Leslie, who although British lived in France. He was a former music journalist who had written for *Melody Maker* and specialised in jazz, and had already been responsible for a television spin-off novel based on ITC's *Danger Man.* He and Macnee were jointly credited with the copyright on *Deadline.*

The plan to issue three hardbacks that would later be published as paperbacks failed to come to fruition. Instead, *Deadline* appeared only in paperback, with an original cover price of three shillings and six old pence (17½ pence in decimal currency). The novel spawned a Portuguese edition in 1967 and was reissued by Titan Books almost three decades later in August 1994 and again in June 1998.

Leslie (who also worked under the pseudonyms Ed Mazzaro and Don Pendleton) would later write various other television tie-in paperbacks based on the American shows *The Man from U.N.C.L.E., The Girl from U.N.C.L.E.* and *The Invaders.*

4.16 – 'The Thirteenth Hole'

Tony Williamson scripted the next episode, 'The Thirteenth Hole', which started filming on Monday 6 September 1965. With Roy Baker in charge of the action, it had the same writer/director combination that had worked so well on 'Too Many Christmas Trees'.

Williamson's screenplay centred around Steed and Mrs Peel investigating strange events at Craigleigh Golf Club and discovering that secrets are being passed to a foreign power via a transmitting station hidden beneath one of the greens. The title – spelt 'The 13th Hole' on the draft script – was an allusion to the superstition surrounding the unlucky number 13. A couple of years previously, *The Avengers'* then producer John Bryce had suggested a scenario where Steed would become involved in a shootout on a golfing green, but it appears that 'The Thirteenth Hole' was not an extension of that idea. Interviewed by *Time Screen* magazine in 1994, Williamson said, 'I always did my own outlines. These would be discussed with the script editor before I went onto the screenplay, either at the studio or just on the telephone.'

The draft script was sent to ABC from the production office at Elstree on Wednesday 21 July, prompting Brian Tesler to reply positively two days later saying, 'I think this is a good one.' The shooting script was then sent from Wintle to Tesler on

Wednesday 1 September.

This was another episode requiring plenty of location footage, most of which was shot at Mill Hill Golf Club, 100 Barnet Way, Mill Hill, London NW7. The clubhouse and car park there are separated from the fairways by the A1 dual carriageway, being accessed through a tunnel along a service road, seen briefly in the end tag scene where Steed and Emma depart aboard an electric golf cart. Footage filmed on the fairways, greens and car park, involving Macnee, Rigg and guest actors Patrick Allen, Francis Matthews, Peter Jones, Victor Maddern and Hugh Manning, was interspersed with close-ups shot against back-projection in the studio.

For the scene toward the end of the episode where the villainous Colonel Watson, portrayed by Manning, attempts to escape, he was filmed crossing the box girder bridge at Stoney Wood Lake on the golf course before falling victim to Steed's well-aimed golf ball, which knocks him unconscious.

Also briefly used to represent the entrance to Craigleigh Golf Club was Dyrham Park Golf Course and Country Club, situated on Trotters Bottom near Barnet. Just a solitary establishing scene was filmed at its back entrance, showing Steed and Mrs Peel – played by doubles – arriving in the 1924 Vauxhall 30/98 (XT 2275) seen previously in 'The Gravediggers'. This location has since undergone some changes: it is no longer used for access, and the two extremities of the large ornate gateway have had some building work done to provide a couple of homes.

For this episode Diana Rigg wore two John Bates-designed outfits: the black leather catsuit called Belt-up, with a white turtleneck sweater and Edward Rayne's white boots with thin black stripe down the front; and a black-and-white-panelled rabbit coney fur coat called Chemin, which retailed for 22 guineas as part of the Jean Varon Avengers Collection. During the '60s, two celebrities associated with the Beatles, Pattie Boyd and Cynthia Lennon, were both photographed wearing a Chemin, and the garment made such an impression that an example now resides in the Fashion Museum in Bath.

In the course of the action Emma exhibits some knowledge regarding astrology and uses a miniature camera to photograph a star chart she finds hidden under the seat of the golf cart. Later, in a telephone conversation with the scientist Professor Minley, she reveals the golf course to be located in Surrey.

Steed wears his riding hat again, as seen in selected episodes, plus a trilby lined with chain-mail, which saves his life by absorbing the impact of a golf ball fired at him at one point.

The studio set of the underground transmitting station incorporated a number of banks of electronic equipment, including the console prop seen previously in 'A Surfeit of H_2O', 'Two's a Crowd' and 'Man-Eater of Surrey Green'. Also included was a pedestal-mounted Pye Mk 2 television camera.

Only weeks after filming took place, construction crews moved onto the west of the Mill Hill course to build the Scratchwood roadside services and lay the southbound extension for the M1 motorway from what is now the Watford turning at junction five. This necessitated some redesigning of the course, as several of its holes were bulldozed and a large amount of land was ultimately lost.

Crew changes

Having gained experience working on '50s film series such as *Colonel March of Scotland Yard* and more recently on *The Saint*, Lionel Banes was now brought onto *The Avengers* to assume control of photography from Ernest Steward. The other significant crew change at this time came about when Lionel Selwyn took a break for a couple of episodes from his position as sound editor and Bert Rule, fresh from working on *Gideon's Way* on adjacent soundstages, moved across to fill in, starting with 'The Thirteenth Hole'.

4.17 – 'Small Game for Big Hunters'

Filming on the next episode, 'Small Game for Big Hunters, was under way by the third week of September 1965. This was another offering from the imagination of Philip Levene, with Gerry O'Hara returning to direct his second and final episode of the series. Investigating the victim of an apparent voodoo curse, Steed and Mrs Peel encounter an ex-colonial who is developing a deadly strain of the tsetse fly virus, which he intends to unleash upon the African state of Kalaya.

The draft script was despatched to Brian Tesler on Tuesday 25 May, and he responded on Wednesday 2 June with the verdict that the finale was most enjoyable, but the first three quarters was too talky and badly needed some action. Wintle replied on Tuesday 22 June, indicating that Levene was rewriting and restructuring the storyline to eradicate the talking heads problem. A revised version was sent for evaluation on Tuesday 29 June. However, Tesler was still not completely satisfied, prompting him to request more alterations, and it appears that the script was retired to the backburner for a time. The final shooting script did not depart from Elstree until Tuesday 14 September. With production on the episode imminent, Tesler wrote back on Thursday 16 September to say that the revisions were a great improvement and overall the screenplay had been tightened up considerably.

The major filming location for this episode was a large house called Starveacres, which stands in its own grounds on Watford Road, Radlett, in the Hertsmere district just over three miles north-west of Elstree Studios. The front of the building was used to represent the residence of the character Dr Gibson, while a shot of the rear, with its extensive gardens, established the nearby Kalayan Ex-Servicemen's Association. The opening teaser sequence, showing a man named Kendrick, played by Peter Thomas, being pursued through undergrowth by unseen assailants, to an incidental accompaniment of jungle drumbeats from Laurie Johnson, was shot in Aldenham Park.

For the now-traditional leaving-by-unusual-transport end tag scene, Macnee and Rigg were again shot in the studio against a large back-projection screen, while their doubles were seen paddling a canoe across Tykes Water Lake.

Mrs Peel arrives at Dr Gibson's home in her Lotus Elan and finds Steed's vintage 1927 3 Litre Bentley (YT 3942) – hired for the duration of the production from Kingsbury Motors – already there. Later the Bentley is ransacked by the Kalayan undercover operative Razafi, who removes some files – the same props previously used as the PZEV files in 'Two's a Crowd.'

During the filming of this episode Diana Rigg once again wore a Chemin, along with the Edward Rayne black and white boots (on sale to the public at 5½ guineas), John Bates' target-motif beret (17 shillings and 11 old pence) and The Avenger wristwatch – a standard Swiss-made Jean Varon timepiece with a target-motif dial supplied by Freedman.

In a sequence where he visits the Kalaya Ex-Servicemen's Association, Steed has his trusty swordstick – also seen briefly in 'The Thirteenth Hole' – and draws the weapon upon encountering Razafi in the grounds. After being caught in an animal net, he regains consciousness only to discover that the principal villain, Trent, has searched through his pockets and located his official ID card, revealing his identity as Major John Steed.

After Emma is captured by overwhelming numbers on the jungle set – a sequence featuring an uncredited Billy Cornelius as one of the Kalayans natives – Steed arrives to even up the odds, swinging in on a rope imitating the call of the well-known fictional character Tarzan. Scattering the opposition, he declares 'Me Steed!' as he punches the conspirator Fleming to the ground. Mrs Peel then adds 'Me Emma!' before executing an over-the-shoulder throw on the native played by Cornelius.

Honey West

At 9.00 pm on Friday 17 September 1965 *Honey West*, a series often compared to *The Avengers*, premiered on the American ABC network, making it the first female-led private detective show to play on primetime television. The title character had been created in the late 1950s for a series of crime novels written by the husband-and-wife team of Gloria and Forrest E Fickling under the pseudonym G G Fickling. The small-screen version had been piloted in an episode of the detective show *Burke's Law*, screened on Wednesday 21 April, called 'Who Killed the Jackpot?', starring Anne Francis as Honey and Gene Barry as Amos Burke, and this had convinced the network that it would work.

Honey West comprised 30 episodes, each of 25 minutes' duration, and entered production on Monday 4 June, with Francis reprising her role and John Ericson portraying the male sidekick Sam Bolt, a newly-invented character not found in the books. Running her own private investigation agency, Honey was proficient with firearms, had expertise in both judo and karate, used cutting-edge surveillance equipment secreted in her lipstick, wore a black skin-tight catsuit and drove a Shelby Cobra sports car.

While developing the series, producer Aaron Spelling had seen *The Avengers* episode 'Death of a Great Dane' and been so impressed by Cathy Gale that he had offered the part of Honey to Honor Blackman, but she had rejected it.

'The Avengers are Back'

Popular press interest in *The Avengers* grew during late September 1965 as the on-air debut of the filmed episodes approached, with everyone eager to see how the new Avengergirl Emma Peel would shape up. Diana Rigg completed a photoshoot for the *Sunday Times Magazine* published on 26 September, modelling some of John Bates' fashions for the series, including the black leather catsuit and both lengths of the snakeskin print jacket. The following day the *Daily Mail* reported that Emma Peel's state-of-the-art clothing would become available off-the-peg at various high street retailers. The *Daily Mirror* also devoted a two page spread to Emma, highlighting the connection to John Bates' creations.

The Jean Varon Avengers Collection finally arrived in retail outlets at the end of the month.[12] These outlets included Selfridges and Harrods in London, branches of Chanel,

---

[12] See Appendix Seven for full details of the collection.

and other well-known stores that have since undergone changes, such as Rackhams and Army and Navy Stores (both acquired by House of Fraser), Richard Shops and Wallis (both acquired by Arcadia) and Peter Robinsons (rebranded as Topshop).

On Wednesday 29 September, both Rigg and Macnee took part in a photoshoot at St Mary's Bay in Dymchurch, Kent, to capture publicity images for the new season. Some monochrome promotional film was also shot of Rigg riding a grey horse.

Transmissions of the fourth season episodes began in the London and Scottish regions at 8.00 pm on Tuesday 28 September when Rediffusion screened their trimmed-down print of 'The Town of No Return' and Scottish Television took their line-feed. That morning, ABC had secured a full page advert in the *Daily Mirror* to promote the series' return, debuting the slogan 'The Avengers are Back on ITV' (aka 'The Avengers are Back'). Two days later, that week's edition of *Kine Weekly* ran an article previewing the filmed season with the headline 'New-Style Avengers Can't Miss'.

The same edited print of 'The Town of No Return' that had been aired by Rediffusion was transported down to Southampton for Southern Television, who transmitted it to their region at 8.25 pm on Friday 1 October, with both Anglia and Ulster also taking the feed.

The majority of the ITV regional companies began their broadcasts of the season the following night. The ABC and TWW dual regions, Channel, Grampian, Tyne Tees and Westward all kicked off with the complete print of 'The Town of No Return' at 8.25 pm.

The editions of *TV Times* and *TV World* published on Thursday 30 September for the week of Saturday 2 to Friday 8 October both featured a cover photograph of Macnee and Rigg to publicise the arrival of *The Avengers* on film. ABC's schedule of Saturday evening programming started with the science fiction series *Lost in Space* and continued with the pop music show *Thank Your Lucky Stars*, the sitcom *The Worker* and the imported Western drama *Laredo*, which was used as the lead-in to *The Avengers*. Both listings magazines were owned by the Rediffusion-controlled TV Publications Limited, and the *TV Times* also carried an advertisement for a new *The Avengers* comic strip that was about to start its run in the Saturday 2 October issue of the same company's *TV Comic*. The black-and-white strip with artwork by Pat Williams would feature Steed and Mrs Peel in ten multi-part storylines, first in a two-page format though later reduced to only a single page per issue, and would continue for almost a year until its conclusion in the issue of Saturday 24 September 1966. The two agents would also appear in a single self-contained escapade in the *TV Comic Holiday Special 1966*, published in May of that year, and in two stories within the pages of the *TV Comic Annual 1967*, published in September 1966 for the Christmas market.

The final ITV region, Border, scheduled the new season on Sunday nights and began its transmissions at 9.35 pm on 3 October with 'The Master Minds'.

4.18 – 'The Girl from Auntie'

Principal filming was under way by the second week of October 1965 on 'The Girl from Auntie', another screenplay from Roger Marshall with direction by Roy Baker – who would depart the series upon the editing of this episode, having fulfilled his in-house contract.

The storyline this time involved Mrs Peel being kidnapped to be auctioned off to the highest bidder, forcing Steed to track down both her and the perpetrators. Julian Wintle forwarded the draft script to Brian Tesler on Thursday 9 September, and Tesler delivered his assessment seven days later, describing it as fast, funny and furious. The shooting script followed the well-worn route to Tesler on Tuesday 28 September, although Marshall has since indicated that Brian Clemens had carried out some major rewriting on it. In fact, so unhappy was Marshall with the end result – an episode played for laughs, with comedy actress Liz Fraser replacing Diana Rigg for the most part as a fake Mrs Peel, allowing Rigg some time away from filming – that he now refuses even to discuss it. Baker, by contrast, stated in his book *The Director's Cut*, published in 2000, that out of all the episodes he directed for *The Avengers*, this was his favourite.

Returning to the back entrance of Dyrham Park Golf Course and Country Club at Trotters Bottom near Barnet, featured previously in 'The Thirteenth Hole', the crew filmed Rigg and guest actress Mary Merrall in a sequence involving Mrs Peel exiting a charity ball. Another location, used to represent the shared premises of Art Incorporated and the Arkwright Knitting Circle, was a building at the junction of Clarendon Road and Shady Lane in Watford, Hertfordshire. This has since been demolished and replaced with contemporary office blocks. A sequence where Steed and Fraser's character Georgie Price-Jones visit the solicitors Barrett, Barrett and Wimpole was filmed at another building situated on Clarendon Road, although this likewise no longer exists owing to redevelopment.

Filming was also executed at what was then the West London Air Terminal on Cromwell Road, Kensington, London SW5, from where BEA (now British Airways) offered a direct bus service to Heathrow Airport. Checking-in at this facility was discontinued in 1973 and the building then remained empty until 1983, when J Sainsbury converted part of it into a superstore. The remainder was later developed into the Point West luxury apartment building. This sequence, shot in rainy weather, contains a continuity error, as the Austin FX4 cab (BGJ 193B) that leaves the terminal becomes an older Austin FX3 cab (VGF 345) when it arrives at Highpoint 2, situated on North Hill, London N6. The Lotus Elan was also on location at Highpoint 2, and this would be the only occasion that the exterior of Emma's apartment block was witnessed this season.

The end tag sequence was once again filmed on Silver Hill, with Emma and Steed squeezed into a Messerschmitt KR200, a German micro car built between 1956 and 1964, coming up behind a vintage Bentley driven by Georgie. Piloting the Messerschmitt, Mrs Peel overtakes the Bentley, and there is an exchange of greetings, with Rigg, Macnee and Frazer all shot in close-up against back-projection in the studio. Reaching a junction, Emma and Steed turn off along High Canons as Georgie continues down the main road heading toward Well End. This sequence was a replacement for Marshall's original tag scene, which would have had Emma flying a Tiger Moth biplane and looping the loop with Steed as a passenger.

Numerous in-jokes were included in the episode. For instance, Steed and Georgie discover two dead advertising men named Bates and Marshall, whose names were obviously inspired by those of fashion designer John Bates and scriptwriter Roger Marshall. The firm of Barrett, Barrett and Wimpole was named after *The Barretts of Wimpole Street*, which over the years has been a play, film and television series. Even more obvious is a reference to the Beatles in the names of the costumiers John, Paul, George and Fred (not Ringo). Steed and Georgie almost break the fourth wall at one point when he asks her, 'Six bodies in an hour and 20 minutes, what do you call that?', and she replies, 'A good first act.'

While at Emma's apartment, Georgie attempts reading some books, but when *Basic Nuclear Physics* proves heavy-going she switches to *Self Defence: No Holds Barred*, credited to the series' stunt arranger Ray Austin – another in-joke. An amusing sequence follows where an assassin, disguised as an old lady, attacks Georgie, who desperately tries to read through the appropriate passages to discover how best to defend herself – and, realising that there is insufficient time to do this, simply uses the heavy tome to strike her assailant!

Having dealt with the villain Ivanoff, Steed quickly produces a .38 Smith and Wesson revolver from his trouser pocket, handing it to Georgie with the instructions, 'If he moves, point this at him … his second button.' 'Second from the top or the bottom?' she enquires. 'Suit yourself,' is the casual reply.

During the auction scene Mrs Peel is described as an expert in ciphers, scented fuels and cybernetics. The set for the Art Incorporated basement, where the auction takes place, was actually the dungeon from 'Castle De'ath' after a complete makeover and redressing.

In a sequence where Steed and Georgie visit the Jacques Brothers theatrical costumiers, the stencilling on their inner glass door reads 'Starr Brothers', suggesting that the set may have been constructed prior to some last-minute amendment to the script.

As an episode title, 'The Girl from Auntie' was obviously inspired by *The Man from U.N.C.L.E.*, the viewing figures for which over on BBC1 were now high enough to see it in the top 20 programmes on a weekly basis.

Crew changes

Lionel Selwyn returned to carry out both sound and film editing duties on 'The Girl from Auntie'. However, he would gain only a few additional credits up to the end of the season. From this point on, Richard Best and Peter Tanner would generally handle alternate episodes as film editor, while Jack Knight (aka Jack T Knight) would take care of the sound editing on six of the remaining eight, with Selwyn and Ken Rolls tackling the other two.

'The Naked Lassie'/'Bayonet'

Having been a regular contributor to the third and final videotaped season, writer Eric Paice now submitted an outline for a screenplay he called 'The Naked Lassie', which had a strong Scottish element and was basically a reworking of his earlier episode 'Esprit de Corps'. Seeing potential in the concept, Clemens and Fennell gave the go-ahead for him to write a draft script. After this came in, they requested two rewrites, and by the time Paice presented the third version, the title had undergone a change to 'Bayonet'. However, it still contained the Scottish element, as it involved the Scots Border Guards regiment taking part in a NATO exercise of a mock attack on London – which, as with 'Esprit de Corps', was going to provide an opportunity for the villains to try to oust the government.

One effect of the rewrites was to increase Mrs Peel's role, by having the additional factor of her going undercover as a Russian Colonel on an exchange programme and being assigned to the Scots Border Guards, from where she reported back to Major Steed. There were scenes of Steed's vintage Bentley coming under artillery fire and being destroyed, and of Steed crawling through a minefield, carefully prodding the ground ahead of him with his umbrella to locate unexploded devices.

The regiment's Fort Charles and its entrance gateway were to have been realised by filming on the Elstree Studios lot, with the battle training ground being provided by the backlot, although Hampstead Heath was specified as a possible location in the screenplay. The episode was to have culminated in a one-on-one tank battle in Hyde Park. However, the production crew quickly realised this was beyond their means; and the lack of eccentric characters and of a bizarre situation sealed the fate of this story, which never got to shooting script stage.

'Gomorrah'

Eric Paice also submitted a five page story outline for another unmade Diana Rigg black and white episode. Titled 'Gomorrah', this incorporates his criminal organisation Bibliotek from the season three episode 'The Little Wonders', though now renamed Synod. There are references to the Archbishop of Winnipeg and the Bishop of Botswana, as Synod, described as a British Commonwealth mafia, move in on another gang's established territory in Carnaby Street, London. This other gang is led by a giant wrestler called Gomorrah, and a battle for supremacy begins in swinging '60s London, centred on the fashion industry. Going undercover, Steed obtains a position in Gomorrah's gang as a getaway driver. Unfortunately Mrs Peel's investigations bring her to the attention of the gang, who then attempt to kill her. Repeating an element from his second season episode 'The Decapod', Paice then has Steed face off against Gomorrah in the wrestling ring, while Mrs Peel is trapped in a car placed into a scrap yard crusher. Arriving in the nick of time, Steed stops the crusher, and the episode concludes with him attempting to free the trapped but unhurt Mrs Peel using oxyacetylene cutting gear.

Although Paice dialled into the Mod fashion movement and emerging pop culture with this story idea, the reuse of concepts from the show's second season probably scuppered 'Gomorrah'.

Scheduling alterations

After screening just a single episode of the new season, Rediffusion, Southern and Anglia all changed their transmission slot for *The Avengers* to Thursday evenings, starting on 7 October 1965 with 'The Gravediggers' at 8.00 pm. This was short-sighted, as it placed the series in direct opposition to *The Man from U.N.C.L.E.* on BBC1. However, such competitive scheduling was not unusual in the years before the invention of domestic recording equipment. The other problem it created had been foreseen on Thursday 23 September, when ABC programme records officer P Mahoney had written to Albert Fennell requesting that a second trimmed-down print be produced every week for use by Scottish Television, who continued to transmit on Tuesdays.

Also on Thursday 7 October, the latest edition of *The Stage and Television Today* saw columnist Bill Edmund review 'The Town of No Return' favourably, but bemoan the fact that the series now clashed with *The Man from U.N.C.L.E.*, which meant he would not be watching it.

Publicity

The Sunday 17 October 1965 edition *The Observer* covered the new season in its television section, 'Briefing/Where and When', and also interviewed Brian Clemens, who discussed the unwritten ground rules that had been introduced.

As a thank you to Lotus Cars for supplying the production with Mrs Peel's personal transport, Diana Rigg spent some time on their stand at the 1965 Motor Show held at Earls Court in London from Wednesday 20 to Saturday 30 October. This then annual event was where car manufacturers showcased their latest models, and with Rigg in attendance, wearing her John Bates-designed lace trouser suit, it became the perfect photoshoot opportunity. Many shots were taken of her reclining on a Lotus Elan just like the one she drove in the series.

4.19 – 'Quick-Quick Slow Death'

Robert Banks Stewart returned to the production with his screenplay 'Quick-Quick Slow Death', which began filming in the last week of October 1965, with James Hill also returning to direct. Inspired by the BBC's *Come Dancing* ballroom dancing show, the storyline opens with the discovery of a dead body dressed in evening wear, which leads Steed and Mrs Peel to investigate a dancing school and uncover a scheme to replace people with foreign agents.

The decision to film 'Quick-Quick Slow Death' had been an eleventh hour one by Julian Wintle when the production team realised that the scheduled episode, Martin Woodhouse's 'A Sense of History', needed more rewriting. The situation was made clear to Brian Tesler when Julian Wintle submitted the draft script – with the title spelt differently as 'Quick, Quick, Slow, Death' – on 13 October, indicating that shooting was scheduled to begin in about a week's time. Tesler promptly replied on 15 October stating that he liked the screenplay very much.

The opening teaser sequence, showing guest actor Michael Peake pushing a pram along, was shot in Borehamwood on Shenley Road, Deacons Hill Road and The Rise.

Mackidockie Street was specified in the script as the location of the firm Purbright and Co, but the street sign seen on screen was a prop as there is actually no such place in London; this scene was probably shot somewhere local to Elstree Studios.

In his first appearance in the episode, Steed shows proficiency with a double-barrelled shotgun, using empty beer cans instead of clay pigeons for target practice – until Mrs Peel arrives and accidentally launches a full can.

Significant alterations to the shooting script were made during principal shooting, with Brian Clemens obviously on hand and co-ordinating with James Hill on a scene-by-scene basis. A number of scenes originally written for the alcoholic Read character were changed, substituting the more obviously villainous Bracewell and thus helping to create a twist-in-the-tail ending. For instance, a scene in a dress hire shop where the assistant is knifed was originally written for Read, but his name was blocked out in the script and Bracewell's handwritten in its place. Similarly, scenes 31 and 32, in which Emma enters a gentlemen's locker room, were changed to have her being found by Bracewell, whereas in the original version she was surprised by a drunken Read, who then offered her a drink. The preceding scene, in which Emma casually points a slightly drunk Read toward some French windows and he leaves the building, was not in the shooting script at all. It may have been added by Clemens to provide some light relief, or else to make up for some running time lost by the omission of the scripted scene 46, which would have seen Read at the dance school talking on the telephone to someone he called his commander: 'Yes sir … Right sir … You'll attend to it.' (This foreshadowed the events of scene 47, in which the character Bernard is killed at Piedi's high quality shoe shop.) Bracewell and Read also swapped places for the big ballroom dance and the following fight scene at the episode's conclusion, from which – in contrast to all the other episodes – Steed and Mrs Peel do not depart via some form of transport, but simply dance into the fadeout.

Scheduling alterations

With the season's on-air run now in full swing, *The Avengers* was still attracting plenty of publicity. The Saturday 23 October 1965 edition of *TV World* presented an interview with stunt arranger Ray Austin, while the same month's edition of the fashion magazine *Vogue* ran a two page feature on John Bates' fashions under the title 'First Facts On Lethal Fashion'. However, having geared the series for an 8.00 pm time slot, ABC mysteriously rescheduled it back to a 10.05 pm start for three episodes, beginning with 'Castle De'ath' on Saturday 30 October, and Tyne Tees – taking the ABC line-feed – followed suit. Rediffusion meanwhile changed their transmission day again to Friday, starting with 'The Murder Market' on 12 November. Two days later Border dropped the series from its usual Sunday slot in favour of *The Royal Variety Performance*, although it resumed its screenings the following week. Grampian switched from Saturdays to Fridays starting from 19 November with 'A Surfeit of H$_2$O'.

On Saturday 20 November both ABC regions and Tyne Tees then rescheduled their screenings again to the earlier time of 9.05 pm, while Channel, Southern, Westward and TWW all moved their start time back by an hour and five minutes to match. This uniformity of scheduling across the regions brought about instant results, with 'A Surfeit of H$_2$O' clocking up the series' highest ratings figure of the year at 7.5 million viewers, making it the sixth most popular programme for the week.

Overall, the average viewing figures for November placed *The Avengers* in tenth place on the popularity chart. However, TWW's Welsh speaking service Teledu Cymru dropped the series from Saturday 20 November to Saturday 11 December, showing instead their own programme *Hwb I'r Galon* and the silent comedy film compilation show *Mad Movies*. Transmissions of *The Avengers* on Teledu Cymru did not resume until Saturday 18 December with 'Two's a Crowd'.

4.20 – 'The Danger Makers'

Roger Marshall's final script for this season, 'The Danger Makers', was being filmed by the third week of November 1965. It had been submitted to Brian Tesler by Julian Wintle as a draft script on Monday 18 October. Tesler's reply three days later had been short and to the point, indicating that he found it to be extremely good. Hence the shooting script had been despatched by Wintle on Monday 1 November, and director Charles Crichton had begun arranging rehearsals.

The story this time focuses on a group of military officers who, having become bored, form a society of thrill-seekers and plan to steal the Crown Jewels from the Tower of London. The teaser sequence, in which a masked motorcyclist recklessly dodges other vehicles at a country crossroads and ultimately crashes into a lorry, was shot at the junction of Wildhill Road and Woodside Lane near Hatfield, Hertfordshire and featured the Triumph motorcycle (452 YMF) seen previously in 'Dial a Deadly Number'. This machine presumably belonged to the stuntman riding it; the owner would receive an additional fee for providing a vehicle used in the filming. All the remaining location footage appears to have been shot in or around what was Grove Park in Watford, as seen when Steed and Emma in his Bentley turn off Hempstead Road onto the access road when visiting the fictional Faversham Military Hospital. Later, one of the officers, Major Robertson, drives Mrs Peel in his Sunbeam Alpine convertible at great speed up the access road and over a humpback bridge. The sports car is then seen travelling along Fir Tree Hill to the junction with Grove Mill Lane. Passing through an old gateway (now disused), the vehicle speeds eastward along the other end of the Grove Park access road, where it narrowly avoids a collision with a Thames Trader lorry (2705 VX) – also used as the lorry involved in the collision with the motorcycle in the teaser sequence, and previously seen in 'Man-Eater of Surrey Green'. Reverting to a westward direction, Robertson powers his vehicle up the final stretch of access road before reaching the fictional Manton House – which is now The Grove Hotel. The episode's end tag scene features Steed and Emma on go-karts departing down the access road toward Hempstead Road, leaving Manton House behind them.

The army grenade bunker featured in the story was created by stacking sandbags along part of the back edge of the smaller concrete-lined water tank on the studio backlot, which had been drained.

When Major Robertson opens a wooden box of medals belonging to the dead motorcyclist, General 'Woody' Groves, a small metal plaque on the inside is seen to bear the inscription 'To Woody from Wing Commander Watson RAF Hamelin' – a reference to the airbase featured in 'The Hour That Never Was'.

In a stock footage mix-up, the Supermarine Swift jet fighter flown by Wing Commander Watson becomes a propeller-driven de Havilland Chipmunk just before it disappears behind some trees, followed by the sound of an explosion and then huge plumes of thick black smoke. Steed and some RAF personnel watch proceedings from beside Stage 5 on the studio lot, with the traffic lights used to facilitate the movement of large pieces of scenery in and out of the soundstage clearly visible.

At one point while held prisoner, Steed occupies himself by reading *The Times*. When Robertson arrives to kill him, he simply points out that there is more danger in stamp collecting than in shooting an unarmed man.

A large-scale fight scene sees Billy Westley doubling for Diana Rigg again, as Mrs Peel leaps the entire length of a long table to take down two of the villains. Both Steed and Mrs Peel show their fencing skills as they fight a trio of the military danger-makers, played by the unbilled stuntmen Romo Gorrara (Army), Terry Plummer (Navy) and Joe Dunne (RAF).

Branding the danger-makers 'A bunch of schizoid paranoid psychopaths' for their constant pursuit of thrills and excitement, Mrs Peel fails to acknowledge a parallel with her own motivation for assisting Steed with his investigations. Although nowhere near as extreme, her own attitude toward danger is not all that different.

This episode marks the arrival of a different Bentley for Steed's transportation in the form of a 1924 3 Litre model, though Kingsbury Motors had affixed to it the registration plate (UW 4887) from the 4½ Litre example used in some previous episodes.

Over-running production schedule

Production on all 26 episodes of season four was originally scheduled to be completed by the end of October 1965, but due to the female lead being recast and the filming of episodes averaging 13 days instead of the expected ten, seven screenplays remained unfilmed at this point. In anticipation of the problem, contracts for the major players and key production personnel had all been extended by 15 weeks. The proposed budget reduction measures had yet to be implemented; and despite ABC having employed various agencies and assorted middle men, all of whom had indicated that they could arrange a sale of *The Avengers* to one of the American networks, no progress had been made on that front whatsoever.

American network sale

Taking a leaf out of Lew Grade's book, Howard Thomas decided to try to gain an American sale of the series in person, flying to New York along with the recently-hired American Robert Norris, who handled overseas sales for ABC. Sales pitches and the screening of episodes at both CBS and NBC aroused interest but ultimately proved unsuccessful, their buyers citing various reasons for not taking the series, such as it being too British and lacking in pace. However, on their last day in New York, Thomas managed to secure a meeting with the ABC network (no connection to ABC Television) through his personal friendship with their president Leonard Goldenson.

Upon viewing the sample episodes, ABC executives were enthusiastic. However, there were a couple of problems to be overcome. With NBC now switching to colour transmissions, both CBS and ABC would have to follow suit – and of course *The Avengers* was in black and white. However, Thomas managed to talk the executives around by suggesting that it could actually be promoted as the last monochrome-produced television show ever sold to an American network. Another problem raised by the ABC executives was that none of them had ever heard of Diana Rigg, but again Thomas's powers of persuasion won them over, convincing them that she was a star in the making.

The two ABCs finalised a deal worth approximately £350,000 for the networking of season four across the United States, with an option for additional episodes – although, if required, this second batch would have to be in colour. This was a great personal achievement for Thomas, who had wanted to get an ABC programme onto one of the three American networks since the ITV regional company had been established in 1956. The story broke on Thursday 25 November, with *The Times*, *Daily Mirror* and *Daily Mail* all covering events. The headline on the latter proclaimed: 'Sold For A Million Dollars: *The Avengers*'. Thomas was quoted in the *Daily Mirror* as saying, 'We have not made any concessions for the American market. The Americans like it because it is different and sophisticated.'

A rumour that has surfaced since 1965 suggests that the US network compared costs and found that buying in the 50-minute episodes of *The Avengers* was less expensive than actually producing the 25-minute episodes of *Honey West*. True or not, *Honey West* was cancelled after the April 1966 screening of its thirtieth and final episode, just as UK transmissions of the series were getting under way in selected ITV regions.

New theme release

A seven-inch single record of Laurie Johnson's *The Avengers* theme, credited to the Laurie Johnson Orchestra, was released on the Pye label, serial number 7N 17015, on Friday 3 December 1965. It came in a photographic picture sleeve featuring a shot of Macnee and Rigg, the latter wearing John Bates' creation Flash, taken from the Wednesday 29 September photoshoot on the beach at Dymchurch in Kent.

Doctor Who

On Saturday 4 December 1965 the *Daily Mail* gave coverage to the latest *Doctor Who* serial with the headline 'A Touch Of *The Avengers*: The New Girl Linking Up With Doctor Who Tonight'. The article spotlighted the Doctor's newest companion, space security agent Sara Kingdom, played by Jean Marsh, whose black jumpsuit and matching leather boots invited instant comparisons to Mrs Peel. Ms Kingdom's time in *Doctor Who* would be short-lived: she would travel in the TARDIS for only part of the 12-part story 'The Daleks' Master Plan' before being killed off in its final episode. However, the character would be revived in 2010, again played by Marsh, for a number of the *Doctor Who* audio plays from Big Finish Productions.

4.21 – 'A Touch of Brimstone'

Having been on file for over a year, Brian Clemens' 'A Touch of Brimstone' (apparently titled 'The Hellfire Club' at one point) was finally scheduled for filming sometime around the middle of December 1965, due to a lack of other screenplays ready for production. Clemens has gone on record as stating that he did not wish to write so many episodes toward the conclusion of season four; but with the team failing to receive the type of submissions they required, he ended up contributing five out of the last six.

In this adventure, Steed and Emma infiltrate a '60s version of the Hellfire Club – an exclusive 18th Century high society fraternity noted for its debauchery – and discover that its members intend implementing a political coup by blowing up a conference of government ministers. James Hill returned to direct and, together with casting director G B Walker, hired amongst his guest cast Peter Wyngarde, Colin Jeavons, Michael Latimer and *Monty Python's Flying Circus* collaborator Carol Cleveland.

A sequence of an aborted dash by Steed and Emma to a new Hall of Friendship in the 3 Litre Bentley (UW 4887) involved the vehicle being filmed travelling at speed on several country roads in the Hertsmere district close to Borehamwood. The first piece of footage had it being driven along Mimms Lane before turning into Deeves Hall Lane and passing Deeves Hall Cottage near the village of Ridge. The second was executed on Rectory Lane in Shenley, with the Bentley travelling past the large triangle of grass that forms the junction with Harris Lane. The third and last piece was captured on the same piece of road, shot from another angle, with the Bentley returning along Rectory Lane before taking a sharp right-hand turn toward Harris Lane.

A night-time establishing shot was filmed of the London Palladium on Argyll Street, Westminster, London W1. The interior of the fictional Queens Theatre was represented by a mixture of stock footage and specially-filmed material shot in one of the viewing theatres at Elstree Studios. Returning home in the Bentley after their night out at the theatre, Steed and Emma pass along Watling Street in Radlett – although Macnee and Rigg were actually filmed in close-up in the studio, with the location appearing to one side of them on back-projection.

The mode of transport used for the end tag scene this time was a large horse-drawn carriage, which was filmed once again on Silver Hill, heading in the direction of Borehamwood.

Brian Tesler's earlier stipulations regarding the draft screenplay had caused Clemens to make some major adjustments. In the final version, the character originally called Bates, now simply an unnamed VIP, is still electrocuted, but the scene is toned down, with the twitching and convulsions caused by the strong electric current deleted, leaving just a few sparks and a little smoke. Likewise, the original idea of Lord Darcy being impaled by a large broadsword is replaced by him disappearing through an elaborate trapdoor in the floor and then drowning off camera in an underground river. The Night of All Sins orgy sequence is allowed to go no further than amorous kissing and heavy drinking; and when Wyngarde's villainous character John Cartney, referring to Mrs Peel, tells his fellow revellers, 'She's yours to do with what you will!', this prompts nothing stronger than her being carried around the room shoulder high amid more drunken revelry. The notion of Willy (Willie in the draft script) having a false hand, the cause of much apprehension in the earlier version, is now dealt with more sensitively, Steed managing to remove the prosthetic during hand-to-hand combat as opposed to hacking it off with his sword. Actor Jeremy Young, portraying Willy, wore a leather glove, and there was no reference to the false hand being made of wood as in the earlier draft.

The spiral staircase that had already seen service in both 'Death at Bargain Prices' and 'The Gravediggers' was reused as the access point to the catacombs where the Hellfire Club meet, and part of the underground structure included the tunnel seen previously in 'The Town of No Return'. As the Queen of Sin, Diana Rigg wore a risqué outfit, comprising a black corset with matching bikini briefs, stiletto-heeled boots, opera gloves, spiked dog collar and a thin-chained leash. This costume was apparently designed by Rigg herself, although Clemens may have had some input into it, as back in December 1964 he had been quoted in the *Daily Express* as saying that she would wear a studded dog collar. For some publicity shots the leash was fastened around James Hill's neck, a laughing Rigg in her Queen of Sin costume pretending to be in control.

The screenplay called for Rigg to work with a young python. Its handler assured her it would not bite, though as soon as she took hold of it he added that it might pee on her. Michael Latimer was absolutely terrified of snakes, but had to assist in carrying Rigg around the set as she held the reptile. More positively, while working on this episode, he established a lasting friendship with Macnee.

When the episode was eventually transmitted, columnist Michael Billington gave it an extremely positive review in the Thursday 24 February 1966 edition of *The Stage and Television Today*, opining that it was vintage stuff. He stated that Macnee's portrayal of Steed could not been improved upon; that Rigg had successfully established the Mrs Peel character; and that talented guest star Peter Wyngarde had given an immaculate performance.

Along with 'Death at Bargain Prices', 'A Touch of Brimstone' was the other episode on which Weintraub Entertainment experimented with colourising portions of footage in the late '80s, though again the master tape of the colourised material apparently no longer exists.

Marvel's Hellfire Club

Just as Brian Clemens drew inspiration from the Hellfire Club societies of the 18th Century for 'A Touch of Brimstone', writers Chris Claremont and John Byrne were clearly heavily influenced by his episode when, years later, they were creating stories for Marvel Comics' *The Uncanny X-Men* comic book. In 1979 they reinvented the existing *X-Men* character Mastermind as Jason Wyngarde – named partly after actor Peter Wyngarde and partly after the Jason King character he played in the television series *Department S* and *Jason King*. Jason Wyngarde first appeared in issue 122 of *The Uncanny X-Men* and was followed shortly afterwards by Marvel's own rendition of the Hellfire Club, an exclusive society that is really the cover for a criminal organisation. Bent on world domination, the Club is ruled by characters codenamed after the pieces on a chessboard, such as the White Queen, alias Emma Frost, whose original costume bears more than a passing resemblance to the outfit worn by Emma Peel in 'A Touch of Brimstone'. Supporting characters Sir Patrick Clemens and Lady Diana Knight were introduced later. Then in 1996 came Emma Steed, alias the Black Queen, created by another pair of Marvel writers, Warren Ellis and Carlos Pacheco, who made her debut in the comic book *Excalibur* issue 96 and initially looked identical to Emma Peel, complete with black leather catsuit.

Whipping scene controversy

'A Touch of Brimstone' has acquired something of a reputation owing to a sequence where Emma Peel is repeatedly attacked by John Cartney with a whip. Rediffusion demanded that their print of the episode be trimmed back even further than usual, this time on the grounds of good taste, considering the subject matter unsuitable for a primetime family audience. They were backed by the Independent Television Authority (ITA), leaving ABC with no alternative if they wanted to see the episode transmitted before 10.00 pm. The whipping scene was consequently reduced, making it conclude very abruptly.

The *Daily Express* of Tuesday 15 February 1966 – three days prior to the episode's airing by Rediffusion – reported on the situation and stated that a total of 38 seconds had been removed. *The Stage and Television Today* weighed in with its version of events on Thursday 3 March, claiming that a full minute's worth of material had been excised – which would in fact have been impossible, as the whole sequence runs for only about 50 seconds in total. Despite all this furore, Telemen Ltd must have felt vindicated when the episode pulled in what turned out to be *The Avengers'* largest audience of 1966, rating 8.4 million viewers and placing it as the fourth most popular programme for the week of its transmission.

Unfortunately the American ABC network also objected to the whipping scene, and this resulted in 'A Touch of Brimstone' being omitted from the initial run of *The Avengers* in the United States. However, according to Brian Clemens, the episode was shown exclusively for ABC network executives at their Christmas party and other private functions.

Eventually the missing footage was reinstated and the complete episode commercially released on the Lumiere Pictures VHS videocassette *The Avengers Volume*

3, issued on Monday 25 October 1993. Unfortunately it was a copy of the edited print that Channel 4 aired on Tuesday 30 April 1985 and Monday 11 August 1997 as part of its network repeats of *The Avengers*. However, the complete version was made available again on the DVD sets *The Avengers: The Definitive Dossier 1966 Files 3 and 4*, released on Monday 9 September 2002 by Contender/Kult TV, and *The Avengers: The Complete Series 4*, released on Monday 5 July 2010 by Optimum.

Christmas schedule

Christmas scheduling considerations saw Rediffusion move *The Avengers* from its usual Friday evening slot and transmit 'Too Many Christmas Trees' a day earlier, on Thursday 23 December 1965, although at the later time of 9.40 pm. However, they then resumed their Friday screenings with 'Silent Dust' on 31 December. Sticking to their established schedule, Anglia Television also transmitted 'Too Many Christmas Trees' on 23 December, at 8.00 pm. Border abandoned their usual Sunday showing in favour of a Christmas Eve slot on Friday 24 December at 8.00 pm. The majority of regions, however, took ABC's feed on Christmas Day at 10.10 pm. Southern was a slight exception, starting five minutes later.

4.22 – 'What the Butler Saw'

Filming on 'What the Butler Saw' began at the end of 1965 and spilled over into January 1966. It was directed by Bill Bain, who had been invited to take on an episode sometime after August in a letter that Julian Wintle wrote to him at his home address on Thursday 8 April. Bain had previously handled a number of the series' videotaped episodes for ABC, and arrangements were made with Brian Tesler and ABC's now Head of Drama George Brightwell to allow him to spend several weeks at Elstree working on this filmed one.

Brian Clemens' story this time involves the butlers of unsuspecting high-ranking military officers stealing secret information from them. The title refers to the Victorian coin-operated amusement known as a Mutoscope, a device that worked on the same principle as a flip book telling a short story via the quick turning of about 850 images in succession. The story, which was often mildly pornographic, would be presented as if the family butler was watching events unfold through a keyhole; hence the Mutoscope acquired the more user-friendly name of a What the Butler Saw machine.

The draft script departed from Elstree on Thursday 1 July 1965, and Tesler responded to Wintle on Thursday 8 July, giving his opinion that it was dull and lacking in action, and adding that the send-up of military officers was territory the series had already covered. Clemens rewrote his material, though it appears this was not considered a priority as the amended version was not forwarded to Tesler until Monday 29 November. The new version was accompanied by a letter from Wintle stating that filming was due to commence in a fortnight's time.

Returning to Edge Grove School on Oakridge Lane in Aldenham, the crew filmed a sequence of Steed posing as Major White arriving in a six-wheeled Alvis Saladin armoured car at the home of Brigadier Goddard. The later scene of the butler Benson, played by guest actor John Le Mesurier, departing from Captain Miles' residence in an Austin FX3 cab (VGF 345) – a vehicle seen previously in 'The Girl from Auntie' – was filmed at the same location, but with the school building behind the camera to disguise this fact. The cab was followed down the drive by Emma's Lotus Elan, which was also filmed parked off the road on Silver Hill near Shenley. The car was equipped with a prop radio telephone, allowing Mrs Peel to receive a message from Steed. Mrs Peel again sports the Jean Varon/Freedman wristwatch in this episode.

Location footage showing a Brantly B-2B helicopter arriving at Group Captain Miles' large house, and later departing in the end tag scene, was filmed at Radlett Preparatory School off Watling Street near Radlett. A segment where Steed, disguised as Commander Red, comes ashore from a small cabin cruiser to the riverside home of Vice Admiral Willows was not shot locally to Borehamwood, but rather on the River Thames in Middlesex. The property was actually a large, distinctive red-brick Georgian house called Monksbridge, situated at 50 Thames Street, Sunbury-on-Thames, where it stands in one and a half acres of ornate grounds.

A sequence of the body of the spying butler Walters being unceremoniously dumped from a rowing boat was filmed on the larger of the two water tanks on the Elstree backlot, actor Peter Hughes going beyond the call of duty by performing the scene himself and sinking under the surface of the water.

The large Avro Lancaster model plane seen on the military bar set had been the bomber aircraft in 'Two's a Crowd', and the smaller wartime airplanes had previously appeared in 'The Town of No Return' and 'Death at Bargain Prices'.

A number of eight-by-ten-inch glossy photographs of Diana Rigg placed around the set of Miles' office were mainly publicity stills, with the addition of a solitary picture of her taken with a Mini Moke during the filming of 'A Surfeit of H$_2$O'.

Laurie Johnson excelled himself with his incidental score for this episode, composing three military-sounding variations on the theme tune plus 'March of the Butlers', a memorable incidental cue that was later included in his CD collection *50 Years of the Music of Laurie Johnson Volume 1*.

The finished episode differed in several respects from the shooting script – which was subtitled 'In which Steed becomes a gentleman's gentleman and Emma faces a fate worse than death'. A scene where Steed visits the barber's was a replacement for one in the script where he pretends to be talking on a telephone in a booth at an airport, waiting for someone to arrive. In the sequence where Major General Goddard is instructed to leave by his son, the Brigadier, the latter's throwaway line '… and don't blow up the roses again' appears to have been improvised on the day of filming, as it was not in the script. As originally scripted, Scene 19C, where Group Captain Miles becomes mesmerised on noticing Emma in the military bar, was supposed to continue with her dropping her sunglasses, him picking them up for her, and her then thanking him in a Marilyn Monroe type voice. The fact that the scene was designated 'C' suggests that it was actually rewritten several times. The beginning of Scene 25, where the trainee butlers are seen polishing shoes, was an unscripted addition. Originally the scene was to have started with the tray-balancing segment that comes directly afterwards. The scripted Scene 30, in which Steed surreptitiously approaches the Butlers & Gentlemen's Gentlemen Association under the cover of darkness, was omitted altogether from the programme. Likewise, some of Sergeant Moran's scripted dialogue in the sequence where he fights with Mrs Peel – 'I was a commando sergeant taught to kill with my hands … my bare hands. It'll just be like the old days' – was not included.

The relatively high humour content of 'What the Butler Saw' – exemplified by Steed's flippant line 'The butler did it', a phrase associated with whodunit mysteries – is representative of the later season four episodes, and indicates the direction in which the series would progress in its next run.

Approach to Richard Bates

In December 1965, *The Avengers* had risen to become the seventh most popular programme on British television, increasing its viewing average substantially to 7.3 million. Around this time, Brian Clemens approached Richard Bates to join the team at Elstree and resume his former position as story/script editor on the series. Despite the proposed salary being far in excess of what he was currently earning as story editor on *Public Eye*, Bates declined the offer, thinking that he had nothing original to contribute. Furthermore, Bates was on the verge of being promoted to producer on *Public Eye*, making any move to another story editor position a backward step in his career.

Scheduling alterations

After the scheduling alterations for 'Too Many Christmas Trees', both ABC regions, Channel, Southern, both TWW regions, Tyne Tees and Westward all reverted *The Avengers* to the standard start time of 9.05 pm on Saturday 1 January 1966 with 'Silent Dust'. Likewise, Border resumed their Sunday transmissions, also with 'Silent Dust', which went out at 9.35 pm on 2 January. Tyne Tees however quickly abandoned their ABC feed, deciding to change to Fridays at 8.00 pm, beginning with 'Room Without a View'. Toward the conclusion of January, Southern had a couple of time variations, screening 'The Girl from Auntie' at 8.55 pm on Saturday 22 January and 'The Thirteenth Hole' at 8.25 pm on Saturday 29 January.

New comic book

The Avengers appeared once again in comic form in January 1966 when Thorpe and Porter published a one-off 68-page British-printed but American-influenced comic book containing four different black and white strips, 'The Mohocks', 'The K Stands for Killers', 'No Jury… No Justice!' and 'Deadly Efficient'. The artwork for the first three was provided by Mick Anglo, while that for the fourth was handled by Mick Austin. These strips would later be repackaged into two comic books for the Dutch market as part of the TV Classics range, and again for German consumption as part of the Krimi Klassiker imprint, which encompassed other television-related material. Besides publishing their own comics and reprinting American comic strips, Thorpe and Porter also imported and distributed both Marvel and DC comic books in the UK in the '60s.

4.23 – 'The House That Jack Built'

During early January 1966, the production crew were occupied filming Brian Clemens' 'The House That Jack Built', essentially a science fiction reworking of his season three screenplay 'Don't Look Behind You'. The claustrophobic nature of the storyline, in which Mrs Peel is enticed into a trap in the form of a nightmarish fully automated house, made it the perfect vehicle for director Don Leaver, who had excelled with this type of scenario on the videotaped episodes.

After reading the draft script, Anthony John sent Brian Tesler a memo dated

Thursday 12 August 1965 expressing his opinion that it was perhaps too scary for an early evening time slot. He suggested that, as a way to lighten things up, when Steed realises that Emma has been enticed to the house, he should not use his Bentley to travel there but should instead catch a bus and have a jovial interlude with one of the passengers. Tesler did not share John's concerns; when he communicated with Julian Wintle by letter on Tuesday 17 August he described 'The House That Jack Built' as absolutely first class and commented that it should make a magnificent episode. There was however one point of contention, which was a lack of motivation for the villainous inventor Professor Keller choosing Mrs Peel as the test subject for his automated house. This suggests that the backstory included in the final episode – in which the young Emma Knight is revealed to have sacked Keller after taking over her family's business, Knight Industries, on her father's death – was not included in this draft. The shooting script – subtitled 'In which Steed takes a wrong turn … and Emma holds the key to all' – was dispatched for Tesler's approval on Wednesday 15 December.

The episode affords the only view of the exterior of Steed's home in season four, in a sequence where Mrs Peel's Lotus Elan was filmed departing from one of the streets of the studio backlot town. Originally constructed in 1961 for the comedy film *Go to Blazes*, this backlot structure was added to, altered and redressed for various productions until its demolition in late 1972. The Lotus was also filmed being driven down Ivinghoe Beacon Road near the village of Ivinghoe in Buckinghamshire, watched by Frederick Withers, played by guest actor Michael Wynne in a boy scout master's uniform, on Beacon Hill. Wynne was also on location for the sequence where Emma has to perform an emergency stop to avoid knocking Withers down, though Rigg was studio-bound in the Lotus against back-projection.

The majority of the footage featuring both the Lotus Elan and the 3 Litre Bentley (UW 4887) was filmed on Rectory Lane, in close proximity to Ridge Hill Farm and the entrance of the access road to Shenley Lodge, Shenley. The cottage seen in a sequence where the Lotus passes a prop B31 road sign has long since been demolished, and Ridge Hill Farm is now a much larger riding school known as Ridge Hill Stud and Riding Centre, with many additional buildings.

The Bentley was driven down the nearby Packhorse Lane, passing the white railings by the house known as Rabley Willow, before crossing the Catherine Bourne Ford – the footbridge over which no longer exists – on Mimms Road heading west toward Shenley. Having arrived at a dead end because of a misleading signpost with moving direction markers – which would have been created by the props department back at the studios – Steed drives back to the junction and, working out the problem, reverses the Bentley into the gateway of Ridge Hill Farm. He proceeds to power the vintage vehicle down the access road to Shenley Lodge, smashing a barrier with a 'Road Closed' sign and in the process damaging the offside front headlight, which appears in the following scene with the bezel hanging off.

After falling foul of a vicious-looking tyre-slashing device in the road – another props department creation – Steed continues on foot and, looking through some bushes, finds Mrs Peel's Lotus, supposedly in front of Seven Pines at Pendlesham in Hampshire – though actually it was Shenley Lodge in Hertfordshire.

Shenley Lodge now houses Manor Lodge School, but from the mid-1960s until 1988 it was a health hydro. It was here that a sequence was filmed of the escaped convict Burton, portrayed by Griffith Davies, breaking into the house to elude his pursuers. Opening one door, Burton finds himself confronted by a lioness that leaps toward him

– actually a short clip from the 1958 film *Nor the Moon by Night*, projected on a screen.

The final location was reserved for the end tag scene, which was once more filmed on Silver Hill, south of Shenley. Steed and Emma, again played by doubles, are seen pedalling a tandem bicycle toward Borehamwood, after a dialogue exchange delivered by Macnee and Rigg against back-projection in the studio.

Various set elements and props featured in other episodes appear again in this one. These include the spiral staircase last seen in 'A Touch of Brimstone' and some metal consoles from the Auntie office set in 'The Girl from Auntie'. Emma sports her Jean Varon/Freedman wristwatch again and is armed with her chrome-plated .38 Webley and Scott mark four revolver, not seen since 'Silent Dust'.

When naming the episode, Clemens obviously had in mind the nursery rhyme 'This is the House that Jack Built', which dates back to the 16th Century. After losing a fight against Mrs Peel, Burton slinks away to a dark corner where he starts slowly reciting the rhyme line by line. Clemens also appears to have been thinking about introducing another regular character to the series, as this and his later episodes 'How to Succeed … at Murder' and 'Honey for the Prince' all mention Steed's colleague Colonel Robertson (referred to simply as the Colonel in 'How to Succeed … at Murder'). The reference to Robertson in 'The House that Jack Built' was clearly inserted at a late stage, as the name does not appear in the shooting script.

There are various other differences between the final episode and the shooting script. For instance, when Steed leaves his apartment in Scene 83 he was originally intended to take his swordstick, as seen in both 'The Thirteenth Hole' and 'Small Game for Big Hunters', rather than his usual umbrella. Also altered slightly was a sequence where Emma finds a small window showing a view of the night sky, but on smashing a hole through the larger frosted glass below it reveals only the revolving electronic mechanism she has come across previously. Originally she was to have tried using Withers' wooden stave to break the window, but to have been unsuccessful. This was probably changed as it would have confused continuity with Scene 105, where Emma discovers another window, with daylight beyond. For the filming, this window became more like an arrow-slit as found in medieval castles – the view from which was actually a shot of Ivinghoe Beacon Road.

Scene 152, set in the main control room of the house, was originally intended to run longer, with everything plunged into darkness, frightening Emma as a rat scuttles across the floor and something (bird or bat) flies around and touches her hair. Running into the unknown, Emma was to have become trapped in a confined space no bigger then a telephone box, the floor of which then gave way beneath her. Eventually she was to have found herself facing the suicide box into which eller is trying to drive her – after which the action would have continued as per the actual episode. These traditional horror elements would arguably have been somewhat out of step with the futuristic science fiction approach of the rest of the episode, so perhaps it is not a surprise that they were purged at the filming stage.

Scenes 164 and 165, comprising further shots of Steed attempting to force open the house's outer door, were similarly dispensed with. The episode's conclusion was also tightened up, reducing from five to two the number of short scenes of the automated house breaking down. In the following scene where Steed starts looking for Emma, the medieval poleaxe to which he helps himself was not mentioned in the shooting script – presumably it was added by Clemens and Leaver on the day of filming.

A working copy of page six of this episode's screenplay, complete with various handwritten notes by Clemens, would later be reproduced in the *TV Times* edition dated Thursday 23 October 1969 as part of a *Diana Rigg Spectacular* supplement. One of the notes indicated the need for special effects for a sequence where the needle on the barometer in Steed's kitchen moves erratically. More jotting – 'Let's talk about this line on shooting', signed by Brian H Clemens – referred to a line where Emma speaks about her uncle Jack. The final note applied to the sequence where Mrs Peel departs from Steed's apartment, instructing Rigg, 'Give that special look'.

The more contemporary *TV Times* dated Thursday 24 February 1966 featured a two-page feature on a day in the life of Diana Rigg. This involved reporter Dave Lanning spending a day with the actress while she worked on this episode at Elstree. Apparently her typical day commenced when her alarm clock sounded at 6.30 am, after which she was driven from her London apartment in Dolphin Square SW1 to Borehamwood, where breakfast consisted of a bacon sandwich and a cup of coffee. Make-up and hairdressing followed, allowing her time to arrive on set on Stage 4 before 8.00 am and a chance to go over the script – which she never practised beforehand, preferring to pick up the dialogue during camera rehearsals. Rigg said that she considered the days spent on a production-line series like *The Avengers* to be very long, but never dull, and confessed to spending her lunchtimes sleeping on a camp bed in her dressing room. Her routine would then continue with some vigorous exercise. Every morning she would order in two pounds of mandarin oranges, which she and the entire crew would share. This camaraderie extended to there always being a box full of sweets on set, to which everybody would contribute. The working day ended at 5.30 pm and, feeling that she had the life of a nocturnal animal, Rigg was driven back home after dark, leaving her to prepare her only full meal of the day.

Crew changes

For 'The House That Jack Built', Lionel Banes returned to take over from Alan Hume on photography. He would retain this position until the end of the season, except on the next episode, 'A Sense of History', which would be handled by Gilbert Taylor. Mirroring this situation, Tony White, who had previously worked on *Gideon's Way*, became the regular camera operator at this point, although he would give way to Val Stewart on 'A Sense of History'

Scheduling alterations

There were few scheduling changes for *The Avengers* around the ITV regions in February 1966. Anglia moved their screening of 'Quick-Quick Slow Death' back by 25 minutes to start at 8.25 pm on Saturday 5 February, but the only other alteration involved both TWW regions dropping the series on Saturday 26 February to make way for a late evening airing of an episode of the spy series *The Rat Catchers* that had been pulled from its usual early evening slot earlier in the week due to unsuitably violent content.

4.24 – 'A Sense of History'

The idea for Martin Woodhouse's final *The Avengers* screenplay, 'A Sense of History', apparently came to him in a dream, where he imagined Diana Rigg in men's clothing as

Robin Hood. However, as with 'A Touch of Brimstone', the draft script remained on file for the best part of a year. It was first presented to Brian Tesler on Friday 26 February 1965, and his response was unenthusiastic, stating that he had read much better screenplays but that it should prove viable after considerable tightening up. The shooting script did not materialise until Monday 4 October, and unfortunately Tesler remained dissatisfied with the scenario and requested amendments. The final shooting script did not depart Elstree until a month later, on Thursday 4 November. This time Tesler was happy when he reported back to Wintle, indicating that the latest version was a huge improvement on the previous ones.

Presented as a mystery, the episode concerns an archivist and his followers plotting to change the course of history by killing an eminent politician whose policies include uniting Europe. Peter Graham Scott was assigned as director.

At the start of the episode, the Rolls Royce belonging to prominent economist James Broom, played by Kenneth Benda, is seen leaving the village of Letchmore Heath and travelling along Butterfly Lane, Elstree, before turning into the gateway of Aldenham Wood Lodge, representing the vehicle entrance to the fictional St Bode's Academy. Establishing shots of St Bode's were a combination of newly-filmed material of the Royal Masonic School on The Avenue in Bushey near Watford and stock footage of Corpus Christi College, Cambridge. The Royal Masonic School would later be used as the United States International University until the early '90s, before lying unoccupied for several years and then undergoing redevelopment into luxury apartments as Royal Connaught Park in 2007.

Rather than being shot on location, the cloisters of St Bode's were realised as a set inside one of the soundstages at Elstree. A sequence of Mrs Peel driving her Lotus Elan into a garage to meet up with Steed was also filmed on the studio lot, in the workshop by the gateway at the north-west corner. The transportation chosen for this episode's tag scene was a BSA motorcycle and enclosed sidecar (FYK 76C), with the Emma and Steed doubles on location as usual on Silver Hill heading toward Borehamwood.

St Bode's Academy was originally scripted as St Bede's College, but the name was changed during the course of filming, in consequence of which several pieces of dialogue delivered by various cast members had to be redubbed in post-production, though the prop folders seen on screen retained the original name. Another change, made during scripting, affected a sequence where Broom's right-hand man Richard Carlyon, played by Nigel Stock, is attacked at his caravan by masked archers – in an earlier draft, the attackers where repelled by Steed producing a gun, whereas in the actual episode they simply retreat.

Going undercover as a lecturer at the Academy, Mrs Peel finds inside a desk in her classroom a copy of the children's comic *Lion* dated Saturday 15 May 1965 – a genuine publication rather than a specially-created prop.

As Woodhouse later confirmed, his names for this episode's guest characters were based on those found in the Robin Hood tradition, which derives from rhymes and ballads dating back as far as the 15th Century. In Woodhouse's script, Robin was represented by Dubouys, a Norman interpretation of Robin's name meaning 'Robin of the woods'; Maid Marion became Marianne; Little John became John Pettit; Much the miller's son was reinvented as Millerson; Alan-a-Dale was represented by Allen; and Richard the Lionheart, aka Richard Coeur de Lion, became Richard Carlyon.

Woodhouse later moved to California for a time before settling in the West Indies for ten years. However, he did not abandon writing completely, penning five espionage novels featuring his character Giles Yoman – who he admitted was an exaggerated version of his own personality. He later commented that no matter how pleasant working on a television show was, he would always have to conform to the will of both producers and directors, and he preferred the creative freedom allowed by simply being a novelist.

Fake Avengers fashions

Meanwhile, the Jean Varon Avengers Collection was proving so popular that, according to a report in the Sunday 23 January 1966 edition of the *People*, copies of the outfits manufactured by rag trade pirates were flooding the shops. Eric West, the Managing Director of Jean Varon, was quoted as saying that legal action was imminent against a company caught pirating the collection. ABC were also involved, warning outlets in writing against stocking the fake items.

Royal Shakespeare Company

On Tuesday 25 January 1966, the *Guardian* reported on a press conference held at the Aldwych Theatre in London, where the Royal Shakespeare Company had announced several upcoming productions, including one of *Twelfth Night* in which Diana Rigg – who attended the conference – would be playing the leading role of Viola. The play would open on Thursday 16 June at the Royal Shakespeare Theatre, Stratford-on-Avon. Rigg had already informed Wintle and ABC that unless she received a substantial salary increase, she would be leaving *The Avengers* upon the completion of season four's filming.

Emma Peel comic strip

A second *The Avengers* comic strip of sorts began on Saturday 29 January 1966 in issue 52 of the girls' comic *June and Schoolfriend*. Entitled 'The Growing up of Emma Peel', it dealt with the adventures of 14-year-old Emma Knight. In licensing this concept, ABC apparently aimed to attract more of a teenage audience to *The Avengers*. The strip ran for 12 instalments in all, ending in issue 63, dated Saturday 16 April.

Corgi die-cast set

Also in January 1966, with *The Avengers* standing at number 12 in the monthly chart of most popular programmes and averaging 6.8 million viewers per episode, Corgi released a die-cast model car set tying in to the series. Numbered Gift Set 40 in their range, this comprised a vintage 3 litre Bentley with a plastic John Steed figure, complete with three accompanying umbrellas, and a white Lotus Elan convertible with a plastic Emma Peel figure. Although the Bentley pictured on the packaging was green, only a small percentage of the models were actually that colour; the majority were red and came with either red or gold wheels, the latter of which were by far the rarer. The set would continue to be produced until 1969, by which time it would have sold 190,000 units.

Dead Duck

The second – and, as it turned out, final – *The Avengers* paperback novel from Hodder and Stoughton also arrived early in 1966 under the title *Dead Duck*. Copies cost three shillings and six old pence and, as with *Deadline*, Patrick Macnee and Peter Leslie were given a joint copyright credit, with only Macnee's name appearing on the cover. Also as with *Deadline*, the novel was later reissued twice by Titan Books – on Tuesday 13 September 1994 and again in September 1998.

4.25 – 'How to Succeed … at Murder'

Filming on season four's penultimate episode, 'How to Succeed … at Murder', was under way by early February 1966. This marked the final involvement with the series for director Don Leaver, who had worked on every season since directing the very first episode, 'Hot Snow'. Leaver always thought that the series would have more scope on film, although he personally preferred the videotaped episodes made mainly in a television studio, because he liked the confined space; the way the episodes were recorded was, in his own words, 'Exciting and left little margin for error. It was like doing a theatre play on several sets.'

Brian Clemens' latest teleplay concerned a secret society of women who begin killing industrialists so that their secretaries and personal assistants can take over the running of large companies, with a view to creating a female business empire. The mastermind is eventually revealed to be a man named Henry, acting through a ventriloquist's doll named Henrietta.

A number of the episode's exterior sequences were shot at Elstree, including one where the character Mary Merryweather, played by Sarah Lawson, leaves her business premises – actually the studios' reception block on Shenley Road – and drives away in her Morris Oxford followed by Mrs Peel's Lotus Elan. Both vehicles are then seen passing the Esso filling station on the junction of Ripon Way and Stirling Way in Borehamwood, before arriving back at the studios. Filmed from the rooftop – with the cameraman's suede shoe visible in the bottom left-hand corner of the picture – Merryweather parks her Morris opposite the sound and post-production building behind Stages 3 and 4. Leaving the Lotus some distance away, Mrs Peel follows Merryweather to the soundstage entrance, where a prop sign on the door, advertising ladies' keep fit classes, indicates her destination. Also seen here is another varnished wooden sign listing the businesses within; a prop reused from Mackidockie Street in 'Quick-Quick Slow Death'.

A further scene shot behind Stages 3 and 4, this one after dark, features the Lotus Elan with Rigg at the wheel and the 3 Litre Bentley (UW 4887) driven by Macnee – who despite his aversion to firearms has Steed packing a .38 Smith and Wesson military and police model revolver.

In a sequence where Henry, played by Artro Morris, leaves the keep fit class venue, Steed is seen keeping watch for him in a parked Morris Mini. No on-screen explanation is given for his use of this vehicle, which was presumably owned by a member of the series' crew – possibly production manager Geoffrey Haine, as fixed to the wall just in front of it is a sign indicating that the parking space is reserved for his use. The same vehicle was also visible in the earlier scene where Merryweather departed from the reception block, but for this later sequence the camera is facing in the opposite direction, with the studio plasterers' shops as a backdrop.

The next sequence begins with both Henry and Steed alighting a London Transport double-decker bus – number 358 from St Albans to Borehamwood – at Black Lion Hill, Shenleybury. With Steed following at a discreet distance, Henry then enters the cemetery of St Boltolphs Church. The cemetery still exists today, although the actual church to the north fell into disuse and underwent conversion to a private residence in 1981.

Unsurprisingly, the episode's end tag scene features the usual location of Silver Hill near Shenley. Filmed on a rainy and misty day, the mode of transport used by Steed and Emma on this occasion is revealed as a caravan, although the towing vehicle, presumably a car, is not seen.

Obviously intended as light relief, a sequence where Emma attempts to paint Steed's portrait results in a piece of abstract art in which his head is square.

Dave Rogers' tome *The Ultimate Avengers*, published in 1995, indicated that this episode had the working title 'How to Succeed at Murder ... Without Really Trying'.

4.26 – 'Honey for the Prince'

Principal filming on the final episode, 'Honey for the Prince', began during February 1966 and concluded on Friday 4 March, bringing the season's production to an end, save for a few weeks of editing. This Brian Clemens story sees Steed enrolling in Quite Quite Fantastic, a company specialising in fulfilling people's fantasies, to assist his investigations into a plot to assassinate a foreign prince from an oil rich state. James Hill was assigned as director.

Macnee and Rigg were filmed crossing the bridge at Tykes Water Lake in Aldenham Park, Elstree, although only a small unit accompanied them as no sound recording was required – the sequence had no dialogue, just an incidental music accompaniment added in post-production. When they depart their adventure at the end, the two agents at first appear to be flying on a magic carpet, though when the camera pulls back this is revealed to be actually mounted on the rear of an Austin A55 pick-up truck going southbound down Silver Hill toward Borehamwood.

The opening teaser sequence at first appears to be set in a Middle Eastern country, but is turned on its head when the Ministry agent Reed, played by Richard Graydon, is shot and slumps down beside a window, out of which there is a view of Big Ben and the Houses of Parliament.

Steed demonstrates an ability to speak French when he talks to a miserable-looking man dressed as Napoleon at Quite Quite Fantastic; and a few notes of the song 'The Yellow Rose of Texas' are heard as another client, dressed as a cowboy, arrives and joins them. Some of Laurie Johnson's incidental music for this episode and the previous one, 'How to Succeed ... at Murder', would form the basis of material he would compose the following season for 'The Winged Avenger'. Other cues in 'Honey for the Prince' were reused from 'Castle De'ath'.

Part-way through the production, censorship problems were highlighted again in a report published in the *Daily Express* of Wednesday 23 February. This stated that a couple of scenes had been cut from the episode. One involved the scantily-clad 21-year-old actress Carmen Dene massaging guest star George Pastell and scratching his back with a stuffed leopard's claw. The other had Diana Rigg performing the Dance of the Seven Veils, which was considered too risqué. The latter scene was reshot as the Dance of the Six Veils, with some added humour content regarding the missing veil, explained by Steed as the undercover Emma having had a poor education.

'The Strange Case of the Missing Corpse'

After the completion 'Honey for the Prince', a three-minute colour promotional film titled 'The Strange Case of the Missing Corpse' was filmed on one of the sets. This was intended to give the American ABC an indication of what the series would look like in colour – or 'In Color', as a red-lettered caption proclaimed. Written by Brian Clemens and directed by James Hill, the team that had been responsible for 'Honey for the Prince', this vignette, scripted as 'Preamble for USA', also tipped American viewers off to the fact that the series would return to their television screens in the not too distant future – provided the network took up its option. Besides Macnee and Rigg, actress Valerie Van Ost made a brief appearance, paving the way for her to return later in a supporting role in the season five episode 'Dead Man's Treasure'.

Never transmitted in Britain, 'The Strange Case of the Missing Corpse' later proved elusive, as consecutive copyright holders of *The Avengers*, Weintraub Entertainment and Lumiere, could not find any prints of it among their inventory. However, in 1999 Ian Potts, an employee of the National Media Museum based in Bradford, was inspecting film cans of television commercials donated by the British Film Institute when he came across one marked up as *The Avengers*. Interested in what was within, he had it placed on a projector and, being something of a television buff, was amazed to find it was a copy of the missing test film. A one-day event showing episodes of *The Avengers*, *The New Avengers* and *The Professionals* was scheduled at the museum's Pictureville cinema a couple of weeks later, and 'The Strange Case of the Missing Corpse' finally received its British premiere there 33 years after being made.

Opening title sequence

A first attempt at creating season four's opening title sequence saw an assortment of stills of Steed and Emma being assembled together with some title graphics. This version was edited onto promotional prints of 'The Murder Market', 'The Master Minds', 'Dial a Deadly Number' and 'Death at Bargain Prices'. However, it was ultimately considered not impressive enough, and so was replaced by another version consisting of a succession of stills showing Steed and Emma plus various other elements associated with the show: a carnation, an umbrella, a bowler hat, a leather catsuit, and – being aimed by Emma – a Walther P38 automatic complete with silencer.

Scheduling alterations

Starting with 'The House That Jack Built' on Saturday 5 March 1966, TWW indulged in some haphazard scheduling for the season's last five episodes, transmitting them all at different times. Anglia also alternated their last four between 8.25 pm and 8.15 pm. ABC appears to have been responsible for some of these variations, as they made alterations to the start time on their final three episodes, forcing some of the other regions taking their line-feed to follow suit.

When the ratings figures were broken down by region, they indicated that Rediffusion's Friday night transmissions in London were extremely popular, with the series being the highest-rated programme of the week nine times, attracting 63 percent of the audience on two occasions. In the Scottish Television region, the series captured the top spot for two weeks running in January 1966. The final half-dozen episodes screened by Tyne Tees all featured amongst the top three positions for that region. Surprisingly, however, the ratings in ABC's North and Midlands regions were not always that impressive, as the series peaked in fourth place locally at the season's conclusion. Overall, *The Avengers* performed well in February and March 1966, standing at number five for both months on the TAM table, with average figures of 8.4 and 7.6 million viewers respectively.

In advance of the ABC network beginning coast-to-coast American transmissions of the series, both Macnee and Rigg flew to the USA on Saturday 12 March for a promotional tour, visiting New York, Chicago, Boston, Philadelphia and Washington. Monday 21 and Tuesday 22 March were spent promoting the series in Montreal, Canada, where the stations that had screened the Blackman episodes had already renewed the series, although they would not start their broadcasts until September.

The Avengers premiered on the ABC network at 10.00 pm eastern seaboard time on Monday 28 March with 'The Cybernauts'. The episode was given a tepid reception the following day in the *New York Herald Tribune*, whose reviewer thought the series relied on gimmicks.

The Blackman episodes had been sold to at least seven countries, but the first filmed season had easily beaten that figure, as 30 nations had already acquired it for television transmission and a further eight, including South Africa, had bought it for showing in cinemas.

Chessboard opening sequence

The lack of any on-screen superior to give Steed and Mrs Peel their assignments, coupled with the fact that the American audience had never seen the earlier videotaped episodes, led the ABC network to request that a short film sequence be shot to establish the series' premise for the US market. This prologue was placed before the opening titles on American prints of the season four episodes. Set on a giant chessboard, it features a man in a waiter's outfit keeling over with a knife in his back as Steed and Emma enter from different directions. Against a background of a Laurie Johnson tom-tom beat, a voiceover by American actor John Brandon begins, 'Extraordinary crimes against the people and the state have to be avenged by agents extraordinary.' Bending down, Steed takes a bottle of champagne from the dead man's hand, and the voiceover continues, 'Two such people are John Steed, top professional, and his partner, Emma Peel, talented amateur' – at which point Emma is seen placing a revolver into the top of one of her boots and smiling. The picture then cuts to a close-up of two glasses being filled with champagne. The narration concludes with '... otherwise known as the Avengers,' as Steed and Emma toast each other, take a sip of their champagne and then walk away.

'Strange Case of the Green Girl'

The April 1966 edition of the magazine *Woman's Journal* included the free supplement *Man's Journal*, featuring a Steed cover photo and a *The Avengers* text story, 'Strange Case of the Green Girl', credited to Brian Clemens and Graham Finlayson.

Season four ends transmission

April 1966 saw both TWW regions again reschedule the series, moving it back to the strange start time of 10.37 pm from 'A Surfeit of H$_2$O'. The final screening of season four's original on-air run came on Tuesday 3 May when Teledu Cymru showed 'Man-Eater of Surrey Green' at 10.55 pm.

Banned vinyl release

Around this time, a Mrs Peel tribute song entitled 'Dearest Emma', performed by the Londonaires, was released on the Decca label as a vinyl single, serial number 12379. The Londonaires, who had done a season in Las Vegas, were three male multi-instrumentalist vocalists, and for stage appearances came complete with their own leather-clad Emma Peel lookalike in the form of 21 year old Susan Evans. Wearing bowler hats and carrying umbrellas, they performed 'Dearest Emma' on the Saturday 14 May edition of ABC's pop show *Thank Your Lucky Stars*. However, the single was withdrawn from sale shortly after this, due to its unauthorised use of the opening fanfare from Laurie Johnson's *The Avengers* theme. Plans to issue the record in the United States on Decca's American label, London Records, were subsequently dropped, although some copies have survived.

Adam Adamant Lives!

Having shown both the first and second seasons of *The Man from U.N.C.L.E.* and several repeats, the BBC unveiled their own home-grown answer to *The Avengers* on Thursday 23 June 1966 in the form of *Adam Adamant Lives!*. This series, which eventually ran for two seasons, featured the adventures of an Edwardian gentleman frozen in ice in 1902 by his arch enemy the Face and thawed out by workmen in the London of 1966, where he was befriended by groovy chick Georgina 'Georgie' Jones.

Having previously appeared in *The Avengers* in both 'Death Dispatch' and 'The Hour That Never Was', Gerald Harper maintained a stiff upper lip as Adam Adamant, whose old-fashioned values were confronted by the swinging '60s. Georgie was portrayed by Juliet Harmer, fresh from her appearance in *The Avengers*' 'The Town of No Return'. Despite Adamant's reluctance to have Miss Jones (as he referred to her) around, she would frequently become involved in the dangerous situations he encountered. The third regular character was Adam's faithful manservant William E Simms, who would spend a great deal of his time providing light relief and discouraging Georgie from visiting Adamant's apartment home built atop a multi-storey car park. Simms was played by Jack May, who had also guest-starred in *The Avengers*, taking a prominent role in 'The Secrets Broker'.

The basic concept of *Adam Adamant Lives!* had been devised by ex-ABC Head of Drama Sydney Newman specifically with a view to competing with *The Avengers* – which is no doubt one reason why its lead characters were similarly a gentlemanly but sometimes ruthless hero with a swordstick and a beautiful young woman, who together become involved in a succession of fantastic and sometimes bizarre escapades. Newman's original inspiration for the series was self-appointed TV 'watchdog' Mary Whitehouse, who he considered was reacting to the swinging '60s with the mind of a strait-laced Victorian. However, Adam himself was conceived as an amalgam of two established fictional sleuths of the Victorian era: Sherlock Holmes and Sexton Blake. In fact Newman at first wanted to make Blake the series' central character, and tried to secure the rights from their then owner, Fleetway Publications. The first two storylines for the series were completed at the beginning of May 1965, when the intended title was *Sexton Blake Lives*. Both were commissioned by BBC script editor Bill Barron from writer Ray Roberts. The first, entitled 'Sexton Blake Dies', established the basic premise, while the second (title unknown) involved Blake in a case involving a Bessemer furnace.

Surviving BBC documentation indicates that on Friday 14 May 1965 – by which point the series title had been shortened to *Sexton Blake* – the BBC's Head of Series Andrew Osborne commissioned frequent *The Avengers* contributor Roger Marshall to provide a different pilot storyline and script. Marshall however recalls that he declined the invitation after attending a meeting with Newman, who wanted him to write the script within a fortnight for a fee of £800, stipulating that if he went a week over deadline this would be reduced to £600, and if he went a further week over it would be reduced again to only £400.

Only a week later, on Friday 21 May, Osborne commissioned another one-time *The Avengers* writer, Philip Chambers, to supply a script called 'The Queen's Surgeon' (although this may have been intended as a later episode rather than a pilot). As the BBC had still not managed to secure the rights to Sexton Blake, *Dick Daring* was now being considered as an alternative series title.[13] Chambers continued to work on the show for several months, writing and developing a storyline for another proposed pilot, 'The First Tycoon'.[14]

In the Autumn of 1965 the series title was changed again, to *Tom Devises*. It was also at around this time that another writer, Donald Cotton, was brought in to provide yet another prospective pilot. He completed his script in November. Based on an outline by Newman, it involved Devises saving the Home Secretary's life. For some reason, this idea was also dropped, so in December – by which time the title had become *Magnus Hawke* – Cotton wrote another, completely different script, based on and retaining the title of Chambers' storyline 'The First Tycoon'. Subsequently, the hero underwent another name change, becoming Damon Kane. Eventually, after trying out a few more ideas, Newman settled on the name Adam Adamant. This was after he saw the word adamant in a dictionary and discovered that adamantine was a substance almost as hard as diamond. The series titles *Adam Adamant* and *Adam Adamant Lives Again* were considered, but ultimately *Adam Adamant Lives!* was chosen.

The producer selected by Newman to launch the new series was Verity Lambert, who had performed the same role on *Doctor Who* in 1963 and on a soap opera entitled *The Newcomers* in 1965 and had previously worked briefly on *The Avengers* when she was an ABC production assistant. By the time Lambert started work on *Adam Adamant Lives!*, much of the development had already been completed, but she did contribute a number of ideas of her own. For instance Newman had originally intended that Adam's arch enemy should be called Mother (a name later used for Steed's superior in

---

[13] HTV eventually produced a *Sexton Blake* series that ran for 60 episodes on ITV between September 1967 and January 1971.

[14] In February 1966, Chambers would also make contributions to two further storylines, 'I Spy Adam Adamant' and 'Whiter than White Adamant' (retitled from 'It's New and Exciting Adam Adamant'), both of which were apparently abandoned. It is unknown who the principal writers of these storylines were.

season six of *The Avengers*), but Lambert considered this an insult to women, so it was changed to the Face.

Early in 1966, *Adam Adamant Lives!* finally reached the studio for recording of a pilot episode. Again retaining the title 'The First Tycoon', this was a rewrite by Richard Harris of Donald Cotton's second script, which he had completed in January. The script editor was Ken Levison, the director William Slater. Unfortunately, for reasons unknown, the completed pilot was judged unsuitable and rejected – and as it no longer exists, its content remains largely a mystery.

Subsequently, yet another different script was commissioned and recorded to form the first transmitted episode. This was 'A Vintage Year for Scoundrels', written by the series' new script editor Tony Williamson – another cross-over from *The Avengers* – and directed by David Sullivan Proudfoot. Several minutes of the abandoned pilot – some introductory scenes set in 1902 and some sequences of a dazed Adam staggering around London's West End – were, however, used as film inserts in the early part of the transmitted episode, hence writers Cotton and Harris and director Slater still received appropriate credits.

As well as being script editor, Williamson also wrote several later episodes, and these commitments on the BBC series would preclude him having any involvement in season five of *The Avengers*. Aside from Williamson and Harris, other *The Avengers* writers who contributed scripts to the first season of *Adam Adamant Lives!* were Brian Clemens and Robert Banks Stewart. John Kruse and Philip Levene were approached too, but neither of them actually gained a credit on the series.

When 'A Vintage Year for Scoundrels' eventually reached the screen, it attracted an impressive 5.2 million viewers. However, the BBC made *Adam Adamant Lives!* mainly with electronic cameras in the television studio, with location exteriors incorporated as film inserts, giving it a visual look more akin to the Blackman episodes of *The Avengers* than to the newer Rigg escapades[15], and in the end it never seriously rivalled the ITV show in the popularity stakes.

Side projects

After season four of *The Avengers* completed filming, Patrick Macnee kept busy by starring alongside Hannah Gordon and Penelope Keith in an episode of ATV's *Love Story* entitled 'The Small Hours', transmitted in the ATV Midlands region on Monday 27 June 1966, and also in an *Armchair Theatre* play called 'The Long Nightmare', screened in both the Midlands and North regions on Saturday 15 October 1966.

Diana Rigg meanwhile appeared in a television commercial extolling the virtues of Lux toilet soap. She was one of several female celebrities that advertising agency J Walter Thompson hired on behalf of Lux to endorse their product, but her commercial was obviously considered successful, as it would be followed in 1967 by a second.

---

[15] The *Adam Adamant Lives!* episode 'Death by Appointment Only', transmitted on Thursday 8 September 1966, did however bear some notable plot similarities to one of the Rigg episodes, 'The Murder Market', which had likewise been written by Williamson. In particular, it involved an agency where a female escort ends her date with a businessman client by killing him. This resulted in a complaint by Julilan Wintle to the BBC, though the situation was quickly resolved with an exchange of solicitors' letters.

Unmade ABC series

ABC had for a couple of years been considering producing some other television film series. Back in October/November 1964, Howard Thomas had attempted to attract international investors for possible co-productions. He had the basic outlines for three potential series, provisionally called *Flight Crew*, *Trans-European Express* and *Charterboat* respectively. However, as no finance was forthcoming, these went no further. Later, in July 1965, correspondence was exchanged between Thomas and Julian Wintle, in which they agreed that at that time there was little to be gained by filming an episode of *The Avengers* in colour, but indicated that plans were afoot to produce a series called *Elephant Boy* in that format. The following month, accountant J M Tennent sent Thomas an enquiry regarding the budget situation on *The Avengers*, hoping that some of the overspend could be transferred across to be borne by the potential series *Elephant Boy* and *The Three Musketeers*.

Apparently Telemen had carried out some preliminary work for both these projects, but ultimately neither would be realised by ABC – although an unrelated *Elephant Boy* series, loosely based on Rudyard Kipling's novel *Toomai of the Elephants*, would be made in 1973 by Portman Productions. During September 1965, Wintle and Brian Tesler exchanged communications mentioning a series idea called *Time Fuse*, on which they had an option. However, this also failed to make it into production.

Had any of these proposals from 1965 been given the go-ahead, it seemed likely that Telemen would have produced them, with Wintle assuming a supervisory position. With this in mind, ABC promoted Wintle to executive producer of *The Avengers* for the forthcoming fifth season, putting him into a position where he could, if necessary, co-ordinate the production of two film series at once.

SEASON FIVE

FROM VENUS WITH LOVE

The Avengers in colour

Having progressed from a videotaped thriller to a fast-moving filmed action show, *The Avengers* moved forward again into glorious colour for its fifth season, as ABC anticipated the American ABC network taking up their option for more episodes. The science fiction elements that had proved so popular in the previous season were expanded on, as crazed madmen plotted futuristic crimes and caused general mayhem in the peaceful English countryside, aka Avengerland. Defending Queen and country as ever were the suave secret agent John Steed and sophisticated woman of means Mrs Emma Peel, who continued their stylish, tongue-in-cheek adventures.

Keeping Diana happy

Diana Rigg had made an enormous impression as Emma Peel in the first filmed season of *The Avengers*, but had quickly become disenchanted with the continuous rigours of making a television film series. Only five months into production, she confided to her co-star Patrick Macnee that she was unhappy making the series and felt that the executives at ABC undervalued her contribution. Eventually, she threatened to leave.

The Avengers being the most successful series ABC had ever made, the last thing they wanted was to lose another leading lady – particularly at a time when the black and white filmed episodes were attracting huge viewing figures on both sides of the Atlantic and they were committed to producing a new season of colour episodes. Managing Director Howard Thomas consequently allocated one of his executives the job of looking after Rigg. While she was at Elstree making the later monochrome episodes, the executive followed her around and acted as her personal assistant, even going so far as to send bouquets of flowers to her dressing room. Happier with the change in attitude, Rigg began negotiations with ABC through her agent to remain with the series for the colour season – though she would require a substantial rise in salary. Eventually she was awarded a 200 percent increase, taking her weekly wage to £450. As a bonus, she was also awarded a small percentage of the series' profits.

New fashion designers

After the success of the Jean Varon Avengers Collection, its designer John Bates had been approached to compile another range of clothing for Emma Peel. However, his connection to the series had given him a much higher profile than before, and an increased workload both as a designer and as the figurehead of the Jean Varon fashion label, and therefore he reluctantly declined the offer to continue his involvement – although he did go on record saying it was *The Avengers* that had really established him in the fashion world.

As an added persuasion to keep her on the show, Rigg was thus promised that she would have a brand new wardrobe designed by Shropshire-born Alun Hughes, whom she had recommended for the job, and that this would be complete before filming commenced – unlike on season four, when her fashions had arrived as and when they were ready. At Rigg's request, the black leather image was discarded and Hughes came up with a wide variety of outfits, including a series of garments he called Emmapeelers. These tracksuit-type catsuits, made from stretch jersey, came in a variety of different colours and styles and were ideal attire for Rigg's fight scenes and the great outdoors. They would eventually retail at eight guineas apiece in the high street.

Meanwhile a deal had been made for the French-based Italian fashion designer Pierre Cardin to supply items of Patrick Macnee's clothing for the upcoming colour season. Both the *Daily Mail* and *Daily Mirror* dated Saturday 30 July 1966 reported that Macnee had attended one of Cardin's fashion shows, where he could inspect at first hand the kind of suits he would be wearing. Some time later, Macnee and Rigg would both pose for publicity photographs outside one of Cardin's upmarket Paris outlets.

Macnee also had a new range of shoes designed for him by Hughes after it was found that the Chelsea Boots he had previously worn as Steed did not match the new Cardin wardrobe. In addition, assorted bowler hats and umbrellas in different colours were purchased from leading gent's hatters Herbert Johnson, based at 54 St James Street, London SW1.

ABC co-productions

Back on Wednesday 18 May 1966, Julian Wintle had written to his wife Anne Francis (not to be confused with the actress of the same name), who was in Canada, informing her that the colour episodes of *The Avengers* would begin filming on Monday 8 August. He also mentioned that ABC intended producing a series of half-hour episodes set in outer space in the 25th Century, and that he was extremely busy as the executive producer of the co-production *Lucy in London*, starring Lucille Ball and the Dave Clark Five.

The Thursday 18 August edition of *The Stage and Television Today* reported that ABC were still looking to embark upon co-productions and were about to enter into a joint venture with American International Pictures. This was the science fiction concept referred to in Wintle's letter, now called *The Solarnauts*, which was to comprise 26 episodes, with a total budget of £750,000, and was envisaged as a live action series with modelwork. The article continued by indicating that ABC considered the popular film and television spy cycle to be burning itself out, hence the villains presented in the new season of *The Avengers* would generally come from the private sector. It was reported that Albert Fennell and Brian Clemens had been promoted to co-producers, with the latter being responsible more than anyone else for the series' style and content. However, initial plans for Steed to relocate to the Hertfordshire countryside and live in a traditional oak-beamed cottage were abandoned in favour of creating a new London apartment for him.

Reassembling the crew

Laurie Johnson would once again provide the incidental music for this season, having also recorded an updated version of the theme tune that now started with a tom-tom beat. He adopted a routine whereby he would watch a rough cut of an episode on a Monday, then aim to have all the incidental music composed for it by Thursday the same week. This allowed a copyist time to write out the score for each individual instrument so that recording could take place the following Monday. If Johnson took too long, the copyist could be rushed and make errors, which would have to be rectified on the day of recording, using up precious studio time. The actual editing of the recorded material onto the finished prints would be undertaken by supervising editor Peter Tanner, who had been promoted from film editor on the previous season. Johnson considered Tanner to be one of the best in the business, though Albert Fennell always kept a watchful eye on this process.

Gordon L T Scott retained his position on the team as assistant to Albert Fennell, but as an ABPC employee he would not be named in the closing credits.

Recording director A W Lumkin returned for the new season, as did regular stunt arranger Ray Austin. Austin had to spend some time teaching Diana Rigg basic martial arts moves, as the producers had decided to change Mrs Peel's fighting style to kung fu. He was also responsible for training her new double, Cyd Child, who had become involved with stunt work at the suggestion of one of her teachers at the Ministry of Aviation, where she had been learning photography. Child was the same height and build as Rigg, had a facial resemblance to her, and with her hair dyed and cut in the same style, made a convincing double. Her predecessor, Billy Westley, departed to become a trainee assistant film director.

Geoffrey Haine also returned to the series as production manager, although only after Ted Lloyd had filled in for several episodes. Dubbing mixer Len Abbott was another crew member retained from the previous season; he managed to work on all the film series in production at Elstree at any one time, sharing the duties with Len Shilton. Karen Heward assumed the newly-credited role of music editor. The film editor credit did not appear on every episode, but when it did it went to Lionel Selwyn, Tony Palk or Bert Rule. Steve Birtles and Walter 'Wally' Thompson were credited individually as the supervising electrician. Initially Charles Hammerton was the construction manager, though later he was replaced by Herbert Worley.

New apartment standing sets

Harry Pottle having vacated the position of art director, he was succeeded by production designer Wilfred Shingleton, whose immediate task was to redesign the interior sets of both Emma's apartment and Steed's. These constructions would be the only standing sets required on the show, but had to be designed with care and attention to reflect the personalities of their owners. Although it was supposed to be the same apartment seen in season four, Steed's abode now looked completely different, with wood panelled walls incorporating a bookcase. There were also military prints and souvenirs dotted around; deep buttoned red leather furniture; and a bunch of yellow flowers in an old tuba. The kitchen and back door could be glimpsed through an open doorway and a spiral staircase led up to the bedrooms. Emma's home, on the other hand, was definitely not the same high-rise apartment of the previous season.

Shingleton's interpretation was of a ground-floor studio flat, sparsely furnished with Victorian-style furniture and a grand piano.

Transports of delight

As before, Lotus Cars of Wymondham in Norfolk saw a chance for some free publicity and supplied the latest Lotus Elan S3 convertible (SJH 499D) for Mrs Peel to drive. The colour of this vehicle was always said to be powder blue – which was obviously how the manufacturer described it – but on screen it appeared silver. Meanwhile, the vintage Bentleys driven by Steed in the season four episodes had aroused great interest and been extremely popular with the viewing public, so these would appear again. In all bar one of the first batch of colour episodes, Macnee would use a 1930 Speed Six Bentley (RX 6180) in British racing green.[16] This was hired from Farmcraft Motors of New Malden, Surrey, although it was actually owned at the time by J N Gooch of Forrest Row near East Grinstead, West Sussex. Farmcraft's driver, Jim Mitchell, would collect the vehicle early in the morning and drive it either to Elstree or directly to wherever the day's location filming was taking place. Later, in 1984, the Speed Six was acquired by vintage Bentley dealer Stanley Mann Racing of Radlett, who sold it for £49,500 to a man named Olle Ljungstrom. Ljungstrom shipped the vehicle to Sweden, where he removed the Le Mans replica bodywork. However, information held by the Driver and Vehicle Licensing Agency (DVLA) indicates that the car has now been returned to the UK.

The Corridor People

On Friday 26 August 1966 a new potential rival to *The Avengers* arrived in the form of Granada's short-lived *avant-garde* series *The Corridor People*, starring Elizabeth Shepherd as Parisian villainess Syrie Van Epp. Designed as an experimental drama set in the world of espionage, the series had no clear protagonist, but instead a collection of oddball characters who could work against each other one week and be allies the next. Unfortunately, producing the show on film was beyond Granada's means at the time, so writer Edward Boyd's creation was videotaped, with exteriors presented on short filmed inserts. In interviews, Shepherd has always maintained that *The Corridor People* was a better show than *The Avengers*, with superior scripts and dialogue. However, only four episodes were ever recorded, and although *The Avengers* was undoubtedly a major influence, Granada really lacked the resources to compete against what was now the most popular film series in the country.

False start

An early obstacle arose when it was discovered that production on season five could not begin at Elstree Studios in Borehamwood, where the monochrome Rigg episodes had been filmed, as all the soundstages there were fully booked until the second week in October 1966. This necessitated a temporary move to Pinewood Studios in

---

[16] The exception was 'The Fear Merchants', the first episode to be produced, in which Steed drives a 1925 Green Label Bentley (YK 6871). This vehicle is still a runner, having taken part in the Lord Mayor's Show in London on Saturday 12 November 2011.

Buckinghamshire to film the first two episodes of the new batch. The delay caused by this meant that the Monday 8 August 1966 start date planned by Julian Wintle came and went with no filming actually taking place.

Originally, Brian Clemens intended to continue with the end tag scenes seen in the previous season, whereby Steed and Mrs Peel would depart from their adventures using a different kind of transport each time. Filming for season five finally got under way on Monday 5 September when three of these sequences featuring vintage cars were shot on location at Lord Montagu's home Palace House in Beaulieu, Hampshire, directed by newcomer Roy Rossotti, who had previously been David Lean's protégé, having worked as second unit director on the epic movie *Lawrence of Arabia*. A selection of colour publicity photographs were also taken, and a short British Pathé news report publicised the filming. Shortly afterwards, however, a decision was made not to continue with the transport tag scenes after all – although the three that were already in the can would be used for the early episodes.

5.01 – 'The Fear Merchants'

Principal filming on the new season of colour episodes, budgeted at £50,000 each, commenced later in September 1966 at Pinewood, with Gordon Flemyng directing Philip Levene's script 'The Fear Merchants.' In this adventure, Steed and Mrs Peel investigate the Business Efficiency Bureau (BEB), which offers a service to companies to eliminate their business rivals by confronting them with their innermost fears and causing a mental breakdown.

Footage supposedly showing a hospital exterior actually featured various small office blocks connected to Pinewood soundstages A, B, C and D (called Main Road). A sequence in which the chauffeur-driven white Rolls Royce limousine of ceramics firm executive Crawley skids to a halt was filmed on the concrete perimeter road on the North Lot.

Some location footage was shot locally of Steed pursuing the Rolls Royce in his Bentley. The Bentley is seen on Pinewood Road and Alderbourne Lane, while the Rolls Royce speeds down Love Green Lane from Bangors Road South. Additional footage was captured on Ivor Lane at nearby Cowley for back-projection purposes, being seen through the rear window of the Rolls Royce as it travels north-west from High Street toward the junction with Palmer's Moor Lane. Crawley's limousine was in fact represented by two different vehicles: a Rolls Royce Silver Cloud III for exterior shots and a Rolls Royce Phantom V for some interiors.

A sequence where Steed investigates a yellow bulldozer blocking his Bentley and then finds himself pushed into a large pit was executed at Springwell Chalk Pit, Springwell Lane in Harefield, Buckinghamshire.

Guest actor Edward Burnham, playing businessman Richards Meadows, was on location in the deserted old Wembley Stadium for the opening teaser, where Meadows awakes to encounter his worst case scenario of a huge wide open space, before collapsing due to the shock.

Later, when the production returned to Elstree, several pick-up shots were filmed on the lot, including one of BEB operative Gilbert arriving in his Humber Super Snipe at the home of the eccentric Jeremy Raven to leave a poisonous spider, and the subsequent one where Emma and Steed pull up there in Emma's Lotus Elan. This footage involved vehicles being parked beside the building containing the plasterers' shops C and D and workshop C, opposite the red-brick maintenance building with Stage 5 in the background. Additional material showing the Lotus Elan was shot toward the rear of the studio lot, showing the vehicle being driven north past the scenery docks.

Together with casting director G B Walker, Flemyng made the decision to have Macnee's close friend Patrick Cargill play the villainous EBE president Pemberton, and also to cast Garfield Morgan as Gilbert and Brian Wilde as Raven. Bernard Horsfall makes a brief appearance as industrialist Martin Fox, who upon seeing a mouse is almost paralysed by fear, despite having just demonstrated his strength by karate-chopping a block of wood in half – an action Horsfall had also performed when playing one of the Cybernauts' victims in the season four episode 'The Cybernauts'. In the background of this sequence, actor Declan Mulholland can be seen struggling to lift a heavy weight in a brief, non-speaking role named as Saunders in the closing credits – surprisingly so, as even minor speaking roles would sometimes go unbilled in later episodes. Clemens' friend, actor/writer Jeremy Burnham was also cast in the episode, as Crawley's colleague White, having previously featured in 'The Town of No Return'. He would return to the series later as the scriptwriter of several episodes.

Wilfred Shingleton's early brief included designing sets that would make the fashions created for Rigg and Macnee stand out, so for 'The Fear Merchants' he devised various neutral-coloured rooms. The BEB office in particular is a very '60s monochrome piece. Mrs Peel sports her now famous dark blue twin cut-out Emmapeeler with gold chain and pocket watch, plus a grey shortie top version with a thin strip of connecting material to cover her navel and keep the American censors happy. She is also seen indulging in her pastime of sculpting, sat in the middle of her apartment on top of a large block of stone armed with a power drill and later a mallet and chisel.

Steed's spitting image, complete with bowler and umbrella, is seen from behind striding down a hospital corridor, although actually this was Macnee's stunt double Rocky Taylor, who also doubled for him in the chalk pit fight scene. Further to this, Taylor doubled for Garfield Morgan for a dangerous sequence where a bulldozer falls on and crushes Gilbert.

Other notable points: a bird sculpture last seen in the offices of Art Incorporated in 'The Girl from Auntie' reappears here as part of the decorations in Mrs Peel's new apartment; Laurie Johnson's incidental cues are now sounding very '60s electric keyboard; and Raven at one point has to leave a message on the undercover Steed's answering machine, which in the '60s could only have been an Ansafone – the world's first commercially-available answering machine, which used magnetic tape to store recordings.

Episode subtitles

A new opening title sequence for the series would not be devised until November 1966, but when edited into place on each episode it would be followed by a teaser scene enticing viewers to keep watching. Then would come an innovation added by Clemens to bring something new to the formula, as the episode title would be followed by a double-barrelled subtitle of the kind he had been including for some time on his scripts. For instance, 'The Fear Merchants' is subtitled 'Steed puts out a light, Emma takes fright'.

'Mrs Peel, we're needed!'

After the subtitle would come another short scene, during which Steed would inform Emma of their impending mission through the words 'Mrs Peel, we're needed!' (or a slight variation on them). To accompany this, Laurie Johnson composed a short piece that could be played by a variety of instruments and that reached a high note just as the message was delivered. In 'The Fear Merchants', the 'Mrs Peel, we're needed!' sequence involves Emma discovering a large box of chocolates in her apartment with a small card informing her that Steed requires her assistance.

Meanwhile, the episodes' end tag scenes would now adopt a more traditional format, with Steed and Emma playing out a light-hearted situation with a witty exchange of dialogue.

5.02 – 'Escape in Time'

By mid-October 1966, filming on Philip Levene's 'Escape in Time' was under way at Pinewood with another new director, John Krish, in control. However, part way through the shoot, the unit would transfer back to Elstree in Borehamwood. Production on ITC's *The Baron* had concluded there on Friday 14 October, thus there was now studio space to accommodate *The Avengers*.

The storyline this time concerns wanted criminals being offered a chance to escape into the past through the use of a time machine invented by the eccentric introvert Thyssen. Krish cast Peter Bowles as Thyssen, and the actor had to have a plastic mould made of his face to enable the creation of busts of the character's ancestors. The guest cast also featured, in the role of Anjali, Imogen Hassall, who at the time was just as well known for attending film premieres and doing pin-up shots as for acting.

A sequence where the man Mitchell, dressed in huntsman's attire, attempts to run Mrs Peel down with a Triumph T120 motorcycle was filmed on scrubland called Clipper Down, off Beacon Road near Dagnall in Buckinghamshire. Doubling for Rigg, Cyd Child narrowly avoided being knocked over by the motorcycle on several occasions, but Krish kept requesting additional takes, thinking that the scene needed to look more realistic. Finally Krish was satisfied, but only after Child had allowed the motorcycle actually to make contact with her. Another problem arose when a new member of the crew thought that stuntman Rocky Taylor, playing Mitchell, had really been injured when he came off the bike, rushing to administer first aid and causing the scene to have to be reshot yet again.

For exterior shots of Thyssen's home, the crew returned to the large residential property Starveacres on Watford Road in Radlett, where footage for 'Small Game for Big Hunters' had been captured the previous year. In another location sequence, Mrs Peel in her Lotus Elan follows a white MGB driven by the character Vesta, played by Judy Parfitt, down Mimms Lane, travelling in a south-easterly direction toward Deeves Hall Cottage. The fictional Yule Tide Turkey Farm was realised by shooting at the farm adjoining Deeves Hall Cottage, with vehicles turning off Earls Lane into Deeves Hall Lane and heading south toward the village of Ridge. Footage of a Rolls Royce hearse was also filmed in this area on Packhorse Lane, with the vehicle heading toward the junction with Mimms Lane.

At some point during pre-production, presumably to save on both time and budget, a decision had been taken to shoot some of the episode's exterior scenes on studio sets.

Consequently the prominently-featured alleyways of Mackidockie Court/Stone Street (Mackidockie Mews in the draft script) were designed by Wilfred Shingleton and assembled on one of the soundstages at Elstree. This practice would become quite common on subsequent episodes, as film studios in the '60s were all four-wallers, meaning that they could meet almost any of their clients' requirements on site. At the time, Elstree employed an army of carpenters, set builders and dressers who could be called upon to create the exterior walls of buildings at short notice.

In another sequence, where Mitchell masquerades as Steed (ironically given that Taylor was Macnee's regular stunt double), Emma follows him from Mackidockie Court, and they are seen on the Elstree backlot heading toward the large structural backdrop for the smaller of the two concrete-lined exterior tanks. After a brief fight with Emma, the tank is where Mitchell ends up – though unfortunately for Taylor all the water had been drained. The real Steed meanwhile continues to follow the criminals' escape route, being shown into the Rolls Royce hearse parked on the studio lot by a barber portrayed by Edward Caddick and named, as indicated on his shop frontage, T Sweeney (obviously after notorious real-life barber Sweeney Todd).

Later, Sweeney has a rifle trained on Steed somewhere in the gardens at Starveacres, but – in a rare example of gadgets being used in the series – the agent activates a knockout gas expellant device in his umbrella, leaving the assailant unconscious. When Vesta also holds him at gunpoint at Tyssen's house, Steed deals with her with similar ease, overpowering her and helping himself to her Browning 1910 automatic.

For a sequence where Steed and Mrs Peel visit the apartment of a man named Pearson, the Bentley was filmed on Randolph Road, London W9, with the Macnee and Rigg doubles alighting and entering number 18.

A *Daily Mail* newspaper stand seen leaning against the wall outside a newsagents carries the headline 'Where Is Blake?'. This referred to the real-life mystery surrounding the disappearance of double agent George Blake, who escaped from Wormwood Scrubs prison on Saturday 22 October 1966. Just as the criminals in 'Escape in Time' were following an escape route, so Blake managed to avoid being recaptured and joined his employers in the Soviet Union, where he was given political asylum.

The 'Mrs Peel, we're needed!' scene for this episode involves Emma in her glad rags preparing to depart from her apartment to a Grand Hunt Ball, when Steed suddenly appears and turns over her invitation card, revealing the lettering, 'We're Needed'.

After Mrs Peel makes a stuffed animal toy, Steed comments that he was not aware she could sew, to which she replies, 'Our relationship hasn't exactly been domestic.'

As with 'The Fear Merchants', Laurie Johnson's incidental music sets the scene impressively, ranging from '60s electronic organ sounds to tinkling piano coupled with heavy brass.

The props department would have had little trouble converting the mechanism of the one-armed bandit representing the time machine to ensure that when the wheels stopped spinning they gave a four digit number indicating the year in the past to which people were about to be transported. The atmospheric trip through time was achieved on screen by adjusting the camera focus to a blur, in conjunction with background music and sound effects.

The humorous closing tag scene featuring both Macnee and Rigg with a red 1908 Unic taxi (MD 1480) was one of the sequences filmed in September at Palace House near Beaulieu.

5.03 – 'From Venus with Love'

On Friday 24 December 1965, Julian Wintle dispatched to Brian Tesler the draft script of an episode from Philip Levene called 'The Light Fantastic', informing him that the title had already been changed, but failing to say what to. As it turned out, it was 'From Venus with Love'. Tesler was apparently unimpressed when he responded in writing to Wintle on the final day of the year, commenting that the script attempted to be kookie too much of the time. Had Tesler responded more positively, it is possible that this episode might have replaced either 'How to Succeed … at Murder' or 'Honey for the Prince' in the season four production schedule. As it was, however, it was held over to season five, when Robert Day was assigned to direct.

Levene's story would in many ways become a blueprint for this period of the series. It centres on an organisation called the British Venusian Society (BVS), whose members are being killed by an unknown force that leaves them bleached white. All the evidence suggests that Venusians have landed and have at their disposal a powerful weapon. The characters include a fair quota of eccentrics: Primble, the visually-impaired optician; Brigadier Whitehead, busy recording his wartime memoirs using several wind-up gramophones; and gentleman chimneysweep Bertram Fortesque Winthrop-Smythe, alias Bert Smith. One of these characters would turn out to be the villain of the piece, and – as in many *The Avengers* episodes – it would be the person the viewer least expected; in this case, Primble.

The exterior location used for the sequence where Mrs Peel meets Bert Smith, played by Jeremy Lloyd, was Radlett Preparatory School off Watling Street, approximately three miles from Elstree. However, when she speeds away in her Lotus Elan in pursuit of the mysterious light that has killed the chimneysweep, the shot where she sees the light disappearing down the wooded driveway was filmed not at the school but on the access road to the large house known as High Canons at Well End near Borehamwood. During her pursuit of the light, Emma is also seen driving the Lotus at speed along Mimms Lane in the direction of Deeves Hall Cottage, but on her arrival there she finds herself dazzled by the increasing brilliance of her quarry and brings the car skidding to a halt directly on the junction. Emma then spies the dangerous light disappearing into the barn of a farm and, running across a field, comes to what is now the RSPCA Southridge Animal Centre on Packhorse Lane, near the village of Ridge.

Macnee and the Bentley also went on location, to Stanmore Hall in Wood Lane, Stanmore, Middlesex, representing the gothic mansion house of Brigadier Whitehead, played by future *Doctor Who* star Jon Pertwee. This property is a Grade 2 listed building, and sometime during the mid-'80s was converted into 23 luxury apartments, complete with an indoor swimming pool.

After acting together on this episode, Rigg and Jeremy Lloyd became good friends. Lloyd later worked in the States, becoming a regular writer and performer on the show that beat *The Avengers* in the Nielsen ratings, *Rowan And Martin's Laugh-In*. Returning to the UK in 1971, he appeared in the short-lived sitcom *It's Awfully Bad for Your Eyes, Darling …*, co-starring with his one-time wife Joanna Lumley (later to rise to fame in *The New Avengers*) and Jennifer Croxton (herself a temporary Avengergirl in season six). During the '80s and '90s, he had a successful collaboration with writer David Croft, which saw them create and script several popular sitcoms including *Are You Being Served?* and *'Allo 'Allo!*.

A silver sports car discovered at Primble's by Mrs Peel was a Ford GT40, complete with prop laser gun mounted on a hydraulic platform courtesy of the electricians at Elstree. Reputedly the GT40 was the fastest road car in the world at the time, and it had won the famous 24-hour motor race at Le Mans in France that year. The scenes with the GT40 were shot inside the garage/workshop at Elstree that would also feature in the next episode, 'The Bird Who Knew Too Much'. Primble's uncredited assistant, Martin, was played by Billy Cornelius, a stuntman/extra who had already appeared as a tribesman in 'Small Game for Big Hunters' in the previous season.

A scene of Steed's Bentley arriving outside Primble's surgery was shot on the backlot town, with the car's nearside front headlamp not working. Evidently someone at Elstree could not spell ophthalmic, as the initial 'h' was omitted from the lettering on the prop lamp outside the premises. Both the wooden farm buildings and the cemetery featured in the episode were examples of exteriors built as sets inside one of the stages.

In a sequence where Emma is talking to Steed on the phone outside the room where Smith is killed, the set features a pair of large white double doors that previously formed part of Thyssen's home in 'Escape in Time'. She is later seen to have a two-way radio secreted in the glove compartment of her Lotus when she reports back to Steed that their out-of-this-world mystery is apparently something more down to earth.

Visiting the scene of astronomer Cosgrove's death, Emma wears an Alun Hughes-designed matching lavender crepe dress and jacket. This would reappear in the later episode 'A Funny Thing Happened on the Way to the Station' and would be made commercially available to purchase for 12 guineas. Another Hughes creation, a tan-coloured mini dress that he called the Little Nothing, is worn by Mrs Peel when she and Steed investigate the death of another astronomer, Sir Frederick Hadley, at his observatory.

The episode's on-screen title caption has the 'O' in 'Love' represented by a heart shape with a small arrow through it. The 'Mrs Peel, we're needed!' sequence involves Emma practising her fencing abilities, as Steed suddenly enters her apartment with the usual message card on the end of his umbrella. The concluding tag scene sees Steed telling Emma that they are going to have 'dinner on Venus' – actually a reference to the character Venus Browne, whose book *Venus Our Sister Planet* was mocked up for the production simply by way of a prop dust jacket placed around an ordinary hardback novel.

Laser effects seen in sequences in Primble's surgery were added during post-production via optical printing, accompanied by the noise of a building power generator followed by a burning laser sound. In a scene where Primble gives Steed an eye test, the test is carried out not with the standard optician's chart, but rather with a trolley containing various different hats, the types of which the agent reels off to amusing effect: 'Trilby, homburg, bowler, cap, jockey, porkpie, topper, boater, busby, fez.'

This was Cyd Child's first episode doubling for Diana Rigg, and literally became a baptism of fire for her when the screenplay required her to pass between some flaming curtains in Venus Browne's office and out onto the balcony beyond. The stunt went without a hitch, although Child has since confessed that she always hated getting anywhere near fire during her work.

Besides Lloyd and Pertwee, other names that Day included amongst his impressive guest cast for 'From Venus with Love' were Philip Locke, Derek Newark and – after using her in the film *Bobbikins* some years earlier – Barbara Shelley.

5.04 – 'The Bird Who Knew Too Much'

Alan Pattillo submitted a storyline that was turned into a shooting script by Brian Clemens called 'The Bird Who Knew Too Much' – a play on the title of Alfred Hitchcock's classic 1956 thriller *The Man Who Knew Too Much*. Peter Graham Scott started out as director of this episode, as evidenced by his appearance in some behind-the-scenes photographs, but for some reason he departed and was replaced by Roy Rossotti, who had previously handled the first day of filming for the season on location at Beaulieu.

This time, Steed and Mrs Peel are searching for an agent known as Captain Crusoe who is passing information to Britain's cold war enemies; but little do they know that he is not human – the culprit is actually a parrot.

The opening teaser sequence was filmed on the Elstree Studios backlot and featured both an elevated guard post also seen in *The Baron* episode 'Enemy of the State' and the larger of the two concrete-lined water tanks.

Guest actors Michael Coles and Clive Colin-Bowler were on location at Clipper Down off Beacon Road near Dagnall in Buckinghamshire for a sequence where their characters, the villains Verret and Robin, spy on the missile installation Muswells Back. This was probably shot while the production was still based temporarily at Pinewood; if it had been done after the return to Elstree, a similar piece of countryside nearer Borehamwood would doubtless have been used instead.

Rigg went on location to Shenley Hall for the scene where Emma visits the home of bird fancier Professor Jordan, played by Ron Moody, and they come under fire from a rifle. The shots of Robin firing the rifle were actually filmed ten miles away, on the diving board at Splashland in Stanborough Park, Welwyn Garden City. This was also the location where a sequence was filmed of Emma having a short fight with Robin – accompanied by Laurie Johnson's incidental cue 'Chase that Car' – and then throwing him into the swimming pool and diving in after him. The dive was actually performed not by Rigg herself but by stuntman/extra Peter J Elliot, who would appear unbilled in various episodes this season. He had previously been both the British springboard diving champion and a recording artist on the Parlophone record label.

The scaffolding featured at one point in the action was a set created inside one of the soundstages. The larger water tank on the lot provided the backdrop for a sequence where Steed has lunch with the young blonde Samantha on board a punt, complete with table and chairs. Also shot at Elstree, in the garage workshop by the gateway at the north-west corner on the lot, was a scene where Verret and Robin stand beside a maroon Austin 1800 and discuss killing Mrs Peel.

Emma is seen to have abandoned her power drill in favour of a hammer and chisel to continue sculpting in her apartment. She is also seen to carry a snub-nosed, pearl-handled .32 Harrington and Richardson revolver, which she entrusts to Professor Jordan to return fire when they came under attack.

Laurie Johnson's incidental music includes pizzicato strings and solo woodwind pieces that are reminiscent of birdsong.

Steed puts his steel-crowned bowler hat to use in dealing with a couple of villains, striking Captain Crusoe's owner Edgar Twitter over the head and then knocking a gun from his assistant George Cunliffe's hand.

While waiting for a pigeon to arrive at fellow agent Mark Pearson's apartment, Steed makes himself comfortable in an armchair with a bottle of champagne and a copy of *The Times*. Telephoning Emma, he leaves her a message on (presumably) her Ansafone.

Part of the Mackidockie Court/Stone Street set seen in the previous episode was reassembled in a new configuration to become the exterior of the studio belonging to photographer Tom Savage. Gagged and tied to a chair inside Savage's studio, Mrs Peel has a gun trained on her that will fire automatically when someone opens the door and thereby unwittingly pulls a string attached to the trigger. Fortunately, Steed enters through a window, announcing, 'New habit, climbing through windows. Lucky for you I'm a devious fellow.'

Additional location filming took place on Silver Hill, showing the Bentley – with the nearside headlamp still not working – speeding in the direction of Shenley, as Steed and Mrs Peel travel to Twitter's home, Heathcliff Hall.

The 'Mrs Peel, we're needed!' opener this time involves Emma drawing back the curtains in her apartment and an arrow flying through the open window and embedding itself in her bird statuette. A small card attached to the card bears the message.

The closing tag scene is a repeat performance with the arrow – with Steed this time climbing in through the window of Emma's apartment – followed by another of the Palace House sequences, this one featuring a 1905 Vauxhall (MV 9942) being reversed around in circles and away – achieved by reversing and partly speeding up some footage of the car being driven forwards.

More rivals for *The Avengers*

On Thursday 20 October 1966 *The Man from U.N.C.L.E.* returned to BBC1 for a new run. Its episodes would alternate weekly with those of the new spin-off *The Girl from U.N.C.L.E.*, starring Stefanie Powers as female operative April Dancer. The parent series had now undergone a change of style, however, departing from straight spy thrillers to encompass more science fiction scenarios and satire; and the spin-off followed suit. This mirrored what was happening on the big screen with the tongue-in-cheek spy movies of the Matt Helm series starring Dean Martin and the Derek Flint series starring James Coburn. It was also part of a wider trend in television, ushered in by the American ABC network's *Batman* series starring Adam West, which had pioneered a more spoofy approach that had proved immensely popular. A number of other already-established television series had quickly adopted a similar style. Irwin Allen's *Voyage to the Bottom of the Sea* and *Lost in Space*, for instance, had abandoned all semblance of scientific accuracy in the pursuit of camp fantasy. *The Girl from U.N.C.L.E.* could have been the biggest rival yet to *The Avengers*, but in following the same trend, it was pitched incorrectly to make maximum impact. As a result it would last only one season before being cancelled. In fact the whole tongue-in-cheek fad would burn itself out in just a couple of years.

Meanwhile, on adjacent soundstages at Elstree, an old rival to *The Avengers* had acquired a new lease of life, as *The Saint* was also currently in production in colour, with star Roger Moore back in the role of Simon Templar. The American NBC network had now bought the series, prompting fresh negotiations with Templar's creator Leslie Charteris, which resulted in newly-commissioned original screenplays being written. In these, Templar was propelled head-on into the swinging '60s, encountering such things as student death games, impregnable underground bank vaults and an experimental suspended animation machine.

Half a mile down the road from Elstree at MGM's Borehamwood Studios, Patrick McGoohan was intricately putting together his television extravaganza *The Prisoner*, which would push the envelope of the British film series to extremes. Originally intended as a six-part serial, it was extended to a planned 26 episodes as Lew Grade wanted a series and provided McGoohan's production company Everyman Films with the necessary funding. In the end, however, delays – usually caused by McGoohan's attention to detail – would cause Grade to lose interest and halt production after only 17 highly innovative episodes.

The swinging '60s

By now the '60s was really swinging, and London was at the forefront of presenting the latest trends in music, fashion and films. In August 1966 the Beatles had released their latest album, *Revolver*, which contained the drugs-influenced track 'Tomorrow Never Knows', heralding the psychedelic era of rock music. Meanwhile, in Los Angeles, Brian Wilson and the Beach Boys were also experimenting, spending hours in recording studios working on the concept album *Smiley Smile*. However, due to Wilson's mental health problems, which were not helped by drug use, the project was later abandoned, and although tracks would appear occasionally, it would take almost 40 years before an official version was issued on CD.

Back in swinging London, Carnaby Street was now the acknowledged fashion capital of the world, and British designers were on the cutting edge, with John Bates, Mary Quant, Ossie Clark, Zandra Rhodes, Vivienne Westwood and Terence Conran leading the way.

The fifth James Bond film, *You Only Live Twice* starring Sean Connery, was currently undergoing production in Japan, and although Ian Fleming's master spy had faced many rivals, he was about to go head to head with the ultimate one: namely himself, as Charles K Feldman's Bond spoof *Casino Royale* was being pieced together from filming at three different British studios.

Change was in the air, and Brian Clemens and Albert Fennell would make certain that *The Avengers* moved with the times, becoming one the fondest-remembered television series from the swinging '60s.

5.05 – 'The See-Through Man'

In front of the cameras around the beginning of December 1966 was another Philip Levene story, 'The See-Through Man', revolving around the Eastern Bloc agent Major Alexander Vazin, who seems to have discovered a way to become invisible. This episode was directed by newcomer Robert Asher. Born in London in 1915, Asher had found employment in the film industry as an assistant director in 1943, and had continued working in that capacity until becoming a director on the movie *Follow a Star* in 1959. He was known as a very patient director, generally addressed as Bob by his colleagues, and had gained credits on a number of comedy films, mainly starring Norman Wisdom, although prior to his arrival on *The Avengers* he had also directed on *The Baron*. During production of 'The See-Through Man', he began rewriting the script during his lunch break, until this came to the attention of Albert Fennell, who gave him a severe verbal reprimand. Unlike on the film projects Asher had handled, the shooting script on an episode of *The Avengers* was regarded as sacrosanct; once Brian Tesler had given his approval, very little alteration was usually allowed – particularly if the script was by co-producer Brian Clemens. The writing burden on this second Diana Rigg season would generally be shared between Clemens and ideas man Levene, who both understood what was required, hence saving time on having to develop and rework unsuitable material.

A sequence where Steed in his vintage Bentley and Emma in her Lotus Elan leave the car park of the Ministry of Defence Records Office, Invention (External Submissions), was actually shot at Watford Central Baths, situated on Peace Prospect in Watford. This red-brick building would be demolished in February 2007 and later replaced by the larger Watford Leisure Centre.

The crew returned to Shenley Lodge, off Rectory Lane near Shenley, which had provided the exterior of the automated house in 'The House That Jack Built', to film Steed's arrival in the Bentley at the residence of eccentric inventor Professor Quilby. Meanwhile, the British Rail Study Centre off Hempstead Road, Watford, doubled as Daviot Hall for a sequence where Emma arrives there, finds the front door open, hears a gunshot from around the side of the building, sees someone speed off in a 3.8 litre Jaguar saloon and then finds Lord Daviot lying dead face down in the ornamental garden pond.

Now sporting the moustache he wore in his famous role as Alf Garnett in the BBC sitcom *Till Death Us Do Part*, Warren Mitchell reprised his role as the vodka-hating diplomat Brodny, first seen in the black and white episode 'Two's a Crowd'. In a nice touch of continuity, the establishing shots of his embassy were filmed, as in that earlier episode, at Edge Grove School on Oakridge Lane, near the village of Aldenham. This location also features in a scene where Brodny's comrade Elena, played by Moira Lister, leaves in her DAF 44 for a rendezvous with Quilby's assistant Ackroyd, discreetly followed by Mrs Peel in her Lotus. Both vehicles were filmed heading away from the centre of Shenley along Rectory Lane, before taking a right into Harris Lane at one of the triangles of grass that make up the double junction there.

Ackroyd, played by Jonathan Elsom, has a cream-coloured customised Austin FX3 cab, complete with purple curtains and two chromed air horns mounted on the roof. Both Elsom and the vehicle were shot on location in Earls Lane, close to Deeves Hall Cottage, along with Lister in the DAF 44 and Rigg in the Lotus. A high-speed car chase ensues, as the Jaguar, driven by Major Vazin, follows the Lotus up Deeves Hall Lane toward Ridge. Vazin then executes some dangerous manoeuvres that cease only when he has to swerve the Jaguar to a halt to avoid an oncoming truck – an action sequence shot almost 25 miles north, on Hexton Road near the village of Lilley in Bedfordshire.

Elsom and Macnee were also filmed at the children's playground in Oxhey Park, Watford, where after Steed is diverted away he returns to find Ackroyd has been murdered.

In dialogue, Brodny, Vazin and Elena are never actually referred to as Russians, although it seems obvious that is intended to be their country of origin. Brodny at one point speaks of his dread of being stripped of his diplomatic status and sent home to the motherland, informing Vazin that he has tickets for the next Beatles concert – which, although Levene and Clemens could not have known it, was an impossibility, as apart from a one-off performance on the roof of the Apple Corp building in London in 1969, the Beatles would never play live again.

During the course of the action, Emma outwits and overpowers Brodny, returning to confront Elena with the diplomat's Walther PPK automatic, which turns out to be unloaded. Diminutive actor Art Thomas went uncredited as Vazin, hidden away under false shoulders and clothing to give the impression of someone whose head is invisible. His face is seen only at the episode's conclusion.

The static robot seen in Quilby's laboratory was an old prop originally constructed for the 1952 film *Old Mother Riley Meets the Vampire*, though for this appearance it had undergone some cosmetic changes including a repaint.

The 'Mrs Peel, we're needed!' sequence has Emma looking at samples through her microscope when Steed places under the lens another slide bearing tiny lettering that conveys his usual message. The end tag scene is the final segment filmed at Palace House near Beaulieu. This time Steed and Mrs Peel have to push-start a 1909 Rolls Royce 40/50 Silver Ghost (R 1909), which fires up and then roars off without them.

The white, full-length rainproof jacket worn by Emma in the sequence where she drives after Elena in the Lotus was manufactured by Dannimac, and as a part of Alun Hughes' The Avengers Pack could be acquired by the public for the sum of £8 19s 6d in old money.

The Americans take up their option

Having obviously been impressed with the Nielsen ratings gained by season four, the American ABC network took up their option of ordering a further 26 episodes of *The Avengers*, this time in glorious colour. This made front page news in the *Daily Mail* of Wednesday 9 November 1966, with the headline 'Avengers for US'. *The Times* also covered the story on the same day, reporting that the contract was worth in excess of $2 million. The following day, *The Stage and Television Today* noted that Rediffusion would begin transmissions of the colour episodes in the London region on Friday 6 January 1967 – though in the event it would actually be a week later. The US transmissions of the new season were also due to begin the same month.

Telemen realised that by the time January arrived they would have completed principal shooting on, at best, only eight of the season's episodes. Given the time taken to shoot and edit each additional episode, this meant that sooner rather than later the broadcasters would run out of material to show. Senior members of the production team knew in advance that 16 episodes was the maximum they could hope to complete before a suspension in transmissions became inevitable by mid-April 1966.

In order to achieve even this, a large amount of overlapping on filming would be necessary, meaning that in some weeks the leads would end up having to work on three different episodes. In general on a television film series, directors were expected to get at least five minutes of finished footage in the can every day. Clemens and Fennell were known to be flexible regarding this rule, as they believed that more time and effort spent on filming would result in higher quality. The question was, could they still afford to be so generous with studio time and turn round 16 episodes in seven months?

Colour opening title sequence

The opening title sequence for this season was planned out in writing by Brian Clemens on Tuesday 15 November 1966. According to author Dave Rogers, it was filmed shortly after that on Stage 6 at Elstree.[17] Rogers has also indicated that the director was Robert Day. However, as 'The See-Through Man' was in production at the time, it is perhaps more likely that it was that episode's director, Robert Asher, who was responsible.

Some compromises and slight alterations were made to Clemens' plan during the filming, but when edited to accompany the new theme tune rendition provided by Laurie Johnson, the sequence epitomised the series perfectly. It did however contain what could be considered a small continuity glitch: Mrs Peel's gold-plated and pearl-handled .38 Webley and Scott mark four revolver makes an appearance in the sequence, but would never actually feature in a colour episode.

ABC Television Films Limited

On Thursday 17 November 1966 *The Stage and Television Today* ran a further report on the sale of the colour episodes to the American ABC network. This revealed that the deal included an option for the network to purchase an additional batch of episodes, worth another $4 million to ABC Television, which could see the series being networked until late 1968. Obviously buoyed by this success and still wanting to develop international filmed co-productions, ABC at this point invested £3.5 million into a new subsidiary company, ABC Television Films Limited, based at Elstree. In anticipation of more filmed television production taking place, a building programme already under way at Elstree would lead to the construction of three new stages, an ancillary building, an underground car park and other facilities, which would all be completed in several months' time.

5.06 – 'The Winged Avenger'

Despite not having written for the series since the first season, Richard Harris supplied the screenplay for the next episode into production. Titled 'The Winged Avenger', this arrived in the soundstage around the middle of December 1966. It appears that Harris had been asked to submit storyline ideas as, like Tony Williamson, he was a close associate of writer/producer Dennis Spooner, who in turn was a friend of Brian Clemens.

During the '60s, Harris was an enthusiast of American comic books like *Superman* and *Batman*, not to mention the *Batman* television series, which had premiered in the UK on ITV on Saturday 21 May 1966. 'The Winged Avenger' was in essence his homage to comic book superheroes; a mystery story in which ruthless businessmen are targeted for murder by an unknown cloaked attacker who can walk up the side of high-rise buildings. In this case though, the title character would be the villain of the piece – comic book artist Arnie Packer – rather than the hero. Clemens readily accepted the script after Harris performed some rewriting at his request.

The director initially assigned to this episode was Gordon Flemyng, who was responsible for some early sequences where the comic book character is not fully seen. However, he was then dismissed from the production, presumably for getting behind with the schedule. Brian Clemens has gone on record as saying, 'Flemyng wasn't a bad

---

[17] Until the building of the enormous Stage 6 at Elstree in 1979 to accommodate extensive sets for the movie *The Empire Strikes Back,* the original Stage 6 was created by simply partitioning Stage 1 down the middle.

director. He just wasn't an *Avengers* director.'

The young newcomer brought in to replace Flemyng was Peter Duffell. This was on the recommendation of producer Jack Greenwood, who had been drafted into the Telemen team in anticipation of him taking responsibility for some innovative working practices that were about to be introduced (see below). Greenwood had worked with Duffell several months previously on *Company of Fools*, one of a series of B-movies grouped under the umbrella title *The Scales of Justice*.

Location filming took place at two eight-storey apartment blocks known as High Sheldon on Sheldon Avenue in Highgate, London N6. These were used to establish the premises of Simon Roberts and Son, Publishers, where Roberts senior becomes the first murder victim. The crew travelled closer to home, returning to the High Canons estate near Well End, to execute some day-for-night shooting featuring an Emma Peel double in long shot, surreptitiously making her way from some woodland up to the home of author Sir Lexius Cray. The exterior of the gothic mansion Stanmore Hall, previously seen in 'From Venus with Love', was utilised again, becoming the residence of eccentric inventor Professor Poole, with actor Jack MacGowran on location in the grounds for a scene where Poole attempts to fly. Since the '60s, most of the extensive grounds around Stanmore Hall have been sold for building land, and although the property still has some surrounding lawns and woods, they are nowhere near the size they were when *The Avengers* was shot there.

Artist Frank Bellamy, who had made his name drawing the adventures of *Dan Dare: Pilot of the Future* in the *Eagle* comic and who was at the time the regular illustrator on the *Thunderbirds* strip in *TV Century 21*, was hired to provide several pieces of artwork for 'The Winged Avenger'. These were copied from 35mm frames, and toward the conclusion of events, some clever editing sees the picture on screen fade into the artwork and *vice-versa*. Bellamy also provided the artwork for the front of *The Winged Avenger* comic featured in the episode, which was actually an issue of a DC Comics comic book with a new cover attached. Besides providing artwork, Bellamy also designed both the Winged Avenger costume and the Winged Avenger Enterprises studio set. In order to concentrate on his contributions to the production, Bellamy took a temporary break from the *Thunderbirds* strip in *TV Century 21*; the edition published on Saturday 22 October saw him temporarily bow out, part-way through the story 'Solar Danger'. He returned several weeks later with a new *Thunderbirds* strip called 'The Big Freeze'.

Also seen in the episode are large scans taken of panels from a copy of the DC Comics comic book *Blackhawk* No. 223, dated August 1966, with newly-drawn giant Winged Avenger images added. However, the style of art indicates that these were not Bellamy's work.

Wearing a pair of anti-gravity books invented by Professor Poole, Emma has to defend herself from Arnie Packer, alias the Winged Avenger – or, as he puts it, 'Creator and creation fused into one, Mrs Peel.' This scene was filmed upside down on the stage floor, with the performers walking about unsteadily, to give the illusion that they were on the ceiling. Rigg wore a large, fashionable cap to hide the fact that her hair was not being affected by gravity. To reinforce the illusion, the collar of her Emmapeeler was stuck up at an odd angle, giving the impression of it pointing to the ground.

Sir Lexius's blackmailing manservant Tay-Ling is seen to read the *Daily Mail* at one point, as is Emma in a scene at Steed's apartment where she sees a report about potential victim Dumayn – who was named after Richard Harris's next door neighbour.

In a sequence where Steed's Bentley is seen *en route* to Professor Poole's abode, the offside front headlight is still defective, as in both 'From Venus with Love' and 'The Bird Who Knew Too Much'. On this occasion, however, the crew were clearly aware of this issue, and to compensate, the centrally-mounted spotlight at the front of the radiator grille was illuminated.

A large eagle was required to be on set for part of the filming. This would also have necessitated the presence of a trained handler for safety reasons, but guest actor Nigel Green, playing Sir Lexius, never flinched when the screenplay called for him to have the bird of prey on his arm.

Also filmed on one of the stages at Elstree were woodland exteriors featuring both Mrs Peel and the stalking Winged Avenger, with the actors in close-up. This episode gives the first glimpse of the new Steed apartment kitchen standing set, featuring a breakfast bar with a black-tiled top, a small wooden table with accompanying chairs and several framed prints on the wall.

The 'Mrs Peel, we're needed!' sequence features Emma indulging in her hobby of abstract painting, until she discovers the words 'Mrs Peel' in small red lettering on her canvas. Then, as if on cue, Steed suddenly appears from behind her easel, announcing, 'We're needed!'

Visiting Winged Avenger Enterprises, Steed finds Packer at work on the comic strip, with a model named Julian posing for him in the Winged Avenger costume. When a dispute arises about the dialogue, the strip's author Stanton rewrites the line to read simply 'Eee-urp!' Amused by this, Steed adopts it as a catchphrase for the remainder of the episode.

'The Winged Avenger' explicitly spoofs the American *Batman* series, especially in its end fight scene. As Emma fights Packer, in his Winged Avenger costume, Laurie Johnson's *Batman*-theme-inspired incidental music starts up. Steed arrives in the nick of time with Stanton, who has several large storyboards of the latest *The Winged Avenger* comic book with him. Grabbing a storyboard, Steed slams it into the Winged Avenger. In true *Batman* style, large animated lettering appears on the screen: POW!, SPLAT! and BAM!. Emma having kicked one of Packer's anti-gravity boots free from the ceiling, a final blow from a storyboard dislodges the other, and Packer falls though a window to his death two storeys below.

Having stepped in to complete 'The Winged Avenger', Duffell was expected to become one of the regular directors on the series. In the event, however, this did not occur. Interviewed in 2003, Duffell explained that someone high up on the series was not happy regarding Greenwood's appointment as production controller and even less happy about him using that position of authority to bring in his own people. Hence the door to *The Avengers* was closed. However, feeling guilty about the situation, Julian Wintle arranged for Duffell to join his old friend Sidney Cole at Pinewood Studios, where he was the producer on ITC's *Man in a Suitcase*. Duffell eventually directed half a dozen adventures of that series featuring ex-CIA agent McGill, and after that did not look back.

Richard Harris was grateful to have the opportunity to write for *The Avengers* again, so long after scripting the first season episodes 'Square Root of Evil' and 'Hunt the Man Down'. He was also delighted with Frank Bellamy's artwork for the episode. He visited Elstree only a couple of times during the production and did not get to interact with the leads, though he came away with the impression that Macnee was a true gentleman. He has since said that there was no writers' guide for *The Avengers*; all the dos and don'ts regarding both the series and the regular characters were in Brian Clemens' head.

5.07 – 'The Living Dead'

The first episode filmed in 1967 was 'The Living Dead', which started out as a storyline by Anthony Marriott and was developed into a shooting script by Brian Clemens to incorporate elements of his earlier episode 'The Town of No Return'. This was similar to the situation on 'The Bird Who Knew Too Much', where Clemens had developed a storyline by Alan Pattillo. However, besides freelancing as both a journalist and a scriptwriter, Marriott was also a Justice of the Peace, and hence had a better-than-average understanding of the law. Somewhere along the line he disputed the authorship of 'The Living Dead', apparently feeling that he should at least have had a 50% credit, and was so aggrieved by the situation that he began legal action against both Brian Clemens and ABC. The matter was not resolved in a satisfactory manner until 1969, *The Stage and Television Today* reporting in its Thursday 24 April edition that all sides now regretted the misunderstanding.

All exteriors for the episode, with the exception of the 'Mrs Peel, we're needed!' sequence, were created as sets on the soundstage. One of these was a cemetery set, complete with headless statue, last seen in 'From Venus with Love', reassembled with added scenery, background and haunted chapel. The responsibility for these designs and acquisitions from the scenery dock rested with Robert Jones, as Wilfred Shingleton had now departed the series. Shingleton would later return to television film series production in 1969 as the designer on ITC's *Strange Report*.

The 'Mrs Peel, we're needed!' sequence features Emma driving her Lotus Elan down a quiet country lane and coming to a set of traffic lights at red. When they change to amber, she notices that the amber light contains the lettering 'Mrs Peel'. Looking over her shoulder, she sees that Steed has pulled up behind her in his Bentley. Then, turning her attention back to the traffic lights, she sees that the bottom light is now illuminated, but instead of green it is turquoise and bears the lettering, 'We're Needed'. The end tag scene, in which Mrs Peel crawls around beneath the Bentley attempting to identify a mechanical problem, was shot at Elstree on one of the stages.

Acronyms abound in this episode, with two societies devoted to the study of paranormal activities: FOG (Friends of Ghosts) and SMOG (Scientific Measurement of Ghosts). After the sceptic Spencer of SMOG is apparently killed by a ghost, Steed and Emma retire to the Duke of Benedict pub, where in the background actor John Cater's character Olliphant plays 'The Death March' on the piano. The agents eventually discover an underground city beneath the local coal mine. This was represented in studio by a square, a street and three buildings, two of which were on a large matte painting designed to give a forced perspective. Establishing shots of the colliery were provided by stock footage. The scenes inside the mine were originally planned to be shot in virtual darkness, but director of photography Alan Hume suggested the introduction of mist onto the set to lighten things up.

A fight scene between Emma and the FOG member Mandy was shot in close-up without the assistance of stunt doubles, showing both women using attacking moves and concluding with Emma applying a sleeper hold to her opponent. However, Cyd Child stood in for Diana Rigg for the filming of a sequence in which Emma fights a guard in the cell where she has been imprisoned, lifting the man on her shoulders and throwing him onto the bunk. Unfortunately, as she turns around, Child's face is clearly visible on camera – a mistake that incurred the displeasure of production controller Jack Greenwood.

The wardrobe department dusted off some of the previous season's fashions for this episode, as Mandy wears Emma's black leather jacket from 'The Cybernauts', then later enters the Duke of Benedict in one of John Bates' Chemin fur coats, as sported by Emma in 'The Thirteenth Hole'. Mrs Peel herself wears her dark blue Emmapeeler with two thin yellow stripes down each arm, looking like an Adidas tracksuit minus the name. The firing squad featured at one point in the action wear black helmets and uniforms that had been created by Nathan's costumiers of London for the book-burning firemen in the film *Fahrenheit 451*.

Innovative working practices

'The Living Dead' marked the introduction of a new production system on *The Avengers*. With time of the essence in order to get the required number of episodes in the can by the deadline for transmission, the old approach of a single crew carrying out ten days' principal filming on each episode in turn was now abandoned. From this point on, Telemen would work on a rolling production pattern that involved many of the crew positions being doubled up, forming two units – A unit and B unit – that would work on alternate episodes.

Alan Hume and Ernest Steward became the directors of photography, after Wilkie Cooper had handled most of the earlier episodes this season. Ted Lewis and Ron Purdie became assistant directors, replacing Malcolm Johnson, who had held the position on the two Pinewood episodes, and Richard Dalton, who had worked on the first few Elstree ones. Tony White and James Bawden took over as camera operators from Frank Drake. Meanwhile, Frank Carter departed the position of art director and was replaced by Len Townsend and K McCallum Tait, sometimes credited as Kenneth Tait.

Continuity would be looked after by various people, including Mary Spain, Eve Wilson and Doreen Soan, although once the new system was established Gladys Goldsmith would gain this credit on more episodes than anyone else. Hairdressing was taken on by Hilda Fox and Jeanette Freeman, after Bill Griffiths had been responsible for this on the first half-dozen episodes. Bill (W T) Partleton was in charge of make-up at Pinewood, but at Elstree was superseded by Jim Hydes, who was then joined by Basil Newall.

Having been the wardrobe supervisor at Pinewood but initially superseded by Hilda Geerdts at Elstree, Jean Fairlie returned for 'The Living Dead' and would then work with both units. Simon Kaye and Ken Rawkins were the sound recordists, the former having already replaced Bill Rowe, who had worked on both of the Pinewood episodes. The sound editors were Jack T Knight and Rydal Love, who would work individually but would not always alternate between episodes and could be attached to either unit.

To assist in making the system work at maximum efficiency, Telemen also introduced seven day working (if necessary) and a small second unit to concentrate on pick-up shots and establishing shots on location. One main unit would be filming with Macnee and Rigg, while the other began preliminary shooting on another episode. Hence, with the A unit, the B unit and the second unit all in operation, three episodes could be in production simultaneously. This meant that the principal shooting on seven episodes could be now completed within three months, whereas under the traditional approach only six could be done within the same period.

Diana comic strip

Issue no. 199 of the girls' weekly comic *Diana*, issued on Saturday 10 December 1966, introduced a new comic strip based on *The Avengers*, promoted with a front cover publicity shot of Diana Rigg and a grey horse taken from the Dymchurch photoshoot. This stylised and impressive full colour strip would present eight multi-part stories until early June 1967, ending with no. 224. Principal artist was the Spaniard Emilio Fréjo Abregon, who was assisted on half of the strips by his fellow countryman González Alacreu.

5.08 – 'The Hidden Tiger'

The next episode to enter production was another Philip Levene script, 'The Hidden Tiger', presenting the scenario of a large jungle cat on the loose and responsible for a number of deaths in the British countryside.

Robert Jones intended to redesign the set of Emma's apartment, so the 'Mrs Peel, we're needed!' scene starts with Emma stripping wallpaper off the living room wall and coming across the words 'Mrs Peel –'. The camera then pans across to the opposite wall, where Steed is also removing wallpaper, revealing the remainder of the usual catchphrase, '– We're needed'. The closing tag scene has Emma and Steed messing about with pots of paint, obviously as a preliminary to redecorating.

Location scouts found three script requirements for this episode locally at North Mymms Park, five miles north-east of Elstree. Shots of North Mymms Mansion House were used to establish the fictional Furry Lodge, headquarters of PURRR (Philanthropic Union for Rescue, Relief and Recuperation of Cats); the nearby Old Vicarage off Tollgate Road represented the home of big game hunter Major Nesbitt; and a sequence involving Steed, the Bentley and various Mini Moke pick-ups making a large milk delivery was executed at the gates of North Mymms Park, again just off Tollgate Road.

The location used for the exterior of the first murder scene, Sir David Harper's large, red-brick stately home Chippenham Manor, was Aldenham Grange, which stands in its own grounds off Grange Lane, just outside the village of Letchmore Heath. However, the exterior of the nearby Experimental Husbandry Farm was constructed back at Elstree on one of the stages.

Additional material was filmed at Rabley Park Lodge off Packhorse Lane, near the village of Ridge, the gatehouse of which served as the exterior of the home of PURRR committee member Walter Bellamy. A mocked-up section of the doorway, including a heavily scratched door, was assembled in the studio.

Venturing into central London, the second unit shot exterior footage of the large block of flats at Boydell Court in St John's Wood, NW8, to provide the backdrop for a sequence where Steed rushes to the home of another PURRR committee member, Samuel Jones.

Sidney Hayers, who had directed four episodes in the previous season, returned to handle this one. Seeing how casually the two leads were now treating the material, he quickly intervened. In response to their objection that they usually performed their two-handed scenes in this manner, he told them that they were not putting any great effort into proceedings, but when he was in charge, they would have to. Macnee and Rigg were not used to directors laying down the law in this fashion but, having received what amounted to a verbal kick up the backside, they knuckled down to the job, giving more effort and gaining a great respect for Hayers in the process.

Together with casting director G B Walker, Hayers assembled a guest cast that included cat lover Gabrielle Drake as PURRR secretary Angora and Ronnie Barker as her boss, the eccentric Edwin Cheshire. During filming, Barker got on extremely well with both Rigg and Macnee.

Besides his usual Bentley, Steed also uses a Land Rover (OPC 104D) while attempting to track the big cat during the hours of darkness. Some of the woodland and shrubbery settings seen here were realised in the studio. The attacking lion footage that Major Nesbitt screens for Steed was taken from the 1958 film *Nor the Moon by Night* (aka *Elephant Gun*). At Furry Lodge, Emma runs along a corridor inhabited by various cats, and cannot resist cracking the one-liner 'Pussies Galore!' The episode has various memorable passages of specially-composed incidental music and also reuses some earlier cues, including the attack music from 'The Winged Avenger' and the undertaker music from 'The Gravediggers'. A powerful cue entitled 'Chase that Car' accompanies the climactic scene where Steed and Emma desperately flick every switch they can on the control panel to shut down the system that sends the cats into a vicious primeval state.

All 15 feline extras featured in the episode were provided by Dorset-based animal trainer John Holmes, who for the duration of filming lived with the cats in a caravan at Elstree. Holmes frequently supplied various types of animals for both film and television productions and was the published author of a number of dog training manuals.

Having previously been credited as assistant director, Richard Dalton now joined Laurie Greenwood as joint unit manager, and this post would henceforth be acknowledged in the closing credits.

5.09 – 'The Correct Way to Kill'

For the next episode, Brian Clemens came up with the idea of reworking his old Honor Blackman story 'The Charmers' into an Emma Peel adventure. The official line was that as the American audience had never seen the videotaped shows, this was an opportunity to acquaint them with some quality television they had missed. However, with transmissions already under way and time now at a premium, this was simply a much quicker way of coming up with a workable script than writing one from scratch. Under its new title 'The Correct Way to Kill', the episode began principal photography in January 1967 under the direction of Charles Crichton.

Having seen Anna Quayle give an over-the-top performance as a Russian in the stage play *Stop the World – I Want to Get Off*, Crichton cast her as the foreign agent Olga, whose mannerisms, catchphrases and jokes were simply variations on those of her character in the play. Also in the strong guest cast were Michael Gough, Philip Madoc, Peter Barkworth and Terence Alexander, who had all appeared in the series before. A number of stuntmen appeared uncredited: Romo Gorrara played another foreign agent, Stanislaus Arkadi; Peter Clay played yet another, Zoric; and Olga's karate sparring partners were Alf Joint, Peter Brace and Terry Plummer. Although it is obvious that the foreign agents are supposed to be Russian, in keeping with the series' usual practice they are never referred to as such, being described only as 'the opposition'.

The 'Mrs Peel, we're needed!' scene, where Emma discovers Steed's message in the form of a newspaper headline, was filmed on the backlot town, although according to the shooting script dated December 1966 this was not the original intention. The message was always going to be conveyed by a newspaper headline, but it was originally to have been pushed under Emma's apartment door one morning, and Emma was then to have opened the door to reveal a smiling Steed holding a recently-delivered bottle of milk.

The opening teaser is a night-time scene filmed on a cobblestone alleyway set that later reappears with daytime lighting, the background in the distance being provided by a large matte painting.

Location footage of a Citroen DS Pallas was shot on Woodchurch Road in the borough of Camden, London NW6, for a scene where the foreign agent Ivan and Mrs Peel arrive at the premises of H Merryweather, chiropodist – who fulfils the same role in this episode as the dentist in 'The Charmers'. While Emma has a consultation with Merryweather, Ivan remains in the waiting room, accidentally knocking a copy of *The Times* onto the floor. The newspaper is picked up and returned by Percy, one of the gentlemen assassins of SNOB (Sociability, Nobility, Omnipotence, Breeding Inc), the organisation behind the plot, who then holds Ivan at gunpoint.

Overall, 'The Correct Way to Kill' follows the basic storyline of 'The Charmers', but has sufficient differences not to be considered a straight remake. There are however some sections of almost identical dialogue – such as early on when the principal villain Nutski repeats virtually word for word a telephone conversation that his counterpart Keller had in 'The Charmers', regarding infiltration of the Horse Guards.

In a scene where Olga and Steed visit a wet weather shop, proprietor J Nathan Winters examines the agent's umbrella and accidentally exposes several inches of the sword hidden within. Upon seeing this, Steed quickly reclaims the umbrella.

Laurie Johnson's striking cue 'March of the Butlers' from the earlier episode 'What the Butler Saw' is reused here, this time as background music for the two gentleman assassins Percy and Algy.

Mrs Peel dons fencing gear for the climactic fight scene in the SNOB headquarters, with Rigg being doubled by Cyd Child in the majority of shots. At the conclusion of events at SNOB, Emma removes a large photograph of Steed from an easel there and replaces it with one of herself. Neither this nor the closing tag scene, in which she and Steed discuss his evening out with Olga, were included in the shooting script.

The Avengers Pack

On Thursday 5 January 1967 the public unveiling of Macnee's and Rigg's fashions for the upcoming colour season took place with a photoshoot at ABC's Teddington Studios, where Rigg was quoted as saying, 'Alun Hughes' clothes are really me.' Besides Macnee and Rigg, also in attendance were stunt man Ray Austin, fashion model Twiggy and several well-known sporting celebrities, namely Formula 1 racing driver Graham Hill, heavyweight boxer Billy Walker, Commonwealth Games swimming gold medallist Linda Ludgrove, national hunt jockey Josh Gifford and Olympic weightlifter George Manners. A news crew from Associated British Pathé were on hand to film a short piece, titled 'Rigg's New Rigs', which would be screened in cinemas throughout the UK.

As with John Bates' earlier Jean Varon Avengers Collection, the various designs created by Hughes would also be made available in the high street. However, preferring not to become involved in the manufacturing side, Hughes following Bates' lead in subcontracting that part of the process to other companies, who would produce the items for what would become known as The Avengers Pack. These companies included Selincourt Ltd, Charnos Ltd and Dent, Allcroft & Co Ltd, all of whom had also been involved with the Jean Varon Avengers Collection. Others were T B Jones Ltd for the Emmapeeler catsuits and stockings; Edward Mann Ltd for hats; Sirela Manufacturing Co Ltd for suede and leather goods; C W Thomas and Co of New Bond Street, London for dresses; L S Mayer Ltd for shoulder bags; Dannimac of Oxford Street, London for rainwear; and L Sheraton Ltd for coats and suits.[18]

Others involved in the new collection were Old England Watches, the British Bata Shoe Company Ltd, Richard Allan Scarves and Associated Tailors Ltd for Macnee, and even Panther Books, who had some spin-off paperback novels in the works (see below). There were four different wristwatches available, all with *The Avengers* lettering on their large dials and chunky thick plastic straps. These could be obtained from retailers for about £5 each.

Having been informed about the photoshoot, both the *Daily Mail* and *Daily Mirror* subsequently ran pieces emphasising the connection between the series and cutting edge fashion.

Panther Books

During January 1967, Panther Books published the first two of four paperback novels based on *The Avengers*, written by John Garforth – actually a pseudonym for Anthony Hussey. Titled *The Floating Game* and *The Laugh was on Lazarus*, these retailed at three shillings and six old pence. Both featured brightly-coloured photographic covers depicting Patrick Macnee as Steed and Diana Rigg as Emma Peel.

An American printing of *The Floating Game* with a different cover was issued by Berkley Medallion in April 1967 and reprinted in February 1969, with another cover depicting Linda Thorson as Mrs Peel's successor Tara King, who did not feature in the story. The novel was translated into French, German and Dutch for printing in those countries, and there was even a South American example published in Chile in 1968.

Berkley Medallion also published an American edition of *The Laugh was on Lazarus* in May 1967, and this was likewise reprinted with an inappropriate Tara King cover in 1969. Once again, French, German, Dutch and Chilean translations were produced.

Unfortunately Garforth had never watched an episode of *The Avengers* before writing these novels, and they were basically just straight thrillers with a little bizarre background. The style and subtleties of the series, the witty repartee between Steed and Mrs Peel, the eccentric characters and the general sense of humour were all missing. Decades later, Garforth acknowledged the shortcomings of the books on his blog, even offering to reimburse anyone who had recently bought any of them from a second-hand bookshop or car boot sale.

---

[18] See Appendix Seven for full details.

Season five begins transmissions

British transmissions of the second Diana Rigg season began on Monday 9 January 1967 at 8.00 pm when 'From Venus with Love' went out in the Southern region. Most of the other ITV regional companies followed suit over the next few days, also with 'From Venus with Love'. TWW's Welsh service Teledu Cymru were second off the blocks, beginning their showings on Wednesday 11 January at 8.00 pm, with Rediffusion getting under way on Friday 13 January, also at 8.00 pm, and line-feeding to the Anglia, Channel and Westward regions. ABC began airing the new episodes in both their Midlands and North regions at 9.10 pm on Saturday 14 January, feeding the transmission through to Tyne Tees, Scottish and TWW. As with the previous season, Border were the solitary company to schedule the series on Sundays, beginning on 15 January. The Grampian and Ulster regions did not transmit the season at all at this time: they held it back until the autumn schedules. Although the episodes had been made in colour for the American market, all these transmissions were in black and white only – colour broadcasting on ITV would not actually begin until November 1969, and then only in selected regions.

To coincide with the season's debut, the then current edition of *TV Times* – no. 585, dated Thursday 12 January – included the fashion article 'Dressed For Danger – That's The Avengers', presenting an interview with Alun Hughes. Meanwhile, the *TV World* edition for the Midlands region, issued on the same date, had a *The Avengers* cover publicising the series' return. The following week's *TV Times* – no. 586, dated Thursday 19 January – also boasted a *The Avengers* cover, although strangely the London and North editions of the magazine used two different, but very similar, colour images from the same photoshoot.

Over on BBC1, competition to *The Avengers'* Saturday screenings was being mounted in the form of the second season of *Adam Adamant Lives!*. This had begun a fortnight earlier, on Saturday 31 December 1966, and had the added advantage that it went out at 9.00 pm, ten minutes earlier than *The Avengers*, giving it a slight head start on capturing viewers. However, it still failed to make any noticeable dent in *The Avengers'* popularity, and this would be its final season.

Across the Atlantic, American television listings magazines were also gearing up for *The Avengers'* return. On Sunday 15 January the series was featured on the covers of both the *TV Magazine* supplement issued with the *Washington DC Sunday Star* and the *TV Roundup* magazine that came with the *Chicago Sunday American*. 'From Venus with Love' heralded the show's arrival in colour across the United States on the ABC network at 10.00 pm on Friday 20 January, in which slot it replaced the Second World War series *Twelve O'Clock High*. It would run until the third week of May.

In the UK, meanwhile, ABC Television struck gold almost immediately with the airing of a second episode, 'The Fear Merchants', on Saturday 21 January. This gained an overall viewing figure of 8 million[19], making it the third highest rated programme of the week, and ultimately the most popular colour Rigg episode of all.

5.10 – 'Never, Never Say Die'

In 'Never, Never Say Die', writer Philip Levene came up with a sequel of sorts to his

---

[19] In the two ABC regions and the others that took the line-feed.

monochrome episode 'The Cybernauts', taking things a step further by presenting a scenario concerning mechanical human duplicates. Director Robert Day and casting director G B Walker secured Macnee's old school friend Christopher Lee to guest star as the amusingly named Professor Frank N Stone, head of the Ministry of Technology's Neoteric Research Unit (NRU), a man who seems able to cheat death. At the time, Lee was virtually typecast in gothic horror roles, having made many films in that genre, including a number of outings as Count Dracula for Hammer Films.

'Never, Never Say Die' was the fourth episode filmed under the newly instigated rolling production system, and it involved a large amount of location work. The opening sequence where the motorist Whittle is seen driving along in his Morris Oxford Traveller was shot on the access road to the British Rail Study Centre at Watford, with the vehicle seen passing the main house. However, the incident moments later where Stone – or, as it later transpires, his duplicate – steps out in front of the car was filmed with it travelling down Silver Hill, heading away from the village of Shenley.

Establishing shots of the hospital to which the duplicate is taken following the accident, showing Whittle examining damage to the headlight of his car, were captured at the newer part of the Haberdashers' Aske's School on Aldenham Road, Elstree, a modern oblong building with a long white canopy over the entrance supported by four uprights. This structure would be demolished sometime during 1995/96.

Filming was also undertaken at the junction of Westfield Lane and Grubbs Lane in Welham Green for a sequence where the Bedford ambulance carrying the duplicate disappears down one road and then the Austin ambulance containing Steed, Emma, Whittle and the hospital's Dr Betty James arrives from another direction. This carefully-choreographed action appears to have been detailed in the shooting script; hence the crew travelled approximately seven miles from Borehamwood to film at this specific junction because of its unusual layout.

When the Bedford ambulance pulls up to give way to other traffic, the duplicate escapes from the rear of the vehicle – a sequence filmed at the junction of St Mary's Church Road and Tollgate Road in North Mymms. The area surrounding Tykes Water Lake in Aldenham Park, Elstree was used for a scene where the duplicate – who is susceptible to radio signals – almost attacks an elderly man, played by Arnold Ridley, who is using a remote control for a model boat. Also filmed in the same vicinity was a scene where the duplicate comes across a man picnicking and listening to his portable transistor radio on some grass beside his parked Triumph TR5 convertible, and also one where he sets upon two soldiers using a two-way radio and appears totally unaffected when shot by a full magazine of bullets from a Sterling submachine gun.

The muddy track leading from Watling Street down to Tykes Water Lake is seen in a sequence where Emma drives her Lotus Elan to Aerial Cottage, and then again in one where Stone's colleague Dr Penrose and his white-smocked assistants search the woods for the Professor. Driving an olive green Land Rover (VX 897), Steed also takes part in the search and discovers Stone's cottage. However, the exteriors and interiors of both cottages were realised as studio sets.

When Steed arrives at Stone's cottage, the blue sky seen through the open outer door was achieved with a large matte painting. The interior set has twin wall-mounted light fittings that appear somewhere in virtually every colour Rigg episode. Macnee's stunt double, Rocky Taylor, took many of the falls in a sequence where Steed is thrown about this set by the duplicate. Saved by the arrival of Penrose and his various assistants, the agent manages to hide in a back room until the duplicate is taken away in the ambulance. Then, as the action shifts back onto location, he returns to his Land Rover – the camera being undercranked to speed up his run through the woods – and follows them back up the track running from Tykes Water toward Watling Street. However, the continuation of this sequence was shot further north, with both vehicles exiting a wooded area via the driveway to Aldenham Wood Lodge on the junction with Butterfly Lane. Steed then follows Penrose's group back to their base at the NRU, represented by the gateway to the Haberdashers' Aske's School.

The 'Mrs Peel, we're needed!' scene has Emma watching 'The Cybernauts' on television in her apartment and Steed breaking into the transmission to doff his bowler and deliver his usual one-liner. The refurbishment of the apartment, started in 'The Hidden Tiger', is now complete. The living room features deep-buttoned leather furniture, including a built-in sofa, different curtains and an assortment of ornaments and pictures hung on the lime green walls. The concluding tag scene involves Steed and Emma both watching television at the apartment when a party political broadcast begins. Emma asks, 'Can you imagine plastic politicians?', to which Steed replies, 'Who'd ever notice the difference!'

Pierre Cardin had the idea of making Steed's bowler hat and umbrella complement his suit by having them all in the same colour – in this episode, grey – hence creating a co-ordinated look. For the sequences filmed at her apartment, Emma wears red and purple silk pyjamas designed by Alun Hughes.

A control panel with red, amber and blue flashing lights on the NRU set had served a similar function on the PURRR base set in 'The Hidden Tiger'.

The shooting script contains quite a number of replacement pages dated Monday 23 January 1967 – the day the episode began principal filming – including three major sequences that do not appear in the finished episode, having probably been dropped for timing reasons. The original Scenes 31 through to 39, leading up to the first commercial break, were set on a military firing range where an army captain supervises a sergeant testing a heavy machine gun. Breaking through the barbed wire perimeter fence and stalking across the range, the Stone duplicate is struck by a hail of bullets and goes down. The captain yells 'Cease fire' and then leaps into a Land Rover with the sergeant. Arriving at the place where they last saw the duplicate, both men are surprised to find no-one present, and even more so to spot him in the distance striding away into the forest. Shocked, the captain and the sergeant retire to their local pub for a strong drink and begin relating their story to the landlord. Also present are Steed and Mrs Peel, who on overhearing the story engage the men in conversation regarding Stone's whereabouts and then depart in separate Land Rovers to try to find him. They split up in their search, taking different tracks, and unlike in the episode itself it is Emma rather than Steed who locates the Professor's cottage and gets herself thrown around by the duplicate. After being saved by the arrival of Penrose and his assistants with a strong net, Emma finds a clue regarding radio ham George Eccles, and the screenplay then returns more or less to what was actually filmed, beginning with Scene 49.

Another scripted segment that does not appear in the actual episode involves Stone surviving a 100,000 volt electrical shock, simply shrugging it off with no ill effects and continuing on his way.

The episode's conclusion also underwent some rewriting. As scripted, Dr James was not to have featured when Steed and Emma have their final confrontation with the duplicates at the NRU, whereas she does in the actual episode.

Between 2.00 pm and 6.00 pm on Tuesday 21 February 1967 – a week after principal photography was completed – Laurie Johnson convened a recording session at Elstree for his group of musicians to lay down incidental tracks for the episode. His powerful marching Cybernauts music would also be given another airing on the soundtrack, accompanying the sequence where Stone goes striding about Avengerland on the rampage, looking for and then destroying sources of radio signals.

Shifting schedules

The fifth season would undergo the most haphazard scheduling since the first across the ITV regions. The first changes came as early as the beginning of February 1967. Having decided to abandon ABC's line-feed, Tyne Tees rescheduled the series into a Wednesday evening slot at 8.00 pm, starting with 'The See-Through Man' on 1 February.

Having abandoned their Monday night screenings, Southern Television rescheduled the series to Wednesday at 8.00 pm, beginning with 'The Bird Who Knew Too Much' on 8 February. Two days later, TWW gave up on their Wednesday showings and joined in with Rediffusion's Friday evening ones.

5.11 – 'Epic'

By the time the B unit finished principal photography on 'Never, Never Say Die' on Tuesday 14 February 1967, filming by the A unit was already under way on the next adventure, 'Epic', having begun on Thursday 2 February.

This Brian Clemens story gave Patrick Macnee a reduced role, leaving the action to be carried mainly by Diana Rigg. It was intended to save on budget, with few location scenes, a small supporting cast and no specially-built sets. Most of the filming was done on the stages and studio lot at Elstree; and in fact this episode more than any other gives a good visual record of both the interior and exterior of ABPC's studio facilities in the '60s, as Clemens' script spoofs the film industry.

Director James Hill, who had a reputation for getting along extremely well with both Rigg and Macnee, cast Peter Wyngarde as faded matinee idol Stewart Kirby, having used him in the controversial 'A Touch of Brimstone' 14 months previously. In 'Epic', the versatile Wyngarde gives a particularly impressive performance, not only as Kirby but also as the various *alter egos* he adopts: a vicar on a bicycle, a cabbie, a priest, an undertaker, Alexander the Great, a Wild West gunfighter, a First World War German soldier, a native American, a '30s gangster, an American civil war Confederate soldier named Edgar, and a horror movie Count.

The graphics used for the episode title lettering make it appear to have been constructed from stone blocks, like a monument in a genuine epic. The 'Mrs Peel, we're needed!' scene has a twist this time: Steed arrives at Emma's home and announces, 'Mrs Peel ...', but before he can finish she replies, 'Sorry Steed, I'm needed elsewhere'.

The Lotus Elan was filmed coming down Elstree Hill North in Elstree before turning left into the fictional Fitzroy Lane and passing Elstree Hill Lodge onto the track that leads to Tykes Water Lake. Both Macnee and Rigg went on location with the Lotus for a sequence where they see Kirby in his vicar-on-a-bicycle disguise.

Having been tricked into using Kirby's Austin cab, Mrs Peel is driven in the vehicle east along Shenley Road, Borehamwood, passing the front of Elstree Studios on the right-hand side before turning into Theobald Street. The journey continues past a swampy area of land on London Road, heading north toward the village of Shenley and then, back in Borehamwood, along Cowley Hill, passing Hertswood Lower School and turning into Gateshead Road. The daily progress report on filming for Tuesday 21 February indicates that footage was also shot within the cab, somewhere on the Aldenham Estate, though this must have been surplus to requirements, as it does not appear in the episode.

The cab then arrives at the locked gateway to the fictional Schnerk Studios – actually a section of internal road situated between the two large outdoor tanks on the Elstree backlot, with the block containing the scenery docks visible in the background. After a scene where Kirby makes a telephone call, the cab is next driven past the large triangle-shaped structure that served as a backdrop for the smaller tank and the scaffolding that supported part of the backlot town standing sets. Along the way the cab also passes a voodoo statue prop that had appeared in *The Saint* episode 'Sibao', plus a wooden sentry box that had featured in *The Champions* escapade 'The Search'.

Turning around the corner of the scenery dock block, which also housed other departments, Kirby proceeds to drive his vehicle past an array of discarded items, some planks of wood and the exterior of Stage 5, before arriving at and entering Stage 4. With the cab now inside the soundstage, the large red light by the outer door begins flashing, illuminating the warning sign 'No entry while red light is on', which indicated when filming was in progress.

Recovering from the effects of a sleeping gas, Mrs Peel initially thinks she is back home in her apartment, but upon opening the bedroom door discovers various film cameras. However, when she leaves the apartment there is a lapse in continuity, as the camera pans around and shows that the apartment set has no fourth wall, so logically Emma should have seen that she was in a film studio before opening the door and reacting to what she found beyond.

Finding the exterior standing set to her home nearby, Emma follows Kirby when he drives past in his Austin cab, and comes across a black Rolls Royce limousine, a prop church lynch gate, a bride's veil and chiming wedding bells.

When a wind machine starts blowing confetti everywhere, the whole scene begins taking on a surreal feel, and is shot partly in slow-motion. Then, after Emma is pushed down a scenery hill by Wyngarde disguised as a priest, the tone changes again. The tolling of the bells becomes a death knell; the Rolls Royce becomes a hearse, behind which is the large matte painting used previously outside the door of Stone's cottage in 'Never, Never Say Die'; every headstone on a cemetery set is seen to be carved with 'RIP Emma Peel'; and the confetti becomes dead leaves. Exploring the studio, Emma discovers a dead actor whom Kirby shot earlier, seated in a director's chair with the name 'John Steed' on the back, placed on the cobbled alleyway set previously seen in 'The Correct Way to Kill'.

Part-way down the left hand side of the alleyway is a painting with a white background, which featured previously in 'From Venus with Love' and would reappear later in 'Wish You Were Here' and in the *Randall and Hopkirk (Deceased)* episode 'When Did You Start to Stop Seeing Things'. Emma then comes across Kirby's fellow faded film star Damita Syn, played by Isa Miranda, sat casually knitting upon an ornate throne with matching cherubs behind her. The throne and cherubs had also appeared in *The Avengers* before, as part of Lovejoy's office at Togetherness in the monochrome episode 'The Master Minds'.

After being knocked out by Syn, Emma recovers in a plush bed, though now with a gun belt strapped to her waist containing two Colt Peacemaker six-shot revolvers. Hearing some noise, she departs to find herself in a Wild West saloon. At the conclusion of the saloon scene, the camera pans to a propped up caption board that reads, 'Meanwhile … back at the ranch'. The picture then cuts to Steed in Emma's (real) apartment.

Investigating further, Mrs Peel walks past a modernist painting that the character Lord Mansford was seen appreciating shortly before his death in 'From Venus with Love'. This painting also appeared in *The Saint* episodes 'The Power Artist' and 'A Portrait of Brenda'.

When the large main door of the soundstage opens unexpectedly, Emma goes outside, only to be confronted by Kirby dressed as a First World War German soldier manning a heavy machine gun behind a wall of sandbags. This scene was filmed between Stage 4 and a white-bricked building nearby. Forced to run for her life under a barrage of bullets, Mrs Peel passes through an outdoor prop store, with Stage 5 providing the backdrop. Trapped with armed enemies approaching from both sides, she is forced to escape through a gap between portions of old sets and large Grecian urns toward the previously-seen scenery dock building.

Entering the backlot town, Mrs Peel is then attacked by Native Americans, accompanied on the soundtrack by some war dance music from Laurie Johnson. She fights with Kirby and defeats him, his final fall being done onto a padded mat resembling cobblestones.

After losing the fight, Kirby suffers the wrath of director Z Z von Schnerk, a character based by Clemens on the famous Austrian actor/director Erich von Stroheim. Von Schnerk, played by Kenneth J Warren, informs Kirby, 'Pink pages. This will mean pink pages. I will have to rewrite the script' – a reference to the common studio practice, as used on *The Avengers* itself, of using pink paper for rewrites added into a script.

Throughout this sequence, portions of the backlot town seen occasionally in other episodes of *The Avengers* and more frequently in various ITC shows produced at Elstree are clearly visible in the background, complete with supporting scaffolding. These include a building on a cobbled ramp, the hoarding of which reads 'The Salmon Fisher' – the name under which it was used as a pub in *The Baron* episode 'The Man Outside', filmed during September/October 1966.

Discovering an electrified perimeter fence, Mrs Peel explores further, arriving on the other side of the backdrop to the smaller outdoor tank, beside which there is a large cat's head prop seen previously in *The Baron* episode 'The Maze'. On the arrival of a policeman – who turns out to be actually only a retired film extra – played by David Lodge, more scaffolding can be seen holding up the backlot town, and the wall of the scene dock is visible once again. As Emma begins telling the policeman her story, directly behind them is a wooden statue seen previously in 'A Touch of Brimstone'. When they head toward the soundstage where Emma found the body, the top of the studio maintenance building is visible above a black shed structure that contained workshop C along with plasterers' shops C and D.

Later, when the policeman extra is sat on the floor, behind him can be seen the undamaged Simon Roberts and Son name plaque from 'The Winged Avenger'. Finally, Emma is captured and bound within the studio, destined to become the major element of the deranged von Schnerk's blockbuster *The Destruction of Mrs Emma Peel*. A shot where the lettering 'A Z Z von Schnerk Production' appears around Emma's head and she growls, imitating the MGM lion logo, pushes the series well beyond the bounds of believability and is probably the most tongue-in-cheek it would ever get – a million miles away from its origins in 'Hot Snow'.

Arriving at Schnerk Studios to the accompaniment of a Laurie Johnson Scottish music cue heard previously in 'Castle De'ath', Steed manoeuvres a mobile ladder stand platform – used at the studios for painting and dressing high sets – so that he can simply step over the electrified fence and walk down a sweeping staircase set element discarded on the backlot.

Surveying the finale of *The Destruction of Mrs Emma Peel*, von Schnerk lines up the shot by looking through the eyepiece of a Mitchell BNC 35mm film camera.

The oblong doorbell seen beside Mrs Peel's outer door in 'The Fear Merchants' has now been replaced with an ornamental oval-shaped one, complete with her name across the centre. Her apartment standing set is shown to be just that when in the concluding tag scene she proceeds to knock part of it down before departing with Steed.

Despite already playing 11 of Kirby's characters in the episode, Wyngarde suggested the addition of both Bluebeard from the classic French fairy tale, performed in the style of American actor George Sanders, and Cyrano de Bergerac, played for laughs as a caricature, complete with exaggerated long nose. He wanted de Bergerac to speak mainly in French with English subtitles, and on just one occasion in English with French subtitles. However, these ideas were ultimately unused. When discussing one of the proposed de Bergerac sequences years later, on the commentary track for 'Epic' on *The Avengers: The Complete Series 5* DVD box set, Wyngarde described something virtually identical to a scene actually included in the episode involving Edgar the Confederate soldier and his mother. This suggests that this part of the screenplay could have been rewritten to substitute Edgar for de Bergerac.

Wyngarde's performance in Kirby's guise of a prohibition gangster, holding a Thompson machine gun and flipping a coin with one hand, was inspired by actor George Raft's performance in the classic 1932 gangster film *Scarface*. Raft, who was reputed to have had genuine Mafia connections, had performed a cameo the previous summer in Charles K Feldman's Bond spoof *Casino Royale*, playing himself stood at a bar during the madcap finale, still flipping his trademark coin.

Performing so many different character parts in the episode meant that Wyngarde had to undergo hours in the make-up chair under the supervision of Basil Newall, with whom he had worked previously on the horror film *Night of the Eagle*. The First World War German soldier was the most technically challenging make-up to achieve, with various facial scars, a false nose and a monocle that refused to stay put until glued into place. The look of the Count was based on modern film interpretations of Dracula, with Wyngarde copying the mannerisms and voice from an Austrian actor named Anton Walbrook.

Wyngarde was full of praise for director James Hill, whom he considered to epitomise the Ealing style of directing. He also greatly approved of the casting of faded Italian film actress Isa Miranda as faded film starlet Damita Syn. Unfortunately during a take on Friday 24 February, the second of two days when the unit filmed on what was described in the daily production and progress reports as the 'Caligari' set on Stage 3 – presumably named after the 1920 silent horror film *The Cabinet of Dr Caligari* – Miranda was accidentally struck with a chair and sustained a cut to her forehead. This might explain why her hairstyle changes several times during the course of the episode, sometimes including a fringe – presumably to hide the injury.

Brian Clemens still owns the clapperboard used in the episode for *The Destruction of Mrs Emma Peel*, although for a time it was part of the decorations in the office he shared with Albert Fennell at Elstree in the early '70s, after *The Avengers* had ceased production.

Publicity and promotion

Alun Hughes' off-the-peg collection, The Avengers Pack, became available throughout the country on Saturday 4 February 1967, receiving extensive publicity in that day's edition of the *Daily Mail*, which devoted three pages to it. Three days later, the *Daily Mail*-sponsored Ideal Home Exhibition began at Olympia, Hammersmith Road, London W14, where the Electricity Council showcased a replica of the fitted kitchen that Diana Rigg was having installed into her new home at Swiss Cottage. Rigg was in attendance promoting the event, along with fashion model Twiggy and comedy actor Frankie Howerd.

The Champions

The Avengers' success had not gone unnoticed by Lew Grade, who sanctioned the production of a new rival in the form of *The Champions*. This went before the cameras at ABPC's Elstree Studios on an adjacent soundstage to *The Avengers* on Wednesday 8 February 1967. Eschewing the solitary hero format used in *Danger Man*, *The Saint* and *The Baron*, *The Champions* was a multi-lead show from the imagination of Brian Clemens' friend and fellow scriptwriter Dennis Spooner, together with producer Monty Berman. It revolved around the adventures of a trio of agents from the international agency Nemesis. The pilot episode, 'The Beginning', saw the lead characters Craig Stirling, played by Stuart Damon, Sharron Macready, played by Alexandra Bastedo, and Richard Barrett, played by William Gaunt, being rescued from a plane crash in the Himalayas by robed members of a long-forgotten civilisation who heal their injuries and endow them with fantastic powers that will assist them greatly during their future Nemesis missions. This larger-than-life scenario resulted in larger-than-life screenplays from writers including Tony Williamson, Brian Clemens and others who would later contribute to *The Avengers*, such as Terry Nation and Donald James.

5.12 – 'The Superlative Seven'

By Monday 27 February 1967 'Epic' was ready for editing and the next episode, 'The Superlative Seven', was before the cameras, having begun filming over a week earlier. This was another episode adapted by Brian Clemens from one of his earlier Honor Blackman ones – in this case, 'Dressed to Kill'. With new elements grafted onto that original plot, 'The Superlative Seven' involves seven experts in fighting methods or particular weapons being invited to a fancy dress party aboard a plane and thereby being enticed to a remote island, where they are informed that one of them is an assassin who will kill all the others. This whodunit scenario with a difference owes more than a nod of respect to the Agatha Christie novel and film *Ten Little Indians*.

Apart from some material shot over two days at Luton Airport in Bedfordshire, there is no major exterior filming in this episode; and, in a reversal of the situation in 'Epic', it is Steed who carries the storyline, with Emma being largely absent.

Sidney Hayers was in the director's chair, bringing together a dream cast that included Donald Sutherland, Charlotte Rampling, Brian Blessed, Hugh Manning and John Hollis. The series' supporting performers were not required to audition or do screen tests for their roles; there were chosen by the director in conjunction with casting director G B Walker, who between them knew what range they had. Clemens has gone on record as saying that the series always got the actors and actresses it wanted, as by this point it had become a major success and everybody wanted to be a part of it.

Some of the tongue-in-cheek silliness exhibited in 'Epic' is also evident in this episode's 'Mrs Peel, we're needed!' sequence. This opens with Steed on a shrubbery set in the studio firing a shotgun at pigeons on stock footage. Thinking he has downed one of them, he discovers instead a yellow plastic duck with his name printed on it. Then Emma appears, parting some bushes and making a quacking sound, and adds 'You're needed'.

The Luton location footage features a twin-prop Handley-Page Herald aircraft on the ground. However, the various pieces of stock footage used to depict supposedly the same aircraft in flight appear to have been obtained from more than one source; some of them show another Handley-Page Herald, sporting a different paint scheme, while others show a twin-engine jet airliner.

Besides Steed, who dresses as a 19th Century military redcoat, the other guests at the fancy dress party are: firearms expert Mrs Hana Wild (played by Rampling) as a cowgirl; experienced guerrilla and self-defence expert Mark Dayton (Blessed) as a medieval hangman; top notch big game hunter Jason Wade (James Maxwell) as a two-faced pirate; expert swordsman Max Hardy (Manning) as a First World War German officer; reputedly the world's strongest man, Freddy Richards (Leon Greene), as a circus strongman; and the best British bullfighter, Joe Smith (Gary Hope), simply wearing his colourful working clothes.

Richards' exclamation 'Kitchener's Valet?' upon seeing Steed's outfit was a reference to the fashionable retail outlet I Was Lord Kitchener's Valet, originally based at 293 Portobello Road, Notting Hill, London W10, which promoted the brightly-coloured military uniforms of the past as fashionable items, reputedly influencing Paul McCartney with regard to the cover of the Beatles' *Sergeant Pepper's Lonely Hearts Club Band* album.[20]

This was one of the episodes filmed mainly by the B unit. Shooting began with the first day of location work at Luton airport, which took place on Sunday 19 February, with Macnee, guest actress Margaret Neale and the Lotus present. On Tuesday 21 and Wednesday 22 February the crew were back at Elstree, where filming took place on sets of a corridor and a training room on Stage 5, with Sutherland, Hollis, stuntman Terry Plummer, the uncredited Cliff Diggins and various extras on call. Then on Thursday 23 February came the second day's work at Luton Airport. This was a long day: the actors were called at 7.00 am and filming ran from the morning through until just after 6.00 pm. The unit took 12 vehicles on location: four unit cars, a hire car for Macnee, a motor coach, a camera car, a sound car, an electrical van, a prop/construction van, a

---

[20] Designed by pop culture artist Peter Blake, the famous cover artwork for this album shows all four Beatles dressed in extremely colourful military outfits, against a background of celebrities and famous figures from history.

shrubbery van and a vehicle – a Land Rover was usually used – to carry the 600 amp generator to power all their equipment. Macnee, Rampling, Maxwell, Blessed, Manning, Hope and Greene were all present. However, the only shots from this day's filming actually to be used in the episode are of Blessed arriving at the plane and of Macnee and Rampling looking out through the windows of the plane prior to it supposedly taking off.

The following day, while the B unit resumed filming on Stages 4 and 5 at Elstree, the second unit travelled to the British European Airways (now British Airways) Flight Simulation Unit at Southall Lane in Heston. There they worked from 5.30 am to midday shooting the automated operation of the cabin controls of a de Havilland Comet airliner. Two days later they returned to take some insert shots of the control panel.

The aircraft passenger interiors were now starting to be filmed on Stage 4 at Elstree, and the following days would be devoted to scenes set inside a dilapidated old house that the characters find on the island, and outside it among the shrubbery.

A scene of Joe Smith being killed by a pitchfork thrown from a runaway cart was filmed on Friday 10 March on a piece of suitable sloping ground on the backlot, mixed in with studio footage. The same day, an accident occurred on Stage 4 when Rocky Taylor sustained a gashed wrist from a knife while rehearsing a fight scene in which he was to double for Macnee. This injury warranted a visit to hospital for Taylor, who received a dozen stitches. A replacement double was called in to film the scene.

Principal filming on the episode was completed on Monday 13 March.

An earlier draft of the screenplay involved the villain Jessel, played by Sutherland, being backed up by gunfire from Mrs Wild and handcuffed by Steed. In the episode as filmed, however, the agent knocks Jessel out from behind using a heavy candelabra.

5.13 – 'A Funny Thing Happened on the Way to the Station'

Filming on the next episode, 'A Funny Thing Happened on the Way to the Station', got under way on Monday 27 February 1967, with the A unit being used and John Krish returning to direct.

This story started life as an 11-page outline titled 'Overkill', dated Monday 9 January 1967, submitted to the production office by Roger Marshall. After discussing the outline with Clemens, Marshall then wrote a shooting script, also titled 'Overkill', dated Friday 24 February. However, Clemens thought this lacked that certain weird quality required for *The Avengers*, so he rewrote sections of it, changing the title to one inspired by the Broadway musical and feature film *A Funny Thing Happened on the Way to the Forum*. Some of the rewrites were dated Monday 6 March and others Tuesday 14 March, indicating that they were actually being done after filming on the episode had already begun.

Having already had scripts rewritten for the previous season, Marshall did not really want to contribute to *The Avengers* anymore, but was under contract to provide two more screenplays, of which 'Overkill' was one. Once again he was far from happy with the rewritten and retitled version, despite it still being credited solely to him, and this time he demanded that his name be removed from the episode. Clemens substituted the pseudonym Brian Sheriff – combining his own first name with another word for marshal.

The basic plot of the finished episode involves Steed and Mrs Peel following clues to locate the killers of a fellow agent, Lucas, and in the process discovering a plan to explode a bomb on a train carrying the Prime Minister. The teaser sequence, in which Lucas, played by Michael Nightingale, flees from a couple of armed men, was filmed on location at railway sidings close to Stonebridge Park railway station, off the North Circular Road, London NW10. A shot involving Nightingale climbing on board a stationary railway carriage caused problems, as the actor found a sharp edge somewhere and cut one of his hands, though the injury was not severe enough to prevent him from working. These scenes were filmed on Monday 27 and Tuesday 28 February, with additional footage of moving trains being captured on the afternoon of the second day at Luton in Bedfordshire.

The second unit filmed at Watford Junction railway station on Monday 6 March. The next day they took pick-up shots at British Rail sidings at Stonebridge Park, and then proceeded to the North Mymms area in Hertfordshire to capture establishing footage. Then on Thursday 9 March they returned to the Watford area for additional filming that included material of the railway tunnel at Gypsy Lane, Hunton Bridge, Kings Langley in Hertfordshire.

All the Elstree-filmed interiors for this episode were done on Stage 2, except for those in Emma's apartment, on Stage 3, and Steed's apartment, on Stage 4. This episode's 'Mrs Peel, we're needed!' scene has Emma entering the living room of her apartment from the bedroom, finding a toy clockwork train going around in circles on her coffee table, then taking from one of the trucks a card with the words 'Mrs Peel' printed on it. Enter Steed into the shot to say simply, 'We're needed.'

The set of the fictional Norborough Junction station was extensively dirtied down and reused for the scenes at the disused Chase Halt station.

A sequence where an assassin in the guise of a bridegroom attacks the railway signal box has him using the Thompson machine gun last seen with Stewart Kirby in 'Epic'. Further signal box scenes featuring Diana Rigg and guest actors John Laurie – playing train-spotter Crewe – and Dyson Lovell – playing Special Branch agent George Warren – were shot on Wednesday 1 March.

All the scenes in the office of Admiral Cartney, the new head of security for VIP travel, were filmed over the next two days. This cabin-like set featuring a galleon-style window frame had been seen previously as part of Vice Admiral Willows' home in 'What the Butler Saw'.

One of Clemens' unwritten rules was broken when an establishing shot of a railway carriage featured two uniformed police constables, obviously assisting in the security inspection of the Prime Minister's transportation.

For this episode Steed has a miniature tape recorder concealed in the handle of his umbrella, and he and Mrs Peel are seen to travel first class when they take the train to investigate Lucas's death. During their journey, Mrs Peel attempts to look inconspicuous by reading the fictional broadsheet newspaper the *Daily Clarion*, while Steed prefers the genuine fishing book *Cheaper Tackle* by Dr Robert Bruce, first published in 1960 by A and C Black.

Principal shooting finished on Wednesday 22 March, two days later than originally scheduled – an overrun caused partly by bad weather experienced on the first day at the sidings near Stonebridge Park.

Laurie Johnson's incidental music this time incorporates bursts of some cues previously heard in 'Escape in Time', including the urgent 'Chase That Car'.

The finished episode generally sticks quite closely to the Marshall-credited – but Clemens-rewritten – shooting script. However, a few further changes were still made to the dialogue here and there – for instance, the line 'Kill the woman', spoken by the ticket collector in the actual episode, was scripted to be delivered by the groom – and toward the conclusion of events some even more notable differences emerge. As scripted, a scene where the groom instructs Mrs Peel to open a carriage door and throw herself from the speeding train has the groom wielding a teapot gun – an interesting concept of a firearm concealed within an innocent, everyday object – whereas in the actual episode he uses a visually more effective automatic pistol. The script then has Emma struggling with the groom and managing to push him from the train, whereas in the filmed version the groom almost drags Emma with him until Crewe intervenes, hauling her back to safety.

In the subsequent scene where Emma fights with both an attendant, played by stunt performer Peter J Elliott, and an uncredited blonde woman referred to in the script as Francis – the male spelling of the name – the episode as filmed has them use cutlery to attack her, whereas in the script they use a gun, which goes off during the fight, alerting the ticket collector in the next carriage, where Steed is held prisoner. In the script, Steed is handcuffed to a kitchen chair – rather than to an overhead steam pipe as in the episode – and as the shot rings out he attacks the ticket collector's assistant George – Georgie in the episode, played by an uncredited extra – knocking him out. Then, as the attendant attacks Steed, the ticket collector produces a gun, only to have it kicked from his hand by Emma as she storms the inner sanctum – whereas in the episode, Steed breaks the steam pipe and the villains are defeated in the ensuing mêlée.

Marshall's original 'Overkill' outline dated Monday 9 January describes the villains as a fascist trouble-making unit, and the 'Mrs Peel, we're needed!' scene is listed as 'Mrs Peel, we're wanted'. Act one is reasonably similar to how it ended up in the finished episode, but act two is very different. Steed and Mrs Peel discover the body of agent Lucas – not named at this point – in his apartment and not at Chase Halt. Following a clue, Emma meets the Memory-Expanding Laboratory's Professor Pierson – a character absent from the finished episode – who proves to have an incredibly bad memory and is explicitly included for comedy effect. Steed and Emma then encounter Crewe – although the outline refers to him only as a 'train enthusiast' – at a deserted railway station.

The plot element of Admiral Cartney's secretary Salt passing on military secrets from the Admiralty is already present at this point, but the character of the Admiral has yet to be fleshed out, and – unlike in the actual episode – he is described as a one-eyed seafaring officer with delusions of being Nelson. As in the actual episode, Salt has a stack of used railway tickets with the O punched through, but Steed and Emma discover these not in his desk at Admiral Cartney's office but in his apartment. The outline has Steed board the train with his pet Great Dane, reminding viewers of the various dogs he owned in the videotaped episodes, although the animal is then stored away in the guard's van and takes no further part in the proceedings. The outline also includes the teapot gun device, indicating that it was Marshall's idea. The plotline element of Steed being taken prisoner and Mrs Peel discovering his umbrella and then effecting a rescue did not feature in the outline; this was one of Clemens' later additions.

Continued success

Averaging 8 million viewers, *The Avengers* tied with *Coronation Street* as the fourth most popular television programme in the UK for February 1967. Amongst television film series, though, it was the number one. However, this still did not stop it suffering further occasional scheduling changes. On Friday 3 March, Teledu Cymru pre-empted their transmission of 'The Hidden Tiger' for no apparent reason with an episode of Rediffusion's spy show *The Rat Catchers*.

5.14 – 'Something Nasty in the Nursery'

The next episode on the schedule was Philip Levene's 'Something Nasty in the Nursery', involving high-ranking officials being drugged with hallucinogens that regress them back to their childhood, causing them to reveal top secret information to their nanny.

Under the direction of James Hill, the B unit began principal filming for the episode on Wednesday 8 March 1967 – a fortnight before the A unit finished work on 'A Funny Thing Happened on the Way to the Station'. The first day's work was on location at Starveacres, off Watford Road in Radlett, as previously featured in 'Small Game for Big Hunters' and 'Escape in Time'. This time the house was used for exterior shots of the residence of Lord William Beaumont. Guest actors Patrick Newell and Paul Hardwick, playing Sir George Collins and Viscount Sir Frederick Webster respectively, were required on location for a scene where Steed and Emma arrive at the house, along with a hired Jaguar and Rolls Royce plus Emma's Lotus. Later in the day the unit moved to the hamlet of Arkley near Borehamwood, where Dennis Chinnery, playing the MoD agent Dodson, was involved in filming exteriors at a house on the junction of Rowley Lane and Rowley Green Road.

The second day's filming saw the crew going on location again, but this time within sight of the production base, at the car park behind the Studio 70 cinema on the corner of Shenley Road and Brook Road, opposite Elstree. Newell was again on site, as was fellow guest actor Trevor Bannister, playing a villain named Gordon, along with Diana Rigg's double Cyd Child and stuntman Arthur Howell driving a Mini van. All concerned reconvened at the same location on Monday 13 March for additional footage. A black E-type Jaguar (140 MPH) seen parked behind the cinema belonged to Brian Clemens at the time, the personalised number plate indicating the top speed the car could achieve. The Studio 70 cinema was demolished in December 1981, to be replaced by two office blocks: Isopad House and Hertsmere House.

Day three saw more location filming, with the unit travelling to The Old Vicarage, off St Mary's Church Road in North Mymms, which served as the exterior of GONN (Guild of Noble Nannies). The sequences shot there involved Bannister and, in the role of GONN secretary Miss Lister, Yootha Joyce. Splitting their time between two locations, the unit also filmed with Hardwick at the now-demolished house known as Hillcrest, which stood in its own grounds off Barnet Road in Arkley. This represented the exterior of Webster's abode.

The following day, footage of Newell was shot at a block of flats called Embassy Lodge on Regent's Park Road, Finchley, London N3, representing Sir George's home, Park Mansions. Newell had previously appeared in the series in the season four episode 'The Town of No Return', and would become Steed's superior Mother in season six.

Filming of the interiors began on Tuesday 14 March, the first studio day on Stage 3 being devoted to capturing some of the hallucination scenes. Production continued on the same stage the following day, with Chinnery and fellow guest actor Dudley Foster, playing the villain Goat, answering their call at 8.00 am and being joined later by Eddington, Hardwick, Newell, Joyce and, playing the MoD's General Wilmot, Geoffrey Sumner. Bannister was the last performer called to Stage 3 that day, keeping his arranged arrival time of 11.00 am. The following day only Joyce and Bannister were required, although Eddington was called at 2.30 pm and waited on standby for over two hours before the director realised that filming would not reach his scene and the actor was dismissed at 4.50 pm. On Thursday 16 March, Bannister was called at 7.30 am and was joined 30 minutes later by Hardwick and George Merritt, playing Webster's butler James, with Diana Rigg participating sometime later during a break in filming with the A unit on 'A Funny Thing Happened on the Way to the Station'.

Also on 16 March, the second unit shot more location footage on Rowley Lane in Arkley. A decision was taken here to remove the 600-amp Mole-Richardson generator from the rear of its transportation Land Rover. It was too heavy for the crew to manhandle, so a block and tackle was used to hoist it off the vehicle. However, this failed to go according to plan, as the generator swung out of control, striking the bonnet of the adjacent Bentley (RX 6180) and damaging the paintwork.

The Thompson machine gun used by the fake Nanny Roberts to attack Steed was hired from props supplier Bapty and Company, which specialised in providing firearms for both television and film productions. Bapty also sent a representative along with the gun to supervise its use.

The eight bullet holes seen in the windscreen of the Bentley were actually novelty stickers given away free when purchasing a certain amount of Regent petrol, as part of a Wild West promotional campaign during 1967. Shortly after this, Regent filling stations were rebranded to their American parent company's name, Texaco.

Gordon's Mini van was filmed on location approaching the junction of Harris Lane and Rectory Lane in Shenley, before arriving in close-up at Shenley Hall to establish the exterior of Steed's London apartment. The action then continues in studio, with Steed picking up a Webley Mark Three revolver as Gordon bounces a black spherical bomb into the apartment. Quickly realising what the device is, the agent removes some flowers from the horn of his tuba and places the bomb into it instead. After a loud explosion, Mrs Peel arrives, concerned for Steed's safety, and finds him okay, but the tuba amusingly blown into a long straight piece of tubing. However, the scene should really have been re-shot, as it can be clearly seen that the bomb actually falls out of the tuba before the explosion occurs.

A Land Rover and a Mini Moke were both adapted with special towing attachments in order that the motorised wheelchair of the elderly Nanny Roberts, played by Enid Lorrimer, could be pulled along at a speed far greater than any electric motor could propel it. The studio carpenters built the large playpen used for some of the sequences where characters revert to their childhood, achieved on screen by a combination of nursery rhyme music and an animated spiralling effect.

In an unusual move, Telemen hired a goat on Wednesday 22 March, obviously for inclusion somewhere in the day's filming (possibly related to the villain being named Goat), but eventually the animal was not used.

Thursday 23 March was James Hill's final involvement with the episode, and saw him directing a variety of scenes on Stages 2 and 3, plus motor vehicle close-ups on the studio lot. According to Telemen's records, production did not recommence on the episode until Tuesday 28 March, when an uncredited Leslie Norman picked up the reins, going onto direct the final five days of shooting. The reason for this is unknown.

Having been cast in the minor role of Nanny Brown, actress Penelope Keith participated in some rehearsals on Stage 3 on Wednesday 29 March and returned on the following two days for some filming, including at least one scene with Macnee. However, this material was obviously considered inessential to the storyline as it was removed by Peter Tanner during final editing. Keith consequently did not appear in the actual episode, although owing to an oversight she was still listed in the closing credits.

An earlier draft of the screenplay had Mrs Peel visiting the toy shop of J W Martin & Son & Son & Son, whereas in the episode as filmed, it is Steed who does this. However, a slip-up was made, as this change was not reflected in the double-barrelled subtitle at the beginning of the episode, which still reads 'Steed acquires a nanny – Emma shops for toys!'

Half way through the episode Mrs Peel arrives at GONN, joining Steed, but no explanation is given as to why she should turn up there, suggesting that a scripted scene either went unfilmed or was removed during editing.

Like the one in 'A Funny Thing Happened on the Way to the Station', the 'Mrs Peel, we're needed!' scene in 'Something Nasty in the Nursery' relates to the actual subject matter of the episode. Discovering a child's toy merry-go-round in her apartment, Emma notices that one of the figures going round is carrying a banner bearing the lettering 'Mrs Peel'. Cut to Steed, who delivers his usual line, 'We're needed.' The toy merry-go-round later turns up in the premises of J W Martin & Son & Son & Son, whose shop exterior was represented by one of the buildings in the backlot town. The red leather chair featured during the series' opening titles is also glimpsed again later on, at General Wilmot's house.

The concluding tag scene, in which Emma tells Steed's horoscope with a crystal ball, finally sees the series break the fourth wall altogether as she ends by saying, '… watch next week'. This comes as no great surprise after the zany interludes in 'Epic' and the surreal 'Mrs Peel, we're needed!' scene in 'The Superlative Seven'. Clearly by this point the series had well and truly embraced the camp antics that had swept through contemporary action shows such as *Batman* and the third season of *The Man from U.N.C.L.E.*. Now *The Avengers* appeared to be sending itself up and not taking anything too seriously.

Meanwhile, Jack Greenwood was absent from the production for at least two weeks in March, as he was acting as producer on the last drama production to be made at Merton Park Studios, the Edgar Lustgarten film *Payment in Kind*.

Further scheduling changes

Teledu Cymru resumed their Friday evening transmissions of *The Avengers* with 'The Correct Way to Kill' at 8.00 pm on 10 March 1967. Westward meanwhile moved their screenings to Wednesday, also at 8.00 pm, beginning with 'Never, Never Say Die' on 15 March. Three days later, Scottish Television ended their first run of season five episodes with 'Never, Never Say Die' on Saturday 18 March at 9.10 pm. Between Monday 20 March and Wednesday 29 March all the remaining 12 regions showing the series dropped it for a week, allowing a little more production time for the crews at Elstree before they ran out of new episodes to show.

Patrick Macnee newspaper ads

The *Daily Express* of Wednesday 15 March 1967 featured Patrick Macnee endorsing the wares of Neville Reed tailors – a now long-defunct chain of retail outlets – in a half-page advertisement. The newspaper would run a further five of these adverts over the course of the next couple of months, Macnee's image as the well-dressed John Steed assisting in promoting a line of gents' wear.

Add-a-Vision

In March 1967, ABPC Elstree became the first major film studio in the world to introduce Add-a-Vision as a standard feature on its productions. This mid-'60s technical innovation allowed for live video feeds of the action to be sent to various monitors around the studios while filming was in progress, so that members of the crew could check their particular areas of production immediately and, among other things, assess if any retakes were needed. This would save ABC Television Films at least ten per cent in overall filming time. Sound recording director A W Lumkin and head of camera department Harold Payne had witnessed the first such system working in Munich in 1965 and, upon returning to Elstree, had recommended that ABPC develop their own version. This was done in conjunction with the Maidenhead-based company Prowest Electronics, who designed a system to function though the American-manufactured 35mm BNC Mitchell film cameras used at the studio. Future plans included adapting a camera vehicle to take Add-a-Vision outside, although a stumbling block with this was the preference of crews to use the lighter, German-made 35mm Arriflex cameras when on location. Initially, Add-A-Vision was also cabled to the production office, allowing Brian Clemens and Albert Fennell to watch scenes being filmed in real time. However, when it was discovered that the system was being left on between takes, the trade unions became unhappy. The situation was resolved by removing the feed to the administration block.

5.15 – 'The Joker'

By the time filming on 'Something Nasty in the Nursery' wrapped on Sunday 2 April 1967, the rolling production schedule ensured that things were already under way on 'The Joker', having begun on Thursday 23 March with Sidney Hayers in the director's chair.

'The Joker' provides another example of Brian Clemens reworking one his earlier Honor Blackman stories – this time, 'Don't Look Behind You', which had already been given a sci-fi twist in the previous season as 'The House That Jack Built'. On this occasion Clemens reverted to basics, having Emma enticed to the remote Rusicana Hall on Exmoor where someone – namely Max Prendergast, played by Peter Jeffrey – lies in wait plotting revenge against her. Like 'Epic', 'The Joker' became an exercise in writing an episode that could be produced inexpensively, with a supporting cast of only four, no extras and only minimal location work.

That minimal location work included the Lotus being filmed on Mimms Lane near Rabley Park, and alongside the Catherine Bourne Lake within the grounds there. However, a studio set was used to represent the exterior of the house, where Emma arrives complete with her 'EP'-stencilled suitcase as seen previously in 'Too Many

Christmas Trees'. A sequence where the Lotus is parked by a strange young woman named Ola Monsey-Chamberlain, played by Sally Nesbitt, was shot on a shrubbery set. Steed's slow driving of the Bentley through dense fog was similarly shot on one of the stages. The scenery department, working to Robert Jones' designs, constructed a large revolving Joker/Ace playing card door and other large playing card decorations seen in the house interior. Sets previously featured with a rundown appearance in 'The Superlative Seven' were extensively redressed to represent Rusicana Hall's dining room and hallway.

This episode's 'Mrs Peel, we're needed!' sequence begins with Steed falling down the spiral staircase in his apartment. This prompts Emma to throw a vase through the frosted glass surround of his outer door in order to gain access, and gives Steed an unusual reason to tell her, in a slight variation on the usual catchphrase, 'Mrs Peel, you're needed!' Emma is revealed to be an expert at the card game bridge, having written a magazine article entitled *Better Bridge with Applied Mathematics*, and is lured to the house by an invitation to meet renowned bridge player Sir Cavalier Rusicana – 'Sounds like an opera,' says Steed, alluding to the Pietro Mascagni opera *Cavelleria Rusticana*. Steed later discovers that his accident was caused by a sophisticated booby trap, actually tying the sequence into the main storyline.

Steed's old tuba having been damaged beyond repair by the bomb explosion in 'Something Nasty in the Nursery', he has acquired himself a new one in this episode. Before setting off for Exmoor after Emma, he checks his swordstick, seen previously in the episodes 'The Thirteenth Hole' and 'Small Game for Big Hunters'.

During the action, Emma is seen to carry a pearl-handled Harrington and Richardson snub-nosed revolver. A pair of the Edward Rayne-designed white boots with a thin black central stripe, as sported by Emma in various episodes the previous season, this time forms part of Ola's costume.

The screenplay called for the inclusion of a German love song on a 78 rpm record. Laurie Johnson composed a suitable tune, and Brian Clemens provided a set of English lyrics that were then translated into German by Leo Birnbaum, the viola player with Johnson's group of session musicians. Mike Sammes of the Mike Sammes Singers supplied the vocals. The song was titled 'Mein Liebling, Mein Rose' and credited to the pseudonym Carl Schmidt.[21] The name of the fictional record label Deutsche Phon was thought up by Clemens.

A 45 rpm seven-inch single version of 'Mein Liebling, Mein Rose', serial number DB 8223, was demoed on the Columbia label in July 1967, some three months after the episode's debut transmission in the ABC regions. The track was later made available on the Laurie Johnson CD collection *Cult TV Themes*, issued on Tuesday 16 November 2004 on the Castle Music label. Some of the episode's incidental music was also expanded upon by Johnson and re-recorded on Friday 15 February 1980 with him conducting the London Studio Orchestra. This re-recording, entitled 'Theme from The Joker', was included as a track on the vinyl album *Music from The Avengers, The New Avengers, The Professionals*, released on the Unicorn-Kanchana label in October 1980.

In a scene where Major George Fancy, played by John Stone, answers the telephone to Steed, he says, 'Wentworth here,' suggesting that the character was renamed at some point during production and a continuity error was made, which should have been

---

[21] Technically speaking, the title should have been spelt slightly differently as 'Mein Liebling, Meine Rose'.

rectified by dubbing in the correct name.

Although 'The Joker' was allocated primarily to the A unit, the B unit assisted by handling some filming on Monday 3 April on the Steed apartment set on Stage 4, featuring both Macnee and his stunt double Rocky Taylor. The B unit was also responsible for some sequences at Rusicana Hall involving Rigg, Nesbitt and Jeffrey, all shot the same day on the dining room and upper landing sets.

The following day, Tuesday 4 April, the second unit was dispatched to execute the aforementioned location work at Rabley Park, while the A unit resumed principal filming on interiors with Rigg and Nesbitt on the upper landing set on Stage 4 and Emma's room on Stage 3. With the episode falling behind schedule, the producers wanted the crew to work overtime. The Electrical Trades Union (ETU) consented for its members to continue for an extra 15 minutes that day, up to 6.15 pm, but no longer. However, an agreement was subsequently reached to have a longer extension on Thursday 6 April, with work beginning at 7.30 am and not concluding until 8.20 pm. Once again this filming was undertaken by the A unit on Stage 4. It encompassed various interiors, including some action scenes in which Cyd Child doubled for Rigg, Rocky Taylor for Jeffrey and Art Thomas for Nesbitt.

In a further effort to make up time, work continued over the weekend. On Sunday 9 April some scenes were filmed on the Mrs Peel apartment set on Stage 3. These included the end tag scene, which was described simply as 'stylised closing' in the shooting script, suggesting that Clemens probably wrote it after filming was already under way. Having previously been in charge of the second unit on this episode, Leslie Norman was recalled to direct the B unit on Stage 4, working with both Macnee and Stone, and in separate footage with Ronald Lacey, playing a strange young man character.

The finished episode is very faithful to the shooting script, which was dated March 1967 and titled simply 'Joker'. One of the few differences is that, instead of breaking the frosted glass to access Steed's apartment in the 'Mrs Peel, we're needed!' scene, Emma was originally to have found the door unlocked. Another is that, in a scene where the strange young man produces a stiletto knife from under his jacket, he was scripted to say 'I'm really Jack the Ripper', but this line was ultimately omitted. The most significant alteration was made to the episode's finale, which was rewritten possibly on the day of shooting. In the sequence as scripted, Prendergast confronts Emma, watched by an armed Ola from the upper landing, as 'Mein Liebling, Mein Rose' begins to play. Ola edges toward the revolving giant playing card door, but is knocked unconscious when Steed comes barrelling through. However, due to his earlier leg injury, Steed finds descending the staircase difficult. Tripping over Ola, he crashes down the stairs. He hears the commotion of Emma and Prendergast fighting in the dining room, then Prendergast appears, holding a knife and clutching his stomach, and collapses to the floor. The finished episode departs significantly from this, with the crisis being resolved by Steed rather than Mrs Peel.

Final Panther Books

Sometime during March 1967, Panther published *The Passing of Gloria Munday* and *Heil Harris!*, its remaining two paperback books based on the series, written by Anthony Hussey under his John Garforth pseudonym. Like the previous examples, these both spawned American editions with different covers from Berkley Medallion, the former in July 1967, with a reprint in February 1969, the latter in September 1967, also with a reprint in 1969. The 1969 reprint covers again pictured Tara King, despite the fact she did not feature in the stories. *The Passing of Gloria Munday* was also translated into French, German and Dutch for editions in those countries, followed by a Chilean printing in 1968. The same was true of *Heil Harris!*, except that there was no German edition, owing to the fact that it utilised the well-worn plotline of Nazi villains.

From strength to strength

As reported in the *Daily Express* of Tuesday 28 March 1967, the American viewing figures for the first eight colour episodes screened by the ABC network had been impressive enough for them to order an additional 16 episodes. In the UK meanwhile the series also remained highly successful. Averaging 7.3 million viewers during March, it retained its joint number four spot in the top 20 television programmes, tying with *Coronation Street* and the detective show *Mr Rose*.

Tyne Tees resumed their Wednesday evening screenings of the series with 'Epic' on at 8.00 pm on 29 March, and Westward followed suit, although they would show only another couple of episodes before taking a break until January 1968. Rediffusion was also back in business at 8.00 pm on Friday 31 March, also with 'Epic', line-feeding their transmission though to Anglia, Channel, Southern and TWW, who were now being joined by Teledu Cymru.

'Epic' was the episode of choice again for both ABC regions and Border when they continued showing the series on Saturday 1 April at 9.10 pm and Sunday 2 April at 8.10 pm respectively, after missing a week. However, Border would then give repeat screenings to 'Death at Bargain Prices' and 'Castle De'ath' over the next couple of weeks before suspending their run of the season five episodes until October.

5.16 – 'Who's Who???'

Even though filming on 'The Joker' finished six days later than scheduled, on Tuesday 11 April 1967, Philip Levene's 'Who's Who???' had already been before the cameras for nine days by that point, having been started on Monday 3 April. The director was John Moxey, making what would be his only contribution to *The Avengers*.

This episode was devised specifically in order to allow Macnee and Rigg some time off. Its plot centres around a mind transfer process through which Steed and Emma have their personalities swapped with those of two enemy agents, Basil and Lola, played by Freddie Jones and Patricia Haines respectively. This device allowed for the two guest actors to carry around half of the screen time, and also made for the inclusion of some very effective humour. The changed Emma, with Lola's thought patterns, acts completely out of character, chewing gum and dancing to pop music played on her Decca 205 record player. Meanwhile Steed, having acquired Basil's personality, smokes a large cigar after biting the end off it. To avoid confusion, after each commercial break a voiceover by actor Richard Bebb informs viewers of the situation, although these announcements are also used to comic effect themselves.

In the opening teaser sequence, Basil and Lola kill a man named Hooper, an agent of the secret Floral network, with a five-shot Smith and Wesson 37 Airweight mini revolver licensed to Emma. They then leave the gun positioned with a single red rose in its barrel as a 'calling card' to attract the attention of Steed and Emma. This was the first time a rose-in-a-gun image had been seen on screen in *The Avengers*, although it had been used as a logo on the cover of the series' shooting scripts for a while. Brian Clemens credits the idea to regular director James Hill, who had apparently made an earlier, unrelated documentary including some footage of young American peace protestors placing flowers into the barrels of National Guardsmen's rifles.[22] The rose-in-a-gun image became associated with *The Avengers* when it was used in an opening caption for the American transmissions of the colour episodes, overlaid with the wording '*The Avengers* – In Color'.

In preparation for their impersonation of Steed and Emma, Basil and Lola use a film projector to screen clips of them. This sequence incorporates footage of Rigg from 'Escape in Time', 'Something Nasty in the Nursery' and the monochrome promotional film shot on Wednesday 29 September 1965 of her riding a grey horse along the beach at Dymchurch in Kent. The clips of Macnee are a mixture of footage from 'The See-Through Man' and publicity material shot on the studio lot behind Stages 3 and 4.

Campbell Singer appears as the Floral network's head, Major B, although some of the imagery seen in the episode suggests that the name had received a subtle alteration from Major Bee. Philip Levene returned to his acting roots by making a cameo appearance as agent Daffodil, while an uncredited Billy Cornelius played Poppy.

Shots of the Bentley arriving at and departing from Steed's London abode were filmed on Thursday 6 April in Duchess Mews, London W1, with Jones, Haines and fellow guest actor Peter Reynolds, playing agent Tulip, all on location.

Three separate filming requirements were met on Nan Clark's Lane, Highwood Hill, London NW7, a quiet leafy country lane that was also a cul-de-sac. A large dwelling called Highwood Park House, which stands in its own grounds, became the exterior of the home of the villainous Dr Krelmar, played by Arnold Diamond, for various scenes of characters arriving there, with the Bentley and the Lotus also featured. In an earlier sequence, Steed and Emma, in the bodies of Basil and Lola, lose the pursuing Tulip by turning the Bentley off Nan Clark's Lane along a single track road – now a private road – leading to Mote End Farm. The third filming location found on Nan Clark's Lane was the distinctive property known as The Barn, which also stands in extensive grounds. This was used for another view of Krelmar's home, when Tulip parts some bushes and sees the parked Bentley.

Additional footage was captured at the junction of Hankins Lane with Stockton Gardens, in nearby Barnet, featuring the Bentley, driven by stuntman Les Crawford, and Tulip's Vanden Plas Princess R, driven by Reynolds' double Joe Farrer. All of this filming was initially executed on Tuesday 11 April by the second unit, with Macnee, Rigg, Jones, Haines, Diamond and Reynolds present on location. Singer was also on standby but not called; in the event, Major B and his men were played by doubles. However, when the rushes of this footage were viewed, some of it was found to be unsatisfactory, so the second unit returned to the location on Tuesday 18 April to film a number of retakes.

Prior to the location work being done, the first day of filming for the episode took place on Stage 2 at Elstree, with the B unit shooting footage on the Major B office set,

---

[22] The most famous instance of this occurring was on 21 October 1967, as captured in the historic still known as 'Flower Power' by *Washington Star* photographer Bernie Boston. If Hill did indeed include such footage in his pre-April 1967 documentary, there must have been at least one earlier, less well-documented instance too.

featuring Haines, Jones, Singer and Reynolds. Day two once again involved the B unit working on Stage 2, filming on the Krelmar's office, consulting room and outer office sets, again with Haines, Jones and Singer, this time along with Diamond.

With a view to making speedier progress, tentative plans were drawn up to film on Sunday 9 April, but both main units and the leads proved to be unavailable, working on 'The Joker', so nothing more was done on 'Who's Who???' until the following day. However, in a further effort to save time, both the B unit and the A unit worked simultaneously on the episode from Wednesday 12 April to Friday 14 April, and then again on Monday 17 April. Moxey directed the B unit while Sidney Hayers took charge of the A unit, as on 'The Joker'. Cyd Child doubled for Haines for some filming on the Monday, while her usual charge Diana Rigg was doubled instead by Annabelle Wise.

This episode's 'Mrs Peel, we're needed!' opener involves Emma at her apartment looking at her reflection in a full-length mirror, before stepping away to reveal in her place a reflection of Steed, who delivers his usual catchphrase.

Seen on the record player in Steed's apartment is the cover for the album *Africa Speaks, America Answers* by Guy Warren with the Red Saunders Orchestra, released in 1956 on the Brunswick label, serial number LAT 8237. Later, when Steed and Emma, in the bodies of Basil and Lola, gain access to the apartment, propped up in the background is the cover of another album, *Ballads for Night People* by June Christy, issued both as a mono and a stereo recording, serial number T & ST 1308, in 1959 by Capitol Records.

While possessing Steed's body, Basil at one point produces a seven-shot 9mm Beretta 1931/4 automatic from a drawer in his apartment to shoot Daffodil.

Rigg decides to leave

Having decided against continuing with *The Avengers*, Diana Rigg informed the producers that she would be leaving upon completion of the next batch of episodes, and that she could not be persuaded to stay for a third season. She later said that, aside from the various concessions she had received, the main reason she had agreed to do season five was her loyalty to close friend Patrick Macnee, whom she affectionately nicknamed Paddynee.

The news that Rigg would be departing the series broke on Friday 14 April, with the *Daily Mail*, the *Daily Mirror* and the *Daily Express* all running reports. The latter's story, headlined 'Diana to Quit', also speculated at to who her replacement might be, the columnist suggesting as possible candidates several of the series' former guest stars: Barbara Shelley, Gabrielle Drake, Pamela Ann Davy and Sally Nesbitt. The *Daily Express* also stated that Rigg had plans to appear later in the year in a feature film version of William Shakespeare's *A Midsummer Night's Dream* – a production that would eventually reach cinemas in 1968, with Rigg in the role of Helena. A few weeks later, on Thursday 11 May 1967, *The Stage and Television Today* reported that producer Irving Allen was planning to film James Mayo's espionage novel *Hammerhead* with Rigg and Vince Edwards in starring roles. Shooting was reported to be scheduled to begin in September 1967 at Shepperton Studios. However, in the event, Rigg was still committed to *The Avengers* at that point, and Judy Geeson took the female lead alongside Edwards.

American influences

After the completion of principal filming on 'Who's Who???' on Tuesday 18 April 1967, both units were stood down for 15 days and did not reconvene at Elstree until Wednesday 3 May. By overlapping the filming of consecutive episodes and undertaking some weekend work, the crew had managed to complete production on 16 scripts in about six-and-a-half months.

Transmissions now having caught up with production, the ITV regional companies that were still running the series had no option but to drop it from their schedules during the first two weeks of May – although some, including the two ABC regions and Tyne Tees, simply substituted repeats of episodes from the previous season. The American ABC network were similarly obliged to conclude their second run of *The Avengers* with 'Who's Who???' on 19 May[23], and would not air any further episodes until January 1968.

However, changes were coming to *The Avengers*, and they would start with the next batch of episodes to be filmed. At the ABC network's request, the 'Mrs Peel, we're needed!' scenes and the opening double-barrelled subtitles – in the format 'Steed does this, Emma does that' – featured in the first 16 colour episodes would both be discarded. This was to allow more time for commercials, which earned the network revenue when *The Avengers* went out coast to coast across the USA. There also appears to have been a conscious decision taken regarding the level of humour and the eccentricity of the characters in the series, which from now on would be toned down in comparison with some of the earlier colour episodes. No longer would the series be allowed to descend into self-parody, as the more outlandish aspects of 'Epic', 'The Superlative Seven' and 'Something Nasty in the Nursery' were relegated to a memory. Although the inclusion of science fiction concepts and bizarre situations would still be allowed, ABC Television obviously felt that taking a step back toward reality would give the series greater longevity and better viewing figures. In the UK viewing chart for April, the series had dropped quite dramatically to joint seventeenth place, tying with *University Challenge* and Rediffusion's anthology *Seven Deadly Virtues* on an average of 5.9 million viewers per episode.

Two units down to one

With the pressure now off to complete further episodes for American networking, the crew was reduced from two main units back to just one. However, the smaller second unit was retained, as was the rolling production schedule approach that had proved so successful. Ernest Steward kept the director of photography position initially, although Alan Hume would handle a couple of episodes toward the conclusion of the season's production. The position of assistant director would change frequently, Ron Carr overseeing the next two episodes, then Ernie Lewis one, Jack Martin a couple, Ron Appleton one and Martin finishing things off by handling the last two. Len Townsend assumed the art directing duties on all of the remaining adventures, likewise Hilda Fox on hairdressing and Jim Hydes on make-up. James Bawden would serve as camera operator on the majority of the upcoming episodes, though Tony White would work on

---

[23] This run had consisted of 15 of the first 16 colour episodes. 'Escape in Time' was held back, and would not be transmitted in the USA until July 1968.

a couple and Kevin Pike would come in for the final one. Gladys Goldsmith would handle continuity for the next three episodes, followed by Mary Spain, Goldsmith again, Elizabeth Wilcox and then Marjorie Lavelly, who would work on both the penultimate episode and the last. Ken Rawkins would be responsible for the sound recording initially, then Cecil Mason and Brian Marshall would work on an episode each, and Mason would finish off the season. The wardrobe department would be under the control of Gladys Jones for three episodes, before Felix Evans took over for the remainder. Russ Hill and Peter Lennard would more or less alternate as sound editor.

5.17 – 'Death's Door'

With the production crew reassembled, filming commenced on Philip Levene's script 'Death's Door', the plot of which involves two government dignitaries – Sir Andrew Boyd, played by Clifford Evans, and Lord Melford, played by Allan Cuthbertson – experiencing vivid nightmares that start to come true and deter them from attending an important international conference. The plot element of remembering things from a nightmare was very similar to one featured in an episode of *The Baron* called 'The Maze', scripted by Brian Clemens under his Tony O'Grady pseudonym, which had been filmed at Elstree ten months previously. Scenes in 'Death's Door' of a nightmare room inside the Temp Storage Company, complete with oversize props, directly mirror sequences in 'The Maze' where the character John Mannering experiences flashbacks as portions of his lost memory return. Therefore it appears that Clemens had a hand in formulating the 'Death's Door' storyline.

With summer now approaching, the majority of the upcoming episodes would feature a large amount of location filming around Hertfordshire, with visits to London, Buckinghamshire and Bedfordshire. In a sequence where Steed's 1930 Bentley Speed Six (RX 6180) runs out of control down the fictional Spout Hill, the vehicle was actually descending Old House Lane near Sarratt, north of Watford. The camera was in the back seat, shooting Steed and Emma from behind, with Rocky Taylor and Cyd Child doubling for Macnee and Rigg, whose close-ups were filmed in the studio and inserted during editing. This sequence was filmed on the first day of production and, as in 'The House That Jack Built', the crew had no qualms about running the vintage Bentley through an obstacle – this time some wooden fencing.

For a scene where Steed and Sir Andrew Boyd depart from the latter's country estate in his chauffeur-driven Daimler Majestic Major, the location used was what is now known as the Great Westwood Equestrian Centre off Old House Lane. As the vehicle travels along, the back-projection view out of the rear window is of Hilfield Lane, heading away from the village of Patchetts Green toward Elstree, with an electricity substation in the background.

The conference centre exteriors were filmed at the Royal Masonic School for Boys – since renamed Royal Connaught Park – off The Avenue in Bushey near Watford. A sequence where Sir Andrew is knocked down and killed was shot on Tuesday 16 May on what is now Royal Connaught Drive, although at the time it was just an internal access road. Stuntman Joe Dunne doubled for Evans, performing a spectacular mid-air somersault after apparently being stuck by a dark blue Alvis 3 Litre. The car was driven by Bill Cummings, doubling for guest actor Terry Maidment in the role of a villain named Jepson. The vehicle sustained minor damage during the stunt, which was promptly reported to the hire company, Kingsbury Motors, who advised that they would obtain an estimate for repairs that Telemen would have to pay for.

A scene was filmed of Steed and Lord Melford departing along Clarendon Road, Watford, in the Daimler after seeing a couple of inept deliverymen drop a wooden packing case from the back of a Bedford pick-up truck. This footage, along with other shots at the same location, was filmed on the afternoon of Tuesday 23 May, with all the vehicles again being supplied by Kingsbury Motors.

The background footage seen behind the Daimler this time shows parts of Letchmore Heath, including the house called Aragon situated on Aldenham Road at the edge of the village. This back-projection material – technically referred to as travelling matte – had been filmed a couple of weeks earlier, on Thursday 11 May, by the second unit. Production paperwork for that day indicates that the unit travelled from Letchmore Heath to Aldenham and then to Watford, also passing through Patchetts Green to obtain the footage by the electricity substation. Kingsbury Motors provided a bicycle that stuntman Cliff Diggins rode for a sequence where his character was almost knocked off by Melford's car, filmed on Hilfield Lane, near Patchetts Green, approximately three miles from Borehamwood.

The main unit was meanwhile busy in central London that day at Duchess Mews, W1, where they filmed exteriors of Steed's apartment, including footage from a first-floor window of Mrs Peel arriving in her Lotus, although this was not Diana Rigg as she was absent from the production on this day due to illness.

In another scene, Steed and Emma are taking a trip to the conference centre in his limousine when they stop at a crossroads and hear what sounds like machine gun fire but is actually the noise made by construction workers building a petrol station. The workmen were filmed at the junction of Pinner Road and Aldenham Road in Watford, although the petrol station has since been replaced by the premises of a power tool manufacturer and retailer called Powertek.

Later, Steed arrives in his Bentley at the residence of the Eastern Bloc observer Becker, finding him at the rear of the buildings indulging in some target practice with a carbine. This sequence was filmed at Little Westwood Farm off Bucks Hill, near Sarratt, close to Old House Lane and the Great Westwood Equestrian Centre. Becker's wooden target was transported to the location by the unit construction van before being assembled on site. However, having recced the terrain in advance, the crew knew that it would be impossible to move their Arriflex 10 camera around smoothly. Consequently, 30 feet of tracking boards and a Wilcox dolly (to mount the camera on) were requisitioned from the stores at Elstree, to ensure a smooth movement when filming shots of Steed trapped behind the wooden target. Also for this day the unit abandoned their usual 600 amp Mole-Richardson generator, preferring the smaller and more mobile 250 amp Brute, hired for the duration from Mobile Generators Ltd.

On Wednesday 17 May the second unit was prevented from location filming by bad weather, adjourning to the nightmare set on Stage 3 at Elstree on standby in case the leads should become available so that they could film there. However, both Macnee and Rigg were occupied with the main unit on Stage 2 all day, leaving the second unit unable to get any footage in the can. The following day, location filming was cancelled again, this time because of a substantial change to the filming schedule, although on this occasion the second unit did manage to capture some footage on the nightmare set.

The rough and tumble shots in the fight scenes that occur in the conference centre at the episode's conclusion feature Rocky Taylor doubling for Patrick Macnee, Cyd Child for Diana Rigg and Joe Dunne for William Lucas in the role of a diplomat named Stapley. The minor role of the aide Haynes was played by a stuntman, Terry Yorke, so he did not require a double. Both Macnee and Rigg participated for close-ups.

Officially, the final day of production on 'Death's Door' was Wednesday 7 June, but this is somewhat misleading as that day's shooting consisted only of some car interiors with travelling matte back-projection shot on Stage 2. The bulk of principal photography was actually completed on Friday 26 May, four days over schedule. The second unit also shot some inserts on Tuesday 30 May and some travelling matte footage the following week.

Other notable points: the winged red leather chair seen with Rigg in the season's opening title sequence puts in another appearance in this episode as part of the furniture in Sir Andrew's home; the prop *Daily Clarion* newspaper that Sir Andrew reads in the Daimler is the same one that Emma reads on the train in 'A Funny Thing Happened on the Way to the Station', shot three months earlier; and there is a nice exchange of dialogue in which Mrs Peel, referring to her two-way radio, tells Steed, 'You know my wavelength', to which he beams, 'Indeed I do', which some viewers have taken to imply that their relationship was a more intimate one than is immediately apparent on screen. Asked in recent years if he considered the two agents were sleeping together, Brian Clemens has said that he always wrote the characters as having previously had an affair but since moved on to being just good friends.

Mission: Impossible

The Stage and Television Today published on Thursday 1 June 1967 devoted column inches to the Europernio TV 67, also known as the Venice Television Festival, reporting that small-screen critics from 16 different European countries had voted the top acting award to Diana Rigg for her performance in *The Avengers*.

Early in May there had also been American Emmy award nominations for *The Avengers* in the Outstanding Dramatic Series category and for Diana Rigg in the Outstanding Continued Performance by an Actress in a Leading Role in a Dramatic Series category. Both Macnee and Rigg flew out to attend the Emmy awards ceremony on Sunday 4 June at the Americana Hotel in New York.[24] However, they were disappointed when *The Avengers* lost out to *Mission: Impossible* and Rigg lost out to the same series' leading actress Barbara Bain.

Mission: Impossible – a drama about an elite group of undercover operatives who use a mixture of elaborate charade, illusion and gadgetry to complete their assignments – had been shown in the United States since September 1966, but would not arrive on British television until 18 months later. Several ITV regions such as Granada would show the first season and some second season material, Rediffusion starting their transmissions in January 1968. However, the independent channel would eventually lose interest and drop the series. Later the BBC would buy selected episodes from the second season through to the seventh, which they would begin screening in June 1970. However, due to the earlier haphazard ITV scheduling, *Mission: Impossible* never really posed any serious competition to *The Avengers* in the UK.

---

[24] Another part of this televised event was hosted at the Century Plaza Hotel in Los Angeles.

5.18 – 'Return of the Cybernauts'

The next adventure, 'Return of the Cybernauts', had started principal photography on Monday 22 May 1967, from another Philip Levene script featuring the robotic adversaries first seen in the black and white Rigg episode 'The Cybernauts'. The director was Robert Day, who with the aid of casting director G B Walker managed to secure the services of big-name guest star Peter Cushing to play the part of Paul Beresford, a man who befriends Steed and Emma so that he can plot their demise as revenge for the death of his brother Dr Clement Armstrong in the earlier Cybernauts episode. Although he had been an actor for many years, Cushing had become known to the public mainly for his numerous appearances in British gothic horror films.

Also amongst the guest cast were Frederick Jaeger reprising his role of Armstrong's assistant Benson from 'The Cybernauts', Charles Tingwell as Dr Neville, Fulton Mackay as Professor Chadwick, Anthony Dutton as Dr Garnett and Aimi MacDonald as Garnett's secretary Rosie.

Michael Gough, who had portrayed Armstrong, visited Elstree on Thursday 4 May to have a cast made of his head. This served as a mould for a plaster-of-Paris bust that was then spray-painted to resemble a bronze. The finished product would be used on the set of Beresford's home. Presumably Diana Rigg put herself through the same ordeal for the bronze of Emma also featured, although there is no record of this.

The initial day of filming involved the second unit being dispatched to the village of Denham in Buckinghamshire, where they took a series of colour plates of Denham Place, a large building that stands in extensive grounds and was owned by ITC at the time. These plates would be shown on screen as a succession of stills, tilted at different angles, to give the impression of the building from the Cybernaut's viewpoint as it walks toward it. With this material in the can, the second unit decamped to Watford, where they took some establishing footage of St John's Church on Sutton Street. Next they moved on to The Avenue in Bushey, filming the clock tower at what was then the Royal Masonic School for Boys, which showed the time as four o'clock.

The second unit continued location filming on day two at Duchess Mews, London W1, executing the beginning of the car chase featured in the episode. Cyd Child drove Mrs Peel's Lotus out into New Cavendish Street, turned right almost immediately into Weymouth Mews and passed the Dover Castle pub, where the crew would often take their lunch break when filming at the Duchess Mews location. Meanwhile, having dived and rolled out of the path of the Lotus, Macnee's stunt double Rocky Taylor quickly set off in pursuit using the Bentley (RX 6160), which he obviously had the measure of, throwing the vintage vehicle about at high speed. Both the Lotus and the Bentley were driven up Holmshill Lane toward the village of Ridge, initially with the heavy traffic of the A1 Barnet by-pass visible in the background.

Having wrapped at midday, the second unit returned to the studios, but departed later for the village of Shenley at 2.00 pm to film footage on the surrounding roads. This included material of both the Lotus and the Bentley travelling along Silver Hill in the direction of Shenley, for a sequence where Steed narrowly avoids an oncoming blue Volkswagen Beetle, driven by stuntman Les Crawford. The Volkswagen was actually Crawford's everyday transport, and thus the day's work would have rewarded him with a double fee.

Wednesday 24 May brought more location filming by the second unit, this time at the large, white-painted mansion house at Woolmers Park, which comprises 250 acres of grounds off Essendon Road in Letty Green, about 12 miles from Borehamwood. Footage of both Steed's Bentley and Emma's Lotus was shot in the driveway by the house. Portions of this would later be played on a monitor on the set of Beresford's control room. The two vehicles were also filmed travelling along the narrow Woolmers Lane in Letty Green, taking a sharp bend, then returning along the same stretch of road in the opposite direction toward the north entrance to Woolmers Park. Here the Lotus smashed through a five-bar wooden gate – which, as the crew could not risk damaging the vehicle, would have been made from lightweight balsa wood and augmented with an appropriate sound effect. Once again on hand were Taylor and Child – who rates this as her favourite episode of the series – to double for Macnee and Rigg and actually drive the vehicles. Also shot at Woolmers Park on the same day was exterior footage of Dr Garnett making a break from his confinement in Beresford's house. The crew erected two props in the grounds in the form of a white birdhouse and a cherub statue, which both had a discreet camera lens fitted to create the impression they were part of a closed-circuit television system. At the time, Woolmers Park was owned by the Lucas family, who not only provided Macnee with refreshments but also allowed him to relax in their home in order to get out of the blazing sun between takes.

What was then the newer part (now partly demolished) of the Haberdashers' Aske's School at Elstree provided the backdrop to the abduction of Dr Neville, when the Cybernaut, dressed all in black, smashes through a trestle fence and begins advancing. Running to his grey Jaguar saloon, Neville attempts to escape, but the immense strength of the automaton stop his vehicle moving, although the rear wheels continue to turn vigorously, causing clouds of smoke. Once again the second unit was responsible for this sequence, filming it on Thursday 25 May, and it took the majority of the day to complete. They then moved at 4.20 pm to Totteridge Park, Totteridge Common in Barnet. This building provided the exterior of the offices of lawyer John Hunt, played by Redmond Phillips, with Jaeger, Terry Richards as the Cybernaut and Taylor doubling Macnee all present on location. However, due to bad weather, filming was not completed on the required scenes. This resulted in a return visit by the second unit on the final day of principal filming, Thursday 15 June, to take pick-up shots and additional footage. They also filmed that day at Duchess Mews and on the Aldenham Estate. They later returned to the Haberdashers' Aske's School to film some further pick-ups on Tuesday 27 June.

Friday 26 May witnessed the initial studio filming for the episode, which occurred on the control room set on Stage 3, featuring Cushing, Jaeger, Mackay, Tingwell, Richards and, in the role of Dr Russell, Roger Hammond. Further studio filming was then done over the next few days. Close-ups were shot of both Rigg and Macnee sat in their cars in front of a large back-projection screen, which when edited together with the location footage previously shot by the second unit would give the impression that they rather than their doubles were driving. Some excerpts from 'The Cybernauts' were played in on the monitor on the control room set, featuring Macnee, Rigg, Gough, Jaeger and the two fighting Cybernauts, concluding with the sequence of Armstrong's demise. The climactic fight sequence in the control room was shot on Friday 2 June, with Taylor and Child performing their usual doubling duties for Macnee and Rigg, Joe Dunne substituting for Jaeger and Joe Farrer taking the lumps for Mackay.

On Tuesday 13 and Wednesday 14 June additional material of the wheel-spinning Jaguar was shot under controlled conditions on the studio lot, featuring Tingwell and Richards. An exterior scene outside Beresford's home, where the hypnotically-controlled Emma confronts Steed before felling him with a single karate chop, was also filmed on 14 June, somewhere among the foliage on the studio backlot.

A note on the daily progress report for the upcoming episode 'Dead Man's Treasure' indicates that some special effects work for 'Return of the Cybernauts' was carried out on Thursday 29 June down the road from ABPC Elstree at MGM Borehamwood Studios, on Elstree Way. However, it is unknown what this work entailed.

In this episode Mrs Peel initially sports one of the chunky, white-strapped Old England Limited timepieces designed by Alun Hughes, but then accepts from Beresford the gift of a dress watch. In a sequence reminiscent of the conclusion of 'The Cybernauts', she pushes the shattered door of Russell's office over with a single finger, though later Steed insists that she allow him to do the same to the deactivated Cybernaut.

During 1968 a Mexican company called Cinematographica Calderon SA produced a movie called *Las Luchadiras vs el Robot Asesino* (aka *Women Wrestlers vs the Robot Killer*), which appears to have been heavily influenced by 'Return of the Cybernauts'. The robot of the title, which is visually identically to the episode's Cybernaut, is programmed by a mad scientist to do his bidding. The Steed equivalent is a police detective called Arturo, played by Joaquin Cordero, whose acting career appears to have been confined to Mexico. The Emma Peel counterpart is Arturo's girlfriend, the lady wrestler Gaby, portrayed by Regina Torné, another performer who restricted her appearances to her homeland. This movie was released in Mexico on 9 January 1969 and appeared in other Spanish-speaking markets during the early '70s.

Blackman declines to return

The *Daily Mail* had a scoop on Tuesday 30 May when it revealed that Honor Blackman had rejected an offer to make return guest appearances in *The Avengers*. Blackman, described as having played 'leather-clad judo expert' Cathy Gale, said 'There's nothing new to get out of it. I want to look forward not backward.' The piece also reiterated that the current Avengergirl, Diana Rigg, would be taking her leave from the series later in the year.

Meanwhile, *The Avengers*' viewing figures were dropping even further. The average ratings for May 1967 were 5.2 million, placing the series at joint nineteenth in the UK television chart, tied with the quiz show *University Challenge*.

5.19 – 'Dead Man's Treasure'

The next episode, 'Dead Man's Treasure', went before the cameras on Monday 5 June 1967 – ten days before principal filming on 'Return of the Cybernauts' was completed – with Sidney Hayers directing. The script was credited to Michael Winder, although when interviewed by the magazine *Time Screen* in 1992 Brian Clemens asserted that he had heavily rewritten it, leaving little of Winder's original save for the concept of a treasure hunt. The finished episode can almost be considered an extended car chase, as Steed and Mrs Peel follow clues in a car rally to obtain the prize treasure chest ahead of the self-serving Major Mike Colborne and enemy agents Alex and Carl, and thus retrieve a despatch box that Steed's murdered colleague Bobby Danvers has concealed within it. The guest actors hired by Hayers included Norman Bowler – a regular in the

BBC's long-running police show *Softly, Softly* and later in the soap opera *Emmerdale* – as Colborne, Edwin Richfield as Alex, Neil McCarthy as Carl and Rio Fanning as Danvers.

When talking about *The Avengers'* filmed episodes, writers and directors associated with the series often use the phrase '50-minute feature film' and 'Dead Man's Treasure' probably epitomises that statement better than any other. In fact, it incorporates more location filming than any other British film series episode produced during the '60s. It was a mammoth undertaking for all involved, and took a month to get in the can. Fortunately, however, location scouts quickly concluded that the majority of the required exteriors could be obtained within four miles of the series' base of operations at Elstree Studios in Borehamwood. As good weather was essential to the location work, the episode was placed in the schedule for mid-summer.

The action opens with some motor vehicle filming on Mimms Lane and Rectory Lane at Shenley, plus footage shot at the junction of Deeves Hall Lane, Earls Lane and Mimms Lane near the village of Ridge. This second unit material was shot day-for-night – a cinematic technique achieved by underexposing the film stock or else placing a blue filter on the camera lens – and involved Les Crawford doubling for Fanning as the driver of an MGB hardtop, stuntman Romo Gorrara replacing McCarthy at the wheel of an E-type Jaguar, and Joe Farrer filling in for Richfield.

The MGB enters the grounds of Shenley Hall via the now disused northern entrance, prior to a studio sequence where Danvers hides the box of secret papers in the treasure chest, which he finds in the study of the High Pines manor house. Picking up an invitation reading 'George Benstead requests the pleasure of [blank space for name] at his Annual Car Rally starting from High Pines, Edgington, August 21st', Danvers scribbles Steed's name onto it, then places both the card and a key into an envelope, hoping that his colleague will be tipped off to come and retrieve the box's contents. Besides the envelopes and invitation cards, Benstead's untidy desk also bears a copy of *Motor* magazine dated 17 June, containing a report on the Le Mans 24 hour race, and the June 1967 edition of the American publication *Road and Track*. *Motor* must have been published at least a few days in advance of its cover date, as Fanning completed the study scene on Wednesday 14 June 1967 on Stage 2. All the day-for-night filming was accomplished a few days earlier, on Friday 9 June, with Fanning on location at Shenley Hall. Completing the sequence were close-ups of Richfield and McCarthy sat in their vehicle in front of a back-projection screen inside Stage 2, filmed almost a month later on Tuesday 4 July.

The following scenes are then set in the small hours and early morning at Steed's London apartment, which is established by second unit footage filmed at Duchess Mews, London W1, on Thursday 15 June. Breaking one of Clemens' unwritten rules, there is blood seen on Danvers' hand, not to mention on the invitation card, the envelope and the white paintwork on the pillar in Steed's home. After receiving the invitation to Benstead's car rally, Steed and Mrs Peel arrive in a 1929 3 Litre Bentley (UW 4887) supplied by Kingsbury Motors. The same vehicle had already seen service in five monochrome Rigg episodes.

Turning off Mimms Lane, the Bentley enters the grounds of Shenley Hall, with Paul Weston doubling for Macnee and Cyd Child for Rigg, in a sequence accompanied by Laurie Johnson's harp and electronic organ cues. This was filmed on the first day of production, Monday 5 June. The scene where Macnee and Rigg then alight from the Bentley on location at Shenley Hall was shot much later, on Monday 26 June.

Benstead, played by Arthur Lowe, allows Steed to have a demonstration run in his single-seater racing car simulator, which faces a back-projection screen showing the motor racing circuit at Brands Hatch in Kent from the driver's viewpoint. This simulator, loaned to the production by Lotus, was based on a Lotus 31 Formula 3 racing car and worked along the lines of the most sophisticated flight simulators of the time. Back-projection footage was shot by a small third unit despatched by Telemen to Brands Hatch on both Thursday 8 and Monday 12 June. The actual simulator, now upgraded with modern software, resurfaced for sale on the internet service Craigslist in November 2008.

As the action continues, there is a fight between Mrs Peel and Carl, the latter stealing invitation cards so that he and Alex can enter the treasure hunt. Meanwhile, the contestants are gathering in another room containing a yellow and black vintage Rolls Royce Phantom I convertible, along with petrol pump-shaped drinks dispensers that cause Benstead to comment 'They've put the super in the standard' – a joke since unfortunately rendered somewhat obsolete by the passage of time and the arrival of four-star and unleaded petrol. As lots are drawn from a crash helmet to determine the rally pairings, Emma finds herself partnered with Colbourne while Steed is teamed up with the blonde, mini-dressed debutante Penelope (Penny) Plain, who arrives with an aristocratic 'Oh darling!' In the role of Penny was Valerie Van Ost, who would go on to appear in the 1973 movie *The Satanic Rites of Dracula* and then decide to become a casting agent.

The various cars are seen lined up outside in front of Shenley Hall as Benstead's butler Bates, played by Ivor Dean, hands the teams their first clue in a sealed envelope. Tricking their new partners, Carl and Alex drive off together in their E-type and open their envelope, revealing the first clue as 'The Vaults at Mithering'.

This beginning of the treasure hunt was also filmed on Monday 26 June by the main unit. The sequence involved 15 extras playing rally participants, of whom eight supplied their own vehicles – two-seater sports cars having obviously been a specified requirement, as these were an MGA, an MGB, an MG Midget, a Triumph TR3, a Triumph TR4A, a Triumph Spitfire, a Sunbeam Alpine and a white E-type Jaguar. The Sunbeam Alpine was filmed leading the cars from the southern gateway of Shenley Hall onto Mimms Lane, turning right and continuing along Rectory Lane, only to be overtaken by Colbourne and Emma in his burgundy Mercedes 250 SE convertible. The rest of the cars followed on behind, with Steed and Penny in the Bentley and Carl and Alex in the Jaguar, quickly establishing themselves in second and third places in the rally.

The road sequences, featuring four sports cars plus the Bentley, the Mercedes, the Jaguar and Bates' Land Rover, had been filmed a couple of weeks previously by the second unit, on Tuesday 13 June. The leading cars pass the northern entrance to Shenley Hall, with Laurie Johnson's incidental music now in full flight. This memorable cue would later be given a different arrangement to become the theme to the following year's Peter Ustinov film *Hot Millions*, for which Johnson also wrote the score. Bates' Land Rover emerges from the northern gateway of Shenley Hall, the butler following the contestants at a distance in his capacity as adjudicator. There is then a short sequence of the Bentley on Crossoaks Lane, passing the track to Crossoaks Farm and continuing down Summerswood Lane heading away from the village of Ridge. Other sequences filmed on 13 June show Steed taking a shortcut across a field off Rectory Lane and the butler driving the Land Rover cross country to keep up with the leading cars.

Also resorting to a shortcut, Carl and Alex mistakenly assume that they have got into the lead, as their Jaguar comes down Deeves Hall Lane and turns right, passing Deeves Hall Cottage before accelerating along Earls Lane in the direction of South Mimms. This footage was captured by the second unit on Tuesday 6 June, with Gorrara and Farrer still standing in, or rather sitting in, for McCarthy and Richfield. Geographically the rally follows no logical route, as Deeves Hall Cottage is about a mile and a half in the opposite direction from where the various cars were last seen travelling, north-easterly along Rectory Lane.

Carl and Alex find that they are still behind the Mercedes and the Bentley when the cars arrive at the fictional village of Mithering – actually the picturesque Letchmore Heath, where The Three Horseshoes pub doubled as the episode's The Vaults. The three teams search for a clue to continue their journey, and it is Mrs Peel who notices the lettering 'Swingingdale, Get A Move On' painted on the pub sign beside the beer garden. The cars leave Letchmore Heath along The Green, Carl and Alex having taken the lead, followed by Colbourne and Emma. This sequence involved Macnee, Rigg, McCarthy, Richfield, Bowler and Van Ost all on location, and was filmed by the main unit on Tuesday 27 June.

Next comes a short sequence showing the E-type Jaguar moving at speed, with the two doubles, passing Melbury Cottage on Caldecote Lane in the built-up area of Bushey. Deciding that it is time he and Alex consolidated their lead, Carl produces a number of spiked wooden blocks, which on the next fast stretch of road he throws out behind the Jaguar, joking 'Bombs away!' Colbourne proves to be an adept driver, swerving his Mercedes in between the blocks, commenting that the following cars will probably come to grief. Steed and Penny soon arrive in the Bentley, and the agent has to perform hasty course corrections to avoid running over any of the blocks, causing the vintage vehicle to come to an abrupt halt with two wheels on the grass verge. Next to meet the hazard is an MG Midget, manned by stuntmen Gerry Crampton and Peter J Elliott. This also swerves from side to side, but the driver is not as skilful as those before him and a loud pop indicates the puncturing of a tyre. The car then goes out of control and disappears off screen, followed by the sound of a collision. All the location shots for this sequence were captured by the second unit as part of the work done on Tuesday 6 June. They were filmed on what is now Hilfield Lane South, which had been separated into two parts the previous year by construction of the M1 motorway southbound extension. With this once-busy road now a cul-de-sac, the production crew found it perfect for their purposes, as they could easily prevent other traffic from entering the filming area. Close-ups of the main cast were again shot against back-projection in the studio for incorporation into the finished sequence.

Driving on, the E-type sweeps around the bend by what is now Ridge Hill Stud and Riding Centre on the northern end of Rectory Lane before disappearing from sight. The Mercedes then arrives but, braking hard, turns left, in a different direction from the E-type, and goes down what was then the narrow access road to Shenley Lodge. Having taken another shortcut, Colbourne drives the vehicle down Bentley Heath Lane, crossing Baker Street and stopping in Sawyers Lane, just south of Potters Bar in the Hertsmere district. Filmed in long-shot, Colbourne then gets out and sprints back to the wooden signpost at the crossroads, where the camera pans to a board showing two miles to Swingingdale. In order to mislead the following contestants, the unseen Colbourne slowly turns the signpost to point in the wrong direction, then runs back to the Mercedes and drives away. Shortly after this, Carl and Alex arrive along Baker

Street and, having the same idea, Carl unknowingly twists the signpost back into the correct position; thus when Steed and Penny arrive, they turn right and continue along the most direct route.

This whole sequence involving the crossroads was again part of the second unit work carried out on Tuesday 6 June, with doubles taking the place of all the main cast members – including Les Crawford standing in for Norman Bowler and Gillian Oldham for Valerie Van Ost. A different location had originally been chosen for the action, but when the crew assembled there early that morning, Sidney Hayers was unhappy with it. Thus at his request – apparently approved by Albert Fennell – the unit moved at 9.40 am to the crossroads on Baker Street. The majority of the day's filming was then occupied with obtaining the required footage there before travelling several miles to Ridge, where additional filming was undertaken between 4.50 pm and 6.30 pm. Later it was discovered that more crossroads material was required, so various pick-up shots were scheduled for Monday 12 June. The Baker Street location would later be changed forever by construction work that took place from May 1973 to September 1975 on the section of the M25 motorway between junctions 23 and 24, reducing the crossroads to a junction and making Bentley Heath Lane a no through road.

Shortly, Carl and Alex come across another signpost showing that they are in fact moving away from Swingingdale. Carl takes out his frustration on his colleague, to which Alex protests, 'Somebody's cheated. It's not my fault if some people are dishonest.' The humour of the situation works ironically, as these two foreign spies, who have no qualms about killing to obtain secret information, are apparently aghast at cheating in a car rally! Both Neil McCarthy and Edwin Richfield were on location for this scene at the junction of Buckettsland Lane, Summerswood Lane and Holmshill Lane, near Well End.

Colbourne and Emma arrive in Swingingdale, and deciphering the earlier clue, drive around the village duck pond to a parked removal lorry, where upon lowering the tailboard Emma discovers the words 'The Village of Galding, Mr Smith's Hammer.' As Carl and Alex arrive from the opposite direction, Steed and Penny also pull up in the Bentley. Seeing the clue, both teams follow Colbourne's Mercedes. This Swingingdale footage was filmed by the second unit on the morning of Wednesday 7 June in Aldbury, near Tring, Hertfordshire, approximately 20 miles north-west of Elstree, using doubles – close-up inserts of the main cast members were shot at an alternative location. The three cars leave the village along Station Road, having to use the wrong side of the road to avoid the camera filming the sequence, which then turns around and shows them driving off into the distance. Having completed this work, the second unit departed Aldbury at 11.50 am for the Hertsmere district, where their afternoon was spent filming in Ridge.

In a car interior scene where Penny tells Steed one of her stories about an unfortunate boyfriend, back-projection behind the Bentley shows them passing a parked Ford Cortina mark two – a repeat use of footage seen before Steed's earlier shortcut across the field. The E-type Jaguar is then seen to drive into the farmyard at the fictional Old Forge Blacksmith at Galding – actually Church Farm on the junction of Deeves Hall Lane and Crossoaks Lane at Ridge – where the Carl and Alex doubles leave their vehicle and enter the barn. The sequence continues with Edwin Richfield and Neil McCarthy on the blacksmith's interior set on Stage 2 at Elstree, as the two spies discover the next clue written word by word on the heads of a number of blacksmith's hammers: 'Barrels of Fun at Tree Top Farm.' Noticing the Bentley arriving, they decide to slow down the opposition. This results in a fight in which, attempting to assist Steed, Penny accidentally strikes him on the head with a horseshoe, allowing Carl and Alex to get away first. However, having spotted one of the spiked wooden blocks in the Jaguar, Penny has decided to stop playing by the rules. As Steed recovers, she confesses that before entering the barn she put sugar in the Jaguar's petrol tank. The exteriors at Ridge – for which Macnee, Van Ost, Richfield and McCarthy were all present on location – were filmed on Wednesday 28 June. The interiors – involving the participation of stuntmen Rocky Taylor and Romo Gorrara – were shot the following week, on Tuesday 4 July.

In a sequence of additional material shot on Wednesday 28 June by the second unit, the Bentley travels along Crossoaks Lane again, away from Ridge, following the road as it becomes Summerswood Lane. It is on a narrow stretch here that Carl and Alex have parked the Jaguar and raised its bonnet to investigate their engine trouble. Leaping to safety, the two spies – still played by the actors' doubles – narrowly avoid being run down as Steed increases the speed of his Bentley.

Suddenly a gunshot rings out and the vintage car's bullet-proof windscreen is covered in a web of cracks, forcing Steed to apply the brakes in an emergency stop, bringing his vehicle to a halt on a loose gravel surface. The location for this was Crossoaks Farm in Ridge, with the usual doubles substituting Macnee and Van Ost, who were sat in the Bentley for close-ups back at Elstree, filmed on Stage 2 by the main unit on Thursday 29 June.

At the fictional Tree Top Farm, Colbourne and Emma begin searching for the next clue in rooms full of large wooden beer barrels. Emma eventually finds it hidden in a shotgun barrel, revealing the message, 'Back at My Place, What a Shocking Place to Hide the Treasure!' The location for Tree Top Farm was Rabley Park Farm situated on Packhorse Lane, near Rabley Park, about halfway between the villages of Shenley and Ridge. Major changes have since taken place at this location, making the layout look somewhat different now. A single-storey building between the farmhouse and the gateway has been demolished and replaced by a red-brick wall. Further demolition work has also occurred on the other side of the gateway, another farm structure having been removed, although the barn used for the sequence where Emma and Colbourne search for 'barrels of fun' is still intact as it is a Grade 2 listed building. The second unit captured the exterior footage on Thursday 8 June, using doubles for Macnee, Rigg, Bowler and Van Ost, but also actor Ivor Dean, who was never doubled during the making of the episode.

Having spoken with Bates at Tree Top Farm, Steed and Penny begin rushing back to High Pines, with back-projection footage seen behind the Bentley in studio shots including views of Lister Cottages on Dagger Road at Elstree. Carl and Alex, however, have now rectified their mechanical problem with the Jaguar, and they start to catch up with the Bentley. The next high-speed action was filmed heading south-east on the half-mile stretch of Aldenham Road, Elstree, with both vehicles passing the entrance and buttressed wall of the Haberdashers' Aske's School and the Dagger Lane road junction. Despite attempts by Steed to prevent the Jaguar coming alongside the Bentley, Carl manages to draw level, and then Alex produces an automatic. Fortunately, a combination of the E-type swerving about and defensive measures taken by Penny with Steed's umbrella cause Alex to miss his intended target, and as he accidentally shoots Carl. Carl's foot then presses the accelerator to the floor and the car charges forward out of control, smashing through a five-bar gate at the entrance to Home Farm on Aldenham Road before disappearing off camera and then colliding with a large tree. For the shots where Steed and Penny arrive on the scene, the E-type was chocked into place with the front of the vehicle higher than normal. The bonnet was part-way open and steam was rising from the engine compartment. Photographic evidence indicates that unscripted material was filmed of Steed checking on the occupants – who appear dead – although this is not included in the finished episode.

The original filming of this crash sequence was also carried out by the second unit on the afternoon of Thursday 8 June. However, things went horribly wrong after stuntman Romo Gorrara really did lose control of the E-type Jaguar (648 CYV) supplied by Kingsbury Motors. Wet conditions after a recent rain shower had made stunt driving difficult at the location, and the film crew had to dive for safety as the Jaguar demolished their tripod-mounted 35mm Arriflex camera. Having witnessed the accident, Rocky Taylor slammed the brakes on the Bentley and ran back to see if he could assist – but then, with everyone's attention focused on the mayhem, the Bentley burst into flames. Fortunately, part of the crew's equipment included a fire extinguisher, which a passer-by used to dowse the flames, though not before the front passenger seat had been damaged. When interviewed some years later, stuntwoman Cyd Child confirmed that the Bentley fire happened because of a leak of petrol, which suddenly ignited. Thankfully no-one was injured and Gorrara was able to walk away from the wrecked E-type, which was replaced by Kingsbury Motors with an identical vehicle for the following day's shooting. This replacement had the registration number JLN 4D, though a set of fake 648 CYV number plates was attached for filming in order to maintain continuity. This vehicle also accompanied the second unit when they returned to Home Farm and Aldenham Road on Friday 16 June and Wednesday 28 June to complete further filming for the episode. However, a third E-type (FED 349D) was also used, again with the fake 648 CYV registration plates affixed, for the filming done on Thursday 15 June at Duchess Mews, having been brought to the production by Romo Gorrara himself. The stuntman had secured a day's loan of the car from a friend who wanted to sell it, on the pretext of him being interested in buying it. After the shoot the car was returned, and apparently the owner was none the wiser that it had been a part of *The Avengers*.

Once back at High Pines, Steed quickly becomes involved in a fight with Colbourne, the more spectacular and dangerous aspects of which were achieved with Macnee and Bowler being doubled by Taylor and Crawford. This sequence was shot by the main unit on Wednesday 21 June on both the simulator room set and the car memorabilia room set on Stage 2.

The considerable amount of location filming required for the episode took longer than envisaged to complete, and principal photography was not finished until Thursday 11 July, five days over schedule, with the final day's shooting of the end tag scene being directed by Robert Day instead of Sidney Hayers. On Wednesday 2 August some post-synch recording took place at the studio, with Pauline Collins (who did not appear in the episode) redubbing the small amount of dialogue originally delivered by fellow actress Penny Bird in the minor role of ousted rally participant Miss Peabody.

The interpretation of the shooting script by cast and crew was extremely accurate, with very few differences apparent in the finished episode. The teaser sequence was originally intended to conclude with a view of the invitation envelopes, with the top one addressed to John Steed Esquire, and not a wide-angled shot of High Pines as seen in the episode. A couple of jokes in the episode – one by Mrs Peel regarding rock cakes, and another by Benstead about quality of petrol – were unscripted and presumably improvised at the filming stage. As scripted, Penny's dialogue was slightly different in the scene where she arrives late at the car rally, referring to her having trouble with her carburettor, rather than her clutch control as in the episode. Finally, the end tag scene as written on Thursday 15 June was about twice the length of what eventually appeared, and did not include the closing joke of Emma giving herself a moustache with Steed's shaver.

Benstead's address of High Pines, Edgington, had also been used for the abode of Dr Armstrong's lawyer John Hunt in 'Return of the Cybernauts', although the actual filming locations were two different places. At one point during the shoot, Cyd Child was unavailable to double Diana Rigg for a sequence of Mrs Peel driving the Mercedes at speed, so the actress's stand-in Diane Enright was requested to take on the task instead. However, feeling that this would be dangerous as she had no experience of driving cars fast, Enright refused. Eventually it was arranged for Child to take part in the sequence after all.

A couple of short clips from 'Dead Man's Treasure' featuring the E-Type Jaguar were shown in an instalment of the Channel 4 documentary series *Equinox* transmitted on Sunday 1 November 1992. 'Dead Man's Treasure' is also notable for having inspired a group of *The Avengers* enthusiasts to host a treasure hunt convention every year since 1987, usually in Borehamwood, though occasionally in Buckinghamshire where the majority of *The New Avengers* was filmed. The weekend event always culminates in a recreation of the treasure hunt/car rally as seen in the episode.

Second film proposal

In its Thursday 29 June 1967 edition *The Stage and Television Today* reported that Julian Wintle was going to produce a full feature-length version of *The Avengers* starring Patrick Macnee. This venture never came about – although two season five episodes, 'The Winged Avenger' and 'Return of the Cybernauts', would be coupled together and given a theatrical release in Europe.

Emmapeelers

Once again the *Daily Mirror* devoted space to the series in its Saturday 15 July edition, which included a two page article spotlighting the Alun Hughes-designed Emmapeelers. This also pointed out that *The Avengers* would be one of the few programmes that would actually be screened in colour when German television changed over from their black and white service in August 1967.

5.20 – 'The £50,000 Breakfast

Roger Marshall was meanwhile still under contract with ABC to provide one final script for *The Avengers*. Preferring to focus more on other projects, he fulfilled this obligation by simply rewriting the Blackman episode 'Death of a Great Dane'. He had always considered this collaboration with Jeremy Scott to be his finest contribution to the show, and reasoned that reworking it would take less time than writing a new script from scratch. The end result was 'The £50,000 Breakfast' – referred to as 'The Fifty

Thousand Pound Breakfast' (minus figures) in all Telemen documentation of the time – the writing credit for which noted 'Based on a story by Roger Marshall and Jeremy Scott', indicating its origins. The plot of the remake remains more or less faithful to the original, involving the aides of rich financier Alex Litoff secretly continuing to run his business empire after his death, allowing them time to steal the assets. One of the only notable differences is that deceased financier's personal assistant was changed by director Robert Day from a male character in 'Death of a Great Dane' to the female Miss Pegram, played by Yolande Turner, in 'The £50,000 Breakfast'. The dogs featured in the action were also changed from Great Danes to Borzois.

Marshall, who had co-created and written many episodes of the gritty private detective show *Public Eye* for ABC, had no regrets about leaving *The Avengers*, considering it to have become too far removed from its videotaped days. Interviewed for the magazine *Action TV* in January 2005, he gave the following summation of his feelings: 'Brian Clemens had fixed ideas on the series and only saw [it] how he wanted to do it. After a while I would say, "I'm just copying down what you want to say; this isn't working," and having *Public Eye* to fall back on, I left.'

The teaser sequence features an Austin Cambridge Countryman, driven by uncredited stuntman Art Thomas doubling for guest actor Richard Curnock in the role of ventriloquist Dusty Rhodes, in a collision with a trailer of hay bales towed by a Land Rover, driven by fellow uncredited stuntman Peter Clay. This sequence was shot by the second unit on Monday 26 June 1967, the first day of filming, on a stretch of road now called Chipmunk Chase, at what was Home Farm on the North Mimms Park estate. Due to bad light and showery weather, the sequence took most of the day to complete. There is no longer a working farm at this location, some of the buildings having been demolished and others having been extensively converted into dwellings.

On Tuesday 27 June, after spending time at the Haberdashers' Aske's School to complete the final pick-ups needed for 'Return of the Cybernauts', the second unit moved into central London to continue work on 'The £50,000 Breakfast', and specifically to get establishing footage for a sequence where Steed visits the Litoff penthouse. Originally they intended to film this at Bilton Towers in Great Cumberland Place, London W1, but this location was changed, possibly at Robert Day's request, and the nearby Bryanston Street used instead. The sequence shows Steed, with actor Eric Woolfe doubling for Macnee, driving the Bentley into what is supposed to be the underground car park at Marble Arch Tower, but was in fact one of two shuttered entrances at the rear of the Odeon Cinema accessed from Edgware Road, Marble Arch. Woolfe was also given a minor role in the episode as one of the assistants to Miss Pegram, although his surname would be spelt 'Woofe' in the closing credits.

The wine-tasting sequence from 'Death of a Great Dane' was reworked for 'The £50,000 Breakfast' to become a cigar party sequence. While Litoff's doctor, the noted surgeon Sir James Arnell, played by David Langton, is attending this party, Emma searches through the boot of his Rolls Royce, which was actually parked in the backlot town. However, she is disturbed by two men – Woolfe's assistant character and an uncredited Romo Gorrara – and a fight ensues. Telemen paperwork indicates that the second unit filmed this scene after 2.15 pm on Wednesday 28 June. It also states that the fictional location is a cul-de-sac called Painter Street, although no close-up of a street sign is featured during the sequence, this obviously having been considered unnecessary. Steed does mention in dialogue that the Rolls will be parked outside the premises of Kerrick Brothers, but this was a last-minute change, as the shooting script gave the name as Jerez Brothers. This shoot also involved the episode's director, Robert Day, 'calling the quarter'; that is, advising the union representatives at the studio by a certain point in the afternoon that he would require the crew to work 15 minutes' overtime to complete a shot.

Ex-*Doctor Who* companion Anneke Wills, who had appeared previously in *The Avengers* in the season three episode 'Dressed to Kill', was cast as Litoff's niece and tie boutique proprietor Judy Chanarin. All her scenes for the episode were also filmed on 28 June by the second unit on Stage 3.

On Thursday 29 June, Diana Rigg and guest actor Alan Tucker spent a whole day with Day and the second unit filming on location at Tykes Water Lake on the Aldenham Estate at Elstree, where eight slates were completed. However, for some unknown reason, none of this material was actually used in the finished episode, and Tucker did not appear on screen or receive a credit.

With the addition of some plaster animal sculptures, the cemetery on the Elstree backlot became The Happy Valley Pet Cemetery. Footage featuring Rigg and guest actors Cecil Parker, playing Litoff's butler Glover, and Cardew Robinson, playing the vicar, was completed there by the second unit on Monday 3 and Tuesday 4 July. An exterior sequence where the assistant portrayed by Eric Woolfe arrives with the Borzoi named Bellhound on a lead, meeting up with Glover driving a Jaguar saloon, was also filmed on the backlot on Friday 7 July. Shuffling Bellhound into the rear passenger seat of the car, Glover drives away, passing a distinctive D-shaped piece of roadway before following the concrete perimeter road along the back fence of the backlot.

Travelling further than usual to undertake location filming, Macnee, Rigg, guest actor Richard Owens, playing a mechanic, and the second unit drove 23 miles up the A5 to the Bedfordshire village of Hockliffe on Wednesday 12 July. Footage was then filmed at the A5 Garage on Watling Street, presumably because they had a badly-damaged grey Austin Cambridge Countryman that matched the one featured in the teaser sequence. The area occupied by the A5 Garage was partly redeveloped in later years and is now home to a small business called the Garage Door Workshop. Returning to the studio at 2.50 pm, Macnee and Rigg filmed a sequence in which Steed and Mrs Peel arrive in the Speed Six Bentley (RX 6180) at Wickham Cottage Hospital, which was actually the road between the administration block and Stages 1 and 2 at Elstree.

ABPC's expansion plans for Elstree had come to fruition earlier in the year, including the construction of three new soundstages numbered 7, 8 and 9, and *The Avengers* used these new facilities for the first time on Tuesday 4 July. The hospital interiors were filmed on Stage 9 beginning at 10.35 am, continuing the following day with material set both in the ventriloquist's dummy shop run by Rhodes' wife and the living room behind the shop. This featured Macnee, Rigg, Gorrara, Woofe, Pauline Delany as Mrs Rhodes and Michael Rothwell as a dog kennel man.

The final confrontation and fight scene on the Litoff bedroom set between Mrs Peel and Miss Pegram underwent filming on Stage 3 on Monday 10 July, with Child performing her usual doubling for Rigg and Jenny Pink standing in for Turner.

A sequence where Miss Pegram's assistant has Rhodes' car crushed was filmed on Tuesday 18 July at the premises of scrap merchants W C Jones and Company on the corner of Britannia Road and Eleanor Cross Road in Waltham Cross, Hertfordshire. This is another area that has since undergone total redevelopment, the scrap merchants having been dissolved in 1987.

When Mrs Rhodes turns on the transistor radio in her living room, the music heard is some of Laurie Johnson's dancehall music from the season four episode 'Quick-Quick Slow Death'. While at Steed's apartment, Emma reads *The Times* newspaper, which is also seen along with the supplement *Times Business News* at the Litoff penthouse.

The two Borzois featured in the production were actually called Dancer and Bellhound – the names used for them in the episode – and were supplied by animal trainer John Holmes from his Formakin Animal Centre near Cranborne in Dorset. The episode concludes with Steed finding Emma and the two Borzois in his apartment, prompting him to inform her that he does not like dogs in his home, or on the tie that she has bought him. However, this is a significant continuity error, as in the videotaped episodes Steed owned several pet dogs.

Also of note is the fact that this episode breaks two of Brian Clemens' unwritten rules for *The Avengers*: first, it depicts the killing of a woman, albeit off camera, when Mrs Rhodes is taken out by two assassins in her shop; secondly, it features a group of black West Indian steel band musicians playing at the cigar party.

5.21 – 'You Have Just Been Murdered'

Philip Levene's next screenplay, 'You Have Just Been Murdered', sees millionaires being targeted by blackmailers who prove that they can be murdered several times over, resulting in high ransom demands. This episode was directed by Robert Asher, and guest cast members included Leslie French as millionaire Lord Rathbone, Robert Flemyng as British Banking Corporation head Lord Maxted, Barrie Ingham as wealthy businessman George Unwin and Simon Oates as the villainous Skelton.[25]

Filming began on Monday 10 July 1967 and followed the usual pattern of location work being scheduled first, so that if adverse weather conditions intervened the crew could always return to shoot at the studio instead. Revisiting the familiar location of Clarendon Road in Watford, the second unit filmed establishing footage of the British Banking Corporation's premises and shots of motor vehicles on the forecourt of the since-demolished Star House. After almost three hours, the unit decamped to Mimms Lane near Ridge, to obtain footage of Lord Rathbone's vintage 1928 Lincoln and Mrs Peel's Lotus passing the junction with Packhorse Lane. Both vehicles were then filmed travelling northbound along Packhorse Lane, before turning left onto a track heading toward the fictional Bridge Farm, about a hundred metres on from Rabley Park Farm seen in the background.

The following day, the second unit once again embarked on a double location shoot. First they filmed exteriors of Unwin's residence outside the Edgwarebury Hotel off Edgwarebury Lane, Elstree, known at the time as the Edgwarebury Country Club. Capturing the required footage extremely quickly, in just over 20 minutes, the unit then moved on, although they would return for further filming on both Friday 14 July and Wednesday 2 August. The second location was the multi-levelled parking garage at a complex of buildings now called Hill House but then known as Blue Star House, situated on Highgate Hill in the London Borough of Islington. There, the remainder of the day was spent filming establishing shots of the Unwin Enterprises premises and a tense scene where Unwin is almost crushed against a concrete wall by Skelton's 3.8 litre

---

[25] Simon Oates would later portray Steed in the short-lived stage play based on the series (see Part Two).

Jaguar.

Keeping the momentum going, the second unit then spent three days on the Aldenham Estate at Elstree, filming numerous scenes in fields and woodland and both in and beside Tykes Water Lake. Rigg, French and Ingham were all on location here, along with stunt performers Les Crawford – who often doubled for Roger Moore in *The Saint* – and Frank Maher – who performed the same function for Patrick McGoohan in *Danger Man* and *The Prisoner* – playing Skelton's fellow blackmailers Morgan and Nicholls. Stuntwoman Cyd Child was also present. As ABC had been inundated with viewer requests for Rigg to wear black leather outfits like she had in season four, Alun Hughes had designed such a catsuit for this episode, complete with a silver belt, collar and decorative chains. However, a fight scene between Maher and Child doubling for Rigg proved problematic, as during the action scenes the leather outfit kept splitting along the seams. A woman from the wardrobe department had to spend most of her day sewing Child back into the garment.

Completing their allocated scenes on the last of the three days, Friday 14 July, the second unit returned to Elstree Studios to begin working on interiors for the episode at 3.00 pm, when Rigg and French reported to Stage 2 for a scene set in Rathbone's fortified living room.

The pedestrian entrance to The Happy Valley Pet Cemetery seen in 'The £50,000 Breakfast' had been dismantled and replaced on the backlot by the double gates and red-brick retaining wall of Rathbone's large home, Barns Hall. It was here that the second unit filmed on Monday 17, Tuesday 18 and Wednesday 19 July. One of these sequences involved Mrs Peel being chased up a tree by Ivan the Alsatian, one of two German Shepherd dogs provided for the episode by regular animal supplier John Holmes.

Meanwhile, the main unit also filmed on Tuesday 18 July, shooting scenes on Stage 2 of an exclusive party thrown by Unwin, involving 23 extras. Macnee was due to be present but was absent due to illness, later submitting a doctor's note indicating that he would not return for a week.

A fight scene with a sword was undertaken on the same set by the main unit on Wednesday 19 July, with Les Crawford and Frank Maher here doubling for Simon Oates and Barrie Ingham.

A shot of Steed firing a tracking device onto a suitcase belonging to Unwin was performed by Macnee among some foliage on a studio set and edited together with the Edgwarebury Hotel location footage of Unwin leaving his residence in his white Reliant Scimitar. Unwin is then seen driving up Packhorse Lane and dropping the suitcase – supposedly containing blackmail money – over the red-brick bridge at Tykes Water Lake, as Rathbone has done previously. Emma retrieves the suitcase, only to become involved in a fight with Morgan. To capture this sequence, the second unit returned to Aldenham Estate on Monday 24 July, together with Rigg, Crawford, Oates, Child and Peter J Elliott. Paperwork indicates that Elliott – a former Olympic diver – was to double for Rigg in the lake fight sequence with Crawford, but Asher obviously thought this would look unconvincing and replaced him with Child.

After Macnee was fully recovered from his illness, the second unit resumed filming at the same location on Thursday 27 July, having secured 30 feet of track and a Wilcox Dolly on which to mount their 35mm Arriflex camera. These acquisitions were used for a tracking shot where Mrs Peel forces Morgan away at gunpoint, using his Colt Combat Commander automatic pistol. Unfortunately, while filming the shot, the camera operator inadvertently allowed one of the dolly wheels to appear in the bottom left-hand corner of the picture. Apparently this was only barely visible on television sets of the time, but it is much more apparent on modern equipment. The majority of the filming on this date was restricted to a field adjacent to the lake, including shots of a horse-drawn caravan and of a haystack with a concealed door. Macnee, Rigg and Oates were joined for this by Ingham and, playing the blackmailers' boss Needle, George Murcell. Les Crawford was also on location again, both playing Morgan and doubling for Ingham, and so was Rocky Taylor, doubling for both Macnee and Murcell.

A type of flock wallpaper commonly seen in other Elstree-produced series of the time, such as *The Baron* and *The Champions*, is evident in a shade of dark green in Rathbone's home. A rampant stone lion previously seen outside the conference centre in 'Death's Door' appears again here, this time directly outside Rathbone's front door. Steed's huge reel-to-reel Ansafone makes another appearance when, together with Mrs Peel, he listens to a telephone message. Later, one of the series' unwritten rules is broken as blood is seen on the shirt of murdered millionaire Gilbert Jarvis, played by Geoffrey Chater, and also when Rathbone is impaled on his own sickle.

On Monday 31 July, while 'You Have Just Been Murdered' was still in production on Stage 2, time was allocated during the afternoon for both Macnee and Rigg to take part in an interview for German television, conducted by actor Joachim Fuchsberger. This did not flow well, as after receiving each reply from Rigg or Macnee the interviewer proceeded to translate it into German for his audience.

Emma Peel replacement screen tests

In preparation for the imminent departure of Diana Rigg, three sets of screen tests were held at Elstree at around this time to try to find a new lead actress. First, director Patrick Dromgoole supervised action tests and close-ups for Susan Engel, Jane Murdoch, Toby Robins and Wanda Ventham, with actor Moray Watson playing Steed in two-handed scenes. The same procedure was then followed for Lyn Ashley, Diane Clare (who had appeared uncredited in 'The Cybernauts'), Susan Travers and Valerie Van Ost, with James Maxwell playing Steed. On this occasion the director was Blackman-era story editor and producer John Bryce. The third set of tests took place on Stage 9 at Elstree on Thursday 20 July 1967 under the direction of Gerry O'Hara. This time, Penny Riley, Jill Melford, Barbara Steele, Gabriella Licudi and Linda Thorson each played out a scene on the Emma Peel apartment set, opposite Charles Stapley as Steed.

Production shake-up

The reason for John Bryce's involvement with the screen tests became apparent when, in its edition of Thursday 27 July 1967, *The Stage and Television Today* reported the surprising news that – despite being a major player in *The Avengers'* success and joint owner of the production company Telemen – Julian Wintle was to leave the series at the end of the current season, to be succeeded by Bryce on the next. This short news item made no mention of current producers Brian Clemens and Albert Fennell – who, according to Dave Rogers' tome *The Complete Avengers*, were at the time in dispute with ABC over the direction of the show – but in the event their contracts would not be renewed. The reason for these changes was that ABC felt that the series was now bordering on fantasy and wanted to take it back to being less extreme, with the science fiction elements replaced with more realistic storylines – a situation reported shortly before this in the Saturday 15 July edition of the trade journal *Kine Weekly*. Another significant contributor who would depart the series at the same time was composer Laurie Johnson, whose contract was likewise not renewed.

Patrick Macnee first became aware of the changes after being summoned to the Hanover Square office of ABC Managing Director Howard Thomas. He was informed that Clemens had allowed the Steed character to become too soft and jokey, and that Bryce would be back in charge as producer for season six. ABC wanted the series to leave the death rays and robot men behind and get back to reality, as in their opinion this would ultimately give it greater longevity; and they saw Bryce as the man to oversee that shift in direction.

In 2010 Clemens recalled a situation during the production of the colour Rigg episodes, when Thomas approached him and requested that he write a screenplay involving Steed and Mrs Peel with intrigue at the FA Cup final. Part of the thinking behind this was that ABC possessed a huge amount of football match footage in their archive, which could be easily incorporated into the episode. Clemens simply responded 'It's not *The Avengers*,' feeling that Thomas failed to understand what made the series a success. However, with hindsight, Clemens believes this was probably held against him and contributed to him and Fennell being ousted.

ABPC claim *The Avengers*

Around July 1967, parent company ABPC took a decision to move *The Avengers* from ABC to come directly under its own control at Elstree Studios. Further to this, with Julian Wintle's departure imminent, the Telemen production company he part-owned with ABC would be wound up upon the conclusion of work on season five. For the next season, Telemen would be seamlessly replaced by the ABC Television Films production company, which since its formation in late 1966 had made only the television special *Lucy in London* with American star Lucille Ball. A second spectacular starring French actress Brigitte Bardot had been planned, but had failed to materialise. The other television film project that ABC had hoped to make, the co-production with American International titled *The Solarnauts*, had had a pilot episode called 'Cloud of Death' filmed at Elstree in August 1966, but had also failed to progress any further.

This move by ABPC was motivated in large part by forthcoming major changes to the ITV network, which would come into effect at the end of July 1968 and would amount to the biggest shake-up in UK commercial broadcasting to date. Lord Hill of the Independent Television Authority (ITA) had first announced the intention to make such changes at the end of 1966, when he had invited applications to run restructured regional franchises. As noted in reports by both the *Daily Mail* and the *Daily Telegraph* on Monday 12 June 1967, the outcome of these applications had now been decided, and would entail a realignment of the established franchisees, plus the creation of some new ones.

In a seemingly unthinkable move, ABC would lose their weekend monopoly in the Midlands and North regions, as Hill had decided to abolish weekend-only contracts with the exception of London. Howard Thomas had consequently set his company's sights on becoming the capital's weekend provider, but in an unforeseen move this franchise had been awarded instead to the newly-formed London Weekend Television (LWT). Thomas and ABC had then put themselves up for consideration for the

Midlands region, but had ultimately lost out to Lew Grade's ATV. Another target had been the newly-created Yorkshire region, but this had always been envisaged as a showcase for a locally-run and financed operation, and from that point of view ABC had never been in serious contention.

Ultimately the only remaining unallocated contract had been the much-sought-after London weekday franchise, which had previously been the domain of Rediffusion. The ITA had thus had two major bidders – ABC and Rediffusion – vying for this lucrative region. Both companies were among the 'big four' ITV programme-makers – the other two being ATV and Granada. In fact, Rediffusion had been the first independent UK television channel to begin transmission in September 1955. The thought of having to lose one of these two prolific and high-profile companies was obviously unappealing to the ITA, and in June 1967 they came up with a solution by strongly suggesting an amalgamation. The two parent companies, ABPC and the British Electric Traction Company, vetoed this move, but instead settled on forming a new joint venture, which would become Thames Television. The resources of both ABC and Rediffusion would be incorporated into Thames, with the profits being shared equally between the two parent companies. However, the former ABC would have a controlling share interest, and Howard Thomas would be installed as chairman. Thames would simply take what it wanted from Rediffusion – including some staff and the children's, schools and current affairs departments – resulting in the former franchise-holder becoming little more than an investor in the new ITV contractor.

ABPC's board of directors, realising that there would no longer be an ABC in 13 months' time, took their decisions regarding *The Avengers*' future within weeks of the franchise negotiations being resolved. They thereby prevented any future profits from overseas sales of the series going to either Thames or the British Electric Traction Company.

5.22 – 'The Positive Negative Man'

By the time the main body of filming on 'You Have Just Been Murdered' was completed a day over schedule on Wednesday 2 August 1967, work on the next escapade was as usual already under way. 'The Positive Negative Man' came from talented scriptwriter Tony Williamson, who had contributed 'The Murder Market', 'Too Many Christmas Trees' and 'The Thirteenth Hole' to season four. His lack of recent contributions to *The Avengers* was due to his commitments as script consultant on the BBC's *Adam Adamant Lives!* and also scriptwriting on ITC's *The Champions*.

'The Positive Negative Man' has Steed and Emma tracking down someone or something that is killing, one by one, a group of people who are all connected. The killer's method of despatching the victims is original, mysterious and intriguing, making the story a perfect fit for *The Avengers*, with various similarities to the earlier episodes 'From Venus with Love' and 'The Winged Avenger'. In short, 'The Positive Negative Man' is a story that could not really have been adapted to any other series … it is pure *The Avengers*.

A number of locations were found in the Bricket Wood area near Watford, around five miles north-west of Borehamwood. These included the Building Research Establishment, a complex of buildings and service roads accessible from either Bucknalls Lane or Bucknalls Drive. This is where Mrs Peel visits the fictional Wavel Electronics, finding that electronics expert Maurice Jubert, played by Sandor Elès, has already undergone a shocking experience. Another part of the site then appears when Steed returns to his Bentley after speaking with electrical researcher Mankin, played by Peter Blythe. As Steed drives away in his 1927 3 litre Bentley (YT 3942) – supplied by Kingsbury Motors and used in the series only once previously, in 'Small Game for Big Hunters' – a blue Morris 1000 van follows him. This footage was filmed by the second unit, with director Robert Day in charge, on Tuesday 25 July 1967 from 8.50 am to 3.15 pm. Afterwards, the unit returned to the studio, where they executed filming in the backlot town, showing a Morris 1000 van arriving outside Mrs Peel's apartment.

Steed receives a lesson in the destructive potential of broadcast power when the ammeter on his Bentley goes haywire and the car's wiring begins to burn out due to the overload in the electrical system. Footage for this sequence was shot by the second unit on Monday 24 July – the first day of filming on the episode – with the Morris van tailing the Bentley, turning off Station Road into Smug Oak Lane, Bricket Wood and then at the entrance to what is now the HSBC Group Management Training Centre. The sequence continues with footage captured earlier the same day at a ford close to Old Moor Mill at Colney Street. Rocky Taylor drove the Bentley in a cloud of smoke and then steered the vintage vehicle into a shallow-bed river for the scene where Steed manages to dissipate the electrical charge. There were substantial changes made at this location shortly after filming, with the footbridge being dismantled and a road bridge being constructed to span the river.

For the exteriors of the Risley Dale Electronic Research Laboratory the crew returned to what was then the British Rail Study Centre in The Grove Park, off Hempstead Road on the outskirts of Watford. However, unlike 'The See-Through Man' and 'Never, Never Say Die' – the other colour episodes to shoot exteriors here – 'The Positive Negative Man' used the rundown area where British Rail employees were given hands-on training. The various single-storey brick and wooden buildings here were demolished long ago, and the railway lines, signals and signal box have also gone, as the area was completely cleared sometime in the mid-'90s.

For a sequence where the electrically-charged Peter Haworth, played by Michael Latimer, touches the railway line with a metal tube on one of his fingers, a trail of gunpowder was lit to indicate that the charge was travelling along the rail toward Mankin. This was augmented in dubbing by the laser blast sound effect heard previously in 'From Venus with Love'. The effect was used a second time in the scene where the unfortunate Mankin attempts to escape by climbing over the wire perimeter fence, being stopped when Haworth emerges from a nearby building and simply touches the fence to electrocute his victim. The small metal tube that Latimer had on his forefinger as a device to discharge electrical energy had previously appeared in the series as one of Willy Frant's false digits in 'A Touch of Brimstone'.

This British Rail Study Centre shoot was the main location work done for the episode, with Macnee, Rigg, Latimer, Blythe and Ray McAnally, playing the villainous Dr Creswell, all on location at some point during the six visits made to the site by the second unit between Wednesday 26 July and Wednesday 16 August.

The exterior of Creswell's abode was represented on location by a house called Hillcrest Cottage, found two miles east of the studio on Barnet Road in Arkley, where the second unit filmed on Monday 7 August and again ten days later. Macnee, Rigg, Latimer and McAnally all spent time on location there, beside the house and also in the reasonably-sized landscaped grounds. This property has since been demolished.

Some humour is brought to the episode by the character of Cynthia Wentworth-

Howe, a jobsworth hush-hush secretary from the Ministry played by Caroline Blakiston, who is featured in a short scene with Steed shot by the second unit at Tykes Water Lake on Friday 11 August. They both stand in the lake, wearing waders, as Cynthia fishes. Then Steed requests the secret files on Project 90 and, much to Cynthuia's amazement, produces from inside the crown of his bowler hat his priority pass proving his top security clearance. The pass reads, 'John Steed 379905 London has been permitted access to all ministry files class A3-C7.'

The episode also manages to generate a sense of menace in a sequence where Steed attempts to gain access to the Morris van and, touching the exterior door handle, receives an electric shock, which causes him to collapse to the ground unconscious. Having been abducted, Emma awakes to find herself bound to a bench and Creswell boasting about creating an army of electrically-charged men who will assist him in ruling the UK, in response to which she quips, 'What happens if there's a power cut?'

The concluding fight scene once again involved Rocky Taylor doubling for Macnee, with Les Crawford performing the same function for Michael Latimer and Dinny Powell providing cover for Ray McAnally. The fight was arranged by Ray Austin, and Robert Day's early experience as a cameraman in the film industry came in useful as he decided to operate one of two handheld Arriflex cameras used to shoot the sequence. With medical staff standing by, Powell sustained minor cuts after being thrown head first through a plate glass window, and under the circumstances Day decided that this was good enough and did not request a second take.

However, Day himself did not escape without injury from filming this episode, as on Friday 11 August, when he was on location with the second unit, he tripped and damaged an ankle. This resulted in a trip to a local hospital for an X-ray, which fortunately showed no broken bones. Day returned to the location and resumed directing, although in his absence the unit had been stood down for an hour and a half.

As a result of their near miss with high voltage, Steed and Emma find themselves magnetically attached to his Bentley in the end tag scene, though an earlier draft of the script had Mrs Peel being stuck to a dustbin lid.

'The Positive Negative Man' concluded principal photography four days over schedule, on Thursday 31 August.

'This'll Kill You'

In the upheaval surrounding the departure of Wintle, Clemens, Fennell and Johnson, season five would fall short of its planned 26 episodes, eventually comprising only 24, and a number of unmade scripts remained on file. One of these was Cyril Abraham's 'This'll Kill You', dated August 1967, concerning a Chinese plot to deluge the UK with almost endless rain, caused by the seeding of clouds from a giant hot air balloon released from an amusement park. Steed and Emma follow a bizarre trail of murders caused by excessive pranks, which involve an Olympic diver, a bumbling private detective named Corker and a joke shop proprietor named Janie who hates her profession.

Offering elements of weather manipulation, this script instantly reminds one of 'A Surfeit of H_2O' from the previous season. Other aspects of the story such as funfairs and lethal practical jokes had also featured previously in the series. 'This'll Kill You' could have become a worthwhile entry in the season, although Brian Clemens would no doubt have wanted to perform some rewrites first. The Chinese Communist Colonel

Zebra would probably have become a home-grown villain; Corker may have been assigned a different career, private detectives being somewhat out of place in the filmed episodes; and Janie would presumably have become more eccentric than gloomy when cutting up horror face-masks in her joke shop. The idea of Colonel Zebra having facial tattoos in the design of the animal, which the script indicated had taken four years to complete, would probably have been changed or dropped completely, as the tattoos would have a been a nightmare for the make-up department to have had to apply every day before filming. A scene where a character called Wright dies after launching himself from a diving board into a swimming pool that has been drained of water also strains credibility, as he would surely have noticed the water level falling, even though the script describes him as being occupied undertaking a rigorous warm-up routine.

Leaving these shortcomings aside, some portions of the screenplay work exceptionally well. These include the teaser, where a character called Sir Basil telephones Steed late at night during a vicious thunderstorm and is apparently killed by a lightning strike inside his building. Upon investigating, Steed and Mrs Peel find that someone has hidden capsules of nitro-glycerine in Sir Basil's cigars, and this was actually the cause of his death. Another clever sequence involves Mrs Peel at the amusement park, where a woman mistakes her for the new assistant in the knife-throwing act. To avoid detection, Mrs Peel allows the woman to rehearse her routine by throwing knives at her, all of which narrowly miss. Only later does the woman reveal that she is not in fact the knife-thrower but the funfair strong lady, attempting to expand her sideshow skills.

After killing meteorologist Professor Parto, Zebra traps Steed inside something called the Zero Cloud Chamber and, turning up the temperature, leaves him to die from heat exhaustion, before returning to the funfair to throw more knives at a helpless Mrs Peel. Effecting an escape from the rehearsal tent where she is being used for target practice, Emma then rescues Steed and they both return to the amusement park to release the owner Mr Jumbo, before taking on Zebra and his cohorts. Zebra escapes to the basket beneath the hot air balloon and, severing the final guide rope with the swordstick hidden in his umbrella, Steed sends the villain skyward. Mrs Peel is resigned to the fact that it might now rain forever, but Steed confesses that during the earlier confusion he managed to disconnect the tubes to the cloud-seeding chemicals, and all is well in Avengerland again.

'It's Bigger than Both of Us'

Another unmade season five script, this one from July 1967, was called 'Its Bigger than Both of Us', from the American husband-and-wife writing team of Pat Silver and Jessie Lasky Jnr. Lasky had established himself as a scriptwriter in Hollywood between the '30s and the late '50s, working on features including *The Ten Commandments*, then drifted into television work and collaborating with his wife. Together they had provided scripts for both *The Saint* and *Danger Man* in the '60s. In the '70s they would go on to contribute episodes of *The Protectors* and *Space: 1999* and a feature-length *Hammer House of Mystery and Suspense*. Little is known about the storyline to 'Its Bigger than Both of Us', except that it was reportedly totally lacking *The Avengers'* usual sense of humour, coming across more like an episode of ITC's *The Champions* – which is probably why it remained unused.

5.23 – 'Murdersville'

The season's penultimate entry, Brian Clemens' 'Murdersville', entered production on Thursday 3 August 1967, ten days after 'The Positive Negative Man', but actually concluded principal photography six days before that episode, on Friday 25 August. Film buff Clemens was apparently inspired by the 1955 movie *Bad Day at Black Rock* in coming up with this story, which involves a whole community hiding a deadly secret – territory he had also explored in his earlier episode 'The Town of No Return'. The action focuses mainly on Emma, and Macnee would be absent for the majority of filming.

The August scheduling of the filming reflected the fact that this was another storyline requiring extensive location work. The picturesque village of Aldbury near Tring in Hertfordshire was chosen to represent the fictional Little Storping in-the-Swuff. The crew were already familiar with Aldbury, as some second unit footage for 'Dead Man's Treasure' had been shot there a couple of months previously.

The teaser sequence is pure Clemens, enticing viewers into another bizarre situation that could happen only in Avengerland. Two local men – Hubert, played by John Ronane, and Mickle, played by Colin Blakely – are seated outside The Happy Ploughman pub – actually The Greyhound in Aldbury – drinking beer, playing dominoes and discussing the weather. Then suddenly a man, played by the uncredited Peter Clay, runs from the pub, followed by another, the uncredited Maxwell Craig, holding a pint of beer and a revolver. The second man calmly shoots the first several times, killing him. Throughout this, the two locals do not react at all, but simply continue their game of dominoes and agree that there might be rain.

On the first day of production Telemen hired an Aerospatiale Alouette II helicopter from RBA Helicopters of Reading, for filming by the second unit in a field adjacent to what was Ridge Hill Farm on the northern end of Rectory Lane at Shenley. Cyd Child doubled for Rigg, being chased around the field by the helicopter. The helicopter was also used to take aerial shots of the open countryside. This particular helicopter, registered as G-AVEE, also appeared in episodes of *The Baron*, *Man in a Suitcase*, *The Champions*, *Department S* and – under its previous registration, F-BNKZ – both *The Saint* and *The Prisoner*. In addition, a Mini Moke was hired from Kingsbury Motors for use as an off-road camera car to assist in capturing the footage for this sequence. Blakely, Ronane and the latter's stunt double Bill Cummins were all on location, directed by Ray Austin.

The following day, Friday 4 August, Austin resumed filming at Shenley with the second unit on both Harris Lane and Silver Hill, with actor John Chandos, playing businessman Samuel Morgan, driving a black Vanden Plas Princess R. Footage involving the Rover of local GP Dr Haymes, played by Ronald Hines, was also executed here, although this was later written off for continuity reasons after the vehicle broke down and had to be replaced by another car several days later for additional filming at Aldbury. It appears that filming was also undertaken at a large house somewhere in the village to represent the new home of Emma's childhood friend Major Paul Croft, played by Eric Flynn, but the car breakdown rendered this useless too and necessitated more re-filming.

Five solid days of further filming at Aldbury began on Monday 7 August, this time carried out by the main unit, with the episode's principal director Robert Asher assuming control and utilising more performers on location than any previous episode of the series. For tracking shots, the unit secured a Wilcox Dolly and 30 feet of rails from Elstree Studios, plus a second 35mm Arriflex film camera. The unit vehicles for the first day of this major undertaking were a camera car, a sound car, a prop van, a construction/electrical van, a motor coach, a mini bus, four unit cars plus the action vehicles: Emma's Lotus Elan; the Citroen Safari belonging to Croft's batman Forbes, played by Norman Chappell; a Wolsley 6/110 police car; the MGB of Morgan's murderer Frederick Williams, played by Andrew Laurence; and Haymes' Rover.

In addition, Telemen hired from Berkhamsted Urban District Council a Land Rover complete with an extended platform. Usually used to work on streetlights, this provided a base for overhead shots. When the Rover, supplied by Kingsbury Motors, had its aforementioned breakdown on Tuesday 8 August, director of photography Alan Hume volunteered his own Ford Corsair for use as a replacement. The unit spent parts of the final two days collecting footage involving this vehicle at Stocks House, a large property that stands in extensive grounds off Stocks Road, just north of the village, to replace the footage shot earlier in Shenley.

For a sequence where Mrs Peel follows Dr Haymes' Ford Corsair back to his surgery, Rigg was sat in the Lotus in the studio against back-projection of Aldbury, passing the pub, the duck pond and the combined library and museum – which has since become a shop. The exterior location for Haynes' surgery was on Trooper Road. Later, when Emma goes on the run from the locals, she is seen venturing into Town Farm, off Stocks Road in the centre of the village. A ducking stool sequence shot at the village duck pond was performed partly by Rigg, but it was her stunt double Cyd Child who braved the underwater aspect. Child arranged with the crew that she would wiggle her toes when she wanted to be brought back to the surface, but to her surprise she was brought up sooner than expected, because the stunt was beginning to make Asher feel ill.

Filming at Elstree got under way on Monday 14 August on Stage 2 on interior sets of the local museum. This played host to 14 performers, three stand-ins and six extras. An exterior scene where Emma discovers the body of the murdered Forbes, and a later one where she takes Dr Haymes to see the body, only to encounter instead a local man called Higgins, played by Joseph Grieg, were both shot among the shrubbery on the studio backlot on Wednesday 16 August. Also on that day, as the second unit was preoccupied with location filming for 'The Positive Negative Man', a small unit was brought in from Pinewood Studios to film travelling matte footage for 'Murdersville', reporting to Telemen at Elstree at 8.30 am to accept the assignment. A couple of days later, Rigg joined the second unit back in the field beside Ridge Hill Farm to complete several action close-ups, which would later be intercut with the existing helicopter footage obtained there earlier.

Stock footage showing Duke's Drive in Burnham Beeches, Buckinghamshire was used as travelling matte behind Haymes and Emma in his car when it was filmed on one of the soundstages. The same footage had previously seen service in 'The Bird Who Knew Too Much' and *The Saint* episode 'Little Girl Lost', and was apparently sourced from a third party.

In a sequence where Emma is held prisoner and forced to make a telephone call to Steed, there is some amusing dialogue as she tips him off to the situation by calling him Johnsey Wonsey and mentions their four supposed children, all named after senior members of the production team: Julian (Wintle), Albert (Fennell), Gordon (L T Scott) and baby Brian (Clemens).

Considering that this is a Clemens episode it is perhaps surprising that it breaks two of his unwritten rules: the deceased Forbes has blood visible on his forehead, and two uniformed police officers are featured – even though they are actually fake.

A wooden sign outside Dr Haymes' surgery incorrectly reads 'Dr J F Haynes MD', suggesting a breakdown in communication somewhere between the production office and the carpenters' shop.

A number of performers went uncredited, including Gareth Thomas – later to play Blake in the BBC's *Blake's 7*, amongst many other notable roles – as an assassin wearing dark glasses, Paul Weston portraying the second fake policeman, and Hilary Dwyer playing telephone operator Hilary, one of a number of villagers held prisoner in the museum and prevented from speaking by having a medieval bridle attached to her head. Apparently the bridle was so tight when first fitted that the actress was almost in tears, resulting in the prop being adjusted on set, after which it was comfortable enough for her to keep it on even between takes. Among the artefacts on show in the museum is an Iron Maiden prop previously seen in 'Castle De'ath'.

5.24 – 'Mission ... Highly Improbable'

The final colour Rigg adventure was 'Mission ... Highly Improbable' by Philip Levene, involving Eastern Bloc agents having a miniaturisation machine at their disposal and causing general havoc with it. It was based on a rejected script of Levene's called 'The Disappearance of Admiral Nelson', submitted to the production office in September 1964 – at which time Brian Tesler had been unimpressed, both because he considered it to be blatant science fiction and because he felt the size-changing aspects would be virtually impossible to achieve in a believable way. Clemens retitled the episode 'Mission ... Highly Improbable' probably as a tongue-in-cheek swipe at *Mission: Impossible*, the American series that had defeated *The Avengers* in the Emmy Awards, although the phrase does actually crop up in the episode's dialogue.

With Robert Day assigned as director, principal photography on the episode kicked off on Wednesday 23 August 1967, two days before the conclusion of that on 'Murdersville', which had overrun by two and a half days. Unlike on most episodes, it started in the studio rather than on location, with Rigg and Macnee on the Emma Peel apartment set on Stage 3. Exterior shooting began a couple of days later, featuring material of Rigg and the Lotus on the backlot. In the finished episode this would be edited together with footage shot by the second unit on Monday 4 September outside The Old Vicarage off St Mary's Road at North Mymms Park. The summer house belonging to the villain General Shaffer, played by Ronald Radd, was also built on the backlot, while the exteriors of his home were shot at the large house at Rabley Park near Ridge; another location visited by the second unit on 4 September.

The teaser, involving a Rolls Royce Silver Cloud and motorcycle outriders, was shot by the second unit on Friday 15 September on parts of the narrow and rarely-used service roads on the North Mymms Park Estate, directed by Sidney Hayers rather than Robert Day, who had already filmed other footage there as part of the work done on 4 September.

A scene where Dr Chivers, played by Francis Matthews, disturbs Steed examining the tyre tread on a Land Rover at the government's Metal Fatigue Division was filmed on the studio lot beside the film vaults. The exterior of the experimental shed was represented by the building that housed the scene docks. The later scene where Colonel

Drew, played by Richard Leech, invites General Shaffer for a closer inspection of the Alvis Saracen FV603 armoured car housed in the shed was also undertaken on the lot, in front of the white-bricked building next to the cutting rooms, used for administration purposes at the time. The second unit captured this footage on Thursday 31 August when, due to the excessive workload, Day called the quarter at lunchtime, enabling the unit to work overtime, but only until 5.20 pm.

The six-wheeled Saracen, built from a specially-developed alloy and able to withstand direct artillery fire, replaced Levene's original concept of a revolutionary one-man tank, the Champion MK39, as outlined in 'The Disappearance of Admiral Nelson'. Like the majority of action vehicles seen in the series, it was sourced through Kingsbury Motors, who also delivered Steed's 3 litre Bentley (YT 3942) to North Mymms Park for two days of filming.

An armoured car demonstration sequence was shot on Thursday 7 September at what was the Ball Lane Sand Pit at London Colney, Hertfordshire. This location later underwent complete redevelopment, the building of the M25 motorway through the area, plus landscaping and the planting of trees, changing it beyond recognition. The sequence was augmented with stock footage of firing artillery pieces and close-ups of the supporting cast shot on the studio backlot that afternoon. A portion of the demonstration footage would later reappear in the *Department S* episode 'Who Plays the Dummy?'

The screenplay required three giant sets for the miniaturised characters to inhabit, prompting the set builders and props department out of their comfort zone to construct larger-than-life everyday items. Steed clambers about an enormous desktop, complete with giant ashtray and smoking cigar, blotting pad, picture frame, fountain pens and telephone, plus the desk calendar last seen in the Temp Storage Company in 'Death's Door'. Music editor Karen Heward would accompany this with various incidental passages and cues drawn from the previous episodes 'Castle De'ath', 'From Venus with Love' and 'The Winged Avenger'.

Prior to filming, guest actor Nicholas Courtney, who played Captain Gifford, had the opportunity to ride the Triumph 650cc his character would use in the episode, but considered the machine too powerful. Borrowing another, less powerful motorcycle, he practiced riding it, but by his own admission still lacked confidence when filming began. However, as the director only required the bike to be ridden slowly, he passed the ordeal.

On the set of the office of Professor Rushton, played by Noel Howlett, the walls were decorated with a number of vintage car prints previously seen at High Pines in 'Dead Man's Treasure' and also in Dr Haymes' surgery in 'Murdersville'.

In one scene, Shaffer's assistant Karl, played by regular 'heavy' actor and stuntman Dinny Powell (credited here with his first name as Denny), is seen sat on guard reading the classic Jane Austen novel *Emma*, obviously intended as an in-joke. Like Penelope Keith in 'Something Nasty in the Nursery', actress Nicole Shelby made it into the closing credits even though her actual performance was edited out of the episode – although she would eventually get to appear in *The Avengers* in the next season's 'They Keep Killing Steed'.

All of Diana Rigg's work on the episode was scheduled for the first five days of filming, her last scenes being shot on Wednesday 30 August, although she did return later to attend the end-of-season wrap party.

The Emma Peel era of *The Avengers* concluded with the final day of production on

'Mission ... Highly Improbable', Friday 22 September, when the main unit shot a mixture of studio scenes and exteriors without performers. Having been cutting and splicing film together into finished episodes since the beginning of this season, supervising editor Peter Tanner took a rare opportunity and left the cutting room to direct this establishing footage.

Although the script of 'The Disappearance of Admiral Nelson' pre-dated by several years Irwin Allen's series *Land of the Giants*, which also featured characters on giant-sized sets, the latter's pilot episode, 'The Crash', was networked across the United States nine days before 'Mission ... Highly Improbable.'

Season five resumes transmission

With the autumn season about to get under way, the ITV regional companies once again regarded *The Avengers* as a major asset, scheduling the resumption of transmissions for late September/early October with 'Return of the Cybernauts'. Grampian, who had not screened any season five episodes so far, were the first to begin, on Wednesday 27 September at 8.00 pm, followed by Rediffusion the following evening at 9.00 pm and then Southern a day later at 8.00 pm. Rediffusion would switch the series between Thursday and Friday evenings, and these transmissions proved extremely popular, *The Avengers* being rated the most watched programme of the week on at least four occasions in the London region. The publicity machine began rolling again, with both *TV World* and Issue 622 of *TV Times* running covers showing Macnee and Rigg in publicity shots taken on the set.

Both ABC regions resumed their Saturday evening transmissions of the series more or less at 9.05 pm on 30 September, with TWW and Teledu Cymru opting for 7.25 pm the following evening. Border also opted for Sunday 1 October, but at the later time of 10.05 pm. The outstanding region yet to transmit any season five episodes, Ulster, finally joined the party on Thursday 5 October, choosing 7.30 pm as their start time. Most of the remaining regions – Anglia, Channel, Tyne Tees and Scottish – waited until Saturday 7 October, when they broke ranks by restarting the season with 'Death's Door' at 9.10 pm. That left just Westward, who would not show any more episodes until the new year.

More Emma Peel replacement screen tests

On 12 September 1967 another round of Mrs Peel replacement screen tests took place under the direction of Patrick Dromgoole. This time Linda Thorson, Valerie Van Ost, Aleta Morrison and Mary Peach all performed opposite Patrick Macnee on the Emma Peel apartment set. Seven days later it was the turn of Jane Merrow, Tracy Reed, Anne Lawson and Christina Taylor to work with Macnee, this time under the direction of Sidney Hayers.

On Tuesday 3 October, Thorson attended the studio for a nine-minute read-through and action test with actors Jeremy Burnham and – in a voice-only capacity – Ian McShane on the Steed apartment set on Stage 3, with Patrick Dromgoole directing. By this time there were just four actresses in the running for the part; in addition to Thorson, Reed, Merrow and Peach all visited Elstree Studios for a further screen test. However, it would be another 16 days before ABC would hold a press conference at their Hanover Square offices to announce the identity of the new Avengergirl.

Undoubtedly season five of *The Avengers* had been the most successful yet, selling to more overseas markets than any of the earlier ones and making it the most profitable series ever produced by ABC. However, with Diana Rigg, Brian Clemens, Albert Fennell, Julian Wintle and Laurie Johnson all now gone, could the series' future ever match what had gone before?

SEASON SIX

MY WILDEST DREAM

The new Avenger girl is announced

Showing just how much influence the American ABC network was now exerting on *The Avengers*, the screen tests for all four actresses still in the running to replace Diana Rigg – namely Linda Thorson, Tracy Reed, Jane Merrow and Mary Peach – were shipped off to them in the United States, where they would make the final decision on who would be Steed's new partner.

The *Daily Express* of Friday 6 October 1967 reported on how the mighty dollar would dictate the future of this most British of British television series, stating that Thorson was the favourite to fill Rigg's kinky boots. However, they emphasised that it was not a done deal, reporting that others under consideration were Gabrielle Drake, Jane Merrow, Valerie Van Ost and Pamela Ann Davy – showing that their information was slightly out of date, as in fact the only one of those still in contention was Merrow. The *Express* also mentioned Aleta Morrison, describing her as having the most beautiful legs in Europe, but in the acting stakes she was only ever a supporting performer.

The ABC network spoke and ABC Television listened, as Linda Thorson was ultimately chosen as the series' new female lead. However, some executives considered her to be slightly overweight, so she spent eight days on a strict diet at Henlow Grange Health Farm in Bedfordshire. After that she was offered a contract, and signed on the dotted line to become the new Avengergirl. Thorson also visited Harley Street, where an eminent doctor placed her on a course of Durophet tablets, which curbed hunger. However, it was later discovered that this drug could have serious side effects and it was banned. Incoming producer John Bryce accepted Thorson's own choice of name for her new character, Tara King, the Tara being inspired by the place of the same name in the classic movie *Gone with the Wind* and King by king and country.

Thorson was announced to the press as Miss Tara King on Thursday 19 October at ABC's London offices. Coverage the following day included a piece in the *Daily Mirror* with the headline 'Enter Tara, The New Avenger', and one in the *Daily Express* where Steed's new partner was described as 'Essentially warm, feminine and sexy.'

It had been decided that Thorson's own long dark hair made her appear too similar to Rigg, so as Tara she should have it curled and dyed blonde. Sporting this new look and wearing a lilac mini dress, she took part with Macnee in a London photoshoot on Sunday 22 October, posing for the cameras at the Savoy Hotel, on the steps of the British Museum and taking a stroll alongside the Thames on the Embankment. A newsreel crew from Associated British Pathé were present to capture the event on film, and incoming producer John Bryce was quoted in the press as saying, 'She'll be more likely to hit her opponents with her handbag than fell them with a karate chop.' Providing more background on the new character, Bryce also indicated that Tara was a wealthy farmer's daughter and would not wear leather, but would appear more feminine, soft and sexy and favour a line in '20s retro fashion.

Colour Diana Rigg season publicity

Meanwhile, throughout October the *TV Times* devoted several pages to Diana Rigg in every issue, including a three-part profile and interview titled 'The Girl Behind Emma Peel'. This interest came about from the then current transmissions, though on Saturday 21 October ABC suffered a delay in both of their regions, resulting in 'Dead Man's Treasure' beginning at 9.10 pm instead of the billed time of 9.05 pm.

'Invitation to a Killing'

Filming on what would turn out to be the final season of *The Avengers*, again budgeted at £50,000 an episode, commenced on location at Starveacres, off Watford Road in Radlett, on Monday 23 October 1967, with Robert Asher directing the main unit. The Donald James-written screenplay, 'Invitation to a Killing', was intended to introduce Tara King – and was also, incidentally, notable for its inclusion of a number of black characters, providing immediate evidence of the ending of Brian Clemens' influence. However, the first day's work did not run smoothly. Shooting was delayed for approximately an hour by the non-arrival of Steed's 3 litre Bentley (YT 3942) from Kingsbury Motors, as it had unfortunately broken down *en route* to the location. More seriously, John Bryce's decision to make Tara a blonde caused problems almost immediately, when the liberal application of peroxide to hide Thorson's dark roots caused the ends of her hair to break off, leaving spiky strands approximately a quarter of an inch long. As a result of this extreme reaction, she would be forced to wear wigs for the filming of the next 11 episodes until her hair grew back. This unfortunate incident cannot have done anything for the confidence of the 20-year-old actress, who later admitted to spending much of her time indoors during that period.

On days three and four of the location shoot, overcast weather caused further filming delays. This prompted Bryce to dispatch the second unit with its director John Hough to work alongside the main unit at Starveacres in an attempt to catch up. On Thursday 26 October, the first studio day at Elstree also failed to run smoothly when the Add-a-Vision system that had been introduced in March 1967 broke down, resulting in an hour's downtime for the crew until it was repaired. Concerned about getting behind schedule again, Bryce repeated his strategy of sending in the second unit to share the workload. This resulted in the main unit under Asher and the second unit under Hough working side by side for six days solid on Stage 3. As the storyline revolved around stolen rifles, an employee of armourers Bapty and Co was unsurprisingly present to advise the cast and crew on the safety aspects of handling the weapons – although, more surprisingly, only on one day, Friday 3 November.

Filming for the episode wrapped on Thursday 9 November. However, unknown to the crew at the time, further problems lay in store for 'Invitation to a Killing', and it would never reach the screen in the form originally intended.

New cars for Tara and Steed

Wanting to retain their association with the series, Lotus Cars provided a red example (NPW 999F) of their new +2 model Lotus Elan, which had been introduced the previous month. This would become Tara's personal transport. Interviewed by *Time Screen* magazine in 1992, Brian Clemens said, 'Lotus later told us that the association with us was worth five million dollars and really sold the car for them in America.'

Seeking a similar product placement, AC Cars of Weybridge in Surrey offered the production one of their AC 428 sports cars. Liking the look of this, Bryce decided to make it Steed's new car and dispense with the vintage Bentleys. As it turned out, the AC 428 would become a very rare vehicle, with only 81 being made before the model was discontinued in 1973. The majority of these were exported to the United States. Of the 81, only 29 were convertibles, and it was one of these, a maroon example (LPH 800D), that would be used in *The Avengers*. It was already a year old when it was delivered in time to feature in the next episode.

Tara King characterisation

The edition of *The Stage and Television Today* published on Thursday 26 October 1967 included a small feature on Tara King and how she would differ substantially from Emma Peel, describing her as a member of the international jet set who would rely on feminine guile more than fighting ability. They added that although she would fight on occasion, she would not be above screaming for help in dangerous situations. John Bryce was confirmed as the producer of the upcoming season, with Jack Greenwood continuing as production controller. Gordon L T Scott was incorrectly named as executive producer, when in fact his title would be executive in charge of production. Also slightly erroneous was the report's statement that the third batch of episodes to be networked in the States would begin transmitting there on Wednesday 13 December 1967, when it would actually be on Wednesday 10 January 1968.

Season five continues on air

Meanwhile, transmissions of the later season five episodes continued across the ITV network; although, as before, not without some scheduling alterations. In particular, after showing only five episodes of the resumed season, Border decided to hold the remainder back until February 1968. On a more positive note, *The Avengers* had now recaptured some of its lost audience, averaging 6.3 million viewers per episode and standing at number eight on the TAM top 20 most popular programmes of October 1967. The series also continued to attract publicity; and on Monday 30 October both *The Times* and the *Daily Mail* ran late stories regarding Rigg's replacement by Thorson.

6.01 – 'Invasion of the Earthmen'

Principal photography on 'Invitation to a Killing' concluded on Tuesday 7 November 1967, although a further sequence of an explosion of a munitions hut was filmed by the second unit, directed by John Hough, two days later on the studio backlot. It was followed into production by Terry Nation's 'Invasion of the Earthmen', in which Steed and Tara pose as man and wife in order to investigate the Alpha Academy, where one of Steed's colleagues has been killed. Filming got under way on Monday 6 November – an indication that new producer John Bryce had chosen at the outset to abandon the rolling production system favoured by his predecessors Albert Fennell and Brian Clemens and revert to the traditional method of producing a British television film series: start an episode, film it and then start another. Assigned to direct was newcomer Don Sharp, who had been at Elstree handling an episode of *The Champions* when he was approached by Gordon L T Scott with an offer to take on the task. Although surprised to discover that he would not be working alongside Fennell and Clemens, Sharp had jumped at the chance, feeling that he could not pass up the opportunity to be a part of the most successful film series in the country.

The first four days' filming for the episode were undertaken on Stage 9 at Elstree, which held the set of a quarry where the trainees take survival tests, complete with fake grass, bushes, rocks and bear traps. Nation's script called for the inclusion of a boa constrictor, but it was considered too dangerous to have a real snake on set, so the prop department made an unconvincing substitute, which could be pulled by a wire along a rail hidden in the long grass. Despite his press statement to the contrary, Bryce apparently made a conscious effort to reintroduce leather to the series, as Tara wears a two-piece tan-coloured leather outfit designed by Harvey Gould, who had been given responsibility for creating her wardrobe. Bryce also attempted to keep Steed in character by having him address Tara as 'Miss King', in the same way he had called Emma 'Mrs Peel' and Cathy 'Mrs Gale.'

Sets of an underground tunnel, a metal tube and a two-storey tunnel entrance were also constructed on Stage 9, and filming on these was undertaken by the main unit on Thursday 9 and Friday 10 November. The following week there was a move to Stage 3 for some scenes in the office of Academy headmaster Brigadier Brett, played by William Lucas, and others in an Academy composite corridor set. The latter were shot on Thursday 16 November, with further material being captured four days later.

On Friday 17 November the second unit went on location to the village of Essendon, approximately nine miles north-east of the series' base of operations at Elstree. With second unit director John Hough calling the shots, a sequence was filmed of Steed and Tara arriving in the AC 428 convertible at a country hotel, in fact The Salisbury Crest pub on West End Lane – which in recent years has closed down, the building becoming a private residence. As they enter the hotel, Steed and Tara come under the surveillance of two Alpha Academy students sat in a blue Land Rover (695 EAC), which had previously appeared in 'You Have Just been Murdered'.

Discovering a brochure for the Academy, Steed and Tara return to the AC. When they depart, they are followed by the Land Rover, and both vehicles are later seen passing St Giles Church in Codicote, situated about six-and-a-half miles from Essendon. For a sequence of the vehicles arriving at the gateway to the Alpha Academy, the location used was a set of gates to Hatfield House on Wildhill Road near the village of Welham Green, only three miles from Essendon. After some of the students are persuaded to open the gates, Steed and Emma drive up to the main building, for which the unit shot not at Hatfield House but at Knebworth House some eight miles to the north.

The AC 428 had been delivered to the production by the manufacturers on Thursday 9 November, and had been tried out by Macnee's stunt double Rocky Taylor prior to being used for filming. However, it was not until the location work on Friday 15 November that anyone thought to look inside the boot. Unknown to the crew, a spare battery had been supplied, and due to the movement of the vehicle, this had overturned in the boot, leaking diluted sulphuric acid and causing a certain amount of damage. As a courtesy, unit manager Laurie Greenwood reported the incident to Mr Wright of AC Cars Limited.

Ray Austin having now assumed the position of second unit director on *The Champions*, Joe Dunne replaced him as the series' stunt arranger. However, things did not always go as planned. On 9 November, while doubling for one of the Alpha Academy students doing a stunt fall, Dunne accidentally hurt himself. He initially declined first aid at the studio, but was still in some pain 90 minutes later and was finally persuaded by the crew to visit the duty nurse, who promptly sent him to a nearby hospital for a check-up. Upon examination it was revealed that Dunne's left shoulder had been temporarily dislocated, but had luckily relocated itself. To relieve his discomfort the medical staff simply placed his arm in a sling, and he returned to work. Meanwhile, having previously been Diana Rigg's regular stunt double, Cyd Child had now visited her hairdresser and undergone a makeover, adopting a shorter hairstyle so that she could perform the same function for Linda Thorson too.

Other notable points: the internal staircase entrance to Professor Quilby's laboratory from 'The See-Through Man' was reassembled and redressed to become the way into the underground tunnel from Alpha Academy; a scene where Tara sees a figure in a spacesuit – a low-tech improvised costume from the wardrobe department – floating in a chamber at the Academy, shot on Stage 3 with the actor being flown on Kirby wires, replaced a scripted but abandoned sequence of her encountering a 'space creature' on the quarry set; and music editor Karen Heward elected to reuse some passages of incidental music heard previously in 'The Fear Merchants' and 'The Winged Avenger'.

While working on the episode, Don Sharp became concerned about the lack of a defined personality for Tara King, and approached John Bryce on more than one occasion to discuss developing some background for her. He could see nothing in the screenplay or series paperwork that outlined any characterisation for the new Avengergirl, and more importantly there was nothing to explain her working relationship with Steed. However, Bryce appeared more concerned with finding a major talking point for the series to replace the interest created by the leather fashions worn by Honor Blackman and Diana Rigg. At the time, ABC Managing Director Howard Thomas had total faith in Bryce, heaping praise on the newly-arrived producer and feeling confident that he would find a new and different direction for *The Avengers*.

Principal filming on 'Invasion of the Earthmen' was completed on Tuesday 21 November. However, although no-one knew it at the time, this was not the last work that would be done on the episode, as additional footage would be ordered in the New Year …

'The Great Great Britain Crime'

The fact that 'Invasion of the Earthmen' contained overt science fiction elements was in a sense surprising, given that John Bryce was supposed to be taking *The Avengers* back to being more of a straight thriller. On the other hand, perhaps it was only to be expected, given that the writer was Terry Nation, who had a recent history of highly successful contributions to the BBC's *Doctor Who*. Having used two new writers in James and Nation, Bryce also entered into long discussions with *The Avengers* novelist John Garforth regarding potential storyline ideas for the new season. However, the two men failed to come to any agreement, leaving Garforth unhappy with the process and feeling that Bryce had wasted his time and was, as he put it, 'Dishing out the new series to the same old gang who wrote everything around that time.'

Garforth's statement was not entirely accurate, though, as for the next screenplay Bryce turned to a couple of writers he was familiar with but who had not contributed to the series since the Honor Blackman seasons. The third episode into production was 'The Great Great Britain Crime', a straight heist yarn written by Terrance Dicks and Malcolm Hulke, who resurrected their criminal organisation Intercrime from the season two episode of the same name. Having directed five episodes of *The Human Jungle*, the experienced Vernon Sewell was well known to ABC when he arrived at Elstree to take charge of the action.

Principal filming for 'The Great Great Britain Crime' began on Stage 9 on Monday 20 November 1967, using sets of both the Intercrime control room and the office of a character named Dunbar. It concluded on Wednesday 6 December. By this point, however, a major behind-the-scenes upheaval was in progress.

Having now had an opportunity to view all of the material shot for season six so far, ABC and ABPC executives realised that it lacked the quirky charm, style and clever scripting that had made *The Avengers* so popular. Horrified by the lacklustre content, they concluded that a mistake of huge proportions had been made. A radical rethink was called for; and one consequence of this was that – although another use would later be found for much of its footage – 'The Great Great Britain Crime' would never reach transmission.

Production rethink

Despite his previous experience on *The Avengers* in its videotaped days, John Bryce had faced a considerable challenge on his return to the series. He had effectively been thrown in the deep end by ABC to produce a film series – something he had never done before – and perform all the duties previously shared between two men, Brian Clemens and Albert Fennell. This included costing everything associated with the series, creating a filming schedule to make best use of cast, sets and locations, assuming overall supervision of two units, plus developing story outlines and draft scripts with potential writers. Bryce did admittedly have the assistance of Philip Levene, who had now been appointed as the series' story consultant/script editor, but his lack of experience of working with film obviously brought great pressures. Seeing the quality of the show slipping, Patrick Macnee had suggested several improvements, but found that Bryce was no longer the supportive and friendly superior he had known several years earlier at Teddington Studios. Instead, this Bryce had simply shouted him down and insisted that everything be done exactly how he wanted it done. The official line to the crew was that Clemens and Fennell had been replaced as a budget-cutting exercise, but everyone disbelieved this, as Fennell was renowned as one of the most cost-effective producers in the television/film business.

Meanwhile, Clemens had simply moved to work with his friend Dennis Spooner in the Filmaker production office, also at Elstree, where he wrote two scripts for *The Champions*. While there, he found that Levene would frequently phone him to seek his advice regarding scripts for *The Avengers*. After a while, Clemens understandably pointed out to Levene that he ought to be liaising with Bryce instead, as Bryce was now the series' producer. Levene apparently took offence at this and stopped calling. Clemens also received a visit from Bryce himself at the Filmaker office, to enquire if he would be interested in writing for his old show. Clemens replied that he not could leave as the producer and return as a writer.

Clemens would have been well aware that there were problems on *The Avengers*, not least because, being based at same studios, he would undoubtedly have had contact with the series' crew, with whom he had been working only months previously. Taking his family on a touring holiday to Wales, he left Spooner the telephone numbers where he could be reached on certain days. When he and his family reached their first destination, he found a message left for him to call ABC, but he decided to make them wait; he called back only when he found another message waiting for him at his second port of call the following day.

ABC were in trouble. They had dismissed both John Bryce and Philip Levene over artistic differences (although Levene would continue to be credited as story consultant on the first 14 episodes to be produced for season six), and with American network transmissions looming, they wanted Clemens to return to the series he had guided to international success. Clemens agreed to return, but only on two conditions. First, Albert Fennell had to be reinstated as well. Secondly, they would have to be given virtually total control of the series. Under the circumstances, ABC had no other choice than to agree.

The new production set-up did not include Julian Wintle, although as a professional courtesy by Clemens and Fennell he would be credited on seven of the Thorson episodes as a consultant to the series. Passages in the 1986 book *Julian Wintle: A Memoir*, written by his wife Anne Francis, indicate that Wintle had made a conscious decision to leave the series, mainly because Diana Rigg was leaving. Other sources state that his contribution toward the final eight Rigg episodes had not been very substantial, although this was probably due to his long battle against haemophilia, which had earlier brought about his hospitalisation for a week in May 1965. During the last few months of season five's production, he had taken to walking with a cane as he gradually became more unwell. Eventually he spent several days in bed, assuring his wife that he would be fine. However, instead of recovering he actually became worse, prompting Francis to call for medical assistance. In late August 1967, Wintle was admitted to The London Clinic, Devonshire Place, London W1, where he would spend the next five weeks undergoing treatment, while back at Elstree 'Mission … Highly Improbable' was being filmed. Upon being discharged, he would have to spend many months convalescing as an out-patent.

Clemens and Fennell returned to Elstree Studios as co-producers of *The Avengers* on Wednesday 6 December 1967. Joining season six mid-stream, they soon realised the enormity of the task they had taken on. They needed seven episodes in the can and fully edited for the third American run by late March 1968, which gave them about four months – and all they had were the three unsatisfactory Bryce-produced episodes. Upon viewing 'Invitation to a Killing', 'Invasion of the Earthmen' and 'The Great Great Britain Crime', they agreed that they lacked that special magic of *The Avengers*. However, they concluded that with additional filming the first two could be salvaged.

Both Clemens and Fennell considered Linda Thorson unsuitable to portray Steed's new partner, but a couple of things prevented her from following Bryce and Levene out of the series. First, she had been selected for the role by the American ABC network, and with the series now dependent on the stateside sale, ABC were extremely reluctant to risk offending the network by recasting. Secondly, although they had encountered a similar situation with Elizabeth Shepherd in 1964, production costs were now much higher than they had been back then, and carrying out more screen tests and then completely re-shooting three episodes would have cost somewhere in the region of £160,000.

While in conversation with this author in the early '90s, Clemens voiced his preference for Jane Merrow as Diana Rigg's replacement. This would also have suited Merrow herself: when interviewed on the retroseller.com website regarding acting roles she had missed out on, her initial response was, 'Well, I would have liked to have done the lead in *The Avengers*.' However, it was not to be, as Thorson was retained in the role of Tara King.

Season five transmissions wind down

Back on Friday 17 November, Rediffusion, Southern and Anglia had concluded their transmissions of the season five episodes with 'Mission … Highly Improbable' at 8.00 pm. Both ABC regions finished their run with the same episode the following evening, at the later time of 9.05 pm. Then, seven days later, Tyne Tees became the sixth ITV region to bring their screenings to an end, when 'Return of the Cybernauts' went out at 9.50 pm.

The average viewing figure had gone up to 6.5 million per episode for November, but the series had fallen three places to stand at number 11 on the TAM chart.

The Grampian region gave the series a miss on Wednesday 6 December, but resumed screenings the following week at 8.00 pm with 'Escape in Time'. Scottish Television was another region that rested the series for a week before getting under way again with 'The Superlative Seven' on Friday 8 December, but now at the earlier time of 8.00 pm.

6.02 – 'The Curious Case of the Countless Clues'

When Brian Clemens and Albert Fennell reassumed control of *The Avengers*, the crew were occupied on the second day of principal photography on a Philip Levene screenplay called 'The Curious Case of the Countless Clues' (working title: 'The Murderous Connection'), involving blackmailers fabricating incriminating evidence against their victim Robert Flanders, who has to meet their demands by parting with valuable items. With Levene himself now out of the picture, Clemens polished up the shooting script, rewriting sections as filming progressed, endeavouring to reinstate some of the quirkiness and oddball qualities for which the series had become famous.

With the restrictions of a straight thriller screenplay and time against him, Clemens struggled to recapture former glories. However, the episode's teaser sequence is exceptional, showing blackmailers Earle, played by Anthony Bate, and Gardiner, played by Kenneth Cope, in an apartment with a chalk outline on the floor, apparently collecting evidence at the scene of a murder that lacks just one thing: a body. The apartment's owner, Dawson, played by Reginald Jessup, arrives and innocently asks who has been murdered. 'You', replies Earle, producing a revolver and shooting him, which results in Dawson falling to the floor and landing exactly inside the chalk outline.

One notable aspect of the script is that most of the action is carried by Steed, with Tara's involvement confined to scenes set inside her apartment, where the story has her recovering from a dislocated ankle sustained in a skiing accident. Linda Thorson was required to do only five days work on the episode, with Nurse Ryan from the studio's first aid station dropping by early in the morning on three of those days to apply a prop bandage to her ankle. As it was too early in production for Thorson to be taking a holiday, it can only be assumed that this was done to allow her more time to work on the episode 'The Forget-Me-Knot', which was being filmed over the same period. It was not something dictated by Clemens and Fennell, as Levene's draft was structured that way from the outset, presumably because he was aware that his episode would be filmed concurrently with another. It was however Clemens' decision to have Tara appear as a brunette rather than a blonde, as a consequence of which Thorson wore a dark wig for her scenes.

On Tuesday 5 December 1967, the first day of filming, the main unit, under the direction of Don Sharp, travelled to the Edgwarebury Hotel at Elstree. In the grounds there they captured footage of the wooden structure known as The Norwegian Barn, which in the story represents the exterior of the home of an elderly murder victim named Scott. Some years later the structure would be totally destroyed by fire and replaced by several larger, red-brick buildings after Edgwarebury Country Club, as the hotel was then known, sold off the plot of land. The crew remained for the following two days at the Edgwarebury Hotel, where the gatehouse on Edgwarebury Lane doubled as the cottage used by Earle and Gardiner and additional material was shot on various stretches of the hotel access road. The main hotel building itself was used for the exterior of the home of Cabinet Minister Sir William Burgess, played by George A Cooper, though this footage was not shot until Thursday 14 December, when Sharp returned to the location with the smaller second unit.

Work on interiors for the episode commenced on Thursday 7 December, with filming on the Dawson's apartment and Burgess's billiards room sets on Stage 9. The following day, extremely bad weather conditions of snow and ice resulted in transport difficulties, preventing several crew members from arriving at the studio on time to meet the unit call of 8.30 am. To compensate for the loss of studio time, production manager Ron Fry brought the second unit in to Stage 9 to double up and work alongside the main unit.

On Saturday 9 December, the main unit moved to Stage 3 to execute footage on the set of the study of blackmail victim Flanders, played by Edward de Souza. This featured Macnee, de Souza, Bate and Cope, plus Tony Selby in the part of blackmail gang member Stanley, and Tracy Reed playing Flanders' sister Janice, an old flame of Steed's. Meanwhile, with John Hough directing in place of Don Sharp, the second unit remained on Stage 9, where they spent the day involved with various make-up, hair and wardrobe tests with Thorson.

On Wednesday 13 December, Flanders' silver-grey Bentley S3 was filmed in Elstree Studios' underground car park, from which the vehicle departed via the ramp in front of the building that housed ABPC's own suite of offices plus the studio canteen and restaurant. The subsequent sequence where Earle and Gardiner follow the Bentley in their Citroen, arriving at the junction of Judges Hill and Well Road near the village of Northaw, was filmed seven days later.

This episode also features the first exterior footage of Tara King's apartment, which was filmed by the second unit on Chalcot Crescent in Primrose Hill, near Regents Park, London NW1 on Friday 15 December.

A sequence where Steed visits Flanders' home was captured on Monday 18 December outside the large white stately house at Woolmers Park in Letty Green, Hertfordshire, where extensive filming had previously been done for the Rigg episode

'Return of the Cybernauts'. Directing the second unit, Sharp spent over ten hours getting these shots and a mixture of motor vehicle footage on the surrounding roads. Some day-for-night material was also obtained on the access road, involving Steed attempting to start the Bentley (YT 3942) with the starting handle after it breaks down. This scene continues with the arrival of Stanley in a red Land Rover recovery vehicle and concludes with a fight in which Steed forces the mechanic to reveal a plot to frame him for Tara's impending murder.

More location work was undertaken on Thursday 21 December when John Hough led the second unit out to The Ridgeway near Northaw to obtain additional vehicle footage featuring the Citroen and the Land Rover breakdown truck towing an accident-damaged BMC 1100.

The final day of principal photography was Friday 5 January 1968. However, Sharp found this a frustrating experience. He had taken the second unit back to the Edgwarebury Hotel, intending to carry out more filming at both the gatehouse and The Norwegian Barn before moving to Little Common in Stanmore, but found that bad weather prevented them from obtaining any footage at all.

The three main antagonists in the blackmail plot, Earle, Stanley and Gardiner, were named after the American crime writer Earle Stanley Gardner, author of the Perry Mason books that formed the basis of the successful early '60s television series and '70s revival of the same name.[26] Similarly, the detective character Sir Arthur Doyle was obviously named after British crime author Sir Arthur Conan Doyle and given a costume based on that of his famous creation Sherlock Holmes, complete with frock coat, deerstalker hat and magnifying glass. For this role, casting director G B Walker chose comedy actor Peter Jones, who had made his name in the BBC sitcom *The Rag Trade* in the early '60s. Jones obviously made an impression, as several months later he would be back in very similar clothing as the Sherlock lookalike Frederick P Waller in an episode called 'The House on Haunted Hill' in the series *Randall and Hopkirk (Deceased)*. In the earlier version of Levene's screenplay, Sir Arthur had a female sidekick called Watson, but she failed to appear in the episode, not having made it through Clemens' rewrite.

Other points of interest: the wall-mounted double light fittings seen in many of the Rigg episodes were requisitioned from the prop store for use in Burgess's home; the weapon with which Earle intends killing Tara is Steed's Smith and Wesson revolver; Kenneth Cope, who would later become a regular at the studio co-starring as Marty Hopkirk in *Randall and Hopkirk (Deceased)*, was allocated the dressing room next to Thorson, who frequently visited him to fill up her kettle as her own room had no running water; Steed again addresses Tara as 'Miss King', something to which Clemens would soon put a stop; the vintage car prints seen in 'Dead Man's Treasure' and other episodes turn up again in Dawson's apartment; Earle and Gardiner use a black and white Citroen DS19 Safari (AYR 141B) featured before in the series as Forbes' transport in 'Murdersville'; and music editor Karen Heward elected to reuse passages of Laurie Johnson's score from 'Escape in Time' – particularly from the Mackidockie Court sequences – giving 'The Curious Case of the Countless Clues' a familiar feel.

Levene's earlier version of the script was more complicated, and Clemens simplified it in a number of ways. He removed an indication that Scott had worked for

---

[26] When *Perry Mason* was resurrected for television again in the early '90s, this time as a series of feature-length television movies, Brian Clemens would contribute three scripts.

Flanders but had been fired due to financial irregularities, so providing a convenient motive for his murder. Also deleted was an entire subplot in which Gardiner and Earle, having discovered that Janice knows they are blackmailing her brother, kidnap her and set a trap for Steed involving a crossbow that will fire automatically when he enters a room – something he survives by donning the breastplate from a suit of armour he comes across in the hallway of the house. Returning to Flanders' home, Steed finds that all the previously missing paintings have been returned along with Janice, who goes along with her brother's insistence that nothing is amiss. Later, he sneaks back and discovers that Flanders' hunting rifle has been switched for another, so the blackmailers still hold the original as incriminating evidence against him. The final change made by Clemens was to the finale: in the draft script, Tara knocks Earle out with a pair of skis, whereas in the actual episode she shoots him with the revolver he was planning to use on her.

In addition to these differences, it appears that some of the footage shot on the first day of production on the Edgwarebury Hotel estate was considered inessential to the storyline and dropped during editing. This was of a scene where, preparing to murder Scott, Gardiner and Earle use a Bentley limousine with identical number plates to Flanders' car and purposely allow it to be seen by a passing cyclist, thus planting more misleading evidence.

Tara King's apartment

Soon after his return to the series, Brian Clemens had production designer Robert Jones create an apartment for Tara that would reflect her personality. Jones came up with a large, two-level standing set with two entrances, an open staircase and a fireman's pole for quick access to the lower level. Decorated in bright colours, it contained various oversized items from business premises, such as an enormous pair of spectacles from an optician's, a giant boot from a shoe shop and a huge padlock from a locksmith's. Three porcelain mannequins from a Victorian clothing outlet were stood on the mantelpiece, over which a penny-farthing bicycle was hung on the wall. Large scatter cushions in various shades were placed on both the floor and the leather furniture, with the large gold letters 'TK' and 'NO' mounted on one wall. The downstairs door incorporated an engraved glass panel, and several period telephones were placed around the room, which also boasted a pink carpet.

6.03 – 'The Forget-Me-Knot'

It appears that even before being approached to return as producer, Brian Clemens had already envisaged how to introduce Steed's new partner and give Emma Peel a decent farewell. With this in mind he came up with the crossover episode 'The Forget-Me-Knot', scripted over Friday 8, Saturday 9 and Sunday 10 December 1967. This story not only explains why Emma stops working with Steed, but also provides something of a background for Tara. It involves Steed suffering amnesia and consulting the one person he can remember, namely trainee agent Tara, who then assists him in locating a traitor in the department for which they both work.

Apparently Diana Rigg's participation in this one-off return was never in doubt, as she had been under contract to appear in 26 colour episodes and only 24 had been filmed for season five. In her book *Diana Rigg: The Biography*, Kathleen Tracy would later explain the situation thus: 'Because of some clause in her contract, Rigg was required to come back for four days' work.'

One problem Clemens and Fennell had to face was that most of the team of directors they had used on season five had now moved on to other projects. Charles Chrichton had recently been directing episodes of *Man in a Suitcase*. Robert Day, having emigrated to the United States, found that his experience directing several Tarzan films in the late '50s and early '60s brought him work on Quinn Martin's *Tarzan* television series starring Ron Ely. John Moxey also felt that there were better opportunities in the States, where he directed episodes of *The Name of the Game* and *Hawaii Five-O*. John Krish had abandoned working on film series to direct the obscure movie *Decline and Fall ... of a Birdwatcher*. Robert Asher would shortly direct *The Saint* episode 'The Scales of Justice'. Sidney Hayers was taking a sabbatical. Roy Rossotti, having worked with Patrick McGoohan on *The Prisoner* episode 'A Change of Mind', found it a challenging process and would not direct again. James Hill, however, was still available, and he added to his previous credits on *The Avengers* – gained on the season five episodes 'Epic' and 'Something Nasty in the Nursery' – by agreeing to direct 'The Forget-Me-Knot', which for the most part would be made at the same time as Don Sharp was shooting 'The Curious Case of the Countless Clues'.

Principal photograph commenced on Thursday 14 December, and Hill made an instant impression with his interpretation of the opening teaser sequence, which features the overhead lights of the set swinging in the darkness and adding to the spectacle of the scene as agent Mortimer, played by Patrick Kavanagh, fights with and defeats an assailant named Karl, played by Alan Lake, who shoots him with a dart. As the action switches to location footage, obtained by the second unit on Weymouth Mews, London W1 on Thursday 28 December, Mortimer escapes into the street and comes upon a black Austin FX4 cab, but on speaking to the cabbie, played by Leon Lissek, suddenly finds that he cannot remember where he wants to go or even his name. The second unit also filmed on the same date and at a cab rank in an unknown location, which failed to appear in the episode.

Later, Mrs Peel is with Steed in his apartment when she notices Mortimer looking confused in the street outside. Recognising him, Steed goes down to find out what is going on, and there is a shot of him opening the yellow outer door of his apartment at 3 Stable Mews, shot not on location but on a small exterior set on Stage 9.

Clemens' device to write Emma Peel out of the series at the end of the episode involved her husband Peter, previously presumed to have been killed in a plane crash, being found alive and well after three years in the Amazon rainforest. In perhaps the most moving scene in the entire series, Emma bids Steed farewell in his apartment, whispering, 'Always keep your bowler on in times of stress. Watch out for diabolical masterminds.' 'I'll remember,' he replies. 'Bye Steed,' she says, and with a kiss to his cheek, she is heading for the door, only to turn around briefly as, for the only time in the series, he calls her by her first name: 'Emma ... thanks!' The scene proved a difficult one for Macnee to film. Rigg had gone for good this time, and he returned to his dressing room and was very upset.

This goodbye scene was filmed on either Thursday 14 or Friday 15 December, but the following action where the exiting Emma passes the entering Tara on the staircase was shot on Tuesday 19 December – the last of Rigg's four days on the episode – on a closed set on Stage 9. This was the only scene the two Avengergirls played together. Originally, they were to have passed without a word, but at the eleventh hour Clemens came up with a piece of dialogue where Emma informs Tara that Steed likes his tea stirred anticlockwise.

A shot of Mrs Peel and her husband, who dresses exactly like Steed, departing in a Rolls Royce convertible as Steed watches from the window of his apartment was filmed on the studio lot on Monday 18 December. However, the following long shot, showing the Rolls turning out of Duchess Mews into Duchess Street, was another part of the location work done by the second unit ten days later.

Before Steed has time to dwell on events, Tara enters the apartment, causing him to exclaim a catchphrase established earlier in the episode, 'Ra-boom-di-ay!'

Production failed to get under way until 10.15 am on Friday 22 December, because Alan Lake missed his 7.40 am call and did not arrive at the studio until 9.40 am.

On Wednesday 27 December, establishing footage for the hospital was shot in front of the cutting rooms on the studio lot, where a prop sign was strategically placed on the grass and then filmed in close-up.

The location that would be used for exteriors of Tara's apartment throughout the season was Chalcot Crescent in Primrose Hill, near Regents Park, London NW1, with the camera usually focusing on No. 19. The fictional address is given as 9 Primrose Crescent, and for the scene in this episode where departmental operative Simon Filson, played by Jeremy Burnham, arrives there in his car, a prop sign was fixed to some railings. This material was shot by James Hill and the second unit on Friday 29 December, until the unit generator broke down. The unit later moved on to Little Common in Stanmore, in the London Borough of Harrow, where John Hough took over from Hill. A replacement generator had been dispatched from Elstree and was waiting for them upon their arrival, enabling them to obtain footage of the Rover 2000 of secret agent trainer Burton, played by Jeremy Young, travelling to the glass factory featured in the story.

Ignoring the national holiday on Monday 1 January 1968, Hill led the second unit back into the capital with the aim of carrying out additional filming at Duchess Mews, although unfortunately heavy rain prevented this being achieved. With the weather set for the day, Hill broke the abortive shoot at 2.30 pm.

On Thursday 4 January the second unit returned to Duchess Mews and captured the footage that they had failed to obtain three days earlier. They then adjourned back to Stage 9 at Elstree to film a number of inserts. The Duchess Mews footage shot that day featured a Steed double driving the Bentley, plus Alan Lake and Douglas Sheldon, playing Karl and Brad, with two motorcycles: a black Triumph (NKH 741) and a red Norton (431 BY) with a black sidecar box. Filming also took place on 4 January on a length of corridor that had been left standing on Stage 3 and heavily redressed from its earlier appearance as Flanders' hallway in 'The Curious Case of the Countless Clues'. In the story, this corridor is part of the home of a senior agent codenamed Mother, a new character written in by Clemens to serve as Steed's superior, who would ultimately become a semi-regular.

The first choice of actor to play the wheelchair-bound Mother was Ken Parry, who had had the minor guest role of effusive honey shop owner Bumble in the season four episode 'Honey for the Prince', but he was unable to accept the part as he was already contracted to the comedy series *Horne A'Plenty*. Consequently the role went to Patrick Newell, who had appeared in different roles in the earlier episodes 'The Town of No Return' and 'Something Nasty In The Nursery'. Newell shot all his scenes for 'The Forget-Me-Knot' on Tuesday 2 January, believing that it was nothing more than a one-off guest-starring role. The phrase 'Mother knows best' crops up in the dialogue at one point, and would subsequently be used as a catchphrase for the character.[27]

On Friday 5 January, the National Association of Theatrical and Kine Employees union forced all filming at Elstree Studios to conclude at 2.50 pm when their members began preparing for a meeting that started at 3.40 pm. At that meeting a vote was taken to ban all overtime, but the union shop steward waited until the following Monday to inform James Hill of the situation, when the main unit were on location at what was then the Eastern Gas works – now the Hemel Hempstead gas holder – on London Road, Hemel Hempstead. The union insisted that filming cease at 4.15 pm, to allow the unit sufficient time to travel back to the studios in Borehamwood before the end of normal working hours at 5.20 pm. As a result of this industrial action, some of the scheduled scenes could not be filmed that day, forcing another visit to the location, this time by the second unit, on Wednesday 17 January.

More problems were encountered on Tuesday 9 January when, due to a heavy snowfall, the cast faced travelling delays and were late reporting to the studio. Filming on Stage 3 thus began much later than usual, at 2.30 pm. The weather was somewhat better the next day, but still caused the vehicle carrying Patrick Macnee to arrive late, this time causing only a slight setback in the production schedule.

On Tuesday 16 January, when John Hough and the second unit were on location at Burnham Beeches to film some action involving Brad on his motorcycle, a further delay occurred as Douglas Sheldon's stunt double informed Hough that he could not actually ride a motorcycle. Eventually the rider who had delivered the vehicle to the location from the hire company was persuaded to don the costume and goggles and ride it for the shoot.

Never happy with the idea of Steed driving a sleek sports car, Clemens had decided to reinstate the agent's beloved Bentley and give the AC 428 to Tara instead. However, the Bentley (YT 3942), supplied by Kingsbury Motors, caused problems for the second unit on their 17 January return trip to the gas works at Hemel Hempstead, proving to be temperamental and causing further considerable delays in filming.

It had been decided to construct the gates and red-brick garden wall of Mother's house on Stage 3 and couple them with the bushes and shrubbery set that had already been used for 'Invitation to a Killing'. This provided the locale for the first on-screen meeting between Steed and Tara King, or Agent 69 as trainer Burton calls her, after she has judo-thrown the organisation's finest to the ground. Paperwork indicates that in addition to the gates and grounds there were plans to construct at least a wall of the house. However, as this does not appear, either it was never done or the shots in which it was seen were considered inessential to the story and removed during editing.

The episode's concluding fight scene sees Mrs Peel out-fight both Karl and Brad in the glass factory. Then, with Karl down, Brad speedily exits the building just as Tara arrives in the AC. The vehicle was filmed with its hood down, so that Tara could stand up and swing her handbag to connect with the villain, knocking him out cold. Steed looks confused until Tara opens the bag and removes a brick. It appears that the brick was originally conceived as a regular part of Tara's armoury, but after this one outing Clemens obviously thought better of it and it never appeared again. The two Avengergirls did not meet during this sequence as it combined footage of Rigg on the

---

[27] This was later picked up on by Don Macpherson when he wrote the 1998 movie based on the series, as it was also included in his screenplay.

glass factory interior set in the studio and of Thorson out on location almost three weeks later.

During the course of the action Steed experiences several flashbacks of a smiling Emma Peel, achieved using footage from 'Escape in Time', 'Return of the Cybernauts' and 'You Have Just Been Murdered'.

ABC statement

In its Wednesday 20 December 1967 edition, *The Stage and Television Today* gave a belated report regarding the return to the series of Brian Clemens and Albert Fennell. The departure of John Bryce took up just four lines, in which he was inaccurately described as the producer responsible for certain creative aspects of the new season. ABC were quoted as saying, 'We are delighted that Clemens and Fennell were available to return to the new season. We are confident that they will maintain and perhaps even enhance the quality for which *The Avengers* is renowned throughout the world.'

Brian Clemens takes stock

Once back in charge of the series, Brian Clemens began a process of change that would continue for several months. Out of all the fashions created for Tara King by Harvey Gould, he considered that the best overall costume consisted of a grey culottes suit, fur coat, black leather thigh boots and elbow gloves. However, he was still far from overjoyed with it. He felt that Bryce and ABC had been trying to mould Tara into an Emma Peel clone, which he believed was the wrong direction to go. He preferred to start with a blank piece of paper and develop the character from scratch, and thus used 'The Forget-Me-Knot' to establish Tara and give her the first sparks of personality that would develop throughout the season.

Also instigated by Clemens shortly after his return was an eight-minute promotional film entitled *Girl about Town*, featuring an athletic Linda Thorson doing a mixture of outdoor activities and talking about herself. Several months later, after filming was completed on the episode 'Get-A-Way!', a second promo would be assembled under the title *Introducing Linda Thorson*, comprising excerpts from several early season six episodes with a voiceover by Patrick Macnee.

Of the three John Bryce-produced episodes, 'The Great Great Britain Crime' was considered the worst. Clemens has gone on record as saying that it made no sense whatsoever and would never have been commissioned by him. It would be put on the shelf for just over a year until he found a use for some of the footage. 'Invitation to a Killing' did not greatly impress either Clemens or Albert Fennell, and they scheduled extensive refilming to be done for it, to start in early February 1968. Despite reservations, Clemens considered the third episode, 'Invasion of the Earthmen', the best of the three, but decided that even this required some replacement scenes to be shot.

'Invasion of the Earthmen' take two

In light of the decision to make Tara a brunette rather than a blonde, the main thing Clemens had to do was to provide a rationale for her having blonde hair in the footage shot for 'Invasion of the Earthmen' the previous November. To this end he wrote several two-handed scenes for Macnee and Thorson and arranged for them to be filmed over two days by the episode's original director, Don Sharp, on Stage 3 at Elstree. The main unit was used on the first day, Thursday 11 January 1968, and the second unit the following morning. A new opening scene was shot on the set of Tara's apartment, where she is practicing judo with a large scatter cushion when Steed arrives with a mission for them. Needing a disguise for the mission, she dons a blonde wig. A second sequence, with Macnee and Thorson being filmed inside the AC 428, was to be slotted into the action after Steed and Tara first leave the Alpha Academy. Here, Tara temporarily removes the blonde wig as the dialogue indicates their intention to return to the Academy later. This was done with the AC parked on the stage against a back-projection screen, with travelling matte of a wooded location visible through the car window. The third scene has Steed arrive back at Tara's apartment to collect her for a late-night continuation of their investigation, and – reinforcing the idea that she is going to be in disguise again – she hands him the blonde wig and says, '… you could do my hair.' Also filmed was a new end tag scene, with Tara practicing judo again, this time on Steed, causing him to consult the fictional tome *Brush Up Your Judo*.

Somewhere along the way, writer Terry Nation's concept of an army of teenagers being prepared for the conquest of outer space became watered down. A scripted scene where Steed discovers dozens of young people in suspended animation, waiting for the day when space travel has advanced far enough for them to be revived ready for blast off, was either never filmed in the original studio sessions or more likely removed during editing to allow space for Clemens' new material. Also absent from the episode is a scripted sequence of Steed discovering an anti-gravity practice room that lifts him into the air with a powerful updraft – explaining the floating spacesuited figure that Tara saw earlier.

First Linda Thorson title sequence

The second unit finished filming the additional 'Invasion of the Earthmen' footage at 10.10 am on Friday 12 January 1968 and by 11.00 am had transferred to Stage 4, where new opening and closing title sequences envisioned by Brian Clemens were committed to celluloid over the next two days under the guidance of post-production coordinator Harry Booth. Londoner Booth had started his career in the early '40s as a sound editor on several movies before assuming the position of dubbing editor on one of the first film series shown on ITV, *Colonel March of Scotland Yard*. He had then got involved in other areas of production, scripting and producing the movies *At the Stroke of Nine* and *The Case of the Mukkinese Battle Horn* and directing for the film series *Sir Francis Drake*, *Man of the World* and *The Sentimental Agent*. He was thus well qualified to stand in as the second unit director on *The Avengers*, as well as to ensure the smooth operation of the editorial department and oversee all dubbing sessions, making him a valuable member of the crew.

A reworked version of Laurie Johnson's theme tune begins with a powerful drumbeat – as opposed to the tom-tom used on the previous version – as the new opening title sequence shows an animated shooting gallery quickly counting down and stopping on the only target figure with a heart shape over its breast. This then briefly becomes two red heart shapes, after which the screen turns completely red, providing a background for *The Avengers* title logo. Another shooting gallery countdown follows, with each of the target figures wearing a bowler hat, and again the animated gun sight stops on the one with a heart shape. Cut to Steed tipping his bowler and the Patrick

Macnee credit caption. This is followed by another shooting gallery in which all the figures are female, and the procedure is repeated. Cut to a red lip print as Tara appears on screen with the Linda Thorson credit caption, at which point a counter-melody is added to the theme tune. Cut to Macnee and Thorson on an orange-lit limbo set. Wearing a two-piece beige outfit and white roll-neck sweater, Tara runs from the gun sight to Steed, who diverts the sight away with his bowler. A gunshot leaves a hole in the crown of the hat. The titles then conclude with the producers' credit for Albert Fennell and Brian Clemens.

The closing title sequence continues from where the opening one stops, with Tara poking a finger through the hole in Steed's bowler. With an unhappy look on his face, Steed replaces the bowler on his head, while Tara applies her lipstick using the reflection in a chrome-plated Smith and Wesson 1917 revolver. The animated gun sight reappears and, firing a shot from her gun, Tara makes it vanish. Then both Steed and Tara are seen in long shot and the credits progress with additional gunshots and more close-ups before they walk away from the camera into the distance.

ITV's final season five transmissions

The Avengers had cemented its position as the nation's favourite television film series of 1967, being rated number 16 in the annual TAM chart with an average of 8.0 million viewers per episode. 1968 however brought more scheduling alterations as the last few season five episodes were shown by those ITV regions that had yet to complete the run. Ulster moved the series from 7.30 pm to 9.00 pm on Thursday 4 January, beginning with 'The Winged Avenger', although less than a month later, on Thursday 1 February, they would revert to 7.30 pm, starting with 'Never, Never Say Die', keeping the series in that slot until concluding the run in March. On Friday 5 January at 7.30 pm, after a break of eight months, Westward resumed their screenings with 'Death's Door'. However, they would soon drop the series again, after 'Mission ... Highly Improbable' on Friday 9 February, and would not start showing the remaining five episodes of the season until July 1968. Border would resume their screenings on Sunday 4 February at 7.25 pm with 'The Superlative Seven', the first of eight episodes they had still to air, again concluding the run in March. After transmitting their penultimate episode, 'The Winged Avenger', at 8.00 pm on Wednesday 6 March, Grampian waited almost four weeks before screening their final one, 'A Funny Thing Happened on the Way to the Station', at the later time of 10.30 pm on Tuesday 2 April.

The Avengers sells worldwide

In its Thursday 11 January 1968 edition, *The Stage and Television Today* reported that *The Avengers* had now been dubbed into French, German, Italian, Spanish, Japanese and Chinese Cantonese, and sold to 70 different counties overall, including Poland. It went on to say that ABC hoped this would provide the breakthrough into Eastern Europe they sought for the series.

More network transmissions in the USA

Also on Thursday 11 January 1968, the American ABC network began its third run of *The Avengers*, comprising the last eight Rigg episodes and first seven Thorson ones, including the crossover adventure 'The Forget-Me-Knot'. This was essentially a stopgap until more episodes were ready for the new autumn season in September 1968, but the network also saw it as the ideal way of introducing Linda Thorson to the American audience.

On Wednesday 17 January the weekly American entertainment trade publication *Variety* ran a positive review of the opening episode, 'Mission ... Highly Improbable', highlighting the well-conceived and executed special effects and praising Patrick Macnee's roguish portrayal of Steed and his delightful foil in the form of Diana Rigg's Mrs Emma Peel. Readers were also informed of Emma's forthcoming departure, and of the ABC network's decision to move the series from its previous 10.00 pm Friday slot to a primetime 7.30 pm Wednesday one.

6.04 – 'Split!'

Needing another script quickly, Brian Clemens realised that he would have to have another weekend session behind the typewriter at his farm in Ampthill, Bedfordshire. Doing so, he wrote the majority of the next episode into production, 'Split!'. Dennis Spooner was staying with him for the weekend and assisted in an uncredited capacity with the plotting of the episode, which was still being written as filming commenced. The storyline concerns mind-controlled agents within the Ministry of Top Secret Intelligence (TSI) who can be triggered at a moment's notice to kill their colleagues. So speedily was the script written that Clemens resorted to giving one of the characters a name, Boris Kartovski, that he had already used previously in the season four episode 'A Touch Of Brimstone'.

As getting this episode in the can was another case of working against the clock, there was only one director considered for the job: Roy Ward Baker, whose reputation for being able to handle projects at extremely short notice went before him. Baker had directed more of the black and white Rigg episodes than anyone else, and from that point of view had been responsible for the early look of *The Avengers* on film.

Upon his arrival, Baker quickly took control of the situation and assembled a strong guest cast including, in the role of departmental operative Major Peter Rooke, Julian Glover, whom he had directed previously in the season four episode 'Two's a Crowd' and in the Hammer Films adaptation of the BBC's *Quatermass and the Pit*. However, evidence of the rushed nature of the production can still be seen in the episode's closing credits, which give the director's name as Roy Baker rather than Roy Ward Baker – the preferred form he had recently adopted in order to avoid confusion with another Roy Baker who worked in the industry as a dubbing editor.

Principal photography commenced on Friday 12 January 1968, the first of six working days spent by the main unit on Stage 9, which culminated in a fight scene in the hospital room of Kartovski, played by Steven Scott, where Steed throws his steel-rimmed bowler to knock a gun out of the hand of the villainous collaborator Hinnell, played by John G Heller. This sequence would be accompanied on screen by Laurie Johnson's fast-moving incidental music cue 'Fisticuffs', first heard in the black and white Rigg episode 'Death at Bargain Prices'.

A large amount of location filming was undertaken on Monday 22 January, when the main unit travelled several miles north-west, initially to the Aldenham Estate. Thorson was present with the AC 428 in a field close to Tykes Water Lake for a sequence where Tara awaits the arrival of Ministry head Lord Barnes in a Hughes 269B helicopter (G-AVZC), which was hired for the production along with the pilot from Gregory Air Services, who at the time were based at Denham Airfield in Buckinghamshire. This is followed on screen by Tara driving Barnes to the Ministry along Pegmire Lane in Patchetts Green. Later, Tara is seen passing Hilfield Farm on Hilfield Road, heading toward Patchetts Green, where she comes across a staged car accident and, taken unawares, is overcome by Hinnell and his assistant Morrell, played by an uncredited Terry Maidment, with a cloth soaked in chloroform. She is taken away in the same Austin ambulance (YLD 259) previously featured prominently in 'Never, Never Say Die', which is seen to emerge from the gateway of Aldenham Grange onto a location that is actually several miles away, Grange Road at Letchmore Heath. Additional material showing the AC turning off Summerhouse Lane onto Primrose Lane near the hamlet of Patchetts Green was also shot, for the later sequence where Tara drives Rooke to Lord Barnes' home. The day's filming was then completed with scenes of Steed's Bentley (YT 3942) crossing the M1 motorway bridge on Sandy Lane, again near Patchetts Green, plus a shot of it going along Radlett Road with the village of Aldenham in the background.

After another day filming back at the studio, on Wednesday 24 January Baker supervised the main unit on a morning's location visit to the large country house called Camfield Place, off Wildhill Road in Wildhill, around ten miles north-east of Borehamwood. This location, which stands in a large wooded area, became the exterior for Lord Barnes' home, where the required footage was captured before 10.50 am, allowing the unit to return to Elstree and film on Stage 9 later in the day. Meanwhile, John Hough and the smaller second unit were at Brocket Hall, near Welwyn Garden City, shooting footage at both the gateway and house to establish the location of the Ministry of TSI. Paperwork indicates that the second unit also filmed material on the studio lot to augment their Brocket Hall footage; if so, however, this does not appear in the episode.

On Thursday 25 January the schedule needed rearranging when the crew arrived to start work and discovered that the wigs worn by Thorson and her stunt double Cyd Child had disappeared overnight. This situation prevented the main unit filming with Thorson until later in the day, by which time a replacement wig had been obtained.

The final location filming for this episode was carried out on Wednesday 31 January, when Baker once again directed material with the second unit at Brocket Hall in the morning, then moved on to the Haberdashers' Aske's School at Elstree, where the more modern school building that had doubled as a hospital exterior in 'Never, Never Say Die' was once again pressed into service as a medical facility, Nullington Private Hospital.

Other points of interest: the hallway set on Stage 3 used in both 'The Forget-Me-Knot' and 'The Curious Case of the Countless Clues' was redressed again to become part of Lord Barnes' large country house; Steed's 1928 3 litre Bentley, furnished by Kingsbury Motors, had several cracks in the windscreen in the top corner of the driver's side; the two German Shepherd dogs seen at the Ministry of TSI were supplied by Zoo-rama, a company specialising in animal performers for film and television productions; and for part of the episode Tara wears the matching beige jacket and miniskirt seen in the Harry Booth-directed opening title sequence.

With both the 'Mrs Peel, we're needed!' scenes and the double-barrelled 'Steed does this, Emma does that' subtitles having been previously dropped from the series at the insistence of the American ABC network, Clemens now decided to have some fun with some of the episode title captions. In this instance, to emphasise the dual personality aspect of the storyline in 'Split!', the title lettering appears on screen and then breaks apart into two pieces, splitting corner to corner.

Having been brought onto the series by John Bryce, fashion designer Harvey Gould – who favoured traditional tweeds, checks and herringbone patterns – had now left the production, and would be credited on only six episodes[28]. Clemens and Fennell had instead reverted to using their own preferred choice: Alun Hughes. Gould and Hughes shared the credit for Thorson's costumes on 'Split!', then Hughes took over fully from the next episode into production, 'Get-A-Way!'.

Jeremy Burnham joins the team

It appears that sometime during early January 1968 Jeremy Burnham – who had acted in the series in both 'The Town of No Return' and 'The Fear Merchants' – was hired on a retainer as an in-house writer for *The Avengers*, with additional fees payable for the completion of shooting scripts. For some time Burnham had desperately wanted to write for the series, and it seems that he reminded Clemens of this fact during the production of 'The Forget-Me-Knot', which resulted in him getting the green light to join the team. During a question-and-answer session at *The Avengers* at 50 event in Chichester in June 2011, Burnham confirmed that his scripts each came about after he was given one of Clemens' 'thumbnails' – a one-line story idea from a list the producer had. Burnham also stated that despite the Emma Peel character having departed from the series, he always wrote the female lead part as if it were her or someone like her.

6.05 – 'Get-A-Way!'

By the time the main body of filming for 'Split!' was completed on Thursday 1 February 1968, 'Get-A-Way!' had already been in production for several days. The teleplay by Philip Levene deals with three Eastern Bloc prisoners at a maximum security facility who simply disappear one by one. Clemens again decided to have some fun with the title caption on this episode, which departs sideways off screen, making its own getaway before Levene's credit appears. Don Sharp returned to direct what would be his third and final episode of the series, and proceedings were given a boost by the casting of accomplished actor Peter Bowles as one of the prisoners, Ezdorf.

Filming began on location on Friday 26 January with the second unit at Ashridge College, a large teaching establishment that stands in the extensive Ashridge Park near Berkhamsted in Hertfordshire, which was used to represent the prison/monastery. Later, Sharp moved the unit back to Warwick Road in Borehamwood, where a large building occupied by National Cash Registers provided the exterior of the premises of the fictional Magnus Importing Company. Since the '60s, this whole area has undergone a major redevelopment, resulting in the demolition of the building in question, although it is believed to have stood partly where Elstree Gate is now located, opposite the car park of the nearby Premier Inn hotel.

Taking charge of the main unit on Stage 4 the following day, Sharp began shooting the episode's interiors. Gunsmith Mr Bapty, of the longstanding film and television

---

[28] Including the two episodes completed later in the season that used footage originally shot for the abandoned 'Invitation to a Killing' and 'The Great Great Britain Crime'.

armourers Bapty and Co, supervised the use of firearms for a couple of days.

On 2 February John Hough led the second unit to Belsize Crescent, London NW3, to film exteriors for a sequence where Tara visits the office of the fictional *Bryant's Natural History Magazine*. Following a studio fight scene between Tara and the escaped prisoner Lubin, played by Robert Russell, in which Lubin falls through the window and down to the street below, the following exterior shot shows Thorson on location as a blue Austin A55 van owned by the Magnus Importing Company drives out of the adjacent Burdett Mews. Belsize Crescent now looks slightly different from how it appears in the episode, however, as the exterior of the building that Tara enters has been refurbished and the opposite side of the road has been redeveloped. Paperwork indicates that additional footage was obtained by the unit at Belsize Park Gardens, NW3 and Boydell Court, NW8, representing the fictional Melrose Court, but neither location actually appears in the episode. One of them could have been intended simply to establish the exterior of the apartment of Steed's old colleague Paul Ryder, played by Neil Hallett, and been omitted for timing reasons. Later in the day, the unit returned to Borehamwood, where Hough directed more material at the National Cash Registers building on Warwick Road.

The aforementioned fight scene between Tara and Lubin in Bryant's office was filmed over Thursday 8 and Friday 9 February at Elstree, with Cyd Child as usual doubling for Thorson and both Dinny Powell and Arthur Howell doing the same for Russell.

Poor weather conditions prevented the main unit from doing more London location work on Wednesday 14 February, forcing Sharp to rearrange the schedule and film on Stage 3 instead. The following day, however, the weather had improved, and Sharp travelled to Duchess Mews where – as for 'The Forget-Me-Knot' – some footage was shot from a first floor window of one of the houses there, revealing the prone body of another of Steed's old colleagues, George Neville, played by Terence Longdon, who has been attacked down in the mews below by the enemy operative Rostov, played by Vincent Harding.

On Tuesday 27 February John Hough and the second unit carried out more location filming at Duchess Mews, before returning to the studio to shoot footage on Stage 3 on the set of Ezdorf's cell. In addition to this, the shooting schedule indicates that at least one scene was filmed on what was described as the Melrose Court passageway set, although this failed to make it into the finished episode.

Ezdorf's abilities with a Beretta automatic are mentioned in the dialogue, but Steed voices a preference for the Smith and Wesson 19 Combat Magnum revolver, and later Tara removes this weapon from a drawer in his apartment. She also reads the tome *Code Breaking for Beginners*. As usual in the series, neither 'Soviet' nor 'Russian' was used to describe the foreign agents, but given their accents and their obvious penchant for vodka, their intended origins are pretty clear.

Still redefining the show, Brian Clemens decided that Steed needed something different in the way of transportation, so in this episode the agent acquires a pale yellow 1923 Rolls Royce 40/50 Silver Ghost convertible (KK 4976). This vehicle, which in the past had apparently been driven by none other than Winston Churchill, had been bought for £200 during the early '50s. It was restored prior to its appearance in *The Avengers*, and would eventually feature in a total of 18 episodes. Afterwards, it would be stored in a garage in Sussex for decades, gradually deteriorating, until being passed on to a new owner who hired classic car expert Charlie Tope to undertake a complete restoration in 2011 that left the vehicle worth £250,000.

Levene's original screenplay differed from the finished episode in a number of details. For instance the office of *Bryant's Natural History Magazine* was originally situated on the fifth floor, hence Lubin's fall was from a far greater height than depicted on screen. As scripted, Tara was bound and gagged in a scene where Ezdorf lies in wait to shoot Steed in the agent's apartment, whereas in the finished episode she is able to call out a warning. The end tag scene was also slightly reworked, although with Steed inspecting his tuba it still incorporated an element of him being camouflaged so that Tara initially fails to see him, as in Levene's version.

6.06 – 'Have Guns – Will Haggle'

Next into production was a remount of the John Bryce-produced episode 'Invitation to a Killing', now under the new title 'Have Guns – Will Haggle'. Rather than do a total rewrite of the screenplay, Brian Clemens had revised just certain portions, which would be filmed to fit in with existing footage. On transmission, the episode would still be credited solely to the original writer, Donald James.

Clemens' version introduced a number of new characters, such as the eccentric ballistics expert Professor Spencer played by Timothy Bateson; the state ordnance depot worker Crayford – actually an inside man for arms dealers Condrad and Adriana – played by actor Jonathan Burn; and the mercenary Brad played by Peter J Elliott. Conversely, a number of characters from the original version did not make it through into the new one and were thus unseen on screen. These were played by guest actors Basil Tang, Thi Ha, Brian Haines and Jennifer Croxton. When later interviewed about her time making 'Invitation to a Killing' in November 1967, Croxton recalled that she had spent two days playing a photographer in a mixture of both interior and exterior scenes, building a rapport with second unit director John Hough.

It was the second unit that would shoot all of the new footage for 'Have Guns – Will Haggle'. Robert Asher, the director of 'Invitation to a Killing', was either unable of unwilling to return for the remount, so Harry Booth stepped in for the first three days of filming, on Tuesday 6, Wednesday 7 and Thursday 8 February 1968. There was then a break of five days while the crew worked on 'Get-A-Way!' before Ray Austin arrived to take over as director on Wednesday 14 February. It was Austin rather than Asher who would receive the director credit on the finished 'Have Guns – Will Haggle'. Having been employed as second unit director on *The Champions*, Austin was presumably still under contract for that series with the Monty Berman and Dennis Spooner production company Filmaker. However, with work on *The Champions* only weeks away from completion, it appears that some dispensation was allowed to let him take on his first full directing job.

The teaser sequence starts with four men wearing clown masks using a large trampoline to vault over the fence of the ordnance depot – actually somewhere south of the studio vaults. The action then switches to the ordnance depot interior set, which incorporates some red fire buckets seen in the Alpha Academy corridor in 'Invasion of the Earthmen'. The intruders are there to steal new, not-yet-off-the-secret-list FF70 rifles, complete with telescopic sight and flared muzzle – though the guns used for the production were actually modified Armalite assault rifles. After the robbery, Steed explains the mystery to Tara, who is busy practicing her skills on the trampoline that the robbers have left behind. Again this scene was filmed on the studio lot behind the vaults, with Stage 5 and prop stores A and B in the background.

Following this there is some of the original 'Invitation to a Killing' footage, shot on location in the grounds at Starveacres at Radlett, where the villainous Conrad, played by Jonathan Burn, and one of Adriana's mercenaries, played by an uncredited Joe Dunne, attempt to outwit each other in the dense bushes. Firing a single shot, Conrad kills his opponent, who falls beside a prop cannon in the garden. In new footage filmed on Thursday 22 February, Adriana, played by Nicola Pagett, then applauds and congratulates her brother from the terrace behind Stokely House.

A sequence where Steed drags the mercenary's body from some water with his umbrella, while he and Tara discuss the victim's identity, was shot using the smaller outdoor tank at Elstree Studios. This is followed by a two-handed scene back at Tara's apartment, which brings viewers up to speed with the plot as Steed deduces that Colonel Nsonga of an unnamed African state is in London attempting to buy weapons to stage a military coup in his homeland.

Returning to 'Invitation to a Killing' material, Nsonga is seen in his hotel suite having a meeting with Conrad and Adriana, who get him interested in the stolen FF70 rifles. Betraying the fact that this is footage from the original shoot, Adriana calls Nsonga 'Osonga' – obviously there had been a change of name for the character between the two versions, and either this was overlooked or it was not possible to reassemble the cast to refilm the scene by the time editor Manuel del Campo came to cut the episode together. Nsonga, played by Johnny Sekka, and his aide Giles, played by Roy Stewart, escort the two arms dealers through the hotel lobby, again in 'Invitation to a Killing' footage. Then it is back to newly-filmed material, as Steed watches from a nearby telephone booth, then bribes the attendant to keep the lift busy, allowing him sufficient time to enter Nsonga's suite and crack open the safe, revealing a large amount of cash. The hotel exterior is meanwhile seen in new night-time footage captured at the entrance to the main studio administration block situated on Shenley Road in Borehamwood.

Back in her apartment, Tara has decided to don a blonde wig. As in 'Invasion of the Earthmen', this was a plot device introduced by Clemens to explain the fact that she has blonde hair in the footage from the original shoot – although, for continuity reasons, she also wears the blonde wig in some of the newly-filmed material. Tara then visits the ballistics establishment – exterior shots of which were filmed at the Haberdashers' Aske's School in Elstree, recently used to represent the hospital in 'Split!' – where she compares bullets with Spencer, firing off several rounds from an FF70 as samples. This was a departure from the equivalent action in 'Invitation to a Killing', which had Steed and Tara attend the ballistics establishment together, parking the Bentley in some woodland on the way to allow Steed to try out the rifle for himself.

Crayford makes a telephone call to Conrad to tip him off about Tara's line of investigation, ensuring that there is a reception committee waiting for her when she leaves. Fighting off one of the mercenaries, Tara starts the engine of her red Lotus Elan +2 (NPW 999F) and, after narrowly avoiding a collision when Conrad drives his Jaguar 3.8 litre saloon straight at her, escapes at speed. First the Lotus and then the Jaguar are seen shooting out of the Haberdashers' gateway, crossing Aldenham Road and then accelerating side by side along Dagger Lane, where Tara's path is blocked by a parked motor coach. At the last moment, Tara finds a little more speed in the Lotus and, swerving in front of the Jaguar, misses the coach. This forces Conrad's car wide on the bend, causing the vehicle to collide with the verge, puncturing a front tyre. As previously mentioned, the Elan +2 was originally to have been Tara's car for the whole season. In the event, however, the only other time it was used was during the filming of 'The Great Great Britain Crime'. It was apparently borrowed back from its suppliers, Lotus Cars of Wymondham, for this final outing in 'Have Guns – Will Haggle', now that the AC had become Tara's regular transport.

After some more exposition, proceedings return briefly to original 'Invitation to a Killing' footage, showing Nsonga in his suite listening to his Decca record player playing part of the incidental music heard in the season four episode 'Small Game for Big Hunters'. Then it is back to new footage, with further scenes on the ordnance depot interior set as Crayford allows Conrad and the mercenaries to pilfer more munitions. Looking out of a window, Crayford sees Tara's car at the ordnance depot security gate – actually the western gateway at the studios – and voices his opinion that Conrad ought to have dealt with her by now. Crayford becomes even more agitated at the sight of Tara's red security pass allowing her access to all areas – something seen previously in 'Split!', with Steed's equivalent having appeared in 'The Positive Negative Man'.

Upon gaining access to the depot, in a sequence of 'Invitation to a Killing' footage, blonde Tara begins looking around and enters a warehouse full of wooden packing cases, where she becomes trapped between two of Conrad's mercenaries. A fight scene follows in which Tara emerges victorious and escapes. A newly-filmed sequence then shows Crayford registering his disgust, only to be killed by Conrad to make this second break-in look more convincing. Another newly-filmed sequence follows, in which the mercenaries' Land Rover is seen pulling away from outside the red-brick maintenance building on the studio lot, turning left and accelerating past the scenery docks. In the next shot the vehicle is passing the production offices, coming toward the front of the lot to depart through the western gateway. It then turns left onto Shenley Road. Shortly afterwards, Tara follows the same route in her Lotus. The viewer then sees some location footage of the car on Chalcot Crescent, London NW1, indicating that Tara has returned home. Back on the studio set, she enters her apartment, removes the blonde wig and goes into another room, but when she returns as a brunette, Conrad is waiting for her with a gun.

Later, in another section of 'Invitation to a Killing' footage, Steed drives up to Stokely House in his Bentley (YT 3942), accepting an invitation from Adriana to attend an auction of the FF70 rifles, much to the dismay of Nsonga, who dispatches Giles to kill him before the auction begins. Unaware that he is a target, Steed notices Nsonga's aide approaching holding a silenced automatic, but then a gunshot rings out. Giles has been shot dead by Conrad, who explains that his sister believes in fair play.

Before the auction can get under way, Adriana announces that there will be a demonstration of the FF70s, and everyone steps outside onto the terrace to watch as – in a newly-filmed sequence – two of the mercenaries have an exchange of fire in the garden, which ends with one killing the other. Another demonstration is announced, and this turns out to be a similar duel between Conrad and Tara – again in a newly-filmed sequence. Reverting to original 'Invitation to a Killing' footage, Steed frantically persuades Adriana to abandon the demo in favour of getting down to business and beginning the auction. The action continues indoors, with new footage of Tara and Conrad together in close-up mixed with original footage of the auction taking place in long-shot.[29]

---

[29] Owing to the way her scenes were scheduled, Linda Thorson was never on set at the same

Nsonga outbids everyone and decides that the duel should continue, so – in newly-filmed material – Conrad and Tara are seen back in the garden at Starveacres while – in 'Invitation to a Killing' footage – Adriana, who calls the colonel 'Osonga' again, watches from the terrace with the bidders, including Steed. A photograph taken during production of 'Invitation to a Killing' seems to show that in the original version of this sequence blonde Tara was to have lost. However, in the new version, brunette Tara knocks Conrad out and escapes into the woods, closely followed by Steed, who narrowly avoids being hit by a hail of bullets.

Proceedings continue with new night-time material shot on the woodland/shrubbery studio set, where Steed finds a shipment of rifles stored in a large wooden hut guarded by two of the mercenaries, played by uncredited stuntmen Frank Maher and Les Crawford. Taking care of both men, Steed then lays a trail of gunpowder leading to several sticks of dynamite, aiming to destroy the FF70 rifles. Along the way, however, Tara becomes imprisoned inside the hut, and Steed is prevented from rushing to her rescue when he gets involved in a fight with Conrad. The mercenary eventually falls on his own knife, allowing Steed to release Tara, using the safety pin from her skirt to unlock her handcuffs.

Adriana and Nsonga arrive nearby just as the hut explodes, causing several rounds of FF70 ammunition to go off and a stray bullet to hit the colonel, killing him instantly, in a scene filmed on Stage 3 on Tuesday 20 February. This ending had been slightly reworked by Clemens, as Donald James' original script had an FF70 rifle being thrown through the air by the blast and striking Nsonga a fatal blow on the head.

Events conclude with the end tag scene, accompanied by Laurie Johnson's tag scene music.

Principal photography on 'Have Guns – Will Haggle' wrapped on Thursday 29 February, having taken 15 days – two days longer than that on 'Invitation to a Killing' – although some additional inserts were filmed 15 days later on Stage 3, under the direction of John Hough. Again the shoot had been beset by problems. On both Thursday 8 and Wednesday 14 February it had proved impossible to complete all of the scheduled scenes because Linda Thorson had been occupied for longer than expected working with the main unit on 'Get-A-Way!'. Roy Stewart had missed his call on Thursday 22 February, arriving 35 minutes late at the studio and holding up shooting for a time. More seriously, Peter J Elliott had accidentally strained a ligament while performing a trampoline stunt at approximately 4.30 pm on the afternoon of Wednesday 28 February, resulting in a trip to the Orthopaedic Hospital at Stanmore.

However, one positive development did come out of the filming of 'Have Guns – Will Haggle'. Like Brian Clemens and Albert Fennell, Patrick Macnee had initially considered Thorson too young and inexperienced to assume the lead female role in *The Avengers*. However, sometime during this episode's production, he voiced his reservations to Ray Austin, and Austin persuaded him to give his new co-star a chance to prove herself, as he thought the Canadian actress definitely had potential. This conversation brought about a change of outlook, as Macnee then tended to look out for Thorson and they became great friends, which also boosted their on-screen relationship.

---

time as Nicola Pagett or Johnny Sekka, so Tara is never seen in the same shot as either Adriana or Nsonga.

6.07 – 'Look – (Stop Me If You've Heard This One) But There Were These Two Fellers ...'

Still short of usable scripts, Clemens turned to his friend Dennis Spooner, who obliged with what was probably the most humorous episode of the season, 'Look – (Stop Me If You've Heard This One) But There Were These Two Fellers ...'. This was in some ways a throwback to the early season five episodes, as it was written for laughs and full of eccentric characters, as Spooner obviously drew inspiration from his own early career as a stand-up comic and gag writer. In fact, Spooner had initially proposed the story when season five was in production, but it had been turned down at that time as being too outrageous. The plot involves the directors of Project Cupid – a scheme to create an emergency underground shelter for the British government's use in the event of war – being murdered one by one by a pair of clowns who object to the fact that it entails the demolition of some old music halls.

The episode's title was taken from a catchphrase used by popular comedians Eric Morcambe and Ernie Wise. Between 1961 and 1968, ATV made six seasons of their *The Morecambe And Wise Show*, a mixture of comedy sketches and stand-up, co-starring the comedians and their writers Sid Green and Dick Mills. At the conclusion of each show, Sid and Dick would be sitting in deckchairs as Eric began telling Ernie a dirty joke. However, Eric never managed to get further than the first line before the show ended. That first line was initially, 'There were these two old men sitting in deckchairs,' but over time evolved into, 'Look, stop me if you've heard this one, but there were these two old men sitting in deckchairs.' This catchphrase became ingrained in the nation's psyche, and so would have been very familiar to viewers when Spooner adapted it for his own use.

James Hill was recalled for his last stint directing on *The Avengers*, and amongst the guest cast were veteran variety performer Jimmy Jewel as the clown Merry Maxie Martin; magician Julian Chagrin as the mime artist Jennings; comedy actor Bernard Cribbins as gag writer Bradley Marler, whose office is shown knee-deep in screwed up pieces of paper containing unfunny jokes from his typewriter; and, fresh from doing sketches on the BBC's satirical show *The Frost Report*, John Cleese as the eccentric Marcus Rugman. Linda Thorson obviously took a shine to Chagrin, as after *The Avengers* ended she became the assistant in his magic act for a time. She also found Cleese highly amusing. This might explain why she considers the episode one of her favourites.

The first day's filming, on Tuesday 20 February 1968, included a novelty bomb explosion that kills the Cupid Project's Brigadier Wiltshire, played by Garry Marsh. This was shot by the main unit in the car park of Wembley Point, a 21-floor building on Harrow Road in Wembley. Despite precautions, including having a trained firefighter on standby, the special effects used in the scene resulted in fire damage to the front seat of the Bentley limousine hired for the day. The unit returned to Wembley Point the following day, but Hill broke the shoot at 11.45 am because heavy rain prevented filming. He planned to resume there the next morning, but in the event this was also cancelled due to bad weather. Instead the unit spent the morning of Thursday 22 February capturing some interior footage on Stage 9 on the Bradley Marler's office set. After things brightened up, however, they were back at Wembley Point by mid-afternoon to complete all the required footage at this location.

Figuring that the next company director earmarked for assassination is Lord

Dessington, played by William Kendall, Steed gives Tara the job of protecting him, along with a .38 Smith and Wesson M40 revolver. However, Maxie still manages to kill Dessington, after which he links arms with Jennings and they exit stage left to the accompaniment of pantomime music, as if at the end of a music hall act. When interviewed by this author in 1985, Spooner pointed out that he could allow Tara to fail in this way as she was an inexperienced trainee agent, whereas he could never have let it happen to the seasoned professional Emma Peel.

An amusing sequence where the honourable Randolph Cleghorn, played by Bill Shine, is duck hunting and finds himself on the receiving end of a gun barrel was shot on Friday 23 February on the wooded bank of Tykes Water Lake on the Aldenham Estate, Elstree. Jewel, Chagrin and Shine were all present at this location, where summer filming had previously taken place for both 'You Have Just Been Murdered' and 'The Positive Negative Man'.

Hill called the quarter before lunchtime on Friday 1 March, to keep the trade unions happy and allow an additional 15 minutes' shooting at the end of the morning.

On Monday 4 March the main unit started filming on Stage 3, before moving across to Stage 9 sometime during the morning, making way for the second unit to replace them on Stage 3 to obtain car interior footage. Then, during the afternoon, John Hough led the second unit out on location to Silver Hill, where Maxie Martin's Austin FX4 cab was filmed heading toward the village of Shenley, being followed by the AC 428. On the same day, Steed's Rolls Royce Silver Ghost (KK 4976) broke down while being driven to the studio and had to be loaded onto a trailer provided by the hire company and transported to Borehamwood, where it was consequently late arriving.

Driving her AC, Tara follows Maxie and Jennings in their Austin cab to the gateway to the fictional Vauda Villa, the exterior of which was represented by Longmeadow, a large dwelling situated on Woodside Lane in Welham Green, about seven miles from Borehamwood. Later, Steed arrives at Vauda Villa – called Greasepaint Grange in the original draft script – in his Rolls, posing undercover as a down-on-his-luck theatrical entertainer introduced as 'Gentleman Jack – a song, a smile and an umbrella.' The main unit carried out all the required location filming at Longmeadow on the morning of Friday 8 March, before returning to the studios in the afternoon and taking over from the second unit, which had been shooting on the Vauda Villa main room set on Stage 9.

Feeling unwell, Patrick Macnee went home an hour after the unit call on the morning of Monday 11 March and was unable to return until two days later, leaving the crew no option but to shoot around him in his absence.

Spooner's depiction of Rugman recording every clown's intricate make-up by painting on eggs was completely true to life, as the writer knew exactly how circus performers' facial designs were kept for reference. In one scene, Rugman and Tara are seen shuffling along the floor so as not to disturb any of the eggs, to the accompaniment of the Scottish-sounding incidental music first heard in 'Castle De'ath'.

The uncredited performer operating the Punch and Judy show puppets featured in the action was magician and all-round entertainer John Styles, who would later play a ventriloquist in the *Randall and Hopkirk (Deceased)* episode 'That's How Murder Snowballs'. Over the years, Styles has found his Punch and Judy show talents called upon for a number of other productions, including *The Goodies*, *Inspector Morse* and the feature film *102 Dalmatians*. Also uncredited on the episode were pantomime performers June and Paul Kidd, playing the two halves of Herbie the Horse. One person who did receive a credit, however, for the final time on the series, was Julian

Wintle.

As in a couple of the videotaped episodes, Steed is seen to be a fan of the adventures of Belgian author Hergé's Tintin character – on this occasion chuckling to himself in his apartment while he reads *Le Lotus Bleu* (aka *The Blue Lotus*), which would not be translated into an English edition until 1983.

'Look – (Stop Me if You've Heard This One) But There Were These Two Fellers ...' finished principal filming on Tuesday 19 March, after which a further ten working days were spent cutting and editing it. This completed the last of the seven Thorson episodes that ABC Television Films had been required to provide in time to round off the third American run of *The Avengers*. Viewers across the United States would get to see the new Avengergirl for themselves when 'The Forget-Me-Knot' was networked on Wednesday 20 March – well in advance of the ITV regions beginning their airings of season six.

To coincide with the earliest transmissions of his long-running sitcom *Nearest and Dearest*, Jimmy Jewel took out a half-page advertisement in the Thursday 22 August 1968 edition of *The Stage and Television Today*. Under the headline 'The Many Faces Of Jimmy Jewel', the ad incorporated five photographs of Merry Maxie Martin as different characters he changed into during the course of the episode, despite the fact that most of the ITV regions would not screen it until December. Obviously hopeful of generating work through this exposure, Jewel also included his manager's name and contact details.

Restoring the style

Now without the pressure of having to meet the American deadline, Brian Clemens, Albert Fennell and the crew could concentrate more on putting the style back into *The Avengers*, working with a new team of writers and directors. Could Patrick Macnee and Linda Thorson continue the series' tradition of high kicks, high thrills and high quality entertainment? The answer appeared to hinge on one factor: could Linda Thorson ever successfully fill Diana Rigg's kinky boots?

Television Wales and the West

The forthcoming restructuring of the ITV regions had already had a knock-on effect. Having earned a dubious place in broadcasting history by becoming the first company ever to lose a UK television franchise, TWW felt victimised and decided against continuing through to the hand-over date at the end of July 1968. Bailing out early, they sold most of their final three months to successor Harlech for £500,000 and made their final transmissions on Sunday 3 March. However, despite having been awarded the contract to replace TWW, Harlech were not yet entirely ready to start their service to the dual region, so the ITA had to step in and arrange a stopgap service. The temporary provider, Independent Television Service for Wales and the West, run by Harlech management and TWW staff, began broadcasting from the latter's Cardiff studio on Monday 4 March. This arrangement allowed Harlech time to prepare their own programming. Quickly getting their house in order, they took over the region on Monday 20 May. Within the week, they had started transmitting the few outstanding season five episodes of *The Avengers* that TWW had failed to screen, with 'A Funny Thing Happened on the Way to the Station' going out on Sunday 26 May at 7.25 pm.

6.08 – 'My Wildest Dream'

Clemens and Fennell had been running out of screenplays when they had given the go-ahead to film 'Look – (Stop Me If You've Heard This One) But There Were These Two Fellers …', but they still had in hand a final Philip Levene script, 'My Wildest Dream'. Unfortunately, this had been written to conform to John Bryce's earlier 'back to basics' approach, so anyone who expected another classic from the writer responsible for 'The Cybernauts' and 'From Venus with Love' was to be disappointed. The end result was a slow-paced affair about people being conditioned by a psychiatrist named Dr Jaeger, played by Peter Vaughan, to commit murder. On the plus side, however, it did mark the initial directorial assignment on the series for its one-time production designer, Robert Fuest.

The initial day of filming, on Monday 11 March 1968, was undertaken by the second unit, with Fuest directing, on location at Mansfield Street, Duchess Street and Weymouth Mews in central London. This was for a car chase sequence in which Tara, driving Steed's vintage Rolls Royce, pursues Dr Jaeger's assistant Dyson, played by Tom Kempinski, in his Volvo 122, losing him at the corner of the fictional Marlin Street, identified by a prop street sign. Thorson was not on location for this filming – her close-ups were shot in the studio, with back-projection behind the Rolls. When it came to the lunch break, the unit visited the Chilton Court Restaurant in Baker Street – something they would do on several occasions during the making of this episode – rather than hiring a catering bus from John Anderson Limited as was more usual.

Production on day two involved the second unit back in the capital, filming on location at both Duchess Mews and Chalcot Crescent for establishing footage of Steed's and Tara's apartments. The third day, Wednesday 13 March, then proceeded with a visit to the four large apartment blocks called Clarendon Court situated in Sidmouth Road, London NW2, where actor Murray Hayne, playing conditioned killer Paul Gibbons, was filmed climbing a fire escape beside some garages at the rear of the site. Later in the day the unit returned to Borehamwood, where some footage was shot at Foster House, then the premises of BSP Industries, on Maxwell Road adjacent to the studios. This was for a scene of Tara arriving at the premises of the Acme Precision Combine Ltd and for the subsequent start of the car chase sequence, which would be accompanied on screen by some incidental music first heard in 'Never, Never Say Die'. The day did not pass without incident, as the catering bus from John Anderson Limited got too close to the Rolls Royce, scratching the paintwork on both nearside mudguards.

On Monday 18 March, Fuest was completely occupied with the main unit on Stage 7, filming scenes on the Jaeger consulting room set, which featured some distinctive walls made up of squares with eight small, different-sized circles in them, seen previously in the hospital operating room in 'Split!'. The second unit meanwhile spent another full day in London, under the direction of John Hough. Filming once again took place on Duchess Mews and Mansfield Street, plus Park Crescent and Marylebone Road, all in London W1, and on Westbourne Terrace Road, London W2. The property at 18 Mansfield Street served as the exterior of Dr Jaeger's consulting room. Once more, production failed to run smoothly. The hired Volvo 122, driven in this instance by Jaeger's nurse Janet Owen, played by Susan Travers, was involved in an accident during filming, resulting in one of the doors becoming detached from the vehicle – although repairs would be quickly undertaken and the car returned to the second unit four days later. Further to this, some wiring under the dashboard of Steed's Rolls Royce ignited on location. Fortunately the fire was quickly extinguished, and on inspecting the damage, the hire driver declared the vehicle fit for continued use.

The following day, Hough led his small team back to Mansfield Street for two hours of location work in the afternoon, but once again there were car problems as the offside front bumper of the AC sustained slight damage during the shoot.

Paperwork indicates that the second unit also planned to do some location filming in Sutherland Avenue, London W9. If this went ahead, however, it must have been dropped at the editing stage, as it does not feature in the finished episode.

In an unprecedented move, Fuest called the quarter twice during filming on Stages 7 and 3 on Wednesday 20 March, allowing him to get an additional 15 minutes' filming time before lunch and then again before the conclusion of normal working hours.

A couple of days later, Hough was out on location again with the second unit at Nan Clark's Lane in Highwood Hill, approximately three miles from the studios, where some footage for 'Who's Who???' had previously been filmed. The shoot went without a hitch – despite there being a number of vehicles on location, none of them was damaged on this occasion!

Principal photography on the episode was completed on Monday 1 April, although editor Manuel del Campo – known as Mike to the crew – supervised the shooting of a number of inserts with a third unit on Thursday 18 April on Stage 3.

One other point of note: during the first scene in Tara's apartment, she is seen flicking through the fashion magazine *Flair* before answering the door to Steed, shortly after which the overhead boom microphone makes an unwanted appearance in shot.

'My Wildest Dream' later proved to be something of a problematic episode when it came to transmission, owing to it including several instances of hypodermic needles being used to administer drugs. With the drug-taking hippy culture rife at the time, there was a feeling within ITV that this could be offensive to some viewers and could even influence people to experiment with drugs. It appears that the regional companies were made aware of the content and, erring on the side of caution, most of them transmitted the episode after 10.30 pm. Only three – Southern, Westward and Channel – broke ranks and went for a 9.00 pm slot.

Composer Howard Blake fills in

Laurie Johnson was invited by Brian Clemens and Albert Fennell to resume his former role as *The Avengers*' regular incidental music provider. However, since the end of production on season five, he had become involved with other projects – such as the musical stage play *The Four Musketeers*, for which he wrote the entire score – so he was unable to give the series his full commitment at this time. Consequently he arranged for fellow composer Howard Blake to fill in and provide additional music for ten episodes, starting with 'My Wildest Dream'. Blake's contributions would be recorded after the episodes were filmed, ready to be dubbed on at the editing stage, but would still be augmented by music editor Karen Heward reusing cues from the extensive library that Johnson had created since the start of his involvement with the series.

Global success

Meanwhile, the Thursday 21 March 1968 edition of *The Stage and Television Today* reported on a Writers' Guild of Great Britain awards ceremony that had taken place the previous week at the Dorchester Hotel on Park Lane in London. Merit awards had been presented both to *The Avengers* and to Philip Levene for his contributions to the series and other scriptwriting endeavours.

The following week, under the headline 'Avengers for Peak American Showing', the same publication revealed that the American ABC network had scheduled a further run of *The Avengers* to form part of their all-important autumn season. They had already promoted the series from a late-evening summer replacement to a primetime attraction, but now they would be placing it in a 7.00 pm Monday slot from 23 September as one of their key weapons in the American ratings war. ABC Television was quick to point out, 'This makes *The Avengers* the most successful British television series ever to appear on the American network.'

Back in the UK, the children's comic *TV Tornado* No. 64, dated 30 March, featured an artwork John Steed cover – though this was somewhat misleading, as coverage of *The Avengers* inside the comic was restricted to a solitary sentence, informing readers that Macnee was filming new episodes.

There was also interest being shown in Linda Thorson's homeland, as the March edition of the *Toronto Star Weekend Magazine* covered the series in an article, which actually concentrated more on Macnee. Brian Clemens was quoted as saying, 'Macnee is the only indispensable character in *The Avengers*. We can't change him, but we can change the girls, we've done it.'

During April the German magazine *Bravo* featured coverage of Macnee and Rigg collecting Gold Otto awards as the top male and female television stars, having been selected by the publication's readers for their roles in *The Avengers*.

Terry Nation joins the team

Aware of the American ABC network's intention to start transmitting their next run of *The Avengers* in late September, Brian Clemens and Albert Fennell drew up their own production plans accordingly. These included a reintroduction of the system of having two main units supported by a second unit, as had been utilised to such positive effect on season five. This change would be implemented in three months' time. Clemens and Fennell also decided that they needed to bring someone else onto the team to serve as a script editor, and to this end they headhunted scriptwriter Terry Nation. Nation had already provided the script for the John Bryce-produced 'Invasion of the Earthmen', but his experience as script supervisor on ITC's *The Baron* and writing duties on both *The Saint* and *The Champions* were what probably clinched the position for him. It is likely that the initial approach to Nation was made in late March 1968, when he had just scripted a couple of early *Department S* episodes for his friend Dennis Spooner, but if so it appears that he did not start work on *The Avengers* straight away, as his first on-screen credit would not come until July, on the episode 'False Witness'. He could well have spent some of the intervening period finishing off three scripts – 'The Desperate Diplomat', 'The Time to Die' and 'Where the Money Is' – for the last season of *The Saint*, which would all be filmed toward the end of the year.

6.09 – 'Whoever Shot Poor George Oblique Stroke XR40?'

Having scripted only a solitary season five episode, 'The Positive Negative Man', Tony Williamson suddenly found himself in demand to contribute to *The Avengers* again after receiving a telephone call from Brian Clemens. The story he came up with, under the unusual title 'Whoever Shot Poor George Oblique Stroke XR40?', involves a man named Jacob attempting to 'murder' a computer known as George just before it can expose its creator, Sir Wilfred Pelly, as a traitor. Giving the action a typical *The Avengers* twist, Williamson wrote the scenes of technicians attempting to repair George as if they were of a medical operation done in a sterile environment, complete with masks and gowns.

Principal photography on the episode began on Thursday 28 March 1968, a few days before the end of that on 'My Wildest Dream'. Following the usual procedure of location work being done first, Hough took the second unit into London to shoot some day-for-night footage on Sutherland Avenue, W9. Actor John Porter-Davison, playing Jacob, was present for this filming, being seen to enter no. 182 after kicking the front tyre of Steed's vintage Rolls Royce.

The small unit returned to Elstree Studios later the same day, where they again used day-for-night shooting for a sequence where the night watchman of the Ministry of Technology, Cybernetics and Computer Division does his rounds, checking a door on the exterior of the building that actually housed the ABPC's own offices, then moving down the west side of the studio lot by the cutting rooms. A small production error is apparent here, as the prop sign on the wire perimeter fencing misspells part of the Ministry's name as 'Computor.' The sequence ends with the watchman being attacked and knocked out by the escaping Jacobs, using the butt of the 12-bore shotgun used to shoot George. This action was filmed under the covered walkway between Stages 7, 8 and 9 and the red-brick ancillaries block.

The second day involved another location visit, this time to the large property at Rossway Park near Berkhamsted, Hertfordshire, approximately 15 miles from the studio. This doubled as the manor house of Sir Wilfred Pelley, played by Clifford Evans. Hough and the second unit filmed outside the house all day, capturing scenes featuring Porter-Davison and fellow guest actor Tony Wright, playing Pelley's chauffeur Keller, along with Steed's Rolls Royce, Tara's AC 428 and Pelley's Rolls Royce limousine.

Experienced director Cyril Frankel arrived to take over on the third day of production, Monday 1 April, when his main unit worked alongside Hough's second unit all day on Stage 7 at Elstree, on the set of the apartment of murdered Ministry official Baines.

Baines was played by Adrian Ropes, while other guest actors in the episode included Anthony Nicholls as cybernetic surgeon Dr Ardmore and Frank Windsor as the duplicitous technician Tobin. Frankel had previously worked with Nicholls on *The Champions*, and would later use Windsor again in the *Randall and Hopkirk (Deceased)* pilot episode. Another casting choice was character actor Dennis Price as fake butler Jason. Frankel obviously considered Price to have done a good job in this role, as he would later cast him as Gene Bradley's butler Brandon in three episodes of *The Adventurer*.

Costume designer Alun Hughes supplied Tara with a black fancy dress catsuit complete with mask, matching leather gloves, kinky boots and green feather boa tail and neckline. The mask was included to hide the fact that it was Thorson's double, Cyd Child, who performed a stunt where Tara falls down the stairwell of Baines' apartment block, filmed on Stage 5 on Tuesday 16 April.

Steed's steel-crowned bowler comes into its own again in a sequence where Jacobs fires a pistol at him in Baines' apartment and the bullet simply ricochets back from the inside of the hat, killing the assailant instantly.

Pelley's study contains the winged red leather chair seen with Diana Rigg and her on-screen caption in the previous season's opening title sequence.

The summerhouse interior set last seen in 'Mission ... Highly Improbable' was brought out of storage and reassembled to appear in a scene toward the end of the episode where Tara is about to be burnt alive but Steed rescues her. This was filmed by Frankel and the main unit on Stage 3 on Tuesday 2 April. Eight days later, Hough and the second unit shot the corresponding exteriors of the summerhouse hidden away among the shrubbery on the backlot.

A number of differences are apparent between Williamson's original shooting script and the finished episode, suggesting that Clemens had some input. Absent altogether from the script is one sequence where, while attempting to pick the lock of Pelley's cellar door, the undercover Tara hands her chrome-plated .45 Smith and Wesson 1917 revolver to Jason, explaining that she is an impostor – in response to which he turns the gun on her and confesses that he is too. Also, instead of attacking Steed at Baines' home as in the finished episode, Jacobs was originally to have stormed the agent's apartment with his shotgun, firing both barrels and leaving a large hole in the wooden outer door. Steed was then to have defended himself by throwing his umbrella sword through the hole so that it embedded itself in Jacobs' chest, killing him. This appears to have been rewritten because, unknown to Williamson, Clemens and Fennell had the attitude that the umbrella sword could be seen but never used in anger.

The Stage and Television Today reports

Meanwhile, the Wednesday 10 April 1968 edition of *The Stage and Television Today* reported that Honor Blackman had returned to ABC's Teddington Studios to record an *Armchair Theatre* instalment titled 'Recount'. This production was transmitted in both ABC regions on Saturday 20 April and marked Blackman's first work for the company since leaving *The Avengers* four years earlier. The same edition of the magazine reported that John Bryce had recently been appointed Head of Drama Series at the newly-formed LWT, which at the end of July would replace ATV as the capital's weekend programme provider.

First original American paperback

Also during April 1968, publishers Berkley Medallion issued the first American-originated novel based on *The Avengers*. Titled *The Afrit Affair*, this came from the typewriter of science fiction author and ex-US diplomat Keith Laumer. The plot had Emma Peel partnering Steed, indicating that Laumer had written it sometime before the first batch of Linda Thorson episodes began transmission across the USA the previous month. The front cover sported a publicity still taken on location at Stapleford Park during the filming of 'The Gravediggers', showing Emma tied to the railway tracks and Steed attempting to free her. No UK edition of this book was ever published.

6.10 – 'All Done With Mirrors'

The next episode to enter production, 'All Done with Mirrors', was written by series newcomer Leigh Vance, who was briefed to allow for the fact that Macnee would be absent on leave for most of the filming dates, requiring Linda Thorson as Tara to carry the main action almost single-handedly. The storyline had Steed being placed under house arrest, while Tara, aided by the somewhat inept Roger Watney, played by Dinsdale Landen, attempts to uncover the culprit leaking top secret information from the Carmadoc Research Establishment. Also in the cast were Michael Trubshawe and, making his sixth guest appearance in the series, Edwin Richfield, playing a pair of enemy operatives impersonating the eccentric lighthouse dweller Colonel Withers and his assistant Barlow. Joe Dunne appeared uncredited as their villainous henchman Sweeno, who after a fight with Tara falls down all 365 steps of the lighthouse. Also uncredited in the role of the giant hit man Gozzo was professional wrestler Big Bruno Elrington, an 18-stone fighter who hailed from Portsmouth.

The inclusion of a lighthouse in the storyline caused John Hough and the second unit to be dispatched on Tuesday 16 April 1968 to Torcross in Devon, from where they had easy access to carry out three days' filming at the nearby Start Point Lighthouse. Joanna Jones, playing reporter Pandora Marshall, was the only cast member to accompany them, although Liz Mitchell also went along in her capacity as Thorson's double. Having completed all her scenes, Jones departed from the location on Thursday 18 April. The crew followed the next day, catching the 12.30 pm train from Plymouth and returning to base via Paddington railway station.

Also on Thursday 18 April Ray Austin arrived as the episode's principal director and took the main unit to Rabley Park, off Packhorse Lane close to the village of Ridge, approximately four miles north-east of the studio. It was here that a fight between Tara and Gozzo was filmed, with stunt double Cyd Child as usual standing in for Thorson. As the fight progresses, Tara is seen tackling her larger opponent with a number of martial arts moves – including karate chops, dropkicks and an impressive monkey flip that sends him rolling head over heels – before knocking him through a wooden shed, where he falls onto the spikes of a garden rake and is killed – a slight departure from Vance's draft script, which had him being impaled on a scythe instead.

The exteriors of the cottage home of a local named Guthrie, played by Desmond Jordan, were shot on the same day a couple of miles to the west, on London Road, close to Well End. Tara carries out her investigations here after arriving in a Morris Mini Moke (LYP 794D) borrowed from the research centre.

On the morning of Monday 22 April, Hough led the second unit on another long-distance location shoot to Peacehaven, East Sussex, where they stayed all week, playing host to various cast members on different days. Thorson, Landen and Jordan all filmed on the clifftop here, as did Peter Copley, playing the research centre's head of security Major Sparshott, and Peter Thomas, playing another enemy agent, Kettridge. A truck-mounted hydraulic platform was used to raise the camera up and give a high angle on the action. It appears that the shoot would have been completed in four days but for the fact that deteriorating weather conditions prevented filming after 10.00 am on Thursday 25 April. After wrapping up all the required scenes by 4.00 pm the following day, the unit returned to Elstree.

Scenes featuring Thorson at the outer door of the lighthouse were shot on a set at Elstree; and a behind-the-scenes photograph exists showing that on one take she was surprised when the door was opened by none other than Roger Moore, who presumably had some time to kill while making *The Saint* on adjacent stages and thought he would play one of the practical jokes for which he was renowned.

The exteriors of the red-brick Carmadoc Research Centre were filmed on Tuesday 23 April at RAF Stanmore Park in Stanmore – an establishment that no longer exists, as in the intervening years the area has undergone total redevelopment to create housing.

Thorson suffered a setback on Wednesday 24 April when she began developing a throat infection that resulted in a doctor being summoned to the studios, though after an examination she elected to continue filming.

Additional second unit footage was obtained on Monday 29 April at Ivinghoe Beacon Road near Ivinghoe, Buckinghamshire for a couple of motor vehicle sequences. One of these involved Watney's black S-Type Jaguar being handbrake-turned to block the road after the agent hears a cry for assistance from Tara. The other showed Steed's vintage Rolls Royce momentarily going out of control in similar circumstances. As at Peacehaven, a hydraulic platform – a 40-foot Simon Snorkel model – was hired and used to film both vehicles in high-angle long shots, giving the impression of them being seen from the vantage point of the top of the lighthouse.

After being absent for the majority of the filming, Patrick Macnee returned on Monday 6 May to take part in some scenes set beside a swimming pool (discussed in more detail below). He would also do some pick-up inserts for this episode the following month. One of these was the end tag scene, featuring the cooking of a steak on the engine of Steed's Rolls Royce, which was filmed in a grassed area on the Aldenham Estate, Elstree.

The Carmadoc interior set featured some of the distinctive walls consisting of squares with eight small, different-sized circles in them, as seen previously in 'Split!' and 'My Wildest Dream'. The revolving device in the centre of the set was also basically made up of four of these squares fixed together.

This was the first episode for which Thorson did not need to wear a wig, as her own hair had now grown back sufficiently after the peroxide incident that had caused so much damage to it at the start of the season's production.

The red leather chair seen in the season five opening titles and more recently in the episode 'Whoever Shot Poor George Oblique Stroke XR40?' appears once more here, on the ground floor of the lighthouse.

Tara at one point brandishes a 9mm Beretta 1934 automatic after liberating it from one of the enemy agents in the lighthouse.

This was another of the episodes on which Howard Blake stood in for Laurie Johnson to supply incidental music, supplemented by existing cues chosen by music editor Karen Heward. One of these existing cues was Johnson's menacing Cybernauts music, which was used to accompany some of the action of Gozzo fighting with Tara.

Its scenic location filming having been undertaken so far from the series' base of operations, 'All Done with Mirrors' must have been one of the most expensive episodes of this season to produce, but the end result was also one of the best.

Mother and Rhonda

The aforementioned swimming pool scenes in 'All Done with Mirrors' were particularly notable for reintroducing the character of Steed's wheelchair-bound superior Mother, played by Patrick Newell, as seen previously in 'The Forget-Me-Knot'.

This move was decided upon by Brian Clemens to provide some additional light relief, as he felt that Thorson could not portray the subtle humour he wanted in the series. Thus Mother is seen here sat in the pool in a floating chair, alongside floating tables containing drinks decanters and telephones. From this point on, Steed and Mother would share a couple of scenes in almost every episode, with Mother's base of operations changing each time – becoming something of a tailored effect within the series, as he would often turn up in the most unusual places.

Macnee was not initially convinced that the series needed a regular character in the mould of James Bond's M, making Steed explicitly answerable to someone in authority – unlike in the Emma Peel episodes. However, he got on very well with Newell both on and off set, and the concept appeared to work largely because of their good rapport.

Making her debut in 'All Done With Mirrors' in the role of Mother's assistant was former professional swimmer Rhonda Parker, who demonstrated her abilities when she was filmed diving into the pool. This was originally intended as nothing more than a walk-on bit part. However, when Parker emerged on location wearing a pale blue swimsuit she instantly turned all heads and captured the full attention of both Macnee and Newell. This resulted in her being put under contract to play the character, who was also given the name Rhonda, on a semi-regular basis, to serve Morther drinks and push his wheelchair – although she would never speak a line of dialogue or receive any on-screen credit.

Born in Australia in 1947, Parker had come to Britain earlier in the '60s and often found work – usually uncredited – due to her tall stature. Aside from *The Avengers*, she also appeared on television in *The Champions*, *Hark at Barker*, *Space: 1999* and *The Two Ronnies*, and on the big screen in the film *Husbands*. The ABC publicity machine went into operation, claiming that Parker's height was six feet two inches. However, when interviewed years later, the actress insisted that it was actually just a whisker under six feet, and that the extra inches had been added to hype up her character.

6.11 – 'You'll Catch Your Death'

Next into production was the first Jeremy Burnham-written episode, initially titled 'Atishoo, Atishoo, All Fall Down', in which Steed and Tara are tasked with investigating the mystery of ear, nose and throat specialists dropping dead after each receiving a seemingly empty envelope that actually contains a virulent form of the cold virus.

Having been given the go-ahead by Brian Clemens to script an episode for the series, Burnham saw his dream start to turn into reality as principal photography got under way on Tuesday 30 April 1968. To establish Walsingham House, the home of the retired Colonel Timothy, played by Ronald Culver, John Hough supervised the second unit on a return visit to Edge Grove School on Oakridge Lane in the village of Aldenham, about four miles north-west of the studio. Footage was also filmed that day at another location seen previously in the series, Shenley Hall on Rectory Lane in Shenley, which provided the exterior of the Anastasia Nursing Academy, the place to which the envelopes were initially delivered after being bought wholesale.

The exterior of the ear, nose and throat consulting rooms featured in the episode was represented by a building in the courtyard toward the northern end of Cumberland Terrace, next to Regents Park in central London. Hough brought the second unit to this particular area on four different occasions to undertake filming not just on Cumberland Terrace, but also on the adjacent Cumberland Place, Chester Close North and Chester Terrace.

The medical consultant Seaton, played by Geoffrey Chater, becomes another victim of the virus after one of the envelopes is delivered to him by the fake postman Preece, played by Peter Bourne. Tara takes to the AC 428 and gives chase as Preece tries to escape in a Rolls Royce limousine driven by co-conspirator Dexter, played by Dudley Sutton, eventually reaching some woodland. This location was actually Burnham Beeches in Buckinghamshire, where footage of the two vehicles was obtained on some of the internal access roads. The crossroads where Tara turns the AC around is where Halse Drive becomes Sir Henry Peakes Drive and is crossed by Lord Mayors Drive. Also shot here was material of Steed's vintage Rolls being driven along Sir Henry Peakes Drive, for use in a sequence earlier in the episode where Steed and Tara go to consult Mother. All of this Burnham Beeches material was captured by the second unit on the second day of filming, Wednesday 1 May.

Driving back to Steed's apartment, Tara fails to notice that the limousine has followed her. This involved more footage being shot at the usual location for this setting, Duchess Mews, London W1, on Friday 3 May.

Director Paul Dickson arrived at Elstree on Monday 6 May to take charge of the main unit on what would be his only outing on *The Avengers*. Filming took place on the studio backlot in the smaller of its two concrete-lined water tanks, which had been drained in order to serve as one of the more bizarre examples of Mother's headquarters, complete with assorted stepladders and with blonde-haired assistant Rhonda on hand. The larger of the two tanks would later be filled in when Elstree's then owners Brent Walker sold off a portion of the site to retail chain Tesco in 1990, but the smaller one would be retained and would eventually become the location of the house used for the *Big Brother* reality television show.

Character actor Royston Tickner was called at 10.30 am on the last day of principal photography, Friday 24 May, to portray a character at the Anastasia Nursing Academy, which involved him staying on stage until 4.00 pm. In the end, however, his role was completely excised during editing.

One final piece of filming for the episode took place on Stage 3 on Wednesday 5 June, when editor Karen Heward supervised a small third unit minus any performers to shoot inserts for three scenes.

Other points of note: the Pelley living room set from 'Whoever Shot Poor George Oblique Stroke XR40?' had been left standing and underwent a light redressing and the addition of a revolving wall to become Colonel Timothy's study; Steed's home address, 3 Stable Mews, London, is clearly visible on the envelope destined for him; the agent uses his steel-crowned bowler hat to good effect again to assist in knocking Dexter out cold; some of the footage of guest actor Andrew Laurence as Dr Herrick having an unfortunate accident in his Wolsley 1885 while sneezing uncontrollably was overcranked, thus making it appear in slow motion in the finished episode; and Mother is revealed to have his own superior, known as Grandma, who gives him a grilling over the telephone due to lack of progress on the case.

To his credit, Burnham seemed to have dialled into the quirky style of *The Avengers* straight away with this far-fetched tale of victims who sneeze themselves to death after exposure to an extreme virus. He also succeeded in giving an apparently harmless everyday public servant, namely a postal worker, a hidden menace – something he would also manage to achieve with milkmen in the upcoming episode 'False Witness'.

The large nose prop seen on the wall of the Anastasia Nursing Academy was also down to the writer. However, Burnham's episode title, 'Atishoo, Atishoo, All Fall Down', did not make it to the screen, being replaced with the more catchy traditional warning about being out in bad weather, 'You'll Catch Your Death'.

Incidental music recordings

Meanwhile, on Monday 6 May 1968, composer Howard Blake had supervised the first of his incidental music recording sessions for *The Avengers*. This took place at Elstree in what was described by *Kine Weekly* at the time as the most modern sound studio in the UK. With various session players hired to perform, cues were laid down for both 'My Wildest Dream' and 'Whoever Shot Poor George Oblique Stroke XR40?' This would be followed a month later to the day by a second such session, this time to record material for 'All Done with Mirrors'.

Patrick Macnee interview

An interview with Patrick Macnee appeared in the *Los Angeles Times* of Wednesday 8 May 1968. In this the actor explained how the production units worked on two episodes of *The Avengers* simultaneously, and said that he would be staying with the series for as long as it continued. He added that he had recently bought the film rights to novelist David Hughes' book *The Major* and planned to star in the project later that year. In the event, however, he would be committed to *The Avengers* until February 1969, and that proposed film would never be made.

6.12 – 'Super Secret Cypher Snatch'

Tony Williamson's next script for *The Avengers* was produced under the title 'Whatever Happened to Yesterday?'. The story this time concerns a firm of fake window cleaners who gain access to a military establishment known as Cypher Headquarters, put its director Webster and other staff into a trancelike state and proceed to pilfer secret information.

Principal photography began on Tuesday 14 May 1968, when John Hough – enjoying a temporary promotion to credited main director on this episode – took the second unit out on a double-header location shoot. The first location used was an apartment block at Boydell Court, a cul-de-sac off St John's Wood Park in St John's Wood, London NW8. This was used for the exterior of the residence of MI12 operative Jarret, played by Clifford Earl. Then, later that day, the unit returned to Borehamwood to undertake some shooting at the since-demolished Franco Signs factory that stood on the corner of Ripon Way and Stangate Crescent. This similarly represented the exterior of the apartment block containing the home of MI12 photographer Peters, played by John Carlisle.

The following morning found the second unit making the first of three visits to the Brookmans Park Transmitting Station, situated on Great North Road, Brookmans Park, Hertfordshire, which became the exterior of the Cypher Headquarters. Shooting continued that afternoon outside BSP Industries on Maxwell Road adjacent to the studios in Borehamwood, which was decked out with prop signs for a scene where Steed visits The Classy Glass Cleaning Co Limited.

Friday 17 May saw the second unit on location again, at Crossoaks Farm in Ridge, to execute sequences involving a telegraph pole and a fleet of five Classy Glass vehicles gathering before invading Cypher HQ. Additional footage showing the Classy Glass vehicles forming a convoy was filmed under Hough's direction on the junction of Buckettsland Lane and High Canons, near the hamlet of Well End, approximately a mile from the studios. During this shoot the crew were stood down for 15 minutes after the fan-belt of their generator snapped, cutting all power to their equipment. Fortunately, the problem was quickly rectified by the fitting of a replacement.

As on 'You'll Catch Your Death', Burnham Beeches was used as the location for a car chase sequence, this one involving Classy Glass operatives Maskin and Vickers, played by Simon Oates and Donald Gee respectively, running Steed's vintage Rolls Royce off the road using an aluminium ladder suspended from their Morris J4 pick-up truck. Narrowly avoiding an accident, Steed chases after the fleeing truck, but the Classy Glass men have a nasty surprise waiting for him, as further along they stop and pull the truck across the road, blocking it. Coming around a blind bend at speed, Steed is confronted by the stationary truck, and the Classy Glass men then extend the ladder, making a collision unavoidable. Steed hits the brakes but it does no good, as the ladder smashes through the windscreen, ending up with Steed's bowler dangling on the end of it. This scene is handled extremely well and provides a chilling ending to the act, leading into the commercial break.

Altogether, Hough and the second unit visited Burnham Beeches four times to shoot motor vehicle material, on Monday 20, Tuesday 21 and Tuesday 28 May and again on Friday 5 July. On the first of these dates, 80 members of the Electrical Trades Union (ETU) took unofficial industrial action over a pay claim, withdrawing their labour. This prevented the main unit from carrying out its first scheduled day of filming at Esltree, so under the direction of Paul Dickson they too went out on location, to Holmshill Lane, Well End in Hertfordshire – although even then they had to make do without lighting.

Further industrial problems arose on Wednesday 22 May when there was a stoppage relating to a pay dispute by 400 members of the National Association of Theatrical and Kine Employees (NATKE), which again brought Elstree to a standstill. In common with the ETU dispute, the strikers were also in conflict with their own union, which had strongly recommended against such action. The workers threatened to stage a one day strike every week until their demands were met. This would play havoc with production not only on *The Avengers*, but also on the other filmed television series, *The Saint* and *Department S*, being made at Elstree at the same time.

Interior filming for the episode did get under way on Thursday 23 May, however, with Hough directing the action on Stage 3 on sets of the Cypher office, Webster's office and the Cypher Headquarters foyer. However, the latter appears to have been judged superfluous to requirements, as no footage featuring this set appears in the finished episode.

Production was disrupted again on Monday 27 May when members of the ETU escalated their unofficial action by staging a lightning strike, failing to return after lunch and beginning an indefinite stoppage. ABPC's management decided to take a hard line in response to this action and immediately issued dismissal notices, pointing out that they had an agreement in place with the ETU to prevent such occurrences. Then, turning their attention to the proposed unofficial one-day-a-week strike threatened by members of NATKE, the company sent these employees a letter indicating that any further industrial action would be looked upon as a breach of contract. They added that ABFC refused to tolerate unofficial strikes and warned that any further walkouts would also result in instant dismissals. This move was successful in persuading the NATKE members to reconsider their position and call off the planned strike action.

More location shooting took place on Wednesday 29 May, when Hough and the main unit journeyed the short distance to Aldenham Park in Elstree to capture material of Steed and Tara meeting with Mother in the same field where footage for 'Split!' had previously been shot. Upon completing this work with Macnee, Thorson, Newell and Parker, the unit also visited an unknown swimming pool location to film some linking scenes for use when the series was transmitted on the German television channel ZDF. These scenes involved Macnee and Hungarian actress Edina Ronay, who had appeared previously in *The Avengers* in the videotaped episode 'The Nutshell' in 1963.

Two days later, assistant director Ron Appleton advised production manager Ron Fry, and through him Brian Clemens and Albert Fennell, that due to the industrial action earlier in the month they were now running five and a half days behind schedule.

Some on-site location filming was done inside the Elstree garage beside the western gateway on Shenley Road for a scene where Steed and Tara break into the Classy Glass premises and discover the body of MI12 operative Ferret, played by Ivor Dean. This had undergone a slight rewrite, as originally it was intended as part of an exterior sequence where the agents stumble across the deceased Ferret in the yard at Classy Glass, who then transport the body to his home as they did previously with Jarret.

In a repeated continuity error, Tara's hair changes style noticeably between shots several times during the episode, including when she is working undercover at Cypher Headquarters. The red crash helmets of the security guards at the Headquarters had recently been worn by the guards at the Carmadoc Research Establishment in 'All Done with Mirrors' and had also been seen in other episodes, including 'Mission … Highly Improbable'.

Attempting to make up for lost time, Hough arranged for an extended working day on Monday 10 June, when the second unit shot on Stage 3 until 8.20 pm. Principal photography on the episode was finally completed on Friday 14 June.

That, though, turned out to be not quite the end of the matter. Early the following month, Hough was tasked with doing three days' additional filming for the episode, which at that point was still titled 'Whatever Happened to Yesterday?'. The first of these days, Friday 5 July, saw him and the second unit shoot material on Stage 9, on the studio backlot and on location at Burnham Beeches. Then, as Clemens and Fennell had apparently concluded that the episode's original teaser sequence (of which nothing is known) failed to work, on Monday 8 July Hough and the third unit filmed a 'new hook' – as it was described on paperwork – at Ivinghoe Beacon and the road there, involving the Hughes 269B helicopter (G-AVZC) seen previously in 'Split!'. Uncredited stunt performer Fred Haggerty portrayed a spy disguised as an old lady on a bicycle, riding past actor David Quilter playing an agent named Wilson. Rocky Taylor was also on hand to double for Quilter in a motorcycle stunt. The final day's additional work, on Tuesday 9 July, saw Hough direct the third unit on Stage 9 on scenes required to augment the new teaser.

It appears that the episode was first retitled 'Secret Cypher File' later in July before the team finally settled on 'Super Secret Cypher Snatch' (though some paperwork gave that title with an initial 'The').

Emmy award nominations

Meanwhile, both Diana Rigg and *The Avengers* had once again been nominated in their respective categories for American Emmy awards. Disappointingly however the award ceremony, held on Monday 19 May 1968 and jointly compèred by Frank Sinatra and Dick Van Dyke, proved to be a repeat of the previous year's, as Barbara Bain and *Mission: Impossible* were declared the winners.

6.13 – 'Game'

The next episode into production was 'Game', from the typewriter of Richard Harris. The story this time involves deranged ex-serviceman Sergeant Daniel Edmund, now known as Monte Bristow, seeking revenge on the one-time officers who court-martialled him in 1946.

The first filming for the episode was done on Thursday 30 May 1968, when director Robert Fuest and the main unit visited the Aldenham Estate for scenes involving some army manoeuvres. However, principal photography did not get under way properly until the following Wednesday, when more location filming was done, this time by the second unit at The Bishops Avenue, London N2 and at Hillcrest on Barnet Road in Arkley. The latter location – previously seen in the season five episodes 'Something Nasty in the Nursery' and 'The Positive Negative Man' – provided the exterior for the home of Steed's former fellow officer Averman, played by Alex Scott.

The main unit undertook another central London visit on Tuesday 11 June, when Fuest organised filming in Duchess Mews, W1, which as usual doubled as Steed's street. Later the same day the unit returned to Elstree to shoot interiors on Stage 5. Bristow's large property, as seen in the picture on a jigsaw puzzle, was in fact the Grim's Dyke Hotel, off Old Redding in Harrow Weald. Just over a ten minute drive away from Elstree, this location was ideally situated for the quick transportation of cast, crew and equipment, and it frequently featured in television shows, including *Doctor Who*, *The Saint*, *The Champions* and *Department S*.

Thursday 13 June saw Fuest supervising the main unit at Oxhey Park in Watford, to film a sequence of Steed and Tara discovering the body of Dexter – who was part of the court martial – on a swing in the children's playground there.

A fight scene in Steed's apartment between Tara and Bristow's manservant, played by Garfield Morgan, involved Cyd Child and Romo Gorrara serving as stunt doubles for the two actors.

Brian Badcoe, playing the first murder victim, racing driver Cooty Gibson, was filmed on Stage 9 at the wheel of a racing car simulator based around a Formula 3 Brabham BT21. In the story, this simulator mimics the movements of a slot car going around a small oval Scalextric track, although the toy was in fact a model BRM. The technique of undercranking the camera was employed to speed up the playback of a sequence where, much to Tara's amazement, the manager of the Jig Creations jigsaw company fully completes a puzzle in under a minute.

Fearing for Steed's safety at one point in the action, Tara barricades him behind items of furniture in his apartment and produces her chrome-plated Smith and Wesson 1917 revolver as seen in 'Whoever Shot Poor George Oblique Stroke XR40?' and the opening title sequence.

Fuest liaised closely with designer Robert Jones over two unusual script requirements, a giant hourglass and a bomb inside a transparent safe, which were both successfully realised with the aid of the studio prop builders. Thorson was not entirely happy being inside the giant hourglass as the sand got in her hair, but she filmed the scene without complaint and Fuest saw her as a true professional and easy to work with.

Steed's reward for cracking the transparent safe and preventing the bomb from exploding is a 9mm Beretta 1934 automatic, although he has to overcome other traps to obtain the magazine and six bullets.

Fuest took an instant dislike to Add-a-Vision and refused to use it. He also found production controller Jack Greenwood to be overly loud, and pedantic when it came to timing. One afternoon Greenwood enquired if the scene Fuest and the crew were working on would be completed by the end of the day. Fuest replied that it would be in the can by 4.00 pm. Greenwood, however, did not want the crew leaving early, and instructed the director to spin things out and not finish until the normal end of the working day at 5.20 pm.

The flock wallpaper seen in many of the film series produced at Elstree Studios throughout the '60s surfaces again in Bristow's home, this time coloured red and white.

Patrick Newell and Rhonda Parker do not appear in this episode, which was evidently written before their characters became regular inclusions.

Principal photography on 'Game' concluded on Tuesday 25 June. However, as with 'Whatever Happened to Yesterday?', the crew was required to revisit the episode and shoot some additional footage the following month. Between Monday 15 and Thursday 18 July Hough worked with both the second and third units to complete all but one of the outstanding scenes on Stage 9. The remaining one entailed a foray onto the foliage area on the studio backlot, where the use of a narrow-angled camera lens gave the impression of being in a field.

6.14 – 'False Witness'

Jeremy Burnham's 'False Witness', originally drafted as 'Lies', concerns a situation where a witness suddenly changes his statement in advance of the upcoming trial of blackmailer Lord Edgefield, played by William Job, and Steed finds that one of his colleagues is highly unreliable.

Filming was under the control of experienced director Charles Crichton, who kicked things off by leading the second unit on a London location visit on Tuesday 18 June 1968. The teaser sequence featuring departmental operatives Melville, played by Barry Warren, and Penman, played by Peter Jesson, was shot on the corner of Townsend Road and Mackennal Street in St John's Wood, NW1, with a prop telephone box. While Melville keeps watch, Penman walks down the ramp of the underground car park at Imperial Court to break in and search through Lord Edgefield's Rolls Royce limousine. Unfortunately bad weather severely hampered the crew's progress, which meant that Crichton had to return to the location to obtain further footage the following day and John Hough had to follow suit with a small third unit a week later. Originally there were also plans to shoot at the same location a sequence of a milk float being followed by Tara in a red Lotus Europa (PPW 999F), but despite both vehicles being present on the first date, along with stuntman Frank Henson to double for Thorson, this did not occur.

The sleek, rear-engined Lotus Europa – a model usually available only for export or for buyers intending to use it solely for motor racing – had been obtained by Brian Clemens from Lotus Cars as a new regular vehicle for Tara to drive in the series. Despite having earlier switched the maroon AC 428 over from Steed to Tara, Clemens had now decided that the large convertible did not complement her style and arranged for it to be returned to AC Cars in Thames Ditton. At this point Thorson had not yet actually passed a UK driving test – although this did not stop her personally acquiring a large American Ford Mustang, in which she was initially driven by an ABC-supplied chauffeur – and while filming 'False Witness' she accidentally damaged one of the front wings of the Lotus after being persuaded by the crew to drive it when it was on private property.

On Friday 21 June, the fourth day of filming, the second unit undertook another London location visit, this one centred around Wilton Crescent, SW1. It was here that a sequence was shot of Lord Edgefield arriving at no. 33 for a meeting with the trial judge Sir Joseph Tarlton, played by Tony Steedman, the witness Plummer, played by Michael Lees, and Steed. Also filmed was the rescheduled sequence of Tara's Lotus trailing the Dreemykreem Dairies Austin J2 milk float, passing from Wilton Place into Wilton Crescent, then from Motcomb Street also into Wilton Crescent. Both vehicles were also shot travelling around Belgrave Square in the same vicinity, although this was done six days later with John Hough directing the same unit.

The 21 June shoot continued with material filmed in Duchess Mews, which once again provided the exterior for Steed's home. Here, Cyd Child doubled for Thorson for a scene of Tara chasing the milk float into Duchess Street. However, the next piece of action on screen, where Tara attempts to hold onto the vehicle – whose driver was played by Rio Fanning – but falls over and does a forward somersault as it increases speed, was actually filmed back at Wilton Crescent.

The second unit completed their workload for the day by returning to the Borehamwood area and filming part of a sequence where Tara parks the Lotus on a triangle of grass beside a prop telephone box, from where she contacts Sir Joseph to try to warn him that the milk has been spiked with a drug that induces lying and erratic behaviour. This triangle of grass forms the junction of Rectory Lane and Harris Lane in the village of Shenley, and the second unit would revisit this location on both Wednesday 26 and Thursday 27 June.

On Monday 24 June, the second unit filmed scenes on the upper deck of a 1954 London Transport Leyland Titan double-decker bus (OLD 666) as it travelled along Cowley Hill in Borehamwood, with its front destination roller indicating that it was on route 707 to Piccadilly Circus. There was a repeat performance the following day on Bell Lane in London Colney to complete these scenes of the vehicle in motion. Later the same day the unit adjourned to Home Farm in Elstree, where the bus was parked in a field and a sequence involving Dr Grant, played by Arthur Pentelow, was captured using a blimped (soundproofed) 35mm Arriflex camera.

On Wednesday 26 June, Crichton and the main unit shot footage of the bus heading southbound on Green Street from the direction of Shenley toward Borehamwood, followed by the sequence earlier in the story that would actually introduce the bus on screen. This involved Steed parking his Rolls Royce by a housing estate on Hartforde Road, north of the centre of Borehamwood, and assembling a portable bus stop sign. When the bus pulls up, Steed promptly gets on board, and the upper deck is revealed to have been converted into Mother's mobile headquarters, complete with Rhonda, drinks decanters and telephones.[30] The conversion was carried out by the Elstree set builders, presumably on the understanding that the original seating would be replaced before the vehicle was returned to the hire company, Kingsbury Motors, who had acquired it from London Transport earlier in the month for use in film work. In went on to appear in the film *Husbands* the following year, but then remained idle until September 1971, when it was sold to LWT, who sprayed it green for use in an episode of their sitcom *On the Buses*. The episode in question, entitled 'No Smoke Without Fire', required the bus to be burnt out, resulting in it being completely written off.

Also on Wednesday 26 June, Hough and the second unit visited Rectory Lane in Shenley before doing some more filming at Home Farm to establish the Dreemykreem Dairy. There were teething problems with the new Lotus as it managed to blow all its electrical fuses while being driven between locations. This caused a delay, which was possibly the reason why the unit apparently failed to film at their final scheduled location for the day, indicated on studio paperwork as being a dual carriageway. It is possible that the intention was to film on the nearby A1 Barnet bypass, but no such footage appears in the finished episode. An auto electrician named Dooley from the London Sports Car Centre was booked to attend the Lotus the following day to investigate and rectify the fault.

Thursday 27 June saw Crichton directing the main unit on the Steed apartment set on Stage 5 at Elstree while Hough with the second unit undertook an ambitious schedule of filming at six different locations. After obtaining footage in central London, Borehamwood and Shenley, including further material of the bus and Steed's DIY bus stop on Hartforde Road, the small crew assembled back at Home Farm, where they filmed the bus exiting the gateway and turning right onto Aldenham Road. A sequence where the bus arrives at Steed's parked Rolls Royce, with the canopy up to protect against the rain, was also filmed on Aldenham Road, but further south, within sight of the red-brick houses known as Butterfield Cottages. An establishing shot of the bus parked in a field surrounded by cows was also filmed at Home Farm, with the camera mounted on the opposite side of the stream that drains into Aldenham Reservoir from Tykes Water Lake.

The main unit toiled away on the Steed apartment set again on Friday 28 June, although there was a disruption sometime during the morning to accommodate a stills session for the forthcoming episode 'Noon Doomsday'.

On Monday 1 July John Hough supervised additional shooting by a small third unit in central London, including material described in the daily progress report as taking place at 'Bus Stop Three' (Bus Stops One and Two having been the settings already filmed on Hartforde Road in Borehamwood). Like the previously-mentioned dual carriageway location, this failed to materialise in the finished episode.

Other notable points: a silhouette example of modern art painting first seen in 'From Venus with Love' and later in 'Epic' surfaces again here as part of the decor in Lord Edgefield's apartment; and Laurie Johnson was able to provide some new pieces of incidental music on this occasion, although these were augmented by Karen Heward reusing cues originally heard in the season five episode 'Escape in Time'.

'False Witness' was the first episode to credit Terry Nation as *The Avengers*' script

---

[30] The idea of Mother's headquarters being on the upper deck of a London Transport double-decker bus would later be copied for the 1998 feature film based on the series.

editor, and the last to credit Philip Levene as its story consultant. Unlike Nation, Levene had had no involvement with the production for some time now, and the fact that he had continued to receive credits appears to have been due partly to his contribution to the three Bryce-produced escapades and partly to a contractual agreement. At the time, the Rediffusion drama series *Sanctuary*, which he had created, was having its second season transmitted across the ITV network, and the Thora Hird-starring *The First Lady*, which he had also been involved in creating, was being screened on BBC1.

ABC meets ABC

The Thursday 20 June 1968 edition of *The Stage and Television Today* reported that top executives of the American ABC network had recently visited Elstree in order to see *The Avengers* in production for themselves. During their visit, network president Elton Rule, vice president of programming Marty Stagger and London representative Dan Boyle also met Brian Clemens, Albert Fennell, Gordon L T Scott and the Managing Director of Associated British Pathé, Robert Norris.

Back in the chart

In June 1968, after an absence of six months, *The Avengers* returned to the TAM top 20 most popular programmes at number 17, with an average of 4.9 million viewers. This was on the strength of some regions showing various repeats, and a couple still finishing off their first run of season five episodes.

Second original American paperback

Meanwhile, in the United States, Berkeley Medallion published another spin-off novel based on the series. *The Drowned Queen*, penned by Keith Laumer, offered a plotline in which Steed and Tara go undercover on the *Atlantic Queen*, the world's first ocean-going luxury submarine liner, to prevent sabotage on her maiden voyage.

6.15 – 'Noon Doomsday'

Terry Nation's second screenplay for *The Avengers*, 'Noon Doomsday', was based on an idea he had developed with Brian Clemens about assassins coming to kill an injured Steed in an isolated agents' rest home, with elements inspired partly by the famous 1952 Western movie *High Noon*. The series had presented pastiches before – 'Man-Eater of Surrey Green' being a sideswipe at *The Day of the Triffids*, for instance – but Nation's was a little more blatant, even borrowing part of the film's title. Upon receiving the screenplay, Clemens was less than impressed to find that he needed to rewrite large sections of it, and he complained bitterly to Nation, saying that as the show's script editor he should be doing far better. The highly experienced Nation was not used to getting such a verbal kick in the pants, so he went away determined to improve.

Principal photography for the episode got under way on Monday 1 July 1968 when director Peter Sykes – a newcomer to the series – began a two-day shoot with the second unit at the disused Stanbridgeford railway station near Dunstable in Bedfordshire, doubling as the story's desolate Langs Halt. Several months after filming took place there the station building would be demolished, then a couple of years later that stretch of railway line would be lifted; the old track bed now forms part of the National Cycle Network.

It appears that throughout the process of the story being developed, Clemens had always envisaged that the majority of the location filming for it could be executed on his own Park Farm at Ampthill in Bedfordshire. This was where Sykes and the main unit worked on Wednesday 3 July, with a Hughes 269B helicopter (G-AVUM) and pilot hired for the day from the Denham-airfield-based Gregory Air Services.

The second unit was back in action on day four, returning that morning to Stanbridgeford Railway Station, where guest actors Ray Brooks and T P McKenna, playing professional assassins Farrington and Grant, were filmed riding horses obtained from George Mossman, supplier of equine performers and extras to the film and television industry. Unfortunately McKenna fell from his horse and had to be driven by Clemens to a local GP, where an examination revealed a mild concussion and two cracked ribs, although the actor was later able to return to the shoot.

In the afternoon, the second unit moved on to Park Farm, where they were scheduled to continue filming every working day until Friday 12 July. However, adverse weather conditions affected their visits on Monday 8 and Wednesday 10 July, and on the latter of those dates Sykes broke the shoot after lunch and returned to Elstree to film on Stage 5 instead. Altogether, the two units would spend eight whole days and two half days filming at Park Farm, which in the story represented the agents' rest home, Department S – a name obviously chosen by Nation as an in-joke at the expense of his and Clemens' good friend Dennis Spooner, who had co-created the ITC film series *Department S* (see below), then in its third month of production on adjacent stages.

Coached by Cyd Child and Joe Dunne, Linda Thorson successfully performed a 16-foot jump onto some cardboard boxes and was proud not to have sustained an injury doing the stunt. However, the more dangerous leaps were still left to her double Child, who recalls, 'Linda didn't like being doubled and wherever possible she would try to avoid that happening. If she could get the storyline changed in some way so she could perform the stunt, rather than me, she would.' Thorson's luck ran out at around 5.20 pm on Tuesday 23 July when she received a rope burn to one of her hands while filming on the barn set on Stage 5. This effectively ended the day's shoot, as the injury was severe enough to require her to visit the studio's first aid station, where the sister recommended a trip to the practice of Dr Carl Hodes in Borehamwood for treatment.

Probably as a measure to save on budget, just for once Mother's temporary headquarters was not some specially-designed and constructed set. Instead, Patrick Newell and Rhonda Parker performed all their two-handed scenes on the Steed apartment set. To guard against forgetting his lines, Newell was known to secrete small pieces of paper around the set to prompt him with his dialogue.

When the traitor Dr Carson, played by David Glover, is accidentally killed in a struggle at the episode's climax, Tara immediately helps herself to his .38 Smith and Wesson revolver. She then shares a strong embrace with Steed after he dispatches Murder International head Gerald Kafka, played by Peter Bromilow, with a spear gun contained in one of his crutches.

This was another of the episodes scored by Howard Blake, although music editor Paul Clay also incorporated snatches of Laurie Johnson's distinctive incidental stings from the episode 'Split!'.

An earlier draft of the script had Department S's Giles Cornwall, played by

Lawrence James, assassinated by Farrington and Grant, whereas in the finished episode he is killed – off camera – by Dr Carson. The draft then had the two assassins depart temporarily to meet their boss Kafka, before all three returned to Department S on horseback. Clemens changed this to have them arrive back by helicopter, thus avoiding the previously-established active minefield around the facility.

With Albert Fennell in hospital suffering from an ulcer, Brian Clemens stepped in to assist Manuel del Campo in cutting and editing the final print of the episode.

Second Linda Thorson title sequences

Transferred away from work on 'False Witness' for a day on Wednesday 3 July 1968, the main unit went on location to the Aldenham Estate and undertook filming of a second season six opening title sequence, devised by Brian Clemens and directed by Robert Fuest. This would be used for the series' fourth American network run, replacing the earlier shooting gallery sequence that had been included on six of the seven Thorson episodes in the third run – the exception being 'The Forget-Me-Knot', which had retained the season five opening sequence featuring Diana Rigg. The new sequence would also be edited onto the British prints of all the season six episodes – again with the exception of 'The Forget-Me-Knot' – before the season began transmission in September, meaning that the shooting gallery opening sequence would not be seen at all by ITV viewers.

The new sequence shows Steed and Tara in action in a large field – previously used during the filming of 'Split!' – with a prop doorway and three immobile suits of armour, one of which falls over and turns out to be full of red carnations. Being extremely athletic and enthusiastic, Linda Thorson asked to perform her own stunt in a shot where Tara runs along the parapet of the nearby red-brick bridge at Tykes Water Lake. This left her stunt double, Cyd Child, who was in attendance at the location, with nothing to do all day. The daily progress report records that Steed's 1923 Rolls Royce Silver Ghost was also involved in the filming, although this footage never made it into the finished titles. Furthermore, a ten ton Fowler steam-powered traction engine (BH 6971) dating from 1897 was on location all day, but went unused.

Fuest returned to the same location with the smaller third unit the following day to film a matching closing credits sequence, which was apparently intended to feature both the Rolls Royce and the traction engine; but again a decision was later made not to use any of this footage.

An additional insert for the new opening sequence was shot on Thursday 11 July, the final day of principal filming on 'False Witness', under the direction of Charles Crichton on Stage 9.

A new closing credits sequence was still needed to replace the shooting gallery one – which in the UK would be seen only at the end of 'The Forget-Me-Knot', although in the US it had been included on all seven of the Thorson episodes in the third run – and material for this was shot by John Hough with the third unit on Stage 9 on Thursday 18 July, a day used primarily for inserts to complete the earlier episode 'Game' (as discussed above). This consisted of close-ups of the hands of Magic Circle member John Wade as he performed various impressive card tricks. As a result of this, Wade is paid several pence every time an episode including this closing sequence is shown anywhere in the world.

Department S

The glossy ITC film series *Department S* had entered production at Elstree on Wednesday 3 April 1968. Its format was based around a specialist Interpol unit called upon to solve mysterious crimes and events after all other attempts have failed. This would provide the springboard for a succession of exotic adventures of the three leads: American team leader Stewart Sullivan, played by Joel Fabiani, outrageous Jason King, played by Peter Wyngarde, and computer analyst Annabelle Hurst, played by Rosemary Nichols.

Dennis Spooner and Monty Berman were credited as co-creators of the series. Berman was a production person who knew filmmaking and how to put a television show together technically, while Spooner was the ideas man who devised the format. Fascinated by strange stories from the Second World War, Spooner had kept notes about Churchill having Dennis Wheatley head a team of fellow authors who dreamed up crazy ideas to win the conflict. Drawing inspiration from another source, he wondered who would investigate the mystery of the *Mary Celeste* if it were to happen today. Putting the two ideas together, he came up with the concept of a team of three people, each with a different approach to solving strange incidents that baffled the authorities.

Each episode began with the *Department S* logo, a large letter 'S' with the small wording 'Department' superimposed on it, accompanied by a musical fanfare. This was followed by an establishing shot complete with a overlaid caption stating the place, country and date of the action, but no year. This led into a pre-titles sequence designed to hook viewers and keep them watching. A man wearing a spacesuit suffocates to death in a London street; a tube train pulls into a station with everyone on board dead; an airliner lands at Heathrow airport, but when boarded is devoid of crew and passengers.

Although interesting, *Department S* never became quite as extreme or stylish as *The Avengers*, usually presenting at the end of each episode a quite plausible explanation for the seeming impossible event witnessed at the beginning. Any hopes of it becoming a major rival to *The Avengers* were short-lived, as haphazard scheduling by the various ITV companies prevented it from making a great impact. Perhaps more disappointing for Spooner, Berman and financial backer Lew Grade of ITC was the failure of *Department S* to attract one of the American networks to pick up the show for primetime coast to coast transmissions across the USA.

6.16 – 'Legacy of Death'

Terry Nation made his next script contribution to the series almost straightaway, with an episode initially called 'Falcon' but quickly renamed 'Legacy of Death'. This is a clever send-up of the classic 1941 film noir *The Maltese Falcon*, as Steed receives an ornate German dagger in the post but quickly finds that numerous unsavoury characters are willing to go to any lengths to acquire it. Brian Clemens had developed the initial concept for this together with Nation, who had now familiarised himself more with the style of the show; and Clemens was delighted to see that the hard line he had previously taken with his script editor was paying dividends, as he had no rewriting to do on this occasion. Clemens and Fennell were beginning to hit their creative and stylish stride again, and the higher standard set with 'Noon Doomsday' would be maintained for 'Legacy of Death'.

Having gained plenty of experience on other television film series, Don Chaffey arrived to direct his first episode of *The Avengers*, and together with casting director G B Walker he assembled an impressive guest cast. This included Stratford Johns, Ronald Lacey, Richard Hurndall, John Hollis, Kynaston Reeves, Norwegian actor/choreographer Tutte Lemkow and an actor previously used by Chaffey on *The Prisoner*, Peter Swanwick. As a further homage to *The Maltese Falcon*, the characters played by Johns and Lacey were named Sidney Street and Humbert Green, after the actor Sydney Greenstreet who played Kasper Gutman in the film.

This was the first episode this season to make extensive use of the backlot town, which provided three different settings: the alley and exterior of a Chinese curio shop; the street where a cherry picker Land Rover is seen after the solicitor Dickens, played by Kynaston Reeves, is shot; and the rear of Tara's apartment.

Filming began on Tuesday 16 July 1968 in central London, where the second unit – which was also working with John Hough that week on additional inserts for the earlier episode 'Game' (see above) – shot exteriors of Tara's apartment on Chalcot Crescent, NW1. These featured Johns, Lacey and an uncredited Romo Gorrara. The following day there was another London location shoot, this time in Sharpleshall Street, NW1, where the Lotus Europa was filmed to establish Tara and Steed leaving the capital. Duchess Mews, W1, also featured again, as usual for the exterior of Steed's mews-based apartment.

On the third day, Thursday 18 July, Chaffey concentrated on filming with the second unit locally to Elstree, doing plenty of shooting around the Shenley area, including on Pound Lane for a sequence where Tara's Lotus is followed by six black cars – a 1937 Humber Pullman, a Rolls Royce Phantom III, a Mercedes Benz, a Wolseley 6/110, a Peugeot 404 and a 1940 Ford Tudor. The pursuing drivers all miss the fact that Tara's Lotus has turned into the entrance to Shenley Hall. Continuing, they arrive at the junction of Harris Lane and Rectory Lane, where some of them proceed north and others go south. Finding the coast clear, Tara reverses her car out onto the road again and continues back in the direction that she and Steed came from.

Additional filming was undertaken along Green Street in Borehamwood and further north, for a sequence where the Lotus is seen turning off the same road into a concealed gateway – actually the entrance to a private dwelling known as Lyndhurst, near the village of Shenley – which on screen leads into a studio scene where Steed and Tara arrive at a deserted nursery that Steed remembers from his childhood – in fact a heavily redressed summerhouse interior set last seen in 'Whoever Shot Poor George Oblique Stroke XR40?'. To conclude the day's work, Chaffey organised filming at The Haberdashers' Aske's School, where an establishing shot was taken of the Aldenham House part of the facility and – in a rare instance of interior filming at a location – some material was also obtained inside the building. However, things did not run entirely smoothly, as during the day both Tara's Lotus Europa and Sidney's Ford Tudor suffered mechanical problems, delaying the shoot.

Returning to London on Friday 19 July, the second unit completed some establishing shots, one of which was intended to provide an exterior for the premises of solicitors Dickens, Dickens, Dickens, Dickens and Dickens, although this was not used in the finished episode.

Production was slowed down on Monday 29 and Tuesday 30 July when a mechanical failure made the Add-a-Vision system at the studios inoperative, forcing the crew to revert temporarily to older working practices.

Principal photography on the episode concluded on Friday 9 August.

6.17 – 'They Keep Killing Steed'

Putting their heads together again, Brian Clemens and Terry Nation worked out the outline of an episode revolving around a staple adventure series idea that Nation would use many times during his career – that of characters having doubles. However, this time it was Clemens rather than Nation who wrote the screenplay, which became 'They Keep Killing Steed', focusing on several Steed lookalikes being created to gain access to a peace conference. Robert Fuest returned to handle direction and together with G B Walker cast Ian Ogilvy as the German character Baron Von Curt.

John Hough handled the first four days of filming, which were all on location. The work began on Monday 29 July 1968 with some motor vehicle footage of a Triumph 2000 being driven at high speed by Steed, followed by Von Curt and Tara in his vintage Mercedes. This fast-moving car chase was shot in the wooded Burnham Beeches area in Buckinghamshire, with both vehicles throwing up clouds of dust as they oversteered around the Morton Drive and Morton Drive/Halse Drive junctions. Having filmed a similar sequence at the same location a couple of years previously for the 'Night of the Hunter' episode of the ITC show *The Baron*, Hough used virtually identical camera angles this time. In more recent years, speed bumps have been incorporated into the road surface here, preventing any further car chase filming from taking place.

Later, Von Curt drives Tara in his Mercedes to the Old London Road – actually the road leading to The Grove Hotel in The Grove Park on the outskirts of Watford – and stops his vehicle on a humpback bridge there, allowing Tara to jump off the parapet into a river – in fact the River Gade. This leads on to a studio sequence, where a wetsuit-attired Rhonda lets a soaked Tara through an airlock door – previously seen as the door on a butter-making machine in 'False Witness' – into Mother's underwater base. Meanwhile, back on location, an unperturbed Von Curt waits until Tara reappears from the water, then helps her to the bank, where they both return to his Mercedes and leave. The exteriors for this sequence were filmed by the third unit on day two, Tuesday 30 July.

On day three, Hough switched to working with the main unit and travelled to the village of Northaw, approximately five miles north-east of Borehamwood, where The Sun pub became the exterior of the story's Ye Olde Sun Hotel. Material was filmed here of enemy agents Arcos and Zerson, played by Ray McAnally and Norman Jones, keeping the hotel under surveillance from across the village green by the St Thomas a Beckett parish church. In later filming at Elstree, the hotel's lobby would be represented by the Department S main room set from 'Noon Doomsday', redressed but still with its white walls.

The Rosary Priory High School at Bushey was used as the location for all the required footage of the conference centre exterior and grounds featured in the episode. Four visits were made there altogether by the main unit – the first with Hough on Thursday 1 August and the other three with Fuest on Wednesday 7, Thursday 8 and Monday 12 August, although on 7 August filming was delayed by intermittent heavy rain and Fuest abandoned the shoot at 2.30 pm in favour of returning to the studios to film interiors on Stage 5. Besides some vehicle footage filmed at this location, there was also material of both the real and the fake Steeds. This included a sequence of the real

Steed grabbing a gavel containing a hidden percussion bomb and disposing of it in the grounds – although the ensuing detonation was achieved with recycled footage originally filmed for the explosion of the ammunition hut at the conclusion of 'Have Guns – Will Haggle'. This was augmented with additional footage filmed on the afternoon of 12 August on the Aldenham Estate, beside the red-brick bridge and lake there. The finished sequence was rather more complex than envisaged in an earlier draft of the script, which had Steed simply throw the gavel out of an open window.

Starting on Friday 2 August, three consecutive working days were spent by Fuest and the main unit at Springwell Chalk Pits in Harefield, Buckinghamshire. After consulting Brian Clemens and Albert Fennell, Fuest deleted from the script three scenes – scenes 32, 165 and 167 – that were supposed to be shot here but were felt by him to be inessential to the telling of the story. A wrecked black Austin FX3 cab was sourced by the production team and transported to the location each day to serve as the concealed entrance to Arcos's underground base. During the filming on Monday 5 August, the Triumph 2000, borrowed by Steed from the conference centre, sustained two small dents to its bonnet. Paperwork fails to indicate how this occurred, but it was probably during shooting of a sequence where Arcos's man Samnoff, played by Frank Barringer, is physically thrown onto the bonnet by Steed. Paul Weston doubled for Macnee in this sequence, and he would also do in the episode's concluding fight scene. The following day, stuntman Bill Cummings received a cut to his forehead while performing another fight scene, requiring first aid to be administered. Despite the time already spent at this location, Fuest and the main unit would return for another day of filming there on Tuesday 13 August.

On Wednesday 14 August, Linda Thorson did not return to the soundstage after lunch as she was feeling unwell and had to go home to recuperate. She returned briefly the following Tuesday to do post-sync work on 'Noon Doomsday', but did not feel sufficiently recovered to recommence shooting until Thursday 22 August.

It was during Thorson's absence that Clemens and Fennell reverted to using both A and B units, augmented by a smaller third unit, similar to the set-up under the rolling production system adopted for some of the colour Rigg episodes. This appears to have been prompted by the added time pressures arising from the fact that transmissions of the season six episodes were shortly to begin in the UK and to resume in the USA.

On Tuesday 27 August the B unit travelled the short distance to Drayton Road in Borehamwood, where Hough directed a couple of short scenes showing Arcos's associate Bruno, played by William Ellis, delivering kits used to change the facial appearance of enemy agents to that of Steed.

Principal photography on the episode was concluded at Elstree on the morning of Thursday 29 August, although as with other recently-produced episodes another couple of days' shooting would be required – three weeks later, in this instance – to finish it off completely. The final piece of filming done was for a sequence of Mother and Rhonda in a small rowing boat that sinks below the water to descend to Mother's temporary headquarters. This was achieved on the larger outdoor tank at Elstree, with Rhonda Parker going beyond the call of duty by remaining seated in the boat until the water went over her head.

Other points of interest: at one point in the action Tara produces a .38 Smith and Wesson revolver, while in another scene Von Curt brandishes a sabre; at the conclusion of events in the quarry, Tara gives Steed a very affectionate embrace on learning that he has not been killed as she feared; the facemask component of the face-changing kit was a duplicate of the front half of the spacesuit headpiece seen in the earlier episode 'Invasion of the Earthmen'; and the security guards at the conference centre wear a mixture of red and white crash helmets seen previously in other episodes including 'Mission ... Highly Improbable' and 'Have Guns – Will Haggle'.

An earlier draft of the script offered a virtually identical storyline set in Spain, and the final version reveals that even at a late stage there were plans to shoot parts of the episode overseas. The title page notes that all European-set scenes to be shot abroad are designated with a capital E. It also includes several sentences of guidance from Clemens to the director, stressing the importance of maintaining *The Avengers'* tradition of showing a depopulated world even when shooting exteriors overseas, so that although the inclusion of a traditionally-dressed passer-by might add local colour to a scene, the temptation must be resisted and wherever possible the streets be kept empty of anyone not directly involved in the plot. Clemens added that he expected the shooting to adhere as closely as possible to the screenplay, and that if any deviation proved necessary, then the director should still aim to maintain the intention.

The most notable difference between the draft script and the finished episode is that Arcos's base was originally intended to be secreted not in a quarry but beneath a bullring, in an area converted from the pens where animals are contained before a bullfight. Another significant change concerned the location of Mother's base: rather than an underwater submersible, he and Rhonda were originally meant to be seen in a gypsy caravan, working undercover in Spain as a travelling fortune teller and his assistant – a sequence that the script noted could be shot either on location or on the Elstree backlot. Other minor differences were that the security liaison contacted by Steed and Tara was originally to have been Captain Jose of the Spanish secret service rather than the finished episode's Captain Smythe; the minor character Zerson was originally to have been called Markin; and although Arcos and all of his other Spanish-named associates were simply transplanted into the British-set version without any further name alterations, in the Spanish-based draft Arcos actually informed Steed that they were *not* Spanish, leaving the audience to guess their true nationality.

Mrs Peel in *The Saint*?

Meanwhile, on an adjacent soundstage, *The Saint* episode 'The Man Who Gambled with Life' was in production. Toward the conclusion of the adventure Simon Templar's female companion Stella Longman uses her karate abilities, exclaiming, 'I saw that on television.' The Saint replies: 'Very good, but keep your voice down, Mrs Peel.'

6.18 – 'Wish You Were Here'

Back on *The Avengers*, the next episode to be filmed was known during production as 'The Prisoner', although it would be renamed 'Wish You Were Here' before transmission. This came from the typewriter of Tony Williamson, and was essentially a solo adventure for Tara, allowing for the fact that Macnee would be absent for most of the filming. The plot involves Tara locating her missing uncle Charles Merrydale, played by Liam Redmond, in the secluded Elizabethan Hotel, but then discovering that the management allows none of its guests to leave.

Don Chaffey returned to helm proceedings, working with the B unit throughout, beginning on Wednesday 21 August 1968 with exterior filming at a couple of previously-used locations: Clarendon Road in Watford and the Edgewarebury Hotel near Elstree. The unit would return to the Edgewarebury on two further dates, Friday 23 August and Tuesday 3 September, to shoot additional material outside the hotel and in the grounds.

The perimeter road on the studio backlot was used for the filming of a sequence where the body of Maple, the chief clerk in the company for which Tara's uncle works, is discovered beside a country lane. This is one of the few scenes in the episode to feature Macnee, along with an uncredited actor playing a doctor plus Steed's Rolls Royce and the Austin ambulance (YLD 259) previously seen in 'Split!'

Principal photography on the episode concluded on Thursday 12 September.

The red and gold variation of the flock wallpaper seen in other episodes appears both in the office of the hotel's desk manager Parker, played by Dudley Foster, and in the hotel's games room. Similarly, the abstract painting seen previously in 'From Venus with Love' and 'Epic' reappears as part of the décor in the office of Maple, played by John Cazabon.

Steed finds Mother in a room of large photographs and cardboard cut-outs, counterbalanced on a large weighing scale. Realising that Tara requires assistance, Mother dispatches his nephew Basil, played by Brook Williams, who arrives at the Elizabethan in a small Austin 7 and then has the staff unload masses of sporting equipment from the vehicle. This was obviously copied from a sequence in 'The Girl from Auntie' where Steed, having returned from a foreign holiday, similarly has a huge number of sporting goods shoehorned into a black cab.

This was another episode for which Howard Blake provided some incidental cues, augmented by library tracks selected by music editor Paul Clay from earlier Laurie Johnson scores such as 'Escape in Time' and 'The Winged Avenger'.

6.19 – 'Killer'

'Killer' was another episode from the imagination of writer Tony Williamson, and would prove to be something of a return to form for the series. The A unit was lined up to start work on it straight after the conclusion of principal photography on 'They Keep Killing Steed'. However, Thorson's recent illness had thrown the schedule into disarray. The actress had returned in time for the making of 'The Prisoner', but had still to complete her scenes for 'They Keep Killing Steed', and consequently it was simply impracticable for her to play a substantial part in 'Killer' as well. The improvised solution adopted by the production team was to bring in a temporary new partner for Steed in the form of Lady Diana Forbes-Blakeney. A scene where Steed and Mother discuss the impending mission – which involves investigating the mysterious deaths of agents whose corpses are turning up gift-wrapped in a graveyard – was rewritten to introduce Forbes-Blakeney as an agent recently transferred from another section, where she spent 18 months organising agents in the Orient. Apart from this, no further background is provided for the character, and it appears that the dialogue went unchanged; she simply speaks the lines originally intended for Tara.

Casting director Gerry Walker decided that the role of Forbes-Blakeney would be perfect for actress Jennifer Croxton, on the strength of her performance over two days' filming on the John Bryce-produced 'Invitation to a Killing'. Croxton's acting career had begun in 1966 with supporting roles for the BBC in *Dixon of Dock Green* and an instalment of the anthology series *The Wednesday Play*. Upon being cast as Forbes-

Blakeney, she worked out a background and mannerisms for the posh, aristocratic Avengergirl, already being familiar with *The Avengers'* history and with the previous heroines Cathy Gale and Emma Peel. Croxton drove her Mini from her home in Virginia Water, Surrey to the studios at Borehamwood or to the filming location every day, finding a friend in fellow guest cast member William Franklyn and discovering that Macnee was polite and charming just like his on screen persona.

Forbes-Blakeney's fashions include a variety of trousers, culottes, coats, shirts and the obligatory kinky boots, in a mixture of pastel mauve and purple colours. Some of these items Croxton was allowed to keep after shooting. On the whole, Croxton was impressed with the number of costumes her character wore, but found a yellow shirt and grey slacks not to her personal taste, though they did match her ash blonde hair.

Experienced director Cliff Owen was assigned to call the shots on 'Killer', in what would be his only association with *The Avengers*. Filming got under way on Thursday 29 August 1968 in Duchess Mews, London W1, once more representing the cobbled mews where Steed's apartment is located. Returning to equally familiar territory the following day, the unit filmed outside one of the newer buildings at The Haberdashers' Aske's School, as previously seen in 'Never, Never Say Die', 'Return of the Cybernauts' and 'Split!'. The Hughes 269B helicopter (G-AVZC) that featured in both 'Super Secret Cypher Snatch' and 'Split!' was hired again for the day from Gregory Air Services. It was filmed doing some low level flying at the school and around the adjacent Aldenham Estate, dropping a body-shaped package into one of the fields there.

Also on Friday 30 August, the unit captured establishing footage of Forbes (as Steed calls his temporary new partner) in her white MGC convertible (BMG 300G) arriving at the house of the architect Wilkington, played by James Bree. The location used for this was Letchmore Lodge on Aldenham Road in Elstree. On screen, this would be followed by a later-filmed studio interior scene where, upon entering the property, Forbes finds Franklyn's enemy agent character Brinstead burning Wilkington's papers. A fight ensues, in which she uses a mixture of high kicks and judo throws and eventually gains the advantage by grabbing a katana she sees hung on the wall. Although Croxton performed some of this fight scene herself, Thorson's usual stunt double Cyd Child stood in for the more dangerous aspects.

Days three, four and five of the shoot were spent on the studio backlot, on both the exterior cemetery set that occupied the south-west corner and on the streets of the standing backlot town, which in the story actually represented a backlot town, described in dialogue as belonging to a bankrupt film company. Guest actor Richard Wattis was suitably droll in the role of the medical examiner Clarke, who informs Steed that the neatly-packaged corpse found in the cemetery was 'Clubbed, poisoned, shot, spiked, stabbed, strangled and suffocated … and his ear drums were damaged.' Closely inspecting the body, Steed replies, 'His neck's broken as well.'

The sixth day, Friday 6 September, involved the unit travelling to The Crown pub in East Burnham in Buckinghamshire, which doubled as The Pirate in Lower Storpington, the same fictional village where the events of 'A Surfeit of H_2O' took place.

For the first and only time on the Thorson episodes, the crew then worked over a weekend – a practice that had been used more often on season five. On Saturday 7 September some initial filming was done at nearby Burnham Beeches, involving Macnee, Croxton and Franklyn, whose character Brinstead is killed after being run down by a large four-wheeled cart. This usually horse-drawn vehicle was supplied to the production by George Mossman, who had also provided the horses for 'Noon

Doomsday' a couple of months earlier. Then, on Sunday 8 September, Owen directed the first of 13 days of interior filming, when Thorson completed her only scenes for this episode on the Steed apartment set on Stage 9, Tara's absence from the rest of the action being explained by her simply going on a week's holiday.

Damaged motor vehicle syndrome struck again on Thursday 19 September, when the A unit were back at The Haberdashers' Aske's School filming material at the main gateway on Aldenham Road near Elstree with a beige Commer HX441 coach (616 BYP). Presumably while being manoeuvred in a tight space, the coach sustained damage to both the nearside front and offside rear mudguards. It is believed that, like most other vehicles used in the series, the coach was sourced from Kingsbury Motors, although for a time during the '60s it was actually owned by the Molins Machine Company, who ran a small fleet of coaches providing staff transport to their cigarette machine manufacturing factory at Saunderton in Buckinghamshire. This same shoot also included a sequence where undercover agent Trancer, played by Michael McState, escapes from the grounds of the factory featured in the story and manages to get himself on board a moving van travelling along Dagger Lane, opposite The Haberdashers' Aske's gateway.

The final three days of principal photography – Wednesday 25, Thursday 26 and Friday 27 September – brought a return to Burnham Beeches. On the Wednesday, Jennifer Croxton unfortunately injured her wrist on being accidentally struck by the four-wheeled cart. The actress elected to continue working, although it appears that she was still in some pain the following day, as an X-ray was arranged at a local hospital. Meanwhile, camera loader Michael Proudfoot had been stung by either a bee or a wasp and was taken to Wexham Hospital for treatment before being driven home by one of the unit cars; and he was unable to report for work the next day.

Like 'Epic', this episode allows viewers an unrestricted view of the extensive scaffolding that supported the street facade of the backlot town, especially in a sequence where the agent Lawson, played by Clive Graham, abseils down the end of the backdrop structure for the smaller outdoor water tank. The shop called Ashley King on the backlot town's Marlin Street, seen briefly in 'Legacy of Death', reappears here.

The destination board of the Commer coach indicates that the company operating the factory is the fictional Camden Goods. When Steed and Forbes enter the Remak (Remote Electro-Matic Agent Killer) control room at the factory, an unwelcome overhead microphone is visible in the top right-hand corner of the picture for several seconds.

Between script and screen there was a major change made regarding Mother's temporary headquarters. These were originally envisaged as being situated in a training facility with various blackboards, where Mother sits in a rocking chair lecturing a class of trainee agents who are also in rocking chairs. On screen, however, the briefing scene instead takes place in a vintner's tasting room. Another difference comes at the episode's conclusion. Whereas in the finished episode the leading enemy operative Merridon, played by Grant Taylor, is killed in an explosion caused by Forbes-Blakeney typing in an instruction for Remak to self destruct, originally he was scripted to lose his life passing through one of the factory's computerised murder rooms.

Thorson reappears in the end tag scene, Tara having returned from her holiday with a present for Steed that he opens before she can stop him, automatically inflating a full-size life-raft that fills the living room of his apartment. Feeling that the characters of Steed and Forbes-Blakeney had worked very well together, Jennifer Croxton was disappointed that she was not included in the tag scene, which would have allowed her a proper farewell to the series. Over the years, there has been some speculation that if *The Avengers* had gone on to another season, then Croxton might have become the show's permanent female lead. The actress enjoyed the experience of making 'Killer' immensely and would have been overjoyed to have done more episodes, or even to have taken over from Thorson should she have left, figuring that she was one of several actresses in the running as a possible successor. However, in a 1992 interview, Brian Clemens put paid to this rumour, stating, 'She just wasn't good enough. She was only a guest star and we couldn't have developed her character into Steed's permanent partner.'

The ITC connection

On the front page of its Thursday 5 September 1968 edition, *The Stage and Television Today* reported that ATV had entered into an agreement with the American NBC network for the production of a new television film series – which would become *From a Bird's Eye View*. Buried down in the small print of this report was the news that Julian Wintle had signed a long-term contract with Lew Grade to produce films and television film series. Initially this agreement included a television project called *The House of Spies*, which had apparently been pre-sold to the American network CBS, although in the event it was never made.

At the turn of the decade, Wintle collaborated with writer Philip Levene, director Sidney Hayers and composer Laurie Johnson on a couple of pilots for ITC. These television movies, *Mister Jerico* – which starred Patrick Macnee – and *The Firechasers*, were both networked across the USA, but neither generated enough interest to warrant the production of a series. *The Firechasers* was a slight reworking of a series outline that Levine had submitted to ITC in 1968 under the title *Fire-Tec*, which had itself been based on a '50s radio show he had written called *Destination-Fire!*.

Levene and Hayers later worked together again on the film thriller *Deadly Strangers*, and once more on the Silhouette production *Diagnosis Murder*, with Johnson handling the musical side of things on the latter.

6.20 – 'The Rotters'

Robert Fuest returned to direct the next episode into production, namely 'The Rotters'. This was written by Dave Freeman, and although it would be his only contribution to *The Avengers*, he succeeded in incorporating all of the series' essential ingredients, including a science fiction one. The story this time involves forestry experts being killed, prompting Steed and Tara to investigate and discover that the experts all possessed knowledge about a virulent form of dry rot.

The B unit was responsible for the filming on this occasion, and began proceedings on Friday 13 September 1968 by travelling approximately eight miles north-west of Elstree to the Hatfield London Country Club at Essendon, which became the exterior of Wainwright Timber Industries. Filming also took place at a couple of other locations on the first day, to establish the Department of Forestry Research and a country cottage, although it is unknown where these were. However, plans to shoot establishing footage of the Institute of Timber Technology were dropped, the scenes in question – scenes 5 and 6 – presumably being considered unnecessary. Instead, footage was filmed at

Elstree on Monday 23 September of a wooden nameplate attached to a gatepost on a recently-landscaped piece of the backlot, thus establishing Tara's visit to the Institute's Professor Palmer, played by John Nettleton. Even this scene was trimmed down a little, as there were initially plans for a uniformed gatekeeper to be seen giving Tara directions.

On Monday 16 September, exterior work continued with the unit shooting between rain showers at the Bell Moor apartment block, accessed from East Heath Road near Hampstead Heath in north London. Later the same day, Fuest led the unit back to Hertfordshire, where the script requirement of a church with a wooden tower was met at St Andrew's in the village of Little Berkhamsted. There was a half-hour delay here when the film jammed in the 35mm wild Arriflex camera[31], blowing an electrical fuse present as a safety measure to avoid damage to the equipment.

The following three days involved extensive filming at Littleworth Common near Burnham in Buckinghamshire, with additional footage being obtained on the nearby Common Road. Shooting also took place on Stoney Lane and East Burnham Lane in East Burnham, between heavy rainfalls that left the narrow country lanes prone to localised flooding and large roadside puddles, through which were driven both Tara's Lotus and the MGB belonging to Sawbow, played by Frank Middlemass.

Devonshire Mews South, London W1, was the location used for Sawbow's antiques restoration workshop, and it was here that a scene was shot on Friday 27 September of Tara beginning to trail him when he departs in his MGB.

A sequence where the woodcutter Sandford, played by Dervis Ward, blocks the road with his truck, chases Tara through some woods wielding an axe and then steals her car was captured the following day at Burnham Beeches.

Principal filming for 'The Rotters' concluded on Tuesday 8 October, though a solitary additional insert was shot on 22 October, directed by Charles Crichton, who was working at that time on the next episode in production, 'The Interrogators'.

There were a number of differences between the shooting script and the finished episode. For instance, the two sardonic upper class Wormdoom assassins Kenneth and George, played by Gerald Sim and Jerome Willis, were originally to have been attired in green tweed suits – to match their Morris 1000 van – and deerstalker hats, whereas they ended up having beige outfits. The on-screen visual joke of Mother listing to one side as Rhonda pumps up his inflatable chair was taken further in the script, which had him accidentally touch the adjacent inflatable table with the lit end of his cigar, causing it to deflate rapidly and spill its contents onto the floor. Some scenes were tightened up and others had slightly different dialogue.

One element discarded during rewrites involved Sawbow being made to start digging his own grave by Sandford and his fellow Wormdoom henchman Jackson, played by John Scott. However, the biggest change related to the way Steed tracks down the missing Tara at Wainwright Timber Industries. In the script, he uses a direction finder supplied by Mother to home in on an emitter in Tara's car, but in the process happens upon a nudist colony in the woods. Dave Freeman noted that this sequence would need to be handled with extreme caution during filming, but in the

---

[31] A wild camera is one with no soundproofing over the reels of film, as no sound recording is required – music, sound effects etc are to be dubbed on later. This is in contrast to a blimped camera, where the reels have a cover over them to prevent the noise of their movement being picked up by microphones.

event it was judged a non-starter. Consequently all the naturist scenes were excluded, and the conclusion of the episode was reworked to have dry rot expert Victor Forsyth, played by John Stone, give Steed some information that leads him to Tara. As with some of the season five episodes, the shooting script was minus an end tag scene, stating simply, 'Tag scene to be written.'

Two other points of note: in one scene, Tara helps herself to Sandford's .38 Smith and Wesson revolver after knocking him out with an empty wine bottle; and once again Paul Clay raided the existing musical library for the episode's score, reusing some of Laurie Johnson's incidental cues from 'The Hidden Tiger'.

Tara King fashions

In anticipation of the new autumn television season and the UK premiere of the Tara King episodes, the Sunday 15 September 1968 edition of the fashion magazine *Vogue* featured Linda Thorson and the Ballantyne's Avenger range of cashmere sweaters associated with Harvey Gould. However, unlike when the extensive ranges of Avengerwear created by John Bates and Alun Hughes had been retailed to coincide with transmissions of the earlier Diana Rigg episodes, the fashion merchandising for the new season would be somewhat low key.

Out Goes Emma, In Comes Tara

The week before transmissions of the season six episodes commenced on ITV, the *TV Times* dated Thursday 19 September 1968 contained a feature titled 'Out Goes Emma, In Comes Tara', looking at the handover between Steed's female partners. For her part, Linda Thorson admitted to being extremely anxious, as although she had been working on the series for a year, she acknowledged that Diana Rigg was still the female face of *The Avengers*. Clearly she was worried about being accepted by the general public, knowing full well that Rigg had commanded great popularity during her time with the series.

Back on TV

Having already screened 'The Forget-Me-Knot' back in March 1968, along with half a dozen other Thorson episodes, the American ABC network kicked off their fourth run of *The Avengers* with 'Game' on Monday 23 September. In its new Monday slot between 7.30 pm and 8.30 pm, the series was competing for ratings against the long-running Western drama *Gunsmoke* and the fantasy comedy *I Dream of Jeannie*.

British viewers finally got their opportunity to see Linda Thorson as Tara when the newly-formed Thames Television showed 'The Forget-Me-Knot' – the episode used by every ITV region to open their season six transmissions – at 8.00 pm on Wednesday 25 September. Tyne Tees, Grampian and the newly-formed Yorkshire Television all joined in by taking the Thames line-feed. ATV began their screenings at 7.00 pm the following evening, along with Anglia, Ulster and Harlech. However, the edition of *The Stage and Television Today* published that day contained a small piece noting that Granada had decided against showing the season as part of their autumn schedule, preferring to hold it in reserve until the new year. Both Westward and Channel got under way on Thursday 3 October at 7.00 pm and, sticking with their traditional Sunday night slot for the series, Border followed up three days later at 8.10 pm.

6.21 – 'The Interrogators'

The next escapade before the cameras was 'The Interrogators', a clever storyline of bureaucracy turned in on itself, where agents of an unnamed foreign power interrogate security personnel on the pretext of it being simply a realistic training exercise. Richard Harris concocted the original draft script, but the finished episode was co-credited to Brian Clemens, who rewrote it not just for content but also for structure, to allow the leads freedom to work on other episodes concurrently. There are only three scenes in the entire screenplay that involve Steed and Tara together: they meet when Steed enters Mother's headquarters, when Tara saves the day at the episode's conclusion, and finally as usual in the end tag scene.

Charles Crichton returned to direct his final episode for the series, working with the A unit, and Hammer Films veteran Christopher Lee was cast as the principal villain, Colonel Mannering.

Principal photography commenced on Monday 30 September 1968, although it is not known what was done that day. On 1 October, the unit filmed in Cavendish Place, London NW3, which provided the location for Mother's headquarters, this time in a plant nursery accessed via a concealed entrance in a prop telephone box. A sequence where the agent Lieutenant Caspar, played by Philip Bond, releases a homing pigeon was also achieved here, although according to the shooting schedule it was originally to have been done on a quiet country road. Filming also took place the same day at the Farm Court apartment block off Watford Way in Hendon, London NW4, establishing Caspar's home.

After completing some interiors on Stages 3 and 5, the unit embarked on another London visit on Friday 4 October with Linda Thorson on location at 182 Sutherland Avenue, W9, which doubled as the apartment exterior of the army officer Minnow, played by David Sumner. Later in the day the unit moved to Hampstead Heath, London NW3, where they shot scenes involving balloon vender Mr Puffin, played by Cardew Robinson, plus part of a sequence where Minnow's contact Fillington, played by an uncredited Ken Jones, meets his demise while practicing his football skills.

Additional location footage was collected five days later at Springwell Chalk Pits – previously seen in 'They Keep Killing Steed' – where an uncredited Johnny Laycock played one-man-band act Izzy Pound and his Incredible Marching Sound. Initially there were also plans to film a Brantly B2B helicopter (G-AVCA), hired from British Executive Air Services Limited, at this location, but although the aircraft was on standby all day, the sequence was rescheduled.

The helicopter was eventually used on Monday 21 October, the penultimate day of principal shooting, although things failed to run smoothly as, after it took off from Oxford Airport at 8.00 am, it ran into heavy fog and was forced to land at Princes Risborough. The unit had arranged to meet up with the Brantly at Brocket Hall near Welwyn Garden City, but with no sign of the weather clearing, they detoured and instead filmed further material for Fillington's death scene at the Aldenham Estate, along with some footage on what was described in studio documentation as Street B, although the latter unknown location would not actually appear in the episode. Conditions having improved sufficiently, the helicopter resumed its journey at midday, and 20 minutes later arrived at Brocket Hall, where it was filmed taking off, doing some low level flying over woodland and landing. Documentation reveals that Crichton (presumably after liaising with Brian Clemens and Albert Fennell) discarded six scenes, probably due to the helicopter's late arrival.

The various pigeons seen throughout the episode were provided and handled in hands-only close-ups by their owner Ron Bede.

Once again Steed's steel-crowned bowler hat saves him from sustaining a serious injury in this episode, bending the blade of a bayonet as it is thrust toward him by the Chinese guard Toy, played by Vincent Wong.

Linda Thorson rates 'The Interrogators' as one of her favourite half-dozen episodes, considering herself privileged to have worked with both Charles Crichton and Christopher Lee, with whom she also later co-starred in the 1988 film *Olympus Force: The Key*. All of Thorson's scenes were completed by day nine of production, Thursday 10 October, and she then embarked on a holiday from the series, not being called again until Monday 28 October to take part in the forthcoming episode 'The Morning After'.

John Bryce at LWT

At around this time, it was announced in the trade press that production of LWT's first drama series, *The Inquisitors* starring Tony Selby and Alan Lake, was under way, with John Bryce as producer. Although planned as a season of 13 episodes, *The Inquisitors* ultimately managed only three before the powers-that-be at LWT decided that it did not match what they had envisaged. Production was stopped and Bryce left the company. He would not return to small screen projects until 1983, when he produced for Thames three segments of the anthology series *Storyboard*, including one called 'Lytton's Diary'.

The Avengers in print

The third original American paperback novel based on the series was published by Berkley Medallion in September 1968. Titled *The Gold Bomb* and written by Keith Laumer, this revolved around Steed and Tara attempting to locate a home-built atomic bomb.

In Britain, meanwhile, after an absence of just over 12 months, *The Avengers* returned to the pages of *TV Comic* in issue no. 877 published on Saturday 5 October. This run would eventually last for about four years and comprise a total of 28 new multi-part stories featuring John Steed and Tara King, drawn by experienced comic strip artists Tom Kerr and John Canning. As before, the series also featured in *TV Comic*'s contemporary annuals and holiday specials, although this time in the form of illustrated text stories rather than comic strips.

Patrick Newell interview

The *TV Times* dated Thursday 10 October featured an in-depth interview with Patrick Newell. Newell revealed that he had trained at the Royal Academy of Dramatic Arts (RADA) alongside such prominent actors as Peter O'Toole and Albert Finney. However, feeling that he lacked the abilities of his classmates, he had hatched a plan that involved him accumulating excessive weight until he was 20 stone, allowing him to corner the market in overweight characters on television. Newell added that he was thoroughly enjoying *The Avengers*, where after playing villains for most of his career, he was now one of the good guys. He confessed that some of his proceeds from the series would be used to purchase a Rolls Royce.

6.22 – 'The Morning After'

Next into production was 'The Morning After', an imaginative and tension-filled Brian Clemens screenplay about a deserted town under martial law where Steed finds himself handcuffed to a master criminal called Jimmy Merlin, played by Peter Barkworth, and encounters some troops who turn out to be mercenaries attempting to construct an atomic bomb on the pretext of dismantling one.

This episode involved extensive location filming, which was undertaken by John Hough – gaining his second credit as a director on the series – mainly with the B unit, although for the final couple of days' shooting he instead utilised the smaller third unit to finish things off. Hough's preferred working method involved having only minimal rehearsal of each scene – usually just a run-through – and then filming it in a single take, although he would do a second or third take if he thought improvements could be achieved.

Filming began on Thursday 10 October 1968 in St Albans with footage of Merlin and his Rover 3 Litre on Fishpool Street, and of a deserted Keyfield Terrace showing the junctions with Sopwell Lane and Pageant Road. This included shots showing part-empty drinking glasses outside the White Hart Tap pub, looking down Pageant Road with the tower of St Albans Cathedral visible in the background.

The second day brought more of the same, with filming at two separate locations on Fishpool Street, including for a sequence where a Thames Trader truck blocks the road near the Lower Red Lion pub house. Further material obtained the same day consisted mainly of establishing shots of deserted streets that would be used for atmospheric effect, plus shots of Steed's Rolls Royce travelling along the narrow Queen Street in the city.

After the usual weekend break, Hough reassembled the crew in Watford on Monday 14 October for the filming of exteriors for The Rostarn Trading Company, situated on the junction of Shakespeare Street and Milton Street. Returning to St Albans later that day, the unit completed scenes involving Major Parsons, played by Donald Douglas, together with his troops and military vehicles on Abbey Mill Lane and Sumpter Yard against a backdrop of the cathedral. Footage was also shot of bystander Cartney, played by Jonathan Scott, fleeing from troops along Wellclose Street, and of the handcuffed Steed and Merlin walking along Thorpe Road.

Day four began further north, the unit having moved to Old Hatfield, where footage obtained included a sequence of Steed and Merlin in a stolen army Land Rover coming down Fore Street and then disappearing along Park Street. The remainder of the working day was spent back in St Albans, filming a sequence where the rogue troops search through terraced houses for anyone left behind on Portland Street.

On the morning of Wednesday 16 October there was a return to Watford, where the unit filmed further exteriors of The Rostarn Trading Company – the building used for which has since been demolished as part of a redevelopment of the area. Upon completion of this, the crew made an initial visit to the army's Regent Street Barracks off Albany Street, London NW1. This military establishment doubled as an old trade commission and was the location used for a black and white interview scene featuring guest cast members Penelope Horner playing television news reporter Jenny Firston, Joss Ackland playing Brigadier Hansing, and Brian Blessed playing Sergeant Hearn, although subsequent footage with Macnee was filmed on a second visit, on Friday 25 October.

The sixth day saw filming take place in both Watford and St Albans. In Watford, more footage was obtained of Steed and Merlin walking, and an exterior scene was shot of the agent entering a red telephone box at the junction of Garfield Street and Milton Street. In St Albans, Macnee and Barkworth performed various scenes on Albert Street, including a segment where Steed is offered a bribe by Merlin. Also filmed was material of deserted houses at the western end of Albert Street on Woodfield Terrace – which is no longer referred to by that name today, the metal nameplate seen on screen having since been removed.

The exterior of the bank featured in the episode was realised back at Elstree by redressing the façade of one of the buildings in the backlot town, with the lot itself providing the backdrop for a sequence where Steed and Merlin encounter the television news crew comprising Jenny Firston and her colleague Yates, played by Philip Dunbar. The interior and exterior of the studio garage doubled as a motor vehicle repair facility, where Cartney hides and is eventually found and shot by Sergeant Hearn.

Unusually, outdoor filming days outnumbered those spent inside the studio, where work did not get under way until Friday 18 October, when material of the bank interior was shot on Stage 3.

A last day's location work in Watford was done on Friday 25 October, when more footage was obtained of the troops searching houses and a sequence was filmed of a black Volkswagen van on Copsewood Road and Stanmore Road.

The final location shoot came on Monday 4 November in St Albans, and was really just a mopping up exercise. Additional filming took place on Portland Street and at the bottom of Fishpool Street at the junction with Branch Road – some of which footage would be flipped during the editing process, as is apparent on screen from the fact that the lettering on The Blue Anchor pub appears in reverse. Further material was also obtained of the Volkswagen van, and of the handcuffed Steed and Merlin on foot at the junction of Black Cut with Old London Road. In order to achieve the completely deserted look required by the script, the crew obviously received a great deal of co-operation from the population of St Albans throughout the filming done there, which entailed streets being closed off and residents resisting the urge to look out of their windows to watch the action.

The population's evacuation of the town was depicted in the episode by the use of stock black and white footage, obtained according to Hough from a film library. The footage in question originated from the 1950 feature film *Seven Days to Noon*, where it showed London being evacuated due to an atomic threat, with scenes of a traffic jam shot on the westbound A40 dual carriageway between Gibbon Road and Perryn Road, London NW3, and a sequence of troops imposing martial law filmed at The Boltons in Chelsea, London SW10 and St John's Gardens in Notting Hill, London W11.

There is a significant continuity error apparent in the episode, as location footage of Steed and Merlin stealing a Land Rover features a vehicle with registration number 22 AP 46, whereas later material filmed between Stages 3 and 4 and the red-brick post-production building on the studio lot uses a different one with registration number KJB 27. A subsequent sequence on screen then shows Sergeant Hearn and his troops on Portland Street in St Albans, disembarking from the supposedly stolen first Land Rover with registration number 22 AP 46.

Other points of note: the Ministry of TSI prop warning signs from 'Split!' were recycled for use in this episode; an early sequence where Merlin outwits the army personnel was shot behind the cutting rooms at Elstree; while waiting at The Rostarn Trading Company for Merlin to arrive, Steed has at the ready his trusty .38 Smith and Wesson revolver complete with wooden stocks; during the interior sequences shot on this set, the usually impeccably-dressed Steed has a large stain on the back of his jacket; and the screenplay was structured so that Linda Thorson played only a minimal part in proceedings.

Overall, 'The Morning After' was an ambitious production that worked extremely well, though the concept of someone searching a deserted urban area was not entirely new, having been used before on television in *The Twilight Zone* episode 'Where is Everybody?'. There are also some obvious similarities to Roger Marshall's season four episode 'The Hour That Never Was' about an abandoned airfield.

The closing tag scene begins with Steed watching the conclusion of a programme on television and then, with a smile, repeating actress Judy Carne's catchphrase 'Sock it to me!' from the zany American music and comedy sketch show *Rowan and Martin's Laugh-In*. This is ironic, as the reason often cited for *The Avengers'* eventual cancellation is that *Rowan and Martin's Laugh-In* had dealt it a heavy blow in the American ratings war, its viewing numbers having increased by approximately 33 percent over the previous year, lifting it from twenty-first to first position in the most popular programme chart.

6.23 – 'Love All'

Jeremy Burnham's 'Love All' involves government secrets being leaked from the Missile Defence Department by top officials who turn out to have been influenced by a message broadcast by microdots contained in romance novels. Burnham wrote the shooting script over a period of three to four weeks, using one of his aunts as the basis for the character Martha Roberts, initially disguised as a charlady but later revealed to be a femme fatale spy, and then writing it as if his actress wife Veronica Strong were playing the part. Upon studying the screenplay, casting director G B Walker considered Strong ideal for the role, and offered it to her after inviting her to Elstree for an interview, at which to begin with she did not realise that the script was one written by her husband. Despite the family involvement, however, Burnham declined to attend any of the filming, as he found the process extremely slow and boring.

Directed by Peter Sykes, the episode entered principal photography on Friday 25 October 1968, having been allocated to the A unit. As had now become standard practice, the first day involved a visit to central London. Establishing footage of the exterior of publishers Casanova Ink was shot on Osnaburgh Street, NW1 – a location that now looks completely different, as in 2007 two new buildings were constructed on that side of the road, opposite the Melia White House Hotel seen in the episode, which gives an indication of where the original premises were. Later the unit returned to Borehamwood, where on Grosvenor Road within sight of the studios a scene was filmed involving Steed falling down an open manhole and straight into Mother's latest temporary headquarters.

The following Monday, Sykes led the unit back to the capital to obtain a small amount of footage of the exterior of Tara's apartment at the usual location on Chalcot

Crescent. They then journeyed back to Hertfordshire later in the day for some filming in front of Watford Town Hall, which in the episode would represent the Ministry building. During this shoot assistant director Ted Lewis was accidentally struck by Steed's vintage Rolls Royce, although fortunately he did not require any medical attention. Another problem was posed by poor weather conditions, which restricted the work that could be done. Eventually Sykes had to call a halt at 4.00 pm due to heavy rain.

On day three, an establishing shot of the upmarket perfume outlet Bellchamber Brothers was filmed outside 73 Grosvenor Street, London W1, featuring Tara's Lotus and the Mercedes of Casanova Ink proprietor Nigel Bromfield, played by Terence Alexander. Later the same day the unit made the first of four visits to Sutherland Avenue, London W9, on this occasion to shoot further motor vehicle footage, including interiors in the Mercedes.

Returning to Sutherland Avenue the following day, the unit shot scenes featuring Martha's front door and the Rolls Royce (MWF 435F) of government official Sir Rodney Kellogg, played by Robert Harris. Filming took place in two different locations on the street and also inside the vehicle, for a sequence where Martha kills Sir Rodney with a gun. Further footage was also obtained of the interior of Bromfield's Mercedes.

On Thursday 31 October, the unit was back on Sutherland Avenue for the third day running to execute even more material. However, production was brought to a halt for approximately half an hour when the main generator broke down. After repairs were carried out, the unit moved back to Watford Town Hall to complete unfilmed scenes from three days earlier.

Monday 4 November brought a fourth visit to Sutherland Avenue, involving both Macnee and Thorson being filmed in Sir Rodney's Rolls Royce. This did not pass without incident, as when parking the vehicle to show exactly how he wanted it positioned, Sykes misjudged the situation and damaged the bodywork. Later the unit adjourned back to Elstree, where they shot on Stages 3 and 5. The afternoon's work gave rise to another problem, however, when Macnee hurt himself while pulling Thorson in through a window on the Casanova Ink office set. Months later, after *The Avengers* had ceased production, the actor would discover when consulting a back specialist regarding another injury that he had actually cracked some ribs in this incident.

Since Clemens' return to the series, his unwritten rules had been by and large adhered to. They were well and truly broken in this episode, however, by the appearance of a uniformed police officer in the form of policewoman Grimshaw, played by Anne Rye.

The spacious, white-painted interior housing the indoor cricket nets used as Mother's latest base had seen service before as his greenhouse headquarters in 'The Interrogators', though earlier still it had been Arcos's underground base in 'They Keep Killing Steed'.

At one point in the action, while besotted with Broomfield due to the influence of one of the microdots, Tara attacks Steed with a large porcelain planter, forcing him to tap her over the head with his steel-crowned bowler hat. Recovering later, she scoops up the unconscious Broomfield's 9mm Beretta 1934 automatic, but then falls victim to the various microdots attached to Steed's waistcoat and instantly falls in love with him, after which she follows his commands. This sequence in many ways epitomises the Tara King version of the Avengergirl, who differed considerably from her two predecessors. The hard woman persona had been generally abandoned in favour of a more feminine and warmer approach. This incorporated elements of her hero-worshipping and being smitten with Steed, in contrast to the attitudes of the confident, self-made Emma Peel and sarcastic Cathy Gale.

Season six comes to France

French screenings of the season six episodes started on Sunday 20 October 1968, when the channel ORTF 2 showed 'The Forget-Me-Knot' at 8.00 pm. Although the Diana Rigg seasons had also been shown in France, this run of Thorson episodes would prove more successful in that country. Shortly afterwards, Thorson's vinyl single 'Here I Am', written by variety entertainer Kenny Lynch, was a massive hit there, whereas in the UK it failed to chart. The same was true of the follow-up single, 'Wishful Thinking', issued two years later on the Ember record label with serial number EMBS 284.

In the USA, however, Rigg remained more popular, and in 1968 a Cleveland, Ohio-based garage band calling themselves Sam and the War Machine recorded and released on the Blue Onion record label an Emma Peel tribute single, 'Spy Girl'.

Scheduling alterations

In the UK, meanwhile, Yorkshire Television became the first of a number of regional companies to bail out of Thames's regular Wednesday evening line-feed, switching the series to Friday evening at 7.35 pm from the episode 'Whoever Shot Poor George Oblique Stroke XR40?' on 1 November. The series' scheduling across the ITV companies would in general be even more fragmented this season than in the past, so it is perhaps no surprise that it struggled to achieve strong ratings, managing to reach only number 15 on the TAM programme chart for October.

Wonder Woman comic book

In the comic book world, DC Comics' superheroine Wonder Woman was at this time evolving in a different direction, choosing to relinquish her superpowers rather than join her fellow Amazons in another dimension. From issue no. 178, published in October 1968, Diana Prince, aka Wonder Woman, became a boutique owner involved in espionage and fantasy storylines as an Emma Peel/Modesty Blaise-style spy chick character, trained in both martial arts and the use of weapons, with a blind Asian mentor and sidekick called I-Ching. The comic book was temporarily renamed *The Incredible I-Ching and The New Wonder Woman*, and the cover of issue no. 180 depicted Prince wearing a purple and yellow Emmapeeler outfit with a zipped front and white boots, although she would eventually adopt a completely white catsuit. The Emma Peel influence would last just over four years, until Wonder Woman had both her superpowers and her original costume restored from issue no. 204, published in February 1973.

6.24 – 'Take Me to Your Leader'

Terry Nation submitted another inspired and cleverly-thought-out screenplay for the next episode into production, 'Take Me to Your Leader', in which Steed and Tara have to track a red suitcase that issues recorded instructions to get passed along a chain of contacts, and contains a bomb to prevent it being opened before it reaches its intended recipient. Assigned to direct was Robert Fuest, who formed a good working relationship with the Welsh writer.

Principal photography got under way on Tuesday 5 November 1968, when the B unit began a three-day location visit to RAF Bovingdon, where a large portion of the season four episode 'The Hour That Never Was' had been filmed. Cyd Child doubled for Thorson in a sequence at the deserted airfield where Tara takes cover behind various large wooden packing crates, including one bearing the motif FF70, which had contained firearms in the episode 'Have Guns – Will Haggle'. Tara also ducks behind the landing gear of a fixed-wing CASA 2.111 aircraft, a Spanish-built version of the Heinkel He 111 bomber, painted in Second World War German markings. This plane was one of many used months earlier in the filming of the movie *The Battle of Britain*, after which a number of them had been stored at Bovingdon awaiting disposal.

A colleague of Tara's named Captain Andrews, played by Hugh Cross, was a last-minute addition to the storyline made part-way through shooting, apparently when someone realised that a scheduling clash would not allow Macnee sufficient time to do all his scenes. Andrews thus appears in some scenes – including at Mother's warehouse headquarters and at the airfield – that according to the shooting script were actually written for Steed, with the dialogue left unchanged. Showing just how late in the day this decision was made, at one point in the airfield action, when Andrews supposedly emerges from a packing case (actually his surveillance post) in his Trojan bubble car, the bowler-hatted figure of Steed – with Alf Joint doubling for Macnee – is incongruously visible through the vehicle's side window. Indeed the daily progress report actually lists the vehicle as 'Steed's bubble car'.

During the filming, the bubble car was used for a stunt collision with a BSA motorcycle, in which both vehicles unfortunately sustained some damage. Also on hand at Bovingdon for two days was a long-haired German Shepherd dog, referred to as Fang the Wonder Dog in the episode's end tag scene but actually called Toby, which had been brought along by its handler Ron Farebrother. An uncredited Joe Dunne doubled for guest actor Bryan Kendrick as the agent Philipson in disguise as a scarecrow, and went beyond the call of duty by agreeing to have Toby attack him, although he prepared thoroughly for this by placing under his clothing a protective arm pad of the type used when training police dogs. Rainy weather plagued the shoot, with Fuest having to stand the unit down earlier than he wanted to on both Wednesday 6 and Thursday 7 November.

The requirements of the screenplay were such that extensive central London filming occupied Fuest and the B unit for three consecutive working days on Friday 8, Monday 11 and Tuesday 12 November. Clifton Gardens, W9 was used for a sequence where, following instructions from the suitcase, Steed takes it to a room in the fictional Cremorne Hotel on Sloane Street. Having made off with the case, the criminal Condon, played by Raymond Adamson, is seen turning his grey Austin Cambridge off Lanark Road and into Elgin Mews South, W9, supposedly seeking somewhere quiet to receive his own taped message. After knocking Condon out with a large spanner, Tara reclaims the suitcase, then she and Steed follow the next set of instructions, which take them to a children's ballet class. Further information leads Tara to visit a telephone box in Cranley High Street – actually Blomfield Road, W9, beside the canal there – before making a detour to her apartment – for which Chalcot Crescent, NW1, once again provided the exterior. Eventually the two agents arrive at the luggage entrance to Kings Cross railway station – actually shot on the studio lot – to see two different contacts leave, both carrying suitcases.

The action continues with Tara following her chosen contact around a block of flats at Maida Vale, W9, before arriving at St Mark's Church on the corner of Hamilton Terrace and Abercorn Place, NW8. Steed's contact meanwhile leads him to Grantully Road, W9, where footage was shot of the vintage Rolls Royce following a red Morris 1100. The Morris eventually arrives at Mother's warehouse – actually Scene Docks B and C back at Elstree. Having escaped a deadly trap in a sealed crypt at a church, Tara borrows the vicar's Mini, leaving him a bottle of champagne as a consolation, before returning to Mother's place.

At one point, Steed uses his .38 Smith and Wesson revolver to wound Cavell, played by Michael Robbins, just as he is about to kill Tara. In another sequence, Tara throws martial arts fighter Captain Tim, played by John Ronane, through a window, making him groggy and unaware that Steed has sneaked up behind him and administered a swift blow over the head with his steel-crowned bowler hat. Captain Tim then concedes that Tara has defeated him, and that she will have to courier the suitcase to the next contact. This differs from Nation's shooting script, in which Tara wins the fight single-handedly, without Steed's aid, and Captain Tim is called Tiny Tim.

At the apartment of a man named Shepherd, played by Michael Hawkins, Steed and Tara discover that only a series of musical notes will activate the audio message to give them their next instructions. Tara's talents with the trumpet fail to work, prompting her to encourage Steed to play a tuba like the one in his apartment. In response, he regretfully informs her that he cannot play the instrument, adding, 'It's to put flowers in.'

Another FF70 packing crate from 'Have Guns – Will Haggle' is seen toward the end of the episode, in a sequence in Mother's warehouse.

The end tag scene involves Fang arriving at Tara's apartment carrying one of the suitcases with a message from Steed. However, having anticipated this, Tara has gone out, leaving another suitcase. The two suitcases then proceed to hold a conversation, replaying recorded messages to each other, in a clever take on the usual conclusion. This scene was filmed on Thursday 28 November, the penultimate day of principal photography, and was Toby's third day at Elstree, his handler having also brought him in for scenes the previous day and seven days earlier.

There were a number of other changes made between the shooting script and the finished episode. The opening in Mother's warehouse was originally completely different. It began with him in a chair appearing to glide across the top of a row of packing cases. It was then revealed that the chair was actually being carried by a forklift truck driven by Rhonda, as she emerged from behind the cases. Commenting that he was in a creative mood, Mother instructed Rhonda to drive the machine back and forth. In the finished episode, this was altered to Mother simply asking Rhonda to trundle his wheelchair. In addition, the numerous changing screens featured on this set were not specified in the script; they would have been an addition furnished by production designer Robert Jones.

Stunt performers Alf Joint, Joe Cornelius, Nosher Powell and Terry Plummer play four martial artists in a scene set in a gym, but in the shooting script they numbered six. The script also had Tara go undercover as another martial arts fighter, Emily

Greensmith, whereas in the finished episode she assumes the name of the previous contact, Cavell.

As scripted, the traitor Colonel Stonehouse, played on screen by Patrick Barr, met his demise when the suitcase with which he was absconding from Mother's warehouse exploded outside. This was amended for the episode to have him die from poisonous gas emitted by the suitcase within the confines of a car.

The scene set in the Cremorne Hotel was originally to have featured a porter, but this role was dispensed with in the episode itself. The end tag scene was also completely different in Nation's shooting script, being a traditional two-hander between Steed and Tara.

John Steed, Emma Peel comic book

During November 1968 the American Gold Key company released their only comic book based on the series, though *The Avengers* name did not feature on the cover as it was marketed under the title *John Steed, Emma Peel*. This was to avoid litigation from rival comic book publisher Marvel, who held the trademark on *The Avengers* name for comics in the USA, using it for their superhero team.

6.25 – 'Stay Tuned'

Tony Williamson's innovative scenario 'Stay Tuned' offers a different type of story for *The Avengers*, in which Steed suffers bouts of amnesia due to an outside influence. The surreal concept of Steed unknowingly repeating certain actions, and being unable to perceive the enemy operative Proctor, played by Gary Bond, who is causing him to do this, was a novel one at the time. Williamson was evidently pleased with it, as he later reworked it for his *Department S* episode 'A Ticket to Nowhere', in which Jason King, Annabelle Hurst and Stewart Sullivan all go through a cycle of forgetting everything they uncover about a mysterious crime.

Don Chaffey returned to direct, working with the A unit. The first day, Tuesday 19 November 1968, involved a location shoot approximately two miles north of Elstree in the village of Shenley, where footage was obtained at Pound Lane and at the junction of Rectory Lane and Harris Lane. Further material with Tara's Lotus Europa was filmed on North Avenue, adjacent to where Shenley Hospital stood, although this has since been demolished and the area redeveloped.

The second day saw Chaffey lead the unit into central London for filming in Weymouth Mews, W1 and Chalcot Crescent, NW1. Just for once, the latter was not used to establish Tara King's apartment. Instead, no. 33 Chalcot Crescent provided the exterior for the consulting room of psychiatrist Dr Meitner, played by Harold Kasket, whom Steed visits when fearing that he is suffering from psychiatric problems. Chaffey also directed filming at two other locations (possibly in London) on the same day, described on the shooting schedule as 'Urban Street' and 'Street A', but neither actually appears in the episode.

The third day of shooting was again on location, though this time nearer to home at Kendal Hall, off Watling Street near Radlett, which had appeared in the series before in 'What the Butler Saw' and 'From Venus with Love'. The unit returned to the same location 15 days later, but lighting conditions were so poor that they were unable to commence filming until 10.45 am, after which the 35mm Arriflex camera began malfunctioning, causing the crew to be stood down for 30 minutes until the problem was rectified. Later they continued shooting on Stage 5, although there were minor delays throughout the afternoon due to excessive noise from set construction outside the soundstage, which temporarily suspended filming on several occasions.

On Monday 9 December there was another visit to Weymouth Mews, W1, which doubled as the fictional Fitzherbert Street for some footage shot after dark involving Macnee and Bond. Four days' work at Elstree followed, with filming concluding on Friday 13 December.

In the early part of the episode, Steed has a temporary superior in the form of a blind woman called Father, played by Iris Russell, although Mother returns toward the conclusion of events. Steed lets off four rounds from his trusty .38 Smith and Wesson with wooden stocks when Mother mentions the Greek mythical figure Bacchus – a post-hypnotic trigger word given to the agent by the seemingly-invisible Proctor.

For a fight scene between Tara and the villain Kreer, played by Roger Delgado, Cyd Child as usual doubled for Thorson, while stunt performer Dave Wilding substituted for Delgado. Similarly, for Tara's other fight scene of the episode, this time against Kreer's associate Lisa, portrayed by Kate O'Mara, Child doubled for Thorson while Dorothy Ford stood in for O'Mara. However, the two actresses participated in segments where their faces would be clearly seen on camera, and this proved problematic as Thorson mistimed an uppercut, leaving O'Mara with a lump on her chin from the blow.[32]

Steed's home telephone number is revealed as Whitehall 9819 when he calls his answering service to advise them that he will be away for a while.

Laurie Johnson's incidental music for the episode includes material heard earlier in 'The Hour That Never Was' and a cue that would become known as 'Theme from Pandora' after being reused in the upcoming episode 'Pandora'. The latter piece would be freshly recorded in February 1980 by Johnson conducting the London Studio Orchestra for the Varese Sarabande-released album *The Avengers*.

6.26 – 'Fog'

Jeremy Burnham's next offering for the series – presumably again based on one of Brian Clemens' one-line story ideas – was a Jack the Ripper pastiche originally titled 'Ripper!' but later renamed 'Fog'. Speaking at *The Avengers* at 50 event held at Chichester University in June 2011, Burnham freely admitted that he carried out very little research regarding Jack the Ripper before writing the screenplay.

The episode was directed in an atmospheric manner by John Hough, with filming carried out by the A unit. Work commenced on Thursday 21 November 1968 with a location shoot at the Hadley Common railway tunnel within sight of Crescent West, Hadley Wood in Hertfordshire, where footage was obtained of both the track and the tunnel. However, this footage, along with some inserts of prop signs filmed by the third unit on a country road on Thursday 9 January 1969, does not appear in the finished episode. It was originally intended to come near the conclusion of events, in a dropped sequence where Mother and Rhonda, travelling in a Rolls Royce, become lost in the fog and find themselves inside a railway tunnel.

---

[32] Kate O'Mara would later feature prominently in the short-lived stage play version of *The Avengers* (see Part Two), as the leather-clad villainess Madame Gerda.

The rest of the filming for 'Fog', making up the entirety of the episode on screen, was realised on studio sets, with a complex of Victorian streets and alleyways constructed on Stage 2 being utilised on eight days.

At one point Tara removes Steed's .38 Smith and Wesson revolver from a drawer in his apartment and then replaces it, during a scene where she attempts to explain disarmament to guest actor Frederick Peisley's character, the Russian disarmament conference delegate Grunner, whose English is not very good.

The props department completely customised a Mini Moke to serve as Mother's personal transport (in place of the Rolls Royce), giving it black and orange stripes and various accessories such as a flashing warning light and a prop radar to navigate through the infamous London 'pea soup' fog. In the episode, a suitably-attired Rhonda drives the car while Mother sits in the back.

In what has by this point become something of running joke in the series, Steed refers to one of his supposed eccentric relatives, commenting 'As my Aunt Clara used to say …' Tara finishes the sentence: 'Life is a bowl of cherries.' 'I didn't know you'd met her!' comments Steed in surprise. The apt and amusing punchline goes to Tara: 'Well, your aunts are so predictable.'

A horse called Planet and a working hansom cab were both hired for the filming from George Mossman, although the other cabs seen in the episode were static props created in the carpenter's workshop at the studio.

An appearance by actor David Lodge as a sword expert named Maskell was omitted from the final edit of the episode, although the character is mentioned in dialogue and he is still included in the on-screen credits.

The closing tag scene involves Steed and Tara in her apartment, where the air conditioning has gone into reverse on a foggy day, filling the room with thick mist. Having poured a drink for Tara, Steed is attempting to locate her when there is the sound of a car horn, then Mother's voice and then a screech of tyres, as the unseen Mini Moke is apparently driven through the apartment.

Being another admirer of the work of Peter Hammond on the videotaped episodes, Hough emulated some his trademark techniques in 'Fog', using a number of overhead shots and at one point filming through Grunner's spectacles. Hough has since acknowledged also being greatly influenced and inspired by others he worked with on *The Avengers*, namely Brian Clemens, Albert Fennell and director of photography Alan Hume.

Burnham's original 'Ripper!' shooting script had a somewhat more complicated storyline than the actual episode, and concluded with Steed rushing to save Tara after she was enticed to Bromley by a '60s version of Jack the Ripper. Clemens apparently considered that the inclusion of a character directly based on most famous serial killer of all was too gruesome and too near reality for *The Avengers* and so concocted a replacement, the episode's Gaslight Ghoul.

Haller was the only one of the story's four East European delegate characters not to undergo a change of name between script and screen – Grunner, Straddlestof and Valarti were originally called Janacek, Streltsov and Vailati respectively.

The screenplay began in a traditional manner with one of the delegates being murdered by a mysterious figure wearing a top hat and wielding a swordstick – an event that occurs a little later in the finished episode. This prompted Steed to give Mother a visit at his latest headquarters, envisaged as being on board a boat moored on a canal, where after being piped aboard by Rhonda, wearing a tight-fitting sailor suit, he went below and found his superior relaxing in a hammock. The investigation then got under way with a sequence retained in the finished episode, of Steed and Tara reconstructing the crime.

This version was minus the episode's exchange of dialogue about Sherlock Holmes and Dr Watson outside the home of Ghoul enthusiast Charles Osgood, played by David Bird. Similarly, the script omitted the episode's reference to horror writer Edgar Allan Poe.

Burnham advised that the Janacek character should meet his demise at the hands of Jack in a bandstand in Greenwich Park, or else in the most Victorian-looking piece of parkland that location scouts could find, whereas in the finished episode the equivalent scene of Grunner being murdered was of course shot in studio. The screenplay also included an additional character, a hansom cab driver called Moneypenny, who was obviously thought to be surplus to requirements. Conversely, however, Clemens wrote in a number of extra background characters in the form of a tinker, an organ grinder, a blind man, a heather seller and a beggar, giving even more mystery to the story. With the action shrouded in fog and played out on the confined set of cobblestone streets and alleyways, the episode became an extremely atmospheric one, and brought a completely different approach to the series.

Original American novel number four

The fourth American *The Avengers* novel and the third featuring Tara King, *The Magnetic Man* by Norman Daniels was published by Berkley Medallion in December 1968. Its cover design, featuring a photograph of Steed and Tara, followed that of the same company's reissues of the John Garforth novels based on the series. Inside, the book also contained a photograph of Mrs Peel, although she is not involved in the story.

Born in 1905, Daniels had written for American pulp magazines throughout the '30s and '40s, producing a mixture of crime and espionage stories, and had then worked intermittently as a scriptwriter during the '50s, contributing instalments to anthology series including *Alfred Hitchcock Presents*. In the '60s he was concentrating on Western and espionage novels, including some television tie-ins.

6.27 – 'Who Was That Man I Saw You With?'

Jeremy Burnham's final screenplay for the series, 'Who Was That Man I Saw You With?', offered a variation on the standard traitor plotline, with Tara becoming the victim of a frame-up by foreign paid agents.

With director Don Chaffey and the A unit assigned, shooting got under way on Monday 16 December 1968 in Hadley Green in the London Borough of Barnet, EN5. This was for a short sequence of Tara gaining entrance to a military establishment's war room via a sentry box. Later that day Tara's Lotus and the departmental operative Jay Fairfax's Austin were shot travelling along Heath Road in Hampstead, London NW3, before turning into the car park there. Steed's personal transport of delight underwent a change, his pale yellow vintage Rolls Royce being forsaken in favour of a 1929 Phantom 1 (UU 3864), which would also appear in some forthcoming episodes.

The second day of filming found the unit working between rain showers at the underground garage of an apartment block called Bellmoor in London NW3, as previously seen in 'The Rotters'. More footage of Fairfax's Austin 3 Litre trailing Tara's

Lotus was captured, showing them speeding down Bakers Hill and into Hadley Wood Road in Barnet, approximately three miles from the studios.

Filming on days three and four included shots of Tara's apartment in Chalcot Crescent, London NW1, giving the series' clearest view of her outer doorway, revealing the number as 19A.

Production proceeded smoothly save for a minor incident on Tuesday 7 January when Rhonda Parker slipped on the soundstage floor, although she was unhurt and declined to visit the studio first aid station. For the final couple of days of principal filming, John Hough stepped in to direct the third unit on location in Duchess Mews for establishing shots of Steed's apartment, while Chaffey finished the interior scenes back at Elstree.

While in his car staking out Tara's apartment, Fairfax, played by William Marlowe, uses a handheld 8mm Elmo Zoom 82 camera to record her apparently meeting with the enemy agent Gregor Zaroff, played by Alan Browning.

When infiltrating the war room, Tara sports a .38 Enfield No 2 mark 1 revolver, although her own firearm – which she is found holding when Steed discovers her standing over the dead Fairfax – is a Beretta 950 automatic. When she later demonstrates to Steed at his apartment how easy it would be to frame someone as a traitor, his .38 Smith and Wesson revolver plays a prominent part in proceedings.

The crypt set from 'Love All' was redressed to become Mother's new temporary headquarters, and part of the streets and alleyways set from 'Fog' was reused with daytime lighting for the teaser sequence.

The shooting script was realised very faithfully in the finished episode, although as was often the case it included no end tag scene, indicating that this was written later by Brian Clemens.

More incidental music recordings

Howard Blake held his final recording session of incidental music for *The Avengers* on Thursday 9 January 1969 on the music stage at Elstree, to provide cues for 'Who Was That Man I Saw You With?'. In the period since his initial compositions for 'My Wildest Dream', 'Whoever Shot Poor George Oblique Stroke XR40?' and 'All Done With Mirrors', Blake had also laid down passages and cues for the following episodes: 'Super Secret Cypher Snatch', 'Game', 'Noon Doomsday', 'Wish You Were Here', 'The Interrogators' and 'Take Me to Your Leader'. Usually he brought together a dozen musicians, drawn from a larger base of session players, including ace bassist Herbie Flowers and Vic Flick, who had played the distinctive guitar riff on the James Bond theme.

Turn-of-the-year developments

In the aftermath of the ITV franchise reassignment, television film series had suffered somewhat from haphazard scheduling as the regional companies struggled to find their feet. The Thorson episodes became something of a casualty of the situation, and perhaps because of this, season six failed to match the high viewing figures of season five. By October 1968, however, the series had managed to hit the top of the ratings chart in the London and Tyne Tees regions. In November there were a couple of weeks when it equalled that achievement in Ulster. Then in December it did likewise in the

Westward region and, after briefly falling away slightly, returned to number one in both London and Tyne Tees.

Also during December, Honor Blackman's recording career appeared ready to take off again when demo copies of the single 'Before Today', backed with 'I'll be Always Loving You', were issued on the CBS label and distributed to disc jockeys and radio stations. Both tracks had been written by John Taylor for Blackman's recent stage success *Mrs and Mrs*, based on the works of Noel Coward, although for the single the actress had freshly recorded them with Geoff Love and his Orchestra. However, non-demo copies of this recording, sporting the standard orange CBS label, are rare in the extreme, suggesting that in the event it received only a limited release.

Meanwhile, in the United States, the religious organisation Christian Science Monitor had been investigating violence on American television throughout the autumn, and now named *The Avengers* as the worst offender. This surprising news made the front page of *The Stage and Television Today* 's Christmas Eve 1968 edition, the report citing the episode 'Game' as containing 22 violent incidents, including six deaths. In the wake of this, Brian Clemens defended the series in the pages of the *Daily Mail*, saying: 'They never take into account the manner of the killings. In fact, the stories are about as violent as the average pantomime or Grimm's fairytale.'

The last ITV regional company to debut the Thorson episodes in 1968 was Southern, which launched its transmissions on Wednesday 4 December. This left only Scottish and Granada yet to join the party. However, all the ITV regions currently screening *The Avengers* temporarily rested it over the Christmas period, Tyne Tees swapping their usual Wednesday night transmission for a one-off Saturday screening of 'Get-A-Way!' on 28 December.

Rescheduling for 1969, Westward and Channel joined Anglia, Harlech and Ulster in taking ATV's Thursday evening line-feed of the series, starting on 2 January with 'The Interrogators'. This line-up of regions changed again the following week, as Anglia dropped out. They would not transmit any further Thorson episodes until May. Grampian was another region to reschedule, opting out of Thames's Wednesday evening line-feed and going for a one-off Thursday screening of 'The Interrogators' at 8.00 pm on 2 January before settling on a regular 7.00 pm Friday slot, starting on 10 January with 'The Morning After'. Also on Friday 2 January, Scottish Television finally began showing the Thorson episodes, with 'The Forget-Me-Knot' at 8.00 pm. Border meanwhile decided to drop their longstanding Sunday night slot for the series in favour of an 8.00 pm Wednesday one, beginning with 'The Interrogators' on 8 January. ATV also abandoned their Thursday evening screenings early in the month and rescheduled to Fridays at 7.30 pm. Retaining their line-feed, Harlech, Ulster, Westward and Channel all did likewise. However, after late February, Westward and Channel would follow Anglia's example in suspending transmissions until May. Yorkshire would meanwhile move the series from Friday evenings to what was virtually its old ABC slot, Saturdays at 8.30 pm, starting on 18 January with 'Invasion of the Earthmen'.

Following the realignment of the ITV franchisees, Granada were usually several months behind the other regions when it came to scheduling any film series, and sure enough they would be the last region to embark on screening the Thorson episodes, airing 'The Forget-Me-Knot' at 8.25 pm on Sunday 12 January.

6.28 – 'Pandora'

As with 'Fog', Brian Clemens instigated a different approach to *The Avengers* with his script for the costume drama 'Pandora', in which Linda Thorson takes centre stage and which she also regards as her all-time favourite episode. The storyline has Tara apparently waking in 1915 to find everyone addressing her as Pandora – although of course it all turns out to be a trick in the end.

Shot mainly on studio sets, the episode harked back to the videotaped era of the series in some ways, with Thorson's friend Robert Fuest – who also rated it as his favourite episode – providing some atmospheric direction.

Having obtained a clue regarding the whereabouts of the missing Tara, Steed consults junior records department official Carter, played by Geoffrey Whitehead, who is initially seen flicking through some suspension files, including those of Mrs Emma Peel and Mrs Cathy Gale. Later, when Carter telephones Steed with additional information, the scene is marred by the inclusion of an overhead microphone, visible for a short time in the top left-hand corner of the picture.

With the B unit assigned, filming on the episode ran from Thursday 2 January to Monday 27 January 1969, and was uneventful throughout.

6.29 – 'Thingumajig'

Automated opponents had proved popular in the series since Philip Levene had invented the Cybernauts and, tapping into this area of thinking, Terry Nation devised the next episode to go into production. Initially titled 'It', it had become 'Little Boxes' by the time Nation submitted a shooting script, and gained its final title after a rewrite. The scenario this time involves a team of archaeologists digging in the crypt of a church when one of them is killed in mysterious circumstances.

The director assigned to handle this episode was Leslie Norman, who was a natural choice to work on *The Avengers*, having previously directed portions of two season five escapades uncredited as well as episodes of *The Saint* and other film series, making him a frequent visitor to Elstree. The initial filming however was done by John Hough with the small third unit on Friday 9 January 1969 at St Margaret's Church off Crossoaks Lane in Ridge, where the crew became unpopular after their heavy vehicles damaged the village green when parking on it. It was on the next filming day, Monday 13 January, that Norman arrived, assuming control of the A unit on Stage 3 at Elstree. Hough and the third unit meanwhile embarked on a further busy location day, visiting Tykes Water Lake in Aldenham Park, Ivinghoe Beacon Road in Buckinghamshire, Mimms Lane near Shenley and, after dark, Hill Farm in Radlett.

On the third day of filming, actor Jack Woolgar, who had previously portrayed Kermit the hermit in 'The Living Dead', answered his call to report to Stage 2 at 10.00 am to participate in some scenes being filmed on tunnel sets. However, as the day went on he found himself waiting for his part to be reached, and in the end this never happened. He was released by Norman at 5.00 pm and never called back, presumably because his small role in proceedings had been removed during a rewrite.

While Norman concentrated on the interiors for the episode, Hough undertook a couple more location shoots on Monday 20 and Tuesday 21 January, returning to Tykes Water Lake and then visiting Springwell Chalk Pit, off Springwell Lane, Harefield in Buckinghamshire. A wrecked blue van seen in the footage shot at the latter site was not a standing feature but rather a prop taken there for filming.

Meanwhile, back at the studio, Linda Thorson had contracted a heavy cold, and the producers called in Dr Carl Hodes from his Borehamwood surgery to examine her. Hodes' opinion was that Thorson would be unavailable for filming the following day, and he was correct. This meant that the episode's production schedule had to be rejigged in order for shooting to continue. Thorson would eventually be absent for three days in all.

On Friday 31 January, crew member Pat Noonan received burns to his face from an arc flash effect (similar to that produced by an arc welder), from equipment that Steed uses to destroy an electricity-craving mechanical box device. This necessitated him consulting the studio medical staff.

The X-rays made of the box earlier in the action were props reused from 'Take Me to Your Leader', where they had represented X-rays taken of the talking suitcase.

A package that Steed dispatches to Tara via British Rail is seen to be addressed to 'Miss T King, 9 Primrose Crescent, London W2.'

Some of Laurie Johnson's incidental music from the episode 'From Venus with Love' is heard again in this one; and to conclude events Tara plays a snatch of the theme tune on the church organ.

Nation's 'Little Boxes' version of the screenplay differed from the finished episode in several ways. Originally the archaeologist Inge Tilson, played by Dora Reisser, was called Liz, and Steed failed to recognise his old associate Revd Teddy Shelley, played by Jeremy Lloyd. The sneezing electronics expert Professor Truman, played by Willoughby Goddard, had an earlier scene with Steed at his apartment, and there was a sequence where Liz and Steed come across a large crater in the countryside where something has burrowed into the soil, tapped into a large electrical cable and then given off a power surge. These were both dropped during rewriting. The scene where Steed and Liz discover the wrecked van also underwent a small change between script and screen, as originally they were to have found three insulated compartments in the van as opposed to only two. However, other parts of this scene – such as Steed removing a brass knob from a bed frame salvaged from the river, because it matches one missing from his own bed – were already present in the script.

Further rewrites appear to have been quickly carried out to accommodate Thorson's illness. Tara was given Thorson's cold, resulting in most of her scenes for the episode being confined to her apartment set at Elstree.

6.30 – 'Homicide and Old Lace'

Brian Clemens finally found a use for much of the footage from the abandoned John Bryce-produced episode 'The Great Great Britain Crime' when he came up with the idea of presenting it within a framing device whereby it appears as a story that Mother makes up to entertain his aged aunts. Originally entitled 'Tall Story', this became 'Homicide and Old Lace' before transmission, the title being a pastiche on that of the play and movie *Arsenic and Old Lace*.

Initially, three days' production was allocated to complete the necessary scenes: Wednesday 15, Thursday 16 and Friday 17 January 1969. Later, though, a fourth day was added: Thursday 23 January. The filming was under the direction of John Hough and carried out by the third unit, using a small cast comprising Patrick Newell, Rhonda Parker and, as Mother's aunts Harriet and Georgina, Joyce Carey and Mary Merrall.

Strangely, two different London locations were specified for the exterior shots required, but eventually they were all obtained at one: Weymouth Mews.

The writers of 'The Great Great Britain Crime', Malcolm Hulke and Terrance Dicks, received the credit on the finished episode – understandably so, as most of the material included was their work. However, besides using plenty of footage from 'The Great Great Britain Crime', the episode also recycled sequences from 'The Bird Who Knew Too Much', 'Murdersville', 'The Fear Merchants', and 'Never, Never Say Die', all of course within Clemens' new framing material.

Back in 1967, location filming for 'The Great Great Britain Crime' began on Thursday 23 November after three days devoted to interiors on Stage 9. John Hough supervised the second unit on a busy schedule in central London, taking establishing shots of several well-known landmarks including Buckingham Palace, Trafalgar Square, Westminster Abbey, the Houses of Parliament, the Thames Embankment and Tower Bridge – only the first two of which were retained in 'Homicide and Old Lace'. Meanwhile, the main unit under director Vernon Sewell was capturing exteriors at the premises of the Bullens Organisation, adjacent to the studios on Maxwell Road in Borehamwood, to represent the super vault in which replicas of the all the nation's greatest treasures are held as a security measure by Colonel Corf, played by Gerald Harper, star of the BBC's intended rival to *The Avengers*, *Adam Adamant Lives!.*

At 9.50 am the following day, Friday 24 November, Sewell began shooting a car chase sequence in the multi-storey Church Car Park in Watford. This saw Cyd Child doubling for Thorson, driving Tara's Lotus Elan +2. Later, Sewell supervised more location filming at the Archway, a collection of office blocks accessed from McDonald Road in Highgate Hill, London N19, which provided the exterior for Intercrime's base of operations. The main unit then concluded their work for the day in Bryanston Street, London W2, where they captured footage to indicate the capital's telephone system being sabotaged.

Meanwhile, Hough's second unit was also busy that day, filming both on Edgware Road, London W2 and on Wood Lane, Little Common, near Stanmore, compiling more footage that ultimately went unused.

The following Monday, 27 November, the second unit completed material for the car chase back in Watford, showing the Lotus being pursued at high speed down the car park's circular off ramp by a pair of Minis driven by stunt personnel Bill Cummings and Romo Gorrara. Unfortunately, while filming the sequence, a road wheel on one of the Minis was damaged after the vehicle was driven at speed over a concrete kerb.

Five days later, the final location shoot, involving a BMC 250 JU minibus and a Jaguar saloon, was carried out on the junction of Crossoaks Lane and Summerswood Lane in the village of Ridge This was for a sequence where, after being ambushed and shot by Intercrime agents, an informant named Freddie Cartwright, played by Donald Pickering, is buried in an adjacent field – though for a later sequence where he claws his way out of the shallow grave, having survived by virtue of having on a bullet-proof vest, Pickering was doubled by stunt performer Billy Dean with his face covered in soil.

The production schedule reveals several studio scenes that were shot for 'The Great Great Britain Crime' but do not appear in 'Homicide and Old Lace', including one set inside the reception of Orpheus Tours (whose minibus does appear), apparently a travel agency used by Intercrime as a cover for illicit activities.

The jeweller's shop heist featured in the episode was originally filmed entirely in the studio, over Thursday 30 November and Friday 1 December on Stage 3. The location footage seen in the finished sequence derives from the new Weymouth Mews shoot – as is apparent from the fact that Steed's vintage Rolls Royce is parked behind the Intercrime getaway car, whereas at the time of the original shoot the agent's regular mode of transport was the AC 428 sports convertible.

On Wednesday 29 November, Sewell directed scenes on the storage space and corridor sets comprising part of Colonel's Corf's vault. This material is all included in 'Homicide and Old Lace'. However, the director also worked with the main unit on what was presumably a large set representing Piccadilly Circus underground station, plus another set described simply as a cell. These do not feature in the finished episode.

The following day saw the main unit shooting on a set described in documentation as Hobson's office, with actor Tom Gill (presumably playing Hobson) answering his call at 10.00 am for his solitary day's work on the project, which again ultimately went unseen. A Hobson's removal truck is featured in 'Homicide and Old Lace', being used to collect the national treasures for storage, but it is not known if Hobson was intended to be an associate of Colonel Corf's or someone aligned to Intercrime.

Further untraceable filming took place on the same day, as records indicate that a sequence involving a country road and a telephone box was undertaken by the second unit somewhere (probably the concrete perimeter road) on the studio lot, but this also failed to make it into 'Homicide and Old Lace'. However, one piece of second unit backlot filming from Thursday 30 November that did get used in the episode was a sequence of Cartwright being killed by Intercrime agents after being mistaken for Steed.

The dialogue of Mother relating the story to his aunts was edited in post-production at around the eight minutes and 21 seconds mark, with some unknown words being deleted and then, after a short pause, 'personally' being substituted. Tara's blonde hair in the material from 'The Great Great Britain Crime' is explained away as being a product of Mother's overactive imagination.

Steed's calling card, which he drops into a cleaner's bucket during the jeweller's shop robbery, gives his telephone number as 460-9618, which is different from the one quoted in 'Stay Tuned', although the 3 Stable Mews, City of London address is consistent with other episodes.

Components of the fitted furniture from the Emma Peel season five apartment set were recycled in a redressed form as part of the office of the European Intercrime head Dunbar, played by Keith Baxter.

In a sequence where Tara fakes a fainting spell in Colonel Corf's underground office, a boom microphone is visible overhead. A similar problem affects a later scene where Steed and Mother discuss Operation Rule Britannia – the scheme to swap all of Britain's treasures for the replicas in the vault in the event of a national emergency.

John Bryce's approach to Steed's umbrella sword was almost casual, and completely different from the policy adopted by Clemens and Fennell of it being seen occasionally but never used in anger. When attacked by Intercrime's knife-throwing African delegate, portrayed by Bari Johnson, Steed draws his sword and takes aim before launching it at his assailant. However, a cut was made to this old footage from 'The Great Great Britain Crime' when it was amalgamated into 'Homicide and Old Lace', hence the weapon is not seen hitting its intended target. The action simply continues with Steed removing a large throwing knife from the side of a wooden packing case.

The soundtrack to this episode's closing credits is somewhat different from usual, beginning with sounds heard previously played by Izzy Pound in 'The Interrogators', then becoming a gripping silent movie piano version of the theme that concludes with the season five fanfare.

Though it had a solid basic concept of criminals contriving to get the nation's most valuable items brought to one location and then stealing them, the screenplay of 'The Great Great Britain Crime' appears to have been overly complicated. Even Clemens' device of having Mother's aunts recap the entire storyline toward the conclusion of 'Homicide and Old Lace' does not really make things any clearer. In addition, the screenplay seems to have included an excessive number of characters. These two factors may help to account for the fact that Vernon Sewell amassed over 63 minutes' worth of film to tell the story, which then required editing back to the standard episode length of approximately 50 minutes. Unfortunately, even when incorporated into 'Homicide and Old Lace', this older footage appears both disjointed and uneven; but under the circumstances this was probably the best thing that could be done with it.

The basic plot of 'The Great Great Britain Crime' was not all that different from what appeared in 'Homicide and Old Lace', and ran as follows. The teaser sequence consisted of Intercrime's ambush of Freddie Cartwright in Ridge. Escaping from his shallow grave, Cartwright went to Steed's apartment but later sneaked away, having helped himself to some of the agent's clothing, including a bowler hat and an umbrella, and having stolen the AC 428 convertible. Seeing Cartwright from a distance and believing him to be Steed, the Intercrime execution squad killed him with machine guns, thinking they had disposed of the agent himself.

This was followed by a sequence of the arrival of the foreign delegates at the Intercrime headquarters. Steed and Tara then foiled the robbery at the jeweller's shop. Having created problems for the criminal organisation, Steed found himself the victim of an abduction attempt by a fake cabbie and accomplice. However, taking control of the situation, the agent disarmed the aggressors and went along to meet Intercrime Europe boss Dunbar. Under the misapprehension that Steed was an upper class criminal, Dunbar offered him the opportunity to work for Intercrime on their latest scheme, described as the crime of the century.

Steed and Tara next visited Colonel Corf to evaluate security measures at the underground vault. Then Tara was kidnapped, after her Lotus was chased down the multi-storey car park by two Minis, and she became Intercrime's prisoner. Faking a national emergency, Dunbar had Steed call Colonel Corf and instruct him to dispatch the Hobson's removal trucks to collect the nation's treasures, leaving the elaborate replicas in their place, and then return to the vault, where Intercrime planned to pilfer everything.

Escaping from Intercrime headquarters, Tara rushed to the vault, warning Colonel Corf of the impending robbery, but found that he paid her little attention. After the treasures arrived and were stored away, the Intercrime gang, delegates and Steed gained access. Then Steed and Tara proceeded to apprehend all the criminals, except for Dunbar, who used a cigarette lighter bomb to blast a way through into Piccadilly Circus underground station. After Dunbar had also been subdued, Steed commented that he was only a couple of stops away from home – which was actually inaccurate, as Piccadilly Circus is the closest that the Piccadilly line gets to Westminster. The concluding tag scene involved Tara convincing Steed that the fake crown jewels that she had were the real thing.

Crew changes

Quite a number of personnel new to *The Avengers* had been engaged prior to the start of filming on season six back in October 1967, taking up key positions within the crew. These included post-production co-ordinator Harry Booth, who worked on the first dozen episodes. There was no on-screen credit for that position on 'Game', but then Ann Chegwidden took over for the remainder of the run. Manuel del Campo was the editor on the first ten episodes until Karen Heward moved across from her position as music editor, then they more or less alternated in the role, although Chegwidden doubled up on 'Pandora' as both post-production co-ordinator and editor. Assisting along the way, both Tom Simpson and Robert Dearberg gained a credit as editor at one point during the season.

Having been the director of photography on *The Baron* for almost half of its run, Gilbert Taylor arrived to perform the same function on *The Avengers*, although Jimmy Harvey stood in on 'Have Guns – Will Haggle', Frank Watts was responsible for 'My Wildest Dream' and then Alan Hume returned for half a dozen adventures. After the reintroduction of the system of having two main units, the position changed from episode to episode, as Hume, Stephen Dade, Peter Jessop, David Holmes and H A R Thomson all took turns.

The assistant director function was carried out by Ron Appleton on 12 of the first 13 episodes, with John O'Conner filling in on 'Have Guns – Will Haggle'. Ted Lewis then assumed the position from 'False Witness' for four episodes, after which he alternated with Ron Purdie for a time, until being succeeded by Colin Lord.

Brian Elvin worked as the camera operator up until 'Game', then Geoff Seaholme and Ernie Robinson stepped in, eventually alternating in the position as they were attached to different units, although Norman Jones stepped in on 'Wish You Were Here'.

Len Townsend became the associate art director, though later he was joined by Kenneth Tait from 'All Done with Mirrors' onwards, though Richard Harrison replaced him on several occasions. Toward the conclusion of the season's production Tait worked solo. Tait's previous position as the series' set dresser was meanwhile assumed by Simon Wakefield, who also stayed through to the end of proceedings.

Felix Evans controlled the wardrobe department until Ivy Baker succeeded him from 'The Rotters' onwards. Two regulars from the Rigg episodes, Len Shilton and Len Abbott, took on the majority of sound dubbing duties, although five episodes were handled by Bill Rowe. Hairdressing was initially supervised by Gordon Bond, then by Janice Dorman from 'Whoever Shot Poor George Oblique Stroke XR40?', and finally by Mary Sturgess from 'Killer', although along the way Betty Sherriff and Pat McDermott each handled a solitary episode.

Continuity was originally entrusted to June Randall, who around this time seemed to bounce back and forth between *The Avengers* and *The Saint*, but she was superseded by Mary Spain, who had worked in this capacity on several season five episodes. Lorna Selwyn was assigned a solitary episode, but once the two main units were functioning independently, additional continuity people became involved, namely Kay Perkins and Kay Fenton.

The second unit photography credit appeared on only about two thirds of the episodes. Jimmy Harvey received it on the first seven, followed by Wilkie Cooper on one, Desmond Dickinson on one, Gerald Gibbs on six, Bob Thompson on six, David

Holmes on two and Bert Mason on the final four.

Russ Hill was sound editor on a couple of early episodes, but Peter Lennard assumed that role on all the others until 'False Witness'. As with many other roles, the sound editor position was then shared as the A and B units took it in turns to undertake the major filming on consecutive episodes, the credits going to Lennard and Bob Dearberg alternately. Later in production, Brian Lintern replaced Dearberg on 'Thingumajig', and Lennard finished things off by sound editing all of the final three episodes.

Cecil Mason was the sound recordist on all of the first 17 episodes, but as with other crew positions, the reinstatement of the twin main unit approach brought about some changes. Sid Rider, Dennis Whitlock, Sash Fisher, Bill Rowe and Claude Hitchcock all handled odd episodes in place of Mason, who returned from time to time to offer an experienced ear.

Herbert Worley was the construction manager on this season, except for a period between August and November 1968 when Len Dunstan fulfilled the duty.

Steve Birtles initially took on the supervising electrician responsibilities, but later Roy Bond handled alternate episodes with him.

6.31 – 'Requiem'

'Requiem' was another screenplay from the typewriter of Brian Clemens. It tells the story of an elaborate deception played on a drugged Tara by members of Murder International – the villainous organisation previously featured in 'Noon Doomsday' – who desperately want to learn the secret location where Steed is acting as bodyguard to a witness willing to give evidence against them in a trial.

Having evidently impressed with his previous assignments, Don Chaffey was recalled to direct what would be the final episode of *The Avengers* to feature extensive location work. Filming by the B unit got under way on Monday 20 January 1969 with another visit to the Bellmoor apartment block situated near Hampstead Heath, London NW3, for an underground garage sequence.

The following day, Chaffey and the unit had a busy schedule in the Letchmore Heath area, shooting a sequence of the Murder International agents Major Firth and Lieutenant Barrett, played by John Cairney and Mike Lewin, driving around and searching for Steed's hideaway.

The third day saw filming take place at the gateways to the Haberdashers' Aske's School off Aldenham Road in Elstree and Camfield Place on Wildhill Road in Wildhill near Hatfield, plus some work closer to home in Borehamwood.

Thursday 23 January brought another challenging day for the unit, beginning at Duchess Mews in London for some footage featuring Steed's vintage Rolls Royce outside his apartment. Later the crew returned to the Hertsmere district, where they filmed at a large private residence called Lyndhurst, situated in its own grounds on Green Street near Shenley. Shooting continued with Cyd Child doubling for Thorson driving Steed's Rolls Royce down a quiet Maxwell Road beside the studio, before paying a return visit to the Haberdashers' Aske's school. The day's schedule concluded back at Elstree, where the Rolls Royce was shot arriving at a warehouse – actually the wood mill and the largest of the three carpenters' workshops on site, toward the rear of the studio lot.

After spending a day filming interiors in the warmth of Stage 5, Chaffey and the unit braved the cold weather again on Monday 27 January at the Heath Brow car park off North End Way, London NW3, for a sequence where Steed collects the witness Miranda Loxton, played by Angela Douglas – who had been one of the hopefuls auditioned by ABC at their Teddington Studios seven years earlier for the semi-regular role of Venus Smith.

Further days of studio interiors followed, then another part-day of location work, beginning with a sequence of Mother's apparent funeral – actually faked by the villains – in the churchyard at St Andrews Church in the village of Totteridge, near Barnet, London N20. This was followed by the shooting of additional material with several cast members on The Rise back in Borehamwood, conveniently close to the studio, where they spent the remainder of the working day.

The final location work undertaken on this episode took place on Monday 3 February, when John Hough and his third unit filmed a small amount of material at Aldenham Reservoir near Elstree. Despite looking altogether authentic, the canon-shaped weathervane featured in this sequence was not real, but rather a prop mounted on the roof of a building in the backlot town.

In a budget-saving move, it was decided on this occasion to have Mother make his temporary headquarters in the absent Steed's apartment, where he engages in raiding the well-stocked drinks cabinet. As the apartment would not feature in the final couple of episodes, the set dressers were allowed to run riot and totally ruin the set for scenes showing the aftermath of a bomb explosion.

At one point in the action, Tara attempts to escape from a locked room by opening the only window, which fails to budge, though unfortunately as she applies pressure the whole wall of the set can be seen to move.

After appearing in the background in the majority of the other season six episodes, Rhonda Parker was finally allowed to become involved in the action, her character knocking out a couple of intruders convinced that Mother's house is Steed's secret location.

When Tara first arrives at Steed's apartment, she finds him checking his .38 Smith and Wesson revolver, which he then pockets as a security measure for his upcoming mission.

As usual on the Thorson episodes, various clips of Laurie Johnson's earlier incidental music were reused, including material originally recorded for 'Castle De'Ath' and 'Something Nasty in the Nursery'.

The Americans pull the plug

In America, the hugely successful *Rowan and Martin's Laugh-In* on NBC was not the only stiff competition that *The Avengers* faced. All the other shows pitted against it by the ABC network's rivals were also performing well in the Neilsen ratings. Over on CBS, the long-running Western *Gunsmoke* was the sixth most popular show of 1968, and another NBC offering, the comedy fantasy *I Dream of Jeannie*, was twenty-sixth. *The Avengers*, by contrast, languished in sixty-ninth place. It was thus no great surprise when on Friday 24 January 1969 the *Daily Mail* ran an article entitled 'Tara's Farewell To Her Steed', including a brief interview with Brian Clemens but more importantly informing readers that production on *The Avengers* would shortly cease. The scries had become a casualty of the American ratings war, the ABC network having informed ABPC that no further episodes would be required beyond the end of season six. Even though the series had been distributed to many other countries – a total of 90 worldwide – the production cost of £50,000 per episode was just too high to be afforded without an American network sale to offset it. Clemens admitted to the *Daily Mail* that he would greatly miss making the series, and working with Patrick Macnee.

6.32 – 'Take-Over'

The penultimate episode, 'Take-Over', was another script contribution from Terry Nation. The plot involves four intruders taking over the country home of Steed's friends Bill and Laura Bassett with the intention of wiping out a nearby peace conference with a rocket, only to have their plans foiled when the agent unexpectedly arrives for a visit.

Filming commenced on Thursday 30 January 1969, with director Robert Fuest taking the third unit on location with a black Rolls Royce Phantom V to Aldenham Road near Elstree, together with guest actors Tom Adams and Keith Buckley playing two of the intruders, Grenville and Lomax. This was for the episode's opening teaser sequence, featuring shots of a handcuffed prisoner, played by an uncredited Art Thomas, running off across some fields near Elstree Cricket Club in the direction Aldenham Reservoir, before being killed by the villains using a remote control device to detonate a miniature phosphor bomb implanted in his neck.

Friday 31 January saw Fuest and the third unit visiting the nearby Aldenham Estate to start filming sequences of a morning hunt during which Steed fakes his own death in a swamp. On Tuesday 4 and Wednesday 5 February, the director returned to the same location, this time with the A unit, which would be responsible for most of the episode's filming, although on the first of those dates rainy weather forced the cancellation of the shoot virtually as soon as the camera started rolling, leaving the crew with no other choice than to return to the studio.

On Friday 7 February John Hough executed a complete day of filming with the third unit, visiting three different unknown country road locations plus a field where material was captured of an ambulance and Steed's vintage Rolls Royce. However, none of this footage appears in the finished episode. Instead, Macnee is seen in some shots where he is sat in the Rolls in front of an unconvincing travelling matte back-projection.

It appears that the shooting script originally incorporated some additional action in which Steed is discovered unconscious in the woods by a peace conference security officer named Hatch, then placed in an ambulance where, on recovering, he works out what Grenville and his associates are planning and commandeers the vehicle to get back to the Bassetts' home. Although none of this material features in the final version, at least some of it was actually filmed, indicating that the shooting script was still being worked on while the episode was before the cameras. The daily progress reports show that actor Walter Gotell and stunt performer Jimmy Lodge appeared in the missing scenes.

On Thursday 13 February, Hough and the third unit visited what is now Radlett Preparatory School, off Watling Street near Radlett, where the main building doubled as the Barretts' home. As scripted, a sequence where the Bassetts' manservant Groom escapes from the house was to have continued with him driving away in a car, only to suffer the effects of one of the phosphor bombs just before reaching the gateway, causing him to lose control of the vehicle and crash. He was then to have been seen staggering from the wreckage with a cloud of white smoke billowing from his mouth, before dying an agonising death. In the finished episode, this action is greatly simplified, Grenville killing Groom almost straightaway as he runs from the house.

There are few other differences between the shooting script and the finished episode, the only notable one being that a conversation between the characters over an evening meal was dropped in favour of some dialogue in which Steed and Grenville engage in a music quiz.

For the sequence where the villains think that Steed has met his doom in the swamp, technicians at the studio devised a piece of equipment they called the mud tank, which could be used either on the stage or out on location. This was used to achieve a close-up shot of Steed's glove being sucked under the surface of the swamp.

Having been cast as another of the villains, Gilbert Sexton, Garfield Morgan made his second guest appearance of the season, the previous one having come in the episode 'Game'.

The concept of criminals seizing a strategically-located property in order to launch an attack on nearby dignitaries was not entirely original, as Brian Clemens (under his Tony O'Grady pseudonym) had already used it for an episode of *The Baron* called 'The Maze'. It appears that Nation, who at that time had been script supervisor on *The Baron*, simply recycled the idea for his screenplay.

EMI takeover

Meanwhile, during January 1969, having decided to relinquish their UK film production arm, Warner Brothers sold their shares in ABPC to EMI, who had already acquired 25 percent of the company. This resulted in EMI taking over ABPC – which it renamed EMI Films – and all of its subsidiaries and properties, including the ABC cinema chain, Elstree Studios and the rights to *The Avengers*.

6.33 – 'Bizarre'

The Avengers' final episode, 'Bizarre', was another offering from Brian Clemens. With a story about supposedly dead men who are actually still alive, it bore some similarities both to his earlier *Adam Adamant Lives!* screenplay 'The Terribly Happy Embalmers' and to his Blackman-era episode 'The Undertakers'. Likewise, the opening teaser of a young woman, Helen Pritchard, wandering aimlessly in her nightgown after falling from a speeding train was drawn from a half-hour *Danger Man* episode he had written at the beginning of the decade, entitled 'The Girl in Pink Pyjamas'.

Filming got under way at the start of February 1969 – a month that would see the series' ongoing ITV transmissions averaging an improved 6.8 million viewers per episode, making it the eighth most popular programme on British television. On Friday 7 February John Hough and the third unit shot material of Steed arriving at the gateway to the fictional Happy Meadows funeral parlour and burial plot – in reality the entrance to Camfield Place in Wildhill – in the 1923 Rolls Royce Silver Ghost (KK 4976) he had driven in numerous earlier episodes. Hough was also responsible for the following day's shooting in the snow-covered fields of Kendall Farm, off Watling Street, near Radlett. Present on location were guest cast members Sally Nesbitt, playing Helen Pritchard, and James Kerry, playing Mother's agent Captain Cordell.

Filling in for the episode's principal director Leslie Norman for a single day, Don

Chaffey took charge of the B unit, with whom he had just been working on 'Requiem', with the intention of carrying out another London location shoot. However, due to adverse weather conditions they instead filmed interiors on Stage 5 and additional footage on the studio lot beside the film vaults.

Norman arrived and took over on the fourth day of principal filming, travelling into London with the B unit on Thursday 13 February to complete the planned footage – the very last piece of location work undertaken for the series – involving Steed getting run down by a Bedford Beagle van in Weymouth Mews, W1, with stuntman Paul Weston doubling for Macnee.

Toward the end of February, Hough's third unit joined Norman's main B unit, working alongside each other at times in order to complete the episode, and with it the entire series.

The moving train footage seen in the episode was reused from a March 1967 shoot for the episode 'A Funny Thing Happened on the Way to the Station', and included material of a steam locomotive and coaches emerging from the tunnel near what is now Warner Brothers Studios, Leavesden, near Watford, filmed from the road bridge on Gypsy Lane.

As part of their costumes, the hostesses welcoming visitors to the exclusive Paradise Plot area of Happy Meadows all wore metallic chain-mail guard girl dresses originally created by Paco Rabanne for Charles K Feldman's 1967 James Bond spoof *Casino Royale*.

Helen Pritchard's dog, seen in the guard's van of the train, was actually called Fred, and he spent a single day at the studios along with his handler and owner, a Mrs Tate.

A professional snooker player named Sydney Lee was employed for a couple of days, presumably to be filmed potting some balls in close-up for a sequence where Steed has a game with Mother at his headquarters, but no such shots are included in the footage in the finished episode.

The closing tag scene, showing Steed accidentally blasting off into outer space with Tara in a rocket he has constructed from a kit, was realised using stock footage of an Atlas SLV-3 being launched by NASA from Launch Complex 14 at Cape Canaveral, Florida circa 1966.

The Avengers in print

Even as production on *The Avengers* drew to a close, the series was still generating magazine articles and features, such as a profile of Linda Thorson in the Thursday 27 February 1969 edition of *TV Times*.

Meanwhile, in the USA, this month also saw the publication by Berkley Medallion of the fifth and final original American novel based on the series. This was *Moon Express* by Norman Daniels, another adventure for Steed and Tara King – although once again they were joined on the cover by Mrs Peel, who plays no part in the plot.

Scheduling alterations

Having screened only seven episodes on Friday evenings, Grampian reverted to their earlier Wednesday evening time slot for *The Avengers*, beginning with 'The Rotters' at 8.00 pm on 26 February 1969. According to ratings research data, the series underwent a slight drop in UK viewing numbers this month, to 6.2 million per episode, although it still managed to achieve nineteenth place in the chart of most watched programmes.

Production wraps on *The Avengers*

Patrick Macnee and Linda Thorson both completed their final scenes for 'Bizarre', and for the series as a whole, on Friday 28 February 1969 on Stage 2 at Elstree. Macnee was released from the shoot by director Leslie Norman at 12.25 pm, although Thorson remained until the end of the working day, being officially released at 5.16 pm.

The following Monday, 3 March 1969, was the last day of principal photography on the series, although this involved only guest actors Roy Kinnear – playing a character known as Bagpipes Happychap – and Michael Balfour and Patrick Connor – playing gravediggers Tom and Bob – on the Paradise Plot set, where Norman called the final shot and was satisfied with the result at 11.25 am. For some unknown reason, after lunch the three actors were kept on set until 2.45 pm before being allowed to return to their dressing rooms, then all the equipment was switched off and the lights went out. *The Avengers* – arguably the most successful British television series ever, having been sold to 90 different countries at the time – had officially ceased production.

Recalling the situation at *The Avengers* at 50 convention at Chichester University in June 2011, Brian Clemens offered the opinion that the Thorson episodes had had the most diverse storylines, that the series had undoubtedly still had potential and that he and Fennell could have easily produced another season.

The closing tag scene of 'Bizarre' ended on an upbeat note, as Mother – who had originally been intended to join Steed and Tara on their impromptu rocket trip into space, until a rewrite had him disembark just before the launch to take a snapshot for his album – spoke directly to camera, saying: 'They'll be back … You can depend on it.'

Yes, *The Avengers* would be back – or at least, John Steed would – but that would be a completely different story.

PART TWO
THE IN-BETWEEN YEARS

THE STAGE PLAY AND RADIO ADAPTATION

WHO'S WHO???

Transmissions continue

Although filming on *The Avengers* had ceased at the beginning of March 1969, it would take several further months for the regional ITV companies to complete their initial screenings of the final season. As in the past, a number of them subjected the series to scheduling changes during the course of the run.

Yorkshire kept their transmissions on Saturdays but moved them to an 8.00 pm slot, beginning on 1 March 1969 with 'Stay Tuned'. Abandoning their 7.30 pm start time, ATV also opted for 8.00 pm from the following week, when they screened 'Fog', forcing Harlech and Ulster, the two remaining regions still taking their line-feed, to do the same.

A problem arose in the Yorkshire region on Wednesday 19 March when the transmitter at Emley Moor near Huddersfield collapsed due to a combination of oscillating winds and a build-up of ice on both the mast and the guide cables. This resulted in Yorkshire being unable to transmit the episode 'Who Was That Man I Saw You With?' in its intended slot three days later, although it would eventually be rescheduled to Saturday 10 May. On Sunday 23 March a temporary, 61-metre mast was erected, allowing a limited-range service to resume in time for the screening of 'Homicide and Old Lace' on Saturday 29 March. Almost a month passed before a new, 204-metre mast was acquired from the Swedish army and assembled in order to reinstate transmissions to outlying areas. A permanent replacement concrete tower and mast would not come on line until January 1971.

Meanwhile, with an average viewing figure of 6.2 million per episode, *The Avengers* tied with *News at Ten* and the BBC police drama *Softly Softly* as the fifteenth most popular programme of March 1969.

On Wednesday 9 April, both Southern and Tyne Tees failed to screen an episode in the series' usual slot. Meanwhile, having shown 'My Wildest Dream' in a late evening slot, Border rescheduled the series to Sundays at 7.25 pm, starting with 'Thingumajig' on 13 April.

Across the Atlantic Ocean, *The Avengers*' American run concluded when the ABC network wrapped up their coast-to-coast transmissions with 'Bizarre' on Monday 21 April.

Ulster dropped the series for one week in April, but reinstated it seven days later with 'Killer' at 9.00 pm, before screening 'My Wildest Dream' at 11.05 pm and then reverting to 8.00 pm for their last two transmissions.

Southern dropped the series again on Wednesday 7 May, this time in favour of the light entertainment special *Frankie Howerd at the Poco a Poco*.

On Saturday 17 May, Westward and Channel recommenced their transmissions of the series at 8.25 pm with 'Game'.

In June, Granada – who up till this point had been extremely consistent in their scheduling of the season – dropped episodes on two occasions, the first on Sunday 1 June for an international football match between England and Mexico, and the second on Sunday 29 June for a documentary about the Royal Family.

MiniKillers

Meanwhile, Diana Rigg was on location on the Costa Brava in Spain, taking the lead in a silent 8mm short entitled *MiniKillers*[33], which ran to almost 28 minutes and was obviously based around her Emma Peel image. This was the brainchild of Wolfgang von Chmielewski, who both directed and co-wrote it with his brother Michael, and its roots could be traced back three years.

Von Chmielewski was an employee of the German television station WDR in Dusseldorf, where his father Christian was in overall control, giving him the opportunity to make short, low-budget films for them, one such example being *Pop Art USA*, shot on location in New York in 1966. On forming his own production company, Accentfilm International, later that same year, von Chmielewski realised that he needed a major name for his first independent film. Diana Rigg's management was thus approached, presumably when the actress was between contracts with ABC for *The Avengers*, and although the project was never intended to be anything more than a low-quality Super 8 movie, a fee was agreed for her appearance. The result was a silent, black and white short called *Das Diadem*, which ran for almost 13 minutes, along with a colour version known as *Der Goldene Schlüssel*. Von Chmielewski took the director credit on both.

Three years later, Rigg was approached again, and after her commitment to the James Bond film *On Her Majesty's Secret Service* had ended with the completion of its production on Monday 23 June 1969, she filmed *MiniKillers* during a six day shoot in the last week of that month.

MiniKillers was always intended only for the home projector market, and then only in France. It was also made available in four separate reels of approximately eight minutes' duration each, individually titled 'Operation: Costa Brava', 'Heroin', 'Macabre' and 'Flamenco'.

The film sees Rigg playing an investigative reporter who learns about a gang of international drug dealers smuggling illegal substances into Spain hidden inside large, clockwork toy dolls that fire poison from their eyes – making them the MiniKillers of the title. The storyline thus allowed Rigg to utilise the stunt fighting abilities she had acquired while filming *The Avengers*.

While on location in Spain, Rigg stayed at the luxury Santa Maria hotel in Lloret Del March and had a Mercedes 600 limousine at her disposal, though she also spent

---

[33] The title was presented on screen as one word, all in capitals.

considerable time at the Hotel Monterrey for filming purposes.

When interviewed as part of a feature on *MiniKillers* in the German magazine *Bravo* dated Monday 18 August 1969, Rigg claimed, 'The salary is not less than what I got for the James Bond movie *On Her Majesty's Secret Service.*' The actress also stated that after the shoot she had no immediate plans to perform in any other productions, as she intended relaxing at her home in Ibiza – though in the event her rest would be short-lived, as sometime during July she would commence work on the film *Julius Caesar.*

Together, *Das Diadem* and *The Goldene Schlüssel* had moved 130,000 units, and Wolfgang von Chmielewski had high expectations for his latest creation, having already signed a licensing agreement with an American company. However, despite his optimism, *MiniKillers* would never be retailed in the United States or in the UK.

Adding even more mystery to that already surrounding this production, cameraman Josef Kaufmann claims that he has the only 16mm print of *MiniKillers* in existence, and that it includes dialogue – which if true would presumably mean that each scene was filmed twice, once without dialogue and once with.

European cinema screening

On 1 October 1969 an unauthorised version of *The Avengers* opened at the Odeon cinema in Lisbon, Portugal. This was another instance of someone simply putting two episodes together and calling the end result a film. 'Never, Never Say Die' was coupled with 'The Superlative Seven' and augmented with part of a promotional film created for overseas markets, in which Steed performs an introduction.

The Black Widow

The comic book world felt *The Avengers'* influence again in 1970, when Marvel Comics decided to overhaul their character Natasha Romanoff, better known as the Black Widow. She emerged in issue no. 86 of *The Amazing Spider Man*, published in July 1970, wearing a dark blue skin-tight catsuit very similar to Emma Peel's trademark attire. Having ditched her old fishnet tights outfit, she now looked the complete super spy. This appearance with Spider Man was simply a taster for her own ongoing comic strip in *Amazing Adventures* nos. 1 to 8, after which she joined the Shield organisation, becoming involved in crime, espionage and science fiction scenarios in a number of other titles. Over the decades, the Black Widow has featured in lengthy runs in *Daredevil, The Champions, The Avengers*[34], *Captain America* and *The Secret Avengers*. In both the 2010 movie *Iron Man 2* and the 2012 blockbuster *Avengers Assemble* the character was played on screen by Scarlett Johansson, still attired in a variation of her Emma Peel catsuit.

The Avengers **on stage**

Considerable interest was generated in April 1971 when an announcement was made indicating that *The Avengers* would enter a new sphere of entertainment in the form of a stage play adaptation. Writers Brian Clemens and Terence Feely, both of whom were experienced contributors to *The Avengers* on television, provided a script that captured

---

[34] The Marvel Comics superhero title, not the television series covered in this book.

the feel of the series, complete with humour and science fiction elements that required elaborate special effects. The venture's producer, John Mather, convinced both writers that with experienced stagehands and clever props, their vision could be successfully realised on stage. All three men were keen to ensure that the play retained the series' familiar ingredients, such as Steed's bowler hat and umbrella, but at the same time wanted it to have a much lighter touch. However, the production, budgeted at £35,000, was to prove technically challenging, as the script had 15 scene changes and included amongst other things a helicopter, Steed's vintage Bentley and a large brainwashing computer.

Initially Mather approached Patrick Macnee to reprise the role of John Steed, but the actor declined, feeling that the theatre was not the correct environment for *The Avengers*. On Tuesday 25 May, the *Daily Mirror* revealed that Simon Oates – who had guested in the television episodes 'You Have Just Been Murdered' and 'Super Secret Cypher Snatch' – would be donning the bowler hat instead. The newspaper added that Steed's female partner Hannah Wild – a character featured in the television episode 'The Superlative Seven' – would be portrayed by Sue Lloyd – who had also guested in the series, in the episode 'A Surfeit of H_2O'.

When first approached regarding the role of Steed, Oates had telephoned Macnee, whom he considered a friend, fearing that he had not been consulted. However, Macnee had provided reassurance and given his blessing to his fellow actor, whose main claim to fame at the time was playing Dr John Ridge in the BBC series *Doomwatch*.

Another actress who auditioned for the Hannah Wild role was Joanna Lumley, who felt that she had failed to get it because at the time she was much better known as a fashion model than as an actress – although she was destined to become an Avengergirl later in *The New Avengers*.

Cast as the play's sultry villainess Madame Gerda and as MI5 operative Carruthers were two other performers whose résumés included *The Avengers* on television, namely Kate O'Mara, who had appeared in 'Stay Tuned', and comedy writer and actor Jeremy Lloyd, who had featured in both 'From Venus with Love' and 'Thingumajig'. John F Landry replaced Patrick Newell for this production as Steed's superior, Mother.

Madame Gerda and her female followers in the story's Forces of Evil organisation were all costumed in shiny PVC outfits designed by Ronald Cobb and made by fetish clothing manufacturer Atomage Ltd, though unfortunately they tended to squeak when the actresses moved. Maintaining the tradition started by Honor Blackman and Diana Rigg, in some scenes Lloyd wore a red leather catsuit/fighting suit designed by theatrical costumier Berkley Sutcliffe and again made by Atomage Ltd. The play's fight sequences, which in some instances were played for laughs, were choreographed by stuntman Tim Condren, who would later appear on screen in an episode of *The New Avengers*.

The Tuesday 25 May 1971 edition of the *Daily Express* reported that performances of *The Avengers* play would begin at the Birmingham Theatre on Thursday 15 July, directed by comedy actor Leslie Phillips, best known for his portrayal of upper class characters on the big screen. Considering the complexities involved in mounting such an ambitious production, and his lack of directing experience, Phillips seemed a strange choice to take on this responsibility.

The Stage and Television Today were slower to report events, although they awarded the play front page status in their Thursday 3 June issue. Keeping the momentum going, they later announced both the venue and the opening night in their Thursday 24

June edition.

The show played for ten days at the Birmingham Theatre – now the Birmingham Hippodrome – with the final performance taking place on Saturday 24 July, prior to a planned relocation to the Prince of Wales Theatre in London. Unfortunately however the production was plagued by problems from the outset, suffering from insufficient advance preparation and some presentation requirements that were too complicated to be successfully achieved with the resources available.

Performance problems

In her book *It Seemed Like a Good Idea at the Time*, Sue Lloyd later recalled how hectic things were behind the scenes on the play's opening night. Earlier, someone in authority had realised that the production was so technically challenging that the theatre's staffing levels were inadequate to cope with it, resulting in the management having to augment their team by drafting in additional stagehands from Birmingham's other main theatre, the Alexandra.

Most of the glitches that occurred on that first night in Birmingham were looked upon mainly as teething troubles. However, an incident where O'Mara was on a rope ladder attached to the helicopter prop and it broke, dropping her centre stage, could have had serious consequences. Luckily the actress suffered only bruising, but on grounds of safety she insisted on wearing a harness for future performances. Another, more minor issue arose when a plastic bottle with which Hannah was supposed to knock someone out slipped from Sue Lloyd's fingers and went bouncing across the stage, leaving her with no option but to improvise – something the play's cast would find themselves having to do quite frequently.

In scripting the play, Clemens and Feely had decided that Madame Gerda should use the power of invisibility in order to secure her dreams of conquest by destroying the world's spy agencies from within. However, this illusion proved more difficult to achieve than first thought, and was the root of many of the production's problems. In her autobiography *Vamp Until Ready*, O'Mara later outlined some of the difficulties caused by special props and sets, including a wall section with two wide rubber strips through which she had to force herself in order to disappear from view in a scene where Madame Gerda became invisible. As she recalled, this proved so difficult to achieve that she would sometimes rebound from the rubber strips into Simon Oates, who as Steed was backing her up against what appeared to be a wall. A number of press reviews of the play mentioned the theatre lighting being momentarily cut to allow O'Mara to vanish seemingly into thin air, in a 'now you see me, now you don't' scenario.

Some scenes in the play were performed against a large projection screen displaying a filmed background – the technique known as back-projection in the film industry – although on one occasion the technician controlling this accidentally rolled the film in reverse.

Another of the play's special props was a mummy case incorporating a secret back door through which O'Mara could exit unseen by the audience in a scene where Madame Gerda uses invisibility in order to escape from an advancing Steed, who brandishes the sword from his umbrella and then plunges it through the sarcophagus. One night, however, a stagehand neglected to unlock the secret back door and O'Mara found herself trapped inside the sarcophagus as Oates prepared to lunge with the sword. She resorted to shaking the prop from side to side to draw Oates' attention to the fact that something was wrong.

The worst offender of all the items on stage was a prop sofa that became notorious for malfunctioning during performances. Its temperamental nature was again due to the incorporation of a mechanism designed to create the illusion of characters becoming invisible. This allowed the prop to open up so that the cast members concerned could pass through it and then wait out of sight behind it until an opportunity arose for them to leave the stage unseen. In her aforementioned book, Sue Lloyd later recounted how during one performance the sofa opened up unexpectedly part-way through a scene, causing Jeremy Lloyd to become trapped in it with only his head and shoulders sticking out. Unable to contain herself, she burst into laughter, as did the audience, prompting the lowering of the curtain. During the unscheduled interlude, two stagehands then released a thankful Jeremy Lloyd. The problem with the prop was that the lever the performers had to use in order to activate the mechanism whenever they wanted their character to vanish did not always return to its original position. Hence when someone else sat on the sofa later on, they could find themselves suddenly ejected out of the back without warning, leaving whoever they were sharing the scene with to attempt to ad-lib their way out of the situation.

A number of decorative columns that appeared to be solid were in fact hollow and – like the section of wall with the rubber strips – elasticated to allow O'Mara to disappear inside them. Once when the actress entered one of these columns, however, the elasticated entrance caught her hairpiece when it snapped shut behind her, leaving it attached to the fake stonework and fully visible to the audience for the remainder of the scene.

The London run

The play's London performances at the Prince of Wales Theatre in the West End got under way on Monday 2 August 1971. However, despite further rehearsals having taken place, mishaps still occurred. Whereas a preview of the production in that day's edition of *The Sun* was positive and upbeat, a review by theatre critic Arthur Thurkell in the following day's *Daily Mirror*, after he had attended the opening night's performance, made it clear that he was less than impressed.

John Mather and others involved obviously hoped for an extended West End run, but due to declining attendances it was actually curtailed after only three weeks, spelling the end of *The Avengers* stage play. Over 20 years later, when interviewed by the magazine *TV Zone*, co-writer Terence Feely said that he and Brian Clemens had been assured by John Mather that the play's special effects could be achieved just by falling back on tried and trusted theatre techniques. It appears however that the effects were actually quite groundbreaking for the theatre of the time, and had not been perfected, needing more preparation and rehearsal time before the cast and crew put themselves on the treadmill of nightly performances.

The Avengers **radio series**

Four months later, at the end of 1971, *The Avengers* entered another different medium when it debuted as an audio drama on Springbok Radio, an English-language station run by the South African Broadcasting Corporation (SABC). For the next two years,

Springbok Radio would present a series of adaptations of screenplays from *The Avengers'* filmed seasons, subdivided into 15-minute segments broadcast every evening from Monday to Friday. The 7.15 pm to 7.30 pm time slot in which the series was placed was sponsored by the multinational company Unilever, promoting their washing powder Cold Water Omo, a brand name also used in the UK at the time.

Two pilot programmes for the series had been recorded earlier at AFS Studios, overseen by producer Dave Gooden, but neither had fulfilled what SABC were looking for, so both had been abandoned and apparently erased without any details of their content being logged. However, when interviewed some years later, actor Donald Monat, who played Steed in the radio series, recalled having portrayed the chief villain in both pilots, opposite someone else as Steed.

The taping of the broadcast episodes took place at Sonovision Studios' Plein Street premises in Johannesburg. Gooden hired British actor Tony Jay both to adapt the television scripts into the required format and to direct the recordings. Jay was also instrumental in casting the leads, Donald Monat as Steed and Diane Appleby as Mrs Emma Peel. Both actors were British expatriates who boasted considerable South African radio drama and comedy experience.

Having received a consignment of shooting scripts from EMI, Jay selected a couple that he thought were less dependent on visuals than the others and began preparing and casting two five-part serials, getting them ready for recording within a fortnight – a speedy turnaround time that was quite standard on South African radio productions in the early '70s. However, Jay quickly realised that there was no way the original dialogue could adequately convey certain aspects of the storylines, and that portions would have to be replaced with more radio-friendly material. Eventually he decided that a narrator would have to be used to provide occasional exposition. Newscaster and actor Hugh Rouse was recruited for this job, and his amusing delivery added an extra element that helped to make the radio series work.

The recording of a five- or six-part serial would be completed in a single afternoon, with the performers usually having no pre-knowledge of the script or any rehearsal time. The cast generally numbered no more than eight, some of whom could find themselves playing up to three different roles, but both they and the technicians would be experienced at working in this manner. Sonovision's policy was to have three personnel occupying the control room during recordings, namely producer David Gooden, director Tony Jay and sound engineer (aka controller) Paul Wright, who would oversee the production. Laurie Johnson's theme from the season five episodes was adopted for the radio episodes, and portions of his *Synthesis* album released on the EMI Columbia record label in 1970 were also used for background music. All sound effects and incidental music cues were played in live during recording.

At the time when he became involved with the project, Jay had actually been planning to return to the UK, but he agreed to remain in Johannesburg for six months to establish the series. He eventually departed sometime in the middle of 1972. Gooden then found a replacement in another actor/director, Dennis Folbigge, who upon arrival discovered that quite a number of the Emma Peel screenplays had already been adapted, leaving mainly Tara King storylines still to be done. Folbigge nevertheless decided to retain Mrs Peel as Steed's partner for these, adapting them accordingly. He also introduced Mother into the series – something Jay had refused to do, as he disliked the character.

Folbigge's interpretations of the shooting scripts tended to result in slightly longer serials, running for six or seven instalments each. He also wrote new adaptations of some of the ones that Jay had already tackled, so in these instances a second version was made from the same source material. Several serials had different titles from their equivalent television episodes, but it is unknown whether this was because the South African production team simply decided to rename them or whether some of the scripts with which they had been provided by EMI were draft versions bearing working titles.

Given the nature of the medium for which they written, the radio serials understandably differed in many respects from the televised episodes, although for a series that was so visual, *The Avengers* transferred extremely well to the spoken word. To take an example, the serial 'A Grave Charge', based on the season six episode 'Bizarre', not only substituted Emma Peel for Tara King, but also introduced a newly-created character, Croaker Waysgoose, and the latest branch of British Intelligence, a section known as Strange and Inexplicable Happenings. Unlike in the televised version, Steed accompanies Captain Cordell to the area where Helen, the young woman in the nightgown, is found wandering in a dazed condition, having been pushed from the speeding train. Unsurprisingly, the radio serial has no rocket blasting off into outer space at its conclusion, just Mother toasting Steed's apparent resurrection from the dead.

Many of the other serials also make interesting departures from their television counterparts or boast noteworthy production features, too numerous to be fully detailed within the scope of this book. The adaptation of 'The Morning After', for instance, includes some particularly effective background music, very reminiscent of composer Edwin Astley's fast-moving theme to the ITC film series *Department S*.

Sonovision were interested in marketing the serials on cassette, but unfortunately they could not secure an extension of the rights from EMI for this purpose. Hence, as they appeared to have no remaining commercial value, the master tapes were all apparently erased or recorded over shortly afterwards, in keeping with standard practice at the time, when magnetic tape was a costly resource. Unfortunately preservation was never considered. However, thanks to radio enthusiasts in South Africa recording them off air at the time on reel-to-reel machines, 19 of the serials do still survive, mainly on quarter-inch tape. Eventually in 2002 all these recordings came under the control of Alan and Alys Hayes of the *Avengers on the Radio* website, who took it upon themselves to completely restore the serials; a mammoth task that took ten years to achieve.

PART THREE
PRODUCTION HISTORY
THE NEW AVENGERS

SEASON ONE

THREE HANDED GAME

A French-led revival

In the summer of 1975, possibly inspired by a recent television commercial for Timex watches in which Macnee appeared dressed as Steed (although the character was not referred to by name), a French director named Rudolph Roffi contacted Brian Clemens wanting to locate Macnee and Thorson to secure their participation in a similar project for him. This resulted in Macnee and Thorson starring in two *The Avengers*-themed commercials for Laurent-Perrier champagne, filmed at Elstree and intended for screening on both French and Spanish television.

Because of their enormous popularity, the Thorson episodes had been continually repeated on French television, and Roffi had been under the impression that the series was still being made. He was aghast when Clemens – who was present for the filming of the commercials – informed him that the show had ceased production in March 1969. Clemens explained that the conclusion of the final episode, 'Bizarre', had been constructed so as to allow for further adventures sometime in the future, in the hope that one day the series could be revived. However, despite *The Avengers* being an extremely popular commodity, Clemens had been unable to obtain funding for such a large-scale film series from any British source.

Roffi was highly enthusiastic about the idea of the series being resurrected, and during the shoot he sounded out both Macnee and Thorson about the possibility of them returning to their familiar roles. Several weeks later he telephoned Clemens again, announcing that he had secured sufficient backing from two French companies, IDTV and Television Productions, to film another batch of episodes. He then posed the question: 'When can we start production?'

Over a hectic three month period, Clemens, his former co-producer Albert Fennell and composer Laurie Johnson devised a plan of action that included forming a production company, The Avengers (Film & TV) Enterprises Ltd. Considering it essential to include Patrick Macnee in their revival, the producers contacted him through his agent John Redway, who advised the actor to accept the role as the remuneration was extremely good and also included five per cent of the profits.

On Thursday 11 December 1975, *The Stage and Television Today* carried the news that *The Avengers* was to be revived in the form of a new series of 30 episodes. This was also reported two days later in *Screen International*, which quoted the production's total budget of almost £4 million. This time around, Steed would apparently share his adventures not only with a female partner but also with a younger male colleague, and it was reported that Brian Clemens was already working on several screenplays – one of which would become the episode 'The Eagle's Nest'.

Filming on the new series was scheduled to commence at Pinewood Studios in April 1976, the producers having discovered that their former production base of Elstree Studios would be unavailable. The whole Elstree facility had been booked for the period from March to July 1976 by the American production company Lucasfilm, to film their science fiction movie *Star Wars*.

An agreement had already been struck between IDTV, The Avengers Enterprises and EMI – who had also invested money in the project – allowing Thames the first option to acquire the new series for UK transmission. However, *Screen International* lamented the fact the series was being payrolled by French companies, pointing out that ITV (perhaps meaning ITC) were no longer playing a very active part in big-budget programme production.

Unmade story outline

Having become aware of the impending revival, scriptwriter Tony Williamson, who had contributed nine episodes to the original series, wrote a letter dated Thursday 18 December to Albert Fennell, suggesting a possible story outline involving the kidnapping of Queen Elizabeth II. Williamson thought this would make for an ideal pilot episode, but it appears that Clemens and Fennell disagreed, and the outline was rejected.

Revising the series format

Sometime during January 1976, Clemens and Fennell assembled a basic two-page document outlining the style of the new series, for distribution to potential writers and directors. Beginning with notes on style, the document acknowledged that *The Avengers* needed to progress with the times and transform into *The New Avengers*. To maintain the pace of the action, characters were not to be filmed arriving somewhere or coming through doors; time would be saved by this, as they would be straight into a scene. Likewise, establishing shots of buildings were said to be undesirable, unless the shot exhibited something else, such as the villain approaching. Fight sequences needed to be handled in a certain manner, with the new Avengergirl shown to have graceful and sexy movements and the new male character filmed as a blur of fast action. Steed, complete with bowler hat and umbrella, would remain in character from the original series, though some expansion of his background would ultimately occur. Another aim of the producers was to develop a different look for *The New Avengers*, which would be created by the increased use of location filming and a faster pace in the narrative. They also warned of the need to maintain good taste, though they promised that major censorship issues would be eradicated at the script editing stage, hence writers and directors could focus on keeping things interesting and entertaining. The document lacked any detailed characterisation of the three leads, failing to indicate what they would or wouldn't do in given situations, although this was probably intentional, as Clemens envisaged writing the majority of the episodes himself.

Casting Charley and Mike Gambit

Sometime early in 1976 the *News of the World*'s showbusiness columnist Ivan Waterman suggested Nina Baden-Semper as the new female star of *The Avengers*, a suggestion echoed by his counterpart Chris Kenworthy in *The Sun*, although he also saw Kate O'Mara, Susan Penhaligon, Lesley-Anne Down and Prunella Gee as obvious candidates. On Monday 19 January the *Daily Express* also reported on the search for the new Avengergirl, which had recently got under way. The following day, Tuesday 20 January, a large number of hopefuls for the role underwent a 15-minute interview with Clemens at Elstree Studios. Those hoping to impress the producer and progress to the next stage in the selection process included Sally Farmiloe and Marilyn Galsworthy.

A week later, on Tuesday 27 January, the producers saw 82 performers, both female and male, for further auditions, this time at Pinewood Studios. A process of elimination took place over the course of the day. This started with all those who clearly failed to meet the producers' requirements being placed on a list and then dismissed. On the female side, this included Lynda Bellingham, Susie Baker, Sharon Duce, Judy Loe, Sharon Maughan and Vicki Michelle. The male side of the list was considerably shorter, though it included David Roper, who at the time was a regular in the Granada sitcom *The Cuckoo Waltz*, and Martin Fisk, who would later win a guest role in the episode 'The Last of the Cybernauts …??'. On a second list were placed the names of all those the producers considered as possible contenders for the two roles, although as the day continued, the high standard of candidates meant that all of these left early as well. Several well-known actresses suffered rejection at this point, including Jan Francis, Jan Harvey, Geraldine James, Barbara Kellerman, Geraldine Moffat, Carolyn Seymour and Jenny Twigge. Male actors who failed to make this cut included Michael Elphick, John Nettles, David Rintoul and Malcolm Stoddard. On a third and final list were the names of the 19 actresses and seven actors who had impressed the most and were still in the running. However, Clemens, Fennell, Johnson and casting director Mary Selway then faced the difficult task of thinning the numbers down even further.

The next stage in the process was to be a script reading, but before that, further cuts were decided upon. Amongst those who lost out at this stage were Jacky Allouis, who had previously appeared in *The Avengers* in the episode 'Whoever Shot Poor George Oblique XR40?', Jill Gascoine, Prunella Gee, Lisa Harrow and Louise Jameson, who would go on to win the role of Leela in *Doctor Who*; plus on the male side John Hug, who would later become a semi-regular on the second season of *Space: 1999*, Tommy Boyle and Robert Tayman.

Thirteen actresses progressed to read for the producers, and those eliminated at this stage included Elizabeth Cassidy, who would later play the female lead in the BBC's *Gangsters*, Sarah Douglas, Rula Lenska, Diana Weston and Trudi van Doorne. Only six got over this hurdle and were then screen tested. These were Gabrielle Drake, Cassandra Harris, Joanna Lumley, Diana Quick, Julia Schofield and Ann Zelda. Only three male actors were screen-tested, namely Lewis Collins, Gareth Hunt and Harry Meacher.

Gabrielle Drake and Lewis Collins were paired up for their three-minute test, obviously to see how they sparked off each other. So too were the two ultimately successful candidates, Joanna Lumley – who at this time had shoulder-length brown hair – and Gareth Hunt, who together played a short, Clemens-scripted action scene with a sprinkling of humour. So well did this go that shots from it would actually be incorporated into the version of the series' opening title sequence used for the later American transmissions (which would differ from the standard version used for the UK – see Part Four for further details).

So that the producers could be confident of Lumley's ability to handle the more physically demanding elements of the role, the actress then underwent a further screen test comprising a short fight scene with stuntman Vic Armstrong.

Eventually the six remaining actresses were whittled down to two: Lumley and Diana Quick. Although Quick was easily the more experienced, the three producers were unanimous in their choice of Lumley for Steed's new female partner, whom Clemens had named Charley.

For the male role, meanwhile, the producers all agreed that Hunt was the best candidate. Stories have since emerged that he was always Clemens' favourite to portray the character he had named Mike Gambit, and after the screen tests it was simply a matter of him convincing Fennell and Johnson.

Purdey

Having attended the Pinewood tests at short notice, Lumley returned to Italy to continue a modelling assignment for catalogue fashion supplier Grattan. Exhausted from her journey, she was relaxing in her hotel room when the telephone rang. It was a call from her London-based agent, who told her that Clemens, Fennell and Johnson had been impressed by her performances and that the female lead in *The New Avengers* was hers. Clemens later admitted that Lumley had been a front-runner from the outset, as he had met and been impressed with her some five years earlier when he had visited director Robert Fuest on the Elstree set of the movie *The Abominable Dr Phibes*, in which she had a minor role that was deleted from the final edit.

Initially it was envisaged that the female Avenger would be Steed's niece – recognising the age difference between them – but this idea was dropped at an early stage in the development of the series. However, it was not until several screenplays had already been written that a decision was made to dispense with the character name Charley. This came about because the producers realised that the cosmetics giant Revlon had a perfume called Charlie, and they wanted to avoid inadvertently giving this free publicity. They gladly accepted Lumley's own suggestion of Purdey as a replacement name. This was always thought to have been solely inspired by the high-quality shotgun-maker James Purdey & Sons, though later, in her book *Stare Back and Smile*, Lumley admitted that fashion model Sue Purdie (different spelling) had also been an influence.

Press conference

On Monday 8 March 1976, a major press conference was held at the Dorchester Hotel in London, where Joanna Lumley and Gareth Hunt were publicly announced as playing Steed's latest partners. In publicity leading up to this event, Brian Clemens' imagination had clearly gone into overdrive, with him stating that the new Avengergirl would be a leggy stockings-and-suspenders girl, displaying glimpses of thigh. Consequently when Lumley attended the launch wearing tights, the assembled reporters and photographers were disappointed to say the least. Feeling misled, they voiced their displeasure at not being able to deliver what their Fleet Street bosses wanted. Fearing that negative coverage would result, Albert Fennell persuaded Lumley to borrow someone else's stockings and suspender belt to pose together with a bowler hat, umbrella and revolver. This was clearly what the popular press wanted, and a photograph from the shoot appeared in the following day's *Daily Mirror*. Details of the casting had obviously been leaked prior to the press conference, however, as the *Daily Mail* got the scoop when it revealed the news on the morning of 8 March itself. Clemens meanwhile generated further interest by encouraging the rumour that one of the earlier Avengergirls would make an appearance in the new series.

Thursday 11 March saw *The Stage and Television Today* give further coverage to *The New Avengers*, confirming that Thames would have the first option of screening the series in the UK. Again this was backed up in a contemporary issue of *Screen International*. Robert Norris, who had assisted Howard Thomas in selling the monochrome Diana Rigg episodes to the American ABC network and was now with the company Film and Television Marketing, was also mentioned as having been enlisted as the consultant for overseas sales. However, after some thought, Thames decided against investing any money in the series, as they already had their own in-house production company, Euston Films, which handled all their television film series requirements.

Pre-production

Pre-production on the new series was meanwhile under way at Pinewood Studios, which at the time were offering free office space to any company willing to make a production there. Clemens, Fennell and Johnson all had separate offices opening into the main production office, where production assistant Linda Pearson and production co-ordinator Patricia Robinson were based. Pearson had plenty of experience for her job, having previously worked as Monty Berman's PA on various ITC film series produced at Elstree during the '60s and early '70s. Robinson, for her part, had enjoyed a long working relationship with Laurie Johnson and would later marry film editor/director Graeme Clifford, who also worked on *The New Avengers*. As Patricia Clifford, she would later progress to being a production manager, and by the late '80s she would be working in the United States as both a producer and an executive producer on television movies.

Also hard at work on preparations for the new series was production supervisor Ron Fry, who was busy recruiting the crew members needed to film the episodes. These would include a number who had been associated with the original series.

Having a background as a production manager, Albert Fennell's son Robert was appointed as the unit manager, while the location manager position went to Nicholas Gillott, who had performed the same function on *The Sweeney*. Despite limited experience, having worked on only four films, Maggie Cartier found this was no barrier to her being made casting director.

Syd Cain took on the responsibility for production design. Robert Bell, who since the early '60s had worked exclusively on Gerry Anderson productions, became the art director. Leon Davis filled the position of construction manager, having already worked in this capacity on a couple of James Bond movies.

Having previously worked in the wardrobe department on ITC's *The Zoo Gang* and on films going back to the early '60s, Jackie Cummins was well qualified to become the new series' wardrobe supervisor. The set dresser and post-production supervisor positions were both filled by people who had also worked on the Thorson episodes, namely Simon Wakefield and Paul Clay.

All of these crew members would work on all 13 episodes of *The New Avengers'* first season, bringing a continuity to the production.

An early logo for the new series appeared on some of the initial scripts, showing the word 'new' being held between the thumb and forefinger of a hand above the title '*The Avengers'*, but either this was just a temporary measure or the producers decided they could improve on it, as it was subsequently dropped. In its place, Clemens came up with a distinctive series emblem, with a Union Jack-themed rampant lion motif. This reflected the fact that he and Fennell had decided that the series should embrace a patriotic British approach.

Vehicles

The patriotic approach would also extend to the vehicles that the characters drove. Although Lotus expressed interest in renewing the association they had with *The Avengers*, the producers wanted to involve a manufacturer that could supply a wide variety of vehicles, and as the only large-scale British-owned car-makers were British Leyland, they were chosen.

The deal struck between The Avengers Enterprises and British Leyland included an agreement for them to provide Steed's new mode of transport – it having been decided that the new series would not feature the vintage cars that had proved so popular back in the '60s episodes. Something different was required, so Jaguar – then part of British Leyland – had the Broadspeed racing team convert for everyday road use an XJ12C coupe (NWK 60P) of the kind they raced in the European Touring Car Championship in 1976 and 1977. The vehicle was first registered on Monday 3 May 1976 with Jaguar Experimental logged as the owners. Then the front bumper was removed, the spoiler and wheel arch extensions fitted and the bodywork resprayed from lavender to olive green. However, something had been overlooked, and that was the unavailability of road-going tyres for the exceptionally wide Kent Avon wheels. Fortunately, a search further afield located some in the United States, but the delay caused by the transportation of these to the UK meant that the Jaguar – which would become a much-talked-about tailored effect in the series – would be unavailable for use in the first two episodes into production, 'The Eagle's Nest' and 'The Midas Touch'.

After the end of production on *The New Avengers*, the road-going racer, nicknamed the Big Cat, was sold off through the classified ads section of the January 1982 edition of the Jaguar Drivers' Club magazine *Jaguar Driver*. Later, in 1985, a West Bromwich car dealer offered the vehicle to Dave Rogers, author of several books about *The Avengers*, but he declined to purchase it. In March 1991 the Big Cat changed hands again, and was then apparently kept in storage for over 15 years. By 2007 it was reported to be in poor condition, but the then owner, who knew of its history, was unwilling to sell it.

As the Big Cat was unable to appear in 'The Eagle's Nest', Steed was instead allocated a beige Rover 3500 (MOC 229P). This would appear in four other episodes, and he would also be seen to drive a five-year-old green Range Rover (TXC 922J).

Mike Gambit's main vehicle for the series was a sleek Jaguar XJS (NRW 875P) model, which appeared in seven episodes, though like Steed, when circumstances dictated he also drove a Range Rover (LOK 537P).

Purdey's regular transportation was a beige-coloured MGB convertible sports car

(MOC 232P). When this was not required for filming, Brian Clemens frequently used it for everyday commuting. However, the first time he drove it was a very frustrating experience as he was unable to engage reverse gear. Eventually he had to get some Pinewood security personnel to push the car out of the parking bay so that he could proceed forwards. In an oversight at the factory, the gear knob from a different model had been fitted, indicating that the lever should be pulled one way to engage reverse when actually it needed to be pushed in the opposite direction.

Fashions

Fashion would be a major factor in the series, and designer Catherine Buckley was chosen to devise an eye-catching wardrobe for Purdey that would be completely different from the black leather image associated with the original series' female leads. In sharp contrast, the initial drawings to emerge from Buckley's small retail outlet on Westbourne Grove, London W11, depicted extravagant and colourful floaty dresses of chiffon and silk. Lumley's suggestion that as an action girl Purdey would wear fashionable sportswear to allow easy movement for fight sequences was completely disregarded.

Buckley's contributions were extremely elaborate, although generally impractical, a good example of this being a patchwork skirt seen in the episode 'House of Cards', which carried the following warning on its label: 'This garment is made from a jacquard material woven between 1905 and 1935. Because of its age, please handle with great care.' Other costumes created by Buckley contained labelling that strongly advised against washing or dry cleaning, which in some cases made their lifespan out on location somewhat limited. Unfortunately, the designer lacked the resources to maintain a constant supply of new outfits and duplicates, and this resulted in her on-screen credit disappearing after the first four episodes.

Meanwhile, Gareth Hunt's preference for his character Gambit to be casually attired in blue jeans and bomber jackets was also rejected in favour of making him a smartly-dressed man in three-piece suits with expensive shirts and ties.

Steed's fine taste in clothing would go unchanged, although Macnee refused to adopt the then-fashionable flared trousers for his suits, preferring his to be cut straight. Famous as a bespoke provider of military officers' dress uniforms, gentlemen's outfitters Gieves and Hawkes of no. 1 Savile Row, London, were responsible for supplying his wardrobe of elegant suits and accessories.

Joanna Lumley and Gareth Hunt prepare for their roles

Brian Clemens and Albert Fennell wanted *The New Avengers* to have a more realistic look than the Thorson episodes and decided on a policy of using fewer stunt doubles. This meant that, although they had both expected their roles to be physically demanding, Lumley and Hunt ended up having to execute more of the potentially dangerous stunts than they had envisaged. In preparation for this, stunt performers Ray Austin and Cyd Child – both of whom had worked extensively on the original series – devised a rigorous training schedule for the two stars. The music stage at Pinewood Studios was converted into a makeshift gym so that Lumley and Hunt could work out on site daily. This involved a couple of hours of stretching exercises, running and karate training. Hunt then lifted weights for an hour, while Lumley practiced ballet and high kicks, incorporating Purdey's balletic fighting style invented by Child and based on the obscure French martial art Panache.

The Purdey hairstyle

Before filming got under way, Lumley paid a visit to her usual hairstylist, John Frieda at Leonard's salon in Mount Street, London W1. She then returned to the studio sporting a short, streaked-blonde bobbed hairstyle. Having been unaware of her intentions, Clemens was unimpressed, but realised that he and his fellow producers would have to accept it. In the event, Lumley's distinctive look would be a huge hit with the viewing public, creating additional publicity for the show as hairdressers across the UK were bombarded with requests from women wanting a 'Purdey cut'.

Patrick Macnee arrives from the USA

Sometime during March 1976 Patrick Macnee and his daughter Jennifer arrived in London from the United States, where the actor was then residing. Jennifer would return shortly afterwards, leaving her father to rent properties in both Beaconsfield and Bosham, near Chichester for the duration of his stay in the UK. From the outset, Brian Clemens and Albert Fennell had felt that securing Macnee's participation would be crucial to *The New Avengers'* success. They had even offered to show him completed shooting scripts before filming began. In fact that might not have been possible – the few screenplays written by that point appear to have been still at the draft stage, 'The Eagle's Nest' for instance undergoing revisions dated Tuesday 16 and Tuesday 23 March – but Macnee had nevertheless agreed to reprise the role of Steed. He was made extremely welcome on his first day at Pinewood Studios by his old friends Clemens and Fennell, and was then taken to a rehearsal room and introduced to Lumley and Hunt by the director assigned to 'The Eagle's Nest', Desmond Davis.

1.01 – 'The Eagle's Nest'

Desmond Davis was arguably a strange choice to direct 'The Eagle's Nest', as he had virtually no experience with film as opposed to video, but this did not prevent him from setting the style that others would follow. With initial French funding deposited in The Avengers Enterprises' bank account, principal photography got under way sometime in early April 1976 on what would be the first of 13 episodes in *The New Avengers'* debut season. This entailed Davis and the three regulars taking a light plane to the Isle of Skye for a location shoot, also involving some guest cast members.

Determined to impress with the new series' initial outing, Brian Clemens had set part of his screenplay in a monastery on a remote Scottish island called St Dorca, which was realised by filming at Eileen Donan Castle, near Dornie, Ross-shire, in the Highlands of Scotland. Additional Scottish filming included some scenes of a quayside and of Purdey coming ashore in a wetsuit. These were filmed approximately six miles west of the castle in the coastal village of Kyleakin on the Isle of Skye. Sequences of a narrow road with some monks walking along it and with Purdey after she talks to Steed through the window of an inn were shot 15 miles north-west in the small settlement of Milton near the village of Applecross. The episode's opening teaser sequence, involving the agent George Stannard, played by Brian Anthony, being chased by men wielding poison-tipped fishing hooks, was also filmed on the Applecross peninsula, at a small settlement called Little Hill of my Heart. Stannard is seen escaping in a boat from the small bay here, until one of his pursuers casts a fishing rod and the poisoned hook breaks his skin, killing the agent.

The location scouts, including Albert Fennell's son Michael, found the remaining outdoor requirements closer to home, not far from Pinewood Studios in Buckinghamshire. Stoke Park House, the clubhouse of Stoke Poges Golf Club, doubled as the building where medical professor von Claus, played by guest star Peter Cushing, gives a lecture on suspended animation. The car park of the same building was also used for a sequence where Gambit helps himself to a Citroen DS21 to give chase after von Claus is kidnapped and taken away in a van. Travelling at speed, the Citroen – actually Fennell's own car – departs from the golf course grounds via the eastern gateway on Stoke Poges Lane. Then, shot from the driver's point of view, the vehicle powers up Hollybush Lane near Denham toward the barns of Hollybush Farm – one of which has since been demolished and the other rendered invisible from the road due to woodland growth since the '70s. Additional material, shot through the small rear window of the van, shows the Citroen in pursuit down a narrow hedgerow-lined country lane. This was also filmed on Hollybush Lane. Further along Hollybush Lane, both vehicles cross the bridge over the M40 motorway, Gambit having to apply the brakes harshly to avoid an oncoming Volvo that suddenly pulls out of Field Road. This is followed by a shot inside the van as it travels down Hawkswood Lane, near Fulmer.

The villains hatch a plan to stop their pursuer, which involves one named Ralph, played by Charles Bolton, bailing out of the moving van and then standing in the middle of the road brandishing a Luger automatic. This was filmed on Southlands Road near Denham. Ralph waits for the Citroen to round the bend before shooting out both the windscreen and a front tyre, causing Gambit to lose control of the vehicle, which swerves across the road into a ditch. Ralph then moves in fast to finish off the driver, but Gambit is nowhere to be seen. Crossing over into the adjacent field, Ralph suddenly finds himself confronted by the man he has just attempted to kill.

The following fight scene adheres closely to the directive set out in Clemens' and Fennell's outline document for the series back in January 1976, Davis directing the action in a series of close-ups that in the finished edit appear in a succession of short, rapid cuts. Overall this gives exactly the impression that the producers were seeking in Gambit's fight scenes – a blur of fast movement. The end result is that Ralph swallows a cyanide pill to avoid being captured.

Filmed on site somewhere in the Pinewood grounds was a sequence where Purdey is in some woods and comes across guest actor Sydney Bromley's character Hara, a hermit with short term memory loss. In one shot the reverse side of a sign is visible in the distance, indicating that the performers were near the studio perimeter fence.

Exteriors of Stannard's home were shot at Bulstrode Court, a collection of four large apartment blocks on Oxford Road in Gerrards Cross, Buckinghamshire, where Steed pulls up in his new-design Rover 3500 SD1. As this vehicle would not actually appear in showrooms until June, British Leyland insisted that it be transported to and from locations on a trailer covered by a lightweight tarpaulin, so that no-one could photograph it in advance and steal their thunder. As soon as filming was completed, the tarpaulin was quickly replaced.

Lumley chose to play Purdey as an exaggerated version of her own personality, proving to have a talent for puns and one-liners that gave the new series some of its humour content. Hunt's interpretation of Mike Gambit was as an agent of no nonsense and few words who is obviously attracted to Purdey. Their first scene together in 'The Eagle's Nest' establishes both their working relationship and their quick banter, as on arriving at her apartment he tips her out of bed. 'Mike Gambit, one of these days …' she threatens, to which he replies with a double meaning, 'I know, I'm looking forward to it.'

During the rest of the episode, however, Purdey works with Steed in a more traditional *The Avengers* pairing, while Gambit pursues his own lines of investigation. Purdey's fighting abilities are exhibited when she and Steed are confronted by four Nazi troopers and she pirouettes into action, delivering several high kicks to disable them. For this sequence, Lumley kept *The Avengers'* tradition alive by wearing red ankle boots and a green Catherine Buckley-designed catsuit, which the actress actually detested and called the Green Slime.

At one point in the action, after it is revealed that the monastery harbours Nazis intent on launching a Fourth Reich by reviving Adolf Hitler from suspended animation, Steed helps himself to the Walther P38 automatic of one of their number who has been rendered unconscious, only to be learn that it is minus ammunition. Meanwhile, Gambit arrives in the nick of time, sporting a .357 Smith and Wesson Model 19 Combat Magnum revolver, which would be his regular firearm throughout the entire series, though occasionally he would use a chrome-plated example. The Nazis' leader Trasker, played by Derek Farr, fires at the agents with a machine pistol, but instead inadvertently kills the comatose Hitler with some stray bullets.

Steed's bowler hat is revealed to incorporate a concealed radio complete with telescopic aerial, and it still retains the steel crown from the original series, as seen when he uses it to deliver a knockout blow to the local publican Jud, played by Ronald Forfar.

Laurie Johnson, who resumed his role as the series' regular composer, provided some exceptional incidental music for this episode. Portions of the score would later be incorporated in 'A Flavour of *The New Avengers*', the B-side of a seven-inch single release of Johnson's theme music for the show (see below). This would also feature much later as a track on the three-CD set *The Music of Laurie Johnson Volume 3*, issued on the Edsel label in 2009.

Appropriately, when the remaining Nazi villains are rounded up and marched across the bridge at Eileen Dona Castle at the episode's conclusion, it is to the sound of Steed, Purdey and Gambit whistling the 'Colonel Bogey March', often used to mock the Nazi leadership during the Second World War.

A number of members of the episode's guest cast, including Cushing and Farr, had previously appeared in *The Avengers*. The role of a German records woman named Gerda went to Trudi Van Doorne, aka Geraldine Gardner, who had obviously impressed the producers when she took part in the final day of auditions for the role of Charley.

Opening titles and closing credits

Each episode of *The New Avengers* begins with a teaser sequence that pauses on a freeze frame at a crucial moment. The distinctive double five-note opening of Laurie Johnson's original *The Avengers* theme is then heard, but this leads instead into a powerful new marching band piece with electric guitar. This accompanies the opening title sequence, consisting of a succession of silhouettes and images of the leads seen through the rampant lion motif. Also included are credits for Macnee, Hunt, Lumley, Fennell, Clemens and Johnson. The action of the episode the resumes from the freeze frame, which now includes the episode title and writer credit, followed by the director credit.

The closing credits are set against a simple two-tone green title background. For 'The Eagle's Nest', they begin with a special 'Guest Star' credit for Peter Cushing, in line with an initial intention on the producers' part to include a famous name in every episode. In the event, however, this plan would be dropped, apparently due to budget limitations, and there would be few other such credits.

Joanna Lumley and taxi drivers

In her biography *Stare Back and Smile*, Lumley recalled that taxi drivers would frequently inform her that either Honor Blackman or Diana Rigg was their favourite Avengergirl, but would never mention Linda Thorson. However, Lumley believed that *The New Avengers'* French backers, although they initially made no attempt to influence the style or format of the series, were a little disappointed that Thorson had not been invited to reprise her role as Tara King; and Lumley herself felt some gratitude toward Thorson, as without her popularity in France there would have been no *The New Avengers*, no Purdey and no female lead role for her in a major television series.

1.02 – 'The Midas Touch'

The second episode into production, 'The Midas Touch', saw the return of director Robert Fuest, who would later tell interviewers that working on *The Avengers* had opened more doors for him than all his other credits combined – although he would also admit to having been less comfortable on *The New Avengers* than on the original series, despite considering Lumley unquestionably exceptional.

Another story from Brian Clemens, 'The Midas Touch' centres around a young man who is a carrier of all known contagious diseases but immune to all of them himself, and the havoc he can cause. The second draft of the screenplay, featuring Charley as opposed to Purdey, was completed by Clemens on Tuesday 23 March 1976.

Patrick Macnee, Joanna Lumley and guest actors Ronald Lacey and Tim Condren all went on location to Terminal 3 at Heathrow Airport to film a sequence where Condren's character, the hit man Boz, attempts to assassinate Lacey's, Hong Kong Harry. Lacey was inadvertently stranded in costume at Heathrow when the crew departed after filming and forgot him.

Exiting quickly from the scene of the crime, Boz departs driving an Aston Martin DBS, pursued closely by Purdey and Gambit in the latter's Jaguar XJS. A lengthy car chase follows. Initially the two vehicles are seen on Rifle Place and Hunt Street, London W11 – both of which would be demolished some years later and replaced by Hunt Close. Speeding along Olaf Street, W11, Gambit is forced to brake heavily to avoid a pedestrian crossing the road. Then both vehicles pass under the railway viaduct on Freston Road, W10, with the Jaguar mounting the pavement. From here they career through an open-air market, causing havoc among the stallholders, in a specially-staged sequence underneath the M40 Westway accessed from Kingsdown Close, W10. The Aston Martin then leads the Jaguar off St Anns Road, W11, passing a red telephone box situated on a traffic island, and into Latimer Road – which now no longer exists due to major redevelopment since the '70s. This is followed by additional material filmed under the Westway, featuring both vehicles on a loose surface, with the Jaguar performing a couple of handbrake turns before the chase continues. Turning left off St Anns Road into Mortimer Square and right into Freston Road, both cars pass The People's Hall, which at the time was occupied by Delta Litho Ltd.

Eventually the chase concludes at a disused gas works on the junction of The Straight and White Street, Southall, London E6, where Boz leaves his Aston Martin and scales the high gates giving access to the premises, followed by Purdey and Gambit. The gas works was also used for a sequence early in the episode where the corrupt scientist Professor Turner, played by David Swift, leads his men in a search for an escaped lab rat, while the down-and-out ex-agent Freddy, played by John Carson, watches them from a safe distance. The same location was frequently used by other television dramas during the '70s, including episodes of *The Professionals*, *Doctor Who*, *The Sweeney*, *Blake's 7* and *Return of the Saint*. Today only a small amount of gas equipment remains at the site, the majority of the area having been turned over to car parking. Furthermore, there is now no access to this area from The Straight and White Street, although the roads are still there.

Later in the episode, Gambit drives himself, Steed and Purdey to the Exhibition of Gold Antiquities, the exterior of which was provided by the Marriott Hotel situated on Ditton Road in Langley near Slough in Berkshire. The Jaguar was filmed speeding southbound and then back in the opposite direction on Wood Lane, Iver Heath, within a mile of the studio, with interior shots of the vehicle allowing Gambit an opportunity to mention his motor-racing experiences. Additional footage for this sequence was captured with a door-mounted camera on the XJS as it was driven off The Straight onto Randolph Road at the junction with The Crescent back in Southall.

Night-time filming was executed at a large building called Oakley Court – now The Windsor Moat House Hotel – in Windsor Road, Bray, Berkshire, for the venue of a fancy dress party featured in the episode. Exteriors had been shot at the same location for various horror films, as Hammer Films' then base of operations, Bray Studios, was virtually adjacent, separated from it only by a field. Having been abandoned years earlier, Oakley Court was extremely run down, although there was free access to the grounds and The Avengers Enterprises realised that they could film there without paying a fee.

Additional after-dark location filming took place outside The Cock Pit restaurant on Windsor Road in Eton, Berkshire, for a sequence where Steed and his date run into Freddy. This establishment has since been renamed the Tiger Garden. After arranging a meeting at an abandoned sand pit, Freddy discovers that he has become infected, and as Steed and Purdey arrive, he climbs into his old Ford Anglia and drives it over a precipice into the quarry. This sequence and the resulting explosion were captured on location at H F Warner's landfill site on Star Lane, Knowl Hill, between Reading and Maidenhead in Surrey.

A sequence featuring an assault course was filmed early one morning with Lumley and guest actor Jeremy Child, portraying an army lieutenant, both on location at Aldershot in Hampshire, with genuine trainee paratroopers appearing as the personnel being put through their paces. The screenplay called for Purdey to swing off a high platform using a rope and drop onto some netting, but when she got to the platform Lumley began to have second thoughts about performing the stunt. A sergeant arrived and advised her how to avoid injury, so on the cry of action she took his advice, clenching the rope and tucking her elbows in as she swung out over the netting and dropped onto it. However, she still landed heavily and bruised a knee.

The registration number of Boz's Aston Martin (MCO 731P) was the same as that of the Citroen borrowed by Gambit in 'The Eagle's Nest', suggesting that the number plate was a false one owned by The Avengers Enterprises.

Other points of note: during the extensive car chase sequence, Purdey and Gambit casually discuss the 1948 feature film *The Treasure of the Sierra Madre* and the identity of its director; during the course of the action, various characters consult page two of *The Times* newspaper; Gambit's martial arts abilities are showcased as he easily bests the large bodyguard Choy, played by professional wrestler Big Bruno Elrington; and it seems somewhat incongruous that not only Choy but also Hong Kong Harry are played by non-Asian actors.

The complete incidental music score for this episode, comprising 14 cues in total, would later be included on *The Music of Laurie Johnson Volume 3* in 2009.

1.03 – 'House of Cards'

The third episode to enter production was 'House of Cards', the first draft screenplay for which was completed by Brian Clemens on Wednesday 28 January 1976, again naming the female lead as Charley. The storyline this time involves Soviet sleeper agents being reactivated and instructed to become assassins.

Calling the shots on the episode was Ray Austin, who would become the in-house director on the series. It is thought that this position was first offered to Cyril Frankel, who during the '60s and early '70s had worked almost exclusively with Dennis Spooner and Monty Berman on *The Champions*, *Department S*, *Randall and Hopkirk (Deceased)*, *Jason King* and *The Adventurer*. However, Frankel was unwilling to become involved with another production-line television series, having had bad experiences on *The Adventurer* – although he would direct the two-part *Return of the Saint* story 'Collision Course', because he considered it to be a film.

Airport footage seen at the beginning of the episode, for a sequence where Steed and fellow agent Roland, played by Frank Thornton, snatch the Russian scientist Professor Vasil, played by Gordon Sterne, with the assistance of Gambit posing as a pop star with a group of screaming teenage fans, was filmed at RAF Northolt, approximately five miles from the studio.

Steed, having obviously moved from his London apartment in Stable Mews, now lives in a large country house and stud farm surrounded by an estate. The location the producers chose for this was Binfield Manor, a collection of buildings and equestrian facilities set in extensive grounds complete with a large lake, off Forest Road in Binfield, near Bracknell in Berkshire.

The isolated St Mary the Virgin church off Village Lane in the small settlement of Hedgerley near Gerrards Cross provided the setting for a sequence where guest actor Lyndon Brook's character Cartney, a Russian agent posing as an undertaker, arrives to deliver a hypnotic trigger in the form of half a playing card to a man named Frederick, played by Anthony Bailey, who is chauffeur to a bishop, played by Derek Francis. Travelling west approximately seven and a half miles from the studio, the crew also filmed in the grounds of the Old School House off Remenham Lane in the small community of Remenham, near Henley-on-Thames in Oxfordshire. Most of the scenes shot at this picture-postcard location were carried by Lumley and guest actress Annette André, portraying the bishop's stepdaughter Suzy, although also in attendance were both Brook and, playing the Russian agent and chief villain Ivan Perov, Peter Jeffrey. The maroon Audi of Perov and Cartney was filmed negotiating the Dolesden Lane and Skirmett Road junction in the small settlement of Fingest, near Turville in Buckinghamshire, travelling at speed toward Steed's home.

Steed's Big Cat Jaguar finally makes its debut in this episode, though its only significant part in the action comes during the final ten minutes, when Perov uses a Bell 47G-5A helicopter to follow it to a safe house where Vasil is stashed. Filmed from the helicopter, the Big Cat is seen travelling through the village of Ibstone along Ibstone Road, proceeding past the junction with Gray's Lane in a south-easterly direction and eventually arriving at the safe house – actually a large property within a converted windmill known as Cobstone Mill, overlooking Turville. At the time of shooting, this was owned by film producer Roy Boulting and his then wife Hayley Mills.

'House of Cards' also features the initial outing of Purdey's MGB convertible, which she and Gambit use to trail Perov's helicopter across country. They too arrive in the village of Turville along Holloway Lane, before turning left between two buildings at the junction with School Lane as they continue their pursuit of the aircraft. This takes them into a field but also, as Purdey points out, onto a track leading up to the windmill.

Later Gambit appropriates Perov's helicopter, and there is a scene where it swoops low over the Russian as Purdey comes in and rugby-tackles him to the ground. While filming this, Lumley somehow managed to strike her chin on something solid, causing some facial swelling. However, the finished sequence was sufficiently impressive that part of it was incorporated into the American opening titles.

Clemens wrote into his screenplay an amusing exchange of dialogue making reference to the three previous Avengergirls. This comes when Steed's girlfriend Jo, played by Geraldine Moffat, asks him about the framed photos of them that he has in his home. Preparing a drink, he replies without looking, 'Oh, just some fillies I've toyed with.' Picking up the Cathy Gale photo, Jo comments, 'She's magnificent.' 'Yes, beautiful', he agrees, still with his back toward her. 'We went through some tricky situations together,' he adds. 'Faithful, reliable.' 'And this one?' Jo enquires, looking at the Emma Peel photo. 'Very spirited and very special,' Steed answers. 'Fantastic creature … I had to take the whip to her though sometimes.' Looking shocked for a moment, Jo moves to the final photograph, of Tara King, 'And the other one?' Steed replies: 'Excellent, great action, liked her oats too much. I sold her to an Arab prince. I think he eventually had to shoot her!' 'Shoot her!' Jo echoes in alarm. Steed then joins her and realises that they have been talking at cross purposes – he thought she was asking him about three framed horse photographs across the room.

The set of an interrogation room where Steed and Gambit question Frederick has some interesting graffiti scrawled on its walls, including, 'You're never alone with a schizophrenic!' and an in-joke at the construction manager's expense: 'Leon Davis slept here 1975.'

In a scene where she confronts Jo, who is attempting to poison Steed, Purdey is armed with a gold-coloured Beretta 70 automatic.

As with 'The Midas Touch', the complete incidental music score for this episode, this time comprising 19 cues, would later be included on *The Music of Laurie Johnson Volume 3* in 2009.

The Purdey apartment set

'House of Cards' allowed viewers their first extensive views of Purdey's basement apartment set. This had been designed by Syd Cain, although Lumley had been consulted regarding what colours she preferred, going for lilac with dashes of purple. The open-plan apartment was furnished with a matching sofa and two easy chairs, a piano, a small metal table, two basket chairs, various sculptures and a coffee table bearing some magazines, including a copy of *Vogue*. Partitioned only by a curtain of stringed beads, the bedroom, containing a metal-framed double bed and wicker furniture, was off to one side.

1.04 – 'The Last of the Cybernauts …??'

The second episode to commence principal filming in May was 'The Last of the Cybernauts …??' As the title suggests, this revived Steed's old mechanical adversaries from the original series. Unfortunately their creator, Philip Levene, had passed away several years earlier, so Clemens decided to write the episode himself. He had a first draft script ready by March 1976, then developed this into a shooting script that would be directed by Sidney Hayers, who had also handled the Cybernauts' debut episode back in March 1965. The cybernetics concept is taken one step further this time, in a story involving a double agent, Felix Kane, using the technology to create artificial limbs for himself after he is injured in an explosive car crash.

A fast-moving teaser sequence culminating in the car crash was filmed under controlled conditions on Car Park 4 in front of the production's allocated Stages J and K at Pinewood. Having learned of a rendezvous between Kane, played by Robert Lang, and a contact, Steed, Purdey and Gambit set a trap for them. Kane's contact Anton de Salles, distracted by Steed throwing the Big Cat about in reverse, loses control of his Peugeot 404 and collides with a parked white Citroen DS21 (MOC 731P) seen previously in 'The Eagle's Nest' and then a Hillman Minx, rendering him unconscious. As both the Big Cat and Gambit's Range Rover move to box him in, Kane attempts to outmanoeuvre his pursuers in his Austin Westminster, until he too loses control. After the opening titles, a shot filmed on the adjacent Studio Drive shows the Austin running into a parked petrol tanker, which promptly explodes, killing Kane – or so Steed, Gambit and Purdey believe.

The red-brick-clad Stages J and K were constructed in 1966 and took a self-contained approach, incorporating sufficient rooms to accommodate administration, dressing rooms and wardrobe/make-up departments. Provision was included so that at a later date control rooms could be added, thus converting the soundstages into television studios, although initially they were used for feature films and some television film series. The two stages were identical, both measuring 8,960 square feet, and had previously been occupied by the film series *Man in a Suitcase*, *Strange Report*, *Shirley's World* and Gerry Anderson's *UFO*. Later, due to increased demand for videotaped television productions, Pinewood executives would decide to make Stages J and K dedicated multi-camera television studios, beginning work in June 2000 and then renaming them TV One and TV Two after more refurbishment in 2005.

After the teaser, the events of which turn out to have occurred a year before the rest of the action, the story continues with guest actor Robert Gillespie's character Frank Goff, a previously unknown assistant to the Cybernauts' original controller Dr

Armstrong, being released from prison. This was filmed on location in front of what remained of the old St Albans Jail on Grimston Road in that city. It is perhaps surprising that Clemens chose to introduce a new character here rather than bring back the established assistant Benson, played by Frederick Jaeger in both 'The Cybernauts' and 'Return of the Cybernauts'. Possibly he was uncertain of Jaeger's availability – although the actor would appear as a different character not long afterwards, in the episode 'Target!'

Having gained admission to Gambit's fully-automated yet basically-furnished multi-level apartment, Purdey insists that he get out of bed immediately, saying, 'I want you to accompany me' – to which he gives the quick-fire response, 'On the piano?' Together they go to the apartment block where the prison warden Foster lives and, dropping Gambit off at the entrance, Purdey drives off in her MGB to locate a parking space, unaware that Kane's Cybernaut is already on the premises. For these scenes the crew shot both inside and outside Blythe House on Blythe Road, London W14, and at one point an unfortunate incident occurred as Gareth Hunt accidentally knocked stuntman Rocky Taylor down one of the stairwells in his full Cybernaut costume.

The Old Place on Lock Path, Dorney, near Bray in Berkshire was used to represent the country cottage residence of cybernetics expert Professor Mason, played by Basil Hoskins, who is placed under round-the-clock guard to protect him from Kane. Footage obtained at this location included a sequence featuring Taylor, Oscar Quitak as Kane's associate Malov and Ray Armstrong as a guard who shoots the Cybernaut with both barrels of a shotgun – to no avail, as the Cybernaut kidnaps Mason with ease.

Emma Peel is mentioned in dialogue spoken by Kane and again when Gambit plays Scrabble with Purdey at her apartment and they discuss looking at old files regarding the Cybernauts. 'I didn't mention Mrs Emma Peel,' says Purdey, showing a first hint of a jealousy that would be expanded on in the second season, to which Gambit replies, 'You never do!'

For firepower, Purdey again relies on a Beretta 70 automatic, although this proves totally ineffective against Kane's metal breastplate.

One of Steed's birthday presents, received at the second of the two parties seen in the episode, is a Dubreq Stylophone; a miniature synthesiser played by moving a handheld stylus over a metal keyboard to create a tune. However, his housekeeper Mrs Weir, played by Pearl Hackney, who makes her only appearance here, seems far better at playing it than he is.

The episode concludes at Purdey's apartment, where the cybernetic Kane attempts to gain his revenge by maiming the ex-ballerina by crushing her legs – one of the most chilling scenarios that would be presented in the series. Exterior shots of the apartment were obtained on location in St Peter's Square, Chiswick, London W6, where Gambit is seen sat in his Jaguar keeping guard, until he is knocked unconscious by Kane pushing a Range Rover into the vehicle. Arriving in the nick of time, Steed distributes aerosol cans of plastic skin, which when sprayed on Kane's mechanical joints jam them solid, causing the circuitry of his cybernetic implants to short out. Showing the motionless Kane the aerosol's label, which boasts 'Good for 100 and 1 uses,' Steed adds the correction: 'Hundred and two.'

This was not how Clemens originally envisaged the episode ending. His first draft involved Steed enticing Kane outside behind Purdey's apartment and causing him to become immobilised in some wet tar being used to resurface the road.

Other changes between draft and final script were mostly slight. For instance, the draft mistakenly credited a man named Professor Dormeuil with having invented the Cybernauts[35]; the surviving Cybernauts were originally to have been found simply buried underground, rather than entombed in the basement of a partly-demolished house; Kane was to have accompanied Malov and the Cybernaut to abduct Mason, instead of remaining behind; and Kane was to have dealt with Gambit outside Purdey's apartment by knocking him unconscious with a single punch – albeit one that had smashed through his car door *en route* – rather than ramming his car. A scene in the finished episode where Ministry man Fitzroy, played by David Horovitch, sneaks up on Steed and his latest girlfriend Laura, played by Sally Bazely, in the gardens of his house – filmed on site at Pinewood around a hedged walkway in the gardens of Heatherden Hall – replaced a similar sequence in the draft. This had Gambit, competing against Purdey in an equestrian time trial, sensing someone hiding in the shrubbery and spurring his horse forward, knocking Fitzroy flat on his back. The reason for this being rewritten may have been that, at the time, Gareth Hunt had never ridden a horse.

The handgun used by Purdey in this episode was actually nothing more than a prop made from hard resin rather than her usual Beretta 70 as seen in previous episodes. At the time of writing, this item, complete with certificate of authenticity, has been up for sale for several years at the Prop Store: Ultimate Movie Collectables in London.

1.05 – 'To Catch a Rat'

Moving into June 1976, the next episode into production was 'To Catch a Rat', from the typewriter of Terence Feely, who had recently worked with Brian Clemens on both *The Avengers* stage play and instalments of ATV's anthology series *Thriller*. Although perhaps not a major player in British film series during the '60s, Feely had also amassed considerable experience with scripts for *The Saint*, *The Prisoner* and Gerry Anderson's *UFO*, and then into the '70s with *The Persuaders!*. The storyline concept he pitched successfully for this episode presented another traitor-in-British-Intelligence scenario, but he also managed to incorporate a '60s Cold War element, including a teaser sequence set in 1960. He completed his second draft script on Tuesday 1 June, suggesting that the shooting script was assembled very quickly after that.

Assigned to direct this episode was James Hill, another veteran of the original series. The story involves an agent named Erwin Gunner, codenamed the Flyer, thought to have been killed 16 years previously while working undercover behind the Iron Curtain, suddenly starting to broadcast his presence on a security service wavelength. In a surprising move, *The Avengers'* original lead actor Ian Hendry was cast as Gunner, although any thought of amending the script to change Gunner to his old character Dr David Keel was apparently a non-starter, mainly due to time restrictions.

A sequence where two flower-arranging members of a church congregation are surprised first by the traitor Cledge, played by Barry Jackson, and then by Gambit and Purdey was filmed at St Bartholomew's on Chequers Lane in the small village of Fingest in Buckinghamshire. Both interiors and exteriors were shot here, as was also the

---

[35] A September 1977 Futura paperback novelisation, *The Cybernauts* by Peter Cave, would be adapted from this early screenplay, hence it too would name the creator of the killer robots as Professor Dormeuil. (See below for further details of *The New Avengers* in print.)

case with St Mary the Virgin Parish Church, off Church Hill, Harefield, in the London Borough of Hillingdon, which was used for a sequence where Cledge tracks Gunner down and attempts to kill him. The script requirement of a church ruin was met by shooting a small amount of footage showing Newark Augustinian Priory, near Pyrford in Surrey.

An East German checkpoint scene where the Volkswagen Beetle of the double agent known as the White Rat crosses over the border was actually filmed on Peace Road in Black Park, adjacent to Pinewood Studios.

Some material in which Gunner watches a white police car arrive at the ornate gates to the large stately home of a Minister named Quaintance, played by Robert Fleming, was filmed at another entrance to the studio lot on Pinewood Road, at the original gateway to Heatherden Hall. A sequence set outside a nursing home where Gunner has an accident with a swing that restores his memory was also filmed on site at Pinewood, under trees directly in front of Heatherden Hall.

The episode's final shot was filmed on location in Wandsworth, London SW15, showing the Big Cat travelling along Bank Lane, passing both the Bank of England Sports Centre and the International Tennis Federation premises.

Catherine Buckley's contract to design and supply her fashions having now been terminated, Purdey's attire takes on a more practical look in this episode, as she wears an outfit of blue jeans and a leather bomber jacket, and also one of a brown velvet suit with a lilac and white shirt and white tie. However, there is also a short stockings-and-suspenders scene to reinforce the image promised in pre-publicity.

On a musical note, Laurie Johnson's incidentals for this episode appear to have been greatly influenced by John Barry's distinctive zither score for the Cold War spy thriller *The Ipcress File*.

Steed at one point informs his younger colleagues that for a time during the early '60s he had the codename the New Doberman, or the New D for short, in response to which Purdey quips 'The nudie!'

In another scene, Steed finds Purdey's automatic inside her purse, and again this is represented by the hard resin prop seen in 'The Last of the Cybernauts ...??'.

This episode is the first since 'The Eagle's Nest' to have its closing credits open with a special 'Guest Star' caption, this time for Hendry.

1.06 – 'Cat Amongst the Pigeons'

The second episode to enter production in June 1976 was 'Cat Amongst the Pigeons', written by Dennis Spooner. Like his close friend Brian Clemens, Spooner admired the work of director Alfred Hitchcock, and it was his movie *The Birds* that inspired this screenplay. The Avengers Enterprises did not have the time or the budget to hire and train hundreds of avian extras, but the production team obviously decided when Spooner submitted his first script in April that the challenges it presented were worth taking on in order to create a very strong *The New Avengers* episode. Ingenuity would clearly play a major part in its realisation, however, and experienced director John Hough was brought on board to make it work.

Spooner's story opens with the bizarre situation of a pet shop proprietor discovering that within the space of a few moments all his caged birds have apparently escaped confinement and disappeared. For the continuation of this teaser sequence, where an agent named Merton, played by Andrew Bradford, crouches by his convertible and nervously radios Steed before being attacked by an unseen something that forces him to fall backwards into a quarry, the crew returned to H F Warner's landfill site at Knowl Hill in Berkshire. Macnee, Hunt, Lumley and Bradford were all present at this location, along with extras playing two ambulance men and a nurse.

Acting on Merton's radioed warning that at noon that day an attempt will be made on the life of ornithologist Hugh Rydercroft, played by Basil Dignam, Steed insists that his light plane be thoroughly checked over before allowing him to take off – a sequence filmed at Wycombe Air Park in Marlow, Buckinghamshire. Despite this, however, with only seconds to go until noon, Rydercroft's plane crashes. The crash site strewn with wreckage was created in Black Park, where a sequence was shot of security officer Turner, played by Matthew Long, discussing events with the first real eccentric to appear in the series so far, lead investigator Lewington, played by Hugh Walters.

A large residence called St Hubert's House, accessed from St Hubert's Lane in Gerrards Cross, approximately a mile and a half from Pinewood, was used to represent the exterior of a bird sanctuary called Sanctuary of Wings.

Steed's horse stud was again represented by Binfield Manor, where the three leads and Long were filmed outside both the main house and the outbuildings for various scenes, including one of Purdey rushing after Steed and Gambit when she discovers a Sanctuary of Wings bird ring, only to see them driving away.

The villain of the piece, a revenge-seeking bird lover named Zarcardi, played by Vladek Sheybal, is revealed to be using a flute-like device to control the birds to do his bidding. The episode's second overtly eccentric character, Ryderscroft's acquaintance Bridlington, played by Gordon Rollings, is also seen to be developing a similar device, although this one can only attract birds, as proven when he demonstrates it for Steed. In this sequence, sound effects and shadowy movement give the impression of a large number of birds attempting to get through a partly-boarded window, while a much smaller number manage to gain access down the chimney. Bridlington actually references *The Birds* here, though not by its title, as he asks Steed, 'Didn't you see that film?'

The crew returned to the junction of The Straight and The Crescent roads in Southall to capture some material involving Gareth Hunt, including some shot through a window from inside the red-brick water tower there, looking down on the street below.

Purdey acquires a new mode of transportation for this episode only, in the form of a yellow Yamaha 250cc motorcycle (LLC 950P). In her autobiography *Stare Back and Smile*, Lumley later recalled spending part of a lunchtime learning how to handle this machine, as she had never ridden one before. However, she was doubled by either Colin Skeaping or Wendy Cooper for the more dangerous shots required.

Fearing for the safety of bird expert Professor Waterlow, played by Peter Copley, Steed and Gambit hurry to his home, which was represented by the large property Fulmer Rise Manor on Fulmer Rise, about a mile north of the studios. The swimming pool seen here has since been filled in and become part of the garden.

A subsequent sequence where Steed is attacked by a large bird of prey hidden by Zarcardi inside his Range Rover was filmed with the vehicle travelling along Southlands Road, near Denham. The attack forces the agent to drive into the empty rear of a removals van parked outside Quarry Cottages there. When the darkness inside the van calms the creature down, Steed is able to cover it with his bowler hat, allowing him to reverse out and resume his journey.

Despite its science fiction elements and eccentric characters, this episode has some chilling aspects – especially Zarcardi's warning to Purdey that his birds of prey are trained to attack their victims' eyes! The finale, in which the massed birds back Purdey up against a door and she uses a wooden table as a shield, is particularly well directed by Hough.

Steed's stud

'Cat Amongst the Pigeons' gives a good view of the living quarters of Steed's manor house, represented by a set furnished with a three-piece leather suite, a grand piano, a coffee table and two occasional tables complete with large table lamps, plus matching green wallpaper and velvet drapes. On one wall is a large Greek frieze, and on a shelf a large porcelain sphinx – although in 'House of Cards' only, it held the three framed photographs of Steed's former partners. The adjoining dining area features white decoration, with a large dark-wood table and eight matching chairs, plus an open staircase leading to the first floor.

Crew changes

There were a couple of changes to the regular crew for 'Cat Amongst the Pigeons'. Roger Simons rather than Ron Purdie assumed the position of assistant director; and after this they would work on alternate episodes for a couple of months, before Purdie took on the responsibility for the penultimate run of three episodes and Simons the final run of three. Having previously handled make-up along with Alan Boyle, Neville Smallwood was now replaced by Peter Robb-King for a couple of episodes, after which Alan Brownie would take over until the end of the season. Boyle however would stay for the whole season, save for the final episode, when Wally Schneiderman would step in instead.

1.07 – 'Target!'

Dennis Spooner's second screenplay for the season was 'Target!', which commenced principal photography in July 1976 under the direction of Ray Austin.

The primary location required by the storyline was a derelict building to serve as the training facility of the agents' department, and this was found 15 miles south-east of the production base at a collection of buildings that made up Pinewood Sanatorium, off Nine Mile Ride at Wokingham Without in Berkshire. Despite them sharing the same name, Pinewood Studios had no connection to this deserted establishment, which had been closed down during the mid-'60s. For the filming, art director Robert Bell dressed the exterior of the location as if it were a standing set, including such items as a telephone box, a police box, a pillar box, a pram and a bus stop sign, plus various street name signs and pieces of graffiti, including 'I luv Purdey'. To represent an automated target range, used to test the agents' shooting abilities, a number of shop window mannequins were dressed and posed with firearms. These included look-alikes of Gambit, Purdey and Steed – although, like the real Steed, the latter had no gun.

Lumley went beyond the call of duty for a sequence where Purdey shins up a drainpipe and traverses the roof of a building on the target range. While this was being filmed, a concerned Ray Austin called out to her, advising that she edge along the rooftop ridge in a seated position. However, going for realism, she ignored him and walked along it. Although the producers wanted both Lumley and Hunt to undertake the majority of their own stunts, the hazards of this particular one were readily apparent. Shortly afterwards, Cyd Child was brought in to become Lumley's stunt double, having previously performed the same service for both Diana Rigg and Linda Thorson.

Purdey's thigh and stocking top are glimpsed once more when she climbs up the drainpipe at the start of the aforementioned sequence, but for the last time, as this element of the character was subsequently discarded.

While undergoing the automated test, all the agents, including Purdey, use a 9mm Browning HP-35 automatic. In fact Gambit uses several, after first quickly firing all six rounds from his Smith and Wesson revolver.

Having first been coached by stunt personnel, Hunt was called upon to perform a running somersault through a full length (sugar) glass door inside one of the Pinewood Sanatorium buildings. However, this was not the scariest moment for him at this location. A sequence of the police box prop being destroyed was accomplished with too large a charge by the special effects team, and the resulting explosion not only took Hunt off his feet but also left him with his face blackened and fragments of blue paint scattered throughout his hair.

Guest actor Frederick Jaeger was initially cast in the role of Bradshaw, the controller of the tests, but when inclement weather conditions delayed filming at the sanatorium location he began running out of time before he needed to leave to fulfil a commitment on another production. Roy Boyd was brought in as a replacement Bradshaw, although the script was amended so that Jaeger could still make a one-scene appearance as a new character called Jones, who prepares Purdey for her test. In reference to this situation, the Thursday 18 November 1976 edition of the *TV Times* later quoted Clemens as saying: 'Sometimes you can't beat the British weather'.

Nine Mile Ride was used as the location for a sequence where Steed, while speeding along in his Range Rover, with Gambit and Purdey as passengers, starts to feel the effects of having been poisoned with curare. The Range Rover was also filmed turning right into New Wokingham Road – something that would be impossible now, as at some point since the '70s a new road layout has been adopted there.

In a sequence where agent George Myers, played by Malcolm Stoddard (one of the actors who had auditioned for the Gambit role), is being driven to the training facility by Purdey in her MGB convertible, the vehicle is seen passing through the village of Fulmer on Windmill Road, with both St James Church and The Black Horse pub visible in the background. Fulmer was only a mile and a half to the north-west of Pinewood, thus making it ideal for the series' location work.

More location work was undertaken at Binfield Manor, where Macnee, Hunt and Stoddard filmed a solitary sequence involving the MGB.

'Target!' evolved from an original idea of Spooner's for a scene where an agent enters a telephone box, dials Steed's number and simply says, 'I'm dead'. With some development, this became the scene in the finished episode where agent David Palmer begins feeling unwell after visiting the training area and calls Steed. This was shot on location at Adelaide Square in Windsor.

A sequence where the secondary villain Klokoe, played by Deep Roy, disguises himself as a child on a bicycle and manages to inject Steed without his knowledge was shot on Ragstone Road in Slough outside a medical examiner's building, although these premises now belong to the Quakers Religious Society of Friends.

The Pinewood Studios lot provided the background for a sequence where the agent McKay, played by stunt performer Marc Boyle, falls down a metal staircase, having just departed from the surgery of Dr Kendrick, played by John Paul. The staircase was in fact the fire escape situated at the western end of the main administration block.

A scene where the agent Potterton, portrayed by an uncredited Peter Brace, falls ill while fishing, causing him to collapse into the water, was shot beside the ornate pond in the gardens at Heatherden Hall.

'Target!' was one of the episodes that Clemens showed potential buyers in the United States in an attempt to secure a network sale of *The New Avengers*. The network representatives were so impressed that this assisted Ray Austin in obtaining directing assignments on some American series.

Crew changes

Like 'Cat Amongst the Pigeons', 'Target!' saw a number of changes occur within the series' production crew. Pat Rambaut replaced Renée Glynn on continuity, although they would more or less alternate on episodes from then on, with Mary Dalison also handling one. James Allen (credited as Jimmy Allen) temporarily took over from Mike Reed as the director of photography, although Reed would return for the following episode and both Ernie Steward and Ian Wilson would also serve in this capacity before the end of the season. Camera operator Jimmy Devis departed, allowing Malcolm Vinson on board to undertake the filming of this episode and others, although later Herbert Smith would assume this role for several episodes.

1.08 – 'Faces'

Deciding to have some fun on the series, Brian Clemens and Dennis Spooner came up with a wheeze whereby one of them would write the first half of a screenplay and then allow the other to complete it, the final credit being shared between them. 'Faces' was the first of two examples of this novel type of collaboration, and was basically an old-fashioned 'doubles' episode, although Clemens expanded the concept a little further than usual in the first half, and Spooner devised a satisfying ending in the concluding half. The initial draft was ready by May 1976, and James Hill was invited to direct his second episode for the season.

This story opens with two poachers named Mullins and Terrison, played by Edward Petherbridge and Richard Leech, seeing a chauffeur-driven limousine carrying a man who looks identical to Terrison, namely Ministry official Craig, also played by Leech. This gives them the idea to kill Craig and have Terrison impersonate him. Five years later, they have teamed up with the plastic surgeon Dr Prator, played by David de Keyser, to perpetrate a more elaborate variation on this scheme, altering the appearance of itinerants from the Mission for the Distressed and Needy so that they can take the places of prominent government and security officials, giving them access to valuable secrets.

The crew returned to one of the locations used for 'The Last of the Cybernauts …??', The Old Place on Lock Path in Dorney, Buckinghamshire, to film an exterior scene where Steed and Lady Sheila Rayner, played by Jill Melford, discuss her late husband. The wooded grassland surrounding this property was also used for some other scenes:

the opening teaser where the two poachers first see Craig; one where Steed's old friend Mark Clifford, played by Neil Hallett, and his wife Wendy, played by Annabel Leventon, have a picnic; and one where Wendy later brings an inquisitive Steed to investigate.

An early sequence where, using his archery skills, Mullins kills Craig as he dives into his swimming pool was filmed on location in the grounds of Radlett Preparatory School, off Watling Street, Radlett in Hertfordshire – a location that had appeared eight years previously in the episode 'All Done with Mirrors' – though since the '70s the swimming pool appears to been abandoned, having now become a large pond.

Macnee and Hallett played out a scene on the wide steps at Prince Consort Road, London SW7, against the backdrop of the Royal Albert Hall, where Steed thinks his friend has suffered a fatal heart attack. Further central London location work took place in Covent Garden, the former site of the famous fruit and vegetable market that had been relocated the previous year. This included filming inside the empty shell of what had been the Jubilee Market, now known as the Jubilee Market Hall shopping area. Both Petherbridge and fellow guest actor David Webb, playing Ministry official Bilston and his double, were present for this shoot.

Purdey attempts to locate Gambit at the department's Base 47 in a sequence that involved Lumley and Petherbridge filming at Pinewood Sanatorium, though in a completely different area than those used for 'Target!'. Some years later, all the sanatorium buildings would be demolished, after which electronics company Hewlett Packard would acquire the entire site and redevelop it into a training facility, before selling it again in 2004. In 2007, Johnson and Johnson Medical would move into a newly-constructed building on the same site, making it their UK base of operations.

The production crew returned to another location used for 'Target!', Ragstone Road in Slough, to shoot a scene of Purdey parking the MGB and using a telephone box to call Steed, all within sight of the medical examiner's building visible in the previous episode.

Steed and Gambit are seen clay pigeon shooting in the gardens at Heatherden Hall, with the bridge leading to the island in the pond clearly visible at the beginning of the sequence. However, for the subsequent sequence where Terrison drops off a double of Steed using his Rolls Royce, Leech and Macnee were filmed on the driveway at Binfield Manor. The same location was used for a shot where Wendy is later seen leaving the main building.

Other notable points: 'Faces' marks the debut of a new closing title sequence, the two-tone green background having been discarded in favour of the credits being run over the red and blue rampant lion motif; some of Laurie Johnson's memorable incidental music from 'The Eagle's Nest' and 'To Catch a Rat' was recycled for the episode's soundtrack; part of a monastery dungeon set from 'The Eagle's Nest' was redressed to form the interior and exterior of a cell in which Gambit is confined; and when Purdey confronts Dr Prator, having adopted the guise of a cockney gangster's moll complete with permed wig, she reinforces her point by sporting a Walther PPK automatic.

Gambit's apartment

'Faces' affords the most detailed look yet at Gambit's white-themed, all-mod-cons apartment, containing an electronically-controlled sofa/bed, a glass-topped table, spotlights and items of furniture covered in sheepskin. The furnishings also include a black leather director's chair, a white television, fitted units incorporating smoked glass sections, and various silhouette prints hung on the walls, one of which consists of plain bricks painted grey. Further to this, there are several firearms hung on one wall, and a couple of crossbows on another.

Scheduling

In the first week of August 1976 *Screen International* reported that ITV would start transmitting *The New Avengers* during the forthcoming autumn season. The following week's edition of the same periodical then carried some quotes from Brian Clemens, who confirmed that production on seven episodes had been completed, with one undergoing editing and another ('The Tale of the Big Why') having just entered principal photography. Clemens also said that the new series was drama with underlying humour, whereas the original series on film had been a humorous spoof with dramatic undertones. The edition of *The Stage* issued on Thursday 12 August confirmed that UK screenings would commence in October. ITV's film series buyer of the time, Leslie Halliwell – the author of a number of film and television reference books, and an enthusiast of *The Avengers* – apparently watched four episodes of *The New Avengers* before sanctioning the buying of the series.

1.09 – 'The Tale of the Big Why'

The Robert Fuest-directed 'The Tale of the Big Why' was the first episode to begin filming in August 1976. Although credited to Brian Clemens, it was based on a Philip Broadley screenplay originally entitled 'The Tale of the Double Cross', which had been rejected at the draft stage. General opinion is that Dennis Spooner had recommended Broadley as a writer for *The New Avengers* on the strength of contributions he had previously made to *The Champions*, *Department S*, *Jason King* and *The Adventurer*. However, it appears that Broadley was paid off by The Avengers Enterprises when 'The Tale of the Double Cross' was deemed unsuitable, on the understanding that his name would not be present on the finished episode. The draft script was clearly written before April 1976, as it named the female lead as Charley (or, to use Broadley's spelling, Charly) throughout. This was naturally one of the things that Clemens changed when he performed a major rewrite.

The story involves a spy named Bert Brandon, played by George Cooper, who is released after a nine-year jail term and then seeks to recover some politically damaging information that he hid years earlier and that he believes will make him rich. Also after the information are disenchanted fellow spy Roach, played by Gary Waldhorne, and his more reluctant comrade Poole, played by Rowland Davis.

A sequence of Brandon and an undercover Gambit being released from jail was filmed on location at Aylesbury Prison on Bierton Road in the town. This was combined with footage of Purdey riding her latest mode of transport, a Honda 125cc trials bike (OLR 471P). Having approached Honda UK for assistance, the producers had been extremely impressed by the Japanese-owned manufacturer's helpful offer to make multiple motorcycles available, and even to produce a special edition Purdey example. This was in complete contrast to the attitude of British Leyland, who were only willing to supply single vehicles and no duplicates – a situation that caused The

Avengers Enterprises some expense, as they then had to scour dealerships throughout London and the Home Counties to hire identical spares to cover breakdowns and late arrivals.

A further problem with British Leyland arose in relation to the annual Motor Show held at the Earls Court exhibition centre from Wednesday 20 to Saturday 30 October 1976. Seeking to capitalise on their association with *The New Avengers*, the company had asked if sometime during the event Macnee, Lumley and Hunt could make a public appearance at their stand. Even though this would cause a financial loss to The Avengers Enterprises, filming was curtailed two hours early one afternoon so that Clemens and the three leads could meet this request. However, upon their arrival they found the British Leyland stand completely deserted. Looking out of place, they were invited for a glass of wine at the nearby Mercedes stand instead. Clemens has since gone on record stating that British Leyland were extremely difficult to work with, and that it is no surprise they subsequently went out of business.

Much of the first quarter of an hour of 'The Tale of the Big Why' is taken up by an extended sequence of Brandon's Renault R16 being followed by Purdey on her red Honda motorcycle, with Poole and Roach in a Citroen Safari behind her and Gambit's Range Rover bringing up the rear. The first three vehicles were filmed passing by a pub on a beautiful sunny day, the level of the beer in a pint glass on a table outside being progressively lowered to indicate the passage of time. This footage was captured in front of The Rainbow Inn on Stonor Road in the remote Oxfordshire village of Middle Assendon, near Henley-on-Thames.

Coming over a humpback bridge on Mansion Lane in Iver, approximately two miles south of Pinewood, Brandon ignores a couple of 'Road Closed' signs and proceeds down Hollow Hill Lane – a site that has since become home to the large Dudley Wharf boating and mooring facility, adjacent to the Grand Union Canal. Purdey however continues along the main road until she comes to a dead end by a stream with a narrow footbridge – a sequence filmed at the junction of Watersplash Lane and The Splash in Warfield near Bracknell, Berkshire.

The subsequent action where Brandon retrieves a small package from its hiding place in a well was filmed at the disused Malders Lane brickworks in Pinkneys Green, Berkshire – a location that no longer exists, the site having since been totally redeveloped.

Purdey meanwhile doubles back and, realising what has happened, she too ignores the 'Road Closed' signs and rides down Hollow Hill Lane.

Having also missed Brandon, Poole and Roach determine that he has taken a no-through track and will ultimately have to return. When he does so, they are waiting for him, and he is killed. They then dismantle his crashed Renault looking for the package, but fail to find it. When Purdey arrives, she is shot at and thrown from her motorcycle, which is damaged in the process, preventing her from giving chase when the two men depart in their Citroen.

Meanwhile, having arrived at the end of the fictitious B97, Gambit radios Steed to advise him of the situation in a scene shot on a disused section of Southlands Road near Denham, about a mile north-east of the studios, though more like three miles when travelling by road. Southlands Road was blocked off at one end after the junction with Denham Road was redeveloped and replaced by a roundabout, resulting in the old stretch of road now leading only to buildings belonging to Copse Hill Farm.

As their investigation continues, Gambit takes Purdey in his Range Rover in search of a cherry orchard, in a sequence filmed in Iver at the junction of Billet Lane and Hollybush Lane – a road that has since become mostly closed to vehicles, with concrete blocks placed part-way down and at the junction to restrict access to pedestrians only. This time, the positions are reversed, as the two agents are followed by Poole and Roach in their Citroen as they enter the fictional village of Neverton, represented on location by Chalfont St Giles in Buckinghamshire.

A small amount of filming was also carried out at Binfield Manor, as usual serving as Steed's large residence, which comes under surveillance from Poole and Roach using a directional microphone to eavesdrop on the conversations within.

In a later sequence, Gambit and Purdey depart from Steed's residence intending to visit a restaurant. However, troubled by events, Gambit instead parks his Range Rover beside a roadside hot dog vendor's van, where Purdey obtains a pint pot of tea and a doorstep sandwich, prompting her to quip, 'Is this one of your favourite restaurants?' and 'I suppose you bring all your girlfriends here?'

Taking their opportunity, Poole and Roach invade Steed's home, hoping to obtain Brandon's package. Once again, Steed's steel-crowned bowler hat saves his life when Poole fires a double-barrelled shotgun at him and it absorbs the impact, the recoil propelling his assailant through some French windows.

As the action continues, the villains render Purdey unconscious with a gas grenade in order to kidnap her, although in a shot where Roach goes to pick her up, he has a struggle to do so, as when performing this scene Waldhorne failed to realise he had inadvertently stood on Lumley's dress.

After the tyres of their Range Rover are shot out, Gambit and Steed begin walking cross country, in footage obtained in the fields leading up to the windmill at Turville, as seen previously in 'House of Cards'. Later, they manage to gain a lift on the back of a manure truck, filmed on Holloway Lane about a mile outside Turville.

The package obtained by Brandon from the well turns out to contain a coded clue to the valuable information's whereabouts, in the form a paperback Western novel called *The Tale of the Big 'Y'* (a slightly different spelling from the title of the episode); and the information itself is ultimately revealed to consist of incriminating photographs of Home Office representative Harmer, played by Derek Waring, being bribed by a foreign agent, Kommissar Verslashky.

Other points of interest: in the scenes where she rides her red Honda motorcycle, Purdey dresses for biking, though not entirely inconspicuously, in a black cotton jumpsuit complete with both her name and the rampant lion motif on the reverse; a small, black cloth bag that Steed substitutes for the novel in the package from the well was a 'laughter bag' of a type that had been available since the mid-'60s, containing a battery-operated, plastic-cased device that emitted laughing sounds; and some of Laurie Johnson's incidental music for this adventure, including for parts of the vehicle footage, sounds like a piece of easy-listening library music.

Two light aircraft are seen during the course of the action. One of these, a red and white de Havilland Tiger Moth biplane, registration G-ANOH, was built in 1942 and is now owned by Nicholas Parkhouse of Haywoods Heath, who has maintained it in an airworthy condition and retained the same livery. The other, a yellow Tiger Moth G-AOMX, poses something of a mystery, as it does not appear on the Civil Aviation Authorities register, indicating that it has probably been either scrapped or exported.

For a short fight scene at the episode's conclusion, Fuest stuck closely to the January 1976 directive from Fennel and Clemens about showing Gambit's combat moves as a flurry of activity. He achieved this by way of some brief, rapidly-intercut shots of Hunt landing various blows in close up against Roy Marsden playing Brandon's contact Frank Turner.

The original Philip Broadley script 'The Tale of the Double Cross' began differently, with a teaser sequence involving Charley being held prisoner in her own home by a pair of self-serving agents called Mac and Pane – the prototypes for the finished episode's Roach and Poole. On discovering a little black book taped beneath a television set, the two men are suddenly disturbed by a character called Hamilton, who takes the book at gunpoint but is later killed. The use of a freeze frame to separate the teaser from the opening titles appears to have been a part of the producers' plans for the series from the outset, as Broadley included one here in his draft.

The storyline continued with a character known as Carling – who later became Brandon – driving around the countryside, followed by Charley on her powerful Yamaha 850cc motorcycle and Gambit using a car. However, the motorcycle sequences were more limited than in the finished episode, in which Purdey rides across grassland and other terrain that would have defeated her MGB convertible.

In Broadley's screenplay, the well from which Carling retrieves his package was on a deserted farm, rather than an abandoned industrial unit as in the episode. A further, more significant difference was that Steed, Gambit and Charley obtained not one paperback novel but two, *The Land of Death* and *The Tail of the Double Cross* – the misspelling of '*Tale*' in the latter turning out to be a clue, indicating that Carling has stashed his valuable information in a remote overgrown cemetery.

Broadley's plot was also more complicated than that of the actual episode, as it had Steed and his current girlfriend, Araminta, accidentally break a code that involved using alternate letters from the text of each of the two novels. The writer's knowledge of the village of Old Sarum in Salisbury, Wiltshire, clearly gave him inspiration for certain events, as on page 54 of the screenplay he pointed out that, from the air, the cross shape of the ruined cathedral there would be perfect for the story's requirements.

The two parties caught in the compromising photographs were named Sir Keith and Kolkov of the KGB in Broadley's version, rather than Harmer and Verslashky, and likewise a lady aviator who turns out to be Brandon's daughter was named Diana, whereas in the finished episode she became Irene, played by Jenny Runacre. The characters of Frank Turner and his wife were newly added during Clemens' heavy rewrite and did not feature in Broadley's original.

'Tell Me About It'

Having had his earlier storyline proposal for the series' opening episode rejected, Tony Williamson suffered a further knock-back when he also submitted a script entitled 'Tell Me About It', concerning a revolutionary gas called PX 400 that compels those who inhale it to tell the truth. An amusing sequence in this has Steed, Purdey and Gambit don gasmasks and attempt to get a man called Keller to reveal what the villains intend doing with the PX400 they have stolen, only to discover that he is suffering from total amnesia. It turns out that the gas is destined to be released at a peace conference, with the aim of forcing the massed group of international politicians to begin telling the truth, thereby wrecking negotiations – or, as Steed puts it, causing a war.

It is uncertain how far Williamson's script progressed toward production. The female lead's name was typed as Charlie (Charley), but at some later point this was amended to Purdey in all her speech cues – although whoever performed this task forgot to check through the actual dialogue, resulting in instances of both Steed and Gambit still referring to their fellow agent as Charlie.

In correspondence with this author in June 1991, Williamson indicated that he had been reluctant to contribute to *The New Avengers* in the first place, stating, 'It simply borrowed the title and prestige of what had already become a classic series.'

1.10 – 'Three Handed Game'

The novel type of writing collaboration begun with 'Faces' concluded with 'Three Handed Game', for which the roles were reversed as Dennis Spooner began the screenplay and then passed it across to Brian Clemens, who brought it all together and devised the ending. The story the two men devised between them has Steed, Purdey and Gambit assigned to protect three agents, each of whom has a photographic memory and holds a third of some secret information that does not make sense without the other two parts. The second draft of the script was completed during August 1976, allowing the shooting script to be written before the second half of the month, when director Ray Austin began pre-production and then filming the episode.

All the exteriors of the theatre featured in the narrative were filmed at the stage door entrance to the New Theatre on Russell Road, Wimbledon, London SW19. The finale to the action, featuring Macnee, Lumley, Hunt and guest actor David Wood as the villainous master spy Juvenator, was shot inside the same building.

A sequence where Gambit, Purdey and their fellow agent Larry, played by Michael Petrovich, stake out a foreign embassy was shot on Peek Crescent, also in Wimbledon; and one where Larry rides a Honda motorcycle in pursuit of a green Jaguar carrying Juventor and Colonel Meroff, played by Terry Wood, was captured along the nearby Marryat Road.

Juventor's temporary base of operations was represented by, and took its name from, an abandoned and generally rundown dwelling called Cantley, situated in 50 acres of parkland off Twyford Road in Wokingham, Berkshire. In 1983, this dilapidated building was converted into the luxury Cantley House Hotel. Besides taking some exterior establishing shots, the crew also filmed inside the building, in an area that is now the hotel foyer and in both the Oak Room and the Ormonde Room, which are now ground floor function suites.

Macnee accompanied the Big Cat Jaguar to Silverstone motor racing circuit off Dadford Road near the village of Silverstone, Northamptonshire, where filming took place both on the track and in the pits area. Two single-seater racing cars owned by Val Musetti, who had performed stunt work on some of *The Avengers'* videotaped episodes, were hired for this shoot via David Price Racing, whose van can be seen in the background. The first of them, a March Cosworth 752 seen in a sequence where Steed pursues and catches up with it in the Big Cat, had been raced by Musetti in conjunction with David Price Racing in the Shellsport Formula 1 Championship in 1976, and would be again in 1977. The second, a March Ford 74B seen to be driven by the agent Tony Fields, played by Noel Trevarthen, had been raced previously by Musetti in the 1975 John Player Formula Atlantic series.

Scenes set in the studio of another of the agents, sculptor Helen McKay, played by Annie Lambert, were filmed in Heatherden Hall's Gatsby Suite, a large conservatory originally constructed for the filming of *The Great Gatsby* at Pinewood in 1973, which allowed excellent views of the surrounding parkland. Although never intended as a permanent addition to the main structure, this would not be removed until 2008, when the avenue in front of Heatherden Hall was restored. Footage was also obtained of McKay's modern art sculptures laid out in a wooded area directly in front of the Hall, and of Gambit chasing down the enemy agent Ivan, played by Tony Vogel, on one of the adjacent lawns. In the exterior sequence, McKay has a hand bandaged, implying a prior accident with her hammer and chisel, although no such incident features in the episode, suggesting that some footage may have been trimmed at the editing stage.

Guest actor John Paul reprised his role of Dr Kendrick (credited this time simply as 'Doctor') from 'Target!', a physician employed by the department Steed works for. Aside from the three regulars, this is the only instance of a recurring character in *The New Avengers*.

1.11 – 'Sleeper'

September 1976 was devoted to the making of Brian Clemens' next offering, 'Sleeper', an extremely ambitious screenplay demanding over 30 different locations, mostly in central London. Having already pushed the boundaries for location filming on a studio-based series with *The Avengers* episodes 'Dead Man's Treasure' and 'The Morning After', the producers committed even greater resources on this occasion. Australian Graeme Clifford, having already served as the editor on four episodes, was given the challenge of cutting his teeth as a director on this location-heavy extravaganza.

The basic plot revolves around a new sleeping gas, S-95, invented by a Professor Marco, who comes to London for a demonstration of its effects but is waylaid *en route* by criminals led by a man named Brady, who absconds with the gas and uses it to put much of the city's population to sleep, intending to take advantage of this to carry out a series of robberies – though fortunately Steed, Purdey and Gambit have been inoculated against the gas and are on hand to thwart them.

The action opens at the London Heliport, situated on Lombard Road, SW11. Then owned by Westland, this location was used for a sequence of Professor Marco's arrival by helicopter. The shooting script then called for an interior sequence where Marco is greeted by Brady, played by Keith Buckley, which was realised by filming in a corridor at the Pinewood Studios sound department, based on Goldfinger Avenue at the complex. Subsequently Brady impersonates Marco to attend the outdoor demonstration of S-95, along with Steed, Purdey, Gambit and military dignitaries, in a sequence shot on location at RAF Northolt.

Masquerading as a London sightseeing tour party, Brady and his villainous associates, including Tina played by Sara Kestelman, are seen on board an AEC Reliance motor coach circling Trafalgar Square, WC2, before arriving at the disused Beckton Gas Works beside the River Thames. It is here that one of their number named Hardy, played by an uncredited Joe Dunne, attempts to abscond, intending to inform Steed of their plot to spray S-95 over part of the capital, but is gunned down by Tina as he runs along an elevated overhead railway.

In a sequence shot at night, Steed and Gambit drop Purdey off outside her apartment in St Peter's Square, W6, then proceed in the Big Cat Jaguar down Waterloo Place, heading for Gambit's abode, where Steed ends up staying overnight, the apartment block exteriors being filmed at the nearby Carlton House Terrace, SW1.

Having departed from the gasworks, the coach is seen in further night-time footage passing through Piccadilly Circus, W1. However, by the following morning it is at Brunel University, Kingston Lane in Middlesex, parked on campus grounds in the north-west corner of the extensive site. Brady rouses his motley band against a backdrop of the buildings housing the Brunel Centre for Advanced Solidification Technology.

Upon receiving an early morning call from Steed, Purdey goes outside in her pyjamas and discovers a kissing couple asleep in a Ford Cortina, and a Mini with its engine left running. She then finds that she has accidentally locked herself out and decides to drive to Gambit's place, borrowing the Mini to do so. Pushing the sleeping driver over into the passenger seat, she sets off, in a sequence filmed at the junction of St Peter's Square and St Peter's Villas.

This is followed by various shots of a deserted central London, starting with one across the River Thames to the Houses of Parliament, SW1, then one of Trafalgar Square, WC2, and one of Cannon Street, EC4, with St Paul's Cathedral in the background. The sequence continues with views of Throgmorton Street, EC2, showing the visitors' entrance to the old London Stock Exchange, Horse Guards Parade, SW1, and Kensington (Olympia) Railway Station, Olympia Way, W14.

Having been cut off because the gang has severed the telephone lines, Gambit and Steed head for Purdey's apartment in the Big Cat, turning left from Aldensley Road into Brackenbury Road, W6, with a screech of tyres. They encounter a uniformed police officer sleeping against a no-entry sign at the junction of Montpelier Walk and Montpelier Place, SW7, which prompts Steed to drive the Big Cat along the one-way street in the wrong direction. Arriving in Black Lion Lane, SW7, they pass by a newspaper delivery boy asleep in the road, having fallen from his bicycle.

In further footage filmed in one of the car parks at Brunel University, Brady details four of his men to patrol designated areas just in case someone has managed to avoid the effects of S-95.

Having arrived at Purdey's apartment in St Peter's Square and got no reply from inside, Gambit kicks the door in. However, upon hearing an explosion – Brady's gang hitting their first bank – he and Steed depart quickly on foot. Meanwhile, having also heard the explosion while at Gambit's apartment, Purdey resumes her journey in the Mini. Upon hearing the vehicle approaching, Steed and Gambit hide from sight, in a sequence filmed in Ennismore Gardens, SW7.

Arriving back in St Peter's Square, Purdey discovers the Big Cat parked outside her apartment, just as there is another explosion in the distance, indicating the gang robbing a second bank. In another sequence filmed at Brunel University, the gang are seen emptying the contents of Payne's Bank Ltd into the back of the coach, which had been hired from Jack Crump, aka Denham Coaches, who operated from the Pinewood Studios lot and whose vehicles had consequently appeared in several early-'70s Pinewood-based comedy films such as *Carry On Camping*, *Carry On at Your Convenience*, *Please Sir!* and *Carry On Abroad*.

Purdey meanwhile encounters two of Brady's men, played by Prentis Hancock and Mark Jones, patrolling the streets in a Volvo. They open up with a Sten gun, shattering the Mini's windscreen. For the more hazardous parts of this sequence, filmed at the junction of The Straight and The Crescent in Southall, E6, as previously featured in 'Cat Amongst the Pigeons', the Mini was driven by Lumley's stunt double Cyd Child. Unfortunately Child accidentally gashed her hand quite badly when delivering a double punch to the shattered windscreen to restore her vision, even though it had been fitted with safety glass. Nevertheless, she still rates this as her favourite episode of *The New Avengers*.

With the Volvo in hot pursuit, the Mini rounds the corner from The Straight into White Street and, colliding with a brick wall, comes to a halt, leaving Purdey with no alternative but to climb over the wall for cover. The two criminals give chase, circumventing the wall by machine-gunning the lock off a set of gates, filmed at Southall Gas Works, as previously seen in 'The Midas Touch'. Purdey then sprints away across a large square, in footage shot at Brunel University.

Breaking into the storage area of a clothing outlet, Purdey hides from her pursuers in plain sight as a shop window mannequin, until given away by her pyjama trousers falling down, forcing her to overcome the two men in a fight scene. This footage was obtained in and outside a dress shop called Marian's in what was then the Bells Hill Shopping Precinct in Stoke Poges, Buckinghamshire – a small arcade area that closed in February 2005 and was later demolished, having been bought by Persimmon Homes for residential development.

Meanwhile, having narrowly missed the bank robbers at Payne's Bank in more footage captured at Brunel University, Steed and Gambit proceed on foot to a canal-side café on location at Camden Lock, NW1, already seen in a couple of brief inserts earlier in the episode.

Purdey then comes across a couple of the robbers, played by George Sweeney and Dave Schofield, helping themselves to the contents of a shop called Montague Jewellers, having first smashed the windows. This sequence was filmed mainly at the Pinewood Studios lot on a Victorian standing street set originally constructed for the Disney film *One of our Dinosaurs is Missing*, although some of the shots of Lumley were obtained on St Peter's Grove, W6.

After Steed and Gambit move off from Camden Lock, having refreshed themselves with bottles of beer, the two gang members played by Sweeney and Schofield arrive at the café and decide to help themselves to some bottles of champagne. In doing so, they fail to spot Purdey running along a wrought iron footbridge on the opposite side of the canal, although she sees one of them brandish a large, chrome-plated revolver and quickly retraces her steps, taking cover behind a wall.

Steed and Gambit are next seen running underneath the railway lines beside The Straight in Ealing, taking the underpass from Spencer Street. They then find the damaged Mini that Purdey drove earlier.

Meanwhile, back at Camden Lock, the two gang members are becoming worse for wear and decided to indulge in some target practice, which occupies their attention. This allows Purdey a chance to edge unseen along the top of the lock gates. With one of the bank robbers inside the café, she easily takes care of the other.

Meanwhile, Brady and the majority of his gang have used a bazooka to gain entrance to the ACC Bank, represented by another of the buildings on the standing street set at Pinewood.

Steed and Gambit come across a stationary black cab with sleeping occupants outside what is now Blakes Hotel on Roland Gardens, SW7, then take cover from the bank robbers' motor coach, filmed at the same junction but from a different direction. Walking along Ennismore Street, SW7, the two agents come to the attention of the two gang members played by Hancock and Jones, who are in the adjacent Ennismore Mews. By the time the gang members round the corner into Ennismore Street with guns ready, Steed and Gambit have already made off. However, the shot showing the empty road is not actually of Ennismore Street, but rather of the nearby Rutland Mews South.

Steed and Gambit quickly pass through the pedestrian archway from Rutland Mews East into Rutland Street, SW7, representing the fictional Downton Street, where they discover further people affected by S-95. Pretending to be further sleeping bystanders, they fool the two gang members and knock them unconscious.

In another part of London unaffected by the gas, two police constables played by Jason White and Tony McHale are instructed to investigate the loss of contact with their colleagues in the city. Starting the siren on their Rover 3500, they pull out of Bigland Street into Cannon Street, E1. The vehicle is next seen turning right from Pearscroft Road into Bagley's Lane and then left into Fulmead Street, SW6. Switching to the perspective of a camera mounted inside the police car, the action proceeds east along Wapping High Street, SW6, passing the junction with Hellings Street – an area that now looks completely different, having been redeveloped since the '70s. The Rover eventually passes a prop nameplate for the fictional Pemberton Street, which is also identified on a map that Purdey finds beside Hardy's dead body at the Beckton Gas Works location – a sequence for which a standard London A to Z street map was doctored with the words 'Pemberton Street' replacing 'Thomas More Street' in Wapping. The officers catch sight of Purdey waving to them as the Rover speeds down Townmead Road, W6, but as they approach her they suddenly fall asleep due to the effects of the gas, and their vehicle collides with some large wooden packing cases.

Having ascended to the top floor of the BT Tower, accessed from Cleveland Mews, W1, Steed and Gambit take full advantage of their elevated position to pinpoint the gang carefully sifting through their ill-gotten gains. They also witness the arrival at the heliport of a Bell Jet Ranger helicopter (G-BBEU), which together with its pilot was hired for the episode from Alan Mann Helicopters Ltd, who at the time were based at Fairoaks Airport in Chobham, Surrey. This aircraft (which was not the same one seen depositing Professor Marco at the beginning of the episode) would be sold in 1978 to a company called International Messages, and then three years later to one called Air Hanson, who would keep it for less than a year before it was permanently exported to Uganda.

Meanwhile, having entered a marshalling yard, Purdey comes under fire from another member of the gang acting as a sniper perched atop a railway wagon. This sequence was filmed at Imperial Wharf Sidings at Sands End in Fulham, SW10, another location that has since undergone complete redevelopment and is now unrecognisable. These extensive sidings were east of the existing railway line, around where Harbour Avenue is now located.

Having managed to infiltrate the gang wearing balaclavas, Steed and Gambit surprise and overpower Brady and Tina in a sequence shot back in the sound department corridor at the studios, again doubling as part of the heliport interior. They then manage to get on board the helicopter, the pilot's seat of which is occupied Purdey, although initially they fail to recognise each other as she too has donned a balaclava, along with a flying helmet. Gambit and Purdey pull 9mm Beretta 1934 automatics on each other before recognition dawns.

Footage showing central London and St Paul's Cathedral in particular was shot from the Jet Ranger, which is shown landing back at RAF Northolt at the episode's conclusion.

In constructing his screenplay, Clemens drew inspiration and situations from the

The same area was used again for a scene at the episode's conclusion where Purdey inadvertently enters a minefield, forcing Gambit to fire several rounds from an Armalite rifle in her direction to make her aware of the situation.

The Longmoor filming was augmented by footage shot on the Pinewood Studios lot, including for a scene where Gambit passes Corporal Keller, played by John Labanowski, who is seen descending the exterior metal stairway on the east side of the studio film vaults. Later, a running Gambit momentarily stops to salute Keller at the same location, with Stage D and the cutting rooms prominent in the background. However, the following fight scene, in which Gambit and Purdey throw the soldier onto the corrugated roof of a walkway, was shot on the other side of the cutting rooms on the edge of Car Park 1. At the time, these structures were covered in terracotta-coloured masonry paint, though they have since been given a coat of brilliant while.

The episode's opening scene, set in what appears to be a tropical rain forest, where a camouflage-suited cameraman named Travis, played by Colin Skeaping, films the rogue unit under the command of principal villain Colonel 'Mad Jack' Miller, played by John Castle, and then escapes under gunfire by crossing a stream, was actually shot in the gardens at Heatherden Hall, the stream being represented by part of the large pond there.

In a throwback to the original series, actor Ballard Berkeley appears as a highly eccentric character, Purdey's uncle Colonel Foster, a retired military officer who enjoys barking amusing orders at his manservant.

A change of fashion for Purdey

Although 'Dirtier by the Dozen' was the last episode of season one, new fashion coordinators Jillie Murphy and Jennifer Hocking were brought on board for it, and they immediately hit the mark, providing Purdey with a number of striking items, including a pair of brown knee-length boots and a long red dress. Hocking was an Australian ex-model who had also served for a time as the editor of the British version of *Harper's Bazaar* fashion magazine.

No American sale

Upon completion of 'Dirtier by the Dozen', the production crew were stood down for almost five months before filming recommenced, amid concerns over budget. However, the biggest disappointment for all concerned was that, despite concerted efforts, *The New Avengers* was still without an American network sale – and, as proven in the past with *The Avengers*, this was essential to the ongoing success of a television film series such as this. Attempting to remedy the situation, The Avengers Enterprises took out a two-page spread advertisement in the Wednesday 27 October edition of the weekly American trade magazine *Variety*, borrowing a quote from the *Daily Mail*, which stated, 'Avenging is even better than before …'

SEASON TWO

K IS FOR KILL

Public image

During November 1976, *The New Avengers* was undergoing regional transmissions across the UK, amid much publicity and tie-in marketing. Spearheading the publicity was the *TV Times*, which in its Thursday 11 November edition ran the first of a two-part feature on Joanna Lumley, which concluded the following week. Independent Television Books Ltd also marketed *The TV Times Souvenir Extra*, a 68-page magazine that celebrated *The New Avengers* and *The Avengers* from the show's beginning, mainly with photo montage pages.

A couple of months earlier, publishers Brown Watson had issued *The New Avengers Annual 1977*, a large-format 64-page hardback book aimed at the Christmas children's market, containing a mixture of comic strips and text. The two strips, 'Fangs for the Memory' and 'Hypno-Twist', were written by Steve Moore and had artwork by John Bolton. Both Moore and Bolton had previously worked on the horror movie comic strip magazine *The House of Hammer*, and Moore had contributed to a vast number of other titles for Brown Watson, whose rates of remuneration were so low that he churned out both text stories and comic strip storylines as fast as possible, never devoting more than 24 working hours to a single project.

As Christmas approached, other assorted toys and games associated with the series became available. These included *The New Avengers* Mission Kit, produced by the company Thomas Salter, who had been retailing similar children's toy spy kits for several years. Arrow Games licensed the rights to market four different 750-piece jigsaw puzzles depicting excellent artwork renditions of Steed, Gambit, Purdey and other elements seen in the series, such as a Cybernaut and the Big Cat Jaguar. However, the toy manufacturer taking the most visible interest in the series was Denys Fisher, who produced a number of items, starting with *The New Avengers* Shooting Game, where the object was to fire pellets from spring-loaded plastic guns at cardboard silhouette targets. Back in the 1960s, some rarely-seen Emma Peel and Tara King toy dolls had been manufactured in the Far East for obscure companies marketing them almost certainly without ABC's official endorsement, and now Denys Fisher also produced a more-readily-available and higher-quality official Purdey example, dressed in an outfit from the episode 'The Eagle's Nest', although its likeness to Joanna Lumley left plenty to be desired. Not content with just Purdey, Denys Fisher also announced Steed and Gambit action figures in their 1977 catalogue, both with the added feature of moving limbs activated by pressing a button on the back. In the event, neither of these items actually made it past the development stage, although over the years, components of their construction have surfaced, such as Steed's black bowler hat and Gambit's head, which was later used on the company's Tom Baker *Doctor Who* doll.

November saw the publication by the now-defunct Futura imprint of a first spin-off paperback based on *The New Avengers*. A novelisation of the episode 'House of Cards', this was written by ex-newspaper reporter Peter Cave, whose career as a novelist had begun with several teenage exploitation paperbacks in the early '70s, and he took considerable liberties with Clemens' original screenplay, greatly expanding it with new material.

Also released the same month was '*The New Avengers* Theme' by The Laurie Johnson Orchestra, a seven-inch vinyl single on the EMI label, marketed in a paper sleeve featuring a publicity photograph of Macnee, Lumley and Hunt. The B-side, 'A Flavour of *The New Avengers*', was a mixture of incidental music and exchanges of dialogue from the first couple of episodes filmed, 'The Eagle's Nest' and 'The Midas Touch'.

The Saturday 4 December edition of the children's magazine *Look-In* – which described itself as the junior *TV Times* – featured an artwork cover depicting the series' three leads and an accompanying two-and-a-half-page article.

Further *TV Times* coverage came in the issue published on Thursday 9 December, which included a three-page feature on Hunt.

Also in December, Futura issued a second paperback based on the series, *The Eagle's Nest* by John Carter. This amalgamated the storylines of both 'The Eagle's Nest' and 'The Midas Touch'.

Lastly, the Christmas edition of the motoring periodical *Autocar* sported a John Steed/Big Cat Jaguar cover and included a two-page feature on the vehicle.

Viewing figures

On the evening of Friday 19 November 1976, 'Cat Amongst the Pigeons' became the most-watched episode of *The New Avengers*' first season, attracting 7.5 million viewers with its partial networking and ranking number eight in the chart of the week's most popular programmes. Throughout November, the series managed reasonable viewing figures, especially in the Scottish region, where it was consistently in the top ten, eventually reaching number one on Friday 10 December with 'The Tale of the Big Why'. Its overall average viewing figure for November was 6.8 million viewers per episode, making it the nation's eighteenth most popular programme. In December, these figures rose to 7.5 million viewers per episode and fourteenth place in the chart.

Christmas scheduling

The ITV regions screening the series on Friday evenings dropped the show on both Christmas Eve and New Year's Eve 1976. ATV, Granada, Southern, Ulster and Westward all resumed with 'Sleeper' on Friday 7 January 1977. However, Border, Grampian, Scottish, Tyne Tees and Yorkshire decided against continuing straightaway, and would not recommence transmissions until Wednesday 2 March. 'Dirtier by the Dozen' became HTV's final *The New Avengers* episode of 1976 on Sunday 19 December, as they also rescheduled the series to March 1977. Thames and Anglia simply missed out Thursday 28 December, then continued in January with the three episodes they had left to air.

Benny Hill spoof

Comedian Benny Hill spoofed *The New Avengers* in a sketch on his *The Benny Hill Show* transmitted on Wednesday 26 January 1977. Complete with bowler hat and umbrella, Hill assumed the role of Steed, with his usual foil Jackie Wright (famous for a visual bald-head-patting gag) playing Gambit and tall blonde Linda Robinson portraying Purdey.

A third novelisation

In February 1977 the third *The New Avengers* paperback, *To Catch a Rat*, became available in retail outlets. Based on the television episode of the same title, this was written by Walter Harris, who had previously worked as a radio interviewer for the BBC, served as motoring correspondent on *Penthouse* magazine and written a number of other novels during the '70s, including adaptations of horror films. As with the other titles in the series, Harris was allowed creative input into proceedings, and he expanded the storyline and added gritty elements that Clemens and Fennell would never have considered for the television series.

Tweaking the format

The start of 1977 saw *The New Avengers'* producers reviewing the series' format and planning for the future. One point they had to consider was that Macnee had been unhappy with the structure of some of the first season's episodes, which in his opinion had relegated Steed to a Mother type role. The format of *The New Avengers* differed from that of *The Avengers* by having the additional male character Gambit, who had been introduced by the producers to handle much of the running, fighting and other physical action, in view of the fact that Macnee was now in his early fifties. They were not the only ones to have identified this as a potential issue: shortly after the series had first been announced, journalist Pat Boxall had written a piece in her column in the 11 January 1976 edition of the *Sunday Mirror*, questioning whether or not Macnee would still be capable of playing Steed in the manner to which the viewing public were accustomed. As a result, the first season's storylines had generally involved Steed as the senior agent issuing instructions to Gambit and Purdey, who then carried them out and became involved in the action. Episodes such as 'To Catch a Rat' and 'Gnaws' had given Macnee considerably less screen time than his co-stars. Macnee discussed his concerns in detail with Clemens, who promised to rectify the situation for the forthcoming second season. There was however no animosity between Macnee and Hunt. On the contrary, Macnee stated that his main reason for staying with *The New Avengers* was the superb working relationship he enjoyed with both Hunt and Lumley. Meanwhile, during the between-seasons hiatus, Macnee spent just over two months in Swaziland working on the film *King Solomon's Treasure* before returning to his California home to pass the rest of the time with his daughter Jenny.

The New Avengers' rivals

British film series were undergoing something of a transition at this time. Thames' production company Euston Films had broken new ground by filming the third and fourth seasons of *Special Branch* on 16mm film mainly on location, and were now taking the same approach on their gritty crime drama *The Sweeney*. This was in contrast to *The New Avengers*, which was shot on the 35mm format traditionally used for film series and was still based at a film studio. However, *The New Avengers* and *The Sweeney* were as different as chalk and cheese, being aimed at completely different markets. The real competitors for Steed and co were the big-budget American imports.

Espionage shows had fallen from grace by this point, with the exception of Universal's *The Six Million Dollar Man*, the ITV transmissions of which began with the pilot film in 1974 and then continued on a regional basis. In this series, Lee Majors portrayed Steve Austin, a man who receives cybernetic implants after being badly injured in an experimental aircraft crash and then uses his enhanced abilities to complete missions as an agent for the OSI (Office of Scientific Research). Encompassing science fiction-themed scenarios as well as basic espionage themes, the series eventually ran to five seasons and a number of television movies.

Meanwhile, across on BBC1, the buddy cop show *Starsky and Hutch* was proving a powerful ratings winner on Saturday evenings. Since its April 1976 debut, this fast-moving action-adventure series, centred around two American police detectives, Dave Starsky played by Paul Michael Glaser and Ken Hutchinson played by David Soul, had become compulsive viewing for millions. Filmed by Spelling-Goldberg for Columbia Pictures Television and featuring a steady stream of car chases and humour, it was popular on both sides of the Atlantic, and benefited from being cross-promoted by Soul's parallel success as a pop singer. It would eventually run for four seasons.

Spelling-Goldberg's other major television offering around this time was *Charlie's Angels*, a series featuring three glamorous undercover private detectives, originally Sabrina Duncan, Jill Munroe and Kelly Garrett, played by Kate Jackson, Farrah Fawcett-Majors and Jaclyn Smith, who receive their cases via an intercom link from the unseen Charles Townsend, voiced by John Forsythe. They arrived on British television in January 1977, when ITV began screening their adventures. Over the years, the line up at the detective agency would change more than once, as angels came and went, but interest would be maintained long enough to produce five seasons, and later to inspire two major Hollywood feature films.

Crew changes

Public relations material issued by The Avengers Enterprises stated that the production values of *The New Avengers* were higher than those of any other television series in the world – a statement that was underlined for emphasis. Budgeted at £125,000 an episode, the series was without doubt an expensive commodity to have in production. Once filming was under way, the overall costs continued to mount up, as the series consumed another screenplay every two or three weeks.

As production on the second season drew closer, Ron Purdie assembled his crew, bringing in Cheryl Leigh to maintain continuity and Ernie Steward as the lighting cameraman. Having been involved with the first season, Malcolm Vinson returned as the camera operator. Others returning to the fold included the make-up department's

Alan Boyle and Alan Brownie and sound recordists Paul Lemare and Ken Barker, although Gordon K McCallum would also take on the latter responsibility for a solitary episode. Newcomer Mark Nelson came in to supervise the hairdressing department. The position of location manager was abolished and Nicholas Gillott moved sideways to replace Robert Fennell as unit manager. Maggie Cartier remained as casting director.

The first season's production designer Syd Cain and art director Bob Bell were both now committed to pre-production on the feature film *The Wild Geese*, so they were replaced by Keith Wilson and Michael Ford, the latter of whom would be credited as assistant art director. Bill Waldron took over from Leon Davis as construction manager, and Maggie Lewin succeeded Jackie Cummins as wardrobe supervisor. Paul Clay retained the post-production supervisor post. Having appeared uncredited in a couple of first season episodes, Joe Dunne became the series' fight arranger, though the previous holder of that position, Cyd Child, remained involved with the production in the capacity of Joanna Lumley's stunt double. Film editing duties would be split between Bob Dearberg and Alan Killick, the latter of whom had served as music editor on various television series during the '60s.

A fourth novelisation

Taking full advantage of their licensing agreement, Futura pressed ahead with their fourth *The New Avengers* novelisation, published in March 1976. This was *Fighting Men* by Justin Cartwright, based on the episode 'Dirtier by the Dozen'. Cartwright was just beginning his career as a writer, and *Fighting Men* was only his second novel. He had previously worked in the advertising industry and directed documentaries and television commercials.

2.01 – 'Hostage'

The edition of *Screen International* published on Saturday 26 March 1977 reported that the second season of *The New Avengers* would commence filming that week, with the Brian Clemens penned episode 'Hostage' directed by Sidney Hayers.

Having dieted during his time in the United States, a slimmer Macnee would play a major role in 'Hostage', as Clemens' screenplay afforded Steed a much meatier part than most of the first season episodes. While it did repeat some elements seen previously, with Purdey being kidnapped and Steed coming under suspicion of being a traitor, Clemens purposely went for a more dramatic scenario involving a conflict of friendship versus the rules. The initial draft script was completed by October 1976, and the shooting script was ready for filming sometime during March to April 1977.

Presumably as a cost-cutting measure, there would be no more trips to Binfield Manor in Berkshire to undertake location shooting for Steed's estate. Instead, the crew would use Fulmer Hall, a whitewashed collection of connected buildings in extensive grounds situated a mile north-west of the studios, with its main access point on the junction of Stoke Common Road and Windmill Road near the village of Fulmer. This was where a sequence was filmed of Steed departing from his residence driving the beige Rover 3500, shadowed by fellow agent Walters, played by Michael Culver, at the wheel of a BMW 3.0S.

A scene where Steed receives instructions from Purdey's kidnappers was achieved with a prop telephone box erected on Lord Mayor's Drive in Burnham Beeches,

Buckinghamshire. The Barn Garage and the Dell tea shop seen later when Steed drives off in the Rover, again followed by Walters in the BMW, were situated nearby at the junction of Sir Henry Peakes Drive and Hawthorne Lane. These buildings have since been demolished and replaced by private homes, and indeed the junction as a whole now looks completely different, as there are far more trees and foliage and Sir Henry Peakes Drive is blocked off to traffic by a barred gate.

Realising that he needs to lose whoever is tailing him, Steed throws the Rover into a gateway at high speed and, performing a 360-degree turn, powers back toward the oncoming BMW. Walters takes evasive action at the last moment, and is then forced to apply the brakes harshly to avoid a collision with some trees. He engages reverse gear, but the BMW spins its wheels on the soft surface, delaying his pursuit. By the time he manages to get his vehicle back on the road, there is no sign of Steed. This sequence was filmed on Pinewood Road in Iver Heath, with both vehicles entering and leaving the studio lot via the Heatherden Hall gateway, which stands beside the South Lodge.

Having ceased production of the MGB, British Leyland supplied a yellow Triumph TR7 (DOM 721R) sports car as a replacement vehicle for Purdey's regular use. This was filmed on the studio lot, passing through Car Park 2 at the Grand Porte-Cochère entrance on the eastern side of Heatherden Hall, for a sequence where Purdey departs from the department's base of operations. A staircase, landing and offices within Heatherden Hall were also pressed into service for interiors of the department's headquarters, thus avoiding the expense of building sets.

As demanded by the kidnappers, Steed places a ransom in a dustbin outside the fictional 14 Edge Street, a sequence actually filmed approximately three miles from the studio on the cul-de-sac Clifton Road in Slough.

In an attempt to blackmail Steed, the villains steal an Enfield number 2 revolver from his desk drawer, but in a later sequence at an abandoned amusement park he has a Walther PPK automatic secreted inside a hidden compartment in his bowler hat.

After the trials and tribulations of *The Avengers* stage play, Simon Oates – an actor rated highly by Clemens – became involved with the franchise again here, being cast as the traitor Spelman. Also in the guest cast, in the role of Ministry man Mackay, was William Franklyn, who was involved in an in-joke in a scene where he is seen holding a file marked 'Top Secret' – which just happened to be the title of his early '60s espionage series made by Associated-Rediffusion.

The exterior of the villain's hideout was represented by a standing set discarded after appearing in another production, while the interior was assembled from the sewer set seen in 'Gnaws'.

Having returned to her hairdresser John Frieda, Lumley now sported a slightly longer and modified version of the Purdey bobbed hairstyle that had proved so popular during the first season.

Fashions

Jillie Murphy would be responsible for Lumley's wardrobe for this season, taking a co-credit on selected episodes with Betty Jackson and Jennifer Hocking. Jackson would shortly become a designer for the Quorum line of fashions before later establishing her own company, Betty Jackson Limited. Later still she would design for Lumley again, providing many of the costumes for the *Absolutely Fabulous* sitcom in which the actress co-starred.

2.02 – 'Trap'

Sometime during April 1977, filming commenced on another Brian Clemens screenplay, 'Trap'. The writer had developed this from a single-page outline dated Monday 3 May 1976 into a first draft script three months later. The story centres around an Asian drugs lord, Soo Choy, who loses face when Steed, Purdey and Gambit intercept a large narcotics consignment and then devises his own brand of revenge. Ray Austin assumed the director's chair and assisted in casting his then wife Yasuko Nagazumi as Soo Choy's assistant Yasko, which incidentally was also the name of the character she played in eight episodes of the second season of *Space: 1999*. Soo Choy himself was played by Terry Wood.

Location scouts discovered that the street and multi-storey car park locations required by the shooting script could all be found in Windsor, Berkshire, a mention of which was then included in the dialogue. Purdey is seen driving CIA operative Marty Brine, played by Stuart Damon, in her Triumph TR7 down Castle Hill in the town, and then along High Street and Frances Road, turning right into Grove Road, to keep a prearranged meeting with Steed and Gambit. Splitting into pairs, the four agents stake out someone posing as a street cleaner working in the narrow Gloucester Place, where they witness a passing car drop off the consignment of drugs. The street cleaner, played by an uncredited Vincent Wong, shoots Brine and then flees, followed by Steed and Gambit, who are later seen on the corner of Russell Street and Alexandra Road. Eventually the street cleaner is chased to the highest level of the Victoria Street multi-storey car park, from which he falls to his death in Alexandra Road after attempting to shoot Gambit.

A sequence in which the blue Land Rover of agent Williams, played by Larry Lamb, is seen travelling to East Anglia was actually shot locally to Pinewood, going along Uxbridge Road and passing the junction with Black Park Road, heading toward the Five Points roundabout in Iver Heath.

Soo Choy's impressive house was represented by Iver Grove, a large dwelling occupying its own grounds on Wood Lane in the Shreding Green area of Iver Heath, not ten minutes' drive south of the studios. However, a scene at the start of the episode where Williams is wounded as he escapes over the house's high barbed-wire fence appears to have been shot at the Pinewood perimeter fence, of which a section had featured previously in 'The Eagle's Nest'.

The site of a plane crash in which Soo Choy tries in vain to kill Steed, Purdey and Gambit was elaborately realised among the trees within Black Park, directly next to Pinewood. This also served as the location for the subsequent scene where soldiers search for the three agents in the wooded area of the drugs lord's estate. In editing, this footage was supplemented by various sequences filmed on the studio lot's South Lodge Drive, where Gambit is captured by soldiers and the three fugitives fashion improvised weapons.

A sequence in which a ninja sneaks into the department to steal a file and is confronted descending a staircase was also filmed at Pinewood, using the fire escape at the western end of the main administration block on Main Road, as seen previously in 'Target!'.

Purdey at one point produces a small Beretta model 70 automatic from her shoulder bag, although both this and Gambit's .357 Smith and Wesson Combat Magnum revolver are later confiscated in a fake customs check at the airport where the agents board the ill-fated plane.

2.03 – 'Dead Men are Dangerous'

On Thursday 14 April 1977, the *TV Times Top 10 Awards* show was transmitted by ITV, revealing that viewers' votes had secured Joanna Lumley the accolade of Most Compulsive Female Character on Television for her role as Purdey in *The New Avengers*. The actress had little time to savour her success, however, as before the month was out, filming was under way on another episode, Brian Clemens' 'Dead Men are Dangerous'. The story this time centres around and gives more background to the character of Steed, revealing that his childhood friend and defector Mark Crayford has returned to the UK, holding a grudge from their schooldays and intending to inflict a final defeat on the agent. However, there is also some character development for Purdey, who starts to show the first signs of an attraction toward Steed. Sidney Hayers returned to direct what would be his final episode for the series.

The opening sequence set in 1967, where Crayford, played by Clive Revill, unexpectedly defects after Steed drives him to the border in a Mercedes, was filmed partly on Peace Road and the surrounding area in Black Park.

Fulmer Hall again served as the exterior of Steed's stud, with Macnee and Lumley filmed on location there along with the Big Cat Jaguar.

The gardens at Heatherden Hall were used for a sequence where Gambit strolls with Steed's former tutor 'Pin Man' Perry, played by Richard Murdoch, until they discover dead goldfish in the ornate pond.

Continuity back to the original series was maintained in a scene where Purdey checks through rows of Ministry folders and comes across those containing information about the cases involving Cathy Gale, Emma Peel and Tara King.

Built in 1935, the 100-foot-tall Farringdon Folly Tower in Farringdon, Oxfordshire was chosen to represent Crayford's hideout and the site of his only victory over Steed. However, only Macnee and Hunt were required to visit this location for filming.

Following the trend started on 'Hostage', the construction of sets was avoided by filming inside Heatherden Hall, this time to represent Steed's old school, where Gambit meets Maths teacher Penny Redfern on what is referred to as the Club House staircase. Scenes in the school trophy room were played out in what was known at the time as the Green Room, although this has since undergone a complete redecoration and is now known as the Paul Hitchcock Room.

Having previously appeared in the fifth season *The Avengers* episode 'The Hidden Tiger', and having also been considered for the roles of both Emma Peel's replacement and Charley, Gabrielle Drake was cast as Redfern, who later visits Gambit at his apartment, the set for which had been redressed to give it an untidy appearance, allowing him to crack a joke about having moved in four years earlier.

The rooftop of Stages J and K at Pinewood was used to film from Crayford's vantage point as he targets Steed with a sniper rifle complete with a telescopic sight. Only grazing Steed with his shot, Crayford then escapes in a waiting car pursued on foot by Gambit, who is seen to emerge from the entrance to Stages L and M, representing a hospital admissions unit. Gambit throws himself onto the boot lid of Crayford's Fiat 132, but is later dislodged by the erratic movement of the vehicle.

Gambit mentions dropping out of school at the age of 15 and joining the merchant navy to sail around the world, which is in fact what Hunt did in real life. Inside

Crayford's hideout, the walls are seen to be scrawled with graffiti thought up by production designer Keith Wilson, including the well known '60s slogan 'Clapton is God,' referring to blues guitarist Eric Clapton. This episode also marks the first appearance of a redecorated Steed living room set, with the walls now terracotta in colour.

A sequence of a martial arts sparring match between Purdey and Gambit was filmed on Lumley's birthday, Sunday 1 May 1977. Behind-the-scenes photographs show Lumley in Purdey's blue silk fighting outfit, cutting her cake with assistance from Macnee and Hunt.

Some amendments were made to the shooting script during filming, although most of these were simply minor dialogue alterations, presumably agreed between Hayers and Clemens. One more significant change was that Purdey was originally to have been just a spectator in a scene where Gambit and Steed play cricket, whereas in the actual episode all three characters are involved in a match filmed on location at Beaconsfield Cricket Club in Wilton Park, just outside Beaconsfield. Another was that at the end of a sequence where Crayford's assistant Hara, played by Terry Taplin, destroys Steed's beloved vintage Bentley, the petrol tank was originally to have been the only component to survive, whereas this was ultimately changed to the more recognisable radiator grille.

Purdey perfume

Around this time, a merchandising licence was agreed between The Avengers Enterprises and Carlo Dini, an Italian opera singer and owner of the Dini perfume brand name, to market a Purdey fragrance. Lumley assisted by appearing in a promotional photoshoot, in a white floral dress that she had worn during 'Dead Men are Dangerous'. The Purdey perfume was then advertised in both *Vogue* and *Harper's Bazaar*. It was described as having been created by Dini for the exciting woman of today, and was accompanied by the slogan, 'Purdey fragrance for the woman with style.'

The Professionals

Upon the completion of work on 'Dead Men are Dangerous', Sidney Hayers threw himself into pre-production on a newly-devised 16mm film series called *The Professionals*, which had been created by Brian Clemens and was being financed by LWT. However, as it had a smaller budget than *The New Avengers*, it was decided that this production should be based at the independent facility Harefield House on Rickmansworth Road in Harefield, Middlesex. In preparation for the making of 13 episodes, the stables block of this new base of operations was converted into a post-production facility, including cutting rooms.

Having moved across from *The New Avengers* to become unit manager on *The Professionals*, Nicholas Gillott was busy assembling a crew for the series. Hayers had agreed to become producer on the understanding that it would be for only the first season. Initial screen tests for the lead actors were undertaken on Tuesday 10 May 1977, at Harefield House in the morning and on Stages J and K at Pinewood in the afternoon, all directed by Hayers.

2.04 – 'Medium Rare'

Meanwhile, back on *The New Avengers*, the next episode into production was 'Medium Rare' from the typewriter of Dennis Spooner. Spooner had submitted his second draft for the producers' consideration in April 1976, and filming got under way in May, with Ray Austin directing. The story concerns a corrupt Ministry official named Wallace, played by John Finch, who murders his colleague Freddy Mason, played by Alan Weston, and tries to avoid exposure by having Steed framed for the crime.

The Heatherden Hall gateway was used for filming again, this time as the entrance to a foreign embassy; and Fulmer Hall once more provided the background for Steed's large home, driveway and ancillary buildings. The scene where Wallace kills Mason by knocking him over the parapet of a bridge was shot on Eton Road near the village of Eton in Buckinghamshire, with Mason landing beside Eton Wick Road,.

Some interiors required by the shooting script were obtained by the crew filming inside Heatherden Hall. Mason's wood-panelled office was represented by a room within the administration section, and the corridor outside this room also appears – for the second time in the series, as it was also used for 'Hostage'. Steed is later witnessed descending the staircase heading for Wallace's office, situated in another corridor located in the Club House portion of the building – which had also appeared previously, in 'Dead Men are Dangerous'.

For a sequence where he is called to a public telephone within an auditorium where he is watching a ballet, Macnee was actually filmed on the first floor landing in the foyer of Stages J and K at Pinewood. Also shot on site was a scene where a courier named Parr, played by an uncredited Marc Boyle, is prevented by Gambit from depositing a package of cash into Steed's bank account, the London Bank building actually being the main entrance to Stages L and M.

At one point in the action, Steed is enticed to a secret meeting with the accounts clerk George Cowley, played by an uncredited Hugh Walters, who is promptly killed by the assassin Richards, played by Jeremy Wilkin, leaving the agent to be found in incriminating circumstances kneeling over the body. This is notable as the character name George Cowley was quickly revived in *The Professionals* for the head of the anti-terrorist organisation CI5, played by Gordon Jackson.

Tapping into the style of the original series, Spooner incorporated into his screenplay a highly eccentric character in the person of the fake psychic medium Victoria Stanton, played by Sue Holderness, who thinks that she has finally managed to receive some genuine premonitions.

Jon Finch was given the special guest star treatment with his own caption in the closing credits. Having gone through a lengthy audition process, he was also offered the leading role of Doyle in *The Professionals*, but strangely turned it down almost immediately, stating that he could never play a police officer. Clemens was staggered that an actor would put himself through a screen test and then, upon being cast, simply reject the part, especially after being briefed in detail beforehand as to what that role entailed.

2.05 – 'Obsession'

Brian Clemens' next offering was originally called 'Missile', although this had been altered to 'Obsession' by the time the final draft was completed on Monday 9 May 1977.

All-rounder Ernest Day was given the opportunity to undertake his first directing assignment on this episode, which expands a little on Purdey's background and gives her a former lover in the person of RAF pilot Larry Doomer, played by Martin Shaw – who, after the casting problem with Jon Finch, had also taken on the role of Doyle in *The Professionals*.

Scenes set at an airbase, including an opening flashback involving Purdey and Doomer in 1970, were shot at RAF Northolt, where material had also been obtained for both 'House of Cards' and 'Sleeper'. On location here were Macnee, Lumley, Shaw and guest actor Tommy Boyle, playing the base's Flt Lt Wolach, plus various extras. Stock footage of SEPECAT Jaguar military aircraft came courtesy of the 1972 RAF training film *The Engineer in the RAF*, showing them taking off from RAF Lossiemouth in Moray, Scotland, with several of them later passing Glen Coe in the Highlands. However, not all of the episode's military aircraft footage features Jaguars; mixed in, there are also some shots of British Aerospace Harrier jump jets with similar camouflage markings, presumably sourced from another RAF training film.

The series' final location shoot at Fulmer Hall was undertaken for a short sequence where General Canvey, played by Mark Kingston, departs in his Jaguar from a party thrown by Steed. Shortly after this, the General comes across Doomer's broken-down Mercedes on the road – actually a trap engineered by Doomer – in a sequence filmed at the gateway of St Hubert's Home Farm on St Hubert's Lane, near Gerrards Cross, a couple of miles north of Pinewood.

Taking Canvey prisoner, Doomer returns to his home, meeting up with ordnance expert Kilner, played by Lewis Collins. This exterior was also filmed on St Hubert's Lane, at a large property called Grayleigh. Purdey is later seen arriving at the same location on her motorcycle, which for this episode is her Honda 125cc trials bike, as seen previously in 'The Tale of the Big Why'. This bike had apparently been given to the production company by the manufacturer, as it would go on to appear in six episodes of *The Professionals* as well. Later still it would be bought by Ron Purdie, whose credit on the second season of *The New Avengers* underwent various charges, from assistant director to unit manager to associate producer to production manager. At the time of writing, it is still owned by him.

Additional material was filmed in the immediate vicinity of Pinewood. This included shots of a military dispatch rider on his BSA Starfire motorcycle turning off Black Park Road adjacent to Black Park, proceeding north-west along Rowley Lane and then travelling in the opposite direction along Black Park Road, passing the junction with Rowley Lane and continuing north, where the rider is dislodged by a washing line strung across the road.

Later, Gambit produces his Smith and Wesson revolver while stood in the middle of Sevenhills Road, near Gerrards Cross, as Kilner and his fellow munitions expert Morgan, played by Anthony Heaton, speed toward him in a Bedford pick-up truck, supplied for the production by Action 99 Cars of Hemel Hempstead. Losing this game of chicken, Kilner swerves the vehicle into the wooded verge, narrowly missing Gambit, who breathes a deep sigh of relief. This action was filmed on Wednesday 25 May, along with footage of a downed missile embedded in what was described on the call sheet for the day as rocky/sandy ground, somewhere nearby in Iver, Buckinghamshire.

A section of the 1970-set footage showing Doomer's father being confronted by three armed militia men who push his Saab 96 estate over a sandy drop was obtained at

Springwell Chalk Pit, Springwell Lane in Harefield, Buckinghamshire.

A day-for-night sequence of Kilner and Morgan starting a blaze at the RAF station involved Collins and Heaton being filmed running past a cleaning department truck parked opposite the carpenters' shop on Carpenters Road on the Pinewood lot, before knocking out a guard patrolling by the cutting rooms. The fire itself was represented by stock library footage.

It was established in the previous episode, 'Medium Rare', that Purdey was in the process of redecorating her apartment and now the end result is revealed. The décor features magnolia walls, wicker furniture and light-coloured soft furnishings, and Purdey's upright piano has been stripped back to bare wood.

During the 1970-set sequence, Purdey finds a copy of the *Daily Telegraph* almost ripped in half. Later, back in the present of 1977, Steed shows her an edition of the *Daily Express* with the headline 'Anglo-Arabian Summit'.

Purdey once again favours the compact Beretta model 70 automatic for this episode's action, firing a single shot to flatten a tyre on Steed's Range Rover and enable her to reach Doomer first. As Doomer holds her at gunpoint, she pleads with him not to implement his plan, which involves levelling the Houses of Parliament with the downed missile in order to kill the foreign dignitary responsible for his father's death in 1970. Gambit meanwhile arrives from another direction and, seeing the situation, acts swiftly, killing Doomer with a single shot, much to Purdey's distress. Then Steed arrives and caps Doomer's makeshift missile silo with his Range Rover, causing the weapon to explode on launch, although destroying his vehicle in the process. This sequence of events – arguably the most dramatic of the entire series – leaves a devastated Purdey to try to come to terms with the death of her former lover.

Recasting on *The Professionals*

The Professionals entered production on Monday 13 June 1977 with the lead roles of William Bodie and Ray Doyle played by Anthony Andrews and Martin Shaw. However, in a situation similar to that encountered with Elizabeth Shepherd on *The Avengers*, it was decided after four days that Andrews was wrong for his part, as the two characters failed to spark off each other. Remembering the good rapport Shaw had had with fellow guest actor Lewis Collins during the making of 'Obsession', Brian Clemens suggested Collins be brought in to replace Andrews. After a screen test, the appointment became official, and Collins joined the shoot on the series' first episode, 'Old Dog with New Tricks' – making it quite prophetic that at one point during the filming of 'Obsession' he had been required to deliver to Shaw the line of dialogue 'Maybe we should work together again.'

2.06 – 'Angels of Death'

Terence Feely and Brian Clemens collaborated on the screenplay for the next episode into production, 'Angels of Death', getting a first draft ready by Saturday 7 May 1977, although at that stage the title was the slightly different 'The Angels of Death'. In this adventure, Steed, Purdey and Gambit investigate the sudden, unexplained deaths of some 47 of their colleagues over a relatively short period of time, and find the common link at a health farm.

Principal photography commenced sometime during June, with Ernest Day directing his second episode in succession – an unusual occurrence for a film series. However, a section of the opening teaser sequence written on Monday 11 July and shot on location in Paris is thought to have been handled by Frenchman Yvon Marie Coulais instead, during the making of the later adventure 'K is for Kill'. It shows Purdey descending the wide steps from the famous Sacré-Coeur Basilica Roman Catholic church and having her silhouette cut by a street vendor on Rue du Cardinal Dubois under surveillance by a Russian agent.

The episode's guest cast brought together three actors who had previously appeared in other roles in *The Avengers*, namely Terence Alexander, Dinsdale Landen and Macnee's friend Michael Latimer, along with Bond girl Caroline Munro and Pamela Stephenson, who was also working concurrently on *The Professionals*.

The unit returned to film material at The Straight in Southall for a sequence where a Mini driven by Munro's character Tammy overtakes a Morris 2200 driven by Alexander's character Peter Manderson. Tammy activates her rear parcel shelf, which lifts up to reveal a maze diagram. Upon seeing this, the stress-conditioned Manderson suddenly dies. This leaves his passenger Steed fighting to control the vehicle as it careers down White Street adjacent to what was then the gasworks. Having avoided colliding with a white Volkswagen Beetle on two occasions, the Morris then careers around the corner in the opposite direction from The Straight into White Street, where it grinds to a halt, having struck several cardboard boxes and dustbins.

Prior to this, both Macnee and Terence Alexander had been filmed on location in the car park of the since-demolished South Buckinghamshire District Council offices on Windsor Road, Slough, which represented the exterior of the Ministry building.

At one point in the action, suffering from the effects of a drug he has been given, Steed finds himself trapped within a maze of small rooms and begins experiencing flashbacks. These are represented by excerpts from the episodes 'Dirtier by the Dozen' and 'Target!'

While discussing events with Gambit, Steed practices putting golf balls around his living room and chipping them into his bowler hat on the sofa, something he had also done in some episodes of *The Avengers*.

A fight scene between Purdey and the female staff of the fictional Briantern Health Farm is accompanied in part by some Laurie Johnson incidental music first heard in the series' opening episode, 'The Eagle's Nest'.

The Leyland Marathon articulated truck driven by agent Martin, played by Christopher Driscoll, was supplied by British Leyland. It was filmed on Peace Road in Black Park for a sequence where it crashes through an East German checkpoint and stops nearby, where the driver is then shot by a concealed assassin just as Steed and Purdey arrive.

When she and Steed are trapped together in the maze and about to be crushed to death, it sounds as if Purdey is about to reveal her true feelings toward her superior, as she begins 'Steed, I must tell you something …' However, before she confesses all, Gambit intervenes, saving their lives.

This episode is also notable for marking the final appearance in the series of the Big Cat Jaguar.

French and Canadian episodes

The New Avengers had by this point run into financial problems so serious that at one point Brian Clemens, Albert Fennell and Laurie Johnson were paying the crew's salaries out of their own bank accounts in order to keep production going. As would later be revealed in a short feature in the *Daily Express* of Friday 16 December 1977, the French funding for the series passed through accounts in several countries, including Guatemala and Switzerland, before arriving with The Avengers Enterprises, resulting in regular hold-ups. To try to rectify the situation, the producers held negotiations with the French backers, and also obtained additional funding from the Canadian company Nielsen-Ferns Incorporated of Toronto. However, there were strings attached, as both the French and the Canadian investors demanded that a number of episodes be filmed on location in their own respective countries. As the additional money was needed in order to complete the season, Clemens, Fennell and Johnson had no option but to agree, hence a production schedule was drawn up to film in both Paris and Toronto. As reported in the *Daily Express* of Thursday 16 June 1977, the French backers also attempted to exert more influence on the style of the series, wanting Purdey to exhibit a sexier image.

Around this time, French designer Yves Saint Laurent was suggested as a provider of fashions for Lumley, as the Parisian backers voiced their opinion that Purdey needed to be styled more akin to the women in *Charlie's Angels*. Lumley was understandably unhappy with this, having left the frilly dresses, stockings and suspenders behind early in the first season in preference for the trouser suits and split skirts she had been wearing in the second. Fortunately for her, the producers totally ignored these demands from the French financiers, whom they blamed for bringing about the series' budget problems in the first place.

On Monday 30 June, the Toronto-based newspaper *The Globe and Mail* reported that seven episodes of *The New Avengers* would be filmed in the city and surrounding area. These were intended to comprise two episodes for the current second season and five for the third, which at that point Brian Clemens was confident would occur, outlining a deal to produce two episodes in West Germany and indicating that negotiations were also under way to film in Australia. Despite these positive statements, *The New Avengers* would never be filmed in either West Germany or Australia, and although some finance would be found for a third season, the full amount required would ultimately prove impossible to obtain.

2.07 – 'The Lion and the Unicorn'

The next episode, 'The Lion and the Unicorn', directed by Ray Austin, was the first of three to be filmed mainly in France. The initial draft of John Goldsmith's screenplay – his only contribution to the series – was completed on Friday 27 May 1977, though this was minus a teaser sequence, which the producers had already decided should be a car chase adapted from a pre-existing Cornish-shot British Leyland television commercial, albeit with additional filming.

The post-production of the three French-filmed episodes would take place as usual at Pinewood, but there were some major changes within the film unit at this point as key personnel moved across to work on *The Professionals*. Continuity person Cheryl Leigh was replaced by both Pat Rambraut, who had worked on the first season, and Eliane Baum, who had worked as a script supervisor on a small number of French films. Gilbert Sarthre, who had been credited as cinematographer on various French movies since the early '60, took over from Ernest Steward as the lighting cameraman.

Paul Le Marinel assumed the make-up department role previously fulfilled by Alan Brownie. The position of location manager was reinstated, and assigned to Ginette Mejinsky, who had started her career as a production secretary on French feature films. Experienced dubbing editor Jack Knight, who had worked on some of the Diana Rigg episodes of *The Avengers*, came in to replace Peter Lennard, and Mamade-Madeleine Demay, credited simply as Mamade, took over from Maggie Cartier as casting director. Production designer Keith Wilson's involvement with *The New Avengers* also concluded – although unlike his colleagues he did not go on to work on *The Professionals* – and the virtually unknown Frenchman Daniel Budin was recruited to take his place.

'The Lion and the Unicorn' opens with Steed and Purdey tracking down an international assassin known as the Unicorn, played by Jean Claudio, by using stethoscopes to eavesdrop against the doors in a hotel corridor. Once again the cost of building a set was avoided by having the unit film this scene within Heatherden Hall on site at Pinewood. This entailed temporarily removing the nameplates from the doors there, leaving small screw holes visible under the room numbers.

As Steed and Purdey beat a hasty retreat, the Unicorn follows them from the hotel and fires a couple of shots in their direction – a sequence for which Claudio was filmed on the administration building fire escape at Pinewood.

The aforementioned car chase teaser sequence incorporating British Leyland's television commercial footage begins in the coastal village of Trebarwith Strand, as Steed's Rover 3500 powers away, followed by the Unicorn's associates in a Mercedes 250, a Volvo 244 and a Ford Granada. Aerial footage shows the Rover leading the other three vehicles along Marine Drive, passing the Widemouth Manor Hotel at Widemouth Bay, continuing along a narrow road between high hedgerows shot adjacent to an area called Voter Run, near Crackington Haven. The chase then continues with all the vehicles rounding a tight, narrow bend before descending toward the small village of Millbrook Haven, where the driver of the Granada loses control, resulting in the vehicle briefly leaving the road.

From here the cars descend another narrow, steep hill, forcing an oncoming Ford Transit to stop, allowing passage for the Rover to speed away over a small bridge. However, the leading pursuer, the Mercedes, fails to negotiate the tight road layout and is ultimately driven into a shallow-bed river – a sequence filmed at the ford on Harpur's Downs, near Camelford. Returning to the Crackington Haven area, the two remaining pursuers follow the Rover round a bend on an unnamed coastal road, then a sharper bend close to cliffs back on Marine Drive in Lower Upton. The conclusion of the chase is played out at the Delabole Quarry, near Delabole village. The driver of the Volvo misjudges a bend on a muddy track and collides with some large boulders, putting him out of action. The Granada then follows Steed's Rover upwards on a muddy track leading to a small plateau, where both vehicles are handbrake-turned to reverse their course. However, this manoeuvre proves the downfall of the Granada's driver, as he is unable to control his vehicle, resulting in it careering off the parapet and falling hundreds of feet to the quarry floor, where it then bursts into flames.

In an early sequence filmed outside Eton College Hall and School Library on Eton High Street in Eton, Buckinghamshire, Gerald Sim portrays a church minister who is apparently killed by a single gunshot fired by the Unicorn. Later, however, it is revealed that the minister was wearing a bullet-proof vest.

While in Paris, Purdey drives a red Mini with a black vinyl roof – a popular form of customisation adopted by most car manufacturers during the '70s.

At the request of Steed, who wants the Unicorn taken alive, Gambit hands over his .357 Smith and Wesson Model 19 Combat Magnum revolver, plus his back-up weapons, a smaller revolver and a compact automatic. However, when later chasing the Unicorn's henchman Ritter, played by Jacques Maury, he withdraws a Beretta that was tucked into his boot, while Purdey favours one of the smallest mass-produced guns ever made, producing a concealed gold-coloured .25 Baby Browning automatic from her shoulder bag. The sequence of Gambit and Purdey chasing Ritter was filmed on the busy Avenue du Président Wilson. Their quarry eludes them by escaping into the d'Iéna Metro station, using a group of nuns as cover.

Going for maximum impact with the Paris location filming, the unit obtained footage of a number of well-known landmarks such as the Eiffel Tower and the Arc de Triomphe, situated on the Avenue des Champs-Elysées, toward which Steed and Purdey are also seen travelling in a car from the perspective of a camera mounted in the back seat. This leads the two agents to a meeting with the Unicorn's former second-in-command Henri DuValle, played by Raymond Bussières, whom they pressurise into parting with some information. This sequence was shot at the junction with Avenue de Friedland, where Purdey impresses Steed with her skill at boules on a gravel-surfaced playing area.

Used to represent the agents' base of operations in Paris was a building known as Place d'Iéna, which stands on the junction of Avenue du Président Wilson and Avenue d'Iéna, with footage being filmed at an entrance on the latter. In one sequence, one of the assassin's men named Grima, played by Henri Czarniak, parachutes onto the roof, intent on gathering information. Discovering that the Unicorn is dead, he escapes in a Saviem truck, pursued by Gambit using a pick-up truck based on a three-wheeler Piaggio scooter. Perched atop the roof of Place d'Iéna, Purdey directs Gambit using a Pye Telecom PF8 two-way radio, after sighting the Saviem heading north on Boulevard de Rochechouart and Gambit driving the pick-up truck down Rue Chappe.

Turning left, Gambit powers his vehicle along Rue Tardieu. A gendarme on traffic duty blows his whistle repeatedly to get him to slow down, but Gambit takes no notice, leaving him in an agitated state and toppling from his raised pedestal. This short sequence was filmed at the multi-junction of Rue de Trois Frères, Rue Chappe, Rue Tardieu and Rue Yvonne le Tac. The chase then moves into the Montemartre quarter of the city, and takes on a humorous slant as a baker's breadsticks are severed as he attempts to cross the road in Place Emile Goudeau and a photographic model loses part of her outfit beside the Restaurant Panoramique on Rue Saint-Eleuthere. Continuing in a similar vein, a postal worker on a bicycle in Rue Norvins is left stationary as his wheels are crushed by the passing pick-up truck, then a diner at a street café in Rue Poulbot unexpectedly loses his table and a waiter is left pouring burgundy into a glass that is no longer there.

After destroying a bed being carried by two delivery men back at Place Emile Goudeau, Gambit finally collides head-on with the Saviem in Rue de la Manutention. Grima escapes on foot up the wide steps toward Avenue du Président Wilson but, giving chase, Gambit catches the Frenchman before he reaches the top. A short fight scene ensues, resulting in Grima being taken prisoner.

The final sequence involves Steed and Gambit showing Purdey the nightlife of Paris, arriving outside the world famous Moulin Rouge club situated at 82 Boulevard de Clichy – though she declines to join them for the show.

2.08 – 'K is for Kill: The Tiger Awakes'

The second and third predominantly French-filmed episodes made up the only two-part *The New Avengers* storyline, initially titled 'The Long Sleep'. This was written by Brian Clemens, who had a draft version of the first part ready by May 1977 and the second by the following month. Shooting scripts were then prepared, and the first part entered principal photography in late June. Director Yvon Marie Coulais was assigned to handle the double-header at the insistence of the French backers, despite the fact that his only previous experience had come on French television commercials. Before reaching the small screen, 'The Long Sleep' was retitled to 'K is for Kill', and the two parts subtitled 'The Tiger Awakes' and 'Tiger by the Tail' respectively.

'The Tiger Awakes' starts with two prequels to the main storyline. The first opens with stock footage captioned 'Tibet, April 21st 1945. 11.22 am.' This shows Buddhist monks taking part in ritual activities, plus the Boudhanath Stupa, an ancient shrine adorned with a distinctive graphic of a pair of eyes, which is actually situated in Kathmandu, Nepal. The scene is thus set for some newly-shot material of a Russian force trying to find the secret of arresting the aging process. The second prequel takes place 20 years later, and features a Second World War Russian soldier suddenly appearing in a remote English village and gunning down members of the local Salvation Army. The establishing shot of the village depicts Turville in Buckinghamshire. However, the footage of the Russian soldier sneaking around was obtained in another village, Sarrett in Hertfordshire. Initially the solider wanders through the churchyard of Holy Cross Church on Church Lane, then he moves around the village duck pond, arriving at The Cricketers pub. The site of the massacre is the local village hall, outside which Steed's 1927 3 litre Bentley (YT 3942) is later seen to be parked. This vehicle had last been featured in season six of *The Avengers*, in the episode 'Have Guns – Will Haggle'.

Given the 1965 setting of this action, the production team took the opportunity to have Steed involve Emma Peel in proceedings, although her appearance is limited to two clips of her answering the phone in her apartment, lifted from the earlier episodes 'The Winged Avenger' and 'The Hidden Tiger', plus a voiceover by an uncredited Sue Lloyd imitating Diana Rigg's voice. In interviews, Clemens has frequently stated that Rigg was too busy with other projects to reprise her role as Emma. However, the actress had actually gone to great lengths since her departure to distance herself from *The Avengers*, so it seems unlikely that she could ever have been enticed back to appear in *The New Avengers*, even for a cameo.

Steed's second phone call to Mrs Peel comes in the 1977 present day material, after he reads in the *Guardian* newspaper of a similar mysterious attack in a small French town. This is much to Purdey's disgust, as she bluntly asks him, 'Calling in reinforcements?'

Sequences set in the former Allied wartime headquarters that serves as the military museum of the elderly General Gaspard, played by Maurice Marsak, were filmed at what is now the luxurious Tiara Château Hotel Mont Royal, situated 22 miles north of Paris and completely surrounded by the Chantilly Forest. The Forest itself afforded more than sufficient filming locations for the episode's scenes of Russian and French troops attacking and counterattacking.

As the action moves to Paris, night-time establishing footage shows a traffic jam on the Avenue de Friedland, with the camera panning across to the Avenue Hoche, apparently from the vantage point of the top of the Arc de Triomphe. Later, Steed and Purdey are seen in disguise as a bishop and a nun departing from the Hotel George V on Avenue George V and then walking around the first corner into Rue Quentin-Bauchart, where they deposit their outfits into a convenient rubbish bin.

2.09 – 'K is for Kill: Tiger by the Tail'

Instead of beginning with a pre-title teaser sequence like all the other episodes of *The New Avengers*, 'Tiger by the Tail' presents a montage of excerpts recapping the events of the previous episode.

For one scene, Macnee, Lumley, Hunt and actress guest actress Christine Delaroche, playing Dr Jeanine Leparge, were all filmed in Paris taking a drink at a street café in Place Dauphine, a tree-lined square on the north-western end of Île de la Cité, the larger of the two islands in the River Seine. This location was also used for a sequence later in the episode when a Russian named Turkov, played by Maxence Mailfort, realises that Stanislav, played by Charles Millot, is his son.

As in 'The Tiger Awakes', Steed has a suite in the George V Hotel on Avenue George V. This was the location used for a scene where the Russian Ambassador Toy, played by Paul Emile Dieber, visits him with a warning regarding the 'K agents' involved in the special anti-aging assignment, though unknown to him an embassy guard has tailed him. However, the subsequent footage where the guard, played by Guy Mairesse, shoots both Steed and Toy from the street below was actually filmed around the corner at the junction of Avenue Pierre the First de Serbie and Impasse du Docteur Jacques Bertillon. The latter, a cul-de-sac containing blocks of expensive apartments, was also used for the following action where the guard holds Purdey at gunpoint and fires a shot at Gambit, who manages to deflect it with the butt of his Smith and Wesson revolver, though not without sustaining an injury. The guard is also seen on the corner of Avenue George V and Avenue Pierre the First de Serbie, within sight of the George V Hotel. Steed, incidentally, survives the attempt on his life by virtue of the bullet being blocked by a cigarette case in his breast pocket.

The Tiara Château Hotel Mont Royal features again in this episode, in a sequence where the K agent Minski, played by Frank Oliver, guns down General Gaspard as he is bugling the last call on the steps of his military museum, then suffers the safe fate himself when Gambit arrives.

The exterior of the building where Steed and Colonel Martin, played by Pierre Verner, have a conference with French government Ministers was represented by the Hôtel de Soubise, a 14th Century manor house surrounded by fortified walls, accessed from Rue des Francs-Bourgeois two miles east of Avenue George V.

Having departed from a nightclub where she fails to appreciate the dancing girls, Purdey accompanies Steed and Gambit across the Pont Neuf bridge at first light, walking south away from Place Dauphine.

Some of the 35mm film footage for 'K is for Kill' was processed as usual at the Rank Organisation's premises on the North Orbital Road in Denham, Middlesex, only ten minutes' drive from Pinewood. While the unit were filming in France, however, it was LTC Laboratories, based in the St Cloud district of Paris, who developed the rushes, enabling the producers to watch each day's filming during the evening.

With its decades-spanning storyline and action set in the UK, Tibet, Russia and particularly France, 'K is for Kill' was obviously intended by Brian Clemens as an epic international adventure, with Steed, Purdey and Gambit taking on a high-stakes mission involving the prevention of a potential Third World War.

Canada beckons

With the influx of additional funding, no expense had been spared during the making of the French-filmed episodes. The leads had been accommodated in the Hilton Hotel, and Rudolph Roffi had entertained Patrick Macnee every weekend with a meal at an expensive restaurant. However, despite getting the series' budget issues resolved, Brian Clemens and Albert Fennell still felt that the move overseas meant that the continuity of production they had established in the UK was lost, thus reducing the quality of the finished episodes; and Macnee agreed with them on this. Nevertheless, the filming in Canada still had to go ahead.

On Tuesday 19 July 1977 the Canadian newspaper *The Gazette* (aka *Montreal Gazette*) reported The Avengers Enterprises' tie-up with Nielsen-Ferns and indicated that shooting on either two or three episodes would commence in early August. By this time, the first transmissions of *The New Avengers* had already taken place in the provinces of Quebec and Saskatchewan, plus the major cities of Montreal, Vancouver, Winnipeg and Saskatoon.

Flying the existing unit to Canada and accommodating them in Toronto was a complete non-starter, not least because the contracts for all the French members concluded with the completion of work on 'K is for Kill'. Also at this point, a number of the British crew such as Malcolm Vinson, Alan Boyle, Ken Barker, Alan Killick and Bob Dearberg were redeployed to join their former colleagues at Harefield House working on *The Professionals*. Brian Clemens was also preoccupied with that newer series, for which he would write the majority of the first season episodes. This left Albert Fennell to oversee production of *The New Avengers* in Canada with a new crew.

Joining Fennell in Toronto were Ray Austin, who had been promoted to co-ordinating producer, and Ron Fry, who continued his associate producer role, along with Dennis Spooner, acting as an uncredited script editor. Most members of the new film unit were Canadian, although the post-production personnel were all British-based, indicating that the cutting and final editing of these episodes took place in the UK, presumably in the converted stables block at Harefield House.

Recruited as a new co-producer was Hugh Harlow, who would be credited on three of the four episodes that were ultimately filmed in Canada. He had entered the film industry as a third assistant director on the 1955 film *A Man on the Beach*, then worked throughout the late '50s and '60s mainly for Hammer Films, gaining promotions to second assistant director and then production manager. Upon completing his time with *The New Avengers*, he would become a production supervisor on various films, including *Octopussy*, *Aliens* and *The World is Not Enough*, plus Gerry Anderson's television series *Space Precinct*.

Canadian Ross McLean would also be credited as a co-producer of the first Canadian episode, 'Complex', having previously served as producer of the obscure television series *Midnight Zone* during the '60s. After *The New Avengers* he would virtually disappear from the industry; it would be almost 20 years before he returned as an executive producer on the feature film *Terminal Justice*.

Despite apparently having no experience whatsoever in either film or television, Jim Hanley would also become a co-producer on the final couple of episodes. *The New*

Avengers would serve as a stepping stone for his career, which would see him go on to become a producer on the mini-series *A Man Called Intrepid*, the series *Chairman of the Board* and the movie *Heartbreak High*.

A basic production unit was assembled, including Karen Hazzard as casting director, Ziggy Galko as construction manager and Allan Bryce (aka Alan Bryce) in the newly-created special effects position. Malcolm Tanner took on responsibility for hairdressing, and Jean Murray and Ken Freeman for make-up. Two stunt co-ordinators were appointed, namely stuntman/actor Dwayne McLean and *The Avengers* veteran Val Musetti, whose racing cars had featured in 'Three Handed Game'.

There was no break in production between the conclusion of 'K is for Kill: Tiger by the Tail' and the beginning of 'Complex'. Joanna Lumley flew out from London's Heathrow Airport on Monday 15 August 1977, the day filming commenced, accompanied by her nine-year-old son Jamie, who would spend his summer break in Canada with her, and film editor Eric Wrate, who would perform the initial cutting of 'Complex' in Canada before the print was sent to Harefield House for final editing. The Lumleys and Gareth Hunt and his son, also named Gareth, would all stay at the Harbour Castle Hotel in Harbour Square, Toronto, overlooking Lake Ontario.

2.10 – 'Complex'

Dennis Spooner completed his first draft screenplay for 'Complex' by June 1977. He then reworked it over a nine day period, substituting replacement scenes on both Wednesday 27 and Friday 29 July, and again on Tuesday 2 and Thursday 4 August. On Thursday 14 July, the *Toronto Star* reported that experienced Canadian director Peter Pearson had been contracted to handle 'Complex', though for some unknown reason this failed to occur. The piece also informed readers that the production would be filming at a disused police station on College Street in the city, hired from Toronto Metro Council for $300 per day, but again this ultimately did not happen.

Another Canadian director, Richard Gilbert, was actually allocated the episode. He had begun his career both producing and directing television material in his homeland during the late '50s and early '60s. He had also spent time in the UK in the early '60s, handling episodes of the crime shows *Boyd Q.C.* and *No Hiding Place*, before returning to Canada to work on more television material such as *Adventures in Rainbow Country*. In the early '70s he had created the Canadian series *The Collaborators*. After *The New Avengers*, however, he would essentially retire from the industry, subsequently directing only a couple of episodes of the revived television show *The Littlest Hobo*.

All of the Canadian episodes of *The New Avengers* would be shot mainly on location, with very few sets being constructed for the production. As reported two days later by *The Windsor Star* newspaper, the cameras started rolling on Monday 15 August in Toronto, on what was originally intended to be the first of seven episodes filmed in and around the city.

In common with all the other Canadian-filmed episodes, 'Complex' opens with a caption of the series' logo against a red background, over which two titles are overlaid, reading: 'Albert Fennell Brian Clemens', 'Present The New Avengers in Canada.' The action then begins with an establishing shot of the buildings that make up the Toronto-Dominion Centre and the distinctive CN Tower, accessed from Front Street West. There follows a sequence of Canadian agent Keith Greenwood, played by David Nichols, taking a succession of photographs of the University Centre, situated at 393 University

Avenue, from the vantage point of the CN Tower. Later, he is seen at Toronto Pearson International Airport, in a scene where a courier departs for the UK with the photographs.

Incorporated into the teaser sequence is an arranged meeting between the courier and Steed, Purdey and Gambit, set in Kent, described on a prop nameplate as the garden of England, although this was actually shot in South Humber Park in Toronto. Additional footage was obtained at Pearson International Airport for a sequence of Steed, Purdey and Gambit arriving and alighting from an Air Canada Lockheed TriStar airliner, before being driven away in a chauffeur-driven Lincoln Continental stretch limousine. The Lincoln then delivers the trio of British agents to the building earlier photographed by Greenwood, representing a Canadian security establishment.

The soviet contact Karavitch, played by Vlasta Vrana, arranges a meeting with the agents outside the since-demolished Pickin' Chicken Bar-B-Q restaurant and takeaway situated on Lake Shore Boulevard. Steed and Purdey wait in Steed's latest car, a yellow Jaguar XJS (MHF 291), while Gambit waits in a red Triumph TR7 (MHF 292), both vehicles having been supplied by British Leyland – with whom The Avengers Enterprises still maintained their connection, at least for the time being, despite filming outside the UK. Before contact can be established, Karavitch is gunned down from a moving *Toronto Star* van – an example of product placement, as additional funding for the production had been obtained not only from Nielsen-Ferns but also from the *Star*, Canada's largest daily newspaper.

Discovering his car blocked by another vehicle, Gambit appropriates a woman's Chevrolet Impala and begins chasing the van. Both vehicles are seen passing a since-closed photographic store on Laird Drive, then progressing down Bayview Avenue, alongside railway tracks, before turning left into Eastern Avenue at a junction that, due to subsequent redevelopment, no longer exists. The van exits the adjacent Trinity Street into Front Street East, still pursued by Gambit's Chevrolet, and both vehicles are then thrown at speed into a sweeping bend on a section of road that, again, has since disappeared, as this area has undergone redevelopment.

Seen from the perspective of a camera mounted inside the Chevrolet, Gambit continues his pursuit of the van along Cypress Street, a road that has since become yet another casualty of urban renewal, along with all the surrounding buildings, including the Federal Cold Store. Speeding through the Vanderhoof Avenue and Brentcliffe Road crossroads a couple of miles north, the Chevrolet then chases the van down the Roxborough Drive junction with Mount Pleasant Road, another couple of miles to the south-west. Temporarily losing his quarry, Gambit stops on the bridge at Lawrence Avenue East and, getting out of his vehicle, looks down onto the traffic on a section of Bayview Avenue three miles north of that seen in its appearance two minutes previously. Catching sight of the van, Gambit resumes the chase.

The van is next seen travelling along a tree-lined residential road known as The Bridle Path, before being brought to a halt by an off-camera collision as Gambit rams it with the Chevrolet, the results of the crash being posed on the junction with Park Lane Circle. Gambit is arrested for causing the accident and transported to a holding facility by a police car, seen being driven north along University Avenue, passing the Canada Life Building. The driver of the van is bailed by the Russian operative Koshev, played by Rudy Lipp.

Later reunited with his Triumph TR7, Gambit keeps the Russian Consulate building under surveillance in a sequence filmed outside 61 Binscarth Road in the Rosedale area of the city. When Koshev leaves the premises driving a Pontiac Parisienne, Gambit follows. Footage of the two vehicles was captured back on The Bridle Path, and was later put to the accompaniment of a piece of incidental music first heard in 'The Tale of the Big Why'. Both vehicles turn left from the cul-de-sac Beaumont Road into Glen Road and proceed over a bridge back in Rosedale, near Binscarth Road, with the CN Tower visible in the distance. The Pontiac then enters the driveway of a large dwelling in its own grounds at 172 The Bridle Path, where Gambit falls foul of a couple of law enforcement officers as a trespasser on the property.

Upon being released from the police cells for a second time, Gambit returns to 172 The Bridle Path, which had been loaned to the production for a solitary day by its absent owner. Director Richard Gilbert thought that having Gambit enter the building by barrelling through a large window would look spectacular; and having performed a similar stunt previously in 'Target!', Hunt felt confident to attempt this. However, Hunt's request to take a long, sprinting approach was denied by Gilbert in favour of a shorter run-up. Gilbert also considered that the whole thing would be even more impressive if the curtains over the window were closed. Ever the professional, Hunt proceeded with the stunt and smashed through the window. However, he had been correct about requiring a longer run-up, as unfortunately he gashed his head on the broken glass; and instead of him simply passing through the curtains as envisaged, the impact brought both curtains down, along with the curtain rail. Upon his return, the property's owner was naturally unhappy with this situation.

Upon discovering that the house Koshev visited belongs to the security building's designer Berisford Holt, played by Gerald Crack, Steed fears for the investigating Purdey's safety and sets off after her. His Jaguar XJS is seen emerging from an unnamed street into Queens Quay West, in front of The Westin Harbour Castle Hotel, and then in the downtown portion of the city on the crossroads of King Street West and York Street, where he attempts to overtake a PCC Tram Car of the Toronto Transit Commission.

The foreign agent known as Scapina, codenamed X41, turns out to be the computer-controlled security building itself, its name being an acronym for the Special Computerised Automated Project in North America. The episode's climatic sequences of Purdey inside the building recall situations and concepts seen previously in *The Avengers* episodes 'The House That Jack Built' and 'Killer', where someone is trapped within an automated environment programmed to kill them. Attempting to escape, Purdey rifles through some drawers in an office and finds a .38 Smith and Wesson revolver, which she fires several times at one of the large windows, only to find that the glass is bullet-proof.

Coming up with an idea, Steed has dozens of matchbooks posted into the building, suggesting to Purdey a way of defeating Scapina by starting a fire to which the building's automatic sprinkler system will respond. When she acts on his suggestion, the abundance of water causes the master computer to shut down. Four takes of this sequence were required before Gilbert was satisfied, resulting in Lumley becoming completely soaked.

For this episode Lumley wore an eye-catching, Jillie Murphy-designed flowing white and red lip-print dress, which had previously appeared as part of Purdey's designer wardrobe in 'K is for Kill: Tiger by the Tail'.

2.11 – 'The Gladiators'

Brian Clemens' 'The Gladiators' was the second Canadian episode to undergo principal filming in early September 1977. The original draft of the screenplay had been completed sometime during July, and revisions had been made on both Thursday 18 and Friday 26 August. The plot involves an elite Russian operative arriving in Canada to train a squad of men in advanced unarmed combat skills, then to attack a Canadian security building to destroy its computers. Canadian all-rounder Claude Fournier was assigned to direct what would be his only episode for *The New Avengers*.

A secluded mansion acquired by the Russians to act as their training headquarters was represented by Valley Halla Villa at 1757 Meadowvale Road in the Scarborough district of Toronto. These premises, situated in woodland, were both owned by and in close proximity to Toronto Zoo, who in later years would use them for a time as office space. Maintaining continuity with the previous episode, 61 Binscarth Road, Rosedale was again used for the building housing the Russian cultural attaché.

The unit filmed on Sewells Road, about 15 miles north-east of central Toronto but less than a mile from Toronto Zoo, for a scene where Canadian agents Rogers and Hartley, played by Dwayne McLean and Michael Donaghue, continue trailing the car of Russian spymaster Karl Sminsky, played by Louis Zorich, by turning their vehicle off the main road at the concealed entrance to a rough track, representing the access point to the secluded mansion.

Hunt and Lumley were filmed a relatively short distance away, at the junction of Old Finch Avenue and Sewells Road, for a sequence where Gambit and Purdey later search for the two missing Canadian agents and a GMC 4x4 passes them carrying a passenger Gambit thinks he recognises. Continuing their search, they travel in Gambit's Triumph TR7 down a forest track and turn right into Meadowvale Road, where they have to pull over to allow passage for an oncoming police car with lights flashing and siren sounding. Deciding to follow the police car and investigate, Gambit executes a three point turn, and is almost involved in an accident with a speeding police motorcycle rushing to the same incident.

The incident in question is a short fight sequence shot on the outskirts of Pickering, approximately 16 miles to the north-east of downtown Toronto, at a convenience store at 490 Whitevale Road – a property that would later be demolished and replaced by a more traditional wooden building, used for both commercial and residential purposes, though this would be partly destroyed by fire in 2011, resulting in an extensive rebuild.

Later, the two British agents are still searching on Meadowvale Road, though about half a mile further south of their previous location, passing over Little Rouge Creek, where Purdey reports seeing some carrion birds. Heading down to the river through dense vegetation, they locate a Pontiac Parisienne, inside the boot of which they find the dead bodies of Rogers and Hartley.

Upon returning to the Triumph TR7, Gambit and Purdey call Steed at the Canadian intelligence headquarters, and he immediately decides to join them, departing in his Jaguar from the Yonge Eglinton Centre in central Toronto onto Orchard View Boulevard. From here the vehicle is seen taking the westbound slip road from Lower Jarvis Street onto the Gardiner Expressway, the film unit making certain to include a spectacular shot of the CN Tower some way off.

Patrolling the area, one of the police officers seen earlier in the convenience store sequence arrives at Little Rouge Creek, where Gambit and Purdey inform him of their gruesome find down by the river. Steed then joins them and they decided to inspect the dead agents' vehicle. Addressing the officer, Steed says, 'Why don't you come along too? After all, it's your country.' They split up to search the area, and the officer comes across Sminsky and his three assassins, whose car has become bogged down while driving across a meadow in an attempt to reach Toronto without being detected. Alerted to the situation by gunfire, Steed, Purdey and Gambit race to the scene in time to see Sminsky's Chevrolet Impala being driven away. Intent on giving chase, Gambit runs back to the road. Discovering his Triumph blocked in by the officer's Plymouth Gran Fury, he elects to use the latter instead, and promptly activates the siren and flashing lights. Filmed in long-shot from a high vantage point, the Plymouth accelerates up Pottery Road heading south-east toward the Greek Town district and away from the Don Valley Parkway (seen in the background), three miles from central Toronto.

Temporarily reverting to the British practice of driving on the left, Gambit narrowly misses an oncoming car before realising his mistake and moving over to the right. The Plymouth is then seen exiting Montcrest Boulevard onto Broadview Avenue, alongside Riverdale Park, back in the heart of Toronto. After this it emerges from the Bayview Avenue underpass, beneath the Queen Street East and King Street East intersection, turns right onto River Street, then left along Queen Street East.

This is followed by material showing Hunt driving the Plymouth in the opposite direction along Queen Street East, back toward the crossroads with River Street, switching off the siren en route. The chase then moves uptown, onto Lower Jarvis Street, with the Gardiner Expressway visible in the background – a view that has since completely changed due to major redevelopment. As the Plymouth turns left into Fore Street East, the local landmark, the triangular shaped Gooderham Building (aka Flat Iron Building), is momentarily visible. The sequence then reverts to Queen Street East as Gambit drives west with the tower of St Paul's Church visible in the background. The chase finally concludes with another change of locale, as the Plymouth turns off Yonge Street into Orchard View Boulevard, where Gambit locates Sminsky's car parked at the Yonge Eglinton Centre – the same location from which Steed's Jaguar was earlier seen departing.

In view of all the car chase material featured in this and the previous episode, Macnee was forced to voice his opinion that *The New Avengers* was beginning to lose its identity by following current trends and becoming something of a *Starsky and Hutch* clone.

Lumley's early suggestion for her character to be dressed in tracksuit-style sportswear, allowing easy movement for her fight scenes, was finally adopted for the Canadian episodes. Her wardrobe now consisted of casual outfits incorporating baggy trousers and lightweight jackets, with flat, trainer-like shoes. This on the whole made filming a more pleasant experience for the actress.

The whip-crack sound effect heard whenever the Cybernaut attacked in 'The Last of the Cybernauts …??' was reused for this episode to accompany some of the martial arts blows administered by Sminsky and his student Nada, played by Doug Lennox. Sminsky's training sessions were filmed at Valley Halla Villa, inside the conservatory and behind the house. Steed and Purdey are later brought to the house at gunpoint by the Russian operative Cresta, played by Jan Muzynski, who has discovered them lurking in the grounds. After a derogatory comment from the Russian official Barnoff, played by Yanci Burtovek, Purdey knocks him out with a single punch. Then, as Cresta moves forward, Steed uses his steel-crowned bowler hat first to knock a Colt

Government automatic from his grip and then to render him unconscious with a blow to the head. As Steed quickly picks up the fallen automatic, one of the Russian recruits challenges him to shoot, intending to use Sminsky's technique of deflecting bullets with his bare hands – which unfortunately for him it turns out that he has failed to master.

The New Avengers in print

The publicity build-up for the start of the second season's on-air run across the various ITV regions began in August 1977, when the latest issue of the magazine *Hot Car* pictured the Big Cat Jaguar on its cover and discussed the vehicle as part of a detailed feature on car customising. The *TV Times* also went for maximum impact, sporting a Joanna Lumley/Purdey cover on its Thursday 1 September edition. The Saturday 10 September edition of *Look-In* then featured a Steed, Purdey and Gambit artwork cover, together with a three-page article covering the series. A little later, issue no. 720 of the girls' teen magazine *Jackie*, published on Saturday 22 October, included a Gareth Hunt interview titled 'Opening Gambit'. Overall, though, the interest generated this time around was far less than for the first season.

Scheduling improvements

In scheduling their transmissions, the ITV companies organised themselves rather better for *The New Avengers*' second season than they had for the first. The episodes would generally be part-networked twice a week. Thames, Granada, Anglia, Westward, Channel, Scottish, Southern and Ulster all began with 'Dead Men are Dangerous' at 8.00 pm on Thursday 8 September 1977. The following evening the same episode was shown in the same time slot by the remaining regions, ATV, Yorkshire, Border, Grampian, HTV and Tyne Tees.

This rethink on transmission strategy brought an instant positive impact on viewing figures, as *The New Avengers* became Britain's sixth most watched television programme of September, averaging 13.4 million viewers per episode. The series' return seems to have gone down particularly well in the HTV region, where 'Dead Men are Dangerous' was the most popular programme of the week and the show would usually feature somewhere in the top ten throughout this run.

Annual, comic strips and other merchandising

In the run-up to Christmas 1977 the Denys Fisher toy company issued *The New Avengers* Board Game, which supplemented their previous tie-ins to the series and was along similar lines to games they had produced for other television shows such as *Space: 1999* and *Are You Being Served?*.

Publisher Brown Watson also catered for the children's Christmas market with *The New Avengers Annual 1978*, which repeated the successful format of the previous year's equivalent title but with a higher photographic content. The two eight-page comic strips featured within this volume were 'Midas Secret' and 'The Cybernauts', adapted by Steve Moore from the television episodes 'The Midas Touch' and 'The Last of the Cybernauts …??' respectively. This time the artwork came courtesy of artist and comic book creator Pierre le Goff. Le Goff also drew another four strips that were collected together with the first two in a 48-page French-published comic album entitled

Collection Télé Junior Number 1.

These four French strips were 'Death Has Wings', an adaptation of 'Cat Amongst the Pigeons'; 'The Mystery of Planet Y', based on 'The Tale of the Big Why'; 'The Eagle's Nest', inspired by the episode of the same title; and the original story 'The Curse of Falkenstein'. None of these strips was ever published in the UK, although the collection was available in Belgium and Switzerland as well as in France, and 'Midas Secret' and 'The Cybernauts' were also reprinted in 1980 as part of the large Belgian compilation comic *Télé Junior Almanac*.

The storyline for an unused comic strip penned by Moore for one of *The New Avengers* annuals would be published over 20 years later in the July 1999 issue of the fanzine *Stay Tuned*. Titled 'Diamonds are for Evil', this revolved around a cursed diamond previously owned by Cleopatra, which has laser-printed information on it regarding British agents operating in Russia and brings Steed, Purdey and Gambit face to face with a live ancient mummy.

2.12 – 'Forward Base'

The penultimate episode to go before the cameras was 'Forward Base', a clever and original Dennis Spooner story concerning a Russian base hidden in Lake Ontario. Spooner had a second draft of the screenplay ready sometime during July 1977, although some rewrites were incorporated on both Thursday 21 July and Friday 12 August, and further revisions were made on both Friday 19 August and Monday 22 August in order to accommodate the actual filming locations. Paperwork indicates that Ray Austin also contributed some pages to the screenplay, although without credit.

Assigned to call the shots on both this and the final episode, 'Emily', was the little-known Canadian director Don Thompson, whose prior experience was limited to a short film, a segment of a horror film and a television movie.

After an opening flashback to events in Vladivostok in 1969, the main action of 'Forward Base' gets under way with a small amount of footage captured at a location seen previously in 'Complex', Pearson International Airport in Mississauga, approximately 14 miles west of central Toronto. Steed is then seen crossing Yonge Street in downtown Toronto, heading for the Eaton Centre shopping mall and office complex, where he is due to keep an appointment with a Canadian agent named Bailey, played by August Schellenberg. While here on location here, Macnee stepped out of a lift and unexpectedly encountered his old friend and fellow thespian Peter O'Toole, who was an enthusiast of the original *The Avengers* series. Naturally he enquired what Macnee was currently working on, and when Macnee told him, he exclaimed, 'But Patrick, you're always working on *The Avengers*!'

The episode's main filming location, however, was the Toronto islands off the coast of the city in Lake Ontario. The largest of these small land masses, the heavily wooded Ward's Island, was the most prominently used. Lumley and Hunt were filmed on the wooden footbridge between Ward's Island and the adjacent Snake Island for a scene where the Russian operative Ivan Halfhide, played by David Calderisi, passes beneath Purdey and Gambit in a motorised swan boat hired from the amusement park at nearby Middle Island. However, the subsequent action, where Purdey carries out an underwater search to try to locate a missile guidance circuit board that Halfhide has mysteriously dropped into the lake, was shot along the shore of the mainland at Ashbridge's Bay Park.

Along the way, Gambit and Purdey meet a fisherman named Hosking, played by American actor Jack Creley, whose inclusion at various points in the episode is a welcome touch, as his bewilderment at the repeated shifting of the coastline reintroduces a note of humour and charm to the series.

Wishing to acquire some postcards of the coastline as it was before Hurricane Agatha struck it in 1969, Steed proceeds to Harper's Trading Post, a sequence realised by filming outside a shop at 2340 Lake Shore Boulevard West in the coastal Mimico region of the city. Steed's steel-crowned bowler hat saves the day yet again here. when he uses it to ward off an attack by the Russian operative Clive, played by Toivo Pyyko.

The since-demolished Silver Moon Motel, found by location scouts nearby at 2157 Lake Shore Boulevard West, was used to represent the exteriors of the motel where Halfhide is staying. After escaping from the motel, Halfhide drives to Humber Bay Park, down the coast from the Toronto islands, followed by Purdey in her yellow Toyota Corolla hatchback (LRM 022), with both vehicles arriving on Humber Bay Park Road East.

With the conclusion of the series in sight, it appears that The Avengers Enterprises made a conscious decision to stop using vehicles supplied by British Leyland in favour of sourcing cars from the Japanese manufacturer Toyota, who had approached them shortly before production began back in 1976. Not only does Purdey have the Corolla in this episode, but Steed also drives a green and white Toyota Land Cruiser 4x4 off-roader (MMZ 300) – though he will be reunited with his Jaguar XJS in the following episode.

In a scene early in the episode where the wounded enemy agent Czibor, played by Ara Hovanessiaan, emerges from some woods brandishing an automatic, Purdey suddenly has him covered with Gambit's .357 Smith and Wesson revolver. Czibor then keels over dead, and while Steed and Bailey deduce that he must have buried the package he was previously carrying, Purdey casually returns Gambit's firearm to him. However, there is no explanation given as to why Purdey has the Smith and Wesson in the first place, suggesting that some scripted material was either omitted from filming or removed, possibly for timing reasons, during the final editing.

Other notable points: the back of Purdey's personalised wetsuit features her name in white lettering, while beneath it she wears a blue T-shirt complete with the Union Jack and rampant lion motif of *The New Avengers*; and snatches of Laurie Johnson's incidental music from the first season episodes 'Cat Amongst the Pigeons' and 'To Catch a Rat' resurface during this episode.

2.13 – 'Emily'

Her son Jamie having returned to the UK, Lumley moved from the Harbour Castle Hotel to the Windsor Arms Hotel at 18 St Thomas Street in the city in time for the filming of the series' final episode, Dennis Spooner's 'Emily'. The concentration on location work was beginning to have drawbacks for the cast as, with the onset of autumn, the temperatures outside were beginning to plummet toward freezing point, in complete contrast to the sunny August days that they had found upon their arrival in Canada. There were other problems too. One morning, the cast and crew arrived on location to find that the chemical toilet in the large Winnebago shared by the wardrobe and make-up departments had overflowed all over the floor, because someone had forgotten to empty it. Worse still, during the night, rainwater had seeped into the vehicle through the roof and soaked all the costumes. Hunt was philosophical about the whole thing, but Lumley was apparently less than impressed, as the vehicle also served to provide shelter from the harsh weather for the entire film unit.

Spooner had a revised draft screenplay for the episode completed by September 1977. However, this underwent revisions on an almost daily basis before it was considered ready for filming, with new pages being substituted on Monday 19, Tuesday 20, Wednesday 21 and finally Friday 23 September. The plot involves a criminal mastermind called the Fox giving Steed and his fellow agents the slip but leaving behind a vital clue to his identity in the form of a palm print on the roof of an antique car – the Emily of the title – owned by a little old lady, Miss Daly. The Avengers then have to preserve and retrieve the palm print at all costs, even if it means driving it across country.

The teaser sequence opens with a panning shot of the Toronto skyline, including the CN Tower and the skyscrapers of the Toronto-Dominion Centre, followed by a cut to Purdey smashing her way through an outer door marked Puck's Circus. This was filmed in the fairground area of Exhibition Place, off Lake Shore Boulevard West, adjacent to Lake Ontario, where the travelling circus known as Puck's was apparently happy to become involved with the production. From here Purdey is seen sprinting past some local landmarks, the Bulova Tower and the wooden-trestle-supported Mighty Flyer rollercoaster, both partly hidden behind a solid fence. She then arrives at the Exhibition Stadium, which at the time was Toronto's major outdoor sports stadium, and begins climbing onto the roof to try to evade the Fox's men Mirschtia and Kalenkov, played by Peter Ackroyd and Peter Torokvei, who are chasing after her. Since filming took place here in 1977, all these structures have been demolished.

The action then shifts a couple of miles away to downtown Toronto, where Purdey quickly descends some steps from Wellington Street West into Royal Bank Plaza North before sprinting across the front of the Royal Canadian Bank headquarters, with the Fox's men still giving chase. The next sequence plays out a couple of miles north, in the residential area of Rosedale. Here Purdey flings a dustbin over as she rushes past it, delaying one of her pursuers, before managing to get to a safe house, the exterior of which was provided by a large dwelling situated on the corner of Chestnut Park Road and Roxborough Street East.

Having discovered that the courier Alkoff, played by Don Corbett, is about to deliver a payoff to the Fox, Purdey keeps his hotel room under surveillance disguised as a cleaner, while outside Gambit and Steed keep watch from the latter's Jaguar XJS. For the filming of this sequence, the hotel was represented by a low-rise apartment block situated at 2341 Lake Shore Boulevard in Mimico, within sight of the shop façade that doubled as the Trading Post in 'Forward Base'.

Alkoff's Chrysler LeBaron departs north-west along Lake Shore Boulevard toward the city centre, followed by Steed and Gambit in the Jaguar and then Purdey in her Toyota Corolla. All three vehicles are then seen heading southbound in downtown Toronto on Bay Street, passing Toronto City Hall, before taking a left-hand turn onto Queens Quay West and then reappearing back on Lake Shore Boulevard. Here Alkoff turns off to enter Humber Bay Park West, while Steed and Gambit go further along and turn into a dusty track beside a filling station. This location would soon afterwards become part of the entrance to Humber Bay Park East, which was in the process of being landscaped to transform it into a recreational area, parkland and butterfly sanctuary. At the time of filming, however, it resembled an uneven gravel pit more than anything else.

Alkoff waits offshore in a speedboat until the payoff is collected by a passing water-skier, who upon reaching land drives away at high speed in a Datsun B210 coupe (also known as the 120Y), with Steed and Gambit in hot pursuit.

The water-skier is none other than the Fox. Thinking that he has managed to elude his pursuers, he parks his car among others at a motor vehicle facility on Burtons Lane in Woodbridge (mentioned in dialogue), approximately 15 miles north-west of Toronto city centre. These small premises would later become known as Hank's Auto Repair, although they now appear to comprise a storage unit for road maintenance rollers and construction equipment. This is the location where Emily – a brown 1941 Plymouth Deluxe – first appears.

All the remaining Woodbridge locations were filmed within sight of each other along Woodbridge Avenue. The Bank of Montreal at 145 Woodbridge Avenue is visible in a scene where Steed, Purdey, Gambit and the Canadian official Phillips, played by Richard Davidson, depart in Emily from what is now Market Street. Almost opposite the bank is Woodbridge Library, which is also seen in the background in a scene toward the conclusion of the episode where Miss Daly is presented with a replacement Plymouth. Since the '70s, both the bank and the library have undergone some refurbishment, so they no longer look the same. Adjacent to the bank, at 137 Woodbridge Avenue, is the historic Wallace House, built in 1873, and this was used to represent Miss Daly's home. This also looks somewhat different today, as it now boasts a fenced garden containing trees and plants.

Across the road from the Wallace House, at 124 Woodbridge Avenue, is the clothing outlet Michele Luisi Couture, which appears in the episode as a shop called Florist in the Valley. Again, this has since undergone changes, now having roof sections supported by columns. However, it is at least still standing, which cannot be said of the distinctive Ray's Car Wash at 119 Woodbridge Avenue, which has since been demolished in a major redevelopment of the immediate area, to make way for a large block containing retail units and low-rise living accommodation. In the episode, after Emily emerges from the car wash and Steed tapes his bowler hat over the palm print on the roof, the rear of Wallace House is visible in the background, showing just how close these two locations actually were.

The palm print has survived the car wash thanks to Purdey throwing herself across the Plymouth's roof, keeping it dry. For this sequence, filmed in Ray's Car Wash, Lumley went beyond the call of duty by allowing herself to be subjected to a complete soaking on an extremely cold day, as she was bombarded by various water jets and soft brushes. She also had to be covered in detergent beforehand, to make her clothing foam when the water hit it. Stunt co-ordinator Val Musetti was on hand to ensure safety, but director Don Thompson was apparently dissatisfied with the first take and called for a second. After that, Lumley was hosed down to remove all traces of soap and then driven seven miles for a hot bath and dry clothing.

According to the book *The Avengers and Me* by Patrick Macnee and Dave Rogers, Lumley became very unhappy while filming on location during 'Emily', so much so that she walked off camera at one point, vowing never to return. Ever the professional, she did eventually complete her scenes for the episode, although it is thought that Ray Austin played a part in persuading her to continue.

With 'Emily' being the series' final episode, Dennis Spooner, Albert Fennell and Don Thompson decided to play up the humorous aspects of the screenplay. For instance, when Emily overheats, Steed helps himself to some eggs from a nearby chicken coop – leaving some money in payment – and uses them to make a traditional repair to the leaking radiator. In a fitting touch, *The New Avengers* concludes with Miss Daly handing Steed a red carnation for his buttonhole.

On Friday 21 October the *Toronto Star* reported that Macnee and Lumley had been filming 'Emily' in and around the city, but that production had now ceased after the completion of only four of the seven episodes originally planned. The newspaper went on to state that this situation had come about because Lumley had declined to extend her contract with the series' producers in order to complete the remaining episodes.

Even if the other three Canadian episodes had been made, this would still have left the production one short of the proposed total of 30 episodes that had been announced back in December 1975.

The life and times of John Steed

October 1977 saw the publication by Weidenfield and Nicholson of the hardback book *John Steed: An Authorised Biography Volume One: Jealous in Honour*, a fictional biography of Steed written by Tim Heald. However, a second volume would never appear.

Viewing figures

On the evening of Thursday 20 October 1977, all the ITV regional companies that normally transmitted *The New Avengers* on Thursdays dropped the series for a week to make way for coverage of the British Phonographic Industry's first ever BRIT awards ceremony, recorded two nights earlier at the Wembley Conference Centre. However, as the series' second season approached its conclusion, it was continuing to perform well in the ratings. The figures for the Granada transmissions were particularly impressive, 'Trap' taking top spot in that region's weekly chart when it screened on Friday 14 October. Another region in which the series enjoyed a healthy audience was Grampian, where 'K is for Kill: Tiger by the Tail' became the most watched programme of the week when it was transmitted in early November. The series also had a large following in London, where *The Avengers* had always gone down well. The early episodes of the season regularly featured in the weekly top ten there, and although the later ones did slightly less well, they still figured in the top 20.

UK-wide, despite increasing its average audience to 13.7 million viewers per episode in October, *The New Avengers* slipped down the monthly chart to number 13. A slight drop in average viewing figures to 13.6 million per episode in November saw it fall a few places further, to number 16.

Scheduling changes

Toward the season's conclusion, there appears to have been some misunderstanding or miscommunication between The Avengers Enterprises and *TV Times*, as the magazine's regional editions for a given week would frequently list different episodes from the ones that were actually shown that week.

A further complication arose when Thames decided to pull 'The Gladiators' from their schedule as they considered some of its content overly violent; the episode would eventually be held back until 1978, when it would be buried away in a one-off late evening time slot. Following Thames's example, some of the other regions, including Anglia and HTV, also dropped 'The Gladiators', wishing to avoid any possible controversy. They too would reschedule it in the following year, when HTV would use it to launch a run of repeats.

On Thursday 24 November 1977 the scheduled episode, 'Emily', was replaced by 'Forward Base', which proceeded to clock up the series' highest rating of the season with 14.1 million viewers, making it the UK's fourth most popular programme of that week. ATV then decided to curtail the season early, having aired only 12 episodes and omitted 'Emily'. As Yorkshire, Border, Grampian, HTV and Tyne Tees all took Thames's weekly line-feed, they had no option but to do likewise. 'Emily' would finally receive its initial transmission in those regions as part of a selection of repeats 12 months later.

The final Futura paperback and the Gareth Hunt record

In December 1977 Futura published their sixth and final paperback novel based on *The New Avengers*. Entitled *Hostage*, it was written by Peter Cave, who as usual grafted additional material onto the plot of the television episode on which it was based.

A further piece of *The New Avengers*-related merchandise appeared at the beginning of this month, when Gareth Hunt released a seven-inch vinyl single entitled 'Sail Away', backed with 'We of All People'. This was marketed in a photographic picture sleeve on the Chrysalis label, serial number PD 1515. However, in a strange move, Chrysalis decided against making it available on home soil in the UK. In fact, the only country in which it was actually released was South Africa, making it an extremely obscure recording.

PART FOUR
AFTERLIFE

AFTERLIFE

SECOND SIGHT

The Avengers may have ceased production, but over the years that followed, it would continue to hold a special place in the viewing public's affections, acquiring a cult status with a large and loyal fan base and generating a considerable amount of further tie-in merchandise. There would also be opportunities to see the surviving episodes again, and even a few attempts to resurrect the series in one form or another.

Dinky die-cast models

With repeat screenings of *The New Avengers* being scheduled in various ITV regions during 1978, the Dinky toy company announced its intention to make available two 1/43 scale die-cast models of vehicles featured in the series. In the event, though, only one of these actually made it into the shops. This was Purdey's yellow Triumph TR7 (no. 112 in the Dinky range), the Purdey connection to which was emphasised by the addition of a capital letter P on the bonnet together with silver flashing. The reverse of the box packaging depicted an action scene that also included the second of the two planned models, Steed's Big Cat Jaguar XJ12C (no. 113). The 1977 Dinky catalogue had announced that this model would be made available later, but this did not occur. The 1978 catalogue then indicated that it would finally appear along with the Triumph TR7 in a *The New Avengers* gift set (no. 307). However, this also failed to materialise. Some sources suggest that this was due to financial problems encountered by Dinky's parent company Meccano, while others indicate that it was because the moulds for the Jaguar were destroyed in a fire.

The Dinky manufacturing centre in Liverpool closed in November 1979, but over the years since then a number of pre-production copies of the Jaguar model have surfaced, complete with a bowler-hatted Steed figure behind the steering wheel. Like some of the die-cast models Dinky made depicting vehicles from various Gerry Anderson series, these examples are in different colours from the one seen on screen. Instead of olive green, they come in either one of two different shades of a lighter metallic green, complete with gold stripes. Due to their rarity, these pre-production models have a high value. Numerous replica Big Cat Jaguars have been modified from other Dinky castings, but these can be easily differentiated from the genuine *The New Avengers* ones because they have slightly different wheel arches.

Escapade

Sometime during the first couple of months of 1978, Brian Clemens found himself headhunted by the American production company Quinn Martin to become involved with a 60-minute pilot episode they wanted to make for a proposed television film series heavily influenced by *The Avengers*. In fact, Quinn Martin and their co-producers Woodruff Productions originally intended to call this *The Avengers USA*, until copyright considerations caused them to rename it *Escapade*. Clemens became both producer and scriptwriter on the project, although by the time he arrived in San Francisco to begin work on it, actors Granville Van Dusen and Morgan Fairchild had already been cast as the two lead characters, agents Joshua Rand and Suzy (no surname).

The director assigned to the production was Jerry London, and a short report in the Thursday 9 March edition of the *San Francisco Chronicle* noted that Quinn Martin himself had accompanied the film crew to shoot it on location in the city. The report also informed readers that *Escapade* would be based on the highly sophisticated style and characterisation of *The Avengers*, and name-checked the leads Van Dusen and Fairchild.

Clemens' screenplay was called 'I Thought It Was Someone I Knew', although on screen only the *Escapade* title appears. The story introduces the characters of Rand and Suzy and establishes that they are answerable to a huge computer they affectionately call Oz, voiced by Jonathan Harris, famous for his role as Dr Smith in *Lost in Space*. Clemens' original intention was that the two agents would have to drive out into the desert to gain access to Oz, which would be housed inside an obelisk there. However, possibly for budgetary reasons, the finished production instead has Oz located just outside San Francisco on the first floor of an elegant stately home. Rand and Suzy are admitted by two business-suited men who open the front door with an electronic device. They are then escorted upstairs by another pair of similarly-attired men. A fifth man opens the door to a study, where Rand and Suzy confirm their identities by using an electronic handprint reader. This results in fitted library shelving sliding back to reveal Oz, or more accurately Computerised Security Initiator Mk 5/K7.

The villain of the piece is an old adversary of Rand's, the self-serving freelance agent Arnold Tulliver, played by Len Birman, who was intended to become a semi-regular character if the pilot was bought by one of the networks and a full series resulted. Intent upon discovering the secret codes used by the organisation for which Rand and Suzy work, Tulliver kidnaps trainee agent Paula Winters, played by Janice Lynde, just prior to her first mission to procure some secret papers. Fortunately Rand and Suzy manage to rescue her and thwart his plans.

Rand is presented as a stylish Martini drinker who drives a brown Mercedes Benz 450SL convertible (865 PCE), while the zany and erratic Suzy uses a rundown white Volkswagen Beetle for her everyday transport.

The theme tune and incidental score for the production were both composed by Patrick Williams (credited as Pat Williams), whose previous television credits included *It Takes a Thief*, *Cannon* and *The Streets of San Francisco*.

Billed as a special presentation, *Escapade* was transmitted by the CBS network on Friday 19 May 1978, little more than ten weeks after filming wrapped. The actual time slot differed between the regional time zones across the country, some receiving it at 9.00 pm and others at 10.00 pm.

In anticipation of the pilot being liked and picked up by CBS for a full season,

Clemens already had on file 24 thumbnail storyline ideas that either he or other writers could flesh out into shooting scripts. He had also written a second screenplay, titled 'Illusion', which incorporated science fiction elements and brought back Tulliver with a device that could project an image onto someone's eyeball, making them see whatever he wanted them to; something he would use to try to gain access to a nuclear installation for sabotage purposes. In a 1992 interview with *Time Screen* magazine, Clemens said he was confident that if *Escapade* had gone ahead as a series, he could have easily handled being the producer and an executive producer on *The Professionals* at the same time. *Escapade*'s Mexican executive producer Philip Saltzman, who had previously worked as both a writer and a producer on various Quinn Martin shows including *The Fugitive*, is also known to have written a number of scripts for the prospective series. However, all this was in vain, as despite the pilot achieving a reasonable share of the ratings, CBS decided against financing a season. It appears that further interest was shown in the project the following year, as Quinn Martin Productions were reported to be back scouting locations in San Francisco, but unfortunately this also came to nothing.

There was some British media interest in the project, as Morgan Fairchild was interviewed in July 1978 by the *Daily Record* newspaper, who described Suzy as the sexiest Avengergirl of them all. Fairchild indicated that she would have preferred Suzy's relationship with Rand to have been more mysterious, and not included sexual innuendos. Another point of contention was that although Suzy exhibited martial arts abilities, she never actually became involved in any fight scenes. Fairchild said that should a series have been developed, she would have insisted on being in the forefront of the action.

On 23 July 1978, the *Sunday Express* also printed a photograph of Fairchild and inaccurately reported that the cool blonde, as they described her, would star in the new series *The Avengers USA*. A couple of months later, on 24 September, the same newspaper published another pin-up shot of the actress with a similar blurb, preferring to ignore the *Escapade* name again in favour of its early working title *The Avengers USA*.

Later in 1978, Quinn Martin sold both his production company and the rights to most of his television series to a group of investors, who quickly turned them around for a profit by selling them on to Taft Entertainment the following year. By this time, only *Barnaby Jones* and *A Man Called Sloane* were still in production, but Taft quickly began selling the Quinn Martin back catalogue for repeat screenings. This included *Escapade*, which received UK airings in various ITV regions in the early '80s. In 1997 Taft Entertainment were acquired by Republic Pictures, a wholly-owned subsidiary of Spelling Entertainment, and two years later they themselves were bought up by Paramount, who now own the rights to *Escapade*.

The CBS Late Movie

Back on 12 March 1978, the *Sunday Express* reported that although *The New Avengers* was now out of production, the long-awaited American sale had finally occurred, as the CBS network had acquired the series for the forthcoming autumn season. While Brian Clemens and Albert Fennell would doubtless have been pleased by this, they would have been disappointed by the 11.30 pm to 12.30 am graveyard time slot the series was given, as part of *The CBS Late Movie* – an umbrella title under which the network typically screened a film, two films, a film and a television episode or two television episodes every weeknight. *The New Avengers* was the first series to undergo its initial networking in this manner – prior to this, all the television episodes shown under *The CBS Late Movie* banner had been repeats – with some sources blaming this on its level of violence, which was considered in excess of that presented in an average American action show of the time. Transmissions began with 'The Eagle's Nest' on Friday 15 September 1978 and continued in an almost unbroken weekly run until a change of day on Thursday 22 March 1979, when the two portions of 'K is for Kill' were amalgamated together for a feature-length screening.

One notable aspect of these American transmissions was that the opening title sequence used for them was completely different from the UK version. Apparently assembled at a very early stage of the series' production, it consists of a montage of clips from the first two episodes to be filmed, 'The Eagle's Nest' and 'The Midas Touch', plus some material from the joint screen test that Lumley and Hunt performed when auditioning for their roles. The series' logo is also different, consisting of the figures of Steed, Purdey and Gambit in semi-silhouette inside a grey circle, with the title overlaid in white lettering. It is possible that this sequence was originally intended to be seen on the original UK transmissions but dropped in favour of the one that was ultimately used. It is unknown why it was included on the American prints.

Ian Hendry: *This Is Your Life*

For the Wednesday 15 March 1978 edition of ITV's *This Is Your Life*, Patrick Macnee assisted presenter Eamonn Andrews in surprising Ian Hendry with the series' famous big red book outside the Sheraton Park Tower Hotel in Knightsbridge, London. Macnee and Andrews were both dressed as Steed in matching grey suits, complete with bowler hats and umbrellas, as they accompanied Hendry to the Royalty Theatre in Portugal Street, London, where the programme was recorded.

Vauxhall cars commercial

1978 also saw Macnee adopt his bowler hat and umbrella again to film a couple of television commercials for Vauxhall Motors, more or less in character as Steed. One of these had him on location at what is now the Luton Hoo Hotel, off The Luton Drive in Luton, Bedfordshire, where he name-checked all the then current models made by the manufacturer. The second, shorter commercial featured the actor sat inside a helicopter, coupled with car footage shot at Vauxhall's Millbrook Proving Ground in Bedford.

Another season of *The New Avengers* ...?

Meanwhile, despite having been hidden away from a primetime American television audience, *The New Avengers* had proved itself a success in *The CBS Late Movie* time slot. The 2 September 1978 edition of the *Sunday People* carried a story indicating that the series was now considered a hot property by the CBS network, which was prepared to provide the majority of the funding for another 26 episodes to be made. The network was willing to commit $140,000 (approximately £64,500 at the time) per episode, while LWT was offering to contribute £30,000 per episode. However, when combined, this still left a shortfall of £30,000 per episode. Brian Clemens and Albert Fennell hoped to attract further investment to make this up, but in the event this was sadly not forthcoming.

Revell model kits

Influenced by *The New Avengers*' American popularity at this time, the Revell hobby company issued 1/25th-scale plastic model car kits of both Gambit's red Jaguar XJS and Purdey's yellow Triumph TR7. The cardboard box packaging, emblazoned with *The New Avengers*' Union Jack and rampant lion emblem, advised that each of the models was easy to assemble, with no gluing required, and came moulded in two colours, avoiding the need for any painting.

The Hardy Boys: 'Assault on the Tower'

On Sunday 15 October 1978, Patrick Macnee returned to American television as a bowler-hatted, umbrella-carrying British agent codenamed S in an episode entitled 'Assault on the Tower' in the ABC network's *The Hardy Boys* series. The format of this series had been altered for its current third season to move it away from the teenage whodunits it had previously presented as part of *The Hardy Boys/Nancy Drew Mysteries*, based on the books of Franklyn W Dixon. The female character had now been dropped, and the Hardy brothers were working for the US Treasury Department.

The storyline of 'Assault on the Tower' revolves around the Hardy brothers investigating the disappearance of their father in London, where they enlist the assistance of S and uncover a plot to undertake the largest robbery in British history. Parker Stevenson and Shaun Cassidy co-starred as Frank and Joe Hardy, although they never actually filmed in London, which was represented by footage of Big Ben, the River Thames, Heathrow Airport, New Scotland Yard and the Tower of London.

Macnee had been persuaded to appear in the episode by its producer, Glen A Larson, who was a friend of his. Copyright considerations prevented his character actually being called Steed, but the intention was quite clear, and was emphasised by the inclusion of incidental music reminiscent of Laurie Johnson's *The Avengers* theme.

The Avengers networked across the USA

On the strength of the positive audience reaction to *The New Avengers*, CBS suddenly rediscovered British television film series. Starting on Friday 21 December 1979, they networked the colour Diana Rigg episodes of *The Avengers* in a weekly double bill with first-run episodes of *Return of the Saint*, again in *The CBS Late Movie* slot. The only episode of *The Avengers*' fifth season to be omitted was 'From Venus with Love', and the run concluded with the Diana Rigg/Linda Thorson crossover adventure 'The Forget-Me-Knot' in July 1980.

Despite having been unwilling to supply quite enough money to enable the making of another season of *The New Avengers*, CBS still saw potential in the concept. On Saturday 9 February 1980 the *Daily Mail* ran a story under the headline 'Steed's A Wanted Man', reporting that the American company had now set its sights on funding a feature film version of *The Avengers* – although later this proposal would be downgraded to a television movie.

After screening 'The Forget-Me-Knot', CBS failed to follow through with the Thorson season, but instead started rerunning the colour Rigg season again. After only half a dozen episodes, however, they then switched to reruns of *The New Avengers*, starting with 'The Eagle's Nest' in the usual late Friday night slot on 9 September 1980. They screened the episodes in the same order as previously, but omitted 'Faces' and this time kept 'K is for Kill' in its original two-part format.

The Saga of Happy Valley

Also in 1980, an Australian enthusiast of *The Avengers*, Geoff Barlow, had his paperback novel *The Saga of Happy Valley* published by the Albion Press. Although clearly based on the series, it was unlicensed, so Barlow avoided using *The Avengers* name and also spelt the lead characters' names slightly differently, as John Steade and Emma Peale. Nevertheless, this did not prevent the book eventually attracting the attention of *The Avengers'* then current copyright owner Thorn-EMI, resulting in it being withdrawn from sale.

The New Avengers theme gets another release

In September 1980, with *The Professionals'* fourth season being transmitted across the ITV network, Laurie Johnson's theme to the series was released on a seven-inch vinyl single. On the B-side was the theme to *The New Avengers*. Both tracks were newly-recorded versions and credited to Laurie Johnson and the London Studio Orchestra. The single came in a glossy picture sleeve, although somewhere along the line there must have been a communications breakdown, as *The New Avengers* was featured on the front of the sleeve while *The Professionals* was relegated to the reverse. Both tracks were also included on the Unicorn-Kanchana album *Music from The Avengers, The New Avengers, The Professionals* (KPM 7009), released on 12-inch vinyl toward the end of 1980 in a gatefold cover. Early in 1982, the Varese Sarabande label in association with the telefantasy magazine *Starlog* would issue an American version of this album, also on vinyl, with a different cover and the title simplified to *The Avengers*. This would be promoted by way of a flexi-disc sampler given away with *Starlog's* issue 55, dated February 1982. However, around the same time, Varese Sarabande would confuse matters by also issuing a CD version, again called *The Avengers*, but featuring a slightly different photographic cover and with the tracks from *The Professionals* replaced by themes and incidental cues from various feature films. Later, in January 1989, soundtrack specialists Silva Screen Records would begin importing this CD into the UK, obviously seeing a market for it.

The First Avengers Movie

Having reached an agreement with CBS, Brian Clemens wrote an initial draft script for their proposed television movie version of *The Avengers*. Completed in January 1981, this was headed *The First Avengers Movie* – although that was obviously as much a descriptor as an actual title. The storyline was devised jointly between Clemens and Dennis Spooner and harked back to the fantastical style of the colour Diana Rigg episodes rather than the more realistic approach of *The New Avengers*. The plot opens with people being mysteriously killed by something that leaves them as nothing more than skeletons. It turns out that a South American military leader called Cavalo has perfected a way of controlling ants and consequently now has the largest army in the world, which he intends to use for global conquest. Inside the villain's secret hideout, the staff move about on Kirby wires to avoid trampling the ants that swarm about underfoot.

Besides including the bizarre scenario of the victims' bodies being picked completely clean, the screenplay also includes some eccentric characters of the kind encountered in Avengerland during the series' heyday. One of these is the madcap miniaturisation expert Bernard Igg, who is said to be developing contact lenses for butterflies. When Steed asks why he is doing this, he replies, 'Because they keep losing the glasses.' Another example is George Ware, a man who realises what devastation the army ants could cause, and consequently lives in a basket strung beneath a helium-filled balloon to prevent them from reaching him. When Gambit enquires why he chooses to spend his life off the ground, Ware answers, 'Because the submarine isn't ready yet.'

Interviewed by this author at the Fan Aid North Convention held at the Griffin Hotel in Leeds in November 1985, Spooner said that he felt Telly Savalas would have been ideal to play Cavalo, while John Cleese would have been approached to portray Bernard Igg. Another casting idea was Rowan Atkinson for the role of George Ware. Spooner confirmed that the title *The First Avengers Movie* was an expression of optimism on his and Clemens' part, as they saw this as the initial entry in a string of television movies continuing the adventures started with *The New Avengers*.

Despite her misgivings regarding *The New Avengers* in Canada, Lumley had greatly enjoyed working with Macnee and Hunt, and she was later quoted in the Tim Ewbank and Stafford Hildred-penned book *Joanna Lumley: The Biography* as saying, 'All three of us would love to have done another 13 episodes.' Like her two co-stars, Lumley had been disappointed that *The New Avengers* largely lacked the humour that they all considered an essential part of *The Avengers'* format, so she might well have appreciated the reinstatement of this element in *The First Avengers Movie*. Surprisingly, however, Purdey was not included in the screenplay, whereas Steed and Gambit were – presumably an indication that Macnee and Hunt had expressed themselves willing to reprise their roles.

In place of Purdey was a new female agent and ex-trapeze artist called Carruthers; and Clemens had Gambit use a variation on the celebrated 'Mrs Peel, we're needed' catchphrase in one scene where he arrives at Carruthers' apartment block and begins talking to her over the intercom, saying, 'Carruthers, we're needed!' The writer also had the three Avengers working alongside a female CIA operative called Suzy Stride. Given that they shared the same first name, it is tempting to speculate that this might have been the same character who featured as the female lead in *Escapade*, but the screenplay gives no indication to that effect.

The opening titles would announce that the movie had a cast of thousands (meaning the ants), though the true nature of the killers would not be revealed until the heroes and heroines had investigated and deduced the facts. Clemens apparently wanted no further association with British Leyland (then known as BL), as Steed would revert to driving a vintage Bentley, and Gambit would be given a Morgan convertible.

In the end, however, despite paying both writers, CBS decided to abandon the project altogether, possibly because the budget required to realise the concept was beyond what they usually allocate to a television movie.

Channel 4 reruns

In the UK, the newly-launched independent television station Channel 4 began transmissions on Tuesday 2 November 1982, having already announced that their programming would include classic '60s shows such as *The Prisoner*, *The Munsters* and *The Avengers*. The channel decided to screen *The Avengers'* fifth season, starting with 'From Venus with Love'. The episodes would of course be seen in colour this time, whereas their initial ITV transmissions had been in black and white only, and this would also be the first ever full networking of *The Avengers* on UK television. The series was initially placed in a five minutes past midnight slot on Sunday mornings, but despite this short-sighted scheduling it still managed to pick up something of a following. This prompted a move to Saturday nights at 11.00 pm from the start of 1983.

The original *TV Choice*

The fourth issue of the original *TV Choice* magazine, published on Friday 26 November 1982, celebrated *The Avengers'* Channel 4 reruns by featuring an airbrushed artwork cover depicting Steed and Mrs Peel, with the eye-catching caption 'Avenging the '60s'. Launched by the London-based TV Choice Ltd, this was an early attempt at producing a television listings magazine to rival the monopoly enjoyed at that time by the *TV Times* and *Radio Times*, who threatened legal action in response, claiming that their schedules were copyright. Bowing to this pressure, *TV Choice* continued for a time minus programme details, but unfortunately this proved unsuccessful and it ceased publication shortly afterwards. A new *TV Choice* would appear in 1999, after the monopoly on television listings magazines had ended, and go on to become one of the highest-selling weekly publications in the UK, but this would have no connection to the earlier magazine of the same title.

Channel 4/CBS reruns

Channel 4 struck gold with their initial Saturday night showing of *The Avengers* on 8 January 1983, as the episode 'Never, Never Say Die' managed to attract 2.05 million viewers, making it the third most popular programme on the channel that week. Seeing even more potential in the series, Channel 4 shifted the show again, this time to 7.15 pm on Sundays, where Steed and Mrs Peel continued to perform so well in the ratings that they were rarely out of the top ten programmes on the channel. Toward the end of March the series was rested for six months, before being reinstated at the beginning of October in its old ABC primetime slot of 8.00 pm on Saturdays for the remaining five colour Rigg episodes. The Tara King introductory episode 'The Forget-Me-Knot' went out on 12 November, followed by the majority of the season six episodes, continuing into the following year. On 21 April 1984, 'The Morning After' clocked up 2.55 million viewers, placing it at number three in the Channel 4 top ten for that week. The weekly transmissions concluded on 2 June with 'Homicide and Old Lace', when – even though they still had seven episodes left to show – Channel 4 once again dropped the series from their schedules, this time for five months.

Meanwhile, in the USA, *The New Avengers* began a short repeat run, replacing *Magnum P.I.* back in *The CBS Late Movie* slot. This consisted of nine episodes, beginning on Tuesday 26 June and concluding on Wednesday 22 August with 'Cat Amongst the Pigeons'.

Michael Sloan's proposed television movie pilot

Meanwhile, Michael Sloan, who had written and acted as supervising producer on *The Hardy Boys* episode 'Assault on the Tower', was interviewed in *Starlog*'s issue no. 70, dated May 1983, and although most of the conversation concerned his involvement with *The Return of the Man from U.N.C.L.E.* television movie 'The Fifteen Years Later Affair' – which included Patrick Macnee in the cast as U.N.C.L.E.'s new boss Sir John Raleigh – it also touched on *The Avengers*. Sloan revealed that he had for a number of years been developing an outline for a two-hour television movie based on the series, and that Patrick Macnee was interested in appearing in it. He added that he also hoped to attract Honor Blackman, Diana Rigg, Linda Thorson and Joanna Lumley to reprise their respective roles, and that he had considered offering the then-untitled production to the CBS network. Having co-created and written many episodes of *The Equalizer* for Universal Television, Sloan also had that company interested in backing the concept as a pilot for a new series. The proposed storyline was to have opened at what appeared to be Steed's funeral, with his pallbearers being Cathy Gale, Emma Peel, Tara King and Purdey – although according to Dave Rogers' *The Ultimate Avengers* book, published in 1995, only Linda Thorson and Honor Blackman had agreed to become involved. Ultimately, however, this was another proposal that petered out and came to nothing.

Channel 4 black and white reruns

On 6 November 1984, Channel 4 resumed their transmissions of *The Avengers*, now in a new time slot of 6.00 pm on Tuesday evenings. However, instead of carrying on with the outstanding Linda Thorson episodes, they decided to screen the black and white Diana Rigg ones instead, starting with 'The Town of No Return'. This latest run followed the previous pattern of continuing through into the following year, at the rate of one episode per week. The Rigg episodes concluded with 'Honey for the Prince' on 4 June 1985, and only then did Channel 4 complete the Thorson season by tagging the seven remaining episodes on to the end. The eighty-third and final filmed adventure, 'Bizarre', brought the run to a close on 23 July .

Patrick Macnee: *This is Your Life*

The subject of the Wednesday 14 November 1984 edition of ITV's *This Is Your Life* was Patrick Macnee. Presenter Eamonn Andrews enlisted the actor's former co-stars Joanna Lumley and Gareth Hunt to assist in surprising him. Just as Macnee was leaving a hotel, a vintage 1919 Bentley 3 litre (BM 8287) pulled up, driven by Hunt and with Lumley as a passenger. Hunt and Lumley then disembarked and engaged Macnee in conversation, allowing Andrews to sneak up behind him with the big red book. Once proceedings adjourned to the television studio, the other guests on hand to share their reminiscences and anecdotes about Macnee included Honor Blackman and Ian Hendry, plus Patrick Cargill, Leslie Phillips and director David Greene. Neither Diana Rigg nor Linda Thorson could be present, but they sent their greetings via filmed messages. This edition of *This Is Your Life* had actually been recorded a couple of months prior to the transmission date, on Sunday 23 September.

The Avengers ... International!

On Friday 15 March 1985 the magazine *Broadcast* carried a story about British producer Sarah Lawson, who was vice president for planning and development of the recently-formed American media company Taft Entertainment Television. Lawson was developing a project together with the Controller of BBC1 Michael Grade – her then husband – and Brian Clemens, from a script written by the latter called 'Reincarnation'. This they hoped would serve as a pilot episode for a proposed revival of *The Avengers*, titled *The Avengers... International!*. Patrick Macnee had been consulted and had promised to keep himself free of commitments from mid-May 1985 onwards, so that he would be available to return once again in the role of secret agent John Steed.

Attempting to recreate the successful Emma Peel era of the series, but realising he could not actually include that character in his screenplay, Clemens went for the next best thing by introducing her daughter-in-law Samantha (which was the original name for Mrs Peel back in 1964). Like her predecessor, this new Mrs Peel would also drive a Lotus Elan and have a missing husband named Peter (named after his father), who disappeared on an espionage mission in Eastern Europe four years previously. The second new lead character was an American operative named Christopher Cambridge, whose inclusion was aimed at attracting interest from one of the US networks in the hope that they might finance the pilot – the first step in getting *The Avengers ... International!* up and running.

The storyline borrowed elements from the Thorson episode 'Split!' and expanded upon them. An old adversary named Lomax returns to exact revenge on Steed – who shot and believed he had killed him years earlier – but now looks completely different. Utilising an advanced brain transplant technique that has fallen into the wrong hands, Lomax keeps coming back from the dead in a new body, the final one being that of a woman. Both Purdey and Cathy Gale receive name-checks in the dialogue.

Although Clemens wanted the production to be more in the style of *The Avengers* than of *The New Avengers*, the screenplay contains fewer eccentric characters than *The First Avengers Movie*. An amusing exception, however, is a man named Weir, who believes in reincarnation and states that in a past life he was an elephant, until he was killed by a hunter, after which he came back as a soldier in Wellington's army at Waterloo.

'Reincarnation' is structured so that Steed is the senior agent instructing Samantha Peel and Chris Cambridge, who then proceed to carry out the investigation and do the majority of the running and fighting. However, this type of set-up, giving Steed a reduced role in proceedings, had been tried before, in the first season of *The New Avengers*, and Macnee had been unhappy with it, so it is uncertain how he would have reacted to the idea, had the project progressed.

With the new line-up of Steed, Samantha Peel and Chris Cambridge established and ready to embark on further adventures, the prospects for the series' own reincarnation looked good. However, although Clemens was paid for his screenplay, none of the American networks thought this proposed new version of the series was a viable one, so the funding required to film the pilot was ultimately not forthcoming.

CBS reruns

On Thursday 11 July 1985, after a break of 11 months, CBS resumed their repeat transmissions of *The New Avengers*, replacing *The Fall Guy* in *The CBS Late Movie* slot. This run began with 'Target!' and generally saw two episodes being networked each week, on Wednesday and Thursday evenings. It concluded on Thursday 19 September with 'The Last of the Cybernauts …??'

A good influence

While all attempts to revive *The Avengers* might have come to nothing, by the 1980s its influence was arguably being felt in a number of other series, particularly North American-produced ones, that adopted a similar approach of having a male lead and a female lead of equal standing – the so-called 'dog and cat' format. The most successful of these was *Hart to Hart*, starring Robert Wagner as multi-millionaire Jonathan Hart and Stefanie Powers as his wife Jennifer. This husband-and-wife team frequently found themselves embroiled in the criminal activities of others for five seasons in a Spelling-Goldberg production for Columbia Pictures Television. Transmissions across the ITV network began with the pilot film on Sunday 27 January 1980, and although the series was cancelled in 1984, a further eight television movies were filmed between 1993 and 1996.

Another series that ran for five seasons was *Remington Steele*, in which Pierce Brosnan played the private detective title character and Stephanie Zimbalist portrayed the detective agency's true owner Laura Holt. The lead characters endured an abrasive relationship while solving their clients' problems, as discovered by British viewers when the series began transmission on BBC1 on Saturday 3 September 1983, switching to Channel 4 for some of its later episodes. Made by MTM Enterprises, *Remington Steele* eventually concluded after 94 episodes, allowing Brosnan the opportunity to become James Bond.

Scarecrow and Mrs King arrived in the UK when ITV began screening it on Tuesday 22 May 1984. In this series, secret agent Lee Stetson (codename Scarecrow), played by Bruce Boxleitner, enlists the assistance of the complete amateur Mrs Amanda King, played by Kate Jackson – very similar in essence to the way Steed recruited first Dr David Keel and later Cathy Gale in *The Avengers*. Overall, 88 episodes were filmed over four seasons by Shoot the Moon Enterprises for Warner Brothers Television.

Where *The Avengers* had been innovative and groundbreaking during the '60s, the same could be said of *Moonlighting* during the '80s. In this series, ex-fashion model Madelyn Hayes, played by Cybill Shepherd, runs the Blue Moon Detective Agency, but the so-called real detective is David Addison, ably portrayed by Bruce Willis, and together they embark on a succession of madcap investigations. UK transmissions began when the pilot film was shown by the BBC on Monday 26 May 1986. Picturemaker Productions in association with ABC Circle Films had found a winning formula that ultimately spanned five seasons, as *Moonlighting* amassed 65 episodes.

Hot Shots was a Canadian-produced 'dog and cat' show featuring a pair of investigative reporters who work for *Crime World* magazine. Jason West (aka Jake), played by Booth Savage, is an ace reporter, whose partner in criminal detection is Amanda Reed, played by Dorothy Parke. Once again the lead characters' different personalities and quirky mannerisms cause friction during proceedings, as British viewers saw when *Hot Shots* premiered in a late night graveyard slot on LWT on Saturday 8 April 1989. In the United States, the series appeared in *The New Avengers'* old slot as part of *The CBS Late Movie*, but proved unsuccessful, and only 13 episodes were made as a co-production between Alliance Communications Corporation and Grosso Jacobson.

On Target: The Avengers

In April 1986 Dave Rogers published his *Look Who's Talking: The Avengers All Interview Special*, containing interviews with Macnee, Blackman, Rigg, Thorson, Newell, Clemens, Lumley and Hunt. This A5-format glossy booklet was the culmination of Rogers' *On Target: The Avengers* fanzine, which he had launched shortly after his first book about the series, titled simply *The Avengers*, was published by ITV Books and Michael Joseph in March 1983. The earliest examples of *On Target: The Avengers* were slim and photocopied in black and white, but it quickly progressed to a higher page count, then glossy paper and eventually colour printing.

'Don't Get Me Wrong'

On Tuesday 5 August 1986, the rock group the Pretenders issued a new single entitled 'Don't Get Me Wrong', the promotional video for which featured lead singer Chrissie Hynde as an Emma Peel/Tara King figure in a pastiche of *The Avengers*.

The video's opening mimics the closing credits of the colour Diana Rigg episodes, in which Steed and Mrs Peel practice their unarmed combat skills, shot with the characters in silhouette against a pale-coloured background. Also copied are the graphics from the commercial break bumpers of the black and white Diana Rigg episodes, with *The Avengers'* logo adapted into the group's name.

With Steed apparently kidnapped, Hynde sets off on a series of short adventures in her red Reliant Scimitar convertible (C691 GOH), unaware that she is under surveillance. Led by a coded message, she arrives at row MI5 in a dimly-lit underground car park, where she finds herself caught in a trap. Just in the nick of time, Steed arrives in his vintage Bentley to effect a rescue. They drive away, but once out in the daylight, Hynde realises that her saviour is not the real Steed, but an impostor – played by Dicken Ashworth, an actor featured in the Channel 4 soap opera *Brookside* – forcing her to bail out of the Bentley onto a grassy verge.

Having recovered her Reliant Scimitar, Hynde is then seen close to Pinewood Studios, going through the ford on Hawkswood Lane near Fulmer in Buckinghamshire. From there she follows a fake diversion road sign and eventually has to abandon her vehicle, arriving on foot at St Hubert's House on St Hubert's Lane in Gerrards Cross, Buckinghamshire, which had been used as a filming location in *The New Avengers* episode 'Cat Amongst the Pigeons'.

The scene then changes to Hynde out on the town at night, receiving another message via an envelope placed under the wiper blade of her convertible, which leads her to a basement nightclub where a rock band is playing. The Pretenders' lead guitarist of the time, Robbie McIntosh, delivers his solo on stage in the club, then the video continues with Hynde, carrying a top hat and a rolled umbrella, walking across Albert Bridge in London.

Arriving outside a building representing Steed's apartment, Hynde sees the real agent looking down at her from an upstairs window – achieved by way of clips of Macnee from the episode 'The Forget-Me-Knot'. Using the end of her umbrella to knock over the ladder of a window cleaner, who is revealed to be the fake Steed she encountered earlier, she enters the premises. There, through clever editing to incorporate more footage from 'The Forget-Me-Knot', she finally comes face to face with Macnee as Steed.

Amplex commercials

During the summer of 1988, two *The Avengers*-themed television commercials for Amplex breath fresheners and roll-on deodorant appeared frequently in Channel 4 programme breaks. These both featured newly-recorded Patrick Macnee voiceovers over clips of him as Steed and Linda Thorson as Tara King from several season six episodes, including 'Game' and 'Look – (Stop Me If You've Heard This One) But There Were These Two Fellers …' . Macnee's catchphrase for these ads was, 'Don't get a complex, get Amplex'.

The New Avengers arrives on VHS

Also in 1988, *The New Avengers* arrived on sell-through VHS video courtesy of Channel 5 Home Video, who issued three cassettes containing two episodes on each. The combinations were 'The Eagle's Nest'/'The Gladiators', 'The Last of the Cybernauts …??'/'Sleeper' and 'Target!'/'Faces' – although the latter actually had the episodes in reverse order from that billed on the packaging.[36] Channel 5 Home Video was one of the innovators in selling television episodes on video for reasonable prices. It was eventually forced to end its own label when swamped by competitors, but at the time of writing still exists as a DVD and games distribution company.

---

[36] This book covers only UK VHS releases of *The Avengers* and *The New Avengers*. There were also releases from other companies elsewhere, including in Europe, the USA and Australia.

PART FIVE
PRODUCTION HISTORY
THE AVENGERS (MOVIE)

THE MOVIE

A SURFEIT OF H$_2$O

The Avengers heads for the big screen

In April 1986, having run into severe financial problems, Thorn-EMI sold off their extensive film and television library, including *The Avengers*, to businessman Alan Bond. The following week, he in turn sold it on to the American-based Cannon Group, who had secured a huge loan for the purpose. On Friday 1 May 1987, Cannon then sold it on for $85 million to producer Jerry Weintraub's recently-formed Weintraub Entertainment Group. Having acquired the rights to *The Avengers* in the process, Weintraub formulated plans to adapt the series for the cinema. Shortly afterwards, on Tuesday 9 June, *The Avengers* author Dave Rogers attended a meeting where he advised the American producer regarding the series' style.

Sometime later, at a dinner party, Weintraub engaged Australian star Mel Gibson in conversation regarding the series. Gibson was extremely positive about it and confessed to being a fan. Later Weintraub leaked a story to the press about having the actor on board to portray Steed in his proposed movie remake. A slightly garbled version of this surfaced on Friday 1 January 1988, when Ivor Davis of the *Daily Express* reported that Gibson had bought the movie rights to *The Avengers* with a view to playing the character of Steed. On Sunday 8 May the Australian newspaper *The Sunday Mail* went further, reporting that Gibson had signed on the dotted line to star as Steed in a big-budget movie, and would probably play the part like his hero Cary Grant. However, Gibson later denied that he had bought the rights to the series and said that he would never consider playing Steed, because in his opinion Patrick Macnee was perfection in the role. Gibson relayed some of this information to his friend Michael Sloan, whose *The Avengers* television movie concept, now called *The Avenging Angel*, had been in limbo for years, and with Weintraub having acquired the rights, would never progress any further than a story outline.

Having created plenty of publicity for his proposed cinema version, Weintraub surprisingly appears to have been in no hurry to commission a script, waiting until the second half of 1989 before hiring writer Sam Hamm. At the time, Hamm had little experience writing for feature films, but his screenplay for Tim Burton's *Batman* had had the desired effect of getting him noticed, and he was now flavour of the month. The writer produced a script, but the project then went into hiatus for several years as Weintraub Entertainment suffered a number of financial flops and funding to back large projects like *The Avengers* became scarce.

Stay Tuned

By the end of the 1980s, Dave Rogers' *The Avengers* fanzine had been renamed from *On Target: The Avengers* to *Stay Tuned*. Rogers had also begun an association with Australian author Geoff Barlow, by virtue of which the latter's previously-withdrawn paperback novel *The Saga of Happy Valley* (see Part Four) now gained authorised status. Copies of the book were shipped to the UK and distributed to readers as a Christmas gift. Working together, Rogers and Barlow then produced in booklet form a *The Avengers* novella called *The Weather Merchants*, which could be obtained only through *Stay Tuned* in 1989. The following year, Barlow alone wrote another example, *The Monster of the Moor*, and then a Tara King solo story, *Before the Mast*, although the latter was presented as simply a photocopied supplement to the fanzine. The final volume contained two different stories, *Moonlight Express* and *The Spoilsports*, again both credited to Barlow, although this did not become available until 1994.

Macnee and Thorson on *Blankety Blank*

Enthusiasts of *The Avengers* were prompted to tune in to the Monday 26 February 1990 edition of the BBC1 game show *Blankety Blank* by the news that both Patrick Macnee and Linda Thorson were to appear on the panel of celebrities. Under the haphazard guidance of compère Les Dawson, the two former Avengers provided possible answers to the questions facing the contestants.

The demise of Weintraub Entertainment

Weintraub Entertainment, the current owner of the rights to *The Avengers*, was declared bankrupt in September 1990. Jerry Weintraub resigned from his own company on Tuesday 25 September, moving on to become a producer of feature films for Warner Brothers.

Steed and Mrs Peel: the comic book

The Avengers returned to the comic strip medium in the Eclipse publication *Steed and Mrs Peel*, the first issue of which became available in October 1990, presenting the debut instalment of a three-part story titled 'The Golden Game'. Written by Grant Morrison, who had previously been responsible for comic strips in *Doctor Who Magazine* and several titles for DC Comics, it followed the style of the colour Diana Rigg episodes. Ian Gibson provided the artwork, taking time out between assignments on the comic *2000 AD*, for which he drew various strips, including *Judge Dredd*. The second issue arrived in January 1991, and this also included a back-up strip titled 'Deadly Rainbow', written by Anne Caulfield, a mainstream author who, having penned a book about travelling in the Middle East, thought she would try something different. Leaving readers thinking that the title had been curtailed prematurely, the third and final issue of the mini-series took over 12 months to appear, finally arriving in 1992.

Too Many Targets

The Avengers returned to the written word format too when American publishers St Martin's Press brought out the paperback novel *Too Many Targets* in December 1990. This was co-written by American-based British writer John Peel and Dave Rogers. The story features Steed once again battling the Cybernauts, assisted by his main partners against crime from the '60s, Dr David Keel, Cathy Gale, Emma Peel and Tara King. Peel had begun writing for *Doctor Who* fanzines in the late '70s before progressing to semi-professional American publications such as *Fantasy Empire* in the '80s. After Target Books came to an agreement with the agent of Dalek creator Terry Nation, he had been given the opportunity to novelise a number of *Doctor Who* serials featuring the creatures, beginning with *The Chase* in 1989.

Cathy Gale comes to America

After decades of waiting, American viewers finally got the opportunity to watch the videotaped second and third seasons of *The Avengers* when the cable channel A&E began screenings in January 1991. The run concluded in April, but curiously omitted the episode 'The Golden Fleece'.

Without Walls documentary

On Tuesday 14 January 1992, Channel 4 transmitted a half-hour documentary spotlighting *The Avengers* in their *Without Walls* series. The production company, Screen First, conducted interviews with Patrick Macnee, Honor Blackman and Linda Thorson to provide a backbone for the presentation. Augmenting this material was archive interview footage featuring Diana Rigg, Brian Clemens, Leonard White, Richard Bates, Roger Marshall, Cyd Child, James Hill, Peter Bowles and Don Leaver. The programme would be repeated on Wednesday 4 October 1995, before reappearing in an extended form on videocassette as *Avenging the Avengers*, released by Contender on Monday 5 June 2000, but minus the Leonard White footage, which had been removed at his request.

TV Heaven on Channel 4

Also on Channel 4, the third season episode 'The Gilded Cage' was transmitted on Saturday 15 February 1992 as part of their *TV Heaven* season, where most of the evening's programming consisted of archive material. 'The Gilded Cage' was the first of a batch of 13 videotaped episodes of *The Avengers* that the station had acquired for screening about six months previously, but had so far failed to schedule. Six weeks later, *TV Heaven* included the only existing *Police Surgeon* episode 'Easy Money', starring Ian Hendry as Dr Geoffrey Brent.

Virtual Murder

Friday 24 July 1992 saw the arrival of the BBC's short-lived 'dog and cat' show *Virtual Murder*, a light thriller with quirky and surreal storylines that appeared to have been significantly influenced by *The Avengers*. Nicholas Clay portrayed psychology lecturer

Dr John Cornelius (J C for short), while his sexy redhead sidekick Samantha Valentine was played by Kim Thomson. Unfortunately, although *Virtual Murder* showed considerable promise, the BBC declined to continue production after showing the half-dozen episodes that comprised the first and only season.

Channel 4 reruns

In 1993, Channel 4 finally began screening the videotaped episodes of *The Avengers* to which they had acquired the rights. The run began on Thursday 7 January with the first season adventure 'The Frighteners' and continued the following week with the Blackman episode 'Immortal Clay'. The channel obviously thought that these produced-as-live black-and-white episodes would have limited audience appeal, as they were relegated to a late slot, beginning at 11.05 pm. They did however go to the trouble of commissioning a series of short, newly-recorded introductions to the episodes, under the umbrella title 'Life in the Past Lane'.

The Avengers arrives on VHS

Meanwhile, the Weintraub Entertainment film and television library, including *The Avengers*, had been bought by the multinational Movie Acquisitions Corporation. On Monday 26 April 1993, the daily edition of *Variety* reported that the French chairman of this company, Jean Cazes, was restructuring and renaming it Lumiere Pictures. It was under this banner that *The Avengers* finally became available on sell-through VHS video.

The initial offering on Monday 20 September was *The Avengers: A Retrospective*, which although described as a documentary was more of a promotional item presenting clips from various episodes linked by newly-recorded material featuring Patrick Macnee. Retailing at £10.99, this cassette was stocked exclusively by F W Woolworth and served as a taster for the avalanche of *The Avengers* material that would be marketed in the UK over the next two and a half years.

With the ground now suitably prepared, the first of the standard releases arrived on Monday 25 October, each bringing together one black and white and one colour Diana Rigg episode. The combinations were as follows: Volume 1: 'The Town of No Return'/'From Venus with Love'; Volume 2: 'The Cybernauts'/ 'Return of the Cybernauts'; Volume 3: 'A Touch of Brimstone'/'The Bird Who Knew Too Much'. Lumiere also targeted the tape rental market by offering 'Murdersville'/'Never, Never Say Die' as a special one-off title available to rent exclusively through the now-defunct Titles video chain.

The following day, Tuesday 26 October, Lumiere threw an extravagant launch party in Chelsea, with Macnee, Blackman, Rigg and Thorson all present for publicity purposes – the only time all four had ever been together in one place. Also in attendance were a number of other performers who had appeared in the show, including Simon Oates, Sue Lloyd, Nigel Davenport, Fenella Fielding and Patrick Cargill, plus fellow actors Barry Morse and Nickolas Grace. From the production side, there were Brian Clemens, Roy Ward Baker, Leonard White and Richard Bates.

Realising that there was an untapped collector's market for *The Avengers*, Lumiere would occasionally produce special sets, and the first of these came in an attaché case-style box set of three videocassettes, called *The Complete Avengers* (aka *The First Ever*

Episodes Collection). Containing an episode from each season, plus 'The Forget-Me-Knot' and an informative booklet, this collection hit the shops on Monday 1 November.

By Monday 29 November another three standard episode releases had been made available – again, each coupling one monochrome and one colour Diana Rigg episode.

The Avengers movie in black and white?

Despite his former company having lost the old Thorn-EMI film and television library, Jerry Weintraub had retained the rights to produce a movie version of *The Avengers*; and having now acted as producer on three films for Warner Brothers, he had convinced them to back it. Interviewed in the *Starburst Special 15: Monsters Special* magazine published in 1993, director David Fincher indicated that there had been some discussion between himself and Weintraub with regard to the project. However, it appears that Fincher's vision of *The Avengers* differed from the American's, as he wanted to create an atmospheric experience by filming in black and white. He also voiced a preference for Charles Dance to play Steed, having previously cast him in *Alien 3*.

Sam Hamm's screenplay for the movie presented the first meeting between Steed and Mrs Peel. However, obviously wanting to craft something that he thought would appeal to a '90s audience, he completely revised the characters. Although their names were unchanged, they were given completely different backgrounds and personalities from the Steed and Mrs Emma Peel of the television series. This approach was exactly what Warner Brothers did not want, so Hamm was paid off and departed the project in the summer of 1993. Weintraub then hired a replacement scriptwriter, the little-known Don MacPherson, who started again from scratch.

For five months beginning in January 1994, Weintraub and MacPherson – a confirmed fan of the series – developed storyline ideas. MacPherson then had a first draft of a new screenplay ready by May. Even at this early stage, it appeared that he had been drawing considerable inspiration from certain episodes of the television series, including the weather controlling aspects of 'A Surfeit of H_2O'.

The Avengers on satellite

The satellite and cable television station Bravo lived up to its 'Timewarp Television' slogan in early 1994 by purchasing *The Avengers*, which it began transmitting on Sunday 6 February with *The Avengers: A Retrospective*. This was followed up with the Ian Hendry episode 'The Frighteners' the following day, then the station continued with the videotaped adventures from seasons two and three, before moving on to the Diana Rigg episodes and then in July those featuring Linda Thorson.

More VHS releases

Thursday 10 February 1994 saw Joanna Lumley and Gareth Hunt reunited for an edition of the regional news programme *London Tonight*, where they promoted the imminent re-release of *The New Avengers* on VHS video. The *Daily Mirror* ran a combined interview with the two actors the following day, highlighting the launch of the series on the Video Gems subsidiary label TV Gems. Hunt said, 'There is the possibility that I will be doing something with Joanna as a spin-off,' suggesting a possible Gambit and Purdey project, although if that was indeed what he meant, unfortunately it never got off the ground.

The first two cassettes in *The Classic Television Collection*, as Video Gems called their releases of *The New Avengers*, became available on Monday 14 February, but disappointingly they contained exactly the same episodes as had been issued in 1988 by Channel 5 Home Video. There would be another two releases later in 1994, with previously-unreleased episodes, but then the range would peter out.

Meanwhile, picking up from where they had left off the previous year, on Monday 28 February Lumiere released another three volumes of *The Avengers*, including their initial Tara King cassette, containing the episodes 'Game' and 'They Keep Killing Steed'. As 1994 progressed, they continued marketing new VHS material. This included, on the final day of October, another box set, *Emma Peel: Six of the Best*, showcasing three black and white and three colour episodes, complete with three collectable Diana Rigg postcards. Also enclosed within the box was a pamphlet/order form for *The Avengers* Collection, a range of memorabilia carrying *The Avengers* motif, including a ceramic drinking mug, various shirts, plus a matching baseball cap and jacket. Further to this, toward the conclusion of November, the Rigg episode 'Honey for the Prince' was coupled with the Thorson episode 'Bizarre' to form the *Special Final Episodes Volume*, retailed exclusively through the HMV chain of shops.

The Avengers Studio Kafé

The *Daily Mirror*'s *TV Weekly* section covering Saturday 23 to Friday 29 April 1994 ran a piece in which reporter Neil Murray outlined Linda Thorson's plans to open a *The Avengers*-themed restaurant in London. Obviously influenced by the successful Planet Hollywood chain that had been established three years earlier, Thorson envisaged her *The Avengers* Studio Kafé as having a huge interactive video wall and a working television studio, which celebrities could visit. The restaurant would include memorabilia not only from *The Avengers* but also from other television series, with the waitresses' outfits being bowler hats, mini dresses and black leather boots. Unfortunately, this ambitious concept never progressed any further than an idea.

The Age of Elegance

Also in 1994, some quality merchandise became available from the company Age of Elegance Fine Art Productions, who created five porcelain statuettes of characters from *The Avengers*. Standing approximately eight inches tall on a circular wooden base, these painted collectables were designed by Marcus Quincey, and depicted Cathy Gale, Emma Peel, Tara King and two different versions of Steed.

Movie developments

Toward the end of 1994, further reports started appearing in the popular press regarding the imminent production of a movie version of *The Avengers*. As noted in the *Daily Express* dated Tuesday 13 December, Weintraub was still sticking to his Mel Gibson story regarding the casting of Steed. Possibly due to the fact that Weintraub's previous movie, *The Specialist*, had co-starred Sharon Stone, her name also became attached to the project as being in the running to assume the Emma Peel role. When consulted regarding the situation, *The Avengers'* former co-producer Brian Clemens suggested that Hugh Grant and Elizabeth Hurley would make a more appropriate Steed and Emma, and was quoted as saying, 'Americans making *The Avengers* is like making *The Godfather* in Watford.'

The planned February 1995 shooting date mooted for the film came and went without anything happening, and it seemed that the project was stuck in production limbo once again. However, a positive development occurred in May, when Nicholas Meyer, who had written and directed both *Star Trek II: The Wrath of Khan* and *Star Trek IV: The Undiscovered Country*, was appointed as the film's director. Meyer promptly rewrote Don MacPherson's screenplay, but Warner Brothers were unimpressed with the new version and rejected it, bringing about Meyer's departure from the production. This sequence of events would later be recalled in edition no. 310 of writer and literary critic Edward Champion's New York-based podcast *The Bat Segundo Show*, broadcast in September 2009.

Seeing his dream of bringing *The Avengers* to the cinema screen receding once again, Weintraub had MacPherson perform another rewrite of his screenplay. This new draft, dated Wednesday 21 June 1995 and running to 105 pages, would provide the backbone for what was eventually shot, although it would undergo further development for another two years before filming finally began.

The New Avengers on Bravo

Meanwhile, back in February 1995, satellite and cable channel Bravo had begun transmitting *The New Avengers*, having obviously been more than pleased with the reaction to their run of *The Avengers* the previous year.

Bugs

On Saturday 1 April 1995 the BBC unveiled their new high-tech action series *Bugs*, which a continuity announcer described as '*The Avengers* of the '90s'. Set in the near future, *Bugs* featured a scenario of cutting-edge technology pushed one step further into science fiction, and had Brian Clemens as a series consultant. Ex-government agent Nick Beckett was played by Jesse Birdsall; computer and electronics expert Ros Henderson was portrayed by Jaye Griffiths; and daredevil pilot Ed Russell was brought to life by Craig McLachlan. Initially the trio worked as an independent unit, providing security measures in a technically advancing world and becoming involved in storylines that included groundbreaking inventions – similar to situations found in the filmed episodes of *The Avengers* 30 years earlier. From the third season onwards, the trio came under the control of the government agency Bureau 2, though their exploits continued unabated. Screened on BBC1 between 1995 and 1999, *Bugs* clocked up a total of 40 episodes over four seasons, for the last of which Steven Houghton took over from McLachlan in the Ed Russell role.

VHS releases continue

Meanwhile, the video rights to *The New Avengers* had passed to another company Pyramid HE, who launched with a mass release of seven cassettes on Monday May 1995, but made the strange decision to issue only one episode per tape, with the exception of 'K is for Kill', where both parts were amalgamated.

The following month saw Lumiere issue their first two VHS cassettes featuring Cathy Gale, with the second season episodes 'Death Dispatch'/'Propellant 23' and 'Mr Teddy Bear'/'Bullseye'.

Network television transmissions

During the autumn of 1995, *The New Avengers* underwent its first ever full UK networking. This came courtesy of BBC2, in a Friday evening time slot previously used for the screening of other nostalgic fare such as *The Champions*. Transmissions commenced with 'Complex' on 8 September, but soon faced competition from the original series, when Channel 4 began showing black and white Rigg episodes on Tuesday 10 October. After only five episodes, Channel 4 switched seasons and substituted the colour Rigg escapades, beginning with 'From Venus with Love' on Tuesday 14 November, but despite this change they could muster only 1.5 million viewers at best. Meanwhile, over on BBC2, *The New Avengers* was proving more popular in its Friday slot, where it regularly attracted 2 million.

Having bought the complete rights to *The New Avengers* from The Avengers Enterprises, Lumiere looked destined to begin a prolonged series of video releases to accompany their *The Avengers* tapes, but this was not to be. Lumiere was acquired by the French-based cinema chain operator UGC in January 1996, and after only a couple of *The New Avengers* tapes and a further four *The Avengers* tapes were released under the Lumiere Pictures banner in March, there was then a halt to video releases for both series for approximately two and a half years.

Jeremiah Chechik

In October 1995, Canadian director Jeremiah Chechik read an early draft of Don MacPherson's screenplay for *The Avengers* movie and was instantly interested in directing and assisting in the development of Weintraub's project. He was consequently appointed as Nicholas Meyer's replacement. Then, in February 1996, after years of delays, Warner Brothers finally gave Weintraub the green light for the movie, putting up the finance and allowing casting to begin.

The speculation over who would win the role of Emma Peel continued, and on Thursday 15 February the Australian newspaper *The Sunday Mail* thought they had gained an exclusive, using the headline 'Nicole The New Avenger' to report that Nicole Kidman would be slipping on the kinky boots. Unknown to them, however, Kidman had actually turned down the part. As Chechik later revealed in an interview with Simon Brew, published on Tuesday 1 February 2011 on the *Den of Geek* website, the actress had been forced to keep her diary free of commitments as she had already signed to appear in Stanley Kubrick's *Eyes Wide Shut*, and the notoriously fastidious director had yet to decide when shooting on that movie would commence. As things transpired, *Eyes Wide Shut* and *The Avengers* would be in production simultaneously at Pinewood Studios during the summer of 1997.

On Friday 23 February 1996 the *Daily Mirror* stole a lead on other publications when they reported that Ralph (pronounced Rafe) Fiennes would be taking the part of John Steed in the movie, although others under consideration for the role had included Hugh Grant, Sean Bean, Alan Rickman and Robbie Coltrane.

The July 1996 edition of *Dreamwatch* magazine indicated that Chechik had eradicated all surreal and science fiction elements from the movie's screenplay, but would be retaining the kooky and crazy aspects of the television series. The storyline was described as a straight crime yarn pitting Steed and Mrs Peel against organised crime in the form of the American Mafia. However, as this bore no relation to Don MacPherson's draft, it can only be assumed that it was a completely different screenplay that was being referred to.

More Channel 4 reruns

Having continued with their Tuesday evening transmissions of *The Avengers*, which had now reached the Thorson episodes, Channel 4 dropped the series for several weeks toward the end of June 1996 to allow coverage of the Tour de France cycling event. The weekly screenings resumed on 23 July, continuing through to 19 November, when they concluded with 'Homicide and Old Lace'.

Uma Thurman

Still finding *The Avengers* movie a newsworthy subject, the *Daily Mail* confidently reported in its Friday 29 November 1996 edition that the production had finally found its leading lady in the person of Gwyneth Paltrow. Like the *Daily Mirror*'s earlier report about Nicole Kidman, this was inaccurate. As Paltrow later told the *Express* in a feature printed on Monday 27 April 1998, she had also refused the role, as she wished to remain in the United States with her then boyfriend Brad Pitt.

On Saturday 8 February 1998, the true identity of the movie's Emma Peel was revealed when the *Express* informed its readers that Uma Thurman had been approached through her agent and had accepted the part. Others actresses considered for the female lead but not approached included Julia Roberts, Polly Walker, Meg Ryan, Elizabeth Hurley and Emma Thompson.

Thurman was the personal dream choice to play Emma Peel for both scriptwriter Don MacPherson and producer Jerry Weintraub. Weintraub had in fact approached her about the project before it was offered to anyone else. Initially she had to decline due to other commitments, but later she agreed to become involved after Kidman and Paltrow passed up their opportunities.

Spy Game

Meanwhile, on Monday 3 March 1997, the ABC network in the USA unveiled *Spy Game*, a stylish series that drew inspiration from the '60s espionage genre, especially *The Avengers*, *The Man From U.N.C.L.E.* and *The Girl From U.N.C.L.E.*. The series centred around the character Lorne Cash, played by Linden Ashby, a retired agent drawn back into service with ECHO (Emergency Counter Hostilities Organisation) and teamed up with the younger Maxine (aka Max) London, portrayed by Allison Smith. In the first episode, 'Why Spy?', Patrick Macnee acted alongside ex-*Mission: Impossible* star Peter Lupus as a pair of assassins, and ex-*I-Spy* lead Robert Culp also made an uncredited appearance, as the series paid homage to its '60s antecedents. In subsequent episodes Macnee then took on the different role of the recurring character Dr Quentin. Sadly, however, the series was cancelled in July 1997 after ABC had transmitted only nine of the 13 episodes that had been filmed. In the UK, Channel 4 later showed all 13 episodes in a late evening time slot from June to September 1999.

Sean Connery

On Friday 11 April 1997 the *Daily Mail* continued its coverage of the forthcoming movie version of *The Avengers* when it revealed the big name casting of Sean Connery as the evil Sir August de Wynter. Intent on securing an A-list performer to play the villain of the piece, Jerry Weintraub had sent a copy of the script to Connery, an old golfing buddy of his. Connery had initially turned it down because he considered the role too small, but further negotiations had then taken place, involving Weintraub and Don MacPherson visiting the actor at his Spanish home, and after several meetings they had thrashed out an agreement. Connery was won over by an undertaking from MacPherson to rewrite the screenplay to increase de Wynter's role, and was also impressed by Weintraub's intention to film at locations such as Blenheim Palace and Stowe House. The actor remembered watching *The Avengers* on television and thought that playing an off-the-wall villain would be fun. It seems however that Connery was not the only candidate for the role, as later, in an interview published in a December 1998 edition of the *Express*, Michael Caine revealed that he too been approached about playing de Wynter, but upon reading the script had decided that it was definitely not for him.

In further casting news, the *Express* pitched in again on Thursday 15 May 1997, reporting that stand-up comedian, writer and actor Eddie Izzard would be featuring in the movie, as would Patrick Macnee, although only in a cameo role and not as Steed.

Back on Channel 4

On 18 May 1997 Channel 4 launched another batch of *The Avengers* reruns in a late Sunday night/early Monday morning time slot, returning to their stockpile of black and white Rigg episodes and beginning with 'The Master Minds'. With their rights to the series due to lapse shortly, the channel also started showing the remaining seven Linda Thorson episodes that had been omitted from the previous year's screenings, scheduling these on Friday evenings at 6.00 p

The feature film enters production

After undergoing extensive development for eight years, Jerry Weintraub's vision of a major motion picture version of *The Avengers* finally became a reality on Monday 2 June 1997, when shooting commenced at Pinewood Studios. However, an early setback occurred on the night of Friday 13 June, when a special effects explosion on E Stage ignited the ceiling, the resulting fire damaging the roof and destroying a set costing a million pounds. Over 60 fire-fighters from the surrounding area battled the blaze, which fortunately occurred while the cast were absent. The following day numerous newspapers, including the *Express*, the *Independent*, the *Sun* and the *Guardian*, all reported the incident, with the *Daily Mail* quoting Jerry Weintraub as saying that he did not know if production would be delayed.

On location in Hambleden

The movie's opening sequence, filmed in early July 1997, shows Fiennes as Steed undergoing a physical training exercise, apparently inspired by *The New Avengers* episode 'Target!'. This was shot on location in the small village of Hambleden in Buckinghamshire. Having narrowly avoided being struck by a falling plant pot, Steed picks himself a white carnation from the debris and places it in his buttonhole, as a readout in the bottom left-hand corner of the screen informs viewers: 'John Steed: Secret Agent, The Ministry.' Taking a relaxed stroll through the village as the exercise continues, Steed is forced to defend himself from a variety of assailants disguised as, respectively, a police officer, a milkman, a nanny and some garage mechanics. Eventually he has to hoist himself clear of a passing car by hooking his umbrella over a gas lamp, the metal frame of which is attached to a red-brick building later revealed to be a fake structure and part of the test course. Throughout filming, Fiennes found that he far preferred smooth, rosewood-handled umbrellas to the traditional bamboo variety that Patrick Macnee had favoured in the television series.

Establishing the scenario

The scene next switches to a dark and dusty underground office where Steed's superior Mother, played by Jim Broadbent, and his glamorous assistant Brenda, played by Carmen Ejogo, are monitoring the Prospero Programme weather shield. This time a readout caption states: 'Codename: "Mother": Head of the Ministry, Elite Intelligence.' Broadbent wore body padding to bulk out his appearance for the movie, but nevertheless interpreted the character of Mother very differently from Patrick Newell in the television series, even smoking unfiltered cigarettes.

In complete contrast to Mother's headquarters, Emma Peel's modern-looking multi-level apartment is all smooth surfaces and lightness. The interiors for this were shot on location in architect Richard Rogers' home on Royal Avenue in Chelsea, London SW3. Here Mrs Peel receives a hand-delivered personal message from Steed requesting her to answer the telephone. Upon her return to the apartment's upper level the telephone promptly rings, and then a recorded message plays, arranging a meeting at Boodles gentlemen's club. A further readout caption states: 'Dr Emma Peel: Former Chief of the Prospero Project.'

Boodles is established by footage filmed both inside and outside the Reform Club at 104 Pall Mall, London SW1. It is here that Mrs Peel locates Steed, sat naked in a sauna reading the *Financial Times* – a scenario allowing Fiennes to crack the joke, 'I was about to throw in the towel.'

As in the television series, Mrs Peel is portrayed in the movie as a widow whose test pilot husband went missing four years earlier – although, in a new twist, it is said that he too worked for the Ministry.

Steed's vintage Bentley

With Mrs Peel accompanying him, Steed goes to meet Mother, travelling east across Lambeth Bridge, London SE1, in his vintage 1928 4½ litre Bentley (RT 4700) and then arriving at a disused tram tunnel in Kingsway, WC2. Some computer-generated imagery was used here, in shots of the Bentley descending a cobblestone roadway, to replace the location background of trees and traffic with a clear road and, in the distance, the River Thames. Stopping at a barrier, Steed presents his personal security pass to an automated card reader that announces, 'You are now entering a restricted area.' Another readout in the bottom left-hand corner of the screen states: 'The Ministry, London.'

As the vintage Bentley used for the production lacked a synchromesh gearbox, the action vehicle coordinator Duncan Barbour had to teach Fiennes how to declutch and double declutch, although the actor never took the vehicle higher than third gear. Barbour already knew Fiennes, having worked with him on another movie, *The English Patient*. Barber would later go on to run Wildtrackers, a company offering a worldwide off-road expedition service plus film tracking equipment and vehicles.

Mrs Peel a traitor?

Emma is accused of sabotaging the top secret Prospero research laboratory but protests her innocence, despite being presented with closed circuit television pictures of her apparently carrying out the deed while wearing a black crocodile-skin PVC catsuit. Mother's response is to team her up with Steed to discover the real saboteur. After Brenda has shown them out, a blind operative codenamed Father arrives, having obviously been eavesdropping on the meeting. For the movie, this character, originally portrayed by Iris Russell in the television episode 'Stay Tuned', was played by Fiona Shaw, although comedienne Dawn French had also been under consideration for the part. The latest readout caption explains: 'Codename: "Father": Second in Command, The Ministry.'

A subsequent sequence of Steed fencing with Emma at his tailor's, Trubshaw and Co, was lifted from the episode 'The Town of No Return', even to the point of including some of the same dialogue. The cobblestone street seen outside Trubshaw and Co was a large standing set constructed on the Pinewood backlot and designed to work in forced perspective, although this effect is not apparent in the final edit of the film, as the scene where Steed and Emma depart appears to have been cut short.

De Wynter's house

Mrs Peel agrees to join Steed on a jaunt in the countryside, and together they take the Bentley to make a social call on Sir August de Wynter, a retired and wealthy ex-Ministry man who oversaw something called the special deception initiative. Steed describes de Wynter as having an absolute fascination with the weather, pointing out that he was also the chairman of BROLLY, standing for the British Royal Organisation for Lasting Liquid Years. The exteriors and some interiors of de Wynter's exceptionally large home, Hallucinogen Hall, were provided by Blenheim Palace and grounds, situated off Oxford Road in the village of Woodstock in Oxfordshire. The establishing interior shot showing an enormous number of snow globes was filmed inside Blenheim's Long Library, which contains over 10,000 books and the largest organ in a private dwelling in the UK. Having worked as a puppeteer on various Gerry Anderson productions, Christine Glanville was instrumental in assembling the globes for this sequence, and each of them contained something different. However, when the director required them all to be shaken up to give the impression of falling snow, a problem occurred as the water inside turned cloudy. It transpired that some detergent used during the manufacturing process was still present, and this had to be thoroughly cleaned out in a time-consuming process before the globes could be refilled with fresh water, allowing shooting to commence.

The interiors of de Wynter's huge tropical greenhouse, where Mrs Peel diverts de Wynter's attention and leaves Steed free to investigate, were filmed not at Blenheim but in the Great Conservatory of Syon Park. This large residence was built in 1547 and stands in 200 acres of parkland in Brentford, Middlesex. The interiors were later redesigned by 18th Century architect Robert Adam.

The extensive gardens of Heatherden Hall at Pinewood were used for the following sequence where, exploring some woodland on de Wynter's estate, Steed comes across the strange sight of a red telephone box, which begins to ring as he approaches. Suddenly from nowhere a gale-force wind erupts, forcing him to seek shelter in the box, where he answers the telephone, only to discover that because of the increased noise level he is unable to hear whoever is on the other end of the line.

Leaving the telephone box, Steed finds the surrounding parkland now covered in snow – another sequence shot in the Heatherden Hall gardens, as described in the book *The Pinewood Story* by Gareth Owen, published in 2000. With snow still falling, Steed watches as a dog sled emerges from the white, drawn by eight huskies under the control of Mrs Peel, wearing dark glasses and a fur coat over her black crocodile-skin PVC catsuit. Taking aim with a spear gun, Mrs Peel fires at Steed, but he instinctively dives for cover. She then produces a fully-chromed Colt King Python revolver with a six inch barrel and shoots him at point blank range.

The plot thickens

Steed regains consciousness in Emma's apartment, where he is unsure if Mrs Peel is really Mrs Peel. He explains his escape from death – his waistcoat was bullet-proof – and they discuss protons, ions and manipulating the weather over a chess match – the moves of which happen to be exactly the same as those of the match played between the characters Rick Deckard and Roy Batty, played by Harrison Ford and Rutger Hauer, in the movie *Blade Runner*. The two agents then get back on the trail of whoever is manipulating the elements, a snow globe leading them to a place called Wonderland Weather.

On arriving, Steed spins a yarn to Tamara the receptionist, played by Keeley Hawes, who begins showing an interest when he mentions de Wynter's name. The muted background music heard over this scene is an instrumental version of 'Raindrops Keep Falling on My Head', written by Burt Bacharach and Hal David back in the '60s. A version with lyrics had reached number one on the American Billboard chart in 1970, sung by B J Thomas.

Meanwhile, in another room at Wonderland Weather, de Wynter is addressing a meeting of his colleagues from BROLLY, who are all dressed in colourful life-size teddy bear costumes to hide their identities from each other. Forecasting that they are about to make history, de Wynter casually enquires if anybody wishes to resign, and promises to pay any takers a million dollars for their valuable contribution to his work. This dialogue was slightly altered in post-production, the word 'dollars' being dubbed over the original 'pounds' delivered by Connery during filming. The yellow and the green teddy bears both raise their hands to take advantage of de Wynter's offer. However, part of the brooch on de Wynter's chest then transforms into a pair of darts, which in one fluid movement he throws at the two men, piercing their costumes and killing them instantly. The whole of this sequence was filmed in a large room at Syon House.

On location at the Lloyd's Building

Tamara having been called away, Steed and Mrs Peel proceed to investigate Wonderland Weather for themselves. For these scenes, filming took place at the futuristic-looking Lloyd's Building at 1 Lime Street, London EC3. Steed and someone in the black teddy bear outfit are seen travelling in glass lifts on the building's exterior. Arriving at ground level, Steed emerges into a metal-lined courtyard where five men dressed in black are disposing of the scarlet teddy bear outfit into a dumpster. Noticing his arrival, the men surround him. Then de Wynter's chief henchman Bailey, played by Eddie Izzard, removes the agent's bowler hat, prompting the remark, 'That was a very silly thing to do.' A fight scene follows, consisting of a succession of brief, rapidly-intercut shots, as the thugs find they are unable to contain Steed, even with the benefit of a large hunting knife brandished by Donavan, played by the Happy Mondays' lead singer Shaun Ryder.

Bailey retreats to Wonderland Weather's nearby black Ford Transit van and departs at speed. Among the oldest examples of the Ford Transit in the country, this vehicle was first registered in 1965. In 2008 it was reported as being in Hertfordshire, undergoing a complete restoration, but still retaining the Wonderland Weather umbrella graphics added to it for the film.

In a sequence shot around several walkways and sections of roof on the Lloyd's Building, Mrs Peel is suddenly attacked by the black-costumed teddy bear. Defending herself, she knocks off the headpiece of her opponent's costume to reveal … Emma Peel! Arriving on the scene, Steed thinks he is seeing things. However, Emma's double – or Bad Emma, as she was called in publicity material for the movie – escapes by leaping off the roof to her apparent death. When in character as Bad Emma, Thurman sported darker make-up and was subjected to wearing amber-coloured contact lenses. However, as she usually wore the black crocodile-skin PVC catsuit, this more obviously gave away her true identity.

Mother's mobile HQ

Mother's mobile headquarters in the movie is represented by a London Transport Routemaster double-decker bus – an idea copied from the television episode 'False Witness'. This vehicle was filmed passing Cornwall Terrace on part of the Outer Circle at Regent's Park, London NW1. On the upper deck, Mother and Father express opposing opinions regarding the Mrs Peel duplicate, while Steed sits silently reading his fictional newspaper, the *City Bulletin*, the headline of which declares 'Heat Bumps and Frostbite All in One Day'. At the beginning of this sequence, a further readout caption appears in the bottom left-hand corner of the screen: 'The Ministry: Mobile Headquarters.'

On location at Hatfield House

Father is then revealed to be a traitor, as she is seen playing croquet with de Wynter in a sequence shot on location in the grounds of Hatfield House. This 17th Century structure stands surrounded by ornate gardens within the Great Park, off Great North Road in Hatfield, Hertfordshire.

Emma's E-type Jaguar

Mrs Peel is then seen driving Steed through the countryside in her pale blue 1970 E-Type Jaguar (439 OJX), when she spots that they are being pursued by a swarm of large mechanical flying insects with machine guns, radio-controlled by Bailey from a black and white Mini Cooper (D453 BBB) with Donavan at the wheel. The Mini was supplied to the production by the Rover Group, formerly known as BL and before that as British Leyland. At the time of writing, it is still in concours (i.e. pristine) condition and frequently appears in classic car shows, complete with a display showing its appearance in *The Avengers*.

Initially it was envisaged that Mrs Peel would drive a Lotus Elan, like her television counterpart, but Jeremiah Chechik preferred the E-Type, considering it a more iconic and nicer-looking car. Four examples were purchased for the production and sprayed pale blue. One was then upgraded with the addition of heavy-duty shock absorbers and a full roll cage to protect the stunt performers should the vehicle overturn while being driven at speed during filming. The preparation of this stunt vehicle was undertaken by an uncredited Paul Ridgeway of Midland Rally Team Services, who at the time were based at Silverstone motor racing circuit. The second Jaguar served as a back-up for the main stunt car; the third was a 'victim vehicle' chosen to sustain damage during the automated insect attack sequence; and the fourth, which had immaculate upholstery, was used only for interior shots.

Since appearing in the film, the main stunt Jaguar has had the safety roll cage removed and undergone a complete restoration, being resprayed to a slightly darker shade of blue. It is now based in Shropshire.

Duncan Barbour came to the production's aid again when it was discovered that Uma Thurman had always driven cars with an automatic gearbox and was unable to use a manual transmission. He initially coached Thurman in an MGF loaned to the production by the Rover Group as part of the same deal involving the Mini Cooper. Gaining confidence under Barbour's instruction, which he later described as fun, the actress mastered changing gear and progressed to driving the faster E-Type Jaguars.

The plague of mechanical insects

In a protracted action sequence (which, as detailed below, was the result of a reshoot), the two agents are attacked by a swarm of mechanical flying insects. One of the insects flies into the rear of the E-Type, where it then lies incapacitated. Disconnecting its machine gun, Steed uses it to shoot down some of the others. Meanwhile, Mrs Peel's evasive driving under a railway bridge and through a wood causes a number of the automated insects to collide with the brickwork and trees, resulting in them exploding or falling to the ground. While navigating her way through a wooded area, Mrs Peel speeds past the stationary Mini and, gunning the engine, Donavan gives chase. Eventually, Bailey manoeuvres the sole surviving insect attacker to fly straight toward the oncoming Jaguar. The E-type deals it a glancing blow, which sends it directly into the windscreen of the pursuing Mini. This causes Donavan lose control to lose control of the vehicle, which leaves the road at speed and somersaults several times over in a field.

Suddenly finding the way blocked by an elderly lady with a bicycle, Mrs Peel brings the E-Type to a tyre-screeching halt. Announcing herself as Alice, the lady politely requests that Steed and Mrs Peel lie flat on the ground. Then, producing a Thompson submachine gun from the basket on her bicycle, she sprays bullets at Bailey and Donavan, who have appeared in the distance. Donavan has an automatic weapon but is hit, although Bailey manages to escape. Alice then explains that Mother dispatched her to provide assistance.

Played by Eileen Atkins on screen, the part of Alice was originally offered to Diana Rigg, who was sent a script for her consideration but declined to become involved. *The Avengers: The Official Souvenir Magazine*, issued by Titan Books around the time of the movie's release, indicates that Joanna Lumley was also offered a chance to appear – although it is unknown in what role – but she too decided against it. Atkins had originally been cast as Father, but saw more scope in the role of Alice and convinced Chechik not only to transfer her into it, but also to enlarge it somewhat.

Exterior shots of Alice leading Steed and Mrs Peel to a back entrance at Hallucinogen Hall show them proceeding through the gardens and past the pond at Heatherden Hall before arriving at a mocked-up section of maze. Further footage for this sequence was obtained in the Marlborough Maze in the grounds of Blenheim Palace.

On location at Stowe House

Taken prisoner by de Wynter, Mrs Peel is held immobile as she undergoes a form of hypnosis, a piece of action filmed in a large, ornate room called the Marble Saloon in Stowe House, off Stowe Avenue, near Buckingham in Buckinghamshire. This location was also used for a sequence where de Wynter dances the dazed Emma toward his bedroom, moving out of the Marble Saloon and into another elaborately-decorated state room called the Music Room.

Meanwhile, back in the maze, Alice has found Steed recovering from another attack by Bad Emma, and together they head toward Hallucinogen Hall – a sequence incorporating further footage from the Blenheim Palace shoot, although taken from a different direction than that seen earlier. Adopting the frontal approach, Alice knocks on the front door and pulls a Smith and Wesson 29 Magnum revolver on de Wynter, forcing her way in.

Having apparently recovered from her hypnosis ordeal, Mrs Peel leaves the Music Room and looks for a way out, but finds herself going around in circles via a marble-lined room and a staircase that always lead her back to the same place – another Stowe House sequence, apparently inspired by a situation encountered by the original, Diana Rigg version of Mrs Peel in the television episode 'The House That Jack Built'.

A storm brewing

Not having managed to gain entrance to the house, Steed is still outside, tapping his umbrella against the darkened windows – footage filmed at Blenheim Palace in the last week of July 1997. Inside, Mrs Peel launches herself against a large mirror on the wall where she hears Steed's tapping, and smashes through the windows beside him outside.

Later Emma is recovering in Steed's apartment, and just as it appears things might get intimate, Mother, Father, Brenda, Dr Darling and two Ministry operatives arrive and take her into custody. The exteriors of Steed's apartment seen here were filmed in York Terrace East, London NW1.

After Brenda promises to arrange a meeting between Steed and Colonel Invisible Jones, dark clouds start rolling over Cornwall Terrace and the agent is seen driving his Bentley underneath Tower Bridge, in the vicinity of the Tower of London. The cloud formations effect was created by the London-based visual effects company Cinesite, who for this purpose developed a computer program that could also project different colours inside the building storm. With snow starting to fall, the Bentley is then witnessed descending the cobbled road of the disused Kingsway Tram Tunnel, heading toward the Ministry headquarters, where Steed proceeds to room 282 of the archives section. The latest readout in the bottom left-hand corner of the screen states: 'The Ministry: Archives.'

Patrick Macnee as Invisible Jones

Don MacPherson had obviously watched 'The See-Through Man' before writing his screenplay, as the following sequence is very reminiscent of that season five episode. When Steed arrives, he watches in amazement as a cup and saucer appear to be floating in midair. This and the other items moved invisibly by Colonel Jones were manipulated by puppeteers David Baker and Christine Glanville, plus a team of marionette performers from Jim Henson Productions, all with the assistance of green screen technology. The Invisible Jones office set was constructed on Stage A at Pinewood. Having put his guest at ease, Colonel Jones, voiced by the original Steed, Patrick Macnee, mentions the accident that resulted in his predicament and proceeds to assist by outlining de Wynter's cloning experiments of the past, thus explaining Bad Emma.

On location at the Old Royal Naval College

With the weather deteriorating, de Wynter arrives in full Highland regalia at a World Council of Ministers meeting – a sequence filmed in the Painted Hall at the Old Royal Naval College on Romney Road in Greenwich, London SE10. There he gives the assembled delegates a forceful speech regarding the consequences of not agreeing to his terms, informing them, 'You will buy your weather from me'. In a nice touch, the meeting is said to take place on 15 July – St. Swithin's Day, celebrating the patron saint of weather.

The return of Alice

Having been coshed from behind by Bailey when she had de Wynter at gunpoint, Alice now returns to Mother's office with the villain's written demands, which if not met by midnight will result in the total destruction of London and beyond. Alice also tips Mother off to Father's betrayal. This scene, which explains what happened to Alice, was a last-minute addition, and did not feature at all in the final revision of the shooting script, dated September 1997.

Having subdued Mrs Peel in the interrogation section, Father and Bad Emma are leaving the facility when they are confronted by Mother sporting a Beretta Tomcat automatic, though they still manage to get away.

Expansion to Shepperton Studios

With Pinewood Studios full to capacity – both Stanley Kubrick's *Eyes Wide Shut* and the Bond movie *Tomorrow Never Dies* also being in production there at this time – *The Avengers'* crew were forced to seek additional filming space at Shepperton Studios in Surrey. Stages J and K at Shepperton were used to house a 1/10th-scale miniature of a snow-covered Trafalgar Square, seen in a sequence where Emma falls from a powered hot air balloon in which Father and Bad Emma are transporting her.

Stages J and K had originally been Stage 6 at Elstree Studios, constructed in 1979 for the making of the second *Star Wars* epic *The Empire Strikes Back*, but had been reassembled at Shepperton in 1996 after being held in storage for the previous five years. The retaining wall between the two stages had recently been removed for the making of the *Lost in Space* movie, making the overall floor space substantially larger and ideal to accommodate *The Avengers'* Trafalgar Square miniature, which was intricately detailed and included Admiralty Arch and the National Gallery. The construction and filming of this miniature were both the responsibility of model unit production supervisor José Granell of the Magic Camera Company, a visual effects contractor based at Shepperton. As the miniature was covered in small polystyrene flakes to simulate the snow, the production crew's call sheets all warned that this material was extremely flammable and that smoking inside the stage was prohibited.

Shepperton's A Stage was meanwhile used for the full-size set of the part of Trafalgar Square where Steed finds Emma, having tracked her by way of a homing device secreted in one of a pair of boots he purchased for her from Trubshaw and Co. The two agents then kiss – something that never occurred during the television series. However, now out of control, the hot air balloon collides with a large illuminated Wonderland Weather sign, resulting in a series of explosions that kill both Father and Bad Emma. In 2008, the balloon's wicker gondola was reported to be still intact, although now being used as a children's playhouse in a garden somewhere in Surrey.

Walking on water

Having been informed by Colonel Jones that de Wynter is controlling the weather from an installation situated on a secluded island in the River Thames, Steed and Mrs Peel place themselves inside transparent inflatable floating spheres and simply walk there across the water. At the time, this effect was achieved by having Fiennes and Thurman inside the spheres walking on a solid surface against a green screen background on a soundstage. Approximately ten years later, however, transparent walk-on-water balls of this kind were actually developed and began being retailed to the general public.

Upon their arrival, Steed and Mrs Peel come across various teddy bear costumes containing dead Prospero personnel, then find the entrance to the installation via a red telephone box, Steed delivering a variation on a familiar catchphrase as he calls out, 'Mrs Peel, you're needed!' Descending into the installation, they decide to separate, with Mrs Peel stopping the weather machine and Steed going further down into the complex to deal with de Wynter.

Catsuits

Having earlier changed into a skintight black leather fighting suit, Mrs Peel is ready when de Wynter dispatches Bailey to intercept her. Precariously balanced on metal guide ropes supporting the weather machine, they battle for supremacy in a fight sequence filmed at Shepperton, which ends with Bailey plunging to his doom. Both Mrs Peel's leather catsuit and Bad Emma's PVC example were designed by film and theatre costume designer Anthony Powell, although Phil Reynolds Costumes were responsible for actually making them, having previously provided outfits for *Batman and Robin* and *Alien 3*. A tie-in was arranged with the high street chain Miss Selfridge for them to retail their own design of black leather catsuit, with labelling that used the film's logo and stated 'Inspired by *The Avengers*.'

The special effects-laden finale

Upon being confronted by de Wynter armed with a duelling staff, Steed produces the sword hidden within his umbrella and a fencing match ensues amidst a raging storm created by the weather machine. De Wynter is eventually bested by Steed, and then finished off by a lightning strike. This sequence was played out on a huge set constructed within the 007 Stage at Pinewood Studios.

Meanwhile, Mrs Peel manages to deactivate the machine, calming the severe weather conditions that have beset London and caused damage to Big Ben. However, de Wynter has incorporated a self-destruct mechanism, and Steed and Mrs Peel are forced to seek refuge in the control pod, which later surfaces in the Thames in front of the Houses of Parliament.

Like the filmed television episodes, the movie includes a closing tag scene, in which Steed, Mrs Peel and Mother are seen drinking champagne in a computer-generated roof garden atop County Hall, on Belvedere Road, London SE1. The camera then pulls back, revealing the River Thames, the Houses of Parliament, a repaired Big Ben and the London skyline, before the closing credits roll.

One Foot in the Past: Patrick Macnee

The production of the movie having put *The Avengers* back in the public eye, on Wednesday 6 August 1997 the BBC documentary series *One Foot in the Past* presented an edition focusing on Patrick Macnee's love of the village of Bosham in West Sussex. Having been stationed there with the Royal Navy during the Second World War, Macnee had returned on numerous occasions over the years, renting on and off a property that he used for weekend breaks while making the filmed episodes of both *The Avengers* and *The New Avengers*.

Latest merchandise

On Friday 12 September 1997, Corgi unveiled a die-cast model version of Steed's vintage Bentley, complete with white metal John Steed figure, which would be in the marketplace when the movie was released. Also around this time, Slow Dazzle Worldwide picked up the rights to feature *The Avengers* amongst their wide range of large, glossy and visually impressive themed calendars for 1998, aimed at the

Christmas 1997 market. This would be just the first of a number of *The Avengers* calendars put out by the company on an annual basis, continuing up to the 2009 example – although Clearway Logistics would pick up the rights for one year part-way through this run, producing the 2004 one. Another calendar specialist, Infocado, would produce a 2010 calendar, and then Titan would step in for a 2012 one, after which the line would be discontinued.

Early in 1998, Juniper Trading produced a 1/6th-scale John Steed resin model kit, although they marketed this as a Patrick Macnee kit as the product was not licensed by *The Avengers'* copyright holders. The company took out an advertisement in the March edition of *Cult TV*, showing both this and examples of the other character construction kits they were producing at the time, which included Mulder and Scully from *The X-Files* and James Bond. Before the year was out, they also had a Diana Rigg (Emma Peel) kit available, which like all their other products was a limited edition of 1000 units.

The movie enters post-production

Principal filming on the movie was completed during October 1997, allowing the post-production team to start work under the supervision of editor Mick Audsley, who together with director Jeremiah Chechik began cutting the film together. This long and intricate operation would take until January 1998 to complete, and was carried out at De Lane Lea Studios at 75 Dean Street, London W1, where over the months Chechik assembled many different versions of the ten reels making up the movie. An internal memo raised by digital assistant editor Mags Arnold on Wednesday 21 January 1998 informed both the sound and picture departments of the current status of the reels – the current reel nine was the ninth version – and advised that all previous examples were now defunct and needed returning to her for recycling.

Impressed with the tongue-in-cheek style of his score for the live action *101 Dalmatians* movie, Chechik had engaged composer Michael Kamen to provide the music for *The Avengers* movie. Kamen had begun working on the project during the autumn of 1997, going on to record incidental passages that December.

Shortly after this, a cut of the movie was screened in Los Angeles for Warner Brothers executives, who voiced concerns regarding its approach and were uncertain of the appeal of a production generally believed to have had a $60 million budget. Despite these forebodings, a National Research Group test screening was arranged for February 1998 at a movie theatre in Scottsdale, near Phoenix, Arizona, to evaluate the reactions of an average American audience. Unfortunately, once their questionnaires were handed in, it became painfully obvious that the majority of those attending disliked the movie.

A second test screening took place in San Diego, California during the last week of February, but this only confirmed the results of the first, as again the audience gave the movie a big thumbs down. Having attended the screening, Jerry Weintraub and Jeremiah Chechik were called to a meeting the following morning with Warner Brothers' co-Chief Executive Officer Terry Semel, plus various research personnel and executives. Having considered the situation, the studio wanted to reduce the movie's running time and remarket it as a traditional action picture, even though it had not been filmed that way.

Eventually, Chechik had to spend months removing certain sections of the movie and re-editing others. This also entailed Kamen reworking parts of his score, which caused him to have to cancel a number of concerts planned to take place at Carnegie

Hall in New York and arrange additional recording sessions during April 1998. However, after working on the project for eight and a half months, Kamen finally walked away from *The Avengers*, taking his score with him, to compose the soundtrack for another Warner Brothers-backed film, *Lethal Weapon 4*. When interviewed by *Soundtrack* magazine in 1998, Kamen described attempting to work on the unfinished film amidst the various different edits with the phrase, 'It was like aiming at a moving target.'

The original opening sequence

One section cut from the movie was the original opening sequence, in which Bad Emma gains access to the Prospero Programme research laboratory, kills a number of the personnel and sabotages the facility, resulting in a large explosion. This was shot partly at RAF Little Rissington in Bourton-on-the-Water, Gloucestershire, where the prop telephone box was positioned beside one of the runways. Bad Emma arrives driving a pale blue E-Type Jaguar, exactly like the one owned by *bona fide* Emma. The only time any of this material is seen in the finished movie is via Mother's CCTV footage of the incident.

Designed to function as the pre-titles sequence, the destruction of the laboratory involved an intricate exterior explosion and visual shockwave effect, supervised by the model unit's director of photography, Nigel Stone. This effect was actually shot three times toward the conclusion of principal filming in October 1997, the crew taking a couple of days between each attempt to refine and improve things. Stone, who would go on to work on most of the Harry Potter movies, later recalled that they had been very much at the mercy of the weather, having to film all three takes at precisely the same time, late in the afternoon, to ensure that the angle of the sun was consistent. Working under special effects supervisor Joss Williams, the team devised a way of making tarmac break up on screen, and this was incorporated into the final version. However, none of this footage made it into the final cut.

More edits

The destruction of the Prospero laboratory was originally to have been followed by a scene with de Wynter playing the organ in the Long Library at Blenheim Palace, which was moved back to a later point in the edit, just prior to Mrs Peel's arrival at Hallucinogen Hall.

Another section of material cut altogether came where Emma goes to keep her appointment to meet Steed at Boodles. Originally filmed for this was a sequence where Emma responds to a porter's attempt to block her progress by using a casual martial arts move to throw him down a staircase. This was one of a number of ultimately cut sequences from which clips were included in the two advance trailers created for the movie, screened in American cinemas from February 1998.

Also removed as unnecessary was some establishing footage of Steed's Bentley travelling through Trafalgar Square, with the camera tracking back and refocusing on the clock tower of Big Ben.

Later, the scene inside Mother's office at the Ministry had a whole passage of dialogue between Mother and Mrs Peel removed, prior to a shot of Brenda raising the blind to reveal the murky water of the River Thames.

Another casualty was a scene in which de Wynter, wearing his teddy bear costume complete with tartan waistcoat, tries to extract top secret information from a scientist by torturing him with what the script described as a razor-sharp baton, scratching his face with this and causing him to groan in pain. The graphic nature of this material perhaps made it an obvious choice for removal – although sadly for Polish actor Christopher Rozycki, who played the scientist, it meant that he went unseen in the final edit. Another actor who apparently lost out in a similar way was Roger Lloyd Pack, who does not appear in the movie but nevertheless listed it on his résumé.

Also deemed surplus to requirements was some material in which Bailey, having watched Steed and Mrs Peel depart from Trubshaw and Co and having followed them in his Mini Cooper, also observes Mrs Peel arriving at Hallucinogen Hall. A photograph of Eddie Izzard on location at Blenheim Palace for this sequence was published in *Starburst* no. 230, dated October 1997, but otherwise it went unseen by the public.

Another piece of deleted footage came after the scene where Steed is shot by Bad Emma in the grounds of de Wynter's house. This showed him recovering momentarily to see the surrounding parkland now devoid of snow, but with the real Mrs Peel present and looking concerned. Again this material features in publicity photographs, but Jeremiah Chechik decided to sacrifice it in favour of tightening up the storyline and progressing more quickly to the following scene set in Mrs Peel's apartment.

Also lost in the extensive editing was some footage of Steed and Mrs Peel starting to explore the Wonderland Winter premises, and some of Brenda wearing a bus conductor's uniform on board the Ministry's mobile headquarters as Steed alights from the vehicle after his meeting with Mother and Father. A colour photograph of Ralph Fiennes and Carmen Ejogo during the filming of the latter scene was subsequently included in *The Avengers: The Making of the Movie* book by Dave Rogers.

Originally the sequence of de Wynter and Father playing their croquet game – in which he takes unfair advantage of her blindness by stepping on her ball and forcing it into the turf – was to have concluded with him sending her off in another direction where there was uneven ground, causing her to lose her footing off-camera, with him calling out a warning far too late. This too was cut.

The reshoot

As outlined in a February 1997 version of the screenplay, a traditional car chase sequence was filmed of Steed and Mrs Peel in her Lotus Elan being pursued through the countryside by three black Minis. These and various stunt replacement vehicles were seen by this author when he visited Pinewood Studios on Saturday 21 June 1997. However, after the test screenings, this entire sequence was replaced by the mechanical insect attack, which had been included in MacPherson's original screenplay but had been dropped in the first instance as being too expensive to achieve.

In writing the attack sequence, MacPherson had suggested that it could be realised using either helicopters or microlight aircraft painted in yellow and black stripes, or else mechanical bees. Warner Brothers, however, decided to go for the more expensive option of using computer-generated insects. Obviously believing that the film would have more box office appeal if this sequence were to be incorporated, they provided another $2 million to mount a reshoot. Fiennes, Thurman, Connery, Atkins, Izzard and Ryder all reassembled sometime between late March and June 1998 to film new material, including the chase sequence.

Production designer Stuart Craig produced a couple of rough sketches of the mechanical insects (described as bees in production documentation), which artist Julian Caldow then interpreted as a stunning visual. Taking the next step, senior modeller Paul Knight designed a mock-up, from which some small preliminary models were made to show Chechik what the finished items would look like. Eventually, the automated insects were created mainly as computer generated images, added to the location footage in post-production, although some animatronic versions were also used in close-ups.

However, it appears that even this expensive sequence was trimmed in the final edit. When Mrs Peel's E-Type Jaguar exits the woods, only the tailgate is missing, but in the following scene the passenger door is also absent and the nearside front wing is damaged. This unexplained additional damage was presumably inflicted in a section of footage edited out of the final version.

Some tracking shots for the mechanical insect attack were achieved by cameras mounted on Duncan Barbour's tracking vehicle, which was equipped with a hydraulic crane. Overhead shooting was also undertaken by a camera carried by a radio-controlled miniature helicopter supplied by a company called Flying-Cam Incorporated, who imported it specially for the production from their headquarters in Belgium.

In the sequence in the finished movie where Alice leads Steed and Mrs Peel toward Hallucinogen Hall, the E-Type Jaguar is mysteriously destroyed in the background off camera, with only the explosion visible. The explanation for this would have come in further material edited out of the final print. The screenplay indicates that the Jaguar's petrol tank was punctured during the automated insect attack, with the perpetrator then being shot down by Steed, crashing to the ground and igniting the trail of fuel behind the vehicle. Once the Jaguar was stationary, the flames were to 'follow petrol trail *toward* car …', the explosion obviously being the result of the fire reaching the petrol tank.

Even more edits

The sequence in the maze on de Wynter's estate was originally somewhat longer, involving Mrs Peel catching sight of Bad Emma and then chasing her around the hedgerows. Steed was also to have spotted the two Mrs Peels, causing him to think that he was seeing double, but this and his single line of dialogue were edited out of the scene.

The same fate also befell a couple of short scenes showing de Wynter's hypnotic disc whirring faster and faster in front of a restrained Mrs Peel, and storm clouds gathering over Hallucinogen Hall.

Originally, after drugging Mrs Peel and dancing her into his bedroom, de Wynter put her onto the double bed and partly unzipped her catsuit, before being interrupted by Alice knocking at the door. Although only seconds long, the unzipping footage was possibly considered too suggestive, and its fate was sealed, leaving it on the cutting room floor.

The sequence where Mrs Peel dives through the mirror inside Hallucinogen Hall and ends up outside the windows was originally a little longer, showing her managing to regain her feet before collapsing into Steed's arms.

Another completely excised scene began with de Wynter winding up a clock in a hall of mirrors at Hallucinogen Hall. The camera angle then changed to reveal a scantily-clad Bad Emma reclining on a double bed. The clone attempted to speak like the real Mrs Peel, repeating words she had said earlier in the film, but suddenly de Wynter turned on her, snapping, 'I don't want you'. He then ranted about how he could manufacture thousands of replicas, and demanded that Bad Emma bring him the real Mrs Peel.

A brief shot showing the homing device secreted inside one of Mrs Peel's boots was ditched as superfluous, as the explanation that Steed had arranged for it to be fitted there by Trubshaw and Co was provided later on.

Some material indicating that Brenda is attracted to Steed was cut from the end of a brief scene between them after Father and her associates escort Mrs Peel away from the agent's apartment.

Also deleted was some material of a straitjacketed Mrs Peel bouncing against the walls of a padded cell, struggling against her bonds, in the sequence where Father interrogates her.

The scripted Scene 151A involved one of de Wynter's men turning on a radio transmitter on the island housing the weather machine, to direct its energy. However, during editing this plot element was completely abandoned.

Shortly after this there were originally three sections of establishing footage showing deserted London streets at dusk, with a strong wind suddenly picking up. Considered inessential to the telling of the story, these went unused.

The revised September 1997 screenplay included some dialogue between delegates at the World Council of Ministers meeting, but this was all absent from the final edit, as was most of the interaction between the delegates and de Wynter. Another deleted shot had the delegates observing the blizzard conditions outside after de Wynter's powerful speech.

Yet another dropped scene involved de Wynter travelling in a snowplough-equipped Rolls Royce – another vehicle witnessed by this author when he visited Pinewood Studios. In the September 1997 screenplay, this was supposed to appear in Scene 165, in a raging blizzard outside the Ministry, with Bailey in the driving seat and de Wynter in the back. Footage showing the movie's second unit filming the vehicle scything through the snow was later featured in a 'making of' documentary entitled *Welcome to Avengersland*, made by Incue Productions (see below for further details). The scene was shot one night after extensive dressing of fake snow on St Martin's Place, London WC2, outside the St Martin's-in-the-Fields church.

Further material deleted as surplus to requirements showed Steed racing to the Ministry building roof and finding that the hot air balloon carrying Mrs Peel is already airborne. Also a victim of the cuts was a succession of brief reaction shots of the two agents in the sequence where Mrs Peel falls from the balloon and hurtles toward the snow-covered ground of Trafalgar Square.

The scripted Scene 186 saw the blizzard and snowdrifts being shot from several different angles on the miniature Trafalgar Square set. However, as the situation had already been established by a sequence of Steed clambering over a felled double-decker bus, this material was dropped in the edit. Also lost was footage shot through the window of a typical London house, where a woman shivers and draws the curtains. This was intended to be intercut with action of Mother talking on a hotline to the Prime Minister.

The action where Steed and Mrs Peel gain access to the island weather machine installation was originally envisaged as being much longer. As scripted, Mrs Peel follows a trail of dead bodies, all in teddy bear costumes, only to encounter their murderer de Wynter. However, after making threats of eternal torment toward her, de Wynter disappears as silently as he arrived, just before Steed looms out of the gloom. Then, having activated the telephone box access lift, the two agents find themselves down inside the instillation and proceed to investigate their surroundings. Most of this footage was purged in favour of simply getting on with the plot.

A comparison between the last 20 pages of the shooting script and the ending of the movie as released reveals many differences, and it appears that anything considered less than absolutely essential was excised in order to tighten up the finale. Completely dispensed with were: Scenes 203, 204 and 205, showing Steed and Mrs Peel staring down into the installation through the multi-faceted giant glass bubble seen briefly in the movie; Scenes 207 and 209, set inside de Wynter's control module; Scenes 209A and 209B, comprising special effects shots of the storm clouds approaching London and the colourful build-up of energy within them; Scene 218, showing the aforementioned radio transmitter on the island beeping to indicate the arrival of de Wynter's deadline; Scene 219, with more special effects shots of white clouds darkening to black; Scene 220, showing de Wynter clearly enjoying himself in the control module and about to wreak havoc on the city; and Scenes 223A and 225, in which de Wynter descends the spiral staircase to the lowest level of the installation and Steed is buffeted by hurricane-force winds being blown upwards toward him, knocking him backwards against the wall.

A small edit was also made to Scene 223, after Bailey plunges to his death, removing Mrs Peel's line of dialogue, 'Poor boy. No head for heights'.

As seen in the longer of the two trailers assembled for the movie, there was originally to have been a second shot of the clock faces of Big Ben simultaneously exploding after being struck by lightning, filmed from a greater distance than the one actually featured in the final edit.

The sword fight between Steed and Sir August de Wynter was assembled from a longer sequence, which originally included a couple of scenes set inside a stairwell separating two gantries. Two of the other scenes, Scenes 237B and 238, were also re-shot. Originally the latter contained dialogue not included in the final edit, and Steed speared de Wynter with the sword from his umbrella, whereas in the final version he uses the Scotsman's own staff. The finished sequence still contains a continuity error, as Steed has blood on his shirt at the end, but at no point during their duel is there any indication of de Wynter inflicting an injury on him.

As originally scripted, after shutting down the weather machine, Mrs Peel was to have performed a high dive from it down into the water surrounding the control module. This was slightly reworked for the revised September 1997 script, with the dive occurring as the weather machine actually exploded, after which there were to be five short scenes filmed from different angles showing the device plummeting into the water. None of this material actually appears in the movie. Scene 240, in which the cyclone breaks up and calm returns to central London, does appear, but has been moved to immediately after scene 238, where Mrs Peel pulls the connection to deactivate the machine.

Scenes 241 and 243, comprising various shots of the storm dying down and the relieved faces of Londoners, were two more that failed to survive the culling of material dictated by Warner Brothers.

Further footage glimpsed in the longer trailer but absent from the movie itself showed a section of lit control panel in de Wynter's control module, displaying the lettering 'Auto Destruct 6.'

Also cut were various scenes of the installation self-destructing, with a firestorm raging through the facility, destroying walls and masonry, before eventually erupting as a large fireball from the water's surface beside the island. This whole sequence was replaced by a short scene in which the installation's two supporting pillars are destroyed and the island miniature is completely engulfed by a number of further explosions.

Minor differences

There are a number of other, more minor differences between the September 1997 revised screenplay and the movie as completed. These include some dialogue changes in the scene where Steed fights Bailey, Donavan and the other Wonderland Weather men, described in the script as 'bully boys'; and a dialogue deletion where Steed was to have informed the receptionist Tamara that he and Mrs Peel represented FLORA, standing for the Flower Lovers of Ross and Cromarty Association.

The fight scene on the balloon originally had a different lead-in in the script, where after being abducted by Father and Bad Emma, Mrs Peel recovers on the roof of the Ministry building and tackles her evil counterpart. According to an interview with special effects supervisor Nick Davis in the July 1998 issue of *Cinefantastique*, this scene was shot on location on a rooftop at the Old Naval College in Greenwich, London SE10. Once the balloon took off, the two Emma Peels were to have continued their fight on a rope ladder dangling beneath it, until they both climbed on board and up to the burners – which is where the fight scene actually begins in the finished movie. Proceedings then continued as per the movie, with Mrs Peel losing her grip and falling down into Trafalgar Square.

De Wynter's island installation was originally to have been not in the River Thames but in the Serpentine lake in London's Hyde Park.

In the scene where Father and her associates arrive at Steed's apartment to arrest Mrs Peel, they were originally to have knocked on the door as opposed to barging straight in. This appears to have been altered to allow Steed the sarcastic one-liner, 'I didn't hear you knock!'

The screenplay also had a different concluding tag scene, in which Steed and Mrs Peel, having pre-booked some sunny intervals from Wonderland Weather, enjoy champagne in a small pocket of tropical temperatures surrounded by a snowscape created by de Wynter's machine.

The 1995 screenplay

There are, unsurprisingly, even more differences between the finished movie and Don MacPherson's earlier script of Wednesday 21 June 1995, which underwent extensive rewrites to become the February 1997 draft and then the September 1997 draft.

This 1995 version features Emma's husband Peter Peel and his brother Valentine, and has them both apparently killed when the Prospero Programme is destroyed during an experiment. Mrs Peel is the solitary survivor to emerge from the wreckage, thus attracting early suspicion from the Ministry that she is a saboteur.

Instead of driving a vintage Bentley, Steed drives a Jaguar SS100, and news reports regarding the weather heard over his car radio assist in telling the story.

Mother exercised by moving around his headquarters holding on to a series of handles secured to the low ceiling – a concept borrowed from the television episode 'The Forget-Me-Knot'.

Some of the storyline is set in the Highlands of Scotland, where Steed and Mrs Peel visit the ancestral home of Sir August Merryweather, rather than Sir August de Wynter. In this draft, Sir August is merely a minor character, though Bad Emma is still a major player, attempting to kill Steed in a desert rather than the snow-covered landscape seen in the finished film.

There is a night-time chase across London rooftops, with Mrs Peel pursuing Bad Emma. The car chase is still present as well, and concludes with Alice producing an Uzi machine pistol and killing Bailey just as he is about to shoot Steed.

This draft is overall much darker in tone than the one eventually filmed. Mrs Peel suffers hallucinations of her deceased husband Peter, raising questions about her sanity that are played down in subsequent versions, and Alice is killed off during the maze sequence.

From approximately half way through, the 21 June 1995 draft bears little resemblance to what appears in the finished film, save for the notion of the weather machine creating catastrophic conditions. Steed is instructed by Mother to kill Mrs Peel, as the Ministry believe her to be unstable and a security threat, but he disobeys orders and they go to visit Invisible Jones together. The World Council meeting takes place in the Palace of Westminster and a delegate is kidnapped by men dressed as butlers, who spirit him away to a waiting helicopter. This leads on to a sequence where Mrs Peel hangs from the helicopter as it flies across London, her actions causing it to crash near Tower Bridge, though she manages to alight without injury. She then departs to confront the villain in the underground installation accessed from the island in the Serpentine, followed by Steed. Father is proven to be a traitor, and the real villain of the piece is revealed to be Valentine Peel, who actually survived the explosion at the Prospero Programme. Valentine has discovered a way to alter his facial appearance and has been working in the Ministry disguised as Dr Darling. He has been changing his face to appear as his brother Peter for the purposes of Mrs Peel's hallucinations, which he has manufactured. All this material was of course discarded in the later rewrites.

The teddy bear costumes

The bulky teddy bear costumes featured in the movie were designed by Anthony Powell, who had been briefed to ensure that they were as flexible and as lightweight as possible, and made by the company Animated Extras at Shepperton Studios. It could be seen as a testament to their effectiveness that some of them would later be reused in other productions. The green one would be seen as a static prop at the beginning of the *Inspector Gadget* movie released in 1999; the pink one would feature in the background of a party scene where everyone is dressed as a furry animal in the first season *She Spies* episode 'The Martini Shot', transmitted by the NBC network in the USA on Saturday 27 July 2002; the yellow one would be put through a vigorous dance routine by Lacey Thornfield in 'The Sino-Mexican Revelation' episode of *The Middleman*, directed by Jeremiah Chechik and screened by the ABC Family channel on Monday 30 June 2008; and the black one would turn up as a child's teddy bear that develops a consciousness and personality, but one of alcoholism and suicidal tendencies, in the fourth season

Supernatural episode 'Wishful Thinking', shown on Thursday 6 November 2008 on the CW network.

London Transport Routemasters

Three Routemaster double-decker buses were acquired for the production from a seller based in Chertsey, Surrey. Upon the completion of filming, he bought two of them back. The remaining vehicle was apparently not sold on because it had been cut open to allow filming inside the upper deck for the scene featuring Mother, Father and Steed on board the Ministry's mobile headquarters. One of the other buses was used for the filming carried out on the Outer Circle at Regent's Park. The remaining one was manoeuvred onto its side on the Pinewood backlot and then partly covered with fake snow for the Trafalgar Square sequence. This proved difficult to achieve, due to the Routemaster's low centre of gravity and weight distribution. Supervising the operation, Duncan Barbour was amazed at the angle the vehicle needed to be tilted to before gravity took over.

No press screenings or premiere

American composer Joel McNeely was drafted in at the eleventh hour to quickly provide a replacement score for the movie, but with re-editing ongoing, it still proved impossible to meet the originally planned release date of Friday 26 June 1998, necessitating a postponement. Eventually, Chechik appeased Warner Brothers by cutting the movie to 89 minutes in length. However, claims that the running time was originally 115 minutes appear exaggerated, as a comparison with MacPherson's final draft of the screenplay suggests that at the most only about 13 minutes of material was removed.

Although both Weintraub and Chechik pleaded the movie's case, Warner Brothers decided against holding any press screenings – a move almost unheard of in the film business, and one that was bound to attract negative publicity. Having now apparently lost confidence in the production, Warner Brothers also refused to fund a premiere on either side of the Atlantic, although they did spend money on advertising and promotion, devising the slogan, 'Saving the World in Style'.

In the weeks leading up to the revised release date in August, the publicity and hype went into overdrive, as numerous magazines ran tie-in features. These included *Cult Times, Starburst, Starlog, SFX, X-posé,* the *Sunday Mirror Magazine, The Times Magazine* and *Flicks,* the latter two also devoting their covers to the movie. Issue no. 147 of the American telefantasy magazine *Cinefantastique,* dated August 1998, gave the subject plenty of coverage, running interviews/features on Ralph Fiennes, Uma Thurman, Sean Connery, Patrick Macnee and Eddie Izzard.

Meanwhile, the lack of press screenings had also started to attract publicity. On Sunday 2 August, *The Observer* reported that Warner Brothers considered the film to be brilliant and wanted the public to see for themselves, without bothering about press reviews. However, Colin Brown, the editor of *Screen International,* was quoted as saying, 'Alarm bells start to ring when no press show is scheduled for a film on the scale of *The Avengers.*' In its Thursday 6 August edition, the *Guardian* gave another perspective, speculating the failure to arrange media screenings was a tactic by Warner Brothers to create their own hype simply in order to arouse the public's curiosity and hopefully attract a larger audience for the movie.

Welcome to Avengersland

One piece of Warner Brothers-sanctioned promotion for the movie was the American mini-documentary *Welcome to Avengersland*. This was assembled by the Los Angeles-based company Incue Productions, who worked almost exclusively on 'making of' specials for the Home Box Office (HBO) channel. Running for 22 minutes, it included many clips from the film, plus interview sections with Ralph Fiennes, Uma Thurman, Patrick Macnee, director Jememiah Checknik, producer Jerry Weintraub and various London bystanders, plus some minor celebrities such as Peter Howarth, who was the then editor of the British edition of *Esquire* magazine. There was also plenty of behind-the-scene footage, including some of the crew filming on location inside Bleinham Palace. The documentary was screened on Australian television as well as in America, but received no UK transmission.

Titan Books

Thinking that *The Avengers* movie was about to be the next big thing, Titan Books invested heavily in merchandising rights and published a range of books to coincide with the release. These were *The Avengers: The Making of the Movie* by Dave Rogers, *The Avengers: Original Movie Screenplay*, credited to scriptwriter Don MacPherson, and a novelisation by American mystery writer Julie Kaewert. In addition to these, Titan published the informative one-off *The Avengers: The Official Souvenir Magazine*.

Kult TV tapes

Meanwhile, the film and television library that includes *The Avengers* had now been acquired by the French corporation StudioCanal, and they used another acquisition, the British film distribution company Contender Entertainment, to take over issuing both *The Avengers* and *The New Avengers* on VHS via their Kult TV video label. Aiming to take advantage of the imminent arrival of the movie version, Contender arranged for the release of a couple of tapes of Emma Peel episodes (which would be marketed as *The M Appeal Collection*) and also a couple of tapes of *The New Avengers*. Unlike the previous examples from Lumiere, which contained only two episodes per tape, the Kult TV videos contained three per tape, all with newly-recorded introductions by Patrick Macnee. Issued at the same time was *The Avengers: Movie Commemoration Special*, a limited edition of 5,000 box sets consisting of 12 assorted episodes over four videocassettes, although this lacked any direct connection to the movie.

Musical tie-ins

Monday 10 August 1998 saw the release on the East West record label of *The Avengers: The Movie*, a compilation CD album containing music from and inspired by the production. The 14 tracks included 'Storm' by Grace Jones and the Radio Science Orchestra, 'Solve My Problems Today' by the indie band Ashtar Command, and 'I Am' by Madness's lead vocalist Suggs, all of which play over the movie's closing credits. Another of the tracks was an arrangement of Laurie Johnson's 'The Avengers Theme' from the television series, put together by the movie's music supervisor Marius de Vries, who also wrote and produced 'Storm' and 'Solve My Problems Today'.

The same day, Suggs' 'I Am' also appeared as a CD single, accompanied by a pop video in which the Madness front man impersonates Steed, wearing an expensive suit and bowler hat and carrying an umbrella. The video incorporates various excerpts from the movie, and Suggs' all-female band are dressed in Emma Peel-inspired shiny black catsuits.

Later, on 30 November, Joel McNeely's score for the movie would also be made available on CD.

Launch party

To mark the release of *The Avengers: The Movie* CD and the 'I Am' single, and that of the movie itself in four days' time, the Warner Music Group's UK division and Jerry Weintraub organised a launch party. Held on the evening of Monday 10 August 1998 at the Leopard Lounge nightclub on Fulham Road, Fulham, London, this event featured live entertainment from Suggs and from dance music band Utah Saints (who also had a track on the album). Unfortunately, none of the movie's cast and very few members of its production crew were present that night at the Leopard Lounge. The attendees numbered around 600, mainly from the worlds of fashion and music. Celebrities making an appearance included Grace Jones, Emma Noble, Malcolm McLaren, Denise van Outen, Jimmy Nail, weather presenter Sian Lloyd, stunt performer Candice Evans (who had worked on the movie) and costumier Phil Reynolds. *Monty Python's Flying Circus* and *Fawlty Towers* writer and actor John Cleese was also present, but at least he could boast a legitimate connection to *The Avengers*, having actually appeared in the series.

The movie opens – and the press are unimpressed

The Avengers movie finally received its debut public screening in Israel on Thursday 13 August 1998. Friday 14 August then brought its long-awaited opening in the UK, the USA and five other countries. Between them, Weintraub, Chechik and MacPherson had succeeded in giving the movie an authentic feel of Avengerland, a realm where the '60s has never ended and – in line with some of producer Brian Clemens' ground rules for the television series – no bystanders or traffic are seen in the exterior shots. The characters of Steed and Mrs Peel also remain largely true to their television counterparts. Unfortunately, however, most of the following day's popular press reviews of the movie were negative, including those in the *Daily Mirror*, the *New York Times* and the *San Francisco Chronicle*. The main bone of contention was the lack of rapport between Steed and Mrs Peel, plus the poor narrative of the storyline – which Chechik chalked up to Warner Brothers' knee-jerk reaction of having material removed after the test screenings, making the plot difficult to follow.

Even allowing for the possibility of critics and correspondents seeking revenge for the lack of press screenings, some of the reviews that appeared over the next few weeks were exceptionally vicious. Any hopes that the box office takings would prove the reviewers wrong were also unfounded, as – according to figures on the Internet Movie Database website – after almost two months on general release, the movie was nowhere near recovering its production costs.

The critical and commercial failure of the movie caused Jeremiah Chechik to re-evaluate his future as a director, while for Jerry Weintraub his 11-year struggle to bring *The Avengers* to the big screen had ended in calamity, putting paid to his dream of building a franchise to rival the James Bond films.

However, despite the bad publicity and poor box office performance, the movie continued to attract media attention for a few more months, with features, articles and cast and crew interviews appearing in magazines such as *Empire*, *Film Review*, *Neon*, *Starburst*, *Total Film*, *Dreamwatch*, *Sci-Fi Universe*, *Sight and Sound*, *Femme Fatales*, *Starlog*, *Sci-Fi Teen* and *X-posé*.

Granada Plus reruns

Meanwhile, *The Avengers* television series was given another airing when the satellite channel Granada Plus scheduled a batch of reruns, beginning on Tuesday 1 September 1998.

More merchandise

The London Postcard Company had previously marketed two nine-card *The Avengers* sets as part of their extensive range of cult television postcards, and in October 1998 they issued a third. Shortly afterwards they expanded their range of *The Avengers*-themed products to include bookmarks and, in January 1999, four different posters, each measuring 24 by 36 inches.

The marketplace having been starved of both *The Avengers* and *The New Avengers* on VHS for quite some time, Contender scheduled new releases every month from September through to December 1998. Given that they were fitting three episodes per tape, one logical approach was to institute a sub-range presenting an episode each of Cathy Gale, Emma Peel and Tara King, and this became a reality on Monday 28 December when the first two entries in *The Parallel Lines Collection* arrived in retail outlets. In a rare example of inter-company co-operation, Contender arranged for Sequel Records to produce a promotional CD single containing 'The Avengers' Theme' and the track that inspired it, 'The Shake', both by The Laurie Johnson Orchestra. This was given away free of charge to those who purchased *The Parallel Lines Collection: Volume 1*, and was never sold separately, making it a scarce item.

On Tuesday 29 December, Warner Home Video released *The Avengers* movie on DVD in the USA. The only extra included was one of the movie's theatrical trailers. A UK release followed on Monday 5 April 1999, this time with no extras at all. Unusually, the movie's VHS release came a little later, with both full-screen and widescreen alternatives appearing simultaneously on Monday 30 August. By that time, the movie had gained its UK television premiere, being broadcast on the Sky Box Office channel at 8.00 pm on Wednesday 11 August.

Throughout 1999, Contender/Kult TV kept up a steady stream of new VHS releases of both *The Avengers* and *The New Avengers*. These were all readily available from high street stockists such as HMV, Virgin, Music Zone, MVC, F W Woolworth, Our Price and Fopp. After finishing off *The Parallel Lines Collection* in June with tapes five and six, a couple of months later Contender began releasing a further themed set, *The Celebrity Guest Collection*, all six entries in which were available before the year was out.

The London Postcard Company re-entered the picture during the first week of

November 1999, when they issued another collection of postcards, this time featuring *The New Avengers*.

Collectables

On Monday 15 November 1999 Channel 4 aired an edition of their *Collector's Lot* programme in which Honor Blackman visited the home of *The Avengers* enthusiast Ian Beazley to survey his enormous collection of memorabilia related to the series. Beazley, who confessed that Cathy Gale was his favourite Avenger, showed Blackman some very rare and valuable items, including a pre-production Dinky Big Cat Jaguar XJ12C in red, as opposed to the usual metallic green. However, in the years after the programme was transmitted, Beazley would lose interest in *The Avengers* and sell off his collection.

Adding to their range of film- and television-related die-cast models, Corgi released two further vehicles from *The New Avengers* in December 1999. These were 1/36th-scale models of Steed's green Range Rover and Gambit's red Jaguar XJS, both complemented by white metal figures of their owners.

In a less positive development, the turn of the decade saw Contender scale back their range of VHS tapes of the series. During the course of 2000 they would release only the *Avenging the Avengers* documentary and the four-tape *The Evolution Collection* – although the latter would offer better value for money than the earlier releases, as the company would excel themselves by putting four episodes on each tape.

The Avengergirls get a BAFTA

Sunday 9 April 2000 saw the annual BAFTA awards ceremony take place at the Grosvenor House Hotel in Park Lane, London, where the academy had chosen *The Avengers* as the recipient of its Special Award. This resulted in BAFTAs for the four main Avengergirls, with Honor Blackman and Joanna Lumley receiving their awards in person and Diana Rigg and Linda Thorson giving acceptance speeches via filmed messages. Patrick Macnee offered his congratulations, also via a filmed insert from Palm Springs, California. These highlights along with others were televised on BBC1 on Sunday 14 May.

PART SIX
THE LEGACY

THE LEGACY

ESCAPE IN TIME

By 2001, the flurry of interest and merchandising arising from the release of the long-awaited *The Avengers* movie had faded away, and there was no serious prospect of any further film or television production appearing. *The Avengers* and *The New Avengers* would not be forgotten by the viewing public, however, and would retain a loyal following, even acquiring many new devotees as the episodes started to become more accessible in the new medium of DVD.

The Avengers comes to DVD

On Monday 2 April 2001 Warner Brothers in the UK reissued *The Avengers* movie on VHS videotape as part of a triple pack, which also contained *The Wild Wild West* feature film and *Batman and Robin*. Struggling a little for ideas, Contender meanwhile devised *The Kinky Boots Collection*, consisting of four videotapes, all of which were available by Monday 23 April. Although the company had plans for further VHS releases, these never appeared, as a management decision brought about a switch the newer DVD format.[37]

The initial Contender/Kult TV DVD set, titled *The Avengers: The Definitive Dossier: 1967 Files One and Two*, comprised six episodes on two discs. This hit the shops on Monday 4 June. The advantages of DVD were apparent straight away, as the format allowed various extras to be included, thus making the release even more desirable. On this first set, the extras included picture galleries and biographies, plus 'The Strange Case of the Missing Corpse' test film. A further attraction was a so-called Follow the Hat function, which led the viewer to a number of Granada Plus Points – short snippets of relevant information given by Patrick Macnee, Brian Clemens, Laurie Johnson, Roger Marshall or Cyd Child, which had been recorded some years earlier to accompany the series' transmissions on the Granada Plus channel.

An agreement was reached between Contender and the since-cancelled *DVD Monthly* magazine for them to assist in promoting the DVD range by giving away a free VCD of 'From Venus with Love' with their June issue.

---

[37] This book covers only UK DVD releases of *The Avengers* and *The New Avengers*. There were also releases from other companies elsewhere, including in Europe, the USA and Australia.

The movie gets a terrestrial screening

The Avengers movie gained its first UK terrestrial screening in a 105-minute slot between 9.00 pm and 10.45 pm on Tuesday 3 July 2001 on Channel 5, a relatively new channel launched in February 1997.

Multiple DVD releases

The second DVD set, *1967 Files Three and Four*, arrived on Monday 3 September 2001, and again came with the Follow the Hat feature along with items of information presented in caption form, sometimes against a still image of the subject matter. *1967 Files Five and Six* followed in December, and *1967 Files Seven and Eight* on Monday 25 February 2002. This completed Contender's releases of the entire colour Diana Rigg season in less than 12 months.

Now turning their attention to the black and white Rigg episodes, the company wasted no time in capitalising on their success, as *The Avengers: The Definitive Dossier: 1965 Files One and Two* appeared on Monday 2 April, *1965 Files Three and Four* on Monday 3 June and *1966 Files One and Two* on Monday 5 August.

Heading into September, this major marketing push continued with the unveiling of *The New Avengers: The Definitive Dossier: 1976/1977 Files One to Seven*, containing all of that series' 26 episodes. The following week saw the release of the final black and white Rigg set, *1966 Files Three and Four*. A week later came the initial Linda Thorson set, *1968 Files One and Two*.

Steed and Mrs Peel action figures

Sometime during 2002, Product Enterprises produced both Steed and Mrs Peel talking and fully poseable 12-inch plastic action figures, which were packaged together under *The Avengers* name and marketed as 'Action Figures with Style …' The Steed figure was dressed in a grey suit and had a matching umbrella and bowler hat, and the attention to detail extended to the inclusion of a red carnation in his buttonhole. The Mrs Peel figure sported her black leather catsuit and boots from season four, but with the gold-plated Webley revolver from the season five opening title sequence. The eye-catching packaging also featured the well known catchphrase, 'Mrs Peel, we're needed!'

More DVD sets

On Monday 7 October 2002 Contender quickly followed up their earlier releases with *The Avengers: The Definitive Dossier: 1968 Files Three and Four*. However, there would then be a delay of five months before both *1968 Files Five and Six* and *1968 Files Seven and Eight* appeared on Monday 10 March 2003, completing the Thorson season. By the end of the same month, Contender also had a complete season three box set on the shelves. However, this would be the final release in their range, as their rights to both *The Avengers* and *The New Avengers* expired on Monday 30 June 2003.

Another set of Steed and Mrs Peel action figures

Another collectable item arrived in 2005, when Product Enterprises announced a second limited edition Steed and Mrs Peel combination of talking action figures, which they referred to as 'The Avengers in Colour'. Whereas the previous figures had been based on the two characters as seen during season four, this later set epitomised the Steed and Mrs Peel of the colour season five episodes. This time around the Steed figure wore a black outfit, complete with concealed sword hidden inside his umbrella, while Mrs Peel was attired in a two-tone blue Emmapeeler, with cut-outs from which the chain of her pocket watch hung, although she was still armed with the Webley revolver.

Documentaries

In 2005, Channel 4 commissioned the production company Talent Television to produce a short series of 30-minute documentaries spotlighting cult television subjects. This went out under the title *Must See TV* and the initial edition, broadcast on Thursday 10 November 2005, featured *The Avengers*. Presented by Joan Collins, the programme gave a loose history of the series, told partly through interviews with Patrick Macnee, Honor Blackman, Linda Thorson, Brian Clemens, Don Leaver, actor Peter Bowles and the co-author of *Halliwell's Television Companion*, Philip Purser. To assist in showing the progression of the series through the '60s, the interview portions of the programme were backed up with liberal excerpts plucked from various different episodes.

Strangely, on the very same evening, the BBC decided to screen its own documentary about the series, *The Avengers Revisited*. This was as a prelude to a run of BBC4 repeats of the colour Rigg episodes, which began the following evening and would continue generally twice-weekly until 'The Forget-Me-Knot' went out at 10.50 pm on Friday 10 August 2007.

The New Avengers complete DVD box set

In 2006, StudioCanal bought the British film distribution company Optimum and began channelling their back catalogue DVD material through the Optimum Classic label in the UK. This included *The Complete New Avengers* box set, which surfaced on Monday 30 October. The 26 episodes were presented across eight discs, and 'The Eagle's Nest' and 'Dead Men are Dangerous' both featured joint audio commentaries by Brian Clemens and Gareth Hunt.

The Avengers and *The New Avengers* original soundtrack recordings

Some of the distinctive, quintessentially '60s incidental music from the colour Diana Rigg season finally became commercially available in October 2006, when Demon Music released the triple-CD set *50 Years of the Music of Laurie Johnson Volume 1*. One disc of this set was completely devoted to cues and background music from *The Avengers*, and while it focused mainly on season five, it also included a small amount of material both from season four and from season six.

A follow-up, *50 Years of the Music of Laurie Johnson Volume 2*, was released in 2008, but focused entirely on music from *The Professionals*. However, on Monday 2 February 2009, Demon brought out a third and final triple-CD set, *50 Years of the Music of Laurie Johnson Volume 3*, which included recordings from *The New Avengers*. These comprised the complete scores from the episodes 'The Midas Touch', 'House of Cards' and 'To

Catch a Rat', along with a track from 'The Last of the Cybernauts...??', plus the material that Johnson had re-recorded with the London Studio Orchestra back in 1980, from the episodes 'Cat Amongst the Pigeons', 'Obsession' and 'The Tale of the Big Why'. Rounding off the collection were both sides of the 1976 EMI theme single.

Pimms television commercial

July 2009 saw the appearance of a television commercial for the alcoholic drink Pimms, in which a group of eccentric characters are seen heading through the streets of London toward a summer garden party, accompanied by the theme to *The New Avengers*. Known as *The Call Up*, this commercial was one of a number devised for Pimms at the London office of the international advertising agency Mother and shot on location by the American production company MJZ.

The Avengers on Optimum DVD

Reaching new heights of quality content, Optimum launched their first digitally-restored DVD box set of *The Avengers* on Monday 5 October 2009.[38] This comprised the entire second season along with the surviving first season material. However, it was in the extras department that this set really excelled. The comprehensive package included: audio commentaries by Leonard White, Roger Marshall, Martin Woodhouse and Julie Stevens; newly-recorded introductions by Stevens to 'The Decapod', 'The Removal Men' and 'Box of Tricks'; the first part of an exclusive interview with Honor Blackman; the edition of *Collector's Lot* in which Blackman appeared with *The Avengers* collector Ian Beazley; the *Police Surgeon* episode 'Easy Money'; a short documentary in which both Julian Bond and Leonard White recalled events at ABC at the time *Police Surgeon* was in production; a booklet reproducing the scrapbook that White had compiled while working on the first season, containing various newspaper and *TV Times* cuttings and numerous John Cura's telesnaps; and a reduced-size reproduction of the brochure that ABC created for the second season to assist in selling *The Avengers* abroad.

Although several months had passed since its release, this box set received detailed coverage in the January/February 2010 issue of the magazine *Video Watchdog*, which also featured a John Steed and Cathy Gale cover.

Monday 15 February 2010 saw the release of Optimum's second DVD box set, *The Avengers: The Complete Series 3*, and like the initial offering this contained an impressive array of extras, including: commentaries by Brian Clemens, Richard Bates, Don Leaver, Jonathan Alwyn and Roger Marshall; the concluding part of the Honor Blackman interview started in the previous set; some of the 'Life in the Past Lane' introductions commissioned by Channel 4 for their 1993 screenings of the season; reconstructions of two of the missing first season episodes, 'A Change of Bait' and 'Double Danger', consisting of a slideshow of John Cura's Tele-snaps accompanied by a voiceover describing the storyline; the final act of the *Armchair Theatre* instalment

---

[38] Some of the discs in the initial pressings of the Optimum DVD sets contained minor mastering/authoring errors, prompting Optimum to launch a replacement programme whereby customers could obtain corrected versions if they sent in their original purchases. However, the errors were all corrected for later pressings of the sets.

'The Importance of Being Earnest', starring Patrick Macnee; and newsreel footage regarding *Honor Blackman's Book of Self-Defence*.

The Avengers part-work

Toward the end of February 2010, Eaglemoss Collections tested the market for a part-work entitled *The Avengers: The Definitive DVD Collection*. The debut release, sold through selected outlets for a special opening price of £2.99, was made up of both a magazine and a DVD of the first season episodes 'Girl on the Trapeze' and 'The Frighteners'. Having launched a website to promote this new venture, Eaglemoss initially planned more second season releases. However, after a rethink they changed direction and came up with another test package, this one comprising a magazine and a DVD featuring the Emma Peel episodes 'The Town of No Return' and 'The Gravediggers', again retailing at £2.99. However, when the next part arrived with 'The Cybernauts' and 'Death at Bargain Prices' included on the DVD, there was a price hike to £7.99. This led to a fall in sales, and Eaglemoss decided against continuing with any further releases.

The Emma Peel and Tara King seasons on Optimum DVD

Optimum scheduled the filmed episodes to undergo digital restoration next, beginning with the black and white Rigg season, the DVD box set of which became available on Monday 5 July 2010. Audio commentaries once again made up the backbone of the extras, as Roger Marshall, Robert Banks Stewart, Don Leaver and Gerry O'Hara all contributed a recording for an episode with which they had been involved. Brian Clemens and Roy Ward Baker provided a joint commentary for 'The Town of No Return', and the first Mrs Peel, alias actress Elizabeth Shepherd, gave an exclusive audio interview about her short time with the series. For this set many extremely rare visual items were brought together, such as the American opening chessboard sequence and colourised test footage from both 'Death at Bargain Prices' and 'A Touch of Brimstone'. There was also the rejected tag scene originally filmed for 'Death at Bargain Prices', and the alternative but unused opening titles, closing credits and commercial break bumpers created for this season. The obscure material continued with the colour promo 'The Strange Case of the Missing Corpse', reconstructions of the missing first season episodes 'Dead of Winter' and 'Kill the King', and the *Armchair Theatre* production 'The Hothouse' featuring Diana Rigg.

The colour Rigg season box set was prepared much more quickly, appearing for sale on Monday 25 October 2010. It offered the now-established extras package of commentaries and archive footage. The commentaries this time around were supplied by Brian Clemens, Richard Harris, Cyd Child and Peter Wyngarde, who all recalled their experiences of working on specific episodes. Clemens also provided his services for filmed introductions to several episodes, and the informative Granada Plus Points seen via the Follow the Hat function on the earlier Contender releases were also incorporated. Never-before-seen material came in the form of footage cut from the final prints of the episodes 'From Venus with Love', 'The Fear Merchants', 'Escape in Time' and 'The See-Through Man'. Vintage '60s newsreel material sourced from the media archive at Leicester University showed Diana Rigg accepting an award for her role as Emma Peel at a large function, then giving a brief interview. Also included was the extremely rare ABC trailer *The Avengers: They're Back*, used to promote this season prior to its transmission.

The final Optimum DVD box set, covering the Linda Thorson season, began retailing on Monday 6 December 2010, and this maintained the extremely high standards established by the previous sets. Introductions originally filmed by Linda Thorson for the Lumiere VHS box set *Tara King: Six of the Best*, issued back in October 1995, were combined here with the corresponding episodes on DVD. Accompanying extras included the short promotional films *Introducing Linda Thorson* and *Girl about Town*, plus a filmed introduction by director Cyril Frankel to the episode 'Whoever Shot Poor George Oblique XR40?'. The audio commentaries featured Brian Clemens and Roy Ward Baker teaming up again on 'Split!', scriptwriter Jeremy Burnham and his wife, actress Veronica Strong, doing likewise on 'Love All' and solo contributions from Robert Fuest, John Hough, Cyd Child and Jennifer Croxton. The remaining extras included the German opening titles and closing credits, plus an extensive stills gallery and further reconstructions of missing first season episodes.

Eventually, Optimum combined all five DVD sets (minus booklets) as *The Avengers: The Complete 50th Anniversary Collection*, with the added attraction of an additional disc of previously unreleased material, making 39 discs in all. The new extras included an interview with director Laurence Bourne that had been screened on French television, a documentary examining London filming locations seen in *The Avengers*, and the Diana Rigg 8mm films *Der Goldene Schlüssel* and – presented in its four-segment format – *MiniKillers*. The comprehensive set was marketed in packaging resembling a large-format hardback book and reached the shops on Monday 9 May 2011.

The Avengers at 50 celebration

Celebrating five decades since *The Avengers* began, *The Avengers* at 50 convention, held over Friday 24, Saturday 25 and Sunday 26 June 2011 at Chichester University, was a unique event that had taken 18 months of intricate planning to put together. An impressive line-up of guests from both in front of and behind the cameras included Honor Blackman, Linda Thorson, Brian Tesler, Brian Clemens, Leonard White, Julie Stevens, Ray Austin, Richard Bates, Jeremy Burnham, Richard Harris, John Hough, Robert Fuest, Cyd Child, Howard Blake, Terrance Dicks and Anneke Wills. Also in attendance as master of ceremonies was *The Avengers* enthusiast and chat show host Paul O'Grady, who had assisted in promoting the event. The Chichester University Big Band and Pops Orchestra kicked things off on the evening of 24 June when, conducted by Crispin Ward, they gave a Laurie Johnson tribute concert, including their renditions of his themes for both *The Avengers* and *The New Avengers*. They also performed an extremely accurate version of the Johnny Dankworth theme used on videotaped episodes of *The Avengers*. The following couple of days presented a mixture of interviews, panels, screenings and an exhibition of rare memorabilia, all against the backdrop of the largest reunion of the cast and crew ever assembled. 25 June was mainly devoted to the videotaped era of the show, and the following day to the later filmed seasons.

Linda Thorson season soundtrack CD

Having found some old tapes in his attic, composer Howard Blake had managed to salvage his incidental cues from the final season of *The Avengers,* and these were released on Monday 8 August 2011 by Silva Screen Records as a double CD set entitled *The Avengers: Original Tara King Season Score,* which also featured Laurie Johnson's theme. This improved upon and effectively superseded an unofficial single CD release called *The Avengers: Original 1969 Season Score,* which had been made available by Blake some years earlier.

The Avengers returns to the world of comic books.

On Saturday 28 January 2012 the Los Angeles-based publisher Boom! Studios began reissuing the three Eclipse *Steed and Mrs Peel* comic books from 1990. With fewer pages per issue than the originals, these extended over half a dozen issues. Having obviously found a market, the company then began its own ongoing series of newly-produced *Steed and Mrs Peel* comic books, which like the reissues were made available with a choice of several different artwork covers. Under the control of writers Mark Waid and Caleb Monroe, these all-new adventures got under way in August 2012 and involved the return of two old television adversaries, the Hellfire Club and the Cybernauts. However, the run was short-lived, concluding just a year later, in August 2013.

ITV reruns

ITV4 gave *The New Avengers* another rerun starting on Monday 11 February 2013 at 4.50 pm, and then yet another starting on Sunday 29 September 2013. In both cases, each episode was generally shown twice within its week of transmission. However, there appears to have been a problem regarding the episode 'Target!', as this was omitted from the run.

The Avengers comes to Big Finish

Towards the end of June 2013, audio specialists Big Finish announced plans to market new recordings of a dozen lost first season episodes of *The Avengers,* in a similar format to their famous *Doctor Who* full-cast audio CD dramas. By the following month the company had completed their casting of the lead roles, with Anthony Howell taking on the mantle of Dr David Keel and Shakespearean actor Julian Wadham recreating the persona of John Steed. Lucy Briggs-Owen would later be chosen to play the recurring character Carol Wilson. The first four adaptations in this Lost Episodes range appeared in a box set in January 2014. The response from listeners was overwhelmingly positive, prompting Big Finish to announce that the project would be expanded to encompass the entire first season. At the time of writing, these releases are still ongoing.

The Avengers' legacy

Overall, no other British television series has managed to epitomise the swinging '60s in quite the way *The Avengers* did. Stylish, sophisticated and action-packed, it revolutionised both the thriller genre and the spy genre by having a woman doing things on screen that previously had been done only by men. *The Avengers* never followed trends and fashions. It was always at the forefront, creating new styles and situations as it progressed from a mainly studio-bound black and white videotaped show to a lavish filmed extravaganza in glorious colour. The series was anchored by the bowler-hatted and umbrella-carrying John Steed, an overtly charming gentleman, who when the need arose could be a ruthless defender of Queen and country. Steed's lethal ladies in the espionage business – Cathy Gale, Emma Peel, Tara King and Purdey – were all suitably strong-willed, fashionable and independent, not to mention devastatingly attractive. Throughout its years in production, *The Avengers* offered high drama, groundbreaking fashion, witty dialogue, distinctive direction, clever storylines, bizarre situations and plenty of action. Along the way it also managed to ooze class, style and quality. Over the years, all these ingredients played a part in making it an extremely popular and immensely successful series, which has now been screened in over 120 different countries around the world. Long may its legacy last!

PART SEVEN
BIOGRAPHIES

PRINCIPAL CAST MEMBER BIOGRAPHIES

Presented below are brief biographies of the principal cast members of *The Avengers*, *The New Avengers*, the US spin-offs and the 1998 movie in alphabetical order by surname. The relevant character names are given in brackets.

DIANE APPLEBY (EMMA PEEL – RADIO VERSION)

British-born Diane Appleby entered the acting profession when she became involved in both repertory theatre and West End productions during the '60s. She also made television appearances in the BBC's *Maupassant* and *The First Lady*. A 20-week-long engagement in the stage play *Chase me Comrade!* brought her to the Academy Theatre in Johannesburg, South Africa. After that, she found further projects that kept her in the country, including a move into radio comedy. Having been cast as Emma Peel in the early '70s Springbok Radio version of *The Avengers*, she was grateful to have seen episodes of the television series when she was in the UK, as this gave her a starting point for her interpretation of the character.

HONOR BLACKMAN (CATHY GALE)

Born on 12 December 1927 in the Plaistow district of Newham in London, Honor Blackman gained an interest in performing while attending the Guildford School of Music and Drama. Upon graduating she became the understudy in a West End play called *The Guinea Pig*. When the leading actress fell ill, Blackman replaced her, and this led to two further plays, this time as the principal, and also an uncredited and non-speaking part in the 1947 film *Fame is the Spur*.

Blackman then joined the Rank Charm School at Pinewood Studios, which brought her plenty of grooming and preparation for various film roles during the early '50s, including *Quartet* and *So Long at the Fair* alongside Dirk Bogarde. In the mid-'50s, the arrival of ITV meant that television would now start to play a major part in Blackman's life, with guest-starring roles in film series as diverse as *The New Adventures of Charlie Chan*, *The Vise*, *African Patrol*, *H G Wells' Invisible Man* and *The Third Man*. In 1959 she was cast as the semi-regular character Iris Cope in nine episodes of ATV's drama *Probation Officer*, and the following year she played Nicole in ten escapades of ITC's *The Four Just Men*.

Back in the world of feature films, Blackman appeared in Ray Harryhausen's *Jason and the Argonauts*. She then continued in the crime/spy genre of television with parts in *The Pursuers*, *Top Secret*, *Ghost Squad* and then of course *The Avengers*.

After her time on *The Avengers*, Blackman memorably played Pussy Galore in the James Bond film *Goldfinger*, which opened the gates for multiple movie appearances throughout the '60s, including in *The Secret of My Success*, *Shalako* and *A Twist of Sand*. Though television work in the remainder of the '60s was rarer, there were still solitary outings in *Play of the Week* and *Armchair Theatre*.

In the '70s, Blackman became more of a global player, appearing in episodes of the American television shows *The Name of the Game* and *Columbo* and the Australian series *Boney*. Film roles continued to come her way, including in *The Last Grenade*, an adaptation of D H Lawrence's *The Virgin and the Gypsy* and the Hammer Horror movie *To the Devil a Daughter*. In 1977/78 there were two performances as Marion Nicholls in an ITV sitcom, *Robin's Nest*, followed several years later by five appearances as Veronica Barton in another, *Never the Twain*.

Blackman next found herself cast in LWT's version of Agatha Christie's *The Secret Adversary*, before moving on to a big-budget television movie from Lorimar Productions called *Lace*. Her talents were brought to the feature-length *Minder on the Orient Express* in 1985, and a year later she graced four episodes of the *Doctor Who* serial 'The Trial of a Time Lord'. Between 1990 and 1996 she had a regular presence on television screens after assuming the role of Laura Weston in the Central TV/Columbia Pictures-produced sitcom *The Upper Hand*, which eventually clocked up 94 episodes.

In the 21st Century, Blackman's career continued unabated on the big screen with a part in *Bridget Jones's Diary* and on the small screen with roles in *Midsomer Murders*, *The Royal*, *Coronation Street* and *New Tricks*.

SEAN CONNERY (SIR AUGUST DE WYNTER)

Thomas Sean Connery was born in Edinburgh, Scotland on 25 August 1930 into a working class background. He tried various occupations, such as driving a truck and being a milkman, before becoming a bodybuilder. Eventually, at the age of 23, he decided against playing professional football and went for a career in acting, going on to portray a police constable in the short film *Simon* in 1954. Finding that television was easier to break into, he then played supporting roles in episodes of *Dixon of Dock Green*, *Sailor of Fortune*, *Sunday Night Theatre*, *Television Playhouse* and *Armchair Theatre*.

By this point, casting scouts were beginning to notice the Scot with regard to feature film parts, leading to appearances in *Hell Drivers*, *Darby O'Gill and the Little People*, *Tarzan's Greatest Adventure* and *The Frightened City*. However, Connery's big break arrived in 1962 when he was cast as Ian Fleming's super-spy James Bond for *Dr. No*, which was popular enough to bring about a sequel, *From Russia with Love*, the following year.

1964 brought two more major feature film projects with Alfred Hitchcock's *Marnie* and a third Bond picture, *Goldfinger*; and in 1965 these were followed by high drama in *The Hill* and, with Bondmania now in full swing, a fourth 007 outing, *Thunderball*.

Bond five number five, *You Only Live Twice*, was completed for 1967, followed by the Western *Shalako*. Connery then gave his last television acting performance in an instalment of *Sunday Night Theatre*, transmitted in February 1969.

United Artists enticed Connery back to Bond in 1971 for *Diamonds are Forever*, after agreeing to his large pay demand and promising to fund two other film projects of his choice. The first of these was *The Offence*, released in 1972; the second was an adaptation of *Macbeth*, but this was abandoned when it was discovered that director Roman Polanski was already filming a version of Shakespeare's classic, which became *The Tragedy of Macbeth*.

After original choice Burt Reynolds fell ill, Connery took over the lead role in the science fiction film *Zardoz*, before becoming part of an all star cast for *Murder on the Orient Express*, released in 1974. Over the next few years he participated in several well-received productions, beginning in 1975 with *The Wind and the Lion* and *The Man Who Would be King* and continuing with *Robin and Marian* and *A Bridge Too Far*.

As the '70s became the '80s, the Scot diversified into new and different roles, starring in *The First Great Train Robbery*, the disaster movie *Meteor*, the sci-fi movie *Outland* and the fantasy film *Time Bandits*.

Eventually, Connery returned to James Bond, appearing in Kevin McClory's reworking of *Thunderball*, *Never Say Never Again*. He then starred impressively in *Highlander*, released in 1986. An Oscar-winning performance followed in *The Untouchables*. Then, toward the conclusion of the '80s, Connery added a humorous touch to *Indiana Jones and the Last Crusade*.

The early '90s provided strong roles for the actor in *The Hunt for Red October*, *Highlander II: The Quickening* and (uncredited) in *Robin Hood: Prince of Thieves*. He also provided the voice of the Dragon in *Dragonheart*. As the decade progressed, there was further feature film work including in *The Rock* and, of course, the movie adaptation of *The Avengers*. His last movie acting part came in *The League of Extraordinary Gentlemen*, released in 2003.

Although formally retired, Connery continues to provide voiceovers for animated features and computer games.

MORGAN FAIRCHILD (SUZY)

Hailing from Dallas, Texas, USA, Patsy Ann McClenny – aka Morgan Fairchild – was born on 3 February 1950. She entered the acting profession with an uncredited role in the 1970 film *A Bullet for Pretty Boy*. However, it then took another six years before she found herself cast in a supporting part in an episode of *Kojak*, which paved the way for further guest-starring roles in other American television series including *Switch* and *Happy Days*. She had now found her feet in this medium, and the credits started to mount, including appearances in *Barnaby Jones*, *Dallas*, *Mork and Mindy* and *The Love Boat*.

During the early '80s Fairchild played Constance in the soap opera *Flamingo Road* for a time and then returned to jobbing acting work, including on episodes of the film series *Magnum P.I.* and *Simon and Simon*. By this time she had achieved celebrity status, and she entered a new sphere of entertainment by presenting television specials and awards programmes, being interviewed for documentaries and taking part in chat shows. In the middle of the decade, she won a role in the mini-series *North and South* and its sequel *North and South, Book II*, before assuming the part of Jordan Roberts in another soap opera, *Falcon Crest*.

As the '90s began, Fairchild concentrated mainly on television movies, before moving into a sitcom in 1992 by playing Marla in three episodes of *Roseanne*. She then worked on various other series, including *The New Adventures of Superman*, *Murder She*

Wrote, the revived *Burke's Law* and *Diagnosis Murder*, before becoming a regular on the hard-hitting drama *The City*. Moving on, she portrayed the recurring character Andrea in four segments of the comedy series *Cybill*, and made five appearances as Chandler's mother Nora Tyler Bing in *Friends*.

Since the millennium, Fairchild's television career has continued, with a regular part in the series *Fashion House* and guest-starring roles in various productions including *Law & Order: Special Victims Unit* and *Bones*. She has also continued her presenting work alongside her acting.

RALPH FIENNES (JOHN STEED – MOVIE VERSION)

Ralph Nathaniel Twisleton-Wykeham-Fiennes – aka Ralph Fiennes – was born in Ipswich on 22 December 1962 and began his on-screen career in 1991 with a part in the television series *Prime Suspect*. Progressing to feature films the following year, he played Heathcliff in an adaptation of *Wuthering Heights*. Then came a role in *Schindler's List* in 1993. However, it was his strong performance in the 1996 movie *The English Patient* that established him as a leading man, bringing him to the attention of Jerry Weintraub and Jeremiah Chechik, who approached him regarding the recreation of John Steed in their adaptation of *The Avengers*. Being an admirer of the television show, Fiennes watched many episodes before deciding against imitating Patrick Macnee's version of the character, preferring to give his own interpretation.

After *The Avengers*, Fiennes continued his career as a jobbing actor on various films, including *Maid in Manhattan* and, as the voice of Victor Quartermaine, in *The Curse of the Were-Rabbit*. In 2005 he assumed the part of Lord Voldemort in *Harry Potter and the Goblet of Fire*, going on to reprise the role in three further Harry Potter films. This paved the way for a string of appearances in high-profile features, including *The Hurt Locker*, *Nanny McPhee and the Big Bang*, the *Clash of the Titans* remake and its sequel *Wrath of the Titans* and, in a major role, the James Bond movie *Skyfall*.

INGRID HAFNER (CAROL WILSON)

Ingrid Elaine Hafner was born in London on 13 November 1936 and first entered the acting profession in the theatre, an early role coming in *Cyrano de Bergerac* at the Old Vic alongside Patrick Stewart and Peter Wyngarde during May 1959. The following year saw her cast in the film *Bluebeards's Ten Honeymoons*. She then appeared in the *Police Surgeon* episode 'Lag on the Run', so Sydney Newman and Leonard White were both well aware of her abilities when they required a female lead for *The Avengers*. As Carol Wilson, Hafner was introduced in 'Brought to Book' and went on to appear in 19 out of the 26 episodes of the show's first season. Although her character was a nurse, the actress herself confessed to having a pet hate about illness. She also bemoaned the fact that she had to move from Cornwall to live in London to be close to Teddington Studios.

After *The Avengers*, Hafner took various television roles in *The Odd Man*, *The Plane Makers*, *Crane*, seven instalments of the anthology show *The Victorians* and an instalment of *The Wednesday Play*. As the '60s gave way to the '70s, she continued taking guest-starring parts in shows such as *Man at the Top*, *The Rivals of Sherlock Holmes* and, alongside Ian Hendry again, *The Lotus Eaters*. She played the recurring character Laura Granton in the last season of *The Main Chance* and appeared in the serial *The Clifton*

House Mystery and an episode of *Robin of Sherwood*.

Hafner's last acting credits came on seven instalments of the 1989 Granada serial *After the War*. She died in 1984 of motor neurone disease.

IAN HENDRY (DR DAVID KEEL)

Ian Hendry was born on 13 January 1931 in Ipswich and found an interest in athletics during his stint of National Service in the British Army, where he also ran a motorcycle stunt team. After being demobbed, he tried his hand at being an auctioneer, working for an estate agent and being a circus performer, but the calling of the acting profession saw him in repertory theatre in both Worthing and Hornchurch, which in turn led to small uncredited film roles. These started in 1955 with the film *Simon and Laura*. His first television appearance came the following year in the medical soap *Emergency-Ward 10* on ITV, and then he moved over to the BBC for an instalment of *Television Playwright*. His association with ABC Television started in 1960 with an episode of the anthology series *Inside Story*, followed by his starring role in *Police Surgeon* and continuing through to *The Avengers*.

During the '60s, the feature films he worked on included *Live Now – Pay Later* (for which he was nominated for a BAFTA), *Children of the Damned*, *The Beauty Jungle*, *The Hill* alongside Sean Connery, and Gerry Anderson's *Doppelganger*. During this period, he also appeared in various television productions such as *Armchair Theatre* for ABC, Granada's *Play of the Week*, ITC's *Danger Man* and *The Saint* and LWT's *The Gold Robbers*. He also played the central character in the Associated-Rediffusion crime series *The Informer*.

The '70s began with Hendry taking on the title character in LWT's short-lived science fiction series *The Adventures of Don Quick*, followed by another BAFTA-nominated performance in the gritty British crime film *Get Carter*. This decade would see more television work than film, but Hendry still managed to appear in a number of features, including *Tales from the Crypt*, *All Coppers are …*, *Theatre of Blood*, *Captain Kronos: Vampire Hunter*, *Damien: Omen 2* (uncredited) and *The Bitch*. His small-screen performances over this time included guest-starring roles in *The Protectors*, *The Sweeney*, *Supernatural*, *Van der Valk*, *Return of the Saint* and *The Persuaders!*. He also took the lead in the BBC's Greek-set drama *The Lotus Eaters*. Perhaps his most interesting role though was his return to the fold (though not as Dr David Keel) in the 'To Catch a Rat' episode of *The New Avengers* in 1976. Additional television work continued into the '80s with *The Enigma Files*, *The Chinese Detective*, *Bergerac*, *Jemima Shore Investigates* and the Channel 4 soap *Brookside*.

Hendry died on Christmas Eve 1984.

GARETH HUNT (MIKE GAMBIT)

Gareth Hunt was born on 7 February 1942 and joined the merchant navy when he was 15. Six years later he returned to the UK, where he dabbled in various different occupations including hairdressing. Eventually he studied acting, and this brought about his initial television appearance in the series *Frontier* in 1968. Regular television work still eluded him until the early '70s, though a spell with the Royal Shakespeare Company helped hone his abilities. Proving himself to be versatile, Hunt progressed into several different genres, including comedy with *Bless This House*, drama with *The*

Hanged Man and *A Family at War* and science fiction with *Doctor Who*. However, the role that really established him was that of the footman Frederick in 11 instalments of *Upstairs, Downstairs*, transmitted during 1974/75. He also had an uncredited part in Gerry Anderson's *Space: 1999*.

Upon completing *The New Avengers*, Hunt managed to break into the world of feature films, appearing in *The World is Full of Married Men* and taking the lead in the spy movie *Licensed to Love and Kill*. Also at this time he had a role in the television sitcom *That Beryl Marston ...!*. Progressing through the '80s, Hunt found himself frequently cast in television productions such as *Minder* and *Hammer House of Mystery and Suspense*, plus the occasional film such as *Bloodbath at the House of Death*. Toward the conclusion of the decade he became involved with Albert Fennell and Laurie Johnson again when he appeared in three television movies they filmed, based on the romance novels of Barbara Cartland.

Through the '90s Hunt had television parts in *The Detectives*, *Sooty & Co*, the American-financed *The New Adventures of Robin Hood* and the BBC sitcom *Side by Side*. He also had the small role of Inspector Masefield in the John Cleese film *Fierce Creatures*. A short stint in *EastEnders* came during 2001, followed by more film and television appearances, up to his final credit on the 2007 film *The Riddle*. He died of pancreatic cancer on 14 March that year.

JOANNA LUMLEY (PURDEY)

Joanna Lamond Lumley was born in Srinagar, Kashmir, India on 1 May 1946. She first came to prominence in the swinging '60s as a fashion model, and spent some time working exclusively with designer Jean Muir. However, her ultimate goal of becoming an actress had manifested itself early on as, barely a teenager, she had appeared in a segment of the soap *Emergency-Ward 10*. Her first feature film came with a short, uncredited performance in the late '60s spy thriller *Some Girls Do*. This was followed by an instalment of *The Wednesday Play* and a bit part in the Bond movie *On Her Majesty's Secret Service*.

Bad luck dogged a number of Lumley's subsequent projects, including the films *The Breaking of Bumbo*, which never received an official release, and *Tam Lin*, from which her scenes were deleted during editing. Her appearance as a laboratory assistant in *The Abominable Dr Phibes* was also ditched before release, and her role in one of the segments of the horror movie *The House That Dripped Blood* went unbilled. However, on the plus side, she appeared in an edition of the BBC's *Comedy Playhouse*, which led on to the short-lived follow-up series *It's Awfully Bad for Your Eyes, Darling*. She was then cast in an episode of *Steptoe and Son* and featured in the cast of the movie adaptation of the stage play *Don't Just Lie There, Say Something!*.

After taking the female lead in the 1973 movie *The Satanic Rites of Dracula*, Lumley found regular television work on the soaps *Coronation Street* and *General Hospital*, following up with a couple of episodes of *Are You Being Served?*. After making her name in *The New Avengers*, she launched herself into another successful television series with the supernatural-based *Sapphire and Steel*, a couple of *Pink Panther* films and the mini-series *Mistral's Daughter*. Attempting something different, she appeared in comedy sketches in half a dozen editions of *The Kenny Everett Television Show*, before being reunited with Albert Fennell and Laurie Johnson for the television movie *A Ghost in Monte Carlo*.

During the '90s Lumley participated in three episodes of *Lovejoy* as the recurring character Victoria Cavero, half a dozen instalments of the game show *Cluedo* as Mrs Peacock, the television movie *Cold Comfort Farm* and Carlton's *Class Act* series as Kate Swift. Her greatest claim to fame, however, came in 1992 when she was cast as Patsy Stone in Jennifer Saunders' sitcom *Absolutely Fabulous*, a role she has continued to play on and off ever since.

Toward the conclusion of the 1990s, Lumley became the regular character Donna Sinclair in Witzend Productions' *Dr Willoughby* and appeared as one of several alternative Doctors in the Comic Relief *Doctor Who* skit 'The Curse of the Fatal Death'. In the new millennium, her talents found a new outlet as a voiceover artist on films including *The Magic Roundabout* and Tim Burton's *Corpse Bride*. Further regular television roles followed in the series *Sensitive Skin* and *Jam & Jerusalem*. More recently she has entered a new sphere of entertainment as both a presenter and an executive producer of documentaries, which together with the revival of *Absolutely Fabulous* has kept her firmly in the public eye.

PATRICK MACNEE (JOHN STEED)

Daniel Patrick Macnee was born on 6 February 1922 in London. He gained his first acting experience as an uncredited extra in a film version of *Pygmalion* in 1938, and in the following decade started getting credited roles in BBC plays. He appeared in the BBC's adaptation of *The Strange Case of Dr Jekyll and Mr Hyde* in 1950, then stayed with the Corporation to take roles in four instalments of *Sunday Night Theatre*. He next went to work in Canadian TV, winning parts in *Tales of Adventure* and the anthology series *Summer Theatre*. He also spent time in Hollywood before returning to the UK to appear in the Second World War film *The Battle of the River Plate*. Then it was back to Los Angeles to gain more experience, acting in live television drama including the *Kraft Television Theatre* strand.

Further work in Canada followed, with no fewer than 12 appearances in *General Motors Presents* dating from 1953 to 1960 and eight appearances in *On Camera* between 1955 and 1958.

In 1959 Macnee returned to the United States, where making television drama on film was beginning to take over from live productions. There he guest-starred in shows such as *Alcoa Presents: One Step Beyond*, *Alfred Hitchcock Presents* and *The Twilight Zone*. The following year saw him back in the UK again to do an *Armchair Theatre* and a *Play of the Week*. He then assumed the role of John Steed in *The Avengers*, which would keep him busy for most of the '60s.

Between his commitments as Steed, Macnee did find time to do a couple of plays for the BBC, three instalments of *Love Story* for ATV and two more segments of *Armchair Theatre*. After *The Avengers*, there was a pilot film for a potential ITC series called *Mister Jerico* and a reasonable amount of television work in the States on shows such as *The Virginian*, *Alias Smith and Jones* and *Night Gallery*. In 1973, he was briefly reunited with Diana Rigg for the episode 'You Can't Go Back' in her American sitcom *Diana*. More television work followed over the next few years, with parts in *Orson Welles' Great Mysteries* and *Columbo*.

In 1976 Macnee played Dr Watson to Roger Moore's Sherlock Holmes in the television movie *Sherlock Holmes in New York*, before donning his bowler hat once again as Steed for *The New Avengers*. No sooner had *The New Avengers* ended production than

Steed was back in all but name as a British agent known only by the codename S in the 'Assault on the Tower' episode of the US series *The Hardy Boys*, produced by his close friend Glen A Larson. In 1978, Macnee then became involved with Larson's *Battlestar Galactica*, not only acting in the series but also providing the voiceover for a character and the opening narration on selected episodes.

The '80s brought various feature film projects such as *The Sea Wolves*, *The Howling*, *The Creature Wasn't Nice*, the rock band spoof *This is Spinal Tap* and – cast on the recommendation of star Roger Moore – the James Bond movie *A View to a Kill*. This decade also provided a steady stream of further television roles, which included working with Robert Urich both in an episode of *Vegas* and on the short-lived spy show *Gavilan*, as well as the television movie *The Return of the Man from U.N.C.L.E.*. Showing great versatility, Macnee played three different roles in an episode of *Magnum P.I.* and then became the character Calvin Cromwell in the big-business series *Empire*. He was the subject of the *This Is Your Life* edition broadcast on 24 October 1984. He then worked with another friend, Robert Wagner, on episodes of both *Hart to Hart* and *Lime Street*, before appearing in the revived *Alfred Hitchcock Presents* toward the end of the decade. Returning to Canada, he appeared in the *War of the Worlds* television series and some television movies based on the works of jockey/author Dick Francis.

The 1990s brought more of the same, with Macnee appearing in no fewer than four Sherlock Holmes television movies – revisiting the part of Dr Watson for the first two before taking on the role of the master detective himself in the others. He had a recurring role in the 1991 private detective show *P.S. I Luv U*; voiced the regular character E B Hungerford in *Super Force*; and a couple of years later took the semi-regular part of Edward Whitaker in Hulk Hogan's television series *Thunder in Paradise*. 1997 saw the arrival of *Spy Game*, and Macnee played both the recurring character Dr Quentin and in one episode the assassin Mr Black. Staying in this vein, he also appeared in a *Diagnosis Murder* episode called 'Discards', which co-starred Barbara Bain, Robert Culp and Robert Vaughan, all of whom had made their names in '60s television espionage series.

Finding himself still much in demand in the late 1990s, Macnee took a semi-regular role in the superhero show *Night Man*, then provided the voiceover for Invisible Jones in the feature film version of *The Avengers*. His most recent acting credits have come with a guest-starring part in a 2001 episode of *Frasier* and the 2003 sci-fi short *The Low Budget Time Machine*.

DONALD MONAT (JOHN STEED – RADIO VERSION)

Londoner Donald Monat was 11 years old when his family relocated to South Africa, and was only 16 when he won his first acting role, quickly progressing to become a regular performer in radio drama. Returning to the UK in 1949, he appeared in various London stage plays, including a production of J B Priestley's *Dangerous Corner* on which he met his wife-to-be, June Dixon. Relocating to South Africa the following year, the couple formed an independent radio production company and recorded an average of 15 programmes every week for Springbok Radio. Leaving this hectic lifestyle behind, the couple returned to London in 1952, subsequently finding work in various different plays and also in films and television, with Monat trying his hand at both producing and directing as well as acting. By 1960 the couple were in Canada, treading the boards, writing documentaries, but mainly working in the spoken word medium again. Later they once more moved back to South Africa, where they became big names starring in a succession of comedy radio shows throughout the '60s and into the '70s. Cast as the radio version of John Steed, Monat put his own spin on the character, giving him a more humorous personality than Patrick Macnee had ever exhibited in the role.

DOUGLAS MUIR (ONE-TEN)

Douglas George Muir was born on 5 November 1904 in London and started acting in movies in the early '50s, although these performances were usually uncredited. In order to gain recognition, he switched across to television for the BBC police series *Fabian of the Yard* and the regular role of Bill Jessel in the dramatised documentary series *Private Investigator*. After his stint on *The Avengers*, Muir resumed his career as a jobbing actor with roles in *Harpers West One*, *No Hiding Place* and as the recurring character Tom Bancroft in *The Plane Makers*. He died in 1966.

DIANA RIGG (EMMA PEEL)

Enid Diana Elizabeth Rigg was born in Doncaster, South Yorkshire on 20 July 1938 and spent the majority of the first eight years of her life in Bikaner, India, where her father was employed as a railway executive. Returning to the UK, she then spent a number of years at a boarding school at Fulneck near Pudsey, West Yorkshire before enrolling in RADA and making her stage debut in 1955 in the play *The Caucasian Chalk Circle*. Between 1959 and 1964 she was involved with the Royal Shakespeare Company, and it was during this period that she began appearing on television in small roles, such as a bit part in a televised theatre production of *A Midsummer Night's Dream*.

Small roles in the comedy film *Our Man in the Caribbean* and an episode of *The Sentimental Agent* followed, then after her stint in *The Avengers* she moved on to mainstream films such as *The Assassination Bureau* and the Bond movie *On Her Majesty's Secret Service*. Continuing to concentrate her talents on the big screen, Rigg also starred in the feature film adaptation of Shakespeare's *Julius Caesar*, *The Hospital* and the horror film *Theatre of Blood*. Then in 1973 she accepted an offer from the American NBC network to star in her own sitcom *Diana* for an initial 15 episodes, with a full season promised if sufficient ratings were generated – which unfortunately did not happen.

Leaving the United States behind, Rigg co-starred in LWT's *Affairs of the Heart*, the television movie *In This House of Brede*, the 1975 *Morecambe and Wise Christmas Show* and the BBC's short story drama *Three Piece Suite*. During this period she began to focus increasingly on theatre projects, where she considered her best work was done, but from time to time she returned to television, taking the title role in Yorkshire TV's adaptation of Henrik Ibsen's *Hedda Gabler* in 1981, and also ventured back to popular cinema with *The Great Muppet Caper* and *Evil under the Sun*.

After appearing in some more television movies and a BBC *Play of the Month*, Rigg took the lead in both the seven-part version of Dickens' *Bleak House* and the television movie adaptation of Roald Dahl's *The Worst Witch*. She was reunited with Albert Fennell in 1987 for the television movie version of Barbara Cartland's novel *A Hazard of Hearts*. Then for the next ten years her small screen endeavours consisted mainly of supporting roles in television movies, including *Running Delilah*, in which she played an experienced spy who mentors a younger operative – to date her only return to the world of espionage and secret agents in the visual medium.

Through to the end of the '90s Rigg continued to restrict her small screen appearances to television movies, although 1998's *Speedy Death* became the first of five whodunits under the overall name *The Mrs Bradley Mysteries*. There was another television role in 2003, in an instalment of the BBC anthology *Murder in Mind*, and further feature film appearances in *Heidi* in 2005 and *The Painted Veil* the following year. In 2013 she appeared alongside her daughter Rachael Stirling in a guest role in the *Doctor Who* episode 'The Crimson Horror' and took on the part of the recurring character Olenna Tyrell in the acclaimed American series *Game of Thrones*.

Rigg was made a CBE in 1988 and a Dame in 1994.

JON ROLLASON (DR MARTIN KING)

Jon Rollason was born in Birmingham in 1932 and entered the world of television acting with a supporting role in *The Children of the New Forest* in 1955 before gaining other small acting roles in the early '60s. After his time on *The Avengers*, he guest-starred in series such as *No Hiding Place*, *The Spies*, *Danger Man*, *The Baron* and *The Troubleshooters*, and had a recurring role in *Coronation Street*. He is perhaps best remembered today for his role as Harold Chorley in the 1968 *Doctor Who* serial 'The Web of Fear'. In the '70s there were appearances in *The Wednesday Play* and later *Crossroads*, for which he also wrote a couple of episodes. Besides being an actor, Rollason was a published author, playwright and radio dramatist, who at the time he was working on *The Avengers* lived about ten and a half miles away from Teddington in Dulwich, South London.

JULIE STEVENS (VENUS SMITH)

Julie Stevens – aka Julia Hucks – was born on 20 December 1936 in Prestwich, near Manchester. She had already been under contract with ABC for several years before joining *The Avengers*, having been involved with the fortnightly religious programme *The Sunday Break*, been a hostess on the game show *For Love or Money* between May and August 1961 and made a couple of appearances in the sitcom *Our House*. However, her contract with the company ran out the day before the auditions for Venus Smith, so she had to sign a new one when she was awarded the role. After *The Avengers*, Stevens continued acting for a while, appearing in *The Human Jungle*, *Z Cars*, one of a series of plays for Granada called *Friday Night* and the feature film *Carry On Cleo*. She then found a new outlet for using her presenting, acting and singing skills, as she became associated with children's television in the form of *Play School*, *Play Away* and *Cabbages and Kings*. Before the latter of these there was a brief return to pure acting in 1970/71 with a recurring role in the short-lived sitcom *Girls About Town*.

LINDA THORSON (TARA KING)

Linda Robinson – aka Linda Thorson – was born in Toronto, Canada on 18 June 1947. She began acting in school plays when she was eight years old and also became an ice skating champion before her teens. Later, she performed in some radio plays and attended the Bishop Strong School, where she became involved with their drama department and impressed one of her tutors, Nancy Piper, sufficiently to recommend her in writing to RADA in London. However, it would be a couple of years before she was invited to the UK for an audition, and during that time she left school, enrolled in a secretarial course and began working in the family confectionary business.

At the age of 18 Thorson was called to RADA, auditioned and was accepted. Two years later she graduated with honours, having secured a prize for the best student in vocal production, studied both music and ballet and gained a singing scholarship. Along the way she had married Barry Bergthorson, but later when this did not work out she took part of his name and became Linda Thorson.

While she had been at RADA, Thorson had caught the eye of American film director John Huston when he visited the academy one day looking for an unknown actress to appear in his forthcoming film *Sinful Davey*. After choosing Thorson for the part, Huston later let her down as he had already cast John Hurt in the lead and, at five foot eight, Thorson was just too tall to play opposite him. To make it up to her, Huston arranged a meeting with ABC's casting director Robert Leonard, who was assisting in the search for Diana Rigg's replacement in *The Avengers*. Thorson impressed Leonard sufficiently to get her involved in a round of screen tests, and ultimately won the part. Before this, her only on-screen work had been in the television movie *A Month in the Country* alongside Ian McShane, and in a toilet roll commercial.

After *The Avengers* it would be several years before Thorson appeared on television again, being cast in 1973 in both an instalment of the feature-length *Thriller* and a BBC *Play of the Month*. Then, as the '70s progressed, she became involved with various different projects such as comedy with Frankie Howerd in an edition of *The Howerd Confessions* and drama with the film *Valentino*. There were also guest-starring roles in the North American television shows *Sidestreet* and *King of Kensington*, the feature film *The Greek Tycoon* and – reuniting her with Ian Ogilvy, with whom she had worked on *The Avengers* episode 'They Keep Killing Steed' – *Return of the Saint*.

By the '80s, Thorson was in even greater demand, and she appeared in various American television series, including *McClain's Law*, *St Elsewhere*, *The Equalizer*, *Spenser: for Hire*, *Moonlighting* and *Dynasty*. These were followed by recurring roles in *The Bronx Zoo* and, as the character Hillary Stonehill, in the comedy series *Marblehead Manor*. Further supporting parts came in *Monsters* and *Star Trek: The Next Generation*.

Through the remainder of the '90s, Thorson continued acting in a mixture of series, television movies and feature films, before going on to play the regular role of Emily Yeager in the sports drama *The Hoop Life*. Around this time she also did a season on the drama *Emily of the New Moon*, then an episode of *Law and Order*. She then returned to the UK, appearing in a two-part *Silent Witness* in 2006 and spending a year on the soap opera *Emmerdale*. More guest-starring roles on American television followed, and also a part in the film *Man on the Train* in 2011.

At the time of writing, Thorson is still in regular work as a film and television actress.

UMA THURMAN (EMMA PEEL – MOVIE VERSION)

Uma Karuna Thurman was born in Boston, Massachusetts, USA. Having decided to pursue a career in acting, she left boarding school at the age of 15 and within two years was cast in the film *Kiss Daddy Goodnight*. Toward the conclusion of the '80s she had parts in the high-profile movies *The Adventures of Baron Munchausen* and *Dangerous Liaisons*, then fell into a routine of appearing in one or two films a year. In the mid-'90s she had a major role in Quentin Tarantino's critically acclaimed *Pulp Fiction*. This was followed by parts in a succession of big-budget productions: *Batman and Robin*, *Gattaca* and, of course, *The Avengers*.

Upon completion of *The Avengers*, Thurman fulfilled a long-held ambition by appearing in a Woody Allen film, *Sweet and Lowdown*, released in 1999. After roles in a few lower-profile productions she returned to prominence in the mid-2000s in two more Quentin Tarantino movies: *Kill Bill: Vol. 1* and *Kill Bill: Vol. 2*. Then came the remake of *The Producers*, and *My Super Ex-Girlfriend*.

More recently, Thurman played the recurring character Rebecca Duvall in five episodes of the television series *Smash* in 2012 and appeared in a segment of the comedy film *Movie 43* in 2013.

GRANVILLE VAN DUSEN (JOSHUA RAND)

Granville Roy Van Dusen Jnr was born on 16 March 1944 in Grand Rapids, Minnesota, USA and received his acting break near the bottom of the cast list of the 1971 feature film *The Statue*. Instead of following a path of acting in films, he then focused on getting regular work on American television series. He played supporting roles in shows such as *Ironside*, *Baretta*, *Switch*, *Harry O*, *The Bionic Woman* and *Kojak*. In the '80s, he appeared in several television movies before returning to guest-starring parts in series as diverse as *Barnaby Jones*, *Magnum P.I.*, *Murder She Wrote*, *Moonlighting* and *Highway to Heaven*. The '90s brought more of the same, as he graced episodes of *Hunter, Space: Above and Beyond, The New Adventures of Superman, Diagnosis Murder* and *Sliders*. Besides acting in a couple of episodes of *Star Trek: Enterprise* in 2003 and 2004, more recently Van Dusen has discovered a new outlet for his talents by voicing characters in computer games.

PRINCIPAL PRODUCTION PERSONNEL BIOGRAPHIES

Presented below are brief biographies of the principal production personnel of *The Avengers*, *The New Adventures* and the 1998 movie in alphabetical order by surname. The relevant production roles are given in brackets.

JONATHAN ALWYN (DIRECTOR)

Jonathan Alwyn broke into television directing in 1955 on the obscure show *The Little Round House*. He then worked on Associated-Rediffusion's early espionage serial *Destination Downing Street*. Staying with the same company, he directed the character Lockhart in both *Murder Bag* and *No Hiding Place*, the courtroom drama *Boyd QC* and the supernatural anthology series *Tales of Mystery*. In 1962, he moved to ABC, and like most other directors who worked on the videotaped episodes of *The Avengers*, he also directed instalments of *Armchair Theatre*. This landed him additional work on other ABC shows such as *Out of this World*, the military police drama *Redcap*, the industrial espionage-themed *Intrigue* and the supernatural series *Haunted*. He then became the producer of *Mystery and Imagination*.

Alwyn went into the '70s directing for various companies on shows such as *Special Branch*, the sci-fi-themed *Doomwatch*, the boardroom drama *Man at the Top* and the blood-in-the-gutter espionage classic *Callan*. For his next assignment, he took on both producing and directing duties on a number of episodes of *The Rivals of Sherlock Holmes*. He then returned to directing only, through to the end of the '70s, including for the BBC on both *Warship* and *The Onedin Line*. He had also been directing episodes of LWT's Second World War series *Enemy at the Door*, paving the way for him to take over as producer for its second season, transmitted in 1980.

Alwyn then tried his hand at producing for the BBC on *When the Boat Comes In*, the crime series *The Enigma Files* and, having first directed a number of episodes, a season of the police drama *Juliet Bravo*. He then took over as producer of *Bergerac* for three seasons, steering it through a successful period, and still found time to produce as well the historical drama *By the Sword Divided*.

Now regarded as a producer rather than a director, Alwyn found a steady stream of work in that capacity, including on the eight-part drama *Chelworth* in 1989 and the second season of the period detective drama *Campion* a year later. He also served as producer on the revived *Maigret* in 1992 and as co-producer on the comedy-drama *Under the Hammer* a couple of years later.

RAY AUSTIN (STUNT ARRANGER, DIRECTOR)

Raymond John DeVere Austin – aka Ray Austin – was born in London on 5 December 1932. In his late teens he found himself called up for National Service in the Army, which he greatly disliked except for the physical training. Upon returning to civilian life, he managed to obtain a position as a chauffeur and eventually found himself driving film star Cary Grant around whenever the actor was in the UK making a film. Having forged a friendship with the American, Austin later travelled to Los Angeles, where he was guaranteed stunt work in films and on many different television series.

Austin performed stunts in the Hollywood movies *North by Northwest* and *Operation Petticoat* (both with Cary Grant) and the epic *Spartacus*, before returning to try his hand in the British film and television industry. Doubling Dermot Walsh on the series *Richard the Lionheart* provided the foothold he needed to keep getting himself cast in small but physically demanding roles on shows such as *The Saint*. Then during 1964 and 1965 he became both the fight arranger and recurring character Billy Clay on *GS5* at ATV's Elstree Studios, where he met Brian Clemens, who was script editing the series. Clemens later recommended that Austin be hired as the stunt arranger on *The Avengers*, feeling his abilities were exactly what the series needed. While carrying out these duties, Austin would also occasionally be allowed to do some second unit directing.

Austin later became second unit director on the final 13 episodes of *The Champions* and, having proved himself, took charge of the main on complete episodes of both *The Avengers* and *The Saint*. Leaving his stunt arranging days behind, he now concentrated on directing, and found a wealth of work waiting for him on *Department S*, *Randall and Hopkirk (Deceased)*, *Shirley's World* and *The Adventures of Black Beauty*. Work continued to flow in throughout the '70s, including on episodes of *Space: 1999*, *The New Avengers*, *The Professionals* and *Return of the Saint*.

Austin then accepted an offer to direct television productions in the USA. Arriving back there in 1978, he worked on many diverse shows, including *The Hardy Boys Mysteries*, private detective drama *Barnaby Jones*, *The New Adventures of Wonder Woman*, *Hart to Hart*, *A Man Called Sloan*, romantic comedy *The Love Boat* and *Magnum P.I.*. In 1983 he was instrumental in resurrecting a classic '60s spy series when he directed the television movie *The Return of The Man From U.N.C.L.E.*. This was followed by a couple of episodes of the Lee Van Cleef martial arts show *The Master*.

Austin later directed other television projects including both *Airwolf* and *The Fall Guy*. Then in 1987 he became involved in reviving another couple of old favourites with the television movie *The Return of The Six Million Dollar Man* and *The Bionic Woman*. Toward the end of the '80s there were directing duties on episodes of the light thriller *A Fine Romance* (retitled *Ticket to Ride* for UK transmissions) and producing and directing on over 50 episodes of *Zorro*.

Austin's final directing work was undertaken in 1999 on another revamped version of an earlier success, *CI5: The New Professionals*.

BILL BAIN (DIRECTOR)

Born in 1930, Australian Bill Bain followed his assignment on *The Avengers* by directing episodes of various other ABC programmes such as the serial *Emerald Soup*, *Armchair Theatre*, the sci-fi serial *Undermind*, *Redcap* and *Mystery and Imagination*. Spreading his wings in 1968, he spent time at the BBC directing a couple of episodes of *Sir Arthur*

Conan Doyle's Sherlock Holmes. This was followed a year later by half a dozen instalments of *The Gold Robbers* for LWT. With ABC and Rediffusion having morphed into Thames in July 1968, Bain started directing on *Public Eye* for that company in 1971. He then moved on to handle period drama on *Upstairs, Downstairs* for LWT and *The Duchess of Duke Street* for the BBC. By 1978 he found himself occupied with the wartime drama *Enemy at the Door*, on which he directed 11 segments, followed by a solitary *Play for Today* and finally in 1982 three instalments of *The Brack Report* for Thames. Bill Bain died in 1982.

ROY WARD BAKER (DIRECTOR)

Roy Horace Baker – aka Roy Ward Baker – was born in London on 19 December 1916. He gained his first job in the film industry at Gainsborough Studios, as an errand boy, but determination had him working as an assistant director within three years. Progressing further, he was an uncredited assistant director to Alfred Hitchcock on the 1938 thriller *The Lady Vanishes*. He then directed two short presentations in 1947 and followed this up with his first feature film, *The October Man*, two years later. Baker directed about one film per year after that, including during a stint in Hollywood, where he worked with Marilyn Monroe and Robert Ryan amongst others. Back in the UK, he first worked with Julian Wintle on the movie *Passage Home*, released in 1955.

Baker then directed several critically acclaimed films, with *The One That Got Away*, *A Night to Remember* and *The Singer Not the Song*, leading to his initial experience on a television film series with *Zero One*. A friendship with star Roger Moore led to directing duties on no fewer that 18 episodes of *The Saint*. Then, working with Julian Wintle again, he handled eight episodes of *The Human Jungle*, which in turn led to *The Avengers*.

Highly regarded on the strength of these early endeavours, Baker gained many more directing assignments in the late 1960s, including on episodes of *Gideon's Way*, *The Baron*, *The Champions*, *Department S* and *Randall and Hopkirk (Deceased)*. Having frequently been mistaken for the dubbing editor Roy Baker, he decided to avoid any further confusion by giving himself the middle name of Ward in 1967, just in time to direct Hammer Films' feature version of *Quatermass and the Pit*. This started an association with the house of horror that included him working on *The Anniversary*, *The Vampire Lovers*, *Scars of Dracula*, the television series *Journey to the Unknown* and, reuniting him with Brian Clemens and Albert Fennell, *Dr Jekyll & Sister Hyde*.

In the '70s, Baker still found himself in demand for film series such as *Jason King*, *The Protectors*, *Return of the Saint*, *Danger UXB* and *The Persuaders!*. There were more Gothic horror films too, followed by a long-running association with the Thames/Euston Films series *Minder*, for which he directed 13 episodes over a ten year period.

The '80s brought the Polish-produced *Sherlock Holmes and Doctor Watson*, the short-lived British-based American series *Q.E.D.*, plus the Channel 4-transmitted shows *The Irish R.M.* and *Fairly Secret Army*. Baker's final credits saw him return to heroic action shows with Central's *Saracen* and Yorkshire TV's *The Good Guys*. He retired in 1992 and died on 5 October 2010.

RICHARD BATES (STORY EDITOR)

Richard Bates was born in July 1937 in Kent. After doing National Service in the RAF, he attempted but failed to gain entry to the Royal Academy of Music. Then, on the suggestion of his father, the writer H E Bates, he took up writing. Initially he wrote for a magazine, but soon he gained employment with a literary agent, for whom he vetted screenplays. It was at this time that he first encountered fellow writer Roger Marshall. Moving on, he began working for ABPC at Elstree Studios, where he was once again involved in reading scripts and reporting back to his superiors about their potential. Cutbacks resulted in him being made redundant, but just two days later he saw a job advertisement in *The Sunday Times* for the position of story editor at ABPC's subsidiary company ABC Television on *The Avengers*.

When *The Avengers* progressed onto film for its fourth season, Bates stayed at Teddington Studios and moved across to become story editor on both *Public Eye* and *Redcap*, eventually progressing to producer on the former in 1966. After this he continued mainly as a producer, including on *Armchair Theatre* for ABC and *A Man of our Times* for Associated-Rediffusion.

At the start of the 1970s, Bates tried something different by taking on the role of co-executive producer on the feature film spin-off from the sit-com *Please Sir!*. However, he returned to television drama in 1973 with LWT's *Helen: A Woman of Today*. He produced various other dramas throughout the rest of the '70s and '80s, including *The Prime of Miss Jean Brodie* and the sci-fi serial *The Tripods*.

More sci-fi followed, as Bates worked first as script supervisor and then as producer on all of Thames's *Chocky* serials of the 1980s. He then produced the period detective drama *Hannay* at the end of that decade. Forging an association with Yorkshire Television, he served as executive producer on their light drama *The Darling Buds of May* in the early 1990s and on the serial *My Uncle Silas* at the beginning of the next decade, while also working with star David Jason again as both producer and executive producer on the long-running *A Touch of Frost* from 1992 to 2010.

PAUL BERNARD (DESIGNER)

Born in London on 20 June 1929, Paul Bernard became involved with television production in 1959, designing sets for several instalments of the anthology series *Television Playhouse* before working for both ABC and the BBC on various shows. Arriving on *The Avengers* for the first season episode 'Girl on the Trapeze', he was the production designer on half a dozen episodes, plus other well known shows of the time including *Maigret*, *Ghost Squad* and *No Hiding Place*. Bernard became a director on *Z Cars* in 1964 and continued his career in this role only from then on, finding his true vocation in science fiction of the early '70s, handling 16 instalments of *Doctor Who* and nine of *The Tomorrow People*. He died on 25 September 1997.

HOWARD BLAKE (COMPOSER)

Howard Blake was born on 12 February 1938 in London. His career in music was assisted greatly when at the age of 18 he gained a scholarship to the Royal Academy of Music, paving the way for him to write scores both for documentaries and for a couple of films. However, his day job was as a session musician for EMI at Abbey Road

Studios, where he played keyboards on both pop recordings and film soundtracks. Later he was invited to play with Laurie Johnson, which led to him being among the session musicians on the 1964 recording of *The Avengers* theme, playing piano.

Over the years he has been involved with a wide variety of music, including scores for feature films, television programmes and commercials, opera, ballet and theatre. His most notable work includes his scores for the animated children's film *The Snowman*, the Hammer adaptation of Dennis Wheatley's *The Lost Continent*, the television serial *The Moon Stallion*, plus films such as *The Riddle of the Sands* and *Flash Gordon*.

JULIAN BOND (*POLICE SURGEON* CREATOR)

Julian Bond was born on 8 December 1930 and entered television by writing for the crime thriller *Shadow Squad* in the '50s. He scripted the feature film *The Witness* in 1959, but then concentrated his efforts on further television shows. After his involvement with *Police Surgeon*, he switched to Midlands weekday provider ATV to work on series such as *Drama 62* and *Probation Officer*, before briefly returning to ABC for the sci-fi show *Out of This World*. From there he became involved with the ITC film series *The Saint*, *Man of the World*, *The Sentimental Agent* and *Espionage*, although he subsequently decided against continuing his career in this area and returned to videotaped productions.

By 1963 Bond was contributing to both ATV's anthology *Love Story* and the Victorian detective series *Sergeant Cork*, before writing for the BBC for the first time on the drama-with-science-fiction-elements series *R3*. Now well-established in the industry, he moved freely from company to company over the next few years, contributing material to ABC for *Redcap* and *Public Eye*, MCA/ITC for *Court Martial* and Associated-Rediffusion for the drama *A Man of Our Times*. Toward the conclusion of the '60s he specialised in writing for anthology series, providing scripts for *Armchair Thriller*, Hammer Films' *Journey to the Unknown*, the BBC's *Out of the Unknown* and ATV's courtroom drama *Crime of Passion*.

During the early '70s Bond worked mainly on period drama, writing for *Upstairs, Downstairs*, *The Edwardians* and *The Rivals of Sherlock Holmes*. In the middle of the decade there was a brief return to feature films with the screenplay for the light thriller *Trial by Combat*, then it was back to television for episodes of *The Duchess of Duke Street* and Southern Television's one-off Sherlock Holmes mystery *Silver Blaze*. Around this time LWT commissioned him to adapt H E Bates' novel *Love for Lydia* into a 13-part serial, which was transmitted in 1977. That year he also began writing for the BBC's First World War series *Wings*.

As the '70s concluded, Bond scripted eight episodes of Southern Television's *Dick Barton: Special Agent* before moving on to the BBC costume drama *Penmarric* and then Anglia's anthology series *Tales of the Unexpected*. Several years later he scripted Yorkshire Television's Indian-based mini-series *The Far Pavilions*, before making another brief return to the film world by writing both *The Shooting Party* and *The Whistle Blower*. His final scriptwriting credits came during the '90s with adaptations for *The Ruth Rendell Mysteries*.

Julian Bond passed away on 14 January 2012.

LAURENCE BOURNE (DIRECTOR)

Irishman Laurence Bourne had previous experience directing plays in repertory theatre before taking an ABC television directors' course. After making his debut on *The Avengers*, he spent the first few years of his television career working on other ABC series such as *Public Eye*, *Undermind*, *Redcap* and *Mystery and Imagination*. Moving to the BBC in 1966, he worked on both *Adam Adamant Lives!* and *The Troubleshooters* before finding his niche on the medical drama *Dr Finlay's Casebook*, for which he directed 16 episodes. After this he returned to his homeland, where he gained his last directorial credit on the television movie *Only the Earth* for the Irish station RTE in 1971.

JOHN BRYCE (STORY EDITOR, PRODUCER)

Scotsman John Bryce came to London specifically to follow his dream of being a scriptwriter. After spending a year with a film company he transferred to working in television for a time, eventually joining the staff of ABC. He served for a while as a story editor on *Armchair Theatre* before getting involved as first story editor and then producer on *The Avengers*, later going onto assume the position of producer on both *Redcap* and *Public Eye*.

JEREMY BURNHAM (WRITER)

John Richard Jeremy Burnham entered the industry as an actor and gained his first television role in an instalment of *Armchair Theatre* in 1956, following this up with appearances in various productions into the early '60s. After performing in half-a-dozen instalments of the soap *Emergency-Ward 10*, he continued with guest-starring parts in *The Human Jungle*, *The Plane Makers*, *No Hiding Place* and *Undermind*. Eventually he came to the attention of film series directors, who cast him in episodes of *Gideon's Way*, *Danger Man*, *The Saint*, *The Baron* and *The Avengers*.

Later, having established himself as a scriptwriter on *The Avengers*, he quickly went on to exhibit his adaptability by providing the screenplays for Hammer Films' *The Horror of Frankenstein* and episodes of the period drama *The Flaxton Boys*.

After playing a supporting role in an episode of *The Persuaders!*, Burnham wrote for the BBC shows *Paul Temple* and *Spy Trap*, and then for the soap *Emmerdale Farm*, as it was known then. He then worked exclusively for the BBC for several years, contributing episodes to the drama series *The View from Daniel Pike*, *Menace*, *Warship* and *The Expert*.

Towards the conclusion of the '70s he collaborated with fellow writer and actor Trevor Ray on two children's fantasy serials, *The Children of the Stones* for Harlech and *Raven* for ATV. Then, moving into the '80s, he returned to film series, writing for *The Professionals*, *Hammer House of Horror* and *Minder*, before becoming involved with the serial *Seagull Island* in 1981. Generally his scriptwriting now centred on drama, such as *The Gentle Touch*, *Mitch*, a feature length *Hammer House of Mystery and Suspense* (in which he also acted) and the television movies *The Miracle* and *Tropical Moon Over Dorking*.

The mid-'80s saw Burnham write three episodes of *C.A.T.S. Eyes*, followed by seven segments of *Howards' Way*. Into the '90s he contributed solitary scripts to *Inspector Morse*, *Bergerac* and *The Good Guys*. His final credit came in 1999 with a *CI5:*

The New Professionals episode called 'Miss Hit', co-written with Brian Clemens.

DON CHAFFEY (DIRECTOR)

Don Chaffey was born on 5 August 1917 in Hastings, East Sussex. He began his career working in the art department at Gainsborough Studios, before progressing to be a director on the 1951 film *The Case of the Missing Scene*. A steady stream of film work occupied him until 1955, when he received his first taste of filmed television with the anthology series *Lilli Palmer Theatre* and the BBC's *The Adventures of the Big Man*. Having found the true outlet for his abilities, Chaffey continued in this vein, directing shows such as *The Adventures of Charlie Chan*, *Assignment Foreign Legion*, *The Errol Flynn Theatre* and *The Adventures of Robin Hood*. However, after completing 14 episodes of *The Four Just Men*, he returned to directing feature films, including *Dentist in the Chair*, *Nearly a Nasty Accident* and, perhaps his greatest achievement, *Jason and the Argonauts*.

His friendship with Patrick McGoohan brought Chaffey directing assignments on 14 episodes of *Danger Man* and the film *The Three Lives of Thomasina*, in which McGoohan starred. Another mid-'60s assignment was Hammer Films' prehistoric extravaganza *One Million Years B.C.*. Work on McGoohan's *The Prisoner* followed, along with episodes of other ITC film series *The Baron* and *Man in a Suitcase*, the film *A Twist of Sand* and Hammer's television show *Journey to the Unknown*.

After directing five episodes of *The Avengers*, Chaffey continued into the early '70s with more television work, directing a couple of segments of the Second World War series *Pathfinders* and nine episodes of *The Protectors*. Like several other British directors in the '70s, he decided that the United States held better prospects at that time. There he found work directing the Disney film *Pete's Dragon*, along with episodes of *Vegas* and *Charlie's Angels*. His talents were constantly in demand during the '80s on more US television series including *Fantasy Island*, *T.J. Hooker*, *Matt Houston*, *Spenser: for Hire*, *Airwolf* and *Hunter*.

Chaffey's busy career came to a conclusion with the late-'80s *Mission: Impossible* revival series, for which he directed a feature length storyline and two regular episodes. He died on 13 November 1990.

JEREMIAH CHECHIK (MOVIE DIRECTOR)

A native of Montreal, Canada, Jeremiah Chechik was born in 1955 and arrived as a film director with the comedy movie *National Lampoon's Christmas Vacation* in 1989. Through the '90s he directed several other films: *Benny & Joon*, *Tell Tale*, *Diabolique* and then *The Avengers*. After this he travelled the world and did not return to directing until 2004, with the television movie *Meltdown*.

Deciding to continue working exclusively in television, Chechik doubled up as both producer and director on *The Bronx is Burning* and *The Middleman*, and started a recurring association as director on the espionage show *Burn Notice*. After working on various other American television shows including *Warehouse 13*, he eventually returned to feature films, directing *The Right Kind of Wrong* during the summer of 2012.

BRIAN CLEMENS (WRITER, STORY EDITOR, ASSOCIATE PRODUCER, PRODUCER)

Brian Clemens, who would develop the concept of *The Avengers* more than anyone else, was born in Croydon, Surrey in 1931. After spending several years in the British Army he then worked in an advertising agency. However, he had always wanted to become a writer, so he submitted a script to the BBC. They considered it too complicated and costly to produce, but producer Dennis Vance invited Clemens to a meeting at Broadcasting House, where he discovered that the BBC did not have a large budget for television production. Having been encouraged, he tried again, writing a play about two men in a railway carriage. This inexpensive concept became *Valid for a Single Journey Only*, which was transmitted by the BBC on 4 October1954 and brought the writer to the attention of American brothers Edward J and Harry Lee Danziger. Becoming a staff writer for the Danzigers, Clemens learnt his craft quickly, writing and rewriting screenplays. He proved especially adept at constructing scripts that utilised multiple sets from previous productions, hence saving on budget. Between 1955 and 1962 he worked on 30 B-movies and almost 70 episodes of the Danzigers' television series *The Vise*, *Saber of London*, *The Man from Interpol* and the insurance investigation show *The Cheaters*.

Finding himself in demand to provide screenplays for other projects, Clemens frequently went moonlighting under the pseudonym Tony O'Grady – O'Grady being his mother's maiden name – to avoid detection by the Danzigers, who had him under contract. It was as O'Grady that he penned three episodes of *Martin Kane: Private Investigator* in 1958, plus half a dozen adventures for the police series *Dial 999*. There were also solitary episodes of *White Hunter* and *Interpol Calling*, followed by a couple of collaborations on the ITP film series *H G Wells' Invisible Man*, where his friendship with fellow scriptwriter Ian Stuart Black subsequently got him involved with *Danger Man*. His association with the Danzigers now over, Clemens reverted to using his own name while plotting the adventures of John Drake in the latter show. He then became a jobbing writer, working on the ITC film series *Man of the World* and *The Sentimental Agent*.

Along the way, Clemens also started his involvement with ABC, writing an instalment of *Armchair Theatre*, scripting two episodes of the first season of *The Avengers* and working on the historical series *Sir Francis Drake*. Before getting heavily involved with *The Avengers*, Clemens spent time writing and script editing ATV's videotaped crime show *GS5*, as well as finding time to work on the series *Riviera Police*. While he was under contract to ABC for *The Avengers*, the O'Grady name managed another couple of outings on scripts for *The Baron*, but for the rest of the '60s and the early '70s Clemens used his own name. Constantly finding his services in demand during this period, he supplied scripts for ABC's *Intrigue*, the BBC's *Adam Adamant Lives!*, plus ITC's *The Champions*, *The Persuaders!*, *The Protectors* and *The Adventurer*.

The '70s witnessed Clemens not just scripting but also creating a number of series. He was responsible for the sitcom *My Wife Next Door*, the anthology show *Thriller* and *The Professionals* as well as *The New Avengers*. Despite the almost constant commitments associated with some of these projects, he still found time to contribute to other series, such as the spy show *Quiller* and the forensic police series *The Expert*.

Diversifying in the '80s, Clemens scripted on the American horror anthology *Darkroom*, the BBC's *Bergerac* and Stateside detective show *Remington Steele*, and also adapted Gavin Lyall's spy novel *The Secret Servant* into a three-part serial. Returning to the anthology format, he then turned out two screenplays for the feature length *Hammer House of Mystery and Suspense* and three for *Worlds Beyond* and also worked on the revived *Alfred Hitchcock Presents*. Toward the conclusion of the '80s, he provided the teleplay for the television movie *Timestalkers* and created the German crime-fighter show *Blue Blood*.

During the '90s Clemens began getting hired not just as a writer but also as a consultant on various television series including the detective shows *Max Monroe: Loose Cannon* and *Father Dowling Investigates*, plus Carnival Films' hi-tech series *Bugs*.

Having storylined the film *Highlander 2: The Quickening*, he continued by penning an episode for the *Highlander* television series. Other projects included three feature-length television movies of the resurrected *Perry Mason* series. Then, just before the millennium, he became the main writer on another television revival, *CI5: The New Professionals*

At the turn of the decade, Clemens wrote for Carlton Television's strong drama *The Wrong Side of the Rainbow*. Then in 2006 he wrote the teleplay *Fallen Idol*, one in a series of occasional television movies featuring the character McBride, a Los Angeles-based lawyer. His most recent credit arrived in 2010, when a consortium remade his 1969 film thriller *And Soon the Darkness*.

GRAEME CLIFFORD (DIRECTOR)

Graeme Clifford was born in Sydney, New South Wales, Australia in 1942. He broke into the film industry by becoming the second unit director on the Canadian-produced feature *The Cold Day in the Park*, released in 1969. Initially, however, he preferred to work as an editor, including during the early '70s on the films *Images*, *Don't Look Now*, *The Rocky Horror Picture Show* and *The Man Who Fell to Earth*. After *The New Avengers*, Clifford spent time in the United States, directing a couple of episodes of the detective show *Barnaby Jones*. During the '80s, however, his credits on both films and television episodes became somewhat sparse, although he did handle a solitary instalment of *Twin Peaks*. In the 1990s and 2000s his workload increased again, encompassing a steady stream of television movies and mini-series. His most recent credit came as director of the 2007 television movie *Write & Wrong*.

CHARLES CRICHTON (DIRECTOR)

Charles Ainslie Crichton was born in Wallasey, Cheshire, on 6 August 1910. He broke into the world of film-making in 1935 as an editor on the film *Sanders of the River*, but it took him a further nine years to become a director, making his debut in that capacity on the film *For Those in Peril*. He then directed one or two features every year until 1951, when he came to prominence with the Ealing comedy *The Lavender Hill Mob*. The following year he worked with Julian Wintle on the drama *Hunted* and went on to direct another classic Ealing comedy, *The Titfield Thunderbolt*.

By 1962 Crichton had arrived in filmed television, starting an association with ITC on *Man of the World* that continued with him directing episodes of *Danger Man*, *Man in a Suitcase*, *Strange Report* and *The Protectors*. He was reunited with Wintle for an episode of *The Human Jungle*, which lined him up for *The Avengers*. Then in the early '70s came episodes of the children's series *The Adventures of Black Beauty* and *Here Come the Double*

Deckers!. These were followed by no fewer than 14 episodes of *Space: 1999* and the pilot film *The Day After Tomorrow*, both for Gerry Anderson, plus various other episodes of British film series up to 1982.

Crichton's final credits came in 1988, when he both directed and provided the original storyline for the successful film *A Fish Called Wanda*. He died on 14 September 1999.

JOHNNY DANKWORTH (COMPOSER)

John William Phillip Dankworth was born on 20 September 1927 in Woodfield, Essex. He became generally known in jazz circles as Johnny Dankworth and it was under this name that he provided music for the television serial *The Voodoo Factor* in 1959. After *The Avengers*, Dankworth got himself involved in the '60s spy movie craze by composing the soundtracks for *Modesty Blaise*, *Fathom* and *Salt & Pepper*. He also made a brief return to television to provide the theme for the BBC's science programme *Tomorrow's World*. However, after the '60s he did very little work for either film or television, preferring to focus his talents on performing and recording.

DESMOND DAVIS (DIRECTOR)

Desmond Davis was born on 24 May 1926 in London and became involved in film-making when he started out as an uncredited camera loader and clapper boy on the 1944 movie *It's in the Bag*. He was promoted to focus puller in 1952, and then to camera operator in 1956. The following year saw him directing an episode of *The Adventures of Sir Lancelot*, followed by three instalments of *Tales of Dickens*. Although he continued as a camera operator until the early '60s, he then appeared to make a conscious decision to concentrate on directing, but found work much harder to come by, managing only five films throughout the decade. Eventually he directed five episodes of Yorkshire Television's *Follyfoot* in the early '70s, as well as solitary outings on *Wessex Tales* and *Play for Today*. After *The New Avengers* there were directing duties on a couple of segments of the BBC's *Wings* and then sporadic television assignments, leading to his crowning glory, directing the 1981 fantasy film *Clash of the Titans*. The '80s provided further regular directing work on various television movies and an instalment of LWT's *The Agatha Christie Hour*. Davis's final directing credit came in 1994 on the television movie *Doggin' Around*.

ERNIE DAY (DIRECTOR)

Ernest Day – aka Ernie Day – was born on 15 April 1927 in Surrey. In entering the film industry he was following in the footsteps of his elder brother Robert, who also later directed episodes of *The Avengers*. Ernie became an uncredited clapper loader on the 1944 movie *Mr Emmanuel*, gained a promotion to focus puller five years later, and then a further promotion to camera operator six years after that, starting on the film *The Cockleshell Heroes*. During the '60s and into the early '70s he worked on major features such as *Lawrence of Arabia*, *She*, *Doctor Zhivago*, *You Only Live Twice*, *Ryan's Daughter*, *A Clockwork Orange* and *The Pink Panther Strikes Again*.

Having cut his directorial teeth on *The New Avengers*, Day also handled a solitary episode of *The Professionals* in 1978. In the years that followed, he worked mainly as a second unit director, including on the Bond films *The Spy Who Loved Me* and *Moonraker* and on *Rambo III*, but also occasionally as a cinematographer. His final assignment involved him doubling up as both director and director of photography of the second unit on the 1996 *Mission: Impossible* film. He died on 16 November 2006.

ROBERT DAY (DIRECTOR)

Robert Day was born in East Sheen, London on 11 September 1922. He progressed through several positions, such as clapper boy and camera operator, before becoming a director on the critically-acclaimed film *The Green Man* in 1956. He continued working in feature films, but also recognised the opportunities offered by television film series, directing episodes of both *The Adventures of Robin Hood* and *The Buccaneers*. By 1962 he had worked alongside Tony Hancock, directing his film *The Rebel*, and started an association with Edgar Rice Burroughs' jungle hero Tarzan on both *Tarzan the Magnificent* and *Tarzan's Three Challenges*.

He found further television work directing episodes of *Danger Man* and then, as one of Julian Wintle's closest friends, *The Human Jungle* and *The Avengers*, where he instantly found the correct style and pace. More Tarzan films followed and then episodes of *Court Martial* and the American *Tarzan* television series, before a permanent move to the USA brought about a succession of directing jobs on such shows as *The Invaders*, *Ironside* and *Barnaby Jones*.

Throughout the '70s it was more of the same, as Day found himself in demand in a busy American television industry, working on series such as *The Streets of San Francisco*, *McCloud*, *Switch*, *Kojak* and *Dallas*. During the '80s he made a conscious move toward directing television movies, and his final credit came on the low-budget offering *Fire: Trapped on the 37th Floor*.

REED DE ROUEN (WRITER)

Born on 10 June 1921 in Wisconsin, USA, Reed de Rouen managed dual careers as a writer and an actor in the film and television industry, though mainly in the UK as opposed to his homeland. Gaining his break as a performer, de Rouen appeared uncredited in the classic film *The Third Man* before receiving a credit for his next movie, *The Strangers Came*, which led to him co-writing and co-starring in the British feature *The Six Men*. Returning briefly to the USA, he acted in an instalment of the anthology series *Fireside Theatre*. He then relocated permanently to the UK, where he appeared in *Television Playhouse* and wrote an episode of *Assignment Foreign Legion*. He co-starred in an episode of *Armchair Theatre* early in 1961 before being drafted into the production team of *The Avengers* in May of that year, shortly before producer Leonard White had a brief stay in hospital, being copied in on memos at Teddington Studios. In later years he concentrated more on acting, putting in appearances in *Z Cars*, *Doctor Who*, *The Troubleshooters* and the films *Billion Dollar Brain* and *Baxter!*. However, there were still some writing assignments, as he worked on screenplays for Associated-Rediffusion's *Crane* and its spin-off *Orlando*, Granada Television's *The Man in Room 17* and ITC's *Man in a Suitcase*. In the early 1970s he collaborated with his friend Jon Pertwee on a proposal for a *Doctor Who* story, which the production team turned down. He died on 11 June 1986.

PAUL DICKSON (DIRECTOR)

Paul Gherzo – aka Paul Dickson – was born on 18 January 1920 in Cardiff and entered the business by directing shorts and documentaries, plus writing several screenplays. He never really managed to break into mainstream feature films, but instead found his niche directing '50s television film series such as *Colonel March of Scotland Yard*, *The Vise* and *Adventure Theatre*.

When this work petered out, Dickson directed a documentary short called *Stone into Street* in 1960 and then disappeared from the industry, only to resurface eight years later working on the Australian television series *The Adventurers*. Returning to the UK, he secured directing duties on Dennis Spooner and Monty Berman's *The Champions* at Elstree Studios. Then, after *The Avengers*, he continued in this vein with *Department S*. Thereafter he worked exclusively for Spooner and Berman, directing episodes of the original *Randall and Hopkirk (Deceased)*, *Jason King* and *The Adventurer*. When these ITC film series ended, Dickson's career did too. He died on 6 October 2011.

PETER DUFFELL (DIRECTOR)

Peter Duffell was born in 1937 in Staffordshire, England, and began his directing career in the early 1960s. After his single assignment on *The Avengers* – on the episode 'The Winged Avenger' – he continued his career with *Man in a Suitcase*, an instalment of Hammer Films' *Journey to the Unknown*, episodes of ITC's *Strange Report* and the American comedy *The Ugliest Girl in Town*, which was produced at Shepperton Studios in Surrey.

During the early '70s, there were a couple of feature film credits on *The House That Dripped Blood* and *England Made Me*, plus assorted television work with ITC's *From a Bird's Eye View* and LWT's *The Adventures of Black Beauty*. In 1975 Duffell had one of his most prominent assignments, directing the big-budget movie *Inside Out*, starring Telly Savalas, Robert Culp and James Mason. He then began an association with Yorkshire Television, starting with a couple of episodes of their period drama *Flambards*. At the turn of the decade he also directed episodes of Southern's *Famous Five* and some plays for the BBC, amongst other projects. As the '80s progressed, he went on location to India for Yorkshire Television's mini-series *The Far Pavilions*, directed a couple of Anglia's *Tales of the Unexpected* and followed these up with a couple of television movies and an *Inspector Morse*.

In the mid-'90s Gerry Anderson called upon Duffell's talents for his science fiction series *Space Precinct*. His final directing work came on a couple of 1996 instalments of *The Bill*.

Throughout his career he also gained occasional scriptwriting credits, the last of these coming on the television movie *Some Other Spring* in 1991.

TERENCE FEELY (WRITER)

Terence John Feely was born in Liverpool on 20 July 1928 and was a Fleet Street journalist before starting his television career by scripting episodes of Associated-Rediffusion's *No Hiding Place*. He then moved onto *The Avengers* and also wrote for the Moroccan-based crime series *Crane*. This was followed by a two-and-a-half year gap before he returned to ABC to take up the position of story/script editor on both

Armchair Theatre and *Mystery and Imagination*. He then became an associate producer on *Callan*. Changing direction, he next entered the film industry, joining Paramount Pictures (UK) Ltd as an executive, although he resigned in November 1968.

Along the way, Feely also managed to script episodes of *The Saint*, *The Prisoner* and *Love Story*. In 1969 he worked on the Australian series *Riptide*, before moving on to script a couple of episodes of Gerry Anderson's *UFO*. Throughout the '70s, he worked on various television projects, including *The Persuaders!*, *The Protectors* and HTV's *Arthur of the Britons*. Then in 1973 came a stint on ATV's *Thriller*, writing scripts from both his own outlines and some created by Brian Clemens. Shortly after this, he became involved with LWT's *Affairs of the Heart*, before returning to scriptwriting on film series, namely *Space: 1999*, *The New Avengers* and *Return of the Saint*.

Feely then tried his hand at an episode of the sitcom *Robin's Nest*, but quickly returned to drama, providing solitary screenplays for both *Shoestring* and *Bergerac* and three episodes of *The Dick Francis Thriller: The Racing Game*. As the '80s arrived, he created the tough lady cop show *The Gentle Touch* for LWT, wrote the script for the mini-series *Minstral's Daughter* and then became a major player in TVS's *C.A.T.S. Eyes*, which featured his character Maggie Forbes from *The Gentle Touch*.

Feely died on 13 August 2000.

ALBERT FENNELL (PRODUCER)

Albert Fennell was born on 29 March 1920 in Chiswick, London and entered the film industry as a production manager in 1947 on the movie *Root of All Evil*. He was associate producer on the movie *Idol of Paris* the following year, but it took another five years for him to achieve full producer status on the 1953 feature *Park Plaza 605*. A further 11 years passed before Fennell encountered Julian Wintle, when the former co-produced the Independent Artists film *Night of the Eagle*. The two men then worked together again on the science fiction movie *Unearthly Stranger*. Aside from producing both *The Avengers* and *The New Avengers*, Fennell also worked in a similar capacity on a number of movies, television movies and series during the '70s and '80s, including *The Professionals*. He died in 1988, shortly after producing the television movie *The Lady and the Highwayman*.

LEONARD FINCHAM (WRITER)

Leonard Fincham began writing for television in 1954 with the BBC's *Running Wild*, the first television series featuring Morecambe and Wise. This provided a springboard for him to write episodes for various other shows in late '50s. Having provided scripts for *White Hunter*, *African Patrol*, *Interpol Calling* and *The Pursuers*, Fincham arrived on *The Avengers*. However, 'Death Dispatch' was his only script for the series and also his last television work.

GORDON FLEMYNG (DIRECTOR)

Glaswegian Gordon Flemyng was born on 7 March 1934. He initially became involved in television during the late '50s, directing episodes of the sitcom *The Army Game*. He then moved on to films and film series, directing a couple of *Edgar Wallace Mysteries*, the pop music-based *Just for Fun* and an episode of *The Saint*. This in turn led to projects at

Shepperton Studios in the mid-'60s, directing the films *Dr. Who and the Daleks* and *Daleks – Invasion Earth: 2150 AD*. In 1967 he spent some time at Elstree Studios, directing the two-part story 'Storm Warning'/'The Island' for ITC's *The Baron*. Two months later came his *The Avengers* episode, 'The Fear Merchants'.

Entering the '70s, Flemyng directed several feature films, including *The Last Grenade*, before returning to television on *Crown Court* and what was then called *Emmerdale Farm*. He gained only sporadic credits for a few years after that, but toward the end of the decade had assignments on an episode of the BBC's gritty police series *Target* and on Granada's Victorian detective drama *Cribb*.

Throughout the '80s and early '90s, Flemyng directed on a mixture of television movies and series including *Bergerac*, *Taggart*, *Lovejoy* and *Minder*. He died on 12 July 1995, and his final credits came as both producer and director on the posthumously-aired Yorkshire Television drama *Ellington* in 1996.

CLAUDE FOURNIER (DIRECTOR)

Claude Fournier was born on 23 July 1931 in Waterloo in the province of Quebec, Canada. In 1959 he gained his first directing credit on a short documentary for the National Film Board of Canada. He also wrote material for the French-language family adventure television series *CF-RCK*. Within a couple of years he had also acquired experience as both a cinematographer and an editor on other documentaries. By the '70s he was frequently writing and directing Canadian-produced French-language films. Rare excursions into English-language productions came in 1974 with the Western *Alien Thunder*, starring Donald Sutherland, and in 1978 – a year after he worked on *The New Avengers* – with the comedy *Pump it Up*. He continued to work as a director of films and television series up to the mid-2000s.

CYRIL FRANKEL (DIRECTOR)

Born in Stoke Newington, London on 21 December 1921, Cyril Frankel always wanted to work in the film industry. He took a job as an assistant in a film processing laboratory just to get a union card, which then allowed him to become a third assistant director. After a time he managed to progress through the ranks and in 1953 he directed his first production, a documentary, which then paved the way to feature films. Having acquired a reputation as a performer's director, Frankel rose to prominence in the '50s on movies such as *It's Great to Be Young!*.

Moving into the '60s, Frankel directed the controversial *Never Take Sweets From a Stranger*. However, like a number of other British film directors at that time, he then moved to work almost exclusively on television film series such as *Gideon's Way*, *The Baron* and *The Champions*. While working at Elstree Studios on the latter, he came into contact with both Brian Clemens and Albert Fennell and was asked to direct an episode of *The Avengers*. Despite thoroughly enjoying the experience and wanting to do more, he never found the time, as he became creative consultant on *Department S* and *Randall and Hopkirk (Deceased)*. Having for several years worked exclusively with Dennis Spooner and Monty Berman on these shows, Frankel maintained his relationship with them on both *Jason King* and *The Adventurer*. However, he still occasionally found time to direct other television projects such as Gerry Anderson's *UFO* and *The Protectors*, followed in 1975 by the feature film *Permission to Kill*.

Having always wanted to work on *The Saint* during the '60s, but having never found the time, at the end of the '70s Frankel accepted an approach to direct the only two-part *Return of the Saint* storyline, 'Collision Course', which he approached as a film. Five years later he also directed a feature-length instalment entitled 'Tennis Court' for *Hammer House of Mystery and Suspense*. He gained his final credit in 1990 on the obscure German film *Eine Frau Namens Harry* (English title: *Harry and Harriet*).

DAVE FREEMAN (WRITER)

Londoner Dave Freeman was born on 22 August 1922. After serving as a petty officer in the Royal Navy and a detective in Special Branch, he became a comedy scriptwriter, primarily for television. Equally adept at writing stand-up material, sketches or sitcoms, his first break came on editions of the BBC series *Great Scott, It's Maynard*, starring Terry Scott and Bill Maynard. Switching to ITV in 1956, he contributed material to *The Idiot Weekly, Price 2d* and *Son of Fred*, both of which starred Peter Sellers and Kenneth Conner among others. He also established a long-running working relationship with comedian Benny Hill that not only involved writing but also appearing in sketches as various different characters.

As a writer, Freeman became associated with some of the all-time greats in the comedy business, including Arthur Askey, Roy Hudd, Tommy Cooper and Frankie Howerd. He also progressed onto scriptwriting on productions such as *Play of the Week* and *Comedy Playhouse*. After a detour into feature films with the screenplay for *Rocket to the Moon*, released in 1967, he again found himself in demand to contribute to sitcoms such as *Mr Aitch*, starring Harry H Corbett, and *The Fossett Saga*, with Jimmy Edwards.

During the early '70s Freeman wrote for Granada's controversial comedy *The Dustbinmen,* the seasonal special *Carry On Again Christmas* and both the television series and film versions of *Bless This House*, starring Sid James. These projects were followed up by several instalments of the sketch show *Thirty Minutes Worth* and half a dozen of the series *Carry On Laughing*, the latter of which led to him being commissioned to script the film *Carry On Behind*. *Robin's Nest* was another sitcom he wrote for at the close of the '70s.

During the '80s Freeman's work included an edition of *The Jim Davidson Show* and several of *Terry and June*. He then found a whole new outlet for his writing abilities on Dutch television, which adapted some of his earlier stage plays for the small screen.

When an attempt was made to revive the *Carry On* films, it was Freeman who provided the screenplay for *Carry On Columbus*, released in 1992. His final credits came on the Dutch sitcom *Ha, die Pa!* in 1993. He died on 28 March 2005.

ROBERT FUEST (DESIGNER, DIRECTOR)

Robert Bernard Fuest was born in the London Borough of Croydon on 30 September 1927. He started out in the graphics field, designing record covers and doing the liner notes for Decca Records. Then one day a conversation with an old school friend persuaded him to apply for an art director position with ABC Television. His application was successful, and this propelled him into designing sets for *Armchair Theatre, Police Surgeon* and *The Avengers*. Initially he worked in conjunction with director Peter Hammond and was greatly inspired by him and his *avant-garde* style, which included odd camera angles, overhead shots and shots through foreground set elements such as bookcases – a style that Fuest would later reintroduce, making it a kind of trademark for *The Avengers*, when he became a regular director on the show, starting with the 1968 episode 'My Wildest Dream'.

Continuing with ABC in the early '60s, Fuest designed on the science fiction anthology *Out of this World*. However, he then went freelance, and designed on BBC shows such as *First Night*, *Festival* and *Teletale*. Showing another talent, he then began writing drama for the BBC's *Festival* and gags for Peter Cook and Dudley Moore in *Not Only ... But Also*.

Changing disciplines again, Fuest began working with director Richard Lester in a company that specialised in making television commercials. After training for six months, he was allowed to take control of one of these, for an antiperspirant. Breaking into feature films in 1967, he captured something of the style of *The Avengers* when he both wrote and directed *Just Like a Woman*, a pop-art run-around featuring Clive Dunn as an eccentric Prussian architect. A chance meeting with director James Hill in an underground car park in Park Lane in London brought *The Avengers* on film to his attention, and a recommendation to contact Brian Clemens and Albert Fennell. The two producers apparently checked out *Just Like a Woman* and, impressed by what they saw, brought Fuest onto their team, making him one of the show's regular directors.

After *The Avengers*, Fuest concentrated on directing films, including Clemens and Fennell's *And Soon the Darkness*, the chiller *The Abominable Dr Phibes*, its sequel *Dr Phibes Rises Again*, *The Final Programme* and *The Devil's Rain*.

Being recalled to work on *The New Avengers* pointed Fuest back toward television work. He went on to direct a solitary episode of *Three Dangerous Ladies* and instalments of the HTV serial *The Doombolt Chase*. He then spent several years in the United States, working in children's television and directing two television movies, *Revenge of the Stepford Wives* and *The Big Stuffed Dog*, though mainstream American series eluded him. Returning to Europe, in the '80s he called the shots on the feature film *Aphrodite* before gaining his final credits on *C.A.T.S. Eyes* and the supernatural anthology *Worlds Beyond*. He died on 21 March 2012.

JAMES GODDARD (DESIGNER)

James Goddard – aka D J Goddard – was born in London on 2 February 1936 and broke into television as a production designer with ABC by doing a segment of *Armchair Thriller*. Then he moved onto other shows, including *The Avengers*.

After disappearing from the scene for a couple of years, Goddard returned as a director, working on the arts programme *Tempo* and the dramas *Public Eye* and *Callan* amongst others. He tended to split his time between Thames Television and LWT. For the former he directed episodes of *Special Branch*, *Man at the Top*, *The Rivals of Sherlock Holmes*, *Van der Valk* and *The Sweeney*. For the latter he worked on *Manhunt*, *Budgie*, *The Guardians*, *Villains* and *New Scotland Yard*.

As the '70s became the '80s, Goddard seemed to specialise in directing crime shows, handling episodes of the hard-hitting *Target* for the BBC, plus *Hazell*, *Out* and *Fox* for Thames. He then went into historical drama with *Smuggler* and Victorian espionage with *Reilly: Ace of Spies*, before returning to crime on the feature-length shows *Inspector Morse* and *The Ruth Rendell Mysteries*.

Toward the end of the '90s and into the new century, Goddard began working exclusively for the BBC, gaining credits on shows such as *Dangerfield*, *EastEnders* and *Holby City*.

JOHN GOLDSMITH (WRITER)

John Allan Goldsmith was born on 9 April 1947 in London and gained his initial break into television scriptwriting on Gerry Anderson's series *The Protectors* and *Space: 1999*. After his involvement with *The New Avengers*, he provided screenplays for both *Return of the Saint* and *The Professionals*. There was then a seven-year gap before he scripted HTV's serial *Return to Treasure Island* in 1986. During the following decades he mainly wrote scripts for television movies, exceptions being a 1994 episode of *Lovejoy* and – his final credit to date – a 2009 drama-documentary, 'Darwin's Darkest Hour', for a US-produced series called *Nova*.

JACK GREENWOOD (PRODUCTION CONTROLLER)

Jack Ryder Greenwood was born in Yorkshire on 16 November 1919. He started out in feature films in Los Angeles as an uncredited second assistant director on the movie *Song of Russia* in 1944. He then worked on 24 films as an assistant director before changing course and becoming a producer in 1953. Returning to the UK, he worked exclusively for many years at the small, three stage Merton Park Studios. Having produced a succession of B-movies and second features, he eventually became Managing Director of the Studios, and made no fewer than 73 dramas based on the works of crime writer Edgar Wallace. Originally produced for cinema consumption over an eight year period, these films would later be packaged together and sold for television under the titles *Scotland Yard*, *The Edgar Wallace Mysteries* and *The Scales of Justice*. He then continued in the industry in executive roles. Greenwood died in April 2004.

PETER HAMMOND (DIRECTOR)

Peter C H Hill – aka Peter Hammond – was born in London on 15 November 1923 and managed not one but two careers in the world of film and television. The first was as an actor, starting out in an uncredited role in the 1945 feature film *Waterloo Road* and then amassing a steady collection of further movie credits until the mid-'50s, when he became involved in television film series. Initially this was in the form of guest-starring roles in both *The Adventures of Robin Hood* and *Sword of Freedom*. Then, with television swashbucklers very popular at the time, he got himself cast as the regular character Lieutenant Beamish in the pirate adventure series *The Buccaneers*. In a similar genre, he next took on the recurring part of Hofmanstahl in *William Tell*, before doing a little more varied film and television work that ended with three episodes of the BBC serial *The World of Tim Frazer*.

Hammond's second and greater claim to fame is as a well-respected director who was involved at the beginning of *The Avengers* and went on to work on several other ABC programmes such as *Armchair Theatre*, *Out of this World* and *A Chance of Thunder*. By the mid-'60s he had begun to get involved in BBC productions, including adaptations of both *The Three Musketeers* and *The Count of Monte Cristo*, an espionage serial called *The White Rabbit* and episodes of the anthologies *Theatre 625* and *The*

Wednesday Play. In the '70s, Hammond directed three episodes of the children's series *Follyfoot* for Yorkshire Television, then gained a steady stream of further credits that included the Anglo-Australian serial *Luke's Kingdom* and a BBC adaptation of *Wuthering Heights*.

The following decade also saw Hammond gain regular television directing work, including on a couple of episodes of the drama show *Funny Man* and five instalments of Anglia Television's *Tales of the Unexpected*. Anthologies such as this, where he could work on standalone storylines that did not involve continuity to other episodes, seemed to be a favourite area for Hammond, who continued in this vein directing two of Granada's *Shades of Darkness*. He then became involved with Granada's long-running *Sherlock Holmes* series, directing eight outings for the master detective. During the same period he also found time to complete three episodes of *Inspector Morse*.

Hammond died on 12 October 2011.

RICHARD HARRIS (WRITER)

Richard Harris was born in London in 1934. Having decided on a career in writing, he managed to have screenplays accepted in 1960 by ABC for *Police Surgeon* and the drama *Inside Story*. Having gained some experience, he then provided a couple of scripts for *The Edgar Wallace Mysteries*, followed by instalments of the soap *Harpers West One*, *The Avengers*, *The Saint*, *Ghost Squad* and *Sergeant Cork*. Around this time, he also began collaborating with Dennis Spooner on a number of comedy projects such as *Hancock*, *Comedy Playhouse*, *Foreign Affairs* and *Pardon the Expression* featuring Arthur Lowe.

Together, Harris and Spooner devised an outline for a proposed series called *McGill* which, although nothing more than a single A4 sheet of paper, was bought by Lew Grade, who later had it developed into *Man in a Suitcase*. Meanwhile, Harris continued scriptwriting solo for drama productions, supplying material for *Redcap*, *No Hiding Place* and *Adam Adamant Lives!*. After contributing 'The Winged Avenger' to *The Avengers*, he wrote episodes of *The Informer* and the BBC's *Sherlock Holmes*. These assignments were followed up by a spell as script editor on Rediffusion's anthology series *The Gamblers*, then a return to writing in the early '70s on *New Scotland Yard* and providing storyline ideas for ATV's *Spyder's Web*.

Harris provided scripts for the hard-hitting crime shows *Target*, *The Sweeney* and *Hazel*, on the latter of which he also performed story editor duties, before getting together with another friend, Robert Banks Stewart, to co-create the private detective series *Shoestring*. In the mid-'80s, there was a return to the master detective with Granada's *The Adventures of Sherlock Holmes*, before Harris forged a connection with Yorkshire Television by adapting stories for *The Darling Buds of May*. This led to him writing several feature-length episodes of *A Touch of Frost*, plus adapting the Leslie Thomas novel *Dangerous Davies: The Last Detective* as the first episode of the Meridian TV series *The Last Detective*, first shown in 2003.

SIDNEY HAYERS (DIRECTOR)

Sidney Hayers was born in Edinburgh on 24 August 1921 and became involved in film production in the early '40s, trying his hand at various different production roles before eventually becoming an editor in 1949. His association with Julian Wintle began on the film *Passage Home* in 1955 and continued after Hayers had graduated to the role of director, with him working on *The White Trap* and *Circus of Horrors*. When Wintle moved into filmed television with *The Human Jungle* and *The Avengers*, Hayers followed. In the '70s he also directed instalments for *Shirley's World*, *Arthur of the Britons* and *The Persuaders!*.

After being recalled by Brian Clemens and Albert Fennell to direct for *The New Avengers*, Hayers assumed the role of producer on *The Professionals* on the understanding that it would be for just the first season. He then produced the second season of Southern Television's *Famous Five*, though by its conclusion he had decided to return to directing, but in the USA rather than the UK. Finding himself in demand, he quickly started running up credits on many diverse shows, including *Galactica 1980*, *The Fall Guy*, *The Greatest American Hero*, *Magnum P.I.*, *Manimal* and *Remington Steele*.

By the mid-'80s Hayers was constantly in work on mainstream American series such as *T.J. Hooker*, *Airwolf*, *Knight Rider*, *The A-Team* and the revivals of both *Dragnet* and *Adam 12*. He had a brief spell in Europe to work on the programme *Blue Blood*, before returning to the States for the science fiction series *Super Force* and the fashion-models-as-spies show *Acapulco H.E.A.T.*.

Hayers' career in the visual medium ended where it started, in the UK, with him directing on Gerry Anderson's *Space Precinct* and David Wickes' *CI5: The New Professionals* at the end of the '90s. He died on 8 February 2000.

JAMES HILL (DIRECTOR)

James Hill hailed from Eldwick, near Bradford in Yorkshire, where he was born on 9 July 1919. He started his career as a writer in 1940, providing the screenplay to the film *Keeping Company*, for which he was credited as James H Hill. Then in 1949 he not only scripted but also directed the film short *A Journey for Jeremy*. Three years later he did the same on his first feature film, *The Stolen Plans*. The treble came in 1958 when he wrote and directed, and also produced, the short film *Skyhook*. By this time he had also ventured into the world of documentary-making.

By the early '60s a new challenge beckoned in the form of television film series, and Hill directed episodes of *The Saint* and *The Human Jungle*, where his association with Julian Wintle led to him also working on *The Avengers*. As the decade went on, he directed the Sherlock Holmes film *A Study in Terror*, the family film *Born Free* and the Brian Clemens-co-scripted spy movie *The Peking Medallion*, as well as the odd documentary and episodes of shows such as *Gideon's Way* and *Journey to the Unknown*. Still much in demand at the turn of the decade, he had further assignments on the feature *Captain Nemo and the Underwater City* and the low-budget secret agent flick *The Man from O.R.G.Y.*.

In the early '70s Hill directed an episode of *The Persuaders!* before assuming both writer and director roles on Wintle's family film *The Belstone Fox*. He then resumed his connection with Brian Clemens and Albert Fennell, directing a couple of episodes of *The New Avengers*. By the conclusion of the decade, however, he was working as both producer and director on *Dick Barton: Special Agent*.

Shortly after this, Hill became heavily involved with Southern's *Worzel Gummidge*, again as both producer and director. When that show concluded in 1981 he returned to freelance directing on TVS's *C.A.T.S. Eyes* and Thames' *Prospects*. When *Worzel Gummidge* was revived as *Worzel Gummidge Down Under* in New Zealand at the end of the 1980s, Hill did not resume his producer role but directed more episodes than anyone else, as well as writing three scripts for the series.

Hill's final directing credit came in 1993 on the obscure German television series *Alaska Kid*. He died on 7 October 1994.

JOHN HOUGH (DIRECTOR)

Londoner John Hough was born on 21 November 1941. He began his career in the early '60s doing uncredited work such as being third assistant director on the comedy movie *The Bargee*. Eventually he managed to get involved in television film series, becoming second unit director on *The Baron* and then *The Champions*. After his time on *The Avengers*, initially as second unit director and then as director, he directed a number of feature films, including *Wolfshead: The Legend of Robin Hood* and the chillers *Twins of Evil* and *The Legend of Hell House*.

Returning to television, Hought then directed on the ITC film series *The Protectors* and *The Zoo Gang*. A period of work in the United States followed, including on the film *Dirty Mary Crazy Larry* and, for Walt Disney Productions, the film *Escape to Witch Mountain*, its sequel *Return from Witch Mountain* and *The Watcher in the Woods*. After returning to direct episodes of *The New Avengers*, Hough saw out the remainder of the '70s with the Second World War film *Brass Target*.

In the '80s Hough directed the science fiction film *Incubus* and *Triumphs of a Man Called Horse*, followed by three instalments of *Hammer House of Mystery and Suspense* and the television movie *Black Arrow*. He then directed the First World War/time travel film *Biggles*, an episode of *Dempsey and Makepeace* and the movie *American Gothic*. After this, reuniting him with Albert Fennell and Laurie Johnson, came four Barbara Cartland television movies, on which he took on the roles of both producer and director.

Hough's association with Sir Lew Grade's company the Grade Organisation brought about another directing assignment on the 1998 film *Something to Believe In*, for which he also contributed to the screenplay. His final directing credit came on the 2002 movie *Bad Karma*, although he has since served as executive producer on a number of documentaries and *The Human Race*, a film directed by his son Paul.

MALCOLM HULKE AND TERRANCE DICKS (WRITERS)

Malcolm Hulke started out in a scriptwriting partnership with Eric Paice. Their first break came in 1958 with a BBC play called *This Day in Fear*, which provided a launch pad for them then to script an instalment of *Armchair Theatre*. After spending time working for Associated-Rediffusion on both *Tell It to the Marines* and *No Hiding Place*, they began writing for ABC, including on the *Pathfinders* serials and more *Armchair Theatre* entries. Hulke's writing work supplemented his main income, which came from running a boarding house, where in 1962 a recently-arrived lodger, Terrance Dicks, heard of his landlord's fame and decided that he really ought to meet him.

Busy with the upkeep of his property, Hulke was painting the hallway one day when Dicks engaged him in conversation regarding the possibility of entering the writing profession. Hulke encouraged Dicks to partner him in supplying a script for *The Avengers*, which became the episode 'The Mauritius Penny'.

Now with two writing collaborators, Hulke completed two further screenplays for *The Avengers* with Dicks, plus feature film and foreign television projects with Paice. Eventually in 1963 he took the plunge and wrote solo on *Sergeant Cork*. Further solo credits followed over the next few years on a variety of different television series, including ABC's *The Protectors* (not to be confused with the Gerry Anderson show of the same name), *Gideon's Way*, *Danger Man*, *No Hiding Place*, the comedy drama *Mrs Thursday* and the football soap *United!*. Then, in 1967, with his third writing collaborator David Ellis, Hulke wrote the *Doctor Who* serial 'The Faceless Ones'.

Dicks arrived at the BBC in 1968 to assume the position of assistant script editor on *Doctor Who*, being promoted to full script editor the following year. This paved the way for him and Hulke to write together again on the last *Doctor Who* serial of the '60s, 'The War Games'. Over the next five years, both men generally devoted their energies to *Doctor Who*, Hulke as a writer and Dicks as script editor. Apart from three episodes of *Crossroads*, Hulke's television career then drew to a close, and he died in July 1979. Dicks however continued his long association with *Doctor Who*, scripting several further serials, and also wrote an episode of *Space: 1999*. In the '80s he rejoined the BBC's staff to script edit various classic serials such as *Great Expectations*, *Jane Eyre* and *The Pickwick Papers*, before progressing to become producer on others such as *David Copperfield* and *Vanity Fair*.

Dicks also acquired a reputation as a novelist of original children's fiction, and adapted more *Doctor Who* serials into book form than any other writer.

DONALD JAMES (WRITER)

Donald James Wheal – aka Donald James – was born in London on 22 August 1931. He began his career as a scriptwriter in 1963, when he provided the screenplay for an episode of Rediffusion's crime show *No Hiding Place*. Gaining a foothold with ITC the following year, he contributed a couple of scripts to their Canadian-produced film series *Seaway*. He also wrote more episodes of *No Hiding Place* and some material for the American series *The Man Who Never Was*. After submitting a draft script to *The Champions'* production office on spec, he was taken on as a regular writer, eventually supplying eight scripts for the show.

James provided one screenplay for *The Avengers*, and it appears that Brian Clemens did not consider his ITC-influenced style of writing correct for the series. However, other commissions flooded in, and James wrote for *The Saint*, *Department S*, *Randall and Hopkirk (Deceased)*, *Mission: Impossible* and *Paul Temple*. For Gerry Anderson he gained credits on *Joe 90*, *The Secret Service* and then into the '70s *UFO*, *The Protectors* and *Space: 1999*. He also contributed to the ITC series *Jason King*, *The Adventurer* and *The Persuaders!*, but a jump across to the BBC for the socially-aware drama *The Befrienders* did not lead to a new avenue for his writing.

When the big-budget television film series concluded in the mid-'70s, James's career in that medium also ended, and he teamed up with fellow scriptwriter Tony Barwick to write Second World War-set novels under the pseudonym James Barwick. Later, he began writing solo again, this time concentrating his efforts on thriller novels. He died on 28 April 2008.

LAURIE JOHNSON (COMPOSER)

Laurence Reginald Ward Johnson – aka Laurie Johnson – was born in Hampstead, London on 7 February 1927. He entered the film industry in the mid-'50s after studying at the Royal College of Music and serving as a guardsman. Later he progressed to arranging with the Ted Heath Orchestra and broke into television by constructing the hard-hitting theme to the police series *No Hiding Place* and then its spin-off *Echo Four-Two*. Over the next few years he created the instrumental piece 'Las Vegas', which was used as the theme to the BBC children's series *Animal Magic*. Some recording for the Pye record label in 1963 brought about a cover version of 'Sucu Sucu', the theme to the espionage series *Top Secret*, and this became a top ten hit single.

Johnson continued writing music that became themes, such as 'Latin Quarter' for Rediffusion's multinational crime series *Riviera Police* and 'West End' for the factual *Whicker's World*. After his time with *The Avengers*, Johnson provided both themes and incidental music for a number of ITC productions: *Mister Jerico*, *The Firechasers*, *Jason King* and *Shirley's World*.

In the '70s Johnson composed for Julian Wintle's final film, *The Belstone Fox*, and followed this up with the Brian Clemens-created ATV anthology series *Thriller*. Later he provided the music for both *The New Avengers* and *The Professionals*, followed by several television movies based on novels by Barbara Cartland, taking him up to the '90s. More recently, he has spent time conducting the London Big Band.

JOHN KRISH (DIRECTOR)

John Jeffrey Krish was born in London on 4 December 1923 and gained his first experience of the film industry as a runner in 1941 before being promoted to assistant editor. Through the late '40s, '50s and early '60s he gradually progressed to become an all-rounder in the roles of editor, writer and director. He worked mainly on documentaries and movie shorts, including five instalments of *Stryker of the Yard*, a series of 34-minute films originally made in 1953/54 to accompany feature films but later amalgamated into a television series of sorts and transmitted in some ITV regions in the early '60s.

With the exception of a couple of film assignments, mainstream success appeared to elude Krish, although he did direct a solitary episode of *The Saint*. However, he understood what was required of him on *The Avengers*, assisting in establishing the look of the colour episodes by pioneering the use of unusual camera angles. After *The Avengers* there were a couple more films and a return to directing documentaries, though after the mid-'70s his output became increasingly sporadic.

QUENTIN LAWRENCE (DIRECTOR)

Nathaniel Quentin Lawrence was born in Gravesend, Kent on 6 November 1920. He became involved with ITV from when it was set up in 1955, serving as both producer and director on shows such as *Television Playhouse*, *The Strange World of Planet X* and *The Trollenberg Terror*. By the late '50s he was focusing on directing assignments, and entered the world of television film series working on both *William Tell* and *H G Wells' Invisible Man*.

Able to switch back and forth between film and videotape productions with apparent ease, in the '60s he gained further credits on shows such as *Emergency-Ward 10*, *Deadline Midnight*, *The Plane Makers*, *Danger Man*, *Gideon's Way* and, of course, *The Avengers*. At the tail end of the decade he spent some time spent in Australia, directing episodes of the series *Riptide*. When he returned to the UK at the beginning of the '70s he again took on the dual roles of producer and director on the children's favourite

Catweazle, the period drama *Albert and Victoria* and *Crown Court*. The '70s brought many more directing assignments too, including on the children's series *The Ghosts of Motley Hall*, the soaps *Emmerdale* and *Coronation Street* and finally Granada's crime show *Strangers*. Lawrence died on 9 March 1979.

DON LEAVER (DIRECTOR)

Londoner Don Leaver was born on 27 September 1929. He was under contract to ABC when he began directing on *The Avengers* in 1960, and had recently handled more episodes of *Police Surgeon* than anyone else. Over the next few years, despite his heavy workload on *The Avengers*, Leaver also directed on various other ABC shows, such as *Out of this World*, *Dimensions of Fear*, *Armchair Theatre* and *Public Eye*. Toward the conclusion of the '60s, he went freelance. He was reunited with star Ian Hendry when he directed four episodes of *The Informer*, then worked on a variety of other series including *The Gold Robbers* and Gerry Anderson's *The Protectors*.

In the '70s Leaver handled entries for ATV's *Thriller* and Nigel Kneale's *Beasts* before taking on both director and producer duties on the Southern children's serial *The Famous Five*. The '80s brought directorial outings on a couple of *Hammer House of Horror* episodes and a *Bergerac* before Leaver again combined director and producer roles on the sitcom *A Fine Romance*. Other directing credits came on the dramas *The Detective* and *The Ruth Rendell Mysteries*. The '90s saw Leaver devoting a lot of time to *A Touch of Frost*, mainly as a producer and occasionally as a director, but he still found time to direct a couple of episodes of both *Lovejoy* and *Hetty Wainthropp Investigates*. His final directing work to date was on a couple of segments of *The Bill* in 1999/2000.

PHILIP LEVENE (WRITER)

Philip Levene was born on 9 June 1926. He started out as an actor, gaining an early television role in an episode of the BBC's *Quatermass II* serial in 1955. He then moved into writing radio drama, most notably a serial called *Ambrose* about an undercover spy who poses as a professional tennis player. Another radio creation was *Destination – Fire!*, about a fire insurance investigator, and in 1970 this provided the basic concept for the feature-length ITC pilot *The Firechasers* (Levene having previously offered it to the company unsuccessfully in the early '60s under the title *Firetec*).

Apart from his radio work, Levene also provided screenplays for a number of television shows, including *The Vise*, *Knight Errant*, *H G Wells' Invisible Man*, *The Pursuers* and *Ghost Squad*. After working on *The Avengers*, he created the religious drama *Sanctuary* for Rediffusion and then in 1968 co-created the BBC drama *The First Lady*. He followed this up with the screenplay for the ITC pilot film *Mr Jerico*, which brought him back together with Patrick Macnee, Julian Wintle, Sidney Hayers and many of the crew who had worked on *The Avengers*.

Levene's final credits came in the mid-'70s, when he provided the original story outlines for the films *Diagnosis Murder* and *Deadly Strangers*. He died in March 1973.

PETER LING AND SHEILAGH WARD (WRITERS)

Peter George Derek Ling was born on 27 May 1926 in Croydon, Surrey and became involved in writing for television in 1950 with the BBC children's variety show

Whirligig, followed by his scripting of a televised version of *Aladdin*. As soon as independent television got under way in 1955, Ling teamed up with Sheilagh Ward to write the play *File on Voronov* for Associated-Rediffusion. This in turn led to another play, *Jim Whittington and his Sealion*, which was written solo and also included an acting role for Ling. Staying with Associated-Rediffusion, he provided scripts for both *Murder Bag* and the spin-off *Crime Sheet* before working on several other shows.

After writing with Ward for *The Avengers*, Ling devised two soaps together with another writer, Hazel Adair. One was the short-lived *Compact* for the BBC, but the second one had far greater longevity. This was ATV's *Crossroads*, which ran for 24 years, sometimes five nights a week.

During the remainder of the '60s, Ling wrote various instalments of *Sexton Blake* for ABC and the *Doctor Who* serial 'The Mind Robber'. In 1972 he scripted a solitary episode of the Second World War series *Pathfinders*. After this, however, his writing was restricted to scripting and planning storylines for *Crossroads*, which he did until 1986. He died on 14 September 2006.

Sheilagh Ward, by contrast, appears to have written very little material on her own, save for the obscure series *Time is the Enemy* in the late '50s.

JOHN LUCAROTTI (WRITER)

John Lucarotti was born in Aldershot, Hampshire, on 20 November 1926. It was while providing radio scripts for the Canadian Broadcasting Corporation in 1956 that he first met Sydney Newman. Breaking into television scriptwriting the following year, he contributed to the Canadian series *Tomahawk* before returning to the UK, where he worked on Associated-Rediffusion's *Murder Bag*. He was brought onto *The Avengers* at around the same time as Reed de Rouen, serving for a time as an uncredited story editor and also being privy to interdepartmental memos and policy decisions. However, this was only a temporary position: Lucarotti turned down the opportunity to become a permanent story editor on the show, preferring to continue as a freelance scriptwriter.

In the early '60s, he went on to provide screenplays for ABC's science fiction serials *City Beneath the Sea* and *Secret Beneath the Sea*. Around this time he also worked on *Ghost Squad*, both writing original material and scripting other writers' outlines. He then began working for the BBC, writing 15 episodes of *Doctor Who* and 22 of *The Troubleshooters*. He still found sufficient time to pen three episodes of Granada Television's detective show *The Man in Room 17* and a solitary outing of Gerry Anderson's *Joe 90*. The '70s brought further BBC credits on series such as *Brett* and *Paul Temple*. Lucarotti then became involved with LWT's *New Scotland Yard* and more science fiction with the BBC's *Moonbase 3*. This theme continued in 1976 with the Anglo-German production *Star Maidens* and a serialisation of *Treasure Island* also for the BBC. Ling ending his career writing on the children's serials *The Ravelled Thread* and *Into the Labyrinth* in 1981. He died on 20 November 1994.

DON MacPHERSON (MOVIE WRITER)

Born on 7 September 1954, Don MacPherson had an early career as a journalist, working on *Screen International*, *Time Out*, *City Limits*, *The Face* and *The Sunday Times*, before becoming employed by the BBC on their television documentary series *Arena*.

His big break into writing for the film business came when he provided the screenplay for the 1976 movie *The Bawdy Adventures of Tom Jones*. He followed this up with another movie, *The Third Front*, a couple of years later. However, it was not until 1986 that he received his third feature film credit, with *Absolute Beginners*. He then wrote the three-part television mini-series *The Dark Angel*, screened in December 1987.

Returning to feature films, MacPherson scripted *Big Man*, released in 1990, and also performed uncredited rewriting duties on *Alien 3*. After the movie version of *The Avengers* in 1998, he specialised in rewriting other writers' screenplays, working uncredited on such films as *Godzilla*, *Entrapment*, *Possession* and *Hippy Hippy Shake*. His most recent screen credit came as writer of the 2014 movie *The Gunman*.

MAX MARQUIS (WRITER)

Max Marquis mainly contributed solitary scripts to the series he worked on in the early '60s, such as *Harpers West One*, *Ghost Squad* and Associated-Rediffusion's ratings-winning crime drama *No Hiding Place*. In the latter half of the decade he worked more for the BBC, performing script editor duties on both the crime anthology show *Detective* and an early forensic scientist crime-buster *The Expert*. As before, there were also one-off screenplays for other television series, including *The Revenue Men* and the science fiction series *Counterstrike*. His final credit came on the Norman Wisdom sitcom *A Little Bit of Wisdom*.

ANTHONY MARRIOTT (WRITER)

Anthony Marriott entered the world of television scriptwriting by penning an episode of *Ghost Squad* in 1961, before writing eight adventures for Gerry Anderson's outer space puppet series *Fireball XL5* and then co-creating *Public Eye*. Screenplays for the films *Every Day's a Holiday* and *The Ghost of Monk's Island* followed, which led to *The Avengers* and then solitary episodes of both *No Hiding Place* and *This Man Craig*, before he received a co-writing credit on the movie *The Deadly Bees*. In the '70s he supplied a script for ITC's *From a Bird's Eye View*, but moving into other areas he then worked on foreign television projects and began writing plays for the theatre, including the successful *No Sex Please: We're British*.

ROGER MARSHALL (WRITER)

Roger Marshall was born in Leicestershire in 1934. He began writing when at university in Cambridge, then began attending interviews for scriptwriting jobs. Being successful with the ABPC, he began working for them at Elstree Studios, where he wrote reports on stage plays and scripts, learnt script construction by watching films and generally improved his writing skills. After a while, he moved to the nearby Neptune Studios and worked on *William Tell*, before his earlier association with an American script editor took him to the USA and a chance to work on the American show *Sea Hunt*. Returning to the UK in 1960, he then worked for Granada on the thriller *Knight Errant Limited*, and this paved the way for him to work with Associated-Rediffusion on their shows *No Hiding Place* and *Top Secret*.

From there Marshall managed to get on board the second season of *The Avengers*, contributing three screenplays, the first two co-written with Jeremy Scott, whom he met while they were both contributing to the series *Knight Errant*. It was Marshall who suggested that they collaborate on scripts for *The Avengers*, which they both considered to be more stylish than the other television thrillers of the time. He has gone on record as saying that he thought writing for the show was a gamble that could go horribly wrong, and if he shared the credit, likewise any blame associated with it would also be shared. However, when interviewed in 2005 for the magazine *Action TV* he stated, 'I only collaborate with people if they can bring something extra to the show as generally I find it hard to work with co-writers.'

Marshall wrote another four scripts for season three of *The Avengers*, one of them with Phyllis Norman. When the series went on to 35mm film he still found himself much in demand, being commissioned to provide seven scripts for Diana Rigg's first year. By 1965 he was well established at ABC, having also worked on *Redcap* and co-created *Public Eye*. Though his involvement with *The Avengers* was coming to an end, he would go on to become one of the all-time great British television writers and was still active up to the mid-'90s, when he was working on series as diverse as *Lovejoy* and *London's Burning*.

RAYMOND MENMUIR (DIRECTOR)

Raymond Menmuir began his career in Australia working on one-off productions in 1960. Then in the early '60s he spent several years directing for Associated-Rediffusion on series including *Tales of Mystery*, *Top Secret*, *Crane* and *No Hiding Place*, before spending some time with ABC on *The Avengers* and *Redcap*. Over the next couple of years, he gained some BBC credits, including on *The Wednesday Play*, *The Troubleshooters* and *The Expert*. He then moved on to direct shows as diverse as ATV's *Fraud Squad* and Thames' *Zodiac*.

Throughout the '70s, Menmuir continued to find himself in demand, directing a dozen episodes of *Upstairs, Downstairs* and following that up with work on the spy series *Quiller* and the period dramas *The Onedin Line* and *The Duchess of Duke Street*.

Accepting a new challenge in 1977, he became the producer of the BBC's short-lived drama *Headmaster*. He then took over as producer on the fast-moving film series *The Professionals* from its second season, guiding it through four successful years. Subsequently he returned to Australia to produce a similar show called *Special Squad*. In 1986, TVS considered Menmuir to be the right person to take over the reins of their action show *C.A.T.S. Eyes*, which in turn led to him also producing the drama *Gentlemen and Players* a couple of years later.

KIM MILLS (DIRECTOR)

Londoner Kim Mills was born in 1931. After gaining a foothold in the business by serving as an assistant director on a couple of films, he joined ABC in 1961 and directed an episode of the serial *Plateau of Fear* and two instalments of *City Beneath the Sea* before starting work on *The Avengers*. Staying with ABC/Thames Television for the majority of his career, he worked as a director, producer and executive producer on a variety of shows, including *Mystery and Imagination*, *Armchair Theatre*, *Zodiac* and *The Gentle Touch*. He died in 2006.

JAMES MITCHELL (WRITER)

James Mitchell was born on 12 March 1926 in South Shields, Tyne and Wear and received his break into the business in 1959 by providing the script for the second feature *Flight from Treason*, a spy drama produced by Leonard White, which was later amalgamated into the first season of the American NBC network's *Kraft Mystery Theatre*. Strengthening his credentials as a writer suitable for *The Avengers*, he had also been penning espionage novels for a number of years, some of which were issued under the pseudonyms Patrick O McGuire and James Munro.

As with most writers associated with ABC, Mitchell also contributed to *Armchair Theatre*. Other credits came on the Granada anthology series *Play of the Week* and the BBC's police show *Z Cars*. After his time on *The Avengers*, Mitchell wrote a solitary script for Associated-Rediffusion's *Crane* and then five episodes of the BBC's oil industry drama *The Troubleshooters*.

Mitchell's greatest creation arrived in 1967 with his second *Armchair Theatre* script, 'A Magnum for Schneider', which served as a pilot for a show featuring his character David Callan, a reluctant professional killer who works for a branch of British Intelligence. Four seasons of *Callan* kept Mitchell busy until the early '70s, although he did find time to script some episodes of Yorkshire's drama series *Justice*.

A number of *Callan* novels followed, then Mitchell moved to the BBC, where he created another long-running series in the form of *When the Boat Comes In*, a period drama set in Tyneside just after the First World War. This kept him occupied until 1981, when he devised another BBC drama, *Goodbye Darling*, and wrote a *Callan* television movie, 'Wet Job'. Following this he wrote the Anglo-Australian mini-series *Spyship*.

Though he did a little more scriptwriting up to the conclusion of the '80s, Mitchell then dropped out of television work, preferring to concentrate on writing novels.

JOHN MOXEY (DIRECTOR)

John Llewellyn Moxey was born on 26 February 1925 in Argentina into a wealthy family who relocated to Surrey when he was about six years old. On returning to civilian life after serving with the British Army during Second World War, he wanted to get involved in movie-making. He initially found work editing, but during the late '40s and early '50s he made his way up through the various levels of assistant director. He made the final leap to being a fully-fledged director in 1955 with the arrival of independent television, working on the drama anthologies *Play of the Week* and *London Playhouse*.

By 1960 Moxey had a steady supply of directing work, including on *Television Playhouse* and *Armchair Theatre*, the films *The City of the Dead* and *Foxhole in Cairo* and the television film series *The Cheaters*. He soon ventured into directing episodes of two of the most popular series of the time, *Coronation Street* and *Z Cars*, and also gained film series assignments on *Man of the World*, *The Saint* and *Gideon's Way*. He then became associated with the television version of *The Third Man*, not only as a director but also as a producer.

More film series directing assignments followed as Moxey's talents were brought to bear on *The Baron*, *The Avengers* and *The Champions*. He then decided to relocate to the United States. In the late '60s and early '70s, directing work on American shows was plentiful, and Moxey soon gained credits on *Judd for the Defence*, *Mannix* and *Mission:*

Impossible. He had been credited on some of his early work under his full name, John Llewellyn Moxey, and adopted this universally in 1971, apparently after being advised to do so by a numerologist during a quiet spell for work.

In the '70s Moxey directed further episodes of American series such as *Hawaii Five-O* and *Kung Fu*, and a number of television movies, including one of his proudest achievements, *Kolchak: The Night Stalker*. Along the way there were an instalment of *Ghost Story*, Gene Roddenberry's pilot film *Genesis II* and an episode of the short-lived *Shaft* series.

The directing assignments kept coming through to the early '80s, mainly on television movies – although, having handled the original *Charlie's Angels* pilot film in 1976, Moxey worked with star Kate Jackson again on an episode of *Scarecrow and Mrs King* in 1983. This return to television series led to Moxey also directing on *Magnum P.I.*, *Miami Vice*, *Matlock* and *Jake and the Fatman*. His final credits came on *Murder She Wrote*, for which he directed 18 episodes between 1984 and 1991.

TERRY NATION (SCRIPT EDITOR, WRITER)

Terry Nation was born in Cardiff on 8 August 1930. He entered the entertainment industry by writing gags for radio, then made the transition to television with contributions to sketch shows like *The Idiot Weekly, Price 2d*. Over the next few years the Welshman proved himself to be a versatile scriptwriter, turning his hand to the comedy film *What a Whopper*, episodes of the science fiction anthology series *Out of this World*, drama with episodes of *No Hiding Place* and sitcom material for *Hancock*. It was after a disagreement with the latter's star Tony Hancock that Nation became involved with the BBC's *Doctor Who*, for which he invented the famous Daleks.

Besides returning from time to time to create new adventures for the Doctor and his adversaries, Nation also began writing for film series, starting with *The Saint* and then *The Baron*, on which he was also the script supervisor. Along the way he also provided screenplays for *Out of the Unknown*, *The Champions* and *Department S*. After his contributions to *The Avengers*, he collaborated with Brian Clemens on the screenplay of the mystery thriller film *And Soon the Darkness*. Shortly after this, he became both script editor and associate producer on ITC's big-budget film series *The Persuaders!*.

Returning to the BBC in 1972, Nation wrote *The Incredible Robert Baldick*: 'Never Come Night', a pilot for a potential series about a Victorian adventurer who deals with the supernatural. However, the series failed to materialise, and Nation returned to being a jobbing writer on *The Protectors*, *Thriller* and the Frankie Howerd comedy mystery movie *The House in Nightmare Park*.

Through the late '70s and into the early '80s Nation worked exclusively for the BBC, creating and writing for *Survivors* and *Blake's 7* as well as scripting the occasional further *Doctor Who* serial. He then moved to the United States, where he spent a short period of time as a producer on the series *MacGyver* but contributed only a small amount of writing to it. His final credits came with the television movie *A Masterpiece of Murder* in 1986 and an episode of the comedy thriller *A Fine Romance* (called *Ticket to Ride* in the UK) three years later. He died on 9 March 1997.

SYDNEY NEWMAN (ABC HEAD OF DRAMA)

Sydney Cecil Newman was born on 1 April 1917 in Toronto, Canada, where he showed an early interest in the moving image by working as a commercial artist designing film and theatre posters in the late '30s. In 1938 he travelled to Hollywood, where he was offered a job by Disney as an animator. However, unable to get an American work permit, he had to return to his homeland. Three years later he joined the National Film Board of Canada, where he found opportunities in abundance to become involved in the making of wartime public information shorts and army training films, giving him experience and skills in various roles, including directing, writing, editing and camera operating.

Newman eventually became executive producer on all Canadian government films, then spent over a year in New York on secondment to the NBC network, studying the techniques for outside broadcasting and making drama productions. This was to his advantage as he was later appointed supervising director of outside broadcasting when the Canadian Broadcasting Corporation (CBC) began transmitting their television service in 1952. In a couple of years he was promoted to supervisor of drama, becoming responsible for the anthology series *Ford Television Theatre*, *General Motors Theatre*, *On Camera* and *First Performance*, where he encouraged new writers to become involved in Canada's television industry.

One of the most successful plays from *General Motors Theatre* was 'Flight into Danger', the storyline of which involved the passengers and crew of an in-flight aircraft being stricken with food poisoning. This was screened in the UK by the BBC and came to the attention of ABC's Managing Director Howard Thomas, who was impressed enough to do some research and discover that Newman had been the supervising producer. Thinking that ABC could do with someone of Newman's abilities, Thomas arranged for the Canadian to join both himself and the then Head of Drama, Dennis Vance, for lunch at The Ivy restaurant in London on Christmas Eve 1957. The end result of this was that a deal was sealed to have Newman cross the Atlantic and take over as the producer of *Armchair Theatre*.

Taking up his post in April 1958, Newman had been with ABC only three days when he was promoted to Head of Drama, taking over from Vance, who was more interested in pursuing his career as a producer and director. In his four years with ABC, Newman established a reputation with *Armchair Theatre* by ditching adaptations of the classics and period dramas and replacing them with gritty stories of everyday people that the viewing public could easily identify with. Besides working on *Armchair Theatre* and being involved in launching both *Police Surgeon* and *The Avengers*, Newman was also the producer on a number of children's science fiction serials in the early '60s, including *Counter-Attack*, *Target Luna* and its sequels *Pathfinders in Space*, *Pathfinders to Mars* and *Pathfinders to Venus*.

With *Armchair Theatre* proving to be a regular ratings-winner, Newman was head-hunted by the BBC's Managing Director, Kenneth Adam, who wanted him to 'change sides' and become their Head of Drama. Although this meant a decrease in salary, Newman saw it as an opportunity to be creative in another environment, and this appealed to him so much that he wrote a letter of resignation to ABC. However, ABC refused to accept this and insisted that he work out the remaining 18 months of his contract. Regretfully he had to advise Adam that he was unavailable; but much to his surprise the BBC had so much confidence in his abilities that they were prepared to wait until he was free.

Newman replaced Michael Barry as the BBC's Head of Drama on 12 December 1962, beginning five years with the Corporation. There he was instrumental in getting various series off the ground, including *The Wednesday Play*, *The Forsyte Saga*, *Adam Adamant Lives!* and the creation for which he is now best known, *Doctor Who*.

When his contract came up for renewal at the end of 1967, the BBC were keen to keep Newman, but instead he decided to join the ABPC as their head of production, keen to take on new challenges working in feature films. Unfortunately this all came to nothing when, after 18 months, EMI bought out the company and he was made redundant. After turning down the chance to work for the BBC again as an executive producer, Newman returned to Canada in 1970 where he became a special advisor to the Canadian Radio-Television Commission, spending the rest of the decade acting as a consultant to official bodies involved with the film industry there.

Returning to the UK in 1981, Newman attempted unsuccessfully to develop a drama series for Channel 4 based on the writers, artists and philosophers of the Bloomsbury Group who worked during the first half of the 20th Century. Then in 1986 he met up with the then Controller of BBC1 Michael Grade, who was disappointed with the current state of *Doctor Who* and enquired if he would be interested in revamping the series. A discussion was arranged between Newman and the then Head of Drama Jonathan Powell, but it seems the two men did not see eye to eye and the proposals went no further.

Newman died of a heart attack in Toronto, Canada, in 1997.

LESLIE NORMAN (DIRECTOR)

Leslie Norman was born in London on 23 February 1911. He made his way into the film business as an editor on the 1930 feature film *Compromising Daphne*, then remained mainly in that area of production despite also trying his hand at scriptwriting. His initial directing credit came in 1939 on the film *Too Dangerous to Live*. However, for the time being he concentrated on being an associate producer, then progressing to taking full control as a producer. By the mid-'50s Norman had made a conscious decision to specialise in directing, taking charge of the action on Hammer Films' science fiction movie *X: The Unknown*, released in 1956.

After averaging a film a year for the next few years, Norman transferred to television film series in 1964, directing episodes of both *Gideon's Way* and *The Saint* – eventually handling as many as 21 of the latter. He then began clocking up credits on various different series such as *The Baron*, *The Champions*, *The Avengers*, *Randall and Hopkirk (Deceased)* and *Department S*.

In the '70s, further assignments came on *Shirley's World*, *The Persuaders!* and the Thames' series *Pathfinders*. At the end of the decade Norman gained his final credits on episodes of *Return of the Saint*. He died on 18 February 1993.

GERRY O'HARA (DIRECTOR)

Gerry O'Hara was born in 1924 in Boston, Lincolnshire and began his career in the film business in 1946 as assistant director on the movie *Loyal Heart*, credited as Gerald O'Hara. He kept busy throughout the '50s on various films and several episodes of the early BBC film series *Stryker of the Yard*, now generally billed with his first name as

Gerry and occasionally even as Jerry. He became a fully-fledged film director in 1963 on the feature *That Kind of Girl*, and two years later both directed and scripted another film, *The Pleasure Girls*.

After working on *The Avengers*, O'Hara directed the crime film *Maroc 7* and solitary episodes of both *Man in a Suitcase* and the horror anthology *Journey to the Unknown*. In the '70s he focused mainly on film projects, although at the end of the decade he returned to television, forming a partnership with Raymond Menmuir on the fast-moving action series *The Professionals*, on which he served as script editor for four seasons. He then assumed the same position on the Australian equivalent, *Special Squad*.

Along the way, O'Hara found time to provide the screenplays for the Joan Collins film *The Bitch* and an episode of *Bergerac*. Then he became executive story editor on the last two seasons of TVS's *C.A.T.S. Eyes*.

In the '90s O'Hara continued both writing and the directing, providing the storyline for the television movie *Incident at Victoria Falls* and calling the action on an episode of *Press Gang* and the feature film *The Mummy Lives*.

CLIFF OWEN (DIRECTOR)

Having been born in London on 22 April 1919, Cliff Owen worked his way up from the bottom of the ladder in the film industry, starting out as an uncredited third assistant director on the 1947 feature *Brighton Rock*. After progressing to uncredited second assistant director, he became assistant director on the 1951 feature film *The Magic Box*, for which he was finally credited on screen.

With the arrival of independent television in 1955, Owen transferred to work on the small screen, and in the process became a fully-fledged director, initially on *London Playhouse* and then on the courtroom drama *Boyd QC*. Between 1957 and 1961 his talents were much in demand, especially on the anthologies *Television Playhouse* and *Play of the Week*, plus *The Third Man* television series and *Knight Errant Limited*.

Owen then made a conscious effort to focus his directing abilities back toward the cinema, working on films such as *The Wrong Arm of the Law* and *A Man Could Get Killed* and collaborating with Morecambe and Wise on *That Riviera Touch* and *The Magnificent Two*. After *The Avengers* there was a little more television directing work on *The Adventures of Don Quick*, then another return to the big screen for projects including the feature film versions of *No Sex Please: We're British*, *Steptoe and Son* and *The Bawdy Adventures of Tom Jones*, which gave him his final credit in 1976. Owen died in November 1994.

ERIC PAICE (WRITER)

Born on 13 November 1926 in Pevensey, East Sussex, Eric Paice first became involved in scriptwriting in 1958 when he co-wrote with Malcolm Hulke a one-off drama for the BBC called *This Day in Fear*. This led to them trying their hands at sitcoms, writing for both *Gert and Daisy* and *Tell It To The Marines*, before changing tack and giving crime drama a go with an episode of *No Hiding Place*. Moving to ABC brought considerably more work in the form of several scripts for *Armchair Theatre* and the children's serial *Target Luna* and its various *Pathfinders* sequels. Following this came the screenplay for the B-movie *The Man in the Back Seat*.

There were writing assignments in both Germany and Sweden before Paice and

Hulke decided to go their separate ways. It was around this time that Paice became involved with *The Avengers*, for which he would continue producing screenplays for the next three years. He also found time to contribute to the BBC's soap *Compact* and ATV's Victorian detective drama *Sergeant Cork*.

In 1963, Paice started writing for the BBC's long-running police series *Dixon of Dock Green*, where over the next 11 years he would provide scripts for 42 episodes and act as the script editor/supervisor on 29 more. Along the way he continued to accumulate other writing credits, including on a couple of episodes of *The Expert*, the Australian detective show *Boney* and five episodes of the Anglo-German sci-fi show *Star Maidens*, which he also created.

At the conclusion of the '70s, Paice delivered two scripts for the BBC's *Secret Army* and also co-created the airline series *Buccaneer*. His final scriptwriting came on the 1986 drama *Strike it Rich!*.

ALAN PATILLO (WRITER)

Alan Pattillo became involved with the visual medium in 1958 as sound editor on the feature film *No Time to Die*. Two years later he became a director on Gerry Anderson's puppet series *Four Feather Falls*. Continuing to direct, he gained further credits on the later Anderson puppet shows *Supercar*, *Fireball XL5*, *Stingray* and *Thunderbirds*. For the latter of these he also scripted various adventures, which led to his one-off writing assignment on *The Avengers*.

After this there were more scriptwriting duties on both *Captain Scarlet and the Mysterons* and *UFO*, and editing work on *Strange Report* and another Anderson show, *Space: 1999*.

Throughout the '80s, Pattillo concentrated on editing a succession of television movies, although he was drawn back to directing again on Anderson's puppet offering *Terrahawks*. In 2008 he co-directed a 'new' *Stingray* episode, 'The Reunion Party', assembled from newly-discovered unused footage shot in the '60s and excerpts from existing episodes.

LUDOVIC PETERS (WRITER)

Ludovic Peters was the pseudonym of Peter Ludovic Brent, who was born on 26 July 1931 and wrote a number of crime thriller novels during the '60s and into the early '70s. He began his scriptwriting career in 1962 with an episode of Associated-Rediffusion's smuggling drama *Crane*. After his contribution to *The Avengers*, he wrote several more scripts for *Crane* and then a couple for its spin-off *Orlando*, followed by a solitary episode of *The Man in Room 17* for Granada. From this point forward he worked exclusively for the BBC on their dramas *Champion House*, *The Troubleshooters* and *Detective*, ending his scriptwriting career in 1972 with an episode of the police series *Dixon of Dock Green*.

GORDON L T SCOTT (PRODUCTION EXECUTIVE)

Born on 3 January 1920 in Edinburgh, Scotland, Gordon L T Scott served as an officer in the British Army, attaining the rank of Major, before breaking into the film industry as an uncredited second assistant director on the 1947 film *Frieda*. Two years later, he had risen to be an assistant director on the film *Passport to Pimlico*, and by 1959 he had become a producer on both the film *Don't Look Back in Anger* and the television series *International Detective*. After gaining further producer credits on several ABPC films in the early '60s, he moved upstairs, becoming an executive. He returned to the studio floor for *The Avengers*, then continued his career during the '70s as an associate producer on various films. He produced Gene Roddenberry's television pilot *Spectre* in 1977, and his last credit came on the movie *Out of the Darkness* in 1985. He died on 2 April 1991.

PETER GRAHAM SCOTT (DIRECTOR)

Peter Graham Scott, born in East Sheen, Surrey on 27 October 1923, became one of the true all-rounders of the film and television world. Assistant director, director, producer, writer, editor and production manager; he performed all of these functions at various times during his career, and was seemingly just as comfortable recording live to videotape as he was controlling a full film crew. He started out as an uncredited third assistant director in 1940 on the film *Room for Two* before trying his hand as a scriptwriter on the 1942 feature *C.E.M.A.*. By 1948 he had progressed through the production ranks to become a director on the film *Panic at Madame Tussaud's*. Then in 1955 he branched into television as a producer on *London Playhouse*.

By now he was directing at least two films a year, and one of these assignments was on Julian Wintle's *Breakout*, released in 1959, which led on to further collaborations on the features *Devil's Bait*, *The Big Day* and *Father Came Too*. Ever versatile, Scott became involved in directing studio television drama with six instalments of *Television Playhouse*, plus film series with seven 25-minute episodes of *Danger Man*.

Juggling his various talents, Scott became producer on the serial *The Citadel* and then the horror anthology series *Tales of Mystery*, and directed more video material on *Play of the Week* and *Redcap*. However, he found himself particularly in demand for directing film series, resulting in stints on *Sir Francis Drake*, *Zero One*, *The Avengers*, *Court Martial* and *The Prisoner*.

From the late '60s onwards, Scott usually took the dual roles of producer and occasional director on the various television series he worked on, starting with the BBC dramas *That Man Craig*, *The Troubleshooters* and *The Borderers*. He followed these up with six shorts under the collective title of *The Magnificent 6½*, only ever screened as supporting features in cinemas. Returning to the BBC, he took control of *The Onedin Line* and then *Quiller*. Later, he joined HTV to both produce and direct on the children's serials *Children of the Stones*, *Follow Me* and *The Doombolt Chase*.

At the start of the '80s Scott was producer on the HTV/Columbia television movie *The Curse of King Tut's Tomb*. He then not only produced but also wrote and directed for the HTV fantasy serial *Into the Labyrinth*. Throughout the rest of the decade he worked mainly on a succession of television movies, taking his final credit in 1988 on *Freedom Fighter*. He died on 5 August 2007.

VERNON SEWELL (DIRECTOR)

Born in London on 4 July 1903, Vernon Campbell Sewell entered the film business in 1933 as a director, though he also dabbled in scriptwriting. He worked throughout the '40s and '50s on a mixture of shorts, documentaries and B-movies, but his only credit on a television film series came on an episode of *Sailor of Fortune*. In the '60s he became associated with low-budget films, including the horror movies *The Blood Beast Terror* and *Curse of the Crimson Altar*, before the episode 'The Great Great Britain Crime' gave him his only directing credit on *The Avengers*.

Sewell's final directing credit was on another horror movie, *Burke and Hare*, released in 1972. He then retired to live in South Africa, where he died on 21 June 2001.

DON SHARP (DIRECTOR)

Don Sharp originally hailed from Hobart, Tasmania, where he was born on 14 April 1922. He entered the film industry in 1950 as the producer of the movie *Ha'penny Breeze*, but quickly got more strings to his bow by trying his hand at both directing and acting. Finally, he decided that being a director was his chosen path, and he worked in that capacity on various '60s gothic horror films, usually starring Christopher Lee, as well as episodes of ITC's *Ghost Squad* and ABC's *The Human Jungle*. His career also encompassed directing a couple of Harry Alan Towers' *Fu Manchu* films during the '60s, the *Callan* feature film released in 1974 and an instalment of *Hammer House of Horror*. He both directed and collaborated on the script of the movie version of Alistair MacLean's *Bear Island* made in 1978/79, before finishing off his career in the '80s directing a mixture of television movies, series episodes, mini-series and the film *What Waits Below*. He died on 14 December 2011.

DENNIS SPOONER (WRITER)

Dennis Spooner was born on 1 December 1932 in Tottenham, London and, despite little in the way of education or qualifications, became one of the all-time great writers of British television film series. Leaving school in 1945 he continued to learn part-time, but took his first job working for the Post Office as a telegram delivery boy. Along the way he became interested in writing, performing and football, playing for Leyton Orient as a teenager. He also got involved in Ralph Reader Gang Shows being rehearsed in a Mission Hall just across the street from where he lived, making various appearances in these until he was called up to do National Service in the RAF. Posted to Egypt, he began organising entertainment at the camp where he was stationed, and eventually he came to the attention of the Combined Services Entertainments, which led to both concert party and radio work. After being demobbed, he returned to the UK and became a stand-up comedian, also performing as half of a double act with straight man Leslie Darbon, who later wrote for *Department S*.

Although his self-written material was good, his performances were not, so Spooner soon settled into writing gags for other comedians, mainly for radio. By 1955 he had progressed to television, providing jokes and sketches for Val Parnell's *Showtime* and *The Arthur Haynes Show* and scripts for the sitcom *Tell It to the Marines* – the latter type of work paying substantially better. Spooner had now acquired himself an agent based at Associated London Scripts, which is where he met fellow writers Johnny Speight and Terry Nation. From there his writing abilities were brought to bear on *Coronation Street*, and in 1961 on a couple of the early videotaped episodes of *The Avengers* and the police series *No Hiding Place*.

Shortly after this Spooner became acquainted with Gerry Anderson. He scripted eight puppet space adventures for *Fireball XL5* and also worked on the next two

Supermarionation series, *Stingray* and *Thunderbirds*. Early in 1963 he teamed up with another writer, Richard Harris, and over the next three years they contributed scripts to *Hancock*, *Comedy Playhouse*, *Foreign Affairs*, *Pardon the Expression* and *Six of the Best*. They also devised a drama/action format they called *McGill*, which later became *Man in a Suitcase*.

When not working with Harris, Spooner was writing mainly historical serials for the BBC's *Doctor Who*, a show on which he became story editor in 1965. It was while working at the *Doctor Who* production office that he received a phone call from Terry Nation, who had recently been appointed script supervisor on *The Baron* at ABPC's Elstree Studios. Nation offered Spooner a writing job on the new series and, seeing this as a positive career move, he accepted. Spooner was informed that he would have to provide only half a dozen scripts, but in the event almost all of the remaining episodes were written by him, Nation or jointly between the two of them.

Spooner's duties on *The Baron* went beyond being just a contracted writer, as he also provided the screenplay for the pilot episode, 'Diplomatic Immunity', and served as an uncredited associate script supervisor. Perhaps most importantly he also met producer Monty Berman, and together they went on to invent a succession of other television film series backed by Lew Grade's ITC, beginning with *The Champions* and continuing with *Department S* and *Randall and Hopkirk (Deceased)*. Then in the '70s there came *Jason King* and *The Adventurer*. Still keeping his hand in as a writer, Spooner also contributed scripts to both *Paul Temple* and *Doomwatch* for the BBC.

The demand for Spooner's services continued during the remainder of the decade as he wrote for both *UFO* and *The Protectors* for Gerry Anderson and collaborated with Brian Clemens on episodes of *Thriller*, *Comedy Premiere* and *The New Avengers*. Later, he both wrote and spent some time script editing on both *The Professionals* and *Bergerac*, although he later stated that neither was really his kind of series.

Spooner's final credits came during the '80s on the anthology *Hammer House of Mystery and Suspense*, the American series *Remington Steele* and the children's show *Dramarama*. He died on 20 September 1986.

FREDERICK STARKE (HONOR BLACKMAN'S WARDROBE DESIGNER)

Having been born into a family of clothing producers, Frederick Starke started up his own manufacturing label in the late 1920s and followed this up with his own retail outlet in Bruton Street, London after the Second World War. Eventually he became the director of the Fashion House Group of London, a consortium of 38 individual companies that promoted their wares via television exposure, having worked with Lew Grade's ITC since supplying fashion items for *Man of the World* in 1962. In addition to being credited for designing Honor Blackman's wardrobe, Starke arranged a deal with the Clarks footwear company to start supplying her black leather kinky boots – although her original pair had been specially made by Anello and Davide of Covent Garden, London.

ROBERT BANKS STEWART (WRITER)

Scotsman Robert Banks Stewart was born in Edinburgh on 16 July 1931. He began his career as a story editor at Pinewood Studios before breaking into television scriptwriting on the crime show *Knight Errant Limited*. From the early to mid-'60s, he worked as a jobbing writer, providing screenplays for various series including *Danger Man*, *Ghost Squad*, *Top Secret* and *The Human Jungle*, which paved the way for his writing on *The Avengers*. Up to this point he had been credited simply as Robert Stewart, but around 1963 he acquired a new agent, Beryl Vertue, who pointed out that there were several other industry professionals with the same surname and suggested that in future he should use his middle name as well.

As the '60s continued, Stewart worked as script consultant on ABC's science fiction show *Undermind*, script edited several instalments of *Armchair Theatre* and wrote episodes of various other series including *Adam Adamant Lives!*, *Callan* and *Public Eye*. He then spent some time in Australia, becoming both the associate producer and a writer on *Riptide* in 1969.

Returning to the UK in the '70s, Stewart quickly picked up where he had left off, scripting episodes of *Fraud Squad*, *Special Branch*, *Jason King*, *Arthur of the Britons*, *The Protectors* and *The Sweeney*. For the BBC he wrote a couple of *Doctor Who* serials, while for Thames he served as script editor on the soap *Rooms* and the mystery series *Armchair Thriller* and devised the children's serial *Jukes of Piccadilly*. He then wrote all six episodes of *Charles Endell Esq* for Scottish Television.

In the '80s Stewart resumed his association the BBC, inventing two successful detective shows in *Shoestring* and *Bergerac* and two not so successful ones in *Call Me Mister* and *Moon and Son*. He also served as producer on the first seasons of both *Lovejoy* and *Hannay*. His final writing credits came at the start of the 2000s on Yorkshire Television's adaptation of *My Uncle Silas*.

PETER SYKES (DIRECTOR)

Peter Sykes was born on 17 June 1939 in Melbourne, Australia. He furthered his dreams of becoming involved in film-making by moving to the UK, where he devised the documentary *Interlude* in 1965. Progressing in the industry, he became a production assistant on the feature film *Herostratus*, then directed the obscure 1968 film *The Committee*, featuring the music of Pink Floyd. This got him noticed and led to him directing on *The Avengers*. After this he called the shots on the horror movies *Demons of the Mind* and *Venom* and turned his hand to comedy on *Steptoe and Son Ride Again*. Making a brief return to television, he directed five instalments of the anthology series *Orson Welles' Great Mysteries* and a number of episodes of the soap *Emmerdale Farm*. Another film credit came on Hammer Films' *To the Devil a Daughter*.

By the early '80s Sykes had returned to working on documentaries, but he gained his final directing credits on three episodes of the comedy drama *The Irish R.M.* in 1984. He died on 1 March 2006.

HOWARD THOMAS (ABC MANAGING DIRECTOR)

Howard Thomas was born in Monmouthshire, Wales on 5 March 1909, but at the age of nine moved with his family to Manchester, where some years later he commenced employment as an accounts typist with an industrial company. He wrote both newspaper articles and plays as a hobby, and this brought him a promotion to the company's advertising department. Socialising with others in the advertising industry put him in a position to move to a Manchester agency, F John Roe, and then later a London one, F C Prichard Wood and Partners.

Throughout this time, Thomas continued writing articles, contributing regularly to the *Manchester Evening News*. This brought him to the attention of the London Press Exchange, who gave him a position working in radio. His job was to assemble radio shows as commercial packages that served as advertising for large companies such as Cadburys. These were broadcast on Radio Luxemburg and other long-wave stations.

During the Second World War, Thomas became involved with BBC radio, producing several variety and entertainment shows. He also co-created the successful panel game *The Brains Trust*, which after almost a decade on radio eventually became a television show as well.

Resigning from the BBC in 1944, Thomas found himself approached by the ABPC with an offer to run their newsreel service Pathé Pictures Ltd (later British Pathé), which he accepted. By his own later admission, it took him about three years to bring in new ideas, re-equip and reorganise Pathé, making them a major player in the world of news reporting, whose newsreels were shown in cinemas until 1970.

Having served as Managing Director of first ABC and then Thames, Thomas was compulsorily retired in 1984 at the age of 75. However, he was then appointed chairman of Thames Television International (formerly EMI Films), and continued in that role until his death on 6 November 1986.

LEIGH VANCE (WRITER)

Donald Anthony Hunter Leigh Vance was born on 18 March 1922 and became involved in writing for television in the mid-'50s on shows such as *Douglas Fairbanks Presents*, before going on to script various films. By the mid-'60s he had become one of the writers on *The Saint*, and this perhaps more than anything else got him the job on *The Avengers*.

After *The Avengers*, he wrote an instalment of *Armchair Theatre*, the Roger Moore film *Crossplot* and an episode of ITC's *Strange Report* before moving to the United States, where he saw better opportunities. Once established there, he began turning out screenplays for *Mission: Impossible* and *Mannix*, then progressed into the production side of American television, becoming an associate producer on the private detective show *Cannon*. After a spell as an executive producer on the police drama *Baretta*, he began an association with Robert Wagner as both a writer and producer on his shows *Switch* and *Hart to Hart*, the latter of which gave him his final screen credits in 1984. He died on 15 October 1994.

JERRY WEINTRAUB (MOVIE PRODUCER)

Hailing from Brooklyn, New York, Jerry Weintraub was born on 26 September 1937. He entered showbusiness during the early '60s as the manager of musical acts including the pop group the Four Seasons. Later, he had major success as the manager of singer John Denver. He then progressed into promoting music concerts featuring a wide variety of acts, including Elvis Presley, Led Zeppelin, Frank Sinatra, Neil Diamond, the Carpenters and the Moody Blues. Along the way, he also managed to get some of these concerts televised, receiving an executive producer credit on them. In 1977 he produced his first film, entitled *September 30, 1955*.

In 1984 Weintraub hit major success as the producer of the film *The Karate Kid*, which spawned a successful franchise. Then, leaving his musical connections behind, he concentrated his efforts on the movie world, acting as producer or executive producer on various projects. He was involved with *My Stepmother is an Alien* and, toward the conclusion of the '80s, *Vegas Vacation*. After *The Avengers* movie he was the producer on the all-star trilogy *Ocean's Eleven*, *Ocean's Twelve* and *Ocean's Thirteen*, in which he also took cameo acting roles. In 2010 he was instrumental in remaking *The Karate Kid* for a new generation and with a new cast, including Jackie Chan. He remains active in the film and television world.

LEONARD WHITE (PRODUCER)

Leonard George White was born in Newhaven, Sussex, on 11 May 1916, and like many people involved in the production side of television, he started his career on the other side of the camera as an actor. His first televised performance came in the BBC play *Good Friday* in 1950. He then moved into feature films such as *The Dark Man* and *Hunted*. Having established himself in the profession, he went on to appear in productions in Germany and then Canada, where he gained credits on episodes of *General Motors Theatre* and *First Performance*. It was also in Canada that he first met Sydney Newman. Back in the UK, meanwhile, he continued to win further acting roles, including in the feature films *Passage Home* and *Sailor of Fortune* and ABC's *Armchair Theatre* (which he would later produce).

For some time, White had wanted to switch over to the production side of television, but had been unable to enrol in any BBC training schemes as he lacked university qualifications. However, while in Toronto in 1957 he managed to get himself onto a CBC director/producer course that would prove vital to his future, especially when he later joined ABC. Originally he intended staying in Canada, but family commitments forced his return to the UK, where he took a relief director position with TWW in their Cardiff studios, directing a mixture of light entertainment, quiz shows and advertisement magazine programmes, aka ad-mags.

After a short time, White moved to a Southmapton-based production company who were contracted to produce ad-mags for Southern, but his time there was even briefer than his stay with TWW. His next move took him to Newcastle, where he once again worked as a relief director, covering in-house staff absences and holidays for Tyne Tees Television, working on various different kinds of programmes.

Then one Friday afternoon in January 1960, White received a telephone call from Sydney Newman at ABC, wanting to know what he was doing in Newcastle. In a hurry to catch a southbound train home to Sussex, he did not have time to give a lengthy explanation, so Newman suggested they meet for lunch the following Monday. Much to White's surprise, at that lunch Newman offered him a position with ABC as a producer. The Englishman thought he lacked the necessary experience and started making excuses, but Newman was both very persuasive and confident he had chosen the right man for the job. White reconsidered and accepted the offer, as producing drama was what he really wanted to do.

White's first day with ABC was 29 February 1960. Initially he became involved with finishing off *Inside Story*, a series of plays about the occupants of a block of flats. His first producer credits appeared on the 13-part *Armchair Mystery Theatre*, which began transmitting in June 1960. This was followed by *Police Surgeon* and *The Avengers*.

When *The Avengers* was off the air during the summer of 1962, White also produced the 13 episodes of *Out of This World*. Later he assumed the reins on *Armchair Theatre*, going on to produce an impressive 125 instalments, four of which later went out under the *Playhouse* banner.

After ten years with ABC, White decided to leave. There were no personality clashes or disagreements; White later noted, 'I just found I was not getting enough out of it.' As someone who had received great critical acclaim for his work, including an International Emmy Award in 1968 for the *Armchair Theatre* instalment 'Call Me Daddy', he did not rush straight into another television project, but rather waited a couple of years before starting again. Resurfacing in 1972 at HTV, he produced and did a little directing on the costume drama *Pretenders*. He then moved to Granada to take on some producing work on the anthology show *Late Night Drama*. Returning to HTV, he produced and occasionally directed on four children's fantasy serials between 1975 and 1978. These were *Sky*, *The Georgian House*, *King of the Castle* and *The Clifton House Mystery*. During this period he also found time to be the guiding hand on another couple of HTV serials, *Westway* and the five-part *Murder at the Wedding*.

White then moved north to Scotland. Having previously worked with scriptwriter Allan Prior on *Armchair Theatre*, he proceeded to produce the writer's television play *Bookie* for Scottish Television. The pair then collaborated again two years later on the children's serial *Stookie*. In 1987, there was another fantasy serial of six parts for Scottish Television called *Shadow of the Stone*.

White's final work came as the producer of the second season of the BBC Scotland drama *Strathblair* in 1993.

TONY WILLIAMSON (WRITER)

Tony Williamson was born in Manchester, Lancashire on 18 December 1932. He started his career as a writer of fiction, before progressing to magazine articles and then being a journalist with the *Evening Chronicle* in Newcastle. His first television writing experience came when he collaborated with Dennis Spooner on some comedy sketches for Tyne Tees, but then he moved to Canada, where he landed a position as a television news reporter. Changing course again, he tried scriptwriting, and managed to sell over 20 television plays. Convinced that he had now found his true vocation, he returned to the UK, where he secured a contract writing for *Coronation Street*.

As the '60s progressed, Williamson contributed scripts to a wide variety of series, including *The Plane Makers*, *Compact*, *Armchair Mystery Theatre* and *No Hiding Place*. With BBC assignments becoming increasingly prevalent, he wrote for *Dr Finlay's Casebook*, *The Mask of Janus* and *The Spies* and served as script consultant on both seasons of *Adam Adamant Lives!*. He later created the basic concept of ABC's industrial spy show *Intrigue*, wrote a two part *Z Cars* and in 1968 began working with Dennis Spooner again, initially on *The Champions*. This association with his old friend also led to him writing for *Department S*, *Randall and Hopkirk (Deceased)*, *Jason King* and *The Adventurer*. All these credits on ITC film series, along with episodes of *Danger Man*, *Ski Boy*, *Return of the Saint* and *The Persuaders!*, gained him a reputation of being something of a specialist on this type of show. However, along the way he found time to script three episodes of the BBC's spy show *Codename* and was also credited as the creator of their science fiction series *Counterstrike*.

In 1972 Williamson collaborated with Brian Clemens on the script of the American television movie *The Woman Hunter*. Also during that decade he moved into another area, writing a short series of espionage novels featuring the FBI agent character Lee

Corey. In the '80s he wrote the scripts for two Scandinavian mini-series and four instalments of the anthology *Worlds Beyond*. His final credit came in 1990 for the screenplay of the Roger Moore-starring film *Fire, Ice & Dynamite*. He died on 19 June 1991.

JULIAN WINTLE (PRODUCER)

Francis Julian Wintle was born on 17 October 1913 in Liverpool. By 1941 he was working in one the BBC's engineering departments at Wood Norton in Worcestershire. Seeking a career in film-making, he entered the business in 1946 by producing the short documentary *This is China*. Then, the following year, he formed the production company Independent Artists. Through the '50s and into the early '60s he continued producing films both for his own company and for others. These included the critically acclaimed *Tiger Bay*.

Jumping at the opportunity to control an entire production facility, Wintle and his then business partner Leslie Parkyn leased Beaconsfield Studios from Sydney Box Productions in 1958, and managed keep them ticking over with film production. Around this time, Independent Artists were responsible for three well-know comedies, *Crooks Anonymous*, *The Fast Lady* and *Father Came Too*, which all utilised the talents of James Robertson Justice, Leslie Phillips and Stanley Baxter. Other films with which Wintle was involved during the early '60s at Beaconsfield included the horror movie *Night of the Eagle* and the drama *This Sporting Life*.

By 1962 Wintle had discovered the limitations of Beaconsfield, and he used the much larger Pinewood Studios to film *Waltz of the Toreadors* starring Peter Sellers. Realising that the industry was moving toward larger productions, he honoured his remaining commitments at Beaconsfield, including the first 13 episodes of his television series *The Human Jungle*, but then moved Independent Productions out to ABPC's larger Elstree Studios, while Parkyn retired to Spain. At Elstree, Wintle continued making *The Human Jungle* and then moved onto *The Avengers*. He gained a number of further producer and executive producer credits at the end of the '60s and start of the '70s, the last coming on *The Belstone Fox* in 1973. He died on 8 November 1980.

APPENDIX ONE

THE AVENGERS: PRODUCTION DETAILS

The information presented below differs in format slightly depending on the details that are actually available for particular episodes. As throughout this book, the episodes are listed in production order rather than transmission order. The director on each recording or filming date is noted against that date in the 'Production Schedule' entry for each episode (in view of the fact that occasionally someone other than the episode's credited director was responsible). The main director credits are as per on screen. Where 'Main', '2nd', '3rd', or 'A Unit', 'B Unit' appear in a 'Production Schedule' entry, these refer to the different film crews that worked on the episode in question. Where 'Quarter called' is indicated, this means that the director sought agreement from the film crew's trade union representatives to continue working for 15 minutes beyond the time usually allowed, in order to complete a shot either before lunch or at the end of the afternoon. (This would have involved the crew being paid overtime.) Sources for the information presented include ABC Television, Telemen and ABC Television Films documentation, *The Daily Cinema* and internet resources such as IMDb and the website The Dissolute Avengers (http://www.dissolute.com.au/the-avengers-tv-series/).

The original transmission dates given are the ones for the ABC Midlands and North regions, except for season six, which are the ones for their successor, the Thames region.

SEASON ONE

An Iris Productions production for ABC Television
26 black and white episodes on videotape
Permanent Crew: Leonard White (Producer), Johnny Dankworth (*The Avengers* theme composed and played by).

1.01 – 'HOT SNOW'
Episode 1
Original Transmission Date: Saturday 7 January 1961
Production No: 3365
Videotape No: VTR/ABC/1040

Writer: Ray Rigby, based upon a story by Patrick Brawn
Director: Don Leaver
Cast: Ian Hendry (Dr David Keel), Patrick Macnee (John Steed), Philip Stone (Dr Richard J Tredding), Catherine Woodville (Peggy Stevens), Godfrey Quigley (Spicer), Murray Melvin (Charlie), Charles Wade (Johnson), Alister Williamson (Detective Superintendent Wilson), Moira Redmond (Stella), Astor Sklair (Detective Sergeant Rogers), June Monkhouse (Mrs Simpson), Robert James (The Big Man).
Crew: Alpho O'Reilly (Designed by).
Uncredited Crew: Patrick Brawn (Story Editor), Barbara Forster (Production Assistant), Patrick Kennedy (Floor Manager), Nansi Davies (Stage Manager), Bob Simmons (Lighting Director), Tom Clegg (Senior Cameraman), John Tasker (Sound Supervisor), Del Randall (Vision Mixer).

Production Schedule:
Friday 30 December 1960: Don Leaver
Recording: 18.00-19.00: ABC Teddington Studios, Studio 2

1.02 – 'BROUGHT TO BOOK'
Episode 2
Original Transmission Date: Saturday 14 January 1961
Production No: 3366
Videotape No: VTR/ABC/1054

Writer: Brian Clemens, based upon a story by Patrick Brawn
Director: Peter Hammond
Cast: Ian Hendry (Dr David Keel), Patrick Macnee (John Steed), Ingrid Hafner (Carol Wilson), Lionel Brns (Prentice), Redmond Bailey (Lale), Clifford Elkin (Pretty Boy), Neil McCarthy (Bart), Charles Morgan (Nick Mason), Godfrey Quigley (Spicer), Philip Stone (Dr Richard J Tredding), Joyce Wong Chong (Lila), Robert James (Ronnie Vance), Alister Williamson (Detective Superintendent Wilson), Michael Collins (Detective Sergeant), Carol White (Jackie), Anna Shan-Khoo (2nd Chinese Girl), Charles Bird (Peters), Laurence Archer (Johns).
Crew: Robert Fuest (Designed by).
Uncredited Crew: Patrick Brawn (Story Editor), Paddy Dewey (Production Assistant), Patrick Kennedy (Floor Manager) Barbara Sykes (Stage Manager), David Granger (Call Boy), Bob Simmons (Lighting Director), Peter Wayne (Operational Supervisor), Michael Baldock (Senior Cameraman), Peter Cazaly (Sound Supervisor), Del Randall (Visor Mixer).

Production Schedule:
Thursday 12 January 1961: Peter Hammond
Recording: 18.00-19.00: ABC Teddington Studios, Studio 2

1.03 – 'SQUARE ROOT OF EVIL'
Episode 3
Original Transmission Date: Saturday 21 January 1961
Production No: 3367
Videotape No: VTR/ABC/1089

Writer: Richard Harris, based upon a story by John Bryce
Director: Don Leaver
Cast: Ian Hendry (Dr David Keel), Patrick Macnee (John Steed), Ingrid Hafner (Carol Wilson), Heron Carvic (Five), Cynthia Bizeray (Secretary), John Woodvine (Steve Bloom), George Murcell (Hooper), Vic Wise (Warren) Alex Scott (The Cardinal), Delphi Lawrence (Lisa).
Crew: Patrick Downing (Designed by).
Uncredited Crew: John Bryce (Story Editor), Barbara Forster (Production Assistant), Geoff Smith (Floor Manager), Nansi Davies (Stage Manager), Peter Kew (Lighting Director), Peter Wayne (Operational Supervisor), Mike Baldock (Senior Cameraman), Pater Cazaly (Sound Supervisor), Del Randall (Vision Mixer).

Production Schedule:
Saturday 21 January 1961: Don Leaver
Live: 22.00-23.00: ABC Teddington Studios, Studio 2

1.04 – 'NIGHTMARE'
Episode 4
Original Transmission Date: Saturday 28 January 1961
Production No: 3368
Videotape No: VTR/ABC/1098

Writer: Terence Feely
Director: Peter Hammond
Cast: Ian Hendry (Dr David Keel), Patrick Macnee (John Steed), Ingrid Hafner (Carol Wilson), Gordon Boyd (Williams), Helen Lindsay (Faith Braintree), Michael Logan (Commander Reece), Robert Bruce (Dr Brown), Redmond Bailey (Dr Jones), Robert Sansom (Dr Miller).
Crew: Robert Fuest (Designed by).
Uncredited Crew: John Bryce (Story Editor).

Production Schedule:
Saturday 28 January 1961: Peter Hammond
Live: 22.00-23.00: ABC Teddington Studios, Studio 2

1.05 – 'CRESCENT MOON'
Episode 5
Original Transmission Date: Saturday 4 February 1961
Production No: 3369
Videotape No: VTR/ABC/1113

Writers: Geoffrey Bellman and John Whitney, based on a story by Patrick Brawn
Director: John Knight
Cast: Ian Hendry (Dr David Keel), Patrick Macnee (John Steed), Patience Collier (Senora Mendoza), Harold Kasket (Bartello), Bandana Das Gupta (Carmelita Mendoza), Nicholas Amer (Luis Alvarez), Eric Thompson (Paul), Jack Rodney (Fernandez), Roger Delgado (Vasco), George Roderick (Carlos the Policeman).
Crew: Alpho O'Reilly (Designed by).

Uncredited Crew: Patrick Brawn (Story Editor).

Production Schedule:
Saturday 4 February 1961: John Knight
Live: 22.00-23.00: ABC Teddington Studios, Studio: 2

1.06 – 'GIRL ON THE TRAPEZE'
Episode 6
Original Transmission Date: Saturday 11 February 1961
Production No: 3370
Videotape No: VTR/ABC/1123

Writer: Dennis Spooner
Director: Don Leaver
Cast: Ian Hendry (Dr David Keel), Ingrid Hafner (Carol Wilson), Kenneth J Warren (Zibbo), Delena Kidd (Vera), Howard Goorney (Superintendent Lewis), Edwin Richfield (Stefan), Mia Karam (Anna Danilov), Ivor Salter (Police Sergeant), David Grey (Dr Sterret), Dorothy Blythe (Box Office Clerk), Ian Gardiner (Policeman), Andy Alston (Turek).
Uncredited Cast: Mia Karam (Anna Danilov), Patricia Haines (Katrina Sandor).
Crew: Paul Bernard (Designed by).
Uncredited Crew: John Bryce (Story Editor), Barbara Forster (Production Assistant), Geoff Smith (Floor Manager), Barbara Sykes (Stage Manager), Peter Kew (Lighting Director), Peter Wayne (Operational Supervisor), Tom Clegg (Senior Cameraman), John Tasker (Sound Supervisor), Esther Frost (Vision Mixer).

Production Schedule:
Saturday 11 February 1961: Don Leaver
Live: 22.00-23.00: ABC Teddington Studios, Studio 2

1.07 – 'DIAMOND CUT DIAMOND'
Episode 7
Original Transmission Date: Saturday 18 February 1961
Production No: 3371
Videotape No: VTR/ABC/1141

Writer: Max Marquis
Director: Peter Hammond
Cast: Ian Hendry (Dr David Keel), Patrick Macnee (John Steed), Ingrid Hafner (Carol Wilson), Douglas Muir (One-Ten), Sandra Dorne (Fiona Charles), Hamlyn Benson (Dr Collard), Joy Webster (Stella Creighton).
Crew: Robert Fuest (Designed by).
Uncredited Crew: Patrick Brawn and John Bryce (Story Editors).

Production Schedule:
Saturday 18 February 1961: Peter Hammond
Live: 22.00-23.00: ABC Teddington Studios, Studio: 2

1.08 – 'THE RADIOACTIVE MAN'
Episode 8
Original Transmission Date: Saturday 25 February 1961
Production No: 3372
Videotape No: VTR/ABC/1156

Writer: Fred Edge, adapted by Patrick Brawn
Director: Robert Tronson
Cast: Ian Hendry (Dr David Keel), Patrick Macnee (John Steed), Ingrid Hafner (Carol Wilson), Arthur Lawrence (Dr Graham), George Pravda (Marko Ogrin), Blaise Wyndham (Campbell), Christine Pollon (Mary Somers), Barry Shawzin (Milan Radosevick), Mira Tomek (Frane), Madeline Kasket (Inica), Marie Devereux (Dora Radosevick), Dane Howell (Peter Somers), Basil Beale (Inspector Tudor), John Gayford (1st Police Constable), Paul Grist (2nd Police Constable), John Kelland (3rd Police Constable).
Crew: Alpho O'Reilly (Designed by).
Uncredited Crew: Patrick Brawn (Adapted by), John Bryce (Story Editor), Peter Bailey (Floor Manager), Barbara Sykes (Stage Manager), Sylvia Langdon-Down (Production Assistant), Peter Wayne (Technical Supervisor), Peter Kew (Lighting Supervisor), Michael Baldock (Senior Cameraman), Peter Cazaly (Sound Supervisor).

Production Schedule:
Saturday 25 February 1961: Robert Tronson
Live: 22.00-23.00: ABC Teddington Studios, Studio 2

1.09 – 'ASHES OF ROSES'
Episode 9
Original Transmission Date: Saturday 4 March 1961
Production No: 3373
Videotape No: VTR/ABC/1170

Writers: Peter Ling and Sheilagh Ward
Director: Don Leaver
Cast: Ian Hendry (Dr David Keel), Patrick Macnee (John Steed), Ingrid Hafner (Carol Wilson), Olga Lowe (Olive Beronne), Mark Eden (Jacques Beronne), Peter Zander (Johnny Mendelssohn), Heidi Erich (Denise), Edward Dentith (Maurice Roffey), Barbara Evans (Linda Chapman), Maureen Beck (Jean), Nina Marriott (Avril), Gordon Rollings (Sleeping Car Attendant), Juno (Puppy).
Crew: Patrick Downing (Designed by).
Uncredited Crew: John Bryce (Story Editor), Verity Lambert (Production Assistant), Geoff Smith (Floor Manager), Nansi Davies (Stage Manager), Bob Simmons (Lighting Director), Peter Wayne (Operational Supervisor), Mike Baldock (Senior Cameraman), Peter Cazaly (Sound Supervisor), Esther Frost (Vision Mixer).

Production Schedule:
Unknown Date: Don Leaver
Small Unit: London Victoria Station, Victoria Street, London, SW1 [Int: Railway Station]
Saturday 4 March 1961: Don Leaver

Live: 22.00-23.00: ABC Teddington Studios, Studio 2

1.10 – 'HUNT THE MAN DOWN'
Episode 10
Original Transmission Date: Saturday 18 March 1961
Production No: 3374
Videotape No: VTR/ABC/1211

Writer: Richard Harris
Director: Peter Hammond
Cast: Ian Hendry (Dr David Keel), Patrick Macnee (John Steed), Ingrid Hafner (Carol Wilson), Maurice Good (Paul Stacey), Nicholas Selby (Frank Preston), Melissa Stribling (Stella Preston), Susan Castle (Nurse Wyatt).
Crew: Robert Fuest (Designed by).
Uncredited Crew: Patrick Brawn and John Bryce (Story Editors).

Production Schedule:
Unknown Date: Peter Hammond
Small Unit: Wood Street, London, EC2 [Ext: Manhole cover scenes]
Sunday 12 March 1961: Peter Hammond
Recording time unknown, Studio: 2

1.11 – 'PLEASE DON'T FEED THE ANIMALS'
Episode 11
Original Transmission Date: Saturday 1 April 1961
Production No: 3375
Videotape No: VTR/ABC/1217

Writer: Dennis Spooner
Director: Dennis Vance
Cast: Ian Hendry (Dr David Keel), Patrick Macnee (John Steed), Ingrid Hafner (Carol Wilson), Tenniel Evans (Felgate), Harry Ross (Kollakis), Alistair Hunter (Renton-Stephens), Carole Boyer (Christine), Genevieve Lyons (Sarah), Catherine Ellison (Yvonne), Mark Baker (Barman), Richard Neller (Evans), Charles Bird (Harrigan).
Crew: Patrick Downing (Designed by).
Uncredited Crew: Patrick Brawn (Story Editor), Peter Bailey (Floor Manager), Barbara Sykes (Stage Manager), Sylvia Langdon-Down (Production Assistant), Peter Wayne (Operational Supervisor), Peter Kew (Lighting Supervisor), Peter Cazaly (Sound Supervisor), Tom Clegg (Senior Cameraman).

Production Schedule:
Thursday 30 March 1961: Dennis Vance
Recording: 18.00-19.00: ABC Teddington Studios, Studio 2

1.12 – 'DANCE WITH DEATH'
Episode 12
Original Transmission Date: Saturday 15 April 1961
Production No: 3376

Videotape No: VTR/ABC/1241

Writers: Peter Ling and Sheilagh Ward
Director: Don Leaver
Cast: Ian Hendry (Dr David Keel), Patrick Macnee (John Steed), Ingrid Hafner (Carol Wilson), Diana King (Mrs Marne), Geoffrey Palmer (Philip Anthony), Ewan Roberts (Major Caswell), David Sutton (Trevor Price), Caroline Blakiston (Elaine Bateman), Angela Douglas (Beth Wilkinson), Pauline Shepherd (Valerie Marne), Norman Chappell (Porter), Neil Wilson (Police Sergeant), Raymond Hodge (Plainclothes Man), Graeme Spurway (Hotel Receptionist), Alan Barry (Barman), Ian Hobbs (Teenage Boy), Alan Clare (Pianist).
Uncredited Cast: Dancers (The Ken Bateman Formation Dance Team).
Crew: James Goddard (Designed by)
Uncredited Crew: John Bryce (Story Editor), Barbara Forster (Production Assistant), Peter Bailey (Floor Manager), Barbara Sykes (Stage Manager), Louis Bottone (Lighting Director), Peter Wayne (Operational Supervisor), Mike Baldock (Senior Cameraman), Peter Cazaly (Sound Supervisor), Esther Frost (Vision Mixer).

Production Schedule:
Thursday 13 April 1961: Don Leaver
Recording: 18.00-19.00: ABC Teddington Studios, Studio 2

1.13 – 'ONE FOR THE MORTUARY'
Episode 13
Original Transmission Date: Saturday 29 April 1961
Production No: 3377
Videotape No: VTR/ABC/1263

Writer: Brian Clemens
Director: Peter Hammond
Cast: Ian Hendry (Dr David Keel), Patrick Macnee (John Steed), Ingrid Hafner (Carol Wilson), Peter Madden (Benson), Ronald Wilson (Scott), Dennis Edwards (Pallaine), Malou Pantera (Yvette Declair), Frank Gatliff (Dubois), Irene Bradshaw (Maid), Toke Townley (Bernard Bourg).
Uncredited Cast: Steven Scott (Hotel Concierge).
Crew: Robert Fuest (Designed by).
Uncredited Crew: Patrick Brawn (Story Editor), Paddy Dewey (Production Assistant), Patrick Kennedy (Floor Manager), Barbara Sykes (Stage Manager).

Production Schedule:
Thursday 27 April 1961: Peter Hammond
Recording: 18.00-19.00: ABC Teddington Studios, Studio 2

1.14 – 'THE SPRINGERS'
Episode 14
Original Transmission Date: Saturday 13 May 1961
Production No: 3411
Videotape No: VTR/ABC/1283

Writers: John Whitney and Geoffrey Bellman
Director: Don Leaver
Cast: Ian Hendry (Dr David Keel), Patrick Macnee (John Steed), Arthur Howard (Groves), Donald Morley (Neame), Charles Farrell (Straker), David Webb (Pheeney), Douglas Muir (One-Ten), Ann Saker (Melanie), Barbara Evans (Lisa), Brian Murphy (Haslam), Michael Forrest (Elton), Ian Ainsley (Prison Governor), Margo Andrew (Caroline Evans), Max Miradin (Arthur), Charles Saynor (Skewer), Tom Payne (Jessup).
Crew: Alpho O'Reilly (Designed by).
Uncredited Crew: Patrick Brawn and John Bryce (Story Editors), Barbara Forster (Production Assistant), Harry Lock (Floor Manager), Barbara Sykes (Stage Manager), Peter Kew (Lighting Director), Peter Wayne (Operational Supervisor), Mike Baldock (Senior Cameraman), Mike Roberts (Sound Supervisor), Esther Frost (Vision Mixer).

Production Schedule:
Thursday 11 May 1961: Don Leaver
Recording: 18.00-19.00: ABC Teddington Studios, Studio 2

1.15 – 'THE FRIGHTENERS'
Episode 15
Original Transmission Date: Saturday 27 May 1961
Production No: 3412
Videotape No: Unknown

Writer: Berkely Mather
Director: Peter Hammond
Cast: Ian Hendry (Dr David Keel), Patrick Macnee (John Steed), Ingrid Hafner (Carol Wilson), Willoughby Goddard (The Deacon), Philip Gilbert (Jeremy de Willoughby), Philip Locke (Moxon), Doris Hare (Mrs Briggs), Stratford Johns (Sir Thomas Weller), Dawn Beret (Marylin Weller), David Andrews (Nigel), Godfrey James (Nature Boy), Neil Wilson (Beppi Colissimo), Eric Elliot (Butler), Ann Taylor (Secretary), Ralph Tovey (Waiter), Benn Simons (Inspector Charlie Foster), Eleanor Darling (Flower Seller), Benny Nightingale (Grekio), Frank Peters (Street Sweeper), Charles Wood (1st Plainsclothes Officer), Victor Charrington (Fred the Cabbie).
Crew: Robert Fuest (Designed by).
Uncredited Crew: John Bryce and Reed de Rouen (Story Editors).

Production Schedule:
Thursday 25 May 1961: Peter Hammond
Recording time and studio unknown

1.16 – 'THE YELLOW NEEDLE'
Episode 16
Original Transmission Date: Saturday 10 June 1961
Production No: 3413
Videotape No: VTR/ABC/1318

Writer: Patrick Campbell; adapted by Reed de Rouen
Director: Don Leaver

Cast: Ian Hendry (Dr David Keel), Patrick Macnee (John Steed), Ingrid Hafner (Carol Wilson), Margaret Whiting (Jacquetta Brown), Andre Daker (Sir Wilberforce Lungi), Bari Johnson (Chief Bai Shebro), Wolfe Morris (Ali), Dolores Mantez (Judith), Eric Dodson (Inspector Anthony), Christian Holder (Asiedu), Michael Barrington (Head Waiter), Humphrey Heathcote (Police Sergeant), Harold Holness (Porter), Juno (Puppy).
Crew: Alpho O'Reilly (Designed by).
Uncredited Crew: Reed de Rouen (Story Editor), Barbara Forster (Production Assistant), Alan Davidson (Floor Manager), Barbara Sykes (Stage Manager), Louis Bottone (Lighting Director), Peter Wayne (Operational Supervisor), Mike Baldock (Senior Cameraman), Mike Roberts (Sound Supervisor), Esther Frost (Vision Mixer).

Production Schedule:
Thursday 8 Jun 1961: Don Leaver
Recording: 18.00-19.00: ABC Teddington Studios, Studio 2

1.17 – 'DEATH ON THE SLIPWAY'
Episode 17
Original Transmission Date: Saturday 24 June 1961
Production No: 3414
Videotape No: Unknown

Writer: James Mitchell
Director: Peter Hammond
Cast: Ian Hendry (Dr David Keel), Patrick Macnee (John Steed), Peter Arne (Kolchek), Frank Thornton (Sir William Bonner), Nyree Dawn Porter (Liz Wells), Paul Dawkins (Sam Pearson), Sean Sullivan (Fleming), Redmond Bailey (Geordie Wilson), Robert G Bahey (Jack), Barry Keegan (Inspector Georgeson), Tom Adams (PC Butterworth), Douglas Muir (One-Ten), Gary Watson (Pardoe), Patrick Conner (PC Geary), Hamilton Dyce (Sergeant Brodie), Billy Milton (Chandler), Juno (Puppy).
Crew: Robert Fuest (Designed by).
Uncredited Crew: John Bryce and Reed de Rouen (Story Editors).

Production Schedule:
Thursday 22 June 1961: Peter Hammond
Recording time and studio unknown

1.18 – 'DOUBLE DANGER'
Episode 18
Original Transmission Date: Saturday 8 July 1961
Production No: 3415
Videotape No: VTR/ABC/1340

Writer: Gerald Verner
Director: Roger Jenkins
Cast: Ian Hendry (Dr David Keel), Patrick Macnee (John Steed), Ingrid Hafner (Carol Wilson), Peter Reynolds (Al Brady), Vanda Hudson (Lola Carrington), Kevin Brennan (Leonard Bruton), Ronald Pember (Bert Mills), Charles Hodgson (Mark Crawford),

Robert Mill (Harry Dew), Gordon Phillott (John Bartholomew), Blaise Wyndham (Taxi Driver), Howard Daley (Ted Mace).
Crew: James Goddard (Designed by).
Uncredited Crew: John Lucarotti (Writer), John Bryce and Reed de Rouen (Story Editors), Izabella Lubicz (Production Assistant), Patrick Kennedy (Floor Manager), John Wayne (Stage Manager), Ken Brown (Lighting Director), Peter Wayne (Technical Supervisor), Michael Baldock (Senior Cameraman), Michael Roberts (Sound Supervisor), Gordon Hesketh (Vision Mixer).

Production Schedule:
Thursday 6 July 1961: Roger Jenkins
Recording: 18.00-19.00: ABC Teddington Studios, Studio 2

1.19 – 'TOY TRAP'
Episode 19
Original Transmission Date: Saturday 22 July 1961
Production No: 3416
Videotape No: VTR/ABC/1347

Writer: Bill Strutton
Director: Don Leaver
Cast: Ian Hendry (Dr David Keel), Patrick Macnee (John Steed), Sally Smith (Bunty Seton), Nina Marriott (Alice), Hazel Graeme (May Murton), Mitzi Rogers (Ann), Tony Van Bridge (Henry Burge), Ann Tirard (Mrs McCabe), Brian Jackson (Johnny), Brandon Brady (Freddie), Tex Fuller (Lennie Taylor), Lionel Burns (Photographer), with extras Jill Brooke, Dorothy Watson, George Betton, Felicity Peel, Peter Fenton.
Crew: Douglas James (Designed by).
Uncredited Crew: John Bryce and Reed de Rouen (Story Editors), Michael Vardy (Floor Manager), Valerie Brayden (Production Assistant), John Wayne (Stage Manager), John Cooper (Call Boy), Ken Brown (Lighting), Peter Wayne (Technical Supervisor), Tom Clegg (Cameras), John Tasker (Sound), Esther Frost (Vision Mixer).

Production Schedule:
Thursday 20 July 1961: Don Leaver
Recording: 20.00-21.00: ABC Teddington Studios, Studio 2

1.20 – 'TUNNEL OF FEAR'
Episode 20
Original Transmission Date: Saturday 5 August 1961
Production No: 3417
Videotape No: Unknown

Writer: John Kruse
Director: Guy Verney
Cast: Ian Hendry (Dr David Keel), Patrick Macnee (John Steed), Ingrid Hafner (Carol Wilson), Stanley Platts (Maxie Lardner), John Salew (Jack Wickram), Anthony Bate (Harry Black), Doris Rogers (Mrs Black), Douglas Muir (One-Ten), Nancy Roberts (Madame Zenobia), Miranda Connell (Claire), Douglas Rye (Billy), Morris Perry

(Sergeant).
Crew: James Goddard (Designed by).
Uncredited Crew: John Bryce and Reed de Rouen (Story Editors).

Production Schedule:
Thursday 3 August 1961: Guy Verney
Recording time and studio unknown

1.21 – 'THE FAR DISTANT DEAD'
Episode 21
Original Transmission Date: Saturday 19 August 1961
Production No: 3418
Videotape No: Unknown
Writer: John Lucarotti
Director: Peter Hammond
Cast: Ian Hendry (Dr David Keel), Katharine Blake (Dr Ampara Alverez Sandoval), Reed de Rouen (Luis Garcia), Francis de Wolff (Hercule Zeebrugge), Guy Deghy (Inspector Gauvreau), Tom Adams (Rayner), Andreas Malandrinos (Godoy), Michael Mellinger (Mateos).
Crew: Robert Fuest (Designed by).
Uncredited Crew: John Bryce and Reed de Rouen (Story Editors).
Production Schedule:
Tuesday 14 August 1961: Peter Hammond
Recording: 18.00-19.00: ABC Teddington Studios, Studio 2

1.22 – 'KILL THE KING'
Episode 22
Original Transmission Date: Saturday 2 September 1961
Production No: 3419
Videotape No: VTR/ABC/1390

Writer: James Mitchell
Director: Roger Jenkins
Cast: Ian Hendry (Dr David Keel), Patrick Macnee (John Steed), Ingrid Hafner (Carol Wilson), Bert Kwouk (King Tenuphon), Patrick Allen (General Tuke), Lisa Peake (Mei Li), Moira Redmond (Zoe Carter), Carole Shelley (Ingrid Storm), Peter Barkworth (Crichton-Bull), James Goei (Prince Serrakit), Ian Colin (Major Harrington), Andy Ho (U Meng), Eric Young (Suchong), Myo Toon (Ta Pai), Victor Charrington (Detective), Jerry Lee Yen (Servant), Douglas Muir (Voice of One-Ten), Unity Bevis (Concubine), Sarmukh Singh (Steward Assassin), Jean Woo Sam (Servant), with extra Eugene Che.
Crew: Paul Bernard (Designed by).
Uncredited Crew: John Bryce and Reed de Rouen (Story Editors), Sylvia Langdon-Down (Production Assistant), Patrick Kennedy (Floor Manager), John Wayne (Stage Manager), Louis Bottone (Lighting Director), Campbell Keenan (Operational Supervisor), Tom Clegg (Senior Cameraman).

Production Schedule:
Thursday 30 August 1961: Roger Jenkins

Recording: 18.00-19.00: ABC Teddington Studios, Studio 4

1.23 – 'THE DEADLY AIR'
Episode 23
Original Transmission Date: Saturday 16 December 1961
Production No: 3420
Videotape No: Unknown

Writer: Lester Powell
Director: John Knight
Cast: Ian Hendry (Dr David Keel), Patrick Macnee (John Steed), Ingrid Hafner (Carol Wilson), Ann Bell (Barbara Anthony), Michael Hawkins (Dr Philip Karswood), Keith Alexander (Heneager), Richard Butler (Herbert Truscott), Allan Cuthbertson (Dr Hugh Chalk), John Stratton (Dr Owen Craxton), Douglas Muir (One-Ten), Cyril Renison (Dr Harvey), Anthony Cundell (Ken Armstrong), Geoffrey Bayldon (Professor Kilbride).
Crew: Robert MacGowan (Designed by).
Uncredited Crew: John Bryce and Reed de Rouen (Story Editors).

Production Schedule:
Thursday 7 September 1961: John Knight
Recording: 18.00-19.00: ABC Teddington Studios, Studio 2

1.24 – 'A CHANGE OF BAIT'
Episode 24
Original Transmission Date: Saturday 23 December 1961
Production No: 3421
Videotape No: VTR/ABC/1445

Writer: Lewis Davidson
Director: Don Leaver
Cast: Ian Hendry (Dr David Keel), Patrick Macnee (John Steed), Ingrid Hafner (Carol Wilson), Victor Platt (Archie Duncan), John Bailey (Lemuel Potts), Henry Soskin (Peter Sampson), Robert Desmond (Herb Thompson), Graham Rigby (Nat Fletcher), Gary Hope (Barker), Arthur Barrett (Andre), Norman Pitt (Bryan Stubbs), Gillian McCutcheon (Ivy), Harry Shacklock (Charlie), Michael Hunt (Steed's Helper).
Crew: James Goddard (Designed by).
Uncredited Crew: John Bryce and Reed de Rouen (Story Editors), Barbara Forster (Production Assistant), Patrick Kennedy (Floor Manager), Barbara Sykes (Stage Manager), Peter Kew (Lighting Director), Peter Cazaly (Operational Supervisor), Michael Baldock (Senior Cameraman), Michael Roberts (Sound Supervisor), Gordon Hesketh (Vision Mixer).

Production Schedule:
Wednesday 20 September 1961: Don Leaver
Recording: 18.00-19.00: ABC Teddington Studios, Studio 2

1.25 – 'DRAGONSFIELD'
Episode 25

Original Transmission Date: Saturday 30 December 1961
Production No: 3422
Videotape No: Unknown

Writer: Terence Feely
Director: Peter Hammond
Cast: Patrick Macnee (John Steed), Sylvia Langova (Lisa Strauss), Alfred Burke (Saunders), Ronald Leigh-Hunt (Reddington), Barbara Shelley (Susan Summers), Thomas Kyffin (Jack Alfred), Keith Barron (Technician), Amanda Reeves (Secretary), Eric Dodson (One-Fifteen), Steven Scott (Boris), Michael Robbins (Landlord), Herbert Nelson (Peters), Morris Perry (Second Technician).
Crew: Voytek (Designed by).
Uncredited Crew: John Bryce and Reed de Rouen (Story Editors).

Production Schedule:
Wednesday 27 September 1961: Peter Hammond
Recording time unknown, Studio: 2

1.26 – 'DEAD OF WINTER'
Episode 26
Original Transmission Date: Saturday 9 December 1961
Production No: 3423
Videotape No: VTR/ABC/1469

Writer: Eric Paice
Director: Don Leaver
Cast: Ian Hendry (Dr David Keel), Patrick Macnee (John Steed), Ingrid Hafner (Carol Wilson), John Woodvine (Harry), Blaise Wyndham (Syd), Carl Duering (Schneider), David Hart (Dr Brennan), Sheila Robins (Inez), Michael Sarne (Willi), Zorenah Osborne (Margarita), Neil Hallett (Weber), Norman Chappell (Ted), Arnold Marle (Kreuzer).
Crew: Robert Fuest (Designed by).
Uncredited Crew: John Bryce (Story Editor).

Production Schedule:
Wednesday 18 October 1961: Don Leaver
Recording: 18.00-19.00: ABC Teddington Studios, Studio 2

SEASON TWO

An Iris Productions production for ABC Television
26 black and white episodes on videotape, later copied onto 16mm film
Permanent Crew: Leonard White (Producer, 'Mission to Montreal' to 'The Big Thinker'), John Bryce (Story Editor, 'Mission to Montreal' to 'The Big Thinker'; Producer, 'Intercrime' to 'Killer Whale'), Richard Bates (Story Editor, 'Intercrime' to 'Killer Whale'), Johnny Dankworth (*The Avengers* theme composed and played by).

2.01 – 'MISSION TO MONTREAL'
Episode 27
Original Transmission Date: Saturday 27 October 1962
Production No: 3500
Videotape No: VTR/ABC/1747 & 1747A

Writer: Lester Powell
Director: Don Leaver
Cast: Patrick Macnee (John Steed), Jon Rollason (Dr Martin King), Patricia English (Carla Berotti), Iris Russell (Sheila Dowson), Mark Eden (Alec Nicholson), Gillian Muir (Judy), Harold Berens (Film Director), Alan Curtis (Brand) John Bennett (Guido Aloysius Marson), Gerald Sim (Budge Jackson), Eric McCaine (Pearson), John Frawley (Passenger), Malcolm Taylor (First Reporter), Terence Woodfield (Second Reporter), Leslie Pitt (Third Reporter), Pamela Ann Davy (Peggy), William Buck (Photographer), Angela Thorne (Receptionist), Peter MacKriel (First Steward), William Swan (Second Steward), Allan Casley (Barman).
Uncredited Cast: Richard Pescud (Actor and Royal Canadian Mounted Police Officer), Howard Kingsley (Assistant Director and Passenger), Melvyn Mordant (Photographer and Passenger), Paul Blomley (Cameraman and Passenger), Robin Kildare (Focus Puller and Passenger), David Low (Focus Puller and Passenger), David Low (First Electrician and Passenger), Alan Crouch (Second Electrician and Passenger), with extras Margot Lane, Perry Leigh, Bill Richards, Joan Smith, Barbara Straight, Dorothy Watson.
Crew: Terry Green (Designed by).
Uncredited Crew: Peter Bailey (Floor Manager), Nasi Davies (Stage Manager), Sylvia Landon-Down (Production Assistant), John Cooper (Call Boy), H W Richards (Lighting Supervisor), Peter Cazaly (Technical Supervisor), John Tasker (Sound Supervisor), Tom Clegg (Senior Cameraman), Lee Halls (Wardrobe Supervisor), Audrey Riddle (Make-Up Supervisor).

Production Schedule:
Friday 11 May 1962: Don Leaver
VT Insert: 10.35-10.50: ABC Teddington Studios, Studio 2 [Int: Opening scene on film set]
Saturday 12 May 1962: Don Leaver
Recording: 18.00-19.00: ABC Teddington Studios, Studio 2

2.02 – 'DEAD ON COURSE'
Episode 28
Original Transmission Date: Saturday 29 December 1962
Production No: 3501
Videotape No: VTR/ABC/1778

Writer: Eric Paice
Director: Richmond Harding
Cast: Patrick Macnee (John Steed), Jon Rollason (Dr Martin King), John McLaren (Freedman), Liam Gaffney (Michael Joyce), Donal Donnelly (Vincent O'Brien), Peggy Marshall (Mother Superior), Elisabeth Murray (Deidre O'Conner), Janet Hargreaves (Sister Isobel), Nigel Arkwright (Hughes), Bruce Boa (Bob Slade), Margo Jenkins

(Margot), Trevor Reid (Pilot), Edward Kelsey (Gerry), Mollie Maureen (Kiosk Woman), Denis Cleary (Ambulance Man), Wilfred Grove (Male Nun).
Crew: Robert Fuest (Designed by).
Uncredited Crew: Barbara Forster (Production Assistant), Peter Bailey (Floor Manager), Barbara Sykes (Stage Manager), Paddy Dewey (Timing Production Assistant), Louis Bottone and Brian Turner (Lighting), Campbell Keenan (Operational Supervisor), Tom Clegg (Senior Cameraman), John Tasker (Sound Supervisor), Gordon Hesketh (Vision Mixer), Bob Godfrey (Racks).

Production Schedule:
Saturday 26 May 1962: Richmond Harding
Recording: 18.00-19.00: ABC Teddington Studios, Studio 2

2.03 – 'THE SELL-OUT'
Episode 29
Original Transmission Date: Saturday 24 November 1962
Production No: 3502
Videotape No: VTR/ABC/1807

Writers: Anthony Terpiloff and Brandon Brady
Director: Don Leaver
Cast: Patrick Macnee (John Steed), Jon Rollason (Dr Martin King), Gillian Muir (Judy), Anne Godley (Lilian Harvey), Carleton Hobbs (Monsieur Roland), Arthur Hewlett (One-Twelve), Frank Gatliff (Mark Harvey), Michael Mellinger (Fraser), Anthony Blackshaw (Policeman), Cyril Renison (Customer), Storm Durr (Gunman), Richard Klee (Plumber), Ray Browne (Price).
Uncredited Cast: Henry Rayner (Party Guest and Reporter), Victor Harrington (Party Guest and Reporter), Diane Bester (Party Guest and Reporter), Yvonne Walsh (Party Guest and Reporter), Colin Fry (Chef), with extras Philip Webb, Lance George, James Darwin, Jack Roland, Graham Cruickshank, Jeff Shane, John Roland, Gordon Lang, Albert Grant.
Crew: Terry Green (Designed by).
Uncredited Crew: Peter Bailey (Floor Manager), Mary Lewis (Stage Manager), Sylvia Landon-Down (Production Assistant), John Cooper (Call Boy), Ray Knight (Racks), Louis Bottone (Lighting Supervisor), Campbell Keenan & Peter Cazaly (Technical Supervisors), Mike Roberts (Sound Supervisor), Mike Baldock (Senior Cameraman), Del Randall (Vision Mixer).

Production Schedule:
Saturday 9 June 1962: Don Leaver
Recording: 18.00-19.00: ABC Teddington Studios, Studio 2

2.04 – 'DEATH DISPATCH'
Episode 30
Original Transmission Date: Saturday 22 December 1962
Production No: 3503
Videotape No: VTR/ABC/1821

Writer: Leonard Fincham
Director: Jonathan Alwyn
Cast: Patrick Macnee (John Steed), Honor Blackman (Cathy Gale), Douglas Muir (One-Ten), Richard Warner (Miquel Rosas), David Cargill (Monroe), Valerie Sarruf (Anna Rosas), Gerald Harper (Travers), Hedger Wallace (Baxter), Michael Forrest (Rico), Maria Andipa (Singer) Geoff L'Cise (Thug), Arthur Griffiths (Thug), Bernice Rassin (Chambermaid), Jerry Jardin (Customer).
Uncredited Cast: Steed's Date (Caron Gardner).
Crew: Anne Spavin (Designed by).
Uncredited Crew: Jill Horwood (Production Assistant), Robert Reed (Floor Manager), John Wayne (Stage Manager), H W Richards (Lighting), Peter Cazaly (Technical Supervisor), Mike Baldock (Cameras), Mike Roberts (Sound), Del Randall (Vision Mixer).

Production Schedule:
Saturday 23 June 1962: Jonathan Alwyn
Recording: 18.30-19.30: ABC Teddington Studios, Studio 2

2.05 – 'WARLOCK'
Episode 31
Original Transmission Date: Saturday 26 January 1963
Production No: 3504
Videotape No: VTR/ABC/1854 and 1854A

Writer: Doreen Montgomery
Director: Peter Hammond
Cast: Patrick Macnee (John Steed), Honor Blackman (Cathy Gale), Peter Arne (Cosmo Gallion), John Hollis (Markel), Pat Spencer (Julia), Douglas Muir (One-Ten), Olive Milbourne (Mrs Dunning), Alban Blakelock (Peter Neville), Brian Vaughan (Doctor), Gordon Gardner (Pathologist), Philip Mosca (Mogom), Susan Franklin (Barmaid), Herbert Nelson (Pasco), Christina Ferdinando (Miss Timson), Bill Haydn, Anna Sharkey, Roy Gunson, Maggie Lee, Fred Evans, Gillian Bowden (Gallion's Followers).
Uncredited Cast: Bill Bradley (Apparition).
Crew: Michael Whittaker (Special wardrobe for Honor Blackman designed by), Terry Green (Designed by), Pat Kirshner (Dance Direction by).
Uncredited Crew: Valerie Brayden (Production Assistant), Robert Reed (Floor Manager), Nansi Davies (Stage Manager), John Cooper (Call Boy), H W Ritchie (Lighting), Campbell Keegan (Technical Supervisor), Tom Clegg (Cameras), John Tasker (Sound), Gordon Hesketh (Vision Mixer).

Production Schedule:
Friday 6 July 1962: Peter Hammond
VT Insert: 20.45-21.00: ABC Teddington Studios, Studio Lot [Ext: Having driven Steed home in her car Cathy dropped him off outside his apartment]
Saturday 7 July 62: Peter Hammond
Recording: 18.30-19.30: ABC Teddington Studios, Studio 2
Thursday 24 January 1963: Unknown director
VT Insert: ABC Teddington Studios [Int: Replacement material set at the British

Museum and pub]

2.06 – 'PROPELLANT 23'
Episode 32
Original Transmission Date: Saturday 6 October 1962
Production No: 3505
Videotape No: VTR/ABC/1871 and 1871A/B/C/D

Writer: Jon Manchip White
Director: Jonathan Alwyn
Cast: Patrick Macnee (John Steed), Honor Blackman (Cathy Gale), Justine Lord (Jeanette), Catherine Woodville (Laure), Geoffrey Palmer (Paul Manning), Ralph Nossek (Roland), Barry Wilsher (Pierre), John Crocker (Lieutenant Curly Leclerc), Trader Faulkner (Jacques Tissot), John Dearth (Siebel), Frederick Schiller (Jules Meyer), Nicholas Courtney (Captain Legros), Michael Beint (Co-Pilot), John Gill (Baker), Graham Ashley (Gendarme and HQ Voice), Deanna Shenderey (Shop Assistant).
Uncredited Cast: Deanna Shenderey (Announcer).
Crew: Michael Whittaker (Special wardrobe for Honor Blackman designed by), Paul Bernard (Designed by).
Uncredited Crew: Peter Bailey (Floor Manager), Paddy Dewey (Production Assistant), Mary Lewis (Stage Manager), John Cooper (Call Boy), Gordon Hesketh (Vision Mixer), Peter Kew (Lighting Supervisor), Peter Cazaly (Technical Supervisor), Tom Clegg (Senior Cameraman), John Tasker (Sound Supervisor), Bob Godfrey (Racks Supervisor).

Production Schedule:
Friday 20 July 1962: Jonathan Alwyn
VT Insert: 19.00-21.00: ABC Teddington Studios, Scenery Dock [Int: Four scenes in Cathy's car featuring her and Steed]
Saturday 21 July 1962: Jonathan Alwyn
Recording: 17.00-18.00: ABC Teddington Studios, Studio 2

2.07 – 'MR TEDDY BEAR'
Episode 33
Original Transmission Date: Saturday 29 September 1962
Production No: 3506
Videotape No: VTR/ABC/1907 and 1907A

Writer: Martin Woodhouse
Director: Richmond Harding
Cast: Patrick Macnee (John Steed), Honor Blackman (Cathy Gale), Douglas Muir (One-Ten), Kenneth Keeling (Colonel Wayne-Gilley), Tim Brinton (Interviewer), John Horsley (Dr Gilmore), Michael Collins (Technician), Bernard Goldman (Mr Teddy Bear), Michael Robbins (Henry Farrow), Sarah Maxwell (Café Girl), John Ruddock (Dr James Howell).
Uncredited Cast: Freckles the Dalmatian
Crew: Michael Whittaker (Special wardrobe for Honor Blackman designed by), Terry Green (Designed by).
Uncredited Crew: Peter Bailey (Floor Manager), Valerie Brayden (Production

Assistant), Shirley Cleghorn (Stage Manager), Campbell Keenan (Technical Supervisor), Louis Bottone (Lighting), Michael Baldock (Cameras), Mike Roberts (Sound), Del Randall (Vision Mixer).

Production Schedule:
Friday 3 August 1962: Richmond Harding
VT Insert: 20.45-21.00: ABC Teddington Studios, Studio 3 [Int: The death of Colonel Wayne-Gilley]
Saturday 4 August 1962: Richmond Harding
Recording: 18.30-19.30: ABC Teddington Studios, Studio 2

2.08 – 'THE DECAPOD'
Episode 34
Original Transmission Date: Saturday 13 October 1962
Production No: 3507
Videotape No: VTR/ABC/1979

Writer: Eric Paice
Director: Don Leaver
Cast: Patrick Macnee (John Steed), Julie Stevens (Venus Smith), Paul Stassino (Yakob Borb), Philip Madoc (Stepan), Wolfe Morris (Ito), Lynne Furlong (Edna Ramsden), Raymond Adamson (Harry Ramsden), Harvey Ashby (Guards Officer), Pamela Conway (Borb's Secretary), Stanley M Ayers (Big Man in Audience), Douglas Robinson (Giorgi), Valentine Musetti (Czarko), Valerie Stanton (Cigarette Girl), The Dave Lee Trio (Themselves).
Uncredited Cast: Melvyn Mordant (Chauffeur), Victor Harrington (Wrestling Fan and General at Conference), Alison Leggatt (Wrestling Fan), Richard Cuthbert (Wrestling Fan and General at Conference), John Dennison (Wrestling Fan and General at Conference), Rosemary Chalmers (Girl at Club).
Crew: Terry Green (Designed by).
Uncredited Crew: Barbara Crowe (Stage Manager), Sylvia Langdon-Down (Production Assistant), David Granger (Call Boy), Ray Knight (Racks), Louis Bottone (Lighting Supervisor), Peter Cazaly (Technical Supervisor), Mike Roberts (Sound Supervisor), Mike Baldock (Senior Cameraman), Del Randall (Vision Mixer).

Production Schedule:
Thursday 13 September 1962: Don Leaver
Recording: 18.30-19.30: ABC Teddington Studios, Studio 1

2.09 – 'BULLSEYE'
Episode 35
Original Transmission Date: Saturday 20 October 1962
Production No: 3508
Videotape No: VTR/ABC/1986

Writer: Eric Paice
Director: Peter Hammond
Cast: Patrick Macnee (John Steed), Honor Blackman (Cathy Gale), Ronald Radd (Henry

Cade), Charles Carson (Brigadier Williamson), Judy Parfitt (Miss Ellis), Felix Deebank (Young), Mitzi Rogers (Jean), Robin Wentworth (Foreman), Fred Ferris (Inspector), Bernard Kay (Karl), Laurie Leigh (Dorothy Young), John Frawley (Reynolds), Graeme Bruce (Shareholder).

Uncredited Cast: Henry Rayner (Shareholder).

Crew: Michael Whittaker (Special wardrobe for Honor Blackman designed by), Robert Macgowran (Designed by).

Uncredited Crew: Valerie Brayden (Production Assistant), Denver Thornton (Floor Manager), Ursula Franklin (Stage Manager), Ken Brown (Lighting), Peter Cazaly (Technical Supervisor), Tom Clegg (Camera), John Tasker (Sound).

Production Schedule:
Thursday 20 September 1962: Peter Hammond
Recording: 18.30-19.30: ABC Teddington Studios, Studio 1

2.10 – 'THE REMOVAL MEN'
Episode 36
Original Transmission Date: Saturday 3 November 1962
Production No: 3509
Videotape No: VTR/ABC/2056 and 2056A

Writers: Roger Marshall and Jeremy Scott
Director: Don Leaver
Cast: Patrick Macnee (John Steed), Julie Stevens (Venus Smith), Edwin Richfield (Bud Siegel), Reed de Rouen (Jack Dragna), Patricia Denys (Cecile Dragna), George Roderick (Binaggio), Hira Talfrey (Charlie), Edina Ronay (Nicole Cauvin), Douglas Muir (One-Ten), Donald Tandy (Godard), Ivor Dean (Harbour Officer) Hugo de Verner (Jailer), George Little (Waiter), The Dave Lee Trio (Themselves).

Uncredited Cast: Vincent Charles, Roy Denton, Joan Mane, Michael Moore, Andrea Lawrence (Tourists), with extras Fran Brown, , Paul Duval, Monica Dwyer, Ivor Ellis, Valerie Gold, Michael Hamer, Helen Hancock, Paddy Kent, Umberto Lambardi, Cornelia Lucas, Steve Patrick.

Crew: Patrick Downing (Designed by).

Uncredited Crew: Harry Lock (Floor Manager), Shirley Cleghorn (Stage Manager), Sylvia Langdon-Down (Production Assistant), John Cooper (Call Boy), Frances Hancock (Wardrobe Supervisor), Peter Wayne (Technical Supervisor), Peter Kew (Lighting), John Tasker (Sound), Tom Clegg (Cameras), Bob Godfrey (Racks), Gordon Hesketh (Vision Mixer).

Production Schedule:
Wednesday 3 October 1962: Don Leaver
VT Insert: 14.15-14.30: ABC Teddington Studios, Reception, Foyer & Stairwell [Int: Steed leads Nicole to safety]
Thursday 4 October 1962: Don Leaver
Recording: 18.30-19.30: ABC Teddington Studios, Studio 1

2.11 – 'THE MAURITIUS PENNY'
Episode 37

Original Transmission Date: Saturday 10 November 1962
Production No: 3510
Videotape No: VTR/ABC/2075

Writers: Malcolm Hulke and Terrance Dicks
Director: Richmond Harding
Cast: Patrick Macnee (John Steed), Honor Blackman (Cathy Gale), Alfred Burke (Brown), David Langton (Gerald Shelley), Richard Vernon (Lord Matterley), Sylvia Langova (Sheila Gray), Edward Jewesbury (Maitland), Harry Shacklock (Peckham), Philip Guard (Goodchild), Alan Rolfe (Inspector Burke), Grace Arnold (Charlady), Edward Higgins (P C Andrews), Delia Corrie (Miss Power), Raymond Hodge (Porter), Edwin Brown (Lorry Driver), Anthony Blackshaw (Lorry Driver's Mate), Theodore Wilhelm (Foreign Delegate), Anthony Rogers (Boy).
Uncredited Cast: Freckles the Dalmatian
Crew: Michael Whittaker (Special wardrobe for Honor Blackman designed by), Philip Harrison (Designed by).
Uncredited Crew: Robert Reed (Floor Manager), Diana Gibson (Production Assistant), Barbara Crawford (Stage Manager), Peter Wayne (Technical Supervisor), Del Randall (Vision Mixer), Louis Bottone (Lighting), Michael Roberts (Sound), Michael Baldock (Cameras), Frances Hancock (Wardrobe), Lee Halls (Make-Up).

Production Schedule:
Thursday 18 October 1962: Richmond Harding
Recording: 18.30-19.30: ABC Teddington Studios, Studio 1

2.12 – DEATH OF A GREAT DANE
Episode 38
Original Transmission Date: Saturday 17 November 1962
Production No: 3511
Videotape No: VTR/ABC/2093 and 2093A

Writers: Roger Marshall and Jeremy Scott
Director: Peter Hammond
Cast: Patrick Macnee (John Steed), Honor Blackman (Cathy Gale), Frederick Jaeger (Getz), Leslie French (Gregory) John Laurie (Sir James Arnell), Clare Kelly (Mrs Miller), Dennis Edwards (1st Assistant), Anthony Baird (2nd Assistant), Billy Milton (Minister), Eric Elliott and Roger Maxwell (Winetasters), Herbert Nelson (Gravedigger), Michael Moyer (Policeman), Frank Peters (George Miller), Kevin Barry (Kennels Man), Junia (Dancer), Heidi (Bellhound).
Uncredited Cast: Benn Simons (Waiter).
Crew: Michael Whittaker (Special wardrobe for Honor Blackman designed by), Patrick Downing (Designed by).
Uncredited Crew: Valerie Brayden (Production Assistant), Harry Lock (Floor Manager), Barbara Sykes (Stage Manager), Frances Hancock (Wardrobe), Del Randall (Vision Mixer), Ken Brown (Lighting), Peter Cazaly (Technical Supervisor), Michael Baldock (Cameras), Mike Roberts (Sound), John Cooper (Call Boy).

Production Schedule:
<u>Wednesday 31 October 1962</u>: Peter Hammond
VT Insert: 17.30-18.00: ABC Teddington Studios, Studio 1 [Int: Steed and Cathy discuss Litoff's charitable donations in her apartment]
<u>Thursday 1 November 1962</u>: Peter Hammond
Recording: 18.30-19.30: ABC Teddington Studios, Studio 1

2.13 – 'DEATH ON THE ROCKS'
Episode 39
Original Transmission Date: Saturday 1 December 1962
Production No: 3512
Videotape No: VTR/ABC/2161 and 2161A

Writer: Eric Paice
Director: Jonathan Alwyn
Cast: Patrick Macnee (John Steed), Honor Blackman (Cathy Gale), Meier Tzelniker (Samuel Ross), Gerald Cross (Fenton), Ellen McIntosh (Liza Denham), Naomi Chance (Mrs Daniels), Hamilton Dyce (Max Daniels), Richard Clarke (Van Berg), David Sumner (Nicky), Toni Gilpin (Jackie Ross), Douglas Robinson (Sid), Annette Kerr (Mrs Ross), Haydn Ward (Painter), Jack Grossman (Diamond Dealer Van Klee), Vincent Charles (Diamond Dealer Sid Jacobs).
Crew: James Goddard (Designed by).
Uncredited Crew: Harry Lock (Floor Manager), Paddy Dewey (Production Assistant), Betty Crowe (Stage Manager), John Cooper (Call Boy), Carol Armstrong (Timing Production Assistant), Frances Hancock (Wardrobe Supervisor), Launa Bradish (Make-Up Supervisor), Peter Cazely (Technical Supervisor), Ken Brown (Lighting Supervisor), Tom Clegg (Senior Cameraman), John Tasker (Sound Supervisor), Bob Godfrey (Racks Supervisor), Gordon Hesketh (Vision Mixer), Michael Westlake (Grams Operator).

Production Schedule:
<u>Wednesday 14 November 1962</u>: Jonathan Alwyn
VT Insert: 11.45-12.00: ABC Teddington Studios, Studio 1 [Int: Cathy's gunfight with Liza and Daniels]
<u>Thursday 15 November 1962</u>: Jonathan Alwyn
Recording: 18.30-19.30: ABC Teddington Studios, Studio 1

2.14 – 'TRAITOR IN ZEBRA'
Episode 40
Original Transmission Date: Saturday 8 December 1962
Production No: 3513
Videotape No: VTR/ABC/2171 and 2171A/B/C*

Writer: John Gilbert
Director: Richmond Harding
Cast: Patrick Macnee (John Steed), Honor Blackman (Cathy Gale), John Sharp (Rankin), Richard Leech (Joe Franks), Noel Coleman (Captain Nash), Jack Stewart (Dr Richard Thorne), Ian Shand (Lieutenant Mellors), William Gaunt (Sub-lieutenant Ken Graham), June Murphy (Maggie), Katy Wild (Linda), Danvers Walker (Sub-lieutenant Crane),

Richard Pescud (Williams), Michael Browning (Wardroom Steward).
Uncredited Cast: Melvyn Mordant (Scientist).
Crew: Terry Green (Designed by).
Uncredited Crew: John Russell (Floor Manager), Mary Lewis (Stage Manager), Diana Gibson (Production Assistant), Robert Simmons (Technical Supervisor), Gordon Hesketh (Vision Mixer), H W Richards (Lighting), John Tasker (Sound), Tom Clegg (Cameras), Frances Hancock (Wardrobe), Launa Bradish (Make-Up).

Production Schedule:
Wednesday 28 November 1962: Richmond Harding
VT Insert: 20.15-21.00: ABC Teddington Studios, Studio 1 [Int: Opening in Nash's office/Steed talked with Crane in his cell] [*The third insert, in which Nash admits that Crane is innocent of the spying charge, was not used in the episode.]
Thursday 29 November 1962: Richmond Harding
Recording: 18.30-19.30: ABC Teddington Studios, Studio 1

2.15 – 'THE BIG THINKER'
Episode 41
Original Transmission Date: Saturday 15 December 1962
Production No: 3514
Videotape No: VTR/ABC/2217 and 2217A/B

Writer: Martin Woodhouse
Director: Kim Mills
Cast: Patrick Macnee (John Steed), Honor Blackman (Cathy Gale), Anthony Booth (Dr Jim Kearns), Walter Hudd (Dr Clemens), David Garth (Dr Farrow), Tenniel Evans (Dr Hurst), Allan McCelland (Broster), Penelope Lee (Clarissa), Marina Martin (Janet Lingfield), Ray Browne (Blakelock), Clive Baxter (Nino).
Uncredited Cast: Sheba the Whippet.
Crew: James Goddard (Designed by).
Uncredited Crew: John Russell (Floor Manager), Michael Pearce (Stage Manager), John Cooper (Call Boy), Eileen Cornwell (Production Assistant), Ruth Parkhill (Timing Production Assistant), Frances Hancock (Wardrobe Supervisor), Lee Halls (Make-Up Supervisor), Peter Wayne (Technical Supervisor), Peter Kew (Lighting Supervisor), Michael Baldock (Senior Cameraman), Michael Roberts (Sound Supervisor), Del Randall (Vision Mixer), Ray Knight (Racks Supervisor).

Production Schedule:
Wednesday 12 December 1962: Kim Mills
VT Insert: 20.00-20.30: ABC Teddington Studios, Studio 1 [Int: Dr Brensall's death/Steed and Cathy meet at the amusement arcade]
Thursday 13 December 1962: Kim Mills
Recording: 18.30-19.30: ABC Teddington Studios, Studio 1

2.16 – 'INTERCRIME'
Episode 42
Original Transmission Date: Saturday 5 January 1963
Production No: 3515

Videotape No: VTR/ABC/2271 and 2271A

Writers: Terrance Dicks and Malcolm Hulke
Director: Jonathan Alwyn
Cast: Patrick Macnee (John Steed), Honor Blackman (Cathy Gale), Kenneth J. Warren (Felder), Julia Arnall (Hilda Stern), Angela Browne (Pamela Johnson), Patrick Holt (Manning), Alan Browning (Moss), Jerome Willis (Lobb), Paul Hansard (Kressler), Donald Webster (Palmer), Rory MacDermot (Sewell), Bettine Milne (Prison Officer Sharpe), Charlotte Selwyn and Jean Gregory (Trustees).
Crew: Richard Harrison (Designed by).
Uncredited Crew: John Russell (Floor Manager), Paddy Dewey (Production Assistant), Michael Pearce (Stage Manager), John Cooper (Call Boy), Eileen Cornwell (Timing Production Assistant), Sally Russell (Wardrobe Supervisor), Lee Halls (Make-Up Supervisor), Bob Simmons (Technical Supervisor), Peter Kew (Lighting Supervisor), Dickie Jackman (Senior Cameraman), John Tasker (Sound Supervisor), Bill Marley (Racks Supervisor), Gordon Hesketh (Vision Mixer).

Production Schedule:
Friday 28 December 1962: Jonathan Alwyn
VT Insert: 20.15-21.00: ABC Teddington Studios, Studio 1 [Int: Gunfight in Felder's office and surrounding rooms]
Saturday 29 December 1962: Jonathan Alwyn
Recording: 18.30-19.30: ABC Teddington Studios, Studio 1

2.17 – 'IMMORTAL CLAY'
Episode 43
Original Transmission Date: Saturday 12 January 1963
Production No: 3516
Videotape No: VTR/ABC/2298 and 2298A

Writer: James Mitchell
Director: Richmond Harding
Cast: Patrick Macnee (John Steed), Honor Blackman (Cathy Gale), Paul Eddington (Richard Marling), James Bree (Harry Miller), Bert Palmer (Josh Machen), Gary Watson (Allen Marling), Steve Plytas (De Groot), Rowena Gregory (Anne Marling), Didi Sullivan (Mara Little), Douglas Muir (One-Ten), Frank Olegario (Blomberg).
Uncredited Cast: Leonard Kingston (Waiter).
Crew: James Goddard (Designed by).
Uncredited Crew: Denver Thornton (Floor Manager), Diana Lyddon (Stage Manager), Diana Gibson (Production Assistant), Peter Cazaly (Technical Supervisor), Gordon Hesketh (Vision Mixer), Kenneth Brown (Lighting), Richard Jackman (Sound), Michael Roberts (Cameras), Ambren Garland (Wardrobe), Launa Bradish (Make-Up), Alan Fowler and William Marley (Racks).

Production Schedule:
Wednesday 9 January 1963: Richmond Harding
VT Insert: 20.30-21.00: ABC Teddington Studios, Studio 1 [Int: Concluding fight scene in the pottery works]

Thursday 10 January 1963: Richmond Harding
Recording: 18.30-19.30: ABC Teddington Studios, Studio 1

2.18 – 'BOX OF TRICKS'
Episode 44
Original Transmission Date: Saturday 19 January 1963
Production No: 3517
Videotape No: VTR/ABC/2299 and 2299A

Writers: Peter Ling and Edward Rhodes
Director: Kim Mills
Cast: Patrick Macnee (John Steed), Julie Stevens (Venus Smith), Jane Barrett (Kathleen Sutherland), Maurice Hedley (General Sutherland), Edgar Wreford (Dr Gallam), Ian Curry (Gerry Watson), April Olrich (Denise), Dallas Cavell (Manager), Jacqueline Jones (Henriette), Gregory Scott (Nino), Royston Tickner (Harry), Gail Starforth (Mary), Lynn Taylor (Valerie), Robert Hartley (Maitre d'), Gregory Scott (Doorman), The Dave Lee Trio (Themselves).
Uncredited Cast: Yvette Herries (Hostess), Vernon Duke (Club Patron and British General).
Crew: Ann Spavin (Designed by).
Uncredited Crew: John Russell (Floor Manager), Michael Pearce (Stage Manager), John Cooper (Call Boy), Eileen Cornwell (Production Assistant), Paddy Dewey (Timing Production Assistant), Margaret Morris (Wardrobe Supervisor), Lee Halls (Make-Up Supervisor), Peter Cazaly (Technical Supervisor), Bob Simmons (Lighting Supervisor), Dickie Jackman (Senior Cameraman), Michael Roberts (Sound Supervisor), Gordon Hesketh (Vision Mixer), Alan Fowler (Racks Supervisor).

Production Schedule:
Wednesday 16 January 1963: Kim Mills
VT Insert: 20.30-21.00: ABC Teddington Studios, Studio 1 [Int: Fight scene involving Steed, Dr Gallam and Kathleen Sutherland beneath the stage of the nightclub]
Thursday 17 January 1963: Kim Mills
Recording: 18.30-19.30: ABC Teddington Studios, Studio 1

2.19 – 'THE GOLDEN EGGS'
Episode 45
Original Transmission Date: Saturday 2 February 1963
Production No: 3518
Videotape No: VTR/ABC/2321

Writer: Martin Woodhouse
Director: Peter Hammond
Cast: Patrick Macnee (John Steed), Honor Blackman (Cathy Gale), Peter Arne (Redfern), Pauline Delaney (Elizabeth Bayle), Donald Eccles (Dr Ashe), Gordon Whiting (DeLeon), Robert Bernal (Hillier), Irene Bradshaw (Diana DeLeon), Louis Haslar (Campbell), Charles Bird (Hall).
Crew: Douglas James (Designed by).
Uncredited Crew: Jill Horwood (Production Assistant), Denver Thornton (Floor

Manager), Betty Crowe (Stage Manager), Peter Wayne (Technical Supervisor), Ken Brown (Lighting Supervisor), Dickie Jackman (Senior Cameraman), John Tasker (Sound Supervisor), Del Randall (Vision Mixer), Ambren Garland (Wardrobe Supervisor), Lee Halls (Make-Up Supervisor).

Production Schedule:
Thursday 31 January 1963: Peter Hammond
Recording: 18.30-19.30: ABC Teddington Studios, Studio 1

2.20 – 'SCHOOL FOR TRAITORS'
Episode 46
Original Transmission Date: Saturday 9 February 1963
Production No: 3519
Videotape No: VTR/ABC/2322

Writer: James Mitchell
Director: Jonathan Alwyn
Cast: Patrick Macnee (John Steed), Julie Stevens (Venus Smith), Melissa Stribling (Claire Summers), Anthony Nicholls (Dr Shanklin), John Standing (Ted East), Richard Thorp (Jeff Roberts), Reginald Marsh (Higby), Frank Shelley (Professor Aubyn), Frederick Farley (One-Seven), Terence Woodfield (Green), Ronald Mayer (Proctor), Janet Butlin (Barmaid), The Kenny Baker Trio (Themselves).
Crew: Maurice Pelling (Designed by).
Uncredited Crew: John Wayne (Floor Manager), Harry Lock (Floor Manager Supervisor), Paddy Dewey (Production Assistant), Barbara Sykes (Stage Manager), David Read (Call Boy), Jill Horwood (Timing Production Assistant), Sally Russell (Wardrobe Supervisor), Peter Cazaly (Technical Supervisor), Peter Kew (Lighting Supervisor), Dickie Jackman (Senior Cameraman), John Tasker (Sound Supervisor), Gordon Hesketh (Vision Mixer), Alan Fowler (Racks Supervisor), Lee Halls (Make-Up Supervisor).

Production Schedule:
Saturday 9 February 1963: Jonathan Alwyn
Recording: 18.30-19.30: ABC Teddington Studios, Studio 2

2.21 – 'THE WHITE DWARF'
Episode 47
Original Transmission Date: Saturday 16 February 1963
Production No: 3520
Videotape No: VTR/ABC/2366

Writer: Malcolm Hulke
Director: Richmond Harding
Cast: Patrick Macnee (John Steed), Honor Blackman (Cathy Gale), George A Cooper (Maxwell Barker), Philip Latham (Professor Cartright), Peter Copley (Henry Barker), Bill Nagy (Mervin Johnson), Vivienne Drummond (Elizabeth Fuller), Daniel Thorndike (Minister), Constance Chapman (Miss Tregarth), George Roubicek (Luke Richter), Keith Pyott (Professor Richter), Paul Anil (Professor Rahim), John Falconer (Butler).

Uncredited Cast: Sheba the Whippet.
Crew: Terry Green (Designed by).
Uncredited Crew: Pat Kennedy (Floor Manager), Shirley Cleghorn (Stage Manager), Iris Frederick and Pamela Bedford (Production Assistants).

Production Schedule:
Saturday 16 February 1963: Richmond Harding
Recording: Unknown time: ABC Teddington Studios, Studio 2

2.22 – 'MAN IN THE MIRROR'
Episode 48
Original Transmission Date: Saturday 23 February 1963
Production No: 3521
Videotape No: VTR/ABC/2426

Writers: Geoffrey Orme and Anthony Terpiloff
Director: Kim Mills
Cast: Patrick Macnee (John Steed), Julie Stevens (Venus Smith), Daphne Anderson (Betty), Ray Barrett (Strong), Julian Somers (Michael Brown), Rhoda Lewis (Jean Trevelyan), Haydn Jones (Victor Trevelyan), Michael Gover (One-Six), David Graham (Producer), Frieda Knorr (Iris), The Kenny Powell Trio (Themselves).
Uncredited Cast: Ray Browne (Dead Man), Sheba the Whippet.
Crew: Ann Spavin (Designed by).
Uncredited Crew: Robert Reed (Floor Manager), Michael Pearce (Stage Manager), David Granger (Call Boy), Eileen Cornwell (Production Assistant), Carol Armstrong (Timing Production Assistant), Ambren Garland (Wardrobe Supervisor), Lee Halls (Make-Up Supervisor), Bob Simmons (Technical Supervisor), Louie Bottone (Lighting Supervisor), Mike Baldock (Senior Cameraman), Mike Roberts (Sound Supervisor), Del Randall (Vision Mixer), Bert White (Racks Supervisor), Brian Hibbert (Grams Operator).

Production Schedule:
Friday 22 February 1963: Kim Mills
Recording: 18.30-19.30: ABC Teddington Studios, Studio 1

2.23 – 'CONSPIRACY OF SILENCE'
Episode 49
Original Transmission Date: Saturday 2 March 1963
Production No: 3522
Videotape No: VTR/ABC/2451

Writer: Roger Marshall
Director: Peter Hammond
Cast: Patrick Macnee (John Steed), Honor Blackman (Cathy Gale), Robert Rietty (Carlo), Sandra Dorne (Rickie Bennett), Alec Mango (Sica), Roy Purcell (Gutman), Tommy Godfrey (Arturo), John Church (Terry), Artro Morris (James), Willie Shearer (Professor), Ian Wilson (Rant), Elizabeth and Collins (Knife Throwing Act).
Uncredited Cast: Sheba the Whippet.
Crew: Stephen Doncaster (Designed by).

Uncredited Crew: Jill Horwood (Production Assistant), Patrick Kennedy (Floor Manager), Betty Crowe (Stage Manager), Peter Cazaly (Technical Supervisor), H W Ritchie (Lighting Supervisor), Michael Baldock (Senior Cameraman), Michael Roberts (Sound Supervisor), Del Randall (Vision Mixer), Sally Russell (Wardrobe Supervisor), Lee Halls (Make-Up Supervisor).

Production Schedule:
Friday 1 March 1963: Peter Hammond
Recording: 18.30-19.30: ABC Teddington Studios, Studio 1

2.24 – 'A CHORUS OF FROGS'
Episode 50
Original Transmission Date: Saturday 9 March 1963
Production No: 3523
Videotape No: VTR/ABC/2488 and 2488A/B

Writer: Martin Woodhouse
Director: Raymond Menmuir
Cast: Patrick Macnee (John Steed), Julie Stevens (Venus Smith), Eric Pohlmann (Archipelago Mason), Yvonne Shima (Anna Lee), Colette Wilde (Helena), John Carson (Ariston), Frank Gatliff (Dr Pitt-Norton), Michael Gover (One-Six), Alan Haywood (Jackson), Makki Marseilles (Andreas Stephanopolulus), Norman Johns (First Officer), Steve Cory (Barman), Colin Fry (Bracken), The Kenny Powell Trio (Themselves).
Uncredited Cast: Steve Cory (Stunt Double for Jackson).
Crew: James Goddard (Designed by).
Uncredited Crew: Ruth Parkhill (Production Assistant), Robert Reed (Floor Manager), Shirley Cleghorn (Stage Manager), Peter Cazaly (Technical Supervisor), Louis Bottone (Lighting Supervisor), Richard Jackman (Senior Cameramen), John Tasker (Sound Supervisor), Gordon Hesketh (Vision Mixer), Frances Hancock (Wardrobe Supervisor), Lee Halls (Make-Up Supervisor), Douglas Robinson (Fight Arranger).

Production Schedule:
Thursday 7 March 1963: Raymond Menmuir
VT Insert: 10.00-13.00: ABC Teddington Studios, Studio 1 [Int: Anna kills Jackson with a harpoon gun/Fight in the experimental area to rescue Venus]
Friday 8 March 1963: Raymond Menmuir
Recording: 18.30-19.30: ABC Teddington Studios, Studio 1

2.25 – 'SIX HANDS ACROSS A TABLE'
Episode 51
Original Transmission Date: Saturday 16 March 1963
Production No: 3524
Videotape No: VTR/ABC/2508

Writer: Reed R de Rouen
Director: Richmond Harding
Cast: Patrick Macnee (John Steed), Honor Blackman (Cathy Gale), Guy Doleman (Oliver Waldner), Campbell Singer (George Stanley), Philip Madoc (Julian Seabrook),

Edward de Souza (Brian Collier), John Wentworth (Charles Reniston), Sylvia Bidmead (Rosalind Waldner), Frank Sieman (Bert Barnes), Stephen Hancock (Draughtsman), Freda Bamford (Lady Reniston), Gillian Barclay (Miss Francis), Ilona Rodgers (Receptionist), Ian Cunningham (Butler).
Uncredited Cast: Valantine Musetti (Stunt Double for Julian Seabrook).
Crew: Paul Bernard (Designed by).
Uncredited Crew: Christine Thomas (Production Assistant), Harry Lock (Floor Manager), Barbara Sykes (Stage Manager), Peter Cazaly (Technical Supervisor), Peter Kew (Lighting Supervisor), Dickie Jackman (Senior Cameraman), John Tasker (Sound Supervisor), Gordon Hesketh (Vision Mixer), Sally Russell (Wardrobe Supervisor), Lee Halls (Make-Up Supervisor).

Production Schedule:
Friday 15 March 1963: Richmond Harding
Recording: 18.30-19.30: ABC Teddington Studios, Studio 1

2.26 – 'KILLER WHALE'
Episode 52
Original Transmission Date: Saturday 23 March 1963
Production No: 3525
Videotape No: VTR/ABC/2517 and 2517A/B

Writer: John Lucarotti
Director: Kim Mills
Cast: Patrick Macnee (John Steed), Honor Blackman (Cathy Gale), Patrick Magee (Pancho Driver), John Bailey (Fernand), Kenneth Farrington (Joey), Morris Perry (Harry), John Tate (Willie), Julie Paulle (Angela), Christopher Coll (Laboratory Assistant), Robert Mill (Brown), Frederic Abbott (Sailor), Lyndall Goodman (Receptionist), Brian Mason (Tiger).
Uncredited Cast: June Hodgson, Diane Keys, Elaine Little (Models), Terry Brewer and Valentine Musetti (Boxers).
Crew: Douglas James (Designed by).
Uncredited Crew: Patrick Kennedy (Floor Manager), Nansi Davies (Stage Manager), David Granger (Call Boy), Eileen Cornwell (Production Assistant), Diana Gibson (Timing Production Assistant), Audrey Riddle (Wardrobe Supervisor), Lee Halls (Make-Up Supervisor), Peter Wayne (Technical Supervisor), Ken Browne (Lighting Supervisor), Michael Baldock (Senior Cameraman), Michael Roberts (Sound Supervisor), Del Randall (Vision Mixer), Ray Knight (Racks Supervisor), Brian Moray (Grams Operator).

Production Schedule:
Thursday 21 March 1963: Kim Mills
VT Insert: 19.30-20.15: ABC Teddington Studios, Studio 1 [Joey and Tiger in the boxing ring/End tag scene in Cathy's apartment]
Friday 22 March 1963: Kim Mills
Recording: 18.30-19.30: ABC Teddington Studios, Studio 1

SEASON 3

An Iris Productions production for ABC Television
26 black and white episodes on videotape, later copied onto 16mm film
Permanent Crew: John Bryce (Producer), Richard Bates (Story Editor), Johnny Dankworth (*The Avengers* theme composed and played by).

3.01 – 'BRIEF FOR MURDER'
Episode 53
Original Transmission Date: Saturday 28 September 1963
Production No: 3600
Videotape No: Unknown

Writer: Brian Clemens
Director: Peter Hammond
Cast: Patrick Macnee (John Steed), Honor Blackman (Cathy Gale), John Laurie (Jasper Lakin), Harold Scott (Miles Lakin), Helen Lindsay (Barbara Kingston), Alec Ross (Ronald Henry Westcott), June Thody (Dicey), Anthony Baird (Wilson), Alice Fraser (Miss Prinn), Fred Ferris (Inspector Marsh), Michael Goldie (Bart), Robert Young (Judge), Pamela Wardel (Maisie), Walter Swash (Foreman of the Jury).
Crew: James Goddard (Designed by).

Production Schedule:
Thursday 11 April 1963: Peter Hammond
Recording: ABC Teddington Studios, Unknown Studio

3.02 – 'CONCERTO'
Episode 54
Original Transmission Date: Saturday 7 March 1964
Production No: 3601
Videotape No: VTR/ABC/2644

Writers: Terrance Dicks and Malcolm Hulke
Director: Kim Mills
Cast: Patrick Macnee (John Steed), Honor Blackman (Cathy Gale), Nigel Stock (Zalenko), Sandor Elés (Stefan Veliko), Dorinda Stevens (Darleen Lomax), Bernard Brown (Peterson), Geoffrey Colvile (Burns), Carole Ward (Receptionist), Valerie Bell (Polly White), Leslie Glazer (Robbins) and Junia (Steed's Great Dane).
Uncredited Cast: Lynn Taylor (Stripper), Valentine Musetti (Thug), Howard Kingsley (Club Patron), Richard Cuthbert (Club Patron and Concerto Guest), Benn Simons (Concerto Waiter and Club Patron), Victor Harrington (Club Patron and Concerto Guest), Caroline Hall (Hostess), Terry Brewer (Thug), Rex Rashley (Club Patron and Concerto Guest), John Dennison (Trade Minister), Coreen Burford (Concerto Guest), Gregory Scott (Club Patron and Concerto Guest), with extras Lauderdale Beckett, John Cabot, Daphne Davey, Dorothy Robson.
Crew: Robert Macgowran (Designed by).
Uncredited Crew: Ian Little-Smith (Floor Manager), Michael Pearce (Stage Manager),

David Granger (Call Boy), Eileen Cornwell (Production Assistant), Pat Sparks (Timing Production Assistant), Margaret Morris (Wardrobe Supervisor), Lee Halls (Make-Up Supervisor), Peter Cazaly (Technical Supervisor), Louie Bottone (Lighting Supervisor), Michael Baldock (Senior Cameraman), Michael Roberts (Sound Supervisor), Del Randall (Vision Mixer), Ray Knight (Racks Operator), David Hounsell (Grams Operator).

Production Schedule:
Friday 26 April 1963: Kim Mills
Recording: 18.30-19.30: ABC Teddington Studios, Studio 1

3.03 – 'THE NUTSHELL'
Episode 55
Original Transmission Date: Saturday 19 October 1963
Production No: 3602
Videotape No: VTR/ABC/2675

Writer: Philip Chambers
Director: Raymond Menmuir
Cast: Patrick Macnee (John Steed), Honor Blackman (Cathy Gale), Charle Tingwell (Venner), John Cater (Disco), Patricia Haines (Laura), Christine Shaw (Susan), Edina Ronay (Elin Strindberg), Ian Clark (Anderson), Ray Browne (Alex), Jan Conrad (Jason), Edwin Brown (Military Policeman).
Uncredited Cast: Henry Rayner, Frank Peters, Bob Raymond, Guy Graham (Security Guards).
Crew: Philip Harrison (Designed by).
Uncredited Crew: Pat Sparks (Production Assistant), Barbara Sykes (Stage Manager), John Russell (Floor Manager), John Cooper (Call Boy), Frances Hancock (Wardrobe Supervisor), Lee Halls (Make-Up Supervisor), Peter Wayne (Technical Supervisor), Peter Kew (Lighting Supervisor), Dickie Jackman (Senior Cameraman), John Tasker (Sound Supervisor), Gordon Hesketh (Vision Mixer), Alan Fowler (Racks Operator), Mike Harrison (Grams Operator).

Production Schedule:
Friday 10 May 1963: Raymond Menmuir
Recording: 18.30-19.30: ABC Teddington Studios, Studio 1

3.04 – 'THE GOLDEN FLEECE'
Episode 56
Original Transmission Date: Saturday 7 December 1963
Production No: 3603
Videotape No: VTR/ABC/2715

Writers: Roger Marshall and Phyllis Norman
Director: Peter Hammond
Cast: Patrick Macnee (John Steed), Honor Blackman (Cathy Gale), Warren Mitchell (Captain George Jason), Tenniel Evans (Major Ruse), Barry Linehan (Sergeant Major Wright), Robert Lee (Mr Lo), Yu Ling (Mrs Kwan), Lisa Peake (Esther Jones), Ronald

Wilson (Private Holmes), Michael Hawkins (Jimmy Jones).
Uncredited Cast: Yvette Herries (Hostess), Junia (Steed's Great Dane).
Crew: Anna Spavin (Designed by).
Uncredited Crew: Harry Locke (Floor Manager), Shirley Cleghorn (Stage Manager), Christine Thomas (Production Assistant), Bob Godfrey (Technical Supervisor), Peter Kew (Lighting Supervisor), Mike Baldock (Senior Cameraman), Mike Roberts (Sound Supervisor), Del Randall (Vision Mixer), Ambren Garland (Wardrobe Supervisor), Lee Halls (Make-Up Supervisor).

Production Schedule:
Friday 24 May 1963: Peter Hammond
Recording: 18.30-19.30: ABC Teddington Studios, Studio 1

3.05 – 'DEATH A LA CARTE'
Episode 57
Original Transmission Date: Saturday 21 December 1963
Production No: 3604
Videotape No: VTR/ABC/2716 and 2716A

Writer: John Lucarotti
Director: Kim Mills
Cast: Patrick Macnee (John Steed), Honor Blackman (Cathy Gale), Robert James (Mellor), Henry Soskin (Emir Abdulla Akaba), Paul Dawkins (Dr Spender), Ken Parry (Arbuthnot), Gordon Rollings (Lucien), David Nettheim (Umberto), Coral Atkins (Josie), Valentino Musetti (Ali).
Crew: Richard Harrison (Designed by).
Uncredited Crew: Denver Thornton (Floor Manager), Michael Pearce (Stage Manager), Eileen Cornwall (Production Assistant), Jacqueline Davis (Timing Production Assistant), Sally Russell (Wardrobe Supervisor), Lee Halls (Make-Up Supervisor), Louie Bottone (Lighting Supervisor), Dickie Jackman (Senior Cameraman), John Tasker (Sound Supervisor), Gordon Hesketh (Vision Mixer), Alan Fowler (Racks Supervisor), Dave Hounsell (Grams Operator).

Production Schedule:
Thursday 6 June 1963: Kim Mills
VT Insert: 19.30-21.00: ABC Teddington Studios, Studio 1 [Steed climbing up exterior of the building]
Friday 7 June 1963: Kim Mills
Recording: 18.30-19.30: ABC Teddington Studios, Studio 1

3.06 – 'MAN WITH TWO SHADOWS'
Episode 58
Original Transmission Date: Saturday 12 October 1963
Production No: 3605
Videotape No: VTR/ABC/2799 and 2799A/B/C/D/E/F

Writer: James Mitchell
Director: Don Leaver

Cast: Patrick Macnee (John Steed), Honor Blackman (Cathy Gale), Daniel Moynihan (Bill Gordon), Paul Whitsun-Jones (Charles), Philip Anthony (Frank Cummings), Gwendolyn Watts (Julie Clitheroe), Geoffrey Palmer (Dr Terence), Anne Godfrey (Miss Quist), George Little (Sigi), Douglas Robinson (Rudi), Terence Lodge (Borowski), Robert Lankesheer (Holiday Camp Official).
Uncredited Cast: Patrick Macnee (John Steed Double).
Crew: Paul Bernard (Designed by).
Uncredited Crew: Harry Lock (Floor Manager), Barbara Sykes (Stage Manager), Anne Summerton (Production Assistant), Paddy Dewey (Timing Production Assistant), David Granger (Call Boy), Frances Hancock (Wardrobe), Peter Cazaly (Technical Supervisor), Peter Kew (Lighting Supervisor), John Tasker (Sound Supervisor), Dickie Jackman (Senior Cameraman), Gordon Hesketh (Vision Mixer).

Production Schedule:
Thursday 20 June 1963: Don Leaver
VT Insert: 17.15-18.00: ABC Teddington Studios, Studio 1 [Int: A: The real Gordon before being shot/C: The fake Gordon/D: Steed double and Cummings/E: Steed double and Sigi/F: Steed double enters chalet and hides in shower/Int & Ext: B: Steed arrives at chalet]
VT Insert: 19.00-21.00: ABC Teddington Studios, Studio 1 [Completion of inserts]
Friday 21 June 1963: Don Leaver
Recording: 17.15-18.30: ABC Teddington Studios, Studio 1

3.07 – 'DON'T LOOK BEHIND YOU'
Episode 59
Original Transmission Date: Saturday 14 December 1963
Production No: 3606
Videotape No: VTR/ABC/2829 and 2829A

Writer: Brian Clemens
Director: Peter Hammond
Cast: Patrick Macnee (John Steed), Honor Blackman (Cathy Gale), Janine Gray (Ola Monsey-Chamberlain), Kenneth Colley (Young Man), Maurice Good (Martin Goodman).
Crew: Terry Green (Designed by).
Uncredited Crew: Jill Watts (Production Assistant), Denver Thornton (Floor Manager), Shirley Cleghorn (Stage Manager), Peter Cazaly (Technical Supervisor), Michael Baldock (Senior Cameraman), Michael Roberts (Sound Supervisor), Peter Kew (Lighting), Del Randall (Vision Mixer), Ambren Garland (Wardrobe Supervisor), Lee Halls (Make-Up Supervisor).

Production Schedule:
Thursday 4 July 1963: Peter Hammond
VT Insert: 19.30-21.00: ABC Teddington Studios, Studio 1 [Montage of cut-up stills]
Friday 5 July 1963: Peter Hammond
Recording: 18.30-19.30: ABC Teddington Studios, Studio 1

3.08 – 'THE GRANDEUR THAT WAS ROME'
Episode 60
Original Transmission Date: Saturday 30 November 1963
Production No: 3607
Videotape No: VTR/ABC/2869

Writer: Rex Edwards
Director: Kim Mills
Cast: Patrick Macnee (John Steed), Honor Blackman (Cathy Gale), Hugh Burden (Sir Bruno Luker), Colette Wilde (Octavia), John Flint (Marcus), Ian Shand (Eastow), Raymond Adamson (Lucius), Kenneth Keeling (Appleton), Colin Rix (Barnes).
Uncredited Cast: David Anderson (Penrose), Victor Harrington (Board Member and Senator), Bob Raymond (Board Member, Farmer and Senator), Richard Cuthbert (Senator), Brian Mason and Rocky Taylor (Roman Soldiers).
Crew: Stan Woodward (Designed by).
Uncredited Crew: John Wayne (Floor Manager), Betty Crowe (Stage Manager), David Granger (Call Boy), Eileen Cornwell (Production Assistant), Sally Russell (Wardrobe Supervisor), Lee Halls (Make-Up Supervisor), Bob Godfrey (Technical Supervisor), Ken Brown (Lighting Supervisor), Michael Baldock (Senior Cameraman), Michael Roberts (Sound Supervisor), Del Randall (Vision Mixer), Bill Marley (Racks Supervisor), Peter Wilcox (Grams Operator).

Production Schedule:
Friday 19 July 1963: Kim Mills
Recording: 18.20-19.30: ABC Teddington Studios, Studio 1

3.09 – 'THE UNDERTAKERS'
Episode 61
Original Transmission Date: Saturday 5 October 1963
Production No: 3608
Videotape No: VTR/ABC/2899

Writer: Malcolm Hulke
Director: Bill Bain
Cast: Patrick Macnee (John Steed), Honor Blackman (Cathy Gale), Lee Patterson (Lomax), Jan Holden (Paula), Lally Bowers (Mrs Renter), Patrick Holt (Madden), Mandy Miller (Daphne), Howard Goorney (Green), Marcella Markham (Mrs Lomx), Ronald Russell (Wilkinson), Helena McCarthy (Mrs Baker), Denis Forsyth (Reeve).
Uncredited Cast: Valentino Musetti, Richard Turner, Leonard Kingston, John Dennison (Undertakers).
Crew: David Marshall (Designed by).
Uncredited Crew: John Wayne (Floor Manager), Paddy Dewey (Production Assistant), Dennis Redwood (Stage Manager), David Granger (Call Boy), Carol Armstrong (Timing Production Assistant), Audrey Riddle (Wardrobe), Lee Halls (Make-Up), Bob Godfrey (Technical Supervisor), H W Richards (Lighting Supervisor), Dickie Jackman (Senior Cameraman), Michael Roberts (Sound Supervisor), Muriel Holmes (Vision Mixer), Alan Fowler (Racks Supervisor), Tony Morley (Grams Operator).

Production Schedule:
Friday 2 August 1963: Bill Bain
Recording: 18.20-19.30: ABC Teddington Studios, Studio 1

3.10 – 'DEATH OF A BATMAN'
Episode 62
Original Transmission Date: Saturday 26 October 1963
Production No: 3609
Videotape No: Unknown

Writer: Roger Marshall
Director: Kim Mills
Cast: Patrick Macnee (John Steed), Honor Blackman (Cathy Gale), Andre Morrell (Lord Teale), Philip Madoc (Van Doren), Katy Greenwood (Lady Cynthia), David Burke (John Wrightson), Geoffrey Alexander (Gibbs), Kitty Attwood (Edith Wrightson), Ray Browne (Cooper).
Uncredited Cast: Katie (Steed's Great Dane).
Crew: Paul Bernard (Designed by).
Uncredited Crew: Peter Bailey (Floor Manager), Nansi Davies (Stage Manager), Eileen Cornwell (Production Assistant).

Production Schedule:
Wednesday 14 August 1963: Kim Mills
Recording: 18.30-19.30: ABC Teddington Studios, Studio 1

3.11 – 'BUILD A BETTER MOUSETRAP'
Episode 63
Original Transmission Date: Saturday 15 February 1964
Production No: 3610
Videotape No: VTR/ABC/2930

Writer: Brian Clemens
Director: Peter Hammond
Cast: Patrick Macnee (John Steed), Honor Blackman (Cathy Gale), Athene Seyler (Cynthia Peck), Nora Nicholson (Ermyntrude Peck), Harold Goodwin (Harris), John Tate (Colonel Wesker), Alison Seebohm (Caroline), Donald Webster (Dave), Marian Diamond (Jessy), Allan McClelland (Stigant), David Anderson (Gordon).
Uncredited Cast: Sheila Dunn (Biker Girl).
Crew: Doulas James (Designed by).
Uncredited Crew: Jill Watts (Production Assistant), John Russell (Floor Manager), Betty Crowe (Stage manager), Peter Cazaly (Technical Supervisor), Dickie Jackman (Senior Cameraman), John Tasker (Sound Supervisor), Louis Bottone (Lighting), Del Randall (Vision Mixer), Margaret Morris (Wardrobe Supervisor), Lee Halls (Make-Up Supervisor), Alan Fowler (Racks Supervisor), Tony Morley (Grams Operator).

Production Schedule:
Wednesday 28 August 1963: Peter Hammond
Recording: 18.30-19.30: ABC Teddington Studios, Studio 1

3.12 – 'NOVEMBER FIVE'
Episode 64
Original Transmission Date: Saturday 2 November 1963
Production No: 3611
Videotape No: VTR/ABC/2965

Writer: Eric Paice
Director: Bill Bain
Cast: Patrick Macnee (John Steed), Honor Blackman (Cathy Gale), Ruth Dunning (Mrs Dove), David Davies (Arthur Dove), Ric Hutton (Mark St John), David Langton (Major Swinburne), Iris Russell (Fiona), Gary Hope (Michael Dyter), Joe Robinson (Max), Aimée Delamain (First Lady), John Murray (Returning Officer), Frank Maher (Farmer).
Uncredited Cast: Richard Cuthbert (Member of Parliament).
Crew: Frederick Starke (Honor Blackman's wardrobe designed by), Douglas James (Designed by).
Uncredited Crew: Carol Armstrong (Production Assistant), John Wayne (Floor Manager), Nansi Davies (Stage Manager), Bob Godfrey (Technical Supervisor), Richard Jackman (Cameras), H W Richards (Lighting), John Tasker (Sound), Gordon Hesketh (Vision Mixer), Ambren Garland (Wardrobe), Lee Halls (Make-Up).

Production Schedule:
Thurday 26 September 1963: Bill Bain
VT Insert: 19.30-21.00: ABC Teddington Studios, Studio 1 [Ext: House of Commons Terrace/Int: House of Commons lobby]
Friday 27 September 1963: Bill Bain
Recording: 18.30-19.30: ABC Teddington Studios, Studio 1

3.13 – 'SECOND SIGHT'
Episode 65
Original Transmission Date: Saturday 16 November 1963
Production No: 3612

Videotape No: VTR/ABC/3033
Writer: Martin Woodhouse
Director: Peter Hammond
Cast: Patrick Macnee (John Steed), Honor Blackman (Cathy Gale), Peter Bowles (Neil Anstice), Judy Bruce (Dr Eve Hawn), John Carson (Marten Halvarssen), Ronald Adam (Dr Spender), Steven Scott (Dr Vilner), Terry Brewer (Steiner).
Crew: Frederick Starke (Honor Blackman's wardrobe designed by), Terry Green (Designed by).
Uncredited Crew: Jill Watts (Production Assistant), Ian Little-Smith (Floor Manager), Betty Crowe (Stage Manager), Peter Cazaly (Technical Supervisor), Dickie Jackman (Senior Cameraman), John Tasker (Sound Supervisor), Louis Bottone (Lighting), Gordon Hesketh (Vision Mixer), Margaret Morris (Wardrobe Supervisor), Lee Halls (Make-Up Supervisor).

Production Schedule:
Friday 11 October 1963: Peter Hammond

Recording: 18.30-19.30: ABC Teddington Studios, Studio 1

3.14 – 'THE SECRETS BROKER'
Episode 66
Original Transmission Date: Saturday 1 February 1964
Production No: 3613
Videotape No: VTR/ABC/3094 & 3094A

Writer: Ludovic Peters
Director: Jonathan Alwyn
Cast: Patrick Macnee (John Steed), Honor Blackman (Cathy Gale), Avice Landon (Mrs Wilson), Jack May (Waller), Ronald Allen (Allan Paignton), John Stone (Frederick Paignton), Patricia English (Marion Howard), John Ringham (Cliff Howard), Brian Hankins (Jim Carey), Jennifer Wood (Julia Wilson), Valentino Musetti (Bruno).
Crew: Frederick Starke (Honor Blackman's wardrobe designed by), Anne Spavin (Designed by).
Uncredited Crew: Peter Bailey (Floor Manager), Paddy Dewey (Production Assistant), Mary Lewis (Stage Manager), David Granger (Call Boy), Eileen Cornwell (Timing Production Assistant), Ambren Garland (Wardrobe), Lee Halls (Make-Up), Bob Godfrey (Technical Supervisor), H W Richards (Lighting Supervisor), Dickie Jackman (Senior Cameraman), John Tasker (Sound Supervisor), Gordon Hesketh (Vision Mixer), Alan Fowler (Racks Supervisor), Tony Morley (Grams Operator).

Production Schedule:
Friday 18 October 1963: Jonathan Alwyn
VT Insert: 20.30-21.00: ABC Teddington Studios, Studio 2 [Int: Concluding fight scene in the wine shop and cellar]
Saturday 19 October 1963: Jonathan Alwyn
Recording: 18.30-19.30: ABC Teddington Studios, Studio 2

3.15 – 'THE GILDED CAGE'
Episode 67
Original Transmission Date: Saturday 9 November 1963
Production No: 3614
Videotape No: Unknown

Writer: Roger Marshall
Director: Bill Bain
Cast: Patrick Macnee (John Steed), Honor Blackman (Cathy Gale), Patrick Magee (J P Spagge), Edric Connor (Abe Benham), Norman Chappell (Fleming), Margo Cunningham (Wardress), Fredric Abbott (Jack Manley), Alan Haywood (Westwood), Martin Friend (Hammond), Terence Soall (Peterson), Geoff L'Cise (Gruber), Douglas Cummings (Barker), Neil Wilson (Groves).
Uncredited Cast: Katie (Steed's Great Dane).
Crew: Frederick Starke (Honor Blackman's wardrobe designed by), Robert MacGowan (Designed by).

Production Schedule
Friday 25 October 1963: Bill Bain
Recording: Unknown time: ABC Teddington Studios, Studio: Unknown

3.16 – 'THE MEDICINE MEN'
Episode 68
Original Transmission Date: Saturday 23 November 1963
Production No: 3615
Videotape No: VTR/ABC/3135 and 3135A/B/C

Writer: Malcolm Hulke
Director: Kim Mills
Cast: Patrick Macnee (John Steed), Honor Blackman (Cathy Gale), Peter Barkworth (Geoffrey Willis), Newton Blick (John Willis), Harold Innocent (Frank Leeson), Joy Wood (Miss Dowell), Monica Stevenson (Fay), John Crocker (Taylor), Peter Hughes (Edwards), Brenda Cowling (Masseuse), Lucille Soong (Tu Hsiu Yung).
Uncredited Cast: Elizabeth Villiers (Baths Attendant), Norman Lambert (Thug), Max Latimer (Thug).
Crew: Frederick Starke (Honor Blackman's wardrobe designed by), David Marshall (Designed by).
Uncredited Crew: John Russell (Floor Manager), Nansi Davies (Stage Manager), John Cooper (Call Boy), Eileen Cornwell (Production Assistant), Marian Lloyd (Timing Production Assistant), Margaret Morris (Wardrobe), Lee Halls (Make-Up), Bob Godfrey (Technical Supervisor), Peter Kew (Lighting Supervisor), Michael Baldock (Senior Cameraman), Michael Roberts (Sound Supervisor), Del Randall (Vision Mixer), William Marley and Robert White (Racks), Brian Moray (Grams Operator).

Production Schedule:
Thursday 7 November 1963: Kim Mills
VT Insert: 19.30-21.00: ABC Teddington Studios, Studio 1 [Int: Tu Hsiu Yung murdered at the Turkish baths/Cathy and Fay at the Turkish baths/End Tag Scene: Steed and Cathy see Fay off from his apartment]
Friday 8 November 1963: Kim Mills
Recording: 18.30-19.30: ABC Teddington Studios, Studio 1

3.17 – 'THE WHITE ELEPHANT'
Episode 69
Original Transmission Date: Saturday 4 January 1964
Production No: 3616
Videotape No: VTR/ABC/3168 & 3168A/B

Writer: John Lucarotti
Director: Laurence Bourne
Cast: Patrick Macnee (John Steed), Honor Blackman (Cathy Gale), Godfrey Quigley (Noah Marshall), Edwin Richfield (Lawrence), Scott Forbes (Lew Conniston), Bruno Barnabe (Fitch), Judy Parfitt (Brenda Paterson), Rowena Gregory (Madge Jordan) Toke Townley (Joseph Gourlay), Martin Friend (George).
Uncredited Cast: Roy Powell (Welder).

Crew: Frederick Starke (Honor Blackman's wardrobe designed by), Philip Harrison (Designed by).
Uncredited Crew: Peter Bailey (Floor Manager), Marian Lloyd (Production Assistant), Betty Crowe (Stage Manager), Margaret Morris (Wardrobe), Lorna Bradish (Make-Up), John Cooper (Call Boy), Anne Summerton (Timing Production Assistant), Bob Godfrey (Technical Supervisor), H W Richards (Lighting), Dickie Jackman (Senior Cameraman), Gordon Hesketh (Vision Mixer), Mike Roberts (Sound Supervisor), Bill Rawcliffe (Grams Operator), Alan Fowler (Racks Supervisor).

Production Schedule:
Tuesday 21 November 1963: Laurence Bourne
VT Insert: 19.30-21.00: ABC Teddington Studios, Studio 1 [Int: Steed fights welder in factory/Ext: End fight scene at the zoo]
Wednesday 22 November 1963: Laurence Bourne
Recording: 18.30-19.30: ABC Teddington Studios, Studio 1

3.18 – 'DRESSED TO KILL'
Episode 70
Original Transmission Date: Saturday 28 December 1963
Production No: 3617
Videotape No: VTR/ABC/3194

Writer: Brian Clemens
Director: Bill Bain
Cast: Patrick Macnee (John Steed), Honor Blackman (Cathy Gale), Leonard Rossiter (Robin Hood), Alexander Davion (Napoleon), Richard Leech (Policeman), John Junkin (Sheriff), Anneke Wills (Pussy Cat), Anthea Wyndham (Highwaywoman), Leon Eagles (Newman), Frank Maher (Barman), Peter Fontaine (First Officer).
Uncredited Cast: Richard Pescud (Second Officer).
Crew: David Marshall (Designed by).
Uncredited Crew: John Wayne (Floor Manager), Joan Bradford (Production Assistant), Shirley Cleghorn (Stage Manager), Sally Russell (Wardrobe), Lee Halls (Make-Up), Peter Cazaly (Technical Supervisor), H W Richards (Lighting Supervisor), Dickie Jackman (Senior Cameraman), Gordon Hesketh (Vision Mixer), Mike Roberts (Sound Supervisor).

Production Schedule:
Thursday 5 December 1963: Bill Bain
VT Insert: 19.45-21.00: ABC Teddington Studios, Studio 3 [Int: Steed and Cathy at his apartment/End tag scene: Steed and Cathy at his apartment]
Friday 6 December 1963: Bill Bain
Recording: 18.30-19.30: ABC Teddington Studios, Studio 2

3.19 – 'THE WRINGER'
Episode 71
Original Transmission Date: Saturday 18 January 1964
Production No: 3618
Videotape No: VTR/ABC/3231

Writer: Martin Woodhouse
Director: Don Leaver
Cast: Patrick Macnee (John Steed), Honor Blackman (Cathy Gale), Peter Sallis (Hal Anderson), Paul Whitsun-Jones (Charles), Barry Letts (Oliver), Gerald Sim (Lovell), Terence Lodge (The Wringer), Neil Robinson (Bethune), Douglas Cummings (Murdo).
Crew: Frederick Starke (Honor Blackman's wardrobe designed by), Philip Harrison (Designed by).
Uncredited Crew: John Russell (Floor Manager), Mary Lewis (Stage Manager), John Cooper (Call Boy), Eileen Cornwell (Production Assistant), Carol Armstrong (Timing Production Assistant), Anne Salisbury (Wardrobe), Lorna Bradish (Make-Up), Peter Cazaly (Technical Supervisor), H W Richards (Lighting Supervisor), Michael Baldock (Senior Cameraman), Michael Roberts (Sound Supervisor), Del Randall (Vision Mixer), William Marley (Racks), Brian Moray (Grams Operator).

Production Schedule:
Thursday 19 December 1963: Don Leaver
VT Insert: 19.30-21.00: ABC Teddington Studios, Studio 1 [Ext: Steed and Cathy escape from the interrogation facility/Int: End tag scene: Steed, Cathy and Lovell in Steed's apartment]
Friday 20 December 1963: Don Leaver
Recording: 18.25-19.30: ABC Teddington Studios, Studio 1

3.20 – 'THE LITTLE WONDERS'
Episode 72
Original Transmission Date: Saturday 11 January 1964
Production No: 3619
Videotape No: VTR/ABC/3254 and 3254A/B

Writer: Eric Paice
Director: Laurence Bourne
Cast: Patrick Macnee (John Steed), Honor Blackman (Cathy Gale), Kenneth J Warren (Fingers), David Bauer (Bishop), Lois Maxwell (Sister Johnson), Tony Steedman (Beardmore), Harry Landis (Harry), John Cowley (Big Sid), Rosemary Dunham (Gerda), Frank Maher (Hasek), Alex MacDonald (Porter), Mark Heath (Coalman), Christopher Robbie (Mal), Rick Jones (Ricky).
Crew: Frederick Starke (Honor Blackman's wardrobe designed by), Richard Harrison (Designed by).
Uncredited Crew: Denver Thornton (Floor Manager), Marian Lloyd (Production Assistant), Betty Crowe (Stage Manager), Sally Russell (Wardrobe), Lorna Bradish (Make-Up), Anne Summerton (Timing Production Assistant), Peter Wayne (Technical Supervisor), Ken Brown (Lighting Director), Mike Baldock (Senior Cameraman), Del Randall (Vision Mixer), John Tasker (Sound Supervisor), Brian Moray (Grams Operator), Bill Marley (Racks).

Production Schedule:
Thursday 2 January 1964: Laurence Bourne
VT Insert: 19.30-21.00: ABC Teddington Studios, Studio 1 [Int: Sister Johnson's machine gun attack/Shoot out conclusion in the class room]

Friday 3 January 1964: Laurence Bourne
Recording: 18.30-19.30: ABC Teddington Studios, Studio 1

3.21 – 'MANDRAKE'
Episode 73
Original Transmission Date: Saturday 25 January 1964
Production No: 3620
Videotape No: VTR/ABC/3255

Writer: Roger Marshall
Director: Bill Bain
Cast: Patrick Macnee (John Steed), Honor Blackman (Cathy Gale), John Le Mesurier (Dr Macombie), George Benson (Rev. Wyper), Madge Ryan (Eve Turner), Philip Locke (Roy Hopkins), Annette André (Judy), Robert Morris (Benson), Jackie Pallo (Sexton).
Crew: Frederick Starke (Honor Blackman's wardrobe designed by), David Marshall (Designed by).
Uncredited Crew: John Wayne (Floor Manager), Joan Bradford (Production Assistant), Mary Lewis (Stage Manager), Margaret Morris (Wardrobe), Lee Halls (Make-Up), Bob Godfrey (Technical Supervisor), Ken Browne (Lighting Supervisor), Dickie Jackman (Senior Cameraman), John Tasker (Sound Supervisor), Gordon Hesketh (Vision Mixer).

Production Schedule:
Wednesday 15 January 1964: Bill Bain
VT Insert: 19.30-21.00: ABC Teddington Studios, Studio 1 [Ext: Funeral/Cathy and the Sexton fight/Finale in the churchyard]
Thursday 16 January 1964: Bill Bain
Recording: 18.30-19.30: ABC Teddington Studios, Studio 1

3.22 – 'TROJAN HORSE'
Episode 74
Original Transmission Date: Saturday 8 February 1964
Production No: 3621
Videotape No: VTR/ABC/3352 and 3352A/B

Writer: Malcolm Hulke
Director: Laurence Bourne
Cast: Patrick Macnee (John Steed), Honor Blackman (Cathy Gale), Basil Dignam (Major Ronald Pantling), T P McKenna (Tony Heuston), Derek Newark (Johnson), Geoffrey Whitehead (Right Hon Lucian Ffordsham), Arthur Pentelow (George Meadows), Lucinda Curtis (Ann Meadows), John Lowe (Lynton Smith), James Donnelly (Kirby), Marjorie Keys (Tote Girl).
Uncredited Cast: Brown (Jackie Cooper), John Lynn and Wilfred Boyle (Ambulance Men), Colin Vancao, Eric Green, Brian McNeil (Stable Hands), Bob Manning, Benn Simons, Bob Raymond, Peter Thompson (Bookie's Assistants), Winifred Sabine and Cecilia May (Barmaids), Walter Swash, Coreen Burford, Stephanie Lacey (Race Track Crowd).
Crew: Frederick Starke (Honor Blackman's wardrobe designed by), Richard Harrison (Designed by).

Uncredited Crew: John Russell (Floor Manager), Marian Lloyd (Production Assistant), Nansi Davis (Stage Manager), Ann Salisbury (Wardrobe), Lee Halls (Make-Up), D Wyndham Reid (Call Boy), Eileen Cornwell (Timing Production Assistant), Peter Wayne (Technical Supervisor), Peter Kew (Lighting Supervisor), Mike Baldock (Senior Cameraman), Del Randall (Vision Mixer), Mike Roberts (Sound Supervisor) Peter Wilcox (Grams Operator), Bill Marley (Racks).

Production Schedule:
Wednesday 29 January 1964: Laurence Bourne
VT Insert: 20.30-21.00: ABC Teddington Studios, Studio 1 [Fight in harness room]
Thursday 30 January 1964: Laurence Bourne
Recording: 18.30-19.30: ABC Teddington Studios, Studio 1

3.23 – 'THE OUTSIDE-IN MAN'
Episode 75
Original Transmission Date: Saturday 22 February 1964
Production No: 3622
Videotape No: VTR/ABC/3394 and 3394A/B/C

Writer: Philip Chambers
Director: Jonathan Alwyn
Cast: Patrick Macnee (John Steed), Honor Blackman (Cathy Gale), Ronald Radd (Quilpie), James Maxwell (Mark Charter), William Devlin (Ambassador), Basil Hopkins (Major Zulficar), Beryl Baxter (Helen Rayner), Arthur Lovegrove (Michael Lynden), Virginia Stride (Alice Brisket), Philip Anthony (Sharp), Anthony Dawes (Edwards), Ronald Mansell (Jemkins), Valentino Musetti (Guard), Eddie Powell (Guard).
Uncredited Cast: Paul Bromley (Butcher).
Crew: Frederick Starke (Honor Blackman's wardrobe designed by), David Marshall (Designed by).
Uncredited Crew: John Wayne (Floor Manager), Paddy Dewey (Production Assistant), Betty Crowe (Stage Manager), David Wyndham-Read (Call Boy), Eileen Cornwell (Timing Production Assistant), Ambren Garland (Wardrobe), Lee Halls (Make-Up), Peter Cazaly (Technical Supervisor), H W Richards (Lighting Supervisor), Dickie Jackman (Senior Cameraman), Peter Sampson (Sound Supervisor), Del Randall (Vision Mixer), Bill Marley (Racks Supervisor), Michael Harrison (Grams Operator).

Production Schedule:
Thursday 11 February 1964: Jonathan Alwyn
VT Insert: 20.30-21.00: ABC Teddington Studios, Studio 3 [Int: Chater on the telephone at the cottage/Cathy and Chater fight the two embassy guards/Major Zulficar discovers Chater hidden in the embassy garage]
Friday 12 February 1964: Jonathan Alwyn
Recording: 18.30-19.30: ABC Teddington Studios, Studio 2

3.24 – 'THE CHARMERS'
Episode 76
Original Transmission Date: Saturday 29 February 1964
Production No: 3623

Videotape No: VTR/ABC/3400

Writer: Brian Clemens
Director: Bill Bain
Cast: Patrick Macnee (John Steed), Honor Blackman (Cathy Gale), Fenella Fielding (Kim Lawrence), Warren Mitchell (Keller), Brian Oulton (Mr Edgar), Vivian Pickles (Betty Smythe), John Barcroft (Martin), Malcolm Russell (Horace Cleeves), Frank Mills (Harrap), John Greenwood (Sam), Peter Porteous (Vinkel).
Uncredited Cast: Trevor Ainsley, Howard Kingsley, Leonard Kingston, Paul Mead (Men at Charm School), Brian McNeil, James Darwin, Derek Hunt (Crate Movers).
Crew: Frederick Starke (Honor Blackman's wardrobe designed by), Richard Harrison (Designed by).
Uncredited Crew: John Wayne (Floor Manager), Betty Crowe (Stage Manager), John Cooper (Call Boy), Eileen Cornwell (Production Assistant), Marian Lloyd (Timing Production Assistant), Margaret Morris (Wardrobe), Lee Halls (Make-Up), Peter Wayne (Technical Supervisor), Ken Brown (Lighting Supervisor), Michael Baldock (Senior Cameraman), John Tasker (Sound Supervisor), Del Randall (Vision Mixer), Michael Harrison (Grams Operator), William Marley (Racks Supervisor).

Production Schedule:
Wednesday 26 February 1964: Bill Bain
VT Insert: 19.30-21.00: ABC Teddington Studios, Studio 1 [Int: Charm school office/Fencing sequence/Keller's death]
Thursday 27 February 1964: Bill Bain
Recording: 18.30-19.30: ABC Teddington Studios, Studio 1

3.25 – 'ESPIRIT DE CORPS'
Episode 77
Original Transmission Date: Saturday 14 March 1964
Production No: 3624
Videotape No: VTR/ABC/3481 and 3481A/B/C/D/E/F/G

Writer: Eric Paice
Director: Don Leaver
Cast: Patrick Macnee (John Steed), Honor Blackman (Cathy Gale), Duncan Macrae (Brigadier General Sir Ian Stuart-Bollinger), Joyce Heron (Lady Dorothy Stuart-Bollinger), Roy Kinnear (Private Jessop), John Thaw (Captain Trench), Pearl Catlin (Mrs Craig), Douglas Robinson (Sergeant Marsh), Hugh Morton (Admiral), Anthony Blackshaw (Pivate Asquith), James Falkland (Signaller), George Alexander (Piper), Tony Lambden (Drummer), George Macrae (Highland Dancer).
Uncredited Cast: Billy Cornelius (Private Collins), Terry Brewer (Soldier).
Crew: Frederick Starke (Honor Blackman's wardrobe designed by), David Marshall (Designed by).
Uncredited Crew: John Russell (Floor Manager), Mary Lewis (Stage Manager), Anne Summerton (Production Assistant), Pam Bedford (Timing Production Assistant), David Granger (Call Boy), Audrey Riddle and Sally Russell (Wardrobe), Peter Wayne (Technical Supervisor), Peter Kew (Lighting Supervisor), John Tasker (Sound Supervisor), Dickie Jackman (Senior Cameraman), Gordon Hesketh (Vision Mixer).

Production Schedule:
Unknown date: Don Leaver
VT Insert: Unknown time: ABC Teddington Studios, Studio Lot [Ext: Corporal Craig's execution/Steed marched to his court martial/Captain Trench walking through the camp/Steed's execution]
Tuesday 10 March 1964: Don Leaver
VT Insert: 19.30-21.00: ABC Teddington Studios, Studio 2 [Int: Cathy arrives to join the training course/Cathy and Trench practise unarmed combat/Cathy shoots Marsh and Jessop shoots Trench]
Wednesady 11 March 1964: Don Leaver
Recording: 18.20-19.30: ABC Teddington Studios, Studio 2

3.26 – 'LOBSTER QUADRILLE'
Episode 78
Original Transmission Date: Saturday 21 March 1964
Production No: 3625
Videotape No: Unknown

Writer: Richard Lucas
Director: Kim Mills
Cast: Patrick Macnee (John Steed), Honor Blackman (Cathy Gale), Leslie Sands (Captain Slim), Burt Kwouk (Mason), Gary Watson (Bush), Jennie Linden (Katie), Norman Scace (Dr Stannage), Corin Redgrave (Quentin Slim), Valentino Musetti (Jackson).
Crew: Frederick Starke (Honor Blackman's wardrobe designed by), Patrick Downing (Designed by).

Production Schedule:
Friday 20 March 1964: Kim Mills
Recording: Unknown time: ABC Teddington Studios, Unknown studio

SEASON 4

A Telemen Limited production for ABC Television
Copyright: Associated British Productions
26 black and white episodes on 35mm film
Permanent Crew: Julian Wintle (Produced by), Albert Fennell (In Charge of Production), Laurie Johnson (Music by), Brian Clemens (Associate Producer), Geoffrey Haine (Production Manager), G B Walker (Casting Director), June Randall (Continuity), George Blackler (Make-Up), Jackie Jackson (Wardrobe), Simon Kaye (Sound Recording), Len Abbott (Dubbing Mixer), A W Lumkin (Recording Director), Ray Austin (Stunt Arranger).

'THE TOWN OF NO RETURN'
Initial filming
Original Transmission Date: Not transmitted

Writer: Brian Clemens
Director: Peter Graham Scott

Production Schedule:
Thursday 29 October to Friday 13 November 1964: Peter Graham Scott

4.01 – 'THE MURDER MARKET'
Episode 79
Original Transmission Date: Saturday 13 November 1965

Writer: Tony Williamson
Director: Peter Graham Scott
Cast: Patrick Macnee (John Steed), Diana Rigg (Emma Peel), Patrick Cargill (Mr Lovejoy), Suzanne Lloyd (Barbara Wakefield), Naomi Chance (Mrs Stone), Peter Bayliss (Dinsford), John Woodvine (Robert Stone), Edward Underdown (Jonathan Stone), Barbara Roscoe (Receptionist), John Forgham (Beale).
Uncredited Cast: Roger Milner (J G Henshaw), Colin Vancao (Groom), Penelope Keith (Bride), George Hilsdon (Pallbearer), Billy Westley (Stunt Double for Emma Peel).
Crew: Gerry Turpin (Photography), Harry Pottle (Art Director), Richard Best (Film Editor), Claude Watson (Assistant Director), Ronnie Taylor (Camera Operator), Pearl Orton (Hairdresser), Lionel Selwyn (Sound Editor).

Production Schedule:
Monday 23 November 1964 to Friday 4 December 1964: Wolf Rilla
Wednesday 16 December 1964 to Friday 18 December 1964: Peter Graham Scott

4.02 – 'THE MASTER MINDS'
Episode 80
Original Transmission Date: Saturday 6 November 1965

Writer: Robert Banks Stewart
Director: Peter Graham Scott
Cast: Patrick Macnee (John Steed), Diana Rigg (Emma Peel), Laurence Hardy (Sir Clive Todd), Patricia Haines (Holly Trent), Bernard Archard (Desmond Leeming), Ian McNaughton (Dr Fergus Campbell), John Wentworth (Sir Jeremy), Georgina Ward (Davinia Todd), Manning Wilson (Major Plessy).
Uncredited Cast: Harvey Hall (Raid Leader), Harry Hutchinson (Sir Clive's Butler), Frank Mills (Sir Clive's Doctor), Martin Miller (Professor Spencer), Nigel Lambert (Lieutenant Hardcastle), Elizabeth Reber (Attractive RANSACK Girl), Paddy Ryan (RANSACK Member and Archer), James Copeland (Gymnast).
Crew: Gerry Turpin (Photography), Harry Pottle (Art Director), Peter Tanner (Film Editor), Richard Dalton (Assistant Director), Ronnie Taylor (Camera Operator), Pearl Orton (Hairdresser), Lionel Selwyn (Sound Editor).

Production Schedule:
Thursday 17 December 1964 to Friday 8 January 1965: Peter Graham Scott

4.03 – 'DIAL A DEADLY NUMBER'
Episode 81
Original Transmission Date: Saturday 4 December 1965

Writer: Roger Marshall
Director: Don Leaver
Cast: Patrick Macnee (John Steed), Diana Rigg (Emma Peel), Clifford Evans (Henry Boardman), Jan Holden (Ruth Boardman), Anthony Newlands (Ben Jago), John Carson (Fitch), Peter Bowles (John Harvey), Gerald Sim (Frederick Yuill), Michael Trubshaw (The General), Norman Chappell (Macombie), John Bailey (Warner), Edward Cast (Waiter).
Uncredited Cast: Michael Barrington (Norman Todhunter), Tina Packer (Suzanne), Paddy Smith (Boardman's Butler).
Crew: Gerry Turpin (Photography), Harry Pottle (Art Director), Richard Best (Film Editor), Claude Watson (Assistant Director), Ronnie Taylor (Camera Operator), Pearl Orton (Hairdresser), Lionel Selwyn (Sound Editor).

Production Schedule:
Monday 11 January 1965 to fourth week in January 1965: Don Leaver[39]

4.04 – 'DEATH AT BARGAIN PRICES'
Episode 82
Original Transmission Date: Saturday 23 October 1965

Writer: Brian Clemens
Director: Charles Crichton
Cast: Patrick Macnee (John Steed), Diana Rigg (Emma Peel), Andre Morell (Horatio Kane), T P McKenna (Wentworth), Allan Cuthbertson (Farthingale), George Selway (Massey), Harvey Ashby (Marco), John Cater (Jarvis), Peter Howell (Professor Popple), Ronnie Stevens (Glynn), Diana Clare (Julie).
Uncredited Cast: Arthur Gross (Moran).
Crew: Gerry Turpin (Photography), Harry Pottle (Art Director), Peter Tanner (Film Editor), Richard Dalton (Assistant Director), Ronnie Taylor (Camera Operator), Pearl Orton (Hairdresser), Lionel Selwyn (Sound Editor).

Production Schedule:
Fourth week in January 1965 to Wednesday 17 February 1965: Charles Crichton[40] (2)

4.05 – 'TOO MANY CHRISTMAS TREES'
Episode 83
Original Transmission Date: Saturday 25 December 1965

Writer: Tony Williamson
Director: Roy Baker
Cast: Patrick Macnee (John Steed), Diana Rigg (Emma Peel), Mervyn Johns (Brandon

---

[39] 'Dial a Deadly Number' still in production, *The Daily Cinema*, 22 January 1965
[40] 'Death at Bargain Prices' in production, *The Daily Cinema*, 29 January 1965

Storey), Edwin Richfield (Dr Felix Teasel), Jeanette Sterke (Janice Crane), Alex Scott (Martin Trasker), Robert James (Jenkins), Barry Warren (Jeremy Wade).
Crew: Gerry Turpin (Photography), Robert Jones (Art Director), Richard Best (Film Editor), Claude Watson (Assistant Director), Ronnie Taylor (Camera Operator), Pearl Orton (Hairdresser), Lionel Selwyn (Sound Editor).

Production Schedule:
Friday 19 February 1965 to first week in March 1965: Roy Baker[41] (3)

4.06 – 'THE CYBERNAUTS'
Episode 84
Original Transmission Date: Saturday 16 October 1965

Writer: Philip Levene
Director: Sidney Hayers
Cast: Patrick Macnee (John Steed), Diana Rigg (Emma Peel), Michael Gough (Dr Clement Armstrong), Frederick Jaeger (Benson), Bernard Horsfall (Jephcott), Burt Kwouk (Tusamo), John Hollis (Sensai), Ronald Leigh-Hunt (Lambert), Gordon Whiting (Hammond).
Uncredited Cast: John Franklyn-Robbins (Gilbert), Katherine Schofield (Oyuka), Rocky Taylor (Martial Artist), Alan Chuntz (Martial Artist), Lucille Soong (Miss Smith), Billy Cornelius (Martial Artist), Mike Reid (Martial Artist).
Crew: Alan Hume (Photography), Harry Pottle (Art Director), Peter Tanner (Film Editor), Richard Dalton (Assistant Director), Godfrey Godar (Camera Operator), Pearl Orton (Hairdresser), Lionel Selwyn (Sound Editor).

Production Schedule:
Tuesday 2 March 1965 to the fourth week in March 1965: Sidney Hayers[42]

4.07 – 'THE GRAVEDIGGERS'
Episode 85
Original Transmission Date: Saturday 9 October 1965

Writer: Malcolm Hulke
Director: Quentin Lawrence
Cast: Patrick Macnee (John Steed), Diana Rigg (Emma Peel), Ronald Fraser (Sir Horace Winslip), Paul Massie (Dr Johnson), Caroline Blakiston (Miss Thirlwell), Victor Platt (Sexton), Charles Lamb (Fred), Wanda Ventham (Nurse Spray), Ray Austin (Baron), Steven Berkoff (Sager), Bryan Mosley (Miller), Lloyd Lamble (Dr Marlow).
Uncredited Cast: Aubrey Richards (Dr Palmer), Billy Cornelius (Pallbearer), Cliff Diggens (Pallbearer), Alan Chuntz (Pallbearer).
Crew: Alan Hume (Photography), Harry Pottle (Art Director), Richard Best (Film Editor), Richard Dalton (Assistant Director), Godfrey Godar (Camera Operator), Pearl Orton (Hairdresser), Lionel Selwyn (Sound Editor).

---

[41] 'Too Many Christmas Trees' still in production, *The Daily Cinema*, 1 March 1965
[42] 'The Cybernauts' still in production, *The Daily Cinema*, 19 March 1965

Production Schedule:
Fourth week in March 1965 to Monday 12 April 1965: Quentin Lawrence[43]

4.08 – 'ROOM WITHOUT A VIEW'
Episode 86
Original Transmission Date: Saturday 8 January 1966

Writer: Roger Marshall
Director: Roy Baker
Cast: Patrick Macnee (John Steed), Diana Rigg (Emma Peel), Paul Whitsun-Jones (Max Chessman), Peter Jeffrey (Varnals), Richard Bebb (Dr Cullen), Philip Latham (Carter), Peter Arne (Pasold), Vernon Dobtcheff (Pushkin), Peter Madden (Dr Wadkin).
Uncredited Cast: Jeanne Roland (Anna Wadkin), Anthony Chinn (Interrogator), Romo Gorrara (Guard and Laundryman), Michael Chow (Laundryman), Fred Stone (Head Waiter), Aleta Morrison (Day Receptionist), Terry Plummer (Guard), Billy Westley (Stunt Double for Emma Peel).
Crew: Alan Hume (Photography), Harry Pottle (Art Director), Peter Tanner (Film Editor), Richard Dalton (Assistant Director), Godfrey Godar (Camera Operator), Pearl Orton (Hairdresser), Lionel Selwyn (Sound Editor).

Production Schedule:
Tuesday 13 April 1965 to Thursday 29 April 1965: Roy Baker

4.09 – 'A SURFEIT OF H$_2$O'
Episode 87
Original Transmission Date: Saturday 20 November 1965

Writer: Colin Finbow
Director: Sidney Hayers
Cast: Patrick Macnee (John Steed), Diana Rigg (Emma Peel), Noel Purcell (Jonah Barnard), Albert Lieven (Dr Sturm), Sue Lloyd (Joyce Jason), Talfryn Thomas (Eli Barker), John Kidd (Sir Arnold Kelly), Geoffrey Palmer (Martin Smythe).
Uncredited Cast: Terry Plummer (Frederick), Charles Rayford (Heckler).
Crew: Alan Hume (Photography), Harry Pottle (Art Director), Richard Best (Film Editor), Richard Dalton (Assistant Director), Godfrey Godar (Camera Operator), Pearl Orton (Hairdresser), Lionel Selwyn (Sound Editor).

Production Schedule:
Friday 30 April 1965 to second week in May 1965: Sidney Hayers[44]

4.10 – 'TWO'S A CROWD'
Episode 88
Original Transmission Date: Saturday 18 December 1965

Writer: Philip Levene

---

[43] 'The Gravediggers' in production, *The Daily Cinema*, 2 April 1965
[44] 'A Surfeit of H$_2$O' still in production, *The Daily Cinema*, 7 May 1965

Director: Roy Baker
Cast: Patrick Macnee (John Steed), Diana Rigg (Emma Peel), Warren Mitchell (Brodny), Maria Machado (Alicia Elena), Alec Mango (Shvedloff), Wolfe Morris (Pudeshkin), Julian Glover (Vogel), John Bluthal (Ivenko), Eric Lander (Major Carson).
Uncredited Cast: Royston Farrell (Man in Audience).
Crew: Alan Hume (Photography), Harry Pottle (Art Director), Peter Tanner (Film Editor), Richard Dalton (Assistant Director), Godfrey Godar (Camera Operator), Pearl Orton (Hairdresser), Lionel Selwyn (Sound Editor).

Production Schedule:
Second week in May 1965 to fourth week in May 1965: Roy Baker[45]

4.11 – 'MAN-EATER OF SURREY GREEN'
Episode 89
Original Transmission Date: Saturday 11 December 1965

Writer: Philip Levene
Director: Sidney Hayers
Cast: Patrick Macnee (John Steed), Diana Rigg (Emma Peel), Derek Farr (Sir Lyle Peterson), Athene Seyler (Doctor Sheldon), Gillian Lewis (Laura Burford), William Job (Alan Carter), David Hutcheson (Wing Commander Davies), Joe Richie (Publican), Donald Oliver (Bob Pearson), Joby Blanchard (Joe Mercer).
Uncredited Cast: John G Heller (Lennox), Edwin Finn (Professor Taylor), Ross Hutchinson (Dr Connelly), Harry Shacklock (Professor Knight), Alan Chuntz (Soldier), Billy Westley (Stunt Double for Emma Peel), Fred Peck (Workman), Jim Brady (Workman).
Crew: Alan Hume (Photography), Harry Pottle (Art Director), Richard Best (Film Editor), Richard Dalton and Frank Hollands (Assistant Directors), Godfrey Godar (Camera Operator), Pearl Orton (Hairdresser), Lionel Selwyn (Sound Editor).

Production Schedule:
First week in June 1965 to third week in June 1965: Sidney Hayers[46]

4.12 – 'SILENT DUST'
Episode 90
Original Transmission Date: Saturday 1 January 1966

Writer: Roger Marshall
Director: Roy Baker
Cast: Patrick Macnee (John Steed), Diana Rigg (Emma Peel), William Franklyn (Osgood), Jack Watson (Juggins), Conrad Phillips (Mellors), Norman Bird (Croft), Hilary Wontner (Minister), Isobel Black (Clare Prendergast), Charles Lloyd Pack (Sir Manfred Fellows), Joanna Wake (Miss Beryl Snow), Aubrey Morris (Quince), Robert Dorning (Howard).
Uncredited Cast: Ray Austin (Horse Riding Double for Diana Rigg), Cliff Diggins

---

[45] 'Two's a Crowd' in production, *The Daily Cinema*, 28 May 1965
[46] 'Man-Eater of Surrey Green' in production, *The Daily Cinema*, 4 and 11 June 1965

(Stunt Double for John Steed), Ray Austin (Stunt Double for Croft).
Crew: Ernest Steward BSC (Photography), Harry Pottle (Art Director), Peter Tanner (Film Editor), Frank Hollands (Assistant Director), James Bawden (Camera Operator), Pearl Orton (Hairdresser), Lionel Selwyn (Sound Editor).

Production Schedule:
Monday 14 June 1965 to Friday 2 July 1965: Roy Baker

4.13 – 'THE HOUR THAT NEVER WAS'
Episode 91
Original Transmission Date: Saturday 27 November 1965

Writer: Roger Marshall
Director: Gerry O'Hara
Cast: Patrick Macnee (John Steed), Diana Rigg (Emma Peel), Gerald Harper (Geoffrey Ridsdale), Dudley Foster (Philip Leas), Roy Kinnear (Hickey), Roger Booth (Porky Purser), Daniel Moynihan (Barman Corporal), David Morrell (Wiggins), Fred Haggerty (Milkfloat Driver).
Uncredited Cast: Ray Austin (Dead Milkman), Cliff Diggins (Thug), Charles Rayford (Base Cook), Royston Farrell (Darts Player), Jim Tyson (Party Guest).
Crew: Ernest Steward BSC (Photography), Harry Pottle (Art Director), Richard Best (Film Editor), John Bates (Diana Rigg's wardrobe designed by), Edward Rayne (and her shoes), Anne Trehearne (Fashion Consultant), Frank Hollands (Assistant Director), James Bawden (Camera Operator), Pearl Orton (Hairdresser), Lionel Selwyn (Sound Editor).

Production Schedule:
Monday 5 July 1965 to Tuesday 20 July 1965: Gerry O'Hara

4.14 – 'THE TOWN OF NO RETURN'
Episode 92
Original Transmission Date: Saturday 2 October 1965

Writer: Brian Clemens
Director: Roy Baker
Cast: Patrick Macnee (John Steed), Diana Rigg (Emma Peel), Alan MacNaughton (Mark Brandon), Patrick Newell (Jimmy Smallwood), Terence Alexander (Piggy Warren), Jeremy Burnham (Rev Jonathan Amesbury), Robert Brown (Saul), Juliet Harmer (Jill Manson), Walter Horsbrugh (School Inspector).
Uncredited Cast: Rocky Taylor (Stunt Double for John Steed), Ray Austin (Stunt Double for Rev Jonathan Amesbury).
Crew: Ernest Steward BSC (Photography), Harry Pottle (Art Director), Peter Tanner (Film Editor), John Bates (Diana Rigg's wardrobe designed by), Edward Rayne (and her shoes), Anne Trehearne (Fashion Consultant), Frank Hollands (Assistant Director), James Bawden (Camera Operator), Pearl Orton (Hairdresser), Lionel Selwyn (Sound Editor).

Production Schedule:
Wednesday 21 July 1965 to first week in August 1965: Roy Baker[47]

4.15 – 'CASTLE DE'ATH'
Episode 93
Original Transmission Date: Saturday 30 October 1965

Writer: John Lucarotti
Director: James Hill
Cast: Patrick Macnee (John Steed), Diana Rigg (Emma Peel), Gordon Jackson (Ian De'ath), Robert Urquhart (Angus De'ath), Jack Lambert (McNab), James Copeland (Roberton), Russell Waters (Controller).
Uncredited Cast: Ray Austin (Stunt Double for Angus De'ath).
Crew: Ernest Steward BSC (Photography), Harry Pottle (Art Director), Richard Best (Film Editor), John Bates (Diana Rigg's wardrobe designed by), Edward Rayne (and her shoes), Anne Trehearne (Fashion Consultant), Frank Hollands (Assistant Director), James Bawden (Camera Operator), Pearl Orton (Hairdresser), Lionel Selwyn (Sound Editor).

Production Schedule:
Second week in August 1965 to Friday 20 August 1965: James Hill[48] (10)

4.16 – 'THE THIRTEENTH HOLE'
Episode 94
Original Transmission Date: Saturday 29 January 1966

Writer: Tony Williamson
Director: Roy Baker
Cast: Patrick Macnee (John Steed), Diana Rigg (Emma Peel), Patrick Allen (Frank Reed), Hugh Manning (Colonel Watson), Peter Jones (Dr Adams), Victor Maddern (Jackson), Francis Matthews (Jerry Collins), Donald Hewlett (Waversham), Norman Wynne (Professor Minley), Richard Marner (Man on TV Screen).
Crew: Lionel Banes BSC (Photography), Harry Pottle (Art Director), Peter Tanner (Film Editor), John Bates (Diana Rigg's wardrobe designed by), Edward Rayne (and her shoes), Anne Trehearne (Fashion Consultant), Frank Hollands (Assistant Director), Godfrey Godar (Camera Operator), Pearl Orton (Hairdresser), Bert Rule (Sound Editor).

Production Schedule:
Monday 6 September 1965 to third week in September 1965: Roy Baker[49]

4.17 – 'SMALL GAME FOR BIG HUNTERS'
Episode 95
Original Transmission Date: Saturday 15 January 1966

---

[47] 'The Town of No Return' still in production, *The Daily Cinema*, 30 July 1965
[48] 'Castle De'Ath' in production, *The Daily Cinema*, 13 August 1965
[49] 'The Thirteenth Hole' in production, *The Daily Cinema*, 13 September 1965

Writer: Philip Levene
Director: Gerry O'Hara
Cast: Patrick Macnee (John Steed), Diana Rigg (Emma Peel), Bill Fraser (Colonel Rawlings), James Villiers (Simon Trent), Liam Redmond (Professor Swain), A J Brown (Dr Gibson), Peter Burton (Fleming), Paul Danquah (Lieutenant Razafi), Tom Gill (Tropical Outfitter), Esther Anderson (Lala), Peter Thomas (Kendrick).
Uncredited Cast: Billy Cornelius (Tribesman).
Crew: Lionel Banes BSC (Photography), Harry Pottle (Art Director), Richard Best (Film Editor), John Bates (Diana Rigg's wardrobe designed by), Edward Rayne (and her shoes), Anne Trehearne (Fashion Consultant), Frank Hollands (Assistant Director), Godfrey Godar (Camera Operator), Pearl Orton (Hairdresser), Bert Rule (Sound Editor).

Production Schedule:
Thursday 16 September 1965 to Friday 1 October 1965: Gerry O'Hara

4.18 – 'THE GIRL FROM AUNTIE'
Episode 96
Original Transmission Date: Saturday 22 January 1966

Writer: Roger Marshall
Director: Roy Baker
Cast: Patrick Macnee (John Steed), Diana Rigg (Emma Peel), Liz Fraser (Georgie Price-Jones), Alfred Burke (Gregorio Auntie), Bernard Cribbins (Arkwright), David Bauer (Ivanoff), Mary Merrall (Old Lady), Sylvia Coleridge (Aunt Hetty), Yolande Turner (Receptionist), Ray Martine (Taxi Driver), Maurice Browning (Russian), John Rutland (Fred Jacques).
Uncredited Cast: Royston Farrell (Marshall), Romo Gorrara (Guard), Alan Meacham (Auction Hand), Art Thomas (Man Disguised as Old Lady).
Crew: Lionel Banes BSC (Photography), Harry Pottle (Art Director), Lionel Selwyn (Film Editor), John Bates (Diana Rigg's wardrobe designed by), Edward Rayne (and her shoes), Anne Trehearne (Fashion Consultant), Frank Hollands (Assistant Director), Godfrey Godar (Camera Operator), Pearl Orton (Hairdresser), Lionel Selwyn (Sound Editor).

Production Schedule:
Monday 4 October 1965 to Tuesday 26 October 1965: Roy Baker

4.19 – 'QUICK-QUICK SLOW DEATH'
Episode 97
Original Transmission Date: Saturday 5 February 1966

Writer: Robert Banks Stewart
Director: James Hill
Cast: Patrick Macnee (John Steed), Diana Rigg (Emma Peel), Eunice Gayson (Lucille Banks), Maurice Kaufmann (Ivor Bracewell), Carole Gray (Nicki), Larry Cross (Chester Read), James Belchamber (Peever), John Woodnutt (Captain Noble), Michael Peake (Willi Fehr), Alan Gerrard (Fintry), David Kernan (Piedi), Colin Ellis (Bernard), Graham

Armitage (Huggins), Charles Hodgson (Syder), Ronald Govey (Bank Manager).
Uncredited Cast: Fred Wood (Pallbearer), Gerry Judge (Dancer), Alan Meacham (Dancer), Philip Stewart (Dancer), Pauline Chamberlain (Dancer).
Crew: Alan Hume (Photography), Harry Pottle (Art Director), Richard Best (Film Editor), John Bates (Diana Rigg's wardrobe designed by), Edward Rayne (and her shoes), Frank Hollands (Assistant Director), Godfrey Godar (Camera Operator), Pearl Orton (Hairdresser), Jack Knight (Sound Editor).

Production Schedule:
Fourth week in October 1965 to second week in November 1965: James Hill[50]

4.20 – 'THE DANGER MAKERS'
Episode 98
Original Transmission Date: Saturday 12 February 1966

Writer: Roger Marshall
Director: Charles Crichton
Cast: Patrick Macnee (John Steed), Diana Rigg (Emma Peel), Nigel Davenport (Major Robertson), Doulas Wilmer (Dr Long), Fabia Drake (Colonel Adams), Moray Watson (Colonel Peters), Adrian Ropes (Lieutenant Stanhope), Richard Coleman (RAF Officer), John Gatrell (Gordon Lamble).
Uncredited Cast: Joe Wadham (Van Driver), Royston Farrell (RAF Airman), Terry Plummer (Navy Danger Maker), Romo Gorrara (Army Danger Maker), Joe Dunne (RAF Danger Maker), Billy Westley (Stunt Double for Emma Peel).
Crew: Alan Hume (Photography), Harry Pottle (Art Director), Peter Tanner (Film Editor), John Bates (Diana Rigg's wardrobe designed by), Edward Rayne (and her shoes), Frank Hollands (Assistant Director), Godfrey Godar (Camera Operator), Pearl Orton (Hairdresser), Jack Knight (Sound Editor).

Production Schedule:
Third week in November 1965 to second week in December 1965: Charles Crichton[51]

4.21 – 'A TOUCH OF BRIMSTONE'
Episode 99
Original Transmission Date: Saturday 19 February 1966

Writer: Brian Clemens
Director: James Hill
Cast: Patrick Macnee (John Steed), Diana Rigg (Emma Peel), Peter Wyngarde (John Cartney), Colin Jeavons (Lord Darcy), Carol Cleveland (Sara Bradley), Robert Cawdron (Horace), Michael Latimer (Roger Winthrop), Jeremy Young (Willy Frant), Bill Wallis (Tubby Bunn), Steve Plytas (Kartovski).
Uncredited Cast: Art Thomas (Pierre), Alan Meacham (Theatre-goer), Lewis Alexander (VIP).
Crew: Alan Hume (Photography), Harry Pottle (Art Director), Richard Best (Film

---

[50] 'Quick-Quick Slow Death' in production, *The Daily Cinema*, 29 October 1965
[51] 'The Danger Makers' in production, *The Daily Cinema*, 19 November and 13 December 1965

Editor), John Bates (Diana Rigg's wardrobe designed by), Edward Rayne (and her shoes), Frank Hollands (Assistant Director), Godfrey Godar (Camera Operator), Pearl Orton (Hairdresser), Jack Knight (Sound Editor).

Production Schedule:
Third week in December 1965 to fourth week in December 1965: James Hill

4.22 – 'WHAT THE BUTLER SAW'
Episode 100
Original Transmission Date: Saturday 26 February 1966

Writer: Brian Clemens
Director: Bill Bain
Cast: Patrick Macnee (John Steed), Diana Rigg (Emma Peel), Thorley Walters (Hemming), John Le Mesurier (Benson), Denis Quilley (Captain Miles), Kynaston Reeves (Major General Goddard), Howard Marion Crawford (Brigadier Goddard), Humphrey Lestocq (Vice Admiral Willows), Ewan Hooper (Sergeant Moran), Leon Sinden (Squadron Leader Hogg), David Swift (Barber), Norman Scace (Reeves), Peter Hughes (Walters).
Uncredited Cast: Pamela Davies (Wren).
Crew: Alan Hume (Photography), Harry Pottle (Art Director), Richard Best (Film Editor), John Bates (Diana Rigg's wardrobe designed by), Edward Rayne (and her shoes), Frank Hollands (Assistant Director), Godfrey Godar (Camera Operator), Pearl Orton (Hairdresser), Lionel Selwyn (Sound Editor).

Production Schedule:
Fourth week of December 1965 to first week in January 1966: Bill Bain

4.23 – 'THE HOUSE THAT JACK BUILT'
Episode 101
Original Transmission Date: Saturday 5 March 1966

Writer: Brian Clemens
Director: Don Leaver
Cast: Patrick Macnee (John Steed), Diana Rigg (Emma Peel), Michael Goodliffe (Professor Keller), Griffith Davies (Burton), Michael Wynne (Frederick 'Pongo' Withers), Keith Pyott (Pennington).
Crew: Lionel Banes BSC (Photography), Harry Pottle (Art Director), Richard Best (Film Editor), John Bates (Diana Rigg's wardrobe designed by), Edward Rayne (and her shoes), Frank Hollands (Assistant Director), Tony White (Camera Operator), Pearl Orton (Hairdresser), Jack T Knight (Sound Editor).

Production Schedule:
First week in January 1966 to third week in January 1966: Don Leaver

4.24 – 'A SENSE OF HISTORY'
Episode 102
Original Transmission Date: Saturday 12 March 1966

Writer: Martin Woodhouse
Director: Peter Graham Scott
Cast: Patrick Macnee (John Steed), Diana Rigg (Emma Peel), Nigel Stock (Richard Carlyon), John Barron (Dr Henge), John Glyn-Jones (Grindley), John Ringham (Professor Acheson), Patrick Mower (Duboys), Robin Phillips (John Petit), Peter Blythe (Millerson), Peter Bourne (Allen), Jacqueline Pearce (Marianne Grey).
Uncredited Cast: Kenneth Benda (James Broom), Rocky Taylor (Student).
Crew: Gilbert Taylor BSC (Photography), Harry Pottle (Art Director), Peter Tanner (Film Editor), John Bates (Diana Rigg's wardrobe designed by), Edward Rayne (and her shoes), Frank Hollands (Assistant Director), Val Stewart (Camera Operator), Pearl Orton (Hairdresser), Ken Rolls (Sound Editor).

Production Schedule:
Fourth week in January 1966 to first week in February 1966: Peter Graham Scott

4.25 – 'HOW TO SUCCEED … AT MURDER'
Episode 103
Original Transmission Date: Saturday 19 March 1966

Writer: Brian Clemens
Director: Don Leaver
Cast: Patrick Macnee (John Steed), Diana Rigg (Emma Peel), Sarah Lawson (Mary Merryweather), Angela Browne (Sara Penny), Anne Cunningham (Gladys Murkle), Zeph Gladstone (Liz Purbright), Artro Morris (Henry Throgbottom), Jerome Willis (Joshua Rudge), Christopher Benjamin (J J Hooter), Kevin Brennan (Sir George Morton), David Garth (Barton), Robert Dean (Jack Finlay), Sidonie Bond (Annie).
Crew: Lionel Banes BSC (Photography), Harry Pottle (Art Director), Richard Best (Film Editor), John Bates (Diana Rigg's wardrobe designed by), Edward Rayne (and her shoes), Frank Hollands (Assistant Director), Tony White (Camera Operator), Bob Griffiths (Hairdresser), Jack T Knight (Sound Editor).

Production Schedule:
Second week in February 1966 to third week in February 1966: Don Leaver

4.26 – 'HONEY FOR THE PRINCE'
Episode 104
Original Transmission Date: Saturday 26 March 1966

Writer: Brian Clemens
Director: James Hill
Cast: Patrick Macnee (John Steed), Diana Rigg (Emma Peel), Ron Moody (Ponsonby Hopkirk), Zia Mohyeddin (Prince Ali), George Pastell (Arkadi), Roland Curram (Vincent), Bruno Barnabe (Grand Vizier), Ken Parry (Bumble), Jon Laurimore (Ronny Westcott), Reg Pritchard (Postman), Peter Diamond (Bernie), Carmen Dene (Eurasian Girl), Richard Graydon (George Reed).
Uncredited Cast: Charles Rayford (Napoleon).
Crew: Lionel Banes BSC (Photography), Harry Pottle (Art Director), Lionel Selwyn (Film Editor), John Bates (Diana Rigg's wardrobe designed by), Edward Rayne (and her

shoes), Richard Dalton (Assistant Director), Tony White (Camera Operator), Bob Griffiths (Hairdresser), Jack T Knight (Sound Editor).

Production Schedule:
<u>Third week in February 1966 to Friday 4 March 1966</u>: James Hill

'THE STRANGE CASE OF THE MISSING CORPSE'
Promotional Film
Original Transmission Date: Not transmitted.

Writer: Brian Clemens
Director: James Hill
Uncredited Cast: Patrick Macnee (John Steed), Diana Rigg (Emma Peel), Valerie Van Ost (Girl).

Production Schedule:
<u>During or directly after 'Honey for the Prince'</u>: James Hill

<u>**SEASON FIVE**</u>

A Telemen Limited production for ABC Television
Copyright: ABC Television Films Ltd
24 colour episodes on 35mm film
Permanent Crew: Albert Fennell and Brian Clemens (Produced by), Julian Wintle (Executive Producer), Laurie Johnson (Music by), Peter Tanner (Supervising Editor) Pierre Cardin (Principal Items of Mr Macnee's Wardrobe Designed by), Alun Hughes (Miss Rigg's Costumes Designed by) Ray Austin (Stunt Arranger), G B Walker (Casting Director), A W Lumkin (Recording Director), Karen Heward (Music Editor).

5.01 – 'THE FEAR MERCHANTS'
Steed puts out a light, Emma takes fright
Episode 105
Original Transmission Date: Saturday 21 January 1967

Writer: Philip Levene
Director: Gordon Flemyng
Cast: Patrick Macnee (John Steed), Diana Rigg (Emma Peel), Patrick Cargill (Pemberton), Brian Wilde (Jeremy Raven), Annette Carell (Dr Voss), Garfield Morgan (Gilbert), Andrew Keir (Crawley), Jeremy Burnham (Gordon White), Edward Burnham (Richard Meadows), Bernard Horsfall (Martin Fox), Ruth Trouncer (Dr Hill), Declan Mullholland (Saunders), Philip Ross (Hospital Attendant).
Uncredited Cast: Rocky Taylor (Steed Lookalike).
Crew: Wilfred Shingleton (Production Designer), Wilkie Cooper (Director of Photography), Ted Lloyd (Production Manager), Malcolm Johnson (Assistant Director), Frank Drake (Camera Operator), Fred Carter (Art Director), Ted Tester (Set Dresser), Peggy Spirito (Continuity), Bill Griffiths (Hairdressing), Bill (W T) Partleton (Make-Up),

Jean Fairlie (Wardrobe), Bill Rowe (Sound Recordist), Len Abbott (Dubbing Mixer), Jack T Knight (Sound Editor), Charles Hammerton (Construction Manager).

Production Schedule:
October 1966: Gordon Flemyng

5.02 – 'ESCAPE IN TIME'
Steed visits the barber, Emma has a close shave
Episode 106
Original Transmission Date: Saturday 28 January 1967

Writer: Philip Levene
Director: John Krish
Cast: Patrick Macnee (John Steed), Diana Rigg (Emma Peel), Peter Bowles (Thyssen), Geoffrey Bayldon (Clapham), Judy Parfitt (Vesta), Imogen Hassall (Anjali), Edward Caddick (Sweeney), Nicholas Smith (Parker), Roger Booth (Tubby Vincent), Richard Montez (Josino), Clifford Earl (Clyde Paxton), Rocky Taylor (Mitchell).
Uncredited Cast: Joe Dunne (Redcoat), Terry Plummer (Executioner).
Crew: Wilfred Shingleton (Production Designer), Wilkie Cooper (Director of Photography), Ted Lloyd (Production Manager), Richard Dalton and Laurie Greenwood (Unit Managers), Richard Dalton (Assistant Director), Frank Drake (Camera Operator), Fred Carter (Art Director), Ted Tester (Set Dresser), Gladys Goldsmith (Continuity), Bill Griffiths (Hairdressing), Jim Hydes (Make-Up), Hilda Geerdts (Wardrobe), Simon Kaye (Sound Recordist), Len Shilton (Dubbing Mixer), Jack T Knight (Sound Editor), Charles Hammerton (Construction Manager), Wally Thompson (Supervisory Electrician).
Uncredited Crew: Roy Rossotti (Tag Scene Director).

Production Schedule:
October 1966: John Krish

5.03 – 'FROM VENUS WITH LOVE'
Steed is shot full of holes, Emma sees stars!
Episode 107
Original Transmission Date: Saturday 14 January 1967

Writer: Philip Levene
Director: Robert Day
Cast: Patrick Macnee (John Steed), Diana Rigg (Emma Peel), Barbara Shelley (Venus Browne), Philip Locke (Primble), Jon Pertwee (Brigadier Whitehead), Derek Newark (Crawford), Jeremy Lloyd (Bertram Smith), Adrian Ropes (Jennings), Arthur Cox (Professor Clarke), Paul Gillard (Ernest Cosgrove), Michael Lynch (Sir Frederick Hadley), Kenneth Benda (Lord Mansford).
Uncredited Cast: Billy Cornelius (Martin).
Crew: Wilfred Shingleton (Production Designer), Wilkie Cooper (Director of Photography), Ted Lloyd (Production Manager), Richard Dalton (Assistant Director), Frank Drake (Camera Operator), Fred Carter (Art Director), Ted Tester (Set Dresser), Gladys Goldsmith (Continuity), Bill Griffiths (Hairdressing), Jim Hydes (Make-Up),

Hilda Geerdts (Wardrobe), Tony Palk (Editor), Simon Kaye (Sound Recordist), Len Abbott (Dubbing Mixer), Jack T Knight (Sound Editor), Charles Hammerton (Construction Manager), Wally Thompson (Supervisory Electrician).

Production Schedule:
November 1966: Robert Day

5.04 – 'THE BIRD WHO KNEW TOO MUCH'
Steed fancies pigeons, Emma gets the bird
Episode 108
Original Transmission Date: Saturday 11 February 1967

Writer: Brian Clemens, based upon a story by Alan Pattillo
Director: Roy Rossotti
Cast: Patrick Macnee (John Steed), Diana Rigg (Emma Peel), Ron Moody (Professor Jordan), Ilona Rodgers (Samantha Slade), Kenneth Cope (Tom Savage), Michael Coles (Verret), John Wood (Edgar Twitter), Anthony Valentine (George Cunliffe), Clive Colin-Bowler (Robin), John Lee (Mark Pearson).
Uncredited Cast: Peter Brace (Percy Danvers), Pat Judge (Morgue Attendant).
Crew: Wilfred Shingleton (Production Designer), Wilkie Cooper (Director of Photography), Geoffrey Haine (Production Manager), Richard Dalton (Assistant Director), Frank Drake (Camera Operator), Fred Carter (Art Director), Gladys Goldsmith (Continuity), Bill Griffiths (Hairdressing), Jim Hydes (Make-Up), Hilda Geerdts (Wardrobe), Simon Kaye (Sound Recordist), Len Abbott (Dubbing Mixer), Rydal Love (Sound Editor), Charles Hammerton (Construction Manager), Wally Thompson (Supervisory Electrician).

Production Schedule:
November 1966: Roy Rossotti

5.05 – 'THE SEE-THROUGH MAN'
Steed makes a bomb, Emma is put to sleep!
Episode 109
Original Transmission Date: Saturday 4 February 1967

Writer: Philip Levene
Director: Robert Asher
Cast: Patrick Macnee (John Steed), Diana Rigg (Emma Peel), Warren Mitchell (Brodny), Moira Lister (Elena Vazin), Roy Kinnear (Professor Ernest Quilby), Jonathan Elsom (Ackroyd), John Nettleton (Sir Andrew Ford), Harvey Hall (Ulric), David Glover (Wilton).
Uncredited Cast: Roy Everson (Embassy Guard), Art Thomas (Major Alexander Vazin).
Crew: Wilfred Shingleton (Production Designer), Wilkie Cooper (Director of Photography), Geoffrey Haine (Production Manager), Richard Dalton (Assistant Director), Frank Drake (Camera Operator), Fred Carter (Art Director), Peggy Spirito (Continuity), Bill Griffiths (Hairdressing), Jim Hydes (Make-Up), Hilda Geerdts (Wardrobe), Simon Kaye (Sound Recordist), Len Abbott (Dubbing Mixer), Jack T

Knight (Sound Editor), Charles Hammerton (Construction Manager), Wally Thompson (Supervisory Electrician).
Uncredited Crew: Roy Rossotti (Tag Scene Director).

Production Schedule:
<u>December 1966</u>: Robert Asher

5.06 – 'THE WINGED AVENGER'
Steed goes bird watching, Emma does a comic strip
Episode 110
Original Transmission Date: Saturday 18 February 1967

Writer: Richard Harris
Directors: Gordon Flemyng and Peter Duffell
Cast: Patrick Macnee (John Steed), Diana Rigg (Emma Peel), Nigel Green (Sir Lexius Cray), Jack MacGowran (Professor Poole), Neil Hallett (Arnie Packer), Colin Jeavons (Stanton), Roy Patrick (Julian), John Garrie (Tay-Ling), Donald Pickering (Peter Roberts), William Fox (Simon Roberts), A J Brown (Dawson), Hilary Wontner (Dumayn), John Crocker (Fothers), Ann Sydney (Gerda).
Crew: Wilfred Shingleton (Production Designer), Alan Hume (Director of Photography), Ted Lloyd (Production Manager), Richard Dalton (Assistant Director), Frank Drake (Camera Operator), Fred Carter (Art Director), Gladys Goldsmith (Continuity), Bill Griffiths (Hairdressing), Jim Hydes (Make-Up), Hilda Geerdts (Wardrobe), Tony Palk (Editor), Simon Kaye (Sound Recordist), Len Abbott (Dubbing Mixer), Jack T Knight (Sound Editor), Charles Hammerton (Construction Manager), Wally Thompson (Supervisory Electrician).
Additional Credit: Frank Bellamy (Cartoon Drawings by).

Production Schedule:
<u>December 1966</u>: Gordon Flemyng and Peter Duffell

5.07 – 'THE LIVING DEAD'
Steed finds a mine of information, Emma goes underground
Episode 111
Original Transmission Date: Saturday 25 February 1967

Writer: Brian Clemens, based upon a story by Anthony Marriott
Director: John Krish
Cast: Patrick Macnee (John Steed), Diana Rigg (Emma Peel), Julian Glover (Masgard), Pamela Ann Davy (Mandy Mackay), Howard Marion Crawford (Geoffrey 16th Duke of Benedict), Jack Woolgar (Kermit), Jack Watson (Hooper), Edward Underdown (Rupert 15th Duke of Benedict), John Cater (Olliphant), Vernon Dobtcheff (Spencer), Alister Williamson (Tom).
Uncredited Cast: Cyd Child (Stunt Double for Emma Peel).
Crew: Jack Greenwood (Production Controller), Robert Jones (Production Designer), Alan Hume (Director of Photography), Geoffrey Haine (Production Manager), Richard Dalton (Unit Manager) Ted Lewis (Assistant Director), Tony White (Camera Operator), Fred Carter (Art Director), Gladys Goldsmith (Continuity), Hilda Fox (Hairdressing),

Jim Hydes (Make-Up), Jean Fairlie (Wardrobe), Lionel Selwyn (Editor), Simon Kaye (Sound Recordist), Len Abbott (Dubbing Mixer), Jack T Knight (Sound Editor), Charles Hammerton (Construction Manager), Wally Thompson (Supervisory Electrician).

Production Schedule:
December 1966/January 1967: John Krish

5.08 – 'THE HIDDEN TIGER'
Steed hunts a big cat, Emma is badly scratched
Episode 112
Original Transmission Date: Saturday 4 March 1967

Writer: Philip Levene
Director: Sidney Hayers
Cast: Patrick Macnee (John Steed), Diana Rigg (Emma Peel), Ronnie Barker (Edwin Cheshire), Lyndon Book (Dr Manx), Gabrielle Drake (Angora), John Phillips (Major Nesbitt), Michael Forrest (Peters), Stanley Meadows (George Erskine), Jack Gwillim (Sir David Harper), Frederick Treves (Dawson), Brian Haines (Samuel Jones), John Moore (Williams), Reg Pritchard (Walter Bellamy).
Crew: Jack Greenwood (Production Controller), Robert Jones (Production Designer), Ernest Steward (Director of Photography), Geoffrey Haine (Production Manager), Richard Dalton and Laurie Greenwood (Unit Managers) Ron Purdie (Assistant Director), James Bawden (Camera Operator), Len Townsend (Art Director), Mary Spain (Continuity), Hilda Fox (Hairdressing), Basil Newall (Make-Up), Jean Fairlie (Wardrobe), Tony Palk (Editor), Ken Rawkins (Sound Recordist), Len Abbott (Dubbing Mixer), Rydal Love (Sound Editor), Charles Hammerton (Construction Manager), Steve Birtles (Supervisory Electrician).

Production Schedule:
January 1967: Sidney Hayers

5.09 – 'THE CORRECT WAY TO KILL'
Steed changes partners, Emma joins the enemy
Episode 113
Original Transmission Date: Saturday 11 March 1967

Writer: Brian Clemens
Director: Charles Crichton
Cast: Patrick Macnee (John Steed), Diana Rigg (Emma Peel), Anna Quayle (Olga), Michael Gough (Nutski), Philip Madoc (Ivan), Terence Alexander (Ponsonby), Peter Barkworth (Percy), Graham Armitage (Algy), Timothy Bateson (Dr Merryweather), Joanna Jones (Hilda), Edwin Apps (Winters), John G Heller (Groski).
Uncredited Cast: Romo Gorrara (Stanislaus Arkadi), Peter Clay (Zoric), Alf Joint (Olga's Sparring Opponent), Peter Brace (Olga's Sparring Opponent), Terry Plummer (Olga's Sparring Opponent).
Crew: Jack Greenwood (Production Controller), Robert Jones (Production Designer), Alan Hume (Director of Photography), Geoffrey Haine (Production Manager), Richard Dalton and Laurie Greenwood (Unit Managers) Ted Lewis (Assistant Director), Tony

White (Camera Operator), Kenneth Tait (Art Director), Gladys Goldsmith (Continuity), Hilda Fox (Hairdressing), Jim Hydes (Make-Up), Jean Fairlie (Wardrobe), Lionel Selwyn (Editor), Simon Kaye (Sound Recordist), Len Abbott (Dubbing Mixer), Rydal Love (Sound Editor), Charles Hammerton (Construction Manager), Wally Thompson (Supervisory Electrician).

Production Schedule:
January 1967: Charles Chrichton

5.10 – 'NEVER, NEVER SAY DIE'
Steed meets a dead man, Emma fights the corpse
Episode 114
Original Transmission Date: Saturday 18 March 1967

Writer: Philip Levene
Director: Robert Day
Cast: Patrick Macnee (John Steed), Diana Rigg (Emma Peel), Christopher Lee (Professor Stone), Jeremy Young (Dr Penrose), Patricia English (Dr Betty James), David Kernan (George Eccles), Christopher Benjamin (Whittle), John Junkin (Sergeant), Peter Dennis (Private), Geoffrey Reed (Carter), Alan Chuntz (Selby), Arnold Ridley (Elderly Gent), David Gregory (Young Man), Karen Ford (Nurse).
Uncredited Cast: Terry Plummer (Security Man), Gerry Crampton (Security Man), Rocky Taylor (Stunt Double for John Steed), Cyd Child (Stunt Double for Emma Peel), Eddie Powell (Stunt Double for Professor Stone).
Crew: Jack Greenwood (Production Controller), Robert Jones (Production Designer), Ernest Steward (Director of Photography), Geoffrey Haine (Production Manager), Richard Dalton and Laurie Greenwood (Unit Managers) Ron Purdie (Assistant Director), James Bawden (Camera Operator), Len Townsend (Art Director), Mary Spain (Continuity), Hilda Fox (Hairdressing), Jim Hydes (Make-Up), Jean Fairlie (Wardrobe), Ken Rawkins (Sound Recordist), Len Abbott (Dubbing Mixer), Jack T Knight (Sound Editor), Charles Hammerton (Construction Manager), Steve Birtles (Supervisory Electrician).
Uncredited Crew: D Fitzgibbon (Focus Puller), Val Stewart (Camera Operator).

Production Schedule:
Monday 23 January 1967 to Tuesday 14 February 1967: Robert Day

5.11 – 'EPIC'
Steed catches a falling star, Emma makes a movie
Episode 115
Original Transmission Date: Saturday 1 April 1967

Writer: Brian Clemens
Director: James Hill
Cast: Patrick Macnee (John Steed), Diana Rigg (Emma Peel), Peter Wyngarde (Stewart Kirby), Isa Miranda (Damita Syn), Kenneth J Warren (Z Z Von Schnerk), David Lodge (Policeman), Anthony Dawes (Actor).
Uncredited Cast: Rocky Taylor (Stunt Double for John Steed), Joe Dunne (Stunt Double

for Stewart Kirby).

Crew: Jack Greenwood (Production Controller), Robert Jones (Production Designer), Alan Hume (Director of Photography), Geoffrey Haine (Production Manager), Richard Dalton and Laurie Greenwood (Unit Managers) Ted Lewis (Assistant Director), Tony White (Camera Operator), Kenneth Tait (Art Director), Gladys Goldsmith (Continuity), Hilda Fox (Hairdressing), Basil Newall (Make-Up), Jean Fairlie (Wardrobe), Tony Palk (Editor), Simon Kaye (Sound Recordist), Len Abbott (Dubbing Mixer), Rydal Love (Sound Editor), Charles Hammerton (Construction Manager), Wally Thompson (Supervisory Electrician).

Uncredited Crew: M Morris (Make-Up), J Beck (Make-Up), Ray Atcheler (Second Assistant Director).

Production Schedule:
Thursday 2 February 1967 to Monday 27 February 1967: James Hill
Filming details available for only six days:
Tuesday 14 February 1967: Day 10: James Hill
A Unit: 09.13 to unknown time: ABPC Elstree Studios, Studio Lot [Ext: Von Schnerk Studios]
A Unit: Unknown time: Silver Hill, Shenley, Herts [Ext: Mrs Peel's taxi ride]
A Unit: 16.12-17.30: ABPC Elstree Studios, Stage 3 [Int: Von Schnerk Studios]
Tuesday 21 February 1967: Day 15: James Hill
A Unit: 09.14 to unknown time: ABPC Elstree Studios, Stage 4 [Ext: Mews]
A Unit: Unknown time to 09.52: ABPC Elstree Studios, Stage 3 [Int: Emma's apartment]
A Unit: 11.07-13.45: Aldenham Estate, Elstree, Herts [Int: Black cab]
A Unit: 15.00-17.20: Aldenham Estate, Elstree, Herts [Ext: Fitzroy Lane]
Wednesday 22 February 1967: Day 16: James Hill
A Unit: 09.17-16.50: ABPC Elstree Studios, Stage 3 [Int: Emma's apartment]
A Unit: 16.55-17.20: ABPC Elstree Studios, Stage 3 [Int: Caligari set]
Thursday 23 February 1967: Day 17: James Hill
A Unit: 09.17-17.20: ABPC Elstree Studios, Stage 3 [Int: Caligari set]
Friday 24 February 1967: Day 18: James Hill
A Unit: 09.00-17.10: ABPC Elstree Studios, Stage 3 [Int: Caligari set]
Monday 27 February 1967: Day 19: James Hill
2nd: 09.30-10.45: ABPC Elstree Studios, Stage 4 [Int: Von Schnerk Studios]

5.12 – 'THE SUPERLATIVE SEVEN'
Steed flies to nowhere, Emma does her party piece
Episode 116
Original Transmission Date: Saturday 8 April 1967

Writer: Brian Clemens
Director: Sidney Hayers
Cast: Patrick Macnee (John Steed), Diana Rigg (Emma Peel), Charlotte Rampling (Mrs Hana Wild), Brian Blessed (Mark Drayton), James Maxwell (Jason Wade), High Manning (Max Hardy), Leon Greene (Freddy Richards), Gary Hope (Joe Smith), Donald Sutherland (Jessel), John Hollis (Kanwitch), Magaret Neal (Stewardess), Terry Plummer (Toy Sung).
Uncredited Cast: Cliff Diggins (Killer), Royston Farrell (Killer), Malcolm Taylor (Killer),

Rocky Taylor (Stunt Double for John Steed), Les Crawford (Stunt Double for Jason Wade), Cyd Child (Stunt Double for Emma Peel).

Crew: Jack Greenwood (Production Controller), Robert Jones (Production Designer), Ernest Steward (Director of Photography), Geoffrey Haine (Production Manager), Richard Dalton and Laurie Greenwood (Unit Managers) Ron Purdie (Assistant Director), James Bawden (Camera Operator), Len Townsend (Art Director), Eve Wilson (Continuity), Jeanette Freeman (Hairdressing), Jim Hydes (Make-Up), Jean Fairlie (Wardrobe), Lionel Selwyn (Editor), Ken Rawkins (Sound Recordist), Len Shilton (Dubbing Mixer), Jack T Knight (Sound Editor), Charles Hammerton (Construction Manager), Steve Birtles (Supervisory Electrician).

Uncredited Crew: G Monet (Wardrobe), Eamon Duffy (Second Assistant Director), Ernie Lewis (Assistant Director), Majorie Lovelly (Continuity), Gerald Gibbs (Lighting Cameraman), Ray Sturgess (Camera Operator), Geoff Glover (Focus Puller), R Smith (Clapper Loader), Anthony Waye (Second Assistant Director), Bob Stillwell (Focus Puller), Renée Glynne (Continuity), Roger Inman (Second Assistant Director), J Buckle (Focus Puller), Jimmy Harvey (Lighting Cameraman), J Aarons (Clapper Loader), Terry Plummer (Fight Arranger).

Production Schedule:

Sunday 19 February 1967: Day 1: No Details Available

Tuesday 21 February 1967: Day 2: Sidney Hayers

B Unit: 09.15-17.20: ABPC Elstree Studios, Stage 5 [Int: Corridor/training room]

Wednesday 22 February 1967: Day 3: Sidney Hayers

B Unit: 08.45-17.20: ABPC Elstree Studios, Stage 5 [Int: Training room/control room]

Thursday 23 February 1967: Day 4: Sidney Hayers

B Unit: 11.20-18.10: Luton Airport, Luton, Beds [Ext: Airport]

Friday 24 February 1967: Day 5: Sidney Hayers/Director Unknown

B Unit: 09.00-11.20: ABPC Elstree Studios, Stage 4 [Int: Control room]

B Unit: 12.40-17.30: ABPC Elstree Studios, Stage 5 [Ext: Island undergrowth]

B Unit: 05.30-12.00: BEA Flight Simulation Unit, Southall Lane, Heston, London [Int: Plane cockpit]

Cockpit footage filmed by part of the B Unit who rejoined the team at Elstree Studios later in the day

Sunday 26 February 1967: Day 6: Sidney Hayers

B Unit: 10.35-17.20L ABPC Elstree Studios, Stage 4 [Int: Plane passenger area]

Monday 27 February 1967: Day 7: Sidney Hayers/James Hill

B Unit: 09.55-17.30: ABPC Elstree Studios, Stage 4 [Ext: Island undergrowth and ruins/house main door/Int: Dining room/hallway]

A Unit: 10.45-16.50: BEA Flight Simulation Unit, Southall Lane, Heston, London [Int: Plane cockpit]

Tuesday 28 February 1967: Day 8: Sidney Hayers

B Unit: 08.45-17.45: ABPC Elstree Studios, Stage 4 [Int: Dining room/Ext: Island undergrowth and ruins]

Quarter called pm

Wednesday 1 March 1967: Day 9: Sidney Hayers

B Unit: 10.00-20.20: ABPC Elstree Studios, Stage 4 [Int: Plane passenger area]

Thursday 2 March 1967: Day 10: Sidney Hayers

B Unit: 09.05-17.30: ABPC Elstree Studios, Stage 4 [Int: Plane passenger area]

Friday 3 March 1967: Day 11: Sidney Hayers
B Unit: 09.25-17.30: ABPC Elstree Studios, Stage 4 [Int: Plane passenger area/Pilot's cabin/Ext: Island undergrowth/house]
Monday 6 March 1967: Day 12: Sidney Hayers
B Unit: 09.25-17.30: ABPC Elstree Studios, Stage 4 [Ext: House/Int: Hallway/dining room]
Tuesday 7 March 1967: Day 13: Sidney Hayers
B Unit: 08.45-20.30: ABPC Elstree Studios, Stage 4 [Int: Dining room]
Wednesday 8 March 1967: Day 14: Sidney Hayers
B Unit: 09.05-17.30: ABPC Elstree Studios, Stage 4 [Int: Dining room/Steed's apartment/Ext: Island undergrowth]
2nd: Unknown time to 17.20: North Mymms Park, North Mymms, Herts [Ext: Unknown footage]
The second unit footage did not appear in the episode
Thursday 9 March 1967: Day 15: Sidney Hayers
B Unit: 09.00-17.30: ABPC Elstree Studios, Stage 4 [Int: Dining room/Ext: Shrubbery]
Friday 10 March 1967: Day 16: Sidney Hayers
B Unit: 09.20 to unknown time: ABPC Elstree Studios, Stage 4 [Int: Dining room]
B Unit: Unknown time to 17.30: ABPC Elstree Studios, Studio Backlot, [Ext: Cart rolling down hill]
Sunday 12 March 1967: Day 17: Sidney Hayers
B Unit: 08.45-17.20: ABPC Elstree Studios, Stage 4 [Int: Dining room/Ext: Island undergrowth and ruins/Island undergrowth/ravine]
Monday 13 March 1967: Day 18: Sidney Hayers
B Unit: 09.05-17.30: ABPC Elstree Studios, Stage 4 [Ext: Ravine/island undergrowth]

5.13 – 'A FUNNY THING HAPPENED ON THE WAY TO THE STATION'
Steed goes off the rails, Emma finds her station in life
Episode 117
Original Transmission Date: Saturday 15 April 1967

Writer: Brian Sheriff
Director: John Krish
Cast: Patrick Macnee (John Steed), Diana Rigg (Emma Peel), James Hayter (Ticket Collector), John Laurie (Crewe), Drewe Henley (Groom), Isla Blair (Bride), Tim Barrett (Salt), Richard Caldicot (Admiral Cartney), Dyson Lovell (Warren), Peter J Elliott (Attendant), Michael Nightingale (Lucas), Noel Davis (Secretary).
Uncredited Cast: John Doye (Bart), Jack Arrow (Passenger at Norborough), John Tatum (Passenger at Norborough), Tamsin Millard (Female Agent).
Crew: Jack Greenwood (Production Controller), Robert Jones (Production Designer), Alan Hume (Director of Photography), Geoffrey Haine (Production Manager), Richard Dalton and Laurie Greenwood (Unit Managers) Ted Lewis (Assistant Director), Tony White (Camera Operator), K McCallum Tait (Art Director), Gladys Goldsmith (Continuity), Hilda Fox (Hairdressing), Basil Newall (Make-Up), Jean Fairlie (Wardrobe), Tony Palk (Editor), Simon Kaye (Sound Recordist), Len Shilton (Dubbing Mixer), Rydal Love (Sound Editor), Charles Hammerton (Construction Manager), Wally Thompson (Supervisory Electrician).
Uncredited Crew: Ray Atcheler (Second Assistant Director), Anthony Waye (Assistant

Director), Renee Glynn (Continuity), Bob Stillwell (Focus Puller), Ray Sturgess (Camera Operator), Jimmy Harvey (Lighting Cameraman), J Buckle (Focus Puller), S Aarons (Clapper Loader), Mike Tomlin (Clapper Loader), John Lambourne (Clapper Loader).

Production Schedule:
Monday 27 February 1967: Day 1: John Krish
A Unit: 10.00-16.00: Stonebridge Park railway station and sidings, North Circular Road, Wembley, Brent, London [Ext: Railway sidings]
Tuesday 28 February 1967: Day 2: John Krish
A Unit: 10.10-15.45: Stonebridge Park railway station and sidings, North Circular Road, Wembley, Brent, London [Ext: Railway sidings]
A Unit: 17.10-18.12: Luton railway line, Bedfordshire [Train footage]
Wednesday 1 March 1967: Day 3: John Krish
A Unit: 10.12-17.20: ABPC Elstree Studios, Stage 2 [Int: Signal box]
Thursday 2 March 1967: Day 4: John Krish
A Unit: 09.42-17.20: ABPC Elstree Studios, Stage 2 [Int: Admiral's office]
Quarter called am
Friday 3 March 1967: Day 5: John Krish
A Unit: 08.42-17.20: ABPC Elstree Studios, Stage 2 [Int: Admiral's office/Train compartment/corridor]
Monday 6 March 1967: Day 6: John Krish
A Unit: 09.03-17.25: ABPC Elstree Studios, Stage 2 [Int: Train compartment/restaurant car]
Quarter called pm
2nd: Unknown time: Watford Junction railway station, Station Road, Watford, Herts [Ext: Trains]
Tuesday 7 March 1967: Day 7: John Krish/Director Unknown
A Unit: 09.25-20.20: ABPC Elstree Studios, Stage 2 [Int: Restaurant car/Ext: Norborough platform]
2nd: Unknown time to 17.20: Stonebridge Park railway station and sidings, North Circular Road, Wembley, Brent, London [Ext: Railway sidings]
Wednesday 8 March 1967: Day 8: John Krish
A Unit: 09.32-17.20: ABPC Elstree Studios, Stage 2 [Int: Just Married compartment]
Thursday 9 March 1967: Day 9: John Krish
A Unit: 08.40-17.20: ABPC Elstree Studios, Stage 2 [Int: Just Married compartment/train compartment/restaurant car/corridor/train]
2nd: Unknown time: Gypsy Lane, Watford, Herts {Ext: Train exiting tunnel]
Friday 10 March 1967: Day 10: John Krish
A Unit: 09.35-17.15: ABPC Elstree Studios, Stage 2 [Int: Corridor/Just Married compartment/train compartment]
Monday 13 March 1967: Day 11: John Krish
A Unit: 09.35-17.20: ABPC Elstree Studios, Stage 2 [Int: Corridor/train/waiting room/Ext: waiting room/Chase Halt platform]
Tuesday 14 March 1967: Day 12: John Krish
A Unit: 09.20-10.45: ABPC Elstree Studios, Stage 2 [Int: Train]
A Unit: 10.55-17.06: ABPC Elstree Studios, Stage 4 [Int: Steed's apartment]
A Unit: 17.16-17.20: ABPC Elstree Studios, Stage 2 [Int: Train]
Wednesday 15 March 1967: Day 13: John Krish

A Unit: 08.45-17.20: ABPC Elstree Studios, Stage 2 [Int: Train/Chase Halt station/Ext: Chase Halt platform]
Thursday 16 March 1967: Day 14: John Krish
A Unit: 08.45-16.25: ABPC Elstree Studios, Stage 2 [Int: Train/Just Married compartment/Ext: Norborough platform/Chase Halt platform]
A Unit: 16.35-20.20: ABPC Elstree Studios, Stage 3 [Int: Emma's apartment]
Friday 17 March 1967: Day 15: John Krish
A Unit: 09.50-17.20: ABPC Elstree Studios, Stage 2 [Int: Train/corridor/guard's van]
Sunday 19 March 1967: Day 16: John Krish
A Unit: 08.55-17.20: ABPC Elstree Studios, Stage 2 [Int: Galley/Ext: Norborough Station]
Monday 20 March 1967: Day 17: John Krish
A Unit: 08.45-17.20: ABPC Elstree Studios, Stage 2 [Int/Ext: Galley]
Tuesday 21 March 1967: Day 18: John Krish
A Unit: 09.08-17.20: ABPC Elstree Studios, Stage 2 [Int: Galley/guard's van/corridor/ticket office]
Wednesday 22 March 1967: Day 19: John Krish
A Unit: 08.50-17.20: ABPC Elstree Studios, Stage 2 [Int: Galley/Ext: Chase Halt platform/Norborough platform/shrubbery]
Quarter called am

5.14 – 'SOMETHING NASTY IN THE NURSERY'
Steed acquires a nanny, Emma shops for toys!
Episode 118
Original Transmission Date: Saturday 22 April 1967

Writer: Philip Levene
Director: James Hill
Cast: Patrick Macnee (John Steed), Diana Rigg (Emma Peel), Dudley Foster (Mr Goat), Yootha Joyce (Miss Lister), Paul Eddington (Lord William Beaumont), Paul Hardwick (Webster), Patrick Newell (Sir George Collins), Geoffrey Sumner (General Wilmot), Trevor Bannister (Gordon), Clive Dunn (Martin), George Merritt (James), Enid Lorimer (Nanny Roberts), Louie Ramsay (Nanny Smith), *Penelope Keith (Nanny Brown), Dennis Chinnery (Dobson).
*Does not appear in episode
Uncredited Cast: Cyd Child (Stunt Double for Emma Peel), Arthur Howell (Stunt Double for Nanny Roberts), Cliff Diggins (Stunt Double for Unknown Performer), Rocky Taylor (Stunt Double for John Steed), Art Thomas (Stunt Double for Unknown Performer), Paul Weston (Stunt Double for Unknown Performer).
Crew: Jack Greenwood (Production Controller), Robert Jones (Production Designer), Ernest Steward (Director of Photography), Geoffrey Haine (Production Manager), Richard Dalton and Laurie Greenwood (Unit Managers) Ron Purdie (Assistant Director), James Bawden (Camera Operator), Len Townsend (Art Director), Eve Wilson (Continuity), Jeanette Freeman (Hairdressing), Jim Hydes (Make-Up), Jean Fairlie (Wardrobe), Lionel Selwyn (Editor), Ken Rawkins (Sound Recordist), Len Shilton (Dubbing Mixer), Jack T Knight (Sound Editor), Charles Hammerton (Construction Manager), Steve Birtles (Supervisory Electrician).
Uncredited Crew: Anthony Waye (Assistant Director), Ray Sturgess (Camera

Operator), Mary Sturgess (Hairdresser), Roger Inman (Second Assistant Director), R Smith (Clapper Loader), Renée Glynne (Continuity), Bob Stillwell (Focus Puller, J Craig (Make-Up), J Buck (Continuity), Chick MacNaughton (Focus Puller), Stephen Dade (Lighting Cameraman), D Engleman (Clapper Loader), S Turner (Make-Up), Mike Tomlin (Clapper Loader), G Garfath (Make-Up), Doreen Soan (Continuity), S Freeman (Assistant Director), Michael Meaghan (Second Assistant Director), J Buckle (Focus Puller), Roma Gorrara (Fight Arranger), T Fletcher (Camera Operator), P Hazel (Focus Puller), Geoff Glover (Focus Puller), K Paton (Boom Operator).

Production Schedule:
Wednesday 8 March 1967: Day 1: James Hill
B Unit: 08.30 to unknown time: Starveacres, Watford Road, Radlett, Herts [Ext: Beaumont's house and grounds]
B Unit: Unknown time to 14.50: Rowley Lane, Rowley Green Road, Arkley, Herts [Ext: Wilmott's house]
Thursday 9 March 1967: Day 2: James Hill
B Unit: 09.40-17.20: Studio 70 Cinema Car Park, Shenley Road, Borehamwood, Herts [Ext: Park Mansions car park]
Friday 10 March 1967: Day 3: James Hill
B Unit: 10.15 to unknown time: North Mymms Park, St Mary's Church Road, North Mymms, Herts [Ext: Guild of Noble Nannies]
B Unit: Unknown time to 17.20: Hillcrest, Barnet Road, Arkley, Herts [Ext: Viscount Webster's home]
Monday 13 March 1967: Day 4: James Hill
B Unit: 08.50 to unknown time: Studio 70 Cinema Car Park, Shenley Road, Borehamwood, Herts [Ext: Park Mansions car park]
B Unit: Unknown time to 16.50: Embassy Lodge, Regents Park Road, London [Ext: Park Mansions]
Tuesday 14 March 1967: Day 5: James Hill
B Unit: 09.25-17.30: ABPC Elstree Studios, Stage 3 [Int: Hallucination sequence/reception hall]
Wednesday 15 March 1967: Day 6: James Hill
B Unit: 08.58-17.30: ABPC Elstree Studios, Stage 3 [Int: Reception hall/training room/ Beaumont's study/dream nursery]
Thursday 16 March 1967: Day 7: James Hill/Director Unknown
B Unit: 09.25-17.30: ABPC Elstree Studios, Stage 3 [Int: Webster's study/cellar/dream nursery]
2nd: 08.45-17.00: Rowley Lane, Rowley Green Road, Arkley, Herts [Ext: Wilmott's house/road/shrubbery]
Friday 17 March 1967: Day 8: James Hill
B Unit: 08.45-17.30: ABPC Elstree Studios, Stage 3 [Int: dream nursery/cellar/ training room]
Quarter called am
Monday 20 March 1967: Day 9: James Hill
B Unit: 09.20 to unknown time: ABPC Elstree Studios, Stage 3 [Int: Training room/Gordon's car]
B Unit: Unknown time to 17.30: ABPC Elstree Studios, Studio Lot [Ext: Car park/Beaumont's driveway/Webster's driveway]

<u>Tuesday 21 March 1967</u>: Day 10: James Hill

B Unit: 09.05 to unknown time: ABPC Elstree Studios, Stage 3 [Int: Webster's study/Emma's apartment/Wilmot's den]

B Unit: Unknown time to 17.45: ABPC Elstree Studios, Studio Lot [Ext: Door in car park/Int: Emma's car]

<u>Wednesday 22 March 1967</u>: Day 11: James Hill

B Unit: 09.25 to unknown time: ABPC Elstree Studios, Stage 3 [Int: Wilmot's den/Emma's apartment]

B Unit: Unknown time: Rectory Lane, Shenley, Herts [Ext: Dobson looking down lane]

B Unit: Unknown time: Shenley Hall, Rectory Lane, Shenley, Herts [Ext: Steed's apartment]

B Unit: Unknown time: Rowley Lane, Rowley Green Road, Arkley, Herts [Ext: Wilmott's house]

B Unit: Unknown time to 20.30: ABPC Elstree Studios, Backlot Town [Ext: Toy shop]

<u>Thursday 23 March 1967</u>: Day 12: James Hill

B Unit: 08.55 to unknown time: ABPC Elstree Studios, Stage 3 [Int: Wilmot's den/Emma's apartment]

B Unit: Unknown time: ABPC Elstree Studios, Stage 2 [Int: Steed's apartment]

B Unit: Unknown time: ABPC Elstree Studios, Studio Lot, [Int/Ext: Collins' Rolls Royce/Emma's Lotus]

<u>Tuesday 28 March 1967: Day 13</u>: Leslie Norman

B Unit: 08.45 to unknown time: ABPC Elstree Studios, Stage 2 [Int: Steed's apartment]

B Unit: Unknown time to 17.30: ABPC Elstree Studios, Stage 3 [Int: Training room/toyshop]

<u>Wednesday 29 March 1967</u>: Day 14: Leslie Norman

B Unit: 08.44-17.35: ABPC Elstree Studios, Stage 3 [Int: Toyshop/Wilmot's den]

<u>Thursday 30 March 1967</u>: Day 15: Leslie Norman

B Unit: 08.44-17.20: ABPC Elstree Studios, Stage 3 [Int: Wilmot's den/training room]

<u>Friday 31 March 1967</u>: Day 16: Leslie Norman

B Unit: 08.42-17.30: ABPC Elstree Studios, Stage 3 [Int: Training room/reception hall]

<u>Sunday 2 April 1967</u>: Day 17: Leslie Norman

B Unit: 09.23-17.30: ABPC Elstree Studios, Stage 3 [Int: Beaumont's den]

Quarter called pm

<u>Monday 3 April 1967</u>: Day 18: Leslie Norman

B Unit: 08.35-17.20: ABPC Elstree Studios, Stage 3 [Int: Steed's apartment/inserts]

5.15 – 'THE JOKER'
Steed trumps an ace, Emma plays a lone hand
Episode 119
Original Transmission Date: Saturday 29 April 1967

Writer: Brian Clemens
Director: Sidney Hayers
Cast: Patrick Macnee (John Steed), Diana Rigg (Emma Peel), Peter Jeffrey (Max Prendergast), Sally Nesbitt (Ola Monsey Chamberlain), Ronald Lacey (Strange Young Man), John Stone (Major George Francy).
Uncredited Cast: Rocky Taylor (Stunt Double for John Steed), Cyd Child (Stunt Double for Emma Peel), Art Thomas (Stunt Double for Ola Monsey Chamberlain), Rocky

Taylor (Stunt Double for Max Prendergast).

Crew: Jack Greenwood (Production Controller), Robert Jones (Production Designer), Alan Hume (Director of Photography), Geoffrey Haine (Production Manager), Richard Dalton and Laurie Greenwood (Unit Managers) Ted Lewis (Assistant Director), Tony White (Camera Operator), K McCallum Tait (Art Director), Gladys Goldsmith (Continuity), Hilda Fox (Hairdressing), Basil Newall (Make-Up), Jean Fairlie (Wardrobe), Simon Kaye (Sound Recordist), Len Abbott (Dubbing Mixer), Jack T Knight (Sound Editor), Charles Hammerton (Construction Manager), Wally Thompson (Supervisory Electrician).

Uncredited Crew: Gerald Gibbs (Lighting Cameraman), Ray Atcheler (Second Assistant Director), Frank Nesbitt (Assistant Director), Stephen Dade (Lighting Cameraman), Ray Sturgess (Camera Operator), Geoff Glover (Focus Puller), R Smith (Clapper Loader), Elizabeth Wilcox (Continuity), Tony Palk (Editor), Michael Meighan (Second Assistant Director), Lillian Lee (Continuity), A Thorne (Boom Operator), J Buckle (Focus Puller), M Francis (Clapper Loader), R Allen (Sound Mixer), Claude Hitchcock (Sound Mixer), Fred Tomlin (Boom Operator), H Fairbairn (Boom Operator), Mary Sturgess (Hairdressing), Mike Frift (Clapper Loader), Tom Staples (Boom Operator), John Lambourne (Clapper Loader).

Production Schedule:
Thursday 23 March 1967: Day 1: Sidney Hayers
2nd: 09.58-17.20: ABPC Elstree Studios, Stage 4 [Int: Hallway/hallway and grounds/Ext: shrubbery]
Tuesday 28 March 1967: Day 2: Sidney Hayers
2nd: 08.55-17.20: ABPC Elstree Studios, Stage 4 [Int: Shrubbery/front of house/hallway]
Wednesday 29 March 1967: Day 3: Sidney Hayers
2nd: 09.30-17.20: ABPC Elstree Studios, Stage 4 [Int: Hall/front door/hall and staircase/Ext: Front door and hall]
Thursday 30 March 1967: Day 4: Sidney Hayers
2nd: 09.20-17.25: ABPC Elstree Studios, Stage 4 [Int: Hall/hall and staircase]
Quarter called am and pm
Friday 31 March 1967: Day 5: Sidney Hayers
2nd: 08.42-17.20: ABPC Elstree Studios, Stage 4 [Int: Hall/dining room]
Sunday 2 April 1967: Day 6: Sidney Hayers
A Unit: 09.07-17.20: ABPC Elstree Studios, Stage 4 [Int: Dining room/hall and dining room]
Quarter called am
Monday 3 April 1967: Day 7: Sidney Hayers
A Unit: 09.00-17.20: ABPC Elstree Studios, Stage 4 [Int: Dining room/upper landing/Steed's apartment]
Tuesday 4 April 1967: Day 8: Sidney Hayers/Leslie Norman
A Unit: 08.55 to unknown time: ABPC Elstree Studios, Stage 3 [Int: Emma's room]
A Unit: Unknown time to 18.15: ABPC Elstree Studios, Stage 4 [Int: Upper landing]
2nd: 09.00-12.00: Rabley Park, Mimms Lane, Ridge, Herts [Ext: Sir Cavalier Rusicana's home]
Wednesday 5 April 1967: Day 9: Sidney Hayers
A Unit: 09.45-15.27: ABPC Elstree Studios, Stage 3 [Int: Steed's apartment]

A Unit: Unknown time to 17.20: ABPC Elstree Studios, Stage 4 [Int: Upper landing]
Thursday 6 April 1967: Day 10: Sidney Hayers
A Unit: 09.08-20.20: ABPC Elstree Studios, Stage 4 [Int: Small room/hall/dining room]
Friday 7 April 1967: Day 11: Sidney Hayers/Leslie Norman
A Unit: 08.50-17.20: ABPC Elstree Studios, Stage 4 [Int: Hall/dining hall and hall/front of house]
2nd: 11.00-17.20: ABPC Elstree Studios, Stage 3 [Int: Emma's room/Steed's apartment]
Saturday 8 April 1967: Day 12: Sidney Hayers
A Unit: 11.40-17.20: ABPC Elstree Studios, Stage 3 [Int: Emma's room]
Sunday 9 April 1967: Day 13: Sidney Hayers/Leslie Norman
A Unit: 08.50-17.20: ABPC Elstree Studios, Stage 4 [Int: Emma's apartment]
B Unit: 08.53-17.35: ABPC Elstree Studios, Stage 3 [Int: Steed's apartment/Ext: Undergrowth]
Quarter called pm
Monday 10 April 1967: Day 14: Sidney Hayers/John Moxey/Leslie Norman
A Unit: 10.02-17.20: ABPC Elstree Studios, Stage 4 [Int: Scullery/outhouse/Ext: Outside scullery/shrubbery]
B Unit: 09.02-09.10: ABPC Elstree Studios, Stage 2 [Int: Steed's Bentley]
2nd: Unknown time: ABPC Elstree Studios, Stage 2 [Inserts]
Tuesday 11 April 1967: Day 15 Sidney Hayers
A Unit: 09.32-16.18: ABPC Elstree Studios, Stage 4 [Int: Scullery/outhouse]

5.16 – 'WHO'S WHO???'
Steed goes out of his mind, Emma is beside herself
Episode 120
Original Transmission Date: Saturday 6 May 1967

Writer: Philip Levene
Director: John Moxey
Cast: Patrick Macnee (John Steed), Diana Rigg (Emma Peel), Patricia Haines (Lola), Freddie Jones (Basil), Campbell Singer (Major B), Peter Reynolds (Tulip), Arnold Diamond (Dr Krelmar), Philip Levene (Daffodil), Malcolm Taylor (Hooper).
Uncredited Cast: Billy Cornelius (Poppy), Charles Rayford (Bluebell), Les Crawford (Driving Double for Basil [John Steed]), Joe Farrer (Driving Double for Tulip), Rocky Taylor (Stunt Double for John Steed), Cyd Child (Stunt Double for Emma Peel), Joe Dunne (Stunt Double for Unknown Performer).
Crew: Jack Greenwood (Production Controller), Robert Jones (Production Designer), Ernest Steward (Director of Photography), Geoffrey Haine (Production Manager), Richard Dalton and Laurie Greenwood (Unit Managers) Ron Purdie (Assistant Director), James Bawden (Camera Operator), Len Townsend (Art Director), Doreen Soan (Continuity), Jeanette Freeman (Hairdressing), Jim Hydes (Make-Up), Jean Fairlie (Wardrobe), Tony Selwyn (Editor), Ken Rawkins (Sound Recordist), Len Abbott (Dubbing Mixer), Jack T Knight (Sound Editor), Charles Hammerton (Construction Manager), Steve Birtles (Supervisory Electrician).
Uncredited Crew: Stephen Dade (Camera Operator), Frank Nesbitt (Assistant Director), Ray Sturgess (Camera Operator), F Smith (Clapper Loader), Michael Sarafian (Focus Puller), Lillian Lee (Continuity), David Wimbury (Second Assistant Director), Mary Sturgess (Hairdressing), Ray Sturgess (Camera Operator), T Garrett (Clapper

Loader), J Buckle (Focus Puller), Gerald Gibbs (Lighting Cameraman), Doreen Soan (Continuity), Elizabeth Wilcox (Continuity), EaMonday Duffy (Second Assistant Director), Leslie Hammond (Sound Mixer), Godfrey Godar (Camera Operator), C Davidson (Clapper Loader), Mike Roberts (Focus Puller).

Production Schedule:
Monday 3 April 1967: Day 1: John Moxey
B Unit: 09.45-17.22: ABPC Elstree Studios, Stage 2 [Int: Major B's Office/door of Major B's office]
Quarter called pm
Tuesday 4 April 1967: Day 2: John Moxey
B Unit: 09.10-17.20: ABPC Elstree Studios, Stage 2 {Int: Krelmar's office/consulting room/outer office]
Wednesday 5 April 1967: Day 3: John Moxey
B Unit: 09.28-11.33: Duchess Mews, London [Ext: Steed's mews]
B Unit: 13.45-17.20: ABPC Elstree Studios, Stage 2 {Int: Consulting room/Ext: Krelmar's house]
Thursday 6 April 1967: Day 4: John Moxey
B Unit: 08.40-17.20: ABPC Elstree Studios, Stage 3 [Int: Steed's apartment and hallway]
Friday 7 April 1967: Day 5: John Moxey
B Unit: 08.52 to unknown time: ABPC Elstree Studios, Stage 3 [Int: Steed's apartment]
B Unit: Unknown time to 17.20: ABPC Elstree Studios, Stage 2 {Ext: Krelmar's house/stilt shop/Int: stilt shop]
Monday 10 April 1967: Day 6: John Moxey
B Unit: 09.30-17.20: ABPC Elstree Studios, Stage 2 [Int: Stilt shop]
Tuesday 11 April 1967: Day 7: John Moxey/Leslie Norman
B Unit: 09.00-17.20: ABPC Elstree Studios, Stage 2 [Int: Stilt shop/warehouse]
2nd: 09.10 to unknown time: Highwood Park House, Nan Clark's Lane, Highwood Hill, London [Ext: Krelman's house]
2nd: Unknown time: The Barn, Nan Clark's Lane, Highwood Hill, London [Ext: Tulip spots Steed's Bentley]
2nd: Unknown time to 17.20: Nan Clark's Lane, Highwood Hill, London [Ext: Steed's Bentley being followed by Tulip's car]
Wednesday 12 April 1967: Day 8: John Moxey/Leslie Norman
B Unit: 09.27-17.20: ABPC Elstree Studios, Stage 2 [Int: Stilt shop/Major B's office/warehouse/Ext: Stilt shop]
A Unit: 09.27-17.20: ABPC Elstree Studios, Stage 2 [Int: Stilt shop/Major B's office/warehouse/Ext: Stilt shop]
Thursday 13 April 1967: Day 9: John Moxey/Director Unknown
B Unit: 08.50-20.20: ABPC Elstree Studios, Stage 2 [Int: Major B's office/Krelmar's office/consulting room]
A Unit: 08.50-20.20: ABPC Elstree Studios, Stage 2 [Int: Major B's office/Krelmar's office/consulting room]
Quarter called am
Friday 14 April 1967: Day 10: John Moxey/Sidney Hayers
B Unit: 09.55-17.20: ABPC Elstree Studios, Stage 3 [Int: Warehouse/Emma's apartment]
A Unit: 10.58-17.22: ABPC Elstree Studios, Stage 2 [Int: Stilt shop]
Quarter called pm

Sunday 16 April 1967: Day 11: John Moxey
B Unit: 09.49-17.20: ABPC Elstree Studios, Stage 3 [Int: Emma's apartment/Emma's hall/Steed's apartment]
Monday 17 April 1967: Day 12: John Moxey/Sidney Hayers
B Unit: 09.03-19.30: ABPC Elstree Studios, Stage 3 [Int: Steed's apartment/consulting room]
A Unit: 09.20-17.20: ABPC Elstree Studios, Stage 2 [Int: Stilt shop/shrubbery]
Tuesday 18 April 1967: Day 13: John Moxey/Sidney Hayers
B Unit: 09.04 to unknown time: ABPC Elstree Studios, Stage 2 [Int: Consultation room]
B Unit: Unknown time to 15.37: ABPC Elstree Studios, Stage 3 [Int: Steed's apartment]
A Unit: 14.45-16.15: Highwood Park House, Nan Clark's Lane, Highwood Hill, London [Ext: Krelman's house]

5.17 – 'DEATH'S DOOR'
Episode 121
Original Transmission Date: Saturday 7 October 1967

Writer: Philip Levene
Director: Sidney Hayers
Cast: Patrick Macnee (John Steed), Diana Rigg (Emma Peel), Clifford Evans (Sir Andrew Boyd), William Lucas (Stapley), Allan Cuthbertson (Lord Melford), Marne Maitland (Becker), Paul Dawkins (Dr Evans), Michael Faure (Pavret), Peter Thomas (Saunders), William Lyon Brown (Dalby), Terry Yorke (Haynes), Terry Maidment (Jepson).
Uncredited Cast: Gerry Judge (Diplomat), Lewis Alexander (Diplomat), Royston Farrell (Diplomat), Cliff Diggins (Cyclist), Cyd Child (Stunt Double for Emma Peel), Rocky Taylor (Stunt Double for John Steed), Joe Dunne (Stunt Double for Stapley), Bill Cummings (Stunt Double for Jepson), Joe Dunne (Stunt Double for Clifford Evans).
Crew: Jack Greenwood (Production Controller), Robert Jones (Production Designer), Ernest Steward (Director of Photography), Geoffrey Haine (Production Manager), Richard Dalton and Laurie Greenwood (Unit Managers) Ron Carr (Assistant Director), James Bawden (Camera Operator), Len Townsend (Art Director), Gladys Goldsmith (Continuity), Hilda Fox (Hairdressing), Jim Hydes (Make-Up), Gladys James (Wardrobe), Tony Palk (Editor), Ken Rawkins (Sound Recordist), Len Shilton (Dubbing Mixer), Russ Hill (Sound Editor), Wally Thompson (Supervisory Electrician).
Uncredited Crew: Michael Meighan (Second Unit Director), Eve Brody (Make-Up), E Medhurst (Wardrobe), Ernie Lewis (Assistant Director), P Noon (Continuity), Al Burgess (Second Assistant Director), Gerald Gibbs (Lighting Cameraman), C Davidson (Clapper Loader), A Brody (Make-Up), Peggy Spirito (Post Production), Lillian Lee (Continuity), J Irwin (Wardrobe), M Flaherty (Wardrobe), Bob Kindred (Camera Operator), Mike Roberts (Focus Puller), J Sandler (Clapper Loader), G Davidson (Clapper Loader), Renee Claff (Make-Up), Tony White (Camera Operator), M Arnold (Focus Puller), Ricky Coward (Second Assistant Director), K Nightingale (Boom Operator).

Production Schedule:
Wednesday 3 May 1967: Day 1: Sidney Hayers
Main: 09.40 to unknown time: Great Westwood Equestrian Centre, Old House Lane,

Sarrett, Herts [Ext: Boyd's Country Estate]
Main: Unknown time to 17.42: Old House Lane, Sarrett, Herts [Ext: Sprout Hill]
Thursday 4 May 1967: Day 2: Sidney Hayers
Main: 09.42-17.20: ABPC Elstree Studios, Stage 2 [Int: Ministerial suite/nightmare sequence]
Friday 5 May 1967: Day 3: Sidney Hayers
Main: 09.07-17.15: ABPC Elstree Studios, Stage 2 [Int: Nightmare sequence]
Monday 8 May 1967: Day 4: Sidney Hayers
Main: 09.40-17.20: ABPC Elstree Studios, Stage 3 [Int: Steed's apartment]
Tuesday 9 May 1967: Day 5: Sidney Hayers
Main: 09.00-17.20: ABPC Elstree Studios, Stage 3 [Int: Steed's apartment/conference centre entrance hall/conference room]
Wednesday 10 May 1967: Day 6: Sidney Hayers
Main: 09.12-17.30: ABPC Elstree Studios, Stage 3 [Int: Conference centre entrance hall]
Quarter called pm
Thursday 11 May 1967: Day 7: Sidney Hayers/unknown director
Main: 08.57 to unknown time: ABPC Elstree Studios, Stage 3 [Int: Conference centre entrance hall]
Main: Unknown time to 17.20: ABPC Elstree Studios, Stage 2 [Int: Bedroom]
2nd: 09.24 to unknown time: Duchess Mews, London [Ext: Steed's mews]
2nd: Unknown time: Aragon, Elstree Road, Letchmore Heath, Herts [Int: Back-projection seen from Melford's car]
2nd: Unkown time: Grange Road, Letchmore Heath, Herts [Int: Back-projection seen from Melford's car]
2nd: Unknown time: Hilfield Lane, Padgetts Green, Herts [Ext: Back-projection of electricity substation seen from Boyd's limousine/cyclist almost knocked off bicycle]
2nd: Unknown time to 17.20: Melton House, Clarendon Road, Watford, Herts [Ext: Melford's car leaves for the conference centre]
Friday 12 May 1967: Day 8: Sidney Hayers/unknown director
Main: 10.17-17.20: ABPC Elstree Studios, Stage 3 [Int: Conference centre entrance hall/conference room]
2nd: Unknown time to16.30: ABPC Elstree Studios, Studio Lot, {Ext: Driveway/conference building/Int: Medford's car]
Monday 15 May 1967: Day 9: Sidney Hayers
A Unit: 09.42-17.20: ABPC Elstree Studios, Stage 3 [Int: Conference centre entrance hall/conference room]
Tuesday 16 May 1967: Day 10: Sidney Hayers/unknown director
Main: 09.42-18.55: Royal Connaught Park, The Avenue, Bushey, Herts [Ext: Conference building]
2nd: 12.02-16.04: ABPC Elstree Studios, Stage 3 [Int: Conference centre entrance hall and conference room/conference room]
Wednesday 17 May 1967: Day 11: Sidney Hayers
Main: 09.13-10.16: ABPC Elstree Studios, Stage 3 [Int: Conference room]
Main: 00.00-17.20: ABPC Elstree Studios, Stage 2 [Int: Boyd's study]
Quarter called am
Thursday 18 May 1967: Day 12: Sidney Hayers/unknown director
Main: 08.42-17.20: ABPC Elstree Studios, Stage 2 [Int: Conference room/Boyd's study)
2nd: 09.20-17.10: ABPC Elstree Studios, Stage 2 [Int: Nightmare sequence]

Friday 19 May 1967: Day 13: Sidney Hayers
Main: 09.27-17.15: ABPC Elstree Studios, Stage 2 [Int: Ministerial suite/office/corridor]
Monday 22 May 1967: Day 14: Sidney Hayers
Main: 09.22-17.10: ABPC Elstree Studios, Stage 2 [Int: Bathroom/passageway/nightmare sequence]
Tuesday 23 May 1967: Day 15: Sidney Hayers
Main: 09.00-12.43: Royal Connaught Park, The Avenue, Bushey, Herts [Ext: Conference building]
Main: Unknown time to16.36: Melton House, Clarendon Road, Watford, Herts [Ext: Melford's car leaves for the conference centre]
Main: Unknown time to 19.05: Great Westwood Equestrian Centre, Old House Lane, Sarrett, Herts [Ext: Boyd's country estate]
Wednesday 24 May 1967: Day 16: Sidney Hayers
Main: 09.30-17.20: ABPC Elstree Studios, Stage 2 [Int: Storage company/nightmare sequence]
Thursday 25 May 1967: Day 17: Sidney Hayers
Main: 08.45-17.15: ABPC Elstree Studios, Stage 2 [Int: Nightmare sequence/Steed's Bentley/Emma's Lotus/storage company/Ext: Storage company]
Friday 26 May 1967: Day 18: Sidney Hayers
Main: 10.10 to unknown time: Little Westwood Farm, Bucks Hill, Sarrett, Herts [Becker's home]
Main: Unknown time to 18.50: Royal Connaught Park, The Avenue, Bushey, Herts [Ext: Conference building]
Sound crew from The Champions *B Unit*
Tuesday 30 May 1967: Day 19: Sidney Hayers
2nd: 10.10-17.10: ABPC Elstree Studios, Stage 2 [Inserts]
Wednesday 7 June 1967: Day 20: Sidney Hayers
Main: 10.05 to unknown time: ABPC Elstree Studios, Stage 2 [Travelling matte]
Tuesday 13 June 1967: Day 21: Sidney Hayers
2nd: Unknown time to 17.55: ABPC Elstree Studios, Unknown Stage [Bentley brake pedal (insert)]

5.18 – 'RETURN OF THE CYBERNAUTS'
Episode 122
Original Transmission Date: Saturday 30 September 1967

Writer: Philip Levene
Director: Robert Day
Cast: Patrick Macnee (John Steed), Diana Rigg (Emma Peel), Peter Cushing (Paul Beresford), Frederick Jaeger (Benson), Charles Tingwell (Dr Neville), Fulton Mackay (Professor Chadwick), Roger Hammond (Dr Russell), Anthony Dutton (Dr Garnett), Noel Coleman (Conroy), Aimi MacDonald (Rosie), Redmond Phillips (John Hunt), Terry Richards (Cybernaut).
Uncredited Cast: Michael Gough (Dr Clement Armstrong), Rocky Taylor (Stunt Double for John Steed], Cyd Child (Stunt Double for Emma Peel), Les Crawford (Stunt Driver in Volkswagen), Joe Dunne (Stunt Double for Benson), Joe Farrar (Stunt Double for Professor Chadwick).
Crew: Robert Jones (Production Designer), Ernest Steward (Director of Photography),

Geoffrey Haine (Production Manager), Richard Dalton and Laurie Greenwood (Unit Managers) Ron Carr (Assistant Director), James Bawden (Camera Operator), Len Townsend (Art Director), Gladys Goldsmith (Continuity), Hilda Fox (Hairdressing), Jim Hydes (Make-Up), Gladys James (Wardrobe), Lionel Selwyn (Editor), Ken Rawkins (Sound Recordist), Len Shilton (Dubbing Mixer), Peter Lennard (Sound Editor), Herbert Worley (Construction Manager), Wally Thompson (Supervisory Electrician).

Uncredited Crew: Ernie Lewis (Assistant Director), Gerald Gibbs (Lighting Cameraman), Lillian Lee (Continuity), C Davidson (Clapper Loader), Ricky Coward (Second Assistant Director), Mike Roberts (Focus Puller), Renee Claff (Make-Up), J Irwin (Wardrobe), Val Stewart (Camera Operator), J C White (Assistant Director), R Gaff (Make-Up), Peggy Spirito (Post Production), Michael Meighan (Second Assistant Director), A Brody (Make-Up), D Robertson (Assistant Director), Brian Lawrence (Second Assistant Director).

Production Schedule:
Monday 22 May 1967: Day 1: Robert Day
2nd: 09.05-10.45: Denham Place, Village Road, Denham, Bucks [Ext: Cybernauts view of Russell's home]
2nd: Unknown time: Sutton Road, Watford, Herts [Ext: St John's Church]
2nd: Unknown time to 16.10: Royal Connaught Park, The Avenue, Bushey, Herts [Ext: Clock tower showing four o'clock]
Tuesday 23 May 1967: Day 2: Robert Day
2nd: 10.10-12.00: Duchess Mews, London (Ext: Steed's mews)
2nd: Unknown time: Holmshill Lane, Ridge, Herts (Ext: Lotus and Bentley on country lane]
2nd: Unknown time to 18.35: Silver Hill, Shenley, Herts [Int: Steed's Bentley, following Lotus]
Wednesday 24 May 1967: Day 3: Robert Day
2nd: 09.45 to unknown time: Woolmers Park, Essenden Road, Letty Green, Herts [Ext: Beresford's large house and grounds]
2nd: Unknown time to17.05: Woolmers Lane, Letty Green, Herts [Ext: Lotus and Bentley on country lane]
Thursday 25 May 1967: Day 4: Robert Day
2nd: 09.45-16.20: Haberdashers' Aske's School, Aldenham Road, Elstree, Herts [Ext: Neville's office]
2nd: Unknown time to 18.30: Totteridge Park, Totteridge Common, Mill Hill, London [Ext: High Pines]
Friday 26 May 1967: Day 5: Robert Day
2nd: 09.30-17.16: ABPC Elstree Studios, Stage 3 [Int: Control room]
Tuesday 30 May 1967: Day 6: Robert Day
2nd: 09.30-17.20: ABPC Elstree Studios, Stage 3 [Int: Control room/Beresford's studio]
Wednesday 31 May 1967: Day 7: Robert Day
2nd: 09.17-17.30: ABPC Elstree Studios, Stage 3 [Int: Beresford's studio]
Quarter called pm
Thursday 1 June 1967: Day 8: Robert Day
2nd: 08.55-17.20: ABPC Elstree Studios, Stage 3 [Int: Control room]
Friday 2 Jun 1967: Day 9: Robert Day
2nd: 09.27-17.20: ABPC Elstree Studios, Stage 3 [Int: Control room]

Monday 5 June 1967: Day 10: Robert Day
2nd: 09.30-17.20: ABPC Elstree Studios, Stage 3 [Int: Control room]
Tuesday 6 June 1967: Day 11: Robert Day
2nd: 09.00-17.22: ABPC Elstree Studios, Stage 3 [Int: Control room/cell corridor]
Quarter called am and pm
Wednesday 7 June 1967: Day 12: Robert Day
Main: 08.48-12.25: ABPC Elstree Studios, Stage 3 [Int: Cell corridor/Chadwick's cell/Beresford's studio/Russell's hallway]
Main: Unknown time to 17.16: ABPC Elstree Studios, Stage 2 [Int: Steed's Bentley/Emma's Lotus/Benson's Rover/Ext: Driveway]
Main: Unknown time to 17.20: ABPC Elstree Studios, Stage 3 [No filming]
Thursday 8 June 1967: Day 13: Robert Day
Main: 09.00-17.25: ABPC Elstree Studios, Stage 3 [Int: Control room/Russell's hallway/Russell's study]
Quarter called am and pm
Friday 9 June 1967: Day 14: Robert Day
Main: 09.07-17.20: ABPC Elstree Studios, Stage 3 [Int: Russell's study/Steed's apartment]
Monday 12 June 1967: Day 15: Robert Day
Main: 08.45-17.20: ABPC Elstree Studios, Stage 3 [Int: Steed's apartment/Steed's kitchen/Emma's apartment]
Tuesday 13 June 1967: Day 16: Robert Day
2nd: 09.11-15.38: ABPC Elstree Studios, Stage 3 [Int: Reception hall and Garnet's office]
2nd: Unknown time to 17.20: ABPC Elstree Studios. Studio Lot [Int Neville's car]
Wednesday 14 June 1967: Day 17: Robert Day
Main: 09.07-12.35: ABPC Elstree Studios. Studio Lot [Int Neville's car/Ex: Beresford's house]
Main: Unknown time to 17.20: ABPC Elstree Studios, Stage 3 [Int: Hunt's office]
Thursday 15 June 1967: Day 18: Robert Day/Sidney Hayers
Main: 08.50-09.35: ABPC Elstree Studios, Stage 3 [Int: Hunt's office]
2nd: 12.30 to unknown time: Duchess Mews, London [Ext: Steed's apartment]
2nd: Unknown time: Totteridge Park, Totteridge Common, Mill Hill, London [Ext: High Pines]
2nd: Unknown time to 16.45: Aldenham Estate, Elstree, Herts [Ext: Cybernaut walking across field]
Tuesday 27 June 1967: Day 19: Robert Day
2nd: Unknown time: Haberdashers' Aske's School, Aldenham Road, Elstree, Herts [Ext: Inserts]

5.19 – 'DEAD MAN'S TREASURE'
Episode 123
Original Transmission Date: Saturday 21 October 1967

Writer: Michael Winder
Director: Sidney Hayers
Cast: Patrick Macnee (John Steed), Diana Rigg (Emma Peel), Norman Bowler (Mike Colbourne), Valeria Van Ost (Penny Plain), Edwin Richfield (Alex), Neil McCarthy (Carl), Arthur Lowe (Sir George Benstead), Ivor Dean (Bates), Rio Fanning (Bobby

Danvers), Gerry Crampton (First Guest), Peter J Elliott (Second Guest).

Uncredited Cast: Royston Farrell (Guest), Paul Weston (Stunt Double for John Steed), Cyd Child (Stunt Double for Emma Peel), Rocky Taylor (Stunt Double for John Steed), Gillian Oldham (Stunt Double for Penny Plain), Les Crawford (Stunt Double for Mike Colbourne), Joe Farrar (Stunt Double for Alex), Romo Gorrara (Stunt Double for Carl), Peter J Elliott (Stunt Double for Alex), Les Crawford (Stunt Double for Bobby Danvers), Joe Farrar (Stunt Double for Bobby Danvers).

Crew: Robert Jones (Production Designer), Ernest Steward (Director of Photography), Geoffrey Haine (Production Manager), Richard Dalton and Laurie Greenwood (Unit Managers) Ernie Lewis (Assistant Director), James Bawden (Camera Operator), Len Townsend (Art Director), Gladys Goldsmith (Continuity), Hilda Fox (Hairdressing), Jim Hydes (Make-Up), Gladys James (Wardrobe), Tony Palk (Editor), Ken Rawkins (Sound Recordist), Len Shilton (Dubbing Mixer), Russ Hill (Sound Editor), Herbert Worley (Construction Manager), Wally Thompson (Supervisory Electrician).

Uncredited Crew: Ricky Coward (Second Assistant Director), Gerald Gibbs (Lighting Cameraman), Lillian Lee (Continuity), A Leaming (Focus Puller), Brian Bilgorri (Third Assistant Director), J Buckle (Focus Puller), Peggy Spirito (Continuity), D Engleman (Clapper Loader), A Brody (Make-Up), P Evans (Clapper Loader), Geoff Seaholme (Lighting Cameraman), T Garrett (Clapper Loader), Brian Lawrence (Second Assistant Director), D Robertson (Assistant Director), Michael Meighan (Second Assistant Director), Terry Coles (Focus Puller), John Deaton (Focus Puller), R Smith (Clapper Loader), Y Richards (Continuity), L Parrot (Clapper Loader).

Production Schedule:

Monday 5 June 1967: Day 1: Sidney Hayers
2nd: 09.25 to unknown time: Mimms Lane, Shenley, Herts [Ext: Steed and Emma arrive at Benstead's home]
2nd: Unknown time: Mimms Lane, Harris Lane and Rectory Lane, Shenley, Herts [Ext: Cars leave on treasure hunt]
2nd: Unknown time to 17.05: Back Lane and The Green, Letchmore Heath, Herts [Ext: Village of Mithering]
Tuesday 6 June 1967: Day 2: Sidney Hayers
2nd: 10.00 to unknown time: Deeves Hall Lane and Earls Lane, Ridge, Herts [Ext: Carl and Alex in the E-Type turn right at a road junction]
2nd: Unknown time: Summerswood Lane, Ridge, Herts [Ext: Steed's Bentley goes past the broken down E-Type]
2nd: Unknown time: Bucketsland Lane, Well End, Herts [Ext: Carl and Alex realise they have been going the wrong way]
2nd: Unknown time: Hilfield Lane South, Bushey, Herts [Ext: Bombs away sequence]
2nd: Unknown time to 18.10: Caldecote Lane, Bushey, Herts [Ext: Carl and Alex in their E-Type Jaguar]
Wednesday 7 June 1967: Day 3: Sidney Hayers/unknown director
2nd: 09.40-11.50: Toms Hill Road, Stocks Road and Station Road, Aldbury, Herts [Ext: Village of Swingingdale]
2nd: 12.50-19.20: Church Farm, Crossoaks Lane/Deeves Hall Lane, Ridge, Herts [Ext: Blacksmiths]
3rd: 16.05 to unknown time: Shenley, Herts [Ext: Background plates]
3rd: Unknown time to 19.00: Ridge, Herts [Ext: Background plates]

Thursday 8 June 1967: Day 4: Sidney Hayers/unknown director

2nd: 09.15 to unknown time: Rabley Park Farm, Packhorse Lane, Ridge, Herts [Ext: Tree Tops Farm]

2nd: 14.30-21.15: Aldenham Road, Elstree, Herts [Ext: Steed's Bentley and Carl's E-Type Jaguar]

2nd: Unknown time: Home Farm, Aldenham Road, Elstree, Herts [Ext: E-Type Jaguar smashes through wooden gate]

3rd: 10.20-17.00: Brands Hatch Circuit, Colin Chapman Way, Longfield, Kent [Ext: Racing car simulator screen footage]

Friday 9 June 1967: Day 5: Sidney Hayers

2nd: 08.50 to unknown time: Shenley Hall, Rectory Lane, Shenley, Herts [Ext: Benstead's manor house and grounds]

2nd: Unknown time: Mimms Lane, Harris Lane and Rectory Lane, Shenley, Herts [Ext: Alex and Carl in their E-Type Jaguar chase after Bobby Danvers' MGB]

2nd: Unknown time to 17.45: Deeves Hall Lane and Earls Lane, Ridge, Herts [Ext: E-Type does a U-turn on road junction]

Monday 12 June 1967: Day 6: Sidney Hayers/unknown director

2nd: 09.15 to unknown time: Shenley Hall, Rectory Lane, Shenley, Herts [Ext: Benstead's manor house and grounds]

2nd: Unknown time: Sawyers Lane, Bentley Heath Lane and Baker Street, Bentley Heath, Herts

[Ext: Crossroads where signpost is moved]

2nd: Unknown time: Summerswood Lane, Ridge, Herts [Ext: Steed and Penny in the Bentley round a bend]

2nd: Unknown time to 18.55: Aldenham Road, Elstree, Herts [Ext: Steed's Bentley]

3rd: 06.30-12.30: Brands Hatch Circuit, Colin Chapman Way, Longfield, Kent [Ext: Racing car simulator screen footage]

Tuesday 13 June 1967: Day 7: Sidney Hayers

2nd: 10.15 to unknown time: Shenley Hall, Rectory Lane, Shenley, Herts [Ext: Benstead's manor house and grounds]

2nd: Unknown time to 17.10: Rectory Lane, Shenley, Herts [Ext: Cars leave on treasure hunt/Steed drives his Bentley into a field/Bates crosses over the road from one field to another in his Land Rover/Land Rover/Int: Land Rover]

Crew returned to Elstree Studios to film insert for 'Death's Door'

Wednesday 14 June 1967: Day 8: Sidney Hayers

2nd: 10.00-16.20: ABPC Elstree Studios, Stage 2 [Ext:/Int: Danvers' MGB/Int: Benstead's study]

2nd: 16.45-18.30: Sawyers Lane, Bentley Heath Lane and Baker Street, Bentley Heath, Herts [Ext: Crossroads where signpost is moved]

Thursday 15 June 1967: Day 9: Robert Day/Sidney Hayers

Main: 09.37-17.20: ABPC Elstree Studios, Stage 3 [Int: Steed's apartment]

2nd: 09.40-11.50: Duchess Mews, London [Ext: Steed's mews]

Friday 16 June 1967: Day 10: Sidney Hayers/unknown director

Main: 10.24-17.20: ABPC Elstree Studios, Stage 2 [Int: Benstead's car memorabilia room]

2nd: 08.55 to unknown time: Home Farm, Aldenham Road, Elstree, Herts [Wrecked E-Type Jaguar]

2nd: Unknown time to 16.40: Ridge Hill Stud and Riding Centre, Rectory Lane, Shenley, Herts [Ext: Colbourne and Emma take a short cut in the Mercedes]

Monday 19 June 1967: Day 11: Sidney Hayers
2nd: 08.56-17.20: ABPC Elstree Studios, Stage 2 [Int: Benstead's car memorabilia room/simulator room]
Tuesday 20 June 1967: Day 12: Sidney Hayers
2nd: 09.27-17.20: ABPC Elstree Studios, Stage 2 [Int: Simulator room]
Wednesday 21 June 1967: Day 13: Sidney Hayers
2nd: 09.05-17.20: ABPC Elstree Studios, Stage 2 [Int: Simulator room]
Thursday 22 June 1967: Day 14: Sidney Hayers
2nd: 09.15-17.20: ABPC Elstree Studios, Stage 2 [Int: Switch room/hallway/study/Benstead's car memorabilia room]
Quarter called am
Friday 23 June 1967: Day 15: Sidney Hayers
2nd: 08.40-17.20: ABPC Elstree Studios, Stage 2 [Int: Study/store room/Tree Tops Farm]
Monday 26 June 1967: Day 16: Sidney Hayers
Main: 10.10 to unknown time: Shenley Hall, Rectory Lane, Shenley, Herts [Ext: Benstead's manor house and grounds]
Main: Unknown time to 18.30: Sawyers Lane, Bentley Heath Lane and Baker Street, Bentley Heath, Herts
[Ext: Crossroads where signpost is moved]
Tuesday 27 June 1967: Day 17: Sidney Hayers
Main: 09.25 to unknown time: Back Lane and The Green, Letchmore Heath, Herts [Ext: Village of Mithering]
Main: Unknown time to 18.14: Toms Hill Road, Stocks Road and Station Road, Aldbury, Herts [Ext: Village of Swingingdale]
Wednesday 28 June 1967: Day 18: Sidney Hayers
Main: 09.08 to unknown time: Home Farm, Aldenham Road, Elstree, Herts [Ext: Wrecked E-Type Jaguar]
Main: Unknown time: Summerswood Lane, Ridge, Herts [Ext: Steed and Penny in the Bentley pass the broken-down E-Type]
Main: Unknown time to 15.48: Church Farm, Crossoaks Lane/Deeves Hall Lane, Ridge, Herts [Ext: Blacksmith's]
Thursday 29 June 1967: Day 19: Sidney Hayers
Main: 10.08-17.20: ABPC Elstree Studios, Stage 2 [Int: Steed's Bentley against back-projection]
Friday 30 June 1967: Day 20: Sidney Hayers
Main: 09.52-17.20: ABPC Elstree Studios, Stage 2 [Int: Carl's E-Type Jaguar]
Monday 3 July 1967: Day 21: Sidney Hayers
Main: 09.40 to unknown time: ABPC Elstree Studios, Stage 2 [Int: Mike Colbourne's Mercedes against back-projection/Steed's Bentley against back-projection]
Tuesday 4 July 1967: Day 22: Sidney Hayers
Main: 09.25-17.30: ABPC Elstree Studios, Stage 2 [Int: Carl's E-Type Jaguar against back-projection/Mr Smith's hammer]
Quarter called pm
Wednesday 5 July 1967: Day 23: Sidney Hayers
Main: Unknown time to 17.35: ABPC Elstree Studios, Stage 2 [Int: Simulator room/store room/Steed's Bentley]
Tuesday 11 July 1967: Day 24: Robert Day

Main: 11.15-12.45: ABPC Elstree Studios, Stage 3 [Int: Steed's apartment tag scene]
<u>Wednesday 2 August 1967</u>: Day 25: Robert Asher
Main: Unknown time: ABPC Elstree Studios, Stage 2 [Int: Treasure chest (insert)]

5.20 – 'THE £50,000 BREAKFAST'
Episode 124
Original Transmission Date: Saturday 14 October 1967

Writer: Roger Marshall, based on a story by Roger Marshall and Jeremy Scott
Director: Robert Day
Cast: Patrick Macnee (John Steed), Diana Rigg (Emma Peel), Cecil Parker (Glover), Yolande Turner (Miss Pegram), David Langton (Sir James Arnell), Pauline Delaney (Mrs Rhodes), Anneke Wills (Judy), Cardew Robinson (Minister), Eric Woofe (First Assistant), Philippe Monnet (Second Assistant), Richard Curnock (Dusty Rhodes), Jon Laurimore (Security Man), Richard Owens (Mechanic), Michael Rothwell (Kennel Man), Yole Marinelli (Jerezina), Christopher Greatorex (First Doctor), Nigel Lambert (Second Doctor).
Uncredited Cast: Romo Gorrara (Henchman), Peter Clay (Land Rover Driver), Les Crawford (Farmhand), Janice Hoye (Hostess), John Baker (Mourner), Art Thomas (Stunt Double for Dusty Rhodes), Eric Woofe (Driving Double for John Steed), Cyd Child (Stunt Double for Emma Peel), Romo Gorrara (Stunt Double for First Assistant), Jenny Pink (Stunt Double for Miss Pegram), Russ Henderson, Sterling Betancourt, Max Cherrie (Steel Band Musicians).
Crew: Robert Jones (Production Designer), Ernest Steward (Director of Photography), Geoffrey Haine (Production Manager), Richard Dalton and Laurie Greenwood (Unit Managers) Jack Martin (Assistant Director), James Bawden (Camera Operator), Len Townsend (Art Director), Mary Spain (Continuity), Hilda Fox (Hairdressing), Jim Hydes (Make-Up), Felix Evans (Wardrobe), Ken Rawkins (Sound Recordist), Len Abbott (Dubbing Mixer), Peter Lennard (Sound Editor), Herbert Worley (Construction Manager), Wally Thompson (Supervisory Electrician).
Additional Credit: Russ Henderson and his Trinidad Steel Band (Additional Music by).
Uncredited Crew: Gerald Gibbs (Lighting Cameraman), A Garrett (Clapper Loader), A Brody (Make-Up), F Davies (Sound Mixer), Brian Bilgorri (Third Assistant Director), D Bough (Clapper Loader), Brian Lawrence (Second Assistant Director), Peggy Spirito (Continuity), Terry Coles (Focus Puller), Y Richards (Continuity).

Production Schedule:
<u>Monday 26 June 1967</u>: Day 1: Robert Day
2nd: 11.00-17.30: Chipmunk Chase, North Mymms Park, North Mymms, Herts [Ext: Car accident]
<u>Tuesday 27 June 1967</u>: Day 2: Robert Day
2nd: Unknown time: Bryanston Street, London [Ext: Steed visits Litoff's penthouse]
<u>Wednesday 28 June 1967</u>: Day 3: Robert Day
2nd: 10.00-14.15: ABPC Elstree Studios, Stage 3 [Int: Tie boutique]
2nd: Unknown time to 17.30: ABPC Elstree Studios, Backlot Town [Ext: Painter Street]
Quarter called pm
<u>Thursday 29 June 1967</u>: Day 4: Robert Day
2nd: 10.05-16.30: Aldenham Estate, Aldenham Road, Elstree, Herts [Ext: Woodland and

lake]
None of this day's shoot appeared in the episode
Friday 30 June 1967: Day 5: Robert Day
Main: 10.00-16.20: ABPC Elstree Studios, Stage 3 [Int: Steed's apartment]
Main: 16.20-17.20: ABPC Elstree Studios, Studio Backlot [Ext: Cemetery (setting up)]
Monday 3 July 1967: Day 6: Robert Day
Main: 08.40-17.20: ABPC Elstree Studios, Studio Backlot [Ext: Cemetery]
Tuesday 4 July 1967: Day 7: Robert Day
Main: 08.50 to unknown time: ABPC Elstree Studios, Studio Backlot [Ext: Cemetery]
Main: 10.35-17.20: ABPC Elstree Studios, Stage 9 [Int: Hospital]
Wednesday 5 July 1967: Day 8: Robert Day
Main: 08.30-17.35: ABPC Elstree Studios, Stage 9 [Int: Puppet shop/living room at puppet shop]
Thursday 6 July 1967: Day 9: Robert Day
Main: 08.50-12.50: ABPC Elstree Studios, Stage 9 [Int: Puppet shop/living room at puppet shop/hospital room]
Main: Unknown time to 17.20: ABPC Elstree Studios, Stage 3 [Int: Litoff's penthouse]
Friday 7 July 1967: Day 10: Robert Day
Main: 09.00-10.20: ABPC Elstree Studios, Studio Backlot [Ext: Cemetery]
Main: 12.15-17.20: ABPC Elstree Studios, Stage 3 [Int: Litoff's penthouse]
Monday 10 July 1967: Day 11: Robert Day
Main: 08.30-17.20: ABPC Elstree Studios, Stage 3 [Int: Litoff's penthouse]
Tuesday 11 July 1967: Day 12: Robert Day
Main: 08.30 to unknown time: ABPC Elstree Studios, Stage 3 [Int: Litoff's penthouse/Litoff's bedroom]
Main: 11.15-12.45: ABPC Elstree Studios, Stage 3 [See entry for 'Dead Man's Treasure']
Quarter called am
Main: 13.45-15.50: ABPC Elstree Studios, Backlot Town [Ext: Painter Street]
Main: 16.30-17.35: ABPC Elstree Studios, Stage 3 [Int: Entrance hall]
Wednesday 12 July 1967: Day 13: Robert Day
Main: 08.30-14.10: A5 Garage, A5, Hockcliffe, Beds [Ext: Garage]
Main: 14.50-16.10: ABPC Elstree Studios, Studio Lot [Ext: Cottage hospital]
Main: 16.30-17.20: ABPC Elstree Studios, Stage 3 [Int: Litoff's penthouse]
Thursday 13 July 1967: Day 14: Robert Day
Main: 08.30-17.20: ABPC Elstree Studios, Stage 3 [Int: Litoff's penthouse]
Friday 14 July 1967: Day 15: Robert Day
Main: 08.50-17.20: ABPC Elstree Studios, Stage 3 [Int: Litoff's penthouse]
Monday 17 July 1967: Day 16: Robert Day
Main: 08.30-17.20: ABPC Elstree Studios, Stage 3 [Ext: Window and Litoff's bedroom/Int: Litoff's penthouse/cigar party]
Tuesday 18 July 1967: Day 17: Robert Day
Main: 10.10-10.45: W.C. Jones and Co, Britannia Road, Waltham Cross, Herts (Ext: Car crusher in scrapyard)
Main: Unknown time to 16.00: ABPC Elstree Studios, Stage 3 [Int: Litoff's bedroom/inserts]

5.21 – 'YOU HAVE JUST BEEN MURDERED'
Episode 125

Original Transmission Date: Saturday 28 October 1967

Writer: Philip Levene
Director: Robert Asher
Cast: Patrick Macnee (John Steed), Diana Rigg (Emma Peel), Barrie Ingham (George Unwin), Robert Flemying (Lord Maxted), George Murcell (Needle), Leslie French (Rathbone), Geoffrey Chater (Gilbert Jarvis), Simon Oates (Skelton), Clifford Cox (Chalmers), John Baker (Hallam), Les Crawford (Morgan), Frank Maher (Nicholls), Peter J Elliott (Williams).
Uncredited Cast: Les Crawford (Stunt Double for Skelton), Rocky Taylor (Stunt Double for George Unwin), Cyd Child (Stunt Double for Emma Peel), Frank Maher (Stunt Double for George Unwin), Rocky Taylor (Stunt Double for John Steed), Rocky Taylor (Stunt Double for Needle).
Crew: Robert Jones (Production Designer), Alan Hume (Director of Photography), Geoffrey Haine (Production Manager), Richard Dalton and Laurie Greenwood (Unit Managers) Jack Martin (Assistant Director), Tony White (Camera Operator), Len Townsend (Art Director), Mary Spain (Continuity), Hilda Fox (Hairdressing), Jim Hydes (Make-Up), Felix Evans (Wardrobe), Lionel Selwyn (Editor), Ken Rawkins (Sound Recordist), Len Shilton (Dubbing Mixer), Russ Hill (Sound Editor), Herbert Worley (Construction Manager), Wally Thompson (Supervisory Electrician).
Uncredited Crew: E Lawrence (Make-Up), N Francis (Clapper Loader), Elizabeth Wilcox (Continuity), Michael Meighan (Second Assistant Director), P Aherne (Camera Operator), J Bennett (Focus Puller), Ernie Lewis (Assistant Director), Jane Royal (Make-Up), Anthony Burns (Second Assistant Director), F Tomblin (Boom Operator), Brian Lawrence (Second Assistant Director), A Leeming (Camera Operator), Leslie Hammond (Sound Mixer), Terry Coles (Focus Puller), O Mills (Hairdressing), D Vollmer (Make-Up), Isobel Byers (Continuity), Gerald Moss (Lighting Cameraman).

Production Schedule:
Monday 10 July 1967: Day 1: Robert Asher
2nd: 08.45-11.30: Star House, Clarendon Road, Watford, Herts [Ext: Rathbone's bank]
2nd: 12.30-17.20: Packhorse Lane/Mimms Lane, Ridge, Herts [Ext: Emma's Lotus follows Rathbone's Lincoln]
Tuesday 11 July 1967: Day 2: Robert Asher
2nd: 08.50 to unknown time: Edgewarebury Hotel, Edgewarebury Lane, Elstree, Herts [Ext: Unwin's home]
2nd: Unknown time to 18.00: Hill House, Highgate Hill, Highgate, London [Unwin Enterprises]
Wednesday 12 July 1967: Day 3: Robert Asher
2nd: 10.03 to unknown time: Aldenham Estate, Aldenham Road, Elstree, Herts [Ext: Woodland, lake and bridge]
Thursday 13 July 1967: Day 4: Robert Asher
2nd: 08.50-18.00: Aldenham Estate, Aldenham Road, Elstree, Herts [Ext: Bridge]
Friday 14 July 1967: Day 5: Robert Asher
2nd: 09.10 to unknown time: Aldenham Estate, Aldenham Road, Elstree, Herts [Ext: Bridge/bank]
2nd: Unknown time: Edgewarebury Hotel, Edgewarebury Lane, Elstree, Herts [Ext: Unwin's home]

2nd: 15.00-17.20: ABPC Elstree Studios, Stage 2 [Int: Rathbone's room]

Monday 17 July 1967: Day 6: Robert Asher

2nd: 08.35-16.10: ABPC Elstree Studios, Stage 2 [Int: Rathbone's room/hallway and study]

2nd: 16.20-17.20: ABPC Elstree Studios, Studio Backlot [Ext: Gateway to Rathbone's estate]

Tuesday 18 July 1967: Day 7: Robert Asher

2nd: 08.50-11.20: ABPC Elstree Studios, Studio Backlot [Ext: Gateway to Rathbone's estate/Emma's Lotus]

Main: 11.30-17.20: ABPC Elstree Studios, Stage 2 [Int: Unwin's party]

Wednesday 19 July 1967: Day 8: Robert Asher/unknown director

Main: 08.30-17.20: ABPC Elstree Studios, Stage 2 [Int: Unwin's room]

2nd: 09.50-17.20: ABPC Elstree Studios, Studio Backlot [Ext: Rathbone's estate]

Thursday 20 July 1967: Day 9: Robert Asher

Main: 08.20-17.30: ABPC Elstree Studios, Stage 2 [Int: Unwin's room/Needle's HQ]

Friday 21 July 1967: Day 10: Robert Asher

Main: 08.30-17.20: ABPC Elstree Studios, Stage 2 [Int: Needle's HQ/Unwin's hall and room]

Quarter called am

Monday 24 July 1967: Day 11: Robert Asher

Main: 09.00 to unknown time: Aldenham Estate, Aldenham Road, Elstree, Herts [Ext: bridge and lake/field with haystack and caravan]

Tuesday 25 July 1967: Day 12: Robert Asher

Main: 08.30-17.20: ABPC Elstree Studios, Stage 2 [Int: Needle's H.Q./Unwin's hall and room]

Wednesday 26 July 1967: Day 13: Robert Asher

Main: 08.30-17.20: ABPC Elstree Studios, Stage 2 [Int: Unwin's room/Steed's apartment]

Thursday 27 July 1967: Day 14: Robert Asher

Main: 08.40-19.00: Aldenham Estate, Aldenham Road, Elstree, Herts [Ext: Field with haystack and caravan]

Friday 28 July 1967: Day 15: Robert Asher

Main: 08.30-17.20: ABPC Elstree Studios, Stage 2 [Int: Steed's apartment]

Monday 31 July 1967: Day 16: Robert Asher

Main: 08.40-17.20: ABPC Elstree Studios, Stage 2 [Int: Unwin's room/Jarvis's study/ Steed's apartment (insert)]

Tuesday 1 August 1967: Day 17: Robert Asher

Main: 09.10-17.20: ABPC Elstree Studios, Stage 2 [Int: Jarvis' study]

Quarter called am

Wednesday 2 August 1967: Day 18: Robert Asher

Main: 09.00 to unknown time: ABPC Elstree Studios, Stage 2 [Int: Jarvis's study/Ext: Unwin's house/Steed's Bentley]

Main: Unknown time to 17.20: ABPC Elstree Studios, Studio Lot [Ext: Steed's Bentley]

Wednesday 16 August 1967: Day 19: Robert Day

Main: 14.15-17.30: ABPC Elstree Studios, Stage 3 [Inserts]

Quarter called pm

Tuesday 22 August 1967: Day 20: Unknown director

2nd: Unknown time: ABPC Elstree Studios, Studio Backlot [Insert]

5.22 – 'THE POSITIVE NEGATIVE MAN'
Episode 126
Original Transmission Date: Saturday 4 November 1967

Writer: Tony Williamson
Director: Robert Day
Cast: Patrick Macnee (John Steed), Diana Rigg (Emma Peel), Ray McAnally (Dr Creswell), Michael Latimer (Peter Haworth), Caroline Blakiston (Cynthia Wentworth-Howe), Peter Blythe (James Mankin), Sandor Elès (Maurice Jubert), Joanne Dainton (Miss Clarke), Bill Wallis (Charles Grey), Ann Hamilton (Receptionist).
Uncredited Cast: Rocky Taylor (Stunt Double for John Steed), Denny Powell (Stunt Double for Peter Hayworth), Les Crawford (Stunt Double for Peter Hayworth), Denny Powell (Stunt Double for Dr Creswell).
Crew: Robert Jones (Production Designer), Ernest Steward (Director of Photography), Geoffrey Haine (Production Manager), Richard Dalton and Laurie Greenwood (Unit Managers) Ron Appleton (Assistant Director), James Bawden (Camera Operator), Len Townsend (Art Director), Elizabeth Wilcox (Continuity), Hilda Fox (Hairdressing), Jim Hydes (Make-Up), Felix Evans (Wardrobe), Bert Rule (Editor), Cecil Mason (Sound Recordist), Len Abbott (Dubbing Mixer), Peter Lennard (Sound Editor), Herbert Worley (Construction Manager), Wally Thompson (Supervisory Electrician).
Uncredited Crew: Anthony Burns (Second Assistant Director), A Leeming (Focus Puller), D Engleman (Clapper Loader), Geoff Seaholme (Camera Operator), Jimmy Harvey (Lighting Cameraman), June Royal (Make-Up), Elizabeth Wilcox (Continuity), Leslie Hammond (Sound Mixer), Wilkie Cooper (Lighting Cameraman), F Tomblin (Boom Operator), Michael Higgins (Second Assistant Director), A Garrett (Clapper Loader), P Taylor (Clapper Loader), E Lawrence (Make-Up), D Vollmer (Hairdressing).

Production Schedule:
Monday 24 July 1967: Day 1: Robert Day
2nd: 09.05 to unknown time: Smug Oak Lane, Colney Street, Radlett, Herts [Ext: Bentley driven into shallow bed river]
2nd: Unknown time to 17.20: Station Road and Smug Oak Lane, Bricket Wood, Herts [Ext: Morris 1000 van follows Steed's Bentley]
Tuesday 25 July 1967: Day 2: Robert Day
2nd: 08.50-15.15: Building Research Establishment, Bucknalls Lane, Bricket Wood, Herts [Ext: Wavel Electronics Limited/James Mankin's office]
2nd: 15.55-17.00: ABPC Elstree Studios, Studio Lot [Ext: Emma's apartment]
Wednesday 26 July 1967: Day 3: Robert Day
Main: 08.40-18.30: The Grove, Hempstead Road, Watford, Herts [Ext: Risley Dale]
Thursday 27 July 1967: Day 4: Robert Day
Main: 09.20-18.30: The Grove, Hempstead Road, Watford, Herts [Ext: Risley Dale]
Friday 28 July 1967: Day 5: Robert Day
Main: 08.40-17.20: ABPC Elstree Studios, Stage 3 [Int: Jubert's inner office/Jubert's outer office]
Monday 31 July 1967: Day 6: Robert Day
Main: 08.45-11.38: The Grove, Hempstead Road, Watford, Herts [Ext: Risley Dale]
Main: Unknown time to 17.20: ABPC Elstree Studios, Stage 3 [Int: Jubert's inner office/Jubert's outer office]

Tuesday 1 August 1967: Day 7: Robert Day
Main: 08.35-17.20: ABPC Elstree Studios, Stage 3 [Int: Emma's apartment/Risley Dale electronics lab]
Wednesday 2 August 1967: Day 8: Robert Day
Main: 08.35-17.20: ABPC Elstree Studios, Stage 3 [Int: Risley Dale electronics lab]
Thursday 3 August 1967: Day 9: Robert Day
Main: 08.35-17.20: ABPC Elstree Studios, Stage 3 [Int: Risley Dale electronics lab]
Friday 4 August 1967: Day 10: Robert Day
Main: 08.35-17.35: ABPC Elstree Studios, Stage 3 [Int: Risley Dale electronics lab]
Quarter called pm
Monday 7 August 1967: Day 11: Robert Day
Main: 08.30-12.40: Hillcrest, Barnet Road, Arkley, Herts [Ext: Dr Cresswell's home]
Main: 14.00-17.20: ABPC Elstree Studios, Stage 3 [Int: Risley Dale electronics lab]
Tuesday 8 August 1967: Day 12: Robert Day
Main: 08.45 to unknown time: The Grove, Hempstead Road, Watford, Herts [Ext: Risley Dale]
Wednesday 9 August 1967: Day 13: Robert Day
Main: 08.35-17.20: ABPC Elstree Studios, Stage 3 [Int: Grey's office/Ext: Emma's apartment]
Thursday 10 August 1967: Day 14: Robert Day
Main: 08.35-17.20: ABPC Elstree Studios, Stage 3 [Int: Emma's apartment/Ministry of Science office]
Friday 11 August 1967: Day 15: Robert Day
Main: 08.30 to unknown time: Aldenham Estate, Aldenham Road, Elstree, Herts [Ext: Lake]
Main: Unknown time to 18.10: The Grove, Hempstead Road, Watford, Herts [Ext: Risley Dale]
Monday 14 August 1967: Day 16: Robert Day
Main: 08.30-17.20: ABPC Elstree Studios, Stage 3 [Int: Vault/reception/Mankin's lab]
Tuesday 15 August 1967: Day 17: Robert Day
Main: 08.35-17.20: ABPC Elstree Studios, Stage 3 [Int: Dr Cresswell's lounge/Risley Dale electronics lab (insert)]
Wednesday 16 August 1967: Day 18: Robert Day
Main: 08.30 to unknown time: The Grove, Hempstead Road, Watford, Herts [Ext: Risley Dale]
Main: 14.15-17.30: ABPC Elstree Studios, Stage 3 [Inserts]
Thursday 17 August 1967: Day 19: Robert Day
Main: 08.30-16.00: ABPC Elstree Studios, Stage 3 [Int: Grey's office/Morris 1000 van/cabinet/Ext: Electronics building/fence/Dr Cresswell's home (inserts and pick-up shots)]
Friday 18 August 1967: Day 20: Robert Day
Main: 15.15.16.15: ABPC Elstree Studios, Stage 2 [Int: Steed's apartment]

5.23 – 'MURDERSVILLE'
Episode 127
Original Transmission Date: Saturday 11 November 1967

Writer: Brian Clemens

Director: Robert Asher
Cast: Patrick Macnee (John Steed), Diana Rigg (Emma Peel), Colin Blakely (Mickle), John Ronane (Hubert), Ronald Hines (Dr Haymes), John Sharp (Prewitt), Sheila Fearn (Jenny Prewitt), Eric Flynn (Major Paul Croft), Norman Chappell (Forbes), Robert Cawdron (Banks), Marika Mann (Miss Avril), Irene Bradshaw (Maggie), Joseph Gieg (Higgins), Geoffrey Colville (Jeremy Purser), Langton Jones (Chapman), Tony Caunter (George Miller), John Chandos (Samuel Morgan), Andrew Laurence (Frederick Williams).
Uncredited Cast: Hilary Dwyer (Hilary), Paddy Ryan (Farmer), Paul Weston (Second Policeman), Peter Clay (Martin), Maxwell Craig (Wilson), Gareth Thomas (Assassin in Sunglasses), Romo Gorrara (Man Thrown from Car), Bill Cummings (Stunt Double for Hubert), Cyd Child (Stunt Double for Emma Peel), Denny Powell (Stunt Double for Banks), Romo Gorrara (Stunt Double for Hubert), Les Crawford (Stunt Double for Dr Haymes), Rocky Taylor (Stunt Double for John Steed), Joe Dunne (Stunt Double for Mickle), Joe Dunne (Stunt Double for Hubert).
Crew: Robert Jones (Production Designer), Alan Hume (Director of Photography), Geoffrey Haine (Production Manager), Richard Dalton and Laurie Greenwood (Unit Managers) Jack Martin (Assistant Director), Tony White (Camera Operator), Len Townsend (Art Director), Marjorie Lavelly (Continuity), Hilda Fox (Hairdressing), Jim Hydes (Make-Up), Felix Evans (Wardrobe), Brian Marshall (Sound Recordist), Len Shilton (Dubbing Mixer), Peter Lennard (Sound Editor), Herbert Worley (Construction Manager), Wally Thompson (Supervisory Electrician).
Uncredited Crew: June Royal (Make-Up), D Vollmer (Make-Up/Hairdressing), Isobel Byers (Continuity), J Buckle (Focus Puller), Bill Lodge (Make-Up), E Lawrence (Make-Up), John Deaton (Focus Puller), Denis Fitzgibbons (Focus Puller), Peter Pardo (Boom Operator), B Buckley (Sound Mixer), Brian Lawrence (Second Assistant Director), Geoff Glover (Camera Operator), L Parrot (Focus Puller), A Jones (Focus Puller).

Production Schedule:
Thursday 3 August 1967: Day 1: Ray Austin
2nd: 09.10-18.25: Field at Ridge Hill Stud and Riding Centre, Rectory Lane, Shenley, Herts [Ext: Helicopter chasing Mrs Peel]
Friday 4 August 1967: Day 2: Ray Austin
2nd: 09.00-15.10: Harris Lane/Silver Hill, Shenley, Herts [Ext: Croft's house/country roads]
Some material from this shoot not used in the episode
Monday 7 August 1967: Day 3: Robert Asher
Main: 10.25-18.10: Aldbury, Herts [Ext: The village]
Tuesday 8 August 1967: Day 4: Robert Asher
Main: 09.45-18.18: Aldbury, Herts [Ext: The village]
Wednesday 9 August 1967: Day 5: Robert Asher
Main: 09.50-18.30: Aldbury, Herts [Ext: The village]
Thursday 10 August 1967: Day 6: Robert Asher
Main: 09.30 to unknown time: Stocks House, Stocks Road, Aldbury, Herts [Ext: Croft's house]
Main: Unknown time to 17.52: Aldbury, Herts [Ext: The village]
Friday 11 August 1967: Day 7: Robert Asher
Main: 09.40 to unknown time: Aldbury, Herts [Ext: The village]

Main: Unknown time to 18.25: Stocks House, Stocks Road, Aldbury, Herts [Ext: Croft's house]
Monday 14 August 1967: Day 8: Robert Asher
Main: 10.00-17.20: ABPC Elstree Studios, Stage 2 [Int: Museum]
Tuesday 15 August 1967: Day 9: Robert Asher
Main: 08.45-17.20: ABPC Elstree Studios, Stage 2 [Int: Museum/Dr Haymes' surgery]
Wednesday 16 August 1967: Day 10: Robert Asher
Main: 08.50 to unknown time: ABPC Elstree Studios, Stage 2 [Int: Dr Haymes' surgery and morgue/Emma's Lotus/Dr Haymes' car]
Main: 15.50-17.20: ABPC Elstree Studios, Studio Backlot [Ext: Shrubbery]
Thursday 17 August 1967: Day 11: Robert Asher
Main: 09.25-17.20: ABPC Elstree Studios, Stage 2 [Int: Steed's apartment/museum]
Friday 18 August 1967: Day 12: Robert Asher/unknown director
Main: 08.47-17.20: ABPC Elstree Studios, Stage 2 [Int: Museum/library]
2nd: Unknown time to 17.30: Field at Ridge Hill Stud and Riding Centre, Rectory Lane, Shenley, Herts [Ext: Mrs Peel close ups]
Monday 21 August 1967: Day 13: Robert Asher
Main: 09.25-17.20: ABPC Elstree Studios, Stage 2 [Int: Pub]
Tuesday 22 August 1967: Day 14: Robert Asher/unknown director
Main: 08.37-17.20: ABPC Elstree Studios, Stage 2 [Int: Pub/library]
2nd: 09.00-16.30: ABPC Elstree Studios, Studio Backlot [Ext: Shrubbery]
Quarter called am
Wednesday 23 August 1967: Day 15: Robert Asher
Main: 08.50-17.25: ABPC Elstree Studios, Stage 2 [Int: Library/pub]
Quarter called am and pm
Thursday 24 August 1967: Day 16: Robert Asher
Main: 08.45-17.20: ABPC Elstree Studios, Stage 2 [Int: Library/pub]
Friday 25 August 1967: Day 17: Robert Asher
Main: 09.10-12.22: ABPC Elstree Studios, Stage 2 [Int: Library/pub/telephone exchange/Ext: Sky]

5.24 – 'MISSION HIGHLY IMPROBABLE'
Episode 128
Original Transmission Date: Saturday 18 November 1967

Writer: Philip Levene
Director: Robert Day
Cast: Patrick Macnee (John Steed), Diana Rigg (Emma Peel), Ronald Radd (Shaffer), Jane Merrow (Susan Rushton), Noel Howlett (Professor Rushton), Francis Matthew (Dr Chivers), Richard Leech (Colonel Drew), Stefan Gryff (Josef), Nicholas Courtney (Captain Gifford), Kevin Stoney (Sir Gerald Bancroft), Peter Clay (Sergeant), Nigel Rideout (Corporal Johnson), Cynthia Bizeray (Blonde), *Nicole Shelby (Brunette), Nosher Powell (Hendrick), Denny Powell (Karl).
*Does not appear in episode
Uncredited Cast: Cyd Child (Stunt Double for Emma Peel), Paul Weston (Stunt Double for Dr Chivers), Anthony Marlowe (Second Lieutenant).
Crew: Robert Jones (Production Designer), Ernest Steward (Director of Photography), Geoffrey Haine (Production Manager), Richard Dalton and Laurie Greenwood (Unit

Managers) Jack Martin (Assistant Director), Kevin Pike (Camera Operator), Len Townsend (Art Director), Marjorie Lavelly (Continuity), Hilda Fox (Hairdressing), Jim Hydes (Make-Up), Felix Evans (Wardrobe), Lionel Selwyn (Editor), Cecil Mason (Sound Recordist), Len Shilton (Dubbing Mixer), Russ Hill (Sound Editor), Herbert Worley (Construction Manager), Wally Thompson (Supervisory Electrician).

Uncredited Crew: Ernie Robinson (Focus Puller), Brian Lawrence (Second Assistant Director), D Vollmer (Hairdressing), Gerald Moss (Lighting Cameraman), Peggy Spirito (Continuity), Renée Glynne (Continuity), Peter Carmody (Clapper Loader), Y Richards (Continuity), D Crozier (Boom Operator), K Nightingale (Boom Operator), Ernie Lewis (Assistant Director), R Smith (Focus Puller), J Smith (Clapper Loader), Wilkie Cooper (Lighting Cameraman), J Martin (Assistant Director), A Brody (Make-Up), Simon Wakefield (Art Department Assistant), Ken Softly (Assistant Director), James Alloway (Focus Puller), P Taylor (Clapper Loader).

Production Schedule:
Wednesday 23 August 1967: Day 1: Robert Day
Main: 08.40-17.20: ABPC Elstree Studios, Stage 3 [Int: Emma's apartment]
Thursday 24 August 1967: Day 2: Robert Day
Main: 08.30-17.15: ABPC Elstree Studios, Stage 3 [Int: Rushton'soOffice/skirting board in Shaffer's office/desk with giant items]
Friday 25 August 1967: Day 3: Robert Day
Main: 09.00 to unknown time: ABPC Elstree Studios, Studio Backlot [Ext: Rushton's house/summer house]
Main: 12.00-17.20: ABPC Elstree Studios, Stage 3 [Int: Shaffer's house]
Tuesday 29 August 1967: Day 4: Robert Day
Main: 08.55-17.20: ABPC Elstree Studios, Stage 3 [Int: Shaffer's study/Shaffer's hallway]
Wednesday 30 August 1967: Day 5: Robert Day
Main: 09.00 to unknown time: ABPC Elstree Studios, Stage 3 [Int: Shaffer's study]
Main: 14.10-16.55: ABPC Elstree Studios, Studio Backlot [Ext: Summer house]
Thursday 31 August 1967: Day 6: Robert Day
Main: 09.34-17.20: ABPC Elstree Studios, Studio Lot [Ext: Metal fatigue division]
Quarter called am
Friday 1 September 1967: Day 7: Robert Day
Main: 10.06-17.00: North Mymms Park, North Mymms, Herts [Ext: Motorcycles follow Rolls Royce]
Monday 4 September 1967: Day 8: Robert Day
2nd: Unknown time to 17.20: North Mymms Park, North Mymms, Herts [Ext: Guard post]
2nd: Unknown time: The Vicarage, St Mary's Church Road, North Mymms, Herts [Ext: Rushton's house]
2nd: Unknown time to 17.20: Rabley Park, Packhorse Lane, Ridge, Herts [Ext: Shaffer's house/field]
Tuesday 5 September 1967: Day 9: Robert Day
Main: 09.15-17.45: ABPC Elstree Studios, Stage 3 [Int: Rushton's office/giant photoframe and telephone]
Quarter called pm
Wednesday 6 September 1967: Day 10: Robert Day
Main: 09.05-17.25: ABPC Elstree Studios, Stage 3 [Int: Giant photoframe and

telephone/Shaffer's study, door and doorframe/skirting board]
Quarter called pm
Thursday 7 September 1967: Day 11: Robert Day
Main: 09.00-16.45: Bell Lane Sand Pit, London Colney, Herts [Ext: Testing range]
Main: Unknown time to 17.15: ABPC Elstree Studios, Studio Backlot [Ext: Testing range]
Friday 8 September 1967: Day 12: Robert Day
Main: 09.05 to unknown time: ABPC Elstree Studios, Studio Lot [Ext: Experimental shed]
Main: Unknown time to 17.20: ABPC Elstree Studios, Stage 2 [Int: Summer house/experimental shed]
Monday 11 September 1967: Day 13: Robert Day
Main: 08.55-17.35: ABPC Elstree Studios, Stage 2 [Int: Experimental shed]
Quarter called pm
Tuesday 12 September 1967: Day 14: Robert Day
Main: 09.05-17.30: ABPC Elstree Studios, Stage 2 [Int: Experimental shed]
Quarter called pm
Wednesday 13 September 1967: Day 15: Robert Day
Main: 11.45-17.15: ABPC Elstree Studios, Stage 3 [Int: Rushton's office]
Thursday 14 September 1967: Day 16: Robert Day
Main: 09.05-17.20: ABPC Elstree Studios, Stage 3 [Int: Schaffer's study]
Friday 15 September 1967: Day 17: Robert Day/Sidney Hayers
Main: 08.45 to unknown time: ABPC Elstree Studios, Stage 3 [Int: Schaffer's study and hallway/experimental shed/giant grass]
Main: Unknown time to 17.15: ABPC Elstree Studios, Studio Backlot [Ext: Car/country road/guard post/net and grass]
2nd: 09.25-15.50: North Mymms Park, North Mymms, Herts [Ext: Country road]
Monday 18 September 1967: Day 18: Robert Day
Main: 09.50-16.55: Rabley Park, Packhorse Lane, Ridge, Herts [Ext: Shaffer's house]
Friday 22 September 1967: Day 19: Peter Tanner
Main: 10.10 to unknown time: ABPC Elstree Studios, Stage 3 [Int: Schaffer's study and hallway]
Main: Unknown time to 15.15: ABPC Elstree Studios, Studio Backlot [Ext: Road]

SEASON SIX

An ABC Television Films production for the Associated British Corporation
Copyright: ABC Television Films Ltd
33 colour episodes on 35mm film
Permanent Crew: Albert Fennell and Brian Clemens (Produced by), Gordon L T Scott (Executive in Charge of Production), Jack Greenwood (Production Controller), Robert Jones (Production Designer), Ron Fry (Production Manager), Pierre Cardin (Principal items of Mr Macnee's wardrobe designed by), G B Walker (Casting Director), Laurie Greenwood (Unit Manager), Jim Hydess (Make-Up), Lionel Selwyn (Editor), A W Lumkin (Recording Director), Joe Dunne (Stunt Arranger).

'INVITATION TO A KILLING'
Reworked into 'Have Guns – Will Haggle'

Writer: Donald James
Director: Robert Asher
Cast: Patrick Macnee (John Steed), Linda Thorson (Tara King), Nicola Pagett (Adriana), Johnny Sekka (Colonel Nsonga), Roy Stewart (Giles), Jonathan Burn (Conrad), Rocky Taylor (Mercenary), Terry Richards (Mercenary), Terry Plummer (Mercenary), Robert Gillespie (Lift Attendant), Jennifer Croxton (Photographer), Basil Tang (Unknown Role), Thi Ha (Unknown Role), Brian Stan Haines (Unknown Role).
Uncredited Cast: Cyd Child (Double/Driving Double for Tara King), Joe Wadham (Driving Double for Conrad), Romo Gorrara (Driving Double for Tara King), Rocky Taylor (Double for John Steed), Terry York (Double for Unknown Performer), Terry Plummer (Double for Unknown Performer).
Crew: Unknown.
Uncredited Crew: John Bryce (Producer), Philip Levene (Script Editor) Isobel Byers (Continuity), Peter Carmodie (Clapper Loader), C Davidson (Focus Puller), Bob Kindred (Camera Operator), Ron Appleton (Assistant Director), James Alloway (Focus Puller), J Stillwell (Focus Puller), S Harris (Clapper Loader), Brian Lawrence (Second Assistant Director), Ann Brodie (Make-Up), R Burns (Second Assistant Director), J Lamborn (Clapper Loader), Terry Glover (Focus Puller), Jack Smith (Clapper Loader).

Production Schedule:
Monday 23 October 1967: Day 1: Robert Asher
Main: 09.20-18.10: Starveacres, Watford Road, Radlett, Herts [Ext: Stokely House/driveway/ornamental garden]
Tuesday 24 October 1967: Day 2: Robert Asher
Main: 09.15-17.15: Starveacres, Watford Road, Radlett, Herts [Ext: Stokely house/driveway/woodlands]
Wednesday 25 October 1967: Day 3: Robert Asher/John Hough
Main: 09.50-16.30: Starveacres, Watford Road, Radlett, Herts [Ext: Stokely house/driveway/ornamental garden/rifle range]
2nd: 09.50-16.30: Starveacres, Watford Road, Radlett, Herts [Ext: Stokely house/driveway/ornamental garden/rifle range]
Thursday 26 October 1967: Day 4: Robert Asher/John Hough
Main: 09.35-17.20: ABPC Elstree Studios, Stage 3 [Int: Hotel composite/hotel corridor/Colonel Nsonga's room/hotel lift]
2nd: 09.35-17.20: ABPC Elstree Studios, Stage 3 [Int: Hotel composite/hotel corridor/Colonel Nsonga's room/hotel lift]
Friday 27 October 1967: Day 5: Robert Asher/John Hough
Main: 09.05-17.30: ABPC Elstree Studios, Stage 3 [Int: Hotel room/Colonel Nsonga's room/hotel lobby]
2nd: 09.05-17.30: ABPC Elstree Studios, Stage 3 [Int: Hotel room/Colonel Nsonga's room/hotel lobby]
Monday 30 October 1967: Day 6: Robert Asher/John Hough
Main: 09.25-17.20: ABPC Elstree Studios, Stage 3 [Int: Hotel lobby/hut/Ext: Wood hut compound]
2nd: 09.25-17.20: ABPC Elstree Studios, Stage 3 [Int: Hotel lobby/hut/Ext: Wood hut

compound]
Tuesday 31 October 1967: Day 7: Robert Asher/John Hough
Main: 09.47-17.12: ABPC Elstree Studios, Stage 3 [Int: Hut/Ext: Wood hut compound/Stokely House terrace]
2nd: 09.47-17.12: ABPC Elstree Studios, Stage 3 [Int: Hut/Ext: Wood hut compound/Stokely House terrace]
Wednesday 1 November 1967: Day 8: Robert Asher/John Hough
Main: 08.45-17.20: ABPC Elstree Studios, Stage 3 [Int: Main drawing room/Ext: Stokely House terrace]
2nd: 08.45-17.20: ABPC Elstree Studios, Stage 3 [Int: Main drawing room/Ext: Stokely House terrace]
Thursday 2 November 1967: Day 9: Robert Asher/John Hough
Main: 09.20-17.20: ABPC Elstree Studios, Stage 3 [Int: Drawing room/Gladiator's room/Steed's apartment]
2nd: Unknown time to 18.20: ABPC Elstree Studios, Studio Lot [Ext: Hotel forecourt]
Friday 3 November 1967: Day 10: Robert Asher/John Hough
Main: 09.00-17.15: ABPC Elstree Studios, Stage 3 [Int: Gladiator's room/Steed's apartment/Ext: Shrubbery set/Open Road B]
2nd: 09.30 to unknown time: ABPC Elstree Studios, Studio Backlot [Ext: Testing range/ordnance factory]
2nd: Unknown time to 17.20: ABPC Elstree Studios, Studio Lot [Ext: Factory gates/Int: Ballistic research centre]
Monday 6 November 1967: Day 11: Robert Asher
2nd: Unknown time: ABPC Elstree Studios, Studio Backlot [Ext: Ordnance factory]
2nd: Unknown time to 17.20: ABPC Elstree Studios, Studio Lot [Int: Ordnance factory]
Quarter called am.
Tuesday 7 November 1967: Day 12: John Hough
2nd: Unknown time to 17.20: Starveacres, Watford Road, Radlett, Herts [Ext: Woodland fringe and ornamental garden]
Thursday 9 November 1967: Day 13: John Hough
2nd: Unknown time: ABPC Elstree Studios, Studio Backlot [Ext: Hut explosion]

6.01 – 'INVASION OF THE EARTHMEN'
Episode 129
Original Transmission Date: Wednesday 15 January 1969

Writer: Terry Nation
Director: Don Sharp
Cast: Patrick Macnee (John Steed), Linda Thorson (Tara King), William Lucas (Brigadier Brett), Christian Roberts (Huxton) Lucy Fleming (Emily), Christopher Chittell (Bassin), Warren Clarke (Trump), Wendy Allnutt (Sarah), George Roubicek (Grant).
Uncredited Cast: Paul Weston (Double for John Steed), Cyd Child (Double for Tara King), Rocky Taylor (Double for John Steed), Clifford Diggens (Double/Driving Double for Huston), Peter Pocock (Double for Bassin), Joe Dunne (Double for Alpha Academy Student), Richard Grayden (Double for Alpha Academy Student), Steve Cory (Double/Driving Double for Trump), Liz Mitchell (Double for Tara King), Bill Morgan (Double for Brigadier Brett).
Crew: Laurie Johnson (Music by), Philip Levene (Story Consultant), Julian Wintle

(Consultant to the Series), Gilbert Taylor BSC (Director of Photography), Harry Booth (Post Production Co-ordinator), Manuel del Campo (Editor), Harvey Gould (Miss Thorson's Costumes Designed by), Ron Appleton (Assistant Director), Brian Elvin (Camera Operator), Len Townsend (Associate Art Director), Kenneth Tait (Set Dresser), June Randall (Continuity), Gordon Bond (Hairdressing), Felix Evans (Wardrobe), Jimmy Harvey BSC (Second Unit Photography), Cecil Mason (Sound Recordist), Len Shilton (Dubbing Mixer), Peter Lennard (Sound Editor), Karen Heward (Music Editor), Herbert Worley (Construction Manager), Steve Birtles (Supervisory Electrician).

Uncredited Crew: John Bryce (Producer), Terry Glover (Focus Puller), Jack Smith (Clapper Loader), Ken Softley (Assistant Director), Peggy Spirito (Continuity), Bob Kindred (Camera Operator), Mike Roberts (Focus Puller), J Shillingford (Clapper Loader), Brian Elvin (Camera Operator), Kevin Hall (Driving Instructor for Linda Thorson), Dudley Lovell (Camera Operator), C Davidson (Clapper Loader), Anthony Burns (Second Assistant Director), Kay Freeborn (Make-Up), I Lawrence (Third Assistant Director), H Fairburn (Boom Operator).

Production Schedule:
Monday 6 November 1967: Day 1: Don Sharp
Main: 09.45-17.15: ABPC Elstree Studios, Stage 9 [Ext: Quarry section]
Quarter called am
Tuesday 7 November 1967: Day 2: Don Sharp
Main: 08.40-17.15: ABPC Elstree Studios, Stage 9 [Ext: Quarry section]
Quarter called am
Wednesday 8 November 1967: Day 3: Don Sharp
Main: 08.55-17.15: ABPC Elstree Studios, Stage 9 [Ext: Quarry section]
Thursday 9 November 1967: Day 4: Don Sharp/John Hough
Main: 08.40-17.05: ABPC Elstree Studios, Stage 9 [Ext: Tunnel entrance/tunnel]
2nd: 08.40-17.05: ABPC Elstree Studios, Stage 9 [Ext: Quarry section – inserts]
Friday 10 November 1967: Day 5: Don Sharp/John Hough
Main: 09.15-17.10: ABPC Elstree Studios, Stage 9 [Ext: Tunnel/tube]
2nd: 09.15-17.10: ABPC Elstree Studios, Stage 9 [Ext: Quarry section/tunnel – inserts]
Monday 13 November 1967: Day 6: No details available.
Tuesday 14 November 1967: Day 7: Don Sharp
Main: 09.00-17.15: ABPC Elstree Studios, Stage 3 [Int: Brett's study]
Wednesday 15 November 1967: Day 8: Don Sharp/John Hough
Main: 08.55-16.15: ABPC Elstree Studios, Stage 3 [Int: Brett's study]
2nd: Unknown time: Woodside Lodge, Windhill Road, Welham Green, Herts [Ext: Alpha Academy gateway]
Thursday 16 November 1967: Day 9: Don Sharp/John Hough
Main: 09.00-17.10: ABPC Elstree Studios, Stage 3 [Int: Alpha Academy corridors]
Friday 17 November 1967: Day 10: Don Sharp/John Hough
Main: 09.10-16.15: ABPC Elstree Studios, Stage 3 [Int: Cryobiology room/Steed's apartment/hotel room/Steed's car]
2nd: 09.10 to unknown time: The Salisbury Crest, West End Lane, Essendon, Hatfield, Herts [Ext: Country hotel and road]
2nd: Unknown time: Knebworth House, Old Knebworth Lane, Old Knebworth, Herts [Ext: Alpha Academy]
2nd: Unknown time to 16.15: Church Close/Bury Lane, Codicote, Stevenage, Herts

[Ext: Country roads A and B]
Monday 20 November 1967: Day 11: Don Sharp
2nd: Unknown time: ABPC Elstree Studios, Stage 3 [Int: Alpha Academy corridors/Steed's car/Ext: High wire fence and country road]
Tuesday 21 November 1967: Day 12: Don Sharp
2nd: Unknown time: ABPC Elstree Studios, Stage 3 [Int Alpha Academy classroom/Ext: High wire fence and country road – inserts]
Thursday 21 December 1967: Day 13: John Hough
2nd: 15.15-17.10: ABPC Elstree Studios, Stage 9 [Int: Insert for Scene 61]
Thursday 11 January 1968: Day 14: Don Sharp
Main: 09.15-17.05: ABPC Elstree Studios, Stage 3 [Int: Steed's apartment/Tara's apartment/Steed's car]
Friday 12 January 1968: Day 15: Don Sharp
2nd: 09.30-10.10: ABPC Elstree Studios, Stage 3 [Int: Steed's car]
On completion of scenes the second unit moved to Stage 4 to work on opening titles.
Tuesday 23 January 1968: Day 16: John Hough
2nd: Unknown time: ABPC Elstree Studios, Stage 3 [Int: Insert on quarry set]

'THE GREAT GREAT BRITAIN CRIME'
Amalgamated into 'Homicide and Old Lace'

Writers: Malcolm Hulke and Terrance Dicks
Director: Vernon Sewell
Cast: Patrick Macnee (John Steed), Linda Thorson (Tara King), Keith Baxter (Dunbar), Edward Brayshaw (Fuller), Donald Pickering (Freddie Cartwright), Mark London (American Delegate), Stephen Hubay (Russian Delegate), Bari Jonson (African Delegate), Kristopher Kum (Asian Delegate) Kevork Malikyan (Rossi), Gertan Klauber (Kruger), Ann Rutter (Controller), Dinny Powell (Guard), John Rapley (Taxi Driver), Gerald Harper (Colonel Corf), Bryan Mosley (Sergeant Smith), Tom Gill (Hobson), Jennifer White (Unknown Role), Rosemary Reede (Unknown Role), Bill Sawyer (Unknown Role).
Uncredited Cast: Cyd Child (Double/Driving Double for Tara King), Sadie Evan (Double for Rosemary Reed's Character), Rocky Taylor (Double for John Steed), Joe Dunne (Double for Fuller), Romo Gorrara (Mini Driver), Bill Cummings (Mini Driver), Billy Dean (Double for Freddie Cartwright).
Crew: Unknown
Uncredited Crew: John Bryce (Producer), Philip Levene (Script Editor), I Lawrence (Third Assistant Director), Julian White (Third Assistant Director), Peter Ernst (Unit Runner), Jack Dooley (Stills Cameraman), Richard Gill (Second Assistant Director), B Clark (Make-Up), Ken Softley (Assistant Director), Anthony Burns (Second Assistant Director), Iris Karney (Production Secretary), C Jamison (Hairdresser), Ernie Robinson (Camera Operator), Mike Roberts (Focus Puller), C Davidson (Clapper Loader), Isabel Byers (Continuity), Michael Meagan (Second Assistant Director), Janet Lucas (Wardrobe Assistant), Ron Appleton (Assistant Director), B Royston (Make-Up), Peter Carmody (Clapper Loader), Derek Gibson (Third Assistant Director), A Lemming (Focus Puller).

Production Schedule:

Monday 20 November 1967: Day 1: Vernon Sewell
Main: 09.40-17.10: ABPC Elstree Studios, Stage 9 [Int: Dunbar's office/Intercrime control room]

Tuesday 21 November 1967: Day 2: Vernon Sewell
Main: 09.20-17.15: ABPC Elstree Studios, Stage 9 [Int: Intercrime control room]

Wednesday 22 November 1967: Day 3: Vernon Sewell
Main: 09.05-19.55: ABPC Elstree Studios, Stage 9 [Int: Dunbar's office/Intercrime control room/Orpheus Tours reception, lift and stairs]

Thursday 23 November 1967: Day 4: Vernon Sewell/John Hough
Main: 09.50-16.00: Bullens Organisation, Maxwell Road, Borehamwood, Herts [Int: Packing yard/Ext: Wall]

2nd: Unknown time: Buckingham Palace, The Mall, London, SW1 [Ext: Establishing shots]

2nd: Unknown time: Trafalgar Square, London, WC2 [Ext: Establishing shots]

2nd: Unknown time: Westminster Abbey, London, SW1 [Ext: Establishing shots]

2nd: Unknown time: Houses of Parliament, London, SW1 [Ext: Establishing shots]

2nd: Unknown time: Thames Embankment, London, WC2 [Ext: Establishing shots]

2nd: Unknown time: Tower Bridge, Tower Bridge Road, London, SE1 [Ext: Establishing shots]

Friday 24 November 1967: Day 5: Vernon Sewell/John Hough
Main: 09.50 to unknown time: Church Car Park, Exchange Road, Watford, Herts [Int: Multi-storey car park]

Main: Unknown time: Archway, McDonald Road, Highgate Hill, London, N19 [Ext: Office block and car park]

Main: Unknown time to 15.45: Bryanston Street, London, W1 [Ext: West End street]

2nd: Unknown time: Edgware Road, London, W2 [Ext: Street A]

2nd: Unknown time: Wood Lane, Little Common, Stanmore, Middlesex [Ext: Country road]

2nd: Unknown time: Bullens Organisation, Maxwell Road, Borehamwood, Herts [Ext: Street A]

Monday 27 November 1967: Day 6: Vernon Sewell/John Hough
Main: 09.35-17.12: ABPC Elstree Studios, Stage 3 [Int: Colonel Corf's office/vaults]

2nd: 10.00-16.10: Church Car Park, Exchange Road, Watford, Herts [Int: Multi-storey car park]

Tuesday 28 November 1967: Day 7: Vernon Sewell
Main: 09.05-17.10: ABPC Elstree Studios, Stage 3 [Int: Colonel Corf's office and lift/Ext: Storage space]

Wednesday 29 November 1967: Day 8: Vernon Sewell
Main: 09.20-17.15: ABPC Elstree Studios, Stage 3 [Int: Vaults and corridor/Piccadilly Underground/cell]

Thursday 30 November 1967: Day 9: Vernon Sewell/John Hough
Main: 09.05-17.16: ABPC Elstree Studios, Stage 3 [Int: Hobson's office/jeweller's shop/cell]

2nd: Unknown time: ABPC Elstree Studios, Studio Backlot Town [Ext: Soho type restaurant]

2nd: Unknown time: ABPC Elstree Studios, Studio Backlot [Ext: Country road and telephone box]

Quarter called am
Cat supplied by Zoo-Rama
Friday 1 December 1967: Day 10: Vernon Sewell
Main: 08.55-17.15: ABPC Elstree Studios, Stage 3 [Int: Jeweller's shop/Steed's apartment]
Thorson's double Cyd Child called at 10.00am to model some of Tara's outfits.
Monday 4 December 1967: Day 11: Vernon Sewell
2nd: 09.15 to unknown time: ABPC Elstree Studios, Studio Backlot Town [Ext: Loading treasures National Gallery, Tower of London and Buckingham Palace]
2nd: Unknown time: ABPC Elstree Studios, Stage 3 [Int: Steed's apartment/Steed's car/Intercrime control room]
Tuesday 5 December 1967: Day 12: Vernon Sewell
2nd: 09.30 to unknown time: Crossoaks Lane/Summerswood Lane, Ridge, Herts [Ext: Country roads/field]
Wednesday 6 December 1967: Day 13: Vernon Sewell
2nd: 09.30 to unknown time: ABPC Elstree Studios, Studio Lot [Ext: National Gallery staff entrance/Tower of London service entrance/Buckingham Palace service entrance]

6.02 – 'THE CURIOUS CASE OF THE COUNTLESS CLUES'
Episode 130
Original Transmission Date: Wednesday 5 February 1969

Writer: Philip Levene
Director: Don Sharp
Cast: Patrick Macnee (John Steed), Linda Thorson (Tara King), Anthony Bate (Earle), Kenneth Cope (Gardiner), Tony Selby (Stanley), Peter Jones (Sir Arthur Doyle), Tracy Reed (Janice Flanders), Edward de Souza (Robert Flanders), George A Cooper (Sir William Burgess), Reginald Jessup (Dawson).
Uncredited Cast: Rocky Taylor (Stunt Double for John Steed), Billy Cornelius (Stunt Double for Stanley), Cyd Child (Stunt Double for Tara King), Paddy Ryan (Stunt Double for Earle), Romo Gorrara (Stunt Double for Gardiner).
Crew: Laurie Johnson (Music by), Philip Levene (Story Consultant), Julian Wintle (Consultant to the Series), Gilbert Taylor BSC (Director of Photography), Harry Booth (Post Production Co-ordinator), Manuel del Campo (Editor), Harvey Gould (Miss Thorson's Costumes Designed by), Ron Appleton (Assistant Director), Brian Elvin (Camera Operator), Len Townsend (Associate Art Director), Kenneth Tait (Set Dresser), June Randall (Continuity), Gordon Bond (Hairdressing), Felix Evans (Wardrobe), Jimmy Harvey BSC (Second Unit Photography), Cecil Mason (Sound Recordist), Len Abbott (Dubbing Mixer), Russ Hill (Sound Editor), Karen Heward (Music Editor), Herbert Worley (Construction Manager), Steve Birtles (Supervisory Electrician).
Uncredited Crew: Ernie Robinson (Camera Operator), Terry Coles (Focus Puller), Peter Carmody (Clapper Loader), Anthony Burns (Second Assistant Director), B Royston (Make-Up), Derek Gibson (Third Assistant Director), Richard Bird (Sound Mixer), K Nightingale (Boom Operator), Ken Softley (Assistant Director), Isobel Byers (Continuity), Peter Plumstead (Production Runner), Leslie Hammond (Sound Mixer), A Carpenter (Third Assistant Director), Peggy Spirito (Continuity).

Production Schedule:

Monday 4 December 1967: Day 1: Don Sharp

Main: 09.20 to unknown time: Grounds of the Edgewarebury Hotel, Edgewarebury Lane, Elstree, Herts [Ext: Side road and trees]

Main: 09.20 to unknown time: The Norwegian Barn, Edgewarebury Lane, Elstree, Herts [Ext: Scott's cottage]

Tuesday 5 December 1967: Day 2: Don Sharp

Main: 08.30 to unknown time: The Norwegian Barn, Edgewarebury Lane, Elstree, Herts [Ext: Scott's cottage]

Main: Unknown time to 16.00: Grounds of the Edgewarebury Hotel, Edgewarebury Lane, Elstree, Herts [Ext: Country roads]

Wednesday 6 December 1967: Day 3: Don Sharp

Main: 09.05 to unknown time: Grounds of the Edgewarebury Hotel, Edgewarebury Lane, Elstree, Herts [Ext: Country road]

Main: Unknown time to 16.15: Edgewarebury Gatehouse, Edgewarebury Lane, Elstree, Herts [Ext: Earle's cottage]

Thursday 7 December 1967: Day 4: Don Sharp

Main: 09.30-20.17: ABPC Elstree Studios, Stage 9 [Int: Billiards room/Dawson's apartment]

Friday 8 December 1967: Day 5: Don Sharp/John Hough

Main: 11.00-17.15: ABPC Elstree Studios, Stage 9 [Int: Dawson's apartment/Flanders Finance Corporation]

2nd: 11.00-17.15: ABPC Elstree Studios, Stage 9 [Int: Dawson's apartment/Flanders Finance Corporation]

Tuesday 12 December 1967: Day 6: Don Sharp

Main: 08.40-17.00: ABPC Elstree Studios, Stage 3 [Int: Flanders' study]

Wednesday 13 December 1967: Day 7: Don Sharp/John Hough

Main: 09.15 to unknown time: ABPC Elstree Studios, Studio Lot [Int/Ext: Underground car park]

Main: Unknown time to 17.10: ABPC Elstree Studios, Stage 3 [Int: Flanders' study and hallway/Land Rover breakdown truck/Citroen Safari/Car by bushes/telephone box/garage]

2nd: 09.15 to unknown time: ABPC Elstree Studios, Studio Lot [Int/Ext: Underground car park]

2nd: Unknown time to 17.10: ABPC Elstree Studios, Stage 3 [Int: Flanders' study and hallway/Land Rover breakdown truck/Citroen Safari/Car by bushes/telephone box/garage]

Second unit spent the day working alongside main unit

Thursday 14 December 1967: Day 8: Don Sharp

2nd: 09.00 to unknown time: Edgewarebury Gatehouse, Edgewarebury Lane, Elstree, Herts [Ext: Earle's cottage]

2nd: 00-00-15.00: Grounds of the Edgewarebury Hotel, Edgewarebury Lane, Elstree, Herts [Ext: Citroen Safari]

Friday 15 December 1967: Day 9: Don Sharp

2nd: 09.55-14.30: Chalcot Crescent, London, NW1 [Ext: Tara's apartment]

Monday 18 December 1967: Day 10: Don Sharp

2nd: 10.00-16.45: Woolmers Park, Lower Hatfield Road, Letty Green, Herts [Ext: Flanders' home/country lane/country road and telephone box]

Tuesday 19 December 1967: Day 11: Don Sharp
2nd: 10.50-15.00: Deeves Hall Lane, Ridge, Herts [Ext: Flanders' Bentley/Road B]
Wednesday 20 December 1967: Day 12: Don Sharp/John Hough
Main: 09.45-17.00: ABPC Elstree Studios, Stage 3 [Int: Tara's apartment]
2nd: 10.30-15.40: Well Road, Judges Hill and The Ridgeway, Northaw, Herts [Ext: Country roads]
Thursday 21 December 1967: Day 13: Don Sharp/John Hough
Main: 08.45-05.12: ABPC Elstree Studios, Stage 3 [Int: Tara's apartment]
2nd: 09.50-14.45: Northaw, Herts [Ext: Country roads]
2nd: 15.15-17.10: ABPC Elstree Studios, Stage 9 [Int: New material and inserts for Scenes 37 and 114]
Friday 22 December 1967: Day 14: Don Sharp
Main: 08.50-17.00: ABPC Elstree Studios, Stage 3 [Int: Tara's apartment]
Wednesday 27 December 1967: Day 15: Don Sharp
Main: 09.08-15.05: ABPC Elstree Studios, Stage 3 [Int: Tara's apartment – inserts for Scenes 138, 139, 140, 141, 142, 143, 144, 146, 147, 148 and 150]
Thursday 28 December 1967: Day 16: Don Sharp
Main: 09.25 to unknown time: The Norwegian Barn, Edgewarebury Lane, Elstree, Herts [Ext: Scott's Cottage]
Main: Unknown time to 13.20: Edgewarebury Gatehouse, Edgewarebury Lane, Elstree, Herts [Ext: Earle's Cottage]
Main: 13.50-17.10: ABPC Elstree Studios, Stage 3 [Int: Tara's apartment]
Friday 29 December 1967: Day 17: Don Sharp
Main: 09.25 to unknown time: Woolmer's Park, Lower Hatfield Road, Letty Green, Herts [Flanders' home and grounds/Int: Flanders' stables]
Main: Unknown time to 07.10: ABPC Elstree Studios, Stage 3 [Int: Tara's apartment]
Monday 1 January 1968: Day 18: Don Sharp
Main 09.05-17.19: ABPC Elstree Studios, Stage 3 [Int: Tara's apartment/telephone box]
Wednesday 3 January 1968: Day 19: Don Sharp
Main: 09.45-14.50: Woolmer's Park, Lower Hatfield Road, Letty Green, Herts [Flanders' home]
Friday 5 January 1968: Day 20: Don Sharp
No filming today due to bad weather conditions. Planned schedule was:
2nd: Unknown time: The Norwegian Barn, Edgewarebury Lane, Elstree, Herts [Ext: Scott's cottage]
2nd: Unknown time: Edgewarebury Gatehouse, Edgewarebury Lane, Elstree, Herts [Ext: Earle's cottage]
2nd: Unknown time to 14.15: Wood Lane, Little Common, Stanmore, Middlesex [Country road D/road]

MAKE UP, HAIR AND WARDROBE TESTS
Uncredited Crew: Peter Carmody (Clapper Loader).
Tuesday 12 December 1967: Day 1: John Hough
2nd: Unknown time: ABPC Elstree Studios, Stage 9 [Int: Linda Thorson]

6.03 – 'THE FORGET-ME-KNOT'
Episode 131
Original Transmission Date: Wednesday 25 September 1968

Writer: Brian Clemens
Director: James Hill
Cast: Patrick Macnee (John Steed), Diana Rigg (Emma Peel), Linda Thorson (Tara King), Patrick Kavanagh (Sean Mortimer), Patrick Newell (Mother), Jeremy Burnham (Simon Filson), Jeremy Young (George Burton), Alan Lake (Karl), Douglas Sheldon (Brad), John Lee (Dr Soames), Beth Owen (Sally), Leon Lissek (Taxi Driver), Tony Thawnton (Jenkins), Edward Higgins (The Gardener).
Uncredited Cast: Patrick Macnee (Peter Peel), Paul Weston (Peter Peel in Car) Gerry Crampton (Stunt Double for Brad), Rocky Taylor (Stunt Double for John Steed), Joe Dunne (Stunt Double for Karl), Cyd Child (Stunt Double for Emma Peel), Fred Haggerty (Stunt Double for Brad), Fred Haggerty (Stunt Double for Sean Mortimer), Joe Dunne (Stunt Double for George Burton), Cyd Child (Stunt Double for Tara King), Ken Hall (Stunt Double for Karl).
Crew: Laurie Johnson (Music by), Philip Levene (Story Consultant), Julian Wintle (Consultant to the Series), Gilbert Taylor BSC (Director of Photography), Harry Booth (Post Production Co-ordinator), Manuel del Campo (Editor), Alun Hughes (Miss Rigg's Costumes Designed by), Harvey Gould (Miss Thorson's Costumes Designed by), Ron Appleton (Assistant Director), Brian Elvin (Camera Operator), Len Townsend (Associate Art Director), Kenneth Tait (Set Dresser), June Randall (Continuity), Gordon Bond (Hairdressing), Felix Evans (Wardrobe), Jimmy Harvey BSC (Second Unit Photography), Cecil Mason (Sound Recordist), Len Shilton (Dubbing Mixer), Peter Lennard (Sound Editor), Karen Heward (Music Editor), Herbert Worley (Construction Manager), Steve Birtles (Supervisory Electrician).
Uncredited Crew: Stan Haines (Boom Operator), Peter Plumstead (Unit Runner), Anthony Burns (Second Assistant Director), Ernie Robinson (Camera Operator), B Royston (Make-Up), Derek Gibson (Third Assistant Director), Peter Carmody (Clapper Loader), A Carpenter (Third Assistant Director), Don Wortham (Boom Operator), Isobel Byers (Continuity), Richard Bird (Sound Mixer), Peggy Spirito (Continuity), Mike Roberts (Focus Puller), Colin Jameson (Assistant Hairdresser), Cecil Mason (Sound Mixer) Margaret Nichols (Production Secretary), Mary Gibson (Wardrobe), Claude Gresset (Third Assistant Director), Ken Softley (Assistant Director).

Production Schedule:
Thursday 14 December 1967: Day 1: James Hill
Main: 09.35-17.20: ABPC Elstree Studios, Stage 3 [Int: Steed's apartment]
Friday 15 December 1967: Day 2: James Hill
Main: 09.12-17.12: ABPC Elstree Studios, Stage 3 [Int: Steed's apartment/Ext: Steed's car]
Monday 18 December 1967: Day 3: James Hill
Main: 09.20-17.08: ABPC Elstree Studios, Stage 9 [Int: Glass factory]/Studio Lot [Ext: Steed's apartment]
Tuesday 19 December 1967: Day 4: James Hill
Main: 09.03-17.05: ABPC Elstree Studios, Stage 9 [Int: Glass factory/Steed's stairs/Ext: Steed's front door]
Thursday 21 December 1967: Day 5: John Hough
2nd: 15.15-17.10: ABPC Elstree Studios, Stage 9 [Int: Insert for Scene 38]
Friday 22 December 1967: Day 6: James Hill
2nd: 10.15-17.20: ABPC Elstree Studios, Stage 9 [Int: Glass factory/hospital]

Wednesday 27 December 1967: Day 7: James Hill
2nd: 09.00-12.45: ABPC Elstree Studios, Stage 9 [Int: Hospital]/Studio Lot [Ext: Hospital]
Thursday 28 December 1967: Day 8: James Hill
2nd: 09.36 to unknown time: Duchess Mews, London, W1 [Ext: Steed's mews]
2nd: Unknown time to 13.20: Weymouth Mews, London, W1 [Ext: Cab rank/Int: Cab}
Friday 29 December 1967: Day 9: James Hill/John Hough
2nd: 10.00 to unknown time: Chalcot Crescent, London, NW1 [Ext: Tara's apartment]
2nd: Unknown time to 15.25: Wood Lane, Little Common, Stanmore, Middlesex [Ext: Country road B]
Monday 1 January 1968: Day 10: James Hill
No filming due to bad weather conditions. Planned schedule was:
2nd: Unknown time to 14.30: Duchess Mews, London, W1 [Ext: Steed's mews]
Tuesday 2 January 1968: Day 11: James Hill
Main: 10.26-17.20: ABPC Elstree Studios, Stage 3 [Int: Mother's room]
Wednesday 3 January 1968: Day 12: James Hill
Main: 09.25-17.15: ABPC Elstree Studios, Stage 3 [Int: Waiting area/hallway/Mother's room]
Thursday 4 January 1968: Day 13: James Hill/John Hough
Main: 08.35-17.06: ABPC Elstree Studios, Stage 3 [Int: Waiting area/hallway/Tara's apartment]
2nd: 09.05-13.35: Duchess Mews, London, W1 [Ext: Steed's mews]
2nd: Unknown time: ABPC Elstree Studios, Stage 9 [Inserts for Scene 32]
Friday 5 January 1968: Day 14: James Hill
Main: 08.56-14.50: ABPC Elstree Studios, Stage 3 [Int: Tara's apartment/Ext: Shrubbery set/Steed's car]
Monday 8 January 1968: Day 15: James Hill
Main: 09.35-16.10: Hemel Hempstead Gas Holder, London Road, Hemel Hempstead, Herts [Ext: Glass factory]
Tuesday 9 January 1968: Day 16: James Hill
Main: 14.30-16.35: ABPC Elstree Studios, Stage 3 [Ext: Shrubbery set]
Wednesday 10 January 1968: Day 17: James Hill
Main: 09.45-16.50: ABPC Elstree Studios, Stage 3 [Int: Steed's apartment/Ext: Shrubbery set/Tara's car/Burton's car]
Tuesday 16 January 1968: Day 18: John Hough
2nd: 10.55-15.00: Burnham Beeches, Burnham, Bucks [Ext: Wooded country road/country roads A and B]
Wednesday 17 January 1968: Day 19: James Hill
2nd: 09.15 to unknown time: Hemel Hempstead Gas Holder, London Road, Hemel Hempstead, Herts [Ext: Glass factory]
2nd: Unknown time to 15.45: Wood Lane, Little Common, Stanmore, Middlesex [Ext: Country roads]
Thursday 18 January 1968: Day 20: James Hill
2nd: 10.00-17.00: ABPC Elstree Studios, Stage 3 [Ext: Mother's gates, grounds and house]
Friday 19 January 1968: Day 21: John Hough
2nd: Unknown time to 11.41: Burnham Beeches, Burnham, Bucks [Ext: Vehicle footage]

6.04 – 'SPLIT!'
Episode 132
Original Transmission Date: Wednesday 23 October 1968

Writer: Brian Clemens
Director: Roy Baker
Cast: Patrick Macnee (John Steed), Linda Thorson (Tara King), Nigel Davenport (Lord Barnes) Julian Glover (Major Peter Rooke), Bernard Archard (Dr Constantine), John G Heller (Hinnell), Jayne Sofiano (Petra), Steven Scott (Boris Kartovski), Maurice Good (Harry Mercer), Iain Anders (Frank Compton), Christopher Benjamin (Swindin), John Kidd (Miller the Butler).
Uncredited Cast: Terry Maidment (Morrell), Harry Fielder (Guard), Rocky Taylor (Stunt Double for John Steed), Terry Plummer (Stunt Double for Hinnell), Fred Haggerty (Stunt Double for Dr Constantine), Leslie Crawford (Stunt Double for Hinnell), Cyd Child (Stunt Double for Tara King), Leslie Soden (Pianist Double for Lord Barnes), Cliff Diggins (Stunt Double for John Steed), Bob Anderson (Stunt Double for Lord Barnes).
Crew: Laurie Johnson (Music by), Philip Levene (Story Consultant), Julian Wintle (Consultant to the Series), Gilbert Taylor BSC (Director of Photography), Harry Booth (Post Production Co-ordinator), Manuel del Campo (Editor), Alun Hughes (Miss Thorson's Costumes Designed by), Harvey Gould (Miss Thorson's Costumes Designed by), Ron Appleton (Assistant Director), Brian Elvin (Camera Operator), Len Townsend (Associate Art Director), Kenneth Tait (Set Dresser), June Randall (Continuity), Gordon Bond (Hairdressing), Felix Evans (Wardrobe), Jimmy Harvey BSC (Second Unit Photography), Cecil Mason (Sound Recordist), Len Shilton (Dubbing Mixer), Peter Lennard (Sound Editor), Karen Heward (Music Editor), Herbert Worley (Construction Manager), Steve Birtles (Supervisory Electrician).
Uncredited Crew: Don Wortham (Boom Operator), Ernie Robinson (Camera Operator), Claude Gresset (Third Assistant Director), Mary Gibson (Wardrobe), A Carpenter (Assistant Director), Peter Carmody (Clapper Loader), Isabel Byers (Continuity), Doreen Soan (Continuity), Ken Rawkins (Sound Mixer), Harry Raynham (Sound Camera), Ann Brodie (Make-Up), Fred Tomlin (Boom Operator), Peggy Spirito (Continuity), Keith Batten (Boom Operator), K Lund (Third Assistant Director).

Production Schedule:
Friday 12 January 1968: Day 1: Roy Baker
Main: 11.00-17.15: ABPC Elstree Studios, Stage 9 [Int: Corridor/executive rest room]
Monday 15 January 1968: Day 2: Roy Baker
Main: 09.20-17.18: ABPC Elstree Studios, Stage 9 [Int: Executive rest room]
Tuesday 16 January 1968: Day 3: Roy Baker
Main: 10.45-17.15: ABPC Elstree Studios, Stage 9 [Int: Executive rest room]
Wednesday 17 January 1968: Day 4: Roy Baker:
Main: 09.35-17.19: ABPC Elstree Studios, Stage 9 [Int: Executive rest room/corridor/lift]
Thursday 18 January 1968: Day 5: Roy Baker
Main: 09.30-17.10: ABPC Elstree Studios, Stage 9 [Int: Operating theatre]
Friday 19 January 1968: Day 6: Roy Baker
Main: 09.35-17.15: ABPC Elstree Studios, Stage 9 [Int: Operating theatre/hospital reception]

Quarter called am
Monday 22 January 1968: Day 7: Roy Baker
Main: 09.20 to unknown time: Aldenham Estate, Elstree, Herts [Ext: Helicopter landing]
Main: Unknown time: Hillfield Lane, Pegram Lane, Sandy Lane, Primrose Lane and Summerhouse Lane, Patchetts Green, Herts [Ext: Country roads]
Main: Unknown time: Grange Road, Letchmore Heath, Herts [Ext: Country road]
Main: Unknown time to 15.40: Radlett Road, Aldenham, Herts [Ext: Country road]
Tuesday 23 January 1968: Day 8: Roy Baker
Main: 09.10-17.18: ABPC Elstree Studios, Stage 9 [Int: Operating theatre]
Wednesday 24 January 1968: Day 9: Roy Baker/John Hough
Main: 09.30-10.50: Camfield Place, Wildhill Road, Wildhill, Hatfield, Herts [Ext: Lord Barnes' home]
Main: 11.20-17.20: ABPC Elstree Studios, Stage 9 [Int: Operating theatre/hospital reception]
2nd: 09.30 to unknown time: Brocket Hall, Marford Road, Lemsford, Welwyn Garden City, Herts [Ext: Ministry of Top Secret Intelligence]
2nd: Unknown time to 15.10: ABPC Elstree Studios, Studio Lot [Ext: Ministry of Top Secret Intelligence]
Thursday 25 January 1968: Day 10: Roy Baker
Main: 09.45 to unknown time: ABPC Elstree Studios, Stage 3 [Int: Barnes' car/Steed's car/Tara's car]
Main: Unknown time: ABPC Elstree Studios, Stage 9 [Int: Swindin's office]
Main: Unknown time to 17.05: ABPC Elstree Studios, Stage 3 [Int: Barnes' study]
Friday 26 January 1968: Day 11: Roy Baker
Main: 08.50-17.05: ABPC Elstree Studios, Stage 3 [Int: Barnes' study]
Monday 29 January 1968: Day 12: Roy Baker
2nd: 09.20-17.10: ABPC Elstree Studios, Stage 3 [Int: Barnes' study/Steed's apartment]
Tuesday 30 January 1968: Day 13: Roy Baker
2nd: 09.30-16.55: ABPC Elstree Studios, Stage 3 [Int: Steed's apartment/Steed's car]
Wednesday 31 January 1968: Day 14: Roy Baker
2nd: 09.37-12.10: Brocket Hall, Marford Road, Lemsford, Welwyn Garden City, Herts [Ext: Ministry of Top Secret Intelligence]
2nd: 12.40-15.37: Haberdashers' Aske's School, Aldenham Road, Elstree, Herts [Ext: Hospital]
Thursday 1 February 1968: Day 15: Roy Baker/John Hough
2nd: 08.55-09.00: ABPC Elstree Studios, Stage 3 [Int: Steed's apartment]
2nd: 09.30 15.05: Patchetts Green, Herts [Ext: Country roads]
Tuesday 6 February 1968: Day 16: Harry Booth
2nd: Unknown time: Haberdashers' Aske's School, Aldenham Road, Elstree, Herts [Ext: Hospital]
Monday 12 February 1968: Day 17: John Hough
2nd: Unknown time: ABPC Elstree Studios, Stage 3 [Int: Insert]

OPENING TITLES: FIRST VERSION
Cast: Patrick Macnee (John Steed), Linda Thorson (Tara King).
Uncredited Crew: Ken Softley (Assistant Director), A Carpenter (Second Assistant Director), D Pollard (Hairdresser), Ernie Robinson (Camera Operator), Peggy Spirito (Continuity).

Production Schedule:
Friday 12 January 1968: Day 1: Harry Booth
2nd: 15.05-17.15: ABPC Elstree Studios, Stage 4 [Int: Limbo Set]
Monday 15 January 1968: Day 2: Harry Booth
2nd: 09.45-19.30: ABPC Elstree Studios, Stage 4 [Int: Limbo Set]
Stylised artwork of Tara's lips still to be shot

6.05 – 'GET-A-WAY!'
Episode 133
Original Transmission Date: Wednesday 14 May 1969

Writer: Philip Levene
Director: Don Sharp
Cast: Patrick Macnee (John Steed), Linda Thorson (Tara King), Andrew Keir (Colonel James), Peter Bowles (Ezdorf), Peter Bayliss (Professor Dodge), Neil Hallett (Paul Ryder), Terence Longdon (George Neville), William Wilde (Major Baxter), Michael Culver (Price), Michael Elwyn (Lieutenant Edwards), Barry Lineham (Magnus), John Hussey (Peters), Robert Russell (Lubin), Vincent Harding (Rostov), James Belchamber (Bryant).
Uncredited Cast: Arthur Howe (Double for Lubin), Cyd Child (Double for Tara King), Dinny Powell (Double for Lubin), Rocky Taylor (Double for John Steed), Terry Plummer (Double for Magnus), Rocky Taylor (Double for George Neville).
Crew: Laurie Johnson (Music by), Philip Levene (Story Consultant), Julian Wintle (Consultant to the Series), Gilbert Taylor BSC (Director of Photography), Harry Booth (Post Production Co-ordinator), Manuel del Campo (Editor), Alun Hughes (Miss Thorson's Costumes Designed by), Ron Appleton (Assistant Director), Brian Elvin (Camera Operator), Len Townsend (Associate Art Director), Kenneth Tait (Set Dresser), June Randall (Continuity), Gordon Bond (Hairdressing), Felix Evans (Wardrobe), Jimmy Harvey BSC (Second Unit Photography), Cecil Mason (Sound Recordist), Len Shilton (Dubbing Mixer), Russ Hill (Sound Editor), Karen Heward (Music Editor), Herbert Worley (Construction Manager), Steve Birtles (Supervisory Electrician).
Uncredited Crew: Mike Frift (Focus Puller), Ernie Robinson (Camera Operator), A Strachan (Clapper Loader), Doreen Soan (Continuity), Claude Gresset (Third Assistant Director), A Carpenter (Second Assistant Director), Ann Brodie (Make-Up), Peter Carmody (Clapper Loader), A Box (Hairdresser), B Phillips (Make-Up), K Lund (Third Assistant Director), Godfrey Godar (Camera Operator).

Production Schedule:
Friday 26 January 1968: Day 1: Don Sharp
2nd: 09.40 to unknown time: Ashridge College, Ringshall Drive, Berkhamstead, Herts [Monastery]
2nd: Unknown time to 16.05: National Cash Registers Print Division, Warwick Road, Borehamwood, Herts [Magnus Importing Company Ltd]
Monday 29 January 1968: Day 2: Don Sharp
Main: 09.20-17.15: ABPC Elstree Studios, Stage 4 [Int: Passageways/cells]
Tuesday 30 January 1968: Day 3: Don Sharp
Main: 08.50-17.17: ABPC Elstree Studios, Stage 4 [Int: Passageways/Ezdorf's cell]
Wednesday 31 January 1968: Day 4: Don Sharp

Main: 08.40-17.15: ABPC Elstree Studios, Stage 4 [Int: Ezdorf's cell / cell / passageway / Ryder's apartment]
Thursday 1 February 1968: Day 5: Don Sharp
Main: 08.35-17.15: ABPC Elstree Studios, Stage 4 [Int: Ryder's apartment / corridor / passageway]
Friday 2 February 1968: Day 6: Don Sharp/John Hough
Main: 08.50-17.00: ABPC Elstree Studios, Stage 4 [Int: Ezdorf's cell/passageway]
2nd: 09.35 to unknown time: Belsize Crescent, Princess Mews and Burdett Mews, London, NW3 [Bryant's office]
2nd: Unknown time: Belsize Park Gardens, London, NW3 [Road]
2nd: Unknown time: Boydell Court, London, NW8 [Melrose Court]
2nd: Unknown time to 15.35: National Cash Registers Print Division, Warwick Road, Borehamwood, Herts [Magnus Importing Company Ltd]
Belsize Park Gardens and Boydell Court do not appear in the episode
Monday 5 February 1968: Day 7: Don Sharp
Main: 08.55-17.17: ABPC Elstree Studios, Stage 4 [Int: Ezdorf's cell]
Tuesday 6 February 1968: Day 8: Don Sharp
Main: 09.00-17.15: ABPC Elstree Studios, Stage 4 [Int: Ezdorf's cell/Rostov's cell/James' office]
Wednesday 7 February 1968: Day 9: Don Sharp
Main: 08.50-17.35: ABPC Elstree Studios, Stage 4 [Int: James' office/corridor/Dodge's testing room]
Quarter called pm
Thursday 8 February 1968: Day 10: Don Sharp
Main: 09.25 to unknown time: ABPC Elstree Studios, Stage 4 [Int: Peter's office]
Main: Unknown time to 17.15: ABPC Elstree Studios, Stage 3 [Int: Bryant's office]
Friday 9 February 1968: Day 11: Don Sharp
Main: 09.15-17.08: ABPC Elstree Studios, Stage 3 [Int: Bryant's office/Magnus warehouse]
Monday 12 February 1968: Day 12: Don Sharp
Main: 09.45-17.17: ABPC Elstree Studios, Stage 3 [Int: Steed's apartment]
Tuesday 13 February 1968: Day 13: Don Sharp
Main: 09.25-16.40: ABPC Elstree Studios, Stage 3 [Int: Steed's apartment]
Wednesday 14 February 1968: Day 14: Don Sharp
Main: 09.00-16.50: ABPC Elstree Studios, Stage 3 [Int: Steed's apartment and passageway]
Thursday 15 February 1968: Day 15: Don Sharp
Main: 09.30 to unknown time: Duchess Mews, London, W1 [Ext: Steed's mews]
Main: Unknown time to 19.35: ABPC Elstree Studios, Stage 3 [Int: Steed's apartment/Tara's apartment]
Tuesday 27 February 1968: Day 16: Don Sharp
2nd: 09.22 to unknown time: Duchess Mews, London, W1 [Ext: Steed's mews]
2nd: Unknown time to 17.15: ABPC Elstree Studios, Stage 3 [Int: Passageway, Melrose Court/Ezdorf's cell]
Melrose Court passageway set does not feature in the episode
Thursday 29 February 1968: Day 17: John Hough
2nd: Unknown time: ABPC Elstree Studios, Stage 3 [Int: Steed's apartment]

6.06 – 'HAVE GUNS – WILL HAGGLE'
Episode 134
Original Transmission Date: Wednesday 11 December 1968

Writer: Donald James
Director: Ray Austin
Cast: Patrick Macnee (John Steed), Linda Thorson (Tara King), Nicola Pagett (Adriana), Johnny Sekka (Colonel Nsonga), Roy Stewart (Giles), Jonathan Burn (Conrad), Timothy Bateson (Spencer), Michael Turner (Crayford), Robert Gillespie (Lift Attendant), Peter J Elliott (Brad).
Uncredited Cast: Joe Dunne (Smith), Rocky Taylor (Mercenary), Terry Plummer (Mercenary), Terry Richards (Mercenary), Leslie Crawford (Mercenary), Frank Maher (Mercenary), Gerry Crampton (Mercenary), Maxwell Craig (Guard), Stephen Hubay (Bidder), Hugh Elton (Guard), Rocky Taylor (Stunt Double for John Steed), Roy Vincente (Stunt Double for Crayford), Cyd Child (Stunt Double for Tara King), Peter J Elliott (Stunt Double for Conrad), Peter J Elliott (Stunt Double for Tara King), Joe Dunne (Stunt Double for Brad).
Crew: Laurie Johnson (Music by), Philip Levene (Story Consultant), Julian Wintle (Consultant to the Series), Jimmy Harvey BSC (Director of Photography), Harry Booth (Post Production Co-ordinator), Manuel del Campo (Editor), Harvey Gould (Miss Thorson's Costumes Designed by), John O'Conner (Assistant Director), Brian Elvin (Camera Operator), Len Townsend (Associate Art Director), Kenneth Tait (Set Dresser), Doreen Soan (Continuity), Gordon Bond (Hairdressing), Felix Evans (Wardrobe), Cecil Mason (Sound Recordist), Len Shilton (Dubbing Mixer), Peter Lennard (Sound Editor), Karen Heward (Music Editor), Herbert Worley (Construction Manager), Steve Birtles (Supervisory Electrician).
Uncredited Crew: Peggy Spirito (Continuity/Post Production), A Carpenter (Second Assistant Director), Keith Batten (Boom Operator), Ann Brodie (Make-Up), K Lund (Third Assistant Director), D Hyde (Wardrobe), Dudley Lovell (Camera Operator), B Phillips (Make-Up), Peter Carmody (Clapper Loader), A Box (Hairdresser), Malcolm Stamp (Second Assistant Director), J Wadeson (Assistant Hairdresser), Graham Freeborn (Make-Up), Terry Coles (Focus Puller), Godfrey Godar (Camera Operator), Bert Pearl (Assistant Director), B Clarke (Make-Up), Geoff Seaholme (Lighting Cameraman).

Production Schedule:
Tuesday 6 February 1968: Day 1: Harry Booth
2nd: 09.10 to unknown time: Haberdashers' Aske's School, Aldenham Road, Elstree, Herts [Ballistics establishment]
2nd: Unknown time: Aldenham Road/Dagger Lane, Elstree, Herts [Car chase]
2nd: Unknown time to 16.50: ABPC Elstree Studios, Stage 3 [Int: Tara's apartment/lift/telephone booth]
Wednesday 7 February 1968: Day 2: Harry Booth
2nd: 11.20-16.30: ABPC Elstree Studios, Stage 3 [Int: Ballistics establishment]
Thursday 8 February 1968: Day 3: Harry Booth
2nd: 09.35-16.45: ABPC Elstree Studios, Stage 3 [Int: Tara' apartment]
2nd: Unknown time: ABPC Elstree Studios, Studio Lot [Ext Hotel entrance/ordnance depot perimeter fence]

Wednesday 14 February 1968: Day 4: Ray Austin
2nd: 09.35-17.17: ABPC Elstree Studios, Stage 4 [Int: Crayford's office/warehouse]
Thursday 15 February 1968: Day 5: Ray Austin
2nd: 09.00-15.05: ABPC Elstree Studios, Stage 4 [Int: Ballistics establishment/Ext: warehouse]
Friday 16 February 1968: Day 6: Ray Austin
2nd: 08.56 to unknown time: ABPC Elstree Studios, Stage 4 [Int: Ballistics establishment]
2nd: Unknown time to 16.40: ABPC Elstree Studios, Studio Lot [Ext: Ordnance depot gateway/warehouse/ordnance depot]
Monday 19 February 1968: Day 7: Ray Austin
2nd: 10.10-16.52: Starveacres, Watford Road, Radlett, Herts [Ext: Stokely House/driveway ornamental garden]
Tuesday 20 February 1968: Day 8: Ray Austin
2nd: 09.27-17.15: ABPC Elstree Studios, Stage 3 [Ext: Woodland and grounds of Stokely House]
Wednesday 21 February 1968: Day 9: Ray Austin
2nd: 09.02-17.12: ABPC Elstree Studios, Stage 3 [Ext: Woodland and hut/Int: Hut]
Thursday 22 February 1968: Day 10: Ray Austin
2nd: 09.10-17.08: ABPC Elstree Studios, Stage 3 [Ext: Terrace of Stokely House/Int: Hut/corridor and Nsonga's room/drawing room]
Friday 23 February 1968: Day 11: Ray Austin
2nd: 09.23-17.06: ABPC Elstree Studios, Stage 3 [Int: Land Rover/section of terrace/Steed's apartment/Tara's apartment]
Monday 26 February 1968: Day 12: Ray Austin
2nd: 09.00 to unknown time: ABPC Elstree Studios, Stage 3 [Int: Tara's apartment/Ext: Terrace of Stokely House]
2nd: Unknown time to 16.45: ABPC Elstree Studios, Studio Lot [Ext: Ordnance depot perimeter fence]
Wednesday 28 February 1968: Day 13: Ray Austin
2nd: 09.55 to unknown time: Chalcot Crescent, London, NW1 [Ext: Tara's apartment]
2nd: Unknown time to 16.45: ABPC Elstree Studios, Studio Lot [Ext: Ordnance depot perimeter fence]
Thursday 29 February 1968: Day 14: Ray Austin
2nd: Unknown time: ABPC Elstree Studios, Stage 3 [Int: Steed's Bentley/Steed's apartment]
Friday 15 March 1968: Day 15: John Hough
2nd: Unknown time: ABPC Elstree Studios, Stage 3 [Int: Hut – inserts/Ext: Woodland – inserts]

6.07 – 'LOOK – (STOP ME IF YOU'VE HEARD THIS ONE) BUT THERE WERE THESE TWO FELLERS …'
Episode 135
Original Transmission Date: Wednesday 4 December 1968

Writer: Dennis Spooner
Director: James Hill
Cast: Patrick Macnee (John Steed), Linda Thorson (Tara King), Jimmy Jewel (Merrie Maxie Martin), Julian Chagrin (Jennings), Bernard Cribbins (Bradley Marler), John

Cleese (Marcus Rugman), William Kendall (Lord Dessington), John Woodwine (Seagrave), Garry Marsh (Brigadier Wiltshire), Gaby Vargas (Miss Charles), Bill Shine (Cleghorn), Richard Young (Sir Jeremy Broadfoot), Robert James (Merlin the Magnificent), Talfryn Thomas (Fiery Frederick), Jay Denyer (Tenor), Johnny Vyvyan (Escapologist), Len Belmont (Ventriloquist).

Uncredited Cast: John Styles (Punch and Judy Man) June and Paul Kidd (Herbie the Horse), Jeff Silk (Stunt Double for Cleghorn), Dinny Powell (Stunt Double for Dressington), Rocky Taylor (Stunt Double for John Steed), Cyd Child (Stunt Double for Tara King), Max Faulkner (Stunt Double for Merrie Maxie Martin), Frank Maher (Stunt Double for Seagrave).

Crew: Laurie Johnson (Music by), Philip Levene (Story Consultant), Julian Wintle (Consultant to the Series), Gilbert Taylor BSC (Director of Photography), Harry Booth (Post Production Co-ordinator), Manuel del Campo (Editor), Alun Hughes (Miss Thorson's Costumes Designed by), Ron Appleton (Assistant Director), Brian Elvin (Camera Operator), Len Townsend (Associate Art Director), Kenneth Tait (Set Dresser), June Randall (Continuity), Gordon Bond (Hairdressing), Felix Evans (Wardrobe), Jimmy Harvey BSC (Second Unit Photography), Cecil Mason (Sound Recordist), Len Shilton (Dubbing Mixer), Peter Lennard (Sound Editor), Karen Heward (Music Editor), Herbert Worley (Construction Manager), Steve Birtles (Supervisory Electrician).

Uncredited Crew: Malcolm Stamp (Second Assistant Director), Ernie Robinson (Camera Operator), Colin Lord (Assistant Director), Claude Gresset (Third Assistant Director), Penny Spirito (Continuity/Post Production), Denny Lewis (Assistant Director), Terry Coles (Focus Puller), Peter Carmody (Clapper Loader), Doris Martin (Continuity), Godfrey Godar (Camera Operator), A Carpenter (Second Assistant Director/Third Assistant Director), Doreen Soan (Continuity), B Clarke (Make-Up), R Macdonald (Clapper Loader), Gladys Goldsmith (Continuity), Peter Pardo (Boom Operator).

Production Schedule:
Tuesday 20 February 1968: Day 1: James Hill
Main: 10.00-15.45: Wembley Point, Harrow Road, Wembley, Middlesex [Ext: The Caritol Land and Development Corporation]
Wednesday 21 February 1968: Day 2: James Hill
Main: 09.40-11.45: Wembley Point, Harrow Road, Wembley, Middlesex [Ext: The Caritol Land and Development Corporation]
Thursday 22 February 1968: Day 3: James Hill
Main: 09.25 to unknown time: ABPC Elstree Studios, Stage 9 [Int: Bradley Marler's office]
Main: 14.40-16.40: Wembley Point, Harrow Road, Wembley, Middlesex [Ext: The Caritol Land and Development Corporation]
Friday 23 February 1968: Day 4: James Hill
Main: 09.50-16.10: Tykes Water Lake, Aldenham Estate, Elstree, Herts [Ext: Cleghorn hunting scene]
Monday 26 February 1968: Day 5: James Hill
Main: 09.55-17.25: ABPC Elstree Studios, Stage 7 [Int: Conference room/Sir Jeremy's office]
Tuesday 27 February 1968: Day 6: James Hill
Main: 09.35-17.16: ABPC Elstree Studios, Stage 7 [Int: Dressington's office/conference

APPENDIX ONE

room]
<u>Wednesday 28 February 1968</u>: Day 7: James Hill
Main: 08.45-16.55: ABPC Elstree Studios, Stage 7 [Int: Ante-room/hallway/conference room]
<u>Thursday 29 February 1968</u>: Day 8: James Hill
Main: 09.05 to unknown time: ABPC Elstree Studios, Stage 7 [Int: Conference room]
Main: Unknown time to 17.00: ABPC Elstree Studios, Stage 9 [Int: Bradley Marler's office]
<u>Friday 1 March 1968</u>: Day 9: James Hill
Main: 09.05 to unknown time: ABPC Elstree Studios, Stage 9 [Int: Bradley Marler's office]
Main: Unknown time to 16.45: ABPC Elstree Studios, Stage 3 [Int: Steed's apartment]
Quarter called am
<u>Monday 4 March 1968</u>: Day 10: James Hill/John Hough
Main: 09.15 to unknown time: ABPC Elstree Studios, Stage 3 [Int: Steed's apartment]
Main: Unknown time to 17.15: ABPC Elstree Studios, Stage 9 [Int: Main room, Vauda Villa]
2nd: 11.45 to unknown time: ABPC Elstree Studios, Stage 3 [Int: Steed's car/Martin's cab/Tara's car]
2nd: Unknown time to 16.50: Silver Hill, Shenley, Herts [Ext: Tara's AC follows Martin's cab]
Quarter called am
<u>Tuesday 5 March 1968</u>: Day 11: James Hill
Main: 09.15-17.07: ABPC Elstree Studios, Stage 9 [Int: Main room, Vauda Villa]
<u>Wednesday 6 March 1968</u>: Day 12: James Hill
Main: 09.00-17.15: ABPC Elstree Studios, Stage 9 [Int: Main room, Vauda Villa]
<u>Thursday 7 March 1968</u>: Day 13: James Hill
Main: 08.55-17.15: ABPC Elstree Studios, Stage 9 [Int: Main room, Vauda Villa]
<u>Friday 8 March 1968</u>: Day 14: James Hill/John Hough
Main: 09.20-13.40: Longmeadow, Woodside Lane, Welham Green, Herts [Ext: Vauda Villa]
2nd: 09.40-14.15: ABPC Elstree Studios, Stage 9 [Int: Main room, Vauda Villa]
Main: 14.30-17.25: ABPC Elstree Studios, Stage 9 [Int: Main room, Vauda Villa]
<u>Monday 11 March 1968</u>: Day 15: James Hill
Main: 09.10-17.15: ABPC Elstree Studios, Stage 9 [Int: Main room, Vauda Villa/back room, Vauda Villa]
<u>Tuesday 12 March 1968</u>: Day 16: James Hill
Main: 09.15-17.16: ABPC Elstree Studios, Stage 9 [Int: Back room, Vauda Villa/registration room]
<u>Wednesday 13 March 1968</u>: Day 17: James Hill
Main: 09.15-17.25: ABPC Elstree Studios, Stage 9 [Int: Registration room/back room, Vauda Villa]
<u>Thursday 14 March 1968</u>: Day 18: James Hill
Main: 09.06 to unknown time: ABPC Elstree Studios, Stage 9 [Int: Back Room, Vauda Villa]
<u>Friday 15 March 1968</u>: Day 19: James Hill
Main: 08.50-16.40: ABPC Elstree Studios, Stage 9 [Int: Main Room, Vauda Villa]
<u>Tuesday 19 March 1968</u>: Day 20: John Hough

648

2nd: 08.55-11.22: ABPC Elstree Studios, Stage 3 [Int: Main Room, Vauda Villa]

6.08 – 'MY WILDEST DREAM'
Episode 136
Original Transmission Date: Monday 7 April 1969

Writer: Philip Levene
Director: Robert Fuest
Cast: Patrick Macnee (John Steed), Linda Thorson (Tara King), Peter Vaughan (Dr A Jaeger), Derek Godfrey (Frank Tobias), Edward Fox (The Hon Teddy Chilcott), Susan Travers (Nurse Janet Owen), Philip Madoc (Slater), Michael David (Dr Reece), Murray Hayne (Paul Gibbons), Tom Kempinski (Dyson), John Savident (Henry Winthrop), Hugh Moxey (Aloysius Peregrine).
Uncredited Cast: Mark McBridge (Stunt Double for Chilcott), Andre Cameron (Stunt Double for Nurse Janet Owen), Cyd Child (Stunt Double for Tara King), Paul Weston (Stunt Double for Dyson), Frank Maher (Stunt Double for Paul Gibbons), Paul Weston (Stunt Double for John Steed), Clifford Diggens (Stunt Double for Frank Tobias).
Crew: Laurie Johnson (Music Supervision by), Howard Blake (Additional Music by), Philip Levene (Story Consultant), Frank Watts (Director of Photography), Harry Booth (Post Production Co-ordinator), Manuel del Campo (Editor), Alun Hughes (Miss Thorson's Costumes Designed by), Ron Appleton (Assistant Director), Brian Elvin (Camera Operator), Len Townsend (Associate Art Director), Kenneth Tait (Set Dresser), June Randall (Continuity), Gordon Bond (Hairdressing), Felix Evans (Wardrobe), Jimmy Harvey BSC (Second Unit Photography), Cecil Mason (Sound Recordist), Len Shilton (Dubbing Mixer), Peter Lennard (Sound Editor), Karen Heward (Music Editor), Herbert Worley (Construction Manager), Steve Birtles (Supervisory Electrician).
Uncredited Crew: Doreen Soan (Continuity), A Carpenter (Third Assistant Director), John O'Conner (Assistant Director), Godfrey Godar (Camera Operator), B Clark (Make-Up), Peter Carmody (Clapper Loader), R Cox (Third Assistant Director), Peggy Spirito (Post Production), Lillian Lee (Continuity), Janice Dorman (Hairdresser), Wilkie Cooper (Lighting Cameraman), P Burke (Focus Puller), Anthony Burns (Second Unit Director), K Brown (Clapper Loader).

Production Schedule:
Monday 11 March 1968: Robert Fuest: Day 1
2nd: 09.44 to unknown time: Mansfield Street/Duchess Street, London W1 [Ext: Jaeger's consulting room/Marlin Street/street 'B']
2nd: Unknown time to 16.46: Weymouth Mews, London, W1 [Int: Steed's Rolls Royce/Dyson's Volvo]
Tuesday 12 March 1968: Robert Fuest: Day 2
2nd: 09.45-00-00: Duchess Mews, London, W1 [Ext: Steed's mews]
2nd: Unknown time to 16.27: Chalcot Crescent, London, NW1 [Ext: Tara's apartment]
Wednesday 13 March 1968: Robert Fuest: Day 3
2nd: 10.08 to unknown time: Clarendon Court, Sidmouth Road, London, NW2 [Penthouse and fire escape]
2nd: Unknown time to 15.40: BSP Industries, Maxwell Road, Borehamwood, Herts [Acme Precision]
Thursday 14 March 1968: Robert Fuest: Day 4

2nd: 10.15-17.30: ABPC Elstree Studios, Stage 7 [Int: Jaeger's consulting room]
Quarter called pm.
Friday 15 March 1968: Robert Fuest: Day 5
2nd: 08.53-17.15: ABPC Elstree Studios, Stage 7 [Int: Jaeger's consulting room]
Monday 18 March 1968: Robert Fuest/John Hough: Day 6
Main: 09.17-17.25: ABPC Elstree Studios, Stage 7 [Int: Jaeger's consulting room]
2nd: 09.00 to unknown time: Duchess Mews, London, W1 [Ext: Steed's mews]
2nd: Unknown time: Mansfield Street, London, W1 [Ext: Marlin Street]
2nd: Unknown time: Park Crescent/Marylebone Road, London, W1 [Ext: Tara follows Dyson's Volvo]
2nd: Unknown time to 17.30: Westbourne Terrace Road, W2 [Ext: Dyson's Volvo]
Quarter called pm
Tuesday 19 March 1968: Robert Fuest/John Hough: Day 7
Main: 08.50-17.15: ABPC Elstree Studios, Stage 7 [Int: Jaeger's consulting room]
2nd: 14.30-16.30: Mansfield Street, London, W1 [Ext: Marlin Street]
Wednesday 20 March 1968: Robert Fuest/John Hough: Day 8
Main: 09.06 to unknown time: ABPC Elstree Studios, Stage 7 [Int: Jaeger's consulting room/Gibbon's office]
Main: Unknown time to 17.30: ABPC Elstree Studios, Stage 3 [Int: Peregrine's penthouse]
2nd: 09.06 to unknown time: ABPC Elstree Studios, Stage 7 [Int: Inserts]
Quarter called am and pm
Thursday 21 March 1968: Robert Fuest: Day 9
Main: 09.15-17.05: ABPC Elstree Studios, Stage 3 [Int: Peregrine's penthouse/Slater's office/Ext: Peregrine's penthouse]
Friday 22 March 1968: Robert Fuest/John Hough: Day 10
Main: 09.00-17.19: ABPC Elstree Studios, Stage 3 [Int: Slater's office]
2nd: Unknown time: The Barn, Nan-Clark's Lane, Highwood Hill, London, NW7 [Ext: Windthrop's house/Int: Steed's Rolls Royce/Dyson's Volvo/Tara's AC]
Monday 25 March 1968: Robert Fuest: Day 11
Main: 09.15-16.55: ABPC Elstree Studios, Stage 3 [Int: Slater's office/dark room]
Quarter called am
Tuesday 26 March 1968: Robert Fuest/John Hough: Day 12
Main: 10.00 to unknown time: ABPC Elstree Studios, Stage 9 [Int: Observation unit]
Main: Unknown time to 17.15: ABPC Elstree Studios, Stage 3 [Int: Steed's apartment]
2nd: 09.20-15.05: The Barn, Nan-Clark's Lane, Highwood Hill, London, NW7 [Ext: Windthrop's house]
Wednesday 27 March 1968: Robert Fuest: Day 13
Main: 09.50-11.20: ABPC Elstree Studios, Stage 9 [Int: Observation unit]
Main: 14-30-17.28: ABPC Elstree Studios, Stage 3 [Int: Steed's apartment]
Quarter called pm
Thursday 28 March 1968: Robert Fuest: Day 14
Main: 08.55-19.35: ABPC Elstree Studios, Stage 3 [Int: Steed's apartment/Tara's apartment]
Friday 29 March 1968: Robert Fuest: Day 15
Main: 08.50-17.15: ABPC Elstree Studios, Stage 3 [Int: Tara's apartment]
Monday 1 April 1968: Robert Fuest: Day 16
Main: 09.00-14.10: ABPC Elstree Studios, Stage 3 [Int: Tara's apartment]

Thursday 18 April 1968: Manuel del Campo: Day 17
2nd: 08.57-11.22: ABPC Elstree Studios, Stage 3 [Int: Jaeger's Consulting room/Tara's apartment/Steed's apartment – inserts for Scenes 103, 137, 140, 142 and 181]

6.09 – 'WHOEVER SHOT POOR GEORGE OBLIQUE STROKE XR40?'
Episode 137
Original Transmission Date: Wednesday 30 October 1968

Writer: Tony Williamson
Director: Cyril Frankel
Cast: Patrick Macnee (John Steed), Linda Thorson (Tara King), Dennis Price (Jason), Clifford Evans (Sir Wilfred Pelley), Judy Parfitt (Loris), Anthony Nicholls (Dr Ardmore), Frank Windsor (Tobin), Adrian Ropes (Baines), Arthur Cox (Anaesthetist), Tony Wright (Keller), John Porter-Davison (Jacobs), Jacky Allouis (Jill), Valerie Leon (Betty).
Uncredited Cast: Joe Dunne (Stunt Double for Jacobs), Paul Weston (Stunt Double for John Steed), Cyd Child (Stunt Double for Tara King), Bill Sawyer (Stunt Double for Jason), Lynn Marshall (Stunt Double for Loris).
Crew: Laurie Johnson (Music by), Howard Blake (Additional Music by), Philip Levene (Story Consultant), Alan Hume BSC (Director of Photography), Harry Booth (Post Production Co-ordinator), Manuel del Campo (Editor), Alun Hughes (Miss Thorson's Costumes Designed by), Ron Appleton (Assistant Director), Brian Elvin (Camera Operator), Len Townsend (Associate Art Director), Kenneth Tait (Set Dresser), June Randall (Continuity), Janice Dorman (Hairdressing), Felix Evans (Wardrobe), Wilkie Cooper BSC (Second Unit Photography), Cecil Mason (Sound Recordist), Len Shilton (Dubbing Mixer), Peter Lennard (Sound Editor), Karen Heward (Music Editor), Herbert Worley (Construction Manager), Steve Birtles (Supervisory Electrician).
Uncredited Crew: Wilkie Cooper (Lighting Cameraman), Godfrey Godar (Camera Operator), A Carpenter (Second Assistant Director), Colin Lord (Assistant Director), B Clark (Make-Up), Peter Carmody (Clapper Loader), Anthony Burns (Second Assistant Director), R Cox (Third Assistant Director), Lillian Lee (Continuity), Peggy Spirito (Post Production), Ann Besserman (Continuity), Robin Vidgeon (Focus Puller), Frank Nesbitt (Assistant Director), L Parrot (Clapper Loader), John Deaton (Focus Puller).

Production Schedule:
Thursday 28 March 1968: John Hough: Day 1
2nd: 08.50 to unknown time: Sutherland Avenue, London, W9 [Ext: Baines' apartment]
2nd: Unknown time to 16.40: ABPC Elstree Studios, Studio Lot [Ext: Ministry of Technology, Cybernetics and Computer Division]
Friday 29 March 1968: John Hough: Day 2
2nd: 09.10-16.20: Rossway Park, Rossway, Berkamstead, Herts [Ext: Pelley's mansion]
Monday 1 April 1968: Cyril Frankel/John Hough: Day 3
Main: 09.25-17.15: ABPC Elstree Studios, Stage 7 [Int: Baines' apartment]
2nd: Unknown time to 17.15: ABPC Elstree Studios, Stage 7 [Int: Baines' apartment]
Tuesday 2 April 1968: Cyril Frankel: Day 4
Main: 08.45 to unknown time: ABPC Elstree Studios, Stage 7 [Int: Baines' apartment]
Main: Unknown time to 17.30: ABPC Elstree Studios, Stage 3 [Int: Summerhouse/Steed's apartment]

Quarter called pm
Wednesday 3 April 1968: Cyril Frankel: Day 5
Main: 08.50-17.00: ABPC Elstree Studios, Stage 3 [Int: Steed's apartment/waiting area]
Thursday 4 April 1968: Cyril Frankel: Day 6
Main: 09.15-19.40: ABPC Elstree Studios, Stage 3 [Int: Waiting area and corridor/computer lab]
Extended Day
Friday 5 April 1968: Cyril Frankel: Day 7
Main: 09.35-17.15: ABPC Elstree Studios, Stage 3 [Int: Computer lab]
Monday 8 April 1968: Cyril Frankel: Day 8
Main: Unknown time: ABPC Elstree Studios – No details available
Tuesday 9 April 1968: Cyril Frankel: Day 9
Main: 09.55-17.28: ABPC Elstree Studios, Stage 5 [Int: Pelley's hallway and study]
Wednesday 10 April 1968: Cyril Frankel/John Hough: Day 10
Main: 09.25-17.15: ABPC Elstree Studios, Stage 5 [Int: Pelley's hallway and study]
2nd: 09.10 to unknown time: ABPC Elstree Studios, Stage 3 [Int: Steed's apartment/computer lab]
2nd: Unknown time to 16.35: ABPC Elstree Studios, Studio Backlot [Ext: Summerhouse]
Unknown Date: Day 11: No details available
Tuesday 16 April 1968: Cyril Frankel: Day 12
Main: 09.10-17.15: ABPC Elstree Studios, Stage 5 [Int: Pelley's hallway/upper landing/staircase – Baines' apartment]
Wednesday 17 April 1968: Cyril Frankel: Day 13
Main: 08.50-15.45: ABPC Elstree Studios, Stage 5 [Int: Staircase – Baines' apartment/blue room/cellar/study/hallway – Pelley's mansion]
Wednesday 1 May 1968: Harry Booth: Day 14
3rd: 08.35-15.00: ABPC Elstree Studios, Stage 3 [Int: Computer bab – inserts]
6.10 – 'ALL DONE WITH MIRRORS'
Episode 138
Original Transmission Date: Wednesday 13 November 1968

Writer: Leigh Vance
Director: Ray Austin
Cast: Patrick Macnee (John Steed), Linda Thorson (Tara King), Dinsdale Landen (Watney), Peter Copley (Major Sparshott), Edwin Richfield (Barlow), Michael Trubshawe (Colonel Withers), Patrick Newell (Mother), Joanna Jones (Pandora Marshall), Nora Nicholson (Miss Emily), Tenniel Evans (Professor Carswell), Liane Aukin (Miss Tiddiman), Anthony Dutton (Dr Seligman), Peter Thomas (Kettridge), Graham Ashley (Markin), Michael Nightingale (The real Colonel), Robert Sidaway (The real Barlow), Desmond Jordan (Guthrie), David Grey (Williams), Peter Elliott (Arkin), John Bown (Roger).
Uncredited Cast: Rhonda Parker (Rhonda), Bruno Ellrington (Gozzo), Joe Dunne (Sweeno), Paul Weston (Fake Lighthouse Man), Liz Mitchell (Double for Tara King), Cyd Child (Stunt Double for Tara King), Jack Silk (Stunt Double for Kettridge), Decima Rickard (Double for Tara King), Joe Dunne (Stunt Double for Guthrie), Joe Furrow (Stunt Double for Watney), Arthur Howells (Stunt Double for Markin), Les Crawford (Stunt Double for Ketteridge), John Farrer (Stunt Double for Barlow), Les Crawford (Stunt Double for Barlow), John Farrer (Stunt Double for Ketteridge), Harry Fielder,

Maxwell Craig (Guards).

Crew: Laurie Johnson (Music Supervision by), Howard Blake (Score by), Philip Levene (Story Consultant), Alan Hume BSC (Director of Photography), Harry Booth (Post Production Co-ordinator), Manuel del Campo (Editor), Alun Hughes (Miss Thorson's Costumes Designed by), Ron Appleton (Assistant Director), Brian Elvin (Camera Operator), Len Townsend and Kenneth Tait (Associate Art Directors), Simon Wakefield (Set Dresser), Mary Spain (Continuity), Janice Dorman (Hairdressing), Felix Evans (Wardrobe), Gerald Gibbs (Second Unit Photography), Cecil Mason (Sound Recordist), Len Shilton (Dubbing Mixer), Peter Lennard (Sound Editor), Karen Heward (Music Editor), Herbert Worley (Construction Manager), Steve Birtles (Supervisory Electrician).

Uncredited Crew: Sally Ball (Continuity), Alan Anzarut (Second Assistant Director), R Cox (Third Assistant Director), Ernie Robinson (Camera Operator), Peter Carmody (Clapper Loader), D Lichfield (Focus Puller), Ken Worringham (Clapper Loader), Peggy Spirito (Post Production), Frank Nesbitt (Assistant Director), Godfrey Godar (Camera Operator), L Parrot (Clapper Loader), John Deaton (Focus Puller), Denny Lewis (Assistant Director), Jackie Green (Third Assistant Director), Bert Pearl (Assistant Director), Ernie Lewis (Assistant Director), Geoff Seaholme (Camera Operator), B Jordan (Focus Puller), R Clarke (Make-Up).

Production Schedule:
Tuesday 16 April 1968: Day 1: John Hough
2nd: 08.30 to unknown time: Unit travelled to Torcross, Devon.
Wednesday 17 April 1968: Day 2: John Hough
2nd: 09.30-17.00: Start Point Lighthouse, Salcombe, Devon [Ext: Lighthouse and access road]
Thursday 18 April 1968: Day 3: Ray Austin/John Hough
Main: 09.10 to unknown time: Rabley Park, Packhorse Lane, Ridge, Herts [Ext: Williams' house]
Main: Unknown time to 18.30: The Thatched Cottage, London Road, Well End, Herts [Ext: Guthrie's cottage]
2nd: 08.57-17.00: Start Point Lighthouse, Salcombe, Devon [Ext: Lighthouse, sea and rocks]
Friday 19 April 1968: Day 4: Ray Austin/John Hough
Main: 09.40-18.00: Aldenham Estate, Elstree, Herts [Ext: Wooded area and open clearing]
2nd: Unknown time: Start Point Lighthouse, Salcombe, Devon [Ext: Lighthouse]
Monday 22 April 1968: Day 5: Ray Austin/John Hough
Main: 08.40-17.10: ABPC Elstree Studios, Stage 3 [Int: Guthrie's living room/Williams' work room]
2nd: 14.55 to unknown time: Peacehaven, East Sussex [Ext: Cliff top, sea and rocks]
Tuesday 23 April 1968: Day 6: Ray Austin/John Hough
Main: 08.40-15.30: RAF Stanmore Park, London Road, Stanmore, Middlesex [Ext: Carmadoc research establishment]
2nd: 10.50-18.50: Peacehaven, East Sussex [Ext: Cliff top, sea and rocks]
Wednesday 24 April 1968: Day 7: Ray Austin/John Hough
Main: 08.35-17.15: ABPC Elstree Studios, Stage 3 [Int: Williams' work room/security area and corridor]
2nd: 09.00-19.00: Peacehaven, East Sussex [Ext: Cliff top]

Thursday 25 April 1968: Day 8: Ray Austin/John Hough
Main: 08.30 to unknown time: ABPC Elstree Studios, Stage 3 [Int: Security area and corridor/test laboratory/Watney's car]
Main: Unknown time to 16.15: ABPC Elstree Studios, Stage 7 [Int: Lamp room]
2nd: 08.40-10.00: Peacehaven, East Sussex [Ext: Cliff top]
Friday 26 April 1968: Day 9: Ray Austin/John Hough
Main: 08.35-16.35: ABPC Elstree Studios, Stage 7 [Int: Lamp room]
2nd: 08.45-16.00: Peacehaven, East Sussex [Ext: Cliff top]
Monday 29 April 1968: Day 10: Ray Austin/John Hough
Main: 08.30-17.20: ABPC Elstree Studios, Stage 7 [Int: Lamp room/stairs and ground floor]
2nd: 10.30-17.55: Ivinghoe Beacon, Ivinghoe Beacon Road and The Ridgeway, Ivinghoe, Bucks [Ext: Country road A and B]
Tuesday 30 April 1968: Day 11: Ray Austin
Main: 08.30-17.17: ABPC Elstree Studios, Stage 7 [Int: Stairs and ground floor/stairs]
Wednesday 1 May 1968: Day 12: Ray Austin/Manuel del Campo
Main: 08.35-17.20: ABPC Elstree Studios, Stage 7 [Int: Stairs/lamp room/base room/ Ext: Lighthouse door]
3rd: 08.35-15.00: ABPC Elstree Studios, Stage 3 [Int: Guthrie's den/Williams' work room – inserts]
Thursday 2 May 1968: Day 13: Ray Austin
Main: 08.45 to unknown time: Rabley Park, Packhorse Lane, Ridge, Herts [Ext: Williams' house/cliff top]
Main: Unknown time to 20.15: ABPC Elstree Studios, Stage 7 [Int: Stairs and ground floor/base room]
Friday 3 May 1968: Day 14: Ray Austin
Main: 08.35-17.15: ABPC Elstree Studios, Stage 7 [Int: Base room/lamp room]
Quarter called pm
Monday 6 May 1968: Day 15: Ray Austin
2nd: 10.15-19.32: Radlett Preparatory School, Watling Street, Radlett, Herts [Ext: Swimming pool]
Tuesday 7 May 1968: Day 16: Ray Austin
2nd: 11.02-17.20: ABPC Elstree Studios, Stage 7 [Int: Lamp room/stairs]
Wednesday 8 May 1968: Day 17: John Hough
2nd: Unknown time: ABPC Elstree Studios, Stage 7 [Int: Unknown sets]
Friday 17 May 1968: Day 18: Ray Austin
Main: 14.00-15.06: ABPC Elstree Studios, Stage 9 [Int: Steed's Rolls Royce]
Wednesday 5 June 1968: Day 19: John Hough
Main: 13.35-18.40: Aldenham Estate, Elstree, Herts [Ext: Cooking a steak on the engine of Steed's Rolls Royce, end tag scene]
Thursday 13 June 1968: Day 20: John Hough
2nd: 08.30-18.00: Aldenham Estate, Elstree, Herts [Ext: Wooded area and country road]

6.11 – 'YOU'LL CATCH YOUR DEATH'
Episode 139
Original Transmission Date: Wednesday 16 October 1968

Writer: Jeremy Burnham

Director: Paul Dickson

Cast: Patrick Macnee (John Steed), Linda Thorson (Tara King), Roland Culver (Colonel Timothy), Valentine Dyall (Butler), Fulton Mackay (Dr Glover), Sylvia Kay (Matron), Patrick Newell (Mother), Dudley Sutton (Dexter), Peter Bourne (Preece), Charles Lloyd Pack (Dr Fawcett), Henry McGee (Maidwell), Hamilton Dyce (Dr Camrose), Bruno Barnabe (Farrar), Fiona Hartford (Janice), Geoffrey Chater (Seaton), Jennifer Clulow (Georgina), Emma Cochrane (Melanie), Willoughby Gray (Dr Padley), Andrew Laurence (Dr Herrick), Douglas Blackwell (Postman).

Uncredited Cast: Rhonda Parker (Rhonda), Arthur Howell (Stunt Double for Herrick), Cyd Child (Stunt Double for Tara King), Frank Maher (Stunt Double for Dexter), Mark McBride (Stunt Double for Preece), Max Faulkner (Stunt Double for Dr Glover), Jenny Lefre (Stunt Double for Matron), Eden Fox (Test Subject).

Crew: Laurie Johnson (Music by), Philip Levene (Story Consultant), Alan Hume BSC (Director of Photography), Harry Booth (Post Production Co-ordinator), Karen Heward (Editor), Alun Hughes (Miss Thorson's Costumes Designed by), Ron Appleton (Assistant Director), Brian Elvin (Camera Operator), Len Townsend and Kenneth Tait (Associate Art Directors), Simon Wakefield (Set Dresser), Mary Spain (Continuity), Janice Dorman (Hairdressing), Felix Evans (Wardrobe), Gerald Gibbs (Second Unit Photography), Cecil Mason (Sound Recordist), Len Abbott (Dubbing Mixer), Peter Lennard (Sound Editor), Vivienne Collins (Music Editor), Herbert Worley (Construction Manager), Steve Birtles (Supervisory Electrician).

Uncredited Crew: Ernie Robinson (Camera Operator), D Litchfield (Focus Puller), Ken Warringham (Clapper Loader), Denny Lewis (Assistant Director), Anthony Burns (Second Assistant Director), R Cox (Assistant Director/Third Assistant Director), Sally Ball (Continuity), R Clarke (Make-Up), D Sonnis (Second Assistant Director) John O'Conner (Assistant Director), Peggy Spirito (Post Production) Renée Glynne (Continuity), Jackie Green (Third Assistant Director), D McMurray (Clapper Loader).

Production Schedule:

Tuesday 30 April 1968: Day 1: John Hough

2nd: 09.35 to unknown time: Edge Grove School, Oakridge Lane, Aldenham, Herts [Ext: Walsingham House]

2nd: Unknown time to 17.00: Shenley Hall, Rectory Lane, Shenley, Herts [Ext: Anastasia Nursing Academy]

Wednesday 1 May 1968: Day 2: John Hough

2nd: 09.55-18.15: Burnham Beeches, Burnham, Bucks [Ext: Tara's AC following Rolls Royce limousine/Steed and Tara in his vintage Rolls Royce]

Thursday 2 May 1968: Day 3: John Hough

2nd: 09.50 to unknown time: Cumberland Terrace, London, NW1 [Ext: The ear, nose and throat practice]

2nd: Unknown time to 19.30: Chester Terrace, London, NW1 [Ext: City street B]

Friday 3 May 1968: Day 4: John Hough

2nd: 09.30 to unknown time: Duchess Mews, London, W1 [Ext: Steed's mews/Int: Rolls Royce limousine in Steed's mews]

2nd: Unknown time: Cumberland Place, London, NW1 [Ext: Camrose's house]

2nd: Unknown time to 17.35: Chester Close North, London, NW1 [Ext: City street A]

Monday 6 May 1968: Day 5: Paul Dickson

Main: 08.35-17.15: ABPC Elstree Studios, Stage 5 [Int: Camrose's consulting room]

Tuesday 7 May 1968: Day 6: Paul Dickson
Main: 08.40-17.15: ABPC Elstree Studios, Stage 5 [Int: Camrose's consulting room/ Camrose's house hallway/Steed's apartment]
Wednesday 8 May 1968: Day 7: Paul Dickson/John Hough
Main: 11.30 to unknown time: ABPC Elstree Studios, Backlot Tank [Ext: Mother's place]
Main: Unknown time to 17.20: ABPC Elstree Studios, Stage 5 [Int: Steed's apartment]
2nd: 09.40 to unknown time: Cumberland Terrace, London, NW1 [Ext: The ear, nose and throat practice]
2nd: Unknown time: Chester Terrace, London, NW1 [Ext: City streets B and C]
Thursday 9 May 1968: Day 8: Paul Dickson/John Hough
Main: 08.35-17.35: ABPC Elstree Studios, Stage 5 [Int: Steed's apartment]
2nd: 09.40-17.15: Cumberland Terrace, London, NW1 [Ext: City street C]
Friday 10 May 1968: Day 9: Paul Dickson
Main: 08.35-17.35: ABPC Elstree Studios, Stage 5 [Int: Steed's apartment/Anastasia Nursing Academy]
Monday 13 May 1968: Day 10: Paul Dickson
Main: 08.35-17.20: ABPC Elstree Studios, Stage 5 [Int: Anastasia Nursing Academy/ Herrick's consulting room/tunnel and nose/Colonel's study]
Tuesday 14 May 1968: Day 11: Paul Dickson
Main: 08.35 to unknown time: ABPC Elstree Studios, Backlot [Ext: Mother's place]
Main: Unknown time to 20.20: ABPC Elstree Studios, Stage 5 [Int: Colonel's study]
Wednesday 15 May 1968: Day 12: Paul Dickson
Main: 08.35 to unknown time: ABPC Elstree Studios, Stage 5 [Int: Colonel's study]
Main: Unknown time to 17.18: ABPC Elstree Studios, Stage 9 [Int: Cold cure clinic]
Thursday 16 May 1968: Day 13: Paul Dickson
Main: 08.35-19.40: ABPC Elstree Studios, Stage 9 [Int: Cold cure clinic/deep freeze room]
Friday 17 May 1968: Day 14: Paul Dickson
Main: 08.35-14.00:
Main: 15.06-17.20: ABPC Elstree Studios, Stage 9 [Int: Rolls Royce limousine/Tara's car/Steed's car/allergy room]
Monday 20 May 1968: Day 15: Paul Dickson
No studio filming carried out on this date for this episode because of Electrical Trades Union industrial action. Unit filmed material on location for 'Super Secret Cypher Snatch' instead.
Tuesday 21 May 1968: Day 16: Paul Dickson
Main: 08.35-17.20: ABPC Elstree Studios, Stage 9 [Int: Telephone box/deep freeze room/allergy room]
Wednesday 22 May 1968: Day 17: Paul Dickson
No studio filming carried out on this date for this episode because of National Association of Theatrical and Kine Employees industrial action.
Thursday 23 May 1968: Day 18: Paul Dickson
2nd: 09.00 to unknown time: ABPC Elstree Studios, Stage 9 [Int: Allergy room]
2nd: Unknown time to 17.20: ABPC Elstree Studios, Stage 5 [Int: Seaton's consulting room/hallway]
Friday 24 May 1968: Day 19: Paul Dickson
2nd: 08.45 to unknown time: ABPC Elstree Studios, Stage 5 [Int: Padley's consulting room/hallway]
2nd: Unknown time to 17.15: ABPC Elstree Studios, Stage 9 [Int: Cold cure clinic/deep

freeze room]
<u>Wednesday 5 June 1968</u>: Day 20: Karen Heward
3rd: 09.30 to unknown time: ABPC Elstree Studios, Stage 3 [Int: Consulting room board/inserts for Scenes 7, 73 and 91]

6.12 – 'SUPER SECRET CYPHER SNATCH'
Episode 140
Original Transmission Date: Wednesday 9 October 1968

Writer: Tony Williamson
Director: John Hough
Cast: Patrick Macnee (John Steed), Linda Thorson (Tara King), Allan Cuthbertson (Webster), Ivor Dean (Ferret), Angela Scoular (Myra), Patrick Newell (Mother), Simon Oates (Maskin), Donald Gee (Vickers), John Carlisle (Peters), Nicholas Smith (Lather), Alec Ross (Masters – 1st Guard), Lionel Wheeler (2nd Guard), Anne Rutter (Betty), Clifford Earl (Roger Jarret), Anthony Blackshaw (Davis), David Quilter (Wilson).
Uncredited Cast: Rhonda Parker (Rhonda), Fred Haggerty (Agent), Arthur Howell (Warren), Jonathan Newth (James), Frank Barringer (Classy Glass Man), Paddy Ryan (Classy Glass Man), Billy Cornelius (Classy Glass Man), Ken Buckle (Classy Glass Man), Jack Arrow (Clerk), Cyd Child (Stunt Double for Tara King), Joe Farrar (Stunt Double for Vickers), Terry York (Stunt Double for Maskin), Paul Weston (Stunt Double for John Steed), Bob Anderson (Stunt Double for Maskin), Rocky Taylor (Stunt Double for Wilson).
Crew: Laurie Johnson (Music Supervision by), Howard Blake (Score by) Philip Levene (Story Consultant), Alan Hume BSC (Director of Photography), Harry Booth (Post Production Co-ordinator), Tom Simpson (Editor), Alun Hughes (Miss Thorson's Costumes Designed by), Ron Appleton (Assistant Director), Brian Elvin (Camera Operator), Len Townsend and Kenneth Tait (Associate Art Directors), Simon Wakefield (Set Dresser), Mary Spain (Continuity), Janice Dorman (Hairdressing), Felix Evans (Wardrobe), Gerald Gibbs (Second Unit Photography), Cecil Mason (Sound Recordist), Len Abbott (Dubbing Mixer), Peter Lennard (Sound Editor), Vivienne Collins (Music Editor), Herbert Worley (Construction Manager), Steve Birtles (Supervisory Electrician).
Uncredited Crew: John O'Conner (Assistant Director), K Warringham (Clapper Loader/Focus Puller), Ernie Robinson (Camera Operator), Sally Ball (Continuity), G Phillips (Third Assistant Director), D Lichfield (Focus Puller), Godfrey Godar, (Camera Operator), A Davis-Gough (Continuity), Peggy Spirito (Post Production), J Foley (Focus Puller), Jackie Green (Third Assistant Director), B Jordan (Focus Puller), E Stewart (Continuity), B Ryan (Clapper Loader), Bert Pearl (Assistant Director), Anthony Burns (Second Assistant Director), Peter Carmody (Clapper Loader), D Martin (Continuity), R Clarke (Make-Up), Geoff Seaholme (Camera Operator), Lorna Selwyn (Continuity), M Bell (Second Assistant Director), E Bonnichon (Assistant Director), T Simpson (Editor).

Production Schedule:
<u>Tuesday 14 May 1968</u>: Day 1: John Hough
2nd: 09.35 to unknown time: Boydell Court, London, NW8 [Ext: Jarret's apartment block]
2nd: Unknown time to 18.03: Franco Signs, Ripon Way, Borehamwood, Herts [Ext: Peters' apartment]

<u>Wednesday 15 May 1968</u>: Day 2: John Hough

2nd: 09.28 to unknown time: Brookmans Park Transmitting Station, Great North Road, Brookmans Park, Herts [Ext: Cypher headquarters]

2nd: Unknown time to 18.00: BSP Industries, Maxwell Road, Borehamwood, Herts [Classy Glass Cleaning Company]

<u>Thursday 16 May 1968</u>: Day 3: John Hough

2nd: 09.12-17.05: Brookmans Park Transmitting Station, Great North Road, Brookmans Park, Herts [Ext: Cypher headquarters]

<u>Friday 17 May 1968</u>: Day 4: John Hough

2nd: 09.00 to unknown time: Crossoaks Farm, Crossoaks Lane, Ridge, Herts [Ext: Lay-by and telegraph pole]

2nd: Unknown time to 17.25: Bucketsland Lane and High Canons, Well End, Herts [Ext: Country road B]

<u>Monday 20 May 1968</u>: Day 5: Paul Dickson/John Hough

Main: Unknown time: Holmshill Lane, Well End, Herts [Ext: Country road C]

2nd: 09.30-18.00: Burnham Beeches, Burnham, Bucks [Ext: Country road A]

Unable to film interiors at the studio due to industrial action by the Electrical Trades Union, hence both units filmed on location.

<u>Tuesday 21 May 1968</u>: Day 6: John Hough

2nd: 09.45-18.00: Burnham Beeches, Burnham, Bucks [Ext: Country road A]

<u>Wednesday 22 May 1968</u>: Day 7: John Hough

No filming carried out on this date for this episode because of National Association of Theatrical and Kine Employees industrial action.

<u>Thursday 23 May 1968</u>: Day 8: John Hough

Main: 08.35-17.15: ABPC Elstree Studios, Stage 3 [Int: Cypher headquarters foyer/Webster's office/Cypher office]

<u>Friday 24 May 1968</u>: Day 9: John Hough

Main: 08.35-17.20: ABPC Elstree Studios, Stage 3 [Int: Cypher office]

<u>Monday 27 May 1968</u>: Day 10: John Hough

Main: 08.35 to unknown time: ABPC Elstree Studios, Stage 3 [Int: Cypher office]

Main: Unknown time to 16.55: ABPC Elstree Studios, Studio Lot {Ext: Classy Glass Cleaning Company]

Members of the Electrical Trades Union did not return to work after lunch, staging a lightening strike.

<u>Tuesday 28 May 1968</u>: Day 11: John Hough

Main: 08.30 to unknown time: Burnham Beeches, Burnham, Bucks [Ext: Country road A and woods]

Main: Unknown time to 17.20: Brookmans Park Transmitting Station, Great North Road, Brookmans Park, Herts [Ext: Cypher headquarters]

<u>Wednesday 29 May 1968</u>: Day 12: John Hough

Main: 09.00 to unknown time: Aldenham Estate, Elstree, Herts [Ext: Cars in field]

Main: Unknown time to 18.20: Unknown Location [Ext: Swimming pool: link scenes for German TV]

<u>Friday 31 May 1968</u>: Day 13: John Hough

Main: 08.35-17.20: ABPC Elstree Studios, Stage 3 [Int: Cypher office]

<u>Tuesday 4 June 1968</u>: Day 14: John Hough

Main: 09.00-17.20: ABPC Elstree Studios, Stage 5 [Int: Steed's apartment]

<u>Wednesday 5 June 1968</u>: Day 15: John Hough

Main: 08.35-11.15: ABPC Elstree Studios, Stage 5 [Int: Steed's apartment]
Thursday 6 June 1968: Day 16: John Hough
2nd: 08.40-17.35: ABPC Elstree Studios, Stage 3 [Int: Webster's office]
Quarter called pm.
Friday 7 June 1968: Day 17: John Hough
2nd: 08.35 to unknown time: ABPC Elstree Studios, Studio Lot [Int: Classy Glass garage]
2nd: Unknown time to 17.20: ABPC Elstree Studios, Stage 3 [Int: Peters' apartment]
Monday 10 June 1968: Day 18: John Hough
2nd: 08.35-20.20: ABPC Elstree Studios, Stage 3 [Int: Webster's office/Cypher office/Peters' apartment/Classy Glass Cleaning Company]
Tuesday 11 June 1968: Day 19: John Hough
2nd: 08.30-17.20: ABPC Elstree Studios, Stage 3 [Int: Jarret's apartment/Classy Glass Cleaning Company/Cypher office]
Wednesday 12 June 1968: Day 20: John Hough
2nd: 08.35-17.20: ABPC Elstree Studios, Stage 3 [Int: Jarret's apartment/Ext: Jarret's apartment block]
Friday 14 June 1968: Day 21: John Hough
2nd: 08.55 to unknown time: ABPC Elstree Studios, Stage 3 [Int: Jarret's apartment/Classy Glass Cleaning Company/Cypher office/Steed's apartment]
2nd: Unknown time to 16.45: ABPC Elstree Studios, Studio Backlot [Ext: Country road]
Friday 5 July 1968: Day 22: John Hough
2nd: 09.00 to unknown time: ABPC Elstree Studios, Stage 9 [Int: Jarrett's apartment/Steed's apartment]
2nd: Unknown time: ABPC Elstree Studios, Studio Backlot [Ext: Field]
2nd: Unknown time to 18.15: Burnham Beeches, Burnham, Bucks [Ext: Country road A]
Monday 8 July 1968: Day 23: John Hough
3rd: 09.20-18.30: Ivinghoe Beacon, Ivinghoe Beacon Road, Ivinghoe, Bucks [Two stretches of country road/open country/sky]
Tuesday 9 July 1968: Day 24: John Hough
3rd: 10.25-17.20: ABPC Elstree Studios, Stage 9 [Int: Mother's place]
Model vehicles supplied by Kingsbury Cars, after originally being built by Mastermodels for the film Billion Dollar Brain.

6.13 – 'GAME'
Episode 141
Original Transmission Date: Wednesday 2 October 1968

Writer: Richard Harris
Director: Robert Fuest
Cast: Patrick Macnee (John Steed), Linda Thorson (Tara King), Peter Jeffrey (Bristow), Garfield Morgan (Manservant), Anthony Newlands (Brigadier Wishforth-Browne), Alex Scott (Averman) Aubrey Richards (Professor Witney), Desmond Walter-Ellis (Manager), Geoffrey Russell (Dexter), Archilles Georgiou (Student), Brian Badcoe (Cooty Gibson).
Uncredited Cast: Max Faulkner (Dice Man 2), Terry Richards (Dice Man 3), Romo Gorrara (Dice Man 5), Joe Cornelius (Dice Man 6), Paul Weston (Stunt Double for John Steed), Cyd Child (Stunt Double for Tara King), Joe Dunne (Stunt Double for Brigadier

Wishforth-Browne), Frank Barringer (Stunt Double for Manservant), Romo Gorrara (Stunt Double for Manservant), Romo Gorrara (Stunt Double for Dexter).

Crew: Laurie Johnson (Music Supervision by), Howard Blake (Score by), Philip Levene (Story Consultant), Alan Hume BSC (Director of Photography), Manual del Campo (Editor), Alun Hughes (Miss Thorson's Costumes Designed by), Ron Appleton (Assistant Director), Brian Elvin (Camera Operator), Len Townsend and Kenneth Tait (Associate Art Directors), Simon Wakefield (Set Dresser), Mary Spain (Continuity), Janice Dorman (Hairdressing), Felix Evans (Wardrobe), Desmond Dickinson (Second Unit Photography), Cecil Mason (Sound Recordist), Len Abbott (Dubbing Mixer), Peter Lennard (Sound Editor), Deveril Goodman (Music Editor), Herbert Worley (Construction Manager), Steve Birtles (Supervisory Electrician).

Uncredited Crew: Peggy Spirito (Post Production), Ernie Robinson (Camera Operator), Jackie Green (Third Assistant Director), Bert Pearl (Assistant Director), Lorna Selwyn (Continuity), P Taylor (Clapper Loader), Len Harris (Camera Operator), G Altman (Clapper Loader), L Barnett (Boom Operator), Terry Cole (Focus Puller), J Pointer (Third Assistant Director), E Bonnichon (Assistant Director), Peter Jessop (Lighting Cameraman), N Thompson (Third Assistant Director), Bert Pearl (Assistant Director), J Buckle (Focus Puller), M Oliffe (Clapper Loader), Kay Perkins (Continuity).

Production Schedule:
Thursday 30 May 1968: Day 1: Robert Fuest
Main: 08.50-18.50: Aldenham Park, Elstree, Herts [Ext: Manoeuvres ground]
Wednesday 5 June 1968: Day 2: Robert Fuest
2nd: 08.55-00-00: The Bishops Avenue, London, N2 [Ext: University building]
2nd: Unknown time to 00-00: Hillcrest, Barnet Road, Arkley, Herts [Ext: Averman's house]
2nd: Unknown time to 13.10: Unknown Location [Ext: Country road]
Thursday 6 June 1968: Day 3: Robert Fuest
Main: 09.13-17.20: ABPC Elstree Studios, Stage 5 [Int: Bristow's home]
Friday 7 June 1968: Day 4: Robert Fuest
Main: 09.05-17.20: ABPC Elstree Studios, Stage 5 [Int: Bristow's home]
Monday 10 June 1968: Day 5: Robert Fuest
Main: 09.06-17.20: ABPC Elstree Studios, Stage 5 [Int: Bristow's home/Bristow's hallway/Averman's office/Ext: Averman's french windows]
Tuesday 11 June 1968: Day 6: Robert Fuest
Main: 08.50 to unknown time: Duchess Mews, London, W1 [Ext: Steed's mews]
Main: Unknown time to 17.22: ABPC Elstree Studios, Stage 5 [Int: Averman's office/Ext: Averman's french windows]
Quarter called pm
Wednesday 12 June 1968: Day 7: Robert Fuest
Main: 08.35-17.20: ABPC Elstree Studios, Stage 5 [Int: Averman's office/Bristow's hallway/Bristow's home]
Thursday 13 June 1968: Day 8: Robert Fuest/John Hough
Main: 08.40 to unknown time: Oxhey Park, Watford, Herts [Ext: Children's playground]
Main: Unknown time to 17.20: ABPC Elstree Studios, Stage 5 [Int: Bristow's home]
2nd: Unknown time: Grim's Dyke Hotel, Old Redding, Harrow Weald, Herts [Ext: Bristow's home]

The TVR sports car provided by Kingsbury Motors broke down on location and was replaced by one of the unit cars.

Friday 14 June 1968: Day 9: Robert Fuest
Main: 08.35-17.20: ABPC Elstree Studios, Stage 5 [Int: Averman's office/reading room/Steed's car/Steed's apartment/Ext: Foxhole]
Monday 17 June 1968: Day 10: Robert Fuest
Main: 08.35-20.00: ABPC Elstree Studios, Stage 5 [Int: Steed's apartment]
Tuesday 18 June 1968: Day 11: Robert Fuest
Main: 08.35 to unknown time: ABPC Elstree Studios, Stage 5 [Int: Steed's apartment/jigsaw shop]
Main: Unknown time to 17.35: ABPC Elstree Studios, Stage 9 [Int: Games area]
Quarter called pm
Wednesday 19 June 1968: Day 12: Robert Fuest
Main: 08.35-17.35: ABPC Elstree Studios, Stage 9 [Int: Games area]
Quarter called pm
Thursday 20 June 1968: Day 13: No details available
Friday 21 June 1968: Day 14: Robert Fuest
Main: 08.35-17.20: ABPC Elstree Studios, Stage 9 [Int: Games area/six-sided room]
Monday 24 June 1968: Day 15: Robert Fuest
Main: 08.35-17.20: ABPC Elstree Studios, Stage 9 [Int: Games area]
Tuesday 25 June 1968: Day 16: Robert Fuest
Main: 08.35-17.35: ABPC Elstree Studios, Stage 9 [Int: Games area]
Quarter called pm
Monday 15 July 1968: Day 17: John Hough
2nd: 09.00-17.20: ABPC Elstree Studios, Stage 9 [Int: Steed's apartment/outside Steed's apartment door]
Tuesday 16 July 1968: Day 18: John Hough
3rd: 08.45 to unknown time: ABPC Elstree Studios, Stage 9 [Int: Limbo/Bristow's home/games area/six-sided room/reading room]
3rd: Unknown time to 17.20: ABPC Elstree Studios, Studio Backlot [Ext: Field]
Wednesday 17 July 1968: Day 19: John Hough
3rd: 08.45-17.20: ABPC Elstree Studios, Stage 9 [Int: Limbo/games area/six-sided room]
Thursday 18 July 1968: Day 20: John Hough
3rd: 08.35-15.50: ABPC Elstree Studios, Stage 9 [Int: Limbo/games area – inserts for scenes 99 and 109]
This shoot incorporated the shooting of footage for the new closing credits.

6.14 – 'FALSE WITNESS'
Episode 142
Original Transmission Date: Wednesday 6 November 1968

Writer: Jeremy Burnham
Director: Charles Crichton
Cast: Patrick Macnee (John Steed), Linda Thorson (Tara King), John Bennett (Sykes), Barry Warren (Melville), Tony Steedman (Sir Joseph Tarlton), Patrick Newell (Mother), William Job (Lord Edgefield), Dan Meaden (Sloman), Michael Lees (Plummer), Simon Lack (Nesbitt), Arthur Pentelow (Dr Grant), Peter Jesson (Penman), Rio Fanning (Lane), John Atkinson (Brayshaw), Larry Burns (Gould), Jimmy Gardner (Little Man at Bus

Stop), Terry Eliot (Amanda).

Uncredited Cast: Rhonda Parker (Rhonda), Frank Henson (Stunt Double for Tara King), Cyd Child (Stunt Double for Tara King), Paul Weston (Stunt Double for John Steed), Joe Dunne (Stunt Double for Lane), Alf Joint (Stunt Double for Sloman), Fred Haggerty (Stunt Double for Sykes), Paddy Ryan (Stunt Double for Sykes), Terry Maidment (Stunt Double for Lord Edgefield).

Crew: Laurie Johnson (Music by), Terry Nation (Script Editor), Philip Levene (Story Consultant), Alan Hume BSC (Director of Photography), Karen Heward (Editor), Ann Chegwidden (Post Production Co-ordinator) Alun Hughes (Miss Thorson's Costumes Designed by), Ted Lewis (Assistant Director), Geoff Seaholme (Camera Operator), Len Townsend and Kenneth Tait (Associate Art Directors), Simon Wakefield (Set Dresser), Lorna Selwyn (Continuity), Janice Dorman (Hairdressing), Felix Evans (Wardrobe), Gerald Gibbs (Second Unit Photography), Cecil Mason (Sound Recordist), Len Abbott (Dubbing Mixer), Bob Dearberg (Sound Editor), Karen Heward (Music Editor), Herbert Worley (Construction Manager), Steve Birtles (Supervisory Electrician).

Uncredited Crew: Anthony Burns (Second Assistant Director), Jackie Green (Third Assistant Director), Peter Carmody (Clapper Loader), D Litchfield (Focus Puller), B Clarke (Make-Up), S Rider (Sound Mixer), Peggy Spirito (Post Production), P Taylor (Clapper Loader), Bert Pearl (Assistant Director), B Clarke (Make-Up), Denis Fitzgibbon (Focus Puller).

Production Schedule:

Tuesday 18 June 1968: Day 1: Charles Crichton
2nd: 08.40-17.05: Mackennal Street, Townsend Road and Imperial Court Underground Garage, London, NW1 [Ext: City street A and telephone box/another street/Int: Underground garage]
Wednesday 19 June 1968: Day 2: Charles Crichton
2nd: 08.40-17.00: Imperial Court Underground Garage, London, NW1 [Int: Underground garage]
Thursday 20 June 1968: Day 3: No details available
Friday 21 June 1968: Day 4: Charles Crichton
2nd: 08.45 to unknown time: Wilton Place/Wilton Crescent, London, SW1 [Ext: Sir Joseph's house]
2nd: Unknown time: Matcomb Street/Wilton Crescent, London, SW1 [Ext: Lotus follows milkfloat]
2nd: Unknown time: Unknown Location [Ext: Fire escape]
2nd: Unknown time: Duchess Mews, London, W1 [Ext: Steed's mews]
2nd: Unknown time to 17.05: Rectory Lane, Shenley, Herts [Ext: Country road B and telephone box]
Monday 24 June 1968: Day 5: Charles Crichton
2nd: 08.40-17.00: Cowley Hill, Borehamwood, Herts [Int: Top deck of bus]
Tuesday 25 June 1968: Day 6: Charles Crichton
2nd: 09.20 to unknown time: Bell Lane, London Colney, Herts [Int: Top deck of bus]
2nd: Unknown time to 18.10: Home Farm, Aldenham Road, Elstree, Herts [Int: Top deck of bus]
Wednesday 26 June 1968: Day 7: Charles Crichton/John Hough
Main: 08.30 to unknown time: Warren Lane, Stanmore, Greater London, HA7 [Ext: Vintage Rolls Royce through wooded country]

Main: Unknown time: Green Street, Borehamwood, Herts [Ext: Bus over brow of hill]

Main: Unknown time to 17.20: Hartforde Road, Borehamwood, Herts [Ext: Street B and bus stop]

2nd: 09.10 to unknown time: Rectory Lane, Shenley, Herts [Ext: Country road B and telephone box]

2nd: Unknown time: Home Farm, Aldenham Road, Elstree, Herts [Ext: Dairy and country road C]

2nd: Unknown time to 16.15: Unknown Location [Ext: Dual carriageway]

The 2nd unit ran out of time and did not film at their final location

Thursday 27 June 1968: Day 8: Charles Crichton/John Hough

Main: 08.35-17.20: ABPC Elstree Studios, Stage 5 [Int: Steed's apartment]

2nd: 09.50 to unknown time: Belgrave Square, London, SW1 [Ext: Lotus follows milk float/city street C]

2nd: Unknown time: Hartforde Road, Borehamwood, Herts [Ext: Street B and bus stop/bus stop 2]

2nd: Unknown time: Rectory Lane, Shenley, Herts [Ext: Country road B and telephone box]

2nd: Unknown time: Aldenham Road, Elstree, Herts [Ext: Country road D/narrow country lane]

2nd: Unknown time to 18.35: Home Farm, Aldenham Road, Elstree, Herts [Ext: Field]

Friday 28 June 1968: Day 9: Charles Crichton/John Hough

Main: 08.35-17.20: ABPC Elstree Studios, Stage 5 [Int: Steed's apartment]

2nd: 09.20-17.45: Home Farm, Aldenham Road, Elstree, Herts [Ext: Dairy and country road C]

Monday 1 July 1968: Day 10: Charles Crichton/John Hough

Main: 09.55 to unknown time: ABPC Elstree Studios, Stage 5 [Int: Steed's apartment]

Main: Unknown time to 17.20: ABPC Elstree Studios, Stage 3 [Int: Dairy warehouse/milk vat room]

3rd: 11.00-17.35: Mackennal Street, Townsend Road and Imperial Court Underground Garage, London, NW1 [Ext: City street A and telephone box/another street/Int: Underground garage]

3rd: Unknown time: Unknown Location [Ext: Bus Stop 3]

Tuesday 2 July 1968: Day 11: Charles Crichton

Main: 08.35-17.20: ABPC Elstree Studios, Stage 3 [Int: Dairy warehouse/milk vat room]

One and half hours lost because actor Dan Meadon arrived late at the studio

Thursday 4 July 1968: Day 12: Charles Crichton

Main: 09.15-17.45: ABPC Elstree Studios, Stage 3 [Int: Dairy warehouse/milk vat room]

Friday 5 July 1968: Day 13: Charles Crichton

Main: 09.10-17.20: ABPC Elstree Studios, Stage 3 [Int: Telephone box/dairy warehouse/milk vat room/Plummer's apartment]

Monday 8 July 1968: Day 14: Charles Crichton

Main: 09.20-17.20: ABPC Elstree Studios, Stage 3 [Int: Plummer's apartment/milk vat room/dairy warehouse/Sykes' office]

Tuesday 9 July 1968: Day 15: Charles Crichton

Main: 09.05-17.20: ABPC Elstree Studios, Stage 3 [Int: Sykes' office/Edgefield's apartment and corridor/dairy warehouse]

Wednesday 10 July 1968: Day 16: Charles Crichton

Main: 08.43-17.20: ABPC Elstree Studios, Stage 3 [Int: Edgefield's apartment and

corridor/Sir Joseph's study]
Thursday 11 July 1968: Day 17: Charles Crichton
Main: 08.30-17.20: ABPC Elstree Studios, Stage 9 [Int: Sir Joseph's study]

OPENING TITLES/CLOSING CREDITS: SECOND VERSION
Cast: Patrick Macnee (John Steed), Linda Thorson (Tara King).
Uncredited Crew: Ted Lewis (Assistant Director), E Bonnichon (Assistant Director), D Warrington (Second Assistant Director), P Hammond (Focus Puller), Isabel Byers (Continuity), J Uttley (Clapper Loader), Peter Jessop (Lighting Cameraman), N Thompson (Third Assistant Director), Bert Pearl (Assistant Director), J Buckle (Focus Puller), M Oliffe (Clapper Loader), Kay Perkins (Continuity).

Production Schedule:
Wednesday 3 July 1968: Day 1: Robert Fuest
Main: 08.35-18.50: Tykes Water Lake, Aldenham Estate, Elstree, Herts [Ext: Bridge and field]
Thursday 4 July 1968: Day 2: Robert Fuest
3rd: 09.15-18.25: Tykes Water Lake, Aldenham Estate, Elstree, Herts [Ext: Bridge and field for opening titles and unused closing credits]
Thursday 11 July 1968: Day 3: Charles Crichton
Main: Unknown time: ABPC Elstree Studios, Stage 9 [Ext: Insert for opening titles]
Thursday 18 July 1968: Day 4: John Hough
3rd: Unknown time: ABPC Elstree Studios, Stage 9 [Int: Card ticks for closing credits]

6.15 – 'NOON DOOMSDAY'
Episode 143
Original Transmission Date: Wednesday 27 November 1968

Writer: Terry Nation
Director: Peter Sykes
Cast: Patrick Macnee (John Steed), Linda Thorson (Tara King), Ray Brooks (Farrington), T P McKenna (Grant), Griffith Jones (Sir Rodney Woodham-Baines), Lyndon Brook (Roger Lyall), Peter Bromilow (Gerald Kafka), Patrick Newell (Mother), Peter Halliday (Perrier), Anthony Ainley (Sunley), John Glyn-Jones (Dr Hyde), David Glover (Dr Carson), Lawrence James (Giles Cornwall), Alfred Maron (Taxi Driver).
Uncredited Cast: Rhonda Parker (Rhonda), Max Faulkner (Riding Double for Farrington), Bill Cumming (Stunt/Riding Double for Farrington), David Brandon (Riding Double for Grant), Joe Dunne (Stunt Double for Grant), Cyd Child (Stunt Double for Tara King), Paul Weston (Stunt Double for John Steed), Max Faulkner (Stunt Double for Giles Cornwall).
Crew: Laurie Johnson (Music Supervision by), Howard Blake (Score by), Terry Nation (Script Editor), Stephen Dade BSC (Director of Photography), Manual del Campo (Editor), Ann Chegwidden (Post Production Co-ordinator), Alun Hughes (Miss Thorson's Costumes Designed by), Ted Lewis (Assistant Director), Ernie Robinson (Camera Operator), Richard Harrison and Kenneth Tait (Associate Art Directors), Simon Wakefield (Set Dresser), Mary Spain (Continuity), Janice Dorman (Hairdressing), Felix Evans (Wardrobe), Gerald Gibbs (Second Unit Photography), Cecil Mason (Sound Recordist), Bill Rowe (Dubbing Mixer), Bob Dearberg (Sound Editor), Paul Clay (Music

Editor), Herbert Worley (Construction Manager), Steve Birtles (Supervisory Electrician).
Uncredited Crew: D Gibson (Second Assistant Director), H Richards (Make-Up), M Bell (Second Assistant Director), Bert Pearl (Assistant Director), B Ryan (Clapper Loader), Jackie Green (Third Assistant Director), A Besserman (Continuity), Geoff Seaholme (Camera Operator), D Lichfield (Focus Puller), B Lipman (Second Assistant Director), B Clarke (Make-Up), Peggy Spirito (Post Production), M Carmody (Production Runner), A Grant (Lighting Cameraman), E Treacher (Fireman), M Taylor (Fireman), Kay Perkins (Continuity), L Steward (Wardrobe), C Barrett (Nurse), N Whorlow (Nurse), B Rule (Cutting Room), N Coggs (Sound Mixer), M F Rule (Editor), Isobel Byers (Continuity).

Production Schedule:
<u>Monday 1 July 1968</u>: Day 1: Peter Sykes
2nd: 09.40-18.35: Stanbridgeford Railway Station, Stanbridge Road, Lower End, Beds [Ext: Disused railway station]
<u>Tuesday 2 July 1968</u>: Day 2: Peter Sykes
2nd: 09.20-19.00: Stanbridgeford Railway Station, Stanbridge Road, Lower End, Beds [Ext: Disused railway station]
<u>Wednesday 3 July 1968</u>: Day 3: Peter Sykes
Main: 09.40-17.30: Park Farm, Hazelwood Lane, Ampthill, Bucks [Ext: Department S]
<u>Thursday 4 July 1968</u>: Day 4: Peter Sykes
2nd: 09.05 to unknown time: Stanbridgeford Railway Station, Stanbridge Road, Lower End, Beds [Ext: Disused railway station]
2nd: Unknown time to 20.45: Park Farm, Hazelwood Lane, Ampthill, Bucks [Ext: Department S]
<u>Monday 8 July 1968</u>: Day 5: Peter Sykes
2nd: 09.15-18.20: Park Farm, Hazelwood Lane, Ampthill, Bucks [Ext: Department S]
<u>Tuesday 9 July 1968</u>: Day 6: Peter Sykes
2nd: 09.15-18.00: Park Farm, Hazelwood Lane, Ampthill, Bucks [Ext: Department S]
<u>Wednesday 10 July 1968</u>: Day 7: Peter Sykes
2nd: 09.15 to unknown time: Park Farm, Hazelwood Lane, Ampthill, Bucks [Ext: Department S/Int: Cornwall's office]
2nd: Unknown time to 17.35: ABPC Elstree Studios, Stage 5 [Int: Baines' room]
Quarter called pm.
<u>Thursday 11 July 1968</u>: Day 8: Peter Sykes
2nd: 09.30-18.30: Park Farm, Hazelwood Lane, Ampthill, Bucks [Ext: Department S]
<u>Friday 12 July 1968</u>: Day 9: Peter Sykes
Main: 09.15-18.15: Park Farm, Hazelwood Lane, Ampthill, Bucks [Ext: Department S]
<u>Tuesday 16 July 1968</u>: Day 10: Peter Sykes
Main: 09.00-00-00: ABPC Elstree Studios, Stage 9 [Int: Steed's apartment]
Main: Unknown time to 17.20: ABPC Elstree Studios, Stage 5 [Int: Common room]
<u>Wednesday 17 July 1968</u>: Day 11: Peter Sykes
Main: 08.35-17.20: ABPC Elstree Studios, Stage 5 [Int: Common room]
<u>Thursday 18 July 1968</u>: Day 12: Peter Sykes
Main: 08.35-17.20: ABPC Elstree Studios, Stage 5 [Int: Common room]
<u>Friday 19 July 1968</u>: Day 13: Peter Sykes
Main: 08.35-17.10: ABPC Elstree Studios, Stage 5 [Int: Common room]
<u>Monday 22 July 1968</u>: Day 14: Peter Sykes

Main: 08.45-17.20: ABPC Elstree Studios, Stage 5 [Int: Common room/upper corridor and Lyall's room/Baines' room]
Tuesday 23 July 1968: Day 15: Peter Sykes
Main: 08.35-17.25: ABPC Elstree Studios, Stage 5 [Int: Baines'room/Lyall's room/Perrier's room/Sunley's room/barn]
Wednesday 24 July 1968: Day 16: Peter Sykes
Main: 08.35-17.10: ABPC Elstree Studios, Stage 5 [Int: Barn/well shaft and base]
Thursday 25 July 1968: Day 17: Peter Sykes
Main: 08.45-16.20: ABPC Elstree Studios, Stage 5 [Int: Barn/well shaft and base/Baines' room/Lyall's room/Perrier's room/Sunley's room]
Friday 26 July 1968: Day 18: Peter Sykes
Main: 10.35-18.45: Park Farm, Hazelwood Lane, Ampthill, Bucks [Ext: Department S]
Monday 29 July 1968: Day 19: Peter Sykes
Main: 09.10-18.15: Park Farm, Hazelwood Lane, Ampthill, Bucks [Ext: Department S]
Tuesday 30 July 1968: Day 20: Peter Sykes
Main: 10.00-18.25: Park Farm, Hazelwood Lane, Ampthill, Bucks [Ext: Department S/open countryside]

6.16 – 'LEGACY OF DEATH'
Episode 144
Original Transmission Date: Wednesday 20 November 1968

Writer: Terry Nation
Director: Don Chaffey
Cast: Patrick Macnee (John Steed), Linda Thorson (Tara King), Stratford Johns (Sidney Street), Ronald Lacey (Humbert Green), Ferdy Mayne (Baron Von Orlak), Kynaston Reeves (Dickens), Richard Hurndall (Henley Farrer), John Hollis (Zoltan) Leon Thau (Ho Lung), Tutte Lemkow (Gorky), Peter Swanwick (Oppenheimer), Vic Wise (Slattery), Teddy Kiss (Winkler), Michael Bilton (Dr Winter).
Uncredited Cast: Romo Gorrara (Gregor), Bill Reid (Villain), Paddy Ryan (Stunt Double for Gorky), Paddy Ryan (Stunt Double for Dickens), Paul Weston (Stunt Double for John Steed), Cyd Child (Stunt Double for Tara King), Joe Dunne (Stunt Double for Baron Von Orlak), Alf Joint (Stunt Double for Sidney Street), Terry Maidment (Stunt Double for Humbert Green).
Crew: Laurie Johnson (Music by), Terry Nation (Script Editor), Peter Jessop (Director of Photography), Karen Heward (Editor), Ann Chegwidden (Post Production Co-ordinator) Alun Hughes (Miss Thorson's Costumes Designed by), Ted Lewis (Assistant Director), Ernie Robinson (Camera Operator), Len Townsend and Kenneth Tait (Associate Art Directors), Simon Wakefield (Set Dresser), Mary Spain (Continuity), Janice Dorman (Hairdressing), Felix Evans (Wardrobe), Gerald Gibbs (Second Unit Photography), Cecil Mason (Sound Recordist), Bill Rowe (Dubbing Mixer), Peter Lennard (Sound Editor), Paul Clay (Music Editor), Herbert Worley (Construction Manager), Steve Birtles (Supervisory Electrician).
Uncredited Crew: Bert Pearl (Assistant Director), J Jympson (Footsteps), E Bonnichon (Assistant Director), N Thompson (Third Assistant Director), B Ryan (Clapper Loader/Focus Puller), A Besserman (Continuity), Michael Murray (Third Assistant Director), B Lipman (Second Assistant Director), Jackie Green (Third Assistant Director), B Clarke (Make-Up), Ron Purdie (Assistant Director), Geoff Seaholme

(Camera Operator), D Litchfield (Focus Puller/Camera Operator), A Grant (Lighting Cameraman), James Allaway (Focus Puller), M Temple (Focus Puller), D Worley (Clapper Loader), A Cotton (Make-Up).

Production Schedule:
<u>Tuesday 16 July 1968</u>: Day 1: Don Chaffey
2nd: 09.15-18.00: Chalcott Crescent, London, NW1 [Ext: Tara's apartment]
<u>Wednesday 17 July 1968</u>: Day 2: Don Chaffey
2nd: 09.15 to unknown time: Duchess Mews, London, W1 [Ext: Steed's mews]
2nd: Unknown time to 17.30: Sharpleshall Street, London NW1 [Ext: Tara's Lotus leaves the back of her apartment]
<u>Thursday 18 July 1968</u>: Day 3: Don Chaffey
2nd: 09.15 to unknown time: Pound Lane, Shenley, Herts [Ext: Tara's Lotus followed by various cars]
2nd: Unknown time: Rectory Lane, Shenley, Herts [Ext: Tara's Lotus]
2nd: Unknown time: Mimms Lane/Gateway to Shenley Hall, Shenley, Herts [Ext: Road and gateway]
2nd: Unknown time: Mimms Lane/Harris Lane/Rectory Lane/Gateway to Shenley Hall, Shenley, Herts [Ext: Various cars take different turnings]
2nd: Unknown time: Green Street, Shenley/Borehamwood, Herts [Ext: Tara's Lotus enters a gateway]
2nd: Unknown time to 17.55: Aldenham House, The Haberdashers' Aske's School, Aldenham Road, Elstree, Herts [Ext/Int: Farrer's home]
<u>Friday 19 July 1968</u>: Day 4: Don Chaffey
2nd: 09.25 to unknown time: Unknown Location [Ext: Solicitor's office]
This location does not appear in the episode.
2nd: Unknown time: Belsize Park Gardens, London, NW3 [Ext: London street]
2nd: Unknown time: Butterfly Lane, Elstree, Herts [Ext: Deserted road]
2nd: Unknown time to 16.40: ABPC Elstree Studios, Studio Lot [Int: Sydney's car]
<u>Monday 22 July 1968</u>: Day 5: Don Chaffey
2nd: 09.15-17.20: ABPC Elstree Studios, Stage 9 [Int: Steed's apartment and hallway]
<u>Tuesday 23 July 1968</u>: Day 6: Don Chaffey
2nd: 09.05-17.20: ABPC Elstree Studios, Stage 9 [Int: Steed's apartment]
<u>Wednesday 24 July 1968</u>: Day 7: Don Chaffey
2nd: 08.40-17.27: ABPC Elstree Studios, Stage 9 [Int: Steed's apartment]
<u>Thursday 25 July 1968</u>: Day 8: Don Chaffey
2nd: 08.55-17.12: ABPC Elstree Studios, Stage 9 [Int: Steed's apartment and hallway]
<u>Friday 26 July 1968</u>: Day 9: Don Chaffey
Main: 09.15-17.20: ABPC Elstree Studios, Stage 9 [Int: Steed's apartment]
<u>Monday 29 July 1968</u>: Day 10: Don Chaffey
2nd: 08.55-17.15: ABPC Elstree Studios, Stage 9 [Int: Steed's apartment/solicitor's office]
<u>Tuesday 30 July 1968</u>: Day 11: Don Chaffey
2nd: 09.15 to unknown time: ABPC Elstree Studios, Stage 9 [Int: Steed's apartment/solicitor's office/Steed's car]
2nd: Unknown time to 17.17: ABPC Elstree Studios, Stage 3 [Int: Farrer's home]
<u>Wednesday 31 July 1968</u>: Day 12: Don Chaffey
2nd: 09.00-17.10: ABPC Elstree Studios, Stage 3 [Int: Farrer's home]
<u>Thursday 1 August 1968</u>: Day 13: Don Chaffey

2nd: 08.30-17.20: ABPC Elstree Studios, Stage 3 [Int: Farrer's home]
Hairdresser arrived late at the studio resulting in Linda Thorson arriving on the set 25 minutes late.
Friday 2 August 1968: Day 14: Don Chaffey
2nd: 09.10-17.20: ABPC Elstree Studios, Stage 3 [Int: Farrer's home]
Monday 5 August 1968: Day 15: Don Chaffey
2nd: 09.15-17.20: ABPC Elstree Studios, Stage 3 [Int: Farrer's home/Tara's apartment]
Tuesday 6 August 1968: Day 16: Don Chaffey
2nd: 09.40 to unknown time: ABPC Elstree Studios, Backlot Town [Ext: Tara's back door/Chinese curio shop]
2nd: Unknown time to 17.35: ABPC Elstree Studios, Stage 9 [Int: Steed's apartment]
Quarter called pm
Wednesday 7 August 1968: Day 17: Don Chaffey
2nd: 09.05 to unknown time: ABPC Elstree Studios, Stage 9 [Ext: Summer house/Int: Tara's car]
2nd: Unknown time to 17.27: ABPC Elstree Studios, Stage 3 [Int: Chinese curio shop]
Quarter called pm
Thursday 8 August 1968: Day 18: Don Chaffey
2nd: 08.55-17.30: ABPC Elstree Studios, Stage 3 [Int: Chinese curio shop/backroom curio shop]
Quarter called pm
Friday 9 August 1968: Day 19: Don Chaffey
2nd: 09.02 to unknown time: ABPC Elstree Studios, Stage 3 [Int: Backroom curio shop/Sidney's car/Farrer's home/Tara's apartment]
2nd: Unknown time to 16.15: ABPC Elstree Studios, Backlot Town [Ext: Solicitor's office]

6.17 – 'THEY KEEP KILLING STEED'
Episode 145
Original Transmission Date: Wednesday 18 December 1968

Writer: Brian Clemens
Director: Robert Fuest
Cast: Patrick Macnee (John Steed), Linda Thorson (Tara King), Ian Ogilvy (Baron Von Curt), Ray McAnnally (Arcos), Norman Jones (Zerson), Bernard Horsfall (Captain Smythe), Patrick Newell (Mother), William Ellis (Bruno), Hal Galili (Nadine), Nicole Shelby (Helga), Rosemary Donnelly (Miranda), Gloria Connell (Maid), Michael Corcoran (Hotel Porter), Ross Hutchinson (Chairman), Reg Whitehead (Chief Guard), Anthony Sheppard (Perova), Angharad Rees (Redhead), George Ghent (Taxi Driver).
Uncredited Cast: Rhonda Parker (Rhonda), Arthur Howell (Verno), Bill Cummings (Golda), Frank Barringer (Smanoff), Gerry Judge (Barman), Paul Weston (Stunt Double for John Steed), Cyd Child (Stunt Double for Tara King), Frank Henson (Stunt Double for Baron Von Curt), Fred Haggerty (Stunt Double for Baron Von Curt), Paul Weston (Stunt Double for Steed 4), Paul Weston (Stunt Double for Victim Steed), George Leech (Stunt Double for Zerson), Billy Dean (Stunt Double for Arcos), Cliff Diggins (Stunt Double for Arcos-Steed), Cliff Diggins (Stunt Double for Steed 3).
Crew: Laurie Johnson (Music by), Terry Nation (Script Editor), Stephen Dade BSC (Director of Photography), Manual del Campo (Editor), Ann Chegwidden (Post

Production Co-ordinator), Alun Hughes (Miss Thorson's Costumes Designed by), Ted Lewis (Assistant Director), Ernie Robinson (Camera Operator), Len Townsend and Kenneth Tait (Associate Art Directors), Simon Wakefield (Set Dresser), Mary Spain (Continuity), Janice Dorman (Hairdressing), Felix Evans (Wardrobe), Cecil Mason (Sound Recordist), Len Abbott (Dubbing Mixer), Bob Dearberg (Sound Editor), Paul Clay (Music Editor), Herbert Worley (Construction Manager), Steve Birtles (Supervisory Electrician).

Uncredited Crew: E Bonnichon (Assistant Director), Terry Cole (Focus Puller), Kay Perkins (Continuity), Alan Hume (Lighting Cameraman), H Grigson (Third Assistant Director), M Oliffe (Clapper Loader), M Temple (Focus Puller), A Cotton (Make-Up), B Oates (Editor), M.S. Rule (Editor), L Stewart (Wardrobe), A Fordyce (Hairdresser), Michael Murray (Third Assistant Director), B Clarke (Make-Up), M Jympson (Footsteps), Betty Sherriff (Hairdresser), Peggy Spirito (Post Production), Alan Brownie (Make-Up), Malcolm Vinson (Focus Puller), A White (Camera Operator), Jackie Green (Assistant Director), J Deeble (Clapper Loader).

Production Schedule:
Monday 29 July 1968: Day 1: John Hough
3rd: 10.00-17.25: Burnham Beeches, Burnham, Bucks [Ext: Mercedes following Triumph 2000]
Tuesday 30 July 1968: Day 2: John Hough
3rd: 09.20-14.25: The Grove, Hempstead Road, Watford, Herts [Ext: Bridge and country road]
Wednesday 31 July 1968: Day 3: John Hough
Main: 09.15-17.00: Northaw, Herts [Ext: Hotel and quiet street]
Thursday 1 August 1968: Day 4: John Hough
Main: 09.00-15.55: Rosary Priory High School, Elstree Road, Bushey, Herts [Ext: conference centre]
Friday 2 August 1968: Day 5: Robert Fuest
Main: 08.50-17.20: Springwell Chalk Pits, Springwell Lane, Harefield, Bucks [Ext: Earthworks]
Monday 5 August 1968: Day 6: Robert Fuest
Main: 09.00-17.15: Springwell Chalk Pits, Springwell Lane, Harefield, Bucks [Ext: Earthworks]
Tuesday 6 August 1968: Day 7: Robert Fuest
Main: 09.30-12.50: Springwell Chalk Pits, Springwell Lane, Harefield, Bucks [Ext: Earthworks]
Wednesday 7 August 1968: Day 8: Robert Fuest
Main: 09.20-14.30: Rosary Priory High School, Elstree Road, Bushey, Herts [Ext: Conference centre]
Main: 15.00-17.30: ABPC Elstree Studios, Stage 5 [Int: Taxi/Steed four's car]
Thursday 8 August 1968: Day 9: Robert Fuest
Main: 09.20-16.20: Rosary Priory High School, Elstree Road, Bushey, Herts [Ext: Conference centre]
Friday 9 August 1968: Day 10: Robert Fuest
Main: 08.45-17.20: ABPC Elstree Studios, Stage 5 [Int: Tara's room/hotel corridor/Steed's room]
Monday 12 August 1968: Day 11: Robert Fuest

Main: 09.15 to unknown time: Rosary Priory High School, Elstree Road, Bushey, Herts [Ext: Conference centre]

Main: Unknown time to 17.15: Aldenham Estate, Elstree, Herts [Ext: Bridge and lake]

Tuesday 13 August 1968: Day 12: Robert Fuest

Main: 09.30-16.00: Springwell Chalk Pits, Springwell Lane, Harefield, Bucks [Ext: Earthworks and old cab]

Wednesday 14 August 1968: Day 13: Robert Fuest

Main: 08.30 to unknown time: ABPC Elstree Studios, Stage 3 [Int: Tara's apartment]

Main: Unknown time to 17.35: ABPC Elstree Studios, Stage 5 [Int: Mother's underwater base]

Quarter called pm

Thursday 15 August 1968: Day 14: Robert Fuest

Main: 08.35-17.20: ABPC Elstree Studios, Stage 5 [Int: Villain's headquarters]

Friday 16 August 1968: Day 15: Robert Fuest

Main: 08.35-17.20: ABPC Elstree Studios, Stage 5 [Int: Villain's headquarters]

Monday 19 August 1968: Day 16: Robert Fuest

Main: 08.35-17.20: ABPC Elstree Studios, Stage 5 [Int: Villain's headquarters]

Tuesday 20 August 1968: Day 17: Robert Fuest

Main: 08.35-17.35: ABPC Elstree Studios, Stage 5 [Int: Villain's headquarters/seedy hotel room/dusty hotel room]

Wednesday 21 August 1968: Day 18: Robert Fuest

A Unit: 08.35 to unknown time: ABPC Elstree Studios, Stage 5 [Int: Dingy hotel room/dusty hotel room/fusty hotel room]

Main: Unknown time to 17.20: ABPC Elstree Studios, Stage 9 [Int: Conference room]

Thursday 22 August 1968: Day 19: Robert Fuest

A Unit: 08.35-17.20: ABPC Elstree Studios, Stage 9 [Int: Conference room/entrance foyer/palace]

Friday 23 August 1968: Day 20: Robert Fuest

A Unit: 08.35-17.20: ABPC Elstree Studios, Stage 9 [Int: Conference foom/entrance foyer/palace/side room/second side room]

Monday 26 August 1968: Day 21: Robert Fuest

A Unit: 08.35-17.35: ABPC Elstree Studios, Stage 5 [Int: Tara's room/Arcos' taxi/Nadine's room/Ext: Earthworks]

Quarter called pm

Tuesday 27 August 1968: Day 22: Robert Fuest/John Hough

A Unit: 08.35-17.15: ABPC Elstree Studios, Stage 5 [Int: Tara's room/Nadine's room/ Mother's underwater base/hotel corridor/Triumph 2000 conference car]

B Unit: 08.20 to unknown time: Drayton Road, Borehamwood, Herts [Ext: House exteriors]

B Unit: Unknown time to 17.00: ABPC Elstree Studios, Studio Backlot [Ext: Conference centre/earthworks]

Wednesday 28 August 1968: Day 23: John Hough

A Unit: 08.35 to unknown time: ABPC Elstree Studios, Stage 5 [Int: Nadine's room/hotel foyer/Baron Von Curt's car]

A Unit: Unknown time to 17.20: ABPC Elstree Studios, Studio Backlot [Ext: Bridge and country road]

Thursday 29 August 1968: Day 24: John Hough

A Unit: 10.00 to unknown time: ABPC Elstree Studios, Stage 5 [Int: Earthworks]

A Unit: Unknown time to 11.40: ABPC Elstree Studios, Studio Backlot [Ext: Earthworks]
Thursday 19 September 1968: Day 25: John Hough
3rd: 08.40-17.20: ABPC Elstree Studios, Stage 9 [Int: Villain's headquarters/conference centre – inserts for Scenes 23, 25, 28, 42, 86, 102, 110, 117, 128 and 138]
Friday 20 September 1968: Day 26: Robert Fuest
B Unit: 09.00-15.40: ABPC Elstree Studios, Studio Backlot Tank {Ext: Open water]

6.18 – 'WISH YOU WERE HERE'
Episode 146
Original Transmission Date: Wednesday 12 February 1969

Writer: Tony Williamson
Director: Don Chaffey
Cast: Patrick Macnee (John Steed), Linda Thorson (Tara King), Liam Redmond (Charles Merrydale), Robert Urquhart (Maxwell), Brook William (Basil), Dudley Foster (Parker), Patrick Newell (Mother), Gary Watson (Kendrick), Richard Caldicot (Mellor), Derek Newark (Vickers), David Garth (Brevitt), Louise Pajo (Miss Craven), John Cazabon (Mr Marple), Sandra Fehr (Attractive Girl).
Uncredited Cast: Rhonda Parker (Rhonda), Paddy Smith (Waiter), Martin Lyder (Waiter), Victor Harrington (Guest), Cyd Child (Stunt Double for Tara King), Arthur Howell (Stunt Double for Maxwell), Cliff Diggins (Stunt Double for Parker), Billy Dean (Stunt Double for Vickers), Dorothy Ford (Stunt Double for Miss Craven), Arthur Howell (Stunt Double for Maxwell), Joe Dunne (Stunt Double for Porter A), Paddy Ryan (Stunt Double for Charles Merrydale).
Crew: Laurie Johnson (Music Supervision by), Howard Blake (Additional Music by), Terry Nation (Script Editor), Alan Hume BSC (Director of Photography), Karen Heward (Editor), Ann Chegwidden (Post Production Co-ordinator) Alun Hughes (Miss Thorson's Costumes Designed by), Ron Purdie (Assistant Director), Norman Jones (Camera Operator), Richard Harrison and Kenneth Tait (Associate Art Directors), Simon Wakefield (Set Dresser), Kay Perkins (Continuity), Betty Sherriff (Hairdressing), Felix Evans (Wardrobe), Sid Rider (Sound Recordist), Len Abbott (Dubbing Mixer), Peter Lennard (Sound Editor), Paul Clay (Music Editor), Len Dunstan (Construction Manager), Roy Bond (Supervisory Electrician).
Uncredited Crew: A Fordyce (Hairdresser).

Production Schedule:
Wednesday 21 August 1968: Day 1: Don Chaffey
B Unit: 08.45 to unknown time: Clarendon Road, Watford, Herts [Ext: Office block]
B Unit: Unknown time to 15.30: Edgewarebury Hotel, Edgewarebury Lane, Elstree, Herts [Ext: The Elizabethan Hotel]
Thursday 22 August 1968: Day 2: Don Chaffey
B Unit: 08.35-17.28: ABPC Elstree Studios, Stage 3 [Int: Hotel composite]
Friday 23 August 1968: Day 3: Don Chaffey
B Unit: 08.35-17.15: ABPC Elstree Studios, Stage 3 [Int: Hotel composite/Parker's office]
Monday 26 August 1968: Day 4: Don Chaffey
B Unit: 08.45-18.15: Edgewarebury Hotel, Edgewarebury Lane, Elstree, Herts [Ext: The Elizabethan Hotel and country road]
Wednesday 28 August 1968: Day 5: Don Chaffey

B Unit: 08.45-17.25: ABPC Elstree Studios, Stage 9 [Int: Mother's room]
A 20 minute delay caused by camera problems.
Thursday 29 August 1968: Day 6: Don Chaffey
B Unit: 08.35-17.20: ABPC Elstree Studios, Stage 9 [Int: Mother's room/Steed's apartment/outer office]
Friday 30 August 1968: Day 7: Don Chaffey
B Unit: 08.35 to unknown time: ABPC Elstree Studios, Studio Backlot [Ext: Country road A]
B Unit: Unknown time: ABPC Elstree Studios, Studio Lot [Int: Steed's car]
B Unit: Unknown time: ABPC Elstree Studios, Stage 9 [Int: Outer office]
B Unit: Unknown time to 17.20: ABPC Elstree Studios, Stage 3 [Int: Hotel composite/Charles' room]
Tuesday 3 September 1968: Day 8: Don Chaffey
B Unit: 08.35 to unknown time: Edgewarebury Hotel, Edgewarebury Lane, Elstree, Herts [Ext: The Elizabethan Hotel]
B Unit: Unknown time to 17.20: ABPC Elstree Studios, Stage 3 [Int: Charles' room]
Wednesday 4 September 1968: Day 9: Don Chaffey
B Unit: 08.35-17.25: ABPC Elstree Studios, Stage 3 [Int: Charles' room/outside kitchen door/kitchen]
Quarter called pm
Thursday 5 September 1968: Day 10: Don Chaffey
B Unit: 08.35-17.20: ABPC Elstree Studios, Stage 3 [Int: Kitchen/hotel composite]
Friday 6 September 1968: Day 11: Don Chaffey
B Unit: 08.35-17.20: ABPC Elstree Studios, Stage 3 [Int: Hotel composite]
Monday 9 September 1968: Day 12: Don Chaffey
B Unit: 08.35-17.20: ABPC Elstree Studios, Stage 3 [Int: Hotel composite]
Tuesday 10 September 1968: Day 13: Don Chaffey
B Unit: 08.40-17.30: ABPC Elstree Studios, Stage 3 [Int: Hotel composite/Tara's room]
Quarter called pm
Wednesday 11 September 1968: Day 14: Don Chaffey
B Unit: 08.35-17.20: ABPC Elstree Studios, Stage 3 [Int: Hotel composite/Tara's room/corridor/hotel games area]
Thursday 12 September 1968: Day 15: Don Chaffey
B Unit: 08.35-16.40: ABPC Elstree Studios, Stage 3 [Int: Brevitt's room/basement and laundry chute]

6.19 – 'KILLER'
Episode 147
Original Transmission Date: Wednesday 22 January 1969

Writer: Tony Williamson
Director: Cliff Owen
Cast: Patrick Macnee (John Steed), Linda Thorson (Tara King), Jennifer Croxton (Lady Diana Forbes-Blakeney), Grant Taylor (Merridon), William Franklyn (Brinstead), Richard Wattis (Clarke), Patrick Newell (Mother), Harry Towb (Paxton), John Bailey (Ralph Bleech), Michael Ward (Freddie), James Bree (Wilkington), Michael McStay (Trancer), Anthony Valentine (Calvin), Charles Houston (Gillars), Jonathan Elsom (Chattell), Clive Graham (Lawson), Oliver MacGreevey (Barman).

Uncredited Cast: Rhonda Parker (Rhonda), Cliff Diggins (Stunt Double for Trancer), Paul Weston (Stunt Double for John Steed), Alf Joint (Stunt Double for Paxton), Alf Joint (Stunt Double for Lawson), Joe Dunne (Stunt Double for Trancer), Alf Joint (Stunt Double for Brinstead), Les White (Stunt Double for Merridon), Paul Weston (Stunt Double for Trancer), Cyd Child (Stunt Double for Lady Diana Forbes-Blakeney), Joe Dunne (Stunt Double for Ralph Bleech).

Crew: Laurie Johnson (Music by), Terry Nation (Script Editor), Peter Jessop (Director of Photography), Ann Chegwidden (Post Production Co-ordinator), Alun Hughes (Miss Thorson's Costumes Designed by), Ted Lewis (Assistant Director), Ernie Robinson (Camera Operator), Len Townsend and Kenneth Tait (Associate Art Directors), Simon Wakefield (Set Dresser), Mary Spain (Continuity), Mary Sturgess (Hairdressing), Felix Evans (Wardrobe), Cecil Mason (Sound Recordist), Len Abbott (Dubbing Mixer), Bob Dearberg (Sound Editor), Paul Clay (Music Editor), Len Dunstan (Construction Manager), Steve Birtles (Supervisory Electrician).

Uncredited Crew: Keith Batten (Boom Operator), Kay Perkins (Continuity), Betty Sherriff (Hairdresser), B Daly (Make-Up), A Fordyce (Hairdresser), Geoff Seaholme (Camera Operator), Ann Besserman (Continuity), Terry Allen (Boom Operator), F A Smith (Make-Up), Julian White (Clapper Loader), Peter Plumstead (Unit Runner), Derek Gibson (Second Assistant Director), S Valentine (Production Buyer), Ivy Baker (Wardrobe), C Sharp (Make-Up), Peggy Spirito (Post Production/Continuity), Malcolm Vinson (Focus Puller), P Nash (Camera Operator), Jackie Green (Assistant Director/Third Assistant Director), Geoff Glover (Focus Puller), S Allen (Clapper Loader), T Garnett (Focus Puller), P Taylor (Clapper Loader), F Gell (Focus Puller), Michael Proudfoot (Clapper Loader).

Production Schedule:
Thursday 29 August 1968: Day 1: Cliff Owen
A Unit: 13.15-18.45: Duchess Mews, London, W1 [Ext: Steed's mews]
Friday 30 August 1968: Day 2: Cliff Owen
A Unit: 10.00 to unknown time: The Haberdashers' Aske's School, Aldenham Road, Elstree, Herts [Ext: Factory]
A Unit: Unknown time: Letchmore Lodge, Aldenham Road, Elstree, Herts [Ext: Wilkinton's home]
A Unit: Unknown time to 18.15: Aldenham Estate, Elstree, Herts [Ext: Helicopter in flight]
Tuesday 3 September 1968: Day 3: Cliff Owen
A Unit: 08.35-17.25: ABPC Elstree Studios, Studio Backlot [Ext: Cemetery}
Quarter called pm
Wednesday 4 September 1968: Day 4: Cliff Owen
A Unit: 08.35 to unknown time: ABPC Elstree Studios, Studio Backlot [Ext: Cemetery]
A Unit: Unknown time to 17.30: ABPC Elstree Studios, Studio Backlot Town [Ext: Deserted film set]
Quarter called pm
Thursday 5 September 1968: Day 5: Cliff Owen
A Unit: 08.35 to unknown time: ABPC Elstree Studios, Studio Backlot Town [Ext: Deserted film set]
A Unit: Unknown time to 17.20: ABPC Elstree Studios, Studio Backlot [Ext: Trees]
Friday 6 September 1968: Day 6: Cliff Owen

A Unit: 12.15-18.00: The Crown Public House, Crown Lane, East Burnham, Bucks [Ext: The Pirate at Lower Storpington]
Saturday 7 September 1968: Day 7: Cliff Owen
A Unit: 09.30-17.15: Burnham Beeches, Burnham, Bucks [Ext: Woods]
Sunday 8 September 1968: Day 8: Cliff Owen
A Unit: 09.50-17.20: ABPC Elstree Studios, Stage 9 [Int: Steed's apartment]
Monday 9 September 1968: Day 9: Cliff Owen
A Unit: 09.50-17.30: ABPC Elstree Studios, Stage 9 [Int: Mother's headquarters]
Quarter called pm
Tuesday 10 September 1968: Day 10: Cliff Owen
A Unit: 09.15 to unknown time: ABPC Elstree Studios, Stage 9 [Int: Mother's headquarters]
A Unit: Unknown time to 17.55: ABPC Elstree Studios, Stage 5 [Int: Fancy Frills Limited]
Quarter called pm
Wednesday 11 September 1968: Day 11: Cliff Owen
A Unit: 09.05-17.26: ABPC Elstree Studios, Stage 5 [Int: Fancy Frills Limited/The Pirate public house]
Thursday 12 September 1968: Day 12: Cliff Owen
A Unit: 08.35-20.20: ABPC Elstree Studios, Stage 5 [Int: Factory reception area/ factory room one/foyer and factory room two]
Friday 13 September 1968: Day 13: Cliff Owen
A Unit: 09.05-17.20: ABPC Elstree Studios, Stage 5 [Int: Foyer and factory room two/ foyer and factory room three/factory room four/tunnel area and processing room/Remak control room]
Monday 16 September 1968: Day 14: Cliff Owen
A Unit: 08.35 to unknown time: ABPC Elstree Studios, Stage 9 [Int: Mother's headquarters]
A Unit: Unknown time to 17.20: ABPC Elstree Studios, Stage 5 [Int: Factory reception area]
Tuesday 17 September 1968: Day 15: Cliff Owen
A Unit: 08.35-17.35: ABPC Elstree Studios, Stage 5 [Int: Factory reception area]
Quarter called pm
Wednesday 18 September 1968: Day 16: Cliff Owen
A Unit: 08.35-17.20: ABPC Elstree Studios, Stage 5 [Int: Factory reception area/The Pirate public house/Ext: The Pirate public house window section]
Scenes 9, 11 and 12 deleted
Thursday 19 September 1968: Day 17: Cliff Owen/John Hough
A Unit: 09.10 to unknown time: The Haberdashers' Aske's School, Aldenham Road, Elstree, Herts [Ext: Factory and gates]
A Unit: Unknown time to 17.20: Dagger Lane, Elstree, Herts [Ext: Trancer escapes in van]
3rd: 08.40-17.20: ABPC Elstree Studios, Stage 9 [Int: Steed's apartment/Merridon's car – inserts for Scenes 4N and 95]
Friday 20 September 1968: Day 18: Cliff Owen
A Unit: 08.35-17.35: ABPC Elstree Studios, Stage 5 [Int: Merridon's car/factory reception area/Remak control room/factory room one]
Monday 23 September 1968: Day 19: Cliff Owen

A Unit: 08.30-17.35: ABPC Elstree Studios, Stage 5 [Int: Tunnel area and processing room/factory room one and two composite]
Quarter called pm
Tuesday 24 September 1968: Day 20: Cliff Owen
A Unit: 08.40 to unknown time: ABPC Elstree Studios, Stage 5 [Int: Wilkington's study]
A Unit: Unknown time to 17.35: ABPC Elstree Studios, Studio Backlot Town [Ext: Deserted film set]
Quarter called pm
Wednesday 25 September 1968: Day 21: Cliff Owen
A Unit: 09.30-17.30: Burnham Beeches, Burnham, Bucks [Ext: Woods/country road B]
Thursday 26 September 1968: Day 22: Cliff Owen
A Unit: 10.30-16.45: Burnham Beeches, Burnham, Bucks [Ext: Woods]
Friday 27 September 1968: Day 23: Cliff Owen
A Unit: 09.40 to unknown time: Burnham Beeches, Burnham, Bucks [Ext: Woods/country roads A and B]
A Unit: Unknown time to 18.30: Silver Hill, Shenley, Herts [Ext: Diana in her MGC follows coach]
Wednesday 9 October 1968: Day 24: Cliff Owen
B Unit: 09.45 to unknown time: Location Unknown [Ext: Inserts]
B Unit: Unknown time: ABPC Elstree Studios, Studio Lot [Int: Inserts]
B Unit: Unknown time to 17.16: ABPC Elstree Studios, Stage 9 [Int: Inserts]
Inserts for the following scenes were filmed today: 4, 4F, 4G, 19, 52, 55, 74, 84 and 93
Monday 14 October 1968: Day 25: Charles Crichton
A Unit: Unknown time: ABPC Elstree Studios, Stage 5 [Int: Mother's headquarters – insert]

6.20 – 'THE ROTTERS'
Episode 148
Original Transmission Date: Wednesday 8 January 1969

Writer: Dave Freeman
Director: Robert Fuest
Cast: Patrick Macnee (John Steed), Linda Thorson (Tara King), Gerald Sim (Kenneth), Jerome Willis (George), Eric Barker (Reginald Pym), John Nettleton (Professor Palmer), Patrick Newell (Mother), Frank Middlemass (Mervyn Sawbow), Dervis Ward (Sandford), Harold Innocent (Parbury), Toni Gilpin (Sonia), Amy Dalby (Mrs Forsythe), John Stone (Victor Forsythe), Charles Morgan (Wainwright), Harry Hutchinson (Manservant), Noel Davis (Carter), John Scott (Jackson).
Uncredited Cast: Rhonda Parker (Rhonda), Garry Marsh (Sir James Pendred), Cyd Child (Stunt Double for Tara King), Rocky Taylor (Stunt Double for Mervyn Sawbow), Alf Joint (Stunt Double for Sandford), Gerry Crampton (Stunt Double for Professor Palmer), Fred Haggerty (Stunt Double for George), Paul Weston (Stunt Double for John Steed), Arthur Howell (Stunt Double for Wainwright), Fred Haggerty (Stunt Double for Jackson), Gerry Crampton (Stunt Double for Kenneth), Jenny LeFre (Stunt Double for Sonia), Alf Joint (Stunt Double for Sandford), Alf Joint (Stunt Double for Parbury), Terry Maidment (Stunt Double for Kenneth).
Crew: Laurie Johnson (Music by), Terry Nation (Script Editor), Alan Hume BSC (Director of Photography), Manuel del Campo (Editor), Ann Chegwidden (Post

Production Co-ordinator) Alun Hughes (Miss Thorson's Costumes Designed by), Ron Purdie (Assistant Director), Geoff Seaholme (Camera Operator), Richard Harrison and Kenneth Tait (Associate Art Directors), Simon Wakefield (Set Dresser), Kay Perkins (Continuity), Mary Sturgess (Hairdressing), Ivy Baker (Wardrobe), Bob Thompson (Second Unit Photography), Dennis Whitlock (Sound Recordist), Len Abbott (Dubbing Mixer), Peter Lennard (Sound Editor), Paul Clay (Music Editor), Len Dunstan (Construction Manager), Roy Bond (Supervisory Electrician).
Uncredited Crew: Jackie Green (Third Assistant Director), B Royston (Make-Up), Geoff Glover (Focus Puller).

Production Schedule:
Friday 13 September 1968: Day 1: Robert Fuest
B Unit: 08.45 to unknown time: Unknown Location [Ext: Department of Forestry Research]
B Unit: Unknown time: Hatfield London Country Club, Bedwell Park, Essendon, Herts [Ext: Wainwright Timber Industries]
B Unit: Unknown time to 17.05: Unknown Location [Ext: Thatched cottage]
Monday 16 September 1968: Day 2: Robert Fuest
B Unit: 09.20 to unknown time: Bell Moor, East Heath Road, London, NW3 [Ext: Block of flats]
B Unit: Unknown time: St Andrew's Church, Church Road, Little Berkhamstead, Herts [Ext: Country church]
B Unit: Unknown time to 18.30: Unknown Location [Ext: Steed's Rolls Royce – country road A]
Tuesday 17 September 1968: Day 3: Robert Fuest
B Unit: 10.50 to unknown time: Common Lane, Burnham, Bucks [Ext: Wooded country road]
B Unit: Unknown time to 18.30: Littleworth Common, Burnham, Bucks [Ext: Woods and wooden hut]
Wednesday 18 September 1968: Day 4: Robert Fuest
B Unit: 09.45-17.45: Littleworth Common, Burnham, Bucks [Ext: Woods and wooden hut]
Thursday 19 September 1968: Day 5: Robert Fuest
B Unit: 09.30 to unknown time: Littleworth Common, Burnham, Bucks [Ext: Woods and wooden hut]
B Unit: Unknown time to 18.25: Stoney Lane/East Burnham Lane, Burnham, Bucks [Ext: Road junction]
Monday 23 September 1968: Day 6: Robert Fuest
B Unit: 08.55-17.10: ABPC Elstree Studios, Studio Backlot [Ext: Institute of Timber Technology]
Tuesday 24 September 1968: Day 7: Robert Fuest
B Unit: 08.35-17.30: ABPC Elstree Studios, Stage 9 [Int: Pendred's apartment and front door]
Wednesday 25 September 1968: Day 8: Robert Fuest
B Unit: 08.40 to unknown time: ABPC Elstree Studios, Stage 9 [Int: Pendred's apartment and front door]
B Unit: Unknown time to 17.28: ABPC Elstree Studios, Stage 3 [Int: Laboratory at Wainwright Timber Industries]

Thursday 26 September 1968: Day 9: Robert Fuest
B Unit: 08.38-17.35: ABPC Elstree Studios, Stage 3 [Int: Laboratory at Wainwright Timber Industries/hallway at Wainwright Timber Industries]
Quarter called pm
Friday 27 September 1968: Day 10: Robert Fuest
B Unit: 09.15 to unknown time: Devonshire Mews South, London, W1 [Ext: Sawbow's mews]
B Unit: Unknown time to 17.15: ABPC Elstree Studios, Stage 3 [Int: Hallway at Wainwright Timber Industries/Ext: Road junction]
Monday 30 September 1968: Day 11: Robert Fuest
B Unit: Unknown time: Burnham Beeches, Burnham, Bucks [Ext: Woods and country road]
Tuesday 1 October 1968: Day 12: Robert Fuest
B Unit: 08.40 to unknown time: ABPC Elstree Studios, Stage 3 [Int: Laboratory at Wainwright Timber Industries/Mother's plastic furniture room/Steed's car/Ext: Church belfrey]
B Unit: Unknown time to 20.20: ABPC Elstree Studios, Stage 9 [Int: Steed's apartment]
Wednesday 2 October 1968: Day 13: Robert Fuest
B Unit: 08.40-16.30: ABPC Elstree Studios, Stage 9 [Int: Steed's apartment]
Thursday 3 October 1968: Day 14: Robert Fuest
B Unit: 08.35-17.17: ABPC Elstree Studios, Stage 9 [Int: Steed's apartment/Sawbow's workshop/Department of Forestry Research corridor/Pendred's office]
Friday 4 October 1968: Day 15: Robert Fuest
B Unit: 08.33 to unknown time: ABPC Elstree Studios, Stage 9 [Int: Pendred's office]
B Unit: Unknown time to 17.15: ABPC Elstree Studios, Stage 3 [Ext: French windows/Int: Sitting room]
Monday 7 October 1968: Day 16: Robert Fuest
B Unit: 08.35-17.20: ABPC Elstree Studios, Stage 3 [Int: Sitting room/Church belfrey]
Tuesday 8 October 1968: Day 17: Robert Fuest
B Unit: 08.35-16.35: ABPC Elstree Studios, Stage 3 [Int: Church belfrey/belfrey tower/Pendred's apartment/Pendred's office/Wainwright Timber Industries entrance hall/Ext: Road junction]
Tuesday 22 October 1968: Day 18: Charles Crichton
A Unit: Unknown time: ABPC Elstree Studios, Stage 5 [Int: Insert for Scene 23]

6.21 – 'THE INTERROGATORS'
Episode 149
Original Transmission Date: Wednesday 1 January 1969

Writers: Richard Harris and Brian Clemens
Director: Charles Crichton
Cast: Patrick Macnee (John Steed), Linda Thorson (Tara King), Christopher Lee (Colonel Mannering), David Sumner (Minnow), Philip Bond (Lieutenant Roy Casper), Patrick Newell (Mother), Glynn Edwards (Sergeant Blackie), Neil McCarthy (Rasker), Neil Stacey (Mullard), Neil Wilson (Norton), Cardew Robinson (Mr Puffin), Cecil Cheng (Captain Soo), Mark Elwes (Naval Officer), David Richards (RAF Officer).
Uncredited Cast: Rhonda Parker (Rhonda), Vincent Wong (Toy), Eric Chung (Ling Ho), Ken Jones (Fillington), Johnny Laycock (Izzy Pound), Guy Standeven (Forensics Man),

Maxwell Craig (Forensics Man), Paul Weston (Stunt Double for Minnow), Cyd Child (Stunt Double for Tara King), Alf Joint (Stunt Double for Sergeant Blackie), Frank Barringer (Stunt Double for Captain Soo), Paul Weston (Stunt Double for John Steed), Terry Richards (Stunt Double for Colonel Mannering), Frank Barringer (Stunt Double for Ling Ho), Joe Dunne (Stunt Double for Izzy Pound).

Crew: Laurie Johnson (Music Supervision by), Howard Blake (Score by), Terry Nation (Script Editor), Peter Jessop (Director of Photography), Karen Heward (Editor), Ann Chegwidden (Post Production Co-ordinator) Alun Hughes (Miss Thorson's Costumes Designed by), Ted Lewis (Assistant Director), Ernie Robinson (Camera Operator), Len Townsend and Kenneth Tait (Associate Art Directors), Simon Wakefield (Set Dresser), Mary Spain (Continuity), Mary Sturgess (Hairdressing), Ivy Baker (Wardrobe), David Holmes (Second Unit Photography), Sash Fisher (Sound Recordist), Len Abbott (Dubbing Mixer), Bob Dearberg (Sound Editor), Paul Clay (Music Editor), Len Dunstan (Construction Manager), Steve Birtles (Supervisory Electrician).

Uncredited Crew: Basil Newall (Make-Up), M Wharlow (Nurse), Jackie Green (Third Assistant Director/Unit Runner), F Adair (Make-Up), F Smith (Make-Up), Peggy Spirito (Post Production), P Taylor (Clapper Loader), F Gell (Focus Puller), Sash Fisher (Sound Mixer), P Nash (Camera Operator), J Hutchins (Footsteps), B Harris (Focus Puller), R Clarke (Make-Up), Cecil Mason (Sound Recordist).

Production Schedule:
Monday 30 September 1968: Day 1: No details available
Tuesday 1 October 1968: Day 2: Charles Crichton
A Unit: 09.15 to unknown time: Cavendish Place, London, NW3 [Ext: Street with telephone box/Int: Casper's car]
A Unit: Unknown time to 17.20: Farm Court, Watford Way, Hendon, London, NW4 [Ext: Casper's apartment block]
Wednesday 2 October 1968: Day 3: Charles Crichton
A Unit: 08.40-17.20: ABPC Elstree Studios, Stage 5 [Int: Interrogation room]
Thursday 3 October 1968: Day 4: Charles Crichton
A Unit: 10.25 to unknown time: ABPC Elstree Studios, Stage 5 [Int: Interrogation room]
A Unit: Unknown time to 17.35: ABPC Elstree Studios, Stage 3 [Int: Tara's apartment]
Quarter called pm.
Friday 4 October 1968: Day 5: Charles Crichton
A Unit: 09.00 to unknown time: Sutherland Avenue, London, W9 [Ext: Minnow's apartment]
A Unit: Unknown time: Hampstead Heath, London, NW3 [Ext: Mr Puffin and Tara attacked by Blackie]
Monday 7 October 1968: Day 6: Charles Crichton
A Unit: 08.35-17.20: ABPC Elstree Studios, Stage 5 [Int: Interrogation room/reception/corridor]
Tuesday 8 October 1968: Day 7: Charles Crichton
A Unit: 08.35-17.20: ABPC Elstree Studios, Stage 5 [Int: Casper's apartment/Minnow's apartment]
Wednesday 9 October 1968: Day 8: Charles Crichton
A Unit: 08.35-12.10: ABPC Elstree Studios, Stage 3 [Int: Tara's apartment]
A Unit: Unknown time to 16.15: ABPC Elstree Studios, Stage 5 [Int: Bar]
Thursday 10 October 1968: Day 9: Charles Crichton

A Unit: 08.35-17.10: ABPC Elstree Studios, Stage 5 [Int: Bar/Mother's headquarters]
Friday 11 October 1968: Day 10: Charles Crichton
A Unit: 09.20-16.40: Springwell Chalk Pits, Springwell Lane, Harefield, Bucks [Ext: Quarry]
Monday 14 October 1968: Day 11: Charles Crichton
A Unit: 08.35-17.15: ABPC Elstree Studios, Stage 5 [Int: Mother's headquarters]
Scene 34 was shot at the director's request although it had been deleted from the shooting script.
Tuesday 15 October 1968: Day 12: Charles Crichton
A Unit: 08.35-17.15: ABPC Elstree Studios, Stage 5 [Int: Mother's headquarters]
Wednesday 16 October 1968: Day 13: Charles Crichton
A Unit: 08.35-17.10: ABPC Elstree Studios, Stage 5 [Int: Mother's headquarters/Steed's car/Casper's apartment and front door]
Thursday 17 October 1968: Day 14: Charles Crichton
A Unit: 08.35-17.35: ABPC Elstree Studios, Stage 5 [Int: Casper's apartment and front door/Minnow's apartment/interrogation room]
Quarter called pm
Friday 18 October 1968: Day 15: Charles Crichton
A Unit: 08.35-17.35: ABPC Elstree Studios, Stage 5 [Int: Bar/corridor/reception/interrogation room]
Quarter called pm
Monday 21 October 1968: Day 16: Charles Crichton
A Unit: 09.40 to unknown time: Unknown location – did not appear in episode [Ext: Street B]
A Unit: Unknown time: Aldenham Estate, Elstree, Herts [Ext: Field]
A Unit: Unknown time to 16.45: Brocket Hall, Marford Road, Lemsford, Welwyn Garden City, Herts [Ext: Country house and grounds/Int: Helicopter]
Tuesday 22 October 1968: Day 17: Charles Crichton
A Unit: 08.35-16.55: ABPC Elstree Studios, Stage 5 [Int: Reception/bar/interrogation room/Minnow's apartment/Casper's apartment]
Thursday 31 October 1968: Day 18: Peter Sykes
A Unit: Unknown time: ABPC Elstree Studios, Stage 3 [Int: Tara's apartment – insert for tag scene]

6.22 – 'THE MORNING AFTER'
Episode 150
Original Transmission Date: Wednesday 29 January 1969

Writer: Brian Clemens
Director: John Hough
Cast: Patrick Macnee (John Steed), Linda Thorson (Tara King), Peter Barkworth (Jimmy Merlin), Penelope Horner (Jenny), Joss Ackland (Brigadier Hansing), Brian Blessed (Sergeant Hearn), Donald Douglas (Major Parsons), Philip Dunbar (Yates), Jonathan Scott (Cartney).
Uncredited Cast: Nosher Powell (Guard), Fred Haggerty (Soldier), Frank Barringer (Soldier), Arthur Howell (Soldier), Bill Cummings (Soldier), Terry Richards (Soldier), Alf Joint (Soldier), Sadie Eddon (Stunt Double for Jenny), Paul Weston (Stunt Double for John Steed), Max Faulkner (Stunt Double for Jimmy Merlin), Gerry Crampton (Stunt Double for Major Parsons), Gillian Aldam (Stunt Double for Jenny), Alf Joint (Stunt

Double for Major Parsons), Terry Plummer (Stunt Double for Sergeant Hearn), Cyd Child (Stunt Double for Tara King), Gerry Crampton (Stunt Double for Brigadier Hansing), Terry Plummer (Stunt Double for Soldier), Terry Richards (Stunt Double for Soldier).

Crew: Laurie Johnson (Music by), Terry Nation (Script Editor), H A R Thompson (Director of Photography), Manuel del Campo (Editor), Ann Chegwidden (Post Production Co-ordinator) Alun Hughes (Miss Thorson's Costumes Designed by), Ron Purdie (Assistant Director), Geoff Seaholme (Camera Operator), Len Townsend and Kenneth Tait (Associate Art Directors), Simon Wakefield (Set Dresser), Kay Perkins (Continuity), Mary Sturgess (Hairdressing), Ivy Baker (Wardrobe), Dennis Whitlock (Sound Recordist), Len Shilton (Dubbing Mixer), Peter Lennard (Sound Editor), Paul Clay (Music Editor), Len Dunstan (Construction Manager), Roy Bond (Supervisory Electrician).

Uncredited Crew: Sash Fisher (Sound Mixer), Ted Lewis (Assistant Director), Richard Bird (Sound Mixer), Peggy Spirito (Post Production), R Clark (Make-Up), Jackie Green (Assistant Director/Third Assistant Director), Brian Ellis (Focus Puller), D Worley (Clapper Loader), P Nash (Camera Operator), A Edwards (Continuity).

Production Schedule:
Thursday 10 October 1968: Day 1: John Hough
B Unit: 09.20 to unknown time: St Albans, Herts [Ext: Establishing shot of town]
B Unit: Unknown time: Fishpool Street, St Albans, Herts [Ext: Merlin hides in his Rover]
B Unit: Unknown time to 16.30: Keyfield Terrace/Sopwell Lane/Pageant Drive, St Albans, Herts [Ext: Two deserted cars on junction – deserted area]
Friday 11 October 1968: Day 2: John Hough
B Unit: 09.25 to unknown time: Queen Street, St Albans, Herts [Ext: Steed's Rolls Royce turns into narrow street – thoroughfare]
B Unit: Unknown time: Albert Street/Keyfield Terrace, St Albans, Herts [Ext: Street one]
B Unit: Unknown time: Spicer Street/George Street, St Albans, Herts [Ext: Public toilets]
B Unit: Unknown time: Fishpool Street, St Albans, Herts [Ext: Truck blocking road – street two]
B Unit: Unknown time to 16.40: Branch Road/Fishpool Street, St Albans, Herts [Ext: Junction – street four]
Monday 14 October 1968: Day 3: John Hough
B Unit: 09.00 to unknown time: Shakespeare Street/Milton Street, Watford, Herts [Ext: Street A]
B Unit: Unknown time: Portland Street, St Albans, Herts: [Ext: Steed and Merlin walk – street three]
B Unit: Unknown time: Sumpter Yard/Abbey Mill Lane, St Albans, Herts [Ext: Major Hearn and troops – street five]
B Unit: Unknown time: Thorpe Road, St Albans, Herts [Ext: Steed and Merlin walk – street six]
B Unit: Unknown time to 17.15: Welclose Street, St Albans [Ext: Cartney chased by troops/Ext: Street seven]
Tuesday 15 October 1968: Day 4: John Hough
B Unit: 09.15 to unknown time: Fore Street/Park Street/Salsbury Square, Old Hatfield, Herts [Ext: Steed and Merlin in Land Rover – deserted street]

B Unit: Unknown time to 16.15: Portland Street, St Albans, Herts: [Ext: Troops search – street three]

Wednesday 16 October 1968: Day 5: John Hough

B Unit: 09.10 to unknown time: Shakespeare Street/Milton Street, Watford, Herts [Ext: Street A]

B Unit: Unknown time to 16.27: Regents Park Barracks, Albany Street, London, NW1 [Ext: Commission building]

Thursday 17 October 1968: Day 6: John Hough

B Unit: 09.00 to unknown time: Garfield Street/Milton Street, Watford, Herts [Int: Telephone box/deserted street]

B Unit: Unknown time: Fishpool Street, St Albans, Herts [Ext: Truck blocking road – street two]

B Unit: Unknown time to 17.12: Albert Street, St Albans, Herts [Ext: Merlin offers Steed a bribe – street one]

Friday 18 October 1968: Day 7: John Hough

B Unit: 08.35-17.20: ABPC Elstree Studios, Studio Lot [Ext/Int: Garage]

Monday 21 October 1968: Day 8: John Hough

B Unit: 08.45 to unknown time: ABPC Elstree Studios, Backlot Town [Ext: Bank]

B Unit: Unknown time to 17.10: ABPC Elstree Studios, Studio Lot [Int: Garage]

Tuesday 22 October 1968: Day 9: John Hough

B Unit: 08.30 to unknown time: ABPC Elstree Studios, Backlot Town [Ext: Bank/bank doorway/Int: Bank]

B Unit: Unknown time to 17.02: ABPC Elstree Studios, Studio Lot [Ext: Car park/Int: Van]

Wednesday 23 October 1968: Day 10: John Hough

B Unit: 08.45-17.17: ABPC Elstree Studios, Stage 3 [Int: Bank/Ext: Bank doorway]

Thursday 24 October 1968: Day 11: John Hough

B Unit: 08.30-17.10: ABPC Elstree Studios, Studio Lot [Ext: Car park/Int: Van]

Friday 25 October 1968: Day 12: John Hough

B Unit: 09.20 to unknown time: Regents Park Barracks, Albany Street, London, NW1 [Ext: Commission building]

B Unit: Unknown time to 17.16: Copsewood Road/Stanmore Road, Watford, Herts [Ext: Troops search/TV van – side road/concealed area]

Monday 28 October 1968: Day 13: John Hough

B Unit: 08.50-17.32: ABPC Elstree Studios, Stage 9 [Int: Office]

Tuesday 29 October 1968: Day 14: John Hough

B Unit: 08.40-17.25: ABPC Elstree Studios, Stage 9 [Int: Office and corridor]

Quarter called pm.

Wednesday 30 October 1968: Day 15: John Hough

B Unit: 08.30-17.17: ABPC Elstree Studios, Stage 9 [Int: Office and corridor]

Thursday 31 October 1968: Day 16: John Hough

B Unit: 08.33-17.22: ABPC Elstree Studios, Stage 9 [Int: Office and corridor/Steed's apartment/cellar/van cab]

Friday 1 November 1968: Day 17: John Hough

B Unit: 08.45 to unknown time: ABPC Elstree Studios, Studio Lot [Ext: Section of streets two, three, four and five]

B Unit: Unknown time: ABPC Elstree Studios, Studio Lot [Ext: Brick wall]

B Unit: Unknown time to 17.20: ABPC Elstree Studios, Stage 9 [Int: Cellar]

Monday 4 November 1968: Day 18: John Hough
B Unit: 08.45 to unknown time: Portland Street, St Albans, Herts [Ext: Street three]
B Unit: Unknown time: Branch Road/Fishpool Street, St Albans, Herts [Ext: Junction – street four]
B Unit: Unknown time: Black Cut/Old London Road, St Albans, Herts [Ext: Volkswagen van – empty street]
B Unit: Unknown time to 17.20: ABPC Elstree Studios, Studio Lot [Ext: Brick wall]
Tuesday 5 November 1968: Day 19: John Hough
3rd: 09.12 to unknown time: ABPC Elstree Studios, Stage 3 [Int: Van cab/telephone box]
3rd: Unknown time to 16.04: ABPC Elstree Studios, Stage 9 [Int: Office and corridor/garage]
Monday 11 November 1968: Day 20: John Hough
3rd: 09.45-16.30: ABPC Elstree Studios, Studio Lot [Ext: Secret establishment area]

6.23 – 'LOVE ALL'
Episode 151
Original Transmission Date: Wednesday 19 February 1969

Writer: Jeremy Burnham
Director: Peter Sykes
Cast: Patrick Macnee (John Steed), Linda Thorson (Tara King),Veronica Strong (Martha Roberts), Terence Alexander (Nigel Bromfield), Robert Harris (Sir Rodney Kellogg), Patrick Newell (Mother), Patsy Rowlands (Thelma), Brian Oulton (Tait), Frank Gatliff (George Fryer), Ann Rye (Policewoman Grimshaw), Zulema Dene (Athene), Peter Stephens (Bellchamber), Norman Pitt (Basil Roxby), John Cobner (Security Man), Robin Tolhurst (Secretary), Larry Taylor (Freeman), David Baron (Metcalfe).
Uncredited Cast: Rhonda Parker (Rhonda), Paul Weston (Stunt Double for John Steed), Cyd Child (Stunt Double for Tara King), Fred Haggerty (Stunt Double for George Fryer), Romo Gorrara (Stunt Double for Nigel Bromfield).
Crew: Laurie Johnson (Music by), Terry Nation (Script Editor), David Holmes (Director of Photography), Karen Heward (Editor), Ann Chegwidden (Post Production Co-ordinator) Alun Hughes (Miss Thorson's Costumes Designed by), Ted Lewis (Assistant Director), Ernie Robinson (Camera Operator), Len Townsend and Kenneth Tait (Associate Art Directors), Simon Wakefield (Set Dresser), Mary Spain (Continuity), Pat McDermott (Hairdressing), Ivy Baker (Wardrobe), Cecil Mason (Sound Recordist), Len Abbott (Dubbing Mixer), Bob Dearberg (Sound Editor), Paul Clay (Music Editor), Len Dunstan (Construction Manager), Steve Birtles (Supervisory Electrician).
Uncredited Crew: Jackie Green (Assistant Director), R Clark (Make-Up), Peggy Spirito (Post Production), Kay Perkins (Continuity), D Martin (Hairdresser), P Nash (Camera Operator), J Stillwell (Focus Puller), Godfrey Godar (Camera Operator), D Worley (Clapper Loader), Lillian Lee (Continuity), B Knott (Boom Operator), Brian Ellis (Focus Puller).

Production Schedule:
Friday 25 October 1968: Day 1: Peter Sykes
A Unit: 09.40 to unknown time: Osnaburgh Street, London, NW1 [Ext: Casanova Ink]
A Unit: Unknown time to 17.00: Grosvenor Road, Borehamwood, Herts [Ext: Entrance to Mother's headquarters]

Monday 28 October 1968: Day 2: Peter Sykes
A Unit: 09.30 to unknown time: Chalcott Crescent, London, NW1 [Ext: Tara's apartment]
A Unit: Unknown time to 16.00: Watford Town Hall, Rickmansworth Road, Watford, Herts [Ext: Ministry building]
Tuesday 29 October 1968: Day 3: Peter Sykes
A Unit: 08.45 to unknown time: Grosvenor Street, London, W1 [Ext: Bellchamber Brothers]
A Unit: Unknown time to 16.45: Sutherland Avenue, London, W9 [Ext: Street B/Int: Broomfield's car]
Wednesday 30 October 1968: Day 4: Peter Sykes
A Unit: 09.30-17.05: Sutherland Avenue, London, W9 [Ext: Martha's front door/street B/quiet street/Int: Sir Rodney's car/Bloomfield's car]
Thursday 31 October 1968: Day 5: Peter Sykes
A Unit: 09.15 to unknown time: Sutherland Avenue, London, W9 [Ext: Quiet street/Int: Sir Rodney's car]
A Unit: Unknown time to 17.10: Watford Town Hall, Rickmansworth Road, Watford, Herts [Ext: Ministry building]
Friday 1 November 1968: Day 6: Peter Sykes
A Unit: 08.35 to unknown time: ABPC Elstree Studios, Stage 3 [Int: Tara's partment]
A Unit: Unknown time to 17.10: ABPC Elstree Studios, Stage 5 [Int: Tait's office]
Monday 4 November 1968: Day 7: Peter Sykes
A Unit: 09.20 to unknown time: Sutherland Avenue, London, W9 [Ext: Quiet street/Int: Sir Rodney's car]
A Unit: Unknown time: Osnaburgh Street, London, NW1 [Ext: Casanova Ink]
A Unit: Unknown time: ABPC Elstree Studios, Stage 3 [Ext: Window of Casanova Ink]
A Unit: Unknown time to 17.20: ABPC Elstree Studios, Stage 5 [Int: Mother's headquarters]
Tuesday 5 November 1968: Day 8: Peter Sykes
A Unit: 08.45 to unknown time: ABPC Elstree Studios, Stage 9 [Int: Steed's apartment]
A Unit: Unknown time to 17.20: ABPC Elstree Studios, Stage 5 [Int: Mother's headquarters]
Wednesday 6 November 1968: Day 9: Peter Sykes
A Unit: 08.35 to unknown time: ABPC Elstree Studios, Stage 9 [Int: Steed's apartment]
A Unit: Unknown time to 17.35: ABPC Elstree Studios, Stage 5 [Int: Mother's headquarters]
Thursday 7 November 1968: Day 10: Peter Sykes
A Unit: 08.35-17.35: ABPC Elstree Studios, Stage 5 [Int: Mother's headquarters/Casanova Ink office]
Friday 8 November 1968: Day 11: Peter Sykes
A Unit: 08.35-17.35: ABPC Elstree Studios, Stage 5 [Int: Bellchamber Brothers/Ministry corridor/Tait's office]
Quarter called pm
Monday 11 November 1968: Day 12: Peter Sykes
A Unit: 08.35-17.35: ABPC Elstree Studios, Stage 5 [Int: Casanova Ink office]
Quarter called pm
Tuesday 12 November 1968: Day 13: Peter Sykes
A Unit: 08.55-17.20: ABPC Elstree Studios, Stage 5 [Int: Tait's office/Casanova Ink

office/Corridor outside Casanova Ink office]
Wednesday 13 November 1968: Day 14: Peter Sykes/John Hough
A Unit: 08.45-16.50: ABPC Elstree Studios, Stage 5 [Int: Tait's office/Casanova Ink office/corridor outside Casanova Ink pffice/printing room/Sir Rodney's office]
3rd: Unknown time: ABPC Elstree Studios, Stage 5 [Int: Inserts for Scenes 39, 47, 54, 63, 81, 91 and 95]
Thursday 14 November 1968: Day 15: Peter Sykes
A Unit: 08.55-17.35: ABPC Elstree Studios, Stage 5 [Int: Sir Rodney's office/Ministry corridor]
Friday 15 November 1968: Day 16: Peter Sykes
A Unit: 08.35-16.40: ABPC Elstree Studios, Stage 5 [Int: Ministry corridor/Fryer's office/Casanova Ink office/Ministry corridor with telephone]
Monday 18 November 1968: Day 17: Peter Sykes
A Unit: 08.45-14.00: ABPC Elstree Studios, Stage 5 [Int: Casanova Ink office/Roxby's office]
Friday 22 November 1968: Day 18: Don Chaffey
A Unit: Unknown time: ABPC Elstree Studios, Stage 3 [Int: Insert for Scene 81]

6.24 – 'TAKE ME TO YOUR LEADER'
Episode 152
Original Transmission Date: Wednesday 5 March 1969

Writer: Terry Nation
Director: Robert Fuest
Cast: Patrick Macnee (John Steed), Linda Thorson (Tara King), Patrick Barr (Colonel Stonehouse), Patrick Newell (Mother), John Ronane (Captain Tim), Michael Robbins (Cavell), Henry Stamper (Major Glasgow), Penelope Keith (Audrey Long), Hugh Cross (Captain Andrews), Elisabeth Robillard (Sally Graham), Michael Hawkins (Shepherd), Sheila Hammond (Ministry Doctor), Bryan Kendrick (Phillipson/Scarecrow), Raymond Adamson (Condon), Mathew Long (Holland), Cliff Diggins (Howard Trent), Wilfred Boyle (Vicar).
Uncredited Cast: Rhonda Parker (Rhonda), Nosher Powell (Martial Artist), Terry Plummer (Martial Artist), Alf Joint (Martial Artist), Joe Cornelius (Martial Artist), Rupert Evans (Jackson), Mary Burleigh (Little Girl), Joe Dunne (Stunt Double for Phillipson/Scarecrow), Alf Joint (Stunt Double for John Steed), Cyd Child (Stunt Double for Tara King), Paddy Ryan (Stunt Double for Cavell), Gerry Crampton (Stunt Double for Captain Tim), Paul Weston (Stunt Double for John Steed), Alf Joint (Stunt Double for Colonel Stonehouse), Gillian Aldam (Stunt Double for Audrey Long), Gerry Crampton (Stunt Double for Shepherd).
Crew: Laurie Johnson (Music Supervision by), Howard Blake (Score by) Terry Nation (Script Editor), H A R Thompson (Director of Photography), Ann Chegwidden (Post Production Co-ordinator) Alun Hughes (Miss Thorson's Costumes Designed by), Ron Purdie (Assistant Director), Geoff Seaholme (Camera Operator), Len Townsend and Kenneth Tait (Associate Art Directors), Simon Wakefield (Set Dresser), Kay Perkins (Continuity), Mary Sturgess (Hairdressing), Ivy Baker (Costume Supervisor), David Holmes (Second Unit Photography), Bill Rowe (Sound Recordist), Len Shilton (Dubbing Mixer), Peter Lennard (Sound Editor), Paul Clay (Music Editor), Herbert Worley (Construction Manager), Roy Bond (Supervisory Electrician).

Uncredited Crew: Jackie Green (Unit Runner), B Clarke (Make-Up), D Martin (Hairdresser), Terry Cole (Focus Puller), Godfrey Godar (Camera Operator), Peggy Spirito (Post Production/Continuity).

Production Schedule:
Tuesday 5 November 1968: Day 1: Robert Fuest
B Unit: 09.10-16.40: RAF Bovingdon, Chesham Road, Bovingdon, Herts [Ext: Deserted airfield]
Wednesday 6 November 1968: Day 2: Robert Fuest
B Unit: 09.15-14.45: RAF Bovingdon, Chesham Road, Bovingdon, Herts [Ext: Deserted airfield]
Thursday 7 November 1968: Day 3: Robert Fuest
B Unit: 09.35-15.15: RAF Bovingdon, Chesham Road, Bovingdon, Herts [Ext: Deserted airfield]
Friday 8 November 1968: Day 4: Robert Fuest
B Unit: 09.00 to unknown time: Unknown Location [Ext: Heston Avenue]
B Unit: Unknown time: Grantully Road, London, W9 [Ext: Steed follows contact's car]
B Unit: Unknown time: Maida Vale, London, W9 [Ext: Tara follows contact past flats]
B Unit: Unknown time: Blomfield Road, London, W9 [Ext: Cranleigh High Street]
B Unit: Unknown time to 16.05: Chalcott Crescent, London, NW1 [Ext: Tara's apartment]
Monday 11 November 1968: Day 5: Robert Fuest
B Unit: 09.15 to unknown time: Clifton Gardens, London, W9 [Ext: Sloane Street]
B Unit: Unknown time to 16.00: Hamilton Terrace, London, NW8 [Ext: Churchyard]
Tuesday 12 November 1968: Day 6: Robert Fuest
B Unit: 09.15 to unknown time: Lanark Road/Elgin Mews South, London, W9 [Ext: London mews]
B Unit: Unknown time: Blomfield Street, London, W9 [Ext: Cranleigh High Street]
B Unit: Unknown time to 17.23: ABPC Elstree Studios, Stage 3 [Int: Crypt]
Wednesday 13 November 1968: Day 7: Robert Fuest
B Unit: 09.00-16.40: ABPC Elstree Studios, Stage 3 [Int: Crypt/Tara's apartment and other side of front door]
Thursday 14 November 1968: Day 8: Robert Fuest
B Unit: 08.35-17.20: ABPC Elstree Studios, Stage 3 [Int: Tara's apartment and other side of front door/judo room/outer office]
Friday 15 November 1968: Day 9: Robert Fuest
B Unit: 08.50-17.05: ABPC Elstree Studios, Stage 3 [Int: Tara's apartment/judo room/outer office]
Monday 18 November 1968: Day 10: Robert Fuest
B Unit: 08.30-17.19: ABPC Elstree Studios, Stage 3 [Int: Tara's apartment/hotel bedroom and section of corridor/Steed's car]
Tuesday 19 November 1968: Day 11: Robert Fuest
B Unit: 08.40-17.05: ABPC Elstree Studios, Studio Lot [Ext: Street and warehouse/luggage entrance Kings Cross Station/timber store/urban street B/Int: Telephone box]
Wednesday 20 November 1968: Day 12: Robert Fuest
B Unit: 09.20 to unknown time: Blomfield Street, London, W9 [Ext: Cranleigh High Street]

B Unit: Unknown time: Clifton Gardens, London, W9 [Ext: Sloane Street]
B Unit: Unknown time to 17.15: ABPC Elstree Studios, Stage 3 [Int: Steed's car]
Thursday 21 November 1968: Day 13: Robert Fuest
B Unit: 08.30-05.18; ABPC Elstree Studios, Stage 3 [Int: Shepherd's apartment/warehouse]
Friday 22 November 1968: Day 14: Robert Fuest/Don Chaffey
B Unit: 08.35-17.14: ABPC Elstree Studios, Stage 3 [Int: Giant crate/rehearsal room]
A Unit: 08.30-17.20: ABPC Elstree Studios, Stage 3 [Int: Crypt/Shepherd's apartment]
Monday 25 November 1968: Day 15: Robert Fuest
B Unit: 08.45-16.40: ABPC Elstree Studios, Stage 3 [Int: Rehearsal room and doorway/Shepherd's apartment]
Tuesday 26 November 1968: Day 16: No details available
Wednesday 27 November 1968: Day 17: Robert Fuest
B Unit: 08.35-17.20: ABPC Elstree Studios, Stage 3 [Int: Shepherd's apartment/warehouse}
Thursday 28 November 1968: Day 18: Robert Fuest
B Unit: 08.38-17.07: ABPC Elstree Studios, Stage 3 [Int Shepherd's apartment/rehearsal room/Tara's apartment]
Friday 29 November 1968: Day 19: Robert Fuest
B Unit: 08.30-10.30: ABPC Elstree Studios, Stage 9 [Int Shepherd's apartment/giant crate/warehouse]

6.25 – 'STAY TUNED'
Episode 153
Original Transmission Date: Wednesday 26 February 1969

Writer: Tony Williamson
Director: Don Chaffey
Cast: Patrick Macnee (John Steed), Linda Thorson (Tara King), Gary Bond (Proctor), Kate O'Mara (Lisa), Patrick Newell (Mother), Iris Russell (Father), Duncan Lamont (Wilks), Howard Marion-Crawford (Collins), Denise Buckley (Sally), Roger Delgado (Kreer), Harold Kasket (Dr Meitner), Ewan Roberts (Travers), Patrick Westwood (Taxi Driver).
Uncredited Cast: Rhonda Parker (Rhonda), Paul Weston (Stunt Double for John Steed), Roma Gorrara (Stunt Double for Tara King), Dorothy Ford (Stunt Double for Lisa), Dave Wilding (Stunt Double for Kreer), Rupert Evans (Stunt Double for Wilks).
Crew: Laurie Johnson (Music by), Terry Nation (Script Editor), Peter Jessop (Director of Photography), Karen Heward (Editor), Ann Chegwidden (Post Production Co-ordinator) Alun Hughes (Miss Thorson's Costumes Designed by), Colin Lord (Assistant Director), Ernie Robinson (Camera Operator), Len Townsend and Kenneth Tait (Associate Art Directors), Simon Wakefield (Set Dresser), Kay Fenton (Continuity), Mary Sturgess (Hairdressing), Ivy Baker (Costume Supervisor), Cecil Mason (Sound Recordist), Len Shilton (Dubbing Mixer), Bob Dearberg (Sound Editor), Paul Clay (Music Editor), Herbert Worley (Construction Manager), Steve Birtles (Supervisory Electrician).
Uncredited Crew: Peggy Spirito (Post Production), B Clarke (Make-Up), Terry Cole (Focus Puller), Wally Byatt (Camera Operator), C Barnett (Nurse).

Production Schedule:

Tuesday 19 November 1968: Day 1: Don Chaffey

A Unit: 10.45 to unknown time: North Avenue, Shenley, Herts [Surburban street]

A Unit: Unknown time: Rectory Lane/Harris Lane, Shenley, Herts [Road junction country road A]

A Unit: Unknown time to 16.25: Pound Lane, Shenley, Herts [Country road B]

Wednesday 20 November 1968: Day 2: Don Chaffey

A Unit: 10.15 to unknown time: Unknown Location [Ext: Urban street] Does not appear in episode

A Unit: Unknown time: Unknown Location [Ext: Street A] Does not appear in episode

A Unit: Unknown time: Chalcott Crescent, London, NW1 [Ext: Psychiatrist's consulting room]

A Unit: Unknown time to 17.00: Weymouth Mews, London, W1 [Ext: Fitzherbert Street]

Thursday 21 November 1968: Day 3: Don Chaffey

A Unit: 09.10-12.40: Radlett Preparatory School, Watling Street, Radlett, Herts [Ext: Mother and Father's headquarters]

Monday 25 November 1968: Day 4: Don Chaffey

A Unit: 09.35-17.20: ABPC Elstree Studios, Stage 5 [Int: Study]

Tuesday 26 November 1968: Day 5: No details available

Wednesday 27 November 1968: Day 6: Don Chaffey

A Unit: 09.35 to unknown time: ABPC Elstree Studios, Stage 9 [Int: Forensics garage]

A Unit: Unknown time to 17.15: ABPC Elstree Studios, Stage 5 [Int: Study]

Thursday 28 November 1968: Day 7: Don Chaffey

A Unit: 09.20-17.20: ABPC Elstree Studios, Stage 5 [Int: Steed's apartment/study]

Friday 29 November 1968: Day 8: Don Chaffey/Robert Fuest

A Unit: 09.40 to unknown time: ABPC Elstree Studios, Stage 3 {Int: Tara's apartment]

A Unit: Unknown time to 17.22: ABPC Elstree Studios, Stage 5 [Int: Steed's apartment]

B Unit: Unknown time: ABPC Elstree Studios, Stage 9 [Int: Insert for Scene 24]

Quarter called pm

Monday 2 December 1968: Day 9: Don Chaffey

A Unit: 09.00-17.15: ABPC Elstree Studios, Stage 5 [Int: Steed's apartment/Father's study/study]

Tuesday 3 December 1968: Day 10: Don Chaffey

A Unit: 09.50-17.05: ABPC Elstree Studios, Stage 5 [Int: Conditioning room]

Wednesday 4 December 1968: Day 11: Don Chaffey

A Unit: 09.10-17.20: ABPC Elstree Studios, Stage 5 [Int: Conditioning room/Ext: Fitzherbert Street]

Thursday 5 December 1968: Day 12: Don Chaffey

A Unit: 08.55-17.20: ABPC Elstree Studios, Stage 5 [Int: Hallway/conditioning room/Ext: Kreer's house]

Friday 6 December 1968: Day 13: Don Chaffey

A Unit: 10.45 to unknown time: Radlett Preparatory School, Watling Street, Radlett, Herts [Ext: Mother and Father's headquarters]

A Unit: Unknown time to 17.24: ABPC Elstree Studios, Stage 5 [Int: Conditioning room]

Quarter called pm.

Monday 9 December 1968: Day 14: Don Chaffey

A Unit: 10.30-17.50: Weymouth Mews, London, W1 [Ext: Fitzherbert Street]

Tuesday 10 December 1968: Day 15: Don Chaffey

A Unit: 09.40-17.18: ABPC Elstree Studios, Stage 5 [Int: Conditioning room/Father's study/psychiatrist's consulting room]
Wednesday 11 December 1968: Day 16: Don Chaffey
A Unit: 09.30-17.25: ABPC Elstree Studios, Stage 5 [Int: Psychiatrist's consulting room/Steed's apartment]
Quarter called pm
Thursday 12 December 1968: Day 17: Don Chaffey
A Unit: 08.55-19.45: ABPC Elstree Studios, Stage 5 [Int: Steed's apartment/Father's study]
Friday 13 December 1968: Day 18: Don Chaffey
A Unit: 09.30-14.40: ABPC Elstree Studios, Stage 5 [Int: Hallway/conditioning room/Steed's apartment]

6.26 – 'FOG'
Episode 154
Original Transmission Date: Wednesday 12 March 1969

Writer: Jeremy Burnham
Director: John Hough
Cast: Patrick Macnee (John Steed), Linda Thorson (Tara King), Nigel Green (Sir Geoffrey Armstrong), Guy Rolfe (Mark Travers), Patrick Newell (Mother), Terence Brady (Carstairs), Paul Whitsun-Jones (Sanders), *David Lodge (Maskell), Norman Chappell (Fowler), David Bird (Osgood), Patsy Smart (Mrs Golightly), John Garrie (Wellbeloved), Frederick Peisley (Grunner), Arnold Diamond (Haller), John Barrard (Valarti), Frank Sieman (Concierge), Virginia Clay (Lavender Seller), Bernard Severn (Tinker), Stanley Jay (Organ Grinder), William Lyon Brown (Blind Man).
*Does not appear in episode
Uncredited Cast: Rhonda Parker (Rhonda), Freddy Sommers (Club Member), John Clifford (Club Member), Dido Plumb (Beggar), Peter Rigby (Club Member), H Kempson (Club Member), M Lieder (Club Member), Cyd Child (Stunt Double for Tara King), Peter Brace (Stunt Double for Mark Travers), Paul Weston (Stunt Double for John Steed), Peter Brace (Stunt Double for Sir Geoffrey Armstrong), Joe Dunne (Stunt Double for Osgood).
Crew: Laurie Johnson (Music by), Terry Nation (Script Editor), David Holmes (Director of Photography), Manuel del Campo (Editor), Ann Chegwidden (Post Production Co-ordinator) Alun Hughes (Miss Thorson's Costumes Designed by), Ron Purdie (Assistant Director), Geoff Seaholme (Camera Operator), Kenneth Tait and Richard Harrison (Associate Art Directors), Simon Wakefield (Set Dresser), Kay Perkins (Continuity), Mary Sturgess (Hairdressing), Ivy Baker (Costume Supervisor), Claude Hitchcok (Sound Recordist), Len Shilton (Dubbing Mixer), Peter Lennard (Sound Editor), Paul Clay (Music Editor), Herbert Worley (Construction Manager), Roy Bond (Supervisory Electrician).
Uncredited Crew: Lillian Lee (Continuity), N Jones (Camera Operator), M Arnold (Focus Puller), Jackie Green (Second Assistant Director), P Rigby (Coachman), J Claxton (Horse Handler).

Production Schedule:

Thursday 21 November 1968: Day 1: John Hough

A Unit: Unknown time: Hadley Common Railway Tunnel, Hadley Wood, Herts [Ext: Tunnel and railway line] *Not used in episode.*

Monday 2 December 1968: Day 2: John Hough

B Unit: 09.00-14.35: ABPC Elstree Studios, Stage 2 [Ext: Streets and alleys complex]

Wednesday 4 December 1968: Day 3: John Hough

B Unit: 08.32-17.24: ABPC Elstree Studios, Stage 2 [Ext: Streets and alleys complex/Tara's apartment]

Thursday 5 December 1968: Day 4: John Hough

B Unit: 08.35-00-00: ABPC Elstree Studios, Stage 2 [Ext: Streets and alleys complex]

B Unit: Unknown time to 17.05: ABPC Elstree Studios, Stage 3 [Int: Hamsom cab garage]

Friday 6 December 1968: Day 5: John Hough

B Unit: 08.30 to unknown time: ABPC Elstree Studios, Stage 3 [Int: Mask and face/Tara's apartment/Ext: Mask and face]

B Unit: Unknown time to 17.20: ABPC Elstree Studios, Stage 2 [Ext: Streets and alleys complex]

Monday 9 December 1968: Day 6: John Hough

B Unit: 08.45-07.18: ABPC Elstree Studios, Stage 2 [Ext: Streets and alleys complex/Int: Gaslight Ghoul Club/Black Museum]

Tuesday 10 December 1968: Day 7: John Hough

B Unit: 08.30-17.05: ABPC Elstree Studios, Stage 2 [Int: Black Museum/President's study]

Wednesday 11 December 1968: Day 8: John Hough

B Unit: 08.30-17.20: ABPC Elstree Studios, Stage 2 [Ext: Streets and alleys Complex]

Hansom cab and horse called Planet supplied by George Mossman

Thursday 12 December 1968: Day 9: John Hough

B Unit: 08.30-17.18: ABPC Elstree Studios, Stage 2 [Ext: Streets and alleys complex]

Hansom cab and horse called Planet supplied by George Mossman

Friday 13 December 1968: Day 10: John Hough

B Unit: 09.35-17.30: ABPC Elstree Studios, Stage 2 [Ext: Osgood's house/Int: Osgood's house]

Quarter called pm

Monday 16 December 1968: Day 11: John Hough

B Unit: 08.30-17.20: ABPC Elstree Studios, Stage 2 [Int: Black Museum/Osgood's house]

Tuesday 17 December 1968: Day 12: John Hough

B Unit: 08.30-17.18: ABPC Elstree Studios, Stage 2 [Int: Black Museum/Ext: Streets and alleyways – Gunthorpe Street/Mini Moke]

Wednesday 18 December 1968: Day 13: John Hough

B Unit: 08.30 to unknown time: ABPC Elstree Studios, Stage 2 [Ext: Mini Moke/Int: Mini Moke/Ext: President's house]

B Unit: Unknown time to 17.16: ABPC Elstree Studios, Stage 5 [Int: Steed's apartment]

Thursday 19 December 1968: Day 14: John Hough

B Unit: 08.30 to unknown time: ABPC Elstree Studios, Stage 5 [Int: Steed's apartment]

B Unit: Unknown time to 17.15: ABPC Elstree Studios, Stage 2 [Int: Gaslight Ghoul Club]

Friday 20 December 1968: Day 15: John Hough

B Unit: 08.30-17.15: ABPC Elstree Studios, Stage 2 [Int: Gaslight Ghoul Club/Black Museum]
Monday 23 December 1968: Day 16: John Hough
B Unit: 08.32-17.20: ABPC Elstree Studios, Stage 2 [Int: President's study/Ext: Streets and alleyways/railway station/hotel/Ext: Gaslight Ghoul Club]
Hansom cab and horse called Planet supplied by George Mossman
Tuesday 24 December 1968: Day 17: John Hough
B Unit: 08.30-17.00: ABPC Elstree Studios, Stage 2 [Ext: Streets and alleys complex/Master Cutler'room/Mini Moke/Int: Mini Moke]
Monday 30 December 1968: Day 18: John Hough
B Unit: 08.32-17.13: ABPC Elstree Studios, Stage 2 [Ext: Streets and alleys complex/railway station/Mini Moke/Int: Mini Moke]
Hansom cab and horse called Planet supplied by George Mossman
Tuesday 31 December 1968: Day 19: John Hough
B Unit: 08.30-17.03: ABPC Elstree Studios, Stage 2 [Int: Mini Moke/Ext: Mini Moke/streets and alleys complex/Int: Osgood's house/Gaslight Ghoul Club]
Hansom cab and horse called Planet supplied by George Mossman
Thursday 9 January 1969: Day 20: John Hough
3rd: Unknown time to 15.55: ABPC Elstree Studios, Stage 2 [Ext: Country road – inserts of signs]

6.27 – 'WHO WAS THAT MAN I SAW YOU WITH?'
Episode 155
Original Transmission Date: Wednesday 19 March 1969

Writer: Jeremy Burnham
Director: Don Chaffey
Cast: Patrick Macnee (John Steed), Linda Thorson (Tara King), William Marlowe (Jay Fairfax), Ralph Michael (General Hesketh), Alan Browning (Gregor Zaroff), Alan MacNaughton (Gilpin), Patrick Newell (Mother), Alan Wheatley (Dangerfield), Bryan Marshall (Aubrey Phillipson), Aimée Delamain (Miss Gladys Culpepper), Richard Owens (Perowne), Nita Lorraine (Kate), Ralph Ball (Corporal Hamilton), Ken Howard (Corporal Powell), Neville Marten (Pye).
Uncredited Cast: Rhonda Parker (Rhonda), Peter Brace (War Room Guard), Terry York (War Room Guard), Kevin Smith (Tara's Friend), Cyd Child (Stunt Double for Tara King), Paul Weston (Stunt Double for Corporal Powell), Joe Dunne (Stunt Double for Corporal Hamilton), Rocky Taylor (Stunt Double for Corporal Powell), Cliff Diggins (Stunt Double for Aubrey Phillipson), Gerry Crampton (Stunt Double for Perowne), Fred Haggerty (Stunt Double for Dangerfield), Alf Joint (Stunt Double for Gregor Zaroff), Paul Weston (Stunt Double for John Steed).
Crew: Laurie Johnson (Music Supervision by), Howard Blake (Score by), Terry Nation (Script Editor), Peter Jessop (Director of Photography), Karen Heward (Editor), Ann Chegwidden (Post Production Co-ordinator) Alun Hughes (Miss Thorson's Costumes Designed by), Colin Lord (Assistant Director), Ernie Robinson (Camera Operator), Kenneth Tait and Len Townsend (Associate Art Directors), Simon Wakefield (Set Dresser), Kay Fenton (Continuity), Mary Sturgess (Hairdressing), Ivy Baker (Costume Supervisor), Cecil Mason (Sound Recordist), Len Abbott (Dubbing Mixer), Bob Dearberg (Sound Editor), Paul Clay (Music Editor), Herbert Worley (Construction

Manager), Steve Birtles (Supervisory Electrician).

Uncredited Crew: Derek Hyde (Wardrobe), B Clarke (Make-Up), Peggy Spirito (Post Production), B Garforth (Make-Up), Jackie Green (Second Assistant Director/Third Assistant Director/Unit Runner), B Phillips (Make-Up), M Arnold (Focus Puller), N Jones (Camera Operator), M Morris (Make-Up), Sash Fisher (Sound Mixer), P Taylor (Clapper Loader), John O'Conner (Assistant Director), C Davidson (Clapper Loader), Bob Kindred (Camera Operator), Bert Mason (Camera Operator), C Leigh (Continuity), Ron Appleton (Assistant Director).

Production Schedule:
Monday 16 December 1968: Day 1: Don Chaffey
A Unit: 10.45 to unknown time: Hadley Green, Barnet, Greater London, EN5 [Ext: Tara breaks into war room]
A Unit: Unknown time to 16.20: East Heath Road, Hampstead Heath Car Park, London, NW3 [Ext: Fairfax trails Tara on suburban road/Steed in Rolls]
Tuesday 17 December 1968: Day 2: Don Chaffey
A Unit: 12.00 to unknown time: Bell Moor, East Heath Road, London, NW3 [Ext: Underground garage]
A Unit: Unknown time: East Heath Road, Hampstead Heath Car Park, London, NW3 [Ext: Fairfax trails Tara on suburban road/Steed in Rolls]
A Unit: Unknown time to 14.20: Bakers Hill/Hadley Wood Road, Barnet, Greater London, EN5 [Ext: Fairfax trails Tara on urban road to telephone box]
Wednesday 18 December 1968: Day 3: Don Chaffey
A Unit: 11.00-16.20: Chalcott Crescent, London, NW1 [Ext: Tara's apartment]
Thursday 19 December 1968: Day 4: Don Chaffey
A Unit: 10.20 to unknown time: Chalcott Crescent, London, NW1 [Ext: Tara's apartment]
A Unit: Unknown time to 18.02: Bell Moor, East Heath Road, London, NW3 [Int: Underground garage]
Friday 20 December 1968: Day 5: Don Chaffey
A Unit: 10.10-17.18: ABPC Elstree Studios, Stage 3 [Int: War room/reception and sentry box]
Monday 23 December 1968: Day 6: Don Chaffey
A Unit: 08.55-17.20: ABPC Elstree Studios, Stage 3 [Int: War room/reception and sentry box/lift]
Tuesday 24 December 1968: Day 7: Don Chaffey
A Unit: 08.59-16.55: ABPC Elstree Studios, Stage 3 [Int: Reception and lift/ventilator shaft/Tara's apartment and corridor]
Monday 30 December 1968: Day 8: Don Chaffey
A Unit: 09.10 to unknown time: ABPC Elstree Studios, Stage 3 [Int: Tara's apartment]
A Unit: Unknown time to 17.00: ABPC Elstree Studios, Stage 5 [Int: Steed's apartment]
Tuesday 31 December 1968: Day 9: Don Chaffey
A Unit: 09.30-17.15: ABPC Elstree Studios, Stage 5 [Int: Steed's apartment]
Wednesday 1 January 1969: Day 10: Don Chaffey
A Unit: 10.15 to unknown time: ABPC Elstree Studios, Stage 5 [Int: Steed's apartment]
A Unit: Unknown time to 17.20: ABPC Elstree Studios, Stage 3 [Int: Tara's apartment and corridor]
Thursday 2 January 1969: Day 11: Don Chaffey

A Unit: 08.55-17.12: ABPC Elstree Studios, Stage 3 [Int: Tara's apartment and corridor/telephone box/Tara's car]
Friday 3 January 1969: Day 12: Don Chaffey
A Unit: 10.32-17.18: ABPC Elstree Studios, Stage 3 [Int: Boxing club]
Monday 6 January 1969: Day 13: Don Chaffey
A Unit: 08.30-17.20: ABPC Elstree Studios, Stage 3 [Int: Boxing club/dungeon]
Tuesday 7 January 1969: Day 14: Don Chaffey
A Unit: 09.30-17.05: ABPC Elstree Studios, Stage 3 [Int: Dungeon/corridor outside Tara's apartment]
Wednesday 8 January 1969: Day 15: Don Chaffey
A Unit: 09.05-17.35: ABPC Elstree Studios, Stage 3 [Int: Tara's apartment/underground garage/reception/boxing club]
Quarter called pm
Thursday 9 January 1969: Day 16: Don Chaffey/John Hough
A Unit: 10.10-17.15: ABPC Elstree Studios, Stage 3 [Int: Tara's apartment/dungeon/corridor outside Tara's apartment/war room]
3rd: 09.30 to unknown time: Duchess Mews, London, W1 [Ext: Steed's mews]
Friday 10 January 1969: Day 17: Don Chaffey/John Hough
A Unit: 10.10-17.19: ABPC Elstree Studios, Stage 3 [Int: Boxing club/dungeon/corridor outside Tara's apartment/Tara's apartment/war room/Steed's apartment]
3rd: 09.15 to unknown time: Duchess Mews, London, W1 [Ext: Steed's mews]

6.28 – 'PANDORA'
Episode 156
Original Transmission Date: Wednesday 30 April 1969

Writer: Brian Clemens
Director: Robert Fuest
Cast: Patrick Macnee (John Steed), Linda Thorson (Tara King), Julian Glover (Rupert Lasindall), James Cossins (Henry Lasindall), Kathleen Byron (Miss Faversham), Patrick Newell (Mother), John Laurie (Simon Henry Juniper), Anthony Roye (Hubert Pettigrew), Geoffrey Whitehead (Carter), Peter Madden (Gregory Lasindall), Reginald Barrett (Xavier Smith), Raymond Burke (Young Gregory Lasindall).
Uncredited Cast: Rhonda Parker (Rhonda), Paul Weston (Stunt Double for John Steed), Frank Barringer (Stunt Double for Henry Lasindall), Gerry Crampton (Stunt Double for Rupert Lasindall), Dorothy Ford (Stunt Double for Miss Faversham).
Crew: Laurie Johnson (Music by), Terry Nation (Script Editor), David Holmes (Director of Photography), Ann Chegwidden (Editor and Post Production Co-ordinator) Alun Hughes (Miss Thorson's Costumes Designed by), Ron Purdie (Assistant Director), Geoff Seaholme (Camera Operator), Kenneth Tait (Associate Art Director), Simon Wakefield (Set Dresser), Kay Perkins (Continuity), Mary Sturgess (Hairdressing), Ivy Baker (Costume Supervisor), Claude Hitchcok (Sound Recordist), Len Abbott (Dubbing Mixer), Peter Lennard (Sound Editor), Paul Clay (Music Editor), Herbert Worley (Construction Manager), Roy Bond (Supervisory Electrician).
Uncredited Crew: Ron Appleton (Assistant Director), John O'Conner (Assistant Director), C Davidson (Clapper Loader), M Arnold (Focus Puller), Bob Kindred (Camera Operator), Bert Mason (Lighting Cameraman), M Morris (Make-Up), C Leigh (Continuity), Jackie Green (Assistant Director/Second Assistant Director), N Jones

(Camera Operator).

Production Schedule:
Thursday 2 January 1969: Day 1: Robert Fuest
B Unit: 08.32-17.19: ABPC Elstree Studios, Stage 5 [Int: Dining room]
Friday 3 January 1969: Day 2: Robert Fuest
B Unit: 08.35-17.20: ABPC Elstree Studios, Stage 5 [Int: Dining room/the new room/hallway]
Monday 6 January 1969: Day 3: Robert Fuest
B Unit: 08.35-17.20: ABPC Elstree Studios, Stage 5 [Int: File room/upper landing]
Tuesday 7 January 1969: Day 4: Robert Fuest
B Unit: 08.33-20.20: ABPC Elstree Studios, Stage 5 [Int: Upper landing/forbidden area/the room]
Wednesday 8 January 1969: Day 5: Robert Fuest
B Unit: 09.20-17.05: ABPC Elstree Studios, Stage 5 [Int: Dining room]
Thursday 9 January 1969: Day 6: Robert Fuest
B Unit: 08.45-17.16: ABPC Elstree Studios, Stage 5 [Int: The room/antique shop]
Friday 10 January 1969: Day 7: Robert Fuest/John Hough
B Unit: 08.30-17.20: ABPC Elstree Studios, Stage 5 [Int: Antique shop/Steed's apartment]
3rd: Unknown time to 15.17: Unknown Location,[Ext: Country road]
Monday 13 January 1969: Day 8: Robert Fuest
B Unit: 08.30-16.50: ABPC Elstree Studios, Stage 5 [Int: Steed's apartment/file room]
Tuesday 14 January 1969: Day 9: Robert Fuest
B Unit: 08.30 to unknown time: ABPC Elstree Studios, Stage 5 [Int: File room]
B Unit: Unknown time to 17.18: ABPC Elstree Studios, Stage 3 [Int: Tara's apartment/clock shop/Rupert's car]
Wednesday 15 January 1969: Day 10: Robert Fuest
B Unit: 08.35-17.00: ABPC Elstree Studios, Stage 5 [Int: Dining room/hallway]
Thursday 16 January 1969: Day 11: Robert Fuest
B Unit: 08.30-17.20: ABPC Elstree Studios, Stage 5 [Int: Bedroom]
Friday 17 January 1969: Day 12: Robert Fuest
B Unit: 08.40-17.20: ABPC Elstree Studios, Stage 5 [Int: Bedroom/the room/hallway and upper landing/dining room]
Monday 27 January 1969: Day 13: John Hough
3rd: Unknown time: ABPC Elstree Studios, Stage 3 [Int: Tara's apartment – inserts for Scene 24]

6.29 – 'THINGUMAJIG'
Episode 157
Original Transmission Date: Wednesday 2 April 1969

Writer: Terry Nation
Director: Leslie Norman
Cast: Patrick Macnee (John Steed), Linda Thorson (Tara King), Dora Reisser (Inge Tilson), Jeremy Lloyd (The Rev. Teddy Shelley), Iain Cuthbertson (Kruger), Willoughby Goddard (Professor Harvey Truman), Hugh Manning (Major Star), John Horsley (Dr Grant), Edward Burnham (Brett), Vernon Dobtcheff (Stenson), Russell Waters (Pike),

Michael McKevitt (Phillips), Neville Hughes (Williams), John Moore (Greer), Harry Shacklock (Bill Reston).

Uncredited Cast: Paul Weston (Stunt Double for John Steed), Terry Richards (Stunt Double for Kruger), Cyd Child (Stunt Double for Tara King).

Crew: Laurie Johnson (Music by), Terry Nation (Script Editor), Peter Jessop (Director of Photography), Robert Dearberg (Editor), Ann Chegwidden (Post Production Co-ordinator) Alun Hughes (Miss Thorson's Costumes Designed by), Colin Lord (Assistant Director), Ernie Robinson (Camera Operator), Kenneth Tait and Len Townsend (Associate Art Directors), Simon Wakefield (Set Dresser), Kay Fenton (Continuity), Mary Sturgess (Hairdressing), Ivy Baker (Costume Supervisor), Bert Mason (Second Unit Photography), Cecil Mason (Sound Recordist), Bill Rowe (Dubbing Mixer), Brian Lintern (Sound Editor), Paul Clay (Music Editor), Herbert Worley (Construction Manager), Steve Birtles (Supervisory Electrician).

Uncredited Crew: N Jones (Camera Operator), M Arnold (Focus Puller), Jackie Green (Second Assistant Director), Ron Appleton (Assistant Director), Peggy Spirito (Post Production), Sash Fisher (Sound Mixer), Bob Kindred (Camera Operator), K Mackay (Make-Up), C Davidson (Clapper Loader), Terry Cole (Focus Puller), A Ross (Third Assistant Director), Ray Sturgess (Camera Operator), B Stevens (Fireman), Betty Sherriff (Hairdresser), M Morris (Make-Up), P Carter (Second Assistant Director), Leslie Hammond (Sound Mixer), F Fay (Sound Camera Operator), K Nightingale (Boom Operator), C Leigh (Continuity), John O'Conner (Assistant Director), Mike Roberts (Focus Puller), M Whorlow (Nurse), A Crofton (Nurse), D Martin (Hairdresser), H Bevan (Hairdresser), Bert Mason (Lighting Cameraman), Brian Ellis (Focus Puller), B Clarke (Make-Up), S Valentine (Production Buyer), B Royston (Make-Up), B Lipman (Second Assistant Director), Paul Jordan (Clapper Loader).

Production Schedule:
Thursday 9 January 1969: Day 1: John Hough
3rd: Unknown time: St. Mary's Church, Crossoaks Lane, Ridge, Herts [Ext: Country church]
Monday 13 January 1969: Day 2: Leslie Norman/John Hough
A Unit: 09.35-17.30: ABPC Elstree Studios, Stage 3 [Int: Tara's apartment]
3rd: 11.25 to unknown time: Tykes Water Lake, Aldenham Estate, Elstree, Herts [Ext: Roadway]
3rd: Unknown time: Invinghoe Beacon, Invinghoe Beacon Road and The Ridgeway, Ivinghoe, Bucks [Ext: Steed's Rolls Royce – country road B]
3rd: Unknown time: Mimms Lane, Shenley, Herts [Ext: Car and caravan parked on verge – country road A]
3rd: Unknown time to 15.45: Hill Farm, Oakridge Lane, Radlett, Herts [Ext: Steed's Rolls Royce departs for the railway station]
Quarter called pm
Tuesday 14 January 1969: Day 3: Leslie Norman
A Unit: 09.20-17.16: ABPC Elstree Studios, Stage 2 [Int: Wall telephone/tunnel entrance/section of tunnel]
Wednesday 15 January 1969: Day 4: Leslie Norman
A Unit: 09.25-17.10: ABPC Elstree Studios, Stage 2 [Int: Section of tunnel}
Thursday 16 January 1969: Day 5: Leslie Norman
A Unit: 09.25-17.16: ABPC Elstree Studios, Stage 2 [Int: Section of tunnel/Entrance of

tunnel]

Friday 17 January 1969: Day 6: Leslie Norman

A Unit: 08.30-17.00: ABPC Elstree Studios, Stage 2 [Int: Section of tunnel/church]

Monday 20 January 1969: Day 7: Leslie Norman/John Hough

A Unit: 09.30-17.18: ABPC Elstree Studios, Stage 3 [Int: Tara's apartment]

3rd: 10.13-16.50: Tykes Water Lake, Aldenham Estate, Elstree, Herts [Ext: Lake]

Tuesday 21 January 1969: Day 8: Leslie Norman/John Hough

A Unit: 08.55-17.15: ABPC Elstree Studios, Stage 3 [Int: Tara's apartment]

3rd: 10.05-15.38: Springwell Chalk Pits, Springwell Lane, Harefield, Bucks [Ext: Disused quarry]

Wednesday 22 January 1969: Day 9: Leslie Norman

A Unit: 10.50-17.16: ABPC Elstree Studios, Stage 2 [Int: Church]

Thursday 23 January 1969: Day 10: Leslie Norman

A Unit: 08.50-17.05: ABPC Elstree Studios, Stage 2 [Int: Church]

Friday 24 January 1969: Day 11: Leslie Norman

A Unit: 09.05-17.10: ABPC Elstree Studios, Stage 2 [Int: Church]

Monday 27 January 1969: Day 12: Leslie Norman/John Hough

A Unit: 09.20 to unknown time: ABPC Elstree Studios, Stage 2 [Int: Church]

A Unit: Unknown time to 17.22: ABPC Elstree Studios, Stage 5 [Int: Steed's apartment]

3rd: Unknown time: ABPC Elstree Studios, Stage 3 [Int: Tara's apartment – inserts for Scenes 116, 118, 120, 122]

Tuesday 28 January 1969: Day 13: Leslie Norman

A Unit: 09.30-17.25: ABPC Elstree Studios, Stage 2 [Int: Church/bedroom]

Quarter called pm

Wednesday 29 January 1969: Day 14: Leslie Norman

A Unit: 09.12-17.18: ABPC Elstree Studios, Stage 2 [Int: Church/section of tunnel]

Thursday 30 January 1969: Day 15: Leslie Norman

A Unit: 08.55-17.30: ABPC Elstree Studios, Stage 2 [Int: Section of tunnel]

Quarter called pm

Friday 31 January 1969: Day 16: Leslie Norman

A Unit: 09.10-17.05: ABPC Elstree Studios, Stage 2 [Int: Section of tunnel/caravan]

Monday 3 February 1969: Day 17: John Hough

3rd: Unknown time to 17.16: ABPC Elstree Studios, Stage 3 [Int: Tara's apartment – inserts for Scenes 75A, 116, 120, 122]

6.30 – 'HOMICIDE AND OLD LACE'
Episode 158
Original Transmission Date: Wednesday 26 March 1969

Writers: Malcolm Hulke and Terrance Dicks

Director: John Hough

Cast: Patrick Macnee (John Steed), Linda Thorson (Tara King), Patrick Newell (Mother), Joyce Carey (Harriet), Mary Merrell (Georgina), Gerald Harper (Colonel Corf), Keith Baxter (Dunbar), Edward Brayshaw (Fuller), Donald Pickering (Freddie Cartwright), Mark London (Jackson), Kristopher Kum (Osaka), Bari Johnson (African Delegate), Stephen Hubay (Federov), Bryan Mosley (Sergeant Smith), Gertan Klauber (Kruger), Kevork Malikyan (Rossi), John Rapley (Taxi Driver), Ann Rutter (Controller).

Uncredited Cast: Rhonda Parker (Rhonda), Dinny Powell (Guard), Maxwell Craig

(Wilson), Michael Coles (Verret), Clive Colin-Bowler (Robin), Peter Brace (Percy Danvers), Paul Clay (Martin), John Ronane (Hubert), Colin Blakely (Mickle), Garfield Morgan (Gilbert), Christopher Lee (Professor Stone), Paul Weston (Stunt Double for John Steed), Cyd Child (Stunt Double for Tara King).

Crew: Laurie Johnson (Music by), Terry Nation (Script Editor), Gilbert Taylor BSC (Director of Photography), Ann Chegwidden (Post Production Co-ordinator), Karen Heward (Editor), Harvey Gould (Miss Thorson's Costumes Designed by), Ron Appleton (Assistant Director), Brian Elvin (Camera Operator), Kenneth Tait and Len Townsend (Associate Art Directors), Simon Wakefield (Set Dresser), June Randall (Continuity), Gordon Bond (Hairdressing), Felix Evans (Wardrobe), Bert Mason (Second Unit Photography), Cecil Mason (Sound Recordist), Bill Rowe (Dubbing Mixer), Peter Lennard (Sound Editor), Paul Clay (Music Editor), Herbert Worley (Construction Manager), Steve Birtles (Supervisory Electrician).

Uncredited Crew: Jackie Green (Second Assistant Director), Bob Kindred (Camera Operator), Bert Mason (Lighting Cameraman), C Davidson (Clapper Loader), C Leigh (Continuity), Keith Batten (Boom Operator), Leslie Hammond (Sound Mixer), Terry Cole (Focus Puller), John O'Conner (Assistant Director), Mike Roberts (Focus Puller).

Production Schedule:
Wednesday 15 January 1969: Day 1: John Hough
3rd: 09.33 to unknown time: Weymouth Mews, London, W1 [Ext: Mother arriving by car/heist]
3rd: Unknown time to 16.10: Unknown Location [Ext: Street B] *Not used in episode.*
Thursday 16 January 1969: Day 2: John Hough
3rd: 09.10-17.20: ABPC Elstree Studios, Stage 3 [Int: Room]
Quarter called pm
Friday 17 January 1969: Day 3: John Hough
3rd: 08.35-17.03: ABPC Elstree Studios, Stage 3 [Int: Mother's headquarters/room]
Thursday 22 January 1969: Day 4: John Hough
3rd: 08.40-17.18: ABPC Elstree Studios, Stage 3 [Int: Room]

6.31 – 'REQUIEM'
Episode 159
Original Transmission Date: Wednesday 16 April 1969

Writer: Brian Clemens
Director: Don Chaffey
Cast: Patrick Macnee (John Steed), Linda Thorson (Tara King), Angela Douglas (Miranda Loxton), John Cairney (Major Firth), John Paul (Dr Wells), Patrick Newell (Mother), Denis Shaw (Murray), Terence Sewards (Rista), Mike Lewin (Lieutenant Barrett), Kathja Wyeth (Jill), Harvey Ashby (Bobby Cleaver), John Baker (Vicar).
Uncredited Cast: Rhonda Parker (Rhonda), Terry Maidment (Bodyguard), John Laurimore (Photographer), Joe Dunne (Stunt Double for Murray), Cyd Child (Stunt Double for Tara King), Les Crawford (Stunt Double for Rista), Paul Weston (Stunt Double for John Steed), Dorothy Ford (Stunt Double for Jill), Peter Brace (Stunt Double for Dr Wells), Joe Dunne (Stunt Double for Major Firth), Cliff Diggins (Stunt Double for Lieutenant Barrett), Rupert Evans (Stunt Double for Bodyguard).
Crew: Laurie Johnson (Music by), Terry Nation (Script Editor), David Holmes (Director

of Photography), Karen Heward (Editor), Ann Chegwidden (Post Production Co-ordinator) Alun Hughes (Miss Thorson's Costumes Designed by), Ron Purdie (Assistant Director), Geoff Seaholme (Camera Operator), Kenneth Tait (Associate Art Director), Simon Wakefield (Set Dresser), Kay Perkins (Continuity), Mary Sturgess (Hairdressing), Ivy Baker (Costume Supervisor), Bert Mason (Second Unit Photography), Cecil Mason (Sound Recordist), Len Abbott (Dubbing Mixer), Peter Lennard (Sound Editor), Paul Clay (Music Editor), Herbert Worley (Construction Manager), Roy Bond (Supervisory Electrician).

Uncredited Crew: D Worley (Clapper Loader), M Arnold (Focus Puller), Jackie Green (Second Assistant Director), N Jones (Camera Operator), K Nightingale (Boom Operator), Bert Mason (Lighting Cameraman), Gerry Altman (Clapper Loader), Peggy Spirito (Continuity), C Leigh (Continuity), Paul Jordan (Clapper Loader), B Lipman (Second Assistant Director), Terry Cole (Focus Puller), Bob Kindred (Camera Operator), John O'Conner (Assistant Director), F Fay (Sound Camera Operator).

Production Schedule:
Monday 20 January 1969: Day 1: Don Chaffey
B Unit: 09.30-16.50: Bell Moor, East Heath Road, London, NW3 [Int: Underground car park]
Tuesday 21 January 1969: Day 2: Don Chaffey
B Unit: 09.35 to unknown time: Aldenham Road, Letchmore Heath, Herts [Ext: Quiet road/Int: Firth's car]
B Unit: Unknown time: Hilfield Lane, Elstree, Herts [Ext: Firth's car passes electricity pylon]
B Unit: Unknown time: Letchmore Heath, Herts [Ext: Firth's car goes around village green]
B Unit: Unknown time to 14.50: Aldenham Grange, Grange Road, Letchmore Heath, Herts [Ext: Firth's car stops by large house]
Wednesday 22 January 1969: Day 3: Don Chaffey
B Unit: 09.40 to unknown time: The Haberdashers' Aske's School Gateway, Aldenham Road, Elstree, Herts [Ext: Fake house]
B Unit: Unknown time: The Rise, Borehamwood, Herts [Ext: Cranbrook Road]
B Unit: Unknown time to 15.47: Camfield Place Gateway, Windhill Road, Windhill, Hatfield, Herts [Ext: Real house]
Thursday 23 January 1969: Day 4: Don Chaffey
B Unit: 09.05 to unknown time: Duchess Mews, London, W1 [Ext: Steed's mews]
B Unit: Unknown time: Lyndhurst, Green Lane, Shenley, Herts [Ext: Steed and Loxton arrive at gateway on country road]
B Unit: Unknown time: Maxwell Road, Borehamwood, Herts [Ext: Tara drives Rolls Royce down quiet street]
B Unit: Unknown time: The Haberdashers' Aske's School Gateway, Aldenham Road, Elstree, Herts [Ext: Gateway decorated]
B Unit: Unknown time to 16.35: ABPC Elstree Studios, Studio Lot [Ext: Warehouse area]
Friday 24 January 1969: Day 5: Don Chaffey
B Unit: 08.35-17.25: ABPC Elstree Studios, Stage 5 [Int: Playroom]
Quarter called pm
Monday 27 January 1969: Day 6: Don Chaffey
B Unit: 09.20-15.40: Heath Brow Car Park, North End Way, London, NW3 [Ext: Car

park]
Tuesday 28 January 1969: Day 7: Don Chaffey
B Unit: 08.35-17.17: ABPC Elstree Studios, Stage 5 [Int: Steed's apartment/corridor outside Steed's front door/playroom]
Patrick Newell went home sick at 10.03 am
Wednesday 29 January 1969: Day 8: Don Chaffey
B Unit: 08.45-17.26: ABPC Elstree Studios, Stage 5 [Int: Playroom]
Quarter called pm
Thursday 30 January 1969: Day 9: Don Chaffey
B Unit: 09.15 to unknown time: St Andrew's Church, Totteridge Village, Totteridge, London, N20 [Ext: Church and cemetery]
B Unit: Unknown time: The Rise, Borehamwood, Herts [Ext: Cranbrook Road/Int: Hearse]
B Unit: Unknown time: ABPC Elstree Studios, Studio Lot [Ext: Car park/Int: Cars]
B Unit: Unknown time to 17.12: ABPC Elstree Studios, Stage 2 [Int: Playroom]
Friday 31 January 1969: Day 10: Don Chaffey
B Unit: 08.40-17.20: ABPC Elstree Studios, Stage 5 [Int: Steed's apartment/playroom/locked room]
Monday 3 February 1969: Day 11: Don Chaffey/John Hough
B Unit: 08.30-17.24: ABPC Elstree Studios, Stage 5 [Int: Locked room/corridor outside/hospital corridor/hospital room]
3rd: 09.30-17.16: Aldenham Reservoir, Elstree, Herts [Ext: River area]
Tuesday 4 February 1969: Day 12: Don Chaffey
B Unit: 08.35-16.50: ABPC Elstree Studios, Stage 5 [Int: Hospital room]
Wednesday 5 February 1969: Day 13: Don Chaffey
B Unit: 08.35-17.32: ABPC Elstree Studios, Stage 5 [Int: Hospital room/hospital corridor]
Quarter called pm
Thursday 6 February 1969: Day 14: Don Chaffey
B Unit: 08.33-17.20: ABPC Elstree Studios, Stage 5 [Int: Hospital corridor/Steed's wrecked apartment/Steed's wrecked corridor]
Friday 7 February 1969: Day 15: Don Chaffey
B Unit: 08.55 to unknown time: ABPC Elstree Studios, Studio Lot [Ext: Warehouse area/Int: Tara's car]
B Unit: Unknown time to 17.20: ABPC Elstree Studios, Stage 5 [Int: Steed's wrecked apartment/Steed's wrecked corridor]
Monday 10 February 1969: Day 16: Don Chaffey
B Unit: 08.45-15.39: ABPC Elstree Studios, Stage 5 [Int: Deserted room and outside corridor]
Thursday 13 February 1969: Day 17: John Hough
3rd: Unknown time to 16.52: ABPC Elstree Studios, Stage 5 [Int: Inserts for Scenes 38, 64, 65, 93]

6.32 – 'TAKE-OVER'
Episode 160
Original Transmission Date: Wednesday 23 April 1969

Writer: Terry Nation

Director: Robert Fuest
Cast: Patrick Macnee (John Steed), Linda Thorson (Tara King), Tom Adams (Fenton Grenville), Elizabeth Sellers (Laura Bassett), Michael Gywnn (Bill Bassett), Hilary Pritchard (Circe Bishop), Garfield Morgan (Gilbert Sexton), Keith Buckley (Ernest Lomax), John Comer (Sergeant Ronald Groom), Anthony Sagar (Norman Clifford).
Uncredited Cast: Art Thomas (Handcuffed Man), Paul Weston (Stunt Double for John Steed), Cliff Diggins (Stunt Double for John Steed), Cyd Child (Stunt Double for Tara King), Les Crawford (Stunt Double for Fenton Grenville), Romo Gorrara (Stunt Double for Gilbert Sexton), Joe Dunne (Stunt Double for Ernest Lomax), Dorothy Ford (Stunt Double for Circe Bishop).
Crew: Laurie Johnson (Music by), Terry Nation (Script Editor), Peter Jessop (Director of Photography), Robert Dearberg (Editor), Ann Chegwidden (Post Production Co-ordinator) Alun Hughes (Miss Thorson's Costumes Designed by), Colin Lord (Assistant Director), Ernie Robinson (Camera Operator), Kenneth Tait (Associate Art Director), Simon Wakefield (Set Dresser), Kay Fenton (Continuity), Mary Sturgess (Hairdressing), Ivy Baker (Costume Supervisor), Bert Mason (Second Unit Photography), Claude Hitchcock (Sound Recordist), Bill Rowe (Dubbing Mixer), Peter Lennard (Sound Editor), Paul Clay (Music Editor), Herbert Worley (Construction Manager), Steve Birtles (Supervisory Electrician).
Uncredited Crew: John O'Conner (Assistant Director), Terry Cole (Focus Puller), Jackie Green (Unit Runner/Third Assistant Director), H Bevan (Hairdresser), N Jones (Camera Operator), Bert Mason (Lighting Cameraman), B Royston (Make-Up), K Nightingale (Boom Operator), B Lipman (Second Assistant Director), Leslie Hammond (Sound Mixer), Paul Jordan (Clapper Loader), S Valentine (Production Buyer), Michael Adelman (Third Assistant Director), Betty Sherriff (Hairdresser), Peggy Spirito (Post Production), P Dobson (Assistant Dubbing Editor), M Morris (Make-Up), A Lee (Stills Cameraman), M Jympson (Sound Effects), K Mackay (Make-Up), B Royston (Make-Up), C Davidson (Clapper Loader), Mike Roberts (Focus Puller), C Leigh (Continuity), George Claff (Make-Up), J Lee Wright (Sound Effects), P Taylor (Clapper Loader), F Fay (Sound Camera Operator).

Production Schedule:
Thursday 30 January 1969: Day 1: Robert Fuest
3rd: 09.43-17.13: Aldenham Road, Elstree, Herts [Ext: Country road and field/Int: Car]
Friday 31 January 1969: Day 2: Robert Fuest
3rd: 08.58-16.58: Aldenham Estate, Elstree, Herts [Ext: Countryside and woods]
Monday 3 February 1969: Day 3: Robert Fuest
A Unit: 09.40-16.42: Aldenham Estate, Elstree, Herts [Ext: Countryside, woods and swamp]
Tuesday 4 February 1969: Day 4: Robert Fuest
A Unit: 10.10-10.12: Aldenham Estate, Elstree, Herts [Ext: Swamp]
A Unit: Unknown time to 17.16: ABPC Elstree Studios, Stage 3 [Int: Steed's bedroom/landing]
Wednesday 5 February 1969: Day 5: Robert Fuest
A Unit: 09.50-17.45: Aldenham Estate, Elstree, Herts [Ext: Swamp/Int: Land Rover/Ext: Countryside and woods]
Thursday 6 February 1969: Day 6: Robert Fuest
A Unit: 10.10-17.05: ABPC Elstree Studios, Stage 3 [Int: Landing/the Bassetts' bedroom]

Friday 7 February 1969: Day 7: Robert Fuest/John Hough
A Unit: 08.40-17.20: ABPC Elstree Studios, Stage 3 [Int: Dining – sitting room]
3rd: Unknown time to 16.08: Unknown Location [Country road/fields and country roads A and B]
The 3rd Unit footage not used in the episode
Monday 10 February 1969: Day 8: Robert Fuest
A Unit: 08.50-17.30: ABPC Elstree Studios, Stage 3 [Int: Dining – sitting room/hall]
Quarter called pm
Tuesday 11 February 1969: Day 9: Robert Fuest
A Unit: 10.05-17.10: ABPC Elstree Studios, Stage 3 [Int: Hall]
Wednesday 12 February 1969: Day 10: Robert Fuest
A Unit: 09.30-17.29: ABPC Elstree Studios, Stage 3 [Int: Hall/dining – sitting room]
Quarter called pm.
Thursday 13 February 1969: Day 11: Robert Fuest/John Hough
A Unit: 09.40-17.20: ABPC Elstree Studios, Stage 3 [Int: Tara's apartment/turret room/hall]
3rd: 09.43 to unknown time: Radlett Preparatory School, Watling Street, Radlett, Herts [Ext: The Barretts' home]
3rd: Unknown time: Aldenham Estate, Elstree, Herts [Ext: Swamp]
Friday 14 February 1969: Day 12: Robert Fuest
A Unit: 09.05-17.15: ABPC Elstree Studios, Stage 3 [Int: Hall]
Monday 17 February 1969: Day 13: Robert Fuest
A Unit: 09.10-17.12: ABPC Elstree Studios, Stage 3 [Int: Hall]
Tuesday 18 February 1969: Day 14: Robert Fuest
A Unit: 09.00-17.20: ABPC Elstree Studios, Stage 3 [Int: Hall]
Wednesday 19 February 1969: Day 15: Robert Fuest
A Unit: 08.35-17.12: ABPC Elstree Studios, Stage 3 [Int: Dining – sitting room/turret room/landing]
Thursday 20 February 1969: Day 16: Robert Fuest
A Unit: 09.05-17.18: ABPC Elstree Studios, Stage 3 [Int: Turret room/hall/Ext: Mud tank]
Friday 21 February 1969: Day 17: Robert Fuest
A Unit: 10.00-14.25: ABPC Elstree Studios, Stage 3 [Int: Mud tank/Tara's apartment]

6.33 – 'BIZZARE'
Episode 161
Original Transmission Date: Wednesday 21 May 1969

Writer: Brian Clemens
Director: Leslie Norman
Cast: Patrick Macnee (John Steed), Linda Thorson (Tara King), Roy Kinnear (Bagpipes Happychap), Fulton Mackay (Master), Patrick Newell (Mother), Sally Nesbitt (Helen Pritchard), James Kerry (Captain Cordell), George Innes (Shaw), John Sharp (Jonathan Jupp), Sheila Burrell (Mrs Jupp), Michael Balfour (Tom), Patrick Connor (Bob), Ron Pember (Charley).
Uncredited Cast: Rhonda Parker (Rhonda), Frank Maher (Bradney Morton), Rosemarie Chalmers (First Hostess), Paul Weston (Stunt Double for John Steed), Cyd Child (stunt Double for Tara King), Max Faulkner (Stunt Double for Master), Joe Dunne (Stunt

Double for Shaw), Paddy Ryan (Stunt Double for Charley), Bill Sawyer (Stunt Double for Jonathan Jupp), Roy Scammell (Stunt Double for Helen Pritchard) Peter Brace (Stunt Double for Unknown Performer).

Crew: Laurie Johnson (Music by), Terry Nation (Script Editor), David Holmes (Director of Photography), Karen Heward (Editor), Ann Chegwidden (Post Production Co-ordinator) Alun Hughes (Miss Thorson's Costumes Designed by), Ron Purdie (Assistant Director), Geoff Seaholme (Camera Operator), Kenneth Tait and Len Townsend (Associate Art Directors), Simon Wakefield (Set Dresser), Kay Perkins (Continuity), Mary Sturgess (Hairdressing), Ivy Baker (Costume Supervisor), Cecil Mason (Sound Recordist), Bill Rowe (Dubbing Mixer), Peter Lennard (Sound Editor), Paul Clay (Music Editor), Herbert Worley (Construction Manager), Roy Bond (Supervisory Electrician).

Uncredited Crew: Michael Adelman (Third Assistant Director), Leslie Hammond (Sound Mixer), Terry Cole (Focus Puller), Paul Jordan (Clapper Loader), John O'Conner (Assistant Director), Bert Mason (Lighting Cameraman), N Jones (Camera Operator), Jackie Green (Third Assistant Director/Unit Runner), C Davidson (Clapper Loader), B Lipman (Second Assistant Director), C Leigh (Continuity), Doreen Soan (Continuity), Colin Lord (Assistant Director), B Royston (Make-Up), H Bevan (Hairdresser), Betty Sherriff (Hairdresser), George Claff (Make-Up), Peggy Spirito (Post Production/ Continuity), Michael Proudfoot (Clapper Loader), A McDonald (Focus Puller), Nick Gillott (Second Assistant Director), D Dickinson (Lighting Cameraman), Ernie Robinson (Camera Operator), Kay Fenton (Continuity), F McManus (Wardrobe Assistant), Derek Hyde (Wardrobe Assistant), E Fletcher (Make-Up), T Burns (Second Assistant Director), M Murphy (Third Assistant Director), David Holmes (Lighting Cameraman), D Litchfield (Focus Puller), R McDonald (Clapper Loader), Charles Wheeler (Boom Operator).

Production Schedule:

Friday 7 February 1969: Day 1: John Hough

3rd: 09.04 to unknown time: Camfield Place Gateway, Windhill Road, Windhill, Hatfield, Herts [Ext: The Happy Meadows]

Monday 10 February 1969: Day 2: John Hough

3rd: 09.28-13.36: Kendall Hall Farm, Watling Street, Radlett, Herts [Ext: Bleak open ground]

Tuesday 11 February 1969: Day 3: Don Chaffey

B Unit: 09.16 to unknown time: ABPC Elstree Studios, Stage 5 [Int: Wife's room/Mystic Tours]

B Unit: Unknown time to 16.35: ABPC Elstree Studios, Studio Lot [Ext: Hospital/Int: Car]

Wednesday 12 February 1969: Day 4: Leslie Norman

B Unit: 09.25-17.30: ABPC Elstree Studios, Stage 5 [Int: Mystic Tours/Mystic area]

Quarter called am and pm

Thursday 13 February 1969: Day 5: Leslie Norman

B Unit: 10.05 to unknown time: Weymouth Mews, London, W1 [Ext: Steed run down by van]

B Unit: Unknown time to 16.20: ABPC Elstree Studios, Stage 5 [Int: Mystic area/Mother's headquarters]

Friday 14 February 1969: Day 6: Leslie Norman

B Unit: 09.08-16.51: ABPC Elstree Studios, Stage 5 [Int: Mother's headquarters]

Monday 17 February 1969: Day 7: Leslie Norman

B Unit: 08.55 to unknown time: ABPC Elstree Studios, Stage 5 [Int: Mother's headquarters/wife's room]

B Unit: Unknown time to 17.20: ABPC Elstree Studios, Stage 2 [Int: Paradise]

Tuesday 18 February 1969: Day 8: Leslie Norman

B Unit: 08.50-17.20: ABPC Elstree Studios, Stage 2 [Int: Paradise]

Wednesday 19 February 1969: Day 9: Leslie Norman

B Unit: 08.50-17.20: ABPC Elstree Studios, Stage 2 [Int: Paradise]

Thursday 20 February 1969: Day 10: Leslie Norman

B Unit: 09.10-17.20: ABPC Elstree Studios, Stage 2 [Int: Paradise/Ext: Grave/Int: Hospital room]

Friday 21 February 1969: Day 11: Leslie Norman

B Unit: 09.16-17.20: ABPC Elstree Studios, Stage 2 [Int: Hospital Room/Rocket/Int: and Ext: Sky backing]

Monday 24 February 1969: Day 12: Leslie Norman

B Unit: 08.35-17.20: ABPC Elstree Studios, Stage 2 [Int: Hospital room/Ext: Fire escape]

Tuesday 25 February 1969: Day 13: Leslie Norman/John Hough

B Unit: 09.00-17.15: ABPC Elstree Studios, Stage 2 [Int: Section of Mystic Tours/Happychap's office]

3rd: 09.45 to unknown time: ABPC Elstree Studios, Stage 3 [Int: Guard's van]

3rd: Unknown time: ABPC Elstree Studios, Stage 2 [Int: Hospital room/Ext: Fire escape]

3rd: Unknown time to 17.20: ABPC Elstree Studios, Stage 3 [Int: Mother's headquarters]

Wednesday 26 February 1969: Day 14: Leslie Norman/John Hough

B Unit: 08.55-17.19: ABPC Elstree Studios, Stage 2 [Int: Happychap's office/Paradise plot]

3rd: 08.40-11.00: ABPC Elstree Studios, Stage 3 [Int: Mother's headquarters]

Thursday 27 February 1969: Day 15: No details available

Friday 28 February 1969: Day 16: Leslie Norman/John Hough

B Unit: 08.45-17.16: ABPC Elstree Studios, Stage 2 [Int: Paradise Plot]

3rd: 11.20-12.00: ABPC Elstree Studios, Backlot Town [Ext: Street]

Monday 3 March 1969: Day 17: Leslie Norman

B Unit: 09.00-11.25: ABPC Elstree Studios, Stage 2 [Int: Paradise Plot]

APPENDIX TWO

THE NEW AVENGERS: PRODUCTION DETAILS

The episodes are listed below in production order rather than transmission order. The director on each recording or filming date is noted against that date in the 'Production Schedule' entry for each episode.

SEASON ONE

An Avengers (Film and TV) Enterprises Ltd production for TV Productions and IDTV Paris
13 colour episodes on 35mm film
Permanent Crew: Albert Fennell and Brian Clemens (Produced by), Laurie Johnson (Music Composed by), Ron Fry (Production Supervisor), Robert Fennell (Unit Manager), Nicholas Gillott (Location Manager), Maggie Cartier (Casting Director), Syd Cain (Production Designed by), Robert Bell (Art Director), Simon Wakefield (Set Dresser) Leon Davis (Construction Manager), Jackie Cummings (Wardrobe Supervisor), Paul Clay (Post-Production Co-ordinator).
Transmission Dates: Granada region

1.01 – 'THE EAGLE'S NEST'
Episode 162
Original Transmission Date: Friday 22 October 1976

Writer: Brian Clemens
Director: Desmond Davis
Cast: Patrick Macnee (John Steed), Gareth Hunt (Mike Gambit), Joanna Lumley (Purdey), Peter Cushing (Dr von Claus), Derek Farr (Father Trasker), Frank Gatliff (Karl Bury), Sydney Bromley (Hara), Trevor Baxter (Brown-Fitch), Joyce Carey (Lady with Dog), Neil Phillips (Main), Brian Anthony (George Stannard), Ronald Forfar (Jud), Jerold Wells (Barker), Trudi van Dorne (Gerda), Peter Porteous (Nazi Corporal), Charles Bolton (Ralph).
Uncredited Cast: Sammie Windmill (Barmaid), Raymond Mason (Man loading Car), Maggy Maxwell (Dowager).

Crew: Ron Purdie (Assistant Director), Renée Glynn (Continuity), Catherine Buckley (Joanna Lumley's costumes designed by), Mike Reed (Lighting Cameraman), Jimmy Devis (Camera Operator), Neville Smallwood and Alan Boyle (Make-Up), Helene Bevan and Joyce James (Hairdressing), Ralph Sheldon (Editor), Denis Whitlock and Ken Barker (Sound Recordists), Peter Lennard and Bob Dearberg (Dubbing Editors).
Second Unit: Jimmy Allen (Lighting Cameraman), Malcolm Vinson (Camera Operator), Nicholas Gillott (Assistant Director), Pat Rambaut (Continuity).
Uncredited Crew: Bryn Siddall (Property Buyer), Don Retzer (Transport Co-ordinator).

1.02 – 'THE MIDAS TOUCH'
Episode 163
Original Transmission Date: Friday 19 November 1976

Writer: Brian Clemens
Director: Robert Fuest
Cast: Patrick Macnee (John Steed), Gareth Hunt (Mike Gambit), Joanna Lumley (Purdey), John Carson (Freddy), Ed Devereaux (Vann), Ronald Lacey (Hong Kong Harry), David Swift (Professor Turner), Jeremy Child (Lieutenant Henry), Robert Mill (Curator), Ray Edwards (General Garvin), Gilles Millinaire (Midas), Pik-Sen Lim (Madame Sing), Chris Tranchell (Doctor), Lionel Guyett (Tayman), Geoffrey Bateman (Simpson), Tim Condren (Boz), Peter Winter (Morgan), Bruce Bould (Froggart), Bruno Elrington (Choy).
Uncredited Cast: Kenneth Gilbert (Rostock), Tania Mallett (Sara), Pola Churchill (Princess), John Tatum (Museum Operative).
Crew: Ron Purdie (Assistant Director), Renée Glynn (Continuity), Catherine Buckley (Joanna Lumley's costumes designed by), Mike Reed (Lighting Cameraman), Jimmy Devis (Camera Operator), Neville Smallwood and Alan Boyle (Make-Up), Helene Bevan and Joyce James (Hairdressing), Graeme Clifford (Editor), Denis Whitlock and Gordon K McCallum (Sound Recordists), Peter Lennard and Bob Dearberg (Dubbing Editors).
Second Unit: Jimmy Allen (Lighting Cameraman), Malcolm Vinson (Camera Operator), Roger Simons (Assistant Director), Pat Rambaut (Continuity).
Uncredited Crew: Bryn Siddall (Property Buyer), Don Retzer (Transport Co-ordinator).

1.03 – 'HOUSE OF CARDS'
Episode 164
Original Transmission Date: Friday 29 October 1976

Writer: Brian Clemens
Director: Ray Austin
Cast: Patrick Macnee (John Steed), Gareth Hunt (Mike Gambit), Joanna Lumley (Purdey), Peter Jeffrey (Ivan Perov), Frank Thornton (Roland), Lyndon Brook (Cartney), Derek Francis (The Bishop), Mark Burns (Spence), Geraldine Moffatt (Joanna Harrington), Annette André (Suzy Miller), Ina Skriver (Olga Perinkov), Murray Brown (David Miller), Gordon Sterne (Professor Vasil), Dan Meaden (Boris), Jeremy Wilkin (Tulliver), Anthony Bailey (Frederick).
Uncredited Cast: Terry Plummer (Kristos).
Crew: Ron Purdie (Assistant Director), Renée Glynn (Continuity), Catherine Buckley

(Joanna Lumley's costumes designed by), Mike Reed (Lighting Cameraman), Jimmy Devis (Camera Operator), Neville Smallwood and Alan Boyle (Make-Up), Helene Bevan and Joyce James (Hairdressing), Cyd Child (Fight Arranger), Ralph Sheldon (Editor), Denis Whitlock and Ken Barker (Sound Recordists), Peter Lennard and Bob Dearberg (Dubbing Editors).

Second Unit: Jimmy Allen (Lighting Cameraman), Malcolm Vinson (Camera Operator), Roger Simons (Assistant Director), Pat Rambaut (Continuity).

Uncredited Crew: Ron Purdie (Production Manager), Dushko Indjic (Sound), Bryn Siddall (Property Buyer), Don Retzer (Transport Co-ordinator).

1.04 – 'THE LAST OF THE CYBERNAUTS …??'
Episode 165
Original Transmission Date: Friday 5 November 1976

Writer: Brian Clemens
Director: Sidney Hayers
Cast: Patrick Macnee (John Steed), Gareth Hunt (Mike Gambit), Joanna Lumley (Purdey), Robert Lang (Felix Kane), Oscar Quintak (Malov), Gwen Taylor (Doctor Marlow) Basil Hoskins (Professor Mason), Robert Gillespie (Frank Goff), David Horovitch (Fitzroy), Sally Bazely (Laura), Pearl Hackney (Mrs Weir), Martin Fisk (2nd Guard), Eric Carte (Terry), Ray Armstrong (1st Guard), Rocky Taylor (Cybernaut), Davina Taylor (Tricia).
Crew: Ron Purdie (Assistant Director), Renée Glynn (Continuity), Catherine Buckley (Joanna Lumley's costumes designed by), Mike Reed (Lighting Cameraman), Jimmy Devis (Camera Operator), Peter Robb King and Alan Boyle (Make-Up), Helene Bevan and Joyce James (Hairdressing), Cyd Child (Fight Arranger), Graeme Clifford (Editor), Denis Whitlock and Ken Barker (Sound Recordists), Peter Lennard and Bob Dearberg (Dubbing Editors).
Second Unit: Jimmy Allen (Lighting Cameraman), Malcolm Vinson (Camera Operator), Roger Simons (Assistant Director), Pat Rambaut (Continuity).
Uncredited Crew: Bryn Siddall (Property Buyer), Don Retzer (Transport Co-ordinator).

1.05 – 'TO CATCH A RAT'
Episode 166
Original Transmission Date: Friday 3 December 1976

Writer: Terence Feely
Director: James Hill
Cast: Patrick Macnee (John Steed), Gareth Hunt (Mike Gambit), Joanna Lumley (Purdey), Ian Hendry (Erwin Gunner), Edward Judd (Cromwell), Robert Flemyng (Quaintance), Barry Jackson (Cledge), Anthony Sharp (Grant), Jeremy Hawk (Finder), Bernice Stegers (Operator), Jo Kendall (Nurse), Dallas Cavell (Farmer), Sally-Jane Spencer (Mother).
Uncredited Cast: Genevieve Allenbury (Bridget), Anita Graham (Helga), Corrie Hendry (Little Girl).
Crew: Roger Simons (Assistant Director), Renée Glynn (Continuity), Mike Reed BSC (Director of Photography), Jimmy Devis (Camera Operator), Peter Robb King and Alan Boyle (Make-Up), Helene Bevan (Hairdressing Supervisor), Joyce James (Assistant

Hairdresser), Cyd Child (Fight Arranger), Ralph Sheldon (Editor), Denis Whitlock and Ken Barker (Sound Recordists), Peter Lennard (Dubbing Editor).
Second Unit: Jimmy Allen BSC (Lighting Cameraman), Malcolm Vinson (Camera Operator), Pat Rambaut (Continuity).
Uncredited Crew: Bryn Siddall (Property Buyer).

1.06 – 'CAT AMONGST THE PIGEONS'
Episode 167
Original Transmission Date: Friday 12 November 1976

Writer: Dennis Spooner
Director: John Hough
Cast: Patrick Macnee (John Steed), Gareth Hunt (Mike Gambit), Joanna Lumley (Purdey), Vladek Sheybal (Zarcardi), Matthew Long (Turner), Basil Dignam (Rydercroft), Peter Copley (Waterlow), Hugh Walters (Lewington), Gordon Rollings (Bridlington), Joe Black (Hudson), Patrick Connor (Foster), Kevin Stoney (Tomkins), Andrew Bradford (Merton), Brian Jackson (Controller).
Uncredited Cast: George Hilsdon (Removal Man).
Crew: Ron Purdie (Assistant Director), Renée Glynn (Continuity), Mike Reed BSC (Director of Photography), Jimmy Devis (Camera Operator), Peter Robb King and Alan Boyle (Make-Up), Helene Bevan (Hairdressing Supervisor) Joyce James (Assistant Hairdresser), Cyd Child (Fight Arranger), Graeme Clifford (Editor), Denis Whitlock and Gordon K. McCallum (Sound Recordists), Peter Lennard and Mike Hopkins (Dubbing Editors).
Second Unit: Jimmy Allen BSC (Lighting Cameraman), Malcolm Vinson (Camera Operator), Roger Simons (Assistant Director), Pat Rambaut (Continuity).
Uncredited Crew: Bryn Siddall (Property Buyer).

1.07 – 'TARGET!'
Episode 168
Original Transmission Date: Friday 26 November 1976

Writer: Dennis Spooner
Director: Ray Austin
Cast: Patrick Macnee (John Steed), Gareth Hunt (Mike Gambit), Joanna Lumley (Purdey), Keith Barron (Draker), Robert Beatty (Colonel Ilenko), Roy Boyd (Freddy Bradshaw), Frederick Jaeger (Jones), Malcolm Stoddard (George Myers), Deep Roy (Klokoe), John Paul (Dr Kendrick), Bruce Purchase (Lopez), Dennis Blanche (Talmadge), Robert Tayman (Palmer).
Uncredited Cast: Marc Boyle (McKay), Susannah MacMillan (Susie), Peter Brace (Potterton), John Saunders (Titherbridge).
Crew: Roger Simons (Assistant Director), Pat Rambaut (Continuity), Cyd Child (Fight Arranger), Jimmy Allen BSC (Director of Photography), Malcolm Vinson (Camera Operator), Alan Brownie and Alan Boyle (Make-Up), Helene Bevan (Hairdressing Supervisor) Joyce James (Assistant Hairdresser), Ralph Sheldon (Editor), Danny Daniel and Ken Barker (Sound Recordists), Peter Lennard (Dubbing Editor).
Uncredited Crew: Bryn Siddall (Property Buyer).

1.08 – 'FACES'
Episode 169
Original Transmission Date: Friday 17 December 1976

Writers: Brian Clemens and Dennis Spooner
Director: James Hill
Cast: Patrick Macnee (John Steed and John Steed Double), Gareth Hunt (Mike Gambit), Joanna Lumley (Purdey), David de Keyser (Dr Prator), Edward Petherbridge (Mullins), Richard Leech (Craig and Terrison), Neil Hallett (Mark Clifford and Mark Clifford Double), Annabel Leventon (Wendy Clifford), David Webb (Bilston and Bilston Double), Donald Hewlett (Torrance), J G Devlin (Tramp), Jill Melford (Lady Sheila Rayner), Michael Sheard (Peters), Robert Putt (Attendant).
Crew: Ron Purdie (Assistant Director), Renée Glynn (Continuity), Cyd Child (Fight Arranger), Mike Reed BSC (Director of Photography), Herbert Smith (Camera Operator), Alan Brownie and Alan Boyle (Make-Up), Helene Bevan (Hairdressing Supervisor) Joyce James (Assistant Hairdresser), Graeme Clifford (Editor), Dennis Whitlock and Ken Barker (Sound Recordists), Peter Lennard and Mike Hopkins (Dubbing Editors).
Second Unit: Jimmy Allen BSC (Lighting Cameraman), Malcolm Vinson (Camera Operator), Roger Simons (Assistant Director), Pat Rambaut (Continuity).
Uncredited Crew: Bryn Siddall (Property Buyer).

1.09 – 'THE TALE OF THE BIG WHY'
Episode 170
Original Transmission Date: Friday 10 December 1976

Writer: Brian Clemens
Director: Robert Fuest
Cast: Patrick Macnee (John Steed), Gareth Hunt (Mike Gambit), Joanna Lumley (Purdey), Derek Waring (George Harmer), Jenny Runacre (Irene Brandon), George Cooper (Bert Brandon), Roy Marsden (Frank Turner), Gary Waldhorne (Roach), Rowland Davis (Poole), Geoffrey Toone (Minister), Maeve Alexander (Mrs Turner).
Crew: Roger Simons (Assistant Director), Renée Glynn (Continuity), Cyd Child (Fight Arranger), Mike Reed BSC (Director of Photography), Herbert Smith (Camera Operator), Alan Brownie and Alan Boyle (Make-Up), Helene Bevan (Hairdressing Supervisor) Joyce James (Assistant Hairdresser) Eric Boyd-Perkins (Editor), Danny Daniel and Ken Barker (Sound Recordists), Peter Lennard and Mike Hopkins (Dubbing Editors).
Second Unit: Jimmy Allen BSC (Lighting Cameraman), Malcolm Vinson (Camera Operator), Pat Rambaut (Continuity).
Uncredited Crew: Bryn Siddall (Property Buyer).

1.10 – 'THREE HANDED GAME'
Episode 171
Original Transmission Date: Friday 14 January 1977

Writers: Dennis Spooner and Brian Clemens
Director: Ray Austin

Cast: Patrick Macnee (John Steed), Gareth Hunt (Mike Gambit), Joanna Lumley (Purdey), David Wood (Tap Ranson), Michael Petrovitch (Larry), Stephen Greif (Juventor), Tony Vogel (Ivan), Gary Raymond (Masgard), Terry Wood (Colonel Meroff), Annie Lambert (Helen), Ronald Leigh-Hunt (General), John Paul (Doctor), Hugh Morton (Professor), Noel Trevarthen (Tony Fields), Bill Bailey (Cary).
Uncredited Cast: Joe Dunne (Intelligence Agent).
Crew: Ron Purdie (Assistant Director), Mary Dalison (Continuity), Cyd Child (Fight Arranger), Mike Reed BSC (Director of Photography), Herbert Smith (Camera Operator), Alan Brownie and Alan Boyle (Make-Up), Helene Bevan (Hairdressing Supervisor) Bob Dearberg (Editor), Danny Daniel and Ken Barker (Sound Recordists), Peter Lennard and Mike Hopkins (Dubbing Editors).
Second Unit: Jimmy Allen BSC (Lighting Cameraman), Malcolm Vinson (Camera Operator), Pamela Mann (Continuity).

1.11 – 'SLEEPER'
Episode 172
Original Transmission Date: Friday 7 January 1977

Writer: Brian Clemens
Director: Graeme Clifford
Cast: Patrick Macnee (John Steed), Gareth Hunt (Mike Gambit), Joanna Lumley (Purdey), Keith Buckley (Brady), Arthur Dignam (Dr Graham), Mark Jones (Chuck), Prentis Hancock (Bart), Sara Kestelman (Tina), Gavin Campbell (Fred), Dave Schofield (Ben), George Sweeney (Phil), Peter Godfrey (Pilot), Leo Dolan (Bill), Jason White (Policeman), Tony McHale (Policeman).
Uncredited Cast: Joe Dunne (Frank Hardy), Peter Richardson and Denise Reynolds (Couple in Car), Anulka Dubinska (Woman in Taxi), Maxwell Craig (Member of Gang).
Crew: Roger Simons (Assistant Director), Pat Rambaut (Continuity), Cyd Child (Fight Arranger), Ernie Steward BSC and Ian Wilson BSC (Lighting Cameramen), Malcolm Vinson (Camera Operator), Alan Brownie and Alan Boyle (Make-Up), Helene Bevan (Hairdressing Supervisor), Ralph Sheldon (Editor), Paul Lemare and Ken Barker (Sound Recordists), Peter Lennard and Mike Hopkins (Dubbing Editors).
Uncredited Crew: Bryn Siddall (Property Buyer).

1.12 – 'GNAWS'
Episode 173
Original Transmission Date: Friday 28 January 1977

Writer: Dennis Spooner
Director: Ray Austin
Cast: Patrick Macnee (John Steed), Gareth Hunt (Mike Gambit), Joanna Lumley (Purdey), Julian Holloway (Charles Thornton), Peter Cellier (Carter), Jeremy Young (Chislenko), Patrick Malahide (George Ratcliff), Keith Marsh (Tramp Joe), Ken Wynne (Tramp Arthur), Morgan Shepherd (Walters), John Watts (Harlow), Keith Alexander (Malloy), Ronnie Laughlin (Mechanic).
Crew: Ron Purdie (Assistant Director), Renée Glynne (Continuity), Cyd Child (Fight Arranger), Mike Reed BSC (Director of Photography), Herbert Smith (Camera Operator), Alan Brownie and Alan Boyle (Make-Up), Helene Bevan (Hairdressing

Supervisor), Bob Dearberg (Editor), Danny Daniel and Ken Barker (Sound Recordists), Peter Lennard and Mike Hopkins (Dubbing Editors).

1.13 – 'DIRTIER BY THE DOZEN'
Episode 174
Original Transmission Date: Friday 21 January 1977

Writer: Brian Clemens
Director: Sidney Hayers
Cast: Patrick Macnee (John Steed), Gareth Hunt (Mike Gambit), Joanna Lumley (Purdey), John Castle (Colonel Mad Jack Miller), Shaun Curry (Sergeant Bowdon), Stephen Moore (Major Prentice), Alun Armstrong (George Harris), Ballard Berkeley (Colonel Foster), Michael Barrington (General Stevens), Michael Howarth (Captain Tony Noble), John Forbes-Robertson (Doctor), Brian Croucher (Terry), John Labanowski (Corporal Keller), David Purcell (Orderly), Francis Mughan (Freddy).
Uncredited Cast: Colin Skeaping (Peter Travis), Richard Derrington (Turner), John Challis (Soldier), Rocky Taylor (Soldier).
Crew: Roger Simons (Assistant Director), Pat Rambaut (Continuity), Jillie Murphy and Jennifer Hocking (Joanna Lumley's wardrobe by), Cyd Child (Fight Arranger), Ian Wilson BSC (Director of Photography), Malcolm Vinson (Camera Operator), Alan Brownie and Wally Schneiderman (Make-Up), Helene Bevan (Hairdressing Supervisor), Ralph Sheldon (Editor), Paul Lemare and Ken Barker (Sound Recordists), Peter Lennard and Mike Hopkins (Dubbing Editors).

SEASON TWO

An Avengers (Film and TV) Enterprises Ltd production for TV Productions and IDTV Paris
9 colour episodes on 35mm film
Permanent Crew: Albert Fennell and Brian Clemens (Produced by), Laurie Johnson (Music Composed by), Paul Clay (Post-Production Co-ordinator).
Transmission Dates: Granada region

2.01 – 'HOSTAGE'
Episode 175
Original Transmission Date: Thursday 17 November 1977

Writer: Brian Clemens
Director: Sidney Hayers
Cast: Patrick Macnee (John Steed), Gareth Hunt (Mike Gambit), Joanna Lumley (Purdey), William Franklyn (Thomas McKay), Simon Oates (Tony Spelman), Michael Culver (Clive Walters), Anna Palk (Suzy Pilkington), Barry Stanton (Packer), Richard Ireson (Vernon), George Lane-Cooper (Marvin).
Uncredited Cast: Denny Powell (Symonds).
Crew: Ron Fry (Production Supervisor), Nicholas Gillott (Unit Manager), Ron Purdie (Assistant Director), Cheryl Leigh (Continuity), Maggie Cartier (Casting Director), Keith

Wilson (Production Designed by), Michael Ford (Assistant Art Director), Bill Waldron (Construction Manager), Maggie Lewin (Wardrobe Supervisor), Jillie Murphy (Fashion Co-ordinator), Ernie Steward BSC (Lighting Cameraman), Malcolm Vinson (Camera Operator), Alan Boyle and Alan Brownie (Make-Up), Mark Nelson (Hairdresser), Joe Dunne (Fight Arranger), Ian Wilson (Second Unit Director), Bob Dearberg (Editor), Paul LeMare and Ken Barker (Sound Recordists), Peter Lennard and Mike Hopkins (Dubbing Editors).

2.02 – 'TRAP'
Episode 176
Original Transmission Date: Thursday 13 October 1977

Writer: Brian Clemens
Director: Ray Austin
Cast: Patrick Macnee (John Steed), Gareth Hunt (Mike Gambit), Joanna Lumley (Purdey), Terry Wood (Soo Choy), Ferdy Mayne (Arcarti), Robert Rietty (Dom Carlos), Kristopher Kum (Tansing), Yasuko Nagazumi (Yasko), Stuart Damon (Marty Brine), Barry Lowe (Henry Murford), Annegret Easterman (Miranda), Bruce Boa (Mahon), Larry Lamb (Williams), Maj-Britt (Girlfriend).
Uncredited Cast: Vincent Wong (Courier).
Crew: Ron Fry (Production Supervisor), Ron Purdie (Unit Manager), Dominic Fulford (Assistant Director), Cheryl Leigh (Continuity), Maggie Cartier (Casting Director), Keith Wilson (Production Designed by), Michael Ford (Assistant Art Director), Bill Waldron (Construction Manager), Maggie Lewin (Wardrobe Supervisor), Jillie Murphy and Jennifer Hocking (Joanna Lumley's Wardrobe by), Ernie Steward BSC (Lighting Cameraman), Malcolm Vinson (Camera Operator), Alan Boyle and Alan Brownie (Make-Up), Mark Nelson (Hairdresser), Joe Dunne (Fight Arranger), Alan Killick (Editor), Paul Lemare and Ken Barker (Sound Recordists), Peter Lennard and Mike Hopkins (Dubbing Editors).

2.03 – 'DEAD MEN ARE DANGEROUS'
Episode 177
Original Transmission Date: Thursday 8 September 1977

Writer: Brian Clemens
Director: Sidney Hayers
Cast: Patrick Macnee (John Steed), Gareth Hunt (Mike Gambit), Joanna Lumley (Purdey), Clive Revill (Mark Crawford), Richard Murdoch ('Pin Man' Perry), Gabrielle Drake (Penny Redfern), Terry Taplin (Hara), Michael Turner (Dr Culver), Trevor Adam (Sandy), Roger Avon (Headmaster), Gabor Vernon (Russian Doctor).
Crew: Ron Fry and Ron Purdie (Associate Producers), Al Burgess (Assistant Director), Cheryl Leigh (Continuity), Maggie Cartier (Casting Director), Keith Wilson (Production Designed by), Michael Ford (Assistant Art Director), Bill Waldron (Construction Manager), Maggie Lewin (Wardrobe Supervisor), Jillie Murphy (Fashion Co-ordinator), Ernie Steward BSC (Lighting Cameraman), Malcolm Vinson (Camera Operator), Alan Boyle and Alan Brownie (Make-Up), Mark Nelson (Hairdresser), Joe Dunne (Fight Arranger), Ian Wilson (Second Unit Director), Bob Dearberg (Editor), Paul Lemare and Ken Barker (Sound Recordists), Peter Lennard and Mike Hopkins (Dubbing Editors).

2.04 – 'MEDIUM RARE'
Episode 178
Original Transmission Date: Thursday 22 September 1977

Writer: Dennis Spooner
Director: Ray Austin
Cast: Patrick Macnee (John Steed), Gareth Hunt (Mike Gambit), Joanna Lumley (Purdey), Jon Finch (Wallace), Mervyn Johns (Elderly Man), Jeremy Wilkin (Richards), Sue Holderness (Victoria Stanton), Neil Hallett (Roberts), Maurice O'Connell (McBain), Diana Churchill (Dowager Lady), Celia Foxe (Model Girl), Steve Ubels (Young Man at Séance), Allen Weston (Mason).
Uncredited Cast: John Tatum (Usher), Hugh Walters (George Cowley), Marc Boyle (Parr).
Crew: Ron Fry (Associate Producer), Ron Purdie (Production Manager), Dominic Fulford (Assistant Director), Cheryl Leigh (Continuity), Maggie Cartier (Casting Director), Keith Wilson (Production Designed by), Michael Ford (Assistant Art Director), Bill Waldron (Construction Manager), Maggie Lewin (Wardrobe Supervisor), Jillie Murphy and Betty Jackson (Joanna Lumley's Wardrobe by), Ernie Steward BSC (Lighting Cameraman), Malcolm Vinson (Camera Operator), Alan Boyle and Alan Brownie (Make-Up), Mark Nelson (Hairdresser), Joe Dunne (Fight Arranger), Alan Killick (Editor), Paul Lemare and Gordon K. McCallum (Sound Recordists), Peter Lennard and Mike Hopkins (Dubbing Editors).

2.05 – 'OBSSESION'
Episode 179
Original Transmission Date: Thursday 6 October 1977

Writer: Brian Clemens
Director: Ernest Day
Cast: Patrick Macnee (John Steed), Gareth Hunt (Mike Gambit), Joanna Lumley (Purdey), Martin Shaw (Larry Doomer), Mark Kingston (General Canvey), Terence Longdon (Commander East), Lewis Collins (Kilner), Anthony Heaton (Morgan), Tommy Boyle (Flight Lieutenant Wolach), Roy Purcell (Controller).
Uncredited Cast: Alf Joint (Arabic Soldier) Richard Graydon (Stunt Double for Purdey), Bill Weston (Stunt Double for Mike Gambit), Eddie Stacey (Stunt Double for Kilner), Graham Krenver (Stunt Double for Morgan), Walter Henry (Bodyguard).
Crew: Ron Fry (Associate Producer), Ron Purdie (Production Manager), Al Burgess (Assistant Director), Cheryl Leigh (Continuity), Maggie Cartier (Casting Director), Keith Wilson (Production Designed by), Michael Ford (Assistant Art Director), Bill Waldron (Construction Manager), Maggie Lewin (Wardrobe Supervisor), Jillie Murphy and Betty Jackson (Joanna Lumley's Wardrobe by), Ernie Steward BSC (Lighting Cameramen), Malcolm Vinson (Camera Operator), Alan Boyle and Alan Brownie (Make-Up), Mark Nelson (Hairdresser), Joe Dunne (Fight Arranger), Bob Dearberg (Editor), Paul Lemare and Ken Barker (Sound Recordists), Peter Lennard and Mike Hopkins (Dubbing Editors).

2.06 – 'ANGELS OF DEATH'
Episode 180

Original Transmission Date: Thursday 15 September 1977

Writers: Terence Feely and Brian Clemens
Director: Ernest Day
Cast: Patrick Macnee (John Steed), Gareth Hunt (Mike Gambit), Joanna Lumley (Purdey), Dinsdale Landen (Coldstream), Terence Alexander (Peter Manderson), Caroline Munro (Tammy), Michael Latimer (Reresby), Richard Gale (Charles Pelbright), Lindsay Duncan (Jane), Pamela Stephenson (Wendy), Annette Lynton (Pam), Moira Foot (Cindy), Christopher Driscoll (Martin), Melissa Stribling (Sally Manderson), Anthony Bailey (Simon Carter), Hedger Wallace (Colonel Tomson), Jennie Goossens (Mrs Pelbright).
Crew: Ron Fry (Associate Producer), David Munro (Unit Manager), Al Burgess (Assistant Director), Cheryl Leigh (Continuity), Maggie Cartier (Casting Director), Keith Wilson (Production Designed by), Michael Ford (Assistant Art Director), Bill Waldron (Construction Manager), Maggie Lewin (Wardrobe Supervisor), Jillie Murphy and Betty Jackson (Joanna Lumley's Wardrobe by), Ernie Steward BSC and Jack Atcheler BSC (Lighting Cameramen), Malcolm Vinson (Camera Operator), Alan Boyle and Alan Brownie (Make-Up), Mark Nelson (Hairdresser), Joe Dunne (Fight Arranger), Alan Killick (Editor), Paul Lemare and Ken Barker (Sound Recordists), Peter Lennard and Mike Hopkins (Dubbing Editors).

2.07 – 'THE LION AND THE UNICORN'
Episode 181
Original Transmission Date: Thursday 29 September 1977

Writer: John Goldsmith
Director: Ray Austin
Cast: Patrick Macnee (John Steed), Gareth Hunt (Mike Gambit), Joanna Lumley (Purdey), Jean Claudio (Unicorn), Maurice Marsac (Leparge), Raymond Bussières (Henri), Jacques Maury (Ritter), Raoul Delfosse (Marco), Gerald Sim (Minister), Henri Czarniak (Grima), Jean-Pierre Bernard (1st Bodyguard), Ludwig Gaum (2nd Bodyguard).
Crew: Ron Fry (Associate Producer), Philippe Lefebvre (Production Manager), Bernard Grenet (Assistant Director), Eliane Baum and Pat Rambaut (Continuity), Mamade (Casting), Daniel Budin (Production Designer), Patrick Danon (Unit Manager), Ginette Mejinsky (Location Manager), Jacky Budin (Wardrobe Mistress), Jillie Murphy (Fashion Co-ordinator), Gilbert Sarthre (Lighting Cameraman), Malcolm Vinson (Camera Operator), Paul Le Marinel and Alan Boyle (Make-Up), Mark Nelson (Hairdresser), Bob Dearberg (Editor), Paul Lemare and Ken Barker (Sound Recordists), Peter Lennard and Mike Hopkins (Dubbing Editors).

2.08 – 'K IS FOR KILL Part 1: THE TIGER AWAKES'
Episode 182
Original Transmission Date: Thursday 27 October 1977

Writer: Brian Clemens
Director: Yvon Marie Coulais
Cast: Patrick Macnee (John Steed), Gareth Hunt (Mike Gambit), Joanna Lumley

(Purdey), Pierre Verner (Colonel Martin), Maurice Marsac (General Gaspard), Charles Millot (Stanislav 1977), Paul Emile Deiber (Ambassador Toy), Christine Delaroche (Jeanine Leparge), Sacha Pitoëff (Kerov), Eric Desmaretz (Ivan), Sylvain Clément (Vassili), Krishna Clough (Soldier), Kenneth Watson (Salvation Army Major), Tony Then (Monk), Eric Allen (Penrose).

Uncredited Cast: Diana Rigg (Emma Peel), Charles Millot (Russian Colonel).

Crew: Ron Fry (Associate Producer), Philippe Lefebvre (Production Manager), Jean-Claude Garcia (Assistant Director), Eliane Baum and Pat Rambaut (Continuity), Mamade (Casting), Daniel Budin (Production Designer), Patrick Danon (Unit Manager), Ginette Mejinsky (Location Manager), Jacky Budin (Wardrobe Mistress), Jillie Murphy and Betty Jackson (Joanna Lumley's Wardrobe by), Gilbert Sarthre (Lighting Cameraman), Malcolm Vinson (Camera Operator), Paul Le Marinel and Alan Boyle (Make-Up), Mark Nelson (Hairdresser), Jean-Michel Lacor (Second Unit Director), Alan Killick (Editor), Paul Lemare and Ken Barker (Sound Recordists), Jack Knight and Mike Hopkins (Dubbing Editors).

2.09 – 'K IS FOR KILL Part 2: TIGER BY THE TAIL'
Episode 183
Original Transmission Date: Thursday 3 November 1977

Writer: Brian Clemens
Director: Yvon Marie Coulais
Cast: Patrick Macnee (John Steed), Gareth Hunt (Mike Gambit), Joanna Lumley (Purdey), Pierre Verner (Colonel Martin), Maurice Marsac (General Gaspard), Charles Millot (Stanislav 1977), Paul Emile Deiber (Ambassador Toy), Christine Delaroche (Jeanine Leparge), Maxence Mailfort (Turkov), Sacha Pitoeff (Kerov), Alberto Simono (Minister), Jacques Monnet (Waiter), Frank Oliver (Minski), Guy Mairesse (Guard), Cyrille Besnard (Secretary).

Crew: Ron Fry (Associate Producer), Philippe Lefebvre (Production Manager), Jean-Claude Garcia (Assistant Director), Eliane Baum and Pat Rambaut (Continuity), Mamade (Casting), Daniel Budin (Production Designer), Patrick Danon (Unit Manager), Ginette Mejinsky (Location Manager), Jacky Budin (Wardrobe Mistress), Jillie Murphy and Betty Jackson (Joanna Lumley's Wardrobe by), Gilbert Sarthre (Lighting Cameraman), Malcolm Vinson (Camera Operator), Paul Le Marinel and Alan Boyle (Make-Up), Mark Nelson (Hairdresser), Jean-Michel Lacor (Second Unit Director), Alan Killick (Editor), Paul Lemare and Ken Barker (Sound Recordists), Jack Knight and Mike Hopkins (Dubbing Editors).

An Avengers (Film and TV) Enterprises Ltd production for TV Productions and IDTV Paris/Nielsen-Ferns Inc, Toronto
4 colour episodes on 35mm film
Permanent Crew: Albert Fennell and Brian Clemens (Present *The New Avengers* in Canada), Laurie Johnson (Music Composed by), Ray Austin (Co-ordinating Producer for Avengers (Film and TV) Enterprises Ltd), Ron Fry (Associate Producer), Karen Hazzard (Casting Director), Ziggy Galko (Construction Manager), Jean Murray and Ken Freeman (Make-Up), Malcolm Tanner (Hairdresser), Val Musetti and Dwayne McLean (Stunt Co-ordinators), Allan Bryce (Special Effects), Paul Clay (Post-Production Co-ordinator).

2.10 – 'COMPLEX'
Episode 184
Original Transmission Date: Thursday 10 November 1977

Writer: Dennis Spooner
Director: Richard Gilbert
Cast: Patrick Macnee (John Steed), Gareth Hunt (Mike Gambit), Joanna Lumley (Purdey), Cec Linder (Paul Baker), Harvey Atkin (Sergeant Talbot), Vlasta Vrana (Karavitch), Rudy Lipp (Koschev), Jan Rubes (Patlenko), Michael Ball (Cope), David Nichols (Greenwood), Suzette Couture (Miss Cummings), Gerald Crack (Berisford Holt).
Uncredited Cast: Dwayne McLean (Contact).
Crew: Hugh Harlow and Ross McLean (Produced in Canada by), Don Buchsbaum (Production Manager), Colin Smith (2nd Unit Director), Ian McDougall (Assistant Director), Diana Parsons (Continuity), Seamus Flannery (Production Designer), Keith Pepper (Assistant Art Director), Linda Kemp (Wardrobe Mistress), Jillie Murphy (Fashion Co-ordinator), Henry Fiks (Director of Photography), Karol Ike (2nd Unit Director of Photography), Fred Guthe (Camera Operator), Eric Wrate (Editor), Peter Shewchuk and Ken Barker (Sound Recordists), Jack Knight and Mike Hopkins (Dubbing Editors).

2.11 – 'THE GLADIATORS'
Episode 185
Original Transmission Date: Thursday 8 December 1977

Writer: Brian Clemens
Director: Claude Fournier
Cast: Patrick Macnee (John Steed), Gareth Hunt (Mike Gambit), Joanna Lumley (Purdey), Louis Zorich (Colonel Karl Sminsky), Neil Vipond (Chuck Peters), Bill Starr (Tom O'Hara), Peter Boretski (Tarnokoff), Yanci Bukovec (Barnoff), Jan Muzynski (Cresta), Michael Donaghue (Hartley), George Chuvalo (Jed), Dwayne McLean (Rogers), Patrick Sinclair (Ivan), Doug Lennox (Nada).
Crew: Albert Fennell and Brian Clemens (Produced by), Don Buchsbaum (Production Manager), Rene Bonnière (2nd Unit Director), Tony Lucibello (Assistant Director), Susan David (Continuity), Seamus Flannery (Production Designer), Keith Pepper (Assistant Art Director), Judy Gellman (Wardrobe Mistress), Jillie Murphy and Betty Jackman (Joanna Lumley's Wardrobe by), Henry Fiks (Director of Photography), Karol Ike (2nd Unit Director of Photography), Fred Guthe (Camera Operator), Bob Dearberg (Editor), Peter Shewchuk and Bill Rowe (Sound Recordists), Mike Hopkins and Pete Keen (Dubbing Editors).

2.12 – 'FORWARD BASE'
Episode 186
Original Transmission Date: Thursday 24 November 1977

Writer: Dennis Spooner
Director: Don Thompson
Cast: Patrick Macnee (John Steed), Gareth Hunt (Mike Gambit), Joanna Lumley

(Purdey), Jack Creley (Hosking), August Schellenberg (Bailey), Marilyn Lightstone (Ranoff), Nick Nichols (Captain Malachev), David Calderisi (Halfhide), Maurice Good (Milroy), John Bethune (Doctor), Anthony Parr (Glover), Les Rubie (Harper), Toivo Pyyko (Clive), Ara Hovanessiaan (Czibor), Richard Moffat (Radio Operator).
Uncredited Cast: Dwayne McLean (Diver), Val Musetti (Diver).
Crew: Hugh Harlow and Jim Hanley (Produced in Canada by), Samuel Jephcott (Production Manager), Rene Bonnière (2nd Unit Director), Ian McDougall (Assistant Director), Diane Parsons (Continuity), Keith Pepper (Art Director), Mary Jane Grant (Assistant Art Director), Judy Gellman (Wardrobe Mistress), Jillie Murphy (Fashion Co-ordinator), Henry Fiks (Director of Photography), Karol Ike (2nd Unit Director of Photography), Stephen Lawrence (Editor), Peter Shewchuk and Ken Scrivener (Sound Recordists), Mike Hopkins and Jack Knight (Dubbing Editors).

2.13 – 'EMILY'
Episode 187
Original Transmission Date: Thursday 1 December 1977

Writer: Dennis Spooner
Director: Don Thompson
Cast: Patrick Macnee (John Steed), Gareth Hunt (Mike Gambit), Joanna Lumley (Purdey), Jane Mallett (Miss Daley), Les Carlson (Douglas Collings/The Fox), Richard Davidson (Kenneth Phillips), Brian Petchey (Reddington), Peter Aykroyd (Mirschtia) Peter Torokvei (Kalenkov), Jack Duffy (Radio Operator), Ed McNamara (Chicken Farmer), Don LeGros (Mechanic), Sandy Crawley (1st Policeman), John Kerr (2nd Policeman), Pat Patterson (3rd Policeman), Bill Ballentine (4th Policeman).
Uncredited Cast: Don Corbett (Alkoff).
Crew: Hugh Harlow and Jim Hanley (Produced in Canada by), Samuel Jephcott (Production Manager), Peter Rowe (2nd Unit Director), Tony Lucibello (Assistant Director), Susan David (Continuity), Seamus Flannery (Art Director), Tina Boden (Assistant Art Director), Judy Gellman (Wardrobe Mistress), Jillie Murphy (Fashion Co-ordinator), Dennis Miller (Director of Photography), Robert Fresco (2nd Unit Director of Photography), Eric Wrate (Editor), Peter Shewchuk and Ken Barker (Sound Recordists), Mike Hopkins and Pete Keen (Dubbing Editors).

APPENDIX THREE

US SPIN-OFFS: PRODUCTION DETAILS

ESCAPADE
A Quinn Martin/Woodruff Productions co-production for CBS
Colour pilot episode on 35mm film

Writer: Brian Clemens
Director: Jerry London
Cast: Granville Van Dusen (Joshua Rand), Morgan Fairchild (Suzy), Len Birman (Arnold Tulliver), Janice Lynde (Paula Winters), Alex Henteloff (Wences), Gregory Walcott (Seaman), Charlie Webster (Bart).
Uncredited Cast: Jonathan Harris (Voice of Oz).
Crew: Brian Clemens (Producer), Philip Saltzman (Executive Producer), Jack Swain (Cinematography), Patrick Williams (Music), James Gross (Film Editing).

THE HARDY BOYS: 'ASSAULT ON THE TOWER'
A Glen A Larson Productions production for Universal
Colour episode on 35mm colour film

Writers: Christopher Crowe and Michael Sloan
Director: Winrich Kolbe
Cast: Shaun Cassidy (Joe Hardy), Parker Stevenson (Frank Hardy), Edmund Gilbert (Fenton Hardy), Dana Andrews (Townley), Victor Holchak (Carstairs), James Booth (Lieutenant Buckley), Leon Ames (The Messenger), Patrick Macnee (S), Pernell Roberts (Detective Superintendant Molly), Peter Ashton (Wakefield), Ian Abercrombie (Sergeant Landen), Shepherd Sanders (Clerk), Joi Staton (Woman), Cort Brackett (Black).
Crew: Michael Sloan (Supervising Producer), Christopher Crowe and Ben Kadish (Produced by), Joyce Brotman and Arlene Sidaris (Co-Producers), Glen A Larson (Developed for Television by), Franklin W Dixon (Based on the 'Hardy Boys' books by), Andrew Mirisch (Associate Producer), Steven E DeSouza (Story Editor), Stu Phillips (Music Score), Glen A Larson (Theme), Sy Hoffberg (Director of Photography), Roy Steffensen (Art Director), Sam Gross (Set Decorations), Joseph Z Reich (Casting by), Buford F Hayes (Film Editor), Jean G Valentino (Sound), Universal Title (Titles and Optical Effects), Les Berke (Unit Production Manager), Michael Massinger (1st Assistant

Director), Louis Muscate (2nd Assistant Director), Tom McMullen (Sound Effects Editor), Herbert D Woods (Music Editor), George R Whittaker (Costume Designer), Glen A Larson (Executive Producer).

APPENDIX FOUR

THE AVENGERS (MOVIE): PRODUCTION DETAILS

Jerry Weintraub Productions production for Warner Brothers
Movie on 35mm colour film

Writer: Don MacPherson
Director: Jeremiah Chechik
Certificate: U

Cast: Ralph Fiennes (John Steed), Uma Thurman (Dr Emma Peel), Sean Connery (Sir August de Wynter), Patrick Macnee (Invisible Jones), Jim Broadbent (Mother), Fiona Shaw (Father), Eddie Izzard (Bailey), Eileen Atkins (Alice), John Wood (Trubshaw), Carmen Ejogo (Brenda), Keeley Hawes (Tamara), Shaun Ryder (Donavan), Nicholas Woodeson (Dr Darling), Michael Godley (Butler), Richard Lumsden (Boodle's Porter), Daniel Crowder (Messenger), Nadim Sawalha, Christopher Godwin, David Webber (World Council of Ministers).
Uncredited Cast: Marc Cass (Stunt Double for Bailey), Sarah Franzl (Stunt Double for Dr Emma Peel), Sy Hollands (Stunt Double for Dr Emma Peel), Eunice Huthart (Stunt Double for Dr Emma Peel), Gabe Cronnelly (Stunt Double for Sir August de Wynter).

Crew: Jerry Weintraub (Produced by), Susan Ekins (Executive Producer), Susie Figgis (Casting), Anthony Powell (Costume Design), Nick Davis (Visual Effects Supervisor), Joel McNeely (Music Composed and Conducted by), Laurie Johnson (The Avengers Theme Composed by), Mick Audsley (Editor), Stuart Craig (Production Design), Roger Pratt BSC (Director of Photography), Gerry Toomey (Unit Production Manager), Terry Needham (First Assistant Director), Adam Somner (Second Assistant Director), Marc Boyle (Stunt Co-ordinator), Gary Jones (Financial Controller), William Hobbs (Swordfight Arrangements), Anna Worley (Script Supervisor), Erica Bensly (Production Co-ordinator), Caroline Moore (Production Secretary), Max Brown, Thomas Guard, Christopher Mullane (Third Assistant Directors), Gary Nixon (Production Accountant), Matthew O'Toole (Assistant Accountant), Kim Pinkstaff, Eth Ibrahim Maynard, Julee Weintraub, Jamie Weintraub, Jody Weintraub, Sarah Weintraub, Joseph Weintraub, Rachel Weintraub, Ari Weintraub (Assistants to Mr. Weintraub), Kirsten Welles, Tania Powell, Allan Bradshaw (Assistants to Mr Chechik), Becky Veduccio (Assistant to Mr. Fiennes), Emma Tillinger (Assistant to Ms Thurman), Nicola Armstrong (Assistant to

Mr Connery), Sarah Waldron, Debbie Moseley (Production Office Assistants), Kate Bryden (Casting Assistant), Alan Martin (Chief Lighting Technician), Jason Martin (Assistant Chief Lighting Technician), David Hughes (Rigging Gaffer), Matthew Desorgher (Boom Operator), Stephen Gilmore (Cable Person), Barry Wilkinson (Property Master), Simon Wilkinson, Gary Ixer, Jamie Wilkinson (Standby Props), Keith Hatcher, Terry Blyther (Location Managers), Nick Waldron (Assistant Location Manager), Maurice Newsome (Transportation Co-ordinator), Duncan Barbour (Action Vehicle Co-ordinator), Rosie Bedford-Stradling, Kate Teakle (First Aid), Jennifer Collen-Smith (Unit Publicist), Julia Wilson-Dickson (Dialogue Coach), 1st Unit Catering (Catering by), Imaginary Forces (Main Titles Designed by).

Uncredited Crew: Chris Steenolsen (Assistant Director), Phil Stoole (Third Assistant Director), Stuart Wilson (Sound Effects Recordist), Gerry Turner (Driver and Transportation), Richard Bonehill (Assistant Sword Master), Kyle Cooper, Karin Fong (Title Designers), Lori Freitag-Hild (Compositor Main Titles), Marcel Valcarce (Artist: Titles), Rob Seager (Assistant Accountant), John J. Tomko (Production Executive), Justin Owen (Computer and Video Systems), Steve Hancock (Studio Sound Technician) Paul Knight, Richard Gregory (Prop Making Senior Modellers).

Stunts: Jamie Edgell, Candice Evans, Gabe Cronnelly, Eunice Huthart, Paul Jennings, Marc Cass, Ray De-Haan, Paul Herbert, Sy Hollands, Vincent Keane, Paul Lonergan, Tony Lucken, Rachael Stephens, Steen Young.

Uncredited Stunts: Shelly Benison, Dave Fisher, Dorothy Anne Ford, Sarah Franzl, Mark Mottram, Ray Nicholas, Adrian O'Neil, Dickey Beer, Joss Gower, Lee Sheward.

Art Department: Neil Lamont (Supervising Art Director), Michael Lamont, Andrew Ackland-Snow, Mark Harris (Art Directors), Stephanie McMillan (Set Decorator), Jim Morahan, Dominic Masters, Lucinda Thomson (Assistant Art Directors), Brian Bishop (Scenic Artist), Michael Redding (Construction Co-ordinator), Sara-Jane Valentine (Art Department Co-ordinator), Brian Reid, Miraphora Mina (Assistant Set Decorators), Alex Walker, Alastair Bullock, Nicola Levinsky (Art Department Assistants), Tony Wright, Denis Rich (Storyboard Artists), Carol Kupisz (Graphic Designer), Kenny Pattenden (Construction Foreman), Kavin Hall (Paint Foreman).

Uncredited Art Department: Michael Boone, Peter Dorme, Alan Gilmore, Stephen Morahan, Cyrille Nomberg (Draughtsmen), Peter Francis (Assistant Art Director), Bill Stallion (Storyboard Artist), Daniel Thompson (Carpenter), Sylvain Despretz (Concept Artist and Storyboard Artist), Julian Caldow (Concept Artist).

Editorial Department: Russ Woolnough (Visual Effects Editor), Kate Higham (1st Assistant Editor), Mags Arnold (Digital Assistant Editor), David Burrows (2nd Assistant Editor), Amy Quince (3rd Assistant Editor), Paul Elman (Assistant Visual Effects Editor), Clive Winter (Production Sound Mixer), Adrian Rhodes, Mike Prestwood Smith (Re-Recording Mixers), Peter Joly (Supervising Sound Editor), Adrian Rhodes (Sound Effects Editor), Michael Connell (Supervising Music Editor), Craig Pettigrew (Music Editor), Danny Longhurst (Dialogue Editor), Ian Wilson (Foley Editor), Mark Rose, Guy Hake (Assistant Sound Editors), Stephen Barker (Post-Production Supervisor), Peter Hunt (Colour Timer), Sylvia Wheeler (Negative Cutter).

Uncredited Editorial Department: Bill Daly (Post-Production Executive), Fred Fouquet (Editor: Title Sequence), Asha Radwan (Assistant Editor).

Visual Effects: Alexandra Day (Visual Effects Co-ordinator).

Uncredited Visual Effects: Kevin Campbell (Softwear Developer), Dayne Cowan, John Lockwood (Digital Effects Artists), Adrian De Wet, Elizabeth Moore, Fedele Rinaldi, Charles Tait (Digital Compositors), Paddy Eason, Mark Nelmes (Digital Effects Designers), Dan Harrod (Data Operations), Oliver James (Research and Development), Thomas Lopatka (Digital Compositing Support: Title Sequence), Jon Meakins, Bill Thomas (Model Makers), Paula Pope (Digital Trainee), Candice Scott (Lead Digital Compositor: Title Sequence), Simon Staines, Gavin Toomey (Computer Graphics Designer), Pete Williams (Scanning and Recording Manager), Mark Gardiner (Process Plate Cameraman).

Camera Crew: Simon Ransley, Peter Robertson (Camera Operators), Simon Hume, John Foster (First Assistant Camera), Mik Allen, Ciro Candia (Second Assistant Camera), David Appleby (Still Photographer and Dolly Grips), Chris Warren (Video Playback Operator), Philip Murray (Dolly Grips).

Uncredited Camera Crew: Darren Bailey (Remote Camera Technician), Adam Dale (Aerial Director of Photography and Aerial Camera Operator), Laurence Edwards (Crane Technician), Danny Espey, Alan Grayley, Eugene Grobler (Electricians), Pat Garrett, Phil Murray, Ron Nicholls (Grips), Spencer Murray (Second Assistant Camera), Marc Wolff (Camera Pilot), Martin Kenzie (Camera Operator: Car Chase Unit), Jonathan Taylor (Director of Photography: Car Chase Unit), Howard Smith (Steadicam Operator).

Wardrobe and Hairdressing Departments: Kenny Crouch (Wardrobe Supervisor), Natalie Duerinckx (Assistant Costume Designer), Mark Holmes (Wardrobe Master), Jane Lewis (Wardrobe Mistress), David Croucher, Janet Lucas-Wakely (Wardrobe), Daniel Parker (Key Make-Up Artist), Jeremy Woodhead (Make-Up Artist), Peter King (Ms. Thurman's Makeup and Hair), Paolo Mantini (Key Hairstylist), Kay Georgiou (Hairstylist).

Special Effects Crew: Joss Williams (Special Effects Supervisor), Mike Dawson, Brian Morrison, Kevin Mathews, Jonathan Angell, John Brown, Kevin Draycot, Rodney Fuller, John Holmes, Rob Malos, Roger Nichols (Special Effects).

Uncredited Special Effects Crew: Mark Wollard (Supervising Modeller: Props), Mitch Barnes, Brian Best, Peter Norcliffe, Paul Scotson (Model Makers), Duncan Capp, Paul Dunn, Matthew Roberts (Special Effects), Paul Clancy, Garry Cooper, Manex Efrem, Andy Simm (Special Effects Technicians), Dave Crownshaw (Snow Effects Supervisor), Keith Dawson, Jody Taylor, Neil Teddy Todd (Special Effects Assistants), Doug McCarthy (Special Effects Technician: Model Unit), Benjamin Palmer (Animatronic Engineer), Mark E Raymond (Snow Effects Technician), Colin Shulver (Sculptor), David Watkins (Model Unit Technician), Andy Williams (Action Unit Supervisor), Mark Beverton (Modeller).

Music: Shawn Murphy (Music Score Recorded by), David Slonaker, Joel McNeeley, Jeff Atmajian (Orchestrators), Marius De Vries (Musical Supervision).

Uncredited Music: Ron Aston (Musician: Percussion Programming), Steve Browell (Assistant Music Editor), Chris Elliott (Conductor and Music Arranger).

2nd Unit: Vic Armstrong (Second Unit Director), Arthur Wooster (Second Unit Director), Harvey Harrison BSC (Second Unit Director and Director of Photography), Michael Murray (Production Manager), Peter Bennett Snr (Assistant Director), Eddie Stacey (Stunt Director), David Budd, Peter Taylor (Camera Operator), Mike Evans, John Fletcher (1st Assistant Camera), Sharon Mansfield (Script Supervisor), Simon Lamont (Art Director), Steve Foster (Gaffer), Ian Wingrove, Paul Whybrow (Special Effects Co-ordinators).

Uncredited 2nd Unit: Phil Stoole (Assistant Director), Emma Mager (Production Co-ordinator).
Cinesite (Europe) Ltd (Digital Special Effects and Computer Graphics Animation by).

Cinesite Crew: Alex Bicknell (Digital Effects Producer), Catherine Duncan (Production Co-ordinator), Lubo Hristov (Art Director), Sue Rowe, Niki Wakefield (Digital Composite Supervisors), Chris Gibbons, Matthew Johnson, David Man, David Williams (Digital Compositors), Charles Cash, Dave Child, Chris George (3D Computer Animation).
Uncredited Cinesite Crew: Keith Barton (Technical Support), Nathalie Buce (3D Animator), Sonia Calvert (Digital Compositor), Clare Norman (Lineup and Editorial), Courtney Vanderslice (Head of Production).

The Magic Camera Company (Miniature and VFX by).

The Magic Model Company (Model Construction by).

Model Unit: José Granell (Production Supervisor), Anthony Hunt, Roger Lofting (Model and Visual F/X Producers), Suzie Ford (Production Manager), Brenda Coxon (Production Accountant), Sarah Robinson (Production Co-ordinator), Katherine Lofting (Model Co-ordinator), Tori Martin, Charity Hobbs-Woods (Production Assistants), Nigel Stone (Director of Photography), John Morgan (Camera Operator), Karl Morgan (Focus Puller), Andrew Stevens (Clapper Loader), Joe Felix (Camera Grip), David Carrigan (Assistant Production Supervisor), Gary Blowfield (Video Operator), John Rogers (Gaffer), Frank Sheekey (Best Boy), Andrew Jeffery (Film Controller), John Grant (Film Scanning and Recording), Ian Biggs (SPX Floor Supervisor), Dave Poole (SPX Workshop Supervisor), Nik Cooper, Jacqui Mitchell, Ken Kittens (SPX Technicians), Chris Martin, Roy Scott, Robbie Scott, Nigel Blake, Tracy Curtis (Model Supervisors), Chris Greenwood (H.O.D. Plasterer), Gary Coulter, Caroline Garrett, Adam McInnes (Model Animators), Max Dennison (Model Artist).

Digital Unit: Angus Cameron (Digital Supervisor), Daniel Pettipher (Domino Artist), Steve Begg (FX Animation Designer), Robin Huffer, Helen Ball (2D Digital Artists).

The Computer Film Company Limited: Alison O'Brien, Sharon Lark (Visual Effects Producers), Dan Glass (CG Lead Animation).
Uncredited Crew: Pete Hanson (Studio Manager), Dennis Michelson (Visual Effects), Kevin Phelan (Scanning and Recording Producer), Tim Wellspring (Visual Effects Co-ordinator).

Mill Film Limited, London.

'Raindrops Keep Falling on My Head': written by Burt Bacharach and Hal David.

'Storm': written by Bruce Woolley, Chris Elliott, Marius De Vries, Betsy Cook, and Andy Caine; produced by Marius De Vries, Bruce Woolley and Chris Elliott; performed by Grace Jones with the Radio Science Orchestra.

'Solve My Problems Today'; written by Chris Holmes and Brian Liesegang; produced by Marius De Vries and Ashtar Command; performed by Ashtar Command; Chris Holmes appears courtesy of Atlantic Recording Corp; Louise Post appears courtesy of Geffen Records.

'I Am'; written by Suggs and Nick Feldman; produced by Stephen Lironi; performed by Suggs; courtesy of Warner Brothers UK Ltd.

Soundtrack Album on Warner Sunset Records/ Atlantic Recording Corp.

Inspired by the Thorn EMI Television Series *The Avengers*.

Lighting Equipment Supplied by Lee Lighting Ltd.

Close Range Aerial Photography: Flying-Cam Inc.

Filmed with Panavision Cameras and Lenses Supplied by Panavision UK.

Processing and Prints by Technicolour Film Services.

Kodak Motion Picture Products.

Mini Provided by Rover Group.

Filmed at Pinewood Studios and Shepperton Studios, London, England and Local Locations.

Blenheim Palace Scenes by Kind Permission of his Grace the Duke of Marlborough.

APPENDIX FIVE

FEATURED MOTOR VEHICLES

The details presented below have been compiled from various different sources and so are not uniform. Where 'No records available' is indicated, it means that the Government's Driver and Vehicle Licensing Agency (DVLA) have no information regarding the vehicle in question, suggesting that it has been scrapped. However, in one instance, vintage Bentley YK 6871, although no details are available from the DVLA, images on the internet show the vehicle being recently driven in the Lord Mayor's Show in London, so obviously there are exceptions to the rule. 'Last registered' shows what year a vehicle's latest road tax ran out; this suggests that the vehicle is currently in storage somewhere, possibly awaiting restoration. Unfortunately it has not been possible to locate any information regarding the vehicles driven by the cast in either the French or Canadian episodes.

THE AVENGERS

JOHN STEED

AC Greyhound (880 OPA).
Seen in 'The Sell-Out'.
No records available.

Triumph Herald (7061 MK).
Seen in 'Warlock'.
No records available.

1935 Alvis Speed 25 (CPT 75).
Seen in 'Traitor in Zebra'.
No records available.

1930 Lagonda 3 Litre (GK 3295).
Seen in 'Don't Look Behind You'.
First registered 21 October 1930.

Still registered for UK roads 2013.

1924 Vauxhall 30-98 (XT 2276).
Seen in 'The Gravediggers', 'The Thirteenth Hole'.
First registered 2 May 1924.
Last registered 1998.

1927 Bentley 4½ Litre (UW 4887).
Seen in 'The Master Minds', 'Too Many Christmas Trees'.
No records available.

1927 Bentley 3 Litre (YT 3942).
Seen in 'Small Game for Big Hunters', 'The Positive-Negative Man', 'Mission … Highly
Improbable', 'The Curious Case of the Countless Clues', 'The Forget-Me-Knot', 'Split!',
'Have Guns – Will Haggle'.
First Registered 10 August 1927.
Last registered 1985.

1927 Bentley 3 Litre (UW 4887).
Seen in 'The Danger Makers', 'A Touch of Brimstone', 'The House that Jack Built', 'How
to Succeed at … Murder', 'Dead Man's Treasure'.
No records available.
Note: This vehicle carried the same registration number as the Bentley 4½ Litre (see
above), although it actually appears to have been YT 3942.

1924 Bentley 3 Litre (XR 6056).
Seen in 'The Hour That Never Was', 'Man-Eater of Surrey Green'.
First registered May 1924
Exported to the United States during the 1960s or early 1970s.

Land Rover (VX 897).
Seen in 'A Sense of History', 'Never, Never Say Die'.
No records available.

1925 Bentley 3 Litre Green Label (YK 6871).
Seen in 'The Fear Merchants'.
First registered July 1925
Still in running order, owned by Maurice Avent and Vera Forsyth in the UK.

1930 Bentley Speed Six (RX 6180).
Seen in 'Escape in Time', 'From Venus With Love', 'The Bird Who Knew Too Much',
'The See-Through Man', 'The Winged Avenger', 'The Living Dead', 'The Hidden Tiger',
'Epic', 'Something Nasty in the Nursery', 'The Joker', 'Who's Who???', 'Death's Door',
'Return of the Cybernauts', 'The £50,000 Breakfast', 'You Have Just Been Murdered'.
First registered March 1930.
Exported to Sweden in 1984.
Back in UK and registered for use according to the DVLA in 2013

Land Rover (OPC 104D).
Seen in 'The Hidden Tiger'.
No details available

AC 428 (LPH 800D).
Seen in 'Invasion of the Earthmen'.
No details available.

1923 Rolls Royce Silver Ghost 40/50 (KK 4976)
Seen in 'Get-A-Way!', Look – (Stop Me If You've Heard This One) But There Were These Two Fellers …', 'My Wildest Dream', 'Whoever Shot Poor George Oblique Stroke XR40?', 'All Done with Mirrors', 'You'll Catch Your Death', 'Super Secret Cypher Snatch', 'Game', 'False Witness', 'Legacy of Death', 'Wish You Were Here', 'The Rotters', 'The Interrogators', 'Love All', 'Take Me to Your Leader', 'Stay Tuned', 'Fog', 'Bizarre'
First registered December 1923.
Still registered for UK roads 2013.

1929 Rolls Royce New Phantom Mark 1 (UU 3864).
Seen in 'Who Was That Man I Saw You With?', 'Thingumajig', 'Homicide and Old Lace', 'Requiem', 'Take-Over'.
First registered 19 June 1929.
Still registered for UK roads 2013.

CATHY GALE

MGA (RVB 115).
Seen in 'Mr Teddy Bear', 'Warlock'.
No details available.

Triumph Twin motorcycle (987 CAA).
Seen in 'Build a Better Mousetrap'.
No details available.

EMMA PEEL

Lotus Elan (HNK 999C).
Seen in 'The Cybernauts', 'Two's a Crowd', 'Man-Eater of Surrey Green', 'Castle De'ath', 'Small Game for Big Hunters', 'The Girl from Auntie', 'What the Butler Saw', 'The House That Jack Built', 'How to Succeed … at Murder'.
No details available.

Austin Mini Moke (BOX 656C).
Seen in 'A Surfeit of H₂O'.
Last registered 1987.

Lotus Elan (SJH 499D).
Seen in 'The Fear Merchants', 'Escape in Time', 'From Venus with Love', 'The Bird Who

Knew Too Much', 'The See-Through Man', 'The Winged Avenger', 'The Living Dead', 'The Hidden Tiger', 'Never, Never Say Die', 'Epic', 'The Superlative Seven', 'Something Nasty in the Nursery', 'The Joker', 'Death's Door', 'Return of the Cybernauts', 'You Have Just been Murdered', 'The Positive-Negative Man', 'Murdersville', 'Mission … Highly Improbable'.
Currently located in the Dezer Collection car museum, in Miami, Florida, United States.

TARA KING

Lotus Elan +2 (NPW 999F).
Seen in 'The Great Great Britain Crime', 'Have Guns – Will Haggle'.
No details available.

AC 428 (LPH 800D).
Seen in 'The Forget-Me-Knot', 'Split!', 'Get-A-Way!', 'Look – (Stop Me If You've Heard This One) But There Were These Two Fellers …', 'My Wildest Dream', 'Whoever Shot Poor George Oblique Stroke XR40?', 'You'll Catch Your Death', 'Super Secret Cypher Snatch'.
No details available.

Lotus Europa (PPW 999F).
Seen in 'False Witness', 'Legacy of Death', 'Wish You Were Here', 'The Rotters', 'Love All', 'Stay Tuned', 'Who Was That Man I Saw You With', 'Pandora', 'Thingumajig', 'Requiem'.
No details available.

MOTHER

Bentley Continental (3 HKM).
Seen in 'Super Secret Cypher Snatch'.
No details available.

1954 Leyland Titan double-decker bus (OLD 666).
Seen in 'False Witness'.
Destroyed in *On the Buses* episode 'No Smoke without Fire'.

BMC Mini Moke (THX 77F).
Seen in 'Fog'.
No details available.

LADY DIANA FORBES-BLAKENEY

MGC (BWM 300G).
Seen in 'Killer'.
No details available.

THE NEW AVENGERS

JOHN STEED

Rover 3500 (MOC 229P).
Seen in 'The Eagle's Nest', 'The Midas Touch', 'Hostage', 'Medium Rare', 'The Lion and The Unicorn'.
First registered 22 April 1976.
Last registered 1985.

Jaguar XJ12C (NWK 60P).
Seen in 'House of Cards', 'The Last of the Cybernauts …??', 'To Catch a Rat', 'Three Handed Game', 'Sleeper', 'Angels of Death'.
First registered 5 May 1976.
Last registered 1987.
In storage somewhere in the UK.

Range Rover (TXC 922J).
Seen in 'Cat Amongst the Pigeons', 'Target!', 'The Tale of the Big Why', 'Obsession'.
First registered 1 May 1971.
Last registered and permanently exported from the UK in 1995.

1927 Bentley 3 Litre (YT 3942).
Seen in 'K is for Kill part 1'.
First registered 10 August 1927.
Last registered 1985.

PURDEY

MGB (MOC 232P).
Seen in 'House of Cards', 'The Midas Touch', 'The Last of the Cybernauts …??', 'Target!', 'Faces', 'Three Handed Game', 'Sleeper', 'Dirtier by the Dozen'.
First registered 1 May 1976.
Last registered 1995.

Yamaha DT250 Enduro motorcycle (LLC 950P).
Seen in 'Cat Amongst the Pigeons'.
First registered 28 August 1975.
Last registered 1983.

Honda 125 motorcycle (OLR 471P).
Seen in 'The Tale of the Big Why', 'Obsession'.
Owned by ex-*The New Avengers* production manager Ron Purdie.

Triumph TR7 (OGW 562R)
Seen in 'Hostage', 'Trap', 'Medium Rare'.
No details available.

MIKE GAMBIT

Jaguar XJS (NRW 875P).
Seen in 'The Eagle's Nest', 'The Midas Touch', 'The Last of the Cybernauts …??', 'Cat Amongst the Pigeons', 'Three Handed Game', 'Hostage', 'Medium Rare', 'The Lion and the Unicorn'.
No details available.

Range Rover (LOK 537P).
Seen in 'To Catch a Rat', 'Cat Amongst the Pigeons', 'The Tale of the Big Why', 'Trap'.
First Registered 2 February 1976.
Last registered 1992.

APPENDIX SIX

A BRIEF HISTORY OF ABC TELEVISION

The genesis of ABC Television

The 1954 Television Act provided for the formation of the ITA (Independent Television Authority), which had the task of supervising the creation of Britain's first independent television network, ITV (Independent Television). Beginning operations on 4 August 1954, the ITA under Chairman Sir Kenneth Clark allocated ITV franchises on a regional basis, starting with the London, Midlands and North regions.

Clark approached the Associated British Picture Corporation (ABPC), a film company founded in 1927, with a view to them taking on the Midlands franchise. However, they initially rebuffed him, fearing that an independent television channel would take patrons away from their ABC cinema chain. Also in contention was a consortium from Kelmsley Newspapers and Winnick Entertainment, who were interested in providing weekend programming for both the Midlands and the North. However, Maurice Winnick was eventually forced to inform the ITA that they had failed to attract the finance they needed to run a television station. With the Kelmsley-Winnick Television group out of the running, Clark approached ABPC once again. This time, he had an insurance policy on hand, in the form of a purse of £750,000 government money that, in the event of ITV failing, would be shared out between the companies that had taken on the franchises.

The decision went to a vote by the ABPC board of directors. With foresight, senior executive Howard Thomas persuaded enough of them that this was the right time to get into independent television, just as it was starting up. Thus on 21 September 1955 ABPC signed to take the Kelmsley-Winnick group's place, immediately forming ABC (Associated British Corporation) Television to handle weekend transmissions in both the Midlands and the North. Three more ITV companies were awarded their franchises at the same time: Associated-Rediffusion, Lew Grade's ATV and Granada Television. Together these made up 'the big four', which would provide the great majority of home-grown ITV programming until a regional reshuffle took place in 1968.

Having rejected offers from the other fledgling ITV companies, Howard Thomas took up an appointment as the Managing Director of ABC Television. After some five months of preparations, its Midlands service went on the air on Saturday 18 February 1956. Its transmissions in the North then began on Saturday 5 May 1956, initially covering just the Lancashire area; they were extended to the Yorkshire region six months later.

Teddington Studios

In November 1958, ABC TV acquired what had once been Warner Brothers' film studios on Broom Road at Teddington, near Twickenham, Middlesex, after Howard Thomas had viewed the property and considered the four-acre site to be exactly what the company needed as a programme production base. Up until then, the company had improvised by turning disused cinemas in both Birmingham (shared with ATV as Alpha Television) and Manchester into small makeshift studios.

Filming originally began at Teddington late in the 19th Century, when the owner of Weir House, a large mansion that stood on the site later occupied by the studios, took an interest in the then fledgling medium of cinema and allowed a film crew to use his large greenhouse as a makeshift studio. However, serious film making did not get under way until the next century, and it was not until 1912 that Ec-Ko Films produced several comedies in the ground of the house. Another production company, Master Films, arrived four years later to construct the first purpose-built stage, which would be used up to 1922.

In 1927, Gaumont British merged with the Ideal Film Company and together they leased the property for a couple of years until a fire caused major damage and closed down all film-making there. The site then remained unused up to 1931, until a partnership between established film-maker E G Norman and silent screen actor Henry Edwards renamed the property Teddington Film Studios Ltd and totally refurbished it, adding all the facilities required to make it into a working studio. A second soundstage was added, the latest sound recording equipment and cameras were brought in, and a building programme was undertaken that provided new editing rooms, a scenery and props workshop, dressing rooms and a boiler room.

The major American film company Warner Brothers was so impressed that it leased the studios as its British base of operations, using it to produce a large number of low-budget and tight-schedule 'quota quickies' – films that British cinemas were obliged to screen. Under the name Warner Brothers First National Productions Ltd, the company went through a successful period and eventually committed the funding to actually buy the studios and instigate another round of building plus the total refurbishment of Weir House, which was turned into offices and guest rooms. Teddington was one of the few studios to remain working during the Second World War, and even a direct hit by a German V1 flying bomb on 5 July 1944, which partially destroyed the facility including the stages, did not halt production.

The studio complex was fully restored by 1948, but in the meantime Warner Brothers had acquired a large stake in the ABPC. As a result, their pictures were now in the main being filmed at ABPC's Elstree Studios at Borehamwood in Hertfordshire. Some filming still took place at Teddington for a time, but nothing like the volume that had been done there previously. Perhaps not surprisingly, the industry journal *Kinematograph Weekly* eventually reported in its 23 November 1952 edition that Teddington was being mothballed. Aircraft manufacturer Hawker leased the complex to use the buildings for storage, and feature film production would never take place there again.

When ABC Television took over the site in 1958, they followed the previous owners' example by undertaking upgrading and alterations, resulting in the seating being removed from the viewing theatre that stood alongside Broom Road and the installation of a control room, which was initially for both Studios 2 and 3. Studio 2 was an unusual T-shaped structure offering 5,705 square feet of operating space, while the adjacent Studio 3 was smaller at 2,097 square feet and was originally built for sound recording. These two small studios on the north-west corner of the lot were converted from film to television production, with lighting grids installed and new floors laid, ready for the arrival of a number of pedestal-mounted Marconi MK III Image Orthicon cameras.

Further to this, ABC had managed to obtain a million pounds' worth of equipment from Pye, originally ordered by Kelmsley-Winnick Television, which due to the circumstances came at a discounted price. However, one of the most important pieces of equipment came from the United States. This was the first RCA TRT-1B videotape recorder used in the UK; a large bank of technology weighing in at approximately 660 kilos. Consequently, in the early summer of 1959, ABC's flagship drama production *Armchair Theatre* was relocated from its home in what had been the Capital Cinema at Didsbury in Manchester, where it had gone out live, to Teddington, where instalments could now be recorded at the company's convenience and shown as and when required. Other dramas such as *The Avengers* would follow suit.

The demise of ABC Television

As part of the shake-up of the ITV network in 1968, ABC's former regional franchises effectively disappeared, leaving it without a role. However, the ITA recommended that ABC and Rediffusion (as Associated-Rediffusion was renamed) merge and form a new company, which would provide the London weekday service. In practice, the two broadcasters' parent companies formed a joint subsidiary, Thames Television, which took over all of ABC's staff from Teddington and a minority of staff from Rediffusion, with Howard Thomas remaining as Managing Director. ABC thus ceased weekend broadcasting in the Midlands and North regions on 22 July 1968, and resumed in the London region eight days later as weekday company Thames.

APPENDIX SEVEN

COMMERCIAL CLOTHING LINES

The Jean Varon Avengers Collection
Launched 1965

Suppliers:
Jean Varon (Dresses)
Mr Reginald/Reginald Bernstein (Coats and Suits)
Simon Ellis Limited (Jersey, Crepe and Lace Catsuits)
Paul Blanche (Leather and PVC Rainwear)
Selincourt Limited (Fur Coats)
Charnos Limited (Lingerie)
Echo brandname of T B Jones Limited (Stockings)
Dent, Allcraft and Co Limited (Gloves)
Freedex (Handbags)
Kangol (Berets)
Jean Varon/Freedman (Watches)
Rayne-Delman Shoes/Edward Rayne (Shoes and Boots)

The Avengers Pack
Launched 1967

Suppliers:
Echo brandname of T B Jones Limited (Stockings)
Kashmoor brandname of T B Jones Limited (Catsuits)
Selincourt Limited (Fur Coats)
Edward Mann Limited (Hats)
Sirela Manufacturing Co Limited (Suede and Leatherwear)
Dent, Allcroft and Co Limited (Gloves)
C W Thomas and Co (Dresses)
Bagcraft brandname of L S Mayer (London) Ltd
Old England Watches Limited
British Bata Shoe Co Ltd
Dannimac Limited (Rainwear)
Charnos Limited (Lingerie)

Richard Allen Scarves
L Sheraton Limited (Coats and Suits)

RESOURCES

BOOKS

Honor Blackman's Book of Self-Defence, Honor Blackman, Joe and Doug Robinson, Andre Deutsch, December 1965

With an Independent Air, Howard Thomas, Weidenfeld and Nicolson, April 1977

The Avengers, Dave Rogers, ITV Books and Michael Joseph, March 1983

Elstree: The British Hollywood, Patricia Warren, Elm Tree Books, April 1983

The Avengers Anew, Dave Rogers, Michael Joseph, July 1985

The Avengers: 'Look Who's Talking', Dave Rogers, On Target, April 1986

Julian Wintle a Memoir, Anne Francis, Dukeswood, December 1986

Blind in One Ear, Patrick Macnee and Marie Cameron, Harrap, September 1988

The Complete Avengers, Dave Rogers, Boxtree, March 1989

Stare Back and Smile, Joanna Lumley, Viking, October 1989

40 Years of British Television, Jane Harbord and Jeff Wright, Boxtree, October 1992

Television's Greatest Hits, Paul Gambaccini and Rod Taylor, Network Books, October 1993

The Ultimate Avengers, Dave Rogers, Boxtree, August 1995

British Film Studios: An Illustrated History, Patricia Warren, Batsford, September 1995

The Avengers and Me, Patrick Macnee and Dave Rogers, Titan, May 1997

The Avengers, Toby Miller, BFI Publishing, October 1997

The Avengers: The Official Souvenir Magazine, Marcus Hearn and Andrew Pixley, Titan, August 1998

The Avengers: Original Movie Screenplay, Don Macpherson, Titan, August 1998

The Avengers: The Making of the Movie, Dave Rogers, Titan, August 1998

It seemed like a Good Idea at the Time, Sue Lloyd and Linda Dearsley, Quartet, October 1998

The Gross, The Hits, The Flops: The Summer That Ate Hollywood, Peter Bart, St Martin's Press, February 1999

Joanna Lumley: The Biography, Tim Ewbank and Stafford Hildred, Andre Deutsch, October 1999

Director's Cut: A Memoir of 60 Years in Film and Television: Roy Ward Baker, Reynolds and Hearn, March 2000

The Pinewood Story, Gareth Owen with Brian Burford, Reynolds and Hearn, May 2000

Noises in the Head, Laurie Johnson, Bank House Books, September 2000

Saints and Avengers: British Adventure Series of the 19', James Chapman, I B Tauris, April 2002

RESOURCES

Armchair Theatre: The Lost Years, Leonard White, Kelly Publications, August 2003
Vamp until Ready: A Life Laid Bare, Kate O'Mara, Robson Books, October 2003
Diana Rigg: The Biography, Kathleen Tracy, First BenBella Books, April 2004
The Avengers Files, Andrew Pixley, Reynolds and Hearn, August 2004
Uma Thurman: The Biography, Bryony Sutherland and Lucy Ellis, Aurum Press,
     September 2004
Still Getting Away With, Nicholas Courtney and Michael McManus, Columbian Press,
     January 2005
The Avengers on Location, Chris Bentley, Reynolds and Hearn, October 2007
John Bates: Fashion Designer, Richard Lester, ACC Editions, October 2008
The Avengers: Series One Episode Guide, Jaz Wiseman, Optimum, October 2009
The Man Who Invented the Daleks: The Strange Worlds of Terry Nation, Alwyn W Turner,
     Aurum Press, May 2011
The Tale of the Double Cross: The Unmade Script, Philip Broadley, The Morning After,
     September 2012

MAGAZINE ARTICLES

Timescreen no. 4 revised, British Telefantasy Book Guide 1953-1989, Engale Marketing,
     Andrew Pixley 1989
Primetime no. 15, Under The Influence of the Avengers, WTVA, Michael Richardson
     September 1989
Primetime no. 16, Under The Influence of the Avengers, Box Publishing, Michael
     Richardson January 1991
DWB no. 101, Real Action, Andrew Pixley, May 1992
DWB no. 102, Real Action, Andrew Pixley, June 1992
Timescreen no. 19, The Avengers Man, Anthony McKay and Michael Richardson,
     Engale Marketing October 1992
Record Collector no. 171, The Avengers, Michael Richardson, Diamond Publishing
     Group Ltd October 1993
Timescreen no. 20, Tony Williamson, Michael Richardson, Engale Marketing May 1994
Action TV no. 6, Steed Rallies Around and Emma Drives for Her Life, Michael
     Richardson, April 2002
Action TV no. 7, 'Mrs Peel, We're Needed!', Michael Richardson, August 2002
Action TV no. 10, Cool Britannia, Michael Richardson, May 2004
Action TV no. 11, With Umbrella, Charm and Bowler, Michael Richardson, January 2005
Action TV no. 14, With Umbrella, Charm and Bowler, Michael Richardson, August 2007

NEWSPAPERS AND OTHER PUBLICATIONS

Amazing Adventures (Marvel Comics)
The Amazing Spider Man (Marvel Comics)
Autocar (Haymarket Group)
Bravo (Bauer Media Group)
Broadcast (Top Right Group)
Cinefantastique (Frederick S. Clarke)
Cinema TV Today (Cinema Press Ltd)
Cult TV (Future Publishing)

The Daily Cinema (Cinema Press Ltd)
Daily Express/The Express (Northern and Shell Media)
Daily Mail (Daily Mail and General Trust PLC)
Daily Mirror (Trinity Mirror Group)
Daily Telegraph (Telegraph Media Group)
Dreamwatch (Gary Leigh/Titan Magazines)
Excalibur (Marvel Comics)
The Financial Times (Pearson PLC)
The Gazette (Alan Allnutt)
The Globe and Mail (The Globe and Mail Inc)
The Guardian (Guardian Media Group)
Harper's Bazaar (Hearst Magazines)
Hot Car (AGB Business Publications Limited)
The Independent (Alexander Lebedev)
International Projectionist (J.S. Finn Publications)
Jackie (D C Thompson)
Kine Weekly (Odhams Press Ltd)
Look-In (IPC Magazines)
Look Westward (The Dickens Press)
Los Angeles Times (Tribune Company)
Manchester Evening News (Trinity Mirror Group)
News of the World (News International)
The New Wonder Woman (DC Comics)
New York Herald Tribune (Whitney Communications Corporation)
The Observer (Guardian Media Group)
On Target: The Avengers (Dave Rogers)
The People (Trinity Mirror Group)
Radio Times (BBC Magazines)
The Register-Guard (Guard Publishing Co)
Reveille (Reveille Newspapers)
San Francisco Chronicle (Hearst Corporation)
Screen International (Emap Media Ltd)
SFX (Future Publishing)
Soundtrack (Luc Van de Ven)
The Stage and Television Today (The Stage Newspaper Limited)
Starburst (Visual Imagination)
Starlog (Starlog Group Incorporated)
The StarPhoenix (Postmedia Network Inc)
Stay Tuned to The Avengers (Bowler Enterprises)
The Sunday (News International)
Sunday Mail (News Limited)
Sunday Mirror (Trinity Mirror Group)
Sunday People (Trinity Mirror Group)
The Times (News UK)
Toronto Star (Star Media Group)
TV Times (Times Newspapers Ltd/ITP)
TV World (Aston Publications)
TV Zone (Visual Imagination)

Ultimate DVD (Visual Imagination)
The Uncanny X-Men (Marvel Comics)
Variety (Reed Business Information)
Video Watchdog (Tim Lucas)
The Viewer (The Dickens Press)
Vogue (Condé Nast Publications)
The Weekly News (D C Thompson)
The Windsor Star (Postmedia Network Inc)
Woman's Journal (IPC Magazines)

WEBSITES

ABC at Large, Russ J Graham
A Guide to Avengerland, Anthony McKay
Anew, J Z Ferguson
An Incomplete History of London's Television Studios, Martin Kempton
The Avengers Declassified, Alan and Alys Hayes
The Avengers Forever! David K Smith
The Avengers Illustrated, Mike Noon
Avengers on the Radio, Alan and Alys Hayes
The Avengers: The International Fan Forum, Kimberly Thompson and Allard Postma
Dead Duck, Mike Noon
Deadline, Mike Noon
The Dissolute Avengers, Piers Johnson
Steedumbrella, Denis Kirsanov

ABOUT THE AUTHOR

Michael Richardson is a cult television and film enthusiast, writer and researcher who has previously contributed articles and features to various publications including *TV Zone*, *Book and Magazine Collector*, *Record Collector* and *007 Magazine*. Between 1999 and 2007, he edited and was the main writer on the cult television magazine *Action TV*. He has also written booklets and sleeve notes for television theme tune CD compilations, including *The Avengers and Other Top TV Themes*. As a result of developing an interest in television locations around the Elstree/Borehamwood area, in 1987 he originated the only regular event based on *The Avengers*, the Dead Man's Treasure Hunt convention, which has taken place annually ever since.

INDEX

OTHER TELOS TITLES AVAILABLE

TV/FILM GUIDES

DOCTOR WHO

THE HANDBOOK: THE UNOFFICIAL AND UNAUTHORISED GUIDE TO THE PRODUCTION OF *DOCTOR WHO* by DAVID J HOWE, STEPHEN JAMES WALKER and MARK STAMMERS
Complete guide to the making of *Doctor Who* (1963 – 1996).

BACK TO THE VORTEX: THE UNOFFICIAL AND UNAUTHORISED GUIDE TO *DOCTOR WHO* 2005 by J SHAUN LYON
Complete guide to the 2005 series of *Doctor Who* starring Christopher Eccleston as the Doctor

SECOND FLIGHT: THE UNOFFICIAL AND UNAUTHORISED GUIDE TO *DOCTOR WHO* 2006 by J SHAUN LYON
Complete guide to the 2006 series of *Doctor Who*, starring David Tennant as the Doctor

THIRD DIMENSION: THE UNOFFICIAL AND UNAUTHORISED GUIDE TO *DOCTOR WHO* 2007 by STEPHEN JAMES WALKER
Complete guide to the 2007 series of *Doctor Who*, starring David Tennant as the Doctor

MONSTERS INSIDE: THE UNOFFICIAL AND UNAUTHORISED GUIDE TO *DOCTOR WHO* 2008 by STEPHEN JAMES WALKER
Complete guide to the 2008 series of *Doctor Who*, starring David Tennant as the Doctor.

END OF TEN: THE UNOFFICIAL AND UNAUTHORISED GUIDE TO *DOCTOR WHO* 2009 by STEPHEN JAMES WALKER
Complete guide to the 2009 specials of *Doctor Who*, starring David Tennant as the Doctor.

CRACKS IN TIME: THE UNOFFICIAL AND UNAUTHORISED GUIDE TO *DOCTOR WHO* 2010 by STEPHEN JAMES WALKER
Complete guide to the 2010 series of *Doctor Who*, starring Matt Smith as the Doctor.

RIVER'S RUN: THE UNOFFICIAL AND UNAUTHORISED GUIDE TO *DOCTOR WHO* 2011 by STEPHEN JAMES WALKER
Complete guide to the 2011 series of *Doctor Who*, starring Matt Smith as the Doctor.

WHOGRAPHS: THEMED AUTOGRAPH BOOK
80 page autograph book with an SF theme

TALKBACK: THE UNOFFICIAL AND UNAUTHORISED DOCTOR WHO INTERVIEW BOOK: VOLUME 1: THE SIXTIES edited by STEPHEN JAMES WALKER

Interviews with cast and behind the scenes crew who worked on *Doctor Who* in the sixties

TALKBACK: THE UNOFFICIAL AND UNAUTHORISED *DOCTOR WHO* INTERVIEW BOOK: VOLUME 2: THE SEVENTIES edited by STEPHEN JAMES WALKER

Interviews with cast and behind the scenes crew who worked on *Doctor Who* in the seventies

TALKBACK: THE UNOFFICIAL AND UNAUTHORISED *DOCTOR WHO* INTERVIEW BOOK: VOLUME 3: THE EIGHTIES edited by STEPHEN JAMES WALKER

Interviews with cast and behind the scenes crew who worked on *Doctor Who* in the eighties

WIPED! *DOCTOR WHO'S* MISSING EPISODES by RICHARD MOLESWORTH
The story behind the BBC's missing episodes of *Doctor Who*.

TIMELINK: THE UNOFFICIAL AND UNAUTHORISED GUIDE TO THE CONTINUITY OF *DOCTOR WHO* VOLUME 2 by JON PREDDLE
Timeline of the continuity of *Doctor Who*.

WHOSTROLOGY: A TIME TRAVELLERS ALMANAC by MICHAEL M GILROY-SINCLAIR. Illustrated by Deborah Taylor
Whostrology is a book of daily readings, zodiac signs and explanations, and other *Who*-based astrological elements, designed to allow every *Who* fan to lead a life of peace and ordered calm.

THE COMIC STRIP COMPANION: THE UNOFFICIAL AND UNAUTHORISED GUIDE TO *DOCTOR WHO* IN COMICS: 1964 – 1979 by PAUL SCOONES
Your comprehensive guide to *Doctor Who* in the comics.

THE TELEVISION COMPANION: THE UNOFFICIAL AND UNAUTHORISED GUIDE TO *DOCTOR WHO* 1963 – 1996 by DAVID J HOWE and STEPHEN JAMES WALKER
A two-volume guide to the classic series of *Doctor Who*.

ROBERT HOLMES: A LIFE IN WORDS by RICHARD MOLESWORTH
Whether writing scripts for the far-flung fantasies of *Doctor Who* or *Blake's 7*, or for the more everyday gritty reality of *Bergerac*, *Shoestring*, *Juliet Bravo* or *Public Eye*, Robert Holmes was one of television's most innovative, creative, respected – and least lauded – of talents from the '60s, '70s and '80s. Now, for the first time, this book examines his work in detail.

50 FOR 50: CELEBRATING 50 YEARS OF THE DOCTOR WHO FAMILY by
PAULA HAMMOND
50 previously-unpublished interviews covering all five decades of the show's
history.

TORCHWOOD

INSIDE THE HUB: THE UNOFFICIAL AND UNAUTHORISED GUIDE TO
TORCHWOOD SERIES ONE by STEPHEN JAMES WALKER
Complete guide to the 2006 series of *Torchwood*, starring John Barrowman as
Captain Jack Harkness.

SOMETHING IN THE DARKNESS: THE UNOFFICIAL AND UNAUTHORISED
GUIDE TO *TORCHWOOD* SERIES TWO by STEPHEN JAMES WALKER
Complete guide to the 2008 series of *Torchwood*, starring John Barrowman as
Captain Jack Harkness

24

A DAY IN THE LIFE: THE UNOFFICIAL AND UNAUTHORISED GUIDE TO *24*
by KEITH TOPPING
Complete episode guide to the first season of the popular TV show.

TILL DEATH US DO PART

A FAMILY AT WAR: THE UNOFFICIAL AND UNAUTHORISED GUIDE TO
TILL DEATH US DO PART by MARK WARD
Complete guide to the popular TV show.

SPACE: 1999

DESTINATION: MOONBASE ALPHA: THE UNOFFICIAL AND
UNAUTHORISED GUIDE TO *SPACE: 1999* by ROBERT E WOOD
Complete guide to the popular TV show.

SAPPHIRE AND STEEL

ASSIGNED: THE UNOFFICIAL AND UNAUTHORISED GUIDE TO *SAPPHIRE
AND STEEL* by RICHARD CALLAGHAN
Complete guide to the popular TV show.

THUNDERCATS

HEAR THE ROAR: THE UNOFFICIAL AND UNAUTHORISED GUIDE TO THE
HIT 1980S SERIES *THUNDERCATS* by DAVID CRICHTON
Complete guide to the popular TV show.

SUPERNATURAL

HUNTED: THE UNOFFICIAL AND UNAUTHORISED GUIDE TO
SUPERNATURAL SEASONS 1-3 by SAM FORD AND ANTONY FOGG
Complete guide to the popular TV show.

CHARMED

TRIQUETRA: THE UNOFFICIAL AND UNAUTHORISED GUIDE TO *CHARMED*
SEASONS 1-7 by KEITH TOPPING
Complete guide to the popular TV show.

THE PRISONER

FALL OUT: THE UNOFFICIAL AND UNAUTHORISED GUIDE TO *THE
PRISONER* by ALAN STEVENS and FIONA MOORE
Complete guide to the popular TV show.

BLAKE'S 7

LIBERATION: THE UNOFFICIAL AND UNAUTHORISED GUIDE TO *BLAKE'S 7*
by ALAN STEVENS and FIONA MOORE
Complete guide to the popular TV show.

BATTLESTAR GALACTICA

BY YOUR COMMAND: THE UNOFFICIAL AND UNAUTHORISED GUIDE TO
BATTLESTAR GALACTICA by ALAN STEVENS and FIONA MOORE
A two volume guide to the popular TV show.

A SONG FOR EUROPE

SONGS FOR EUROPE: THE UNITED KINGDOM AT THE EUROVISION SONG
CONTEST by GORDON ROXBURGH
A five volume guide to the popular singing contest.

THE AVENGERS

BOWLER HATS AND KINKY BOOTS: THE UNOFFICIAL AND
UNAUTHORISED GUIDE TO THE AVENGERS by MICHAEL RICHARDSON
This is the most in-depth reference work about the show. It covers all aspects,
going through the production episode by episode, with full behind-the-scenes
details.